THE JEWS
OF CORNWALL
— A History —
Tradition and Settlement to 1913

KEITH PEARCE

**With an Introduction by David Giddings
and a Postcript by Harvey Kurzfield**

*"Judge fairly between man and man, whether he is a fellow Israelite or a
stranger…you too must befriend the stranger, for you once lived as
strangers in the land of Egypt."*
Deuteronomy Ch. 1 v. 16 and Ch. 10 v. 19.

*"A man is thy Neighbour, by his Humanity, not by his Divinity,
by his Nature, not by his Religion."*
John Donne

HALSGROVE

First published in Great Britain in 2014

British Library Cataloguing-in-Publication Data
A CIP record for this title is available from the British Library

ISBN 978 0 85704 222 4

HALSGROVE
Halsgrove House,
Ryelands Business Park,
Bagley Road, Wellington, Somerset TA21 9PZ
Tel: 01823 653777   Fax: 01823 216796
email: sales@halsgrove.com

Part of the Halsgrove group of companies.
Information on all Halsgrove titles is available at: www.halsgrove.com

Printed and bound in China by Everbest Printing Co Ltd

Contents

For my dear friends
Godfrey and Winifred

Acknowledgements

Some sections of this text first appeared in *The Lost Jews of Cornwall* (co-edited by Keith Pearce and Helen Fry) published by the Redcliffe Press of Bristol (2000), with the support of Evelyn Friedlander (The Hidden Legacy Foundation) and John and Godfrey Simmons. I am grateful to John and Angela Sansom of Redcliffe for that publication, and for their encouragement to publish this new book independently.

This publication has been made possible through the generous sponsorship of the Jewish Community of Cornwall *Kehillat Kernow*, and through individual donations from:

The Tanner Trust, David Bishop, Caroline Carter, Martin and Ruth Dunitz, Eileen Essam, Anthony and Josh Fagin, Joanna and James Girdwood-Simmons, Keith and Marian Harper, David Hearle and Anne Sicher Hearle, David Jacobs, Gerry and Wendy Jevon, Dr. Michael Jolles, David Lang, Dr. Elaine Leader, Leslie and Patricia Lipert, Professor Peter Mittler, Dr. Barry Monk, Estelle Moses, Dr. Venetia Newall, Jean Owen, Dr. Anthony Phillips, Stuart and Gail Raine, Adrienne Ross, David Samuelson, Bernard and Barbara Simmons, Betty Spector, Professor Charles and Mrs. Jessica Thomas, Jonathan and Alison Wolf, Brian and Paul Yule.

Without the support, patience and constant encouragement of my wife, Mandy, who has proof read the whole text, and endured with stoicism and kindness the many hours which I have had to spend in my study preparing this book, it would not have been possible to revisit, revise and complete this text.

I owe a unique debt of gratitude to my friend and colleague Godfrey Simmons, to whom this book is dedicated. He has made available extensive material from his research archive, and has advised and supported me in this project over many years. I am especially grateful to him that he has encouraged me to revise and expand the chapters which we previously co-authored, and to publish them independently.

I am also grateful to Anthony Joseph who has continued to advise and assist me in the complex genealogical aspects of this subject, and to David Giddings for his permission to republish his essay "Mediaeval Jewry and Cornish Tin", from "The Lost Jews of Cornwall", as an Introduction to this book.

Since our collaboration on *The Lost Jews of Cornwall*, I have been grateful for information from Helen Fry, especially relating to her research into Jewish Wills. Her books on the history of the Jewish Communities of Plymouth and Exeter are available from Halsgrove.

I would like to give special thanks to those who, since 2000, have also sent me a significant range of information from their records and research: Ena Black, Rebecca Coutts (nee Walker), Jackie Hill, Michael Jolles, Trudy Martin, George Rigal, Angela Shire, and Phoebe Walker.

Prior to the publication of *The Lost Jews of Cornwall*, Eric Dawkins (for many years custodian of the Falmouth Jewish cemetery) provided me with information from his research into the Falmouth Jewish Community, and we co-authored the brief introductory section on the Penryn cemetery in 2000. I remain grateful for his earlier information, which has been retained in the corresponding section of this book, and I have accredited him in the various attached source references. The original introduction has been extensively revised and considerably expanded with new research which I carried out from 2001.

I am also inbebted to H. C. Faulkner and to David Thomas for their help in tracing further original source documents relating to Falmouth and the Penryn cemetery, to Tony Pawlyn for his help and information on maritime and shipping matters, and to Justin Brooke and Allen Buckley for their advice on various aspects of mining.

I would like to thank Dr. Hermann Zeffertt for his translations of the complete cemetery headstone inscriptions, and Yissochor Marmorstein for checking a range of Hebrew dates and his assistance in translating numerous sections of the Penzance Congregational Minute Book from the original Hebrew and Yiddish. My thanks also Rabbi Dr. Nichloas de Lange and Dr. Jennifer Speake for permission to reproduce their 1975 surveys of the Falmouth and Penzance Jewish cemeteries.

I must also thank those who hold copyright to various articles, research and archival material for permission to reproduce or extract from them in this book, and for their generosity in doing so without charge.

The following people and institutions have also helped me with information and assistance: Christine North, Alison Campbell, Steven Hobbs, Alison Spence, David Thomas, Deborah Tritton, Archivists, County Record Office, Truro; Angela Broome (Librarian), Margaret Morgan (Documentation Officer) and Leslie Douch, Courtney Library, Truro; Hilary Bracegirdle (Director) and Sarah Lloyd-Durrant (Curator of Social History) the City Museum, the Royal Institution of Cornwall, Truro; Peter Gilson and the Historical Research Unit, Royal Cornwall Polytechnic, Falmouth; Philip Payton of the Institute of Cornish Studies, University of Exeter, Penryn; the Cornwall Family History Society, Truro; Alison Bevan (Director) and Katie Herbert (Curator) The Penlee House Museum and Art Gallery, Penzance; the Staff of the Morrab Library, Penzance, the Penzance Reference Library, and the Cornish Studies Library, Redruth; the Trevithick Society, Steve Ottery, Curator, Isles of Scilly Museum; Edward Bolitho and Sheila Wilson of the Bolitho Estate Office, Penzance; W.H. White, the Regimental Museum, Bodmin; Joanne Liddle and Simon Reeves of Allied Domecq; Josephine Parker, Achivist, Waltham Forest Archives; John Lee and Diane Pryce of the Office for National Statistics, Southport; Esra Kahn, Head Librarian, Jews' College, London; Edgar Samuel and Jennifer Marin (formerly) of the Jewish Museum, London; the Jewish Memorial Council; Charles Tucker, Record-Keeper, the London Beth Din; Malcolm C. Davis (former) Assistant Librarian, and Richard High, the Brotherton Library, University of Leeds (Roth Collection); C. M. Woolgar, Archivist & Head of Special Collections, Hartley Library, the University of Southampton; John Simmons (formerly) Librarian and Fellow of All Souls College, Oxford; Geoff Pick, the London Metropolitan Archives; the Staff of the British Library, London, and the Bodleian Library, Oxford; the Jewish Historical Society of England; A. J. Brown and J. M Wraight, Admiralty

ACKNOWLEDGEMENTS

Librarian, Ministry of Defence, Whitehall, London; Wendy Tomlin, Librarian, Britannia Royal Naval College, Dartmouth; Alan Giddings, the National Maritime Museum Library, Greenwich; the Royal Naval Museum, Portsmouth; Michael Duffy, the Centre for Maritime Studies, Roger Burt, Mining History, and Stuart McWilliam, History Librarian, the University of Exeter; the British Newspaper Library, London; E. A. Churchill, Genealogy Officer, the Society of Genealogists; Richard Cooper, George Rigal and Sidney Moss of the Jewish Genealogical Society; Liz James of the Australian Jewish Historical Society; T. Knowle, the Probate Registry, York; the Archivists of the Penzance and Falmouth Masonic Lodges, and Peter Aitkenhead and Diane Clements of the Library and Museum of Freemasonry, London.

The following have provided me with information or have given me assistance and advice:

Eric Ackstine, Roger Ainsworth, Lesley Aitchison, Evelyn Armitage, Kathryn Atkin, Keith Austin, Andy Baker, D. B. and R. M. Barton, Karsten Berg, Andy, David and Victor Bishop, Barrie and Sandra Bishop, Elizabeth Brock, Angela Broome, Gordon Brown, Malcolm Brown, John Burn, Roger Burt, Alison Campbell, Harry Carter, Sara Chambers, Paul Cheifitz, Anne Chappell, Rita Collier, Kim Cooper, Derek G. Cousins, David Dale, Dr and Mrs H.A. Davis, Eric Dawkins, Julyan Drew, Alfred Dunitz, Julian Essam, Anthony Fagin, Leslie and Naomi Falkson, Ingrid Fevere, David Fielker, Cyril and Judith Fisher, Esther Fishman, Cyril Fox, Evelyn Friedlander, Michael Gandy, Frank Gent, Peter Gilson, David Giddings, Eva Grabherr, Marilyn Graham, Linda Graicher, Barry Green, Geoffery Green, R. John Hall, Keith and Marian Harper, John Harris, David and Anne Sicher Hearle, Viv Hendra, Alison Hodge, Rachel Hollow, Philip Hosken, Jill Hyams, Peter Hyman, Saul Issroff, Phoebe Isaacs, David Ivall, David M. Jacobs, Henrietta Jacobs, David James, Ron James, Edward Jamilly, Michael Jolles, Judith Joseph, Michael Joseph, Peter Joseph, Sharman Kadish, Sonia Kemelmager, Gary Kent, Terry Knight, Neil Kraft, Harvey Kurzfield, David Lang, Leatrice Levene, Norman Levine, Elkan Levy, Philip Levy, Arnold Lewis, Leslie and Patricia Lipert, David Liss, Stephen Leach, Peter Luscombe, Neil Marcuson, Kenneth Marks, Yissochor Marmorstein, Joanna Mattingly, Stephen Massil, Charlotte Mackenzie, Michael Michell, Monty Miller, Peter Mittler, Barry and Mark Monk, Claire Morgan, Betty Naggar, Eileen Nethercott, Venetia Newall, Martin Nicholson, Elliott Oppel, June Palmer, Hedy Parry-Davies, Barbara Pearce, Mandy Pearce, Harold Pollins, Peter Pool, Ann Preston-Jones, John Probert, Gail and Stuart Raine, David Ricardo, Christopher Richards, Pat Robson, Graham Rogers, Joseph Roth, Edgar Samuel, Judith Samuel, David Samuelson, Sidney Schultz, Ivan and Sheila Segal, Lily Segal, Jack Schofield, Arnold Schwartzman, Michael Shapiro, Angela Shire, Bernard Simmons, John Simmons, Verena Smith, Keith Solomon, David Sonin, Susan Soyinka, Penelope and Richard Strannack, Mrs. B. Susser, Kenneth Teacher, Charles Thomas, Brian Torode, Peter Towey, Charles Tucker, Alan Tyler, Malcolm Veal, Herbert A. Walford, Barbara Warwick, Michael Westerman, Syma Weinberg, Malcolm Weisman, Jonathan Wolf, Joseph Wolfman, Michael Wohl, Brian, John and Paul Yule, Hanna Yaffe, and Hermann Zeffertt.

List of Illustrations

Where possible, accreditation has been given to accompany the illustration.

The Hart portraits (artist unknown) are from a Private Collection and are courtesy of Mrs. Penelope Strannack, daughter of Sir Francis Edmund Turton-Hart.

Other commercial Lemon Hart ® illustrations were supplied courtesy of Allied Domecq plc. (1999), and Mosaiq Inc. of Quebec (2013).

The portraits of Rabbi Barnett Asher Simmons and his wife Mrs. Flora Simmons (Jacob), oil on canvas, by Richard T. Pentreath (1806-1869) are from the Private Collection of Bernard Simmons, on loan to Penlee House Gallery and Museum, Penzance. Other photographs of Penzance traders are also courtesy of Penlee House.

The images of the Lanlivery-Bodwen figurine, of the Earl of Cornwall's armorial shield, and the South Condurrow mine are reproduced with the permission of the Royal Institution of Cornwall, Truro (R.I.C.).

The various photographs and other illustrative materials of the Jacob family, and of members of the Falmouth community are from the Archive of the late Alex M. Jacob, courtesy of his executor, Philip Levy QC, and the Jewish Museum, London.

The plans of the Falmouth and Penzance synagogues are reproduced with the kind permission of the late Edward Jamilly.

Photographs of the Harris family are courtesy of Brian Yule.

The photograph of Alfred Aaron de Pass is from the Archive of Phoebe Walker, and is courtesy of Mrs. Walker and her daughter Rebecca Coutts.

Photographs of the Falmouth cemetery are by the late David Sonin (*The Jewish Chronicle*), and others are by the late Karsten Berg, courtesy of Rachel Hollow.

The photographs of the Penzance cemetery headstones are by Mandy Pearce, Maurice Minsky, Michael Shapiro and David Sonin.

Drawings of the Armorial shields and the Fifteen Bezants represent artwork by the late D. Endean Ivall from his book *Cornish Heraldry and Symbolism* (Dyllansow Truran 1988) and are reproduced by kind permission of David Ivall and his family.

Photographs of the Levin Family are courtesy of the Morrab Library, Penzance.

Photographs of the Oppenheim Family are courtesy of David Jacobs.

Photographs of the Bischofswerder Family are courtesy of the late Victor Bishop and Ivor Segal.

Photographs of Michael Leinkram and his family are courtesy of Gail and Stuart Raine and Esher Fishman.

Preface

This book represents research carried out over thirty years, and it has taken me almost fifteen years to prepare and complete. Through my friendship with Godfrey and Winifred Simmons, descendants of Rabbi B. A. Simmons of Penzance and his wife Flora Jacob of Redruth, I first learned of Godfrey's research into the history of the Jews of Cornwall, which he began as a young man some seventy years ago. At first I assisted him in his ongoing research, and I learned much from him, not only in terms of information, but also about the wider field of Anglo-Jewish history, the evaluation of evidence, and the subtleties of Jewish genealogy. Later, he encouraged me to strike out on my own, and since then his knowledge, advice and perception have continued to be invaluable to me. We shared some of our joint material in the chapters which we co-authored in *The Lost Jews of Cornwall* in 2000 (which I co-edited with Helen Fry). Those chapters contained only a small proportion of the records we held at the time, and an even smaller proportion of material I have since accumulated and which has now found its way into the current text. After the publication of *Lost Jews,* aspects of which required amendment and revision, I continued my research, unearthing much new information. Many people who had seen the earlier book, were also prompted to send me further material from their own records, especially relating to their own families, for which I have been much indebted. In some cases this input has been significant and crucial, in that it might not have come my way from any other source, and I have tried to fully acknowledge these contributions throughout this text, whether they were substantial or modest.

This book covers the story of the Jewish presence in Cornwall up to the demise of the historic communities, and not beyond 1913, after which there was only a gradual, uneven and fragmented settlement of Jewish families in Cornwall. The book begins with a critical examination of the putative role of Jews, and others, in Cornwall's ancient and medieval history, as preserved in Cornish tradition and folklore. It is my belief that too much attention and credence have been given to these traditions in relation to Jews. Although it will be obvious that I take a sceptical view of their validity, and although I regard them as having little or no intrinsic historical or objective value, I do feel that they are of considerable interest from a subjective, social and cultural perspective. It has not been my intention to present this section of the text as in any way a specialist study of either the Cornish language or of Cornish archaeology, and I claim no expertise in these fields, but I have tried to give due attention and respect to these specialist areas and also to the writers who seem to me to be most relevant to my subject both in Cornish and Anglo-Jewish historical studies. I hope that I have given a sufficient overview to allow the general reader a sense of the relevant sources and how they have been and may be interpreted in varying ways.

Throughout this text I have tried as best I can to exclude purely anecdotal detail (from both the ancient and later history of Cornwall) and to distinguish unsubstantiated claims from facts that can be established or reasonably inferred from concrete documentary evidence and from reputable, identifiable and accessible sources. All history, literature and scripture has at some time existed in a purely oral form, but the preservation of tangible documentary material, and advances in scholarship have made it possible to test oral traditions and earlier written accounts against credible evidence and newly discovered sources. In the right hands, oral history can play a vital and indispensable role, as it has done in the case of Holocaust Studies, but it can also be fraught with difficulties. Human memory and oral transmission are by their very nature characterised and limited by the vagaries of imperfect recall, decay, distortion and embellishment, and as such they are as capable of invention as they are of veracity. Oral traditions and purely anecdotal claims can be confirmed to have been largely or substantially correct by the emergence of new and tangible evidence, but those traditions which flourish, as they do best, in its absence can pass on to future generations and the historical process itself, a dubious, defective and even pernicious legacy (the anti-Semitic blood libel is an obvious historical example in point). So virile are these tendencies in the oral form that they are sometimes capable of survival even if their substance has effectively been demolished by incontrovertible evidence, and they can even re-emerge, seemingly unscathed, in published form.

However, even the identification, evaluation and interpretation of tangible and credible documentary sources can be an arduous and difficult procedure, and the potential for error, omission and misunderstanding will always permeate the enterprise. In the first part of this book I examine the various traditions which have linked Jews (and others) to Cornwall's past. In the greater body of the second and third parts of the text I have tried to present documentary evidence for the identities and activities of the Jews who did indeed comprise a distinct community within Cornwall from the 18th century to the close of the 19th century. I am acutely aware of the need to investigate and evaluate the great range of sources given here with extreme care, and I am also aware that in the end this approach can never bring perfect resolution or coherence to the panorama of details which serves to make up a portrait of these communities.

I have concentrated in this book on cultural and social matters in the historical periods which precede and then comprise the rise and fall of the historic Jewish communities in Cornwall up to the end of the 19th century. The people are at the centre. Those with an interest in the Jewish religious artefacts and buildings of the period can find numerous sources which provide expert guidance in these fields, and I have referenced them accordingly. I have made some passing mention of these matters, but I would refer the reader interested in pursuing these facets to the specialist published studies mentioned in the source-notes and the Bibliography. I have also been conscious that this book will be read and used in different ways and for different reasons, and that its readership is likely to be both among those well versed in Cornish Studies, and others whose primary field of interest lies elsewhere in the wider arena of national Anglo-Jewish history. Both of these areas represent dynamic and expanding fields of research and publication. Consequently, I have tried to place the story of the Cornish Jews of the 18th and 19th centuries against aspects of the contemporaneous Cornish and National cultural and historical background. Other readers may look through this book mainly to identify members of their own family. It is with the knowledge that some may use this text primarily as a reference work, rather than a history, that I have also chosen to break off from a strictly narrative approach in the commercial sections, which I have deliberately presented in the form of Trade Directories, in a roughly chronological order. I have adopted the same approach in the sections on Freemasonry.

The genealogies of the Cornish Jews are especially complex, with identical names often attaching to different people from different generations, or even within the same generation. The frequency of these namesakes increases the potential for confusion between Jews from separate families, and sometimes from within the same family. It can also give rise to the erroneous allocation of Jewish identity to those indigenous Cornish people who also bore Hebrew names, adopted from the Bible. By giving as many dates as possible, and by sometimes repeating information (I hope judiciously) it has been my aim that such confusion should be minimised, if not eradicated entirely, and that the reader will find it possible to cross-reference details from separate chapters with relative ease. The public records which do exist for parishes and in the Decennial Census returns (from 1841) are a vital source of information, but even these under-represent how many Jews may have lived in or visited the County, some as transient peddlers and hawkers. This is especially true for the Census records, in that they offer a snapshot for one brief period in one month of one year only out of every ten. The names of numerous Jewish people will, therefore, have been lost, but, sadly, this cannot be remedied.

I have chosen to call this book A History, rather than The History, of the Jews of Cornwall, and in reality it is a thematic and synthetic historical study rather than a conventional chronological history. I would not presume to suggest that the text is a definitive study of this subject, and it may well be superseded by other works in the future, but I hope that it will become the standard, comprehensive treatment of this little-known aspect of Cornish and Anglo-Jewish history, for some time at least. If time and opportunity permit, and new information should present itself about the communities of the 18th and 19th centuries, there may, perhaps, be a revised edition of this book at some point in the future. Like those who have given their time and labour to the study of the Cornish language and to Cornish history and culture, whether in Mining, Maritime studies, Archaeology or Cornwall's Celtic and Christian history, I hope that I have been able to produce something of interest and value relating to this circumscribed, relatively short-lived, but notable feature of Cornwall's social and economic history. My motivation has been above all to bring these people to general notice, to let them live again within these pages both as individuals and as members of a distinctive community alongside their Cornish neighbours, so that they will not be forgotten.

Keith Pearce, Penzance, November 2013

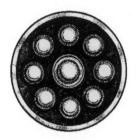

Introduction
David Giddings

Herodotus, writing in the fifth century BCE, was uncertain about the reality of the Cassiterides, or Tin Islands, but he knew that amber and tin came to Greece from the ends of the earth.[1] In his time the Carthaginians may have been the Greeks' immediate suppliers, however this Semitic people guarded its commercial secrets so that the precise origins and trade route of their tin remain unknown. Nor do we know whether the Carthaginians or their cousins, the Phoenicians, tapped the trade at its putative Cornish source. In the well known account of Pytheas of Massilia, the fourth century BCE navigator, whose extraordinary voyage to Norway is probably preserved by Diodorus Siculus, we are told that the inhabitants of Belerion (Land's End) are: "very fond of strangers, and, from their intercourse with foreign merchants are civilised in their manner of life ....Here then the merchants buy the tin from the natives and carry it over to Gaul, and after travelling over land for about thirty days they finally bring their loads on horses to the mouth of the river Rhone."[2] Unfortunately, nowhere do we learn the identity of these merchants.

Since the sixteenth century CE the notion that Cornwall's first Semitic visitors were the Phoenicians has gained a convinced following by reason of frequent repetition. The mythopoeic moment can be traced to 1590 when John Twynne's book, *De Rebus Albionicus,* was printed by his son, Thomas. In it the Phoenicians joined the crush of Trojans, Druids and lost tribes of Israel who were already jostling to fill the void before the beginning of recorded history following the Roman conquest. Subsequently it has been claimed that the joint voyage of Solomon and Hiram, King of Tyre, to Tarshish (?Spain) in the tenth century BCE may have taken them further to Cornwall.[3] Not only Bible reading but also philological temptation has encouraged an enduring belief in early Semitic connections with Cornwall. From the seventeenth century CE it was believed that *Berat-Anach* or *Bartanac,* country of tin in the Phoenician language, was the origin of the name Britain.[4] William Borlase, the great Cornish antiquary, derived 'tin' from the Phoenician for mud or slime,[5] although just over one hundred years later, while allowing the Phoenicians their place, Richard Edmonds was of the opinion that Britain took its name from *Bretin* which, he says, is the Cornish for tin mount, i.e. St. Michael's Mount.[6]

Toponymy has also been employed to suggest Cornish-Jewish links from early times. Marazion, supposedly 'bitterness of Zion', has done great service in this respect.[7] Cairo, evocative of Levantine traders, actually derives from *kerrow* or forts in Cornish; Menheniot has been ascribed a Hebrew origin, *min oniyot*, meaning 'from ships', but is readily construed in Cornish as *ma* (plain) with a personal name.[8] Approximation of the common pronunciation of Mousehole as *Muzzle* to the Hebrew *mazel*, or 'luck' in English, has also excited comment,[9] although both topography, in the form of a cave in the cliff, and the earliest recorded written form,

Pertusum muris, 1242,[10] suggest a more prosaic derivation. Ostensibly more helpful in establishing a Jewish connection is the place name Landjew in the Parish of Withiel and a nearby *Jew's House* smelting hearth. At, or before, the date of Diodorus' account of tin-smelting in Belerion the casting of white tin into astragali (roughly H shaped blocks) shows that the furnaces were tapped to permit the metal to be run off into moulds. This improvement in smelting technology has been attributed to the Jews,[11] and continued to be used into the Mediaeval period. *Jews' Houses* are widely distributed throughout the metalliferous districts of Cornwall; in Penwith at the County's westernmost extremity, a total of five, either extant or documented, are known.[12]

Nevertheless care is needed with the nomenclature because of the virtual extinction of Cornish as a mother tongue; its place names have become the archaeology of human speech and difficult to interpret outside the language and culture of those who speak or spoke it because of anglicising influences. 'Landjew' probably transliterates Cornish *lyn du* which means 'black pool'. Similarly, other suggestive sounding place names become commonplace topographical features, for example: *Baldhu*, black mine, and *Cardew*, black fort.[13] A seventeenth century CE account of tin working may give some cause for doubt about *Jews' Houses* as evidence for a Jewish presence in Cornwall. Thomas Fuller describes the later tin 'blowing-house' as being periodically burned down in order to save tin particles driven by the bellows blast into the thatch of the roof.[14] On the reasonable assumption that the rough granite walls would have been reused, we may infer the origin of the term *Jews' House*. It lay in the Cornish *chy du*, 'black house', a name which was perhaps extended generically to all smelting hearths including earlier examples which had fallen into disuse. Even personal names of a resounding biblical character and the occasional Hannibal have been adduced as evidence of early Semitic connections, so also have the use of saffron in cooking and physical appearance but these are more likely to be wishful thinking than sound surmise.

Christian era folklore would have us believe that Cornwall received various Jewish visitors, even Jesus himself. Joseph of Arimathea, a wealthy Essene Jew and a merchant, came to Cornwall, it is said, with Jesus in his boyhood. Stories abound of their travels from Looe in the east to Ding Dong mine in the far west; at St Just in Roseland, a stone upon which Joseph stepped on landing, used to be pointed out to visitors. Tinners used to sing:

> "Joseph was a tin man
> And the miners loved him well."[15]

Legend further has it that St Paul came to Britain as a missionary to found the British Church, a journey which, if its historicity could be proven, might presuppose a Jewish community given his zeal to convert Jews. However, his execution, traditionally dated to 66 CE, would have precluded exertions among any Jews in Cornwall who may have been working tin as Roman slaves as a consequence of their revolt in Palestine four years later when, according to St Jerome, "an incredible number of Jews were sold like horses and dispersed over the face of the whole earth."[16]

In his contemporary account of the Jewish Wars, Flavius Josephus relates that in the aftermath of the fall of Jerusalem in 70 CE: "as for the rest of the multitude, that were about seventeen years old, he [Fronto] put them into bonds and sent them to the Egyptian mines." Titus, commander of the Jerusalem campaign, sent many captives to the provinces to suffer sentence *ad gladium* or *ad bestias*, "but those under seventeen years of age were sold for slaves."[17] It is at least possible that some of these Jews were employed in tin extraction in the recently pacified lowland zone of Britannia. On the slender archaeological evidence of coins minted in Judaea and found in England there were some links between Britain and Palestine in the first and second centuries CE.[18] Another of the early Church Fathers, St. John Chrysostom, tells of how the fourth century CE emperor Constantine created a new diaspora of enslaved Jews, sending them into "all the territories of his empire."[19] Very likely the Romans were interested in Cornish tin, as discoveries of ingots, ornaments, coin caches and milestones attest, yet whether they employed slave labour or had any direct supervision of the works, which had been conducted by the native population for more than two thousand years, it is impossible to say.

During the fourth century CE we have references to a Solomon, Duke of Cornwall, who was so named even before his conversion to Christianity.[20] His father, Geraint, was a Christian and, while the name may be evidence of Jewish influence from earlier times, there must be a possibility that it stems from the work of Christian missionaries, Jewish converts or otherwise. As the Dark Age Saxon conquest extended inexorably westward, Celtic Christianity in Cornwall pursued its own forms and observances, apparently retaining a regard for biblical names. Evidence from the Bodmin Manumissions shows that between 940 CE and 1040, of 122 liberated slaves 98 were Cornishmen with names such as Noah, Isaac and Jesu. Firm conclusions from such evidence are difficult to make.

Discoveries of bracelets and other ornaments in old workings suggest that the Saxons,[21] who completed their conquest of Cornwall under Athelstan during the first half of the tenth century CE, continued to exploit tin. Folklore is, by its fanciful nature, insusceptible to accurate dating but subscribers to the view that folklore is a damaged version of history might locate tales of Jews' workings in the Saxon period, although descriptions of discoveries of crude wooden and horn implements by Carew in his survey of Cornwall[22] and others could apply to almost any time until the recent past. Polwhele[23] cites Norden's Topographical and Historical Description of Cornwall (1758) on tools found in "old-forsaken workes which to this day retayn the name Attall Sarazin: the Jews cast-off workes, in their Hebrew speache." To John Norden the language may have resembled Hebrew but was, in fact, Cornish and as another antiquary, Thomas Tonkin, pointed out meant "leavings of the Saracins and from thence infers, that the Saxons did not work the mines, but employed the Saracins for that purpose."[24] Among the thickets of language and ethnicity Polwhele,[25] sounding a wise note of caution, quotes from 'Pearce's Preface' which, referring to Attall Sarazin as *Jews' Feast*, continues: "but whether they [the Jews] had liberty to work and search for tin does not appear because they had their dwellings chiefly in great towns and cities."

Such stories, with their outlandish conflation of Saxons, Jews and Saracens among a devout, mostly illiterate and uneducated people, speak of the otherness of times remote and unrecorded but also of a familiarity with poverty which could be ascribed to the exploitation of Cornwall's natural wealth by outsiders. Through the perceived alienness of the Jews in almost every respect they, particularly, were qualified to be objects of speculation and suspicion. This is shown in the folk-tales of the *knockers* who were said to inhabit the subterranean levels of tin mines in the spirit form of Jews who had incited the crucifixion of Jesus and needed to be propitiated by tinners.[26] Charles Henderson,[27] on the other hand, plausibly proposes that *knocker* derives from *Nicor*, a Saxon water sprite, but folklore tells us what people were capable of believing, wished to believe and did believe rather than what is true.

Under the Norman kings the Jews take on a concrete historical existence in England although at what precise point it is uncertain. Since the early eleventh century CE there had been a Jewish settlement in Rouen and John Stow,[28] probably following the mediaeval chronicler, William of Malmesbury, declares: "King William brought the Jewes from Rhoane to inhabit here." There is, however, no authentic reference to a Jewish presence during William's reign, so perhaps the incentive to settle away from Normandy was provided by the massacre of Rouen's Jews by knights crusader in 1096 CE. Under William Rufus (1087-1100 CE) and his successor, Henry I (1100-1135 CE), Jews were offered royal protection and communities began to develop but there is no evidence to confirm settlement in Cornwall nor involvement in tin extraction until the end of Richard I's reign (1189-1199 CE) and perhaps not even then. Nevertheless records show that by 1188 CE there were enough Jews in Exeter to form a distinctive community[29] at a time when the Dartmoor area of Devon was a major tin producer within the stannaries (those districts of Devon and Cornwall where John's Charter of 1201 CE recognised the special rights and immunities of tinners).

Although secure proof of Jewish participation from an early date in Cornish, or for that matter Devonian, tin production is lacking, some insight into either possibility or probability can be gained by examining the role of the Jews under the Norman and Angevin monarchs. Societies which function beyond the level of a subsistence economy require both coinage and credit. Norman England, which had undergone the systematic infeudation of society, had little of either but the king preferred to have his vassals pay their dues not in kind but in coin; in this way he could readily meet his military necessities in Normandy, Ireland, France or Palestine; he could acquire luxuries and have great buildings constructed. In their turn, on the strength of their own accumulation, the barons could reliably meet their obligations to their lord and satisfy their own acquisitiveness. Should there be a shortage of coin for immediate expenditure credit, secured against future revenue, would meet the need.

As yet there was no middle class in England but the Jews took on some of its attributes. Debarred from most other activities wherever they settled, the Jews had been obliged to become merchants and financiers. Their success in these spheres, though tax records show that there were many poor Jews in England, was assisted by the Church which imposed stringent laws against usury, a term which included not only money-lending but also commercial speculation. Thus the way was left open to the Jews who were, of course, not constrained by canon law. They brought capital; facilitated government by advancing funds; contributed to some of the great abbatial and cathedral building of the age; and financed military expeditions such as Richard Strongbow's against Ireland in 1170 CE. They were also a source of income through amercements and regular forms of feudal exaction for their lord the king. They were the king's Jews and the relationship was mutually advantageous until Angevin rapacity removed its simple arithmetical foundations. Finally the Jews themselves were removed in 1290 CE.

Requirements for capital certainly existed in the stannaries, although the shallow working of stream (i.e. alluvial) tin deposits in open cast fashion, in 'coffins' (trenches) or by costeaning (the sinking of pits up to about twelve feet deep linked by horizontal drifts) meant that fixed capital was relatively modest. Wooden shovels, possibly iron-shod, and picks were the basic tools;[30] elaborate deep rock mining which necessitated blasting and steam pumping came much later. However, if the profitability of the stannaries was to be realised for tinners, landholders and, through taxation and pre-emption, the king, finance was needed because of the hazards and delays which characterised the work. Shoding, the search for tin stones, was a lengthy, labour intensive process involving extensive excavation and large-scale diversion of water courses. A group of tinners or a landlord, stirred by the promise of mineral wealth, might be compelled to wait a considerable period before white tin began to flow into ingot moulds. Such a delay could oblige borrowing against the future to meet present needs or attracting non-working shareholders.

It is difficult to believe that Jewish capital did not find its way into the stannaries; yet the evidence for it is elusive, as it is for any direct participation in the work or actual settlement in Cornwall up to the moment of the Expulsion. To complicate the matter further, it was the case by 1290 that other sources of capital had become available. Whether these displaced Jewish finance or were the original source is uncertain. At the close of the twelfth century CE, in the reign of Richard I, we seem to come close to evidence of a Jewish connection with the stannaries through the *Liber Rubeus* (The Red Book) of the Exchequer which contains the Capitula concerning the smelting, assay and taxation of tin in Cornwall. Bannister unequivocally asserts, "That during, and before the reign of Richard, Jews had to do with the tin trade of Cornwall is evident from the Capitula, or Ordinances, respecting tin and the stannaries, made by William de Wrotham, Chief Warden [of the Stannaries] and others, 1197-8."[31] Part of it reads:

"Also neither man nor woman, Christian nor Jew, shall presume to buy or sell any tin of the first smelting, nor to give or remove any of the first smelting from the Stannary, or out of the place appointed for weighing and stamping, until it shall be weighed and stamped in the presence of the keepers and clerks of the weight and stamp of the farm.

Also neither man nor woman, Christian nor Jew, shall presume, in the Stannaries or out of the Stannaries, to have in his or her possession any tin of the first smelting beyond a fortnight, unless it be weighed and stamped by the keepers and clerk of the weight and farm stamp.

Also neither man nor woman, Christian nor Jew, in market-towns and boroughs, on sea or on land, shall presume to keep beyond thirteen weeks tin of the first smelting weighed and stamped, unless it be put into the second smelting and the mark discharged.

Also neither man nor woman, Christian nor Jew, shall presume in any manner to remove tin, either by sea or by land, out of the counties of Devon and Cornwall, unless he or she first have a licence of the Chief-Warden of the Stannaries."

A motive for creating a more efficient stannary bureaucracy is not far to seek. Richard, a lavish and extrovert monarch, incurred huge expenses during the Third Crusade; his ransom from Emperor Henry VI is said to have cost the country a quarter of its income. His outlay on Château Gaillard was great and his defeat of the French at Gisors in 1198 also consumed the royal substance. Furthermore, he spent a fortune on arranging the election of his nephew, Otto, to the dignity of the King of the Romans. Since he died in pursuit of an alleged treasure trove at Chaluz it is reasonable to assume that the king would wish for his treasure in tin to fructify. Nevertheless, it would be unwise to assume from the Capitula alone that Jews had played, or were to play, a part in the drive to improve the king's income from the stannaries. If the phrases: "...neither man nor woman, Christian nor Jew," were a legal coverall meaning "nobody whosoever" or "neither Christian nor non-Christian", it would be difficult to draw firm conclusions from the *Liber Rubeus*. Even if there was an intention to regulate specifically Jewish participation in the mediaeval tin trade, de Wrotham's ordinances do not presuppose a settled Jewish community; he may have been concerned with individual itinerant Jews or their agents. Certainly claims of the Jews' direct activity in tin-working under the Angevins are persistent. It is true that Camden's Britannia (1586)[32] is emphatic that in John's reign (1199-1216 CE) the mines were farmed for one hundred marks; a later editor adds that the Jews themselves were the farmers but it is not clear on what evidence this claim is based. In his *Natural History of Cornwall* (1758) Borlase, describing small blocks of white tin found in old workings, writes that they are "probably as old as the time when the Jews had engrossed the tin manufacture in the time of King John."[33] Polwhele's *History* (1808) follows suit,[34] as does Gilbert's *Survey* (1817).[35] William Hals, in his *Compleat History of Cornwall* (1703)[36] declares that in the Angevin period Jews were employed in the mines as slaves while Carew's *Survey of Cornwall* (1602) also refers to the consequences of the Expulsion which "left the mines unwrought". However, Carew's mention of "the cut throate and abominable dealing" of "the merchants of London" in relation to tinners is clearly a contemporary Elizabethen reference to gentiles and not a mediaeval one to Jews.[37] All or some of these propositions could be true but they are unlikely to be so as will later appear. If positive evidence of Jewish enslavement is lacking there are also difficulties arising from statements about the farm of stannary revenues.

During a reign when Jewry was tallaged severely as never before it is extremely unlikely that John would have permitted Jews to enjoy his revenues from tin at a price of only one hundred marks for the farm. Production in Cornwall did decline from eight hundred thousand pound weight in 1200 CE to six hundred thousand in 1209 but then it rose to a record one million two hundred thousand pound weight of tin (*c*.600 long tons) in 1214.[38] In such circumstances a payment of one hundred marks (£66. 13s. 4d) would have exposed contractors to the needy John's savagery, but of this we have no record. John's Stannary Charter of 1201 may have served to revive confidence among the tinners to an extent which explains the rise in output in Cornwall; on the other hand the incentive could have come, if the anti-quaries are to be believed, from tinners being squeezed by the Jews who, in turn were being pressed by the King. Bannister[39] seems to argue for both possibilities when he quotes from John's Charter which, among other concessions, granted that the tinners should be, "liberi et quieti de placitis *nativorum*." By the use of italics his implication is that despite allowing tinners immunity from lawsuits brought by those belonging to a place (nativi) the Charter did not permit immunity from legal proceedings initiated by others, that is to say Jews. In the context of the document, however, it is beyond doubt that the King is referring to the perennial problem of local landowners seeking to restrain the widespread and disruptive activities of the tinners. In such a context Jews were neither likely to be landowners in Cornwall nor to be exempted from recognising tinners' immunities if they were. As a final point on this vexed matter it may be significant that for the period from de Wrotham's reforms until 1220 the farm of tin revenues fell into abeyance and tinners paid dues directly to royal treasurers.[40] In this way John's Jewish tax farmers may be laid to the rest which Jewish mine slaves richly deserve.

While it is apparent that there is a paucity of straightforward evidence connecting mediaeval Anglo-Jewry and Cornish tin there does exist a fascinating, enigmatic artefact which is as difficult to explain as it is to ignore. In 1853 a hollow tin alloy figurine was discovered three metres below ground surface on Bodwen Moor in the parish of Lanlivery and, curiously enough, near a *Jews' House*. Fourteen point two centimetres high and four point four kilos in weight, the piece portrays a bearded man sitting on a high backed chair; until it was lost in a fire during the late nineteenth century CE there was a crown on the head. Scattered over the cloak or gown of the figure are four incised Hebrew letters: *Nun, Resh, Shin* and *Mem*. Unfortunately no certain archaeological context for the 'tin king' exists but it has been tentatively dated as early as the thirteenth century CE which would place it in the reign of John or possibly the earldom of Richard (1227-1272 CE), younger brother of Henry III (1216-1272 CE). Though hardly flattering, the representation has been claimed to be that of Richard, King of the Romans and Earl of Cornwall. It has also been proposed that the object was made by a Cornish tinner and given as a pledge to a Jew, that it was used in pseudo-Cabbalistic rites or even that it served as a mediaeval chess piece.[41] Nicholas de Lange has made a number of very cautious suggestions about the figurine. He distinguishes three Hebrew characters: *nun, resh* and *shin*. These could form the initials, but without the characteristic 'son of', which would designate a Jew. They might be some kind of code or, with numerical values attaching to Hebrew letters, a chronogram. In the latter case, the total yielded would be 550; as a year this sum would represent 1789-90 in Christian reckoning, although de Lange is at pains to point out that these particular characters would not normally be employed in such a calculation. He concludes on the subject of the significance of the letters that perhaps the most attractive solution is a haphazard choice made for exotic effect. As to the nature of the letters, de Lange tentatively proposes that the formality of the incised characters with their serifs is unlike the more typical cursive style of Jews versed in Hebrew script from an early age. Although a Jewish hand cannot be ruled out, it is conceivable that Christian masons, who are known to have carved Hebrew tombstones in the late eighteenth and nineteenth centuries, their names inscribed in some cases at the base of head-stones in the Jewish cemeteries in Penryn and Penzance, would be familiar with formal and ornamental Hebrew lettering and might have had a hand in that appearing on the tin king. Needless to say the date of the lettering has no bearing on the date of the object.

During the regency years of Henry III's reign and the ascendancy of William the Marshal and Hubert de Burgh, English Jewry recovered from the depredations of John, being once again offered the protection of the Crown. Henry, who assumed power in 1232, was a lavish patron of the arts with a passion for building. At home he faced civil war with the barons but he was also concerned to pursue an elaborate foreign policy to outflank the Capetians by recovering the lost dominions in France and the Hohenstaufen by promoting the candidacy of his brother, Richard, for the Holy Roman Empire. Given a combination of high ambition and financial ineptitude on the King's part it was not long before the Jews were once again suffering repeated tallages.

Both Richard and his son, Edmund, were resident Earls of Cornwall and were indeed the last to be so, but their presence was rare. As far as can be known, Richard spent three or four brief periods of months rather than years in the County.[42] Advanced by Henry to the lands and revenues of the earldom in 1225 CE then to the title two years later, Richard was evidently an able man and a more competent financial administrator than his older brother. Twice in his life, in 1255 CE and around 1270 CE, Richard was granted the Jews of England as a pledge against loans he had made to the King. His concerns for his revenues from the stannaries and his moderation in dealings with the Jews[43] suggest a degree of humanity tempered by an awareness of economic self-interest. It may be that the mortgaging of English Jewry to Earl Richard is the origin of the later belief that enslaved Jews were compelled to work in the tin mines. Jews were, after all, *servi camerae regis*, but *servi* in the feudal context is better translated as 'vassals' of the royal chamber rather than slaves. They would have been of greater profit to Richard in the role of financiers whose bonds would provide a sound basis for amercement.

Already in 1237 CE Jews had been mulcted of three thousand marks so that Richard could go on crusade to the Holy Land, but twenty years later his election as King of the Romans, followed by years of sterile efforts among the German states to give meaning to this title, also necessitated large sums of money. Unfortunately evidence for a close association between Jewry and Cornish tin is not sufficient to claim that it was through their efforts in the County that Richard was able to further his imperial ambition. By the thirteenth century CE there were sources of credit other than the Jews, for instance the first initiatives towards the Hanseatic League took place in Lübeck and Hamburg early in the century. "....Quite contrary to popular tradition about the Jews, it was the Hansa which, in Henry III's time, came to dominate commerce in tin. By the time Richard actively bent himself towards his Earldom the two German towns had an agent in Falmouth."[44] On the other hand this is not necessarily to say that the Hansa's mercantile interest in tin extended to the extraction process. Quickening of commerce had brought a diminishing of conscience on the point of usury so, with resort to convenient, obscuring fictions, wealthy Christians became moneylenders and suffered no qualms over dealing in Jewish bonds.[45] Around 1235 CE the Cahorsin merchants appeared in England from Italy as moneylenders in all but name and were followed by Florentines, Venetians and Genoans.

Questions as to the financial operations of the Jews in Cornwall are made more difficult by the fact that, up to the time of the Expulsion in 1290 CE there was no *archa* in the County. These triple-locked chests, containing copies of all Jewish financial transactions and administered by both Jewish and Christian chirographers, had been instituted shortly after the anti-semitic outrages of 1190 CE primarily to protect the Crown's pecuniary interest. *Archae* do not presuppose a large community; indeed there is an instance of one being set up for a single Jew,[46] so their non-existence in Cornwall casts into doubt any notions of a permanent Jewish presence there in the thirteenth century CE. An *archa* was established in Exeter early in the century but even here the Jewish community was neither large nor conspicuously wealthy, facts which may have limited their role in tin across the river Tamar. In 1221 CE seventeen Jewish centres paid a total fine of £564 towards a dowry for Henry III's sister, Joan. Exeter's share in this amounted to £8 5s. 8d and was met by six people. Two years later fifteen Exonian Jews contributed £78 10s. 6d to a tallage on English Jewry totalling £1,680. These were the prosperous years of England's Jews, but under Henry III's personal rule they were brought low by his repeated demands. By 1276 there seem to have been only two Jews actively engaged in money-lending in Exeter; numbers rose again but by 1290 the community was reduced to a solitary Jewess, Comitissa.[47]

Despite question marks over a settled community in Cornwall and the activities of Jews in neighbouring Devon in connection with advancing funds against Cornish tin, a Jewish financial presence cannot be discounted. In discussing "a few prominent consortia" of Jews dealing with the Treasury in the twelfth century, Roth[48] mentions Isaac fil' Rabbi of London and Aaron of Lincoln: "Between the two of them English Jewry was organised to a certain extent into a great co-operative banking association spread throughout the country." Evidently this level of financial organisation in respect of advances to the Crown could have been translated into the stannaries and have worked at a remove with little in the way of a Jewish presence in the far south-west. Aaron's example provides some insight into what might have happened. When he died in 1186 CE his property escheated to the Crown and his loans of £20,000 were so extensive and complicated that it took a specially created Exchequer department nearly five years to sort them out. "He [had] advanced money to private individuals on corn, armour, estates, and houses, acquiring thus important interests in twenty five counties (especially in the east and the south-east of England), in at least seventeen of which he maintained his agents." While there is no record of the existence of a Jewish community in Rutland, Aaron's agents had evidently been at work there since we have a full account of eleven bonds from that county and ample evidence from elsewhere that Aaron counted Jews among his clients (probably for re-lending) as well as Christians.[49]

In the next century Aaron of York occupied a similar position as the greatest financier among Anglo-Jewry with some twenty co-religionists serving as his local agents.[50] Another powerful figure in Henry III's reign was the dubious character, Abraham of Berkhamsted, with debtors in half the counties of England, who, charged with profaning an image of the Virgin and the murder of his wife, was saved by the intervention of Richard of Cornwall. If the *archae* accounts were preserved in full we might know the details about any outlays by Jews in Cornwall, but when there was unrest, during the Barons' Wars of Henry III's reign, for instance, the chests were sought out so that records of indebtedness could be destroyed. Complementary evidence on the administrative side is also lacking: "This confused history of grants, resumptions and re-grants from 1231 to 1300, taken in connection with the passing of Cornwall into the hands of Richard Plantagenet and his son Edmund, helps to explain why no entries for the Cornish stannaries appear in the Pipe Rolls for the above mentioned period, and why in consequence, the fiscal history at this point remains obscure."[51]

After the *Statutum de Judeismo*, banning loans at interest, was promulgated at Winchester in 1275 Anglo-Jewry was brought to ruin by further tallages. There were also accusations and two hundred and ninety three hangings for coin clipping, a hardening of Papal attitudes and the revival of ritual murder allegations, all of which served further to undermine the very existence of Jews in England. Preparatory to one of these late tallages a writ was issued in 1283 CE to twenty sheriffs with Jews under their jurisdiction to inspect the chests of the chirographers of the Jews whose transactions would have had a life extending well past the date of the *Statutum*. Interestingly, the sheriff of Cornwall received a writ and it is a pertinent question as to why he did if there were no Jews in his county.[52] If they were in Cornwall, however, it was not for much longer. On July 18th 1290, Edward I, by an act in Council, took the final step of expelling the Jews on pain of death.

Hints of an elusive, unverifiable Jewish presence, perhaps in the form of Christian converts, remained. In the *White Book of Cornwall*, the Council Book of the Duchy, during the time of Edward, the Black Prince, we read of John Jeu's suit to end his wardship exercised by the royal Duke so as to inherit his father's, Sir Roger Jeu's, Cornish estate. In the twelfth century CE variants of Jew appeared as *Giw, Gyu, lu, luw* and *leu*. From Edward III's reign the name is rendered *le Jeu*.[53] A little later in 1358, "Abraham, a tinner, complains of imprisonment by the Sheriff for working to the nuisance of the haven of Fowey. He states that he employs three hundred men in the stream works of Brodhok, Tremorwode, Greystone, and Dosmery. The prince issues his mandate to W. de Spridlington, one of his auditors, to enquire into the facts." Although the name is highly suggestive it is impossible to be certain that Abraham the tinner was not a Christian; there is the example of Abraham of Felmingham, who received a land grant from Henry II, and his son Isaac who, from other references and contrary to appearances, were not Jews.[54] Similarly the Jeu's surname may have been a variant spelling of *lew*, which is *yew* in Cornish, and a name mentioned in that form by Carew in a list of those who had married into the Arundell family.[55]

Figures for post-Expulsion tin production have been used in order to suggest a causal relationship between the events of 1290 and a declining output,[56] but this argument can only be adduced by selective presentation of statistics. Between 1291 and 1296 it is true that production was more than halved in the Devon stannary. While there are no year on year figures available for Cornish output until 1301, when, in round figures, five hundred and sixty thousand weight were produced in contrast with Devon's fifty three, thereafter Cornwall shows annual increase until the era of the Black Death, 1348-1351. Although there are gaps in Devon's statistics it is abundantly clear that not only was the eastern stannary in relative decline against the west's performance but that it was also in absolute decline, a process which had probably begun in the thirteenth century CE but was marked in the fourteenth and owed more to geological circumstances than the absence of Jewish capital.[57]

Eventually, after an interval of nearly three hundred years, we do encounter a Jew of some solidity in the historical record of Cornwall and its metals. A German-Jewish mining engineer, Joachim Ganz, or Gaunze, was invited by the Company for the Mines Royal to advise on copper extraction. He went to Keswick to inspect copper mines and produced a report on the treatment of copper ores, then he is said to have spent three years in Cornwall from 1586 to 1589 CE, until he was expelled after drawing too much unfavourable attention to his religious beliefs.[58] Between the Expulsion of 1290 and these events not even a tenuous connection linked the Jews with Cornwall through the mediaeval and early modern periods. Even before 1290 any association seems to have been highly uncertain, probably impermanent and only insecurely recorded. Philology, folklore, tradition, historical documentation — none of these provides a satisfactory footing to establish firmly the activities of Jews in Cornwall. All this, as subsequent chapters will testify, would change with the Resettlement under Cromwell during the Interregnum and especially in the eighteenth century CE when Cornwall experienced a great age of tin production.

---

[1] *Herodotus: The Histories* (London: Penguin, 1972), Book 3, 115, p.250.

[2] Cited by J. Hatcher (1973, p.12).

[3] Hyamson (1908, p. 1).

[4] Samuel Bochart, *Geographica Sacra, 1640*: cited by R. D. Penhallurick in *Tin in Antiquity* (London: Institute of Metals, 1986), p.125.

[5] Borlase (1758, reprinted 1970, p.164).

[6] Edmonds (1862, p.8). For a traditional account of the Phoenicians and British tin, see R. Hunt (1884, chapter 1). R. D. Penhallurick, *op. cit.*, presents a well reasoned dissenting view on any such connection.

[7] See the first chapter by Keith Pearce which explains this further.

[8] Padel (1988, p.119).

[9] Susser (1993, p. 2).

[10] Padel, *op. cit.*, p.125.

[11] For a description of a *Jew's House*, see G. R. Lewis (1908, reprinted 1965, p. 16).

[12] Russell (1971, p.64).

[13] Padel (1985, p.244, 250 & 276).

[14] *History of the Worthies of England* (1811, p.195).

[15] Deane & Shaw (1975, p. 63).
[16] Quoted by J. Bannister (1867, p. 329. ft.14).
[17] Josephus, *History of the Jewish Wars*, (trans. Whiston. London, 1811) vol IV, book VI, chapter IX.2. p.267.
[18] Roth (1964, p.1)
[19] Quoted by Bannister, *op. cit.*, p.329.
[20] Susser (1993, p.4).
[21] Lewis, *op. cit.*, p.33.
[22] Carew (1602, reprinted 1953, p.89).
[23] Polwhele (1808, p. 8). See also part 2 of this chapter.
[24] Cited by C. S. Gilbert (1817, p.208).
[25] *op. cit.*, p.8.
[26] Deane and Shaw, *op. cit.*, p.69.
[27] Henderson (1935, p.202).
[28] Stow (1631), fol.103, 2, 8.
[29] Susser, *op. cit.*, p. 5.
[30] G. R. Lewis (1906, p.546).
[31] *Op. cit.*, p.326.
[32] Camden (1695 ed, p.19). See also an abstract from Camden's Britannia with editorial addenda, editor and date uncertain but probably eighteenth century CE, pp.10-11, in the Cornish Studies Library, Redruth.
[33] Borlase (1970, *op. cit.*, pp.163-184).
[34] Polwhele, *op. cit.*, pp.7-8.
[35] C. S. Gilbert, *op.cit.*, p.208.
[36] Hals - entry for St Ewe in Gilbert (1838, vol. 1, p.414).
[37] Carew, *op. cit.*, p.99. Bannister (1867, p. 327) and his antagonist, Professor Max Müller, appear to have misread Carew.
[38] G. R. Lewis (1906, p.540).
[39] *Op. cit.*, p. 327.
[40] G. R. Lewis (1908, pp.134-136).
[41] Susser, *op. cit.*, p.24. A personal communication from Nicholas de Lange, Reader in Hebrew and Jewish Studies at the University of Cambridge (1999).
[42] Denholm-Young (1947, pp.38, 39, 40, 72-3).
[43] Roth, *op. cit.*, p.57.
[44] V. Newall in Deane and Shaw, *op. cit.*, p.20.
[45] H. G. Richardson (1960, chapters 3 & 4).
[46] Susser, *op. cit.*, p.7.
[47] Susser, *op. cit.*, pp.7-9
[48] Roth (1964, p.14-15).
[49] Richardson (1960, pp.68-69).
[50] Roth, *op. cit.*, p.49.
[51] Lewis (1908, p.136).
[52] Transactions of the Jewish Historical Society of England, iv, 1899, cited by Susser (1993, p. 24).
[53] C.f. Onions' *Oxford Dictionary of English Etymology* & Lysons (1814, p.646).
[54] Roth, *op. cit.*, n. p. 15.
[55] Carew, *op. cit.*, 1602 ed. fol. 145.
[56] Susser, *op. cit.*, p.5.
[57] Figures from G. R. Lewis, *op. cit.*, App. J, p.252.
[58] Susser, *op. cit.*, p.25.

PART ONE
Jews in Cornish Tradition and Folklore

———✦◆✦———

CHAPTER 1
Jews, Mining and the Death of Cornish

Cornwall was the first region of the Celtic countries of the British Isles to be conquered and annexed by the English, and so the first to lose its indigenous language. The term *Celtic* carries no racial or anthropological significance, and covers peoples spread across Europe and beyond, and, in particular, within Britain and Ireland, who comprise separate nations identifiable by their history and linguistic distinctiveness. The notion of a Celtic nation is, therefore, purely topographical, historical and cultural.[59] Whilst there are many factors that contribute to a sense of national or regional consciousness, such as a shared history, territory, and religion, it is arguable that a collective and distinctive language is a major, if not the fundamental defining factor in nationalistic awareness. The decay and loss of a shared language, therefore, whilst it may not destroy this feeling altogether, can seriously and irreparably undermine, weaken and modify it, and, at the very least create a climate of cultural and linguistic confusion and of historical misunderstanding. The death of Cornish was clearly a tragedy from a cultural perspective, but it did not annihilate a sense of distinctiveness amongst the Cornish people. It was not only linguistic change which affected Cornwall's history. Other forces also served to weaken a fixed and continuous pattern of cultural identity. Celtic religion and Celtic Christianity gave way to Catholicism, and this was superseded by the English Reformation, and later the spread of Methodism and other nonconformist churches. Economic and industrial change, emigration and advances in travel and communication were also powerful influences which produced a degree of cultural dislocation and fracture. Despite all of this, Cornwall's pre-Christian Celtic past and its subsequent history continued to be rediscovered, celebrated and reinterpreted by each succeeding generation. Cornwall's history, archaeology and language have been the subject of extensive scholarly scrutiny, and its Celtic heritage has not been overlooked in the process.[60] The enterprise of rediscovery and reassessment has grown in scope and self-confidence, but it is not without its difficulties. In the attempt to unearth such ancient roots, the persistence and wealth of Cornish traditions and heritage requires patient and sensitive evaluation. Where historical fracture has occurred, the evaluative process is all the more difficult, in that whilst subsequent traditions may conserve the past, they can also distort it, or even invent spurious historical elements. The separation of historical certainty from invention is not a problem that can be avoided or easily resolved. I turn initially to a brief examination those aspects of language which have some bearing on the issue of the presence of Jews in Cornwall's ancient history.

The Celtic languages reside within the Indo-European group of languages that stretch from Ireland to parts of Asia, and include Latin, Greek, Sanskrit, English, French, Spanish and Russian. Linguistically, as "first cousins" the ancient Cornish were closer to the Welsh and Bretons, than they were to their "second cousins" the Irish, Scots and Manx.[61] The latter languages, Manx, Irish and Scottish Gaelic, are known as *Goidelic Celtic*, and the former, Welsh, Breton and Cornish as *Brythonic* ("British") *Celtic*. The Brythonic languages differ from the Goidelic. The former are simpler in form than the latter. Brythonic Celtic has also substituted *P* for the Goidelic *Q*, so that the former is also known as "P" Celtic and the latter as "Q" Celtic (in which the sound *q* was later given by the letter *c*). A different and contrasting vocabulary also distinguishes the two branches of Celtic.[62] As far as Cornish is concerned its content, forms and scope will have been subject to the same historical modification, variation, development and decay that would be expected of any language with ancient roots.

Ancient (Old) Cornish (*c*.800-1250) is largely a matter of conjecture, but from the 9th and 10th centuries, glimpses of the language can be had from glosses and annotations in Cornish of Latin texts. From the 12th century a manuscript known as the *Vocabularium Cornicum* has survived that has been said to represent "almost the whole body of Old Cornish".[63] As its Latin title suggests, this manuscript is a vocabulary of ancient Cornish nouns and some adjectives, covering about seven pages, together with a calendar and lives of Cornish (and Welsh) saints, giving almost a thousand words in all. Of Medieval (Middle) Cornish (*c*. 1250-1550) it has been observed that "Between us and it there is the barrier of a lost language and perhaps a lost literature as well" (Henry Jenner) and the extent to which Cornish was used in the Medieval period is uncertain and a matter of speculation (Elliott-Binns), although fragmentary details can be identified from 14th century mottos found on the coats of arms of some of the landed gentry. In the same period, Cornish was used in church services.[64] However, the first complete sentence in Cornish comes from a 15th century manuscript from Penryn, where Middle Cornish miracle plays also seem to have been written, the most ambitious, the cycle of three dramas in verse, known as the *Ordinalia*, having originated there somewhere between 1275 to 1450. In Cornwall, these dramas, that have been described by A. L. Rowse as giving "an extraordinary insight into the mental life of the people, moulded as it largely was by the Catholic faith" were performed in the village amphitheatre, the *plen an gwary*, one of which still exists in St. Just-in-Penwith (near Land's End) where the plays are still performed today. Cornish scripts of some these plays have survived, and represent the main body of early Cornish literature, although they have been regarded as having no great literary merit. The tone of these plays is more sober than their English equivalents, although some elements are coarse, which does not preclude a comic element in their performance. Sadly, Cornish literature effectively ended with these plays, and, unlike Breton, did not proceed to become an expanding printed literature, a factor that was to prove fatal to the survival of the Cornish language.

During the Tudor period evidence of the Cornish language becomes more plentiful. The thirty years that marked the Wars of the Roses ended with the landing of Henry Tudor in Wales in 1485. During his exile in Brittany, he was supported by the Cornish, and after his victory over Richard III (with an army largely comprised of Welshmen) at the battle of Bosworth, he rewarded his Welsh and Cornish supporters with positions of high office at his English court. This led to many adopting the English language, the process of Anglicisation being essential to further advancement. The opening up of the sea routes to the Americas and elsewhere gave many Cornishmen a cosmopolitan experience of how small their county was, and how much of the seas were dominated by England.[65] The Tudors, however, began to impose laws and taxes upon Cornwall, which resulted in widespread discontent within the County and prompted the two rebellions of 1497,[66] and in particular the insurrection of an army of some 15,000 Cornish rebels, led by Myghal Josep (Michael Joseph, who, despite his surname, was not a Jew) from St. Keverne, on the Lizard peninsula, a blacksmith named after his trade *An Gof*. Together with Thomas Flamank, a lawyer of Bodmin, he proceeded to march from St. Keverne to London, collecting numerous supporters on the way, to protest against Henry VII's taxes, which were levied to finance the King's campaign against the Scots. The Cornish rebels were inadequately armed and were easily defeated by the King's army. Both of the Cornish leaders were hung, drawn and quartered at Tyburn as traitors. Despite the king's subsequent leniency towards the Cornish, the rebellion and further discontent marked the county out as a significant threat, and led to a determination that it should no longer enjoy a separate status or language.

Cornish may have been widely spoken at the start of the Reformation in 1533, but with the introduction of the first Act of Uniformity in 1549, which introduced the use of English in all church services, and the Prayer Book Rebellion of the same year, which was a cultural and social disaster for Cornwall, the reprisals seeing the effective elimination of around 10% of the population, the decline of Late Cornish was accelerated, and the period "saw the start of an attack on the language that was to be responsible for its eventual extinction".[67] Indeed, as a result, even the etymological roots of the modern name *Cornwall* (in Cornish *Kernow*) are difficult to identify with absolute certainty: "Kernow may have derived from the name of a tribe (such as the Cornavi – a Celtic tribal name that occurs frequently – the Celts of Caithness and Chester were also called Cornavi as well as Carnabi). The name could also derive from 'the Rock land', 'land of Carns' or 'the Horn Shaped land'. Whatever its original meaning, to the Celtic word *Kern* or *Corn*, the Saxons fixed the name 'weahlas' (foreigners) and arrived at Kearn or Corn-weahlas or Cornwall"[68], hence "the horn or promontory of foreigners". It has also been suggested that the Germanic word *walh*, used variously of both Celtic and Latin speakers, and which also came to refer to serfs and slaves, has survived in the names of Wales and Cornwall, and of other places such as Walton, Walsall, Walcot and Walthamstow.[69]

It has often been assumed that the decline of the Cornish language can be taken as a parallel to the pattern of diminution of usage and westward retreat in the face of the invasion of English that afflicted Gaelic in Ireland, Gallic in Scotland and Cymric in Wales. This, however, is misleading, in that these other indigenous Celtic languages declined but did not disappear altogether, a factor that has been of great benefit to their modern revival, in that where vernacular spoken and written practice continued, it retained a tradition and memory of the language's vocabulary, grammar and pronunciation, from which meaning and etymological understanding could be derived with relative ease. Cornish, however, was extinguished, and English became the *lingua franca* of a whole population which was eventually estranged from the origins and meaning of the few vestigial traces of the forms that survived in place-names and a few common expressions. Understanding of these was sought in phonetic adaptation or conversion to English, or to figurative and imaginative interpolation of the terms, usually of a spurious and misbegotten nature, and this, as a consequence, was productive of a fanciful body of folklore and mythology, which included notions that the Cornish were racially descended from Phoenicians, Spaniards, and, as a Lost Tribe of Israel, from Jews, all of whom were said to have been resident in Cornwall in ancient times. The adoption of terms from this folklore, and of personal and topographical names from Biblical sources also played an important role in the transition from Cornish to English, and especially after the Cornish language had effectively been replaced by English, and ceased to be spoken or understood.

From such tendencies, Venetia Newall has identified a range of expressions and terms that came to birth in Cornish usage, and which seemed to link Jews with the tin-mines, such as *Jew's House*, for disused smelting-works, *Jew's Bowels*, for the fragments of tin found in them, *Jew's Tin*, for larger specimens in block form, and *Jew's Leavings*, for the tin refuse from the mines. Redundant or decayed tin-workings were originally known as *Jew's Offcasts*, and later as *Jew's Workings* or *Jew's Whidn*. West Country expressions, that may have extended to Cornwall, were *Jew's Eye*, for something regarded as very valuable, and the offensive term *To Jew*, meaning "to cheat". In Cornwall (and Devon) the term *Jew's Ear* applied to a type of red fungus, *Jew's Fish* for halibut, supposedly a favourite Jewish delicacy, and *Jew's Beetle* for one of its kind that expelled a reddish or pink fluid, most likely linked with the ancient and infamous "blood libel" that Jews drank, and then spit out the blood of Christian infants they had murdered as a form of evil sacrifice. This *Jew's Beetle* was said to be held in the hand while the person called out "Jew, Jew, spit blood!", most likely as a form of anti-Semitic curse, or as a charm to ward off the evil that was assumed to proceed from the Jews.[70] A hooded crow, which was felt to have had an ugly appearance, which fed off the local crops, and, most likely, homed in on the edible produce at the Thursday market, was known as a *Market Jew Crow*. Of these various expressions, and those that link Jews to tin-mining, it can be shown that they have been the product of linguistic confusion, misinterpretation and erroneous projection, whilst others can be linked with the prevalence of prejudicial anti-Semitic assumptions and beliefs.

Other strands in Cornish mythology and folklore have sought with enthusiasm and through other means to link the Cornish, as a lost tribe of Israel, with near eastern and semitic peoples. The Phoenicians and, later, Jesus in childhood days, Joseph of Arimathea, and St. Paul have featured in legends of visits to Cornwall. It has been suggested that the specifically Christian elements in these legends may have originated in the preaching of merchants and soldiers converted on the continent, who then arrived in Cornwall, but that as tales "they belong more to devotional speculation than to historical fact. There is no evidence which actually contradicts them, so no doubt they will continue to have a hold on the minds of some."[71] Clearly, the longevity and persistence of a tradition does not in itself increase or confirm its historical legitimacy. Nor does its survival eliminate the possibility that it has not at some point in the past been the product of pure invention. The value and allure of a tradition resides not in its veracity but in its utility, and in the particular purpose it serves, and has served within a given culture and context. In the case of the linkage between the Phoenicians, Joseph of Arimathea and Cornish tin, both academic historical and archaeological writings from the 19th century and also Masonic traditions have played their part. In these instances various Biblical accounts have tended to be read literally as accurate and reliable contemporaneous records. The Biblical descriptions of the artefacts of ancient Canaan and the building of the first Temple by Solomon are two cases in point. Today, Biblical historians and archaeologists view these ancient accounts as having been written many centuries after the events they portray, and, commonly used by the rulers of the ancient empires as rhetorical and hyperbolic devices to promote a grandiose but exaggerated image of their regal power and accomplishment. Hence the vast dimensions and embellishments of Solomon's Temple, and the multitude of his horses and captives. In these traditions, however, the considerable amounts of tin and copper needed to fashion the bronze (an alloy of copper and zinc) and brass (an alloy of copper and tin) could allegedly only be found in ancient Cornwall, where it is taken as axiomatic that the mines could readily supply such a demand, originally to Phoenician traders, and later to Jewish merchants, such as Joseph of Arimathaea. Even if such vast amounts of tin were not produced by the Cornish mines, it is likely that the mines of West Cornwall were a major factor in the Bronze Age economies of Western Europe.

The travels of Pytheas (as described by Diodorus Siculus in the first century CE) have sometimes been cited as evidence of the production and exportation of Cornish tin to the Continent some three centuries before the Roman period. Pytheas was a Greek from Marseille who came to Britain around 330CE. There is no original record from Pytheas himself, but "only broken quotations, cited by geographers who knew less of Britain than we do, and were so much more sure that Pytheas was a liar".[72] Pytheas claimed to have seen both the extraction and smelting of Cornish tin, apparently on the Land's End peninsula, and also its overland transportation by pack-animal to the coast, where, at low tide, it was transferred into wagons to the island of *Ictis* (sometimes taken to be Saint Michael's Mount, opposite the town of Marazion). From the island the cargo was taken over by continental merchants and sent by ship to the west Gallic coast, thence to Narbo (Narbonne) and then overland to the mouth of the Rhone and the markets of the Mediterranean.[73] This story has taken hold in Cornish tradition, but even if the account of Pytheas is to be believed, there is no confirmation that any of the tinners who produced the metal, or the pack-horse drivers who transported it, or the merchants who shipped it were Jews. Cicero (106-43 BCE), it seems in ignorance, believed that in Britain there was "not so much as a scruple of silver". However, the geographer Scarbo (writing *c*.14-38 CE) did refer briefly to the earlier and contemporaneous exportation of tin and other exports from Britain, and we could well infer that the tin was from Cornwall. The Romans were also aware of the open-cast mining of lead in Britain. Indeed, the Romans imported to the Continent many resources from there, including corn, cattle, hides and hunting dogs, mainly from Sussex, Kent and Essex. The locations where metals were also extracted can also be inferred from archaeological artefacts: silver from the lead deposits of the Mendips or the Derbyshire Peak District, gold and iron from Wales (and also iron from the Weald), and copper from Caernarvonshire. Of other materials, coal was mined in various locations, shale marble from Purbeck, jet from Whitby, and pearls, the latter most likely from Scotland. The potteries of the Nene and the New Forest were also exploited, as were various tileries throughout the country. Stone was obtained from Bath, slate from Yorkshire, and salt from Worcestershire and Cheshire.[74] Apart from the Cornish traditions relating to tin, in none of these places have Jews been closely linked with the production of the materials.

The legend of Joseph of Arimathea is of medieval origin, and its sole intrinsic historical value lies in its indication of Glastonbury as an early centre of Christianity. Writers on Masonic tradition (and others) have taken Joseph of Arimathaea of the first century CE to have been James Justus, the younger brother of Jesus. Joseph sometimes appears as an overseer of mining estates and as an established and wealthy merchant in the tin trade between Cornwall and the Mediterranean.[75] In some later tales, Joseph of Arimathaea is said to have come to Cornwall himself to trade in tin, purportedly landing at Marazion and establishing there a settlement of Jews, from whose language its name is said to have derived. Attempts have also been made to forge earlier, etymological links between King Solomon (who is said to have sent his ships specifically to Cornwall for tin to use in the construction of his Temple, and in particular for its two main pillars, named *Jachin* and Boaz[76]), and King Hiram of Tyre, and Marazion. Those kings sailed their trading vessels from the Red Sea port of *Ezion Geber*. It has been held that *geber* is a form of the Phoenician *ghizbon* or *ghazbon*, words which may refer to a tin-market, and that variant spellings have absorbed *ezion* into *Marazion*, and *ghazbon* into *Marghasbian*, one form of the name of the place, which, it has been asserted, was a tin-market.[77] Solomon's and Hiram's *Tarshish* fleets sailed widely, and would have docked and traded at many places throughout the Mediterranean, and, possibly, beyond. If they traded for tin or other metals at known market-ports, it could be expected that numerous other places would have been similarly named either by them, or by the inhabitants, but no such evidence exists. The theory rests, therefore, upon an exceptional example, which, in any case, remains unsubstantiated. Clearly, the names of Marazion can be found in numerous variants,[78] and some of these may, indeed, bear some superficial phonetic resemblance (not to the Cornish for "Jew") but to the English *Jew*, but even so, etymology can suggest meanings entirely lacking in any semitic connotation or origin. Cornish families with the name *Iew*, have been taken as Jewish, in that the name is also found in the form of *le Jeu*. The latter, of course, is not the French form of "Jew", which is *Juif*, and a French variant would suggest an amusement or game. Neither is it to be derived from the Latin for "Jew", that is *Judaeus*. If *le Jeu* is to be derived from French, it could be understood as an abbreviation of *le Jeune*, that is "the Younger". The examples of Roger and John le Jeu, who are not known to have been Jewish, have been mentioned in relation to a suit to expedite possession of an estate during the time of Edward the Black Prince (1330-1376) the elder son of Edward III (1312-1377). Despite the fact that variant spellings and forms for "Jew" existed in England from the twelfth century, including *le Jeu* and *le Jew*, it has been mentioned that *Jeu* could be construed as a variant of the Cornish *Iew*, for *Yew*, rather than as "Jew" which, in Cornish, would have been *Yed(th)owen*. An Adam le Jew was rector of St. Ervan (inland from Trevose Head and south of Padstow) in 1309, and despite the assumption (from his name) that he was Jewish and the claim that he "clearly changed his religion",[79] this is by no means self-evident, and there is no corroboration of Jewish descent or conversion on his part. Likewise, the Nicholas le Jeu of St. Winnow (south of Lostwithiel) of 1321,[80] is not known to have been Jewish.

It has also been assumed that Cornish families with Hebrew forenames, and especially surnames, even if practising Christians, must have been descended from an ancient Cornish population of Jews, and that "some of them also having unmistakeably Jewish features is equally certain". It has even been supposed that "Physiognomists also have discovered others, besides these", including the "sturdy fishermen of Mount's Bay" who have been claimed as "having the sharply marked features….of this peculiar people", being "known to be true Cornishmen" having taken names (*Tre, Ros, Pol, Lan, Caer* and *Pen*) "being territorial or local, just as was the case with Isaac of York, Reuben of Tadcaster, &c.".[81] The analogy between these putative "hidden Jews" and those of explicit Jewish ancestry identifying themselves by their place of residence is thoroughly spurious. Despite the fact that the comparison lacks credibility, the case has been pressed further in the ludicrous claim that a 19th century Mayor of Truro, Thomas Solomon, "is an instance in point. He has a fine type of Jewish features". The Mayor, and even a medical practitioner are pressed into the service of the argument, and the former writes that "I never heard of my ancestors being of Hebrew extraction: nothing was known of such to my father. I have always considered one of my daughters to resemble in features the chosen people, and many intelligent Israelites have been of the same opinion. Some years ago, Dr. Jago, of this town, told me he could distinctly see traces of what had been Jewish in the gait of one of my brothers".[82] Leaving aside the outlandish, and to modern sensibilities, the irrational and prejudicial nature of these stereotypical musings, the prevalence of many Hebrew names amongst the Cornish can be explained simply by the fact that over many generations Cornish Gentile families (amongst whom there was a high degree of illiteracy) adopted names directly from the only substantial source familiar to them as read in church, the Bible. This was a practice widespread long before the 18th century, by which time it had become both fashionable and commonplace, and was to continue into the 19th century. These Hebrew names came over time to be used amongst many of the Cornish as both forenames (Christian names) and surnames, and even in Cornish families with non-Hebrew surnames, the use of Hebrew forenames was a traditional feature. Even though some preaching and reading in church may have taken place in Cornish from early times, the fact that the Bible did not exist in a complete Cornish translation was also of great significance, hastening and enabling the process of Anglicisation still further. Despite the fact that the incipient timing, speed and extent of the process will always be a matter of historical debate, its progress was inexorable and Cornwall (or at least parts of it) may have been effectively Anglicised much earlier than has been supposed. One result was a reduction in the use of Cornish nomenclature, or the adaptation of Cornish names towards English forms, and the adoption of Biblical names was part of this phenomenon. It is striking that derivative Hebrew names appear most frequently among the Gentile population from the late 17th and early 18th centuries at precisely the time when Cornish was in rapid and terminal decline. That the use of Hebrew names was derivative rather than direct can be seen in that it is mainly the Biblical (Anglicised) forms of these names which appear rather than their original Hebrew forms: for example, *Solomon* and *Jacob* rather than *Schlomo* and *Yakov*. A writer as late as Arthur Symons (1865-1945) claimed in 1918, in relation to Erisey, near Ruan Minor that "If you hear people talking to one another in the lane, you will notice that they speak and reply in phrases out of the Bible, as in a language of which they can catch every allusion".[83]

Strands of Cornish tradition have held that some of the indigenous Cornish families have assimilated not only Breton, but also Spanish-Iberian blood. It is of special interest that Iberian and Jewish elements in these traditions inter-connect and over-lap to a degree, in that a few families of Cornish descent have claimed or suspected descent from Iberian Jews who had converted to Catholicism, either as *Conversos*, abandoning Jewish practice altogether and embracing Christianity, or as *Marranos*, outwardly observing Catholicism, but secretly maintaining Jewish practice and tradition. When the Jews were expelled from Spain in 1492, and from Portugal in 1496, many fled to the Netherlands, and also to England, where some are known to have settled in the South-West. The proximity of both France and the Iberian peninsula to Cornwall, and the accessibility of those countries by sea might well suggest that such traditions are plausible. Certainly, Iberian commercial links did exist, and in 1582, after a particularly plentiful harvest, corn was exported from Cornwall to Spain. However, oral traditions have often attached themselves, in parasitic fashion, to unusual or dramatic historical events to which, in reality, they bear little if any actual relation. Cornish-Iberian descent has been linked both to the Spanish Armada, defeated in 1588, and to the Spanish Raid on Mount's Bay of 1595. Spanish prisoners, including Jewish sailors from the Armada may have settled in the South-West at this time, but any putative linkage to the later Raid is most unlikely. The sacking and burning of Mousehole, Paul, Newlyn and Penzance by the crew of four Spanish ships on 23rd to 25th July 1595 has been extensively documented in Cornish history. The Spanish landed some 400 men during the attacks, and they left as suddenly as they had arrived, aided in their departure by an auspicious change in the direction of the winds. None of the perpetrators are known to have remained or settled on Cornish soil. The later arrival of Iberian visitors to Cornwall aboard merchant and passenger vessels is well-documented in shipping records, but the settlement of such visitors cannot be established so readily from contemporary sources, at least before the first Census of 1841. The development of the Packet Boat Service from 1689 led to numerous weekly sailings between Falmouth and Gibraltar, Cadiz, Corunna and Lisbon, as well as the Indies, South America and Mexico. If Iberian Jews came to Cornwall, it was most likely to have been during this later period. Earlier than this, a few isolated cases can be glimpsed. One of these may have been the marriage of a Lazarus (or Lazari) Burno (or Bueno) to a Tampsina Peter in Gulval, near Penzance on 7th November 1619. Their daughters, Sara, Johanna and Juliana were also baptised in the same church, and their family descendants may have lived in the village for the next 300 years. It seems likely that the groom was Spanish, but this is not certain, and it is not clear that he was a Marrano. Burno and Bueno (likely variants) are Sephardic Marrano names which appear in the records of the Bevis Marks Synagogue in London. However, both names, especially Bueno, were common among the general Iberian non-Jewish population. In addition, it would seem that the surname Perrow or Perro came to be attached to this Gulval family. Perro is Spanish for "dog", and it has been considered possible by his descendants that this name may have reflected Lazarus Burno's occupation as a Spanish sailor, or "sea-dog". Whilst Bueno might well imply a Spanish connection, the variant spelling as Lazari Burno could equally suggest an Italian origin. Moreover, Perro and Perrow are names found among the indigenous Cornish. The place-name Polperro has been interpreted as some reference to a beach, cove, safe haven or, possibly, a harbour. Perro has also been linked to a container or "crock", or a cauldron, which encloses its contents safely. Various Hebrew forenames, adapted or otherwise, have always been common among Iberian non-Jews, and thus Lazarus remains ambiguous, especially as it too was found among the Cornish population both at this time, and later. The Burno case serves at least to illustrate the difficulties involved in evaluating these issues of ethnicity, religious affiliation and background.[83a]

Parish baptismal, marriage and burial records, headstones in both church and municipal cemeteries, as well as later census records from 1841 reveal many hundreds of Cornish Christians with Hebrew names, where there is no independent evidence that family members were of Jewish descent. A few examples may serve to illustrate this phenomenon. On 20th October 1765 at St. Anthony, Lazarus (a variant of Eleazar) Steel Roberts, son of Abraham and Rachel Roberts, was baptised, and on 20th February 1786, Lazarus Solomon, son of Margery Busset (the father is not identified), was baptised in Penzance.[83b] Parish registers from 1607-1837 record over 150 church marriages where the groom's forename was *Moses,* but where both groom and bride bore standard Cornish surnames. Nor does *Moses* as a surname necessarily indicate a Jew. For example, the 1861 Census lists *Moses* 39 times as a surname, and none of those listed are known to have been Jews. The Cornish surname *Moyse* is often assumed to indicate Jewish descent, and although it may be derived from the Hebrew *Moyshe,* it is a very old Cornish surname, and like *Moses,* was very common amongst Christians. Likewise, the names *Moyse* and *Moise* have always been common in France among Jews and Gentiles alike, and the prevalence of the name in Brittany would suggest that Breton variants may have played a part in the name's dissemination in Cornwall, where, as in England, other forms occur such as *Moyce* and *Moyes.* The Cornish surname *Boase* (which is found among Jews) might suggest a derivation from the Biblical *Boaz,* but in Cornwall the earliest spellings were as *Bores,* from *bos-res,* the dwelling (or those who dwelt) by the ford. The fact that the name first appears in the Camborne Parish Register as early as 1599, suggests its indigenous origins. The surname came to be largely concentrated in West Cornwall: Henry Boase (1763-1827) was Mayor of Penzance in 1816, and a Francis Boase occupied that office in the town on seven occasions between 1859 and 1880. Another J. J. A. Boase was a banker in Penzance,[84] and a *Boaze* traded as a butcher in the High Street, Falmouth in 1815.[85] None of those people are known to have been of Jewish descent.

The Cornish name *Abel*, found mostly in South East Cornwall, has obvious Biblical connections, but it is derived from *a-bel*, far-off. *Jose* may appear similar to *Joseph* (a surname found amongst Cornish Christians) but it is in fact a Romano-Celtic surname borrowed at the time of the Roman occupation from the Latin *Joseus*, and it was common in Cornwall as early as the 14th century. The surname *Lavin*, found mainly in Mid Cornwall, but also in Falmouth and Penzance in the 18th and 19th centuries, may be reminiscent of the Jewish names *Levin* and *Levy*, but it is likely to be derived from *leven* (smooth or even) as in the small town of *Porthleven*, smooth or calm harbour, and named after the stream that runs into it. The name *Leven* or *Levan*, as in the Church of the parish of St. Levan, outside Penzance, can be linked to the Saint *Silvanus* (1327), *Selevan* (1545) and *Sent Levane* (1569). It is derived from the Latin for *Solomon*, a Saint *Salamun* being a Cornish saint in the 10th century, and also in Brittany. In fact, *Levy* itself does appear occasionally as a name amongst the Cornish, as does *Lewin*, which can be understood from the Cornish *lewern* (foxes) and sometimes as *Lewarne*. The surname *Leah* (a Hebrew woman's name) derives from *lyha*, least or smallest, and this occurs in various historical records amongst Cornish Christians. Likewise, the names *Voss, Vos, Vose* and *Vosper* are found amongst Cornish Gentiles. A Jew, Nathan Vos was the last to be buried in the Penryn cemetery, and a man with this surname, is said to have been an Jewish immigrant refugee in North Cornwall in the 15th century. However, the derivation of these Cornish names found for example as *Trevossow, Trevose* and *Vose*, is explicable from the root *fos*, a ditch, embankment or rampart.[86]

The surnames *Jacobs* and *Symons* also appear frequently in Cornish Christian families, as do *Solomon, Joseph, Marks, Abraham* and *Isaacs*. A *Solomon* family of Central-North Cornwall can be traced through several generations. From the 1800s onwards they were settled in Bodmin and Lostwithiel. If they were of Jewish origin, they are only known to have been Christian, with family burials in church-yards in the Lostwithiel area, and others (of a likely related family) at St. Winnow. Christian *Solomon* families were also widespread in Truro as shoemakers, painters, cabinet makers, clerks, greengrocers, maltsters, cordwainers, masons, lead miners, sailors and farmers. *Isaac* men in Truro were masons, painters, scriveners, cord-wainers and gardeners. *Marks* appears amongst copper miners in the Camborne and Redruth areas, and as tin miners in the St. Ives area. In Penzance, a *Marks* family (some of whom were blind) were basket weavers. *Jacobs* and *Abraham* men in St. Ives were fishermen. Such names (and such occupations) do not, therefore, confirm Jewish identity, and they were also widespread among the travelling Romany families, as they have been amongst Afro-Caribbean families. The trades mentioned, above, were not commonly associated with Jews, and this can usually serve to exclude Jewish identity.

What parish and census records also reveal is that, as today, female Hebrew forenames (Rachel, Rebecca, Esther, Naomi, Sarah etc.) were very common

amongst Cornish Christians, as were Hebrew male forenames that were characteristic in Jewish usage, such as Abraham, Moses, Isaac, Jacob, Benjamin, Samuel,
Solomon, Ezekiel, and Aaron. Some less commonly used by Jews, such as *Jeremiah,
Elisha* and *Zephaniah* also were used as "Christian" names. However, more colourful Biblical names, which crucially would not have been used either at all, or at
least exceptionally by Jews, were also adopted by Christians from the Bible. *Maher-
shalhazbaz* (Isaiah Ch. 8) appears in St. Agnes (abbreviated to *Shalal* or *Lal*),
Melchizidech (Genesis 14:18, Psalm 110:4, and from the New Testament, Hebrews
Ch. 7) in Penzance and St. Just-in-Penwith, and *Barzillai* (2 Samuel 19:27, 19:32 &
21:8, 1 Kings 2:7, Ezra 2:61 and Nehemiah 7:63) in Penzance. Sometimes, the forename and trade might both suggest Jewish identity, but other records indicate they
belonged to Christians. Examples of these would be *Zephaniah Job*, General
Merchant (Truro 1861), *Barzillai Major*, Tailor (Penzance 1871) and *Ephraim Symons*,
Draper (Truro 1861). That this adoptive process was not driven by some instinctual
Jewish preference (as proponents of Jewish descent amongst the Cornish might
suppose) is indicated by the fact that names were also taken from the New Testament and from Greek mythology: *Zaccheus Isaac*, Labourer (Truro 1861) and
Hercules Solomon, Farmer (Truro 1871).

Apart from names, culinary elements and products have been linked with
Semitic peoples. The production of clotted cream (which is not an exclusively
Cornish practice, although it is most common in the West Country) has sometimes
been cited as a possible link with the Near East on the dubious grounds that it is
also found in Syria: "When you find clotted cream both in Syria and Cornwall,
there may still be something in the tradition".[87] But one of the most fanciful strands
in the speculative attempts to link Cornwall to Semitic peoples has been the
contention that the spice, saffron, derived from the saffron crocus (*crocus sativus*),
used as an expensive dye in the production of linens and as an additive to cooking,
was introduced to Cornwall in ancient times by a semitic people, sometimes identified as the Phoenicians. One form of this tradition maintains, quite erroneously,
that saffron is only found in the indigenous recipes of Cornwall (saffron cake) and
the semitic areas of the eastern Mediterranean. The historical and topographical
realities are entirely at odds with these notions.

The cultivation and use of saffron dye for linen, silks and cooking was widespread across Asia from Bronze Age Crete to Assyria in the 7th century BCE. Its
name can be derived from the Arabic *zafaran* (from *asfar*, yellow) or from the
Persian *zaparan*. It appears as the Latin *safranum*, the Old French *safran*, the Italian
zafferano, and the Spanish *azafran*. Although saffron is named (only once) in the
Hebrew Bible "with all the chief spices"[88], it was traded widely across the ancient
Mediterranean from Egypt, the regions of north Africa, Tyre, Sidon, Rhodes and
elsewhere. Its use was also widespread in India and China. The Romans brought
it to Southern Gaul, and the spread of Islamic civilization reintroduced it to Spain,
France and Italy. Venice and Genoa became, and remained major ports for its
importation and distribution. Soon after the 14th century CE. its cultivation spread
throughout England, but especially in Norfolk, Suffolk and Essex. In the latter
county, the town of Saffron Walden became England's main centre for the production and distribution of saffron. Later, imports of other spices such as chocolate,

coffee, tea and vanilla, led to a decline in English cultivation and usage of saffron, although it continued on a lesser scale. Saffron was also grown in London, in what is today the borough of Camden, on an estate which lay on either side of Saffron Hill, which stretches from Clerkenwell to Holborn. It was traded by the River Thames, and exported from the East India Dock (*est.* 1803) opposite Greenwich. The Dock was especially famed for the vast quantities of tea processed there and street names around the former dock reflect the various spices that were traded from it: Clove Crescent, Nutmeg Lane, Coriander Avenue, Oregano Drive, Rosemary Drive and Saffron Avenue. Saffron continued to be grown and exported from Italy, Spain, Southern France and Greece, and it was used not only in the traditional recipes of Iran (Persia), Arabic countries and the regions of Palestine and Lebanon, but also in Turkey, Greece, North Africa and the Iberian peninsula. The saffron of the La Mancha region of Spain was renowned and celebrated for its distinctive qualities, and was to become a common ingredient of *paella*, and other dishes.

Cornish tradition has maintained that the introduction of saffron to Cornwall from ancient semitic sources is explicable in that the great cost of the spice made it a suitable currency with which to barter for Cornish tin. The common use to which Cornwall's impoverished population would want to put this expensive saffron would hardly have merited the exchange of ore. Moreover, saffron, by the very nature of the plant from which it is extracted, has always been cultivated in various forms of purity, and hence was priced accordingly, from the relatively inexpensive upwards. Today there are five, laboratory based grades, but the widespread and extensive use of saffron throughout the ancient world, and its availability and common use, attests to its variable market value. It was also traded in adulterated forms, in the ancient world, especially from Iran, the "saffron" robes of Buddhist monks being dyed with tumeric, a spice which the Tamils have also used for over 2000 years. In the Middle Ages in Europe it was mixed with tumeric, or even, as tumeric, sold as saffron. A saffron substitute, "safflower", became known as "Portuguese saffron", or *acafrao*. The putative semitic connection between saffron and Cornish tin remains entirely speculative and unproven, and, moreover, the earliest time from which saffron was used in Cornwall as an additive in cooking its now traditional cake (the spice being restricted largely this culinary item) is unknown. However, the much later arrival of cheap saffron aboard maritime trading vessels into the Cornish ports from the ports of London, East Anglia, Spain, and the wider Mediterranean is entirely credible, and this feature of Cornwall's traditional commercial life intensified during the period of the Packet Boats (1689-1851), together with the development of superior overland routes across England and Europe. It would have been from these plentiful sources that saffron was imported into the County, through its major ports, dotted along its southerly coast, directly connected to those in south and east England, and facing those of eastern France, Portugal and northern Spain. The fact that 19th century census records for Falmouth give such street names as *Saffron Court* and *Saffron Meadow* would suggest that this Cornish port was the main conduit for such importation from the Iberian peninsula, London's East India Dock and elsewhere *via* the Packet Boats and other merchant vessels, and, even local cultivation may have taken place. An ancient Jewish, or at least semitic link with Cornwall's saffron has, therefore, never been established, and, in any event, the tradition remains superfluous to an explanation of the introduction of saffron into the County.

The Phoenicians have played a consistent role in linking the Levant with Cornwall. Writing in 1895 of the need for tin in Canaan in the Bronze age, and allowing that the mines of Cyprus could have "yielded an abundance of copper" and that with the Malayan Peninsula "there are no traces of any commercial intercourse so far to the East", the distinguished archaeologist and philologist, A. H. Sayce wrote: "it is possible that there may be truth after all in the old belief, that the Phoenicians obtained their tin from the isles of Britain" and "it would seem we must look to Cornwall for the source of the tin". The writer is guarded, however, and does not, because he cannot, cite sources which might confirm the idea. It is noticeable that he does not refer to any Biblical texts as support. He was writing at a time when archaeological and Biblical scholarship had developed a more critical view of the issue, and he adds that even if such trade with Cornwall had occurred it "would probably have been overland, like the amber trade from the Baltic" (to such places as Lachish).[89] In fact there is no conclusive archaeological or documentary proof for the notion of trading links between the Phoenicians and Cornwall, and even evidence for later Mediterranean contacts in the late Bronze and Early Iron Ages is modest. What evidence there is points to trade with Greeks from a period after Carthage had lost control of the straits of Gibraltar. The Phoenician connection was first suggested by Camden, and the confusion and conflation of this tradition with the Jews was most likely the result of Camden's view that the Jews controlled and operated the stannaries under King John. In 1870, Max Muller, by applying philological argument was to discredit the Cornish tradition of Jewish tin-mining under King John, and, despite the reservations of Sayce, by the twentieth century at least, historians and archaeologists have viewed the Cornish Phoenician and Jewish traditions as entirely spurious. In his seminal work of 1931, *The Archaeology of Cornwall and Scilly*, H. O'Neill Hencken provided a detailed survey of the problems in assessing Mediterranean contacts, and "the Jewish tradition is not regarded by that author as worthy even of demolition".[90]

In 1832, a workman, John Lawry, who was taking down an old stone-built hedge in the garden of the vicarage of St. Just, some miles west of Penzance, began to dig out a trench, and came across what seemed to be the remains of a much earlier burned structure. Near it he found the statuette of a small bronze bull, which archaeological authorities at the time readily claimed to be of Phoenician origin. Whether this identification was based on sound criteria and reasoning, or on the standard assumption at that time (reflected by Sayce) that Phoenicians did indeed visit West Cornwall, is unclear. The discovery itself, and the subsequent *imprimatur* bestowed on the bull by eminent archaeologists in the 19th century, seemed at the time to confirm the Phoenician connection, and served to reinforce and further encourage the popular espousal of that tradition. However, it was not long before the putative Phoenician origin of the item was disputed by other authorities who, variously, assigned to it Egyptian, Greek, and Roman origin, and bulls, in miniature, figurine form, are not unknown from these ancient cultures. Eventually, opinion began to settle around the notion that the bull of St. Just was, in fact, an "Apis bull",[91] worshipped in, and only in ancient Egypt in the area of

Memphis, as a herald of the god, Ptah, and described by the Greek historian, Herodotus (*c.* 485-425 BCE) as the bull-calf of a cow which is never able to have another, having been rendered sterile by the application of lightning from the heavens. The Apis bull, sacrificed and uncovered in mass burial sites and represented in huge sarcophagi, appears to have been the only deity represented solely as an animal, and another manifestation of the Pharaoh, in the form of the god Osiris, as a symbol of strength and fertility. Egyptologists have been so confident of the identification of the St. Just bull as an Apis bull, that it has been assigned to the late Egyptian period, and to the years from around 747 to 323 BCE., but, in contrast, it has also been allocated to the later Roman period. Other bronze objects and, in particular, Roman coins have been found around the St. Just area and across Penwith.[92] Whether this can be said to be in any sense a definitive or convincing judgement which would link West Cornwall to ancient Egypt, or even to Egyptian visitors in ancient times, is open to debate and interpretation. Like the Lanlivery-Bodwen figurine, it remains possible that, ancient or otherwise, the provenance of the St. Just bull may be purely local, the product of a Cornish fabricant. It is not known for certain if a local fertility cult in the area around St. Just flourished in ancient times, or if this bull was itself a symbol of religious significance. This is, of course, conceivable, but it remains a matter of speculation. It is equally plausible that the figurine was at some time of purely agricultural significance, a good luck talisman, perhaps, believed to promote the fertility of the land and animals. To the possessor, it could also have been a signifier of social status and success within the community of local herdsmen. However, even if it proves to be an ancient artefact, it is not axiomatic that it was brought to West Cornwall in ancient times by foreign visitors. What cannot be excluded is the possibility that it was acquired in more modern times, in the Near East, or even in London, by an enthusiastic collector or amateur archaeologist, who, in view of the location where it was found, could well have been a former incumbent minister of the church (as William Borlase of Ludgvan was a collector of mineralogical specimens, in the 18th century). In any event, bulls, no doubt, were a common sight on the moors of West Cornwall from ancient times, as they are in its fields today.

The Phoenicians, or the people of the ancient lands of Lebanon, Syria and Palestine have, however, been readily employed in the service of the traditions surrounding ancient Cornish mining. Masonic writers have been far less reticent than Sayce in their espousal of this tradition, treating it as historical fact: "it is known that the Phoenicians operated a tin mine in Cornwall, a mine which is still yielding tin to this day."[93] The title of the *Levant* mine, it is said, attests to this semitic connection. Clearly the name itself, in the absence of further substantiating evidence, is insufficient to perform this service, and rather than confirming the tradition, the name Levant simply (and merely) *reflects* it. That these traditions should have been kept alive by the Cornish miners themselves is perhaps not surprising, in that miners (and mariners) comprised a significant proportion of the membership of Masonic Lodges in the 19th century and beyond, especially in West Cornwall. These same men and their families were also members of the many Methodist Chapels which dotted the towns, villages and countryside, and in this context the Old Testament (which contained the story of Solomon and his Temple and his merchant fleets) was read and studied. Cornish mines today, some of which have become museums and tourist attractions, have mentioned the Phoenicians in their promotional literature as if the link was indeed an historical fact. However, the linkage in Cornish tradition between an ancient Jewish presence and Cornwall's tin industry and smelting houses remains unproven and misconceived.

In his paper "Jews Houses"[94], Cecil Roth did not focus exclusively, or even primarily on the Cornish *Jews (smelting) Houses*, but surveyed various sites and buildings in this country and elsewhere (not all of which are strictly "houses" as such, but which he refers to by this term) as putative ancient Jewish landmarks with Jewish nomenclature, having been linked, hypothetically, with Jews. Of the identifiable sites he lists *The Jewry Hall* (Leicester), *Market Jew* (South West Cornwall), *Jews' Mount* (Oxford), *The Jews' Hall* (Winchelsea), *The Jew Gate* (Silver Street, Newcastle), *The Jews' Meadow* (Horsham), *The Jews' House* (Lincoln) and *The Jewry* (Martley, Worcestershire). He goes on to list four "unidentifiable sites...no longer identifiable on the ground but known from historical records". It would be reasonable to assume that his use of "identifiable" can be taken to refer to the original construction in its entirety, and would not exclude previous or subsequent archaeological work at the sites, and his assertion that they are "known from historical records" could include those merely mentioned in these sources. The sites in question are *The Jews Way* (Bury St. Edmunds), *The Jews' Houses* (Southampton), *The Jews' Tower* (Winchester) and *Jews' Tin* and *Jews' Houses* in Cornwall (although, in fact, there has been some minimal identifiable evidence of some of these). There are several *Jews' Houses* that may date from as early as the 12th or even 11th century. It is likely that two of these can be located in Lincoln: one in the High Street, its date being uncertain, and the other on Steep Hill which has been associated with the name of Aaron of Lincoln who died in 1187. Moyse Hall at Bury St. Edmund's (from which the Jews were expelled in 1190) has been known locally as the Jews' Synagogue, and it seems that this building lacked windows at ground floor level, a feature which may have encouraged speculation that Jews using it required privacy and security. These three buildings possess some Norman features. The "Musick House" in Norwich has also been linked with Jews in local tradition, but remains uncertain. Jews were present in Oxford at this time, and were associated with its University, although any connection between them and the Jews' Mount is uncertain. There were also Jews in Cambridge during the thirteenth century. When the Isle of Ely was captured by some barons in 1266, and following a precedent set by King John, they set about victimising both the Prior of Barnwell and capturing the richer Jews for ransom. Henry III, no doubt with a view to securing such sources of revenue for his own treasury, ordered that "no one, under penalty of death or torture, should molest the Jews in Cambridge".[95]

With reference to Continental sites, Roth notes that "In France, there are many place-names embodying the word Juif, or something like it", such as *Villejuif* (near Paris), *Baigneux-les-Juifs* (Cote d'Or) and *La Roche aux Juifs* (Orleans), and that "Similarly there are in Germany many place-names like *Judenberg* or *Judendorf* etc.". Roth does not exclude the possibility that Jews may have formed communities in some of these Continental places, especially Germany. He further gives the example of *Zydaczow* (Poland) and in Greece *Hebraeokastron* (Jews' Castle, on the island of Kythnos, Thermia in the Cyclades), *Evraeonisi* (Jews' Island, in the Saronic Gulf) and *Ovriokastro* (Ebraeokastro, Jews' Town, near Marathon, the ancient Rhamus). Although Jews did live in some of the places of Angevin England, such as Lincoln, Oxford, Bury St. Edmund's and Winchester, Roth maintains that no conclusive evidence exists of an early and contemporaneous Jewish presence in most of these places and that the origins of these topographical features, and in some cases large structures, were unknown. They were ascribed to the Jews for aetiological reasons to confer some ancient mythical origin upon unusual constructions where the identity of the makers remained a mystery and their exact historical context in the distant past had been lost to memory.

Roth points out that the 12th century Arab geographer, Edrisi, called the city of Tarragona in Spain, "a city of Jews"[96] and comments thus: "as far as we know the Jewish settlement there was never of exceptional importance nor large enough in proportion to the total population at any given time to justify this description." Further, Benjamin of Tudela, a younger contemporary of Edrisi, visited Tarragona and did not refer to Jews at all but says that Tarragona "was built by the giant Greeks", which Roth takes to refer to its massive fortification walls which so distinguish the city: "Edrisi's phrase 'a city of the Jews' is the equivalent of Benjamin's 'built by the giant Greeks', both expressions....loosely corresponding to the term 'Cyclopaean'....to describe massive structures of great or even mysterious antiquity."[97] He points out that the *size* of the structures is not the key to the ascriptive process, however, and concludes: "in the Greek islands, the term *Hebraeokastron* was 'applied in contempt by Greek peasants to *any* ancient building whatsoever erected by strangers':[98] this may now be amended to 'any ancient building of unknown origin' ". [99] Susser quotes the first part of the passage above but then omits its crucial conclusion.[100] Thus, without addressing Roth's contention that *any* building could be so ascribed, Susser declines to apply this same explanation to the Cornish *Jews' smelting-Houses* precisely because they *were* small (3ft. high) rather than large structures. Even so, this could involve a misapplication of the term *Jews House* to the smelting-*furnace or oven*, which would have been about 3ft. high instead of its application to the entire structure of the original building, the smelting-*house*, in which it was situated. Moreover, the great number of these buildings, their mysterious origin and unusual structure would have impressed the onlookers as much as their size and could lead to a similar attributive process, especially at a time when the smelting-houses were the only striking constructions to be seen.

The furnaces themselves took different froms. Some were inverted cones of hard clay about 3ft. broad at the top and 3ft. deep. A bellows stoked the furnace in the lower part and molten tin was discharged from a small aperture at the front. Other furnaces were made of granite, and dome-shaped, and one, most likely exceptional, smelting-furnace consisted of a bronze cauldron resting on a large bed of charcoal.[101] At least five *Jews Houses* have been identified in West Penwith, at St. Just (Ballowal), Ludgvan (Marazion Marshes), Madron (Trereife), Paul (Castallack) and Sancreed (Goldherring). At Ludgvan, the structure was of stone, containing a bronze vessel, tin slag, charcoal, and ashes. At Madron, the structure was of clay, and contained a tin ingot. The Paul structure was located near a *Fogou*, completely or partly underground structures, which may also have occurred in an above-ground form.[102] Samples of *Jews House Tin* have also been found in the St. Just area (Portheras and Botallack), Madron (Bosiliack), and Sancreed (Goldherring).[103] The scale of the smelting-houses, none of which survived intact into the early 19th century, also seem to have been underestimated.

In the Annual Report to the Royal Institution of Cornwall,[104] a record from Francis Rodd describes the finding of a stone smelting-ladle and two granite troughs in the 1830s in North Cornwall, on the north-east borders of Bodmin Moor, at Berriow, near Trebartha, in the parish of Northill, south-west of Launceston. The site was "about fifty yards from the River Lynher, which flows through a deep valley at the foot of the Caradon, Cheesewring, and Kilmar range of hills, and near upon the line of junction of the granite and slate", and it was underneath the ruins of an old building (formerly a cottage), known locally as the *Jews House*.[105] The ruin contained two granite "troughs", the larger being some 4ft in length, over 2½ ft wide and almost 1½ ft high, and the smaller about a third of these measurements. The moulds formed in the substance of the blocks were in quadrangular or oblong shape, and had been chiselled with care, presumably to accommodate the molten metal. Of the two moulds, one lay higher, or above the other. The lower, or bottom cavity was "considerably smaller than the upper part "resembling the modern blocks of tin". The ladle itself, which may have been "used as a crucible, or more probably, for dipping into the larger reservoirs of melted metal", was of an uniden-tifiable stone, but it was "lighter than that from the Pollaphant quarry", and it did not "exhibit the brown spots which characterise that particular kind of stone… (which) bears the action of fire very well". (A cover, or crucible made of Pollaphant stone had been found previously with a *celt mould* from Altarnun, north-west of Trebartha). The original mason who built the cottage on the site of the smelting-house confirmed that the space on which the ladle and the troughs lay on a level space "like the floor of a house", and that they had been covered over by "a heap of loose stones overgrown with grass and moss". The blocks of granite appeared to be "unhewn, and of their natural shape and size", and the loose stones had "once formed the end walls of this *Jews House*...he estimated the weight of ...two blocks...at from 10 to 15 cwt." Clearly these dimensions imply an original construc-tion of significant proportions. Even if the granite-block walls and the solidity of their foundations and their construction served, to some extent, to contain the fierce heat from the furnace, they also suggest, together with the extent of the floor area, a height significantly in excess of 3ft. A building of some height and propor-tion would also be necessary for practical reasons to disperse the transmitted heat and so allow safe access to and around the smelting-furnace. To such sites as these, and in the absence of any firm evidence or memory of their genesis, the Cornish people eventually ascribed mythological titles and origins, amongst which, but not exclusively, was the use of the term *Jews Houses*, and "many old stream works….were commonly attributed to Jews".[106] The particular title *Jews House* is, however, of comparatively late usage and, crucially, is in English, a language which did not displace Cornish as the spoken tongue until the 18th century. Long before that, both in the Celtic and Mediaeval world, language and legend evolved to weave a very different story around these artefacts.

In the 16th century, Thomas Beare,[107] compiled a chronicle of the practices, traditions and lore of the Cornish tinners. Beare was a well-read and educated man, proficient in Latin and French, and with a lucid English style. By the time he came to write his manuscript, in his 70s, he had acquired a lifetime's experience of the working of the Cornish tin industry at first hand. Cornwall was divided into four Stannaries (tin-producing districts), each with its principal (coinage) town where the tin was valued and weighed, with a "coin" or corner being removed by a Stannary Officer for assay and identification. The four Stannaries were: Foweymoor (Bodmin Moor), with its coinage town of Liskeard, Blackmoor (the moorland area north of St. Austell), with its town, Lostwithiel, Tywarnhayle (the St. Agnes area), with its town, Truro, and the combined Stannary of Penwith and Kerrier (in the west of Cornwall) with its town, Helston, later Penzance.[108] As a Bailiff of the Blackmoor Stannary district, Thomas Beare was answerable directly to a Steward who had total jurisdiction over his respective stannary and presided over the itinerant Steward's Court which was held every few weeks. Beare's position and work carried considerable legal significance and implications for the proceedings of the Steward's Court, and he was required to have a sound practical knowledge of all aspects of the tin industry. In his case, however, he had also accumulated a deep knowledge and understanding of the tinners' customs and culture. He administered every aspect of the tinners' work throughout his district, regularly visiting hundreds of sites and every smelting house to oversee the production, registration and quality of all aspects and products of the mining process. Not only had Beare learned the basics of the tinners' skills himself, but he had also studied the historical background of the 13th and 14th centuries, how the stannaries had evolved and developed, and how and by whom they were operated.

Beare recorded in his chronicle that the Cornish referred to *all* non-Cornish people, such as Saxons and Danes as "Jewes" (which, in Cornish, would have been *Yedhewon*, likely pronounced as *Yethewon*). The term, *Jew*, therefore, was not used generically, of people of a specific race, but referred to anyone who was perceived to be an outsider or stranger.

> "Off the working in Tinworkes by the Saxons
> which tinners call Jewes working……
> …..the Saxons being heathen people (when
> they inhabited our Country) were skillfull wor=
> kers of and sercers for black tin……
> As they got their tyn and their blowing houses
> and places hard by their works and so made it / white.
> But what so ever they were either
> Saxons or Danes or any other nations our tin
> workers…..call and terme their
> places by the name of the working of Jewes
> which I cannot by any reason judge them to be trew…."

Even today, the native Cornish may refer to a settler not born in the County or from Cornish stock, or even any visitor, as a stranger, and, especially during the tourist season, as an *emmet*, that is a "swarming insect" or ant, a blight upon the land. This deprecatory usage, even if light-hearted, reflects a powerful conscious-ness of distinction and difference in a remote peninsular outpost that, divided from Devon by the River Tamar, was, until the building of the major bridge that carried Brunel's Great Western Railway to Cornwall in the 1860s, virtually an island. In the quotation above it is significant that the word used by Beare to refer to Corn-wall is *Country* and not *County*. It is not clear, however, if the term *heathen*, as applied to Saxons is intended to mean "not a Christian" or "pre-Christian": whilst religious difference may have carried some connotation in the employment of the word, it is more likely that its general sense was "foreign", with linguistic differ-ence as a key component. Beare's "black tin" was the unrefined crude ore that, after smelting, or "blowing", became "white tin". What is obvious from the passage is that Beare took issue with the popular idea (perpetuated by Carew at the beginning of the next century) that Jews worked the stannaries. Whilst he concluded that the Cornish tinners had learned the techniques of the winning and smelting of tin from outsiders, he was clear that they had not done so from Jews. Some two hundred years before its appearance in Polwhele,[109] Beare makes the case that despite the "manifest" presence of Jews in "our Realme" up to the year of their expulsion (1291),

> "…….I never heard
> nor read that they had libertie to seek & worke
> for tyn because they always had their dwellings
> in great towns and cities…. (and that after 1291)
> ……they were never per=
> mitted to dwell in the Realme that I ever read of"

By a similar process of misapplication and misunderstanding, the Saracens have been attributed with an involvement in Cornish tin-working. The term "Saracen" was applied in the early part of the Common Era to obscure tribal peoples who lived on the borders of Egypt, in the Roman province of Arabia, but who were supposed to be distinguished from Arabs, but without themselves possessing any distinctive national character. They have also been allocated to the Sinai peninsula, and to Mesopotamia. They are mentioned by various ancient writers, including Ptolemy, Pliny and Eusebius. By late mediaeval times, the term "Saracen" had acquired derogatory and negative associations, as uneducated and barbaric idolators. Although still viewed as separate from the Arabs, they were, in fact part of the general flux of Arab culture, but they were not identified with Jews. The name "Saracen" has been erroneously derived from *Sarah*, the wife of Abraham, or from Arabic words either indicating robbers or those from an oriental background. The latter notion was expressly contradicted by Ptolemy, who located Saracens on the Western, and not the Eastern fringes of Roman Arabia. The name has also been derived from the Latin and Greek words *sarissa*, a long lance, which would inflict a deep wound, or from the Cornish *tarad* (*pl. taradion*) a piercer or bore, the name of a mining implement. Because in Cornish it is thought that the sound of consonants was spoken more softly than in English, a *t* or a *d* may become *th* or *s*, hence *tharasion* or *sarassion*. "Attal" (or *Atal*) is thought to be a Cornish word, perhaps linked with the French *attelle,* a splint (*pl.* "splinters"), but also similar to the Welsh *adhail,* refuse or left-over waste material. Hence the Cornish *Atal Sarassion* would refer to the refuse or waste from the bore-holes or diggings from the mining process, but in its later pronunciation became confused with the refuse of the "Saracens", who by then had become in Cornish tradition identified with Jews, hence "Jews Leavings". In the same way that "Jew" in fact referred to any outsider, in Cornish both *sarazin* and *sawsen* came to mean "stranger" (and not specifically to "Jew") the word being related to *sarsen,* as sarsen stones on Salisbury Plain, and also to *sassenach,* the Gaelic for a stranger.[110]

Despite this, and Beare's much earlier position on the issue of the Jews, learned authorities continued to perpetuate the traditions linking Saracens with Jews. Carew (1602) states "The Cornish maintain these works to have been very ancient, and first wrought by the Jews with pickaxes of holm, box, hartshorn; they prove this by the names of those places yet enduring, to wit, *Attall-Sarazin;*[111] in English, the Jews' Offcast". Likewise Camden (1695): "the ancient Britons had worked hard at the mines, but the Saxons and Normans seem to have neglected them for a long time, or to have employed the labour of Arabs or Saracens, for the inhabitants call deserted shafts, *Attal-Sarasin,* i.e. the leavings of the Saracens". Pearce, in his (1725) *Laws and Customs of the Stannaries* continued to repeat the erroneous claim "The Tinners call the antient works by the name of the Working of the Jews, and it is most manifest, that there were Jews inhabiting here until 1291; and this they prove by the names yet enduring, viz. Attall Sarazin, in English, "The Jews Feast", although he adds with some caution "But whether they had liberty to work and search for Tin, does not appear".[112] With Pearce, the leavings of the Saracens have now become the "Jews' Feast". Whether this has been influenced by the writings of William Hals (1655-1737) "known to posterity as one of the least reliable of all writers on Cornwall"[113] is uncertain, but Hals (as quoted by Gilbert in his *Parochial History of Cornwall* of 1838) certainly promoted the notion that, in the time of Henry III, his brother, Richard, forced the Jews as his slaves to labour in the tin-mines, some of which, he claims, became known as *Towle* (corrupted to *Attall*) *Sarasin* or (corrupted still further) to *Saracen,* the refuse or outcast of the Saracens, who were those Jews descended from Sarah and Abraham. He further claimed that other workings were called *Whele Etherson* (from *Edhewon,* that is *Ethewon*) the "Jews' Works", which also were called (in Cornish) "Unbelievers' Works". By these means, and by ignoring both the issue of evidence and the vital role of etymology, the identification of Saracens with Jews has been forged and transferred into popular consciousness.

These writers are far removed from the modern concern for and awareness of the crucial role that credible evidence must play in such extravagant claims. Muller's contempt for the approach followed by these writers in this particular instance, and the damage that such an approach can inflict upon posterity as a "verbal myth" is all too evident: "Here we see how history is made; and if our inquiries led to no other result, they would still be useful as a warning against putting implicit faith in the statements of writers who are separated by several centuries from the events they are relating. Here we have men like Carew and Camden [he excludes Hals] both highly cultivated, learned and conscientious, and yet neither of them hesitating, in a work of historical character, to assert as a fact, what, after making every allowance, can only be called a bold guess.....What is Carew's evidence in support of his statement that the Jews first worked the tin mines in Cornwall? Simply the sayings of the people in Cornwall, who support their sayings by the name given to deserted mines, *Attall Sarazin*.....It is difficult, no doubt, to prove a negative, and to show that no Jews ever worked in the mines of Cornwall. All that can be done, in a case like this, is to show that no one has produced an atom of evidence in support of Mr. Gilbert's opinion". In fact, not only does Gilbert fail to produce evidence that Jews were sent by the Earl of Cornwall to work in the mines, but he ignores a vital document relating to the matter, included in Rymer's Foedera, *"De Judaeis Comiti Cornubiae assignatis pro solutione pecuniaea sibi a Rege debitae"*,[114] which indicated that, far from being made slaves, the Jews were "pawned" or mortgaged to Richard for a number of years, purely for the purpose of extorting taxes from them. Crucially, Gilbert does not acknowledge the testimony of Matthew Paris (1200-1259) the historian and Benedictine monk at the Abbey of St. Albans who was the official chronicler of Henry III. Regarding any further form of enslavement, Paris states: *Comes pepercit iis* – "the Earl spared them".

Richard of Cornwall first appears as a patron of the Jews in 1231, when Abraham of Berkhamsted (with Wallingford, one of Richard's chief places of residence) was shown favour.[115] In 1235 Richard was formally allowed to protect the Jews at Berkhamsted as his own. At this time, Richard was contemplating an expedition against the French (which he began in 1240) and he "asked" the Jews to grant him 3,000 marks, which they did in 1237. Despite the fact that Italian merchants and those of Cahors were to supplant the Jews as bankers, Richard chose to retain the Jews as his chief source of profit and he achieved this without losing their goodwill. Abraham of Berkhamsted continued to be shown favour by Richard, and when he fell out of favour with the Crown, he was not allowed to be seized without the consultation and involvement of the Earl. His chattels were confiscated in 1250, but he was allowed to keep a residue through Richard's influence. When in 1254, Abraham murdered his wife, Floria (tradition has it over a religious matter, but Matthew Paris implies that some sexual indiscretion within Richard's household may have been involved) he was imprisoned in the Tower. His position and power over his fellow-Jews could be seen in that he attempted to bargain his release by betraying the financial secrets of "all the other Jews in England". His unpopularity amongst them, if only for this threat alone, was reflected in their offer to pay Richard 1,000 marks to keep Abraham imprisoned. However, he was eventually granted resolution of his offence by the payment of 700 marks in 1255. It was at this time, in order to pay off his debts, that Henry "sold" all the Jews in England to Richard. Also in 1255, Richard intervened to stop the execution of Jews accused of the ritual murder of Hugh of Lincoln. Eighteen were executed at Christmas 1255, but twenty-two others were released at Richard's instance in May 1256. Abraham was by now known formally as Richard's Jew, and all of the debts owing to him, amounting to £1,800, were collected for Richard's use. On 7th December 1256, Richard had all of the Jews committed to him, and partly through his dealings with them, he amassed a fortune, and came to occupy a unique position in the country's financial arrangements. It was only when Richard was away from England in 1267-68 that Henry and his cousins Edward and Edmund used their influence to bring in a provision *Proviso Judaismi* (January 13th 1269) which placed restrictions on the manner in which debts might be contracted with Jews. These restrictions would not have met with Richard's approval, and are in stark contrast to his favourable treatment of them. From then on his influence in relation to the Jews waned, and another ordinance of July 25th 1271, when Richard was present, forbade Jews to hold any freehold property, and "At a stroke their status was virtually reduced to that of pawnbrokers".[116] Richard's treatment and use of the Jews was, therefore, essentially benign and purely financial. Richard visited Cornwall in 1238, 1240, and 1249, and he later raised an army there (or from there). His interests in and revenues from the Stannaries in Cornwall have been well documented, but there is no evidence of his use of Jews there in any capacity.

In fact, it is Thomas Beare's reference to "black" tin, given earlier, which provides the linguistic key to the smelting-houses becoming "Jews houses": the Cornish for "black" was *dhu,* which in pronunciation could become softened to *djew or djoo.* Hence, the smelting-house where the black *(dhu)* tin was refined into white tin, became *chy-dhu,* "black house". Later, the "black houses" were also taken to have been "Jews houses" because of the phonetic proximity of the Cornish *dhu* to the English *Jew.* Moreover, like the English "black", the Cornish *dhu* could be used metaphorically to represent evil,[117] thus overlaying the term "Jews house" with an anti-Semitic veneer. When the much later English term *Jews Houses* did emerge and find currency, it proved deeply persistent and, retrospectively, it encouraged and reinforced legendary traditions and folklore which became entrenched as historical fact; namely that the Jews had even come to Cornwall in Old Testament times and that later they had been brought over by the Romans in large numbers as slaves, either after the Fall of Jerusalem (70 CE) or the Bar Kochba rising (135 CE). It was said that from those times they were forced to work in the mines, introducing a new an unusual method of smelting, eventually acquiring a monopoly over this aspect of tin-production and the construction of the smelting-houses. In reality, little, if any direct evidence for this exists. There is evidence of contact between the Near East from Greek coin-finds and Graeco-Roman bronze pieces in Dorset and Exeter, the former being mainly from the central Mediterranean, and the latter from Syria. The towns from where the Exeter pieces originated (Antioch, Chalcis, Cyyrhus, Hierapolis, Edessa, Samosata, Zeugma and Singara) had sizeable Jewish populations, and it has been said that there is a "high probability of Jewish participation in this traffic".[118] Whilst no inference can be drawn from this regarding Cornwall, it is clear that Exeter and Dorset may have been the earliest ports where Christianity arrived. A jar with a Chi-Ro symbol, **XP**, with the two letters overlaid (XP being the first two letters of the Greek *CHRistos*) was found at Exeter in 1946, and the earliest such symbols on Cornish Christian tombstones (with a closed loop on the P) date from the fourth century CE, from Northern France,[119] and (with an open loop) from the sixth century, from south of the Garonne, from where they also spread to Ireland. There is little evidence of significant Jewish settlement in Northern France before the sixth century or in the

South West of Gaul before the third or fourth centuries, so Jewish participation remains uncertain.

Exemption grants from service in the Roman army were sometimes issued to Jews, but they may not have been intended to have been permanent and may have been a local privilege. Jews who became Roman citizens are likely to have been liable to be called up for service, either to the legions or the auxilia, but this is not certain, although voluntary enlistment was possible. There was a forced enrolment of the Jews of Rome under Tiberius, but "it applied to freedmen and was an exceptional penalisation, part of a general social purge", and "if there were individual Jews in the legions…most of them would have been irrecognisable behind their Latinised or Hellenised names".[120] Even though Jews were more numerous in the Roman army in the fourth century CE, by 404 CE they were excluded by law from service. Any Roman legions entering Cornwall could have had Jews serving in them, but there is no evidence for this, nor that Jewish soldiers were put to work in or were employed to supervise the Cornish mines. Whilst Jewish coins dating from 42-135 CE have been identified in Derbyshire, London and Yorkshire, only the London coin was an official currency, and whilst these finds might suggest a Jewish presence in those places, "they are more likely to have come to Britain as curiosities or mementos…directly with travellers from Judaea".[121] Clearly, none of this provides confirmation of Jews in Cornwall at this time, even if some Jews were by then present in England.

It has been noted that, much earlier, in 325 BCE the Greek merchant Pytheas claimed to have visited Cornwall and watched the inhabitants work the ore and purify the metal,[122] but he made no mention of the involvement of outsiders of near Eastern or Semitic origin. Indeed, far too much has subsequently been read into the term *Jews' House* and its derivative connotations. The term *Jews House* may conjure and convey ready images of material resemblance, but it bears no meaning which follows as a matter of logical necessity. It is a term of considerable ambiguity allowing a range of equally hypothetical and plausible meanings, none of which is rationally preferable and none of which is verifiable. Conservative exegesis has viewed it as causative and historic: that Jews built, owned and ran the smelting-houses at some time, monopolising the tin-trade. The term *Jews House*, however, could equally refer to an idiosyncratic method of oven-smelting which had come to be used by the isolated Cornish miners themselves and the oddity of which, in time, came to be associated with foreign, Jewish origins. This is a form of causative speculation, not of causative verification. The term Jew, moreover, in a non-pluralistic society and age could refer to anyone who was not a Christian, just as the terms *heathen, stranger* or *Gentile* occur in the Bible to denote anyone, without differentiation, whom is not a Jew. Jew, therefore, could operate as an exclusive term rather than a generic-specific category. In this sense, the *Jews Houses* have become an uncharacteristic and mysterious oddity, an ancient importation of the foreign.

The cultural, religious and social life of Jewish communities in France, Spain and Italy during the Middle Ages, from the 13th to the 16th centuries, has been extensively documented.[123] However, there is no evidence of a Jewish presence in England as a class even in Anglo-Saxon times. Bede and the Old English Chronicles (until 1144) do not refer to any Jew. A few references that do occur elsewhere can be read as later interpolations, uncorroborated details, or as copies from Continental Codes. The Anglo-Saxon economy was based upon guilds (which the Jews could not join) and barter (which gave no scope for usury). Neither do Jews feature before the Norman Conquest. William the Conqueror (1066-1087) is said to have brought Jewish slaves over from Rouen, and Jews from Normandy may have come to England at this time, and, if so, these new English Jews would have been French in language and culture. There are only fragmentary traces of the existence of English Jews under the Norman Kings, and it is only with the accession of Henry II (1154-1189) that references to Jews become more frequent,[124] when their relatively temporary presence (up to about 1206) was a reflection of a financial experiment of the Norman Kings who were restricted by the policy of the Church that condemned usury and capital. The cost of this experiment proved too great, however, and popular anti-Jewish feeling, fuelled by reports of the violence against the Jews upon the capture of Jerusalem in 1099 during the Crusades, led to restrictions being placed upon the English Jews by the Church, so that no Jew could engage in agriculture, trade, or public office, and their sole purpose came to be that of usurers and providers of capital to the smaller barons and monasteries as they sought a change of architecture from wood to stone. Ironically, it was precisely these two classes that became the chief persecutors of the Jews.

The estates of the Jews became those of the King, who fined them for any significant event in their lives: to marry, to be divorced, to travel, to enter a partnership with another Jew, and as a windfall tax upon the heir of a deceased Jew. The English Jews became the King's financial agents, and the King himself was effectively the "sleeping-partner" in all Jewish capital, with a full record of all Jewish business being kept in the King's hands. By 1187, the Jews were reckoned by the Court to have one quarter of the moveable wealth of the kingdom, and the King was able to bring pressure to bear upon the barons through the fact that they were indebted to the Jews. At one time during the reign of Henry II, there was some consideration given to the idea of making the Jews the King's official tax-gatherers, as they were in Spain, but this plan was never put into widespread practice. Instead it was restricted only to certain Jews, whose responsibilities were limited to the collection of revenues, and not to the direct management of commercial and industrial concerns within the counties (such as the operations and production of the Cornish mines). The extract from the Charter of William of Wrotham (c. 1197-8), the *Liber Rubeus* of the Treasury of Richard I,[125] a letter regarding the tin-works, has been set out in the Introduction to this book, and it is often read literally as confirming that Jews can either be identified as the architects of the smelting-houses and as practitioners in the Stannaries, or that they were involved in some technical or administrative way. Elliott-Binns (citing the authority of Carew) claimed that "The Jews certainly had their effect in Cornwall, even if they did not live there, for they took their share in the business side of the tin trade".[126] However, even this is unsubstantiated. When Richard I left England in 1194 to engage in a war in France, the responsibility of government devolved to his Judiciar, Hubert Walter, who did not send a Jewish agent, but William de Wrotham to the West Country to see how much tax could be raised from the tin-mines of Devon and Cornwall to finance the king's war. Wrotham, who was appointed Warden of the Stannaries, found the revenues to be greater in Devon than in Cornwall, but by 1198 he had raised significant sums. Wrotham's expression "neither man or woman, Christian or Jew" has been taken to indicate the presence of Jews in Devon and Cornwall, and although there is independent evidence of Jews in Devon at the time, there is no comparable evidence for Cornwall. Even if Wrotham's expression should taken as referring to a Devon Jewry, it is also open to an entirely different interpretation to a literalistic one. It may, in fact, be a stereotypical legal term which meant 'everybody'. If this was so then no inference can be drawn from the *Liber Rubeus* about medieval Jewish tin-trading in Cornwall (or Devon).[127] In this sense the term *Jew* can be seen to function as part of a comprehensive formula, as an inclusive rather than an exclusive, generic term. In any event, neither the *Liber Rubeus* nor any other source from this period can unequivocally locate a community of Jews in Cornwall, nor identify any individual Jew by name as resident in the County.

The term *Jews Houses* can also be understood from the perspective of prejudice and superstition. It could operate as an antisemitic reference, to the vulgarity of the product, or the crude and irregular construction of the smelting-houses. The unusually fierce, white heat could evoke notions derived from Christian preaching and embedded in Christian consciousness of the recalcitrant Jews burning in Hell. Much later, the eerie subterranean noises deep within the mines (at times indicative of imminent disaster) assume the identity of the goblin-type *Knockers* (or *Knackers*) of Cornish mining legend. They sometimes appear in folklore as separate and distinctive spirits, but they are also linked with the *Bockles* (scallywags), *Buccas* (imps, sometimes ascribed with the powers of poltergeists). The *Smae People,* and *Old Jews' Sperrats,* thus become lumped together with the *Sprig-gans* and "all the underground spirits", in a community of wraiths and spectres.[128] The *Knockers* (or *Nuggies*) of Cornish mythology came to be identified specifically with the tormented spirits of Jewish slaves who were said to have been compelled to work the mines from Roman times for the sin of their race in crucifying Christ[129], a notion repeated on the lips of a Cornish character in Charles Kingsley's *Yeast*. These mischievous, malevolent and vindictive Jewish counterparts to the Cornish Pixies, are also called the *Bucka Dhu*, "Black (or Evil) Spirits".[130] From this term, it is all too obvious that the black (*dhu*) spirits could become *Jew* spirits.They have been characterised as "very ugly beings…withered, dried-up creatures, no bigger, apparently than a young baby… They had big disproportionate heads, with faces like old men, and their limbs were disproportionate and clumsy".[131] That the inconsistent strands which make up these legends were once separate and contradictory can be seen in the incongruous portrayal of the status of these beings as, at one and the same time, both free spirits and slaves. On the one hand they are never heard to work on Saturdays (the Jewish Sabbath) or on any of the Jewish festivals, but on the other, they are compelled to sing carols at Christmas time.[132] In this way, the confusion between mythology, archaeology and age-old anti-Jewish prejudice can be established and reinforced in oral tradition and popular written accounts of the folklore. Charles Henderson linked the word "knocker" to the Anglo-Saxon, "Nicor", a water sprite, or underground fairy, found as early as the poem *Beowulf*, sometimes depicted as a female monster or dragon, which haunts a bottomless pool, without inlet or outlet. Such a pool near Lyminster, in Sussex, was known as the *Knucker*, or *Nucker Hole*, and in the west part of the parish of St. Germans in Cornwall, there was a "wayside holding" named *Narkurs*, pronounced locally as Nackers. In 1621 it was written as *Knackers Hole*, and in 1659 as *Knocker's Hole*. Likewise, the Tithe Apportionment Award for Cardinham parish in 1839, mentions a field at Tupton called *Knocker's Hole*. In Camborne parish is a place named *Knave-go-by*, with a lane in Nancherrow, in St Just-in-Penwith named identically, although the latter appears on a map of 1840 as *Nackaby*. Henderson's view was that the derivation of *Knacker* may well have been the result of the importation of the word *Nicor* "over the Tamar"[132a]. Moreover, that elements of the *Knocker* legends are both late and retrospective, can be seen from their overt anachronistic character, in that they presume an ancient system of underground, deep-shaft mining, which is not known to have existed before relatively modern times: "Throughout the Medieval period, tin-working meant mostly streaming the moors for alluvial tin, and, to a lesser degree, searching for "shode" or eluvial deposits. Digging into the outcrop of mineralised structures (lodes/veins) for the tin ore, although undoubtedly an ancient practice, was not a usual or common method until well into the fifteenth century - As alluvial streaming produced less tin, the tendency to seek out the source lodes increased."[133]

In fact, one of the earliest known references to the word "shaft" is from 1536 (on Roslyn mine, Wendron),[134] and by about the time of Thomas Beare, in the middle of the fifteenth century, lode mining by means of open works (trenching) or by shafts and levels was becoming more common, especially in West Cornwall, although the transition from streaming to subterranean mining continued right up to the twentieth century.[135] The *Knocker* legends, therefore, are synthetic, anti-semitic anachronisms, representing as they do, the spirits of Jewish slaves entrapped deep in the mines from ancient times, when, in fact, mining was worked exclusively on the outcrops at the surface of mineralised deposits, or in shallow pits. Indeed, the popular writers, such as Bottrell, inadvertently reveal the fragility and artifice of the folklore, in that while these spirits are said to remain under-ground for most of the time, occasionally venturing to the surface, "they so rarely make their appearance that we hardly know what they are like." [136] Moreover, these legends are the product of a society rife with superstition and fancy. Dr. John Davy (1790-1868), recounting the recollections of his mother, Grace Davey, when she was a girl (around 1770), says: "The lower class then was extremely ignorant, and all classes were very superstitious; even the belief in witches maintained its ground, and there was an almost unbounded credulity respecting the supernatural and monstrous".[137]

The Knocker legends fall well within this general culture of superstition, which incorporated (along with other parts of Britain and Ireland) Cornish traditions concerning "Changelings". Typically, these were children or young women, usually afflicted with serious physical and mental disabilities or disease, whose handicaps were believed to have resulted from their having been stolen or kidnapped by "fairies (or equivalent creatures)" with a fairy substitute left in their place. These tales were often "set in the distant past, or on the edges of human memory".[137a] From Hals, Bottrell, Hunt, Margaret Courtney and others, it is clear that such stories circulated well into the 19th century, and have been associated with Sennen Cove, near Land's End, the Devon-Cornwall borders, Launceston, Polperro, Breage, near Helston, the parish of St. Allen, north of Truro, and Penzance (the Trevelyan case of 1843). Some stories from Ireland, Wales and Scotland suggest that, to "exorcise" the substitute spirits, changelings were habitually subjected to extreme abuse, cruelty and torture, and some may even have been put to death. Whilst such mistreatment may have been applied to Cornish changelings at some point in the past, with the exception of a case in the parish of Breage (likely from the early 1800s) their abuse is markedly absent from the Cornish traditions.

Whatever the administrative system which operated over the Cornish tin-mines in the 13th century, it is possible but not certain that, both before and after the expulsion of 1291, the Crown chose to exempt selected Jews, and to allow them to be employed as its agents in financial matters. However, it is not axiomatic that if some Jews were thus involved (in numbers impossible to determine) that they would ever have been *present* in Cornwall. In a concise but penetrating analysis, Venetia Newall has traced the sources of the confusion of Jews with worsening exploitation in the Cornish mines. After the Norman Conquest, Cornwall became a Norman Earldom, and King William granted the County to his half-brother, Robert, Count of Mortain. Henry III, son of King John, came to the throne in 1216, and in 1225, he gave Cornwall and its tin mines to his brother, Richard, who was then only 16, but who became Earl of Cornwall from around 1225-7 to 1272, and who also assumed the title of Earl of Poitou.[138] Upon his death, his son, Edmund, acquired the title, until 1299. Both Richard and Edmund took up residence in the County, but only for brief periods. From around 1230, the administrative arrangements for the Stannaries are, in fact, obscure, and documentary sources less plentiful. Richard did not give the Cornish tin industry any serious attention until near the end of his life, in 1265, when he "privatised" metal production to various entrepreneurs as his business managers, including some Jews such as Abraham of Berkhamsted, who he had known for some fifteen years. In 1255, Richard had mortgaged the whole of English Jewry as a human pledge against his debts. However, though the Jews were at Richard's mercy, there is no evidence for the tradition that he put them to work in the Cornish tin mines, nor that he farmed the tin mines out to Jews to manage. Newall: "In fact, Jewish merchants seem to have had little to do with the tin trade. Among others they are mentioned as buying tin in Prague three centuries earlier, but there is no hint that their activity exceeded that of other purchasers, and it need not, incidentally, have been British tin."[139] From this it follows that the tin purchased in Prague need not have come from Cornwall.

In his time, Richard appears to have established centres to which the Cornish miners had to bring the ore for smelting and stamping and to pay taxes to the King on the products. Moreover, Edgar Samuel has observed: "Anyone could mine tin, but all smelting had to be done in designated smelteries, where it was weighed and stamped by the officers of the Stannary, once charges for the smelting had been paid. Only stamped tin could be legally sold. This is typical of medieval estate management. All corn had to be ground in the landlord's mill. All cloth had to be fulled in the landlord's fulling mills. In each case, the owner of the estate charged accordingly (& the) Jews.....were engaged in collecting the revenue from the smelteries, first for the king, and then later in the thirteenth century for the Earl of Cornwall. When Richard of Almain, brother to Henry III was Earl of Cornwall, his Jew, Abraham of Berkhamsted was one of his business managers."[140] Despite the fact that Samuel assumes that the Jews were involved in the collection of revenues from the Stannaries, when it is uncertain, this an excellent account of a feudal-based system, and it also affords a basis for an interpretation quite distinct from that which has often been applied to the *Jews Houses*.

The traditional, uncritical perspective is to be found in Coulthard, complete with Carew's prejudicial interpolation: "It was in the days of Earl Richard that the tin mines of Cornwall came to be developed on a large scale, and they became for him a source of immense wealth…a golden key…to unlock the doors of attainment both in Palestine and Germany. We gather that this Earl was most kindly disposed towards the Jewish race; which assertion lends colour to the statement of Carew that the tin trade of Cornwall in ancient times was largely in the hands of Jews, who grievously exploited the Cornish Tinners".[141] This, however, remains little more than unsubstantiated rhetoric, and neither the officers who regulated the smelting-centres *in situ* nor those who physically collected the revenue (if distinct from the former), nor those who operated the smelting-process at the smelteries were necessarily Jews. The King, or the Earl of Cornwall, owned the smelteries some of which may have become known as *Jews Houses* because *a Jew or Jews*, such as Abraham of Berkhamsted, laid claim (through his agents, who need not themselves have been Jews) to those smelteries and their revenues on behalf of the Earl of Cornwall. Abraham's agent could have been based at Exeter where there was a small, but far from affluent Jewish presence in the 13th century and from where the whole enterprise may have been regulated. Such Jews as Abraham, or his agents, may have run the smelting-houses in an administrative sense on behalf of their owner, although the Stannary's own agents regulated them in practice, in stamping the produce and collecting the revenues. In turn, the Cornish miners would have operated the smelting-process itself. This does not mean, therefore, that there were Jews operating the smelting-houses or indeed that there were any Jews present in Cornwall at the time,[142] but, hypothetically, there could have been an awareness or a belief that the collection of revenue from the mines was ultimately in the hands of Jewish agents appointed by the Crown. It has been mentioned that the crude Lanlivery-Bodwen figurine, the so-called "tin-king", may have represented Richard Earl of Cornwall (or the monarch himself) who laid claim to the tin-mines and their revenues. With its rough, and likely random, Hebrew letters (which do not seem to have any significance in themselves) it could also have been a later anti-semitic representation of the supposedly grotesque Jewish agent or agents who were believed to have controlled and exploited the revenues from the mines. That it was found three metres below the ground, near a former *Jews House* could further suggest a function as a talisman to protect against the "Knockers" or malignant Jewish spirits which were thought to threaten the miners, or those operating the smelting furnace itself. If the object is contemporaneous with the time of Earl Richard, it is far from axiomatic that it was the product of Jewish hands. The Christian priests and scholars of the day were well-versed in Hebrew and other ancient languages, as were their equivalents in the 18th and 19th centuries, and it has been mentioned that the finely-wrought, elaborate and precise Hebrew inscriptions on the headstones in the two Cornish cemeteries were carved by Christian, and not Jewish masons whose names have been preserved on their handiwork.

Borlase, referring to the time of King John, states that "I find the product of tin in this county very inconsiderable, the right of working for tin as yet wholly in the King, the property of tinners precarious and unsettled, and what tin was raised was engrossed and managed by the Jews, to the great regret of the barons and their vassals".[143] Clearly, Borlase understood the production to be in the hands of the Cornish tinners, and its engrossment by "the Jews" to have been the management by his agents of the collection of revenues made directly to the King. In which case, the smelteries were the *"Jews Houses"*, *de facto*, and it is in this sense that they could have been viewed (and possibly named) by the Cornish miners. There is, however, little direct evidence that they were given the English name of *Jews Houses* by the miners at that time. There are linguistic reasons why this is unlikely to have been the case when Cornish, and not English, was the *lingua franca* of Cornwall. The expression *Jews Houses* could, therefore, have been a later, retrospective English appellation at a time when there was an declining use and knowledge of the Cornish language itself, and an increasing historical awareness of how in reality, the feudal system had operated.

It has further been emphasised by Newall that in the thirteenth century a new economic and social system was introduced into the Cornish Stannaries, where it became dominant. It was based on pre-industrial capitalism, and even with some non-working shareholders. Whatever exploitation was suffered by the Cornish miners with the introduction of this new system "its initiation coincided exactly with a period when English Jewry was linked to the Cornish Earldom, an era which culminated in the Jews' notorious expulsion from the country, may help to account for their peculiar place in local tradition [and] the equivocal attitude of Cornish folklore towards the Jews". From this it may well be that the Cornish miners associated their experience of exploitation with the expulsion of the Jews in 1290, for which it was taken that they must have been in some way culpable. There is little doubt that negative attitudes towards the Jews were prevalent in England in the thirteenth century, and these may well have spread to Cornwall. The earliest known caricature of a Jew comes from 1233, and it was drawn in the margin of a public document. It depicts "Isaac of Norwich, a slightly older contemporary of Abraham of Berkhamsted…with his wife and some of his household." Despite the fact that Isaac is known to have been "a notable philanthropist, vicious horned demons are preparing to drag him and his companions down to hell".[144]

There are various references to Jews in early England. Reports of Jews fleeing from persecution in Germany to Spain or France (where *Sepharad* for Spain could be read as *Tsarfath* for France) and England in 810 were made as late as 1575 by Joseph Cohen in a Hebrew document, but Cohen's assertions have not been substantiated. Jews may have appeared in Oxford by 1075, but the Biblical names *Abraham, Isaac* and *Manasses* that occur in the Domesday Book in 1086 may or may not be those of Jews. Jews are mentioned as living in London in 1090 during the reign of William Rufus (1087-1100), engaging in disputes with Christians (according to Anselm) but it is not until 1115 that a "Jews' Street" is mentioned, near St. Olave's, north and south of what came to be known as the "Old Jewry Chambers", and later, the house of "Aaron the Jew" in the parish of St. Lawrence in London.[145] Land in this parish continued to be in Jewish hands, falling to Josce of York and then to a Samuel Hoppecole. It reverted to the King, but it was granted (presumably for a fee) to Ysaac, a bond-clerk or cyrographer, being inherited by his son Sampson, and passed in turn to his son, Abraham. The area, which came to comprise Catte Street (later Gresham Street) housed a synagogue (which may have survived until 1280) and a "Great School of the Jews".

In Angevin England, the names of Jews are found in the various "Rolls" of the Royal Court, connected with the dealings of the Treasury (the Pipe and Liberate Rolls), the Law Courts (the Fine and Oblate Rolls) and the proclamations or orders of the King (Charters, and the Patent and Close Rolls). The Pipe (or abacus) Rolls, which run continuously from the reign of Henry II, were the annual accounts and balance sheets of the Sheriffs, and their payments, collection of fines and returns to the King. The Liberate Rolls detail the sums paid out or documents delivered by the Treasury upon the King's writ (often duplicated on the Patent Rolls). The Fine and Oblate Rolls were a record of the fines paid in Court of the offerings (oblations) made to the King through the Sheriffs to obtain certain privileges or to avoid certain penalties. The Charter Rolls contain formal orders and charters, or grants of privilege from the King, and deal with important matters, such as those concerning the Jews. The Patent Rolls are less formal and more public or open orders and grants in the form of letters, and tend to deal with less important issues. The Close Rolls consist of "closed" or private letters. The names of English Jews appear in all of these sources, as well as Jewish business documents and deeds (contracts of loan and deeds of release from the debt) relating to the lending of money upon security or pledge (often in the form of land or commodity), or sometimes without it. Interest was not always charged by the Jewish money-lender if the security was good, and if so it might be levied at a low level, but in its absence, high interest on the debt was common. The failure of the debtor to repay often led to disputes in the courts, where the Jew could gain seisin or legal possession of the security, including lands, houses and abbeys, and Jews held nearly a hundred properties in their possession at this time, the most prominent financier and landowner being Aaron of Lincoln. In particular, from as early as 1166, he appears to have organised his business interests on a national scale, making Jews throughout the country his agents as money-lenders. Another such Jewish entrepreneur was Isaac fil Rabbi. Each such business was, in effect, a Jewish banking corporation, although the King did not allow these to merge into partnerships, in that, upon the death of the individual Jewish banker, rather than the assets being transferred to a partner, the King could claim them, in whole or in part.

In 1130-1131 Jewish names appear as rendering accounts to the Treasury: Jacob the Jew and his wife, Mannasser the Jew, Abraham the Jew, Rubi Gotsce (Rabbi Josh or Joseph: his son, Isaac fil Rabbi, or Rabijoce, was the most prominent English Jew in the time of Richard I from 1189) and Deuslesalt (Dieu le saut = Isaiah).

Around 1140 the Church began to introduce various laws concerning Jews and Usury, and in 1141 Jews are again mentioned as living in Oxford, where they were said to have been involved in the advancement of learning in the University. In the same year, the house of a Jew of Oxford, Aaron ben Isaac was burnt, possibly with Aaron in it, but if he perished in the fire, it is not certain that his death was intended, in that the house's destruction was a form of recompense for the non-payment of a debt. It is not until 1200 that a Deed of Christ Church College identifies the transfer of lands from John of Iffley and his wife Helena to a Lawrence Kepharm, the lands having been in the possession of Jews in the "Jewry of Oxford", including Mosse Jew of Bristol, Deodatus the Jew, and Benjamin the Jew. In 1144 the "blood accusation" arose in Norwich where the Jews were accused of enticing and capturing a Christian child, William, at Passover time, torturing and crucifying him, and secretly burying his body in a wood on Easter Day. (Boy martyrs were very popular at this time and brought pilgrims and donations to the monasteries that housed such a shrine. Another such murder was ascribed to the Jews "of all England coming together" at Gloucester in 1168). In 1146, a Rabbi Simeon from England is supposed to have been murdered in Germany, because he would not convert.[146]

From 1155 to 1160, the "Pipe Rolls" of Henry II record payments from or relating to Jews in "Canteb." ("for a slain Jew"), Oxford, Essex ("Isaac the Jew, son of Rabb.", or Rubi Gotsce), Lincoln, Cambridge, Norwich, Thetford and Bungay, these most likely being the extent of a Jewish presence outside London at this time. In 1158, a Spaniard, Abraham Ibn Ezra ben Mier is said to have composed his work *Yesod Moreh* in London, and a Gentill the Jewess is noted as owing £15 in the Pipe Rolls (6 Hen. II.). Between 1159 to 1163, Jews appear as money-lenders either at or in connection with Cambridge (Vives), Stafford (Bonenfaunt), Canterbury (Dieu Lacresse, or Deulecresse, the Jew), Newport (Jacob and Mirabella), and London (Benedict) where the Jew Hakelot ("Little Jacob": also found at Reading), and Brun the Jew traded. (Another Benedict, Jew of Norwich appears in the Rolls in 1170).

In 1164, Henry II granted a charter to the Jews of London to administer their own Laws in a *Beth Din*, and soon after, from 1166 to 1169, Jews appear as tax-collectors from some counties, including Aaron the Jew in Lincoln and Isaac the Jew in Buckingham and Bedford. In the same years, several Jews are recorded as liable to render the payment of taxes to the King: Abraham fil Rabbi (brother of the tax-collector Isaac) owed the sum of £2000 (an enormous sum), but was exempted, Samson the Jew owed "3 marks of gold" but "is not to be found", and "Comitissa Jewess of Cambridge and her sons the Jews of Lincoln" were to "render an account of 7 marks of gold for the Lincoln Jewess whom a son of Comitissa married without the King's license". (The names of her sons, David and Isaac are recorded in the Pipe Rolls). In 1170 Josce Jew of Gloucester was fined 100 shillings by the King for financing the unauthorised and expressly forbidden expedition of Richard de Clare (the Earl of Pembroke, known as "Strongbow") in which he conquered Waterford and Dublin, arousing the King's fears that an independent kingdom might be set up in Ireland. The Pipe Rolls again mention Jacob the Jew of Newport, and his wife Avigay, in 1172-1176, together with Jurnet, Jew of Norwich, Isaac fil Rabbi, Aaron of Lincoln, and two Jews, Serfdu and Cresselin (the latter a diminutive of Deulecresse, above). These names, and others, continue to appear in the Pipe Rolls and in private contracts and promissory notes from this time.[147]

Between 1173 and 1175 church plate was redeemed from several Jews. Aaron of Lincoln (1173) had come into possession on pledge of plate and ornaments from the Minster, which had been in severe financial difficulties for several years, and in Peterborough (1175) the abbot, William of Walterville was deposed by the forces of Richard, Archbishop of Canterbury, and the church's sacred relics were pledged with Jews for money. In 1177, Henry II granted licences to Jews to establish cemeteries in any city of England provided that it was beyond the walls of the city. Previously all dead Jews had to be taken to London for burial. Jewish contributions to the Treasury from 1180 onwards include the names of Abraham of Coventry, Jeremias, Nicholas and Isabella (both converts to Judaism, who would have lost their property to the King upon conversion), Beleasez, Jewess of Oxford (who, as Belaset, also appears in a private loan agreement around this time), Ysaac of Rochester, Ysaac from Russia, Yssac of Beverley, and Josce Quatrebuches and his son Hakelin. In 1183, a William (Guillaume) de Tottenham mortgaged his manor against a debt of 100 marks of silver to Avigula, the Jewess of London and her son, Abraham. By 1192, the Pipe Rolls record the names of about forty London Jews who had paid arrears due since 1185, and in 1194 the number has risen to about fifty names. Further Jewish contributions to the Treasury in 1188-1189 include "The Jews of Exeter",[148] Jheremias of Dunstable, Deulebenie of Chichester, Lia (Leah) Jewess of Bristol, and, later, in 1193, Aaron, brother of Leon of Dunstable, Aaron, son of Samuel of Northampton and Ysaac of Bedford.

1190 saw riots and the murder of many Jews at Norwich, Stamford, York, St. Edmunds and Lynn (but not at Winchester), which incurred the displeasure of the king, Richard I (1189-1199) against the "unbridled attack of an undisciplined... promiscuous and numberless mob [that] could not be summoned and be brought to justice" (William of Newbury). The king's outrage was not shared to this extent by his successor, John (1199-1216), but in the wake of these events, Richard issued a Charter (an earlier one had been issued by Henry II, and a later was issued by John in 1201) granting various rights to Jews in legal disputes, where "lawful" Jews could act as witnesses, and the adjudication of "the peers of the Jews" was acknowledged as legitimate where Christians might have a dispute with Jews. There were also measures to protect Jews in the case of pledges and debts. The king's charter ends: "And we order that the Jews through all England and Normandy be free of all customs and of tolls...and we command and order you to ward and defend and protect them". In 1199, King John confirmed by charter that "Jacob, Jew of London, priest of the Jews" was to hold the "presbyterate of all of the Jews of the whole of England...as he is our royal Jew whom we retain specifically in our service [and] our dear friend" to whom the King gave his protection and freedom and security of movement throughout the country. The various charters were reconfirmed by John in 1201. Also in 1199, John agreed to the sale of a manor from Josce son of Isaac the Jew to the Earl of Ferrars, and in 1200 he granted properties to his servants, Simon de Pateshull and Andrew of Winchester, belonging to deceased Jews (Benedict of York and Aaron of Winchester). The previous year, King John had taken Leo of London as his royal goldsmith, but in 1204, the king was forced to issue an order to the Mayor and Barons of London after receiving various reports of anti-Semitic incidents in the capital. The order stated that the protection granted to the Jews "should be observed inviolably" and that if there was any failure to protect the Jews in the city of London "we shall require their blood at your hand".

King John's protection of the Jews arose, however, not through any personal feeling towards them, but through financial self-interest and the sums they brought him. Indeed, two of the clauses of the original text of the Charter of Magna Carta of 1215 (omitted from later reissues) limited the right of Jewish money-lenders to claim back total arrears from the heirs, widows and children of a deceased borrower. The king's treatment of Jewish money-lenders was, therefore, selective. In the Patent Rolls of 1202-1204, King John released various of his "dear and faithful" friends and servants from their debts to Jews, urging his Sheriffs and Constables to "make such and so urgent distraints on the Jews of your bailiwicks for their debts" for "the money which they ought to pay us at once". He was to do the same in the Liberate Rolls (1202-1206), the Close Rolls (1204-1206) and the Fine and Oblate Rolls (1204-1206) although the latter sources also reveal at least one case of a Jew, Jacob, son of Samuel of Northampton where the King ordered the Sheriff of Northampton "to hasten the business of Jacob - by giving him seisin [Old French, *seisine* - possession] for the sureties which Hugo de Lisonis pledged him for the debts he owed him - and to keep and defend the same Jew in his pledges". At this time, the Patent Rolls also show that John forbade any molestation of Morell, Jew of Wells, whilst he was in Normandy, and Hannechin, "our Jew" is stated to possess the King's "sure peace" and freedom of movement "like our other Jews" for his "good service". Such freedoms were clearly not absolute, but at the King's discretion: Morell was subject to "our law and customs" and English Jews might be able to travel, but required a written permit to change their place of residence. King John's personal feeling towards the Jews was far from sympathetic, however, and when in 1204 he issued a general amnesty to clear the prisons, he added to the order "except our Jewish prisoners".

In stark contrast to the wealth of recorded detail of named Jews in 12th century England, no evidence exists from any official source of the names of Jews resident in Cornwall at that time, nor, indeed, at any time before the 18th century. The Fine and Oblate Rolls, above, record the names and location of over thirty Jewish Creditors in England (along with the names of their Christian Debtors). There are Jewish creditors listed in Hampshire, Wiltshire, Somerset, Dorset and Devon,[149] but none in Cornwall. Likewise, there are no references to named Jews from Cornwall in the Pipe Rolls from the time of Henry II, nor in the Treasury Accounts, the Patent, Liberate and Close Rolls, or any other primary source from the Angevin period. When all of these primary sources, including Jewish deeds, are taken into account, over six hundred names of Jews and their location can be identified, together with the additional names of other family members in the case of over a quarter of them, amounting to some 750 named individuals. Many of these names only give the male head of family, and cover some four generations (1100-1153, 1154-1173, 1174-1193 and 1194-1206). The total size of the Jewish population at this time cannot be calculated with any degree of certainty, but it was growing steadily. The numerical occurrence of names in each generation would give a figure beginning at around 20 in 1100, rising to about 400 in 1206, but these are only *known* individuals, whose names happen to appear in records. The total number of Jews killed in the various massacres of 1190 may have been around 500: Jewish accounts give about 150 for York, but other sources mention 500 alone for that city. The names that are known, however, indicate clearly that the demographic density of the Jewish population followed that of the general population, being greatest in the South and East, but sparse in the North (beyond Lincoln) and West. From the known names the largest centres of Jewish population began with London, closely followed by Lincoln, then, with about half of the latter's numbers, Norwich, Gloucester, Northampton, Winchester and Cambridge, followed in decreasing numbers by Oxford, Bristol and others.

The Plea Rolls relate to the administration of the *archae*, or chests where copies of all bonds of debt contracted between Jews and Christians had to be deposited and held in the larger centres of Jewish population (the most southerly of these and that which would have covered Cornwall was located in Exeter). These bonds could be taken into the King's exchequer if taxes were left unpaid by Jews, and they became a desirable commodity and an important part of fiscal administration, often acquired by Christians, because land accompanied the bond as a collateral for the debt.[150] Plea Rolls have survived for most of the years in the period from 1218 to 1281, and in addition there are receipts from the Jews from the reign of Henry III and Accounts of receipts from Jews in the Tower of London from 1275-1278, during the reign of Edward III.[151] The Plea Rolls themselves have been extensively recorded, analysed and published in six volumes by the Jewish Historical Society of England (in 1910, 1929, 1972, 1992 and 2005). All of the different types of Rolls mentioned previously have been subject to particular scrutiny by H. G. Richardson (1960 and 1972). From all of these various sources and studies, it is obvious how widespread was the settlement of Jews in England, but also it is striking that only isolated names can be ascribed to the West Country south of Bristol, and only as far as Exeter, and not a single name can be related conclusively or unequivocally to a Jew resident in Cornwall, or to the existence of a Jewish commune in the County at that time. In fact, the only consistent reference to Cornwall relates to the Earl of Cornwall, or to the fact that Richard Earl of Cornwall was granted the city and castle of Exeter by his brother in 1231. It would be remarkable, therefore, if Jews were indeed intimately involved in the revenues from the Cornish tin industry during this period, that their names should not have been recorded in any of these official documents.

Max Muller (1870) refers to only three Jews in Cornwall in the third year of the reign of King John in 1202, their names, he says, appearing in the *Rotuli Pipae* (Pipe Rolls) published in 1863:[152] Simon de Dena, Deudone son of (*fil*) Samuel, and Aaron, all *praedictus Judeus*. It has been recognised that the later work of Joseph Jacobs in his pioneering and extensive study (1893) of the Jews of Angevin England and in particular of the Pipe Rolls was subject to significant omissions and a degree of error,[153] and he may well have missed these references. Jacobs does not mention the name *Dena* at all. It is possible that it is to be linked with Denmark, or with

Salom. de Edene, but Jacobs locates that man in Lincoln. Of the seven names given by Jacobs for *Simon*, he links them only with Northampton, Worcester, Canterbury, London and Norwich. He lists *Deudone* eight times, the names being associated only with Colchester, London, Lincoln, Northampton, Gloucester and Oxford, with *Duedone fil Samuel* linked specifically with Northampton, and not Cornwall. Jacobs further identifies seventeen men named *Aaron*, in London, Colchester, Northampton, Oxford, Lincoln, Buckinghamshire, Canterbury and Winchester. At least one such *Aaron* can be linked with both *Deudone* and Northampton. Neither Adler (1939) or Richardson (1960) mention the three names given by Muller, nor do they link any names (save Earl Richard) to Cornwall. Muller was careful to say that the three names were of Jews *in* Cornwall. He does not draw the conclusion that they were *of* or *from* the County, and most certainly he does not take them to have been resident members of a Cornish Jewry of the time. He comments only that "Their transactions are purely financial and do not lead us to suppose that the Jews in order to make tin condescended in the time of King John, or at any other time, to the drudgery of working in the mines". Moreover, whatever the financial transactions of the three Jews, Muller found no evidence that these were linked with revenues from the tin-mining industry. From this it seems most likely that these Jews were visitors from other parts of England, and even if, as agents, they were in the County to collect payments on behalf of the Crown, such payments need not have been due from the revenues of the Stannaries, but from some other business interests. In no way, therefore, can such occasional references as these especially from the singular instance of one year, suggest a substantial or settled Jewish presence in Cornwall, or of any form of involvement in the Stannaries.[154] Such involvement is, of course, conceivable, but it remains unsubstantiated. Muller's own verdict is both balanced and judicious. He denies that he holds "that no single Jew ever set foot on Cornish soil", and continues "It would indeed be the most extraordinary fact if Cornwall had never been visited by Jews. If it were so, Cornwall would stand alone as far as such an immunity is concerned among all the countries of Europe". However, it is one thing to hold to this perfectly rational position, and quite another to believe in "a kind of Jewish exodus to Cornwall" in Roman or Mediaeval times, with towns and mines being named and populated by large numbers of Jews, especially in the absence of corroborating evidence.

It has been mentioned that some eighty years later, in 1283 CE, prior to a late taxation upon Jews, and not long before their expulsion, a writ was issued to twenty Sheriffs in England who had Jews under their jurisdiction to examine all of their financial transactions, which were held in the local *archa*. One such writ was issued to the High Sheriff of Cornwall, who at that time was an Alexander de Sabridsworth. Clearly, this would seem to imply that Jews were present in the County at the time. However, if this was the case, how many Jews were present, or for how long they had been resident remains unknown. Moreover, their temporary presence or even their retrospective financial involvement, or current involvement *in absentia* cannot be discounted. The writ may have applied to Jewish financial dealings under the jurisdiction of the sheriff rather than to actual Jews currently within that jurisdiction. No *archa* has been identified for Cornwall, and so it cannot even be known if Sabridsworth was, in effect, required to establish one, albeit of a temporary nature. The audit may also have been administered from Exeter, where there was an archa. The examples given by Roth of Aaron of Lincoln (*c.*1186), and in the next century of Aaron of York,[155] together with Abraham of Berkhamsted illustrates the feature that Jews were often involved financially in places where they were themselves not present. Aaron of Lincoln had interests in 25 counties, with 17 Jewish agents working for him, Aaron of York employed at least 20 agents, and Abraham had debtors "in half the counties of England". These agents may have been based in certain towns and cities, but of necessity they would also have travelled to more remote places to conclude their business. Under such arrangements, there could have been a single such agent for Cornwall, and he may have been based in Exeter. In reality, information from the *archae*, and from the Pipe Rolls themselves is either incomplete or entirely lacking, and it cannot be assumed that the administration of accounts was always efficiently and comprehensively recorded. There are certainly no accounts or entries from either source to confirm the involvement of Jews in the Stannaries.

One or two names do appear subsequently in relation to Cornwall, but they are incidental, ambiguous and inconclusive. There is the much later, isolated, case of *Vosper of St. Neot,*[156] said to have been a Jewish "refugee", who emigrated from Eastern Europe (probably Silesia) and settled at the "Old Hall" Liskeard, in the time of Henry VII (1485-1509). Vosper's extended family pedigree (1555-1873) would indicate an immediate assimilation and marriage into Gentile society. From the first generation (*c.* 1555) various Vosper men were burgesses and mayors of Liskeard, which would suggest conversion to Christianity. A Hebrew root to the name *Vosper* is not clear. The Latin *vespa* is a wasp, of which the Hebrew is *ira*, commonly adopted as a later Jewish forename, of which the 20th century American Ira Gershwin is a famous example. *Vosper* might recall *Vespers,* as Christian Evening Prayer, and could be seen as a parallel to the Jewish evening prayers of *Ma'ariv,* although the latter is not used as a Jewish personal name.[157] *Vos* or *Voss* does, however, function as a Jewish surname, Nathan Vos being the last to be buried in the Penryn Jewish cemetery in 1913, but these names, especially as *Vose*, are also to be found as Cornish surnames, and can be derived from *fos* (ditch or rampart) and the place name of *Vose* is associated with St. Ewe, south of St. Austell. Likewise, *Trevose Head*, on the North Cornish coast near St. Merryn and Padstow, is named after a farm that abutted a "bank" or rampart of a promontory fort on the headland, the adjacent *Dinas Head* (*dinas* = a fort) suggesting this, although no definite remains of this feature can be seen today, except for a "revetment" or bank of uncertain date alongside the road that leads to the farm. The Cornish Celtic surname *Trevossow* appears in Parish Registers in the 17th century, but is no longer evident today, although it may well be used by descendants of Cornish people abroad.[158] It seems most likely that the immigrant Vosper of St. Neot (east of Bodmin and west of Liskeard) may well have adopted the name from a local feature or place, such as a rampart, in that it can be understood as coming from the Cornish *fos-por*, the pasture by the ditch or rampart. The place name *Trevospor* is found as early as 1210, and it is associated with St. Petherwin. The surname Vosper is not uncommon in South East and North Cornwall (the modern chain of

Vosper garages and car salerooms in the South West being the main example). Moreover, the 15th century Vosper of St. Neot can in no way be taken as indicative of a Jewish population in North Cornwall in the 15th century, and, in any event, has no known relevance to the issue of mining .

Earlier than Vosper, it is only possible to glimpse isolated examples of individuals, not all of whom are known to have been Jews:[159] An Abraham "carbonarius", a charcoal-burner, appears in 1201 as party to a dispute over land in Cornwall, and he has been taken to have been a Jew, possibly involved in the tin-works. Later, a Nicholas Abram of Cornwall granted land in a tin-working area to a William de Bodrugan. It is not axiomatic from their names alone that they were Jews, and there is, in fact, no evidence that they were. There was also "Abraham Le Tynnere", a mine-owner and master-tinner around 1342-1357 who was the employer of several hundred men in the royal mines of Devon and a wide area of east Cornwall. He is also mentioned as having been arrested at Fowey in Cornwall. This Abraham most certainly "became a leading figure in the tin-industry".[160] It is understandable that these names can lead the most fastidious and reputable scholars into assuming or even assigning Jewish identity. While such a name as "Abraham" might well suggest that the "Tinner" was a Jew, there is no conclusive evidence that he was, and this particular Hebrew name (and others) were not unknown amongst Christians at the time. Abraham of Felmingham (whose son was named Isaac) was not Jewish: he received a grant from Henry II (1133-1189). There was an Aaron "of Cornwall" in 1244, who may have been a Jew, although this is not certain, and he does not appear in Cornwall itself but in Uxbridge where he was also arrested. "Joachim of Gaunze - a Jewish-German mining engineer" who is said to have spent three years in Cornwall from 1586-1589 supplying copper-ore to Wales, although at least one source[161] which deals with Gaunse's (or Ganz's) career in some detail makes only one reference to Cornwall, saying only that the engineer was "probably" there (at some unspecified time).[162] Whilst it has been suggested that various German mining engineers were brought to Cornwall in Tudor times[163] as surveyors, to sink shafts and to smelt ore, such as the German Burchard Cranach (from 1553-1557), "it is evident that the Cornish tin smelters at least had little or nothing to learn from their continental counterparts",[164] and there is nothing to suggest that any of these foreign engineers were Jews.

Susser also refers to two place-names, as providing "Additional support for the view that Jews in the seventeenth century ranged as far afield as Cornwall".[165] One of these is said to be a "Jews' Lane" in the Parish of Breage, near Helston, where, local tradition has it that "a Jew hanged himself after some outrage done to him by a Squire Sparnon. Soon after the Jew's suicide it was said that the lane was haunted. The Reverend Robert Jago was paid five guineas to exorcise the ghost.". Susser dates this between 1633 ("when Robert Jago was presented to the Vicarage of Wendron and Helston") and 1685 (when he died).[166] He also refers to a "Jews' Wood" near Plymouth, the putative site of a Jew's murder, for which he provides no date. These stories may, of course, be nothing more than anecdotal folklore, and hardly amount to evidence of anything more than the occasional, isolated Jewish traveller, or a Gentile pedlar taken to have been a Jew. It is from the elaboration of such tales and their place-names, however, that the erroneous belief can arise that

Jews must have resided in or near such places. In the case of the Cornish location at Breage, it is obvious that the dark "haunted" lane, in the pitch-black and with its tragic associations, could indeed appear to be a "black" (*dhu*) "Jew's" lane, and that linguistic factors may have been at play in shaping the name and the story. Entirely irrelevant to the issue, in the village of Polperro, there is a single old house that has been known locally as *The Jew's House* or *Jew Bank Cottage* which has been assumed to have been associated with Jewish silversmiths and jewellers who are supposed to have lived in the village. However, no evidence of any early resident Jewish presence in Polperro has been identified. Although it is not inconceivable that the house may have provided shelter for the occasional itinerant pedlar (Jewish or otherwise), the name given to the cottage may have an entirely arbitrary origin, or be derived from an unrelated Cornish word. The fact that the cottage has only been known by this name since the 1920s clearly indicates that the puta-tive origin of its nomenclature may be taken as spurious.[167]

A distinctive Language and Hagiography have also played their part in Corn-wall's past and its traditions, and it is these, rather than any supposed Jewish pres-ence, which can help unravel some of the threads which make up the veil of obscurity and misunderstanding surrounding some of the present-day Cornish place-names which have come to be linked with Jews. In a paper written in 1933 and reprinted in the Journal of the RIC in 1973, R. Morton Nance surveys a wide range of evidence that Cornish may have survived beyond the 18th century and even into the 19th.[168] He concludes that some usage, limited topographically and linguistically, may have been possible but in the form of memorised verses and phrases or dialect terminology. Some people may have been able to lapse into brief, occasional usage but little firm evidence exists of a significant number of fluent Cornish speakers after the death of one of its last exponents, in the late 18th century, Dolly Pentreath of the Parish of Paul near Penzance, whose great age of 102, recorded on a "bogus epitaph"[169], cannot be taken as accurate and whose precise birth-date is uncertain, but most likely 1692. A *Doaryte*, daughter of Nicholas Pentreath, was baptised in Paul Church on 16th May 1692, and is most likely to be identified with Dorothy, and the Dorothy Pentreath who was also baptised there on 17th May 1714, "could hardly have been the very old woman seen by [Daines] Barrington in 1768".[170] The former would have been 76 when seen by Barrington, and 85 at the time of her death in December 1777. (Her portrait was painted by the Cornish artist John Opie c.1777-1779).[171] In any event, in Pool's view, she "enjoyed a rather spurious posthumous reputation as 'the last speaker of Cornish' (which) we know to be incorrect, but she may have been the last native-speaker, brought up to speak nothing but Cornish. She became the subject of many stories and legends, most of them obviously without foundation".[172] William Bodener of Mousehole (who died in 1789) was said to have been able to "converse" with Dolly for hours, but as Nance points out, the "conversation" (which, in the context, would not be a distortion to characterise as "incomprehensible ramblings"[173]) was "scarcely understood by anyone of that place", and it may only have been possible to sustain it at all by the contrivance of avoiding problematical areas, and the strict limitation of usage, and, moreover, it may not have been propelled by a complete facility on Bodener's part. In 1776[174], however, Bodener claimed that there were four or five people in Mousehole (some of whom outlived Dolly) who could still speak *some* Cornish. Much later, the Victorian poet and priest, Gerard Manley Hopkins, noted in his journal, for 25th August 1870, that his father had told him that a "Captain Newman" of the Scilly Isles had known an old lady whose name was "Pendraith" (*sic.*) who "is now some years dead", who could speak Cornish, but "I believe he knew no other".[175] Nevertheless, the fact that the terms "speak" and "converse" are often confused and misused in the reports which have come down to us should not be overlooked. Much of the "speaking" could have consisted of the rote memorisation of a repertory of verses and phrases, and even the ability to count in Cornish, or to exchange a few words or a few concocted sentences "got by heart" is not evidence of fluency or of free conversation. Moreover, the very use of the words "converse" and "conversation", when, effectively, the speaker had no one else to converse with is clearly a misuse of language itself.[176] Cornish was primarily a spoken language before its extinction in the 18th century and for centuries before that, many of those who had spoken it, most likely the majority, would have been illiterate. Pronunciation would have varied considerably from place to place, and possibly from person to person in the same locality. Such factors as these make it difficult to evaluate the authenticity of the contemporaneous claims to have identified "fluent" Cornish speakers, and the possibility of anecdotal reports masquerading as credible evidence cannot be ignored.

The Cornishman, Richard Carew (1555-1620), who "neither knew nor cared much about Cornish…and would have heard it only rarely, living as he did at St. Anthony in South East Cornwall, far from the Western areas [Penwith] where it was still spoken",[177] noted that "Most of the inhabitants can speak no word of Cornish, but few are ignorant of English".[178] He also recorded, with some disdain, that some Cornish speakers, whilst fluent in English, affected not to know it when meeting a "stranger", saying *Meea navidna cowza sawzneck,* which he, mistakenly, took to mean "I cannot speak English", while, in fact, it meant "I *will* not speak English". The non-Cornish John Norden (*c.* 1548-1625)[179] observed that few spoke Cornish except "In the west part of the country, as in the Hundreds of Penwith and Kerrier….But it seems that in a few years the Cornish Language will be little by little abandoned." Indeed, by 1600, Cornish was all but extinct except in the west, and even there "the number of monoglot speakers was small". As early as 1563, when Parliament commissioned a Prayer Book in Welsh, it was deemed pointless to give so small a number of people a Prayer Book in Cornish, even though there were Cornish scholars who could have carried out the task. This decision hastened the death of the language: "Had the decision gone otherwise, in all probability Cornish, like Welsh, would never have died out; certainly many hundreds of words of Cornish would have been preserved, which were in the event lost beyond recall."[180] Willam Scawen had noted that other factors were also at work: the eventual loss of contact with Brittany (Breton and Cornish at one time having been one language), the cessation of Miracle Plays (after 1600) and that, in the absence of any persecution or discouragement of the use of the language, it became undervalued, engendering a general apathy, with the result that English was seen as preferable "for reasons both of practical convenience or social snobbery."

The ever increasing primacy of English at this time, which had been a gradual ongoing process from at least the 1600s, serves as a caution in evaluating the traditions of emigrant Cornish people who claim to have preserved spoken Cornish. Such statements as the following, for example, should be regarded with considerable scepticism: "there is one isolated place, Tangier Island off the coast of Maryland, where a few hundred people still speak in a [Cornish] language they say has not changed since people moved to the island 400 years ago"[181] "400 years ago" places such emigrant settlement at precisely the time that Cornish had declined to such an extent that, by 1600, it was barely understood in the County, as the testimony of Norden shows. Even if Cornish settlers did reach Tangier Island as early as 1600, and brought with them a Cornish language that had "not changed", it is highly unlikely to have been ancient spoken Cornish as such, intact and inviolate from any English intrusion or influence. Such late 16th or early 17th century settlers may well have inherited aspects of a Cornish language, but it would most likely have resembled an Anglicised doggerel mixture, containing forms of Cornish dialect expressions. The fact that, in 1710, William Gwavas wrote in Cornish[182] to a contact in America with a translation of the Apostles' Creed, would seem to indicate that some Cornish emigrants understood it there, although their interest in it may have been born of curiosity and nostalgia rather than proficiency in the language.

Despite the ever increasing primacy of English, Richard Symonds, an officer in the Royalist Army during the Civil War, noted that Cornish was still spoken "beyond Truro" (that is to the south and west) though "at Land's End they speak no English"[183] (or, at least, appeared not to do so). According to William Scawen (who "served in the Royalist army in the Civil War, was imprisoned in Pendennis Castle, and at the Restoration was rewarded by being made Vice-Warden of the Stannaries, an important position in the administration of the Cornish tin trade") there were also Cornish speakers in the Royalist Army.[184] The traditional historical sources do not offer a uniform picture of the usage of Cornish at this time. According to the Cornish historian Hals, in Fowey, up to 1640, the communion was administered in Cornish[185], by the Vicar, William Jackman, "because the aged people did not well understand English". Hals, however, has long been "known to posterity as the most inaccurate of all Cornish historians" particularly in his work on the Cornish language which has been said (by Nance) to have been "an attempt by one who knew next to nothing of Cornish to impose on others who knew even less."[186] Hals' work was also disparaged by his near contemporary, William Pryce (1735-1790) who, in 1792, said of Hals that his Cornish language collection was "a most strange hodge-podge of Hebrew, Greek, Latin and British words, confusedly heaped together." In 1678, William Scawen did record that, at Landewednack, the Rector, Francis Robinson, had "not long since" preached the sermon in Cornish, "being the only language understood by his congregation".[187] During this period, however, in 1662, when the naturalist, John Ray visited Land's End, he could find only one man "Dickan Gwyn" (the local dialect pronunciation of [Richard] "Dick" Angwyn of Bowjewyan) in the parish of St. Just-in-Penwith who could write Cornish, and "We met with none here but what could speak English....so that the language is like, in a short time, to be quite lost."[188]

In the late 1600s a small group of elderly men had set out to "gather the fragments that are left, that nothing be lost".[189] Three of these men were from Penwith in West Cornwall. Firstly, there was Richard Angwyn (-1675), who was described by the Nicholas Boson below as "the greatest and eldest of the late Professors of our Cornish tongue". However, as Pool observes "We cannot now judge Angwin's scholarship, since tragically all his MSS [manuscripts] were destroyed by his relatives after his death". Another was John Keigwin (1641-1716) of Mousehole, who had been baptised and was eventually buried in the Parish of Paul, who was "the greatest scholar among these men", and Nicholas Boson (1624-1703) of Newlyn, who is also buried at Paul. Two men of this name were baptised at Paul, one in 1624 and the other in 1653, but it is normally assumed that he was the former. Three of Boson's short works were *Gerriau Dro Tho Carnoack* (A Few Words about Cornish), the fragmentary *The Duchess of Cornwall's Progress*, described by Pool as "a curious jumble of local folk-lore and topography…probably derived from the visit of Catherine of Braganza to Mount's Bay in 1662… on her voyage from Portugal to marry Charles II", and the Cornish tale *Jowan Chy-an-Horth, py an Try Foynt a Skyans* (John of Tryannor, or the Three Points of Wisdom). The latter work, not unique, in that similar tales can be found in English, Scottish and Breton literature, was written for children, but with the purpose of helping them learn Cornish through John's adventures and three easily memorable maxims.

There were three other men from outside Penwith. One was William Scawen (-1689) of St. Germans (in the north of the County, where some still spoke the language), who was a much older man than Keigwin or Boson. Pool observes that a great deal of Scawen's output consists "of a confused and fanciful account of aspects of Cornish geography and history, but it includes a long list of the causes of the decay of the language…and a small but interesting collection of Cornish proverbs." Scawen observed that, only in confined pockets of the County a few people spoke Cornish, and that they did so very corruptly. Amongst these were a few who were effectively monolingual, including, in the West of the County, a "very ancient woman of Gwithian (named elsewhere as Christian or Chrestan Marchant) who had died in 1676 and had habitually used an interpreter, though she had partly understood English." Amongst Scawen's more credible reasons for the decline of Cornish (some of which have been mentioned earlier) were: a pattern of discouragement from the Gentry who would not speak Cornish, even changing their Cornish names to suggest Norman descent, and marrying into families from outside the County; in North and East Cornwall the proximity of English-speaking Devon influenced the Cornish population and the change in place-names; the influx of outside traders (in tin and fish); amongst the Cornish speakers who were literate, failure to correspond in the language; and the loss of crucial manuscripts of Cornish literature.

Of the two much younger men, William Gwavas[190] (1676-1741), a barrister, originally from Suffolk, was from Gwavas in the Parish of Sithney near Helston. The place should not be confused Gwavas in Paul, in Penwith, although he came to spend much of his life in Penzance, in protracted legal disputes with local fishermen, over the fishing tithes he had inherited, the litigation eventually being settled in his favour by a decision of the House of Lords in 1730. Pool describes him as "an indefatigable writer and collector of letters, verses, proverbs, epitaphs and other passages in Cornish", whose manuscripts (now in the British Museum in London) are "the most important source of such material." Gwavas expressly accredited others who had assisted him and given him information, including Keigwin, John Boson and his cousin Thomas Boson, Oliver Pendar of Newlyn, and James Jenkin of Alverton, Penzance. The last man was, in his day, held in high regard as the last proficient writer of Cornish, although only two of his poems, copied by Gwavas, have survived. Gwavas also included amongst these men a John Odger who lived on the Lizard. Of particular interest is the fact that Gwavas noted that, in the parishes of Paul and St. Just (in Penwith), and at St. Keverne (the Lizard) there were very elderly men and women who could speak the "modern Cornish" but that they "knew not how to write it, or rightly to divide the words and sentences." Lastly, there was Thomas Tonkin[191] (1678-1742) originally from Trevaunace in St. Agnes, but later of Gorran, who did not live in the west of the County, where Cornish was spoken, but who learned much from Gwavas. By 1736, Tonkin was of the view that the Cornish which was still spoken by a very limited section of the population was vulgar, corrupted and confined to the most part to illiterate people.[192] Without the work of these men, says Pool, "our knowledge of Cornish in its final stage would have been small indeed. They saw that the language was dying before their eyes, and that the forces working to that end were irreversible; what they could not save, they set out to record. The language continued to decline throughout the years of their work, and in fact died soon after them; their importance was as witnesses and chroniclers of this decline."[193]

In 1700 the Welsh Celtic scholar Edward Lhuyd[194] (1660-1709) made a visit to Cornwall, meeting John Keigwin, Nicholas Boson and others. He noted that some Cornish was still spoken throughout the West Penwith peninsula, and also along the south coast to St. Keverne, but that, even in those places, many of the inhabitants did not understand it, with English being spoken and understood everywhere. By 1750, Cornish had failed to survive even on the Isles of Scilly.[195] Some still sought to imbue their children with a knowledge of the language, and Arthur Boase (1698-1780) a native of Paul, "retained many phrases in Cornish and taught his children the Lord's Prayer, sundry proverbs, and the numerals".[196] In 1758, Dr. William Borlase, Rector of Ludgvan for fifty years (until 1772), and a renowned and respected scholar, claimed that Cornish had "now altogether ceased, so as not to be spoken anywhere"[197], but he was mistaken, because, as we have seen, it was still spoken in the village of Mousehole by Dolly Pentreath (1692-1777). Of this oversight on the part of Borlase, Pool says that he was "the greatest Cornish scholar of the 18th century...but he made no attempt to collect further material from surviving Cornish speakers at Mousehole, only six miles from his home" and that "It seems unbelievable that a man of immense scholarship, keenly interested in Cornish, who spent a lifetime in accurate observation and recording, could have failed to realise that all this time Cornish was being spoken so close to his home."

The Cornish spoken in Mousehole by Dolly Pentreath, and the fact that it was apparently (at least to some extent) understood there by a few others, did not escape the attention of the non-Cornish antiquary Daines Barrington (1727-1800) in 1768.[198] Barrington's interest in Cornish had begun over twenty years before, in

1746, when his brother, Samuel, a naval Captain, had taken onto his ship a Cornish sailor from Mount's Bay, off Penzance, who is said to have spoken Cornish and seemed able to converse freely with Breton sailors. In Mousehole, Barrington noted that he heard Dolly Pentreath "grumbling to other women in Cornish when she got a poor price for her fish, and (they) said they understood, though they could not speak the language readily, being ten years younger than Dolly." It would seem that this report reflects a situation where elements of the Cornish words and expressions were recognised by the women, or, indeed, that to some extent they may have inferred Dolly's meaning from her manner and tone of delivery. This does not establish that these women possessed a precise, or even general comprehension of the Cornish words themselves, and Barrington's observations appear to have been based solely upon the women's *claims* to have understood Dolly on this occasion. Moreover, Barrington did not record any other usage or exchange of Cornish amongst the inhabitants of the village. At first Barrington's evidence was received with scepticism, contradicting, as it did, the established pronouncement of William Borlase; but after the latter's death, in the summer of 1772, Walter Borlase (William's brother, and the Vicar of Madron) confirmed in a letter to Barrington, that Dolly Pentreath was indeed the last known Cornish speaker,[199] although this was not entirely correct. Three years later Barrington claimed to have located evidence of five other Cornish speakers[200], two of whom, Jane Cock and Jane Woolcock, both of Newlyn, had died. The third was an inhabitant of Truro (unnamed, but mentioned by a London bookseller, James Phillips) who Pool suggests was "probably the mining engineer Tompson, who Polwhele met in 1789 and considered to know more Cornish than Dolly [Pentreath] had ever done",[201] and lastly, John Nancarrow of Marazion (aged 40 in 1777) who later emigrated to America[202], and William Bodinar (-1778) of Mousehole, from whom Barrington printed a letter which is described by Pool as "the last passage of authentic Cornish writing to survive". None of these men, however, are known to have been totally proficient in the language, and although Bodinar possessed some fluency, after his death "there is no evidence of the survival of anyone who could speak Cornish fluently, and no reliable witness claims to have met such a person."[203]

By the late 1700s, John Whitaker, the Rector of Ruan Lanihorne, east of Truro (from 1777-1808) claimed that the Cornish people were totally ignorant of the language and the meanings of Cornish place-names,[204] and his visit to Land's End in 1799 to find Cornish speakers, met with no success. Although the Breton grammarian le Gonidec[205] spent the year 1793 in Penzance, he left no record of ever hearing the Cornish language spoken. It has sometimes been claimed by the proponents of the late survival of Cornish that le Gonidec's silence on the matter of Cornish can be explained in that, during his stay, he found Cornish to be so widely spoken that he saw no need to comment on it. It is hardly credible, however, that such an avid student of language would have failed to note at least some of the distinctive grammatical and phonetic features of the language had he encountered it. Another Breton, la Tour d'Auvergne[206], a prisoner of war at Bodmin in 1795 recorded that, so far as he could discover, Cornish was entirely extinct, except for place-names. At Bodmin itself, Cornish is not known to have survived, so it may not be surprising that d'Auvergne did not hear of it there. However, it is not known if, before or after his incarceration, he travelled more extensively towards the western parts of the County. The Rev. Richard Warner of Bath, who began his 1808 tour of Cornwall by paying a visit to Land's End, hopeful of finding Cornish speakers, and who supposed that Barrington could have been more assiduous in his research and could have traced more Cornish speakers in 1768 than he had done, eventually became convinced that, even by the 1760s, "the faculty of speaking the language was exceedingly limited", and that his own visit had produced no evidence that it was spoken at all.[207] Only the occasional person is said to have possessed some spoken ability in the language by this time, such as William Matthews of Newlyn (who died between 1786-1800)[208], Ann Wallis (c. 1754-1844) and Jane Barnicoat (-1857) both of St. Buryan, and John Davey of Boswednack, Zennor (1812-1891), although these claims (especially the latter) are uncertain or doubtful. Indeed, a Professor John Westlake who "had known Davey well and collected many words from him, never heard from or of him that he could converse in Cornish on any topic."[209] In 1814, Lysons recorded that no one could converse in Cornish but that "some old people are acquainted with many words of it which they have learned from the last generation".[210]

Earlier, in 1790, a work by William Pryce (1735-1790), a mine surgeon from Redruth, had been published which was the first book to attempt a comprehensive survey of material relating to the Cornish language. Pryce's *Archaeologia Cornu-Britannica*,[211] comprised a wide-ranging collection of Cornish grammar, vocabulary, place-names, proverbs, prayers and rhymes, largely drawn from the work of others such as Lhuyd, Nicolas Boson, Tonkin and Borlase. This compendium of the language helped at least to preserve many items of the language which might otherwise have been lost. Such people as John Davey of Boswednack, apart from the Cornish lessons given to him by his father, John Davey (1770-1844) a St. Just schoolmaster, could have taken and learned examples of Cornish sayings from the family copy of Pryce's book.[212] Although the extent of its distribution amongst the Cornish people cannot be known, it may well have been an item for recital and of private study in some of those Cornish homes where literacy had taken root. From such a convenient compilation as this, items of Cornish could be learned by rote, or absorbed, unconsciously and intermittently, and so have some chance of being heard and transmitted to others, if only in passing. In this way, at least some consciousness of the language, if not the comprehension of it, would have remained.[213] But, despite such a resource as this, Nance observes that, by 1800, Cornish "was no longer used in daily speech by anyone, old or young, but remembered only occasionally and in fragments.....which would often be numerous enough to give the impression, to those who understood nothing of them, that... their (speakers) must have been able to 'converse on a few topics'. But these people would have been quite unable to take their words and form new Cornish sentences with them, and still less would they instinctively think in Cornish. They knew some Cornish, but as a language they could not speak it."[214] And so, thereafter, the language survived only in the form of dialect words, place-names and proverbial fragments, many barely understood, and most not at all.

In reality the Cornish language had begun to decline and die over centuries. During this attenuated process, and as, in Max Muller's words, Cornish was "losing its consciousness and vitality" and English began to replace it, at about the time of the Reformation, a "metamorphic process" would have taken place:[215] Cornish words were no longer understood and over time they themselves became slightly changed. These verbal relics created puzzlement and confusion and so it became both necessary and desirable to give them an intelligible meaning. The search for a meaning could be satisfied most easily by drawing upon English near-sounding equivalents (a kind of phonetic transfer, or fusion), or by allocating a reference from legend, history or religion for the same reason. "This new meaning is mostly a mistaken one, yet is not only readily accepted, but the word in its new dress and with its new character is frequently made to support facts or fictions which could be supported by no other evidence."[216] This process, according to Müller, is accelerated wherever two languages come into contact and where one supersedes the other. Cornish, while still spoken, became disturbed and invaded from time to time by Latin, Saxon and Norman: the Celtic language adopted words from them and they from it. This is the "metamorphic process" which continued with English.[217] Names were transformed, legends were born, and these in turn came to acquire the status of generally accepted facts. From such a process the names of *Marazion* and *Market Jew* eventually came into existence, their aetiology forgotten and their significance mistaken. The old name for Falmouth, for example, came to be *Penny-Come-Quick*, from the Cornish *Pen y cwm qwic* (Headland of the Valley Creek, or Head of the Creek Valley), *Bryn whella* (highest hill, or from Padel's reading of the 1576 form, "hill of swallows") became *Brown Willy*, and *Cwm ty goed* (Valley-house-wood) became *Come-to Good*.[218] The two place-names which have given rise to the persistent notion that Jews were resident in Cornwall in ancient times are *Marazion,* the little town opposite St. Michael's Mount, and just across the bay from Penzance, and the latter's main street *Market Jew. Marazion* sounds very similar to two Hebrew words: *Marah,* (bitterness, grief) and *Zion* (of Zion). This has encouraged considerable speculation that Jewish coins found in England from the period of the first Jewish revolt against the Romans (66-70 CE), which ended with the destruction of the Temple on Mount Zion, are evidence of the dispersal of thousands of Jewish prisoners as slaves all over the Roman world. Many of these are said to have ended up in Cornwall working in the tin-mines. These exiled Jewish slaves and their descendants, it is claimed, called the settlement *Marazion* - 'Bitter Zion'.

   Little, if anything of this is verifiable, of course, and such notions have clearly been influenced by the Biblical accounts of the Exile of the Hebrews from the ancient Kingdoms of Israel and Judah to Assyria and Babylon in the period circa 731-536 BCE, reflected also in Psalm 137. Moreover, there are a number of obvious weaknesses in this speculative notion. However intriguing the discovery of some Jewish coins from this period might be, and although such fragmentary material might point to the presence of some Jews attached to a contingent of the Roman army as conscripts or slaves, it cannot be used to postulate the presence of a whole population of Jews, let alone many thousands "working in the tin-mines". Nor is it likely that a settlement named *Marazion* in Roman times would have been variously re-named, with unrelated titles, in 13th and 14th century Cornish (as below), only to revert to the Hebrew name (with its persecutory overtones) in the 17th or 18th centuries when by the 1740s Jews had come to live in Cornwall in conditions of freedom and peace. Moreover, if this term did indeed reflect the grief of dispersed Jewish slaves, as suggested, and Jewish captives of the Roman legions displaced to Britain really originated the name *Marazion* in Cornwall, such captives consigned to other outposts would have been likely to have given other such places around the Roman Empire the same, or a similar name. The evidence for this simply does not exist.[219] As Müller points out,[220] *Mara* could be ascribed just as arbitrarily to a corruption of the Latin *Amara*, "bitter" (which in itself could undermine the "Jewish argument"): "It cannot be too often repeated that inquiries into the origin of local names are, in the first place historical, and only in the second place, philological. To attempt an explanation of any name, without having first traced it back to the earliest form in which we can find it, is to set at defiance the plainest rules of the science of language as well as the science of history." Muller's emphasis upon the *earliest* etymological form of words is, of course, central to the matter of explanation. An added difficulty in assessing the forms of words relating to Cornish place-names is the fact that it was common practice to write and pronounce the names of places in various ways thus increasing the ignorance of their original meanings still further. What came to be *Marazion* had been known variously (from around 1600 back to 1480) as: *Merkiu*,[221] *Marcaiew*,[222] *Markesin*, *Markine*, and *Marasdethyon*,[223] *Markysyoo*, *Marchew*, *Margew*, *Marchasyowe*, and *Markysyow*.[224] In a charter of 1257, Richard Earl of Cornwall calls it *Marchadyon*, possibly the oldest known version. In 1261 this has become *Markesiou* and *Markesion*, in 1309, *Marchasyon*, and in 1337, *Marcasion*. In 1595, a charter of Queen Elizabeth calls it *Marghasiewe*. Other varieties proliferated such as *Marghasion* and *Maryazion*.[225]

What these examples clearly show is the variety of spelling and pronunciation. The varieties and inconsistencies of spoken Cornish, exacerbated by high levels of illiteracy, would have shaped the written words. Although consonants could be alternated as soft or hard, and vowels, dental or nasal, as in Welsh, spoken Cornish is likely to have been characterised by the softening of consonants, with (as mentioned earlier) *d* or *t* becoming *th* or *sh*. Hence, an *s* could become a *z*, a *iewe* become a *dyewe* or *jewe*, or the reverse might happen. Vowels could be retained (*Marachasyowe*) or partially dropped with an extra ending consonant (*Markesin*) and the central sounds, possibly omitted altogether. Such features have survived today in spoken Cornish dialect where place-names such as Saint Ives may become *Snives* or Redruth, *Druth*. "*Marc(g)has*" (most likely pronounced as *maraz*) was the Cornish word for "market", and it can be seen to be comparable to the Latin *mercatus*, the Breton *marchad*, and the French *marche*. Ancient Marazion originally consisted of at least two (possibly three) settlements, the smaller inland known as *Marc(g)has-bighan* (small market) and the larger, by the sea facing the Island, or Mount, as *Marghas Yow* or *Marchas-di(y)ew*, or "Thursday market", the Cornish for Thursday being *yow* or *deyow*.[226] Around 1070, Count Robert of Mortain granted St. Michael's Mount to the Norman *Mont Saint Michel*, the grant included weekly market to be held on a Thursday (Jeudi). It may have been known at times as *Marchas-yow*," southerly or south-facing market, and Marazion does face towards the South and East, as its opposite neighbour, Penzance, faces the North and East. It may also have been called *Marchas-ion* (St.) "John's Market", although Müller suggests that the *ion*, *yon*, or *in* endings may indicate a diminutive termination (little market) also commonly found in Welsh. Some form of *diew* can also suggest "second" (French *deux*), or the "other market". Marazion may well have had two such markets at one time, held on different days of the week, or even an inland and a seaward market. Consequently, as Marazion, at one time the Bay's chief town, gradually diminished into an inferior trading centre to the larger market at *Pensans* across the water, it became, in effect, the second market.

The name *Pensans* is not mentioned in the Domesday Book of 1086, but is first mentioned as such in 1284 and regularly thereafter.[227] Like Marazion, its name acquired variant forms over time, as *Pensanns* (1337), *Pensant* (1368), *Pensauns* (1482), *Pensaunce* (1513), *Pensance* (1555 & 1614), *Pensanse* (1620), *Penzour* (1623)[228], *Pensans* (1686)[229] and both *Penzanz* and *Pensands* (1698). As its name varied so has the understanding of its meaning, which has been interpreted as "The Saint's Head" (Carew 1602), "The Head of the Sand" (Norden *c.* 1605) and "The Head of the Bay" (Tonkin *c.* 1700). It is correctly derived from the Cornish words *pen* (head, top or end) and *sans* or *sant* (holy or sacred), hence (the noun preceding the adjective) as "Holy Headland". *Pen* is found in various Cornish names as headland or head, and *sans* occurs in other place-names such as *Lezant* (*lan sant*, holy enclosure), *Tresant* (either *tre sant*, holy farm, or *tyr sant*, holy land) and *Eglosant* (*eglos sans*, holy church) a former name for Sancreed, outside Penzance. *Pensans* is also associated with two chapels, one built on the end of the headland by the quay, and another further inland where the Chapel of St. Anthony once stood, and on the site of the later St. Mary's Church.[230] Penzance has also been known by the alternative name of *Burryton* (1696) that is, the Borough Town. This name appears never to have become established, but survives within the town in the form of the street or house name of "Buriton".[231]

With the name *Marchas-diew*, however, no one who spoke Cornish would have taken the name's ending to mean *Jew* because the Cornish for *Jew* was (Y)*Edhow*, or *Eth(sh)ow*, and "Jew's Market or Market Jew" would have been *Marchas-Ye(th)(dh)ewon*. Against this, it has been argued that *Marazion* can be derived from *Margha Dzhuon* or *Edzhuon*, "the latter being one of the admissible plural forms of the corruption of *Edhow* into *Ezow*, a Jew",[232] so that *Margha Edzhuon* becomes the "Market of the Jews". At best, this remains in essence a speculative exercise, however alluring it may be, and there is no decisive evidence of the stages of the words' corruption in Cornish pronunciation to some phonetic approximation to "Jew", and consequently this theory cannot be established with any certainty. However, that some process of corruption has been at work in the transition from Cornish to English is entirely credible, and the Thursday (*yow*) market may well have become associated with the *jeudi* market held at Mont Saint Michel. Moreover, to the Saxon (English) ear, *Marchas-diew* could become by association *Market Jew*, and *Marchas-bic(z)han* (where the *ch* or *bic* sounds may have been corrupted through omission, contraction, and the hardening into *z*) could become, by the same metamorphic process, to "Marazion" (which clearly is some kind of name for "market"). The town of Penzance (*Pensans*) or at least its main street, also came to be known as *Marchas-diew* (or *yow*), either because it led directly to what later came to be known as Marazion, or because Penzance had also come to have its own, and now the main Thursday market of the area.

Müller dates the emergence of *Market-Jew* to the period from 1634 when it is mentioned in a State Paper, dated 3rd October 1634.[233] In another State Paper dated 7th February 1634-5, the cargo of a wrecked Spanish galleon off "Gwavas Lake" in Mount's Bay was threatened by an unlawful gathering of inhabitants from "Mousehole and *Marka-jew*". In 1720, *Merkju* is mentioned as a little market-town which had taken its name from the market on Thursdays (*Magna Britannia et Hibernia*) and in 1728, *Marca-iewe* is explained in the same way in Norden's *Specul. Britanniae*. As Norden had been born in 1548, his late work, *circa*. 1610, but not published until 1728, might suggest an even earlier usage. Gibson's 1772 edition of *Camden's Britannia* gives *Market-Jew*. Gough's, of 1789, states that "*Merkiu* signifies the *Market of Jupiter*, from the market being held on a Thursday, the day sacred to Jupiter." The 1769 edition of Carew's *Survey of Cornwall* has: "Over against the Mount fronteth a towne of petty fortune, pertinently named *Marcaiew*, or *Marhas diow*, in English 'the Thursdaies market'". In fact, the process by which the name *Marchas diow* came to be transferred across the Bay from the one settlement to the other is not difficult to trace, even it its timing is open to question: as the population and the Thursday Market (*Marchas diow*) of the newer settlement of *Pen Sans* ("Holy Headland") outgrew those of its more ancient neighbour, then the latter lost its name of *Marchas diow*, becoming *Marchas (b)izion* or Marazion ("Little Market") and the street in Penzance were the locality's largest Thursday market was now held became *Marchas yow*, the chief, and by then most possibly the only Thursday Market, so that eventually this became "Market Jew".

The possibilities for such subtle changes and associations may also have been influenced by external factors and by corruption within Cornish itself. Sea-faring contacts with France may have played a part in this process: "In the sixth century Breton and Cornish were one language, but in the interim Breton had acquired many French, and Cornish almost as many English words; besides which the Cornish intonation, and sounds of consonants as well as vowels, had developed on lines of their own, making them as unlike those of other Celtic languages, as they were unlike the oldest forms of Cornish."[234] Eventually such processes as these may have allowed *Marchas-diew* to be overlaid with the French *Marche de Jeudi*, both meaning "Thursday market" and so "*jeudi*" itself could easily have assisted the process towards *Market Jew*. Moreover, the Cornish for Jew (*Yedhow*) came to be corrupted to *Ezow*, *Ethow* or *Eshow*, so that *Mar(ch)as-bic(z)an* could have been confused with *Mar(ch)as-ez(sh)uon*, and the "little" market could, in this way, have acquired an aural connection with Jews or Zion for both Cornish and English speakers. The castle on St. Michael's Mount in the bay would have reinforced this association by re-calling to Cornish Christians familiar with the Old Testament, the Temple on Mount Zion in Jerusalem. The eventual establishment in the 18th and 19th centuries of a Jewish community and Jewish shops in Penzance (especially along its main market street) likewise strengthened the name Market Jew.

Although the smelting-centres, or *Jews' Houses*, are most likely to have been so-called for the reasons above, a similar process less readily traceable through its main phases, may have occurred here. In Cornish these houses were known as *Chiwidden*, from the Cornish *ty* or *chy* (house), no doubt shortened in pronunciation (as today) to *chi* or *chew,* and the old Cornish *gwyn* (white) which became corrupted to *gwydn*. The original name clearly reflected the distinctive colour and intense heat of the smelting furnaces, but the capacity for the Cornish *chew* to be confused with the later *Jew* is self-evident. Sacred legend also attached to the *Chiwidden* in the form of St. Chiwidden, the companion of St. Piran, the Cornish Miner-Saint (but originally from Ireland) whose name occurs (as Perran) in such places as Perranporth, Perranuthno and Perranarworthal. "The legend relates that St. Piran, when still in Cornwall, employed a heavy black stone as part of his fire-place. The fire was more intense than usual, and a stream of beautiful white metal flowed out of the fire. Great was the joy of the saint, and he communicated his discovery to St. Chiwidden - who soon devised a process for producing this metal in large quantities. The two saints called the Cornishmen together.....they taught them how to dig the ore from the earth, and how, by the agency of fire, to obtain the metal."[235] Needless to say, if these "Pirran" legends were to be read simplistically as affording a glimpse of the historical origins of the smelting-houses, then they could be ascribed as arbitrarily to an Irish origin as they have been to the Jews. The *Chiwidden* were also known by the Cornish *tshey* or *dzhey*, a later form of *ty,* or house. Variations in pronunciation, similar to those seen in the case of *Mar(ch)as- diew,* from which the "Saxon mouth and ...Saxon ear might have elicited a sound ...like the English *Jew,*" could easily have turned *dzhey or dzeyew* into *Jew* so that *Jew* and *house* become phonetically indistinguishable.[236] In contrast to the *white* of the heat in the smelting-furnaces, the smelting houses would have become *blackened* and it is likely that *chy du* (black house), as an alternative name for the smelting houses, also played its part in the transition from *du* to *Jew,* as mentioned earlier.

The pronunciation of the word *ty,* or *chy(ew),* may likewise have influenced the name for *Market Jew Street*. Between what is today the Greenmarket, the imposing Lloyds Bank building with its dome and the statue of Sir Humphry Davy facing down the main street, there was the site of the town's ancient market. The Lloyd's building is known today as Market House and the town's market required then, as now, a "House" where financial and commercial transactions could take place. The combination and phonetic conflation of *Marchas* and *dzey(ew)* would also produce *Market Jew,* even though the *Jew* is more readily understood from *diew* or *dyow,* the "Thursday" (or possibly "Southerly") Market. That Jews came to trade along this street and in this market from the mid-1700s, is not relevant to the derivation of the name, but was a factor which provided a later associative gloss. A similar process to these is decipherable in the present-day name of the road, known as *Jews' Walk* in the south London suburb of Sydenham. Tradition has it that the name is derived from the practice of the road being a favoured strolling area for Jewish musicians who played at the nearby Crystal Palace, which was transferred from Hyde Park in 1854. Another story has it that it was once gated at either end, forming a safe sanctuary for its resident Jews from persecution. However, the name is most likely derived from a South London pronunciation and corruption of *Doo's Wharf,* from *Doo,* an ancient place-name in Kent. From a wharf on the river, boats set out for *Doo,* and from the site of this same wharf, the railway line into central London now runs. The Jewess and socialist activist, Eleanor Marx (the youngest daughter of Karl Marx) came to live at No. 7, Jews' Walk, taking her life there in March 1898. This suicide, like that of the *Jews' Lane* in Breage, and the murder in the *Jew's Wood*, near Plymouth, has, no doubt, also given rise to an association with Jews.[237]

And so the term *Jews Houses* and the ostensible Jewish place-names had no necessary original connection with Jews. They are entirely explicable in terms of their derivation from the Cornish language and its legendary products. The much later need to ascribe meaning to a forgotten and foreign language from which people had become excluded and estranged played a vital creative and imaginative part in this process. This, in turn, gave birth to the Jewish connections and legends which have become attached to them. As Müller writes: "these names had given rise to the assumed presence of Jews in Cornwall, and not that the presence of Jews in Cornwall had given rise to these names."[238] Even if some Jews lived and settled in Cornwall in Medieval times, their numbers and activities are unknown, and their contribution, if any, to topography and nomenclature would have been, at most, incidental, and certainly peripheral to the seminal forces at work in the history, indigenous culture and language of the Cornish People. Despite this, the extravagant and unsubstantiated tradition (often based upon little or no evidence at all, or upon ambiguous references and erroneous interpretation) that there was a sizeable Jewish population in Cornwall in ancient times and a late monopoly over the construction and control of the tin-mining industry in Medieval times, by a comparable *resident* population of Jews, has survived, largely through constant repetition, even though it has flourished in the absence of credible confirmation.

Jews and the Cornish Emblem

A curious and little known legend has been woven around a version of the Cornish emblem (fifteen gold balls in the shape of an inverted triangular shield) linking its origin to Jewish pawnbrokers.[239] On the south aisle wall of Westminster Abbey can be seen the coat of arms of Richard, Count, or Earl of Poitou, King of the Romans (1209-1272), the second son of King John, who was created Earl of Cornwall in 1225-7. It consists of a silver shield and a red lion rampant with a gold crown (a symbol of the House of Anjou, and possibly a memento of Richard's uncle, Coeur de Lion, after whom he was named). The shield's black border is dotted with twenty-two bezants, or gold balls.[240] It has been supposed that these may represent gold peas (French *poix*) as a "punning allusion" to *Poitou*, but that during or after Richard's Earldom, the shield began to acquire usage as Cornwall's emblem. The theory would presuppose that a considerably modified version of the shield was eventually adopted, with Richard's lion and crown excised, and with only fifteen gold discs (perhaps for reasons of spatial economy) being relocated to the shield's centre, arranged in rows of 5, 4, 3, 2 and 1. This emblem appears as a carving in the form of an armorial achievement on the front of the Convocation, or Exchequer Hall of the Duchy Palace in Lostwithiel. The Lostwithiel freestone carving, which is most likely the oldest representation in stone of the shield, is later than the building itself, likely post-17th century, and probably from the post-Restoration period.[241]

In fact, "there is no official precedent for the fixed group of *fifteen* bezants as arms of the Duchy before the early seventeenth century", and before 1607, the number and ordering of the bezants was not regularised, although this was the case by around 1610.[242] Richard of Cornwall's shield of twenty-two bezants was not the only pattern, and others show fourteen, eleven and ten bezants. In the first edition of his *Britannia* (1586) William Camden tells of an Earl of Cornwall named Cadoc, at around the time of the Norman Conquest, who is said to have had a black shield decorated with golden roundels, and the second edition (1607) gives the number as fifteen. Subsequent embellishments of this description, in Philemon Holland's translation from the Latin (1610), have led to this tradition being viewed with scepticism, most notably by Henry Jenner. However, three armorial shields, much earlier than Camden, appear on the hilt of a sword made for the young Edward, Prince of Wales, Duke of Cornwall, later Edward V, who died at the age of twelve (1470-1483). One of these show three lions, and another a black shield with seventeen bezants. This would seem to suggest that such a pattern was indeed the emblem of the Overlord of Cornwall. Another painted Roll of Arms appears around 1480 for "King Burbred Cornubie" of seventeen bezants arranged as 4, 3, 4, 3, 2, & 1, and other patterns of the time have thirteen and twenty-five bezants. A seal of Richard, attached to a deed of *c.*1240 in Magdalen College, Oxford consists (on the reverse) of a lion rampant with fourteen bezants, with a floreated border, marked as *Signillum Ricardi comitis Cornubie*.[243] From this, the number of bezants were always more than eight, but were indefinite in number. Of the pattern of fifteen bezants in triangular form that have become associated with Richard of Cornwall (1225), it has been said that they "are late developments, which possess no real significance, but have given rise to foolish and unworthy fictions".[244]

Clearly, issues of aetiology cannot be established with certainty, and there will be other theories as to the origin of the Cornish emblem, in its form of fifteen bezants. One such theory links the triplicate of five balls to each of the five coinage towns which resulted from the addition of Penzance in 1663 to the medieval towns of the four Stannaries of Foweymoor, on Bodmin Moor (Liskeard), Blackmoor, the moors north of St. Austell, later known as the "white moor" of the china clay industry (Lostwithiel), Tywarnhayle, the St. Agnes area (Truro) and the former combined Stannary area of Penwith and Kerrier (Helston). (Penzance was added, because "Helston had no port facilties (other than at Gweek) and was inconveniently remote from the tin-producing areas of Penwith").[245] But there is an even more colourful explanation attached to the emblems's origin, which may well fall into the category of a "foolish and unworthy" fiction. This theory is based upon a notion that, in Plantagenet times, there were Jewish pawnbrokers in Cornwall who were the most prosperous merchants in England, and that when King John wished to mortgage his crown to finance a war in France, five Jewish pawnbrokers agreed amongst themselves to form a consortium so that they could jointly take over the King's debts. The story supposes that the fifteen inverted gold balls represent the combined symbols (of three inverted balls) of these five pawnbrokers, who were based in five Cornish towns, spread across the County. Their names were apparently found in a manuscript in the British Museum, although the source and the details contained in it have not been authenticated. They are said to have been *Ben Levy* of Truro, *Ben Ezra* of Penzance, *Moses* of Mevagissey, and two others whose names and location are lost (as illegible). Needless to say, their names could be entirely fictional, and even as they stand, suggestive as they may be of a Jewish connection, they could apply to Gentiles. Purportedly, their motto "One and All" (which has since become the motto of Cornwall) signified that no business or financial transaction could be conducted without a quorum of all five pawnbrokers. Accordingly, each pawnbroker's symbol (three inverted balls) was incorporated into the fifteen balls of their emblem and, presumably in time, its familiar appearance across the County led to its adoption as Cornwall's emblem of solidarity. That the five Stannary towns (only two of which are consistent with the pawnbroker story) were the chief cohesive factors in Cornwall's administrative, economic system and in popular consciousness is itself questionable. Certainly in Medieval times the charters of the seven boroughs of Bodmin, Dunheved (Launceston), Helston, Liskeard, West Looe, Lostwithiel and Tintagel were of lasting significance, and in much later times the County's districts fell into six distinct administrative areas, of Caradon, Carrick, Restormel, North Cornwall, Kerrier and Penwith.

The theory of the five pawnbrokers has been dismissed as amusing but quite frivolous, and it may well be that it is based upon the dubious premise that wealthy money-lenders will necessarily be Jews. The three names have not been corroborated from contemporaneous sources from the Angevin period (such as the Pipe Rolls) or from any others. The existence of these Jewish pawnbrokers, and their residence on Cornish soil remains unsubstantiated, and the details are most likely entirely spurious. The tradition may well be a hybrid reflection, conflating and combining the Jewish co-operative banking system mentioned earlier (which Roth refers to as a national phenomenon), with the use of Jewish financial agents by such men as the two Aarons (of Lincoln and York) and Abraham of Berkhamsted, the collection of debts on behalf of the Crown during the Angevin period, and a curious reversal of the tradition of the mortgaging of the Jews *to* Earl Richard (in 1255 and 1270). It is doubtful if the origins of the Cornish emblem will ever be established with certainty, but it would, indeed, be an irony if an emblem which came to represent Cornish solidarity, independence and resistance to external influence and exploitation, could be shown to have been imposed by King John, or by Richard Earl of Cornwall upon the County's inhabitants (with or without the involvement of Jewish intermediaries or their agents) as a symbol of Royal potency and control. In this respect it is noticeable that such anecdotal traditions are often characterised by fluid and even contradictory elements, and another contrasting interpretation of the origins of the emblem derives not from an external imposition of financial levies to the Crown from a reluctant Cornish population, but of their willing subscription, locality by locality during the Crusades, of funds to ransom an Earl of Cornwall who had supposedly been taken hostage by the Moors. This particular tradition of loyal adherence to the Crown may well contain anachronistic elements derived from the much later Royalist stance taken by the Cornish (or at least some of the landed Cornish families) during the English Civil War. Later versions of the emblem have removed from the shield the attendant lions, a symbol of royal potency, and have replaced them with the figures of a miner and a fisherman, both representative of the common Cornishman, and the Cornish chough, a rare type of crow, once on the edge of extinction, a symbol of the County's individuality. The former is clearly a reflection of the County's economic heritage, and the latter, as Venetia Newall has observed, echoes a popular tradition surrounding King Arthur (a hero of Cornish myth, who has been associated with Tintagel) that his soul inhabits the chough.

The oral traditions of history, legend and folklore which have been examined here, have been elaborated over many centuries, and they have become entrenched into a powerful symbiosis, which is often negligent in its attention to verification from substantial and credible documentary sources. Nonetheless, these traditions have been repeated uncritically by respected authorities (such as Carew), thereby influencing later writers (such as Coulthard), and they have been accompanied by an oral history shaped and preserved in popular story-telling and populist writings. In such ways the tradition results in Coulthard's uncritical citation of Carew that "the tin trade in Cornwall in ancient times was largely in the hands of Jews, who grievously exploited the Cornish Tinners", which comes to possess the character of unquestionable fact.[246] Indeed the traditions themselves, have been shaped not only by a history of poverty (recorded, amongst others, by Thomas Beare) but also by an age-old prejudice and latent anti-semitism with its familiar juxtaposition of the Jews as slaves and as eager predators and willing accomplices in exploitation. Indeed, in Cornish tradition, the Jew has become by transference the whipping boy for the many hardships and injustices suffered by the miners at the hands of others.

However, from Tudor times onwards, the ruthless financial treatment of Cornish miners, which justified and fuelled their many grievances, was the product and policy not so much of external forces, but of some of the powerful Cornish families who owned and operated the mines, through an "apt combination of dealing and usury", and in so doing amassed great fortunes. Consequently, in the Elizabethan period (which saw the critical transition from tin-streaming to tin-mining), the exploiters and usurers were the Cornish themselves. One of these was "the nasty Elizabethan lawyer" Ezekiel Grose (1564-1631) of Camborne (who, despite his forename, was not Jewish). Grose specialised in lending money to those he knew would be unable to repay him, and when they failed to honour their debt, he foreclosed on their estates. Most notably there was the Roberts family "who having started as merchants at Truro, by tin-dealing and usury achieved an enormous fortune and bought a peerage from Buckingham", changing their name in the process from the common form of "Roberts" to the more distinguished form of "Robartes".[247] The Robartes family were also astute enough to be on the Parliamentarian side in the Civil War, and, from 1553-1601, there were Puritans from some of the other great Cornish families, most notably Edgcumbe, Grenville, and Killigrew, who became both JPs and MPs, although it is uncertain if they were guilty of such excesses of privilege. Just as the rebellion of Michael Joseph can be seen as a reaction against the forces of external control, the later Royalist position of the Cornish during the Civil War could be viewed to some extent as a similar reflexive protest against the predominance of and exploitation by some of the Cornish families over an impoverished population. It may be that the role that has been fabricated for the Jews in Cornish tradition over time and at different times, whether in the form of Roman slaves, their subterranean spirits, the *Knockers*, or the putative control over the mines by Jewish agents of the Crown, were in part a projection and reflection of the sufferings and poverty of the Cornish people at the hands of others. Anti-Semitic attitudes and stereotypes can most certainly exist and endure within a culture and its folklore even when Jews are absent from it, and this was certainly the case in England from the time of the expulsion in 1290, right up to the arrival of Jews from the continent the 1700s.[248]

It is notable, that the industrialisation that came to Cornwall in the 18th and 19th centuries,[249] the form it took, and particularly its impact upon mining, transformed the age-old relations between the miner and the overlord. By its very nature, mining is an activity contingent upon the geology and geography of the land. Many new mines sprang up where the tin and copper was to be found, in towns, on their outskirts, in villages and near hamlets, on moorland and cliff top. Alongside the mines, a plethora of Methodist chapels also took root. Whatever the continuing hardships, the localism of mining life, both urban and rural, resulted in a degree of democratisation of feeling, of pride in a common enterprise, and a new sense of empowerment. Deference towards the gentry and the mine owner may not have been eroded, but its power had been weakened, and a shift in social relations and attitudes was taking place. The Masonic Lodges opened their membership to working men, the culture of choir, band and youth brigade grew out of the workplace, and, later, often directly from the work-place, there followed the establishment of co-operative societies, savings banks and insurance schemes for working men and their families. Fear, early mortality, poverty and bankruptcy had not been banished, but improvements in education, public health and sanitation were underway. Trade Unionism and socialist political movements did not take hold in Cornwall in the way or to the degree they had done elsewhere, and the Cornish Industrial Revolution took on its own particular form and character. It was into this new Cornish culture of optimism and enterprise that Jews arrived and felt able to settle and trade from the 1750s, when the economy was in the ascendant. Suspicion and ignorance of the stranger and the outsider reduced as, in the port towns in particular, foreign visitors and frequent maritime arrivals injected a degree of cosmopolitanism into Cornish society. Jews were to remain in the South of the Cornwall for the next one hundred and fifty years, making a major contribution to the life and commerce of the County.

No doubt, varying attitudes towards the traditions linking ancient and medieval Cornwall with Phoenicians, Jews, and the peoples of the Levant will continue. Some may hold that there must be an historical reality underpinning the stories, even if it remains concealed and unsubstantiated. Others may espouse the view that these traditions are damaged forms of history, distortions and permutations of historical elements which can be glimpsed through their refractory medium, but not defined or fixed with clarity or certainty: there is, after all, no smoke without fire. In the physical world, perhaps, but in the social and cultural world, and even more so in the world of the imagination, the opposite can be true. Traditions may purport to convey an objective, historical reality, but like folktales the method of their transmission is essentially an oral one, shaped by the inventiveness of the tellers and capable of being modified and transformed in the memory and imagination and preoccupations of the listeners, over many generations. Just as there is a distinction between seeing and visual perception, so that two parties looking at the same object will extract and absorb different aspects of it, there is a comparable difference between speaking and hearing, between oral transmission and auditory reception. What was told to the listener is not invariably what the listener hears, and the telling and listening of the same story may vary in content and character from time to time, and from place to place. Moreover, separate traditions and notions may become overlaid and conflated, connections between entirely independent and disparate elements can be forged into quite new, hybrid forms, producing a beguiling and intractable synthesis. Such tales are, therefore, by their very nature, capable of masquerading as fact, when in reality they are fictive, imaginative creations, devoid of any fundamental historical basis, credibility or coherence, spun upon the merest pronouncement or rumour, and reinforced by the pronouncement of prestigious historians of the past. Even so, these traditions are not without historical interest from the perspective of their cultural origins and likely purpose. It may be a truism that a lie told often enough will eventually be believed, at least by many if not by all, but folklore and traditional tales are, at the very least, art-forms, and like any artistic fabrication, their true character lies, not in their supposed explicit or vestigial historicity, but in their artifice, their power of enchantment, and their usage in popular culture.[250] As David Giddings has emphasised in his Introduction to this book: "folklore tells us what people were capable of believing, wished to believe and did believe rather than what is true". What such tales embody, is not an objective, historical reality, but their own very special, subjective reality which resonates strongly with the personal experience of the listener. In this sense they are myths which may embody an essential truth concerning Cornish culture and popular consciousness .

In the case of the "truth" of Cornwall's folklore and traditional legends, the stories tell of a sense of the mystery of the County's ancient past, its isolation, a sense of uniqueness, and a longing for connection and comprehension. The sacredness of the land itself is also a feature of the stories, with peoples from Biblical lands, such as the Phoenicians, seeking it out for its precious products, even Jesus himself, Joseph of Arimathea, and Saint Paul conferring upon it a blessing by their presence. They also tell of fear and suspicion of the stranger and of resentment of the overlord. Christian consciousness and prejudice have also shaped some of the traditions by placing Jews at the centre of the stories which reflect the hardships and dangers which assailed the people, and especially the miners in their struggle to survive and prosper in the face of exploitation from within and without. The loss of the people's indigenous language, a vestigial sense of alienation, and their Anglicisation and adoption of English undoubtedly created cultural confusion and uncertainty, and Jews became implicated in the linguistic struggles and adaptations that resulted. The source for this was the only source heard or read, the Bible. The arrival of Jews in the 1740s occurred in a new, vibrant cultural, economic and linguistic era in the history of Cornwall, when Jews finally stepped out from the shades of the County's folklore and into the reality and glare of its vibrant social and commercial life. Here they took their place in the streets and markets of its towns, travelling into its rural hinterland, and they were seen, not as caricatures, filtered through the distorting prism of folklore and tradition, but as fellow-workers seeking a better life for themselves and their families in the evolving and colourful world of 18th and 19th century Cornish society.

---

[59] See Nora K. Chadwick, *The Celts* (Penguin 1970) and Jan Filip, *Celtic Civilisation and its Heritage* (Prague 1962).

[60] For two studies, among many, see Craig Weatherhill, *Cornovia: Ancient Sites of Cornwall and Scilly 4000 BC to 1000 AD* (Halsgrove 2009), Alan M. Kent, *Celtic Cornwall* (Halsgrove 2012), Barry Cunliffe, *The Celtic World* (London 1979) and Charles Thomas, *Celtic Britain* (Thames and Hudson 1997).

[61] For an early study of the Manx language by a Cornish philologist, see Henry Jenner, *The Manx Language: its grammar, literature and present state* (Transactions of the Philological Society 1875-76).

[62] F. Berresford Ellis, *The Cornish Language and its Literature* (Routledge & Kegan Paul 1974) pp. 6-7 gives various examples of these differences, and this book is an invaluable introduction to the history of the Cornish language and its scholars. Whilst there has been much progress and research in the study of the Cornish language in the last few decades alone, and numerous publications are now available, the classic works by Henry Jenner are still of great interest and value, including *A Handbook of the Cornish Language* (London 1904). See also by Jenner, *Cornish Place-Names* (Journal RIC vol. xviii 1910-11), *A History of Cornish Place-Names* (Royal Cornwall Polytechnic Society *RCPS* vol. ii (1911-13), *Cornwall – a Celtic Nation* (*Celtic Review CR* vol. I, 1905), *Cornish Drama* (*CR* 1907), *The Cornish Language* (Transactions of the Philological Society *TPS* 1873-74), *Traditional Relics of the Cornish Language in Mount's Bay in 1875* (*TPS* 1875-76), *Descriptions of Cornish Manuscripts* (Journal RIC vol. xix 1912), and *The History and Literature of the Ancient Cornish Language* (Journal of the British Archaeological Society *JBAS* vol. xxxiii 1877)

[63] Berresford Ellis, pp. 29-34ff.

[64] Berresford Ellis, pp. 32-51.

[65] Berresford Ellis, p. 53.

[66] A. L. Rowse, *Tudor Cornwall* (1957) pp. 114-140; John Chynoweth, *Tudor Cornwall* (Tempus 2002) pp. 208-211.

[67] Berresford Ellis, p. 52.

[68] Berresford Ellis, p. 21.

[69] Peter Ackroyd, The History of England Vol 1 *Foundation,* Macmillan (2011) p. 50.

[70] Venetia Newall, *The Jews of Cornwall in Local Tradition*, originally published in the Transactions of the Jewish Historical Society of England and reprinted in *The Lost Jews of Cornwall* (2000), edited Pearce & Fry, pp. 13-17. In this concise and insightful essay, which makes a major contribution to any understanding of this issue, Dr. Newall cites various primary sources for the examples given here.

[71] H. Miles Brown, *The Church in Cornwall*, Truro (1964) p. 13.

[72] T. R. Glover, *The Ancient World* (Penguin 1953) p. 289.

[73] Jacquetta and Christopher Hawkes, *Prehistoric Britain* (Penguin 1958) p. 131; I. A. Richmond, *Roman Britain* (Penguin 1958) pp. 149 & 156.

[74] I. A. Richmond, *Roman Britain* (Penguin 1958) pp. 149-185.

[75] For example, W. M. Don Falconer, *The Square and the Compass – In Search of Freemasonry*. This and other sources can be found on the website freemasons-freemasonry.com.

[76] Another Masonic author, Harvey Lowell, provides a detailed analysis of the purported usage of this Cornish tin in his *Solomon's Temple – The Bronze casting of the Jachin and Boaz Pillars*.

[77] Bannister (1867) pp. 339-40.

[78] Bannister (1867) p. 336.

[79] James Whetter, *Cornwall in the 13th Century* (Lyfrow Trelyspen 1998) p. 220.

[80] *Bibliotecha Cornubiensis* p. 914.

[81] Bannister (1867) pp. 324-325.

[82] Bannister (1867) pp. 324-325.

[83] In A.L. Rowse, *A Cornish Anthology* (Macmillan 1968) p.18, quoting from Symons' *Cities and Sea Coasts and Islands* (W. Collins & Sons Co. Ltd. London 1918).

[83a] Cecil Roth, *A History of the Marranos* (Philadelphia 1932) pp. 190-191 & 252-253; Roth, *History of the Jews of England* (Oxford 1949) pp. 135-139, 154-161, 175-179, 200-211 & 230-232. A. L. Rowse, *Tudor Cornwall* (Jonathan Cape 1947) pp. 75 & 403-406; P. A. S. Pool, *A History of the Town and Borough of Penzance* (1974) pp. 24-28, 30-32, 43 & 183; F. E. Halliday, *A History of Cornwall* (Duckworth 1959) pp. 202-204. Helen Fry, a descendant of Lazarus and Tampsina Burno has provided details of this marriage and her family tradition (October 2013). I am also grateful to Jackie Hill for checking sources for the marriage, and to Alison Spence (Archivist CRO Truro) for accessing the original entry in the Gulval Parish Marriage Register (14th October 2013). G. Pawley White, *A Handbook of Cornish Surnames* (Dyllansow Truran 1999) p. 43; O. J. Padel, *A Popular Dictionary of Cornish Place-Names* (Alison Hodge 1988) p. 140.

[83b] Records of the Cornwall Family History Society, Truro.

[84] Pool (1974) pp. 281-282 & 287 (Index).

[85] *Trathen's Guide* (1815) p. 32.

[86] Entries for all of these names can be found in O. J. Padel's *Cornish Place-Names* (1988), T. F. G. Dexter's *Cornish Names* (1968), G. P. White's *A Handbook of Cornish Surnames* (1999) and Craig Weatherhill's *A Concise Dictionary of Cornish Place-Names* (Evertype 2009).

[87] See ref. Applebaum (1953) p. 189 note 4: citing a reported remark by Professor R. G. Collingwood.

[88] *Song of Songs*, Ch. 4; v. 14.

[89] A. H. Sayce, *Patriarchal Palestine* (London 1895). Ch. VI, pp. 242-43. Sayce's considerable corpus of writings apply an archaeological perspective to Biblical history, and also range widely across Egyptian, Assyrian and Babylonian history, culture and philology.

[90] Shimon Applebaum *Were There Jews in Roman Britain* in *TJHSE* vol. XVII (1953) p. 189; Camden *Britannia* (1607) *Damnonii* 9; Max Muller *Chips from a German Workshop* (1870) III, p. 299; Hencken (1931).

[91] The literature relating to Egyptian Religion, History and Archaeology is plentiful, and the five-volume history by A. H. Sayce himself has become a standard work. Numerous publications and websites give information on the Apis Bull.

[92] For a concise outline of the St. Just Bull see Jane Marley in the RIC Newsletter No. 53 (April 2013) p. 13; see also Applebaum (1953) p. 193; *Victoria Histories of the Counties of England* (1924) Cornwall part v. Roman Cornwall 39; Hencken 168-169 & 300. See also Russell (1971) below, p. 97-99; J. Buller *Statistical Account of the Parish of St. Just in Penwith* (Penzance 1842) p. 6.

[93] Kevin Henderson, *The Middle Chamber of King Solomon's Temple* (Masonic websites). Henderson does not identify the mine by name or location.

[94] "Jews Houses" in *Antiquity*, vol. 25, June 1951, pp. 66-68.

[95] John Steegman, *Cambridge* (Batsford 1949) p. 4.

[96] Roth's reference: Edrisi's *Geography*, II, 235.

[97] Roth's reference: *Itinerary*, ed. Adler, p. 2.

[98] Roth's references: Murray's 'Handbook for travellers in Greece', 1854: W. Ettinghausen (Eytan) in the *Jewish Quarterly Review*, N.S. XXXVI, 1946, 419-21.

[99] Roth, *ibid*, p. 67.

[100] Susser (1993, p. 266).

[101] G. R. Lewis *The Stannaries* (1908: reprinted D, Bradford Barton, Truro 1965) p. 16; A. K. Hamilton Jenkin, *The Cornish Miner* (London 1948) p. 68.

[102] Vivien Russell *West Penwith Survey* (Cornwall Archaeological Society, Truro, 1971) p. 64.

[103] Russell, pp. 98-99, 103 & 107.

[104] RIC (1850) p.58.

[105] For convenience, this term will be given as *"Jews House"* without the use of the conventional apostrophe (*Jew's or Jews'*) to indicate both the singular and plural forms.

[106] Polwhele *The History of Cornwall* (1816) bk. Ii, 10.

[107] *The Bailiff of Blackmoor (1586)*, [*The Harleian Manuscript 6380*]; *edit.* J.A. Buckley (Penhellick Publications, Camborne, 1994). See Buckley's Introduction to the text, pp. xi to xx. The extracts are taken from Buckley's reconstruction of Beare's text.

[108] Pool (1974) pp. 48-51.

[109] In 1808, quoting *Pearce's Preface*: see part 1 of this chapter, note 23.

[110] Letter from Justin Brooke (3rd January 2000) from which I have drawn in this section; see also Hamilton Jenkin (1948) p. 29.

[111] In some editions of Carew only as *Sarazin*.

[112] T. Pearce (London 1725) p.ii.

[113] Pool *William Borlase* (1986) p. 72.

[114] *Reymeri Foedera* (1255) tom. i, p. 543.

[115] N. Denholm-Young, *Richard of Cornwall* (Basil Blackwell Oxford 1947) pp. 4, 9, 11, 13, 21-22, 30, 32, 38-40, 45, 66-67, 69, 72-74, 80-81, 111, 120, 125, 129, 131, 134, 143, 149 & 164-165.

[116] Roth (1964) p. 66.

[117] See the section on the "Knockers", below.

[118] Applebaum (1953) p. 190.

[119] Hencken (1931) p. 211.

[120] Applebaum (1953) pp. 194-95.

[121] Applebaum (1953) p. 199-200.

[122] Ackroyd (2011) p. 19.

[123] Therese and Mendel Metzger, *Jewish Life in the Middle Ages* (Chartwell Books 1982).

[124] Copies of the original primary sources from the Angevin Court are readily accessible in various archival and published forms, either in their entirety or in extract. Joseph Jacobs' assembly of the most important extracts from some of the sources that relate to Jews, *The Jews of Angevin England* (London 1893) represents one of the most accessible such compendium. Despite the omissions and flaws in his work, the scale and range of Jacobs' achievement was remarkable for a man who was not a specialist in medieval studies. See also Patricia Skinner (edit.) *Jews in Medieval Britain: Historical, Literary and Archaeological Perpectives* (Boydell Press 2003); Reva Berman Brown and Sean McCartney *David of Oxford and Licoricia of Winchester: glimpses into a Jewish family in Thirteenth Century England* in *TransJHSE* vol. 39 (2004) pp. 1-34; H. G. Richardson, *The English Jewry under Angevin Kings* (Methuen 1960), & Ackroyd (2011) pp. 225-228.

[125] From the *Capitula de Stannatoribus*, 9 Ric. I.

[126] L. E. Elliott-Binns, *Medieval Cornwall* (Methuen 1955) p. 55 (citing Carew). See also James Whetter (1998) p. 51.

[127] Susser, *op. cit.*, p. 22.

[128] Robert Hunt, *Popular Romances of the West of England* (1881) pp. 90, 346 & 349 (Hunt surveys the wider traditions of the miners pp. 342-355 ; William Bottrell, *Traditions and Hearthside Stories of West Cornwall* (1873: 2nd Series) pp. 186-189. M. A. Courtney, *Cornish Feasts and Folklore* (1890) p. 8, 61 & 120. (It should be noted that Hunt, Bottrell and Courtney all repeat the traditional legends uncritically and naively.) Newall, reprinted in *The Lost Jews of Cornwall* (2000) edit. Pearce & Fry; pp.15 & 16. For a brief but critical outline of the Knocker legends, see Deane and Shawe (Tempus, 2003) pp. 35-42.

[129] Courtney (ibid. p. 61).

[130] Bottrell (1873) p. 245-246.

[131] Courtney (ibid. p. 129).

[132] Courtney (ibid. pp. 128-9).

[132a] Charles Henderson, *Essays in Cornish History* (The Clarendon Press, Oxford 1935) pp. 202-203.

[133] Buckley (1994) p. xvii.

[134] Justin Brooke *op.cit.*

[135] Buckley *op.cit.*

[136] William Bottrell, *Stories and Folklore of West Cornwall* (1880: 3rd Series) pp. 193-194.

[137] J. Davey, *Life of Sir Humphry Davy* (1836) p. 9-11: quoted by Pool (1974) pp. 115-116.

[137a] Simon Young, *Five Notes on Nineteenth-Century Cornish Changelings*, in the RIC Journal (2013) pp. 87-115.

[138] For a detailed study see N. Denholm-Young, *Richard of Cornwall* (Basil Blackwell, Oxford 1947).

[139] Newall (reprinted 2000) p. 14.

[140] Extract from a letter from Edgar Samuel to Keith Pearce (January 24th 1999).

[141] Coulthard (1913) p.42.

[142] Letter from Stephen Massil to Evelyn Friedlander, 4th October 1998.

[143] Borlase, *Natural History*, p. 190.

[144] Newall (2000) p. 15.

[145] Jacobs (1893) pp. 4-13.

[146] Jacobs 1893) pp. 14-23.

[147] Jacobs (1893) pp. 28-57 & various of the following references can be found between pages 57-421.

[148] See Michael Adler, *The Medieval Jews of Exeter*, in the *Transactions of the Devonshire Association for the Advancement of Science, Literature and Art* (1931) Vol. lxiii, pp. 221-240.

[149] Michael Adler's essay (1931), noted earlier, does not identify any Jew from Cornwall.

[150] John M. Shafteseley, in the Foreword to the Calendar of the Plea Rolls of the Exchequer of the Jews Vol. IV (JHSE 1972) pp. vii-ix.

[151] The originals are preserved in the Public Record Office and the British Museum, and have been published, in 1902 and 1910 by J. M. Rigg, in 1929 by Hilary Jenkinson; the later Rolls from 1270 have been compiled by H. G. Richardson *TJHSE* (1972), with further volumes (1992 & 2005).

[152] Muller *Chips from a German Workshop* (2nd edition 1870) 3, XIV pp. 289-329; ref. p. 329, *Rotulus Cancellarii vel Antigraphum Magni Rotuli Pipae de tertio anno Regni Johannis* (PRO 1863 p. 96).

[153] H. G. Richardson (1960) p. viii.

[154] G. R. Lewis & G. Randall (1908) p. 212n.

[155] Roth (1964) pp. 14-15 & 49.

[156] Research by Jo Mattingley (2000) and John Simmons (2000) from J. L. Vivian, *The Visitations of Cornwall, 1530, 1573, 1620* (London 1887; pp. 624-5) and *Burke's Landed Gentry* (1972) Vol. III, p. 922. This information can also be found in the *Edgcumbe Papers* at CRO Truro.

[157] Letter to Godfrey Simmons from George Rigal, 30th May 2000.

[158] O.J. Padel (1988) pp. 171-172; G.P White (1999) p. 61.

[159] Susser, *op. cit.*, pp. 5, 25 & 273.

[166] James Whetter (1998) pp. 47, 51 & 220; S. J. Drake, *Politics and Society in Richard II's Cornwall*, in the Journal of the RIC (2013) p. 27.

[161] Israel Abrahams, "Joachim Gaunse - A Mining Incident in the Reign of Queen Elizabeth"; in Transactions of the Jewish Historical Society, vol. 4, pp. 83-97. Susser, *op.cit.*, p.273.

[162] Abrahams, *op. cit.*, p.89.

[163] A.L. Rowse, *Tudor Cornwall* (London 1941) p. 55.

[164] Andrew Foot, *Burchard Cranach in Cornwall*, JRIC (2002) pp. 64-84.

[165] Susser (1993) pp. 29 & 275. Also Coulthard, *op. cit.* p. 151, and Courtney (1890) p. 93.

[166] See also Coulthard (1913) *op. cit.* p. 151 and Courtney (1890) p. 93.

[167] *London Jewish* News, 23rd September 2000) & Susser (1993) p. 273.

[168] R. Morton Nance (1933; re-printed 1973, pp. 76-82). I have also drawn extensively from Peter Pool's excellent study, *The Death of Cornish* (1982). These two studies can be read together to give a introductory overview of the subject. P. Berresford Ellis' *The Cornish Language and Literature* (1974) Routledge & Kegan Paul, London, represents a wider survey of the history of Old, Middle and Late Cornish, and of its death. This work is also an indispensable guide to its many students and scholars, mentioned in this chapter, and to the revival of interest in Cornish in modern times.

[169] Pool (1982) p. 26.

[170] Pool (1982) p. 26, & ftn. 47); For Barrington, see later. See also Nance (1973) p. 79. Her portrait is owned by the family of Lord St. Levan of St. Michael's Mount, Marazion.

[171] Viv Hendra, *The Cornish Wonder: A Portrait of John Opie* (Truran 2007) pp. 4 & 23. Hendra implies that Dolly Pentreath sat for Opie's portrait (commissioned by the then Lord St. Levan, John St. Aubyn of St, Michael's Mount, in 1779, while Pool, referencing A. Earland's (1911) *John Opie and his Circle* (pp. 20,55 & 306) gives the year as 1777.

[172] Pool (1982) p. 26.

[173] Hendra (2007) p. 23.

[174] Nance (1973) pp. 79-80.

[175] Gerard Manley Hopkins, *Poems and Prose,* W.H. Gardner, Edit. (Penguin 1953) p. 123.

[176] R. M. Nance (1933 / 1973) p. 77.

[177] Pool (1982) p. 6.

[178] R. Carew, *Survey of Cornwall* (1602) pp. 55-56.

[179] J. Norden, *Description of Cornwall* (compiled 1597-1604; not published until 1728) p. 26.

[180] Pool (1982) pp.7 & 17.

[181] Melvyn Bragg, *The Adventure of English* (extract: *Sunday Times, News Review*, p. 2 (19th October 2003).

[182] Pool (1982) p. 17.

[183] Pool (1982) p. 8. n. 11.

[184] Davies Gilbert, *History of Cornwall* IV (1838) p. 127. See Pool (1982) p. 9, n. 12, for the original reference

from William Scawen.

[185] W. Hals, *History of Cornwall* (1750) p. 133.

[186] Pool (1982) p. 21.

[187] Pool (1982) p. 9, n.14.

[188] Pool (1982) pp. 9-10; notes 16 & 17.

[189] Pool (1982) pp. 11-22.

[190] The Gwavas manuscripts are to be found in the British Museum, London [Bm Addnl. MSS 28554]; & also in the RIC Truro as the *Gatley Manuscript*.

[191] See H.L. Douch, "Thomas Tonkin - an Appreciation of a Neglected Cornish Historian", JRIC NS IV 2 (1962).

[192] From the dedicatory letter to William Gwavas in Tonkin's 1736 collection of Cornish material, quoted by Pool (1982) on pp. 17 & 21.

[193] Pool (1982) pp. 10-21 contains a detailed survey of their work, and footnotes individual studies on each of them.

[194] Pool (1982) p. 23, and E. Lhuyd, *Archaeologica Britannica* (1707). p. 253.

[195] R. Heath, *Account of the Islands of Scilly* (1750), p. 173.

[196] C. W., G. C. and F. Boase, *The Family of Boase* (1893) p. 12.

[197] W. Borlase, *Natural History of Cornwall* (1758) p. 315. Pool (1982) p. 24. See also Pool's "William Borlase, the Scholar and the Man", JRIC NS V 2 (1966).

[198] D. Barrington, "On the Expiration of the Cornish Language", in *Archaelologica* III (1776) p. 279. Nance, 1973, p. 80; Pool (1982) p. 25.

[199] Pool (1982) p. 26.

[200] D. Barrington, "Some Additional Information relative to the Continuance of the Cornish Language", in *Archaeologica* V (1779) p. 81. The extravagance of this title relative to the piecemeal nature of his new evidence is obvious.

[201] R. Polwhele, *History of Cornwall* V (1816) p. 43.

[202] As Pool (1982) points out (p. 27) he is probably to be identified with the man of that name who emigrated from Marazion to Philadelphia; see also A.L. Rowse, *The Cornish in America* (1969) pp. 103-4.

[203] Pool (1982) p. 27-28.

[204] Pool (1982) p. 23.

[205] R. Morton Nance, "A Long-ago visit to Penzance", in *Old Cornwall* II 3 (1932) p. 41.

[206] R. Morton Nance (1933 / 1973) p. 80.

[207] R. Warner, *A Tour through Cornwall in 1808* (1809) p. 335.

[208] J.J. Daniell, *Geography of Cornwall* (1854) p. 65. J.H. Stone, *England's Riviera* (1912) p. 242 gives Matthews' death around 1786.

[209] Nance (1933/1973) p. 77, and Pool (1982) pp.29-30; J.H. Matthews, *History of St. Ives* (1892) p. 404; and R. M. Nance on "John Davey of Boswednack and his Cornish Rhyme" in the JRIC XXI 2 (1923) p. 146.

[210] D. and S. Lysons, *Magna Britannia* III (1814), v.

[211] Pool (1982) p. 29.

[212] Pool (1982) pp. 29-30 (following Nance).

[213] R. M. Nance (1933 / 1973) p. 77.

[214] R. M. Nance (1933 / 1973) p. 81.

[215] Müller, *op. cit.* Berresford Ellis (1974) p. 140.

[216] Müller, *op. cit.*, p. 300.

[217] Müller, *op. cit.*, p. 301.

[218] Müller, *op. cit.*, p. 304.

[219] Stephen Massil *ibid*; 14th September 1998.

[220] Müller, *op.cit.*, pp. 305-306.

[221] Camden (c. 1586).

[222] Carew (c. 1602).

[223] Leland (c. 1538).

[224] William of Worcester (c. 1478).

[225] Müller *op.cit.*, p.306-7. See also Henry Hawkins, "The Jews in Cornwall", *op cit.*, pp.125-128.

[226] Elliott-Binns (1955) p. 55.

[227] Pool (1974) pp. 2, 9, 12 & 19; & ref. p. 2, note 2.

[228] The epitaph of Richard Daniell: Pool (1874) p. 34.

[229] The alleged case of the witchcraft of John Tonken: Pool (1974). P. 54.

[230] Pool (1974) p. 2.

[231] Pool (1974) p. 54.

[232] Bannister (1867) p. 335, attributes this interpretation to Borlase. By 1871, and despite his awareness of numerous alternative interpretations, Bannister (*Glossary of Cornish Names* p. 92) continued to give Marazion as "Jews' (*edzhuon*) market (*marhas*) and Market Jew as "Jew (*ezow*) market (*marchad*)", not "Thursday (*yow*) market" (*vide* Leland, Camden, Carew, Norden etc.). He notes that Halliwell gives Marazion as "market on the strand (*zian*), Pryce "market on the sea coast", Hingston "market of the island (the Mount)", and Isaac Taylor "hill by the sea". Bannister appears to reject the view of "others" that the derivation is from "bitter Zion".

[233] All references from Müller, op. cit., pp. 310-311.

[234] Nance, *op. cit.*, p.78.

[235] Müller, op. cit., p. 318.

[236] Müller, op. cit., pp. 311-312, 318-320.

[237] Matthew Gwyther: *Daily Telegraph* (23rd September 2000).

[238] Müller, op. cit., p.328.

[239] An outline of this theory appeared as a brief article, "Duchy's Fifteen Bezants", as part of the Peterborough column in the *Daily Telegraph and Morning Post* on October 7th 1937.

[240] D. Endean Ivall, *Cornish Heraldry and Symbolism* (Dyllansow Truran 1988) p. 91; N. Denholm-Young, *Richard of Cornwall* (Basil Blackwell Oxford), front cover of original dustjacket, and illustration opposite page 10; the image can also be found in Anthony R. Wagner's, *Historic Heraldry of Britain* (Oxford University Press 1939 & 1948). Both images can be found in the article by C. K. Croft Andrew, *The Arms of the Duchy of Cornwall – Some New* Facts, with accompanying photographs taken by the author, in the Journal of the RIC Truro, Vol. XXV Parts 1 & 2 (1937-1938), pp. 75-83 and Plates 1 & 3.

[241] Journal of RIC Truro, Vol. XXV, Plate 3.

[242] Croft Andrew (1937-38) pp. 75-76.

[243] Denholm-Young (1947) p. 171.

[244] Croft Andrew (1937-38) p. 82.

[245] Pool (1974) pp. 49-51.

[246] Ref. earlier, Coulthard's uncritical citation of Carew.

[247] A. L. Rowse, *Tudor Cornwall* (1941-57) pp. 54-66; John Chynoweth (2002) pp. 43, 51-52, 130, 133-134, 244-245 & 313.

[248] See Bernard Glassman, *Anti-Semitic Stereotypes without Jews: Images of the Jews in England 1290-1700* (Detroit 1975) and Frank Felsenstein, *Anti-Semitic Stereotypes: A Paradigm of Otherness in English Popular Culture 1660-1830* (Baltimore USA 1995).

[249] See John Rowe, *Cornwall in the Age of the Industrial Revolution* (Liverpool University Press 1953).

[250] Bruno Bettelheim's *The Uses of Enchantment* (Knopf/Random House, New York 1976 & Penguin 1991) provides a penetrating study of how fairy tales and folklore may operate in individual and social consciousness.

פ נ

אִישׁ הַיָּשָׁר בַּנְּדִיבִים ,אֲשֶׁר הָלַךְ בְּדֶרֶךְ טוֹבִים
צִדְקוֹ לְפָנָיו יְהַלֵּךְ ,בְּשָׁלוֹם יָנוּחַ עַל מִשְׁכָּבוֹ
הָ"ה כה"ו מֹשֶׁה ב'ר יַעֲקֹב זֹל פּו"מ דפה
קְ"ק פַאלמוטה שֶׁנִפְטָר בְּיוֹם ג' כ"א שְׁבָט
שְׁנַת תר"כ לפ"ק ת*נ*צ*ב*ה

אֲהָהּ !

מָ י יִתֵּן רֹאשִׁי מַיִם וְעֵינִי מְקוֹר דִּמְעָה
שָׁ אוֹג אֶשְׁאַג בִּבְכִי וְקוֹל נְהִי אֲרִימָה
הָ ן לֹא לַהוֹלֵךְ, כִּי שָׁלוֹם מְנוּחָתוֹ
בְּ נְוֵה שָׁלוֹם יִשְׁכָּב וְעָרְבָה שְׁנָתוֹ
נִ יָנִיו ,אַךְ הֵם ,כֵּן אִשְׁתּוֹ הַיְּקָרָה
יֹ וֹם יוֹם יִבְכּוּהוּ ,כִּי יְפֻקַּד מְקוֹמוֹ
עַ ל רֹאשָׁם כִּי נִלְקַח, כֵּן הָלַךְ הֲדָרָה
קֹ וֹל נְהִי יַשְׁמִיעוּ, לָאֵל לְמְרוֹמוֹ
בְּ מוֹת אִישׁ יָשָׁר בַּנְּדִיבִים, הָלַךְ בְּדֶרֶךְ טוֹבִים
אִישׁ נֶאֱמָן פַּרְנָם וּמַנְהִיג כהו"

מֹשֶׁה ב'ר יַעֲקֹב ז"ל

שֶׁנִפְטָר בְּעִיר מִשְׁכָּנוֹ פֹּה פַּאלמוּטה בן פ"ז

שָׁנִים בְּיוֹם ג' כ"א שְׁבָט וְנִקְבַּר בְּיוֹם ד' כ"ב בוֹ בִּשְׁנַת

תר"ך לפ"ק

ת נ צ ב ה

Memorial Inscriptions for (top) Moses Jacob of Redruth (*d.* 1807)
and (bottom) his grandson Moses ("Moss") Jacob Jacob of Falmouth
(*d.* 1860). (Jacob Archive)

PART TWO
Community and Commerce
The Jewish Families and their Trades 1740-1913

———◆◆◆———

CHAPTER 2
The Jewish Population Against its Background

The Jews who lived in Cornwall in the 18th and 19th centuries were part of a much wider migration of Jews from the Continent. Some were escaping from persecution, many from discrimination and disadvantage, and they were accustomed to travelling across several countries during their lifetime in search of safety and security. Especially in Eastern Europe, pogroms against Jews were far from uncommon. They were often barred from living amongst Christians, and, in towns and cities, their residence was often restricted to ghettos, or in country areas to settlements and villages, each known as a *shtetl* (a Yiddish word from the German *stadt*, "a little town"), with several neighbouring one another as *stetlach*[1] in which most, if not all of inhabitants would be Jews. The *shtetl* system, which did not end until the First World War, was to be found, together with the *ghetto* system, mainly in Eastern Europe (although Venice did have an historic *ghetto*). Across Germany, France and Holland, residential restrictions for Jews were not practised so widely or systematically. In Russia, Jews were confined to twenty-five provinces, known as the "Pale of Settlement" established by Catherine the Great in 1791. Where such restrictions existed, Jews were often forbidden to move or live outside, unless they had received the permission of the authorities. The entire resettlement of Jewish populations was not unknown. Even in a more favourable climate, Jews were often unable to own land or property, were barred from universities and government employment, and were often banned from practising certain trades, crafts and skills. Where Jews were able to travel, they gravitated towards those countries where conditions were more favourable, and Britain, with its absence of a ghetto system, and its relatively tolerant Hanoverian (Protestant) monarchy, offered freedom for Jews to settle and the opportunity to ply their trades in the rapidly expanding ports, towns and cities during the early period of the Industrial Revolution. Whereas the continental pattern of Jewish settlement was both urban and, to a greater extent rural, Jewish settlement in Britain was predominantly urban.

In the 18th century, Jewish settlement was centred on London, although the occasional Jewish traveller is recorded outside the city, but these, like the murder of a Jew at Borton, in Kent in 1686, represent a visitor rather than a resident. A Broadsheet of 1689, *The Case of the Jews*, stated that there was no Jewish settlement outside of London, and fifty years later, D'Blossiers Tovey, in his *Anglia Judaica* of 1738, repeated this claim, adding that synagogues were not tolerated anywhere apart from the capital. This latter statement would seem questionable, in that some semblance of organised Jewish life was to appear in various places within a few years, at Portsmouth (1742), King's Lynn (1747), Liverpool (1750), Plymouth (1752), Bristol (before 1753), and most likely in both Falmouth and Penzance by the 1740-50s. In Plymouth, it is possible that individual Jews were present from the early 1700s: in 1710, an Isaac ben Isaac Pickas (or Pinchas) was apprenticed to an Edward Hookey, an Apothecary, for £35, and in 1713, an Isaac Pickas "son of Decd." To John Stirling, a Tallowchandler, for £20.[2] From the first half of the 18th century, there was a steady expansion of the Jewish population from the capital. This had begun with the wealthier Sephardic Jews of London, such as the Da Costa, Mendes da Costa and De Medina families, who purchased summer residencies in the surrounding countryside. From the early 18th century, the membership and account books of the Great Synagogue in London record names of members attached to it, and resident in places where significant communities were soon to establish themselves, at Dover, Nottingham, Portsmouth, Bristol and Poole in Dorset. The circumcision register of Rabbi Ash of Dover, from 1768, reveals Jewish families in East Anglia and the coast of South East England, as well as across the Channel in Ostend, while from 1782, that of Myer Solomons of London records families in the counties around London, in Brighton, Ipswich, Yarmouth, Coventry, Oxford, Bristol and Bath. Joseph Joseph's circumcision register, from 1784, records Jewish families in Devon. Early 18th century provincial Masonic registers also list the names of Jews, along with newspapers, magazines and Trade Directories.[3]

It was during the second half of the reign of the Hanoverian King George II (1727-1760) and his successor George III (1760-1820) that the first provincial Jewish communities were established. Half of these were in the thriving sea-ports, including those of the South Coast and the South-West. Some Jews entered the country via Harwich during the 1740s. Of these, Naphtali Benjamin (*arr.* 1745) and Henry Hart (*arr.* 1747), both from Germany, and Moses Isaac, originally from Poland, (*arr.* 1748) settled in Plymouth, and Levy Emmanuel (*arr.* 1748), another German Jew came to Truro in 1748, eventually moving to Plymouth.[4] Sephardic Jews had been in London before the 1750s, but from this time onwards Ashkenazi Jews began to arrive in the capital in considerable numbers. By 1753, their combined population in the country as a whole was estimated at 5,000, but by about 1800, their numbers in London alone were between 15,000 to 20,000. The wealthier, most notably the Sephardim, settled in the City, and the poorer Ashkenazim, in the East End.[5] Others gravitated to provincial centres, and to the ports, such as Falmouth and Penzance, which thrived on maritime trade. Both towns enjoyed the advantage of huge natural harbours, and, in the case of Falmouth this extended to a vast inland river valley, invaded by the sea, allowing direct access for several miles to Penryn and also to the town of Truro, where some Jews also settled. These towns also possessed a flourishing economic hinterland based on fishing, farming and mining. The Jews found that they were welcomed and even encouraged to settle, their skills and trades providing a valuable addition to the towns' facilities. Many migrant Jews were of necessity multilingual, and accustomed to the need for linguistic flexibility and cultural adaptation. To an extent, this influenced the formation of Jewish names, in that Hebrew or Yiddish originals could be shaped towards the conventional forms of the host country. This process was especially marked with Eastern European Jewish migrants moving westwards, where Russian or Polish names would be virtually unpronounceable. Such adaptation could also reduce suspicion and facilitate acceptance. It is to the credit of the indigenous population in 18th century Cornwall that they recognised the Jewish newcomers could enrich the local economy. The Cornish ports at this time were especially cosmopolitan, and for their inhabitants it was a common experience to hear of the sound of the many foreign tongues of the sailors, passengers and migrants who arrived on a regular basis by sea, and also by road.

"Migrant-rich societies have conspicuous records of success…countries which deter, deport or destroy their immigrants, tend to perish or stagnate…Migration is not just beneficial – sometimes it is actually vital. During any process of economic change, niches open that the existing workforce cannot fill."[6] This is particularly pertinent to the case of the Jewish migrants who settled in Cornwall in the mid-18th century, in that such niches were filled by the Jewish traders in Cornish towns to the economic advantage of all concerned. With their shared history of persecution and migration, Jews had by tradition acquired the light skills and mobile trades with which they could easily relocate. These tended to fall into the categories of fine craft and service trades, of which jewellery, watch and clock making and haberdashery are obvious examples. In Cornwall, the Jews did not directly involve themselves in the County's core industries of fishing, farming and mining. Some Jews, however, were involved in maritime activities, as suppliers, money agents and in sea-trading (as co-owners with Gentiles of boats). Many of the incoming Jews had been members of the continental Masonic Guilds, and were admitted to the Cornish Masonic Lodges that were developing rapidly at this time. Some Jews were even founding members of such lodges, and rose to some prominence within them. The support and fraternity of affluent Cornish Freemasons, gentry, landowners and merchants, also facilitated the settlement and commercial establishment of Jewish business. These Jewish trades and occupations can be traced from a wide range of sources, which include Commercial and Trade Directories, census returns, newspaper reports, marriage certificates, cemetery headstones, published studies such as Brown's on the Cornish clockmakers[7], Osborne's on Freemasonry, Masonic members' directories, Customs and Shipping records, and from Wills, records of administration and grants of probate.[8]

Itinerant Jewish pedlars and hawkers were frequent visitors to the County,[9] establishing trading routes throughout the West Country, some settling for a few years in particularly profitable localities, and they would have been a common feature of Cornish life even before any significant Jewish settlement began in either Penzance or Falmouth. The extent to which itinerant Jews would have been regarded with suspicion or, conversely , would have been welcomed by the native Cornish cannot be known. No doubt, relations were primarily commercial as the hawkers sold their items from place to place. The Cornishman Samuel Drew[10] (1765-1833), a self-educated shoemaker, Methodist and political thinker, may have been unusual in his enlightened attitude towards Jews and other foreigners, but he cannot have been unique: "At this period (*c.* 1790) his house was known to all the vagrant train. It was, says his sister, a sort of asylum for foreigners. To the itinerant trader, and the wandering musician, my brother's doors were always open. He delighted to converse with them - to learn their history - and to gather from them such information as they could furnish about their respective countries. If intelligent and well-behaved, they were generally invited to sit at our table, and partake of our fare; and frequently has the Jew or Italian left his box of valuables at our house as a place of safety." Taking into account the fact that Drew's biography was written as a memoir by his son, and based upon the recollections of family members, it remains difficult to assess if Drew, or his sister, used the term *Jew* (or indeed *Italian*) with accuracy, as specific generic terms, or if they were accustomed to applying such terms loosely to foreign itinerants. Such visitors were a common occurrence, especially in the port-towns. It should be emphasised that the numbers of Jewish hawkers and commercial travellers will have been significantly greater than the names which appear on the decennial census returns, capturing as they do only a glimpse of such visitors at the particular time of the census itself. In the ensuing ten years many itinerant Jews will have entered and then left the County, their names unrecorded and their identities lost to us.

Visitors also came to Cornwall from the Eastern Mediterranean. In 1731, in Penzance, the Mayor and Corporation received "the Prince of Cheshroan Abu Gemblat Nassar Abascai, of Mount Libanus in Syria", and in 1737 "the Prince of Canaan". On 29th September 1760, the Penzance Volunteer Force was called out to Newlyn to deal with what was supposed to be an intended attack, but which was in fact a call for help from a sinking vessel: "In the night the town was roused by the firing of guns - a large ship of strange appearance having run on shore on the beach towards Newlyn. Great numbers of persons - were still more astonished and shocked by the sight of men still stranger than their vessel, each armed with a scymetar and with pistols. It was now obvious they were Moslems; and a vague fear of Turkish ferocity, of massacre and plunder seized the unarmed inhabitants… the ship was an Algerine corsair, carrying 24 guns - the captain had steered his vessel into Mount's Bay, and run it against the shore. When it was found safe to visit the strangers, curiosity attracted the whole neighbourhood. Their Asiatic dress, long beards and mustachios, with turbans - the dark complexion and harsh features of the piratical band made them objects of terror and surprise. They were on the whole treated kindly- and - after some delay a ship of war took all the men on board, and conveyed them to Algiers".[11]

In 1784, another Muslim, Mahomet Celiby, from Algiers, was in Falmouth, where he attended a meeting of the Masonic Lodge.[12] Much later census records, from 1841-1871, reveal continental (Gentile) residents of Cornish towns. In Penzance, French and Italian names are especially evident, such as James (Giovanni) Balshari and Augustino Solari (both from Genova), Domenica Garibaldi, a clockmaker (also from Genova), Marie Gerard, a French Governess from Caen (France), Henri and Jules Guillemet (France), and Louis (Luigi) Donemi and Ferdinand Scorza (the latter from Trieste, then part of Austria). Alongside other names, the Recorder's note "born in, [or] from Jamaica [or] India" appears. From the 16th century, the Cornish tin industry had experienced a period of depression, and was in transition from tin-streaming to tin-mining, whilst Germany was the most highly developed mining country. German mining experts, such as Hochstetter (the Elder), Hans Hering, Burchard Cranach, and Ulrich Frose were brought over to advise and oversee the survey of mines, the sinking of shafts, and the development of engines and smelting processes. Dutch miners were also employed at this time in the Cornish mines. Merchant trading vessels, including the Packet Boats, sailed regularly to the Mediterranean and the Iberian peninsula, as well as further afield to the West Indies and the Americas. Cornish sailors and Jewish merchants, like Lyon Joseph of Falmouth, both established strong commercial links with Spain and Portugal, and Philip Samuel of St. Austell (briefly a minister at the Penzance synagogue), and the family of Solomon Solomon of Falmouth lived in Lisbon for some years until 1820. Visitors from these countries were also familiar arrivals at the Cornish ports. Falmouth enjoyed a regular boat service to Lisbon (advertised in the local press and elsewhere), and there were even sea voyages to South America. In his Diary for 19th October 1816, the Mayor of Penzance, Henry Boase (1763-1827) noted: "Granted a pass to a sailor named Manton, landed sick from the *Asp*, the ship in which Capt. Richard Trevithick is embarking for Lima".[13]

A. L. Rowse has emphasised that Cornwall had always been distinctive from other regions of the country, and even from those in the West Country itself, in that its towns had always contained a high proportion of foreigners. Indeed, it would seem that it was not until 1300 that Cornish names begin to appear on the official registers (subsidy rolls) of the towns, suggesting that, previously, foreigners may have outnumbered the indigenous population: "in 1327, Penryn was equally divided between natives and foreigners, while in Tregony and Grampound, the foreign element still predominated. At Fowey as late as 1439, there were twenty-seven alien householders, Irish, French, Dutch, perhaps as much as a third of the town, or at least of the property-holders. Bretons constituted much of the largest foreign element – if indeed they are to be considered as foreigners at all in Cornwall, where they spoke the same language as the people. A Subsidy Roll of the reign of Henry VIII shows that at St. Ives there were twenty-three foreigners, all Bretons, of whom nine were fishermen, seven labourers, four tailors, three smiths."[14] Bretons also lived in the parishes of Zennor, Towednack and Lelant in West Cornwall, and also in the parish of Constantine, on the south coast, where there were fourteen families in 1544 and still nine in 1558. These Bretons had come over "in considerable numbers to serve for higher wages in subordinate capacities…but the Reformation, and the subsequent decline of the Cornish language, cut Cornwall apart from Brittany, and they ceased to come over." It would seem that it was at this time, when the Cornish population was being assimilated into the English, that the towns became inhabited mostly by Cornish people. The Cornish sea-ports were prospering and becoming more populous than the inland towns, the decay of which was a problem recognised by Tudor government by 1540. In 1377 the Poll Tax returns suggest a population of 35-40,000, in the 16th century it may have been 40-50,000, and by 1700, it may have doubled to around 105,800.[15] It was the establishment of Jewish shops in the Cornish sea-ports from the early to mid 18th century onwards, which marked the true beginning of Jewish communal life, and this process would appear to have been assisted by the general tolerance and familiarity which the inhabitants of the two major sea-ports had towards the frequent appearance of foreigners. The Accounts of the Corporation of Penzance from 1791 to 1793[16] contain the following entries:

"December 1st 1791. To a Turkish Gentleman in distress......10(s) 6(d).
February 14th 1792. A poor Turk with a pass from Falmouth to Bristol directed a wrong road.......1(s).
February 24th 1792. Postage of a Letter from the Turkish Minister.....6(d).
June 30th 1792. Relief to some distressed sailors of Genoa passed from Falmouth.....1(s).
October 25th 1792. To eight Danish seamen who were shipwrecked near Cuddan.....5(s)."

Jew-baiting had been a widespread and barbaric practice in England in the 18th century and before, with Jews "hooted, hunted, cuffed, pulled by the beard and spat upon". Samuel Pepys recorded in his diary a visit to a Synagogue on 14th October 1663. The synagogue was most likely that in Cree Church Lane, a Sephardic congregation, which had become something of a tourist attraction for Gentiles. The occasion was that of the Rejoicing in the Law, when the formality of the regular service would be uncharacteristically relaxed, convivial and high-spirited, although it seems that Pepys was not aware of this. The spectacle had attracted a constant steam of visitors and sight-seers, and, in his account, Pepys could barely hide his disdain, even, disgust at what he saw: "But Lord, to see the disorder, laughing, sporting, and no attention, but confusion in all their service, more like Brutes than people knowing the true God....I never did see so much, or could ever imagined there had been any religion in the whole world so absurdly performed as this".[17] Pepys' reaction may well have reflected and reinforced the prejudice of his time. Ninety years later, when an Act of Parliament of 1753 sought to legalize the naturalisation of Jews, there were anti-Semitic riots in London. By this time, however, opinion was beginning to change, and in 1753, the novelist Tobias Smollett (1721-1771) published his *Count Fathom*, in which the benign and virtuous character of the Jew *Joshua Manassah* appears. The novel's publication may have been intended to coincide with the 1753 Act.[18] Byron's poem *Hebrew Melodies* (1815) and Wordsworth's *The Jewish Family* (1828) lament the suffering of Israel and extol Hebrew virtues, and Sir Walter Scott included sympathetic portrayals of the Jew in *Ivanhoe* (1819).[19] In 1830, Coleridge encountered a persistent old Jewish clothes hawker, whose curious, garbled cries provoked the poet to challenge him as to why he used such language when plain English would do. The hawker's dignified, articulate and intelligent response describing the wearisome and dispiriting effect of having to cry out the same wares every minute touched Coleridge's conscience, and led him to record "I was so confounded with the justice of his retort, that I followed and gave him a shilling, the only one I had". It is possible that these instances, and the earlier character of Smollett's virtuous Jew had some influence upon Dickens in *Our Mutual Friend* (1863-65)[20] in his portrayal of the kindly and singular supportive Jewish money-lender, *Mr. Riah*, who gives assistance to *Lizzie Hexam* and *Jenny Wren*, a portrayal which may have been intended by Dickens as amends for his earlier presentation of *Fagin*, in *Oliver Twist* (1837),[21] for which he was criticised at the time. Likewise, George Eliot, in her final novel *Daniel Deronda* (1876)[22] drew upon the more positive attitudes to Jews that had developed since the time of Smollett, in her presentation of the Jew *Mordecai*.

In 1771, three Jews took part in a burglary in Chelsea, which resulted in the death of a manservant. All three were later hanged, but fifty years later, the radical Tailor, Francis Place, recorded his view that the incident caused a backlash against Jews in London, resulting in an increase in Jew-baiting in which neither the public nor the police would intervene.[23] By the 1790s, Jew-baiting appears to have been in significant decline, and Jews began to feel a degree of safety and increasing confidence that "the few who would be disposed to insult them merely because they are Jews would be in danger of chastisement from the passer-by and of punishment from the police".[24] One reason why this change took place was that younger Jews began to take lessons in boxing to defend themselves. There had been popular Jewish boxers in London from the 1770s onwards, but it was the fame and success of Daniel Mendoza (1765-1836), "this humble man who probably contributed more to the return of the exceptionally tolerant climate enjoyed by the Jews of England than any other single individual - it was to him - that Francis Place attributed the end of street baitings and assaults".[25]

In Elizabethan times, when there were no Jews in England at the time "except the occasional Marrano visitor",[26] the Jew had been portrayed as either an ambiguous, suspect or vindictive figure in the forms of *Barabas* in Marlowe's *The Jew of Malta* (1590) and *Shylock* in Shakespeare's *The Merchant of Venice* (1597), although Shakespeare's source seems to have been an Italian story in which a Christian demands a pound of flesh from a Jew. However, the rise in popularity among the general public for synagogue music since the time of Samuel Pepys, was to result in a "fashionable craze", and the Jew came to be depicted on the London stage as a comic figure rather than a monster. In 1760, David Garrick, produced a masque *The Enchanter*, in which he gave prominence to "the fine voice to *Leoni*, a Jew boy", and Richard Cumberland's comedy *The Jew* portrayed *Shevya*, a squalid miser, who performs an, albeit uncharacteristic, act of charity. Even so, popular music and drama alone, could not entirely overcome the prejudice of centuries.[27] At the very beginning of the 19th century, two works by Thomas Witherby were published in London that sought to change anti-semitic attitudes towards Jews, *An Attempt to Remove Prejudices Concerning the Jewish Nation* (1804) and *A Vindication of the Jews* (1809). However, in such a far-flung place as Penzance, attitudes may have lagged behind the metropolis itself, and on Shrove Tuesday 1839, the local press reported the following:

"At a petty sessions, held in Penzance on Monday last, before the borough justices, James Corin jun. was convicted of a most atrocious assault upon a poor German Jew, and fined in the greatest amount the law prescribes, namely GBP 5. It appears that the gentlemen of the mob at Penzance fancy they have a prescriptive right, on Shrove Tuesday, to blacken the faces of persons they meet with burnt cork, and to commit other freaks equally indicative of civilisation and good manners; and accordingly, as the Jew was entering the town that day, with his little travelling box on his back, he was met by Corin, who seized him, and endeavoured to disfigure his countenance in the most approved fashion of the place. The Jew, naturally enough, resisted, for which Corin knocked him down several times, and beat his head against the pavement with such force that the blood flowed from both ears, and it was for a time feared he was killed. Corin, in default of payment, was committed to prison for two months".[28]

Whether this brutal attack, occurring as it did on a festival day, was commonplace or exceptional, even in a less extreme form, is difficult to assess, and Corin's actions may well have been those of a notorious local reprobate, and therefore untypical. What is obvious, however, is the contempt in which the report holds the town of Penzance, and the correspondent adds that "we hope this conviction will teach such brutes that they cannot commit their savage freaks with impunity". The disapproval is all too obvious, but the enlightened attitude may or may not represent the views held at the time by the townspeople themselves. The report goes on to cast doubt on the "propriety of Penzance" and urges the town's authorities "following the example of Truro, by immediately organising an efficient police, which shall be uninfluenced by local feelings", which, if taken at face value, suggests that the Jews of Penzance, or at the very least, travelling Jewish hawkers entering the town, were not entirely free from discrimination or danger.

However, in Penzance, in the early to mid 19th century, its Mayor, Samuel Pidwell (1808-1854)[29] was recollected by George Clement Boase (1829-1897) to have taken an especially positive stance towards the Jews: "Overhearing some boys in the street saying, 'Look at that old Jew going by', he called out, 'How dare you say such a thing? Don't you know that the Jews are God's chosen people?".[30] Clearly, this recollection by Boase of Pidwell's enlightened stance could be regarded as anecdotal, and, even if accurate, it is again not possible to generalise or infer from it that it typified attitudes to Jews in Penzance. Indeed, the prejudice displayed by the boys, although falling far short of Place's description of the Jew-baiting he had witnessed in the mid 18th century, may suggest an attitude more widespread, and Pidwell was himself untypical of the town's inhabitants in that he was a particularly well educated, cultured and well-connected man. A graduate of Worcester College, Oxford, he retained a house in London, but had returned to Penzance to trade as a Brewer, the latter profession being allied to the wine and spirit trade of Lemon Hart (who left the town by 1811) and his relative Lemon Woolf (1783-1848) who continued to run Hart's business in the town. Lemon Woolf's son, Moses (1815-), Samuel Pidwell's contemporary, was also a Brewer in Penzance. Like Lemon Hart, Pidwell and Lemon and Moses Woolf were Freemasons, being members of the same Penzance Masonic Lodge, where Lemon Woolf occupied various important positions, including Master (1818), Treasurer (1827-1831) and Secretary (1822 and 1836). In this Lodge, Pidwell would have met a wide cross section of the town's businessmen and members of the locality's gentry. Members of the Pidwell family were Anglicans and others became Congregationalists, suggesting an espousal of nonconformism that sat quite at ease with an Anglican family tradition. One of the Congregational ministers, John Foxell, was a tenant lodger of the Pidwells, and also acted for his mother-in-law, Mary Borlase, in collecting rental payments from the Jewish congregation for its lease of their cemetery. Samuel Pidwell had the resources to build himself an imposing town mansion in the very centre of the town, Morrab House, surrounded by extensive grounds. Some thirty-five years after his death, the Penzance Town Corporation bought the estate (in 1889) and commissioned the London landscape gardener, Reginald Upcher, to develop the grounds into a municipal park. The original house is now a private library. Samuel Pidwell was twice Mayor of Penzance (in 1844 and 1849) a position that carried considerable social and legal influence at that time. In 1831, Samuel Pidwell's cousin, Mary (1811-1894) had married a Jew, David Hart (1799-1868) in an Anglican Church, All Hallows, Staining, in London. David Hart was the son of the former Penzance Wine and Spirit Merchant, Lemon Hart (1768-1845), and the nephew of Lemon Woolf. Two of David Hart's sisters were also to marry Christians, after the family had left Cornwall. Clearly, Pidwell did not disapprove of his cousin's marriage to a Jew *per se*, in that he left her an annuity in his will, for life. That he was also of a liberal and tolerant disposition and in possession of a generous and independent spirit can be seen in that, at a time when marital break-down and separation carried some considerable stigma, he left similar provisions in his will for his aunt (by marriage) Mary's mother, Elizabeth (-1855) who, for many years, had been estranged from her husband, Thomas Pidwell (1778-1848), Samuel's uncle, a Draper, the latter remaining in Penzance, and his estranged wife moving to Falmouth.

Newspaper extracts, and other legal reports from 19th century Cornwall show a similar tolerance of, concern for and equanimity towards Jews. A number of these can be found in the pages that follow, including the examples of Lemon Wolf, Rabbi B.A. Simmons, Solomon Solomon and Elias Magnus (c. 1817), and other cases involving travelling Jewish pedlars in Penzance (1839) and St. Austell (1845 and 1865). The Cornish Press was consistently sympathetic towards the legal emancipation of the Jews, and scathing in its criticism of the Peers who opposed it. In 1836 it carried the following, strongly worded editorial: "We are gratified at learning that it is the intention of Ministers to propose, as a cabinet measure, the removal of civil disabilities from the Jews. The last time such a Bill was introduced, it was thrown out by the Lords; but one more experiment is to be made to prove whether the noble and right-reverend prejudices of the Upper House are wholly invincible. It is impossible to urge any valid objection against Jewish Emancipation. Even the arguments which were, at one time, opposed to the Catholics – granting, too, they were all sound – are wholly inapplicable to the Jews. Few in number – without any object of political ambition – having no secular admixture in their religion, and eminently peaceable in their conduct – what danger can accrue from admitting them to an equality of civil rights? When the bill was rejected by the Peers, the Bishops contended that, as a Christian State, we ought not to receive Jews into the legislature; and to this contemptible dogma their claims were sacrificed….We would submit to have the question of Jewish disabilities decided by the Sermon on the Mount" (*West Briton*, 25th March 1836). Twelve years later, at the time that another Bill to ease and remove various legal and social disabilities that applied to Jews was being debated in Parliament, the Cornish press seems to have adopted a sceptical view of the opposition to it taken forward by Lord Falmouth. The peer was a very influential man, but his formal petitions were not taken to be genuinely representative of public opinion in the County: "THE JEWS'

DISABILITIES BILL – We observe by the parliamentary reports of the House of Lords, that LORD FALMOUTH has presented two or three petitions against this bill, amongst them one from that most important and influential parish of Ruan-lanihorne, in this county. Our legislators ought, we think, to be informed by the presenters of petitions what sort of places these things emanate (sic.) from, and for the edification of some of them, perhaps it may not be amiss if we state that Ruan contains about 1,900 acres, and about 400 inhabitants, has about 60 houses in it, and there are registered electors for it 17, three of whom are non-resident. We should like now to know how many signatures were appended to this notable petition." (*West Briton*, 17th March 1848)[31]

Settled Jewish life necessitated the acquisition of two cemeteries, one in Falmouth and one in Penzance, and the founding of the two synagogues. This gave the Jewish residents a congregational focus. The total size of the Jewish population in Cornwall at any one time is difficult to estimate. Physical and documentary evidence can prove to be of a limited and superficial value. For example, the two cemeteries each contain about 60 graves, but no inference can be drawn from this because these numbers are cumulative over two centuries, and numerous children and relatives would have moved elsewhere, migration and emigration representing unsettling factors that changed the total numbers periodically. Trade Directories can be helpful but they only give the names of the owners of the business and take no account of their families. Decenniel Census returns have been used in this book to identify many of the Jewish people in Cornwall. The census returns provide an overall computation from the size of each household where each adult and child is named, together with details of age, occupation, and place of birth. There is room for error when using census returns to collect particular data. Although names and families appear on the original census returns, even the expert researcher can miss them amongst the mass of information in which they are contained. The early census returns, particularly for 1841, are often in illegible handwriting making names difficult to decipher. Moreover, it is not always obvious that a particular name is that of a Jew. Likewise, some names are mistakenly taken as being Jewish when in fact they are not. It cannot be assumed that the original census returns and subsequent published editions of them are entirely accurate. Sometimes names are missing from the original returns where particular families were known to have been living in that place at the time. Sometimes there were circumstantial factors or procedural errors at work when the original census data was compiled, such that names were omitted from the official census returns. For example, in 1861 Esther Falkson's name does not appear on the official Census for Falmouth[32] even though it is known that she lived there up to the time of her death in 1863.[33] It is possible that she was away from Falmouth when the census was taken. If so, this would highlight a circumstantial variable not subject to the control of the census collector at the time. However, it would require the physical absence of whole families to explain their statistical omission from the data. If individuals were in fact present at that time, it simply serves to emphasise the potential for procedural error. The joint work of several researchers (and perhaps at least one with a very personal family interest and knowledge) would be necessary to cross-check the registers to be certain of exactitude. Family size varied considerably and so the nominal estimate of the Jewish population of a town from a speculative average would be misleading. Census returns do not assist here either. For example, in 1851 in Penzance, Henry Joseph's family consisted of nine children whilst Rabbi B. A. Simmons' family shows none. The latter, in fact, had had eleven children in all, but most of them had left the town over time, although one had died in 1832, and two, Sarah and Simon, were living in the Joseph household as employees. It is, therefore, the factor of when and not where the census is taken which conspires to frustrate any estimate of population size.

There is no doubt that private research into family history and also expert genealogical research, such as that of Anthony P. Joseph, into the Cornish Jewish families and their descendants play a very important role in any attempt to reconstruct a comprehensive profile of the population. The genealogies of the Cornish Jews are very complex with frequent inter-marriage between Jewish families and the proliferation of identical names. This means that the risk of confusion, duplication and mistaken identity is high if the exercise is not conducted by a specialist with experience. Indeed, a separate publication by such an expert on the genealogy of these families would be a valuable complement to this book, which can only try to give a representative picture and not a definitive record of the population. From the foregoing, it would seem therefore, that the only method which can be used is a synthetic one, where information is drawn from a number of co-existing but disparate sources, and compiled to give at least some overall historical impression of the extent of the Jewish presence in Cornwall during the period from the early 18th to the late 19th centuries. During the two decades from around 1820 to 1840, which may well represent the high point or peak of the Jewish communities, it is unlikely that there were more than a dozen families (50 to 60 individuals, adults and children) in each of Falmouth and Penzance, with a few Jews in other towns. From the mid-19th century these numbers declined steadily. Even if they cannot provide a definitive indication of size, this at least is the demographic pattern which the trade directories, the census returns and the marriage registers would suggest.

Identifying Jewish Names

The experienced historian or genealogical researcher will have developed a sensitivity and a degree of intuition in considering the identification of Jewish names and will have accumulated a range of basic criteria and background knowledge against which to check that a name is indeed that of a Jew. Most of these have been mentioned: headstones in a Jewish cemetery, Congregational records (where available), birth, death and marriage records (only parish, and not Registry based before 1837), private family records, genealogical studies, census returns, specified trades, and so on.

It has been mentioned that a key difficulty in the 18th and 19th centuries is that common Jewish (Hebrew) names were widespread amongst Christians, both as forenames and surnames, as an inspection of headstones in any municipal or church cemetery in the County will show. Hebrew forenames could even be used of several members of the same Gentile family, illustrated by the baptism of Lazarus Steel

Roberts, son of Abraham and Rachel Roberts at St. Anthony on 20th October 1765.[34] At a time when the family Bible might be the only book in the home, read privately to the family and publicly in church each Sunday, familiar Biblical names (sometimes more than one Hebrew name) were often given (as their "Christian" name) to children at their baptism, as was the case with Lazarus Solomon, son of Margery Busset (the father's name is not identifiable) in Penzance (Madron Parish) on 20th February 1786.[35] The process by which these forenames might also come to be adopted as surnames is less easy to trace with any certainty, but the practice (standard amongst Jews, but not uncommon amongst Cornish Christians at that time) of referring to someone as "son of" or "daughter of", may well have facilitated the process, especially as verbal communication and identification was the norm, with high levels of illiteracy in the general population. The Jewish practice of giving both boys and girls a Hebrew forename (often in the form of a living memorial of a grandparent, aunt or uncle) followed by *ben* (son of) or *bat* (daughter of) the *father*, can lead to males bearing (at least) two (or more) Hebrew forenames, the second of which could become a family surname. So, for example, Moses *ben* Jacob may become Moses Jacob, or Israel *ben* Solomon may become Israel Solomon. Likewise, it was not uncommon for Gentiles to use two forenames instead of one forename and a surname: so, for example, a man might be known as Henry Lawrence, rather than Henry Harris (his actual surname). The tendency for such traditional forenames (of which there are a limited number) to be inherited and to proliferate amongst the Jewish population as family names (surnames) can easily lead to confusion of identification amongst identically named individuals both within the same family and from entirely unconnected families. Sometimes Jews used two or more forenames, one being the Hebrew name of their father, sometimes followed by another name popular in the family, such as *Lazarus Israel Solomon*, or *Moses Isaac Joseph*. One of these names might be used on some occasions (*Moses Joseph*) and the second name on others (*Moses Isaac*). The impression might be given of two distinct persons, when the same individual is involved. The frequent occurrence of names such as *Joseph Joseph*, and *Jacob Jacob* could also lead to the use of an additional middle name to distinguish the person from his namesake: *Joseph Isaac Joseph*. Sometimes, an additional 's' might be added in such examples of the above for the same reason (*Jacob Jacobs*) although this variant was a general practice. The reversal of names in records can reflect an habitual clerical practice, although it could also arise through error, being an additional misleading factor. One of the last rabbis in Falmouth appears both as *Marks* (Marcus?) *Morris*, and as *Morris Marks*.[36]

Consequently, any random survey of Cornish registers or census returns will reveal numerous such "Hebrew" names in numbers far in excess of the contemporaneous Jewish population. For example, Parish registers from 1607-1837[37] record over 150 church marriages where the groom's forename is *Moses*. In every case the bride bears a surname common amongst and characteristic of Cornish Gentiles. The reasonable conclusion is that none of the bridegrooms can be taken to have been Jews, especially as the vast majority of them also bear standard Cornish surnames. Nor does *Moses* as a surname necessarily indicate a Jew: the 1861 Census lists *Moses* 39 times as a surname, and of these none are known to have been Jews. There was a Jewish *Moses* family in Falmouth in the early 18th century, that of Alexander Moses

(1715-1791), but most of his children had died before the first Census of 1841. Many Cornish Gentile (Christian) families with the surname *Moses* also appear in parish registers and other civil records. One such is the family of a Henry Moses (age 59) of Falmouth, consisting of six children, appearing in the 1861 census. It is not impossible that they were of Jewish descent, but the family were Christians, and Henry Moses had married Johanna Bristo, a widow and a daughter of a native Cornishman, John Richards of Hayle, in Budock Parish Church in 1840. This Henry Moses had no connection with the Falmouth Hebrew Congregation. Another Henry Moses (48) of Probus (Parish of St. Mewan) appears on the same census, and he was also a Gentile. The Jewish Alexander Moses, above, was also known as *Henry*, an example which shows that care must be taken not to confuse or conflate identities, and how misleading inferences can be drawn when relying on the superficial appearance of names alone. It would, therefore, be both facile and erroneous to assume that the mere occurrence of a "Hebrew" name must in itself identify that individual as Jewish, and this would apply even if the name (as forename or surname) was also one commonly found amongst Jews.

The same Parish registers list *Moses* fifteen times with the surnames *Semons, Simons, Symons, and Simmons,* all common variants as actual Jewish surnames, but all of them Christians. Although it is not impossible that one of more of these men may have been of Jewish origin, then entering into a Christian marriage, it is highly unlikely. Only a check of the full marriage entry in the Parish register could confirm the matter, in that a note would appear to indicate that one party was not a baptised Christian if this did apply. In the absence of such a detail, both parties can be assumed to have been Christians. As with *Moses* and *Symons,* the same criteria should be applied to the appearance of other (apparently) Jewish names in records and registers, such as *Jacob* or *Jacobs,* which, although applying to some Jewish families in Cornwall in the 18th and 19th centuries, are also to be found widely amongst the non-Jewish Cornish population. In 1888, a Dane, Hans Hansen, murdered a Charles Jacobs at Maker. There is no evidence to suggest that Jacobs was a Jew.[38] Official Records of the Corporation of Penzance mention the names of Nathaniel Ternerry, Issacke Spriddle, and Solomon Cerveth (1661), Solomon Cock (1791) and Jacob Corin (1817),[39] none of whom were Jews.

In the rural areas to the north-west and west of Penzance, from Zennor to Saint Just, Saint Buryan, Saint Levan and Sennen, a survey of census records from 1841 onwards, reveal no names of Jews or Jewish pedlars and hawkers, even though it would seem likely that they would have travelled to those places from Penzance. The records do show, however, Cornish families with members with striking names, some derived from Greek, Roman or Christian association, such as *Zachaeus, Zenobia, Archelaus, Athanasius, Philadelphia, Theophilus, Hannibal* and *Onesipherous,*[40] but others are clearly derived from the Hebrew Bible or the Apocrypha, such as *Obed, Noah, Caleb, Jabez, Jedidah, Hephzibah, Zechariah, Ephraim, Elisha, Enoch, Uriah, Tobias, Samson, Abednego* and *Athaliah*. The names *Onesiphorous* and the related *Onesimus* occur in three of the Epistles of Paul in the New Testament: the first in II Timothy 1:16 & 4:19, and the second in Colossians 4:9 & the Letter to Philemon. They are of Greek origin, from the words *onaesis,* usefulness, and *phoros,* he who brings: they were associated with profitable work, and the names may have been given to bring good fortune to the bearer. Jews in Greek and Roman times often bore Greek names, and any of those mentioned above could have been so used by Jews. It is of interest that in the case of at least one family from West Penwith, two men were given names, one from the Hebrew Bible, and the other from the New Testament: (1861) Caleb and Onesiphorous Batten, Tin Dressers. Another man, (1851) Onesiphorous Harvey was a Shoemaker, a trade sometimes taken up by Jews. Despite this, there is no evidence that any of these men were of Jewish descent. Similar Biblical names belonging to Cornish Christians could be found on census records outside West Penwith in any other rural area, such as the Lizard, or the moorland between Helston and Falmouth.

None of the following from this area of West Penwith were Jews: (1841) Abednigo Uren, Carpenter; Zacharias Williams, Engineer Man; Joseph Marks, son of Richard Marks, both Masons; Israel Vingoe, Agricultural Labourer, whose son, Israel was later a Tin Miner (1851); William Sampson, Miller; Samson Boase, Tin Miner; (1851) Samuel Brokensha, Mason (born in Mevagissey) with sons, Samuel, Joseph and Nathaniel; Samson Williams, Tin Miner, with sons Joseph and Isaac; Zacharias Renawden, Tin Dresser; Jeremiah Brown, Tin Dresser; Isaac White, Tin Miner; Melchisidec Boyns, Engineer; Abednigo Mathews, Agricultural Labourer; Israel Prowse, Agricultural Labourer, with sons, Israel, Jacob and Samuel; Israel George, Farm Labourer; Hosea Roberts, Farmer; Josiah Pearce, Farmer; Solomon Grose (Farmer's son); Immanuel Carne, Agricultural Labourer; Abednego Badcock, Farm Labourer (Saint Buryan); Isaac Williams, Tin Miner; Samson Boase, Retired Farmer; Isaac Nankervis, Miner; Isaac Perrow, Miner; Elisha Nicholas, Tin Miner; Absalom Thomas, Tin Miner; Hezekiah Rowe, Tin Miner; Josephus Semmens, Tin Dresser; Isaac Perrow, Green Grocer; Melchizedeck Edwards, Tin Miner; Caleb Batten, Tin Dresser. When the 1851 Ecclesiatical Census was drawn up, those signing the returns in West Cornwall included Abraham Wright (Mousehole Wesleyan), Melchizidec James (Madron Tregavara) and Rev. Isaac White (Ludgvan Primitive).[41]

Where full Census entries (from 1841 onwards) [42] give information of occupation and/or location, this can often help to eliminate a "suggestive" name, in that certain indigenous occupations and trades (fishing, farming, mining etc.) were not undertaken by Jews, who resided in towns, and not in villages or in the countryside. The 1841 Census gives a Josiah Symons of Phillack, *Mason,* and a Samuel Simmons of St. Gluvias, *Woolcomber,*[43] and the 1861 Census for Gwinear (Hayle) gives a Moses Simons, *Mineworker,*[44] and for St. Erth (nearby) a Moses Simons, *Ostler,*[45] none of which are occupations associated with Jews. The 1841 Census also lists a Betsy Simons and Eliza Symons, both Dressmakers, their names and their occupations common to both Jewish and Gentile women at the time, but for neither of these particular women is there a reason to suppose that they were Jewish. The 1861 Census gives an Aaron Symons of St. Ives and a Benjamin Symons of Maker (both children), [46] neither of whom are from Jewish families. The same Census gives Isaac Symons of Liskeard (Railway Labourer), Samuel Symons of Church Street, Helston (Carpenter), his son, also Samuel (Tin Miner), and in the same town, in Meneage Street, another Samuel Symons (Grocer's Labourer).[47] In such cases as these, it would be reasonable to eliminate them as Jews, or at least to file them for reference under "uncertain" or even "very unlikely". Elimination by trade alone cannot be an infallible test, in that a Jew may have taken up a trade not usually associated with Jews, especially if they had severed all links with Jewish religious observance, or maintained minimal observance, or had assimilated or converted to Christianity, although these particular forms of adaptation are not prerequisites for a Jew to have an uncharacteristic occupation. Nathan Vos of Falmouth (albeit a very late and untypical example from a time when the Jewish communities had dispersed from Cornwall) was an Innkeeper, and formerly a Grocer and Ship's Chandler. He died in 1913, and was married to a Gentile, but he was buried in the Jewish cemetery.

Entries in Census records may also suggest a Jewish connection because of the use of names linked with Jews. The 1841 census for Penzance, lists an Edward Rosman, a writer, not born in the County, with his wife, Martha, and his children, Eliza Maria, Edwin and Edgar Samuel, and the 1851 census for the same town, in Leskinnick Terrace (a street with some Jewish residents) lists an Alfred Gee, a House Agent from London, whose wife, however, was born in Helston (where no Jews are known to have lived). Two of the Gee children, Garshom and Ebenizer, were born in Antigua, in the West Indies, and are specified as British Subjects. Their younger siblings were Abraham, Eliz(a) and Hen(e)ry. Neither family can be identified as Jewish or of Jewish descent from these names alone, and the Gee forenames can be viewed as influenced by their earlier period of residence in Antigua, where such Hebrew names (also taken by Christians from the Bible) were common.

The following, and their families, also appear on County Census records (taken from 1841 and 1861) and represent further typical examples of Cornish names where the individuals are not known to have been Jewish[48] - Annie Abrahams, 51; Helston, Upholsterer (1871). Henry Harris, 30; Forrabury, Tailor (1841) & Henry Harris, 25; Camborne, Shoemaker (1841): *Harris* was and is a very common Cornish surname, and these are examples of Gentiles who practised trades associated with or similar to those commonly practised by Jews. The German- Jewish families of Samuel and Henry Harris (father and son) of Falmouth and (later) Truro, traded as jewellers and watch makers, and at the same time (*c.* 1817-1823) a Samuel Harris, a Gentile, also traded in Falmouth, as a Stationer, Printer & Bookbinder. The latter was married to a Gentile Mary *Symons*. John Henry Isaac, 38; Perranzabuloe, Mine Engineer (1871): his four children, David (7), Solomon (5), Reuben (2) and Malachi (6m) have forenames taken from the Old Testament. Whilst the first two names are very common amongst Jews, and the third less so (appearing as *Reuven*), the last name rarely occurs in a Jewish context. Zaccheus Isaac, 56; St. Clement, Truro, Labourer (1861) Benjamin Jacob, 46, St. Teath, Quarryman (1841) Benjamin Jacob(s), 25/47, St. Austell, Mason (1841 & 1861); Thomas Jacob, 29, St. Austell, Tailor (1841); Thomas Jacob, 15; St. Austell, Mason (1861): the forename *Thomas* is rarely, if ever, associated with Jews. Jacob Jacobs, 45; St. Ives, Fisherman (1861); John Jacobs, 45; St. Teath, Shoemaker (1841); William Jacobs, 30; St. Austell, Cordwainer (1841); Thirza Jacobs, 21: Polruan, Charwoman (1861); Benjamin Jacobson, 31; Linkinhorne, Yeoman (1841); Samuel Jacobs, 43; St. Kew, Agricultural Labourer (1861); Samuel Jacob(s), 39, St. Teath, Slate Quarryman (1841 & 1861); Zephaniah Job, 43, Truro, General Merchant (1861); Barzillai Major, 42; Penzance, Tailor (1871: mentioned above); Barzillai Beckerleg, Baker, Penzance (1841); William Marks, 48,

Penzance, Basket-Maker (1871: he had been born in Truro); Benjamin Michael, 70, St. Austell, Watchmaker (1841); Levi Michael, 60, Probus, Pensioner (1861); William Moses, 53, Probus, Agricultural Labourer (1861); William Moses, 25, Truro, Papier Mache Traveller (1861); Solomon Rafael, 30, Sithney, Tin Miner (1841); Abraham Ralph, 31, Gwennap, Copper Merchant's Clerk (1871); George Solomon, 53, Gorran, Farm Labourer (1861); Harriet Solomon, 17,Truro, Kitchen Servant (1861); Samuel Solomon, 57, Newquay, Labourer (1861); Solomon Solomon, 15, Kenwyn, Male Servant (1861); Solomon Stoneman, 26, Illogan, Miner (1841); Aron Symonds, 35, Budock, Tanner (1841); Ephraim Symons, 17, Truro, Draper (1861): his father, Charles (51) was a Tea-Dealer & Draper (trades not unconnected with Jews), born in St. Austell. Samuel Symons, 42, Penzance, Tailor (1871); Samuel Symons, 47, Penzance, Warehouseman (1871); W. B. Symons; Helston, Watch and Clock Maker (1856 Brown); Eli Winter, 33; Penzance, Hotel Keeper (1871); Jacob Wolfe, Falmouth, Mariner (c.1792-98)[49]. In 1864, Nehemiah Broadway and Isaac Hadfield were ministers of the Falmouth Primitive Methodist Chapel (built in 1832).[50]

Even names such as *Solomon,* or *Joseph* are numerous in Cornish records, but having no Jewish connection. A *Solomon* family of central-north Cornwall can be traced through several generations, from the early 1800s onwards, some of whom settled in Bodmin and Lostwithiel. Although they may have been of Jewish origin, the family is known to have been Christian, with burials recorded in Lostwithiel area, together with others of a likely related Solomon family at St. Winnow.[51] The handwritten Family Registers of this family, begun by George Solomon Snr. (1807-) and continued by his second son, George Solomon Jnr. (1841-) list twenty-seven members of this family, of whom George Solomon Snr. was a Grocer and Tea Dealer, his grandson, John Solomon (1880-), a Coach Builder and Wheelwright, and Francis Lennox Solomon (1894-) a Coach Painter. There are also five St. Winnow graves of a Richard Solomon (1794-1871), his wife, Betty (1798-1871) who died within a day of her husband, suggesting, perhaps an accident, William Solomon (1825-1853), who died at Fowey, a child, Catherine Solomon (1835-1843) and Samuel Solomon (1818-1854) who was a Coastguard. John Solomon was a Chemist and Druggist in the Lower Market, Penryn in 1864.[52] In a short story, most likely written in the 1920s, and set at "the greatest of all Cornish mines, Dolcoath", by the Camborne Methodist, John Frederick Odgers (1881-1971), the central character is a Solomon Andrew, most likely based on a real, but unidentified local man, and the "Manager" of the business was based on the real-life managing agent of Dolcoath, Captain Josiah Thomas (1833-1901). Their forenames were common in the area amongst Christians, and neither name implies any Jewish ancestry.[53]

Another example may help to illustrate the fact that apparent Jewish names cannot be taken as such without secondary confirmation from other sources. The name *Jacob* or *Jacobs* is a very characteristic Jewish surname. It was also common in Cornwall as a Gentile name, sometimes combined with an equally "Jewish" forename. The 1841 Census lists 102 people with this surname, of these about 30 have forenames common amongst Jews and Gentiles (such as Benjamin and Samuel), but of these there is only one (Joseph Jacobs of St. Austell) with an occupation commonly undertaken by Jews, that of Tailor, and even this case is uncertain. *Jacob* is a more characteristically Jewish surname than *Jacobs*, although the latter is associated with Jews and is sometimes freely alternated with *Jacob*. Both forms are also commonly found as Gentile names, and common Jewish and Gentile variants are *Jacobson*, *Jackobs* (or *Jakobs*) and *Jackson*.

Continental Jews were not accustomed to the use of fixed surnames, and their adoption by Jews was a comparatively late development. In medieval times, a Jew might be known by his place of origin or residence, such as *Aaron of Lincoln*. Traditionally, the Hebrew patronymic (which appears on headstones) served to identify an individual, but even this cannot be viewed as an inherited and stable surname as such. A father might be *Moses ben Solomon*, and so might be known as Moses Solomon. His son, however, could be named *Jacob ben Moses*, and known as Jacob Moses, and his son, in turn, named *Isaac ben Jacob*, and known as Isaac Jacob. In the course of time, some such forenames, especially if used habitually by the family through the generations, could become attached to or adopted by them as a form of surname. When in the early 1800s, Napoleon Bonaparte (1769-1821) recognised equality of citizenship within his domains, this came to include the Jews, and the status of citizenship carried the legal requirement of the use and registration of surnames. Jews who had not previously carried a surname might then choose a Hebrew name for this purpose, or take as their surname the Hebrew or Yiddish word for their trade. Some Jews randomly chose common colours (*Grun*: Green; *Weiss*: White etc.) or precious metals or stones (*Gold, Silver, Diamond, Ruby*,etc.). The chosen name might be used both in its Hebrew and vernacular form. In an English context, for example, the Hebrew surname *Margolith* (Pearl) might become *Pearlman* or *Pearlson*.[54]

Continental Jews, when entering Britain, or soon after settlement here, might change their surname, adopting an English alternative, or modify and adapt the sound of their name. This is the process of "Anglicization", or phonetic approximation of Hebrew or foreign names (German, Dutch, Russian or Polish) to English equivalents. One conscious motive may have been to lessen confusion and misapplication. Another may have been to reduce potential prejudice and discrimination. The German and Yiddish-inflected accent and pronunciation of some of the immigrant Jews (especially those of the first generation of arrivals) may have influenced the process. Both conscious adoption of English names, and gradual adaptation to equivalent near-sounding English names, from Hebrew to Yiddish to German to English, played a part. Two such examples of adoption may serve to illustrate: in 1825 Francis Cohen became Francis Palgrave, taking the name of his wife's mother's family,[55] and in another case in 1868 a *Moses* family became Beddington.[56] The process of adaptation, which took several forms, affords numerous examples. The Hebrew *Zvi* (a stag or hart) becomes *Hirsch* in Yiddish,[57] *Hart* in German and English, even becoming *Harris*. That *Harris* was a common Cornish name has already been mentioned, but surnames such as *Hart* and *Wolf* (or *Woolf, Woolfe and Wolfe*) that have an obvious Germanic (or Dutch) derivation, found in 18th and 18th century Penzance and Falmouth, were also common amongst Christians. A "Mr. Hart", a Nonconformist Christian minister, was married in Falmouth in 1817, and the bankruptcy of a "Jacob Wolfe, mariner...late of Falmouth", who is not known to have been Jewish, led to his departure from the town.[58] *Mordecai* can become Marks, *Moses* can become Merton, and it has been noted previously that *Levy* could become, or be pronounced as *Lavin* or *Levin,* and in some cases it became *Russell.*[59] The customs, processes and traditional rules which tended to govern and influence the names given by Jewish parents to their children have always in reality been of a very complex nature.[60] Sephardic custom has tended towards naming in a rigid fixed pattern, and with less adaptation to secular or vernacular models. Ashkenazi custom has been more fluid, but naming after the dead (such as an infant sibling) or a deceased relative, and naming after a father, grandparent, aunt or uncle are the most obvious patterns, with a greater degree of adaptation, modification or the adoption of vernacular names.

Susser has identified at least five processes by which Hebrew or Yiddish names were anglicized by immigrant Jews: (i) translation (e.g. *Berg > Hill*); (ii) adoption (of a phonetic equivalent, e.g. *Raussman > Roseman*); (iii) *aphesis*, the loss of an unaccented vowel at the beginning of a word, sometimes an unintentional, and usually a gradual process, and often accompanied by an additional ending, e.g. *Abraham(s)* or *Abramovitz(ch) > Braham, Bramson, Branson* or *Bramley*; (iv) mispelling or mispronunciation, as a result of which names appear in various similar forms (*Kohen, Cohen, Cowen, Cowan, Cohn* etc.); and (v) Biblical association[61] (where an element from a story is recalled). Hebrew forenames tended to be anglicized more quickly than surnames, but Jews from Eastern Europe and Russia (whose surnames were especially difficult for the English speaker to pronounce) were under a particular pressure in this respect. Some examples of anglicized male names common in the South West (as well as the country as a whole) are: *Asher > Angel; Avigdor > Victor; Baruch > Barnett* or *Benedict; Benj(y)amin > Woolf* or *Wolf; Eliezer > Lazarus* or *Lawrence; Elijah (Eliyahu) > Elias; Gershon > George; Hayyim (or Hyman) > Henry* or *Harry; Issachar > Barnett* or *Bernard; Judah > Lion* or *Lionel; Levy > Lewis* or *Louis; Michael > Mitchell; Mordecai > Mark; Moses > Morris* or *Maurice,* etc. [62]

Women's names (from Hebrew and Yiddish) include, *Feigele* ("Little Bird") > *Phoebe; Beila > Bella, Betsy* or *Elizabeth; Eddle* or *Edal > Esther; Telza > Eliza; Yetele > Judith; Killa > Kitty, Kate* or *Catherine; Hindele(a)* or *Henne > Hannah; Yuta* or *Yittel > Julia; Mirele(a) > Amelia; Malka > Milly* (or *Queenie); Zilla > Cicillia* or *Cicelia.*

Most of these names, male and female, can be seen on headstones in the cemeteries in Falmouth and Penzance.

To take three examples of these names:

1. The Hebrew name of Rabbi *Barnett* Asher Simmons of Penzance was Avraham *Issachar.* These phonetic and scriptural associations can be very subtle and fluid.

Issachar is associated with a bear. In Genesis 49:14, Jacob describes him as "strong-boned", that is, like an "ass", capable of "bearing" a heavy load. Barnet Levy (-1791) of Falmouth was also known as *Bernard Beer* or *Issachar Baer*, and by the Hebrew names *Behr ben Joel* (on his headstone in Falmouth: 1:4) and *Issachar Jacob* (on the headstone of his daughter, Shevya: Penzance 6:4). (This Barnet Levy is not to be identified with Barnet Levy of St. Austell , about whom little is known).

2. In Genesis 49:27, Jacob likens Benjamin to a wolf. In 18th Cornwall, in Falmouth, the names *Benjamin* and *Wolf/Woolf* appear together, both as forename and surname. A *Wolf* ("Woolly") *Benjamin* (*d.* 1790) is buried in the Falmouth cemetery

(1:2) and also (in an unmarked grave there) a *Benjamin Woolf*, originally from Holland. The former was distinguished by the additional forename *Isaac*, and was somewhat older than the latter, but both of these men traded as jewellers and pawnbrokers in Falmouth at around the same time. This example clearly shows how easy it can be to confuse the identities of separate individuals.

3. In Genesis 49:9, Jacob compares Judah to a lion. *Lyon* Joseph (1775-1825) of Falmouth, who is buried in Plymouth, had the Hebrew name *Judah ben Joseph*.[63]

Familiar Jewish names, such as *Moses*, *Josephs* and *Solomon*, have, of course, been associated with families of Afro-Caribbean descent, in 18th and 19th century Cornwall, surnames such as *Abrahams, Isaacs* etc. were common amongst (although not exclusive to) Romany Gypsy families,[64] and this can lead to a confusion with Jews, especially where the latter were itinerant peddlers. The only practicable way, therefore, to arrive at a credible identification of Jewish names is to cross-check against a variety of sources and records.

Marriage and Conversion

Marriage to non-Jews or conversion to Christianity can also confuse the issue and may have been more widespread than the available evidence suggests. Several examples of this include the marriage of Isaac Polack of Penryn to Mary Stoughton, the conversion of Harriet Hyman, the family of Henry Moses of Falmouth and the family conversion of John Levi in Truro. Gabriel Abrahams and Thomas Levi, both of whom were from Falmouth, converted to Christianity. On 3rd February 1777, Tobias Phillips,[65] a Jew, born 1712 in Lithuania, was baptised (his burial took place on 6th April 1792). On 4th July 1790 and Edward Cecil Brandon,[66] a Jew (possibly of a Sephardic background), born 4th June 1766 was baptised. *Brandon* may be an Anglicisation of the Spanish or Portuguese *Brandao*, in that the Iberian original is pronounced in a very similar way. Edward Cecil Brandon may have had some connection with Falmouth's maritime trade with the Iberian peninsula and the West Indies, and the name occurs on Jewish headstones in Jamaica. On the 8th April 1791 William Cohen, born in June 1783, was baptised in Falmouth at the age of eight. His parents were Moses and Betsy Cohen. In the baptismal register, it would appear that William is stated to have been "formerly a Jew", although the term may refer to the father, Moses Cohen.[67] (A Rose Cohen, aged 47, and her four children were residents in Falmouth in 1851).[68] On 22nd February 1822, the four children of Jacob and Elizabeth Levy were all baptised in St Mary's Church, Truro.[69] They were called Charles, Anna, Jacob and Elizabeth, born between 1813 and 1822. On 11th August 1840, at Budock Parish Church in the district of Falmouth, a Henry Moses of Budock, then aged 37, married Johanna Bristo of Budock, a widow aged 29. She was originally from Hayle and a daughter of John Richards, a miner. Henry Moses was a hawker and traveller, and has sometimes been taken to have been a Jew,[70] his trade, no doubt, suggesting this, although many hawkers and pedlars were Gentiles. His father (who did not sign the certificate of marriage) is given as *Philip*, and a Philip Moses, son of Alexander Moses (the Hebrew Congregation former President) was buried in the

Jewish cemetery in 1831 (2:2). This Philip Moses' death, nine years earlier, could be read as consistent with the non-appearance of the father's signature. However, Jewish genealogical records do not provide any evidence of a Henry as a son of the Jewish Philip Moses, or link him with the Jewish Moses family of Falmouth.[71] The two witnesses to the marriage were both non-Jews: the bride's father and Mary Ann Polglase. This does not, of course, eliminate the possibility that this Henry Moses was a Jew, and that his Jewish relatives could not, on principle attend such a service. By 1851, Henry Moses had moved with his wife, their four sons and a daughter to Porham Lane Falmouth and were able to accommodate a servant girl, Eliza Martin.[72] On 7th February 1851, the Cornish press reported that a "Mr. Jacobs of Poole, a converted Jew", took part in services , with four Christian ministers, at the anniversary services of the Primitive Methodists, at Penzance, "on behalf of the home and foreign missions of that society". Jacobs was clearly a visitor from Dorset, but his presence in the town as a Christian missionary would not have gone unnoticed within the Jewish community.

These men could be regarded as Jewish (or likely to be so), and their families partly Jewish from a genealogical, if not a strictly religious viewpoint. Whilst this approach has its merits and advantages for historical research, it is not entirely free of interpretative and evaluative problems. There are issues relating to the development of the law governing the registration of marriages and also to any assessment of the attitude and practice of Jewish congregations towards intermarriage (especially in a Church), as well as the baptism of Jewish children and the subsequent religious practice of the Jews concerned.

There are two extensive passages in Susser which merit careful study.[73] He outlines the fact that the marriage of a Jew to a non-Jew is not only contrary to Jewish Law, but, because Jewish identity is defined by matrilineal descent, that the children of a non-Jewish mother would not be regarded as Jews, and that, unless the mother converted to Judaism, the extensive home ceremonials could not be celebrated adequately. In so doing he introduces, although he does not explore, the complicating factor that the view taken by a Jewish community to intermarriage with a Christian might differ according to whether the Jewish partner involved was male or female. These issues of *principle* and practice are contrasted, however, with various examples from the 18th and 19th centuries of inter-marriage and church weddings which reveal a complex pattern of *attitude* and practice. Susser stresses that a Church marriage between a Jew (who had not converted or been baptised) and a Christian was legal: Manasseh Lopes married Charlotte Yeats near Windsor in 1795, but did not abandon his Judaism until 1802. Church marriages involving Jews are not, therefore, conclusive evidence of conversion.

Furthermore it cannot be taken as axiomatic that such a marriage would lead to automatic estrangement or expulsion from the Jewish congregation. Although it might lead to exclusion from certain synagogal rites, it did not invariably lead to the loss of all contact. The following passage deserves to be quoted in full in this context: "....Samuel Ralph was married more than once in Church and yet had a Jewish burial. Isaac Gompertz....married Florence Wattier in Church in 1818 and baptised all his children at birth; yet he was buried in the Jewish cemetery at Exeter." (Samuel Ralph was buried in 1867, although not in the main part of the

Plymouth cemetery).[74] Susser even finds an example of a clear case of conversion, that of Moses Ximenes who was baptised in 1802 and yet remained on friendly terms with the practising Jews of the Lousada family. It would seem that Church marriages involving Jews were common in the 18th century and may even have been tolerated by some congregations. If Jews, (in Susser's words) "strongly desired to be accepted", as Abraham Franco did in a letter of application to the Plymouth congregation in 1829 on behalf of his non-Jewish wife and *Familie Particular*,[75] they might be accepted although it is not known if Franco's application succeeded, and the Plymouth congregation had certainly instituted a rule against Church marriages long before this, in 1779.

Church marriages involving Jews would, however, carry the risk that the children and the Jewish partner would be baptised or formally convert in the future, if not at the time. There was a conflict of loyalties at the very least (subsequent Church attendance would have been an obvious test) and an inevitable long-term loss of members from the Jewish congregations. Some Jews may have undergone Church marriage or had their children baptised for reasons of security rather than religious belief. Jewish experience of the perils and pogroms suffered on the Continent and a desire to ensure the safety and future of their children, even in what appeared ostensibly to be a tolerant and welcoming country, may have played its part. This could be seen as *Anglicization* rather than conversion and could be interpreted as adaptation and adjustment rather than apostasy. Moreover, subjective perception and objective appearance may not have coincided in all cases and the dynamics may have differed from the mechanics of the event. Even so, such Church marriages and baptisms are highly suggestive of a compromise which would often lead to the abandonment of Judaism and they are indicative of conversion, especially as Marriage Law at this time recognised the legality of Jewish marriage in Synagogues.

Since the 16th century, the lack of uniformity and completeness in the administration and recording of marriages and deaths had been recognised as a problem. Various attempts had been made to address this.[76] Apart from a brief period during the Commonwealth when the first attempt at civil registration was introduced, responsibility for record-keeping had rested with Anglican clergy. Roman Catholic Churches continued to grow and the Non-conformist Churches spread rapidly in the 17th and 18th centuries such that the need for effective centralised registration and regulation was pressing. In addition to this, there was an alarming growth in the number of unregulated, clandestine marriages which often took place (without proper safeguards of parental permission, witnesses or registration) not in places of worship but in houses and taverns, sometimes with unscrupulous clergy officiating. The legal implications for legitimacy and inheritance were considerable and these irregular marriages became so prevalent that in 1754 Lord Hardwicke's Marriage Act was passed to enforce strict marriage regulations. The key requirements were:

(i) banns must be proclaimed in the Parish Church or

(ii) a licence obtained;

(iii) the marriage could only take place in the Anglican Parish Church in the presence of at least two witnesses;

(iv) the marriage must be registered in the Parish register;

(v) the only legal proof of marriage was a certificate from the register, and

(vi) all non-conformists, including Roman Catholics, had to marry in the Parish Church, so that it was not possible to be married legally outside the Church of England. Quakers were excluded from the Act. Crucially, Jews were also exempt so that marriages in a Synagogue were recognised as legal. The exemption of these two groups was an acknowledgement of the scrupulous manner in which those congregations were accustomed to publicise, celebrate and register their marriages. The Act did require that if a Jew was to marry a person who had been baptised in the Church of England, this marriage *had* to take place in the Parish Church even if the Jew did not convert through baptism.

In July 1837 a comprehensive system of Civil registration of all births, marriages and deaths was introduced in England and Wales together with the facility for civil marriage in a Register Office. Synagogues were not required to be registered for marriages partly because of their good record-keeping but also because Jewish Law allows Jews to marry in a private location, such as the family home, provided the Secretary from the bridegroom's synagogue is present at the wedding. From 1837 all previous marriages (including Jewish) were to be sent for registration to the Registrar General and all subsequent marriages were to be registered either in Parish Churches, non-conformist or Roman Catholic Churches, Synagogues *and* with the local Register Office, from where they would be sent for centralisation at the regional or county Record Office. Unlike Roman Catholics and non-conformists, who had been placed in a situation of compromise and ambivalence by the law, it had not been a legal requirement for Jews to marry in the local Anglican Church or have a marriage registered there before 1837, and most certainly not after that date when marriage in a Register Office became available as an alternative on a civil basis. However, these advantages had applied to Jews who married Jews. Where a Jew wished to marry a Gentile who was not willing to convert to Judaism, then the marriage would have taken place in the Parish Church as a matter of course. Most of the known converts to Judaism in the South-West were, in fact, women, whereas most of the Church marriages were between Jewish men and Gentile women, patterns that afford various interpretations, including the physical (the deterrent element in the requirement of circumcision for male converts) and the social (advancement).[77] From 1837 a Jewish-Gentile marriage could take place in a civil context, although this would not eliminate the social pressure and preference from the Christian party and their family that it should take place in a Church, as a social if not legal necessity. It is questionable, therefore, whether a Jewish-Gentile marriage in Church signifies conversion on the part of the Jew, in that the event could have been undertaken to secure the legality of the marriage where a Jewish ceremony was not possible. What is crucial is that these marriages can only be taken as conversion by the Jew if information other than the mere fact of the location is available; for example such remarks as "formerly a Jew" as in the case of Henry Moses, or a baptism as in the case of Abraham Levi. The subsequent baptism of children does not in itself prove conversion by or even the complete abandonment of Judaism by the Jewish partner, although it is highly suggestive of a distinctive move towards conversion or at least assimilation into a predominantly Christian culture. Clearly a judgement needs to be made whether to include as a Jew anyone who was married in Church or had their children baptised during this period. Where a person is known to have been of Jewish descent, even if they were no longer associated with the Jewish congregation, they have been included in this book.

Despite the reforms of 1837, the accuracy of Official registers in computing the size and profile of the Jewish population of Cornwall remains doubtful and is problematical. Between 1838 to 1892 there were 17 official Jewish marriages in Penzance, where both parties were Jewish. In the case of the marriage in July 1861 of Frederick Lazarus (who was of Jewish descent) to Emily Cock (who was a Gentile), the ceremony was a civil one, and was not, therefore, a "Jewish" marriage. Frederick Lazarus is not known to have had any connection with the Penzance Hebrew Congregation, nor with the Hyman Lazarus who is listed in the Minute-Book in 1843 and 1845, although some relationship between the two is possible. In the case of the marriage of Marcus Bischofswerder to Emma Hawke in June 1892, the bride had previously converted to Judaism. If she had not done so, a Rabbi (in this case, Michael Leinkram) would not have officiated, as no Rabbi could sanction a marriage, whether in synagogue or in a private home, where only one party was Jewish (as in the case of Frederick Lazarus). After 1837, where the marriage took place in a Synagogue, records would have been copied to the local Registrar. Most of the Jewish marriage registers for Falmouth have been lost as a result of their transfer to the Records Office at Exeter where they were eventually destroyed during the Second World War. With those records has been lost the demographic information which could have been drawn from them. Despite this, some details of Jewish marriages in Falmouth can be gathered from other sources. What should be emphasised is that despite the occurrence of a few marriages between Jews and non-Jews in South Cornwall, the available evidence suggests that inter-marriage in the County was very rare indeed compared with the number of conventional marriages between Jews. Whilst Jews may have integrated into Cornish society, they are not known to have assimilated to any great extent. Rather, it was through commerce, the membership of civic and private societies, such as Freemasonry, or other cultural and literary groups rather than through marriage to non-Jews that Jewish integration took place .

The occupations followed by the Jews in Cornwall, as elsewhere, were largely defined by the requirement that their trade and skills should be mobile and relocatable to any place outside the County. The occupation of a jeweller, silversmith, goldsmith, watch and clock maker, tailor and general merchant could be practised anywhere. Some people remained in Cornwall for several decades, and some families for several generations, and their names are to be found in various records, and the main trade directories from the earliest to some of the later editions: the Joseph,

Solomon and Jacob families of Falmouth, and the Woolf, Joseph and Levin families of Penzance are examples of these, with numerous headstones in the two cemeteries. Some members of these, and other families, for reasons of marriage or self-improvement soon moved away. Thus, migration and emigration took their toll on the remaining numbers in the Jewish communities. Some individuals became more specialised in their occupations, and adapted to the special opportunities of the town, as a "tinman", that is, not a miner, but a dealer in tin and copper plate or pipe (Solomon Ezekiel of Penzance), or as a sideline, a dealer in mineralogical specimens (Moses Jacob of Redruth). Some became established in a flourishing family business, such as the Penzance merchant Lemon Hart, in wines and spirits and in sea-trading and imports, or, in the same town, the Oppenheim family, in what was for its day a superstore for household goods. The Harris family became jewellers by Royal Warrant in Truro. Moss Jacob Jacob of Falmouth became a (multilingual) Money broker and Naval Agent, and at least one of the Jacob family, most likely Issac Jacob of Falmouth (later of Swansea) had wide-ranging investments in mining and shipping, which he continued to pursue after he left the County.

---

[1] See Leo Rostein's *The Joys of Yiddish* (1968: pp. 377-381), for a brief account, from which some of these details have been taken. For a detailed account, see Eva Hoffman, *Shtetl* (Houghton Mifflin, New York, 1997).

[2] Arthur P. Arnold, *Apprentices of Great Britain 1710-1773*, in *TJHSE* Vol. XXII (1970) p. 152.

[3] Roth (1950) pp. 15-25. See also Moses Margoliouth, *The History of the Jews in Great Britain* (London 1851).

[4] V. D. Lipman, *The Plymouth Aliens List* (Transactions JHSE 1962) pp. 187-194.

[5] George Rude, *Hanoverian London 1714-1808* (1971 & 2003) pp. 5, 7-8, & 10.

[6] Felipe Fernandez-Armesto (author of *Civilizations*: Macmillan 2000): *The Sunday Times*, February 11th 2001).

[7] H.Miles Brown (1961 & 1970) *Cornish Clocks and Clockmakers*, is referenced as (Br). Page references are not given on every occasion, but where given they refer to pp. 64-91 of the 1970 edition.

[8] For some of the information on Cornish Jewish Wills (which have not been examined here in detail) I am grateful to Helen Fry for providing examples from her research. Wills etc. prior to 1858 can be found at the Family Record Office, Myddleton Street, London, and after 1858 from the Probate Registry. Records also exist at York, and in Cornwall at Bodmin and the County Record Office, Truro.

[9] Naggar (1992, p.22 & 28-30).

[10] The Biography of Samuel Drew (London & Bodmin 1861). The extract is taken from p. 82. I am grateful to Joanna Mattingly for providing this information (17th February 2000).

[11] D. Gilbert, *Parochial History of Cornwall*, Vol. III (1838) p. 97.

[12] R. John Hall (2001) p. 14.

[13] Pool (1974) p. 260.

[14] A. L. Rowse, *Tudor Cornwall* (1941, reprint 1957, Bedford Historical Series, Jonathan Cape, London) pp. 54-58 & 95-96, ref. Matthews, *History of St. Ives*, 117-20, and Henderson, *History of the Parish of Constantine*, 121-13.

[15] Rowse, (1941-57) pp. 96-97.

[16] Pool (1974) pp. 248-252.

[17] Robert Latham (edit.) *The Shorter Pepys* (Penguin 1993) p. 313; Roth *A History of the Jews in England* (1964) p. 174.

[18] Jeremy Lewis, *Tobias Smollett* (Jonathan Cape 2003) p. 159.

[19] Chapters 28 & 33.

[20] Book II, Chapter V & Book IV, Chapter IX.

[21] Chapter 9.

[22] Chapter XLII.

[23] Gerald Reitlinger, *The Changed Face of English Jewry at the end of the Eighteenth Century,* in *TJHSE* vol. XXIII (1971) p. 36.

[24] Roy Porter, *English Society in the 18th Century*; Penguin (1990) p. 101 and 269, the latter quoting the London tailor, Francis Place. See also George Rude (1971) pp. 157-159 & 210; R. J. Mitchell and M. D. R. Leys, *A History of London Life* (Longmans Green & Co. 1958) pp. 24-27 (*The London Jewry*), and Vivian D. Lipman, *The Development of London Jewry,* in "A Century of Anglo-Jewish Life" (edit. Salmond S. Levin (United Synagogue Publications 1970) pp. 43-56. W. R. Ward's *Religion and Society in England 1790-1850* (London 1972) is also a valuable source.

[25] Reitlinger (1971) p. 39.

[26] Jonathan Romain *The Jews of England* (Michael Goulston & Jewish Chronicle Publications 1988) pp. 68-70, 84-85 & 116-121.

[27] Reitlinger (1971) pp. 38-39.

[28] Barton (1971) p. 57: from a full report in the *West Briton* (8th March 1839).

[29] Pool (1974) pp.191 & 281-2.

[30] George Clement Boase (1829-1897), *Reminiscences of Penzance* (Edit. Peter Pool, 1976) p. 69. I am grateful to Jackie Hill for sharing her research into the Pidwell family, as well as a wide range of other information.

[31] Jackie Hill (2009 & 2013).

[32] PRO ref.RG 9/1565.

[33] Cf. her death certificate; information from which has been provided by Leslie and Naomi Falkson of London (Letter and enclosures to Godfrey Simmons, June 11th 1993). It should be noted that it has not been established conclusively that the family of Leslie Falkson is related to that of Lewis and Esther Falkson of Falmouth.

[34] Records of the Cornwall Family History Society (CFHSoc.) Truro.

[35] CFHSoc. Truro.

[36] *Royal Cornwall Gazette,* 5th November 1860 & Census (1861).

[37] CFHSoc., Truro.

[38] *The West Briton,* on 11th October 1888.

[39] Pool (1974) pp. 228, 229, 254 & 265.

[40] 2 Timothy Ch.I, v.16.

[41] J. C. C. Probert (1988) entries 510, 395, 241 & 245.

[42] In the sections which follow, selected examples have been taken from the 1841 and 1861 Census records. The Census records for 1851, 1871 etc. would reveal similar examples.

[43] Piece 143 folio 50 page 38, and Piece 1567 folio 86 schedule 144. Piece 143 folio 53 page 43, and Piece 140/12 folio 12 page 16).

[44] Piece 1585 folio 59 schedule 156.

[45] Piece 1588 folio 114 schedule 100.

[46] Piece 1590 folio 55 schedule 90, and Piece 1522 folio 49 schedule 24.

[47] Piece 1529 folio 130 schedule 47; Piece 1572 folio 60 schedule 83, and folio 25 schedule 199.

[48] One or two of these names may be listed in the Trades sections as "Uncertain", where their trade or other forenames in the family names are associated with Jews.

[49] Bankruptcy notice *Exeter Flying Post,* 10th May and 8th November 1792, 24th June 1793, and 4th January 1798: Helen Fry (2000).

[50] Warn's *Directory and Guide of 1864,* p. 47.

[51] Letters from Keith Solomon of St. Columb Major to Keith Pearce (27th June & 4th July 2000).

[52] Warn's Directory (1864) p. 140.

[53] J. F. Odgers *Solomon the Tributer* (edit. Allen Buckley and Charles Thomas) Journal RIC (2012) pp. 45-56.

[54] Letter from Dr. Barry Monk (16th July 2009) to Keith Pearce.

[55] *Anglo-Jewish Notabilities,* in Jewish Historical Soc. Journal (1949) p. 112.

[56] W.P.W. Phillimore, *An Index to Changes of Name* (1905) p. 22.

[57] Susser (1993) p. 326, note 67.

[58] Wilfred S. Samuel, "Sources of Anglo-Jewish Genealogy" in *The Genealogists' Magazine,* vi 146-59. HF 2000: *Exeter Flying Post,* 24th July 1817; & 19th May 1792, (subsequent records of bankruptcy, November 1792, February 1793 and February 1798).

[59] See further Paul H. Emden, *Jews of Britain* (1943) pp. 229, 504, 508, & 527.

[60] For a detailed descriptive and analytical study: Edgar R. Samuel, *New Light on the Selection of Jewish Children's Names,* in *TJHSE* vol. XXIII (1971).

[61] Susser (1993) p. 230-232 & 326.

[62] Susser (1993) pp. 230-232. Susser expressly mentions the first four of these processes, and implies the fifth in his list of names.

[63] Susser (1972) p. 8.

[64] Allen Buckley (13th July 2000).

[65] *Register of Baptisms, Marriages, and Burials of the Parish of Falmouth 1663-1812 [RegFaL]* :
(The Devon and Cornwall Record Society: 1914 & 1915) part 1, p. 359 & part 2, p. 892. (Research by H. C. Faulkner).

[66] *RegFal.* Part 1, p. 459. (Research by H. C. Faulkner). Barnett & Wright (Ed. Yoffe) *The Jews of Jamaica, Tombstone Inscriptions 1663-1880* (Jerusalem 1997), e.g. pp. 68-9, entries 590, 624, 630 & 631 (there are over 30 examples: see also pp. 135-6).

[67] Cf. letter from Wilfred S. Samuel of the Jewish Museum to Alex Jacob, dated 12th May 1939 (Jacob Archive). See also *RegFal* part 1, p.464.

[68] C.f. 1851 census returns for Falmouth.

[69] C.f Susser (1993, p.243); and St Mary's Parish Register, Truro, p.654.

[70] Susser (1995) p. 22.

[71] Source: A non-facsimile copy of the certificate (Jacob Archive).

[72] Susser (1995) p. 22, took this family to have been Jewish. .

[73] Susser (1993, p.236-237).

[74] Susser (1993, p.190).

[75] Susser, *op. cit.,* pp. 227, 237, 325.

[76] Much of what follows has been drawn from official information provided by Rita Collier, Superintendant Registrar of Marriages, Penzance (26th January 1999) and from Dianne Pryce of the Office for National Statistics, Southport (9th February 1999): Letters to Keith Pearce.

[77] Susser, *op. cit.,* pp.237-8.

CHAPTER 3
The Jews of Falmouth

Although there was not a settled Jewish community in Cornwall until around the mid 18th century, there is some reason to believe that Jews were trading in or via Falmouth before 1700. In 1685 a pamphlet was published by Samuel Hayne,[78] a former customs officer, who detailed illegal trading discovered in 1680 between Barbadian Jews and Amsterdam, with well connected London Jewish merchants acting as intermediaries. The use of English ships, docking at Falmouth, helped to avoid duty on Dutch goods, and suggests that Dutch-Jewish traders had a representative of their own in Falmouth. There were allegations that Jews tried to bribe Hayne, and also bribed the Jury at the trial of two Sephardic Jews, Gomasero and Losado. However, the case went against Hayne and he was removed from office. What became obvious was that Sir Peter Killigrew, a local landowner with considerable influence and contacts in Royal and government circles, and a Falmouth merchant, Brian Rogers, were implicated in the activities. Rogers was Mayor of Falmouth in 1673, 1678 and 1690. He was related to the Keigwin family of Penzance and to the Godolphin family of Trewarveneth. He held leases from the Arwenack Manor Estate to land and property in Falmouth, where he was involved in the brewing trade. Rogers had, over time, become antagonistic towards the Killigrew family, but he was prepared to co-operate with them when his own advancement and status could be served, and in 1686, he shared the cost with Sir Peter Killigrew of the building of a new gallery at the west end of Falmouth Parish Church.[79] From the Hayne case, it would seem, therefore, that the self-interest of local residents also made them sympathetic to the activities of Jewish traders as early as the 1680s, and may have eased Jewish settlement in Falmouth in the 1740s. It is unlikely, however, that, apart from a few, isolated examples of individuals, familial Jewish settlement in Falmouth occurred before the mid-18th century. (The baptism of "Robert, son of Jerubbaal Gideon" in Falmouth in 1719 does not confirm the child's family as Jewish).[80]

In his *Tour Throughout the Whole Island of Great Britain* (1722), Daniel Defoe, drawing to some extent upon his early travels as a merchant in 1685-90, but also upon further direct experience and fieldwork into the 1720s, described the "inlet of the sea...the famous firth...called Falmouth Haven" as "...certainly next to Milford Haven in South Wales, the fairest and best road for shipping that is in the whole of Britain, when there be considered the depth of water of above twenty miles within land; the safety of riding, sheltered from all kind of winds or storms, the good anchorage, and the many creeks, all navigable, where ships may run in and be safe, so that the like is no where to be found....The Town of Falmouth is by much the richest, and best trading town in this county....which is chiefly owing to the situation, for that Falmouth, lying upon the sea, but within the entrance, ships of the greatest burthen come up to the very quays, and the whole royal navy might ride safely in the road. Falmouth is well built, has abundance of shipping belonging to it, is full of rich merchants, and has a flourishing and increasing trade." [81] Of Penryn, Defoe observed that it "is up the same branch of the haven, as Falmouth, but stands four miles higher towards the west, yet (small) ships come to it of as great a size, as can come to Truro itself; it is a very pleasant agreeable town, and for that reason has many merchants in it". Defoe also notes the "new commerce" of the "English packets" between Falmouth and Lisbon (following the Methuen Treaty in 1703, when four new packets had gone into service) and that the "considerable" trade with Portugal had "carried on to a very great value", although he observes that part of this packet trade "was founded in a clandestine commerce", by the avoidance of customs searches, but that it had since been brought under proper regulation, without detriment to Falmouth's interests.

The frequency with which ships docked at Falmouth, and also at Penzance, meant that in the 18th century, the residents of these ports were more than familiar with foreign accents and foreign faces, including Jews. Precious metals, especially gold from Portugal, arrived in Falmouth on board the Lisbon packet boats. Between January and June 1741, the cargoes of gold were valued at £133,562, of which almost 10% had been consigned to Jews (although one Jew, Francis Salvador, received nearly 70%).[82] On board the packet boat, *Greville*, which left the West Indies in 1781, carrying twenty passengers, was the boy seaman, Samuel Kelly, who recorded that one of them was "...a Jew named Levi, who was going to London to have a cancer cut from his under lip, on which he wore a black plaster, and sat at the table in the steerage with the other passengers, selecting such victuals only as he chose to eat, some of which was provided wholly by himself, *viz*: Jew beef salted and spiced, each piece having a lead ticket fastened to it; he had also a large quantity of rusk and sweet cakes, and always drank out of his own cup on account of his cancer." [83] In July 1784 an Algerian Muslim, Mahomet Celiby, was a visitor at the Falmouth Masonic Lodge,[84] In 1803, the Town Clerk of Falmouth, James Tippett, issued a wanted notice, together with a ten guinea reward, for the apprehension of a Joseph De Gomes, who had recently landed "in violation of the Alien Act, and is supposed to be secreted in or near Falmouth". Gomes is described as being "about 5 feet 11 inches high, of a dark copper-colour complexion, has lost one or more of his fore teeth, and has dark hair tied without powder." This kind of notice was comparatively rare, and was published in *The Royal Cornwall Gazette*. It did not give a reason, other than his unlawful entry, as to why he might be a wanted man, and, despite his name, he may simply have been an Iberian native, and not a Jew.[85] Likewise, the packetman, Thomas Solomon, of the ship *Duke of Marlborough*, who was killed near Barbados during the Napoleonic Wars, from an attack by a schooner privateer, on 27th March 1807, is unlikely to have been Jewish.[86] Much later, early in 1840, references occur in the local press (and in the Journals of Barclay Fox) that "Capt. Muddle" of the convict ship *Mandarin*, from Portsmouth, which was "bound for Van Dieman's Land" had docked at Falmouth with the loss of two top-masts. Amongst the 250 male transportees were "the Jews, convicted of the late gold dust robbery". In 1839, the H.M. Packet *Seagull*, carrying £4,600 of gold dust from the Brazilian Mining Company, and en route to London, had berthed at Falmouth. Three Jews, "the two Caspars, father and son (one of whom was "Caspar Abraham") and "Money Moses", stole the gold dust soon after the *Seagull's* arrival. They were apprehended, and so found themselves in 1840 aboard the *Mandarin* as prisoners.[87] These three Jews appear to have been known in Falmouth, but it is not clear if they were residents of the town, or merely travelling opportunists. Prejudicial towards Jews as these extracts may seem, their appeal may have resided in their exotic character, and the earlier reports are likely to be exceptional, in that from the 1750s onwards, and certainly by 1840 there was a well established and respected Jewish community in the town.

Visitors to Falmouth from the Iberian peninsula and the Iberian countries of South America continued to be a feature in the 19th century. In September 1828, Donna Maria Gloria, the Queen of Portugal, arrived in the town aboard the Brazilian frigate *Imperatriz*, to be met by the Portuguese and Brazilian Ambassadors, and in June 1831, the Emperor and Empress of Brazil arrived off Falmouth to be met by a member of the local Fox family, Alfred Fox, who was the town's Brazilian Vice-Consul. Italians were also visitors to the town, and one, Giovanni Battista Zupelli, had set up as a shipping agent by 1864, in Arwenack Street, where two Jews, Moss Jacob Jacob, outfitter and silversmith, and Nathan Vos, then a Grocer and ships' chandler, also traded.[88] The first Jews who arrived in the town and those who came later to settle would not, therefore, have been an unusual feature amongst the town's foreign visitors and residents, although their Germanic and Dutch backgrounds would have been a contrast to the more frequent arrivals from the Mediterranean areas by ship. Most of the incoming Jews would have entered England via Harwich, and then travelled through London to the West Country. They comprised Jews from Alsace (Moses, Levy and Joseph, the latter from Mulhausen) Holland (Wolf), and from Germany (Harris and Jacob) especially from the Rhineland area, the Solomon family having come from Ehrenbreitstein, high up opposite Koblenz, on the Rhine. Ehrenbreitstein was renowned for its impressive elevated fortifications and its wines, which led to it receiving mention in several 19th century literary works, including two by Herman Melville.[89]

The Moses Family

Alexander (or Henry) Moses ("Zender Falmouth": *c*.1715-1791) was integral in establishing the Falmouth Jewish congregation and providing its community with an economic system which sent Jewish tradesmen from Falmouth out into the surrounding villages and town, thus expanding opportunities and income. He had been born in Alsace, where he married Phoebe, who may have been a relative. Alexander Moses was the son of a Moses Moses, and it appears that Phoebe's family name was also *Moses*. Alexander Moses' headstone in the Penryn cemetery reads *Alexander ben* Moses, and his wife, Phoebe's, *Feigele bat Moses*. He is thought to have come to Cornwall from London around 1740 at the age of 25, and he was certainly in the town in 1751, when he was Warden and a founder member of the Falmouth Masonic Lodge.[90] Philip Moses (*c*.1713-1760), a Tailor of London, who was also a Mason there, is likely to have been Alexander's brother, cousin, or brother-in-law. Philip Moses' son was also named Moses Moses, his namesake

Moses of Falmouth

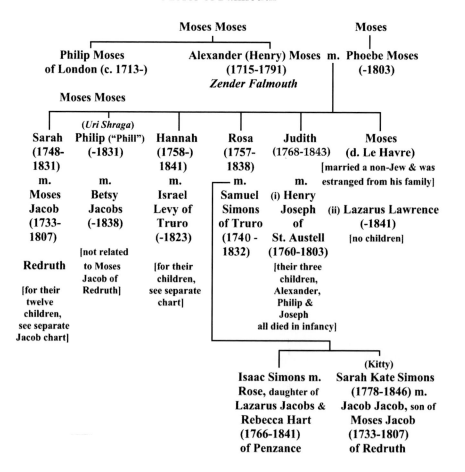

Moses Moses

Philip Moses of London (c. 1713-)

Alexander (Henry) Moses m. Phoebe Moses
(1715-1791)
Zender Falmouth

Moses | Phoebe Moses (-1803)

Moses Moses

Sarah (1748-1831)	*(Uri Shraga)* Philip ("Phill") (-1831)	Hannah (1758-) 1841)	Rosa (1757-1838)	Judith (1768-1843)	Moses (d. Le Havre)
m.	m.	m.	m.	m.	[married a non-Jew & was estranged from his family]
Moses Jacob (1733-1807)	Betsy Jacobs (-1838)	Israel Levy of Truro (-1823)	Samuel Simons of Truro (1740-1832)	(i) Henry Joseph of St. Austell (1760-1803)	(ii) Lazarus Lawrence (-1841) [no children]
Redruth	[not related to Moses Jacob of Redruth]	[for their children, see separate chart]		[their three children, Alexander, Philip & Joseph all died in infancy]	
[for their twelve children, see separate Jacob chart]					

Isaac Simons m. Rose, daughter of Lazarus Jacobs & Rebecca Hart (1766-1841) of Penzance

(Kitty) Sarah Kate Simons (1778-1846) m. Jacob Jacob, son of Moses Jacob (1733-1807) of Redruth

Samuel Simmons may have been the Solomon Simmons who appears in Truro (1777) as a pedlar. Jessop (1951) gives four other children of Samuel and Rosa Simmons: Philip, Joseph, Eliezer and Moses (Morris). Sources: Anthony P. Joseph, Godfrey Simmons, Philip Levy; Plymouth Census and Synagogue records, Records of the Library and Museum of Freemasonry, London. Compiled by Keith Pearce © 2013.

Moses of Falmouth (2)

(Thomas) Henry Moses, a hawker and head of this family is not known to have been of Jewish descent, and neither was his wife. They were Christians and are not known to have had any connection with the Jewish congregation, although connections with members of the Jewish community through trade is likely. They are given here to avoid confusion with the family and descendants of Alexander (Henry) Moses (1715-1791).

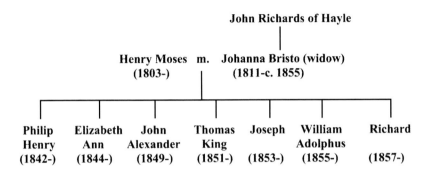

John Richards of Hayle

Henry Moses (1803-) m. Johanna Bristo (widow) (1811-c. 1855)

| Philip Henry (1842-) | Elizabeth Ann (1844-) | John Alexander (1849-) | Thomas King (1851-) | Joseph (1853-) | William Adolphus (1855-) | Richard (1857-) |

The marriage of Thomas Henry Moses to Johanna Bristo took place in Budock Parish Church on 11th August 1840. The two witnesses to the marriage were both Gentiles: the bride's father and Mary Ann Polglase. There is only one baptism in the Falmouth Parish register, that of Elizabeth Ann Moses on 13th November 1844.
It seems that Johanna Moses died in the 1850s: she appears on the 1851 census, but not in 1861.

Source: Census records 1851-1861; research by H.C. Faulkner; records of the Family History Society Truro. Compiled by Keith Pearce © (2013).

being a son of Alexander Moses. Philip Moses became a member of the Masonic *Lodge of Antiquity* in London in 1749. He was its Warden in 1752, and its Master in 1754 and 1759. Alexander Moses visited this London lodge in 1751, 1754 and 1755. On the last occasion (on 17th January), Philip's son, Moses, a junior, but likely to have been near the age for lodge membership (at 21), was also present.

Alexander Moses was a silversmith and, it would seem, recruited pedlars and hawkers both to work for him in return for loans and also to make up the necessary *quorum* for the Sabbath celebrations. It has been said that Alexander Moses became well established in the town and that: "Hawkers would gather at his large brick house (at that time considered quite a luxury). They ate together and said prayers on Saturday..... and on Sunday they would make up their accounts, pay back loans, and be furnished with more goods for their packs. Zender also paid for some of their licences, but only if the hawker agreed to change his original (i.e. *foreign*) name to an English Jewish one, which then became his family name.

Later....(Zender) might introduce them to suitable young girls to marry. As the pedlar saved money, he would buy a shop....and in his turn employ pedlars to sell his goods in the country. In this way, small Jewish communities grew up all over England and Scotland. Other pedlars would travel around Cornwall on pack-horses, lodging at specific Inns, where each innkeeper kept the key to a cupboard containing only kosher cooking utensils. On arrival, the pedlar would find on the frying pan the name of the previous pedlar who had used it, together with the date and a Torah text in Hebrew from the *Sedrah*, all inscribed in chalk. Before the pedlar left he would wash up, write his own name on the frying pan, with the date and a Torah text in Hebrew, from the current week's *Sedrah*, so when the next pedlar arrived he could be sure that everything was kosher." [91]

Whilst these details cannot be confirmed with certainty, and may contain anecdotal elements, such an arrangement to assist the welfare and settlement of incoming Jews is entirely credible. The economic system that it suggests, of commercial focus in the towns, but with the outreach achieved by journeymen trading their wares from their "packs" (which refers to the very heavy loaded boxes, each known as a "marsch", German patois for the buckle that secured it) travelling out into rural settlements, appears to have served the Falmouth Jewish community well. Zender's foresight in applying the practice of the Anglicisation of German names, towards forms more familiar to, and pronounceable by the Cornish inhabitants, would also have assisted accommodation, and so, Israel Behrends became Israel Solomon, and Issachar Baer became Bernard Beer (and Barnet Levy).

Alexander and Phoebe Moses were to have at least six children, of whom four are known to have married into Jewish families in other Cornish towns. There were four daughters. Sarah Moses (1748-1831) married Moses Jacob (1733-1807) of Redruth and they were to have twelve children, most of whom, in turn, married into other local Jewish families: *Joseph, Solomon, Ezekiel, Woolf, Harris and Simmons*. Hannah Moses (1758-1841) married Israel Levy (-1823) of Truro, and Rosa Moses (1757-1838) married Samuel Simons (1740-1832) of Truro. From these marriages alone, most of the Jews who settled in Cornwall over the next century, were able to trace their descent back to Alexander Moses. The fourth daughter, Judith (1768-1843) married, first, Henry Joseph (1760-1803) of St. Austell, but their three sons, Alexander, Philip and Joseph, all died in infancy. She later married Lazarus (Laurance) Lawrence (-1841), but there were no children from this marriage. There were also two sons. Philip ("Phill") Moses (-1831) also known as *Uri Shraga*, who married a Betsy Jacobs (-1838), who may not have been from a local Jewish family, and she was not related to Moses Jacob of Redruth. Moses Moses left Falmouth for France. He married a non-Jew, became estranged from his family, and died at Le Havre.

When he died in 1991, Alexander Moses' will was proved at the Consistory Court in Exeter: "Alexander Moses of Falmouth, dealer in silverware, being weak in body. To each of my several children hereinafter named, that is to say, Sarah Jacob, wife of Moses Jacob of Redruth, Moses Moses, Rose Simons, wife of Samuel Simons of Truro, Hannah Levi, wife of Israel Levi of Truro, and Judith Joseph, wife of Henry Joseph of St. Austle, the sum of 5s. Residue of messauges, land, goods, stock in trade, money, etc. to my beloved wife, Phebe Moses and my son Philip

Moses and the survivor of them equally between them; but in case of my wife shall marry again, then and in such case and not otherwise, all such part and share of my messauges etc., so bequeathed as aforesaid shall become the sole property of the said Philip Moses, and my wife shall be utterly excluded from all advantages etc. which she may have by virtue of said bequest. I appoint my said wife, Phebe Moses and my son Philip Moses Joint executors. Dated 13th April 1791.

Wits. Barto. Incledon. Richd. Bryn. Alex Moses – Seal. 21st November 1793 this will was proved and admin. Was commuted to Phebe Moses and Philip Moses, executrix and executor in the named, sworn by commission, no inventory, 18 Nov. 1793 before R. H. Hit(c)hens, Commissioner…directed to Richd. Hawkin Hitchens, Philip Webber the younger and Robert Dillon, Clerks."

The Woolf Family

Alexander Moses was helped by Benjamin Woolf (sometimes given as Wolf or Wolfe) in founding the Jewish community in Falmouth. Woolf had come from Holland and arrived in Falmouth at about the same time. It would seem that he had previously lived in Penzance. (Barnet Levy from Alsace, was to come to Falmouth some twenty years later). Members of the Woolf family were to settle in Falmouth and Penzance. The names of at least three of Benjamin Woolf's children are known. In 1763, Rebecca Woolf married Eleazar, or Eliezer, (Lazarus) Hart (1739-1803) of Penzance, whose family had been well established there since around 1740. Of their children, Rebecca Hart (1766-1841) married, first, a Lazarus Jacobs (not related to Moses Jacob of Redruth) and after his death, Elias Magnus (1775-1850) of Penzance, with whom she later moved to London. Her brother, Lemon Hart (1768-1845), who also moved to London, in 1811, became a very successful and prosperous wine merchant. Lemon Hart's first wife was a Letitia Michael (-1803) from Swansea, and his sister, Leah Hart (1770-1840) married Letitia's brother, Jacob Michael (1757-1835). Eddle (Edal or Esther) Hart was to marry Benjamin Woolf's son, Hyman (c. 1732-1820) who became a senior member of the Penzance Hebrew Congregation, together with their son, Lemon Woolf (1783-1848) who remained in Penzance and married Rebecca Jacob (1781-1853) a daughter of Moses Jacob of Redruth. Their children, however, were to marry into the *Joseph, Solomon* and *Levy* families of Devon, a pattern of migration of Jews from Cornwall that continued from the early 19th century. Lemon Woolf's daughter, Eliza (Telza) Woolf (1811-1850) married Abraham Joseph II (1799-1868) of Plymouth, although there was no direct familial connection between the Josephs of Plymouth and the Josephs of Cornwall. He had come to Penzance as a Reader in Prayers for a twelve month appointment (August 1826 – September 1827), and remained in the town for several years as a flour dealer, although he later became bankrupt. The couple were to settle in Plymouth. One of their children, Rose Joseph (1829-1887) became the source of a footnote in modern history. She married a Leon Solomon (1811-1879) of Dawlish, and they are said to have had twenty-three children. One son, Ernest Solomon, changed his name to *Simpson*, and his son, also Ernest (1897-1958) was the first husband of Wallis Warfield who, after her divorce

The WOOLF Family of Falmouth and Penzance

Benjamin Woolf from Holland

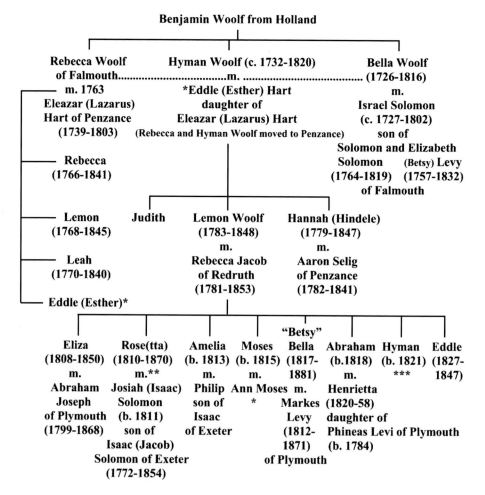

Rebecca Woolf
of Falmouth.................................m. .... (1726-1816)
— m. 1763
Eleazar (Lazarus)
Hart of Penzance
(1739-1803)

Hyman Woolf (c. 1732-1820)
*Eddle (Esther) Hart
daughter of
Eleazar (Lazarus) Hart
(Rebecca and Hyman Woolf moved to Penzance)

Bella Woolf
(1726-1816)
m.
Israel Solomon
(c. 1727-1802)
son of
Solomon and Elizabeth
Solomon   (Betsy) Levy
(1764-1819)   (1757-1832)
of Falmouth

— Rebecca
(1766-1841)

— Lemon   Judith   Lemon Woolf   Hannah (Hindele)
(1768-1845)   (1783-1848)   (1779-1847)
                                    m.   m.
— Leah   Rebecca Jacob   Aaron Selig
(1770-1840)   of Redruth   of Penzance
                                (1781-1853)   (1782-1841)
└─ Eddle (Esther)*

"Betsy"

Eliza   Rose(tta)   Amelia   Moses   Bella   Abraham Hyman   Eddle
(1808-1850)   (1810-1870)   (b. 1813) (b. 1815) (1817-   (b.1818) (b. 1821) (1827-
m.   m.**   m.   m.   1881)   m.   ***   1847)
Abraham   Josiah (Isaac) Philip   Ann Moses m.   Henrietta
Joseph   Solomon   son of   *   Markes   (1820-58)
of Plymouth   (b. 1811)   Isaac   Levy   daughter of
(1799-1868)   son of   of Exeter   (1812-   Phineas Levi of Plymouth
              Isaac (Jacob)   1871)   (b. 1784)
              Solomon of Exeter   of Plymouth
              (1772-1854)

*Jessop gives her surname as Solomon. ** Josiah Solomon lived in Plymouth, where Rosetta is buried. He had moved to New York by 1872. *** Genealogical sources have given his birth year as 1826, but B. A. Simmons' circumcision register confirms the year as 1821.

Source: Anthony P. Joseph & Godfrey Simmons.
Compiled by Keith Pearce © (2013).

from Ernest Simpson, became a catalyst in the abdication of Edward VIII, and subsequently his wife, the couple living out their days in exile, in Paris.[92] A third child of Benjamin Woolf, Bella Woolf (1726-1816) married into another important Falmouth family, of *Solomon*.

The Solomon Family

Israel Solomon (born *c*. 1727, died 1802) was also known as Israel Behrends (or Segal), and was from the Rhineland area of Germany. Of Israel and Bella Solomon's children, three married into local Jewish families, from Falmouth and Redruth. Judith Solomon (1763-1839) married Samuel Harris (1754-1824) of Falmouth. Their son, Henry Harris (1787-1872) moved to Truro, and married Esther Jacob (1784-1871) a daughter of Moses Jacob (1733-1807) of Redruth and Sarah Moses (1748-1831) of Falmouth. A son of Henry and Esther Harris, Morris Hart Harris (1821-1912) also married into the same Jacob family, taking as his wife, Rebecca Jacob (1824-1906) daughter of Jacob Jacob (1774-1853) of Redruth and Sarah Kate (Kitty) Simons (1778-1846) of Truro. Judith Solomon's brother, Simon Solomon, also known as Abraham Simeon Segal (-1825) likewise married another daughter of Moses Jacob of Redruth, Kate (Kitty) Jacob (1772-1854). Simon Solomon was by trade a painter, who produced life-like paintings of subjects from Biblical stories and from nature. He was unsuccessful in his trade, and also suffered from poor health. After his death, his widow went to live in Penzance with relatives. She is buried in the Penryn cemetery.[93] Simon's brother, Solomon Solomon (1764-1819) married a daughter of Barnet Levy (-1791) and Esther Elias (*c*.-1780/86) of Falmouth, Elizabeth (Betsy) Levy (1757-1832). At some point, Solomon Solomon moved his family to Lisbon where he had some business connections, and where Lyon Joseph also had contacts. Lisbon had a large and prosperous Jewish merchant class at this time. When Solomon Solomon died in Lisbon in 1819, his wife moved her family back to Falmouth in 1820, but eventually went with them to Bristol, where her married nephew and niece, Barnet Joseph and his sister, Arabella Levy had settled. Their mother (and Betsy's sister), Judith Levy and her husband Lyon Joseph had previously settled in Bath. Betsy Solomon died in Bristol in 1832.[94] In Bristol, her two sons, Israel (*c*.1803-1893) and Barnet Levy Solomon (1806-) had traded, the former as a Jeweller and Pawnbroker, and the latter as an apprenticed cabinet maker and upholsterer. Soon after their mother's death, the two brothers moved to London, began to wind up their various business transactions, with a view to emigrating to Australia, but, on the advice of a cousin, Benedict (Baruch) Joseph, they decided instead upon New York. However, because of an increase in fares for berths on the clippers bound to New York from Liverpool, only two berths were affordable, and eventually, only Benedict Joseph and Barnet Solomon sailed to New York (a journey which at that time took some nine weeks), leaving Israel Solomon in London.

Barnet Solomon's life in America turned out to be a success story. He arrived in New York at the time of a cholera epidemic, and the social and employment restrictions that resulted from this prevented him from pursuing his trade. After travelling extensively, he returned to New York, at first opening a cigar store for one year, and then, in 1834, he renewed his trade by occupying a store on Broadway. The business was a success, and in 1835 he married Julia, the daughter of John I. Hart of New York, whose family were originally from Portsmouth. (The Hart families of Penzance, Plymouth and Portsmouth were not related). Barnet and Julia Solomon were to have four sons and five daughters, all of whom

Solomon of Falmouth

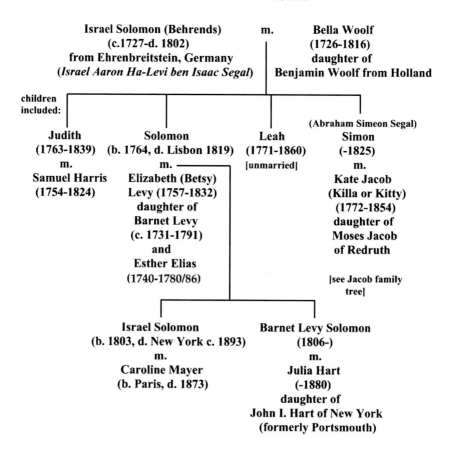

Source: Israel Solomon's *Records of my Family* (1887), Alex Jacob and Godfrey Simmons.
Compiled by Keith Pearce © (2013).

remained in New York. Barnet Solomon carried on his business for nearly fifty years, retiring in 1878, after which his sons took over from him. Julia Solomon died in 1880, and was buried in Salem Fields cemetery, near Brooklyn.

Soon after his brother's departure for New York in 1832, Israel Solomon went to Liverpool, with the intention of following him. A cousin, Barnet Joseph, had come from Bristol to live in Liverpool, and he advised Israel to go to Paris instead to become an agent and commissioner in the thriving trade of purchasing manufactured French goods for importation to England. Upon his arrival in Paris he set up in business as *Joseph & Solomon* (later simply as *Joseph Solomon*). Presumably his cousin, Barnet Joseph was his partner, organising the English side of the import business. The business must have thrived, and soon, Israel Solomon met and married Caroline Mayer, who had been born in Paris. Her parents were natives of Nancy, Lorraine, her father having been a retailer in paper money (known as denominated assignats), the circulation of coins having virtually ceased. The value of such notes was eventually subject to depreciation, and the family sought their fortune in Paris, where Caroline Mayer's uncle, Leon Mayer, was a successful portrait artist, and well-connected with the rich nobility and exiled royalty of Paris. Caroline Mayer had grown up with the Halevy family, then kosher grocers, as neighbours. Two members of this family achieved fame, Jacques Francois Fromental (Elias Levy) Halevy (1799-1862) as a composer of operas, the most famous being *La Juive*, and his brother, the poet Leon Halevy (1802-1883) as a dramatist and librettist of comic operas. Israel and Caroline Solomon had three children. One son died in infancy, and the other son fell seriously ill at three years old with scarlet fever, which left him deaf, dumb and, it would seem, mentally, and possibly physically handicapped. He survived well into adulthood, but spent his life in an institution. A daughter married into a Jewish (Abbenheim) family from Stuttgart, and had four children.

At some point, Israel and Caroline Solomon moved to London, where Israel continued to import goods from France, most notably as an agent for Delicourt wallpaper. He also branched out into the field of optical instruments and photography, manufacturing and patenting a magnesium lamp. Caroline Solomon died in 1873, and was buried in London.

In June of 1881, Israel Solomon, in his own words, "abandoned England forever" and sailed to New York to be with his brother, reuniting them after fifty years. From around 1885 he worked on an account of his family's history. This sketch from memory was published privately in New York in 1887, as *Records of My Family*. An "Addendum" to the *Records* (in fact an earlier draft of 1885) has also survived, and both essays have become key documents in the reconstruction of the history of the Cornish Jews. Israel Solomon died in New York in 1893.

The Joseph and Levy Families[95]

The Joseph family were originally from London. They settled mainly in Falmouth, but also became widely dispersed across Mid and South Cornwall, in St. Austell, Redruth and Penzance. Through marriage and commerce, they migrated to South Wales, Bath, Bristol, Birmingham, London and elsewhere, and emigrated to Australia and America. Being the product of the two marriages of their progenitor, Joseph Joseph, originally of Mulhausen, Alsace, who settled in London in the early 18th century, and died there, and being intermarried both with one another and with the separate and equally large family of Abraham Joseph (1731-1794) of Plymouth (with whom they should not be confused, although the names of individuals are often identical in both families). The genealogies of the various branches of the Cornish Joseph family are, therefore, exceptionally complex. (A non-familial link between Alexander Joseph of Plymouth and Moses Jacob of

Joseph of Cornwall
(1)

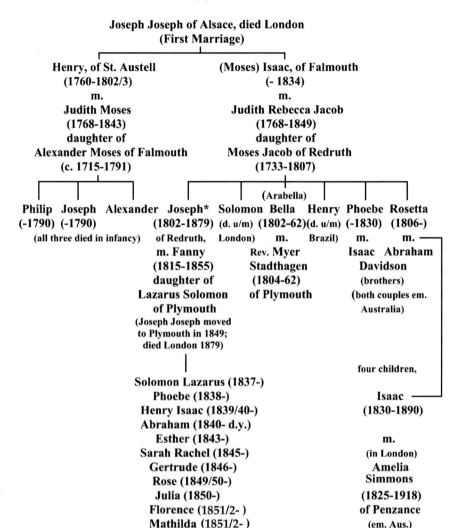

Joseph Joseph of Alsace, died London
(First Marriage)

Henry, of St. Austell	(Moses) Isaac, of Falmouth
(1760-1802/3)	(- 1834)
m.	m.
Judith Moses	Judith Rebecca Jacob
(1768-1843)	(1768-1849)
daughter of	daughter of
Alexander Moses of Falmouth	Moses Jacob of Redruth
(c. 1715-1791)	(1733-1807)

Philip (-1790)   Joseph (-1790)   Alexander   Joseph* (1802-1879)   Solomon (d. u/m)   Bella (1802-62)   Henry (d. u/m)   Phoebe (-1830)   Rosetta (1806-)

(Arabella)

(all three died in infancy)

of Redruth,
m. Fanny
(1815-1855)
daughter of
Lazarus Solomon
of Plymouth
(Joseph Joseph moved
to Plymouth in 1849;
died London 1879)

London)
m.
Rev. Myer
Stadthagen
(1804-62)
of Plymouth

Brazil)
m.
Isaac   Abraham
Davidson
(brothers)
(both couples em.
Australia)

Solomon Lazarus (1837-)
Phoebe (1838-)
Henry Isaac (1839/40-)
Abraham (1840- d.y.)
Esther (1843-)
Sarah Rachel (1845-)
Gertrude (1846-)
Rose (1849/50-)
Julia (1850-)
Florence (1851/2-)
Mathilda (1851/2-)

four children,

Isaac
(1830-1890)

m.
(in London)
Amelia
Simmons
(1825-1918)
of Penzance
(em. Aus.)

Joseph Joseph* outlived his wife, and is recorded, age 59, in the 1861 census for Plymouth. His wife is buried in the Plymouth Hoe cemetery. All of the children were born in Redruth, except for the last three, born in Plymouth. Joseph Joseph moved to London sometime after 1861, where he died in 1879. He is buried in the Willesden cemetery.
Myer and Arabella Stadthagen both died in April 1862 (on 21st & 26th respectively).

Source: Bernard Susser, W.S. Jessop, Anthony P. Joseph, Godfrey Simmons.
Compiled by Keith Pearce © (2013).

Joseph of Cornwall
(2)

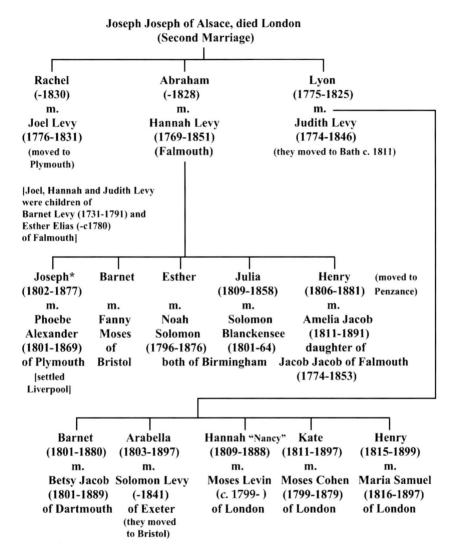

Joseph Joseph of Alsace, died London
(Second Marriage)

Rachel	Abraham	Lyon
(-1830)	(-1828)	(1775-1825)
m.	m.	m.
Joel Levy	Hannah Levy	Judith Levy
(1776-1831)	(1769-1851)	(1774-1846)
(moved to Plymouth)	(Falmouth)	(they moved to Bath c. 1811)

[Joel, Hannah and Judith Levy
were children of
Barnet Levy (1731-1791) and
Esther Elias (-c1780)
of Falmouth]

Joseph*	Barnet	Esther	Julia	Henry	(moved to
(1802-1877)			(1809-1858)	(1806-1881)	Penzance)
m.	m.	m.	m.	m.	
Phoebe	Fanny	Noah	Solomon	Amelia Jacob	
Alexander	Moses	Solomon	Blanckensee	(1811-1891)	
(1801-1869)	of	(1796-1876)	(1801-64)	daughter of	
of Plymouth	Bristol	both of Birmingham		Jacob Jacob of Falmouth	
[settled				(1774-1853)	
Liverpool]					

Barnet	Arabella	Hannah "Nancy"	Kate	Henry
(1801-1880)	(1803-1897)	(1809-1888)	(1811-1897)	(1815-1899)
m.	m.	m.	m.	m.
Betsy Jacob	Solomon Levy	Moses Levin	Moses Cohen	Maria Samuel
(1801-1889)	(-1841)	(c. 1799-)	(1799-1879)	(1816-1897)
of Dartmouth	of Exeter	of London	of London	of London
	(they moved to Bristol)			

[Lyon and Judith Joseph had four other children—
Esther and Joseph, who died young, and Benedict and Frederick who emigrated to America.]
Note: Jessop's (1951) dates (1791-1872) for Joseph Joseph* are incorrect.

Source: Anthony P. Joseph and Godfrey Simmons.
Compiled by Keith Pearce © (2013).

Joseph of Plymouth

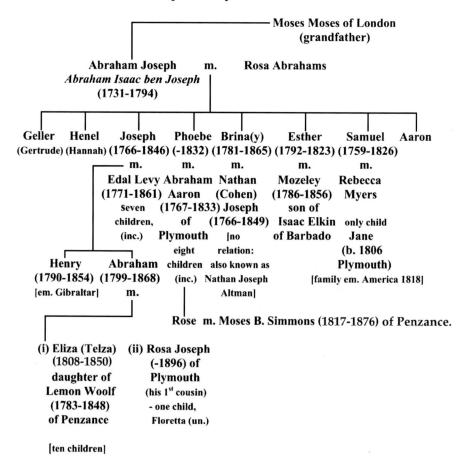

```
                                              Moses Moses of London
                                                  (grandfather)

           Abraham Joseph      m.      Rosa Abrahams
           Abraham Isaac ben Joseph
           (1731-1794)

Geller   Henel    Joseph    Phoebe  Brina(y)    Esther    Samuel   Aaron
(Gertrude) (Hannah) (1766-1846) (-1832) (1781-1865) (1792-1823) (1759-1826)
                      m.        m.       m.         m.        m.
                  Edal Levy Abraham  Nathan    Mozeley    Rebecca
                  (1771-1861) Aaron  (Cohen)   (1786-1856) Myers
                    seven   (1767-1833) Joseph    son of
                  children,    of     (1766-1849) Isaac Elkin  only child
                    (inc.)  Plymouth   [no      of Barbado   Jane
                             eight    relation:              (b. 1806
           Henry    Abraham children  also known as          Plymouth)
           (1790-1854) (1799-1868) (inc.) Nathan Joseph    [family em. America 1818]
           [em. Gibraltar]   m.              Altman]

                                     Rose  m. Moses B. Simmons (1817-1876) of Penzance.

(i) Eliza (Telza)  (ii) Rosa Joseph
    (1808-1850)        (-1896) of
    daughter of        Plymouth
    Lemon Woolf     (his 1st cousin)
    (1783-1848)      - one child,
    of Penzance        Floretta (un.)


    [ten children]
```

Source: W.S. Jessop, Bernard Susser, Anthony P. Joseph and Godfrey Simmons (abridged).
Compiled by Keith Pearce © (2013).

Redruth is provided by the apprentice watchmaker, James Dawson, who worked for both of them: see below).

Joseph Joseph of Alsace lived in London, and it has been assumed that he died there. He married twice, but the names of his wives are not known. From his first marriage there were at least two sons, and from his second, a daughter and two sons. Joseph Joseph may have become estranged from his second wife. Rachel, the daughter from this second marriage, married a Jew from Falmouth (see below), and they settled in Plymouth. This Rachel "with her mother lived & died in Plymouth". This, however, may indicate that the mother came from London to live in Plymouth with her daughter after Joseph Joseph's death.

The First Marriage. The two sons[96] both gravitated to Cornwall and settled there, the family of Alexander Moses having lived in Falmouth for some time. Henry (Harry) Joseph (1760-1802) settled in St. Austell and married Judith Moses (1768-1843) a daughter of Alexander (Henry or Zender) Moses (*c.* 1715-1791) and his wife Phoebe of Falmouth. Henry and Judith Moses are both buried in the Penryn cemetery (2:4 & 4:5) together with their three children, Philip (-1790), Joseph (-1791) and Alexander. Henry's brother, (Moses) Isaac Joseph (-1834) married Judith Rebecca Jacob (1768-1849), a daughter of Moses Jacob (1733-1807) and Sarah Moses (1748-1831) of Redruth. Sarah Moses was an older sister of the Judith Moses, above, and also a daughter of Alexander Moses.[97] Isaac and Judith Joseph had three sons and three daughters. Joseph Joseph (1802-) became a Jeweller and Mineralogist in Redruth, where Moses Jacob was well established. He married into a Plymouth family, traded there, and eventually moved to London. Both of his brothers died unmarried, Solomon in London, and Henry in Brazil. Arabella (Bella) Joseph (1802-1862) married the Rev. Myer Stadthagen (1804-1862) of Plymouth (and onetime minister in Penzance), and Phoebe (-1830) and Rosetta (1806-) each married a brother from the Davidson family, Isaac and Abraham respectively, whose names appear in the Penzance Congregational Minute Book (1825-1826). Both couples eventually emigrated to Australia. Abraham and Rosetta Davidson's son, Isaac (1830-1890) was to marry Amelia Simmons (1825-1919), daughter of Rabbi B. A. Simmons of Penzance, and they too emigrated to Australia.

From his **Second Marriage** there was a daughter, Rachel (-1832), and two sons, Abraham (-1828) and Lyon (1775-1825). These three children left London at some point, and lived in Canterbury, eventually following their half-brothers to Cornwall, and specifically to Falmouth.

The Levy Family

Already resident in Falmouth, from about 1770, was Barnet Levy (1731-1791), from London, originally from Alsace.[98] He was a soap boiler by trade, but finding that the London manufacturers required work on the Jewish Sabbath, he reluctantly became a pedlar, eventually arriving in Falmouth, where he was welcomed by Alexander Moses as an addition to the nascent community's *minyan*, and where

Levy of Falmouth

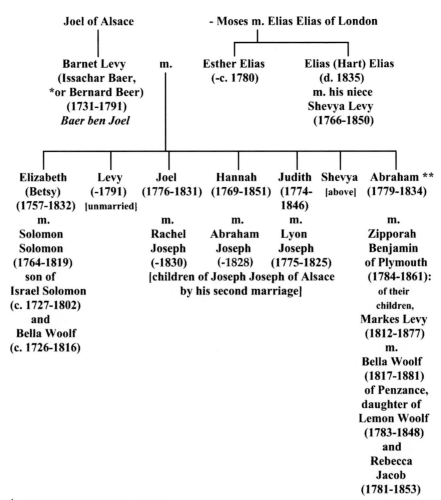

Joel of Alsace — Moses m. Elias Elias of London

Barnet Levy (Issachar Baer, *or Bernard Beer) (1731-1791) *Baer ben Joel*　m.　Esther Elias (-c. 1780)　　Elias (Hart) Elias (d. 1835) m. his niece Shevya Levy (1766-1850)

Elizabeth (Betsy) (1757-1832)	Levy (-1791) [unmarried]	Joel (1776-1831)	Hannah (1769-1851)	Judith (1774-1846)	Shevya [above]	Abraham ** (1779-1834)
m. Solomon Solomon (1764-1819) son of Israel Solomon (c. 1727-1802) and Bella Woolf (c. 1726-1816)		m. Rachel Joseph (-1830)	m. Abraham Joseph (-1828)	m. Lyon Joseph (1775-1825)		m. Zipporah Benjamin of Plymouth (1784-1861): of their children, Markes Levy (1812-1877) m. Bella Woolf (1817-1881) of Penzance, daughter of Lemon Woolf (1783-1848) and Rebecca Jacob (1781-1853)

[children of Joseph Joseph of Alsace by his second marriage]

*   He also used the surname *Jewell.*
** Jessop (1951) also gives an unmarried daughter, Sarah (Sally)

Source: Alex Jacob, Anthony P. Joseph & Godfrey Simmons.
Compiled by Keith Pearce © (2013).

Chapter 1.
The Lanlivery-Bodwen
Figurine. Courtesy of the Royal
Institution of Cornwall, Truro.

Chapter 1.
An Armorial Achievement of a Duke of
Cornwall set in a wall of the Exchequer
Hall at Lostwithiel. Photo copyright C. K. C.
Andrew. Image provided by the RIC Truro.

Chapter 1.
Armorial Shield of Richard Earl of Cornwall and Poitou, carved in the wall of the
South Aisle of Westminster Abbey. A photo
reproduced by C. K. C. Andrew (courtesy of the
Dean and Chapter of Westminter Abbey). The
image courtesy of the RIC Truro.

Plate 1

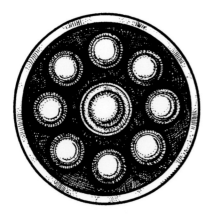

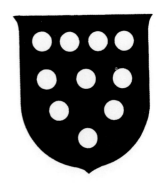

Chapter 1.
Original drawings of Armorial Shields and
Bezants associated with Cornwall by
D. Endean Ivall. Courtesy of David Ivall
and his family.

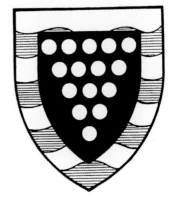

Plate 2

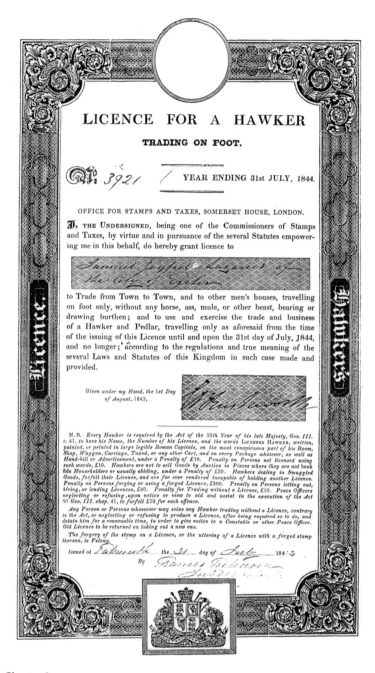

LICENCE FOR A HAWKER

TRADING ON FOOT.

№ 3921 / YEAR ENDING 31st JULY, 1844.

OFFICE FOR STAMPS AND TAXES, SOMERSET HOUSE, LONDON.

I, THE UNDERSIGNED, being one of the Commissioners of Stamps and Taxes, by virtue and in pursuance of the several Statutes empowering me in this behalf, do hereby grant licence to

Samuel Joyful Lazarus of the City of Exeter

to Trade from Town to Town, and to other men's houses, travelling on foot only, without any horse, ass, mule, or other beast, bearing or drawing burthen; and to use and exercise the trade and business of a Hawker and Pedlar, travelling only as aforesaid from the time of the issuing of this Licence until and upon the 31st day of July, 1844, and no longer; according to the regulations and true meaning of the several Laws and Statutes of this Kingdom in such case made and provided.

Given under my Hand, the 1st Day of August, 1843,

N.B. *Every Hawker is required by the Act of the 50th Year of his late Majesty, Geo. III. c. 41, to have his Name, the Number of his Licence, and the words* LICENSED HAWKER, *written, painted, or printed in large legible Roman Capitals, on the most conspicuous part of his Room, Shop, Waggon, Carriage, Taxed, or any other Cart, and on every Package whatever, as well as Hand-bill or Advertisement, under a Penalty of £10. Penalty on Persons not licensed using such words, £10. Hawkers are not to sell Goods by Auction in Places where they are not bonâ fide Householders or usually abiding, under a Penalty of £50. Hawkers dealing in Smuggled Goods, forfeit their Licence, and are for ever rendered incapable of holding another Licence. Penalty on Persons forging or using a forged Licence, £300. Penalty on Persons letting out, hiring, or lending Licences, £40. Penalty for Trading without a Licence, £10. Peace Officers neglecting or refusing, upon notice or view to aid and assist in the execution of the Act 50 Geo. III. chap. 41, to forfeit £10 for each offence.*

Any Person or Persons whosoever may seize any Hawker trading without a Licence, contrary to the Act, or neglecting or refusing to produce a Licence, after being required so to do, and detain him for a reasonable time, in order to give notice to a Constable or other Peace Officer. Old Licence to be returned on taking out a new one.

The forgery of the stamp on a Licence, or the uttering of a Licence with a forged stamp thereon, is Felony.

Issued at *Falmouth* the *31* day of *July* 184:3.

By

Chapter 3.
Hawker's Licence issued in Falmouth to Samuel Joyful Lazarus of Exeter.
Courtesy of the Jewish Museum, London.

Plate 3

Chapter 3.
Lyon Joseph's double-sided headstone in the Plymouth Hoe Jewish Cemetery: "Here lies a G-d fearing gentle man (or "of the water"), Yehuda the son of Yosef of Blessed Memory, Honoured Master amongst the Righteous, He excelled in Good Deeds, Giver of Charity and Doer of Good, Provider to the Poor and Impoverished. He died at his home in the City of Bath on the Tuesday and was buried here on Sunday 19 Sivan 5585 [5th June 1825]. May his Soul be Protected as it was in Life." Courtesy of Helen Fry, Anthony Joseph, Anna Kelly and Jerry Sibley.

Chapter 3.
Jacob Jacob (1774-1853) of Falmouth and his wife Sarah Kate Simons (1778-1846) of Truro.
Jacob Archive

Plate 4

Chapter 3.
Images of Bell's
Court, Falmouth:
the location of the
family home of
Jacob Jacob.
Photo by Alex
M. Jacob (1939).
The Jacob Archive.

Plate 5

Chapter 3.
Moses ("Moss") Jacob Jacob (1811-1860) of Falmouth and his wife, Frances Emanuel (1812-1875) of Portsea. Jacob Archive

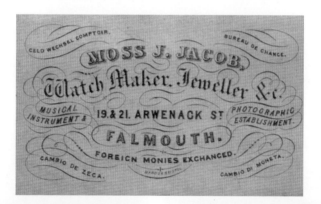

15, MARKET STREET, FALMOUTH.
SAMUEL MARKS,
Auctioneer, Appraiser, Commission Agent,
ETC.,
Has extensive Sale Rooms in the central part of the Town, where every description of Furniture, China, and Glass are received, and sold on Commission.
Upholstery and French Polishing done by First-class Workmen.
DILAPIDATIONS SURVEYED AND VALUED.

MOSS J. JACOB,
FOREIGN MONEY EXCHANGE OFFICE,
19 & 21, Arwenack Street, Falmouth.
GELD WECHSEL COMPTOIR.
BUREAU DE-CHANGE.

Chapter 3.
(Above left) Trade advertisement for Samuel Marks (who may not have been Jewish) and (Above right) Moss J. (Moses Jacob) Jacob (both from an original copy of Warn's Falmouth and Penryn Directory and Guide (1864) in the Jacob Archive.
(Top) Trade Card, Courtesy of the Jewish Museum, London.

Plate 6

Chapter 3.
Frances Jacob (front centre)
then a widow (*c*.1861), with
her children: Samuel and Sarah
Kate (front) and (rear, from
left) Annie, Michael, Alexander
and Lawrence. Jacob Archive

Chapter 3.
Frances Jacob in later life.
Jacob Archive

Plate 7

Chapter 3.
Samuel Jacob (left) with
(below) his sons Michael (left)
and Alexander, all in later
life. The photo of Samuel
was taken in Birmingham,
that of Michael in Paris,
and Alexander in London.
Jacob Archive

Plate 8

Chapter 3.
Samuel Jacob (front left) with three Cornish miners (one named Lanyon), likely just before their departure for British Columbia in 1859. Jacob Archive

Chapter 3.
Samuel Jacob with Joseph (Joe) Joseph, known as "Double Joe" (sitting). The photograph was taken in Penzance. Jacob Archive

Chapter 3.
Alexander Jacob (1841-1903) and his wife, Leah Myer (1846-1933), the daughter of Abraham Myer. The couple were married in Hereford in 1875. Jacob Archive

Plate 9

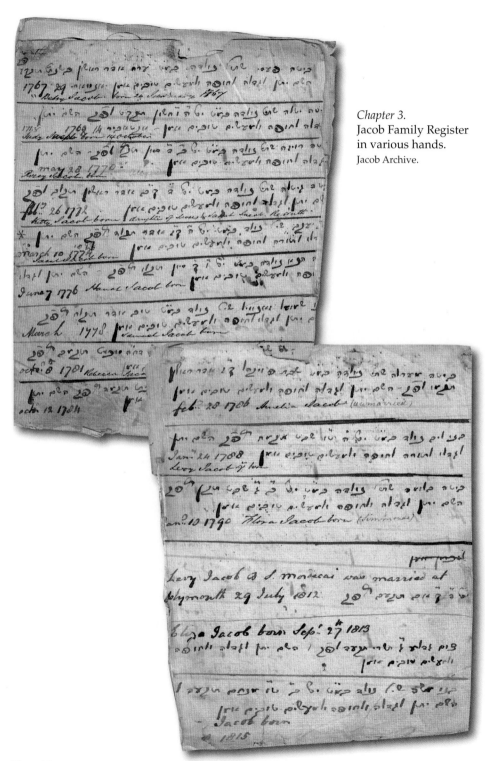

Chapter 3.
Jacob Family Register
in various hands.
Jacob Archive.

Plate 10

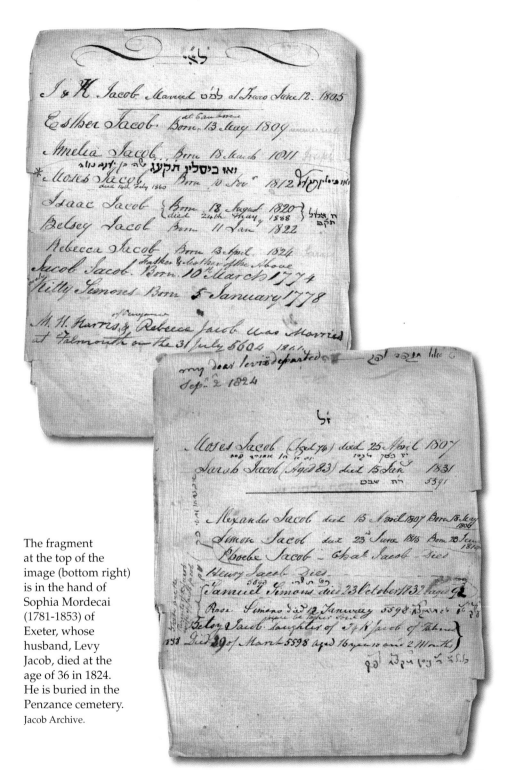

The fragment at the top of the image (bottom right) is in the hand of Sophia Mordecai (1781-1853) of Exeter, whose husband, Levy Jacob, died at the age of 36 in 1824. He is buried in the Penzance cemetery. Jacob Archive.

Plate 11

Chapter 3.
Great Condurrow Mine,
Camborne: the building
of the new engine house
on Woolf's Shaft in 1906.
The mine closed in 1913.
The Condurrow Mine, in
which the Jacob family
had investments was on
or near this site.
Courtesy the Royal Institution
of Cornwall.

Chapter 3.
Swan Pool Mine,
Falmouth, around 1850.
Courtesy the Cornish Studies
Library, Redruth. The Jacob
family also had had investments
in this mine.

Swan Pool Mine. Falmouth

Plate 12

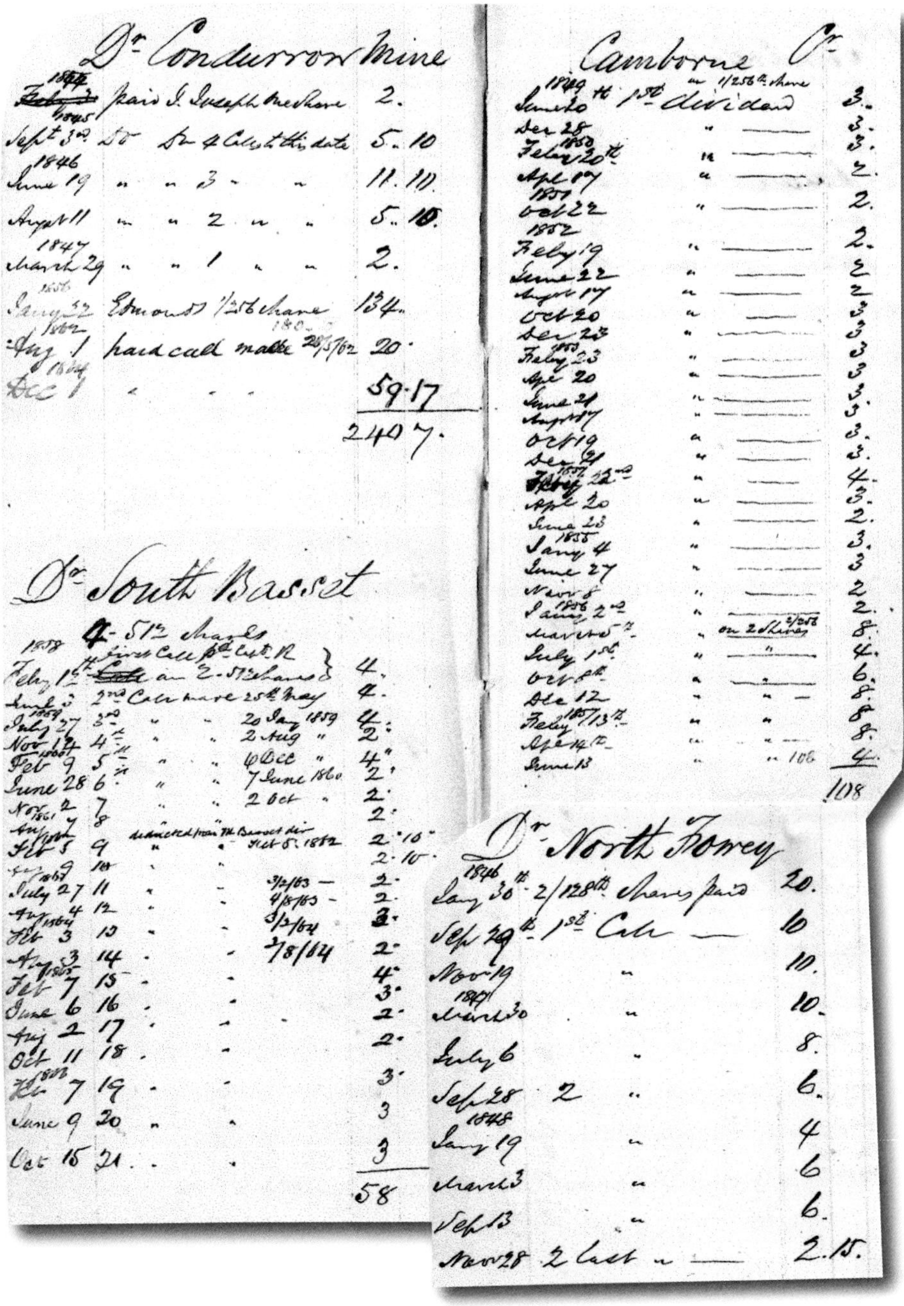

Dr. Condurrow Mine

1844 Feby 3	paid J. Joseph one share	2.
1845 Sept 3rd	Do Dr 4 Calls this date	5..10
1846 June 19	" " 3 " "	11.10
Augst 11	" " 2 " "	5..10
1847 March 29	" " 1 " "	2.
1856 Jany 22	Edmonds 1/256 share	134..
1862 Aug 1	paid call made 28/5/62	20.
1864 Dec 1	" " "	
		59.17
		240 7.

Camborne Cr.

1849 June 20th	1st dividend on 1/256th share	3.
Dec 28	"	3.
1850 Feby 20th	"	3.
Apl 17	"	2.
1851 Oct 22	"	2.
1852 Feby 19	"	2.
June 22	"	2
Augt 17	"	2
Oct 20	"	3
Dec 23	"	3
1853 Feby 23	"	3
Apl 20	"	3
June 21	"	3.
Augt 17	"	3
Oct 19	"	3.
Dec 21	"	3.
1854 Feby 22nd	"	4.
Apl 20	"	3.
June 23	"	2.
1855 Jany 4	"	3.
June 27	"	3
Nov 8	"	2.
1856 Jany 2nd	"	2.
March 5th	" on 2 shares 2/256	8.
July 1st	" "	4.
Oct 8th	"	6.
Dec 12	" "	8.
1857 Feby 13th	" "	8.
Apl 14th	" "	8.
June 13	" 106	4
		108

Dr. South Basset

1858	4 - 512 shares	
Feby 1st	first Call pd. last R. Call on 2 - 512 shares	4.
June 3	2nd Call made 25th May	4.
1859 July 27	3rd " " 20 Jany 1859	4.
Nov 14	4th " " 2 Aug "	2
1860 Feb 9	5th " " 6 Dec "	4.
June 28	6th " " 7 June 1860	2.
1861 Nov 2	7 " " 2 Oct "	2.
Aug	8	2.
Feb 5	9 " " Feb 5. 1862	2.10
Aug 9	10	2.10
1863 July 27	11 " " 3/2/63	2.
Aug 4	12 " " 4/8/63	2.
1864 Feb 3	13 " " 3/2/64	3.
Aug 3	14 " " 2/8/64	2.
1865 Feb 7	15	4.
June 6	16	3.
Aug 2	17	2.
Oct 11	18	2.
1868 Feb 7	19	3.
June 9	20	3
Oct 15	21	3
		58

Dr. North Towey

1846 Jany 30th	2/128th Shares paid	20.
Sep 29th	1st Call	10
Nov 19	"	10.
1847 March 30	"	10.
July 6	"	8.
Sep 28	2 "	6.
1848 Jany 19	"	4
March 3	"	6
Sep 13	"	6.
Nov 28	2 last "	2.15.

Chapter 3.
Extracts from the Jacob Family Investment Book.
Jacob Archive.

Chapter 4.
Portrait: "The Old Jew" by John Opie (*c.* before 1781). Likely to be the image of Rabbi Abraham Hart (Solomon Lazarus) of Penzance. In the private collection of and courtesy of Viv Hendra (The Lander Gallery, Truro).

Plate 14

Chapter 4.
(Top left) Mary Hart (Miriam Solomon), the second wife of Lemon Hart (top right).
(Below) Uncertain, but likely the brothers James Jacob Hart (Jacobs) and Frederick Hart,
both partners in the Lemon Hart firm in London. Artists unknown. Photographs by
Simon Butler, courtesy of Penelope Strannack.

Plate 15

Above left: *Chapter 4.*
Lemon Hart (Artist unknown)
Courtesy of Allied Domecq plc.

Above right: *Chapter 4.*
Lemon Hart's grave in the Brady
Street, Cemetery, London. Photo by
and courtesy of Michael Shapiro.

Right: *Chapter 4.*
A commercial label for Lemon Hart
Rum. Courtesy of Mosaiq Inc. Quebec

Plate 16

Levy of Exeter

This family is not to be confused with the Cornish family of Israel and Hannah Levy of Truro.

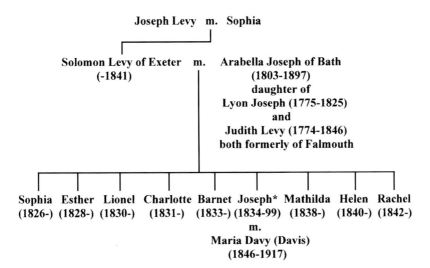

Joseph Levy m. Sophia

Solomon Levy of Exeter m. Arabella Joseph of Bath
(-1841) (1803-1897)
daughter of
Lyon Joseph (1775-1825)
and
Judith Levy (1774-1846)
both formerly of Falmouth

Sophia	Esther	Lionel	Charlotte	Barnet	Joseph*	Mathilda	Helen	Rachel
(1826-)	(1828-)	(1830-)	(1831-)	(1833-)	(1834-99)	(1838-)	(1840-)	(1842-)

m.
Maria Davy (Davis)
(1846-1917)

Jessop (1950-51) confused and conflated the separate Levy families of Exeter and Truro,
assuming that Solomon Levy (-1841) was the son of Israel Levy (-1823) and Hannah Moses
(1758-1841) of Truro, which was not the case. As a result there are serious errors in his pedigree
of "Israel and Hannah Levy of Exeter".

Solomon Levy and Arabella Joseph settled in Bristol. Arabella Joseph had been born in
Falmouth, and by 1871 she was living in Paddington, a widow, age 63, "living on own means".
Contrary to Jessop, their son, Joseph Levy (*above) did not marry Arabella Harris (*c*.1820-1904)
of Truro, as his first wife. Arabella Harris of Truro married another Joseph Levi whose dates are
distinct (1811-1880). One of *their* children, George (1846-1877) married into the Cornish Jacob
family.

Jessop was incorrect, therefore, in ascribing this family to Levy of Exeter.

Source: Anthony P. Joseph and Godfrey Simmons.
Compiled by Keith Pearce © (2013).

Moses, Levy, Jacob & Solomon of Falmouth

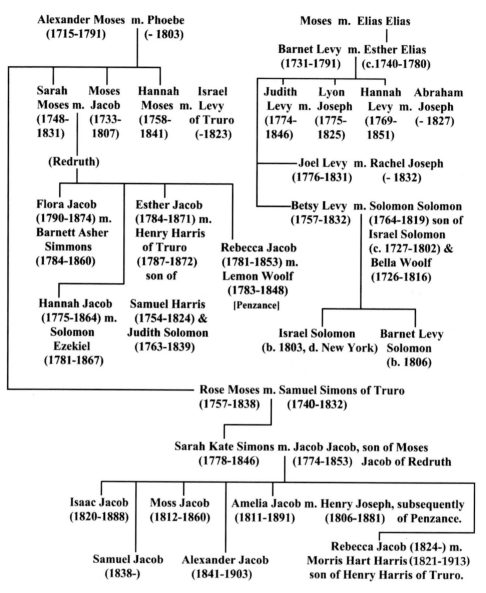

Alexander Moses m. Phoebe
(1715-1791)   (- 1803)

Moses m. Elias Elias

Barnet Levy m. Esther Elias
(1731-1791) (c.1740-1780)

Sarah	**Moses**	**Hannah**	**Israel**
Moses m.	Jacob	Moses m.	Levy
(1748-	(1733-	(1758-	of Truro
1831)	1807)	1841)	(-1823)

(Redruth)

Judith	**Lyon**	**Hannah**	**Abraham**
Levy m.	Joseph	Levy m.	Joseph
(1774-	(1775-	(1769-	(- 1827)
1846)	1825)	1851)	

Joel Levy m. Rachel Joseph
(1776-1831)   (- 1832)

Betsy Levy m. Solomon Solomon
(1757-1832)   (1764-1819) son of
Israel Solomon
(c. 1727-1802) &
Bella Woolf
(1726-1816)

Flora Jacob
(1790-1874) m.
Barnett Asher
Simmons
(1784-1860)

Esther Jacob
(1784-1871) m.
Henry Harris
of Truro
(1787-1872)
son of

Rebecca Jacob
(1781-1853) m.
Lemon Woolf
(1783-1848)
[Penzance]

Hannah Jacob
(1775-1864) m.
Solomon
Ezekiel
(1781-1867)

Samuel Harris
(1754-1824) &
Judith Solomon
(1763-1839)

Israel Solomon	**Barnet Levy**
(b. 1803, d. New York)	Solomon
	(b. 1806)

Rose Moses m. Samuel Simons of Truro
(1757-1838)   (1740-1832)

Sarah Kate Simons m. Jacob Jacob, son of Moses
(1778-1846)   (1774-1853) Jacob of Redruth

| **Isaac Jacob** | **Moss Jacob** | **Amelia Jacob m. Henry Joseph, subsequently** |
| (1820-1888) | (1812-1860) | (1811-1891)   (1806-1881)   of Penzance. |

Rebecca Jacob (1824-) m.
Morris Hart Harris (1821-1913)
son of Henry Harris of Truro.

Samuel Jacob
(1838-)

Alexander Jacob
(1841-1903)

Source: Anthony P. Joseph & Godfrey Simmons.
Compiled by Keith Pearce © (2013 revised).

he obtained a hawker's licence. He was known, variously, as Issachar Baer, Bernard (or Barnard) Beer and Baer Joel (from *Baer ben Joel*, his Hebrew patronymic). He also used the surname, *Jewell*, most likely a phonetic approximation of Joel. It would seem that his adoption of the name *Barnet Levy* was a way to regularise his membership of the Falmouth community. Another *Levy* family, that of Israel Levy (-1823) who had married Hannah Moses (1758-1841) a daughter of Alexander Moses of Falmouth, came to settle in Truro, but does not appear to have been connected with Barnet Levy of Falmouth, and, indeed, another man with the latter's name lived in St. Austell (see below) who is not known to have been connected with either family. Barnet Levy of Falmouth appears to have become well-established in Falmouth with a furnished house and a shop. It had always been his intention to return to London, where, previously, he had met Esther Elias (*c.* 1780) the daughter of Elias Elias a successful London Tailor and Army Clothing Contractor, known by his nickname, "Fine Schneider", who was originally from Germany. Esther's mother was from a *Moses* family, and may have been related to the family of Alexander Moses of Falmouth, although, with such a common Jewish surname, this is speculative. After a lengthy search in London, Barnet Levy eventually located Esther Elias, and they were married. After their marriage, Barnet and Esther Levy made the 300-mile journey from London to Falmouth by road. This journey took several days. The wealthy could afford to hire a private postchaise, or travel by mail coach, but for others, like Barnet and Esther Levy, the common form of transportation to Cornwall was by *Russel's Wagon*, also known as *Russel's Fly*, a huge wagon-like vehicle, which is said to have been "covered by canvas with six heavy horses, a driver and a guard, heavily armed with blunderbusses... who rode on a stout pony either at its head or followed behind the wagon".[99] The passengers would sit at the front of the wagon, in front of the cargo and luggage, on seats of hay and straw. Tradition has it that Esther Elias declined to sit with the others, and, all the way, "she rode behind her husband on...a packsaddle horse". Overnight, the wagon would stop at roadside inns, some of which were chosen because the landlord provided kosher facilities for the Jewish travellers.

Barnet and Esther Levy were to have eight children, two of whom, Levy (-1791) and Sarah (Sally) were unmarried. Levy Levy, like his mother, died of consumption, soon after his father's death in 1791. It has been noted that Elizabeth (Betsy) Levy (1757-1832) married Solomon Solomon (1764-1819), a son of Israel Solomon (*c.* 1727-1802) and Bella Woolf (*c.* 1726-1816), and that the Solomon family (originally *Behrends*) was German, from the Rhineland, and the Woolf family were from Holland. Abraham Levy (1779-1834) married Zipporah Benjamin (1784-1861) of Plymouth and moved there. One of their sons, Markes (1812-1877) married, Bella Woolf (1817-1881), a daughter of Lemon Woolf (1783-1848) of Penzance. Shevya (Sheba) Levy (1766-1850) was to marry her mother's brother, Elias Hart Elias (-1835) of London. He is said to have been a debonair man, well educated, a political agitator and a Hebrew scholar. He declined to go into his father's clothing business, worked as a clerk, book-keeper and letter writer, but failed to find a remunerative career in London or secure a living income. It has been said that his much older sister, Esther, invited him to come to Falmouth to become tutor to her children, which he did, and eventually married his former pupil and niece, Shevya. Israel Solomon's recollections are confused and inconsistent at this point. In his published version (of 1887, but written some years before his addendum of 1885) he says that, after her mother's death, Sheba "remained with her father and the other daughters" and did not go to London until after her father's death "and some time after married [Hart] Elias". In his 1885 addendum to the above, Solomon says that Esther sent for her brother to be her childrens' tutor (in English and Hebrew) "some years after his Marriage with Sheba". The 1887 published version would seem the more credible. The unmarried Hart Elias may have become the childrens' tutor before Esther's death, and may have tutored Shevya as a young girl, but later returned to London. When Shevya went to London to seek her fortune after the death of her father in 1791 (she was then 25) she seems to have spent some time in service to a Jewish family, and later married her uncle. The failure of his various clerical posts, forced them to return to Falmouth, where, as a childless couple, they became dependent on their relatives. Shevya's mother, Esther Elias, is likely to have died (of consumption) early in life, in the 1780s. The date has usually been taken as *c.* 1780, but Israel Solomon (1885) states that Barnet Levy (whose headstone gives his death as 1791) died "within two or three years" of her, that is, she died around 1788. This seems unlikely, in that Solomon also gives her son, Abraham as a "very little boy" at the time of Esther's death, and the youngest child, Sally (Sarah) as "a baby in arms". Abraham Levy was born in 1779, which is confirmed by his head-stone in the Plymouth Hoe cemetery: "died 25th May 1834, aged 55".[100] Around 1780, the oldest child, Elizabeth (Betsy), was then about twenty, Hannah only eleven, with Judith, six, Joel, four, and Abraham, an infant. Shevya was about four-teen. Even before Barnet Levy died "after a knee complaint & poor surgical knowl-edge in those days", the burden of rearing of the children fell to Betsy (Elizabeth) who "became the head & manager of the family & the shop, she was also obliged also to become mother in the case of the two youngest children". Hannah, and Shevya would also have taken their share of the management of the household, and "Sheba…aided in the domestic portion". Other family members helped the family in their dress-making business.[101] So, it is likely that Hart Elias spent some time in Falmouth to help educate the children after the death of his sister, returned to London, but eventually married Shevya and settled in Falmouth with her. Records do not indicate where their marriage took place.[102] Israel Solomon was not born until 1803, and claimed to have known Hart Elias – "I see him now in my mind" – giving a detailed account of his flamboyant manner and dress. Hart Elias died in 1835, and is buried in the Penryn cemetery. Shevya Levy eventually went to live in Penzance with her sister, Hannah Joseph. She died in 1850 and her sister, Hannah, in 1851. Both sisters are buried in the Penzance cemetery.

Barnet Levy did not leave a will, and application was made for probate of his estate. It reads: "Consistory Court, Exeter. Admon. Of Barnet Levy late of Falmouth granted 24 June 1791 to Levy Levy the son and one of the next of kin of the said decd. Bond of Levy Levy of Falmouth, watchmaker, Philip Moses of same, silver-smith, and George Walters of Bredock, husbandman, in £200, dated 24 June 1791. Condit. that said Levy Levy being admitted admr. of Barnet Levy, his father, shall make an invent. etc. signat. of Levy Levy.

Affidavit by Levy Levy that he is the son and one of next of kin of Barnet, 24 June 1791."

Probate was granted to two other executors, one from outside the immediate family, Philip Moses, a member of the Falmouth congregation, and another, a local non-Jew, with whom Barnet Levy may have had business dealings. In the event, the administration of the estate by Levy Levy became a cause for concern, and he died soon after his father in 1791, also without a will. A later codicil administered by the Court reads: "Whereas Barnet Levy late of Falmouth co. [county] Cornwall, shopkeeper decd. Died intestate and admon. of his goods was committed to Levy Levy his son and whereas said Levy Levy did for some time intermeddle in the effects of his father and he is since dead, intestate, leaving some part thereof unadmd., the Vicar General now empowers certain clerks to take oaths of Betsy Levy, Hannah Levy and Judith Levy spinsters, the three daughters and next of kin of sd. Barnet Levy decd. 27 July 1792. They were sworn 14 Aug. 1792. Bond of Betsy, Hannah & Judith Levy of Falmouth. Spinsters, Samuel Russell of same, taylor, and Francis Symons of same, mercer, in £1000. 14 Aug. 1792." Barnet Levy's two sons, Joel (15) and Abraham (12) were deemed minors and, therefore, ineligible to be involved. Russell and Symons, who lived with the three sisters, may have been Jewish, and from outside the County.

The Levy-Joseph Marriages

The three remaining children of Barnet Levy were to marry the three Joseph siblings who had come to Falmouth:

(i) Joel Levy (1776-1831) married Rachel Joseph (-1830), and the couple moved to Plymouth where Joel Levy traded as Navy Agent (1816) and a Silversmith (1822). Joel Levy lost his wife, Rachel, together with his oldest son, Barnet (1812-1830) within a week of one another. He is said to have become mentally unsettled by this trauma, and died some months later, in 1831. He is buried in the Plymouth Hoe cemetery, but the headstones of his wife and son have not survived.[103]

(ii) Hannah Levy (1769-1851) married Abraham Joseph (-1827) and they remained in Cornwall. Of their children, it has been mentioned that Joseph Joseph (1802-1887) moved to Plymouth and then Liverpool, and his brother, Barnet, married Fanny Moses of Bristol. Two daughters married Jews from Birmingham: Esther Joseph married Noah Solomon (1796-1876) and Julia (1809-1858) married Solomon Blanckensee (1801-1864). Henry Joseph (1806-1881) married Amelia Jacob (1811-1891) a daughter of Jacob Jacob (1774-1853) of Falmouth. Henry and Amelia Joseph moved to Redruth, and then to Penzance. They were to have twelve children, six sons and six daughters. Abraham Joseph of Falmouth died in 1827, and is buried in the Penryn cemetery. His wife, Hannah, moved to Penzance to be near her son, and she is buried in the Penzance cemetery. (iii) Judith Levy (1774-1846) married Lyon Joseph (1775-1825). They were to have nine children: Esther died young, and Joseph in infancy. The others became widely dispersed. Arabella Joseph (1803-1897) married a Solomon Levy (-1841) of Exeter, and they moved to Bristol. Three of the children were married to Jews from London: Hannah (Nanny or Nancy) Joseph (1809-1888) to Moses Levin (*c.* 1799-), Kate (Kitty) Joseph (1811-1897) to Moses Cohen (1799-1879), and Henry Joseph (1815-1899) to Maria Samuel (1816-1897) a daughter of Abraham Samuel. Benedict Joseph (-1851) and Frederick Joseph emigrated to America. Benedict married a Jane Feuchtwanger of New York, and Frederick drowned in a bathing accident in the River Schuykill[104] (which runs south-eastwards from the Blue Mountains of Appalachia in Pennsylvania, down to Philadelphia, where it joins the River Delaware). Barnet Joseph (1801-1880) married a Betsy Jacob (1801-1889) of Dartmouth, whose father, Nathan Jacob, was from Fürth in Bohemia. Nathan Jacob's wife was a Miriam Alexander from Devon (various *Alexander* families lived in Exeter and Plymouth),[105] and the couple eventually settled in Sunderland. (Two of their nephews, sons of a sister named *Cohen*, went to London where they were known as Ephraim and Joseph *Bond*. They are said to have founded the once famous gambling club, *Crockfords*, in St. James, and in so doing "they amassed a large fortune, but neither identified himself with the Jewish Community in the Metropolis", although one of the brothers contributed to Jewish charitable causes through an intermediary).[106] Barnet and Betsy Joseph moved to Bristol where he became the president of the Bristol Hebrew Congregation at the age of 24 and traded as a silversmith, jeweller and watchmaker. He left Bristol to live in Liverpool in 1835 where he continued his trade, and became a founder of the Hope Place Synagogue and the Hebrew Schools. The couple retired to Birmingham, where they died. Betsy Joseph gave birth to fourteen children, including Rebecca Joseph (1835-1919) who married Ephraim Joseph (1829-1896) of Swansea, and Rachel Joseph (1831-1891) who married Alexander Levin (1828-1891) from Penzance. The latter's son, Lionel Barnet Levin (1862-1933) settled in Tonga and fathered two daughters by Tongan women.[107]

Lyon Joseph of Falmouth

Lyon Joseph had a colourful and eventful life and was a prominent member of the Falmouth Congregation. His career in some respects replicates that of Abraham, Eleazar and Lemon Hart in Penzance. Compared with Lyon Joseph, the commercial ventures of the Hart family began on a relatively modest scale, but proceeded cautiously and steadily and, eventually, as the Lemon Hart firm, became a considerable success in London. Joseph's ventures began with a dramatic early success, but ended in an equally dramatic and disastrous failure. He started out as a pedlar in buckles for shoes and other items of clothing, and also in cutlery, jewellery, watches and small silver items. He eventually became a shopkeeper and a shipper. During the latter part of the 18th century, Napoleon Bonaparte (1769-1821) had gained control of much of Spain and Portugal, and did much to restrict and damage British trade to those countries, through his control of the Channel Ports. Lyon Joseph, together with other Falmouth merchants, took advantage of the British Government's eagerness to promote free trade by despatching commodities by packet boats to those parts of the Iberian peninsula not occupied by the French. Subsequently, Lyon Joseph became a wealthy man, and, as a result, he was ideally placed to assist and support the Jewish Congregation and the building of its second synagogue around 1808. Eventually, the Government reversed this policy, and ordered that such trade should cease or be declared contraband. Lyon Joseph, however, chose to defy this order, and continued to trade. As a result, his goods were seized, and he is said to have made a loss of some twenty thousand pounds, a considerable fortune for that time, but, it would seem, a sum that did not represent his entire capital, even if it had seriously depleted it.

His situation worsened, in that he also suffered losses in other areas and became involved in a number of disastrous speculations. He had come to be the owner of a merchant vessel, the *Perseverance*, which he had sent with its cargo to Gibraltar, but, *en route*, the captain ran into the port of Lisbon, appropriated some of the goods and absconded. Lyon Joseph was informed of the situation and sailed to Lisbon just in time to reclaim the ship itself, together with part of its original cargo. He was soon to suffer another commercial mishap. Some relatives of his, named Solomon, who had been unsuccessful in business in London, came to Falmouth, and Lyon Joseph sought to help them re-establish themselves. Consequently, he sent them to Gibraltar, where, from the reports that reached Lyon Joseph, they appeared to be trading successfully. Lyon consigned a considerable quantity of goods to them, but they proved dishonest, and disappeared, abandoning the goods, which were seized by various creditors. It took a long and costly litigation for Lyon to recover his goods, and then only £700 of their original value of £8000.

Another unsuccessful commercial venture was to follow as a result of a business connection with a Moses Abecasis, who lived in Malta. Apparently, this man was strongly recommended to Lyon Joseph who decided to send him on consignment "a merchandise to a considerable value".[108] Whatever it was, Abecasis sold the whole of this consignment, and with the proceeds purchased a cargo of Zante (Zakynthos) currants, which, when shipped to him in Malta, turned out to have been salvaged from a wrecked vessel. They were water-logged and ruined, and, to save duty, Abecasis had them destroyed. Even though Lyon Joseph went to Malta to try to recover the value of his original consignment, after three years he had received nothing. Next, he sent commodities to the value of some £3000 to a Victor Levy of Cadiz. When Lyon received no payment for the goods, he went to Cadiz to confront Levy, who, apparently, had converted to Roman Catholicism, and threatened to denounce Joseph to the Inquisition if he did not drop his claim to the goods. It would seem that Lyon left Cadiz empty-handed. Another ship of Lyon's, carrying uninsured goods to the value of £1500 was wrecked off Cork. The partially salvaged cargo was seized by the Government under the law of "Droits of Admiralty", and all that Lyon Joseph recovered from that episode was a mere £60. In 1810, he entered into a partnership with Alexander Cohen, Baruch de Phineas Toledano, and Maurice and Stephen Hart of London to trade between London and Gibraltar, but a dispute led to the partnership being dissolved. All of these various and relentless financial losses reduced his means considerably, and damaged his health. It is likely that around this time Lyon Joseph took employment as a Government Agent for the collection of gold used for the payment of troops and war supplies for the Continental War against Napoleon.

From 1807 to 1815, Lyon Joseph was elected *Parnas* (President) and *Rosh Hakahal* (Head of the Congregation). Towards the end of this period it would seem that a dispute may have occurred within the Congregation that involved Lyon Joseph. It seems to have begun as a controversy over the issue of seating rights in the synagogue for Lyon Joseph's wife, Judith, but eventually extended to further issue of the legal ownership of the synagogue and other adjacent buildings.[109] The Congregation claimed these as communal property, but Joseph appears to have made a personal claim to the buildings, presumably on the basis of the appearance of his name on the lease or the mortgage documents. Whether the dispute led to formal legal proceedings is not known, but Joseph's claims were rejected by the Congregation. It is credible that financial straits may have led Joseph to such a claim, which, as President, and a long-time member, he may have believed would be met with acquiesence, especially as he had been so closely involved in the establishment of the synagogue buildings. This incident may have motivated his departure from Falmouth for Bath, where, it is said, he lived in retirement as a broken man, in circumstances of impoverishment. When he died in Bath on 2nd May, 1825, at the age of only 51, his family did not seek a burial for him in Falmouth burial ground, but in the Plymouth Hoe cemetery, where he was interred on 7th May,[110] "near his mother's tomb" and where, later (in 1846) his wife, Judith, may also have been buried.[111]

The Jacob Family

Like the Harris family, which became established in Truro, the Jacob family are likely to have come from Germany. It is not known when the Jacob family first came to Falmouth, but Moses Jacob (1733-1807) was the child of one of these early settlers, and his year of birth would suggest that he may even have been born in Cornwall. He married Sarah Moses (1748-1831), one of Alexander Moses' daughters, and although he may at first have been reliant upon his father-in-law's franchise, he eventually became commercially independent and settled in Redruth. Moses and Sarah Jacob are known to have had at least twelve children. Two of them, Betsy (1767-) and Amelia (born c. 1785-94; died 1864) were unmarried, but of the other ten, only two Levy Jacob (1788-1824) and Rose Jacob (1770-1846) married into Jewish families from outside the County, although Levy Jacob did settle in Penzance for the remainder of his relatively short life. The others all married into local Jewish families, an opportunity available in these early days of rapid settlement, that was to become a less frequent option for subsequent generations. Judith Rebecca Jacob (1768-1849) married Moses Isaac Joseph (-1834) and her sister, Kate, or " Kitty" Jacob (1772-1854) married Simon Solomon (-1825), both men being of Falmouth. Three of the Jacob children married into Jewish families that had settled in Truro (at that time a thriving port): Jacob Jacob (1774-1853) married Sarah Kate Simons (1778-1846), Samuel Jacob (1778-1860) married Sarah Levy (1784-1868), moving to Penzance, and Esther Jacob (1784-1871) married Henry Harris (1787-1872). Three further children married Jews who established themselves in Penzance: Hannah Jacob (1775-1864) married Solomon Ezekiel (1781-1867), Rebecca Jacob (1781-1853) married Lemon Woolf (1783-1848), and Flora Jacob (1790-1874) married Rabbi Barnet Asher Simmons (1784-1860) who had

The Jacob Family

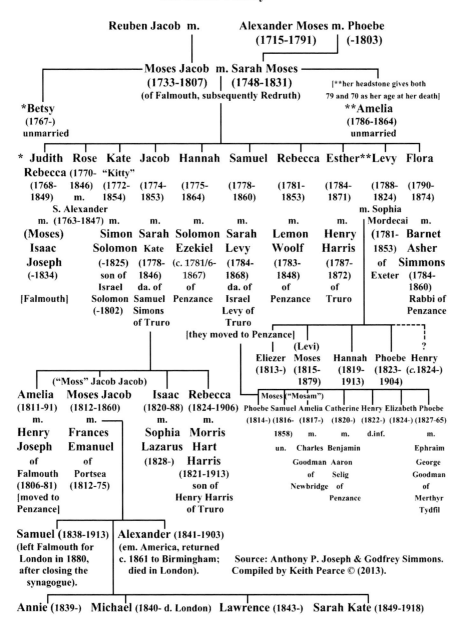

Reuben Jacob m. | Alexander Moses m. Phoebe
(1715-1791) | (-1803)

Moses Jacob m. Sarah Moses
(1733-1807) | (1748-1831)
(of Falmouth, subsequently Redruth)

[**her headstone gives both 79 and 70 as her age at her death]

*Betsy
(1767-)
unmarried

**Amelia
(1786-1864)
unmarried

* Judith Rebecca (1768-1849)
m. S. Alexander (1763-1847)
m. (Moses) Isaac Joseph (-1834)
[Falmouth]

Rose (1770-1846) "Kitty"

Kate (1772-1854)
m. Simon Solomon son of Israel Solomon (-1802)

Jacob (1774-1853)
m. Sarah Kate (1778-1846) da. of Samuel Simons of Truro

Hannah (1775-1864)
m. Solomon Ezekiel (c. 1781/6-1867) of Penzance

Samuel (1778-1860)
m. Sarah Levy (1784-1868) da. of Israel Levy of Truro

Rebecca (1781-1853)
m. Lemon Woolf (1783-1848) of Penzance

Esther (1784-1871)
m. Henry Harris (1787-1872) of Truro

**Levy (1788-1824)
m. Sophia Mordecai (1781-1853) of Exeter

Flora (1790-1874)
m. Barnet Asher Simmons (1784-1860) Rabbi of Penzance

[they moved to Penzance]

Eliezer (1813-)

(Levi) Moses (1815-1879)

Hannah (1819-1913)

Phoebe (1823-1904)

Henry (c.1824-)

?

("Moss" Jacob Jacob)

Amelia (1811-91)
m. Henry Joseph of Falmouth (1806-81) [moved to Penzance]

Moses Jacob (1812-1860)
m. Frances Emanuel of Portsea (1812-75)

Isaac (1820-88)
m. Sophia Lazarus (1828-)

Rebecca (1824-1906)
m. Morris Hart Harris (1821-1913) son of Henry Harris of Truro

Moses ("Mosam")
Phoebe (1814-) 1858 un.

Samuel (1816-) m. Charles Goodman of Newbridge

Amelia (1817-) m. Benjamin Aaron Selig of Penzance

Catherine (1820-) d.inf.

Henry (1822-)

Elizabeth (1824-)

Phoebe (1827-65) m. Ephraim George Goodman of Merthyr Tydfil

Samuel (1838-1913)
(left Falmouth for London in 1880, after closing the synagogue).

Alexander (1841-1903)
(em. America, returned c. 1861 to Birmingham; died in London).

Source: Anthony P. Joseph & Godfrey Simmons. Compiled by Keith Pearce © (2013).

Annie (1839-) Michael (1840- d. London) Lawrence (1843-) Sarah Kate (1849-1918)

137

become the Minister of the Penzance Congregation in 1811, serving it intermittently until his death in 1860.

The later pattern of migration from Cornwall that was to characterise these families can be seen most clearly in this last marriage, which produced eleven children, ten of whom were to leave Cornwall, three of whom went to London, three to South Wales, and three to Australia. Later generations of the Jacob family were also to gravitate to those same places. Moses Isaac Jacob (1820-1888), a son of Jacob Jacob, had moved to Swansea by 1846, in which year he married Sophia, daughter of the late L. Lazarus, the ceremony being conducted by the Chief Rabbi, Dr. Adler.[112] By 1851, Isaac Jacob was trading in Swansea as a Jeweller and Silversmith, but by 1871 he was living in St. Pancras, London.[112] His sister, Rebecca Jacob (1824-1906) married Morris Hart Harris (1821-1913) of Truro, and they too eventually moved to London. Of the four children of Samuel Jacob (1778-1860) and Sarah Levy, only one, Moses ["Mossam"] Samuel Jacob (1816-1858), who was unmarried, remained in Falmouth. Of his siblings, Catherine Jacob (1820-) married Benjamin Aaron Selig (1814-1872) of Penzance, and, subsequently, after the death of the latter's parents, left for Australia, eventually settling in New Zealand. Amelia Jacob (1817-) and her sister, Phoebe (1827-1865) both married into Goodman families in South Wales, where there were various Jewish families with this surname, only some of whom were related. A son of Levy Jacob of Penzance, Moses Levi Jacob (1815-1879) had moved with his family to Birmingham by 1851, where he traded as a Jeweller for many years. The brother of Isaac and Rebecca Jacob, Moses ["Moss"] Jacob Jacob (1812-1860) remained in Falmouth, but four of his sons, Samuel (1838-1913), Michael (1840-), Alexander (1841-1903) and Lawrence (1843-) eventually moved to London (where, as mentioned, their uncle, Isaac Jacob, had settled) by 1881. In 1864, Michael Jacob was both Secretary (Registrar or Treasurer) of the Falmouth Synagogue, and Treasurer of the Falmouth Debating Society (*est.* 1862). For some years after he moved to London, Michael, who was unmarried, lived in Lambeth, but in 1901 he was in Bournemouth, possibly as a visitor. Samuel Jacob was to settle in Hampstead, and both Lawrence[113] and Alexander lived in Paddington, the latter moving to Willesden by 1901. Alexander Jacob is of particular interest in that he emigrated to British Columbia in 1859 at the time of the Gold Rush, together with three Cornishmen, one of whom was a Lanyon, and in the same Falmouth Masonic Lodge as Alexander Jacob's brother, Samuel, and their father, Moses Jacob Jacob. Accompanying them were two brothers of the Falmouth Joseph family, one of whom, Lionel Joseph (1826-1915) had been a Shipping Merchant in Falmouth, but had since moved to Birmingham. On his return to England, around 1861, Alexander Jacob did not move back to Falmouth, but lived for some years in Birmingham. He had settled in London by 1881. His affection for Cornwall, however, can be seen in that he gave traditional Cornish (secondary) names to four of his sons: Alexander *Trelawney* (1876-) who died young, George *Grenville* (1877-1963), Edwin *Ellis* (1878-) and Victor *Vivian* (1883-1903). Of these names, *Trelawney* and *Grenville* are well known in Cornish history, and the Jacob family would have had commercial links with the *Ellis* and *Vivian* families, and were also connected to them through their mutual membership of the Falmouth Masonic Lodge, where various *Ellis* and *Vivian* members had occupied senior positions across several generations.[114]

The spread of the Jacob family into the towns of South Cornwall, Truro, Redruth, Camborne, Hayle, Penzance, and even The Isles of Scilly, meant that, by the 1840s, they had become sufficiently prosperous to engage in a range of business opportunities, and they had diversified their commercial activities both within Falmouth and elsewhere. Their trades included jewellery, watch and clock making, trading in mineralogical specimens, pawnbroking, cabinet making, upholstery, hosiery and tailoring, as well as money broking (as foreign exchange and bullion merchants). One of the most prosperous was Moses ("Moss") Jacob Jacob (1812-1860) of Falmouth, mentioned above, whose wide-ranging business interests are recorded in the Trades section (below). Upon his death on 14th February 1860, his will[115] revealed effects "under £12,000". This in itself suggests a considerable sum for that time, but his entire estate may, of course, have had a total value in excess of this ceiling figure, and would indicate the potential of the family's investments. A ledger of speculative investments made by a member of the Jacob family from 1844 to 1867, written in the same hand throughout, still exists in the Archive of the late Alex Jacob.[116] The name of the investor is not inscribed in the book at any point but clearly it is a member of the Jacob family, most likely Isaac Jacob (1820-1888), son of Jacob Jacob (1774-1853) of Falmouth. Isaac Jacob's dates alone are consistent with the entries in the investment book, although by 1851 he was living in Swansea.[117] It would seem that he came to manage the family portfolio *in absentia*, continuing investments made initially by his father, and later by other family members. His uncle, Henry Harris (1787-1872) originally from Penzance, came to live in Truro, later moving to London. As a shareholder, he made payments to the Jacob ledger in 1855 and 1859. The investments recorded in the ledger were considerable and wide-ranging, and, in the view of Justin Brooke,[118] the Jacob ledger is a unique and invaluable record of shareholding in Cornish mines at this time. Rail transport was also expanding rapidly and there are accounts for the Cornwall Railway (1845-67), the Midland Railway (1848-52), and the Oxford and Worcester Railway (1848-57). Most of the investments, however, were in Cornish enterprises, such as shipping and mining.

The record of the Jacob investments is of great importance for two reasons. Firstly, at that time people did not usually keep records of their investments at all, and certainly not in such meticulous detail as the Jacob family. Secondly, Jacob's purchases show that he not only spread his risk[119] across several distinct industries (railways, shipping, harbour development and mining) but also, in mining, he had a portfolio of shares which struck a balance between sound (dividend-paying) mines, progressive (or "calling") mines, where there was hope for further progress towards profitability and dividends, and new mining concerns that the payments helped to set on foot. The idea of "risk spreading" in shares in several mines at a time had been developing in Cornwall from the early 1800s, but the various shares held by the Jacob family were in "cost-book companies", partnerships in transferable shares, with no limit to the amount that could be called up on each share. Clearly, the Jacob family saw their financial outlay, not only as a form of trade, but also as a social duty to subsidise and support local industry. Where the productive (dividend-paying) mines brought in respectable profits, these (together with other monies) could be reinvested into developing (progressive) mines, and even to establish new ones.

Isaac Jacob's records show that the family was much involved in Falmouth's maritime affairs. Between 1858-1865 he invested in the ships the *Dandy* and the *New Dandy*. The first was a late contemporary of the *Sydney* (first registered at Falmouth in 1848) which was used between the creek port of Devoran to carry tin *via* the Redruth-Devoran railway. The *Sydney* was not a powerful boat and contributed to the wreck of a big full-rigged ship the *Northern Empire*, built in 1854, which was in Falmouth (*en route* for London) and awaiting orders to which port to discharge her cargo of Guano. On the night of Tuesday 2nd March 1858 the tug *Sydney* was used to move the larger ship out of its berth. However when the ship's anchors were up, the tug could not hold her and the ship was wrecked against the rocks. It was later salvaged and sold for £1,200. The accounts relate to the salvage of the *Northern Empire*, from which he made a profit of 5% (£90) in 1859. The first *Dandy* had been built for Edmund Hancock and others, one of whom was the Jacob investor. It first appears in the Parliamentary "Returns of Steam Boats" from 1859. The ship was about 91 feet long and had a similar power to the *Sydney*. The owners ran the ship for five years, gaining about 32% profit at the end of that time (*c.*1858-65). The second *Dandy* mentioned in the accounts replaced the first in 1863. This was a bigger iron tug, about 106 feet long and 126 tons with more powerful engines. His investment records for this tug only go up to 1866. Between 1856-67, Jacob family investments were made in the *Baroness*, a 353 ton ship built at Sunderland in 1851 and registered in London. The principal owner was called Robinson, and throughout the 1860s the ship made voyages to the Mediterranean, Aden, and Port Said. The account book contains a note of Insurance received at Gibraltar, reflecting this use of the ship. The vessel only paid her way from 1860 with a gross return of 385 pounds over the 11 years. There were also shares in the Falmouth Docks Company. These were a long-term investment and directly helped to secure the future of the port. The Jacob accounts do not record any significant return, although the account book only covers the period 1858-62. The Docks Company built three breakwaters, two dry dock basins and twelve warehouses, and the work was completed in 1865. However, income alone was insufficient to sustain the work and 74,500 pounds had to be secured on loan from the Public Works Commissioners. A serious storm in 1867 caused considerable damage and by 1883, the Falmouth Docks were in arrears of their repayments. The Commissioners eventually took possession of the works as Mortgagees. It is doubtful if the Jacob family along with the original shareholders ever received any significant returns from this investment. (One of the Directors of the Falmouth Docks Company, in 1864, was a Frederick Benjamin, but it is uncertain if he was of Jewish descent).[120]

Apart from investing in harbour and port enterprises, between 1844 to 1866 Isaac Jacob was also a shareholder in a number of Tin Mines.[121] Most of the mines were tin, or lead producing, although one (*Wheal Basset*, Illogan) was a copper mine. The dividend-paying mines were mainly on the south side of Carn Brea, and in the Redruth and Illogan parishes. There were at this time several other (unrelated) people with the surname *Jacob(s)* who were connected with Cornish mine management: George A. Jacobs (Secretary, *Wheal Curtis*, Crowan, 1846-1848), M. J. Jacobs (Member of Committee of Management, *North Fowey Consols*, Lanlivery, 1846), and H. Jacob (Member of Committee of Management, *Polberro*, St. Agnes,

The Descendants of Jacob Jacob of Falmouth

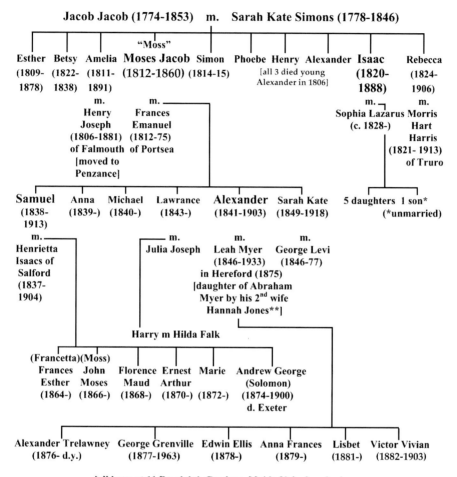

Jacob Jacob (1774-1853)   m.   Sarah Kate Simons (1778-1846)

"Moss"

| Esther (1809-1878) | Betsy (1822-1838) | Amelia (1811-1891) | **Moses Jacob** (1812-1860) | Simon (1814-15) | Phoebe | Henry | Alexander [all 3 died young Alexander in 1806] | **Isaac** (1820-1888) | Rebecca (1824-1906) |

Amelia m. Henry Joseph (1806-1881) of Falmouth [moved to Penzance]

Moses Jacob m. Frances Emanuel (1812-75) of Portsea

Isaac m. Sophia Lazarus (c. 1828-)

Rebecca m. Morris Hart Harris (1821-1913) of Truro

Samuel (1838-1913) — Anna (1839-) — Michael (1840-) — Lawrance (1843-) — **Alexander** (1841-1903) — Sarah Kate (1849-1918)

5 daughters   1 son* (*unmarried)

Samuel m. Henrietta Isaacs of Salford (1837-1904)

Lawrance m. Julia Joseph

Alexander m. Leah Myer (1846-1933) in Hereford (1875) [daughter of Abraham Myer by his 2nd wife Hannah Jones**]

Sarah Kate m. George Levi (1846-77)

Harry m Hilda Falk

| (Francetta)(Moss) Frances Esther (1864-) | John Moses (1866-) | Florence Maud (1868-) | Ernest Arthur (1870-) | Marie (1872-) | Andrew (Solomon) (1874-1900) d. Exeter | George |

| Alexander Trelawney (1876- d.y.) | George Grenville (1877-1963) | Edwin Ellis (1878-) | Anna Frances (1879-) | Lisbet (1881-) | Victor Vivian (1882-1903) |

[all born at 11 Randolph Gardens, Maida Vale, London]

**She was the daughter of Isaiah Groomsfeld from Holland. The Groomsfeld family name changed to Jones soon after they arrived in England in the mid-18th century.
Source: Anthony Joseph & Godfrey Simmons
Compiled by Keith Pearce © (2013).

Jacob of Cornwall and Mordecai of Exeter

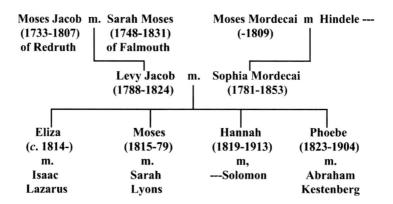

Source: Anthony P. Joseph.
Compiled by Keith Pearce © (2013).

1897). Henry Abraham of Camborne, was under-manager of *South Condurrow* mine from 1869-1880, being recorded as a Mine Agent, age 37, when he was initiated into a Masonic Lodge in 1871. A Michael Abrahams of Camborne was a Hotel Keeper, entering the Freemasons in 1869, age 45. None of these men are known to have been Jewish. Although none of the Cornish Jews in the 18th and 19th centuries are known to have taken up employment in local mining, the mining industry of the time did possess a very open and meritocratic structure, and there is no reason *per se* why a Jew could not have been appointed to a position within it. The Mine Agents were "captains" who had risen through the ranks after acquiring new skills, such as surveying, sometimes acting as investment agents for their mine. As such, Henry Abraham of *South Cundurrow* mine, where the Jacob family held shares, may have had contact of some form with Isaac Jacob. The latter's largest investment, of £2,407 in 1844 (in today's terms over £100,000), was in the successful Condurrow mine, south of Camborne. Its oldest recorded working can be dated to 1712. By 1844 it was sufficiently productive to pay out dividends (from 1849 to 1859). Other dividend–paying mines listed are Consolidated Mines (Consols of Gwennap), Wheal Buller of Redruth, Wendron Consols, Wheal Seaton, Camborne, and the very profitable Wheal Basset and South Wheal Basset, both at Illogan, and East Wheal Basset, at Redruth. New and Developing mines included Trevena, Breage, which had only been worked from about 1844 (the first attempt being unsuccessful as insufficient subscribers came forward), Tolgus, Illogan, worked from 1831, and then 1844-1852, South Wheal Charlotte and Wheal Victoria, both at St. Agnes (worked from 1852 and 1854 respectively), North Fowey Consols, Lanlivery, worked between 1837 to 1849, Wheal Clinton, Flushing (near Falmouth), worked from 1854-1858, and Swanpool, Budock, worked from 1790-93 and in 1814, and then from 1843. The investment book also indicates the extent of contacts with numerous local people who were involved in mining administration and investment, either as managers (or under-managers), pursers (paymasters), accountants or sharedealers. These include: William Bishop (under-manager at Wendron Consols) and John Burgan (a manager of mines in the Wendron district), Edmunds of Falmouth, and Greenwood of Truro (share dealers), Captain Richards, a common name in mining, and probably the under-manager at one of the Basset mines, Tobias Harry Tilly of Falmouth (purser of Wheal Seaton and North Fowey Consols) and Francis Todd (purser and member of the committee of management of Swanpool mine). Another member of the Jacob family, Alexander Jacob (1841-1903), a son of Moss Jacob Jacob, and a nephew of Isaac Jacob, also became involved in the mining industry abroad. It has been noted that, in 1859 he went to British Columbia as a prospector, accompanied by three Cornish miners, and that, upon his return, he lived for a time in Birmingham and then moved to London. In 1875, he married Leah, daughter of Abraham Myer, by his second wife, Hannah Jones (Groomsfeld), the daughter of Isaiah Groomsfeld from Holland. The family had arrived in England in the mid-18th century, and settled in East Anglia, adopting the surname *Jones,* a name said to have been taken by Isaiah Groomsfield from a shop he had seen Norwich.[122] The marriage of Alexander Jacob to Leah Myer took place in Hereford, and the couple were to have six children, all born at their home, 11 Randolph Gardens, Maida Vale, London. Alexander Jacob died in London, where he is buried.

Trades and Occupations

The names of the Jews who traded in Cornish towns in the 18th and 19th centuries can be compiled from various sources, including the published trade directories of the day. The Appendix at the end of chapter 7 explains the abbreviations which are given with each person. The names appear here in approximately chronological order, in that the various source references allow each person to be placed as working in the respective town at the time or during the years given in the directories.[123] It can be assumed in most cases that the people traded in the town for some years before and after the dates given. A trader is given as "Uncertain" where the name may suggest a Jew, but the individual may not have been Jewish.

Barnet Levi (y): Silversmith (Ja. 1776, p. 317) and Dealer in hardware & wearing apparel (1773-1776: Insurance Policies (George Rigal).[124] This is not the **Barnett Levy** who traded at St. Austell from 1758 to 1765 (see St. Austell Trades section).

Insurance Policies are mentioned frequently in these sections on Trades. It should be noted that, sometimes, a number of people were insuring the same address, and that, from 1813, some policies carried a prejudicial "Jews' Clause", being some variation of "No goods paid for which are stolen or lost by removal at or in consequence of a fire or alarm of fire". Such a clause may reflect the frequency with which Jews, as pawnbrokers, might come into possession of stolen goods (albeit inadvertently) and also the insecurity and vulnerability of dwellings. The total value of dwellings, premises and stock insured under these policies do not necessarily reveal, or even reflect, the total value of the assets held by the individuals concerned. In the 18th century especially, fewer than 5% to 8% of the population owned freehold property, or owned it exclusively, and very few owned secure long-term leases. Bankruptcy was a commonplace occurrence in the absence of adequate personal savings or alternative investments to cover total losses incurred. Moreover, hidden, private savings could, in some cases, be significantly in excess of the financial impression given by an insurance policy. It was common to be under-insured, or only partially insured. In Penzance, in 1791, Lemon Hart's business was insured for £500, rising to £800. However, when he set up a branch of his wine and spirit business in London in 1807, he did so with the considerable initial capital of £5,000, although it is not known if this amount was raised entirely from his personal resources, or secured, partially or otherwise, under a loan.

Josiah Abraham (1751). Trade unknown (Falmouth Lodge Masonic records). Uncertain.
It is not known if he is to be connected with the Josiah Abraham (-1810), a Miller in Liskeard, or his namesake (1796-1879) who was a clockmaker there. Josiah Abraham of Falmouth may have been related to the Joseph Abraham (1861) and Sam Abrahams (1889) who later traded in Falmouth.

Alexander Moses (as below), was living in Penryn from at least 1751, when he was recorded as Warden and founder member of the Falmouth Masonic Lodge. It is likely that he had been resident for some years before this date.

Richard Woolfe was apprenticed to Lazarus Hingstone, a Brassmaker, in 1759. Unlikely. It may be that these men have been taken for Jews on the basis of their names.[125]

Isaac Polack of Penryn. (1762 & 1783: Falmouth Masonic records). As his name suggests, he was most likely of Polish extraction, although his family may have come to England via Germany. His trade is not mentioned in the Falmouth Masonic records, but he would be the "Jewish priest" who married a Gentile widow, Mary Strougton, in St. Gluvias church on 15th February 1760. It is not known if he converted to Christianity, and the marriage record does not indicate a simultaneous baptism or that Polack was "formerly a Jew" (as recorded in a few cases of Jewish conversion). He may be buried in the Penryn Jewish cemetery, but, if so, his comparatively early headstone has not survived. He is not known to have been buried at St. Gluvias, where his wife was interred, having died on 16th February 1804, age 78. Isaac Polack's occupation and trade advertisement as a translator of languages from French, German and Dutch for commercial and legal documents, appeared in the *Western Flying Post* in July 1776.[126] It is possible that he was originally from a London family of that name and *Isaac Polack* occurs frequently in the Hawkers' and Pedlars' Office accounts issued there for licences between 1710-1714.[127] The Frances Polack, below, was Isaac Polack's daughter. Isaac Polack is recorded as a member of the Penryn Masonic Lodge. He died *c.* 1794, and letters for the administration of his estate were given to his daughter,[128] presumably Frances. Isaac Polack's connection to his later namesake, Isaac Pollack, mentioned in the Penzance Congregational minutes for 1825 is not known, but a family relationship seems likely, unless the latter was a transient visitor, perhaps from London, where there was a large Polish and Eastern European Jewish community in the East End. Neither is it known if Isaac Polack of Penryn can be connected to the Joshua and Prudence Pollock (whose family name was most likely Jenkins) who lived around the 1780s at Rame-by-Plymouth (not Rame-in-Meneage, between Helston and Falmouth). Their children were all baptised at Rame between 1786-1798, including two daughters, both named Ann, the first born in 1790, who may have died young, and the second Ann Jenkins Pollock in 1798. It is possible that one of these Rame girls could be linked with or even identified with Anna Polack of Penryn (see below), although the latter may have been a daughter of either Frances or Sarah Polack (neither of whom married). The occupation of the Pollock family of Rame may have been that of fishermen (a trade not associated with Jews), in that a much later Joshua Pollock appears as such in the 1841 Census.[129] Another, possibly unconnected and extended Pollock, or Pullock family, some of whom were drapers and tailors, lived at St. Stephen-in-Brannel, in north Cornwall, and were Christians: William and Mary (Bullen) Pullock, from the 1770s, Robert and Mary Pullock, from the 1790s, and Francis and Ann Pollock (originally Gill), from the 1800s.[130] *Pollock* was a relatively common name amongst Cornish Christians in the 18th and 19th centuries: at least twenty baptisms, twelve marriages, ten burials and fifteen headstone inscriptions have been identified. The variation of spelling of names, with the duplication of consonants (Pollack) and the substitution of vowels (Pollack/Pollock/Pullock, or Ann/Anna) was common practice, and *Polack* could readily become Anglicised to *Pollock*. *Polack* itself, however, appears to have been very rare, if not unique, in Cornwall. For Devon, Susser mentions only three, two from London, and the other who may not have been Jewish,[131] and no marriages or burials of this name have been identified there. The fact that the Plymouth Jewish community and congregation was formed by some Jews who were of Eastern European origin, could have led to their presence in a place such as Rame, but any notion that Isaac Polack of Penryn was related to Joshua Pollock of Rame, or to Francis Pollock of St. Stephen remains unsubstantiated. A Henry Charles Polk, "Compositor, formerly of Falmouth" was married to Anne Hicks at Newport in 1844.[132] A Walter Polak was a confectioner in Penzance in 1939, where his son was apprenticed as a municipal and civil engineer,[133] and an "F. G. Pollack" was Secretary of the Falmouth Masonic Lodge as late as 1983, and became its Master in 1986. Any connection with the above is unknown, and all may have been Gentiles.

Jessop (1951), whose survey of the Devonian and Cornish Jewish families can be shown to contain numerous errors, referring to the second half of the eighteenth century, states that a Henry Marx of Exeter was a first cousin of "Isaac Polack of Penrhyn" *sic.,* and that this Henry Marx married an Elizabeth, "daughter of David

Solomon of Exeter".[134] The reference purports to be to an early Solomon family in Exeter, mentioned by Roth, but the connection is uncertain. A much later Exeter Solomon family, members of which moved to Plymouth, appear in the 1851 and 1861 Census records there. A David Solomon of Plymouth, whose mother was from Penzance, and whose children are not known, had a sister, Eliza. A Henry Marx, of Eliza's age, was also resident there. It is possible that Jessop has confused the earlier and later families. His pedigree of the later family is incomplete and shows no awareness of a resettlement in Plymouth. Jessop also states that Isaac Polak (*sic.*) was first cousin to the father of Rosa Abrahams. The latter married Abraham Joseph I (1731-1794) of Plymouth.

Moses Jacob: (1762; Falmouth Masonic records). He later moved to Redruth, where he traded as a watch and clockmaker (see Redruth Trades).

Aaron Delisser: Watchmaker (1768: Falmouth Masonic Lodge Records). Born *c.* 1744, he was the Lodge Master in 1784. These same records also give him as a Jeweller in 1782-1783. It is likely that he was a Sephardic Jew. The surname occurs in Jamaica, where, in Kingston (1795) Nathan, Aaron and Ellis De Lisser were registered as owners of a total of five slaves. In 1819, an Aaron Delisser (deceased) and an Abigail Delisser were registered as owners of four and seven slaves, respectively. A number of later Jewish burials with the name Delisser have also been recorded in Jamaica, in Falmouth, the District of Trelawney (1841-1881).[135] It is not known if Aaron Delisser of Falmouth, Cornwall, was connected with Jamaica.

Samuel Fisher: Actor (1768: Falmouth Masonic Lodge Records). Uncertain.

David Absalom: Mariner (1768: Falmouth Masonic Lodge Records). Uncertain. He had been born in Yarmouth in 1746. Other Mariners listed in the Masonic register of 1768 include Elijah Goldsmith and William Wolfe. Also listed are Benjamin Ostler, Merchant, and William Job, Yeoman. None of these men are known to have been Jewish.

Samuel Higman: Surgeon (1768: Membership Register of the Falmouth Masonic Lodge).[136] It is not certain that he was Jewish, although Higman is found as a variant of *Hyman*. A Jacob Higman (or Hyman: 1763-1841) traded as a Watchmaker in St. Austell.

Samuel and Ann Symons: Mercers, Drapers & Shopkeepers (Ba. 1788; Un. 1791: separate entries). Samuel Simons (1740-1832) married Rosa (Ann) Moses (1757-1838), a daughter of Alexander Moses. It is thought that Samuel Simons may also have traded in Truro as a Jeweller from 1791. Of their children, Sarah Kate (1778-1846) married Jacob Jacob (1774-1853) of Redruth, and Isaac (c. 1796-) married Rose (c. 1800-), daughter of Lazarus Jacobs and Rebecca Hart of Penzance. See Isaac Symons, below. **Francis Symons**, also a Mercer (mentioned earlier in the probate application for the estate of Barnet Levy in 1792) may have been a relative of Samuel Symons.

Emanuel Silver: Mariner, 1785 (Insurance policy).[137] It was not customary to name Mariners in trade directories. This is Emanuel Silva (1750-1800) who married Mary Eathorne (1748-1810) in Falmouth Parish Church on 21st March 1769. Their children, Emanuel (d. infancy, 1770) and Maria (b. 1785, later a schoolmistress: 1851 census) were baptised in the church, where the family is buried.[138] Emanuel Silva (or Silvera) may have been of Sephardic Jewish descent (possibly of Portuguese or Spanish-Marrano extraction). The surname *Siva* or *Da Silva* was common amongst the Christian and Jewish population of Jamaica, where at Falmouth in the Parish of Trelawney, in the 18th and 19th centuries, much of the retail trade was in the hands of Jewish merchants.[139] There were many Jewish investors and shareholders in the Jamaica trade, as well as Jewish companies and families resident in Jamaica in the 17th and 18th centuries. Many of the names found there are of Hebrew and Spanish or Portuguese origin, and were recorded as slave-owners, but it is not possible to be certain how many of these were Jews, or Christians of Jewish descent. Some would have been Gentiles, in that some common Hispanic names (such as *Manuel*) are derived from Hebrew (*Emanuel*) without implying Jewish identity. There were many individuals named with variants of *Silva*, and with traditional Jewish forenames. A confusing, and potentially misleading factor is that the common language of the Jews from an Iberian cultural background was *Ladino*, a conflation of Spanish, Portuguese and Hebrew. The name *Silver* was also found amongst Cornish Christians: a Thomas Anthony Silver, son of Thomas and Dorcas Silver was baptised at Falmouth on 30th July 1763, a Philip Silver, Mariner, was a member of the Penryn Masonic Lodge (*c.* 1795) and a "J. Silver", who may have been related, is mentioned in the Falmouth Masonic records for 1801. A Mary Silva (46) lived in High Street, Falmouth in 1841.[140] A Dorothia Silver, daughter of George Silver, was baptised at St. Kew in October 1611, and in the period 1773-1780, there were five baptisms with this surname in the parish of St. Hilary, near Penzance. Over 150 entries for this surname can be found for St. Endellion from 1876.[141]

Isaac (Wolf) Benjamin: Shopkeeper & Silversmith (1759-1774: Insurance Policies).[142]
The earliest reference to him is in 1754 at the Falmouth Masonic Lodge, where he is also listed in 1768 as a Jeweller, age 56. Born *c.*1712, he died in 1790. His headstone in the Jewish cemetery is one the earliest dated records of a burial there. For his son, Wolf (Isaac) Benjamin, see below. Isaac Benjamin should not be confused with:

Benjamin Wolf: Pawnbroker, (Un. 1791). He was originally from Holland, his children marrying into the Solomon family of Falmouth and the Hart family of Penzance. His son, Hyman (-1821) and grandson Lemon (1783-1848) were prominent members of the Penzance congregation. References in the records of the Falmouth Masonic Lodge from 1754, mention a "Brother Wolfe", and may refer to him, although they may equally be taken to refer to the (unrelated) Jacob Wolfe, who was a Mariner, and who may not have been Jewish. Benjamin Woolf's grandson, Lemon Woolf, was certainly a prominent Freemason in Penzance.

Alexander Moses: Shopkeeper, Silversmith (Insurance Policies, from 1761).[143] Pawnbroker (Un. 1791). He had been Warden of the Falmouth Masonic Lodge in 1751. He died in 1791, but his business may have been continued under his name by his son Philip (d. 1831).

Philip Moses: Silversmith. A son of the above, he was involved in the administration of the estate of Barnet Levy in 1791, and the will of Alexander Moses in 1793.

Levy Levy: Watchmaker, who died in 1791, was a son of Barnet Levy.

William Green: Pawnbroker, (Un. 1793-8). Uncertain.

Samuel Russell: Tailor (*fl.* 1792) and **Francis Symons**: Mercer (*fl.* 1792). They may have been Jewish, and, as noted earlier, they lived with the three spinster daughters of Barnet Levy.

Wolf (Isaac) Benjamin: Jeweller and Pawnbroker, (1794, Insurance Policy).[144] The son of Isaac Benjamin, above. He carried on his father's business after the latter's death in 1790. Wolf Benjamin is listed in the Falmouth Masonic Register of 1768 as a Jeweller, age 24. He eventually moved to Bristol, modifying his name to *Benson*.

Frances Polack: Shopkeeper, Penryn (Un. 1791); *Francis* Polack, Grocer, Penryn (Pg. 1823). Despite the variant spelling of the 1823 entry, these trade entries refer to the same daughter of Isaac and Mary Polack (above). Her father (only) was Jewish. She was baptised in St. Gluvias Church on 28th February 1760, thirteen days after her parents' marriage, and was buried in the same churchyard, having died, age 68, on 28th June 1828. In 1794, she was, presumably, the daughter who was granted letters of administration over her father's estate and property.[145] Frances Polack's sister, Sarah was baptised at St. Gluvias on 1st January 1765. Both Frances and Sarah Polack remained unmarried. It is possible that the Isaac Pollack who is mentioned in the Penzance Congregational records for 1825 (and only that year) was a son of Isaac Polack from an earlier marriage, a nephew or next generation relative of Isaac Polack. He may, however, have been a transient visitor to Penzance, and unrelated to Isaac Polack of Penryn. The Anna Polack, whose age and parentage is not given, and who married a Master Mariner, a widower, Captain William Banks of Newhaven, Sussex (born 1786) at St. Gluvias on 19th September 1820, may have been the illegitimate daughter of Frances or her sister. Anna Banks later named her first child "Frances", which might suggest that Frances Polack was her mother, although this name could have been that of her aunt, or given to her own child in appreciation of the legacy she received as a beneficiary of Frances' Polack's will. No baptismal record for Anna Polack has been found for Cornwall. Illegitimate infants were baptised in Cornish churches (some baptismal records indicating *bastard*) but custom may have varied from parish to parish, and some unmarried mothers could have been reluctant to seek a baptism that would result in the illegitimacy of their child becoming a matter of parochial record. If Anna Polack was illegitimate, it is possible that she was born and baptised outside the County. Frances Polack died on 28th June 1828, and is buried in St. Gluvias churchyard.[146] In her will (which was not proved in the West Country, at Exeter, but at Canterbury, a measure which may reflect a desire for privacy and discretion) Frances Polack, "spinster", left "one moiety or half part of all my money, securities for money, Goods, Chattels and Effects" to her "dear sister, Sarah" (also recorded as "spinster"), and, in trust, the other half, together with "all my wearing apparel, Watches, Trinkets and silver coins…" to Anna Banks, the wife of William Banks of Penryn…Mariner". Anna's name appears throughout the document, but without any term of endearment or indication of her relationship to Frances. This might suggest, but does not establish, a personal connection as a daughter (or niece) and, if such was the case, the document would suggest that any hint of illegitimacy was suppressed, and remained unacknowledged. It is also possible that this Anna Polack was related to the (Penzance) Isaac Pollock of 1825, or she may have been from a London Polack family. Alternatively, she may, in fact, have been one of the daughters of Joshua and Prudence *Pollock* of Rame. Anna Polack and William Banks had two children, Frances Anna (1822-1889) and Edward (1827-1898). Anna Polack, died sometime before 1841, possibly in childbirth, in that the Census for Penryn of that year records that William Banks (50) was living at Broad Street with a Sophia Banks (30) his third wife, Sophia Ann Reece of London, and step mother to Frances Anna (15). Also living in the house was Frances Polack's sister, Sarah, age 75. Sarah Polack was recorded as "Independent", a feature that reflects the legacy from her sister.[147]

Isaac Pollack II, likely of Penryn (Penzance Congregational Records 1825). His offering paid to the congregation may reflect temporary residence and membership in Penzance. His relation to Isaac Polack I, as a son or nephew, is possible, but not certain.

Levy Barnes: Pawnbroker, (Ba. 1788; Un. 1791). He may have been Jewish.

Solomon Solomon: Tailor, Slopseller and Hardwaremen (1800: Insurance Policy).[148]
This is likely to be the Solomon Solomon (1764-1819) son of Israel Solomon (d. 1802). He was married to Betsy (Elizabeth) Levy (1757-1832), daughter of the Barnet Levy, above. Solomon Solomon, who was in partnership with Lyon Joseph by 1802 (Insurance Policy),[149] later acted as a Navy Agent (see below). Lyon Joseph's maritime trade with the Iberian peninsula may have taken Solomon to Portugal, where he died, in Lisbon, in 1819. (For Lyon Joseph, see below).

S. Jacobs: Watch & Clockmaker (in Penzance, as Solomon Jacobs), (Br. *c.* 1800). He died c. 1803, and may have been related to the Jacob family of Falmouth and Redruth, possibly as a brother of Moses Jacob (d. 1807). See Penzance Trades.

Michael Isaac: Hawker and Dealer in Silver & Hardware (1802: Insurance Policy).[150]
It is possible that he was related to Isaac Isaac, Lazarus Isaac or William Issac (see below, and also Masonic records). There are references in the Falmouth Masonic

records to a "Brother Isaac" from 1751, which may refer to a member of this family.

Solomon Solomon: Navy Agent (1809-1819: Green 1989, pp. 150 & 212), and as S. Solomon, Broker, Bullion Office, Market Street (Trathen 1815).

Solomon Ezekiel: Tinman (Ho. 1811). Described as a Tin-Plate Worker and Grocer, his bankruptcy petition, following his imprisonment for debt at Bodmin, was reported in the *Exeter Flying Post* on 3rd August 1815.[151] From 1812, his house in Falmouth had been assessed at 5 shillings and his stock at 1s. 6d. for the purposes of the poor rate.[152] By 1813, he was also trading in Penzance, joining the Masonic Lodge there in 1814, but appears to have retained some business interest in Falmouth up to the time of his bankruptcy. He was originally from Newton Abbot in Devon, and settled in Penzance for the rest of his life. As noted, "tin-man" indicates a small-scale plate worker, but not a miner.

The Benjamin Ezekiel who was born in Falmouth *c.* 1809, may not have been Jewish. He later traded in Plymouth as a Confectioner (1871 census), and as a Tent & Marquee Builder (1881 census).[153] Neither of these trades were associated with Jews. His wife, Amelia, was from Redruth, and in the 1901 census for Plymouth, she was recorded, age 68, as a Nurse. Benjamin Ezekiel is not known to have been related to Solomon Ezekiel. A Benjamin Ezekiel (b. 1805) also traded in Plymouth in 1851 as a Confectioner. From his wife's (Priscilla's) family name, Holmes, it is also uncertain if this family was Jewish, even though one son was named Moses.[154]

Gabriel (George) Abrahams: Druggist (Ho. 1811), Money Broker, Church St. (Pg. 1823/4) and Naval Agent, Fish Strand (Trathen Fal. 1815; 1820; Pg. 1830); Coin & Bullion Merchant, Fish Strand (1820-1829: Insurance Policies).[155] Also listed for 1827-1834, and for 1828.[156] Gabriel Abrahams was born in Germany in 1763, and came to England about 1791. He was of Jewish descent but converted to Christianity soon after his arrival in England. On 31st March 1817 he gave evidence in relation to an unpaid loan at the trial of Robert Sawle Donnall at Launceston for the murder of his mother-in-law, Elizabeth Downing. He married Jane Lovely Symons in Falmouth Parish Church on 16th May 1819 and their three children were all baptised in the same Church. As one of the only two Money Agents in Falmouth he would have been an influential figure in the town.[157]

Lyon Joseph: Merchant (Ho. 1811). Lyon Joseph (1775-1825) was married to Judith Levy (1774-1846). He was President of the Hebrew Congregation.

Lyon (Lionel) Joseph (1826-1905), a grandson of the above was born in Falmouth. He married his second cousin Kate Joseph (1842-1912). Like his grandfather, he was a Shipping Merchant. By the time of the 1851 census he had moved to 25 Bull Street, Birmingham where his occupation was given as Commercial Traveller.

Jacob Levi: Watch & Clockmaker, later at Truro (Ho. 1811). He is not known to have been connected with the family of Barnet Levy of Falmouth or Israel Levy of Truro. Neither is it known if he was related to Samuel Levi, Jeweller, below, or the Benjamin Levi who was alleged to have received stolen silver from a Ruth Goodman in Falmouth in 1852.[158] It seems likely that Jacob Levi was of Jewish descent, but he was married to a local non-Jew, Elizabeth Carnarteon. Their children were all baptised in Truro. He is mentioned in the sections on the Truro Jewish cemetery and Trades (Truro).

Catherine (Kate or Kitty) Solomon: Merchant. Bankruptcy (*Exeter Flying Post* 20th August 1812).[159] A daughter of Moses Jacob of Redruth, she was married to Simon (Abraham Simeon) Solomon (-1825) a son of Israel Solomon (c.1727-1802). Both are buried in the Falmouth cemetery in 3:3 and 5:4. See Kitty Solomon, below.

Levi (y) Jacob(s): Watchmaker and Silversmith (1813: Insurance Policy).[160] Levy Jacob (1788-1824), a son of Moses Jacob of Redruth, had traded there as a dealer in mineral specimens,[161] an aspect of his business which he also pursued in Penzance, where he was living by 1823. He was married to Sophia Mordecai (1781-1853) of Exeter. Their children are thought to have been Eliezar (possibly Eliza, 1814-), Moses Levi (c.1815/17-1879) who moved to Birmingham, who, with his wife, Sarah (1825-) from Portsmouth, had eight children, Hannah (1819-1913), Phoebe (1823-1904) and (possibly) Henry (c.1825-). The latter was born in Penzance, and later, was a fellow lodger with Moses Samuel Jacob in Falmouth. This Henry Jacobs was a sailor, an occupation not associated with Jews. He has not previously been recognised as a son of Levi Jacobs, and he may not have been Jewish. However, if he was a member of this family, he may well have served on one of the merchant vessels that the Jacob family commissioned, or in which they may have had commercial interest.

Jacob Jacob & Co.: Pawnbroker, Cabinet Makers & Upholsterers, Market Street (Fal. 1815; Pg. 1823/4/30). Being a son of Moses Jacob of Redruth, Jacob Jacob (1774-1853) was also known as Moses Jacob Jacob (Jacob ben Moses), but should not be confused with his son of that name (1812-1860). Like his father before him, Jacob Jacob was also a Dealer in Mineral Specimens, and was recommended as a mineral dealer by J. A. Paris in 1816.[162] Also as (John) Jacob Jacob, below.

John Ralph: Navy Agent (1821-1824).[163] It is possible that *John* was an anglicised form of *Jacob*, but it is not certain that he was Jewish.

Abraham Joseph: Clothes Dealer, Pawnbroker and Watchmaker, Market St. (Ho. 1811; Fal. 1815; Pg. 1823/4/30; Br.1827). The brother of Lyon Joseph (1775-1825) above, and the father of Joseph Joseph (1802-1877) below. Abraham Joseph (-1827) was married to Hannah Levy (1769-1851). One of their children, Henry Joseph (1806-1881) married Amelia Jacob (1811-1891) daughter of Jacob Jacob (1774-1853) of Falmouth (later in Redruth and Camborne). Henry and Amelia Joseph settled in Penzance.

Lazarus Lawrence: Watchmaker and Slopseller; Abraham Simon Solomons: Painter & Milliner; T. (Thomas) Solomon: Man's Mercer & Tailor (Holden 1811). The bankruptcy of the first two men, as Merchants, was reported in the *Exeter Flying Post* 6th January 1814.[164] Lazarus Lawrence is to be identified with Moses Lazarus Lawrence, below, and is also likely to be the *Laurance*, watchmaker of Penzance (see Trades for that town, below). Watchmakers, like others with portable skills and wares, would often trade in more than one town. Thomas Solomon may not have been associated commercially with the other two men, and it is not known if he was Jewish, his forename not usually being associated with Jews. A Thomas Solomon, a Jewish convert to Christianity, traded in Penzance, and died there in 1793, being buried in the St. Mary's church cemetery. Another Thomas Solomon, traded in Truro in 1873.

P. Busser: Shoemaker (Trathen 1815). Uncertain.

Boaze: Butcher, High Street (Trathen 1815). Unlikely. As noted earlier, Boase or Boaz is an old Cornish name. Its earliest form occurs as Bores, from *bos-re*, "the dwelling by the ford". The name appears in the Camborne Parish Register as early as 1599, but was most common in Penzance and West Penwith.[165]

R. Osler: Grocer & Tea Dealer, High Street (Trathen 1815). Unlikely. The "B. Osler" who was a Secretary of the Falmouth Masonic Lodge in 1802, may be identical to or a relative of R. Osler. The surname occurs regularly in census records for Falmouth.

Judith Joseph: Earthenware Dealer, Market St. (Pg. 1823/4). This most likely Judith Rebecca (1768-1849), a daughter of Moses Jacob of Redruth. She was the wife of Moses Isaac Joseph (-1834) of Falmouth.

Kitty (Kate) Solomon: Milliner and Haberdasher, Market Street (Trathen 1815); Church St. (Pg. 1823/4). This is Kate Jacob (1772-1854), a daughter of Moses Jacob of Redruth. She was the wife of Simon Solomon (-1825), a son of Israel Solomon (-1802) of Falmouth. Both Simon and Kitty Solomon were artists, but Simon Solomon found it difficult to make a living from his paintings,[166] and the couple may have suffered hardship. After the death of her husband in 1825 she may have gone to Bristol to live with her sister, Elizabeth (Betsy) Solomon, who died there in 1832. Kitty Solomon may have remained in Bristol for some years, and she may be the "Mrs. Solomon" whose nieces went to live with her there, Amelia in 1841, and Phoeby in 1844.[167] Kitty Solomon is buried in Falmouth.

S. Lawrence: Clothes Dealer, Church St. (Pg. 1823), and **Moses Lazarus Lawrence**: Money Broker, Church St. (Pg. 1823/4 & 1830; Philp 1828; Rob. 1839). Lazarus Lawrence was married to Judith Moses, widow of Henry Joseph of St. Austell, who had died in 1803. There were no children of this second marriage. They appear in the 1841 census[168] at Church St. Lazarus, then aged 60 ("not born in county"), and Judith, aged 75. These ages appear to be approximate, in that her death was noted in the *West Briton* (1st December 1843) as "At Falmouth, on Wednesday last, Mrs. Lawrence, relict of the late Mr. Lazarus Lawrence, silver-smith of that town, age 82 years." The S. Lawrence, above, may have been a sister to Lazarus, or a child from a previous marriage. A "Brother J. (or I.) Lawrance is mentioned in the Falmouth Masonic records as early as 1758, although it is not known if this was a member of the family above. Variant spellings appear as *Lawrance* and *Laurance.* Lazarus Lawrence died in 1841, and is buried in the Penryn cemetery. If his marriage to Judith Moses was his second, the **Joseph Lawrance** of 1861 (below) may have been his son.

Samuel Harris: Printer, Stationer & Bookbinder; and **Samuel Harris**: Watch & Clockmaker. References to: High St. (Ho. 1811; Pg. 1823/4; Br. 1823). There were at least two men with this name trading in Falmouth. The first, above, the printer and stationer, married Mary Symons (a daughter of William Symons, an alderman of the borough of Grampound) at Probus in July 1804, subsequently advertising for a "journey-man bookbinder".[169] He was *not* Jewish.[170] He is noted here to avoid confusion with:-

Samuel Harris, who traded as a Watchmaker in Falmouth, also in High St. (1807: Insurance Policy,[171] and Trathan's History of 1815);[172] His family was Jewish. Samuel Harris (1754-1824) married Judith Solomon (1763-1839) of Falmouth, husband and wife being interred in the Jewish cemetery (3:2 & 4:7). Their son was the jeweller and watchmaker, Henry Harris of Truro.

Judith Harris: Dealer in Jewellery, Cutlery and Toys (1825: Insurance Policy).[173] This is the widow of Samuel Harris.

Joseph Joseph: Watch & Clockmaker, Market Strand. (Pg. 1823/4; Br. 1823). This may be **Joseph Joseph** (1802-1879), son of Moses Isaac Joseph (-1834). This Joseph Joseph later moved to Redruth, where he traded from at least 1823 until 1849. Married to Fanny Solomon of Plymouth, he moved there in 1849. His wife died in Plymouth in 1855, and sometime after 1861, Joseph Joseph moved to London, where he died in 1879. However, this may be **Joseph Joseph** (1802-1877), son of Abraham Joseph (-1828) of Falmouth (above). This Joseph Joseph married Phoebe Alexander of Plymouth. They eventually moved to Liverpool where they died (Phoebe in 1869, and Joseph in 1877). The first Joseph Joseph may have moved to Redruth by 1819.

Isaac Symons & Co. : China, Glass & Earthenware Dealers, Market St. (Pg. 1830); Bullion Dealer, Fish Strand (Rob. 1839), Church St. (1881 Census). Isaac Symons (b. 1796), son of Samuel Simons of Truro, was married to Rosetta Jacobs (b. 1800) of Penzance. They had 9 children: Hanna (b. 1823), Eliza (b. 1824), Julia (b. 1825), Solomon (b. 1827), Frederick (b. 1828), Walter (b. 1829), Sarah (b. 1835), Harriet (b. 1838) and Rebecca (b. 1840). Isaac Symons' name appears in the Penzance Congregational Minute Book (1819-1823) alongside an Alex (Alexander) Symons (1820-1824). They are not known to have been brothers, although Alex Symons may have been a son of Samuel Simons from a first marriage, or an uncle or cousin of Isaac Symons. The Mordecai Symons, below, is not known to have been related to Isaac or Alexander Symons. Isaac Symons may also have used the forename of his father, Samuel, and it is possible that he also traded in Penzance, at least before leaving for Falmouth. The Penzance Borough Ward Lists record a "House" for a Samuel Symons in Pendarves Road from 1835 to 1859, and in Leskinnick Terrace by 1871, but this man may not have been a Jew.

Samuel Levi: Jeweller, High Street (1841 Census). Note: see Jacob Levi, above, and Benjamin Levi, below.

Isaac Isaac & Co. : Clothes Dealers, High St. (Ludgate Hill). (Fal. 1815; Pg. 1830; Rob. 1839; 1841 Census). Isaac Isaac was born in 1786 (not in Cornwall), and was married to Judith (b. 1796). There were 5 children: Betza (b. 1821), Harriet (b. 1826), Abraham (b. 1828) who became a shoemaker, Amelia (b. 1829) and Sarah (b. 1832). The 1841 Census also lists a Lazarus Isaac (born *c.* 1816) as a Salesman (see below), who may have been connected with this family. A Rabbi Moses Isaac lived in Penzance from 1808, and a Lawrance Isaacs, who may have been related to Rabbi Moses, appears in the Penzance Masonic membership lists for 1815. It is not known if the Falmouth and Penzance *Isaac* families were related. Isaac Isaac of Falmouth also traded in the town as a shell dealer in 1844 (see below). He left Falmouth soon after, for Ireland, and his death there was noted by the *West Briton* (12th February 1847): "At Dublin, on the 21st *ult.*, Mr. Isaac Isaacs, merchant, late of Falmouth, aged 60 years."[174] There were Isaac families in Truro who were not Jewish.

Joseph Spasshatt and **Alexander Symons**: Wine & Spirit Merchants (Pg. 1830). Uncertain. An Alex(ander) Simmons, Spirit Merchant, was a member of the Penzance Masonic Lodge in 1821, and may have traded there, in that an Alex. Symons also appears in the Penzance Congregational Minute Book (1820-1824). He is likely to be identified with the above. It is not certain that Spasshatt was Jewish, nor if Alex. Symons was related to the Simons family of Truro and Falmouth (see Isaac Symons, above) or to Mordecai Symons, below. In 1861 Spasshatt was trading in Penzance as a Watch and Clockmaker. It is possible that the Spershott of 1864, below, was a relative.

Sarah Abraham: Grocers & Tea Dealers, High St. (Fal. 1815; Pg. 1830).

Abraham Davidson: Watch & Clockmaker, High St. (Pg. 1830),[175] Clothier (1853). He was born in 1801, and married Rosetta. They had five children: Isaac (b. 1830), Eliza (b. 1832), Henry (b. 1834), Arabella (b. 1836) and (possibly) Thomas (b.1839-40). A John Davidson traded as a clockmaker on Ludgate Hill, Falmouth in 1847, but he is not known to have been related to Abraham Davidson. Along with a Solomon Johnson, Abraham and Isaac Davidson (presumably brothers) are recorded as new members of the Penzance Congregation in 1825. They signed their names as *Dawidson*. Their names do not appear for subsequent years, and it is not known if they joined the Falmouth Congregation at a later date. The Isaac Davidson of 1825 is not known to have traded in Falmouth, and may have gone to London, where his nephew, Isaac also lived *c*. 1850, trading as a Watchmaker. In 1853, at the Great Synagogue, Duke's Place, London, the latter married Amelia, daughter of Rabbi B.A. Simmons of Penzance (see Penzance marriages). Abraham Davidson is given as a Clothier on the marriage certificate of his son, Issac. It is possible that Abraham Davidson also moved to London to live. The 1851 Census for Hougham, Kent, lists a Thomas Davidson, age 11, born in Falmouth, as a pupil at the Sussex House School, run by the Rev. Raphael Isaac Cohen from Germany.[176] The school was presumably a boarding institution, and the census suggests that there were numerous Jewish pupils. Another Cornish Jewish pupil at the school at this time, was Samuel (age 13) son of Moses Jacob Jacob of Falmouth. Samuel Jacob was to return to Falmouth. Grace Davidson (below) was also from Kent, and may have been related to Thomas Davidson.

Henry and **Barnett Joseph**: Watch & Clockmakers, Jewellers & Silversmiths, Market St. (Pg. 1830). These are two sons of Abraham Joseph (-1828) and Hannah Levy (1769-1851). Henry Joseph (1806-1881) married Amelia Jacob (1811-1891), daughter of Jacob Jacob (1774-1853) of Falmouth, and Barnet married a Fanny Moses of Bristol.

Mordecai Symons (1841): although his trade is not given, his nickname of "Mordi" suggests that he was well known in the town. He summoned a complaint before the Falmouth magistrates that Lazarus Issacs and Henry Moses had recently "committed a violent assault" against him. Symons was "charged by his brethren with having taken somewhat more than his share in some business he was employed to negotiate, in denying which, he used very provoking and threatening language, amounting, in fact, to a challenge... The magistrates, however, were so satisfied that the parties were equally culpable, that they fined the defendants one shilling each only and costs": (*West Briton,* 10th December 1841).[177] Mordecai Symons is not known to have been related to the Simons family of Truro, nor to Alexander Symons, above.

John Abraham, Corn Meeler, born in Cornwall, and John Solomon, Chemist, who was from outside the County (both 1841 census) are unlikely to have been Jewish. The former lived in Higher Market Street, and had a son, Joseph Abraham, who worked for a local butcher who traded in Lower Market Street.

Samuel "Joyful" Lazarus. He was issued with a hawker's licence for one year (as a foot trader only) in Falmouth on 1st August 1843. He was from Exeter, where he is recorded in the Hebrew Congregational Minute Book for 1818, and as marrying there in 1846. His forename, "Joyful", may well refer to his disposition, or may simply be a translation of the Hebrew *Simcha*, or a derivative. Various *Lazarus* households appear in Census records, although the name itself, as Samuel Joyful Lazarus, does not appear. He may have used another forename, or have been absent, as an itinerant hawker, at the time of the census. He does appear as a householder in Paragon Place (Exeter) on the Voters' Register in 1849. Some years earlier, on 23rd November 1842, an Isaac Lazarus of 4, Paragon Place, Exeter, married an Eliza Jacobs in Plymouth. This Isaac Lazarus was a son of Eleazar and Esther Lazarus of Exeter, and it would seem likely that Samuel Lazarus was a member of this family. Samuel Joyful Lazarus, may have come to the West Country from London or its environs. The original of the hawker's licence is held in the Jewish Museum, London, where it is filed under "Abraham Samuel of Reading". The latter name may refer to S. J. Lazarus himself. Alternatively, Abraham Samuel may have been a Jewish merchant-tradesman, who had employed S. J. Lazarus as his journeyman.[178]

Garson Elias: Itinerant Pedlar. A gold ring was stolen from him (*Royal Cornwall Gazette*, 12th April 1844).[179] *Garson* may be a variant of *Gershon*. See also 1851, below.

John (Jacob) Jacob: Clothier to "Nobility, Gentry & Clergy", Bells Court. (Pg. 1844; Sl. 1852-3; 1841 & 1851 Census). As noted above, he had also been a dealer in Mineral Specimens (*c.* 1816). (Moses) Jacob Jacob (1774-1853) was a son of Moses Jacob and Sarah Moses. He had been born in Redruth in 1774, and was married to Sarah Kate (Kitty) Simons (1778-1846).[180] The 1851 Census records Jacob Jacob as a Retired Pawnbroker, living with his unmarried daughter, Esther (41) and his unmarried sister, Amelia (65) who acted as the family's housekeeper. Jacob and Sarah's daughter, Rebecca (1824-1906) had married Morris Hart Harris (1821-1913), son of Henry Harris (-1872) of Truro, and at the time of the 1851 census, she was visiting her father, with her two children, Sarah (3) and Bessy (8 months).[181] Apart from his daughters, Esther and Rebecca, Jacob Jacob and Sarah Kate Simons had eight other children, four of whom (Simon, Phoebe, Henry and Alexander) died young. Betsy (1822-1838) remained unmarried, Moses Jacob (1812-1860) married Frances Emanuel (1812-1875) of Portsea, and established a thriving business in Falmouth, Amelia (1811-1891) married Henry Joseph (1806-1881) of Penzance, and Isaac (1820-1888) married a Sophia Lazarus (1828-), and moved to South Wales and, later, to London. The death of Sarah Jacob was recorded by the *West Briton* on 4th December 1846: "At Falmouth, on Tuesday last, the wife of Mr. J. Jacobs, a retired Hebrew tradesman, aged 69 years." Jacob Jacob's death was recorded by the *West Briton* on Friday 11th February 1853: "At his residence, Bell's Square, Falmouth, on the 3rd instant - Jacob Jacob Esq. President of the Hebrew Congregation - 78 years."[182]

Moss Jacob Jacob (s): Fancy Repositories, Clothes Dealer & Pawnbroker, 21 Market St. (Pg. 1844; 1851 Census & 1851 [Ecclesiastical] Census; Sl. 1852-3). Moses Joseph (b. 1826, Devonport) resident Shop Assistant: (1851 Census). Moss (Moses) Jacob Jacob (1812-1860) had been born in Camborne. He was married to Frances Emanuel, who was born in Portsmouth in 1812. They had 6 children: Samuel (b. 1838), Hannah (Anne, or Annie, b. 1839), Michael (b. 1840), Alexander (b. 1841), Lawrence (b. 1843) and Sara Kate (b. 1849), all of whom appear in the 1851 Census for Falmouth. This same census records Moses (Jacob) Jacob as a Pawnbroker and Tailor employing five women and three men, together with a shop assistant, Moses Joseph (25) from Devonport. His unmarried cousin, Moses Samuel Jacob (1815-58) worked for Moss Jacob Jacob as a Clerk. Moss Jacob Jacob had several other business interests in Falmouth, which traded collectively under his name, and even after his death in 1860. (See below). Several of Moses Jacob Jacob's children eventually moved to London.

Frances Jacob: Outfitter & Woolen, Jeweller Arwenack St. (1861 Census).[183] This is the business above, continued by Moss Jacob Jacob's widow, which had moved to Arwenack Street by 1854. In 1861, the business employed 8 men and 6 women, including three of Frances' children, Annie, Michael and Alexander. Of her children, Samuel (23) was recorded as a Merchant, and Annie (Anna, then 21), Michael (20) and Alexander (19) as working in the outfitting business. The two other children were Lawrence (17) and Sarah (Kate or Kitty, then 11). Unusually for his age, Lawrence is given as a Scholar, suggesting that the family could afford to continue his education, most likely privately. The oldest son, Samuel, had, in fact, been sent to a Jewish private boarding school for boys (mentioned earlier), Sussex House, in Dover, Kent, run by the Rev.Raphael Isaac Cohen (46) from Germany, who was married to Bloom (Bluma, then 52) who had been born in Dover. She may have lived in Germany, in that Raphael Cohen's daughter, Bertha (21), was born in Hamburg (1851 Census). The school employed two teachers, one from Hamburg, and there were over fifty pupils.[184] Together with Samuel Jacob was another boy from Falmouth, Thomas Davidson. The latter is likely to have been related to the Abraham and Isaac Davidson who are mentioned in the Penzance Minute Book in 1824 and 1825, but who moved to Falmouth.The English pupils were drawn mainly from London and Manchester, but there were also boys from Dublin, Gibraltar, Africa, Sydney, Rome and Paris. Like Falmouth, Dover was a prosperous trading and commercial port as well as a banking centre. At about the time that Samuel Jacob was a boarder at the Sussex House school, Dover's synagogue had an attendance of about 60 at worship, and the town had a number of Jewish traders (Post Office Directory for Kent 1855). By 1871, Frances Jacob had moved from Falmouth to Paddington, London, where, at 60, she is recorded as a Retired Merchant, and her three sons as Merchants. Her son, Samuel, had remained in Falmouth, although he was to leave it, for London, by 1879. Frances Jacob died in 1875.

Moses Jacob: Pawnbroker, Hardware Shop, Market St. (Rob. 1839; Pg. 1844; Wi. 1847). This is Moses Jacob Jacob's cousin, **Moses Samuel Jacob** (1815-1858). He was unmarried, and worked for his cousin, M. J. Jacob. Moses Samuel Jacob was the son of Samuel Jacob (1778-1860) who had settled in Penzance, his son having been born in Hayle. In the 1851 Census for Falmouth, Moses S. Jacob, Outfitter, then 35, was a lodger at the house of the Gentile Vigurs family, who were Mariners and Shipwrights. Also lodging there was a Henry Jacob (26) a Sailor, who had been born in Penzance. The fact that both men bore the same surname might suggest a family connection, but none is known. It is more likely that their coincidental residence at the Vigurs' home as lodgers, reflects the fact that both men were unmarried.

Jonas Heilbron: Jeweller, High Street (1846: Penzance Marriage Registers). He the son of an Isaac Heilbron, a Merchant. The latter is not certain to have traded in Falmouth. Jonas Heilbron married Phoebe, daughter of Rabbi B. A. Simmons, in Penzance in August 1846.

Lewis Falkson: Jeweller, Optician, Watch & Clockmaker, High St. (Ludgate Hill). (Rob. 1839; Pg. 1844; Wi. 1847; Sl. 1852-3; Br. 1852). He was born in London in *c*.1787 and later married Esther, born in Truro *c*.1791 (census records from 1841 vary in their ages). The 1841 Census shows a Mary Palmer living with the Falksons. She was probably a servant or shop assistant. In 1842, Lewis Falkson of Falmouth, "a respectable jew of that town... was sworn in the manner of his people" as a witness at two separate trials of Ann Stevenson of Truro who was accused in the first case of stealing a large number of silver (and other) items from William Davey of Redruth, and, in the second case, of "having feloniously received" certain "articles of plate", also stolen from Davey. The latter had advertised details of the theft of the various items by posting hand-bills in the locality. The accused had come into the shop of "the Jew at Falmouth", who, being suspicious of the items, detained her, and after checking the bills, consulted the town jailer, who advised him to find a constable, which he did. At the first trial (where she was found not guilty) "Mr. Treweeke, the chairman, complimented Mr. Falkson on the judicious and correct manner in which he had acted in the case". At the second trial, Ann Stevenson was found guilty by the jury. Lewis Falkson died of dysentery, a victim of the 1852 cholera epidemic. His headstone in the Penryn Jewish cemetery gives his age as 65 (i.e. born 1787) while the 1851 census gives his age as 61 (i.e. born 1790). In the 1851 census, Esther's age is given as 61 (i.e. born 1790), while in the 1861 census, by then a widow (given as *Hesther Faulkenson*) she is given as 65 (i.e. born 1796). In 1861 she was still recorded as living at High Street, together with Kitty Levey (66) an unmarried domestic servant born in Truro. The latter was Catherine Levy (1791-1864), a daughter of Israel Levy (-1823) and Hannah Moses (1758-1841) of Truro. Esther Falkson was a contemporary of Israel Levy's other daughters, Julia (1792-) and Judith (c.1793-). Esther Falkson died in 1863, and is buried in the Penryn cemetery. Her headstone does not give her age, but she is named as Esther, daughter of *Samuel.* This suggests that she was a daughter either of Samuel Simons (1740-1832) and Rosa (Ann) Moses (1757-1838) of Truro, or of Samuel Harris (1757-1824) and Judith Solomon (1763-1839) of Truro. If the latter, she would have been a sister of Henry Harris (1787-1872), who later moved to London. After Esther's death, Catherine Levy went to live with relatives in Penzance, where she was buried in July 1864.

Jacob Schwerer: Jeweller, Watch & Clockmaker, Market St. (Pg. 1844; Br. 1844). The Jewish Schwerer family were from Germany. A Jacob Schwerer, likely to be the grandfather of the above, was in Cornwall at least by 1786 (see Falmouth Masonic records). Jacob Schwerer was unmarried. He traded both in his own name, and in partnership with the non-Jewish Beringer family, also German, in various Cornish towns (see below). Schwerer's family was related through marriage to Beringer's, and the latter was also related to Joseph Pfaff (1871, below).

Lazarus Isaac: Salesman. High Street. (1841 Census). See Isaac Isaac, above.

Isaac Isaac: Shell Dealer. (Pg. 1844). Likely the same as Isaac Isaac, above. Less lucrative than dealing in mineralogical specimens, shell dealing could be a reasonably profitable trade, and the collection of shells, especially those of an exotic appearance and origin was a popular activity.

Beringer & Schwerer: Watch & Clockmakers. Market St. (Rob. 1839; Wi. 1847; Br. 1847). As noted earlier, this business partnership became located in several Cornish towns. Both families were from Germany: the Beringer[185] family, from the Black Forest, was not Jewish; the Schwerer family was Jewish. The Beringer family traded both in its sole name and in partnership with Schwerer. A Joseph Beringer traded in Meneage Street, Helston (1844) and a John Beringer at the same location in 1847. In Penzance, a John Beringer traded in Alverton Street (1844) and a Fidelis Beringer in the Market Place in 1864. Joseph Beringer & Sons were established in Falmouth by 1873.

At the Falmouth Quarter Sessions (Report in the *West Briton*, Friday 12th 1849): "an indictment against a girl called Tucker, for defrauding her master, **Mr. Yager**, a German Jew, by having booked beer, &c., instead of paying for it, and keeping the money. The evidence, however, was defective, and she was acquitted".[186] "Mr. Yager" can be identified with **Sigmund Yager** from Devon, who had originated from Wiesbaden. It is likely that he had taken up temporary residence in the town. The girl was most likely from Falmouth, and, presumably, worked for him as an assistant. Yager was married to Trephina Levi (*c*.1827-), who, in the 1841 census for Plymouth appears (age 15) as a daughter of John Levi (originally from Portsmouth) and his wife, Elizabeth Levi. In his (1972) survey of the Hoe cemetery, Susser gives Trephina as a daughter of Kitty Levi, wife of Phineas Levi, a silversmith of Devonport, who were also from Portsmouth. It seems likely that John Levi may have been the brother of Phineas, and that Traphina was his niece, resident at his home at the time of the census. In 1851 Yager and his wife, Trephinia, who had been born in Devonport, were in Exeter, and the census records Yager as a Jeweller. By 1861, and at least until 1871, he was living in Plymouth with a large family. He was a travelling hawker and dealer. Trephina Levi's sister, Julia, married Edward Basch (see below).

Grace Davidson: Milliner. 146 Porham St. (1851 Census). She was from Kent. She may have been related to Abraham and Thomas Davidson, above. The latter was also from Kent.

Morris Aarons and **A. G. De (Da) Costa**: Market Strand, Travellers (1851 Census). Both were from London. They were of a similar age, 34 and 33, and were, presumably, travelling together. It is likely that both were of Sephardic origin.

Benjamin Levi, "a jew and dealer in jewellery" was called as a witness in the trial of a Ruth Goodman who, in October 1852, stood accused of stealing "two pieces of silver, the property of Mr. Selley of the Green Bank Hotel, Falmouth". Levi had bought the two items from her at her home. "He saw there was a name on the silver, but said he did not spell it. She told him she had had the silver for some time lying by." Levi sold the items that "afternoon to Mr. John Johns, a jeweller of Falmouth", but he became suspicious of the transaction, and alerted the police. Ruth Goodman (who is not known to have been Jewish, although Jews of that name from South Wales married Cornish Jews) was acquitted for lack of evidence, and Levi, who was suspected of dishonesty as knowingly receiving goods which he should have realised might well have been stolen, was reprimanded by the court, and was told that "he had improperly bought the silver, which had a name on it and having given only tenpence for what was worth half-a-crown".[187]

Samuel Herman: Rabbi of Hebrew Congregation. (res.) 51 Killigrew Street (1851 Census) With Samuel Herman (49) the census lists his wife, Frances (51) from Neustadt, their son, Abraham (23) a bookbinder (in 1852, Slater[188] gives him as the incumbent Rabbi, and his father, Samuel as "clergy"), and daughters Rose (20) and Phoebe (10). Abraham and Rose were born in Konin, and Phoebe in Babiak. Both places were known as "Russian Poland".

Simeon Silverstone: Stationary Traveller (25); 51 Killigrew St. (from Cracow, Poland; resident with the Herman family, above, likewise from Poland; 1851 Census). He may have been related to the large family of Israel Silverstone, a Watchmaker and Jeweller, and his wife, Paulina, of Exeter, who were also from Poland (1841, 1851 & 1861 Census). A Lazarus and Hannah Silverstone lived in Plymouth (1841 Census). The former, a General Dealer, is given as "Foreign", and the latter (a Dealer in Shells and Curiosities) had been born in Redruth in the 1790s (1851 & 1861 Census). She may have been a daughter of one of the earliest Jewish traders there, such as Emanuel Cohen, or of itinerant peddlers. Hannah's daughters were Sarah and Rachel (another may have been Miriam) and they are given as "Joseph", suggesting that Hannah was a widow when she married Lazarus Silverstone. Her first husband may have been a member of the extensive Joseph family of Plymouth. Much later, the family of Myer Silverstone, a Tailor, his wife, Esther, and an Abraham and Rebecca Silverstone, together with others (Leo, Pauline and Sarah) appear either in the Plymouth Congregational Marriage Register or in the Gifford Place Burial Records. The inclusion of photographs of an older Mr. S. Silverstone and his wife (forename not given) in the Jacob Archive, could suggest some familial or commercial connection between Simeon Silverstone and the Jacob Family of Falmouth.

Soloman Sammons: (Solomon Simmons) Pedlar (age 73), Lodging at 209 Fish Strand (1851 Census). He may have been a relative of either Samuel (Solomon) Simons (1742-1832), or of Harman Semmens, both of Truro.

Moses Joseph: the 1851 census records him, then 25, as an assistant at the shop of Moses Jacob Jacob, below. Joseph was from Devonport, and he may be the same as the Moses Joseph who worked as an assistant (shopboy) for Joseph Marks, a silversmith in Exeter (1841 census).[189]

Morris Aarons (34 and unmarried) and **A. G. Da Costa** (33 and married) both appear in the 1851 census at the Market Strand Inn as travellers from London.

Lazarus Hymen (56) a Jeweller, and **Kirshen Elias** (60), likely the pedlar, Garshon Elias of 1844, above, a "Blacking" (boot polish) Maker, appear as lodgers in the 1851 census. Both men were from Poland, but Hymen is also recorded a British Subject. Lazarus Hymen was trading in Penzance in 1856, as a Jeweller and Furrier. *Hyman* may well be a variant of *Herman*, and he may have been related to the family of Rabbi Samuel Herman of Falmouth, also from Poland, several of whose members later became furriers. Elias appears again in the 1861 census (see below).

Rose Cohen: Pedlar's wife, 14 Killigrew St. (1851 Census). She is listed as married, rather than widowed, and as the head of household. Her husband was an itinerant pedlar, only loosely based in Falmouth, and his name does not appear, but he may have been the **Harris Cohen** who appears as living in Penzance in Adelaide Street in 1835 (Penzance Borough Ward Lists: see below). Rose had been born in 1804 in Falmouth, but had lived in Penzance at some point. There were 4 children: Hannah (b. 1837 in Penzance), who was a milliner's apprentice, Sarah (b. 1838 also in Penzance), Phoebe (b. 1839 in Falmouth) and Josiah (b. 1841 in Plymouth). It is possible that this family was related to Emanuel Cohen (1766-1849) of Redruth.

Joseph Abraham: Sugar Boiler, Fish Strand. At the time of the 1861 Census, he lived with George and Alice H. Lemon of Scotland, but it is not certain if they, or Joseph Abraham were Jewish. Joseph Abraham had been born in 1837 in Penryn and had married Isabella Lemon (b. Penryn, 1840) who was a dressmaker. There were two children: John (b. 1859, in Penryn) and William (b. 1860, in Falmouth). There may have been a connection with Josiah Abraham (above 1751) and John Abraham and Sam Abrahams (below).

Gershon Elias: In the 1861 census, his surname has been read as **Giles**. This may be a misreading of a partially decipherable entry, but it is possible that he had adopted an anglicised form of his name. As before he is unmarried, now 65, a Blacking Manufacturer, a British Subject originally from Poland, living in the High Street area.

Zelig Harris: The 1861 census records him as a Jew, unmarried (age 48) a Licensed Hawker from Poland. He was a boarder at the "Duke of Kent" in the Market Strand. He was trading in Truro in 1841. His name, in 1861, has been read as *Zaliff*, but by 1871, he was in Penzance, where he is given as *Zelig*.

Kitty Levey: In 1861 she was an unmarried domestic servant (age 66) at the home of a Hesther Faulkenson (65) a retired jeweller's widow. Both women were from Truro, and it is possible that Hesther Faulkenson was also Jewish. The census record would suggest that her late husband had been a jeweller in London. Kitty Lev(e)y was a daughter of Israel Levy (-1823) and Hannah Moses (1758-1841) of Truro. It has been noted that she died in Penzance in 1864, where she is buried in the area of the cemetery reserved for the poor. This is itself would indicate why she worked in Falmouth as a servant.

Nathan Vos: Ships' Chandler, Arwenack St. (1861 Census); Grocer & Ship Chandler (Warn 1864); Innkeeper of the Marine Hotel (1871 Census). He had been born in Holland in 1833, and he died in 1913, his burial being the last in the Falmouth Jewish cemetery. He was married to Mary Ann (1841-1914) who had been born in Falmouth, and was not Jewish. They had three children: Frederick (b. 1868, in Shropshire), Hermann, also known as Henry (b. 1870) and Rosalie (b. 1873). Mary Ann Vos also ran a public house, the Greyhound (Kelly, 1883). Nathan Vos was a Freemason. His original trade was that of an optician, but it is not known if he traded as such in Falmouth. He was related to the von Bosch family (below).

Morries (Morrice or Morris) Marks: (1861) Minister of Hebrews (34) from Prussia, and a British Subject. He was living at the High Street with his wife, Jebbeth (30) and their three children, Charlotte (9), Willy (5) and Lena (1).

Joseph Lawrance: (1861) a Shoemaker (age 37), living at Synagogue House, who had been born in Falmouth. As noted, he may have been a son of (Moses) Lazarus Lawrence (above), but it is not certain that he was Jewish. Living with Joseph Lawrance was his wife, Eliza Jane (35) and their children, Eliza Jane (7), Emma (5), Angelina (2) and Anna Maria (5 months). With the exception of Anna, the forenames of the children do not suggest that this was a Jewish family, and the other 21 residents of Synagogue House (which was attached to and not part of the synagogue itself) were not Jews.

William Isaac(s): Carver & Turner, Wellington Terrace. (Wa. 1864). He was born in 1830 in Truro, and was married to Susan (b. 1837 in Falmouth). Their son Frederick was born in 1860 (1861 Census), and he was still trading in Falmouth in 1871. Uncertain. It is not known if he was related to Isaac Isaac, Lazarus Isaac or Michael Isaac (above).

Samuel Jacob: Jeweller & Silversmith, Market St. (Wa. 1864). "The entrance to the Royal Hotel was profusely decorated with evergreens; and Mr. Jacobs (*sic*), jeweller displayed a large transparency of the Prince of Wales's plume and the Royal Standard. Mrs. Jacobs displayed a large transparency of the Prince of Wales's plumes, and motto 'Ich Dien'": describing the celebrations at the opening of the railway line to Falmouth).[190] After his father, Moses Jacob Jacob, died in 1860, Samuel Jacob (1838-1913) not only traded under his own name (as above), but also continued the *Moss Jacob Jacob* name with separate Jewellery, Tailoring and Money Exchange branches.

"S. Jacob, Jeweller, &c. Having just finished Taking Stock, and being desirous of reducing the same, will offer at wholesale prices, Gold, Pins, Studs, Sleeve Links, Alberts, Pencil Cases, ladies' and Gentlemen's Finger Rings, Seals, Keys, Masonic Jewels, Brooches, Ear-rings, Lockets, Necklets, Chains, Charms, Hooks, Swivels, Split Rings, Thimbles, Crosses, Watches, Ornaments in Glass and Bronze, Clocks,

Time-Pieces, Plated and Silver Spoons, Forks, Tea Scoops, Snuff Boxes, Cruet Tops, Pickle Prongs, Butter Knives, Cream and Sauce Ladles, Vinaigrettes, Scent Bottles, Aneroids, Spy Glasses, Serpentine, Cruets, Cake Baskets, Violin Material, Musical Boxes, Concertinas, Accordeons, and a Variety of other Articles. Several DIAMOND RINGS, great bargains." The Falmouth Packet, 29th May 1875)[190a].

Samuel Jacob was the last President of the Hebrew Congregation, and was married to Henrietta Isaacs (1837-1904) of Salford, Lancashire. The 1871 Census for Falmouth shows him at Arwennack Street, trading as an Outfitter & Jeweller, together with his wife, Henrietta (Isaacs, 39, from Salford), and his children, Frances (Francetta) Esther (6), John Moss (Moses, 5), Florence Maud (3), and Ernest Arthur (1). Also resident was Henrietta's mother, Sarah Frances Isaac (71). Two further children, Marie (1872-) and Andrew George (1874-1900) were born in Falmouth. Of the latter, who died in Exeter, *Andrew* is not a name often associated with Jews, and it may have been a variant of Alexander, his uncle's name. ("Andrew Jacobs" has been identified, incorrectly,[191] as the Secretary, that is, President of the Falmouth Congregation at the time of the Ecclesiastical Census of 31st March 1851. The census return for Falmouth was completed, with remarks on the recent decrease in the numbers of Jews in the town following the cessation of the "foreign packet establishment", and signed by his grandfather, Jacob Jacob, 1774-1853, as *J. Jacob*). Around 1880, after closing the synagogue, and taking its remaining artefacts, and, presumably its Minute Book and congregational records with him, Samuel Jacob moved to London, living in Hampstead. The 1891 census records him there, as a Merchant, with his son, John, a Silversmith, and his daughter, Florence Maud, an Engraver, and two other daughters as Purcers (that is "piercers") in gold and silver, the whole family being employed in their father's business as a Manufacturing Silversmith by 1901.[192] Samuel Jacob eventually donated some of the more valuable silver artefacts to the Hampstead Synagogue, and the Torah Scrolls and other religious texts to the Royal Cornwall Museum in Truro.

Moses Jacob Jacob: Pawnbroker and Tailor, Market Street (1851 census); Tailor, Watch & Clockmaker, Dealer & Pawnbroker, 19-21 Arwenack St. (Br. 1854; Po. 1862). Tailor & Outfitter, Jeweller & Silversmith, Foreign Money & Exchange Office (Wa. 1864). In 1854 Moses Jacob Jacob (1812-1860), who had been born in Camborne, ran this business himself, but after his death, it was eventually relocated and run by his son, Samuel Jacob and other family members, with the name *Moss J. Jacob* being retained (and possibly transferred to other outlets). In the Post Office Directory of 1873 the business is called "Moss Jacob". A contemporaneous trade card[193] for "Moss J. Jacob, Watch Maker, Jeweller &c" also advertises "Musical Instrument & Photographic Establishment" with "Foreign Monies Exchanged". The card carries the money exchange facility in several foreign languages, a reminder that this particular trade required the ability to communicate effectively with foreign visitors, and it has been noted that Jewish migrants from the continent were often multilingual. The various Jacob entries above indicate the extent to which the family had diversified its commercial interests in Falmouth. Moses Jacob Jacob, like other men of the Jacob family, was a Freemason, and a member of the Falmouth Lodge.

Samuel Marks: Auctioneer & Commission Agent. Furniture, Glass showroom; Upholstery & French Polishing, Market St. (Wa. 1864). Uncertain. The surname, *Marks*, was common among Cornish Gentiles. A Marks family, some of whom were weavers and basket makers, had long been settled in Penzance.

Sam Abrahams (Fisher & Abrahams): Furniture, Pictures & Looking-glasses, 10 High St. (K. 1889).

Thomas Henry Moses: Hawker/Broker, Porham Lane (1851 Census), Allen's Yard (1861 Census); with Thomas King Moses, as Shopkeepers, and Philip Henry Moses, Basket-maker, all of 46 Smithwick Hill (1871 census and K. 1889). The family may have been of Jewish descent. The marriage of Thomas Henry Moses (born 1804, in Falmouth) to a non-Jew, Johanna Bristo of Hayle, at Budock Parish Church on 11th August 1840, has already been noted. The eldest son Philip (above) was born in 1842, and was blind. There is only one baptism in the Falmouth Parish Church Register of Elizabeth Ann Moses on 13th November 1844. She became a dressmaker. It would seem that the family were Christians. There were 5 other children: John Alexander (b. 1849), a shoemaker, Thomas King (b. 1851), Joseph (b. 1853), William Adolophus (b. 1855) and Richard (b. 1857). In 1871, Henry Moses (age 64) then a widower, and his son, Richard (15) appear as Pedlars in Market Street. They may well have been in reduced circumstances, and the street housed several brothels. In one of these, as a lodger, was a John Moses (24) Ostler, who had been born in Falmouth. It is not clear if he is to be identified with John Alexander Moses, above.

Barnet (Nielsen) Falk (Barnes Falck) has sometimes been taken for a Jewish resident of Falmouth. He is listed in the Trade Directories as a Sailmaker (Un. 1799) and a Ship Owner (Fal. 1815).The Nicholas Falck who was a merchant in Falmouth in 1789 may have been a relative.[194] Both *Barnet* (or *Barnett*) and *Falk* (or *Falck* and *Falkson*) are familiar Jewish names from this period, but these were also common Gentile names.

Isaiah (Joshua) Falk Valentine, a money changer and *shochet* from Plymouth, who had originally come from Breslau, was murdered in Fowey in late November 1811.[195] Valentine acted as a money agent for the Joseph family of Plymouth, who, in turn acted for the London bankers, Goldsmid, who bought golden guineas for the Government. He had apparently been enticed to bring £260 to Fowey by William Wyatt, landlord of the Rose and Crown Inn, who murdered him, and dropped his body into the harbour dock . Valentine's body was later found in the river, and taken to Plymouth for burial. Wyatt was convicted of his murder and hanged publicly at Bodmin.[196] Isaiah Falk's headstone in the Plymouth Hoe cemetery reads: "Joshua Falk, son of the late Isaac from Breslau. He was slain in the place of Fowey by the uncircumcised and impure (wicked) man Wyatt, and drowned in the waters. 14 Kislev 5572, and buried on the 17th thereof."[197] Isaiah Falk Valentine may have been related to Martin Valentine, described as a "Cheap John" of the "travelling pack-man fraternity", who died at the Town Arms public house in Camelford in June 1844 and whose body was also taken for burial at the Jewish cemetery in Plymouth, although his headstone has not survived.[198] Neither Valentine nor Martin Falk are known to have been related to the family of Barnet Nielsen Falk, which had come to England from Denmark, and, if they were of Jewish descent, had become Christians, members of the Falk family across five generations were married, baptised and buried in the Parish Church in Falmouth.[199] Some of the Falk family were members of a Trinitarian (Christian) Masonic Lodge. Barnet Falck was exalted to the Order of Knights' Templar on 12th June 1811 at Redruth, and was Master of the Falmouth Lodge in 1827.[200]

Nathaniel Schram: Dealer, Herbalist, Ludgate Hill (1841 Census): subsequently at Truro and Plymouth (1851 Census), and as a Hawker in Jewellery, in Penzance (1861). He was born in the Hague, Netherlands in 1804. His wife, Anna, was born in Gwennap near Redruth in 1816. Three of his five children bore common Jewish forenames: Jacob (b. Falmouth 1842), Henrietta (b. Truro 1845) and Abraham (b. Plymouth 1851).[201] There were two other children: Angelina (b. Truro 1843) and Marianna (or Mary, b. Plymouth 1849). The hamlet of Gwennap might suggest that Anna Schram was from a non-Jewish family (and perhaps she, or Henrietta, did convert upon or after marriage). However, some Jewish pedlars would have found it to their advantage to live outside the main towns (where competition for customers was much greater) and much business was to be derived from the isolated country areas, cut off from the urban shops. Even town-based hawkers travelled into the countryside for much of their business (see Lyon Colman, St. Austell, below) and Gwennap was also well placed for accessing the towns of Redruth, Falmouth and Helston. A Levi family can be connected with Gwennap, in that a Winifred Levi married a William Hugoe there in 1803. However, he was a non-Jew, as his bride may have been, and it is not known if Anna Schram was connected with the family of Winifred Levi. It is not certain that Anna Schram was Jewish, but subsequent marriages and burials of members of the Schram family either suggest or confirm eventual Jewish status. Nathaniel and Anna Schram's daughter, Henrietta married a Jew, Mark Jacobs of Plymouth around 1863-1864. The Schram family were resident in Plymouth at this time, but there is no record of their marriage in the Plymouth congregational register. Both, however, were buried in the Gifford Street Jewish cemetery, Henrietta in 1909 (age 63), and Mark in 1913 (age 74). Their daughter, Catherine (Kate) married Max Bischofswerder, a son of Rabbi Isaac Bischofswerder of Penzance, in the Plymouth synagogue in 1884. Both Catherine and Max were buried in the Jewish cemetery, Max in 1928 (age 69) and Catherine in 1954 (age 90). The Schram family were not long resident in Cornwall. By 1851 they were in Plymouth, at 20 Russell Street, but it would seem that Nathaniel travelled widely as a pedlar. It is possible that he is to be identified with the "Scrann" who appears in the Penzance Congregational records late in 1853. He is not listed in the 1861 census for Plymouth, although his wife (a tailoress) and family appear, at 27 Kinterbury Street, St. Andrews, Plymouth, with a further daughter, Rosina, 8 years of age. In 1871, Nathaniel is recorded as living as a boarder in Helston.[202] Nathaniel Schram's Dutch background would not suggest a connection with Albert Schramm from Germany, below.

Albert Schramm from Prussia, and **Charles Myers**, from Germany, both Bootmakers, and both aged about 30, appear in the 1871 census for Budock, near Falmouth. Schramn was a boarder in the Myers household. It is uncertain if either man was Jewish, and Myers' wife, Elizabeth, who is recorded as having been born at St. Gluvias, is likely to have been a Christian. The Myers' children, Joanna (5), Elizabeth (4) and Paulena (3) were all born at Feock. It is not known if Charles Myers was related to Israel Meyers of Plymouth (b. Bavaria, 1791) and his wife, Zibiah (b. Falmouth, 1788: see below). The firm of Reuben and Mayers, Mercers, had traded in the Market Place, Redruth in 1792. A "Myar" is listed in the Penzance Minute Book in 1828 as contributing two shillings towards a new *Sefer Torah*, but this may the Congregation's Rabbi, Myer Stadthagen, who served there from 1827 to 1829. (See also Redruth trades).

Emanuel Asser: Pedlar. Boarder at Mulberry Square (1861 Census), who had been born in Amsterdam in 1806. He may well have been Jewish, but it is not known if he was related to the family of Gottschalk Ascher (Jeweller) of Plymouth (1841 Census).[203]

Joseph Pfaff: Jeweller, High St. (Wa 1864). Uncertain. Formerly, he had traded as a watchmaker in New Bridge Street Truro (1841 census), and then in Redruth (1851-1861 census records). He was from Germany, but his wife, Elizabeth, was from St. Erth, and he was related through marriage to the Gentile Beringer family. He was still trading in Falmouth in 1871.

Wm. Dymond, Traffic Clerk, and David Volk, Dock-Master, Falmouth Docks (Wa. 1864). Both uncertain. Their occupations would not usually be associated with Jews. While the names of precious stones (silver, gold, diamond etc.) were used by Jews as personal names, *Dymond* (or *Diamond*) was a name found amongst the indigenous Cornish population, and a Samuel Diamond (shoemaker: 1864) and a Letitia Diamond (mariner's widow: 1871) originally from Wales, both lived in Penzance at this time. The murder of a Cornish girl, Charlotte Dymond, in 1844 in north Cornwall has been extensively documented.[204] A memorial stone stands on the place where her body was found on Rough Tor on 14th April 1844, and a Matthew Weeks was hanged for her murder, although many believed in his innocence. Her death gave rise to the belief that her ghost roams the area, and the story was celebrated, much later, by the Cornish poet, Charles Causley.

Elizabeth Hoffmeister (trade unknown) listed as resident at 11, Penwerris Terrace (Wa. 1864). Uncertain.

Harman Spershott (Wa. 1864) was a Municipal Officer of the Borough of Penryn, and the Innkeeper of the *Swan Inn*, Bohill Street, Penryn.[205] He may have been a relative of Joseph Spashatt, a wine and spirit merchant. Neither may have been Jewish.

John Solomon was a Chemist and John Abrahams was a butcher, both in Penryn.

Neither are known to have been Jewish. (Wa. 1864).

By the 1860s, the Jewish population was in rapid decline, and it is noticeable that few Jews appear in the 1871 census.

Abraham Abelson: Teacher of Hebrew and German. It would seem that he or his family were originally from Lithuania,[206] but the 1871 Census for Falmouth gives his birth-place as Neustadt, Poland.[207] He was the Rabbi and *shochet* of the Falmouth Hebrew congregation from around 1868 to 1872. When he left Falmouth he was appointed as minister of the Merthyr Tydfil congregation, which was comprised of Jews from Eastern Europe. Abelson was a witness at a marriage in Penzance in 1869.

Henry Moss: Dentist, 11 Florona (Florence) Place[208] (1877). On 29th August 1877, in the Plymouth synagogue, Henry Moss, son of Moses Moss, General Dealer, married **Sophia Basch**, daughter of **Edward Basch**, Pawnbroker of 10 Whimple Street (Plymouth Hebrew Congregation Marriage Register).[209] The Basch family appear in Census records for Plymouth from 1851 to 1891, at 30 Bilbury Street (1851) and 18 Whimple Street (not "10", as recorded in the Marriage Register) from 1861 to 1891. Edward Basch was from Prussia, whilst his wife, Julia was from Devonport, the daughter of John and Elizabeth Levi, and the sister of the Trephina who married Sigmund Yager, above. Edward Basch traded as a silversmith, jeweller and worker in brass. Henry Moss' surname is likely to be a form of Moses. It is unlikely that Moses and Henry Moss were related to the family of Alexander Moses, and Henry Moss' residence in Falmouth may have been temporary. The Plymouth synagogue marriage entry gives Henry Moss as from Falmouth. However, his place of birth was Hull. He later lived in Highbury (Finsbury Park) London (1881 Census).[210] (A Richard George Moss was a Baptist minister in Falmouth in 1871).

Levi Von Bosch: (1871) a Ship's Chandler (43) from Germany. His wife, Helena (39) was from Holland, and they had a son, Meyer (6). Helena von Bosch was related to Nathan Vos, and like him was from Holland. When Vos died, his nephew, Max von Bosch attended the funeral.

William Henry Solomon: Mayor of Falmouth in 1879.[211] It is not known if he was of Jewish descent. Much earlier, in 1722, Defoe had noted that the "seigniority" of the ancient town of Truro was acknowledged "in some things…that in the corporation of Truro, the person they choose to be their mayor of Truro, is also mayor of Falmouth…" [212] A William H. Soloman traded as a chemist in Penzance in 1871 (Census). He was born in Penryn, and his wife, Ellen, was born in Falmouth.

The following were born in Falmouth:

Caroline Abraham, in 1786. Her family name is not known. She is recorded in the 1891 Census for Plymouth as a widow, living at 1 George Street.

Zibiah Myers, in 1788: she married Israel Meyers, b. 1791 Bavaria. They lived in Plymouth (1841, 1851 & 1861 Census), where all of their children were born: Bessy (b. 1833), Meyer (b. 1836), Isaiah, also known as Frank (b. 1838), Rebecca (b. 1843) and Jacob (b. 1845). She was the oldest daughter of Rabbi Moses Hyman (*c.* 1765-1830). In the Plymouth Census (only) her name is given as Tibiah. It is likely that she died in Plymouth on 16th January 1863,[213] but there is no record of a burial for her in the Hoe cemetery or later Gifford Place burial ground.

Leah (wife of Woolf Solomon of London) was born in Falmouth *c.* 1810. The 1861 Census records her (age 51), a Dressmaker, living at 21 Bell Lane, Spitalfields, London, with her husband (57) a Furniture Dealer.[214] Her original surname is not known.

Eliza Lazarus in 1815. Her original surname is not known. She married Isaac Lazarus, a jeweller, of Exeter, where the couple lived (1851 Census) and where their children were born: Lewis, in 1845) and Julia, in 1847. Her husband, Isaac Lazarus, who was born in 1817, is not known to have been related to the family of Isaac and Rachel Lazarus of Hayle, both of whom were born *c.* 1805.

Bernard Ezekiel in 1815: he married Priscilla, b. Bath 1827. Their son John was born in Redruth in 1840. The family moved to Plymouth (1851 Census) where the other children were born: Elizabeth (1843), Moses (1845) and Benjamin (1849).

Moses Levi Jacob in 1819: he married Sarah, b. Portsmouth 1825. They moved to Birmingham (1851 Census) where their daughter Eleanor was born in 1850.

Lyon J. Joseph in 1827: he later moved to Birmingham (1851 Census).

Andrew George Jacob died in Exeter in March 1900, where he is buried.[215] He was a son of Samuel Jacob (1838-1913) and a grandson of Moses Jacob Jacob (1812-1860) of Falmouth.

Marriages

The destruction of much of the Falmouth records during the War (including those marriages conducted in the synagogue or in Jewish homes) mean that only a fragmentary and tentative outline of Jewish marriages, or marriages involving Jews in or from Falmouth, can be made. Where it is possible that one party to the marriage may have been of Jewish descent, even if their name has not been associated with the Jewish congregation or with genealogical records, and even if the marriage was or may have been in a church, they have been included in this list.

15th February 1760. **Isaac Polack**, "Jewish Priest", to Mary Stoughton, both from Penryn. (Phillimore Parish registers).

December, 1763. **Eleazar Hart** , of Penzance, to **Rebecca Wolf**, of Falmouth.[216]

17th March 1791. **Nathan Cohen**[217] to Aurelia Whitford. Parish of Gerrans, on the Roseland peninsula across Falmouth Bay. His surname suggests Jewish descent. A Nathan Cohen (1769-) from Hamburg, arrived in London in 1791, living there until 1793. From 1793 he lived in Plymouth. It does not seem that the two men can have been connected.

29th October 1803. William Hugoe to **Winifred Levi**, in the Parish of Gwennap (between Redruth and Falmouth).[218] Uncertain.

12th June 1805. **Jacob Jacob** to **Sarah Kate Simons**, at Truro.

7th July 1819. **Henry Harris** of Truro to **Esther Jacob** of Redruth.[219]

10th November 1825. Thomas Pender **Levi** (son of Abraham and Rebecca Levi) to Ann Paskoe, in Falmouth Parish Church. Thomas was baptised the same day.[220] It is not known if the Levi family were of Jewish descent.

28th August 1833. **Henry Joseph** of Bristol to **Amelia**, second daughter of **Jacob Jacob** of Redruth. They were married in Falmouth by the Rabbi of the Synagogue, Joseph Rintel (*Exeter Flying Post*, 5th September 1833).[221]

11th August 1834. **Harriet Elizabeth Hyman** to Edward Pearce Morrall.[222] Both parties were Christians, Harriet Hyman having converted from Judaism in 1830, when she was received into the Methodist Church, where the marriage may have taken place. It was not uncommon for Nonconformists to be married in an Anglican Church.

1st July 1835. **Joseph Joseph**, silversmith, of Redruth, to **Fanny Solomon** of Plymouth, where the marriage is assumed to have taken place (*Exeter Flying Post*, 9th July 1835).[223] Joseph Joseph (who moved to Plymouth in 1849) was the son of Isaac Joseph of Falmouth and Judith Rebecca Jacob of Redruth. Fanny Solomon was born in Poland in 1815.

11th August 1840. **Henry Moses**, of Falmouth, to Joannah Bristo, of Hayle. (Budock Parish Church Registers).

31st July 1844. **Morris Hart Harris**, Jeweller, of Chapel Street, Penzance, son of Henry Harris, Silversmith, to **Rebecca Jacob**, of Bells Court, Falmouth, third daughter of Jacob Jacob. Married at Bells Court, Falmouth by Rabbi Joseph Rintel. Witnesses: Henry Joseph and B. A. Simmons, both of Penzance.[224] Bell's Court was the location of Jacob Jacob's family home, and the notice of the marriage "according to the rites and ceremonies of the Jews" also appeared in the *West Briton* on 2nd August 1844.

April 1846. The *West Briton* (1ˢᵗ May 1846): "In London, on Monday last, at the residence of the bride's uncle, Mr. Levi, Esq., (of) 32 Finsbury Square – Mr. M. J. Jacobs, of 33, Castle Street, Swansea, youngest son of J. Jacobs, Esq., Bell's Square, Falmouth, to Sophia, second daughter of the late L. Lazarus, Esq. The ceremony was performed by the Chief Rabbi, Dr. Adler." The groom (given as "M. J. Jacobs") was, in fact (Moses) Isaac Jacob (1820-1888), who had moved to Swansea. He should not be confused with his older brother, Moses Jacob (M. J.) Jacob (1811-1891) who married a Frances Emanuel (1812-1875) of Portsea.

25ᵗʰ November 1863: **Samuel Jacob** of Falmouth to **Henrietta Rose**, daughter of the late John Michael **Isaacs** of Salford. Married in Manchester.[225]

The Decline of Falmouth's Jewish Community

In 1828, Philp[226] recorded of the Jews of Falmouth that "Their numbers are considerable and respectable, and a great deal of commercial business has been transacted by them for a series of years in this town." By the 1840s there may have been as many as 50 Jewish families in Falmouth but this was the community's peak, soon to decline with surprising speed. Reasons for the community's demise were various and consecutive. In 1850, the removal of the Packet Boat Service, which had operated since 1688, was a major economic disaster for the town, the whole of the mail service being transferred to Liverpool and Southampton. "Falmouth, with its deep harbour, was the main port in the west of England. It was the main packet station for the mail. Large ships would make it their first call, drop anchor and send runners to Lloyd's of London and await instructions from their owners as to the disposal and collection of cargo."[227] There is no doubt that Jewish traders in Falmouth benefited from the Packet Boat Service, but no Jew is listed among the 12 Packet Boat Agents for the period 1689-1845.[228] These boats, which had sailed from the Iberian peninsula, and from as far as the West Indies, would sometimes call at Penzance to unload some of their cargo and passengers, docking in Mount's Bay for a few hours or even a few days. They would then proceed to Falmouth as their first port of call, where they might dock for some weeks. After these long periods at sea, their crew had accumulated considerable amounts in wages and foreign currency, which they were eager to spend. It has been said that some Jewish traders in Falmouth owned small boats known as "Tailor's Cutters" in which they (and, presumably, Gentile traders) would sail out to meet the incoming boats with currency and wares to sell to the sailors, before they proceeded to disembark and spend their money onshore. The cutter owned by the Jacob family is said to have been named "The Synagogue".[229] Some of these details may be based upon local tradition and anecdote, and this may also have influenced the notion that the location of the second synagogue in Falmouth, built in 1808, high up on Parham Hill overlooking the harbour, was chosen for its favourable vantage point from which the worshipping Jews (Lyon Joseph in particular) could keep a look out for the sight of incoming ships during their prayers. The first synagogue, of 1768, had been located by the harbour front itself, and there is no doubt that the position of the second synagogue especially would have offered such opportunities, but observant Jews would not trade on the Sabbath (Saturday), and even if they did attenuate their prayers on a weekday in order not to miss the ships, it is possible that these stories have been shaped by a prejudicial view of the relentless commercial acumen and enthusiasm of the Jew. After the Packet Service was withdrawn, in 1850, the Jewish community continued, but it did so with ever-diminishing numbers. The train of causation which underlay the community's decline was complex, however, but it can be traced through a series of earlier and later physical and economic disasters.

In 1832, the national cholera epidemic reached Cornwall.[230] Penzance and Newlyn were affected with particular severity, where there were at least 64 cholera deaths.[231] The burial register for St. Mary's Church, Penzance for the period September to November 1832 gives a total of 57 names, all being marked as having died of cholera.[232] Newlyn was placed under strict quarantine and a fever field was set aside in the nearby village of Paul to segregate and bury the victims. The epidemic is mentioned on the headstones of two girls buried in the Penzance Jewish cemetery, Pessia Simmons, and her relative Ruth Joseph of Plymouth. They are the only known Jewish victims of the epidemic. The St. Mary's Cholera Register for 1832 lists Ruth Joseph "a jewess", but as a note of her death only, in that she was not buried in Church ground with the other 56 victims. (It is curious, in view of the fact that she died within twenty four hours of Ruth Joseph, and that she was the daughter of a local Rabbi, that Pessia Simmons is not listed. The Joanna Crossman, 45 years, whose name appears on the list, is not known to have been Jewish). In 1833 the epidemic swept Falmouth and Helston, and within four months over 90 victims were recorded, although it is not known how many of these, if any, were Jews or how many people died of secondary illness precipitated by the cholera. Cornwall experienced another outbreak in 1849, with the highest mortality being at St. Germans (236), Liskeard (132), St. Austell (135) and Redruth (133). In Penzance, out of a total population of 50,144, there were 22 deaths, and in Falmouth with a population of 21,700, there were 73 deaths. In both Penzance and Falmouth, there were aggravating topographical factors. Both towns are built on gradients rising from sea level. Together with inadequate sewerage systems this allowed raw effluent to flow downhill contaminating the otherwise pure water-wells.[233] Fatalities may have hit the small Jewish community in Falmouth disproportionately, and some may have been prompted to leave, if only out of fear of recurrence. In 1857 a telegraph service was introduced with the result that ships no longer had to wait in the harbour for instructions from London, which could take at worse several weeks. This new service was another blow to local tradespeople. From 1859 some Jews left for the Gold Rush territories in America: Alexander Jacob of Falmouth went to British Columbia, although he returned after only a few years, but not to Cornwall. (Lionel and Joseph Joseph, whose family had lived in Falmouth, went to California and Hawaii, and eventually bought land for building development on Vancouver Island from the Hudson Bay Company).

Falmouth had long been subject to outbreaks of fire. In October 1824 one such occurrence nearly destroyed two business premises, one of two Jewish partners, and the other of two non-Jews: "On Wednesday last, a fire broke out in the cabinet manufactory of Messrs. Jacob and Soloman, (*sic.*) Falmouth, during the absence of the workmen at dinner, which in a short time communicated with the adjoining premises of Messrs. W. and E. C. Carne, wine and spirit merchants, and so rapid was the conflagration that at one period it was considered that the dwelling house of W. Carne, Esq. in front, could not have been saved. By the great exertions of their friends and the prompt and very efficient working of the six fire engines which were on the spot, the flames were got under about five o'clock in the evening. The greater part of the stock of both Messrs. Carne's and Jacob, by the timely assistance rendered has been saved from destruction, and we are happy to find that the loss will not be so great as was anticipated. The warehouses of Messrs. C. and the workshop of Messrs. J. have been entirely destroyed."[234] Finally, two great fires, the first in High Street on 12th April 1862 destroyed 30 houses and the second broke out in Market Street on 5th June 1870.[235] These were the main commercial areas of the town where Jews had carried on their businesses from some of the shops and premises. The former fire was particularly devastating as it destroyed the centre of the main street which was so narrow (barely a cart's width) that the flames spread quickly. The Town Council resolved that the reconstruction should include the widening of the entire street and proceeded on the compulsory purchase of properties on both sides of the street, paying minimal sums to the residents and shopkeepers based on land values only without regard for loss of trade.[236]

The development and extension of the railways also led to greater mobility and access to London and elsewhere. Even before Cornwall became linked to the Great Western Railway, local lines were being opened in the County.[237] The first to be built was from Hayle to Redruth in 1837, initially as a mineral line, for limited passenger services soon after, and for regular passenger use from 1843. In 1852, Penzance and Truro were connected to Hayle. However, although the line from Paddington had reached Plymouth in 1849, there was still no direct link from Truro to Plymouth, and a journey from Penzance or Falmouth to London, entailed travelling to Hayle, then on by steamer to Bristol, and thereafter by rail to London. By 1859, Brunel's bridge at Saltash crossed the River Tamar, finally linking Plymouth to Truro. It was still not possible to travel directly from Paddington to Penzance in 1859, because the line from London to Plymouth, and across the Saltash Bridge to Truro was built on a broad gauge, and that from Penzance to Truro was on a standard gauge, requiring a change of train at Truro, but, even so, with the arrival of this final link from Truro to London in 1859, Penzance immediately lost its isolation. The broad gauge was not extended to Penzance until 1866. (Ironically, the whole system was converted to narrow gauge in 1892). Falmouth remained relatively isolated from this rail network until 1865, when it acquired its own branch line to Truro.

These improvements in transport between 1859 to 1865 enabled many of the remaining Jews to leave, mainly for Bristol, Birmingham, Plymouth and London, and by 1864 the Falmouth congregation, once significantly bigger in size than Penzance, was unable to find (and possibly could not afford to employ) a *shochet* to provide it with its own kosher meat, and had to pay the Penzance congregation for its regular supply. The Penzance Minute Book records, on 17th April 1864, that

"Mr. Samuel Jacob of Falmouth has agreed to pay the congregation £2 – 2(shillings) per year for the supply of meat & poultry."

All of these factors, together with the fire of 1870, heralded the end of the Falmouth Jewish community. The cumulative and unrelenting weight of these successive blows between 1850-1870 produced effects felt in the Jewish community in Penzance and no doubt played a part in the eventual decline of numbers there. The two communities were inter-related both through marriage, and, eventually, the sharing of resources. That Penzance lasted until the end of the century was due largely to the fact that it had relied to a lesser extent on the Packet Boat trade, suffered no comparable disasters on such an unrelenting scale during this period, and possessed its own economic hinterland. In Falmouth, Samuel Jacob kept the synagogue open for services up to 1879, but in 1880 he left with his family for London after carrying out repairs to the building, which subsequently fell into serious disrepair. And so the Jewish congregation ceased and with it, communal life in Falmouth dwindled to a handful of remaining traders: Moss Jacob, Sam Abrahams, and Mary and Nathan Vos, the latter dying on 23rd October 1913, his burial being the last to take place in the former congregation's cemetery near Penryn.

---

[78] Edgar Samuel, "The First Fifty Years" in Lipman (1961) pp. 27-44; Susser (1993) pp. 29-31.

[79] S. Gay (1903) pp. 191, 203 & 239).

[80] S. Gay (1903) p. 40.

[81] Defoe (1722) Penguin edition (1971) pp. 230-232.

[82] H. E. S. Fisher, in *TJHSE* vol. XXVII (1982) pp. 158-159.

[83] Tony Pawlyn, *The Falmouth Packets 1689-1851* (Truran 2003) p. 89.

[84] R. John Hall, *History of the Falmouth Lodge* (abbrev. title) pub. privately (2001).

[85] Pawlyn, p. 93.

[86] Pawlyn, p. 58.

[87] *The West Briton,* 28th February 1840; Barton (1971) pp. 67-68; *Barclay Fox's Journal* (ed. R.L. Brett, 1979) p. 180. Letter to Keith Pearce from H.C. Faulkner, 15th March 2001.

[88] Warn's (1864) Directory, pp. 14-15, & 84-85.

[89] Herman Melville, *Moby Dick,* Ch. 8, and *Pierre,* Book IV, ii.

[90] Falmouth Masonic Lodge records for 18th June 1751.

[91] Naggar (1992, p.30-31). This book contains a wealth of information on the life and importance of Jewish pedlars in the 18th and 19th centuries.

[92] Anthony Joseph (1975) p. 28-30.

[93] In Row 5:4. Israel Solomon states incorrectly that she was buried in Penzance.

[94] These sections, and those following are drawn largely from Israel Solomon's *Records of my Family* (1887).

[95] Some of the details in this section have been drawn from William Schonfield's (1938) paper, *The Josephs of Cornwall* (1938). Schonfield had married Florence Joseph (1872-1953) a daughter of Lionel Barnet Joseph (1826-1905) and his wife (and second cousin) Katie (1842-1912). Schonfield had received his information from his father-in-law, who, in turn, was in possession of "a lengthy written communication" from his father, B. L. Joseph, "...in the shape of a letter, checked by particulars culled from other sources". This man, Barnet Lyon Joseph (1801-1880) had married a Betsy Jacob (1801-1889) of Dartmouth (who was not related to the Cornish Jacob family). In this "communica-tion", B. L. Joseph had given "a sketch of his own career, together with what he knew of his immedi-

ate and remoter ancestry". Schonfield also received information from a George Jacob of London (Letters of 3rd and 29th November 1936). I am grateful to Jack W. L. Schofield (William Schonfield's grandson) for the information that he was not aware of any subsequent publication of the 1938 paper, and his approval to draw from its contents: Letter to Keith Pearce (8th December 1998). The details here have been drawn partly from Schonfield, not always verbatim, with commentary and correction where necessary. I am also grateful to Anthony Joseph, whose published paper (*JHSE* 1975) and his assistance and advice have proved invaluable in clarifying the complex Joseph genealogies.

[96] Israel Solomon (1885 addendum) states that "There were three brothers, two were of the same Father, but from the Second Wife". It seems likely that Israel Solomon of Falmouth was only counting the three sons who settled in that town, and not Henry Joseph (from the first marriage) who settled in St. Austell. Israel Solomon's *Records of my Family* can be viewed as an anecdotal rather than an historical record in that he was recalling largely what he had been told by his parents, grandparents and others concerning events, some of which had occurred over a hundred years previously, although he was present at the time of some of the later material.

[97] Schonfield is correct in identifying the error in George Jacob's opinion that Henry Joseph's wife, Judith, and Isaac Joseph's wife, Rebecca, were sisters, and that the latter married a *Woolf*. It was Judith Rebecca Jacob's younger sister, also Rebecca Jacob (1781-1853) who married Lemon Woolf (1783-1848) of Penzance. *Judith* Rebecca Jacob was Judith Moses' *niece*, and a granddaughter of Alexander Moses.

[98] Schonfield states that he was from Bohemia (eventually part of Czechoslovakia), but Israel Solomon's *Records of my Family* (1885-1887) gives Alsace.

[99] Israel Solomon (1887): from which these details are drawn. Solomon gives a lengthy account of the social and religious facilities available to Jews at such inns.

[100] Susser (1972) p. 9.

[101] Israel Solomon (1885).

[102] Angela Shire's (1999) compilation of the (London) Great Synagogue Records 1791-1830 does not identify this marriage, which may have taken place elsewhere in London, or in Falmouth, before or around 1791. Falmouth Congregational records of marriages have not survived.

[103] Anthony Joseph (1975) p. 34; Susser (1972) p. 36 (09).

[104] Schonfield gives the spelling *Schkikl*.

[105] Susser (1993) p. 341 & (1995) pp. 75-76.

[106] Schonfield.

[107] Anthony Joseph (1975) pp. 35-36; Judith Samuel (1997) pp. 103-104.

[108] Schonfield's words.

[109] These controversies are examined in more detail in the section on Congregational Life.

[110] Susser (1972) p. 8.

[111] Israel Solomon (*Addendum*) refers to Lyon Joseph being buried "near his mother's tomb", and Schonfield refers to Judith Joseph's burial in the same cemetery. Susser does not record their graves.

[112]*The West Briton* (1st May 1846). The wedding had taken place the previous Monday. The notice gives the groom, incorrectly, as M. J. Jacobs, who was Moses Isaac Jacob's older brother in Falmouth.

[112] Jackie Hill (2004 & 2013) has provided me with some of this information on the Jacob family in Swansea and London from Census records and newspaper reports.

[113] Variously as *Laurence* and *Lawrance* in the census records.

[114] R. John Hall (2001), pp. 20 & 22; Appendices, pp. ii to v.

[115] Helen Fry (2000).

[116] I am grateful to the executors of the Jacob Estate for making this account book available, and especially to Philip Levy for entrusting the Jacob Archive to me. Tony Pawlyn of the Maritime Museum in Falmouth has provided an analysis of the information used here on the Jacob shipping interests (Letter to Godfrey Simmons from Tony Pawlyn, dated 8th December 1998).

[117] 1851 Census Ref. HO 107/2466; Folio 288 Schedule 021 (Jackie Hill 2004).

[118] I have been greatly indebted to the late Justin Brooke, a recognised expert on Cornish mining, especially regarding its economic aspects, for his detailed study of the text of the document, for his comments on information on the mines concerned, and his identification of some of the individuals mentioned in the accounts, much of which has been incorporated *verbatim* into this section.

[119] Letter from Justin Brooke to Keith Pearce (7th November 2000).

[120] Warn's Directory (1864) p. 37.

[121] Records of Justin Brooke; entries from the Masonic records of Dr. Roger Burt of University of Exeter; Letters to Keith Pearce from Justin Brooke and Roger Burt (5th & 13th July 2000, respectively). Communication of 13th July 2000, from Allen Buckley, whose observations on the various mines has been of particular assistance..

[122] Letter from Anthony Joseph to Keith Pearce (20th November 2005).

[123] I am especially grateful to H. C. Faulkner of Illogan, Redruth for information on some of those listed in this section and especially for making available his research into the 1841, 1851 and 1861 Census Returns for Falmouth, and also to Eric Dawkins of Penryn for providing some further information from his records. .

[124] George Rigal (2000) GHL Policy No. 309484. The Guildhall policies cover such insuring companies as Sun Fire, Royal Exchange, Hand in Hand, London Assurance, Globe, Legal & General, Law Life and Metropolitan Life. George Rigal's research on Jewish Insurance Policies has been used extensively in references such as the above, and is referenced as GR. In some cases, information has been also been provided from research by Helen Fry, by Jackie Hill, and by Kathryn Atkin.

[125] Arthur P. Arnold, *Apprentices of Great Britain 1710-1773*, in *TJHSE* vol. XXII (1970) p. 153.

[126] It is given in full in the section on the Rabbis.

[127] PROCL. E.351/1738-9. Naggar (1992) p.15.

[128] Roth (1933) footnote, without a source reference. I have been unable to trace these letters of administration, and they are not in papers of the Roth Collection in the Brotherton Library, University of Leeds: Letter from Richard High, Special Collections, University of Leeds (22nd September 2008).

[129] HO107/135/10 Folio 10 p. 15 (Research by Jackie Hill 2008).

[130] Letters from Trudy Martin to Keith Pearce (17th May 2008) and from Jackie Hill (6th June 2008), from which this information has been drawn. Jackie Hill has identified wills and letters of administration for the St. Stephen family of 1820 (Francis Pollock Ref. AP/P/4489), 1825 (William Pollock Ref. AP/P4598) & 1851 (Ann Pollock Ref. AP/P/5226). She has also identified the 1828 will of Frances Polack of Penryn. It is of interest that, prior to 1857, all wills for the Penryn and Falmouth area were proved in Exeter at the Consistory Court, because these parishes were Peculiar Jurisdiction parishes of the Bishop of Exeter. These early wills were all destroyed by German bombing in the Second World War, and no formal copies survived, other than secondary copies that have occasionally surfaced from private family possession or specialist historical archives, such as the wills of Alexander Moses (13th April 1791) and Barnet Levy (14th August 1792), both of Falmouth. Frances Polack's will was proved at the Prerogative Court of Canterbury, and may reflect the fact that those who wished to avoid the details their estate and bequests becoming a matter of local or regional knowledge, lodged their wills outside of the County.

[131] Susser (1993) pp. 121, 253 & 284.

[132] *West Briton*, 4th October 1844 (Jackie Hill 2008).

[133] CRO Truro Ref. DCPEN/1143 (Jackie Hill 2008).

[134] W. S. Jessop (Chicago 1951). Pub. Gent Exeter 2000, p. 22 & 6.

[135] Eli Faber (1998) *Jews, Slaves and the Slave Trade*, pp. 202 & 232; R. D. Barnett & P. Wright (1997) *The Jews of Jamaica*, pp. 116-117.

[136] Diane Clements, Director of the Library and Museum of Freemasonry, London, has provided details of this register (Letter to Godfrey Simmons 28th October 2004).

[137] GHL No. 495658 (Kathryn Atkin 2000).

[138] Letter from H. C. Faulkner to Keith Pearce (16th December 2000).

[139] Eli Faber, *Jews, Slaves and the Slave Trade* (New York & London 1998): Faber lists about 45 Jamaican variants of *Silva*, all with traditional Jewish forenames (pp. 156-254).

[140] Drawn from Baptismal records and the 1841 Census: Trudy Martin (2004).

[141] Jackie Hill (November 2004).

[142] GHL Nos. 171237, 206458 & 341089 (GR & HF 2000).

[143] GHL No. 28605 (GR 2000).

[144] GHL No. 143020 (George Rigal & Helen Fry 2000).

[145] Roth (1933).

[146] I am grateful to Rev. Canon John Harris, Vicar of St. Gluvias, who has located and reassembled the displaced and broken headstone and has made an accurate reading of the inscription (2008). The name is clearly given as *Frances Pollack*. The spelling of this forename is to be taken as correct over other records. The surname has a second "l", incomplete and without its customary foot. It seems likely that the mason had assumed the second consonant, but had been advised otherwise, too late to modify the error. The inscription contains no reference to any other family member.

[147] Roth (1933). I am indebted to Michael Michell of St. Austell, a descendant of Isaac Polack (Letter of 23rd April & 8th May 2008) for this and other information from his research into the Polack family, and also to Jackie Hill for providing further information from her research.

[148] GHL No. 172582 (GR & HF 2000).

[149] GHL No. 195892 (GR & HF 2000).

[150] GHL No. 188378.

[151] Helen Fry (2000)

[152] Susser (1993) p. 321. n. 29.

[153] RG10/2120 Folio 107 (p. 49) & RG11/2203 Folio 64 (p. 35): research by Jackie Hill (2005).

[154] Susser (1995) pp. 40-41: that Susser records this as the transcription of a "correspondent" suggests that he was also uncertain if the family was Jewish.

[155] GHL Nos. 317108 & 380625 (GR & HF 2000).

[156] Green (1989) p. 210, and in *Philip's Panorama of Falmouth*.

[157] From the family records of H. C. Faulkner of Illogan.

[158] *Royal Cornwall Gazette*, 22nd October 1852, p. 5, col. 5.

[159] Helen Fry (2000).

[160] GHL No. 278461 (George Rigal and Helen Fry 2000).

[161] Cooper (2006) pp. 197-8.

[162] In *A Guide to the Mounts Bay and the Lands End* (1st Edition 1816) later expanded. See also Cooper (2006) pp. 197-8.

[163] Green (1989) p. 212.

[164] Helen Fry (2000).

[165] G. Pawley White, *A Handbook of Cornish Surnames* (Dyllansow Truran 1999, p. 14).

[166] Israel Solomon's *Records of my Family* (1887).

[167] Original Birth Register of the children of Samuel Jacob (1778-1860) in the Jacob Archive.

[168] HO107/154/3 Folio 35, p. 22.

[169] *Exeter Flying Post*, 19th July 1804 and 12th March 1807 (HF 2000).

[170] In the *Lost Jews of Cornwall*, I failed to make this distinction.

[171] GHL No. 260690/1 (GR and HF 2000).

[172] Trathan (1815) p. 84.

[173] GHL No. 349627 (GR and HF 2000).

[174] Jackie Hill (2009).

[175] He is not listed by Brown, who does give John Davidson (1847, Ludgate Hill).

[176] HO 107/1632 Folio 703 p. 9: Jackie Hill (2006).

[177] Jackie Hill (2007).

[178] Ref. Susser (1993) pp. 99 and 293; Susser (1995) Decennial Census records (various). Exeter Congregational Minute Books; Exeter and Plymouth Marriage Registers. I am grateful to Jennifer Marin, the former Director of the Jewish Museum, London for a copy of the original licence.

[179] *RCG*, p. 3, col. 5.

[180] The Census date for her birth, 1781, does not agree with the genealogical date which is generally accepted as 1778; c.f. Anthony Joseph, *ibid*.

[181] See the section on Truro trades, and the Falmouth cemetery (5:2 & 5:3) for details of their family.

[182] Jackie Hill (2005 & 2009).

[183] CFHSoc.,Truro.

[184] Jackie Hill (2006); additional information from Anthony Joseph (Letter to Keith Pearce, 26th March 2006).

[185] Brown (1961 & other editions) give various references.

[186] Jackie Hill (2011).

[187] *West Briton* Friday 22nd October 1852: Jackie Hill (2005).

[188] Slater's *Royal National & Commercial Directory* 1852 (Section on "Places of Worship" and "Clergy").

[189] Susser (1995) p. 13.

[190] E.S. Tregoning, *History of Falmouth* (1865) p. 72. I am grateful to H.C.Faulkner for providing this information (Letter to Keith Pearce, 3rd September 1999).

[190a] I am grateful to the Cornish Studies Library, Redruth, for supplying the original advertisement.

[191] Susser (1993) p. 42, who gives the source reference (p. 279, nt.124) incorrectly as PRO HO 129/12/30*9*. This should read 30*8*, the correct reference for Falmouth (309 being the ref. no for Helston). The name *Andrew* does not appear on the form.

[192] Helen Fry, 2000 (1881 Census), Trudy Martin, November 2005 (1871, 1881 & 1891 Census) and Jackie Hill, 2005-2006 (Census 1851-1901). I am also grateful to Anthony Joseph for information on the Jacob family (November 2005). It should be noted that the standardised transcription of the 1881 census [*Ancestry.com*] gives Andrew *S*. Jacob: the original, however, has a *G*. not an *S*. (Trudy Martin). It is possible that Andrew was also known as *Solomon*. Solomon (1861-) the fifth son of Rev. Isaac Bischofswerder (1822-1899) of Penzance, was also known as George.

[193] The original is in the Jewish Museum, London.

[194] GHL Policy No. 112683 (GR 2000).

[195] Susser (1993) pp. 36, 151 & 165.

[196] Douch (1966) p. 62.

[197] Susser (1972) p. 39: headstone Q24.

[198] *West Briton*, June 1844. Douch (1966) p. 43; Susser (1993) p. 295. In his (1972) survey of the Hoe cemetery, Susser does not record Martin Valentine's grave, but notes that of 95 headstones recorded by Dr. D.M. Berlin in 1900, 45 had since disappeared.

[199] H. C. Faulkner's research into Parish registers.

[200] Osborne (1901) p. 213; R. John Hall (2001) appendix, p. ii. Susan Gay (1903) p. 199 gives further details of Barnet Falk.

[201] Susser (1995) p. 42, assumes that Schram was Jewish.

[202] Piece 2304, folio 14, schedule 109 (*CFHSoc.* Truro: Trudy Martin).

[203] Susser (1995) p. 27.

[204] P. Munn (1978) and S. Bird (2002).

[205] Warn's Directory (1864) pp. 126 & 138.

[206] Wendy Bellany, *The Jews of Merthyr Tydfil* in *Shemot*, Vol. 6:3 (September 1998) p.12.

[207] RCFHSoc. Truro (Trudy Martin).

[208] This is the spelling of the address in the Synagogue records, but it most likely to be Florence Place.

[209] Helen Fry (2000).

[210] Research by Anthony Joseph (2004).

[211] Susan Gay (1903, p. 241).

[212] Defoe (1722) p. 231.

[213] Research by David Liss, Gary Kent and Peter Hyman (2004). It is possible that Zibiah Myers' headstone has not survived, although this would be unusual for her comparatively late burial.

[214] RG9/266 Folio 129 Page 3: Jackie Hill (2005).

[215] The Old Jewish Cemetery, grave 101: headstones transcribed and compiled by Michael Adler (1940) and edited by Bernard Susser (1963). I am grateful to Helen Fry (2000) for providing me with a photograph of the headstone.

[216] Susser (1993) pp. 32 & 276; Anthony Joseph (1975) chart A, p. 26f.

[217] CFHSoc. Truro (Trudy Martin, 2002). Nathan Cohen (1769-): Lipman *Aliens List* 1798 & 1803, Miscellanies VI, p. 190).

[218] CFHSoc Records.

[219] Archive of Alex M. Jacob.

[220] H. C. Faulkner.

[221] Helen Fry (2000); Susser (1972) p. 21, B61.

[222] Eric Dawkins (1998); David Liss, Gary Kent and Peter Hyman (2004).

[223] Helen Fry (2000).

[224] Archive of Alex M. Jacob.

[225] Doreen Berger (2004) p. 171.

[226] *Panorama of Falmouth*, p. 49.

[227] Dunitz (1993) p. 31.

[228] Gay (1903) p. 203.

[229] Alex M. Jacob (1949), pub. Transactions of the JHSE (1951-52) vol. XVII, pp. 63-72, and in *The Lost Jews of Cornwall* (2000) pp. 49-63. These details are based upon an interview with a K. Wills, in the *Cornish Echo* (29th September 1930).,

[230] It has been described comprehensively by John Rowe and C. T. Andrews in their paper, "Cholera in Cornwall" in *The Journal of the RIC*, vol 7, part 2, 1974. Cf. pp.159-162.

[231] The Penzance epidemic is described by G. T. Clark, *Report on the Sanitary Condition of Penzance* (HMSO, 1849) s.21, p.6. See also Pool, *op. cit.*, pp.121-122, & pp. 142-143 & 149.

[232] Letter (6th March 1978) to Godfrey Simmons from Steven Hobbs, Assistant Archivist CRO Truro.

[233] Eric Dawkins: from information supplied by Leslie and Naomi Falkson, 26th May 1993.

[234] Helen Fry (2000): *Exeter Flying Post*, 7th October 1824.

[235] *June* 1870 is confirmed by the report in the *Falmouth Packet* of 11th June 1870 (p. 1; cols. 4-6), and by Gay (1903, p. 236). The date has been given as 5th January 1870 by Fisher Barham (1981) *Yesterday and Today around Falmouth and Penryn* (p. 75), and Gilson (1990) *Old Falmouth in Old Photographs* (p. 47).

[236] Leslie and Naomi Falkson, *op. cit.*

[237] See Pool (1974) pp. 150-153 for the information contained in this section.

CHAPTER 4
The Jews of Penzance

In 1722, Daniel Defoe, noted that "The town of Pensance is a place of good business, well built and populous, has a good trade, and a great many ships belonging to it, notwithstanding it is so remote. Here are also a great many good families of gentlemen, though in this utmost angle of the nation."[238] It is obvious, however, that he found the contrast with Falmouth's visible prosperity striking, and it was his general impression that the people of Penzance "are supposed to be so poor". Defoe found this "yet more strange" in that "the veins of lead, tin and copper ore are said to be seen, even to the utmost extent of land at low water mark, and in the very sea - so rich so valuable a treasure is contained in these parts". It would seem that Defoe's words reflect the emergent economy of the town in the early 18th century, clearly reliant upon its flourishing sea trade, but yet to benefit from the full resources, potential and development of mining. Had he seen the town a few decades later, when the town experienced a rapid influx of population and increase in house-building, he might well have recorded a different impression.

In 1739, the local Congregationalist minister, Risdon Darracott, found that "the town is very rich and populous" and in 1749, *The London Magazine*, in an account by one of the town's residents, whose purpose was to argue that Penzance had "never had justice done to it by any writer", eulogised that "Its situation is both healthy and agreeable - It is extremely commodious for trade, and has a strong and handsome quay - besides the advantages of being one of the Coinage Towns, of having a custom house, of carrying the pilchard trade - it has a large market, and a great inland trade, and is one of the richest most flourishing and best built towns in the County - its wealth is in a great many hands, which constitutes no small part of its happiness". This contrasts with Defoe's impression of the town's poverty, although by 1816, the market was noted for its "goodness, variety and cheapness of its commodities - the delicacy and richness of the pork - the heifer beef is superior, beyond all comparison, to the Scotch. During the winter the market is filled with the greatest variety of wolf-fowl, as woodcocks, snipes etc., which may be purchased for a few pence. Every variety of fish in season is offered for sale every day". Between 1801 and 1871, the town's population tripled from 3,382 to 10,425,[239] and Penzance experienced "a time of almost continual growth and progress". This was not without its deficiencies, however, and in 1849, in an official report of its Public Health, Penzance was described as follows: "In the smaller streets, the paving is very deficient indeed. The narrow lanes are not paved at all, and many of them are in wet seasons impassable, refuse cast into the broad highways, public lights are very inefficient. Public nuisances are numerous. The most considerable are the slaughterhouses, of which there are 14 in the town and nine in one street. In several of the larger squares and courts are open dungheaps and cesspools, and very foul and offensive (with) scarcity of water and absence of drainage, and the prevalence of certain diseases. Dysentry prevails in the lowest part of the town near to the sea, and in certain parts of the higher town remarkable for their filth and want of drainage. It is impossible in words to convey an adequate idea of the filth of the older and more densely peopled quarter of the town near the quay, in which cholera prevailed formerly (that is 1832)".[240]

Also noted were "eight low lodging houses in various parts of the town" whose "dirty and objectionable" inhabitants required "the surveillance of the police", that some public walks and footpaths were "open and stagnant ditches", that the supply of water for extinguishing fires was either "insufficient" or "inapplicable" and some areas had no such supply at all, that there were "no sewers in Penzance, and no house drainage", and that the town's water supply was dependent upon 53 private wells, and six public pumps, and "four were out of order", and in summer the water supply was "quite inadequate".[241] (Numerous such descriptions of the town have survived from the 18th and 19th centuries).[242] The Records and Accounts of the Corporation of Penzance are also revealing in this respect. For the period from October 1661 to October 1662, the Mayor, Thomas Grosse noted payments "To James Newham for clensing the market house [and]…For 15 men to clense the leates", and in September 1793, the Mayor, Thomas Giddy, recorded a payment "To M. Howard for attending at the shute to prevent the cleansing of fish". On 15th August 1817, the Mayor, Henry Boase, heard a "Complaint of Cunnacks against the people committing nuisance against Lescudjack Shoot by cleaning tripe there and fouling the water".[243] Such was the town in which the Jewish community became established in the 18th century and in which it thrived in the 19th century. It was a place of rapid growth and uneven progress, but one where opportunities to trade were abundant, and where the Jewish community could live in security and without fear of persecution, ostracism or extreme destitution.

The Hart Family

The earliest burials in the Penzance Jewish cemetery are either unmarked, their headstones having been lost, or their fragmentary remains preventing identification. These burial plots are clearly visible, however, and the interments are likely to have taken place sometime before 1791, the year of the earliest, anonymous, dated fragment. This in itself implies a Jewish presence in the town for some years, even decades before that date. The Hart family from Weinheim in the Rhineland, Germany, represent some of the earliest settlers, arriving in the early 1700s.[244] The family had lived for generations in Weinheim, where they eventually became known as *Altstadter*. In Germany, and likely upon migration to England, the Hart men assumed a leading role in congregational affairs, and from their forbearer, the first Abraham Hart (-c.1710), they acquired the honorific title of Rabbi or *Rav*. They may have received training in other aspects of rabbinical duties, such as the skills required of a *shochet* and *mohel*. After the death of the second Abraham Hart (1784) in Penzance, the title does not seem to have been adopted by subsequent generations, although it may have been used by them in a limited and purely honorific

sense, by which time the congregation was employing its own incumbent ministers. The earliest known, Asher Hart, and his son, Rabbi Abraham Hart, both died
in Germany, Asher some time before 1682, and his son, Abraham, between 1710-
1720. The family may have been known there as *Altstadter* or *Hart* (or both) and
the forenames *Asher* and *Abraham* continued to pass down in alternation through
the early and subsequent generations of the family.[245]

Rabbi Abraham Hart (-c.1710) had at least three sons, two of whom, Joshua
(-1708) and Lazarus (-1713) died young. It is not known if the third son, Rabbi
Asher (who died around 1745-1752) came to Penzance with his family, but at least
one of his sons, the Rabbi Abraham (-1784) mentioned above, did arrive in the
town around 1740-1750, possibly earlier. Two of his siblings, Lazarus and Vogele,
were to die in the same year (1741) and there were at least two other brothers,
Elchanan (-1776) and Salman, or Solomon (-1779). Two other men of the same
family, who may also have been Abraham's brothers, were Moses (-1764 and Asher
(-1777), although they may have been his cousins, and, if so, most likely sons of
his uncle, Joshua.[246] Some of these men may have accompanied or followed
Abraham Hart to Penzance, although no independent or conclusive local records
of them have been identified. Abraham Hart would have been a very young man
at the time of his arrival in the town, and possibly still a child. He adopted, or
chose to use the family surname *Hart*, but he was also known locally as Solomon
Lazarus. It was common for Jews to alternate between the Hebrew names (including patrinominal identification, *ben*, son of…) by which the person is likely to have
been known in the privacy of the family, in the Jewish community and within the
congregation of the synagogue, and societal names for use in the wider secular
community. Usually, although not always, the former name would be Hebrew or
of foreign (e.g. German) origin, and the latter would be an Anglicised or adopted
English name. The use of a familiar Biblical name (not always related to the
person's Hebrew name) especially where it would be recognised and used by non-
Jews was also common, such as *Solomon* or *Samuel*.

Abraham Hart is the first member of this family for whom there is contemporaneous documentary evidence. This indicates that he traded in Penzance under
the name of Solomon Lazarus. In his Ledger, the West Cornwall historian the Rev.
William Borlase (1696-1772) of Ludgvan records, between 1756 and January 1759:
"Recd from a Jew a toothpick case Birmingham enamel - the same Jew has an eye
glass case abt 7/6 sent to be set in silver etc. to London."[247] In his private accounts
(1734-1772),[248] Borlase had also referred to his dealings with an unnamed Jew some
ten years earlier: "30th December 1748: to a Jew for knives - 8 shillings". Presumably, these unnamed Jews were itinerant pedlars, and unrelated to Abraham Hart,
although it is possible that they include Hart, with whom Borlase was to become
more familiar. From the mid-1750s his account entries relate specifically to dealings
with the Harts in the purchase of a number of small items:

"30th November 1756: to half a dozen knives and forks from Sol. Lazs. 10
(shillings) and 6 (pence); 28th January 1757: To Solomon Lazarus for 4 silver salt
shovels (8s.) and a screw (1s.) - 9 (shillings); July 27th 1758: Paid Solomon Lazarus
for a pencil cap - 2 (shillings); April 23rd 1759: Paid Solomon Lazarus for two razors
- to be returned if not liked....2 (shillings)." William Borlase obviously needed to

be quite satisfied with a product before he eventually accepted them as goods. Abraham Hart was also skilled as a Goldsmith, but the Borlase papers make no further reference to this, nor to him after 1759, and contrary to claims, Borlase did not record in his ledger the purchase of any larger, more valuable items from Abraham Hart, such as silver candlesticks.

It is possible that Abraham Hart's image has survived in a portrait by the renowned Cornish portrait painter John Opie (1761-1807). Opie was born in St. Agnes, and moved to London in 1781, where he established a reputation for himself, including the admiration of the President of the Royal Academy, Sir Joshua Reynolds (1723-1792), who exhibited more than twenty of his paintings at the Academy. Opie was also introduced to King George III and Queen Charlotte, and they bought two of his paintings.[249] Opie remained in London, and died there. Before he left Cornwall, by late 1779 he had moved to Helston, and he began to attract the attention of a number of the local gentry, including the St. Aubyn family, who were living at nearby Clowance, but were preparing to move to St. Michael's Mount, in the bay, opposite Marazion, and near Penzance. For the St. Aubyns, Opie painted several portraits, including a number of their servants, and the old woman, allegedly 102, and said to be the last Cornish speaker, Dolly Pentreath. The Rogers family of Penrose, near Helston, owned a number of Opie's portraits, and it was Canon Rogers who leased the land to the Jews of Penzance for their cemetery. Around 1779-1780, Opie was introduced to the Price family who lived near Penzance. They owned extensive plantations in Jamaica, where Abraham Hart is thought to have travelled, and where he also is also believed to have established business connections, although these details have not been confirmed from primary sources and may be anecdotal. At around this time, Opie painted one of his finest portraits, the "Old Jew", also said to be that of a Rabbi of Penzance, and which was one of the works upon which Opie's reputation came to be founded in London. The canvas is inscribed on the back only as "Jew Rabbi", and although there is no conclusive evidence that would confirm the identity of the subject or the place, if the attribution is valid, then the image would most likely be that of Rabbi Abraham Hart. It would be quite credible that Price introduced Opie to another local man who shared his Jamaican commercial interests, albeit on a much lesser scale. The portrait has been dated sometime before 1781, and Hart was to die only a few years later, in 1784.[250] If "Rabbi of Penzance" is not, in fact, a correct attribution of the subject, Abraham Hart's contemporary, Alexander Moses (1715-1791) President of the Falmouth congregation, would be the most likely alternative candidate as the County's other prominent, and elderly Jew. It is possible, of course, that Opie's portrait was conceived as an imaginative exercise, rather than the depiction of an actual person, but his preference for painting living subjects and local characters in Penzance at this time would suggest otherwise. Opie's connection with Jews may have been rare or occasional, but it is of interest that he married a Jewess, Mary Bunn, the daughter of Benjamin Bunn, a London solicitor and a wealthy money lender and pawnbroker. The marriage took place at Opie's church of St. Martin-in-the-Fields, on 4th December 1782.[251]

Abraham Hart had a number of children, including Mord(e)chai (1736-), Eleazar (1739-1803), Madel (1743), Lemel (1755-) - whose name would be given to his nephew in 1768, also known as Lemon Hart, - Edel (1747-) and Anna (1750-). It is not known if there were other children, or if all of these named children came to live in Penzance. Abraham Hart's son, Eleazar (or Lezar) was also known as Lazarus, and as "Kazanes" amongst those with whom he shared shipping interests. (His name has been given as *Ezekiel*, and his trade given as a "chemist", neither of which was the case). His name first appears in Borlase's accounts on 21st May 1764 when Borlase paid him a guinea "for exchanging a watch upon six months tryal, and buckles." The watch was part-exchanged on 18th July 1765: "Pd Mr. Lazarus Hart besides one guinea pd him May 21st 1764, for changing a watch in part. He to warrant the watch now taken in exchange for two years from this date, and then to receive one guinea more - as per rect. 1. 10. 0d. – pd – D(itt)o for 1/2 pd of tea for Mrs B. Handkerch 3/10 a screw and key 1/6 - 14/4." On 16th August 1767: "pd. Lazarus Hart for screw and cane in full of all - 3/6." and on 29th January 1770: "To Mr. Lazarus Hart for Billy's buckles 14/6 - 2 large tea spoons 10/6 - 1 (pound) 5 (shillings)." The offending time-piece, or a successor (neither having been made by Hart himself) was eventually returned to Hart on 21st August 1770: "Return'd my watch to Mr. Lazar. Hart being long Complain'd of for not going to contract. pa: 80 and promised to be sent to the maker." On 12th February 1772 a similar experience with a pair of spectacles: "Pd. Mr. Laz. Hart for spectacles silver sett but returned as not suiting - 1/6." These are the only items which Borlase specified in his ledger and accounts as purchased from the Harts. Some twenty years later, Hart was still trading in such articles. On 3rd December 1792, Dr. John Tonkin[252] recorded in his diary (which he kept from 1784-1800) that he had "paid Mr. Hart for a pair of plated buckles - 1s 6d.".

From documentary sources such as these, and the shipping records below, Eleazar (or Lazarus) Hart only appears with that surname. It is not known if he ever used his father's alternative forename, *Solomon*, as a surname, but a pocket watch, clearly dated 1775, with a gold movement, contained in a silver case that was set in London, and inscribed on the inside cover with the name *Lazarus Solomon, Penzance*, has survived.[253] It is not clear if the inscription is that of the owner of the watch or its maker. The headstones of Abraham Hart (Solomon Lazarus) and his son, Eleazar (Lazarus) Hart have not survived in the Penzance cemetery. These stones may well have indicated if Eleazar Hart's Hebrew patronymic contained the words *ben Avraham*, or *ben Solomon*, or both names. It is even possible that *Lazarus Solomon* is to be read as *Lazarus, Solomon* (i.e. *Solomon Lazarus* - Abraham Hart). The inversion of names, without the (later) customary use of a *comma* to indicate that the surname is written first, was a common practice in the 18th century, and can lead to a confusion of the name's correct usage and of the person's identity. Abraham Hart may well have possessed the Hebrew patronymic *Solomon ben Eliezar*, and the last name, being that of his grandfather would likely have been taken by Lazarus Hart, who as the son of *Solomon ben Eliezer*, would have been *Eliezer ben Solomon*, Lazarus Solomon. A further confusing factor is that Lemon Hart, Eliezer Hart's son, married as his second wife, Miriam (Mary) a daughter of a *Lazrus Solomon* of London, so that Lemon Hart's father and his father-in-law were namesakes. The congregational records that would contain the names of the synagogue's members, including perhaps a *Lazarus Solomon*, have not been found prior to 1808, nor, as mentioned, any surviving headstones in the Penzance cemetery before 1791. It would seem unlikely that the watch would have been left behind when the Hart family departed for London in 1811, or that it should have returned to Penzance when none of the family ever lived there again. The timepiece of 1775, may, of course, have no direct connection with the Hart family, but with Solomon Solomon, or of Thomas Solomon, both of Penzance (see below), or it may have been the property of a local non-Jew, in that both names can be found in Cornish parish baptismal and marriage registers of the time, occasionally in relation to the same person.

The Borlase papers are of considerable significance in confirming an early Jewish presence in Penzance, and undermines Susser's claim that "there is no evidence of any Jew there [in Penzance] before 1781, when the name of Lemon Hart appears on a clockface, apparently sold by him".[254] The inference that the clock in question, which has survived, had been sold by Lemon Hart, presumably as its maker, is highly unlikely. Lemon Hart had been born only about twelve years before, in 1768, and there is no direct evidence that he, or any other member of the Hart family, was skilled as, or traded as a clockmaker or a watchmaker (although Eleazar Hart did sell second-hand watches). The clock is most likely to have been a piece commissioned by Eleazar Hart for his son, Lemel (or Lemon) on the occasion of his *bar mitzvah* in 1781, when he would have been around twelve years of age. There were a number of Jewish clockmakers in Penzance at this time, and one of them may have made the clock, although a London source is not to be excluded. The premise that there was no evidence of Jewish settlement in Penzance before 1781, has also led to the assumption that the Solomon Solomon who was apprenticed in 1769 to a Gentile, John Sampson, a Penzance watchmaker (from around 1763),[255] could not have been a Penzance resident, and that he was Solomon Solomon of the Solomon family of Falmouth.[256] This identification is erroneous, in that the latter was born in 1764 and he died in Lisbon in 1819. The apprenticed silversmith of 1781 was clearly a Penzance resident, unconnected with the Solomons of Falmouth. Indeed, he could be the Solomon Zalman who died in 1823 and is buried in the Penzance cemetery. A Solomon Solomon, a Silversmith and a Jew, appeared as a formal witness in a Customs case before the Penzance Magistrates around 1781,[257] and he is most likely to be the apprentice of 1769.

During this early period of Jewish settlement, the Jewish community was most likely small in numbers, although by 1768 it had built its first synagogue. Even so, its members are unlikely to have contained a sufficient range of talents to provide advanced training in the skills of watch and clockmaking for its younger men who aspired to be apprentices. Penzance, and other large Cornish towns, contained a number of such skilled Gentile clockmakers. It seems likely, therefore, that the Solomon Solomon who was apprenticed to John Sampson in 1769 was a Jew, and the later Jewish Silversmith, above. It is entirely credible that a local master clockmaker would take on a Jewish apprentice. Moreover, there were other Gentile clockmakers in the town at this time: John Carne (1752), William Pascoe (1758), Henry Sampson (*c.* 1780), Charles Vibert (1750-1809) and, later, Henry Couslon (1772-1834) and William Davey (1791). This flourishing trade enabled a number of Jews to set up their own clock and watch making businesses in the town, and they were able to train their own apprentices, including their own sons. From the early 18th century, these included the following, who may have traded well before the date given here [258] : Solomon Jacobs (1803), Lemon Woolf (1807: silversmith and watchmaker), Levi Jacobs (1823), Joseph Joseph, Henry Levy and Aaron Selig (1830), Abraham Woolf (1841), Morris Hart Harris and Benjamin Selig (1844) and Alexander Levin (1847). It has been mentioned previously, that a third name was sometimes used to distinguish a Jew from others with his namesake, especially where forename and surname (father's name) were identical. It is conceivable that the Solomon Solomon who was John Sampson's apprentice used a third name, such as *Lazarus.* A Solomon (ben) Zalman can be linked with the Hart family as a son, or nephew, of Abraham Hart's brother, and Eleazar (Lazarus) Hart's uncle, Salman (Zalman, Salaman or Solomon) Hart, who died in 1779 (his age is not known), and whose uncle, in turn, was named *Lazarus.* This man could have been the apprentice of 1769, and, possibly the maker of the 1775 watch, by which year he is likely to have served his time. Like the Lemon Hart clock, the watch could also have been a *bar mitzvah* gift to a Lazarus Solomon, if, indeed, the recipient was Jewish. And so, the watch may or may not have been made by a Jewish watch-maker, but by one of the local Gentile traders, or even imported from outside the County.

William Borlase's dealings with local Jewish traders in Penzance may not have been the only contact that he had with Jews. Borlase was a mineral collector, supplier and researcher. Towards the end of Borlase's life, Moses Jacob (1733-1807) of Redruth had established himself as a Jeweller and Clockmaker in Redruth, from around 1769. He was also to become one of the County's most important dealers in mineralogical specimens, although this may have been after Borlase died. The earliest confirmed record of him as a mineralogist is from 1790, but he may have traded as such from an earlier date. Borlase, however, makes no mention of him in his Ledger. The isolation of West Cornwall was a burden to Borlase in his researches, and he sought compensation in correspondence with other naturalists and mineralogists from outside the County. One particularly lasting and fruitful relationship was with a Portuguese Jew, Emanuel Mendes da Costa (1717-1791) of London, a Fellow of the Royal Society, who wrote to Borlase in 1748.[259] At this time, Borlase was researching material for his *Natural History of Cornwall*, that was eventually published in 1758. Emanuel da Costa travelled through Cornwall in 1749, collecting minerals, and stayed with Borlase at the Rectory in Ludgvan. The visit must have proved to be mutually rewarding, and led to a life-long correspondence and sharing of information. That Borlase should have struck up this relationship with a Sephardic Jew reflects the fact that in the mid 18th century a number of Sephardic Jewish families, da Costa, de Medina, Henriquez, Rodriguez, Salvador, Pereira, Ximenes, de Mattos and Gideon had become wealthy London entrepreneurs and businessmen.[260]

In 1754, da Costa was imprisoned for debt, but continued to work on his mineralogical researches, having retained his cabinet (of specimens) and his reference library in his cell. He was eventually to publish a *Natural History of Fossils* (1757) and other works on shells. Soon after his stay with Borlase in Ludgvan in 1749, da Costa had proposed him as a member of the Royal Society, to which he was duly elected in May 1750,[261] after submitting a treatise on *Cornish Diamonds* that he had written in 1739. Borlase and da Costa were to meet in London and to attend the Royal Society together, and in 1763, da Costa was appointed Clerk to the Society with particular responsibility to restore its neglected Museum. Soon after his appointment, however, he began to embezzle sums from the Society's accounts, which, by 1767, amounted to some £1,400. He was expelled and imprisoned for five years. William Borlase had always been generous in his donation of miner-alogical specimens as gifts. He had sent some to da Costa in 1747, even before they had met in person, and he was to deplete "his mineral collection of its finest spec-imens" in a donation to the Ashmolean Museum, Oxford, in 1758. It would seem that Borlase came to regard da Costa's dynamism and single-minded determina-tion in amassing his vast collection of minerals with a degree of awe, and wrote to him in October 1760, acknowledging him as "one who can collect & hoard up with so much Philosophical avarice [but] at the same time…so generous & communica-tive". Clearly, da Costa was "an inexorable enthusiast" and his financial insecurity may well have fuelled his tendency towards greed, but "although he sought to elevate his personal standing through his scientific endeavours, he was also committed to the progress of science and thus to well-being of the wider scientific community".[262] In 1765, Borlase sent further specimens to da Costa, some for his personal collection, and others for the Society's Museum. Despite da Costa's disgrace, and amidst the outrage from the wider community of mineralogists, Borlase acknowledged his fault, but remained loyal to him as a colleague, and in the same year, 1765, Borlase wrote to the Quaker doctor, John Fothergill, who had helped da Costa financially, and had described him as often "necessitous" to him in his own mineralogical research, that da Costa had also "been necessitous ever since I [first] knew him".[263] In 1772, when his health was deteriorating rapidly, Borlase wrote to da Costa when he was released from prison. He did so in a warm and beneficent manner, offering him further specimens and, with great humility, offering him any use da Costa might make of Borlase's "poor opinion" on fossils.

Borlase's business dealings with Abraham Hart and his son, Lazarus Hart, had been at a time when the Harts were only beginning to establish themselves in Penzance. It was Lazarus Hart, however, who was, later, to develop and expand the family business. The 18th century was, for the Cornish port towns a time of rapid expansion, which continued through to the early 19th century, when, in just ten years from 1811 to 1821, the population of Penzance rose from 4,020 to 5,224.[264] The local economy, based on mining, farming, fishing and sea-trade, flourished. It was also a time when there was much interest in the West Indies, and a number of families connected with the West Indies trade came to settle in the South West. Among them were the Prices of Trengwainton, Penzance. Further up-country the Lopes family, who had been long established in Jamaica, put down new roots in Roborough, Plymouth.[265] The Lemon and Daniell families of Truro, whose names have survived in that town's place-names, had Jamaican interests, and Charles Lemon was to become a mining promoter.[266] (A William Lemon, the son of a Germoe-Breage landowner, and unrelated to the Truro Lemon family, had been manager of the Tin-Smelter at Chyandour, Penzance, although little is known of his early life).[267] In view of the Harts' shipping interests and the links between the tin producers and the shippers, it is quite possible that Lazarus Hart knew this particular member of the Penzance Lemon family. The Lemon name occurs in the records of Cornish Masonic Lodges, where Jews such as Lemon Hart and Lemon Woolf were members. Lemon Woolf was Master of the Penzance Lodge in 1818, occupying various positions, including Secretary in 1836, and Sir Charles Lemon became Master of the Falmouth Lodge in 1843. From these various commercial and civic associations, it might seem that Lazarus Hart and Hyman Woolf could have adapted this local surname as forenames for their sons, although an entirely different explanation is possible.

The name *Lemon* pervades the family tree of the Hart family and its connections. Just as the names *Asher* and *Abraham* characterised the earlier generations of the Hart family, the name *Lemon,* a derivative of *Asher,* above, and of *Lemel,* Lazarus Hart's brother (-1755), was passed down through later generations into the 1900s. The name can serve not only to illustrate the subtle phonetic and religious elements that may shape and comprise Hebrew nomenclature, reinforcing familial identification, but may also suggest a means which eased a process of achieving wider social integration and acceptance. In Penzance, only men with the combined forenames *Asher Laemle* ("He/the Man [who is] consecrated (or dedicated / devoted to / loves, or is loved by God") became known as *Lemon.* These were *Asher Laemle ben Eliezar* (Lemon Hart), *Asher Laemle ben Hayim* (Lemon Woolf) and *Asher ben Laemle* (Lemon Jacobs, also known as Frederick Jacobs or Hart). The latter's father, *Laemle ben Solomon Aharon ha-Levi,* was known as Lazarus Jacobs, indicating the *Laemle* did not, on its own, serve to become *Lemon.* This is explicable, in that the "Man Devoted" would be expressed in English as "Devoted Man", a reversal that would suggest a reversal of the Hebrew to *Laemle Asher.* Usage could abbreviate, conflate and partially anglicise this to the phonetic form *Lae-Man,* and familiarity with the Cornish Lemon family name, could lead to the form *Lemon.* It may be supposed that these suggested variations and permutations are essentially fanciful, but, in fact, such processes did operate as commonplace variants in spelling and usage, especially where linguistic collision and fusion acted as factors in the acclimatisation and acculturation of immigrants, like the Jews, whose Yiddish accented pronunciation of English no doubt played a part, as did the irregularities and idiosyncracies of English spelling itself. Lemon Hart's forename, for example, has been written as *Lemon* and *Leman,* in the Penzance Congregational Minutes, as *Lehman,* in victualling records, and his surname as *Heart,* in local shipping records (1802).

Moreover, from at least the 16th century, English colloquial usage had popularised the archaic term *leman* as the "beloved" or "sweetheart", sometimes the devoted spouse, and as the lover or secret paramour. It was also used in a derogatory sense of women, as mistresses or whores, and *Leman Street,* which runs southwards from Whitechapel towards the London Docks may well have been so-called because it was frequented by prostitutes. (It happens to lie a little east of Fenchurch Street, where the Lemon Hart firm became established, but there is no connection with the name *Lemon*). The term *leman* occurs in three of Shakespeare's plays, in Spenser's *Faerie Queene,* and is included in Samuel Johnson's Dictionary of 1755.[268] Such popular usage may well have survived into the 18th century, and have registered with Jewish ears as partially resembling a component of the original Hebrew names. The terms, "my lover" and "my sweetheart" are still used in Cornwall as colloquial, superficial terms of endearment and greeting. The name *Lemon* itself was used by Jews outside Cornwall, and its Hebrew derivation and extraneous associations may have varied from place to place, and from family to family. A Lemon Abraham was a licensed Navy Agent in Plymouth (1814-1815), but his Hebrew names are not known.[269] A Lemuel Hart, who was not related to Lemon Hart of Penzance, and who may have been Jewish, died in Devon in 1747, and in 1825, a Lemuel Lyon was one of the four Jews from Bedford who were involved with the purchase of a burial ground in Nottingham.[270] The name *Lemon* (or *Leman*) modified from *Lemmle* (or *Lemel*) was also used by some Jews as a surname, and can be found, for example, amongst Jews in London and Dublin, and also in Jamaica, where an Israel and a Solomon Lemon were registered in 1817.[271] The Hart family of Penzance passed the name *Lemon* down through the generations both as a forename and as a middle name. Lemon Hart's grandson, Lemon (1831-1886) is given as *Leman*, a Wine and Spirit Merchant, in the 1881 Census for Hampstead, London,[272] and his son, in turn, was also named *Lemon* (1857-1903).

The Hart family from Germany soon married into another Jewish family that had settled in Cornwall, that of Benjamin Woolf and his son, Hyman Woolf. Benjamin Woolf and his wife (whose name is unknown) had come to Penzance from Holland around 1720-30, and later moved to Falmouth, where Benjamin Woolf traded as a pawnbroker. One of their daughters, Bella (1726-1816) married Israel Solomon (*c.* 1727-1802) of Falmouth, a son of Solomon Solomon (1764-1819) and Betsy Levy (1757-1832), and the other daughter, Rebecca married Eleazar (Lazarus) Hart (1739-1803) of Penzance, in Falmouth, in December 1763. The couple settled in Penzance, where Rebecca's brother, Hyman Woolf (*c.* 1732-1820) had remained. He was to marry Eddle (Esther) Hart, who may have been a sister of Lazarus Hart, born *c.* 1747, although she has been taken to be his first cousin, Lemon Hart's sister, and, therefore a daughter of Lazarus Hart and Rebecca Woolf.[273] If the latter was the case, she would have been very much younger than her husband, Hyman, who was 88 when he died in 1820. It would seem far more likely that the Woolf siblings married into the same generation of the Hart family. The two families were to co-operate closely, both in business and in congregational life. While they remained in Cornwall, the Hart family ensured that marriages were contracted with other Jews. On leaving the County, however, members of successive generations were to assimilate and marry non-Jews.

It has been supposed that Abraham (Solomon Lazarus) Hart had started to trade in the import of rum in Penzance around 1740, and that he visited Jamaica from the 1720s.[274] Although Abraham Hart's putative travels to Jamaica have not been confirmed as a matter of certainty, many Jewish traders lived in the West Indies, and it is credible that the Hart family of Penzance could have established commercial links there during the 18th century. Indeed, one of Abraham Hart's great grandchildren, Rebecca (1798-1874), a daughter of Lemon Hart, married a Walter Jacob Levi (d. 1828) from Barbados, on 2nd February 1820, in London.[275] Levi had amassed a considerable fortune from growing cotton and similar crops in the West Indies.[276] He had developed other commercial contacts there, and these may have included the Hart family's suppliers. In 1827, Levi went to New South Wales, Australia, arranging for his wife and family to follow him. (Rebecca Levi's brief stay in the country may well have been the first contact between Cornish Jews and Australia). Walter Levi's failed venture to establish his cotton business there was based on the erroneous assumption that the climate and soil would be suitable, and he died there only a year later. His wife, Rebecca, returned to England, where she married her first cousin, Frederick Jacobs (later as *Hart* in the Lemon Hart family business).

There were Jews named *Hart* either in Jamaica, or connected with it through trade in the 18th century.[277] In England, a Moses Hart had been an investor in the East India Company from 1668 to 1709, in the Royal African Company from 1702-1712, with a Solomon Hart, and in the South Sea Company in 1714. These three companies traded extensively with Jamaica and the West Indies. A Naphtali Hart, of Newport, Rhode Island, was trading with Jamaica from as early as 1746, and he delivered slaves there from around 1755 to 1765. His son, also Naphtali was in St. Eustatius, Jamaica in 1781. Solomon Hart, a landowner of the Parish of St. Dorothy, Jamaica, held 1,085 acres there in 1754. In 1795, a Levy Hart of Kingston, Jamaica was registered there as a resident, together with a John Hart (who may not have been Jewish). Neither are recorded as slave-owners. In 1817, three men, Daniel, Philip and Jonas Hart owned seven slaves there whilst, a Rachel Hart owned thirty-six, and in 1819, thirty-two slaves. In 1817, two people, neither of whom are thought to have been Jewish, a Mary Hart of Kingston (1 slave) and a Thomas Hart of the Parish of St. Elizabeth (12 slaves) appear on local registers. In the same Parish of St. Elizabeth, in 1817, an Elizabeth Hart owned one slave, a Nathan Hart owned two slaves, and Rebecca, Ann, Sarah and Elizabeth Hart owned forty-two between them. This family may have been Jewish. There is mention of a Joseph Hart in the West Indies Commerce Receipt Book of Moses Cohen d'Azevedo (1790-1861). The latter's trade extended to Barbados, where a Joseph Hart and a Nathan Hart were resident in Bridgetown between 1798-1818. Jacob and Joseph Barrow of Barbados, who were Jewish, were involved in the slave trade in the late 18th century[278] and the latter made a donation of £10 to the Penzance Jewish Congregation in 1815.[279] A Daniel Hart, a member of the Jamaican House of Assembly, was the first to free his slaves in 1838.[280]

As slave owners or, rarely, as slave traders, Jews comprised only a small proportion of those involved, as public records clearly indicate, and some Jews in the slave trade, were, in fact, converts to Christianity. Nevertheless, the involvement of Jews in the commercial life of Jamaica and Barbados was very significant. *Hart* was a common name amongst Jews and non-Jews alike, but there is no evidence from the genealogical information available that Abraham Hart of Penzance was directly related to any of the Hart residents of Jamaica, although some connection is possible. Nor is there evidence that Abraham Hart's family were implicated directly in the slave trade at any time, either as slave or plantation owners. Although the Barrow donation of 1815 may suggest some such connection, Lemon Hart (Abraham Hart's grandson) had left Penzance some years previously for London, and if Joseph Barrow had any dealings with him, or his father, Lazarus Hart, these are more likely to have related to the Hart family's importation of rum and other luxury goods from Barbados and Jamaica to England. Clearly, however, even as an importer of rum and other goods from the West Indies, the Hart family may have had an indirect involvement in the slave plantations through commercial links with those who did own them.

Whenever and however it began, the importance of rum from the West Indies to the Hart family's business interests became well established, and Lazarus Hart's commercial ventures widened to include ship-owning, in which capacity he was known as *Kazanes Heart*.[281] In the Penzance Shipping Registers he is given as a shopkeeper and one of five partners co-owning the *Nancy & Betsy*,[282] registered at Penzance on 7th April 1787 as a 78-ton brigantine, 61ft long, 17ft 8 ins. breadth, and 10ft deep in the hold. The ship had been newly built at Mevagissey, and Hart's other partners were Thomas Love, a Merchant, John Stone, Thomas Branwell (whose family had leased the land to the Jews to build their synagogues in 1768 and 1808), and William Woolcock, the last three recorded as "Gentlemen". The first three men were from Penzance, and the last from St. Mary's, Scilly. The proportion of shares held by each is not known. On 18th November 1791 the vessel was issued with a Plantation Certificate by Penzance Customs House for an intended voyage to Jamaica.[283] The last heard of this venture was that the ship foundered near Lundy Island about 15th February 1793 while on passage between St. Ives and Swansea. To be lost so near to her home port was a stroke of misfortune as she had made voyages to Jamaica via Newfoundland, where rum was drunk by the fishermen. This was a serious financial set-back for Lazarus Hart.

Problems had not been confined to overseas trade. Earlier in 1790 Hart had sent 24 *Tea Waiters* by land carriage to Mr. William Basley of Padstow for auction. Only three were sold and Basley returned the unsold balance on the *Mary* sloop from Cork, bound to Plymouth by way of Padstow and Penzance. He fell foul of the Customs House and was accused of trying to avoid duty on imported goods: "To the Honble Commissioners of His Majesty's Customs. The Humble Petetion of Lazarus Hart of the Town of Penzance in the County of Cornwall, Shopkeeper:- Most humbly Sheweth, That your petitioner is a dealer in most kinds of Birmingham and Sheffield wares, and being over Stocked in Japan'd tea Waiters, forwarded by Land Carriage the 19th June last, Twenty four tea Waiters for sale to Mr. William Basley of Padstow, in said County (he being an Auctioneer) with an order to said Mr. Basley to return such part thereof as did not meet with a Ready Sale, supposing by; and Conveyance as forwarded to him - The said Mr. Basely, meeting with an Opportunity by the Mary sloop Captain William Corbett with whom he was acquainted, from Cork bound to Padstow, Penzance & Plymouth with Provisions, ignorantly shipped 21 on said vessel of the said Tea Waiters (having sold three only) with a view to save land carriage, not dreaming any manner of danger, in such trifling Matters, knowing the goods to be realy and bonafide the Manufacture of Great Britain, such is the Real Truth of the whole Transaction without Reserve, and it was not by any Means to defraud the Revenue; In Tender consideration of the premises, your Petitioner most humbly Hopes your Honrs will take this into your most serious Consideration and not blend the honest Dealer who had no manner of Intention to defraud Government, with the Smuggler; but restore the said Twenty one Waiters to your Petitioner, who shall every pray, Laz.s Hart. Lazarus Hart maketh Oath That the Contents of the above Petition are True. Sworn at Penzance the 10th May 1790, before me, J. Batten Jnr. Mayor."[284]

On the 21st May the Commissioners insisted on proof from Hart to support his petition: "The Collector and Comp.r Penzance are to State what proof has been submitted to them to shew that the contents of the Former Petition is True and particularly that the Waiters are of British Manufacture and also to report their Observations on this Petition. By Order of the Commissioners - M. Hutson". Hart was able to satisfy these requirements because he was exonerated. On the 1st June 1790 the Customs Officers at Penzance issued a statement withdrawing their previous accusations: "We beg leave to report that the proof Submitted to Us to Shew that the Contents of the former Petition were true, was by the petitioner Offering to Swear to it (which he has since done) producing at same time his Invoices, from his Correspondent at Birmingham, on the first purchasing of said Waiters, likewise his Correspondence with Mr. Wm. Basley at Padstow, and by our own together with several others examined the Waiters, and we verily believe that they are of British Manufacture, & that no Fraud was intended.

Custom Ho. Penzance. J S Coll.r. J W Comp.r."

A few years later, Lazarus Hart had decided to wind up his business in Penzance. The reasons are not known, but in view of the fact that he continued to trade in the town until 1803, it could be that the desired sale was not forthcoming or that he re-considered. The following advertisement appeared in the *Sherborne Mercury* on 6th May 1793: " NOW SELLING: at prime cost, the entire stock of Mr. Lazarus Hart of the town of Penzance, who begs leave to recommend the same to the public in general, as well worth their attention; consisting of silver tankards, quarts, pints and half-pints; coffee-pots and waiters; tea-pots; quart, pint and half-pint goblets; skewers, polished and common; plain and engraved table and tea-spoons; milk-urns, punch-ladles, sugar-tongs etc. and a great variety of silver shoe-buckles; new and second-hand watches, plated candlesticks,[285] bread baskets, dish-crosses, sugar and cream pails, and a great variety of plated shoe and knee-buckles; some articles in the jewellery line; knives and forks, scissors, razors etc. Also a large quantity of 7/8ths and yard-wide Irishes, printed cottons and chintzes; nankeens, muslins, duroys, velverets, stockings, silk handkerchiefs, black sattins, and some umbrellas. Also a large stock of new and second-hand sea and landsmen's cloaths. Any person in trade inclinable to buy the stock will meet with encouragement, and may have the house, which is well situated in the market-place, and an established shop in the above line for these many years past. Old gold or silver taken in exchange, at its full value."[286] Because there is no mention in this advertisement of Lazarus Hart's interest in the Wine and Spirit business, it may be taken that any shop he used for sales in Penzance was secondary to his main source of income as a wine and spirit importer and a shipping merchant. From the first mention of Lazarus' Hart's trading in 1764 to his death in 1803, it would seem that he sustained a viable business in the town for at least forty years, at a time when bankruptcy was all too common an occurrence. In 1778 his business as a Silversmith & Shopkeeper, with a "dwelling House and Warehouse under One Roof" was insured for £500.[287] By 1786, the valuation of the same business, together with that of a Pawnbroker, had doubled to £1000.[288] In 1799, by which time he may have sold off the bulk of his business, but continued to trade as a Merchant near the Penzance Quay, apparently on a more modest scale, in that his assets were valued at £600.[289]

No more is known about Lazarus Hart's business affairs until 1801 when he registered a complaint with the Customs and Excise against John Julyan, a Tide Waiter (Customs Officer) at Penzance.[290] Writing "as a man of honour - with the greatest respectability" Hart complained of the "constant insults and turbulent conduct of John Julyan", and reported to the Commissioners that Julyan "kept an open shop in this town and deals in Excisable goods in the name of a third party whose name (was) not known in Julyan's house, in the town of Penzance, or in the neighbourhood." Hart also stressed that he was complaining under his own name and not as an anonymous informer. The complaint was duly investigated and the Commissioners pointed out that by an Order dated 6th June 1799, Julyan had been given permission for his wife to carry on a business "provided it did not interfere with his duty". The report went on to state that Julyan had been "searching round a cart which said Hart keeps for conveying (as he says) goods to his customers" and then alleges that Julyan had "positive information" that Hart was "concerned with this illegal traffic". Julyan was clearly a man to be reckoned with. As a Tide Waiter he was part of the Waterguard which was responsible for checking loaded vessels or vessels afloat for contraband. (The Land Waiters on the other hand were responsible for checking goods on the quays before they were loaded into ships, or after they were discharged). Julyan was first appointed as a Boatman in February 1786 and after two years trial, he received a Commission as a Boatman. He was a very active officer who took part in a number of seizures and incidents. He was promoted to the position of Landing and Coast Waiter duties in March 1789 when he was sent to Plymouth for training. In his new role he would have responsibility for both seaside and landside searches. The Penzance officers did not enjoy a very high reputation and a number were dismissed for a variety of irregularities, although they were very rarely prosecuted for dereliction of duty. Since Julyan held office for twenty years or more, he must have been considered a satisfactory officer.[291] It would seem that the Hart complaint was not upheld and matters went no further. When one considers the allegations and counter-allegations, one is left with the feeling that Hart's complaint was not only ill-judged but may well have been a case of "the pot calling the kettle black". As a way of settling personal accounts it was seen as necessary to discourage such complaints if only because it could have endangered a well-established Cornish way of life.

Lazarus Hart died on 5th October 1803, three days after a fire at the home of his son, Lemon Hart (1768-1845), in which the latter's pregnant wife was seriously injured. On 3rd December his shop goods and unredeemed pledges due to him were advertised for sale by auction in the *Royal Cornwall Gazette*:

"Unredeemed Pledges FOR SALE BY AUCTION ON THURSDAY the 15th instant, by Ten o'clock in the Forenoon, at the Dwelling-House of the late MR. LAZARUS HART in Penzance. A GREAT variety of **UNREDEEMED PLEDGES**, whereof the term of 12 months and one day are expired. Also the whole of his SHOP GOODS, consisting of Cloths, Beavers, Checks, Striped Cottons, ready made Men's and Women's Cloaths, Silver and Plated Goods, Watches, Hardware, &c.,

&c.,well worth the attention of the Trade and the Publics' in general. NB. The Pawnbroker's Business will be carried on as usual, in the same House, by his family-Groceries sold Wholesale, as cheap as in London or Bristol. All Persons indebted to the Estate of the said Mr. Lazarus Hart, are destined to pay the same forthwith to Mr. LEMON HART, Wine Merchant, in this Town; the Administrator. Penzance, 1st.Dec.1803".

Letters of Administration had been granted to his son Lemon Hart on 13th October 1803; the Estate being valued at the considerable sum of £3,600, according to the commission executed before the Clerk Master of the Archdeaconry of Cornwall. For Lemon Hart, 1803 became a year of tragedy. Not only did he lose his father, on the 5th October, but also his wife, Letitia ("Letty") Michael of Swansea, on the 10th, both deaths following quickly after a fire at their home on the 2nd October.[292] The event, and the shocking circumstances leading up to her death, were reported locally and were felt to be so dramatic as to be re-printed 65 years later in the monthly journal *One and All* in November 1868:

ACCIDENTS SELDOM COME ALONE, EVEN IN PENZANCE. Sunday evening, Oct. 2nd, 1803, as Mrs. Hart, wife of Mr. Lemon Hart, spirit merchant, Penzance, was in an upper room alone, with a candle, her clothes unfortunately caught fire, and burnt her in a shocking manner. She was pregnant, has since been prematurely delivered, and now lies in a situation so deplorable, that her life is despaired of. In addition to this calamity, Mr. Lazarus Hart, father of the above-named Mr. Hart, died a few days ago in a fit of apoplexy. (Mrs. Hart died Monday, Oct. 10th)."

Letitia Hart is buried in the Penzance cemetery, but the precise location is not known, in that her headstone has not survived. She had come from a family of Jews named *Michael* who were to form a long established line in Swansea, South Wales. Letitia Michael's father, David Michael (1727-1797) had been born in Germany, and had arrived in Swansea in the 1740s.[293] He had married a *Rizpah* (Rachel: 1717-1805) whose family name is not known. The Corporation granted David Michael a plot of land where he established the Jewish Burial Ground in Swansea in 1768, and where he is buried. For some years the community had met for worship in David Michael's house in Wind Street, where he was able to accommodate up to forty people. In 1789, the congregation took possession of a wooden building in the Strand as its synagogue. David Michael's two sons, Levi and Jacob, who were silversmiths, became very successful businessmen, and they were leading members of the Hebrew Congregation. In 1818, a 99-year lease was taken on a plot of land in Waterloo Street, where a synagogue was built that held about sixty to seventy people. The forenames of both Lemon Hart and Letitia Michael were to pass down through both the Hart and Michael families, and the name *Hart* was adopted by members of the Michael family as a middle name for male and female children. Letitia Michael's brother, Levi Michael (1754-1841) was also to marry a *Rose* (1760-1847) whose surname is not known, but who was not a member of the Hart family. Letitia's other brother, Jacob Michael (1758-1835) was to marry Lemon Hart's sister, Leah (1772-1840). Lemon Hart and Letitia Michael were to have five children, Harriet (Harrietta: 1796-1879), Rebecca (1798-c.1875), David (1799-1868), Rose (-1863) and Louisa (Esther or Estelle: -1866). Of the last two, one of these daughters was the child born prematurely a few days before her mother's tragic death on 10th October 1803. Rose Hart was to marry a Jacob Michael (1795-1882) of London, whose connection with *Michael* of Swansea, if any, is uncertain. This Jacob Michael lived at Wandsworth, and died at Northwood.[294] The connection between the Hart family of Penzance and that of David Michael of Swansea may have had its origins in Germany. Levi and Rose Michael had at least two sons, Michael John Michael (-1861) and Frederick David Michael (1780-1870). It was likely to have been the latter, Letitia Michael's nephew, who, as "F. Michael (of) Swansea", is recorded in the Penzance Minute Book Accounts of 9th October 1808 as having made a donation of One Guinea to the congregation (to which he had presumably become attached or affiliated) towards the building of the new synagogue. Frederick Michael may also have been known as Francis, in that a Francis Michael, a son of Levi Michael, founded the Swansea Savings Bank.[295] It is likely that commercial interests had forged links between the Hart and Michael families, in that David Michael and his son Levi Michael were actively involved in the development of the Port of Swansea, and the latter was a proprietor of the Swansea canal, which was forged after 1794 to create a shipping link from Swansea, in Glamorgan, as far as the County of Brecon. From 1802, Lemon Hart had been a co-owner of a shipping vessel, the *Amelia*, that sailed between Penzance and Swansea.

Soon after Letitia Hart's death, Lemon Hart, with the responsibility and prospect of bringing up his children on his own, had found a new wife. It may be that matters of business already took him to London, and on 22nd July 1804, in the Great Synagogue [296] in Duke's Place, London he married a widow, Mary (Miriam) Solomon, the daughter of Lazarus Isaac Solomon of Prescott Street, Goodmans Fields, London.[297] The synagogue's Marriage Registers record the parties as *Hart Lemon Lemle s. Lezar Penzance* (and) *Solomon Miriam d. Mr. Isaac the Chazan, deceased.* It would seem that Mary Solomon's late husband may have been named *Slowman* (possibly a variant of *Solomon*). In his will (proved in 1847) Lemon Hart refers to a stepson, Benjamin Slowman. There were a number of other London Jews named *Lazarus Solomon* at this time, but their connection, if any, with Mary Solomon's father is not known. A Lazarus Solomon married a Catherine Wolf in 1798. Lazarus Solomons married a Trina Lyons in 1802, and another Lazarus Solomons married a Rebecca Woolf in 1825.[298] (This Rebecca Woolf was the daughter of a Benjamin Woolf, but she is not to be confused with her and her father's namesakes. She is not the Rebecca Woolf of Falmouth, the daughter of Benjamin Woolf of Holland, who had married Elieazar (Lazarus) Hart of Penzance in 1763). As with Lemon Hart's first wife, Mary Solomon was not a native or resident of Penzance, and it is not clear how Lemon Hart's connection with the Solomon family of London came about. It is not known if Lazarus Isaac Solomon's family had ever lived in Penzance before settling in London, or if they had always lived in the capital, but the existence of the 1775 watch, mentioned earlier, carrying the inscription, *Lazarus Solomon, Penzance* is intriguing. The absence of Penzance congregational records prior to 1808, which might indicate if a Lazarus Solomon was a member of the congregation around 1775, or if he acted as its *chazan*, renders any such identification with the owner of the watch a matter of speculation. The difficulty of identi-

Hart of Penzance

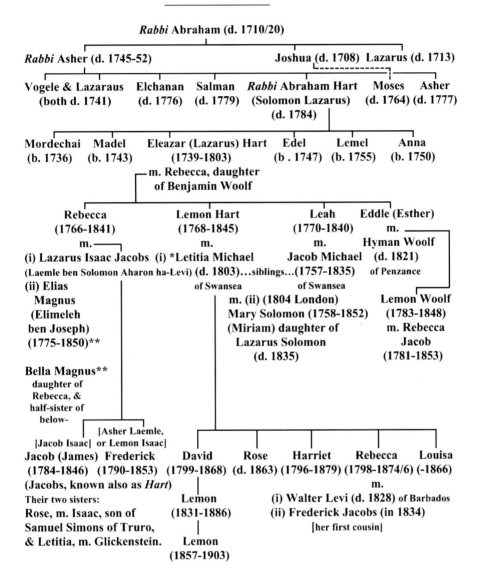

Rabbi **Abraham (d. 1710/20)**

Rabbi **Asher (d. 1745-52)**   **Joshua (d. 1708) Lazarus (d. 1713)**

Vogele & Lazaraus   Elchanan   Salman   *Rabbi* Abraham Hart   Moses   Asher
(both d. 1741)   (d. 1776) (d. 1779) (Solomon Lazarus)   (d. 1764) (d. 1777)
                                           (d. 1784)

Mordechai   Madel   Eleazar (Lazarus) Hart   Edel   Lemel   Anna
(b. 1736) (b. 1743)   (1739-1803)   (b . 1747) (b. 1755) (b. 1750)
                      m. Rebecca, daughter
                      of Benjamin Woolf

Rebecca   Lemon Hart   Leah   Eddle (Esther)
(1766-1841)   (1768-1845)   (1770-1840)   m. ————
m. ————   **m.**   **m.**   **Hyman Woolf**
(i) Lazarus Isaac Jacobs (i) *Letitia Michael   Jacob Michael   (d. 1821)
(Laemle ben Solomon Aharon ha-Levi) (d. 1803)...siblings...(1757-1835) *of Penzance*
(ii) Elias   *of Swansea*   *of Swansea*
Magnus   **m. (ii) (1804 London)   Lemon Woolf**
(Elimeleh   **Mary Solomon (1758-1852)   (1783-1848)**
ben Joseph)   **(Miriam) daughter of   m. Rebecca**
(1775-1850)**   **Lazarus Solomon   Jacob**
                         (d. 1835)   (1781-1853)
Bella Magnus**
daughter of
Rebecca, &
half-sister of
below-
                      [Asher Laemle,
[Jacob Isaac] or Lemon Isaac]
Jacob (James) Frederick   David   Rose   Harriet   Rebecca   Louisa
(1784-1846) (1790-1853) (1799-1868) (d. 1863) (1796-1879) (1798-1874/6) (-1866)
(Jacobs, known also as *Hart*) | **m.**
Their two sisters: **Lemon**   **(i) Walter Levi (d. 1828) of Barbados**
Rose, m. Isaac, son of   **(1831-1886)**   **(ii) Frederick Jacobs (in 1834)**
Samuel Simons of Truro, | [her first cousin]
& Letitia, m. Glickenstein.   **Lemon**
                                     (1857-1903)

*Roth Collection, Leeds (research by Evelyn Friedlander). ** Research by Angela Shire: Bella
married Cerf Cylick in London on 24th October 1838.
Sources: Collyer-Fergusson, Anthony P. Joseph & Godfrey Simmons.
Compiled by Keith Pearce © (2013).

Hart of Penzance - Pidwell of Penzance and Falmouth

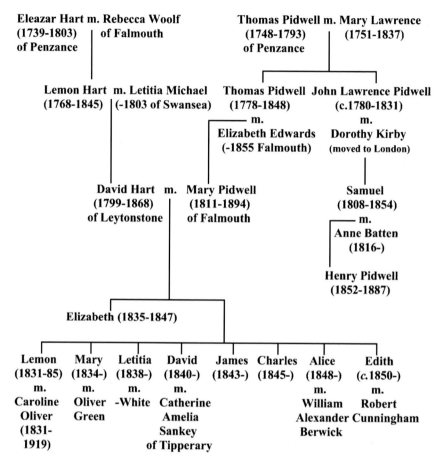

Eleazar Hart m. Rebecca Woolf
(1739-1803) | of Falmouth
of Penzance

Thomas Pidwell m. Mary Lawrence
(1748-1793) | (1751-1837)
of Penzance

Lemon Hart m. Letitia Michael
(1768-1845) | (-1803 of Swansea)

Thomas Pidwell John Lawrence Pidwell
(1778-1848) (c.1780-1831)
m. m.
Elizabeth Edwards Dorothy Kirby
(-1855 Falmouth) (moved to London)

David Hart m. Mary Pidwell
(1799-1868) | (1811-1894)
of Leytonstone | of Falmouth

Samuel
(1808-1854)
m.
Anne Batten
(1816-)

Henry Pidwell
(1852-1887)

Elizabeth (1835-1847)

Lemon	Mary	Letitia	David	James	Charles	Alice	Edith
(1831-85)	(1834-)	(1838-)	(1840-)	(1843-)	(1845-)	(1848-)	(c.1850-)
m.	m.	m.	m.			m.	m.
Caroline	Oliver	-White	Catherine			William	Robert
Oliver	Green		Amelia			Alexander	Cunningham
(1831-			Sankey			Berwick	
1919)			of Tipperary				

[All born in London, except Charles, born Flushing, near Falmouth, Cornwall]

Source: Colyer-Fergusson, Peter Pool (1974), Jackie Hill (2002) & Census (1851 & 1861).

Compiled by Keith Pearce © (2013).

Hart - Michael

of Penzance and London **of Swansea and London**

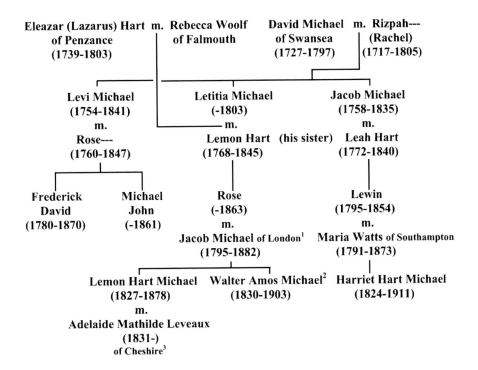

Compiled by Keith Pearce © (2013).

[1] It is not known if he was related to the Michael family of Swansea.
[2] It is possible that he (or another member of this family) is to be identified with the Lieut. Lemon Hart Walter of the 4th, or Royal South Middlesex Regiment, who was serving in Turkey in 1856. Walter Amos Michael died in Ajaccio, Sardinia.
[3] *The Times*, 24th August 1858.

Hart - Levy of Plymouth

There were several unrelated Hart families in Plymouth from the early to mid 18th century..
The Hart families of Plymouth were not related to Hart of Penzance.
The Hart family below were from Ansbach, Germany. Henry Hart entered Harwich in 1747.

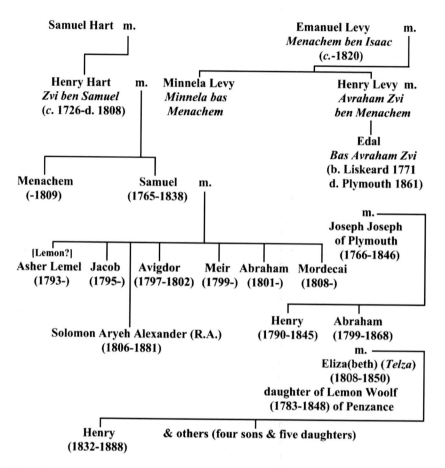

Because *Asher Lemel* (or *Laemle*) was also rendered as *Lemon*, the Asher Lemel Hart of
Plymouth above may have been known by this name. He should not be confused with his
namesake, Lemon Hart of Penzance (1768-1845).

Source: Susser (1972, 1993 & 1995) and Collyer-Fergusson.
Compiled by Keith Pearce © (2013).

fying the town's resident population at a time before the introduction of civil registration (1837) and the decennial census (from 1841) does not help matters. Whether
Mary Solomon had known Penzance as child, or whether she had lived all of her
life in London, she came to live in the town after her marriage in 1804, but for only
seven years, returning to London in 1811 when Lemon Hart relocated his business
there. What is clear is that Lemon Hart's personal connection with London had
been well-established for some years before his move from Penzance. Mary
Solomon was ten years older than her second husband, and she outlived him by
seven years, dying in London at Euston Place on 24th October 1852, at the great
age of 94.[299]

During his father's lifetime Lemon Hart had already pursued business interests
of his own. Lemon *Heart* is recorded as one of six co-owners of the 52-ton sloop
Amelia, some 49ft. long, 16ft. in breadth, and with a hold with a capacity of almost
9ft. The vessel was registered at Penzance on 28th May 1802, its other owners being
John Mathews (Shipwright of Penzance), Arthur Hampton, Joseph Nicholls and
William Richards, "Gentlemen" all of Penzance, and John McFarland (a Victualler
of Plymouth). The *Amelia* was a French prize taken by HMS *Amelia*. Her new
owners employed her in the general coastal trade, mainly sailing between
Penzance and Swansea as a collier. In February 1806 she was employed as a temporary Tin-ship to carry tin between Penzance and London, but on her first run she
was re-taken by the French off Portland Bill on 24th February of that year. (Another
Amelia, also a French prize, was brought into service in 1807, but Lemon Hart was
not one of its owners). On 28th January 1804, in a lengthy advert for the sale of the
Dutch brig *Flora* and her cargo, Lemon Hart is named as the Broker conducting
the sale on behalf of the Admiralty. On 12th November 1805, Lemon *Heart* became
the first named partner in another ship the *Speculation*, a 57-ton sloop newly built
at Penzance, similar in dimensions and capacity to the *Amelia* of 1802. The other
co-owners were Joseph Branwell (butcher), John Mathews (shipbuilder of
Penzance), and three men from St. Ives: James Halse (Gentleman), William Ninnis
(cabinet maker) and Richard Banfield (merchant). The named owners later sold
the vessel to William Bryant, her former master, who is recorded as her sole owner
when her port of register was transferred to St. Ives on 17th October 1808.

Lemon Hart continued his father's business which prospered under his direction, and his own wine and spirit trade was well-established by 1804. He also
played an active role not only in the Jewish community as the first President of
the Hebrew Congregation's new synagogue, but also in the wider social and
community activities of Penzance. The latter years of the 18th century and the early
years of the 19th were times when the fear of invasion from France was ever-
present. Hart served in the Ludgvan and also the Mounts' Bay Volunteers as an
officer. These groups, comprising a form of the civil guard, were relatively small
groups that specialised in carrying out work such as blocking roads, building
defences and constructing batteries. The Ludgvan Pioneers detachment was raised
in 1798 with Captain Lemon Hart as their commander, although he later resigned
in favour of Captain John who had transferred from the Marazion Rangers.[300]
When the Ludgvan and Marazion groups merged, Lemon Hart left and became a
first lieutenant in the Mounts' Bay Fusileers, a two-company corps, established in

1787, although he returned to the re-named Ludgvan and Marazion Volunteers in 1800. Jacob Hart, Lemon's nephew, was also involved in these activities and was appointed to be Ensign of the St. Ives Volunteers in November 1803, at a time when again there was widespread fear of a French invasion.[301] Members of several well-known West Penwith families served in these groups at that time and changing between the various volunteer bodies was by no means uncommon. It is also perhaps an indication that Lemon Hart moved with ease and tolerance between his congregation and the wider community. A similar volunteer army existed in Penryn, under the command of Lieutenant Colonel Sir Francis Basset, Baronet Basset of Tehidy in 1779 and M.P. for Penryn in 1780. It consisted of four companies, with a major, and a number of captains, lieutenants, and ensigns. It had a chaplain, Rev. Robert Dillon, an adjutant, and a surgeon. It consisted of a sergeant major, twelve sergeants, twelve corporals and two hundred privates.[302]

During his years in Penzance, Lemon Hart remained committed to the traditions and values of his Jewish heritage. Both of his wives were Jewish, and his children were raised in the Jewish faith. He appears to have possessed a relatively liberal outlook, however, and, some twenty years after the family's move to London (1811), and, apparently for the first time in the Hart family, at least three of his children were to marry non-Jews, one of whom, Mary Pidwell, was from Cornwall.[303] Further non-Jewish marriages took place in subsequent generations. Although these marriages can be seen as a the beginning of a process of integration and even assimilation into English Gentile society, the marriage of Lemon Hart's son, David, to a Cornish girl does not in any way indicate integration into Cornish society. It took place in London, two decades after the family had settled there, and none of the Hart family returned to Cornwall to live, but only to visit. David Hart (1799-1868) was about twelve when he left Penzance for London in 1811, the year in which his future wife was born. The Hart and Pidwell families of Penzance would have been familiar with one another, and members of both families were to develop business interests in London.[304] The Pidwell family were practising Christians: some attended St. Mary's Anglican Church, situated on the lower stretches of Chapel Street, near the Penzance Quay, where the Hart family business was located, near the church's graveyard. Other members of the Pidwell family were nonconformists, as Congregationalists. Various ministers of that denomination lived with the Pidwells, one being the Rev. John Foxell, who was to marry Mary Borlase of Penzance.[305] She became a sub-lessee to the land that comprised the Jewish cemetery, and Foxell had direct dealings with the Jewish congregation in its rental payments to his wife. Thomas Pidwell (1748-1793) had been a contemporary of Eleazar Hart (1739-1803), and his son, also Thomas (1778-1848), a Draper, was a contemporary of Lemon Hart (1768-1845). He had married an Elizabeth Edwards (-1855) and their children were all baptised at Paul Parish Church, some four miles from Penzance: Thomas (then 18 months old) and Samuel (an infant) on 3rd April 1808, Charles, on 14th October 1810, and Mary, on 6th October 1811.[306] There was also another daughter, Elizabeth. Samuel and Charles Pidwell both settled in Portugal, at Sines (the birthplace of Vasco da Gama) situated on a cape in the Alentejo region. Thomas and Elizabeth Pidwell became estranged, and Elizabeth moved to the Falmouth area with her children. She remained there for the remainder of her life, most likely living at Flushing, across the water from Falmouth, and later at Mylor creek, some miles away. It is unlikely that there was a divorce from her husband, who is recorded in the 1841 Census as living in Penzance alone. He died there in 1855.

Passing reference should be made to another Pidwell family in Falmouth that was, in fact, unrelated to Pidwell of Penzance. A "Joseph Pidwell, linguist" lived in Falmouth in the 1860s in Killigrew Street.[307] This Joseph Pidwell, who had been born in 1811, was the son of Joseph and Mary Pidwell of Truro. The family had moved to Falmouth in 1815. Despite the fact that Joseph Pidwell's mother was named Mary, and that his wife, Amelia Barker, who he married in 1837, was from Lisbon (1841 Census) where she was born (as a British subject), there is no connection with Mary Pidwell of Falmouth (formerly of Penzance). The shared Portuguese connection, between Amelia Pidwell and Mary Pidwell's brothers, Samuel and Charles is entirely coincidental, and Packet Boat services ran frequently between Falmouth and Lisbon.

Of the Pidwell family of Penzance, Thomas Pidwell's brother, John Lawrence Pidwell (c. 1780-1831) who was one of the founder members of the Penzance Library (1818) moved to London, living at Carpenter Buildings, London Wall, near Fenchurch Street, where Lemon Hart traded from 1811. His son, Samuel Pidwell (1808-1854) was a graduate of Worcester College, Oxford. He returned to live in Penzance, where he became a Brewer, and would have come into contact with a trade shared by Moses Woolf (1815-) son of Lemon Hart's relative, Lemon Woolf, the former also being a brewer, and the latter a Wine and Spirit Merchant. Samuel Pidwell retained a family home in London, and was also Mayor of Penzance (1844 and 1849). His son, Henry Pidwell (1852-1887) was initially a Draper in Kensington, but he eventually became a Colonial Broker in the firm *Pidwell, Wilmot & Co.* at Mark Lane, next to Fenchurch Street and Hart Lane, and it would seem likely that the *Lemon Hart* business, with its shipping interests in imports from the Colonies and elsewhere, would, at some point, have come into contact with Henry Pidwell's firm. It is possible that the Lemon Hart firm influenced the street name, *Hart Lane*, but it was not responsible for its origin. *Kent's London Directory* of 1794 lists a number of traders named *Hart* in this vicinity, who had become established well before the arrival of Lemon Hart. An unrelated John Hart, a Perfumier, traded at 20, Fenchurch Street, a few doors from Lemon Hart, at 59.

The connection between the Hart and Pidwell families was sealed when David Hart and Mary Pidwell were married on 3rd January 1831, in London at All Hallows, Staining.[308] The marriage was conducted by the Rector, Lancelot Sharpe, the banns having been published during December 1830. Both the bride and groom signed the register as "of this parish", and the witnesses were J. Michael of Red Lion Yard, and his wife, Rosina, David Hart's sister Rose (-1863) who had married Jacob Michael (1795-1882) in London on 31st December 1824. David and Mary Hart were to live at Park House (or *The Park*) Leytonstone in East London, not far from the location of his father's business interests along the stretch of the River from Tower Hill to Deptford. Park House had extensive grounds, stabling and two tenant-cottages. The 1861 Census reveals that the household was a large one, with a cook, parlour-maid, housemaid, poultry-girl, nurse and a man servant - all in residence. Whereas most of the domestic staff were drawn from London and its environs, at least two, Susan Bassett and Henry Johns, were from Cornwall, from Falmouth and nearby Mylor respectively. The same census records that a Benjamin Pidwell (17) from Penzance, Mary Pidwell's nephew, and son of her brother, Thomas Pidwell was also living in the house. David Hart traded in London as a wine merchant, becoming a wealthy man able to afford to buy land in Leytonstone and Harrow Green. He also became Overseer to the Poor in 1860. David and Mary had at least thirteen children,[309] but only eight names have been identified with certainty, the others, most likely dying young. David and Mary never lived in Cornwall again, but would have returned to visit Mary's mother near Falmouth. At least one son, Charles, was born in Cornwall, at Flushing, near Falmouth on 15th October 1845, and his sister, Elizabeth died prematurely at her grandmother's home at Mylor, in 1847. The *West Briton* recorded (on 24th October 1845) "At Flushing, on the 15th instant, the wife of David Hart, Esq. of Forest Gate, Essex, of a son" (24th October 1845) and (on 12th February 1847) "At the residence of her grandmother, Mrs. Pidwell, Mylor, on 23rd, *ult.*, Elizabeth, second daughter of David Hart, Esq., of Forest Gate, West Ham, Essex, aged 12 years."[310] Their children (eight of whom were born in London) were: Lemon (1831-1885), who married a Caroline Oliver (1831-1919), Mary (1834-) who married an Oliver Green, Elizabeth (1835-1847), [named after her maternal aunt], Letitia (1838-) who married a ... ..White, David (1840-) who married a Catherine Amelia Sankey of Tipperary, James (1843-), Charles (1845-), [named after his maternal uncle (1810-) who, with his brother, Samuel (1808-) settled in Lisbon], Alice (1848-) who married a William Alexander Berwick, and Edith (*c.* 1850-) who married a Robert Cunningham.

Of David Hart's sisters, apart from Rose, one sister was to marry twice, on both occasions to Jews: on 2nd February 1820, Rebecca (1798-1874/6) married Walter (d. 1828, Sydney, Australia), a son of Jacob Levi of Barbados; and then on 25th June 1834 she married her first cousin, Frederick (Lemon) Jacobs (1790-1853), a son of Lazarus Jacobs.[311] Harriet (1796-1879) and Louise (-1866) married non-Jews in Churches in London: on 19th July 1830, Harriet married James McTernan in a church service at Blackheath, and on 12th May 1832, at All Hallows Church, Staining, Louisa (also known as Esther, or Estelle) married a solicitor, Samuel Amos, originally from Evesham.[312] It is possible that Samuel Amos was of Jewish descent, although both of his names are not uncommon amongst Jews and Gentiles. He, or his family, may have been Jewish converts to Christianity. Evesham is not known to have had a Jewish community. At some point Samuel Amos practised as a solicitor in Stoke-on-Trent, and Louisa Hart died at Llanberris, North Wales on 19th August 1866. Louisa Hart's sister, Rose, had two sons, one of whom was named Lemon Hart Michael (1827-1878) and the other Walter Amos Michael (1830-1903). Of the former, it is possible that he, or some other family member is to be connected with the Lieutenant Lemon Hart Walter of the 4th or Royal South Middlesex Regiment who was serving in Turkey in 1856. Walter Amos Michael died in Ajaccio, Sardinia.

The Lemon Hart Tradition

Lemon Hart was one of the most successful businessmen from Penzance in the late 18th and early 19th centuries, and he was a comparatively wealthy man even before he left the town. His rapid rise and continuing success appear to have given rise to an inflated tradition concerning him, elements of which are uncertain and unsubstantiated, and others which are quite simply untrue.[313] Lemon Hart (and his firm) have even been allocated to Plymouth, and not Penzance, as the place where Lemon Hart lived and traded. There was, indeed, a Hart family in Exeter in 1841, that of Moses Hart, a watchmaker, then 55, and his wife, Esther and their four children. They had all been born in Devon.[314] There were also several (unrelated) Hart families in Plymouth, the most notable being that of Henry Hart (*c.*1726-1808), but there was no connection with the Harts of Penzance, and neither the Cornish or Devonian Hart families were related to the Harts of Portsmouth. Fortunately, Susser's study of the Devonian Jewish families, together with his invaluable translation of the surviving headstones in the Hoe Cemetery, allow for a partial reconstruction of these various Hart families, and a clarification of how they may be distinguished from the Hart family of Penzance.

A member of the Joseph family of Plymouth, Joseph Joseph (1766-1846) married an *Edal* (who was born in Liskeard in 1771), and, because her forename was common to two women of the Hart family of Penzance, the genealogist William Jessop inferred, quite erroneously, that she was a member of that family, and, supposedly a daughter of an *Asher*. The latter name was also common in the Hart and Woolf families of Penzance (as *Asher Laemle*, i.e. *Lemon*) and Jessop made the further, tentative suggestion Edal may have been a daughter of Lemon Hart or even a sister of Lemon Woolf.[315] None of the available evidence fits Jessop's thesis. Eliezer Hart's sister (and Lemon Hart's aunt) *Eddle* was born around 1747, and Lemon Hart's sister, also *Eddle* (or Esther) had married Hyman Woolf (*c.* 1732-1880). If there was a sister of Lemon Woolf named *Edal* (in addition to his known sisters, Judith and Hannah), then a birth date for her of 1771 is not impossible, but her existence as such has not been established. Moreover, any daughter of Hyman Woolf would have been *bas Hayyim*,[316] which Edal of Liskeard was not (see below). Lemon Woolf's daughter, *Eddle*, was not born until 1827. Lemon Hart could not have been the father of the *Eddle* of Liskeard in that he was barely four years old at the time of her birth. In view of this persistent notion, a brief account of the Hart families of Plymouth is necessary.

(1) Apart from the Henry Hart mentioned above, there was another Jew in Plymouth also known as Henry Hart, *Yehiel ben Naphtali*, who died in 1821, who was the father of Moses Hart,[317] possibly the same as Moses Hart of Exeter. There were two other Hart men from Mannheim, Germany.(2) Michael Hart (*Yehiel Michael ben Zvi*), a silversmith, was born near Mannheim in 1739; he had entered England *via* Harwich in 1763, and he died in 1819.[318] (3) Joseph Hart (1756-1822), *Joseph ben Jacob Manheim*, known as "Joseph Manheimer", was also a silversmith from Mannheim, entering *via* Harwich in 1770.[319] (4) A Manley Hart, whose name might also suggest family origins in Mannheim, was another silversmith in Plymouth in 1806. He appears as a witness to the will of the miniaturist painter,

Abraham Daniel (1763-1806), one of the executors to the will being Samuel Hart, a son of the (second) Henry Hart, below. (5) Emanuel Hart (*Menasseh ben Zvi*), who died in 1828, was a watchmaker, originally from Biala, near Wroclaw in Southern Poland.[320] Another Joseph Hart, (*ben* Zvi) who died in 1843,[321] may have been his brother. (6) A Nathaniel Hart was in Plymouth in 1860.[322]

The progenitor of the Hart family of Plymouth which relates to the matter of the marriage of Edal of Liskeard to Joseph Joseph of Plymouth was Henry Hart (*Zvi ben Samuel*)[323] who was born around 1726. He was from Bruck, Ansbach, Germany, and he came to England, entering *via* Harwich in 1747. He became a well established merchant in Plymouth,[324] and he married a Minnela (*bas Menachem*)[325] the daughter of an Emanuel[326] (Menachem) Levy (-1820). Minnela's brother, Abraham, or Henry Levy (*Avraham Zvi ben Menachem*)[327] was most likely a pedlar who travelled with his wife (whose name is not known) from Plymouth to Liskeard, where he may have lived briefly, and where his daughter (*Edal bas Avraham Zvi*) was born.[328] It was this Edal Levy who married Joseph Joseph of Plymouth. Henry Hart had a son, Menachem (-1809) and Edal and Joseph Joseph had a son and grandson both named Henry. A final element which has helped to confuse Hart of Plymouth with Hart of Penzance lies with Henry Hart's son, Samuel (1765-1838) who had seven sons, one of whom was *Asher Lemel*, Hebrew forenames which are commonly rendered as "Lemon"; hence an echo of Lemon Hart and Lemon Woolf of Penzance. There were, therefore, two men, both named *Lemon* (*Asher Laemle* or *Lemel*), Lemon Hart (1768-) of Penzance, the son of Eliezar Hart, and Lemon Hart (1793-) a grandson of Henry Hart. These identical names have clearly led to the notion that Lemon Hart's Wine and Spirit business was located in Plymouth.

There are other elements which have combined to create a mistaken picture of Lemon Hart, which relate to his two wives: the first (the Letitia Michael from Wales, who died tragically in a fire) has been named as "Hannah" (Anna was Lemon Hart's aunt) and his second wife (Mary Solomon from London) who he married in 1804, has been assigned to a Penzance family living in Belgravia Street (which in fact was not built until around 1850). Lemon Hart was an only son, but a Jacob Hart (who was his nephew) has been taken as his brother.[329] The commercial aspects of the Lemon Hart tradition appear to be a retrospective embellishment from the later achievements of his London years. These include the notion that he owned vast slave plantations in the West Indies (mentioned earlier) from which he transported rum and other goods in a fleet of privately owned vessels (there is, as we have seen, only evidence of his co-ownership of one or two local ships). By 1804-1807 (or very soon after), it has been supposed that Lemon Hart had moved on from being a merchant importer and distributor of wines and spirits, and had become a manufacturer-distiller, establishing his own firm with Lemon Hart rum ® as his own namesake brand. Moreover, he is said to have been appointed as a victualler to the Royal Navy before moving to London in 1811. In relation to the first decade of the 19th century it has been said of Lemon Hart that he was already "...a distiller, subsequently to become one of the largest spirits merchants in the country, who for many years held the contract for supplying the British Navy with rum....In 1811 [he] removed to London whence he continued in his laudable occupation of supplying the British blue-jackets with rum".[330], but these claims of such early, extensive commercial activity have not been substantiated. More astutely, it has been said of Lemon Hart that "It was possible that he imported the rum and supplied it to Navy agents. One cannot be more specific, as so much of the company's history has come down to us in mythic form with no extant documentation".[331] In fact Lemon Hart, was not the first, or the last, and nor was he ever the sole supplier of rum to the Royal Navy. Moreover, although Lemon Hart was eventually a successful businessman, he was never exceptionally or extraordinarily wealthy when compared with the London Rich[332] of the day, and the level of cover of his insurance policies indicate this.[333] In his will,[334] he left significant, but relatively unremarkable bequests: to his wife, an life-annuity of £500, and an immediate payment of £150; to his stepson, Benjamin Slowman, £20; to his son, David (who was to take control of the family firm), £1000; to each of his four daughters, £100, with an additional £100, to the eldest daughter, Rose: and £1000 to be invested by David in trust for each daughter (payable at 21), and a similar arrangement for his stepson. Compared with Moses Lazarus (1740-1814) of Rochford, who became established in London as a very affluent distiller and wine merchant before Lemon Hart's arrival there, the latter's enterprise was on a more modest scale (and, in fact his firm was to go into liquidation some years after his death). It remains unclear whether all of these commercial strands in the Lemon Hart story are entirely spurious, but they remain anecdotal in that they have not been substantiated for so early a date from formal sources, official documents or primary records. Lemon Hart was not a licensed Navy Agent in Penzance (the only Jewish agent in the town at this time being Henry Ralph, who moved to Plymouth in 1809).[335] It has been held that Lemon Hart operated as a distiller from premises at the top of Jennings Street, near the synagogue, but this has not been confirmed from documentary sources, and the only known premises which he occupied (and insured) were near the Quay.[336] Although he may have imported ready-distilled rum in casks, and bottled it locally, this does not constitute a manufacturer-distiller, and he appears to have concentrated mainly on the bulk importation of rum from the West Indies during his time in Penzance. Even later, Lemon Hart's distillers were based in Jamaica and not England, and labels carried the wording "Original Lemon Hart Imported Jamaica Rum – Distilled in Jamaica under Government Supervision, bottled in Great Britain by Lemon Hart & Son. Ltd., London". (That tradition and anecdote can be unreliable and inconsistent can be seen in the notion that Lemon Hart's Penzance business as an importer declined "following the development of the port of Bristol").[337]

No evidence of contracts to supply rum to the Navy while he lived in Penzance has come to light, but there is some evidence that the Lemon Hart firm became purveyors of rum to the Navy at a much later date, and that by then distilling had become an additional feature of the firm's commercial interests abroad. Moreover, Lemon Hart's appointment as a Naval victualler and the identity of the officials involved in the original and ongoing contractual arrangements have not been confirmed at all from the official Naval victualling records held at Kew and elsewhere. Curiously, neither the name of the Lemon Hart firm, nor even the surname *Hart* itself appears in any of these records, even for the years when Hart Navy rum contracts were reported in the national press (the notices may well have been placed privately by the Lemon Hart firm itself rather than by the Navy or Admiralty). The absence of the *Hart* name from these records is even more puzzling in that the names of other contemporaneous suppliers do appear. The tradition that Lemon Hart was the first to supply rum to the Navy, and that (through an Admiral "Tott") he introduced the sailors' "tot", and acquired a monopoly over the supply is entirely spurious. Long before Lemon Hart was even born (1768), red wine (usually Spanish), brandy and beer had been supplied to the Navy from numerous sources. By 1655, rum, which was cheap, easy to obtain and which improved with age, began to supersede brandy as the favoured spirit, and in 1731 it became the official issue to seamen "the daily half pint being issued in two equal parts, one in the morning and the other in the evening". So potent was the raw rum and so disastrous was it in its effects upon the sailors' capacities to perform their duty, with widespread drunkenness on board ship, that Admiral Vernon (-1757), wrote to the Admiralty in 1740 to inform them that on the ships under his command it would be diluted and strictly rationed. (This policy was eventually adopted). Vernon's unpalatable concoction was known as "grog" (from which the word "groggy" no doubt derives), as a term of resentment against the Admiral who was known as "Old Grog" from the distinctive clothing that he wore, made of grogram.[338] The new rum rendered the sailors "groggy" but not insensible. The "tot" of rum derives from the total (Latin: *totum*) allowed, from the "totting up" of the meagre ration. In Scottish vernacular, a "tottie" is a term for a "wee dram", and is related to "tiny-tot" for a very small child, and both may have a Scandinavian or Icelandic derivation as a variant of *tottr*, "a dwarf". "Admiral Tott" does not appear in the Navy's lists of its officers, but there was a Rear-Admiral Sir Thomas Totty who was a near contemporary of Lemon Hart. Totty's name might suggest some connection with the (much earlier) "tot" of rum, but there was none, and so the notion is anachronistic. He had no responsibility for victualling, and he is not known to have had any connection with Lemon Hart, although the latter's association with senior Naval officers in London who may have recommended him for consideration for contracts is conceivable, but entirely conjectural.[339]

The Development of the Lemon Hart Firm in London

Undoubtedly, Lemon Hart's trade as a successful importer of a range of consumables, such as spirits, and possibly other luxury goods, did flourish during these early Penzance years, although, according to Israel Solomon, in his *Records of my Family*, the wine trade (which may refer to fine wines) was not added to the Lemon Hart business until *after* the move to London. This may be an error on Solomon's part, although it may have been intended to refer to the expansion of the business in a second branch of the company. His commercial success in Penzance, whatever its precise nature, allowed Lemon Hart to expand his interests by setting up a branch of his business in London, whilst, at the same time, retaining a hold on trade in Penzance. Up to 1809, Lemon Hart insured his Penzance business with London firms, but later London-based policies have not been identified.[340] In the

18th century (and 19th) company takeovers and amalgamations were frequent, and policies were often lost. Some traders insured their business and buildings during the crucial early stages of their ventures, but, with increasing prosperity, took the risk of not renewing their premiums, choosing instead to invest their profits and savings as a private safety-net. It is not known if the Lemon Hart firm was uninsured in this way.

To achieve his aim to relocate to London, on 11th October 1806, Lemon Hart drew up a deed of partnership with his nephew, Jacob James Jacobs (1784-1846), who, for commercial reasons, adopted his uncle's surname. (This has led to the erroneous assumption that he was Lemon Hart's brother. Lemon Hart was an only son).[341] Jacob Hart was a great-grandson of Abraham Hart and a son of Rebecca Hart (1766-1841) who had married Lazarus Jacobs. The partnership was to be for 14 years from 1st January 1807. Jacob was to act as Managing Partner and to reside at the premises of the London business where he was to devote his whole personal labour, time and attention to the enterprise. Jacob was also bound to travel as and where directed by his uncle until such time as the partnership could afford to employ staff for that purpose. Lemon Hart, on the other hand, was obliged to act in the business only if he so wished. The initial capital to start the business amounted to £5000, a considerable sum for its time. That all of it was subscribed by Lemon Hart himself was a clear sign of his success and financial strength as well as his confidence in the venture. Jacob undertook to put in his half-share as soon as his financial situation permitted. The deed of partnership also demonstrated quite clearly Lemon's determination to be in control of the future direction of his business. If Jacob Hart acted as the firm's commercial traveller during this initial stage, in later years his brother Frederick (1790-1853), also known as Lemon Jacobs, joined the firm and took over this role, writing business letters to the Hart firm in London from Newark (16th July 1822), Cambridge (14th January 1824) and Spilsbury (22nd May 1825), and in two cases enclosing cash (£173 and £310) from sales secured.[342]

The London business must have been a success from the outset, because Lemon Hart left Penzance for the Capital around the middle of 1811, and his signature appears in the Penzance Congregational Minute Book, apparently for the last time as its President, on 29th July that year. His business, as *Hart, Hart & Co.*, was located successively at 59, Fenchurch Street, Lower Thames Street, Water Lane, and Tower Street. At some point he became resident at or near Fenchurch Street in the City, near Tower Hill and the River. In 1823, an insurance policy,[343] in part for a Solomon Jacob Levi, locates Levi at 57 Fenchurch Street, and also refers to him at 11 Bruton Terrace "in the house of Lemon Hart". It seems likely that Levi was either an employee of Hart's or had business connections with him. Various entries from *The Times* give the Lemon Hart firm's address as Fenchurch Street (*c.*1840s-1850s) but later references (from the 1870s) suggest a move to Great Tower Street, and George Street at Tower Hill. The company's warehouses were located at the West India Docks, up-river from Greenwich. This was at a time when shipments of rum and sugar coming into the country had a high risk of being plundered. To remedy this the Government ensured that the West India Dock was built some years earlier in 1802 in the style of a fortress with guards manning the walls to protect the ships.[344]

Lemon Hart had left his relative, Lemon Woolf (1783-1848) to look after his Cornish interests. (It has been supposed, again incorrectly, that Lemon Hart's "brother" oversaw the Penzance firm). Woolf had already established his own wine and spirit business in Penzance in Market Jew Street, and his son, Moses (1815-) was a Brewer in the town. For some time at least, Lemon Woolf appears to have managed Hart's commercial outlets and remaining business interests in Penzance. Jacob James Hart remained employed in the London branch of the business for some years. Eventually, it is said that he became well-connected as a result of contacts made through supplying wine to the London Clubs and enjoyed the friendship of the young Lord Palmerston, through whose patronage he was eventually appointed Consul-General to the Kingdom of Saxony. He remained unmarried, and his personal wealth allowed him to stipulate in his will that his body was to be taken back to Penzance, where he is buried in the Jewish cemetery (5:3). His grave, with a raised coffin-shaped section (fashionable in some of the Jewish and Christian London cemeteries of that time) possesses a headstone, outstanding in the quality of its material and the scholarship of its inscription (it is Grade II listed).

The success of Lemon Hart's London business eventually enabled him to live in the fashionable area of London's Regent Park, at Cambridge Place.[345] On Monday 13th October 1845, at the age of 76 (a few weeks short of his 77th birthday in November), Lemon Hart died in Brighton, at 20 Marine Parade, Kemp Town, Brighthelston,[346] the latter being the town's ancient name, found in the *Domesday Book*, and sometimes retained on official documents of the time. His death certificate records that a George Smith, of the same address was present, and the cause of death as liver disease.[347] It would seem that Lemon Hart's failing health had prompted him to "take the waters" at Brighton, where George Smith, and others may have been business contacts in the wine and spirit trade. (A Michael Pellatt of Brighton was taken to court by Lemon Hart's son, David, in 1854, for failing to pay for quantities of port wine sold to him on credit).[348] Lemon Hart is interred in the burial ground of the (former) Great Synagogue, in Brady Street. His wife, Mary, died on 24th October 1852, aged 94, at 14 Euston Place, Euston Square. Despite the fact that she was from London, and her late husband had left Penzance over forty years previously, her death was reported in the Cornish press.[349] She was also buried at Brady Street.

David Hart (1799-1868) had been involved in his father's firm, *Hart, Hart & Co.* for some years, during which time it was renamed as *Lemon Hart & Son*. This was the major part of the family business, which appears to have supplied the Navy rum contracts. After Lemon Hart died, David Hart ran this business as the head of firm, and upon his death in turn it passed to his son, also David (1840-), who was eventually involved in the firm's liquidation and bankruptcy proceedings in 1874. At some point, it was decided that the firm's business should diversify, and David Hart's elder brother, Lemon (1831-1885) established the smaller, commercially distinct and independent firm of *Lemon Hart & Company, Distillers*, which seems to have concentrated on the supply of beers, wines and spirits to individual public houses, and this branch of the firm was not involved in the bankruptcy proceedings of 1874.[350] As a measure of the earlier success of Lemon Hart & Son, by the mid 1840s the Royal Navy was taking rum from the firm to a maximum rate of 100,000 gallons. In 1847, *The Times* carried the following: "CONTRACT FOR RUM.- The Government contract for 100,000 gallons of rum for the Navy was again taken this day by Messrs. Lemon Hart & Son, of 59, Fenchurch Street."[351] Clearly, the fact that this contract had been "again taken" by the Lemon Hart firm, confirms that it had been awarded to it previously, although for how long before 1847, or for how many years subsequently, is not known for certain. *The Times* also recorded a contract for 50,000 gallons in January and March of 1849, and in August that same year, *The Jewish Chronicle* reported: "Lemon Hart of Fenchurch Street, 100,000 gallons of rum for Royal Navy; 50 tons of mottled soap for Royal Navy by Mr. L. Cowan of Great Prescott Street. Both supplied against rival competition".

From this notice, some four years after Lemon Hart's death, it is clear that the firm was known by his name alone. It is not known if "Mr. Cowan" (as Cohen) was Jewish. The firm continued to secure further contracts, including one for 50,000 gallons in 1852, and another for 40,000 gallons in 1860. Again, none of these contracts are listed amongst the Royal Navy's official victualling records, even though other contractors are named. As a major importer, the Lemon Hart firm may have sought and promoted the advertisement of its "contracts" in the press, while in fact being suppliers to Navy agents, without being directly contracted to the Navy itself. Neither Lemon Hart, nor any member of his family were registered as Navy Agents after the move to London.[352] If such indirect, private supply was an element in the firm's business, this may have contributed to the notion that Lemon Hart had been contracted to the Navy "for many years".[353] In view of the fact that the firm was soon to decline, it is also possible that these contracts represented a prestigious, lucrative, but relatively brief period of contractual engagement with the Navy. In the absence of substantive documentation, retrospective and anecdotal elements may have entered the Lemon Hart story, and given rise to an inflation of his family's Naval connections. Despite the undoubted commercial success of the firm as importers and distributors from the earliest Penzance days, Lemon Hart (& Son) may not, therefore, have been the continuous and principal contractors to the Navy elaborated in tradition. Whatever the case, the Lemon Hart & Son firm continued to trade for at least another 25 years after the 1847 Navy contract, with sufficient financial security to allow it to contribute to various charitable causes.[354] By 1870, however, the firm had run into trouble and a receiver was appointed when Lemon Hart & Son filed a petition for liquidation.[355] In the event, on 7th January 1871, the firm's shareholders resolved to liquidate by arrangement, rather than by bankruptcy, with a trustee empowered to regulate the firm's affairs.

By July 1871, the firm with its stock-in-trade (except the leasehold premises) was purchased under a deed by which payments were to be made to the trustee by the new owner, George White. White continued to run the firm under its trademark as *Lemon Hart & Son*, with David Hart (1840-) Lemon Hart's grandson, as a partner. In September 1872, the firm secured a much smaller Navy contract for rum, of 15,000 gallons, but payments to the trustee were not sufficient under the terms of the deed. By the end of 1874, George White and David Hart became bankrupt: "Messrs. George White and David Hart, wine and spirit merchants, of 1, 2, and 3 George Street, Tower-Hill, trading as Lemon Hart and Son, have filed a petition for liquidation by arrangement or composition. Their liabilities are returned at £200,000, and their assets - (including) stock in bond of considerable value, besides book debts of large amount, in respect of which remittances are continually being made. Mr. White has also - a separate estate of considerable value. (The Receiver's affidavit) - showed that the business was an extensive one, and that it was material and accessory in the interests of the creditors - that the same should be continued and existing contracts carried on and funds provided for the purpose. His Honour granted the application, an injunction being also allowed to restrain actions by creditors." [356] Official notice of bankruptcy was confirmed on 4th November 1874, with a full statement of assets published in January 1875. The legal proceedings established that the trade-mark name could be treated as a "chattel" of the firm, and could be assigned to a new owner at purchase. The full circumstances of and reasons for the firm's ultimate failing are not entirely clear, although extensive debts and unpaid invoices owing to the firm, some going back to the 1850s, and possibly earlier, were a significant factor.

Subsequently, there were further proceedings, including adjudication against Lemon Hart and Son by individual creditors. To all intents and purposes, this heralded the end of the family firm, although it was at some point taken over, and it may have been able to continue to trade under new ownership. In 1879 it was owned by Norris & Gilby.[357] Even though the separate firm of Lemon Hart & Co., headed by Lemon Hart (1831-1886), was not party to the liquidation, it would have been affected by this blow to the family's income and assets. This Lemon Hart's son, also named Lemon (1857-1903) may have been involved in this branch of the business, but he decided to emigrate to America, and in 1894 he left Queenstown, Cork, on the ship *Campania*, arriving in New York, at Ellis Island, on 13th October that year.[358] Despite all of this, the Hart family had traded successfully in Penzance and London for at least 75 years, at a time when business failure and bankruptcy were all too common. Lemon Hart's name is not likely to be forgotten, and at least until the 1960s advertisements for it could be seen in many city centres, including Piccadilly Circus, where it featured prominently, and was included as such in a painting of the Circus by L.S. Lowry in 1960. Lemon Hart ® rum is still produced under its own label.[359] Anyone drinking it today, drinks to a name with more than two and a half centuries of history.

Lemon Woolf (1783-1848) of Penzance

Before Lemon Hart left Penzance in 1811, he had donated a number of religious artefacts to the synagogue, and with his growing success in London he continued to make donations to the Penzance congregation. His role as President of the congregation was taken up by Hyman Woolf, the father of Lemon Woolf. The Woolf family's origins in Holland, their initial residence in Penzance, and Benjamin Woolf's move to Falmouth, have already been mentioned, together with their marriage into the Solomon family of Falmouth, and the Hart family of Penzance. Hyman Woolf's family supervised and maintained the communal *mikveh* which was attached, not to the synagogue itself, but to his house, which may have been in or at the bottom of Causewayhead, in the vicinity of the Market Place. At this point there was an overground "leat" in the street, which led to a communal pump situated in the Market Place, and this could have supplied fresh water to the Mikveh: "In 1750 a leat or watercourse was constructed to bring water from Madron Well to Causewayhead, and in 1757 a reservoir was constructed at the top of Causewayhead - From the reservoir…the water was taken down Causewayhead to the town shoot ".[360] Hyman Woolf did not enjoy good health in his later years, and his son, Lemon, often substituted for him at the congregation's administrative meetings, and on occasions signed the Minutes for him up to Hyman's death in 1820. Lemon Woolf (1783-1848) married Rebecca Jacob (1781-1853), a daughter of Moses Jacob of Redruth, and his sister, Hannah Woolf (1779-1847) married Aaron Selig (1782-1841) of Penzance, a jeweller, and, briefly one of the congregation's ministers just before and up to 1808. The couple were to remain in the town for the remainder of their lives. Lemon Woolf eventually became the third Warden of the congregation, and, together with Henry Joseph (1806-1881) who had married Amelia Jacob (1811-1891) of Falmouth, a granddaughter of Moses Jacob, negotiated the cemetery leases. At least five of Lemon and Rebecca Woolf's children were to marry into Jewish families in Devon, from Exeter and Plymouth.

Lemon Woolf had originally traded as a watch maker and silversmith, but he also took over the management of Lemon Hart's wine and spirit business when the latter left for London in 1811. Eventually, Woolf ran his own independent wine and spirit business from premises in Market Jew Street and another in Chapel Street. The former shop was located at the top of this street, near the Market House, and not far from the synagogue. The site of this shop continued to be used for this same purpose for many years, and was trading as *Davey* until it closed in the 1980s. It is not known if Woolf stocked wines and spirits that were imported by the Lemon Hart firm, or if he did so on his own behalf. The scale of his ventures in this field are likely to have been much more modest compared with the Hart family business, and he does not appear to have been a registered co-owner of merchant vessels. The local tradition that he also owned a fleet of such vessels can be regarded as spurious. Lemon Woolf also occupied another premises in the Market Place, at the bottom of Causewayhead, as a pawnbroker. In his journal between 1816-17, the Mayor of Penzance, Henry Boase (1763-1827) sitting in his judicial capacity as a magistrate, recorded a number of occasions when Lemon Woolf came before him.[361] Woolf employed at least one servant, which was not at all uncommon. That households registered a servant should not lead to the inference that this was the result of any unusual affluence. Housing stock did not keep pace with population, and even small dwellings could contain up to a dozen people. Where accommodation was used to its maximum capacity, families often needed their older children to lodge elsewhere as servants. Some of these servants might be fortunate to learn a trade, although their wages, in return for bed a board, were very low, and often unpaid. Lemon Woolf's servant entered into a legal dispute with him. On 29th November 1816 she laid a complaint before the Mayor at the Guildhall that Woolf had refused to pay her wages. The Mayor found that the girl had left the service of the family without warning and so dismissed her complaint. "Mr. Woolf stated that he would still pay her the amount on proper apology, otherwise give it to the poor."[362]

In Lemon Woolf's business as a pawnbroker, it would be a matter of course that he accepted goods on the basis of trust, that they were the legal property of the person who placed them in pawn. In at least two cases he is mentioned (entirely without blame) as implicated, by chance, in the circumstances of an illegal pawn. On 4th and 5th June 1817, the Mayor's journal records: "Granted a warrant to arrest Grace Mitchell of this Town, Spinster, servant to Thomas John, for having pawned a waistcoat, his property; Affidavit of Mary Pascoe, Lemon Woolf", and "Granted an arrest to Mr. J. Dennis against a sailor who had pawned a Spy Glass of Mr. W. Dennis at Mr. Woolf's." These same journals also reveal the only recorded incident which could be viewed as a form of harassment of the Jewish congregation. On Monday 22nd September 1817, Woolf and Symmons (Rabbi B. A. Simmons) made a complaint against "boys for disturbing the Syn.", and the Mayor referred the matter to the Town Clerk for a summons, which the next day was granted by the Mayor against John Noy and Mark Row. The matter was heard on the 24th, when the two complainants stated that the boys had thrown "an iron bullet" into the synagogue. Row confessed that he had given the bullet to Noy ("an idiot") and told him to bowl it against the door which was (as a result) broken. "The prosecutors proposed that the parents of Row should be charged to chastize him severely and that he should sign an acknowledgement of his guilt, sorrow, etc. - which was ordered accordingly."[363] The interest in this incident is clearly that the two Jewish complainants were treated with the respect and impartiality which was due to any members of the community.

On the 18th November 1830, Lemon Woolf became involved in a civil suit when Abraham Joseph,[364] a former employee at the synagogue and a "flour dealer" (corn merchant), was made bankrupt .[365] Abraham Joseph II (1799-1868) was the grandson of Abraham Joseph I (1731-1794) of Plymouth, a prosperous mercer and draper, a dealer in goods to the Navy, and the owner of various leasehold and freehold properties in the city,[366] and the third son of Joseph Joseph (1766-1846) of Plymouth, a Naval Agent.[367] Joseph Joseph's bankruptcy in 1816 would have led to difficulties for his family, and his son's employment by the congregation, from August 1826 to September 1827, may well have been a charitable act on their part. His later life suggests that he was an intelligent man of some learning, but he was not a Rabbi as such, although he was paid the same salary as previous ministers. It would seem that his position was as a reader in prayers, and he may also have carried out the duties of a caretaker of the synagogue. His was an interim appointment, of mutual convenience to the parties concerned. In 1828 Abraham Joseph II had married Lemon Woolf's daughter, Eliza (Telza, 1808-1850). Lemon Woolf, signing himself as *Leman*, had made a written guarantee on 23rd May 1827 to cover Abraham Joseph's account for porter with a firm of brewers, and was, as a consequence, sued upon his guarantee. He pleaded in court that the brewers had given Joseph further credit without reference to him (Woolf). The Jury stated that "as practical men" they considered this should not release Woolf, but on Appeal, the decision was reversed. The case of *Coombe v. Woolf* became a leading authority on the law of guarantee into the 20th century.

Trades and Occupations

Solomon Lazarus (Abraham Hart): Goldsmith (Ja. 1757-64: p. 319). Abraham Hart died in 1784.

A John Sampson of Penzance (1769) has been recorded as a Jewish Master crafts-man[368] (jeweller or watchmaker), but this identification is uncertain and unlikely. His surname was common amongst Cornish Christians. A Solomon Solomon was apprenticed to John Sampson in 1769.

Lazarus Solomon: A silver watch with a gold movement dated 1775: Penlee Museum, Penzance (noted earlier). Possibly, an inversion of *Solomon Lazarus* or *Lazarus* (*ben* Solomon) Hart, or connected with Solomon Solomon (previously, and below) or with the Thomas Solomon (below) who converted to Christianity. It has also been noted, above, that a connection with Lazarus Solomon of London, the father of Lemon Hart's second wife (*m.* 1804) Mary Solomon is possible, but spec-ulative. There were various Jewish *Solomon* families in Exeter and Plymouth from the mid 18th century onwards,[369] most of whom appear on later civil registration records (from 1837) and census returns (from 1841), although there are earlier Jewish marriage and burial records for Devon. Although later than the 1775 Penzance watch, a Lazarus (Eliezer or "Lezer") Solomon arrived in Plymouth from Lublin, Poland, sometime before 1802, and was Cantor at the Plymouth synagogue until his death in 1835. He and his wife, Esther, also from Lublin, who died in 1831, are buried in the Plymouth Hoe cemetery.[370] They are not known to be connected with a "Lazarus Solomon" of Penzance.

Lazarus (Eliezer) Hart: Silversmith & Slopseller (1777), Pawnbroker (1785), Merchant, near The Quay (1799): (Insurance Policies) [371]. The 1799 policy refers to his "dwelling house, with cellars and warehouses adjacent". In the 18th century, and before the introduction of the system of address by street and number, it was customary to locate a house or business by its proximity to a notable landmark. The Quay was close to St. Mary's Church in Chapel Street.

Solomon(an) Solomon: Pawnbroker and General Dealer; possibly an apprenticed watchmaker (1769): see below. He was a Silversmith (*c.* 1781; Pro.Cust. 68/11). On 13th June 1781 he made a voluntary deposition before the Penzance Magistrates, John Price and Samuel Borlase, in a Customs case. He is described as "being one of the persons called Jews", and that he had "sworn on the Pentateuch." The case concerned an incident "about the latter end of May or the Beginning of June" involving a Francis Bradley, a Tidewaiter in his Majesty's Customs of St. Michael's Mount, who had approached Solomon to ask if he dealt in indigo, to which Solomon confirmed that he did. It was agreed that Bradley would bring between 150 to 200 lbs. of indigo to Solomon "a few evenings after about twelve O' Clock at night" This did not happen, and the next Sunday Solomon was summoned by Bradley to meet him at the "House of Christ.r Ellis an Innkeeper" in Penzance, where John Dale and Richard Hill, said to own the indigo, promised Solomon that they would bring it to his house a few days later. This appointment was also not kept, and Solomon later heard that a quantity of indigo had been stolen from the Brig *Neptune*, then moored in the harbour of the Mount. Solomon went to the ship's Master, Barend Terkelsen, and relayed his story. Solomon's deposition led to the three men being committed to the Common Gaol on 2nd July to await trial at the next assizes, but "through some mistake of the Attorney for the Prosecution" the case collapsed. He may be the Solomon Zalman (d. 1823) who is buried in the Jewish cemetery (5:4). *Zalman* is a variant of *Zalaman* or Salaman, a spelling of *Solomon* that could suggest a Sephardic origin, although in the Hart family, who were an Ashkenazi family from Germany, Abraham Hart (Solomon Lazarus) had a brother, Zalman (-1779). It is also possible that this Solomon Solomon was a son Zalman Hart. It has been noted earlier that a Solomon Solomon was apprenticed to a Penzance watchmaker and clockmaker, the Gentile John Sampson in 1769. Alternatively, this Solomon Solomon may have been connected with or identical to the Thomas Solomon (below) a convert to Christianity, who died in 1793. Nor is it known if Solomon Solomon was related to the Solomon family of Falmouth. Solomon Solomon of Falmouth was the son of Israel Solomon from Germany (*c.*1727-1802) and Bella Woolf (1726-1816) whose family came from Holland. Their son, Solomon, born in 1764, married Elizabeth Levy (1757-1832) of Falmouth, and, in 1800-1802, traded there as a Tailor, Slopseller and Hardwaremen, and also in partnership with Lyon Joseph as a pawnbroker. Solomon Solomon of Falmouth died in Lisbon in 1819.

Emanuel Hauman (Herman?) who may have been Jewish was born in Penzance in 1788 (Plymouth Census 1841, where he is recorded as a "professor of languages").

Lemon Hart: Wine & Spirit Merchant, Chapel Street and near the Chapel Yard (1791 and 1809: Insurance Policies.[372] The 1791 policy also lists plate, jewellery, watches and china, presumably as part of another aspect of the family business run by his father, although these items may include personal effects. It can be assumed that Lemon Hart continued to trade using Lazarus (Eliezar) Hart's cellars and warehouses near the Penzance Quay, a short distance from Chapel Street. The "Chapel Yard" would be the churchyard or cemetery adjoining St. Mary's Chapel (Church). This is the only location that has been identified with certainty for Lemon Hart's business, which may also have been his home, although this is not certain. It has been noted earlier that a local, anecdotal tradition holds that Lemon Hart also ran a distillery at the top of Jennings Street, just off Market Jew Street. The location of this putative distillery is near that of Lemon Woolf's later wine and spirit business, which Lemon Hart is not known to have occupied himself, although a Hart shop in the town's main street is credible and likely. The Hart "distillery" and the Woolf business may have been confused. George Brown Millett's much later retrospective and speculative plan of the centre of Penzance (*c.* 1805), which he acknowledges "does not pretend to completeness or much accuracy" gives Lemon *Hart's* only business in this part of Market Jew Street, and Lemon *Woolf's* only premises at the top (not the church end) of Chapel St. (then known as Lady Street). It is possible that Millett has confused and exchanged these names and their locations, although Woolf may have taken over Lemon Hart's Chapel Street premises after 1811.

Lemon Hart was President of the Penzance Hebrew Congregation from at least 1807, and until 1811. His Presidency may have run from much earlier than 1807, in that the congregation's surviving records do not commence until May 1807.

Thomas Solomon: Jeweller & Watchmaker (see below). He was a Jew who had either converted to Christianity, or from a family of Jewish Christians. The Burial Register for Penzance (1784-1804),[373] for 4th September 1793, records the burial of "Mr. Thomas Solomon (Jew baptised) by the minister of Penzance, Rev. Coryton" (the Register's compiler). The Rev. George Coryton was the Master of the Latin School (later the Grammar School for Boys) in Penzance, where until 1793, he taught the young Humphry Davy (1778-1829) Latin and Greek, in which the boy "showed great talent in translation". His pupil had little respect for his teacher, "a man of irregular habits", who was "ill-fitted for the office of teaching", and who allowed a climate of "idleness" to flourish in his school. Coryton, likewise, regarded Davy as "idle, impudent and a persistent truant". Although Davy claimed to hold the Classics in low regard, "for the rest of his life his conversation was peppered with quotations from the classical authors".[374] Coryton was also the curate and minister of the Chapelry of St. Mary's from 1789 until September 1804, when he became paralysed after a stroke. His duties were taken over by others, until the appointment of Rev. Charles Valentine Le Grice on 31st July 1806, after Coryton's resignation (he died in 1808). In 1790 and 1794, Coryton had been in dispute with the Vicar of Madron, William Borlase (in whose parish Penzance lay) over the latter's claim that he could take services in the Chapel of St. Mary whenever he chose. The Penzance Corporation supported Coryton against Borlase. Before this, from 1789, Coryton had also maintained a register of baptisms and burials from 1789 (all marriages at this time had to be conducted in Madron Church).[375] Solomon's name does not appear in Coryton's Baptismal Register, and the date and place of his baptism are not clear. *Thomas* is not a forename name associated with Jews, and it may have been given to him in infancy, at his "Christening", or taken by him at his adult baptism. (The significance of such a name upon conversion echoes the story from the Fourth Gospel of the disciple who doubted the reality of the risen Christ, but came to believe).[376] If *Thomas* was this man's adopted Christian name, his previous forename is not known, but if it was *Lazarus*, his retention of that name would have been consistent with his new faith (reflecting the Fourth Gospel's story of Christ's Raising of Lazarus from the dead to new life).[377] It is possible that he was the Lazarus Solomon of the 1775 watch, above.

Two other men with the name Thomas Solomon traded in Cornwall, one in Falmouth in 1811 (Holden's Directory), and the other in Truro in 1873, the latter at 19 King Street as a "Glazier, Church Window Maker, Bell-Hanger, Glass Merchant, Carver and Gilder" as well as a General Contractor (Kelly's Directory). It is not known if these men were related to their earlier namesake of Penzance, and neither have been confirmed as Jews. A Notice from the *Exeter Gazette* of October 22nd

1793 reads: "Penzance, Cornwall-To be Sold by Public Auction at the Star Inn... October 22nd...All the Stock in trade of Thomas Solomon, deceased; consisting of a variety of gold and silver watches, jewellery, plate, and hardware, quite new and of the most modern taste- Mr. Thomas Branwell, his Executor in Trust." Thomas Solomon was also a Watchmaker (Br. 1793).[378]

Solomon Jacobs: Watchmaker, (Br. 1803). Brown records him in relation to a bond upon the administration of goods to Rebecca, his widow. He may be the "S. Jacobs" who Brown lists *c.* 1800 as a clockmaker in Falmouth. It is possible that he was a brother of Moses Jacob of Redruth, who died a few years later in 1807. *Solomon* and *Samuel* were sometimes interchangeable as Jewish forenames. This Solomon Jacobs should not be confused with Moses Jacob's son, Samuel (1778-1860) a Jeweller, who later settled in Penzance.

Henry Ralph: Pawnbroker & Grocer, near The Quay (1804); also a home in Alverton Lane, with Shop and Warehouse in the Market Place (1806): & Tea Dealer, near the Coinage Hall (1808). Insurance Policies[379] (1804-1808); Navy Agent (1809).[380] He remained in the town until at least 1811, and had moved to Plymouth by 1814. Ralph's business success at this time is reflected in the increasing value of the policy valuations from £600 (1804) to £1,000 (1806) to £1,4000 (1808). He was a member of the Penzance congregation, and his name and signature, sometimes as *Hayim ben Abraham*, appear in the Minute Book. An "H. Ralf" is mentioned in the records of the Falmouth Masonic Lodge for 6th March 1801. The surname, *Ralph*, was also common among non-Jews. A Thomas Ralph, originally from Crowan, traded as a Tea dealer in Penzance in 1871. In the same year, an unrelated William Arnold Ralph, who was originally from London, was a High Bailiff of the County Court in Penzance. His wife, Elizabeth, was from a Penzance family.[381]

Lemon Woolf: Watchmaker & Silversmith (1807), and Mercer, Draper & Dealer in Clothes (1809 & 1815), the Market Place: (Insurance Policies).[382] Licensed Navy Agent (1814-1815);[383] Silversmith (Penzance Masonic Lodge records, June 1st 1814); Crockery (1827: Invoice from Dillwyn & Co, Cambrian Pottery, Swansea).[384] These early entries show the diversification that helped Woolf to establish himself in the town, and he continued to trade in the Market Place for the remainder of his life. He is listed in later trade directories as a Pawnbroker. It is not known if he continued his watch making and drapery interests when he expanded into the wine and spirit business (for which see separate entry below).

Jacob Levy: merchant seaman (*c.*1808-1812). Uncertain. He was taken prisoner during the Napoleonic wars when his ship the *Magdalen* (on a voyage from Grenada to Greenock with a cargo of sugar) was seized and then destroyed off Madeira by two French frigates on 29th February 1808. Levy was held prisoner at Cambray. (*Royal Cornwall Gazette;* 25th April 1811, 7th & 14th November 1812).[385] The newspaper reports list numerous Cornish sailors and soldiers held in France, including over 70 men from Penzance, West Cornwall, and the Isles of Scilly. Jacob Levy's ship was a large merchant vessel of 228 tons. It was owned by John Batten, William Carne,

Richard Oxnam and John Mathews. The last named was the Penzance shipbuilder who, in 1802 and 1805 was part owner with Lemon Hart and other men of the ships *Amelia* and *Speculation*. It is possible that Jacob Levy had some connection with Lemon Hart's sea-trade with the West Indies, and the *Magdalen's* presence at Grenada might suggest this. On 19th January 1811, a Petition was presented to Viscount Falmouth to raise a subscription for the Cornish prisoners, to "procure such small comforts as may serve to lessen the weight of imprisonment in a strange and hostile country." By the end of that year £625.0.8. had been raised. In Penzance, the Town Corporation donated over £85. Other donations included those made by members of the Borlase, Branwell, Barham and le Grice families, as well as many donations from local people. From the Jewish community, donations were received from Lemon Hart, H. (Hyman) Wolf and (Elias) Magnus, as senior representatives of the Jewish congregation (*Royal Cornwall Gazette*, 9th March 1811). It is not known for certain if Jacob Levy was Jewish, or if he was a Christian of Jewish descent. Nor is it known if he was related to the "Mr. Levy" (*Leb Hanne*, "Judah from Hanau", or *Judah ben Naphtali*) who was buried, age 100, in the Jewish cemetery (8:1) in 1817. It is possible that he is to be connected with the John Levi who married Eleanor Dash in church in April 1804 (see marriages).

Elias Magnus: Wine Merchant (c. 1808-1819). Born in 1775, he was the grandson of Simon Nathan Magnus (1702-1758) of Holland, and the son of Joseph Simon Magnus (b. 1737 Holland, d. 1815 London).[386] The Magnus family, who were merchants and "money-men", may have come to Amsterdam from Hamburg at the end of the 17th century. Soon after, they moved to the Dutch Hanseatic ports of Zwolle and Elburg, arriving in this country around 1789, first to King's Lynn,[387] and then to London. Elias Magnus was born into a family of about nine children, including an older brother Lazarus, and a younger brother Nathan. It is not known exactly when Elias arrived in Penzance, but he seems to have been of a relatively sound financial status when, as a senior member of the congregation, he became a signatory to its new regulations (*Tikkunim*) in 1808, agreeing to pay a subscription of £4. 10s. (which he later increased). By 1811 he was the congregation's Treasurer, but by 1813 he was falling into debt, and he withdrew from the congregation in 1819, apparently leaving for London soon after. Elias Magnus married Lemon Hart's sister Rebecca (1766-1841) after the death of her first husband, Lazarus Isaac Jacobs. They are only known to have had one child, Bella. Israel Solomon, in his *Records of my Family*, refers to her (without naming her) as the "poor half-sister Magnus", who was shunned by her half-brother Jacob James Jacobs ("Hart"), who "…never mentioned her name or left her any of his money…" when he died in 1846. It would seem that the Magnus family fell on hard times in London. At the time of Rebecca's death in 1841, they were living in Goodman's Fields, where Lemon Hart's second wife, Mary Solomon had also lived some forty years earlier. Like Lemon and Mary Hart, Rebecca Magnus is buried in the Brady Street cemetery of the Great Synagogue. She is interred in the section reserved for *Orchim* (lit. "visitors") that is for those worshippers who did not pay a membership to the congregation. Elias Magnus died in Shoreditch on January 21st 1850. He was a Freemason, and he is mentioned in the Penzance Lodge records for 1813 as a Wine Merchant. The location of his business is not certain, and he does not appear on George Millett's plan of town traders (*c*. 1805). It is not known if he worked for Lemon Hart, or traded independently. Magnus was recorded by the Mayor of Penzance, Henry Boase (1763-1827) in his Journal for 1817 as involved in two legal cases.[388]

"Friday 2nd May: Excise hearing yesterday respecting 4 gallons of British spirits seized from Mr. Magnus, liquor condemned, no penalty." Tuesday 29th July: A search warrant was granted to James Crocker against Thomas Jewell for suspected theft of items of clothing, subsequently found in the place where Jewell had been sleeping. Also found in a chest was a pair of stockings marked "E.M." claimed by Elias Magnus. Wednesday 30th July. Elias Magnus proved he had lost stockings and other items stolen from him several weeks ago. His daughter [i.e. Bella] testified that she had "marked these very stockings".

Amelia Jacobs and **Flora Simmons**: Milliners, Market Place (1814: Insurance Policy).[389] Amelia and Flora Jacob were sisters, daughters of Moses Jacob of Redruth. Amelia (whose birth year is uncertain, *c.* 1785-1794, but who died in 1864) was unmarried, and Flora (1790-1874) was the wife of Rabbi B. A. Simmons. Amelia (-1864) is buried in the Penzance cemetery (3:1). Like her sister, Betsy (1761-) who was also unmarried, and who is buried in the Falmouth cemetery (2:9), she was a deaf mute, a congenital condition that was passed down through the Jacob family to some of its members in various forms and degrees. After the death of her husband, Flora Jacob went to live with a daughter in South Wales, where she died.

"Laurance": Watchmaker (1817). It is possible that this is Moses Lazarus Lawrance from Falmouth. In the Mayor's journal for 12th June 1817 is recorded: "Complaint of Husband of Star Inn & Catian Tresizes for his loss of £8 notes out of his Pocket Book when drunk at his house, they suspected Laurance, watchmaker & Pellow, sawyer." [390]

Levi Jacobs (Levy Jacob, b.1788): Dealer in Mineral Specimens;[391] Watchmaker, (Br. 1823), had previously traded in Redruth and Falmouth.It is not certain where he traded in Penzance, or if he did so continuously. His death was reported in *Exeter Flying Post* on 9th September 1824.[392] He was a son of Moses Jacob of Redruth. Levy Jacob (*Judah ben Moses*) is interred in the Penzance cemetery (4:4). He was a member of the Penzance Masonic Lodge. His widow, Sophia (Mordecai), and his children are given below.

Alex. Simons: Spirit Merchant (1821). His name appears on the membership list of the Penzance Masonic Lodge for this year. It is assumed that he traded in the town, but a business location has not been identified. He is likely to be the same as Alexander Symons who traded with a Joseph Spasshatt as Wine & Spirit Merchants in Falmouth in 1830. He is also likely to be the Alex(ander) Symons who appears in the Penzance Congregational Minute Book (1820-1824), where his name appears along with that of **Isaac Symons** (1819-1823). The latter may have been his son, but it is more likely that he was the son of **Samuel Simons** of Truro (below). Alexander and Isaac Symons were trading in Falmouth by 1830, but it is not known if they were related.

A Samuel Symons is recorded in the Ward Lists of the Burgesses of Penzance with a "House" in Pendarves Road, from 1835 to 1859, and another in Leskinnick Terrace, from 1857. In the 1871 Census he is given as a Warehouseman. He is noted here to avoid confusion with other Symons names, and he was not Jewish.

Samuel (Solomon) Simons of Truro (1740-1832) was married to Rosa (Ann) Moses (1757-1838), a daughter of Alexander Moses of Falmouth. Their son, Isaac (*ben* Samuel) born around 1796, may have used his father's forename. Isaac Simons was married to Rosetta Jacobs, a daughter of Lazarus Jacobs and Rebecca Hart of Penzance, and may have lived in the town.

Lemon Woolf: Pawnbroker, Market Place; Wine & Spirit Merchant, Chapel St. (Pg. 1823/24/30); Wine & Spirit Merchant, Market Place (1841 Census), East St. (Pg. 1844), Market Jew St. (Wi. 1847). The Ward Lists of the Burgesses of the Borough of Penzance (from 1835) record the "House" of named individuals, and the Lists give his place of residence as Market Jew Street.[393] Lemon Woolf (1783-1848) was President of the Penzance Hebrew Congregation from 1820 until his death in 1848. His father, Hyman Woolf had been President from 1811 until his death in 1820. Lemon Woolf was a prominent member of the Penzance Masonic Lodge, and its Master in 1818. Lemon Woolf was married to Rebecca Jacob (1781-1853) a daughter of Moses Jacob of Redruth. After her husband's death, Rebecca Woolf moved to Plymouth, where two of her daughters lived: Rose Woolf (1810-) had married Josiah Solomon of Exeter, and lived at 20 Whimple Street with their eight children (Eliza, daughter of Levy and Sophia Jacob, below, had lived at this address in 1842), and Betsy (Bella: 1817-1881) had married Markes Levy (1812-1871) of Plymouth, and lived with their six children at 50 Bedford Street (later at 38 & 190 Union Street, in 1861 and 1871). The 1851 Census records Rebecca Woolf as a widow annuitant (no address), and she is not included in the households of her daughters. For Lemon and Rebecca Woolf's son, Moses, a brewer, see below.

Henry Jacob: Sailor, was born in Penzance *c.* 1824. It is not likely that he was Jewish (but see Falmouth Trades for 1851). He is not known to have been related to the Jacob family of Falmouth, nor to Sophia Jacob, below.

John Abraham and his wife Phillipa were both born in Penzance c. 1825. John Abraham later traded in Plymouth as an Outfitter (1871 Census). It is not known that they were Jewish, although they have been noted as "People who might be Jews or intermarried with Jews".[394] This John Abraham should not be confused with his namesake, a Yeoman from Crowan (1816-1887) who was a Freemason in the Cornubian Lodge of Hayle (see below).

John Messina: Physician. He was a member of the Penzance congregation from September 1825 to 1827. He is likely to have been an Italian Jew.

Abraham and Isaac Davidson, and Solomon Johnson: trades unknown. They were admitted as members of the Penzance congregation in 1825.

Sophia Jacob: Clothes Dealer, Chapel St. (Pg. 1830). This is Sophia Mordecai (1781-1853) widow of Levy Jacobs. She was the daughter of Moses and Hindele Mordecai of Exeter.[395] Moses Mordecai once lived in London and Portsmouth, but by 1764 he was trading as a silversmith in Dartmouth, and by 1788 as a goldsmith and bookplate printer in Exeter. He was one of the early leaseholders of the Exeter Jewish cemetery, and he died in 1809. His children were Sophia (1781-1853), Mark (1781-), possibly her twin and later a Navy Agent in Devonport, Kitty (1791-) and Esther. It is not known if the Barnett Mordecai, pedlar, who appears in the 1841 census for Exeter was related to this family. Mark Mordecai's wife, also Esther, died in 1833, and her nephew, Jacob Levi (20) lived with him (1841 census). From her marriage to Levy Jacob of Penzance, Sophia Mordecai had a son Moses (c.1815-1879), who married a Sarah Lyons, and three daughters. In 1842, Eliza (1814-, b. Falmouth) married Isaac Lazarus, a jeweller of Exeter, in Plymouth, where Eliza was staying with Rose Woolf of Penzance and her husband Josiah Solomon (see above under Woolf). Isaac Lazarus of Exeter should not be confused with his name-sake of Hayle (see later). Hannah Jacob (1819-1913) married a —— Solomon, and Phoebe Jacob (1823-1904) married, in Exeter (1845), a Polish Jew from Cracow, Abraham Kestenberg (c.1810-) a Commission Agent of Plymouth (1861 Census). The *West Briton* (20th June 1845) recorded her marriage (of the 8th June) to "A. Kestenbury, Esq., of Plymouth, to Phoebe, youngest daughter of the late Mr. Levy Jacob, mineralogist, of Penzance".[396] At Phoebe Jacob's marriage, she was recorded as "of Penzance", and her late father's occupation was given as a "Mineralist", a trader in mineralogical specimens, a profitable activity with which Phoebe's grand-father, Moses Jacob of Redruth had supplemented his main occupation, and that of his son Levy, as watch and clockmakers. Jacob Levi's brother, Simeon Levi, a Navy Agent's clerk from Plymouth, was a witness at the wedding.[397] By 1881, Eliza and Isaac Lazarus were living in Paddington,[398] together with Eliza's sister, Hannah, by then a widow. In the same year, Phoebe, also a widow, was living in the Midlands at Aston, with two unmarried daughters Sarah (34) and Sophia (21). The Birmingham Congregation's Burial Register records Phoebe Kestenberg's death on 22nd August 1904, aged 81.[399] Her mother, Sophia, is likely to have left Penzance for Plymouth by about 1840, where she lived with her widowed brother, Mark Mordecai, in Devonport. She may eventually have returned to Exeter.

Henry Levin: Clothes Dealer, Chapel St. (Pg. 1830); residence at Market Jew Street (Ward Lists from 1835); General Dealer, Sampson's Court (1841 Census); Fancy Repositories, East St. (Pg. 1844); Marine Store Dealer, Jeweller & Hardware, Market Jew St. (Sl. 1852/3). Henry Levin (1798-1877) was married to a Julia (1792-1879) from Truro. She may have been a daughter of Israel Levy of Truro, whose wife, Hannah, and daughter, Catherine (Kitty) are, like Julia Levin, buried in the Penzance cemetery. Julia's headstone reads, *Yuta bat Israel*, and records that she died in 1879, age 87. This would give her birth year as 1792, although, on the 1871 census for Penzance, her age is given as 75, that is, born in 1796. Their children were Mathilda (1826-) who married an Isaac Aron (1811-) of Birmingham, Alexan-der (1828-1891) who married Rachel Joseph (1831-1891) of Bristol, whose parents had originally lived in Falmouth, Israel (1829-1887) who remained unmarried, and

LEVIN of Penzance

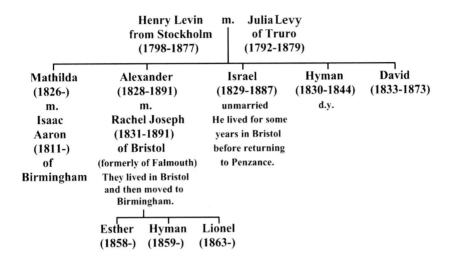

Note: it is not known if Moses Levin of London (b. circa 1799) was related to Henry Levin of Penzance, possibly as brothers. The former married Hannah Joseph (b. Falmouth circa 1809, died London 1879), a daughter of Lyon and Judith Joseph of Falmouth.

Source: Anthony P. Joseph and Godfrey Simmons;
Census records 1841-1891; headstone transcriptions.
Compiled by Keith Pearce © (2013).

who lived in Bristol for a few years, Hyman (1830-1844) whose early death was recorded by the *West Briton* (21st June 1844), and David (1833-1873). When Israel Levin returned from Bristol in the 1850s, the business was run by Henry and Israel Levin jointly. From 1861 the Census returns record Henry Levin as a retired trades-man of 102, Market Jew Street, and his place of birth as Stockholm. He was Presi-dent of the Penzance Hebrew Congregation (1848-49, 1853-54, 1859-60, 1863-65 and 1874-75). He died on 19th October 1877.[400] It is possible that Henry Levin is to be identified with Henry Levy (below). It is not known if Moses Levin (*c.* 1799-) of London was related to Henry Levin of Penzance. Moses Levin married Hannah

Joseph (c. 1809-) of Falmouth, a daughter of Lyon and Judith Joseph. Hannah Levin died in London in 1879.

The family of Henry Levin, Jewellers, should not be confused with the Gentile *Lavin* family of Penzance, even though the Jewish *Levin* family are sometimes recorded in the Hebrew Congregation's Minute Book as *Lavin* (or *Levy*).[401] Various Gentiles named *Lavin* appear in census, parish and trade records for Cornwall. John Lavin (1796-1856) had come from Wales, and had married Frances Roberts of Paul in 1822. He was trading in Chapel Street, Penzance, as a Dealer in Mineral Specimens as early as 1832.[402] John Lavin is recorded as a Mineralogist & Geologist, Chapel St., and his son Edward Lavin, as a Printer, Bookbinder, Bookseller & Stationer, in Chapel St. in the Post Office Directory of 1856.[403] Edward Lavin, also traded as a mineral dealer from the year of his father's death (1856), and he appears at 7, Chapel St. in Cornish's Directory of 1864. An Edward Lavin was a Publican of *The Mount's Bay Hotel* (1871 Census). The Lavin family is said to have built the "Egyptian House" in Chapel St., modelled on a Museum in Piccadilly, London.[404] There was a *Lavin's* Upholstery and General Household Store in central Penzance c. 1880. *Lavin* also appears as a Gentile name in Falmouth.

Abraham Joseph: Flour Dealer. Bankruptcy, December 3rd 1830 (*London Gazette*, reported *Exeter Flying Post*, 9th December 1830;[405] Elwick's Bankruptcy Directory, London 1843, p. 233).[406] Abraham Joseph (1799-1868) was not from the Cornish Joseph family, but was the son of Joseph Joseph (1766-1846) of Plymouth. It has been mentioned that this Joseph Joseph had suffered a bankruptcy in 1816, and his licence as a Navy Agent was revoked in July of 1817.[407] He appears have owned several taverns and inns in Plymouth, one of which was the *Mayflower Inn*, where it is said that he entertained nobility and royalty, including George III and the Duke of Clarence. In 1817, Joseph Joseph went to live in London to try to revive his fortunes, and in 1819 he went to Gibraltar where his son, Henry (c. 1790-1845) had already settled. By 1824 Joseph Joseph had returned to Plymouth, where, presumably, his son, Abraham had carried on some form of business during his father's extended absence. However, the bankruptcy of 1816 led to the family becoming dispersed, and Abraham Joseph's arrival in Penzance in 1826 may not have been his first visit to the town. His employment at the Penzance synagogue for one year (1826-1827) would have afforded him some form of temporary security, and led to his marriage to Eliza (1808-1850), the oldest daughter of Lemon Woolf of Penzance on 31st January 1828.[408] They were eventually to have ten children: Rose (1829-) who married a Leon Solomon of Dawlish, and Hyman (1830-), both of whom were born in Penzance, Henry (1832-1888) who emigrated to Australia, and Moses (1833-) who died young. The 1841 Census records that the first four children were not born in Plymouth. After the bankruptcy, Abraham Joseph's wife, Eliza, lodged with Rabbi B. A. Simmons and his family, while her husband sought to restore his finances elsewhere. He had (most likely) sailed to Gibraltar, where his father had sought and achieved financial recovery, and where Abraham's brother, Henry (1790-1854) had settled, being given a judicial appointment there as a Notary Public around 1821, possibly as a result of royal patronage or influence. Henry Joseph remained in Gibraltar, achieving considerable legal prominence, together with the Presidency of Gibraltar Jewry by 1849. He remained unmarried. Abraham Joseph's absence from Penzance appears to have been relatively brief or intermittent, in that his third and fourth children, Henry and Moses, were born in 1832 and 1833, most likely in Penzance. By 1833, Abraham Joseph had returned to Plymouth, where his wife and family joined him.[409] Abraham and Eliza Joseph's other children were Solomon (1834-1900) who also emigrated to Australia, Sarah (1836-) who married Raphael Harris of Bayswater, London, David (1838-) and Ruth (1840-), both of whom died young, Hannah, who married a David Henry Nathan of Dover, and Eliza (1850-) who married Eliezer Emdon (1841-1900) of Plymouth. Eliza Woolf died in 1850 giving birth to her daughter, Eliza, after which Abraham Joseph married Rosa Joseph (-1896) of Plymouth, his first cousin. From this second marriage, there was one child, Floretta, who remained unmarried. By 1851 Abraham Joseph was trading in Plymouth as a Bill Broker, and became the city's representative to the Board of Deputies of British Jews in London. He also became a partner in the Devon and Cornwall Bank. By 1856, he was able to afford a second home in London, in Savile Row. He died in Plymouth in 1868, and his considerable religious learning was acknowledged in his obituary in the *Jewish Chronicle*, and is reflected by the bequest of his extensive library of religious texts to the Chief Rabbi, Dr. Adler, to whom he was distantly related.[410]

Abraham Joseph of Plymouth was not related to the Joseph Joseph, below, nor to the Henry Joseph who was buried in the Penzance cemetery in 1881, and whose young son, also Abraham, was buried there in 1839. Henry Joseph of Penzance was a prosperous pawnbroker and a prominent member of the Penzance congregation. He was a son of Abraham Joseph (-1827) and a nephew of Lyon Joseph (-1825), both of Falmouth, both of whom were sons of Joseph Joseph of London (by his second marriage).

Joseph Joseph: Watch & Clockmaker, Jeweller, Market Jew St. (Pg. 1830). He also traded in Redruth. He was a grandson of Joseph Joseph of London (from his first marriage), and a son of Moses Isaac Joseph (-1834) of Falmouth and Judith Rebecca Jacob (1768-1849) a daughter of Moses Jacob (1733-1807) of Redruth. He married Fanny Solomon (1815-1855) of Plymouth, moving there in 1849. He later moved to Liverpool, where he died in 1877. This Joseph Joseph's descent from his grandfather's first marriage related him, from the latter's second marriage, to Henry Joseph of Penzance.

Harris Cohen: House in Adelaide Street (Ward List 1835). His occupation is unknown. It is possible that he was related to Emanuel Cohen of Redruth, but his name appears for this year only, and he may have been a transient visitor to the town. The Penzance congregational records name a "J. Cohen" in 1811, a "Cohen" and a "Cohen Redruth" in 1820 (the latter to be identified with the "E. Cohen Redruth" of the following year, and a later" Cohen" in 1853, likely the "Solomon Cohen" of 1854, who was the Rabbi of Penzance until 1856.

Henry Levy: Watch & Clockmaker, Jeweller, Alverton St. (Pg. 1830). This may be a son of Israel Levy of Truro. *Levy* or *Levi* were sometimes alternated with *Levin*.

Israel Levy (-1824) of Truro is thought to have had a son who was known as Henry *Levin*, although he may have been a son-in-law, or a family relative. A Henry Levi (or Levy) was admitted as a member of the Penzance congregation in 1825. He is to be distinguished from Henry Levin, above, who also appears in congregational records as Levy.

Aaron Selig: Watch & Clockmaker, Market Jew St. (Pg. 1830). Residence in Causewayhead (Ward Lists from 1839-1840). Aaron Selig (1782-1841) from London, was employed by the Penzance congregation (as *Rav Aaron ben Pinchas*) sometime before and up to 1808 and then for half a year, from May to October, 1811, as their "shochet and chazan and to teach the children", a ritual slaughterer and reader of prayers.[411] (His headstone in the Penzance cemetery also records that he was qualified, as a *mohel*, to perform circumcisions). Between 1808 to mid-1811, he appears to have returned to London, and his half-year appointment may have been a stopgap, before the arrival of Rabbi B.A. Simmons, also from London. It is not known if Aaron Selig was related to the Rabbi Hyman Selig from London, who served the congregation as its minister from 1815-1817. Aaron Selig was married to Hannah (Hindele) Woolf, a daughter of Hyman Woolf, and sister to Lemon Woolf. Aaron and Hannah Selig's daughter, Maria (1814-) married Solomon Teacher (1811-1856), and for their son, Benjamin Aaron Selig (1814-1872) see below. It is possible that Aaron Selig had another son, in that an Isabella Selig, who had been born in Penzance around 1813, a widow, age 78, with her unmarried daughter, Rosetta, age 39, were living in Chelsea in 1891.[412]

Moses Woolf: Beer Maker (Brewer), Market Place (1841 Census). Moses Woolf (1815-) was a son of Lemon Woolf, and Rebecca Jacob. He was married to Ann Moses, of whom little is known.[413] Moses Wolf appears to have been in partnership with his father. The joint bankruptcy of "Lemon and Moses Wolff, of Penzance, brewers" was recorded in the *West Briton* on 10th March 1847.[414] In the wake of the bankruptcy, a "Mr. John Trevennen Polkinghorne, of Penzance, merchant, was appointed trade assignee". Lemon Woolf died on the 14th March, the following year, and on 12th May 1848, at the Exeter Court of Bankruptcy, the case of "Simon" and Moses Woolf, Brewers, Penzance was heard. (Although the use of *Simon* could be taken as a clerical error, it may well be that Lemon Woolf also used this name, and it has been read as such from the 1841 Census).[415] Upon notification of Lemon Woolf's death, the court issued a certificate of solvency to Moses Woolf.[416] Moses Woolf was a brother of:

Abraham Woolf: Watchmaker, Market Place (1841 Census). By the time of his marriage on 23rd February 1853 to Henrietta Levi (1820-1858), daughter of Phineas Levi,[417] a silversmith and Naval Agent of Plymouth, Abraham Woolf had moved to Aldgate, London, where he lived in Jewry Street. In the marriage register, the groom is given as Abraham *Lemon* Woolf. Phineas Levi (1784-) and his wife Kitty (1788-) were born in Portsea. Phineas Levi arrived in Plymouth sometime before 1810. In 1812 he was trading as a Pawnbroker at 62 North Corner Street, and also as a wholesale slopseller at 48 Queen Street, Plymouth Dock. By 1841 he traded as a silversmith in Catherine Street, Devonport, where, by 1851 he was a Naval Agent. Phineas Levi was one of the first Jews in Plymouth to be elected to civil office as a Commissioner. His headstone in the Hoe cemetery has not survived, but that of his wife still stands. Their children were Henrietta (1820-), David (*c*. 1825-), Rose (*c*. 1825-), possibly his twin, Sophia (*c*. 1828-) and Phoebe (*c*. 1831-). Kitty Levi's headstone appears to mention a "daughter", *Traphina*.[418] Both the 1841 census for Plymouth and the Plymouth Congregational Marriage Register for 12th July 1848, make it clear that *Trephina* Levi was the daughter of a John (and Elizabeth) Levi. John (salesman) and Phineas (silversmith) Levi are clearly distinguished in these records, and the marriage register contains several entries for their respective children. If these Levi families were related, Traphina Levi may have been a niece of Kitty Levi's.

Moses Levy: Silversmith, Market Place (1841 Census). Most likely an itinerant hawker and a skilled journeyman. He was born in Devon, and a **Mark** Levy also appears in this same census and may be the same man, or a brother. There were various Levy (and Levi) families in Exeter and especially in Plymouth (see **Frederick Levy**, below). Their names are to be found throughout the Plymouth Aliens List (Lipman), the Plymouth Congregational Registers of Membership, Marriage and Burials (both in the Hoe and Gifford Street Burial Grounds). Moses Levy is likely to be connected with one of these families, and may be the same as:

Joseph Moses Levy. On Friday 2nd December 1842, the *West Briton* reported a case that had been heard the previous Monday at the Insolvent Debtors' Court in Bodmin. A Penzance man, Hannibal John Boase, aged 79, a butcher who had been declared insolvent was sued by Joseph Moses Levy for incidental expenses or debts owing on an accommodation bill. In the 18th and early 19th centuries, the banking system was relatively undeveloped and did not function as the main source for the raising of credit. Pawnbrokers were an important source of ready credit, and often saved families and small business outlets from insolvency, but most business relations were conducted on the basis of the extension of private credit. Without this the economic and commercial system (which linked manufacturers and suppliers with retailers and shopkeepers, and the latter with customers), could not function. Various forms of private credit arrangements had developed, including bills of exchange, promissory notes and accommodation bills. These were based on trust rather than the valuation of tangible assets as securities. As such, these forms of credit carried considerable risk and were very unstable and unreliable, causing frequent and widespread disruption in economic life. An "accommodation bill" was a form of written credit where a lender or creditor extended a favour to a borrower or debtor by providing the latter with temporary assistance in the form of money, goods or services. Only the creditor (the accommodation party) signed the bill and acted as its guarantor. As such he could not ask for interest or compensation and was liable for the costs if the borrower (the acceptor) failed to repay the debt in whole or in part. Hannibal Boase was clearly in debt to Levy, but he was discharged from the suit by the court on the grounds that the accommodation bill was a purely private arrangement where only one party, Levy, was bound under liability, and as such his suit was inadmissible and lay outside the jurisdiction of the court. Moreover, for the same reasons, the matter also lay outside the remit of the Society for the Relief of Debtors, who had turned down Boase's application to them. *Boase* is a Jewish variant of the Hebrew name *Boaz*,[419] and it was found amongst Jews in Southern France. Despite this, the debtor's name was very common in West Cornwall, and was derived, as mentioned previously, from the Cornish *bos re*, "the dwelling by the ford", and not from Hebrew. Amongst the native Cornish it occurred in a number forms, as *Boas, Bose* and *Bores*, and it was recorded in the Camborne Parish Register as early as 1599.[420]

Zipporah Levy: Pawnbroker, Market Place (1841 Census). She is also recorded in the 1841 census as living with the family of Henry Joseph. She was the sister-in-law of Henry Joseph's mother, Hannah Levy (1769-1851), who was also living in the same household. Zipporah Benjamin (1784-1861) was from Plymouth. She was the widow of Abraham Levy (1779-1834), who had traded in Plymouth, but was originally from Falmouth, and a son of Barnet Levy (1731-1791). Abraham and Zipporah Levy are known to have had six children, Barnet, Mark, Julia, Rebecca, Caroline and Aaron. By 1851 Zipporah Levy had returned to Plymouth, where the Census records her as living at 42 Southside Street with her daughter, Caroline (age 31) and trading as a pawnbroker. Abraham Levy is buried in the Hoe cemetery in Plymouth.[421] There is no record of Zipporah Levy's burial in any South-West Jewish cemetery, although she may be buried in Plymouth in an unmarked grave.

Moses Barnet Simmons: Carver & Gilder, Market Jew Street (1841 Census); Cabinet Maker, Carver & Gilder, East St. (Pg. 1844; Wi. 1847). A son of Rabbi B.A. Simmons, below. He had left the town for London by 1850.

Samuel Oppenheim: Jeweller, Market Place (1841 Census); Clothes Dealer, East St. (Pg. 1844); Slop Warehouse, Market Jew St. (Wi. 1847); Clothes Dealer, Market Jew St. (Sl. 1852/3); Outfitter & General House Furnisher (1861 Census); Clothier, 3, Market Jew St. (Cornish 1864).[422] In 1836, Samuel Oppenheim (1800-1869) established what was to become a prosperous business, which eventually came to occupy premises at Nos. 3, 4 & 8, The Terrace, Market Jew Street on the site of the place where Sir Humphry Davy had been born in December 1778, and opposite the latter's statue that stands at the top of the town's main street today. Samuel Oppenheim was married to Elizabeth (Beila) Levy (1798-1879), a daughter of Israel Levy of Truro and Hannah Moses of Falmouth. He died on 27th May 1869 "by a rupture of a blood vessel"[423] whilst in the Royal Baths on Penzance Promenade. Samuel and Elizabeth Oppenheim are buried in adjacent graves in the Penzance cemetery.

Israel Oppenheim (1843-1913), the (only) son of the above, continued the family business. (His name has been taken, incorrectly, as *Isaac*). The 1871 Census records him as a Merchant (age 27), living at 13 Regent Terrace, with his wife, Mathilda (24), their daughters, Hannah (3), Esther (1) and two servants. Israel Oppenheim was also an investor in the local tin-mining industry, losing most of his money as

Oppenheim of Penzance

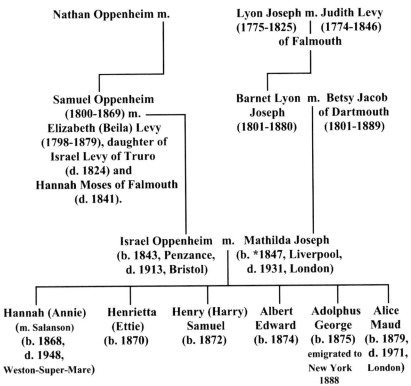

Nathan Oppenheim m.

Lyon Joseph m. Judith Levy
(1775-1825) │ (1774-1846)
of Falmouth

Samuel Oppenheim
(1800-1869) m.
Elizabeth (Beila) Levy
(1798-1879), daughter of
Israel Levy of Truro
(d. 1824) and
Hannah Moses of Falmouth
(d. 1841).

Barnet Lyon m. Betsy Jacob
Joseph of Dartmouth
(1801-1880) (1801-1889)

Israel Oppenheim m. Mathilda Joseph
(b. 1843, Penzance, (b. *1847, Liverpool,
d. 1913, Bristol) d. 1931, London)

Hannah (Annie)
(m. Salanson)
(b. 1868,
d. 1948,
Weston-Super-Mare)

Henrietta
(Ettie)
(b. 1870)

Henry (Harry)
Samuel
(b. 1872)

Albert
Edward
(b. 1874)

Adolphus
George
(b. 1875)
emigrated to
New York
1888

Alice
Maud
(b. 1879,
d. 1971,
London)

all born in Penzance

Israel Oppenheim and his family eventually moved to Bristol.
(This was sometime after 1897, when *Kelly's Directory* records Israel Oppenheim in Penzance).

Source: David Jacobs, Anthony P. Joseph & Godfrey Simmons,
    Research from the 1881 census by Helen Fry.
    Research from the 1901 census by Jackie Hill.
    Compiled by Keith Pearce © (2013).

*Note: the 1881 census gives Mathilda's age as 34, which would give a birth date of 1846/7, and this
    is confirmed by other census records.
    A family tree, in the possession of David Jacobs, gives the year of birth as 1841.

a result of a collapse in the market in the 1890s, when, together, with David Bischof-swerder (see below) he suffered serious losses as a member of the syndicate that had invested in a failing mine near Marazion. Unlike David Bischofswerder, he was not, however, rendered insolvent by the experience, and was able to continue trading in Penzance until the late 1890s, as a "Cabinet maker, complete house-furnisher, upholsterer, carpet maker, and boot and shoe manufacturer, as well as being a contractor and general warehouseman" (*Kelly's Directory 1897*). He adver-tised his "Great Furnishing Mart" extensively in the local press, and in virtually every issue of *The Cornishman* from its first appearance on Thursday 18th July 1878, which carried full column advertisements for his business. He is listed, as a Merchant, in the records of the Penzance Masonic Lodge from 1889 to 1898, and he had also been President of the Penzance Hebrew congregation in 1868-9 and 1872-4. He eventually moved to Bristol, where, by 1901, he had established a furni-ture business, and also traded and travelled across the city as an Agent to a Marble Merchants. The 1901 census for Bristol records Israel Oppenheim as a Boarder at 119 Dove Street, Kingsdown. Curiously, he is given as "Single". Although this might imply that he had separated from his wife, it is more likely a clerical error, or an interpolation, reflecting the fact that he boarded in such houses while trav-elling on business. His wife, Mathilda ("married") and her daughters Ettie (Henri-etta) and Alice (Maud) are recorded at 18, Collingwood Road, Westbury, Bristol, presumably the family's permanent home. Israel's oldest son, Henry (Harry Samuel) was boarding at 105 Redcliffe Hill, Bristol. He was only 29, and already a widower, and he traded as a Commercial Traveller in Clothing Ware. These various details would seem to reflect the fact that the family found it necessary to disperse across the city in the interests of establishing themselves in Bristol. Israel Oppen-heim also became a founder member and Treasurer of the Bristol Cornish Associ-ation.[424] Israel Oppenheim's wife, Mathilda, was a daughter of Barnet Lyon Joseph (1801-1880) formerly of Falmouth, who had moved to Bristol in 1825, and then in 1837 to Liverpool, where Mathilda was born in 1847. They had six children, all born in Penzance, between 1868 and 1879, at a time when Israel and Mathilda Oppenheim were sufficiently prosperous to send their daughters to a private finishing-school in Landau, Germany.[425] Hannah Oppenheim (Annie, 1868-1948) later married Harry Salanson, head of an established Optician's firm in Bristol, who was a prominent Freemason and the President of the Board of Guardians of the Synagogue. Annie Salanson played a significant part in the Jewish Social and Debating Society, and was also President of the Jewish Benevolent Society. She died in Weston-super-Mare. Of her sisters, Henrietta (Ettie, 1870-) married a Solomons of Bristol, who owned a business in Hull, commuting there on a weekly basis (many of the Bischofswerder family were also to settle in Hull). Alice Maud (1879-1971, d. London) worked as a Book-keeper (accounts) and Cashier in the family's Bristol firm. She married a Lowitt. There were three sons, Henry (Harry) Samuel (1872-) a travelling commercial salesman in Clothing, Albert Edward (1874-), of whom little is known, and Adolphus George (1875-). Adolphus, who emigrated to America soon after his Bar Mitzvah at the age of thirteen, settled in New York, where he became a professional actor and theatre producer, taking the stage name of "Mr. George Leonard" in vaudeville. In 1957, at the age of 82, he returned to Penzance for the first time since his departure, becoming the subject of a feature in *The Cornishman* newspaper in which he recalled that his father, Israel, had been instrumental in building a new stage at the St. John's Hall, and had also been involved in theatrical productions there.

Benjamin (Aaron) Selig: Clothes Dealer, & Watch & Clockmaker, North St. (Pg. 1844; Br. 1844); Watchmaker, Causewayhead (1846-7),[426]. ...& China and Glass Warehouse (Wi. 1847). Watchmaker & Pawnbroker (1851 Census; Sl. 1852/3). He was married to Catherine Jacob (1821-), a daughter of Samuel Jacob (1778-1860) of Penzance. The 1851 census for Penzance records their two children, Alfred Aaron (1849-) and Lemon (1850-).[427] Catherine's unmarried sister, Phoebe (23) lived with them as a shop assistant for the pawnbroking side of the business. (This Phoebe Jacob (*b.* 1828) should not be confused with her namesake (born *c.* 1817-20) who was the daughter of Levy Jacob (1788-1824) of Penzance and Sophia Mordecai (1781-) of Exeter. The latter Phoebe Jacob had married Abraham Kestenberg in Exeter in 1845). In 1842, Benjamin Selig appeared as a witness at the Cornwall General Quarter Sessions in the trial of a youth, James Williams, age 15, who was found guilty of the theft of "a silver watch, chain, and key" from the property of Henry Rowe of Newbridge, Sancreed, near Penzance. Williams had entered the house on the pretence of asking the time of Rowe's wife, Mary, who went to a drawer of a dresser, where the watch was kept. Leaving the house briefly, she later found the watch was missing. Henry Rowe subsequently saw the watch in Selig's possession. Williams had taken the watch to Selig, and used it as part exchange of 14 shillings for a jacket, priced at 17s. 6d. James Williams was sentenced to (three months?) hard labour.[428] The incident is typical of the fact that jewellers and pawnbrokers would often inadvertently come into possession of stolen goods (see the two cases below, involving Jacob Schwerer, who was a jeweller in Redruth, and other Cornish towns, including Penzance, and who appeared as a witness at the same sessions). Benjamin Selig (1814-1872) was President of the Penzance Hebrew Congregation from 1852 to 1853, immediately after which he emigrated with his family to become a minister to Jewish congregations in Melbourne, Australia (where a third child, Phineas was born in 1856), and later in Christchurch, South Island New Zealand.[429] Alfred Aaron Selig moved to London, marrying Louisa (1863-) a daughter of Richard Defreig of Islington, a Chemist and Druggist. By 1901, Alfred was trading as a Commercial Traveller in Fancy Goods, and the couple were living in Tottenham, with their daughter, Catherine (16) and son, Alfred (13).[430]

Phoebe Simmons: Milliner, Market Jew Street (1841 Census); Clothes Dealer, East St. (Pg. 1844). Phoebe Simmons (1815-) was a daughter of Rabbi B. A. Simmons (1784-1860) and Flora Jacob (1790-1874). In 1846, Phoebe married Joseph (Jonas Heilbron) a Jeweller of Falmouth.

Henry Joseph: Pawnbroker, Market St. (1841 Census; Pg. 1844; Sl. 1852/3); Chapel St. (Queen's Sq.) (Wi. 1847); Pawnbroker & Outfitter, 5, Market Jew St. (1861 & 1871 Census; Co. 1864, & Cornish 1864, p. 33). Henry Joseph (1806-1881) was originally from Falmouth, but he lived and traded in Penzance for fifty years. The 1841 census lists four children, Hannah Joseph (Levy), Henry Joseph's widowed mother, Zipporah Levy, from the Benjamin family of Plymouth, and Hannah Joseph's widowed sister-in-law, Esther Jacob, sister to Amelia Joseph, Henry Joseph's wife, and Therza Elias, a relative of Henry Joseph's grandmother, Esther Elias. Eventually, Henry Joseph was able to employ a shop, assistant, Simon Simmons, and three servants, Sarah Simmons, domestic servant, Elizabeth Birch, a child's maid, and Nany [Nancy?] Uren, a housemaid.

As one of the largest and most prosperous pawnbrokers in Penzance, in Queen's Square, Henry Joseph, like others in his trade, would come into receipt of goods they suspected to be stolen. Pawnbrokers would also come to know of people and names they associated with having a dubious reputation. In February 1847, Henry Joseph was offered articles of clothing by an Elizabeth Hollow of New Street, Penzance, but he suspected them to be the same items that had recently been stolen from the house of a James Wills of Newlyn. Elizabeth Hollow's husband, Uriah Hollow, was a mason by trade, and the 1841 census for Penzance records the couple living with their infant daughter, Johanna, in the house of a Colin Goldsworthy (also a mason) in the town. In 1843, Uriah Hollow and another man, Abraham Nicholls, had been convicted of theft and sentenced to three months hard labour. Henry Joseph reported Elizabeth to the police. She was taken into custody and committed for trial, a search warrant having found other goods recently stolen from the neighbourhood in her house. Her husband had absconded and had fled the area. At her trial, Henry Joseph testified that Elizabeth Hollow often came to his shop with items to pledge. She, however, testified that she had found the items in her house, and believed that her sister-in-law had sent the items for pledge. The jury was persuaded that her husband had been the true culprit, and she was acquitted.[431]

Henry Joseph died at No. 5 The Terrace, on 20th December 1881.[432] He was married to Amelia Jacob (1811-1891) who had been born in Camborne. She was a daughter of Jacob Jacob (1774-1853), a son of Moses Jacob of Redruth, and Kate (Kitty) Simons (1777-1846) of Truro. Henry and Amelia Joseph had a large family. Abraham (1834-1839) died young, and was buried in the Penzance Jewish cemetery. The other children were Sarah, or Selina (1835-1872: buried in Penzance), Barnet Henry Joseph (1837-1907), who married Isabelle Blanckensee (1839-1912), Rose (1838-1896) who married Ephraim George Goodman (1828-1896) of Merthyr Tydfil (a widower, first married to Phoebe (c.1829-1865) a daughter of Samuel Jacob of Penzance), Lionel (1840-) who died young, Moses, or Morris (1841-) who was unmarried, Esther (1843-) who married Aaron Mark Beirnstein (1848-) of Dowlais, South Wales, Samuel (1844-) who died at five months (buried in Penzance), Joseph (1846-) who married Emily Jacob (1851-1937) a daughter of (Moses) Isaac Jacob (1820-1888) of Falmouth, and later Redruth, Kate (1847-) who married Abraham Freedman of Aberdare, Betsy, also known as Elizabeth, Bessie (1848-1900) who was unmarried and is buried in Penzance, and Julia (1851-1911) who married Morris (1856-) a son of Rev. Isaac Bischofswerder of Penzance. Julia Joseph's burial was the last of a member of the Penzance congregation. Barnet Joseph and his brother,

Joseph of Penzance

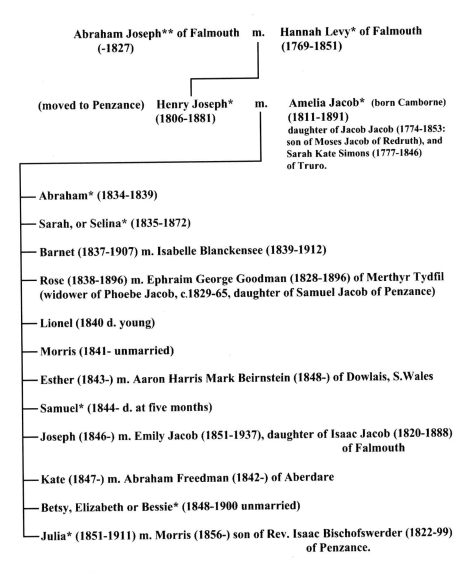

Abraham Joseph** of Falmouth   m.   Hannah Levy* of Falmouth
(-1827)   (1769-1851)

(moved to Penzance)   Henry Joseph*   m.   Amelia Jacob* (born Camborne)
                         (1806-1881)   (1811-1891)
                                                   daughter of Jacob Jacob (1774-1853:
                                                     son of Moses Jacob of Redruth), and
                                                     Sarah Kate Simons (1777-1846)
                                                     of Truro.

— Abraham* (1834-1839)

— Sarah, or Selina* (1835-1872)

— Barnet (1837-1907) m. Isabelle Blanckensee (1839-1912)

— Rose (1838-1896) m. Ephraim George Goodman (1828-1896) of Merthyr Tydfil
(widower of Phoebe Jacob, c.1829-65, daughter of Samuel Jacob of Penzance)

— Lionel (1840 d. young)

— Morris (1841- unmarried)

— Esther (1843-) m. Aaron Harris Mark Beirnstein (1848-) of Dowlais, S.Wales

— Samuel* (1844- d. at five months)

— Joseph (1846-) m. Emily Jacob (1851-1937), daughter of Isaac Jacob (1820-1888)
                                                             of Falmouth

— Kate (1847-) m. Abraham Freedman (1842-) of Aberdare

— Betsy, Elizabeth or Bessie* (1848-1900 unmarried)

— Julia* (1851-1911) m. Morris (1856-) son of Rev. Isaac Bischofswerder (1822-99)
                                                        of Penzance.

*   interred in Penzance Jewish cemetery
** interred in Falmouth Jewish cemetery

Source: Anthony P. Joseph and Godfrey Simmons.
Note: Sources for birth dates may differ. Census returns 1841, 1851, 1861 & 1871, as well as some
headstone inscriptions and marriage certificates have been used to arrive at dates.
In some cases the precise year remains uncertain.
Compiled by Keith Pearce © (2013).

Joseph Joseph moved to Birmingham, where they became successful businessmen. Morris Joseph emigrated to America, where he became a Notary Public, and a contributor of letters to the San Francisco mining and scientific press.[433]

Therza Elias: 75, Independent, living at the home of Henry Joseph in Penzance (1841 Census).

Samuel Jacob: Traveller (Hawker), Market Jew St. (1841 Census); Jeweller, 9 Leskinnick Terrace (1851 Census). Samuel Jacob (1778-1860), who was deaf, was a son of Moses Jacob of Redruth, and traded in various towns in South West Cornwall (see Hayle). Around 1847, he traded in Falmouth, but returned to Penzance. He was married to Sally (Sarah) Levy (*c.* 1784-1868) of Truro. Samuel Jacob's handicap was an inherited trait that was passed down through the Jacob line in several forms. Samuel Jacob's daughter, Betsy, a dressmaker, was deaf and dumb, and another daughter, Amelia, was either born with a hearing impediment or became deaf in later years. She remained unmarried. Of special interest is the fact that an original handwritten **Family Register** for this family has survived,[434] inscribed in a Prayerbook, recording Jacob (and some Levy) births from 1758 up to Samuel Jacob's death. It appears to be in the same hand throughout, and may have been compiled by one of Samuel Jacob's children from memory and family tradition. It appears to have been compiled with great precision, and its general accuracy for the dates of births is likely to be reliable. However, some dates do not coincide with evidence from other sources (public records after 1838) and, in at least two other cases from headstones.

Samuel Jacob's birth is given as 3rd March 1778 (although the *8* could be read as a *3*), and his death as 27th August 1858, but his headstone in the Penzance cemetery clearly records that he died on 30th November 1860, at the age of 83 (his death falling after the new Jewish year). His marriage to Sally (Sarah) Levy is given as taking place in Truro on 16th June 1813. Their seven children are given as:

(i) Ph(o)eby Jacob: born Friday July 19th 1814 at Copperhouse, Hayle (this child may have died young in view of the fact that her namesake is given below).

(ii) Moses Jacob: born on Thursday night (at) 9 o'clock July 15th 1816 (his year of birth has been taken as 1815, and he died on 27th August 1858; he was unmarried). Jacob family tradition held that Moses ("Mossam" for Moses [ben] Samuel) "was rather simple and that practical jokes were always played on him".[435]

(iii) Amelia Jacob: born at one o'clock on Saturday morning October 25th 1817 (her year of birth has usually been taken as 1822 from her declaration on her marriage certificate, but she chose to subtract five years for appearance's sake, in that she was ten years older than the groom).

(iv) Catherine Jacob: born Wednesday morning at seven o'clock on March 8th 1820 (she was to marry Benjamin Aaron Selig), and the register records that "Mrs. C. Selig delivered with two fine boys 1(st) December 1850, Sunday evening eight o'clock…".

(v) Henry Jacob: born Saturday (at) two o'clock on June 29th 1822 "and surrounded by his family". It must have been obvious that he would not survive and he was circumcised by B. A. Simmons the following Tuesday, 2nd July.

(vi) Elizabeth (Betsy) Jacob: born Tuesday morning seven o'clock 10th August 1824.

(vii) Phoeby Jacob: ("the second") born Thursday morning at three o'clock on… August 1827 (or 1829: her marriage in 1853 gave her age as 24).

The register notes that two of Samuel Jacob's daughters went to live with a "Mrs. Solomon" in Bristol, Amelia on November 26th 1841, and Phoeby April 21st 1844. It has been noted earlier that this Mrs. Solomon was most likely Kitty Solomon (Jacob) the widow of Simon Solomon (-1825) of Falmouth. Kitty Solomon's sister, Betsy (Elizabeth), widow of Solomon Solomon (d. 1819 in Lisbon) had gone to Bristol to live, taking her only children, Israel, then 16, and Barnet Levy, then 13 (both men later emigrated to America). Betsy Solomon died in Bristol in 1832. The arrangement with Mrs. (Kitty) Solomon would have been a temporary one, and both girls were later married (see below).

Henry (Hyman) Jacob: Tailor, Market Jew St. (1841 Census). A son of the above. The census records him as a *Taylor*, age 15, although he was born in 1822.

Jacob Moses: Hawker, a lodger in Adelaide Street (1841 Census), from outside the County. An itinerant peddler.

It can be seen from the Samuel Oppenheim and Henry Joseph entries in Coulson's Directory above that from around the 1860s, house and premises numbers begin to be used for some of the chief business and residential streets, although street numbering had already appeared in the 1851 Census. It is likely that it took some time for this to settle into a coherent system of numbering as the postal service and new building expanded rapidly. The numbers for Penzance in Coulson's 1864 directory are street-specific. Around 1878, George Bown Millett attempted an historical reconstruction of the buildings and businesses in the town centre from the beginning of the 19th century, allocating numbers to each site. These numbers are not based on the postal system but upon his own plan and are conjectural. Millett referenced each of his numbers to the town centre as a whole as "Market Jew St." irrespective of the separate names by which the streets had come to be known. The locations on his plan would, however, seem to coincide with the other directory addresses (where known). He indicates other areas, just outside the Market centre itself, such as Alverton and Lady (Chapel) Street, with these distinct names. The historical accuracy of Millett's plan is uncertain.

Morris Hart Harris: Watch & Clockmaker, Chapel St. (Pg. 1844); Watch & Clock Dealer… "advertises American clocks at 17/6d each" (Br. 1844); Jeweller, Silver-smith, Watch & Clock repairs, China & Glass, Chapel St. (Wi. 1847). Morris Hart Harris (1821-1913) was the son of Henry Harris (1787-1872) and the grandson of Samuel Harris (1754-1824), originally from London. Samuel Harris had lived in Penzance, but settled in Falmouth, marrying Judith Solomon (1763-1839). Henry Harris was born in Penzance, but traded in Truro, later returning to London. Henry Harris married a daughter, Esther (1784-1871) of Moses Jacob of Redruth, and their son, Morris Hart Harris married a daughter, Rebecca (1824-1906) of Moses Jacob's son, Jacob Jacob of Falmouth. Morris Hart Harris was President of the Penzance congregation (1849-50), after which he left the town.

Alexander Levin: Watch & Clockmaker, & Dealer in China, Glass etc., & Marine Stores (Wi. 1847). Alexander Levin (1828-1891) was the eldest son of Henry Levin (above). By 1851 he was trading in hardware at 19 Bath Street, Bristol,[436] with his brother Israel as an assistant. The jeweller, Morris Hart Harris, was a visitor, and a Grace Deaton, spinster, age 28, from "Scilly Island" lived with the Levin family as a General Servant. By 1861, Alexander Levin, then 34, had moved to Redcliffe Street, St. Thomas, Bristol, as a jeweller, with his wife Rachel (29), and their children Esther (3) and Hyman (2).[437] Another son, Lionel, was born in Bristol in 1863. Rachel Joseph (1831-1891) was a daughter of Barnet Lyon Joseph (1801-1880) and Betsy Jacob (1801-1889), formerly of Falmouth, who moved to Bristol. By 1871, Alexander and Rachel Levin had moved to Edgbaston, Birmingham, where Alexander traded as a jeweller and pawnbroker.[438] In the year of his death, 1891, the census records his widow at Ladywood, Birmingham, with her unmarried daughter, Esther, and her sister-in-law, Mat(h)ilda (b. *circa.* 1826-), who had married Isaac Aaron (b. *circa.* 1820-) of Birmingham. Matilda's age appears as 44 on the 1871 census, and as 68 in 1891. She is likely to have been born a year to eighteen months before her brother, Alexander (1828).[439] Alexander Levin's son, Lionel Barnet Levin (1862-1933) settled in Tonga.[440]

Rabbi Barnett Asher Simmons: Silversmith (1814) & Jeweller (1821): Penzance Masonic Records (in which he is recorded variously as *Symons, Simmons* and *Semmens*); Slop Warehouse, Market Jew St. (Wi. 1847). He lived at 16 Leskinnick Terrace (1851 Census) with his wife Flora, a daughter of Moses Jacob of Redruth. An elderly relative, Kitty Simons from Redruth and a servant called Grace Read lived with them in 1851. From 1798, Simmons learned his trade as a "Jappaner & Painter" in London from Abraham Jacobs of Denmark Court, completing his Articles in 1804. During this time, it is likely that he lived with his grandfather, Abraham Michel, who was a gold and silver polisher. From these years Simmons may have gained sufficient knowledge to trade in items as a jeweller, although he is not known to have been a watch and clock maker.

Solomon Teacher: Hardware & Jeweller, Market Jew St. and No. 35, Leskinnick Terrace (Wi. 1847; 1851 Census). He was originally from Bavaria, where the family name is likely to have been *Techaur*, and in the 1851 census he is recorded as "Jew". At some point he had lived in St. Ives. He traded in Penzance for most of his life, and was married to Maria Selig, daughter of Aaron and Hannah Selig, and sister of Benjamin (above). Solomon and Maria Teacher's daughter, Annah (b. circa 1850), and a servant called Jane Caday, lived with them. There were also two sons, David (b. 1852), Solomon (the latter born in the same year as his father died, 1856, and named after him). A daughter, Ida, was born in 1854. David Teacher also named one of his sons Solomon. Solomon Teacher took an active part in Congregational affairs and is mentioned in the Minute Books on several occasions. By 1856 the Teacher family's finances were strained, and at a meeting on 13th April 1856, the

Teacher-Selig of Penzance

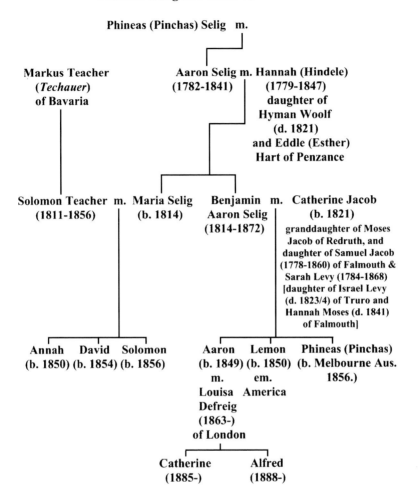

Phineas (Pinchas) Selig m.

Markus Teacher
(*Techauer*)
of Bavaria

Aaron Selig m. Hannah (Hindele)
(1782-1841)   (1779-1847)
daughter of
Hyman Woolf
(d. 1821)
and Eddle (Esther)
Hart of Penzance

Solomon Teacher m. Maria Selig   Benjamin m. Catherine Jacob
(1811-1856)   (b. 1814)   Aaron Selig   (b. 1821)
(1814-1872)   granddaughter of Moses
Jacob of Redruth, and
daughter of Samuel Jacob
(1778-1860) of Falmouth &
Sarah Levy (1784-1868)
[daughter of Israel Levy
(d. 1823/4) of Truro and
Hannah Moses (d. 1841)
of Falmouth]

Annah   David   Solomon   Aaron   Lemon   Phineas (Pinchas)
(b. 1850) (b. 1854) (b. 1856) (b. 1849) (b. 1850) (b. Melbourne Aus.
m.   em.   1856.)
Louisa   America
Defreig
(1863-)
of London

Catherine   Alfred
(1885-)   (1888-)

Note: Benjamin Selig and Catherine Jacob are thought to have had three further children, Hannah,
Sarah and Henry. Aaron Selig (1849-) settled in London, and Lemon Selig (1850-) in Oregon.
The Selig family lived in Melbourne, and then New Zealand, but after 1872, Catherine Selig returned
to Melbourne. Phineas Selig remained in New Zealand.
Source: Kenneth Teacher, Anthony P. Joseph, & Alex Jacob.
Compiled by Keith Pearce © (2013).

Congregation paid out £2 16s. 9d. for Solomon Teacher's funeral expenses. He had died in St. Ives a month earlier. The death certificate, dated 10th March 1856, records the cause of death as "a carcinoma of the stomach, 9 months certified". An Elizabeth Carter was present at the death, which occurred at Fore Street. It is not known if he was visiting the town at the time, or if he had gone there to receive terminal care. The Congregation also paid £2 15s. 6d. for Mr. Staalhagen (*sic*), Rev. Myer Stadthagen of the Plymouth Congregation (from 1829-1862) to come to Penzance to circumcise "Mrs Teacher's child", Solomon. (The Congregation paid £1 15s. 6d. for the funeral of Joseph Barnet, also from St. Ives, at the same time). By 1871, Maria Teacher had moved to Mile End, London. She is recorded as a Needlewoman, living with her married daughter, Ann (Annah) Levy (21), her son, David (19) a Velum Binder, and daughter, Ida (17) a Pupil Teacher.[441]

Joseph Marks: Commercial Traveller, lodging at the Temperance Hotel, Princess Street (1851 Census). He had been born in Portsea (*c*.1804).

Joseph Bloomfield: Musician, age 30, from Germany, listed as a "Stranger" (1851 Census). Uncertain.

Frederick Levy: Commercial Traveller in Cutlery and Jewellery (1851 Census). Aged 30, he was from Plymouth, and was a lodger at an Inn in Market Jew Street.

Nathaniel Schram: Herbalist and Pedlar. A Dutch Jew, he is likely to have been in Penzance in late 1853, when his name appears as "Scrann" in the Congregational records, but not thereafter. He had traded in Falmouth in the 1840s, and then moved to Plymouth, but travelled widely. He is recorded as a Hawker of Jewellery, from Holland, boarding at 95 Market Jew Street (1861), and was in Helston in 1871.

Solomon Isaac Ezekiel: House in Causewayhead (Ward Lists 1835-1839); Tinman (Tin and Copper Plate Worker) North Street (1841 & 1851 Census; Co. 1864); 56, Causewayhead (Cornish 1864, p. 13). He was born in Devon, and was a member of the Ezekiel family of or from that County. His grandfather, Benjamin Ezekiel (-1785) and his brother, Abraham (1726-1799), a silversmith, goldsmith and watch-maker, had come to Exeter, from the continent around 1740-1750. Benjamin Ezekiel's son, Ezekiel Benjamin Ezekiel appears to have settled in Newton Abbot, where his son Solomon was born *c*.1781-6. Roth recorded that he was born there on 7th June 1781, and that he died (in Penzance) at the age of 86 (which accords with the year on his headstone, although this does not record his age). It has been said [442] that Solomon Ezekiel was the son of Ezekiel Benjamin Ezekiel's cousin, the renowned engraver and miniaturist, Ezekiel Abraham Ezekiel (1757-1806), but this is not correct. The latter was unmarried and lived in Exeter. Susser, who correctly identified the original published source of the misinformation that Solomon Ezekiel was a son of Ezekiel Abraham Ezekiel, claimed, erroneously, that Solomon Ezekiel was born in Exeter, in the year 1786, having been recorded on a lease renewal for the Exeter cemetery of 1803 as aged 17.[443] The lease, however, refers to "Solomon Ezekiel son of Ezekiel Benjamin Ezekiel of Newton Abbot....now aged

Ezekiel of Devon and Penzance

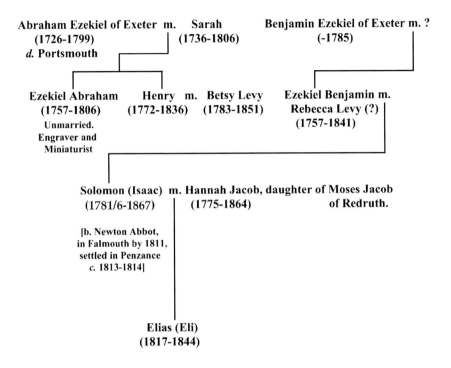

Source: W.S Jessop (1951: modified), Susser (1993), Frank Gent (2000).
Compiled by Keith Pearce © (2013).

about seventeen years…", leaving his precise birth year as uncertain. That Solomon Ezekiel's father lived in Newton Abbot is clear from a later lease of 1827, by which time, Solomon Ezekiel himself was settled in Penzance. An Ezekiel family and a Levy family lived in Newton Abbot between 1780 and 1800, and it is possible that the Rebecca (1757-1841) who has been given incorrectly[444] as a wife of Ezekiel Abraham Ezekiel, may have been a Levy of Newton Abbot, and the wife of Ezekiel Benjamin Ezekiel. The 1827 lease was issued, amongst others, to Solomon's uncle, Henry Ezekiel (1772-1835), who was married to a Betsy Levy (1783-1851), as one of the nominated "lives". It refers to "Solomon Ezekiel now aged about forty one years and son of Ezekiel Benjamin Ezekiel of Newton Abbot".[445] Solomon Ezekiel had moved to Falmouth by 1811 in which year he is listed there in Holden's Directory as a "Tinman" (dealer in metal). It has been noted earlier, that his business in Falmouth was not successful, although he appears to have continued to have retained some trading interest there until 1815, in which year he was imprisoned at Bodmin by a court order as an insolvent debtor.[446] Earlier, by 1813, he had been in Penzance, where he lived in Causewayhead and traded as a plumber and coppersmith, and from 1814 he is listed as a member of the Penzance Masonic Lodge. He married Hannah Jacob (1775-1864) a daughter of Moses Jacob of Redruth. Their only known child, Elias (Eli), was born in 1817, and died in 1844 at the age of 27. He was unmarried, and is buried in the Penzance cemetery as *Eliezer ben Isaac* (6:2).

Solomon Ezekiel was involved in the wider community and was elected to the Penzance Board of Highways as a member of its Committee in 1845, an example that, at the time, the journal *The Voice of Jacob* took to indicate a significant change in attitudes towards Jews, although in the case of Penzance, it is unlikely that the writer possessed local knowledge or familiarity with the climate of tolerance and acceptance that had prevailed in the town for some time: "On March 25th a burgess eulogised the Jewish character for sobriety, loyalty and general good conduct. He proposed Mr. Solomon Ezekiel who was elected unanimously. There has been a great change of late, for 20 years ago such a proceeding would almost have produced a riot." That a riot would have been unlikely in similar circumstances in Penzance in the 1820s, accustomed to the arrival of a cosmopolitan cross-section of sea-faring visitors, does not entirely invalidate the writer's emphasis on the increasing acceptance of Jews in civil society. It has been noted that as early as 1798, Lemon Hart had been a member of local volunteer civilian militia at the time of a potential invasion by the French, and the writer's mention of the burgess' emphasis on the *loyalty* of the Jewish community, echoes and reflects the fact that the oath of loyalty to the Crown would have been recited in English in the synagogue each week. Solomon Ezekiel was also something of a local scholar and lecturer, publishing several pamphlets. His dedication to the civil values of the community in which he lived did not, however, render him a sycophant towards the local gentry, nor was he uncritical of what he regarded as undesirable social developments. He successfully opposed a local landowner, Sir Rose Price of Trengwainton Manor, from establishing in Penzance a branch of the London Society for Promoting Christianity among Jews, that was particularly active in Cornwall at the time. Solomon Ezekiel successfully countered the activities of Price's society locally by founding the Penzance Hebrew Society for the Promotion of Religious Knowledge. As a lecturer, translator and writer on various aspects of the Jewish religion, his published writings were: [447]

(i) "Remarks on the Censures of the authorised version of the Holy Scriptures". (Included in a pamphlet by the Rev. Hart Symons; pub. 1822).
(ii) "The Life of Abraham: a series of three lectures on the Lives of the Patriarchs" (1844).
(iii) "The Life of Issac". Three further lectures (1845).
(iv) "The Hebrew Festivals" (1847).
(v) "A Letter to Sir Rose Price on the Christianizing of the Jews". (31st January 1820).[448]
(vi) "A Lecture on the Passions and Feelings of Mankind". (undated).

Solomon Isaac Ezekiel (*c.*1781/6-1867) and Hannah Jacob (1775-1864) are both buried in the Penzance Jewish cemetery.

Lawrence Jordan: Licensed Hawker, 50, appears as a lodger at 150 Chapel Street (1851 Census), together with Mary Jordan, 50, his wife, Francis Jordan, 42, and a Susan Kelly, 52 (unmarried). All four were from Ireland, and it is unlikely that the Jordans were Jewish (but see 1871, below).

Solomon Cohen: Hebrew reader, 5 Leskinnick Terrace (Post Office Directory 1856);[449] Rabbi and *shochet* of the Penzance congregation from 1853-1856. In the Post Office Directory, his name appears as *Cowen*. He was a son of Eleazar (Elias or Elijah) Cohen from Poland, who later lived in South Wales, and whose three sons, Ephraim, Manasseh and Solomon all became Rabbis.[450] Solomon Cohen is not known to have been related to Emanuel Cohen (1766-1849) of Redruth (who was from Germany), nor to the H. L. Cohen of Warsaw, who married Rosate Moses of Falmouth, in Penzance on 28th February 1833.[451] The surname *Cohen* appears in the Penzance Congregational Minute Book in 1811, 1820, 1821 (the last entry naming Emanuel Cohen of Redruth), 1853 and 1854 (the last naming Solomon Cohen), who was the minister in Penzance from 1853- 1856, and then Rabbi (Reader in Prayers and *shochet*) of the Coventry congregation from 1860-1869.[452] It is of interest that the same 1856 Post Office Directory which lists Solomon Cohen, and the 1871 Census for Penzance record various traders in basket and shoe making with the surname *Marks*. It is not known if any of these were of Jewish descent.

Lazarus Hymen (or Hyman): Furrier & Jeweller, Union Street (PODir. 1856).[453] Lazarus Hymen, who was from Poland, was in Falmouth as a Jeweller in 1851. It is possible that Lazarus Hymen was connected with the family of Rabbi Moses Hyman (also from Poland) who had been the Rabbi of Falmouth until his death there in 1830. At least two of the children of Rabbi Moses Hyman were furriers: Rose (or Rosetta) and Abraham, born in Falmouth in 1822 and 1823. Both later traded in the East End of London. An "L. Hyman" signed the New Penzance Regulations of 1844. It is not known if the below is a reversal of Lazarus Hyman.

Hyman Lazarus: (trade unknown). His name appears in the Penzance Minute Book in 1843 and 1845. Curiously, Hyman Lazarus appears to have signed the minutes of a meeting of 12th March 1843 (unless someone else wrote his name) but in a meeting of 13th April 1845, the minutes record "The Mark of Hyman Lazarus. He is not known to have been related to Frederick Lazarus, below, or to Isaac Lazarus of Hayle. It is possible that the Bella Lazarus, age 55 (Stoke Newington, London), born Cornwall, and Francis Lazarus, age 28, (Southampton), born Penzance, who appear in the 1891 Census, were related to Hyman Lazarus.[454]

Israel Levin: Hardware Dealer & Jeweller (1861 Census), Marine Store Dealer, Levin's Court & 102 Market Jew St. (Co. 1864 & Cornish 1864, p. 38). Toy Warehouse (Cornish 1864, p. 149). The second son of Henry Levin, above. From about

1850, Israel Levin (1829-1887) had moved to work with his brother Alexander in Bristol, but returned to Penzance when the latter moved from Bristol to Birmingham. After Henry Levin's death in 1877, he continued to run his father's Jewellery and Hardware store in Market Jew Street until his own death on 3rd April 1887.[455] Israel Levin was unmarried. He was a contributor to the Penzance Dispensary, which had been established in 1809 in Market Jew Street, moving to Chapel Street in 1813, and then to St. Clare Street in 1871, becoming an infirmary in 1874 with eight beds.[456] Israel Levin was also the Master of the Penzance Masonic Lodge in 1863, and from 1881 to 1887. He also served as President of the Penzance Hebrew Congregation.

Joseph Spasshat: Watch & Clockmaker, and Mary Ann Spasshat, Dressmaker & Milliner, 14 Market Jew Street (1861 Census). It is not certain that they were Jewish. He had been born in Cornwall, and his wife, Mary, in Clerkenwell, London (both c. 1819). No other Jewish family with this surname has been identified in Cornwall. In 1830, Joseph Spasshatt had traded with Alexander Simons in Falmouth as Wine and Spirit Merchants.

Aaron Roeback: a Hawker of Jewellery, from Bavaria (1861 Census). Uncertain.

Samuel Diamond: Shoemaker, Custom House Lane, the Quay (Cornish 1864, p. 25). Uncertain (see Diamond below).

Symon B. Simmons: Commercial Traveller, boarding in a hotel at 60 Chapel Street. His father, Rabbi B.A. Simmons had died in 1860, and his mother, Flora, had left Penzance to live with a daughter in South Wales.

Marcus Spiro: Rabbi, 2 New St. (adjacent to the Synagogue); (Co. 1864 & Cornish 1864, p. 44 & 137); 72, Causewayhead (Cornish 1864, p. 158). Spiro (or Spero) was minister to the Penzance congregation from c. 1862 until April 1865. The Cornish reference to the house adjacent to the synagogue was not Spiro's place of residence, but, by association, where he practised his profession. The synagogue did not have a rabbi's house attached to it.[457]

The 1861 census records that the occupier of 56, Adelaide Street (a Jewish Rabbi) "had died between the day of delivery and the day of collection of the schedule". This was Rev. **Hyman Greenberg**, who was buried in the Penzance cemetery on 8th April 1861. Although the names and dates of the Rabbis who lived in Penzance can be identified from the congregational Minute Book, they are not listed in this section unless they appear in independent records, such as census returns or trade directories.

Josiah Solomon: Tailor, 5 Sandybank (1871 Census). He was born in Liskeard (c. 1833) and his wife Hannah (a Dressmaker) at St. Enoder (c. 1840). The family had lived in Bradford, Yorkshire (c. 1860) where two of their children, Simon and William had been born. Three other children were born at St. Enoder, Truro and

Penzance. Three of the boys were also Tailors. Josiah Solomon was not Jewish, and he is not to be identified with his namesake who was a witness at the marriage of Amelia, daughter of Lemon Woolf, to Phillip Solomon of Newcastle, which took place in Penzance on 10th May 1842.

A **Josiah Solomon**, Jeweller and Furnishing Hardwareman, originally from Exeter, was living in Plymouth in 1881, with his wife, Rose, their five sons and six daughters. This family was Jewish.

Despite their Hebrew forenames (taken from the Old Testament) and their trades (commonly associated with Jews) the following Penzance traders were not Jewish: Abraham Tonkin, Draper, Market Place, Enock Tonkin, Tailor, Victoria Place, and Joseph Tonkin, Tailor, Chapel Street (1856 Post Office Directory).[458]

William H. Soloman: Chemist & Druggist, 61 North Street (1871 Census).
It is not certain if he was of Jewish descent. He was from Penryn, and his wife from Falmouth. It has been noted previously that a William H. Solomon was Mayor of Falmouth in 1879. William Solomon may have been related to John Solomon, a Chemist in Penryn (1864).

Zelig Harris (or *Zeleg Harries*): Hawker, 2, Adelaide Street (1871 Census). He was originally from Poland. *Harris* would have been adopted by him in place of his Polish surname. He was a boarder at this address, suggesting that he may not have been a long-term resident of the town. He was 60 at the time of the census , and unmarried. The note (*Jew*) appears next to his occupation. He is not known to have been connected with the family of Samuel Harris (1754-1824) of Falmouth or his son Henry Harris (1787-1872) of Truro. *Harris* was a common surname amongst Jews, and appears frequently in Cornish census and parish records as a Christian surname. He had previously traded in Truro (1841) and in Falmouth (1861).

Harold Bereshof: a Commercial Traveller from Bristol, boarding at a the Union Hotel in Chapel Street (1871 Census). Uncertain.

Letitia Diamond: Mariner's Wife, 4 Abbey Place (1871 Census). She was from Wales. Her husband's name is not given, and it is not certain that the family was of Jewish descent.

Laurance Jordan: Traveller in Cloth, 6 Alverton Street (1871 Census). It is not certain that he was of Jewish descent. He was 73 in 1871, unmarried, and originally from Ireland. It is possible that he was related to the Lawrence Jordan, above, of 1841. Both Laurance (or Lawrance) and Jordan appear as Jewish names, and the surname occurs amongst Cornish Christians. A William Jordan of Helston has been taken to have been the author of a manuscript in the Cornish language of 1611, a miracle play, *Gwerans an bys* (The Creation of the World) but he is most likely to have been its transcriber, in that the earlier original has been lost, and Jordan may have completed his transcription direct from the play's performance.[459] In 1849, a

Phoebe Aaron (whose name has been read as Jordan) was co-insurer with four Jews of a house in Bodmin (see Bodmin Trades).[460]

John Solomon: Schoolmaster, 48a Chapel Street (Cornish 1864, p. 48, & 1871 Census). He was born in North Cornwall, and he is not known to have been of Jewish descent.

Miceal (Michael) Leinkram: Rabbi, 16 Alverne Buildings (1891 Census). He was originally from Krakow, Poland and he was Rabbi of the Penzance congregation from 1887-1894.[461] After leaving Penzance, Leinkram became a minister in Belfast, lived briefly in America, and died in London.

Berenger & Schwerer: Watch & Clockmakers, 17 Market Jew St. & 27 Market Place; (Br. & PODir. 1856). They appear in several Cornish towns, and in various census records.

The following Penzance Clockmakers are not known to have been Jewish:

Samuel Shortman (1823). A Sarah Shortman (76), originally from Camberwell, and her grandson, William John Shortman (16) born in Kentish Town, London, are listed as living at 13 Union Terrace (1871 Census). Henry Sleeman (1833). Nicholas Daniel (1844) and Michael Daniel (1847). Matthew Kistler (1844), and his sons, George Kistler (1856/73) and Matthias Kistler (1873). The Kistler family were from Germany. Mathias Kistler's wife, Rosina was from a local Madron family (1871 Census).

Richard Hart, an Engineer from Marazion, living in Trewellard, Saint Just (1871 Census) has been, erroneously, connected with Hart of Penzance. His wife was from Germoe, and all of his children, including his sons Samuel and Joseph, were born at Saint Hilary.

Frederick Lazarus: [462] Hawker & General Dealer (1871 & 1891 Census). He was born in Sheffield, Yorkshire (c. 1838), the son of a Jonas Lazarus, a licensed hawker. (It is possible that he was also known as Henry, or that the latter was his brother, or cousin. A birth for a Henry Lazarus has been identified in Sheffield, but not for a "Frederick".) Frederick Lazarus married his wife, a non-Jew, Emily Cock, a domestic servant, then 22, the daughter of the late Thomas Cock, a farmer of Madron, in Penzance in July 1861, at the Registry Office. At the time of the marriage the couple were living in Queen Street, and both witnesses to the marriage were local Christians, William Noy and John Easton Tonkin. (Curiously, another **Frederick Lazarus** of Penzance, married a Julia of Whitechapel, London, in September 1861. It is not known if he was related to this family or that of Hyman Lazarus, above). In August 1862, Frederick and Emily Lazarus were living in Redruth, where their daughter, Annie was born. By 1864, the Lazarus family had moved back to Penzance, where their second daughter, Bessie, was born that same year. The 1871 Census lists the family at 49, North Street, with Frederick (33) as a Hawker, his wife Emily (32) a Greengrocer, and their children Annie (8), Bessie (7), and, all born in Penzance: Fanny (5), Mary [Ellen] (2) and Frederick (3 months). Emily Lazarus bore two more children, Henry, in 1875, and Emily, in 1879. In the 1881 Census, the occupations of the older children are given as: Annie, a Tailoress, Bessie, also a Tailoress, and Fanny, a (sewing) Machinist. By 1886, their mother, Emily had died, and Frederick soon re-married. In 1891, Frederick Lazarus (then 53) was living at 49, Chapel Street, with his second wife, Elizabeth Ann (48), also a Greengrocer, who had been born in the nearby Regent Square, Penzance. Frederick Jnr. (21), General Dealer, and his brother Henry (19), a Driver of a Grocer's Van, are given as having been born at North Street, and a daughter, Emma (12), born in Market Jew Street. Frederick Lazarus' daughter, Bessie, then 24, was living at 33 St. James Street, as a servant. On 5th April 1895, Gertrude, the daughter of Frederick Lazarus (Jnr.) and Ellen Laura Lazarus, was christened at St. Mary's Church, Penzance. By 1901, Emily (Emma) Lazarus was living in a "sheltering home" in Liverpool, and working as a waitress. In the same year, her brother Henry, a house painter, is listed as living as the nephew of William Barnes, (62), formerly of Portsmouth, the Resident Keeper & Port Missionary of the "Gordon Smith Seaman's Institute", in Paradise Street, Liverpool, and his wife Ellen (50) who was from Penzance. Frederick Lazarus Snr. is not known to have been related to Isaac Lazarus of Hayle (1841 Census: see under Hayle Trades) or to Hyman Lazarus. Isaac Lazarus (1828) and Hyman Lazarus (1843 and 1845) appear by name in the Penzance Hebrew Congregational Minute-Book, but Frederick Lazarus does not.

Moses Harman: Glazier (1881 Census). He was a boarder, and was from Danzig, Germany.

Jacob Israel: Glazier (1881 Census). He was also a boarder, and was from Exeter. His father, Aaron Israel, was a Jeweller at 8, Synagogue Place, Exeter, and was from Poland (1851 Census). His wife, Esther was from Prussia. Their children were Sarah (1837-), Rebecca (1835-), Jacob (1842-), Abraham (1845-) and Israel (1849-). Like Harman, Jacob Israel would have been an itinerant trader.

Sidney Ostler: A Commercial Traveller, age 20, from Bristol (1881). Uncertain.

Louis Solomon: An itinerant Hawker, age 32, from "Russia(n) Poland" (1891 Census). He was a lodger at the Duke of Cumberland Inn at 70, Causewayhead.

Amelia Joseph: Pawnbroker at 5 Market Jew Street (1891 Census). She was a daughter of Jacob Jacob (1774-1853) of Falmouth, and the widow of Henry Joseph (1806-1881) of Penzance, who was also originally from Falmouth. Amelia Joseph was 80 at the time of the Census, and died soon after. Living with her was her daughter, Kate Freedman (43) who had married Abraham Freedman of Aberdare in 1870, and she may also have been a widow, in that she is given as an assistant, and not a visitor. Also resident were her unmarried sister, Bessie (42), and Amelia Joseph's niece, Goldie Coppel (21) from Liverpool.

The Bischofswerder Family[463]

Just as the Hart family had been fundamental to the establishment of the Jewish community in Penzance in the early 18th century, the Bischofswerder family were to be one of its last representatives in Penzance, playing a major commercial and charitable role in the town and sustaining the Jewish congregation during the last decades of its final decline.

Isaac Bischofswerder: Jewish Minister, 6 Belgrave Terrace (1871); 6 Belgravia Street (1881); 9, Belgravia Street (Kelly's Directory 1883);[464] 7, Alverton Place, The Hollies (1891 Census). Belgrave Terrace was renamed as Belgravia Street sometime after 1871. Between 1881-1891, it is possible that the houses were re-numbered, although the "9" in Kelly's Directory may be an error (for 6), or for 19, where Isaac's son, David, lived around this time. Isaac Bischofswerder was from Vansburg in West Prussia (or Posen, later known as Wiecbork in Bydgoszcz Voivoidship, Poland). His German surname is unlikely to have been the family's original name. By the early 18th century, across much of Prussia, local parliaments had issued decrees enabling all Jews who were not already citizens of the area to take out citizenship. This was conditional upon a life-style of law-abiding civic responsibility and morality, the ability to use German in business matters, the acceptance of a specific German family name, evidence of residence (in Posen, where such a decree was issued in 1833, it was since 1st June 1815), and current financial security. Any Jew who did not take up this offer, or could not qualify for it, could be seriously penalised and disadvantaged. In 1836, to facilitate the effective conduct of business, an official book was published containing the names of Jews who had become citizens, listing them by occupation. In Posen, only 5.5% of Jews were on this list.[465] This situation encouraged many Jews to adopt the German language, but eventually many Jews were prompted to leave Prussia and migrate westwards in search of better opportunities, and by 1854, Isaac Bischofswerder and his family were in Hamburg. Well before that, however, he had been officiating as a Rabbi for some years. His headstone in the Penzance cemetery suggests that he had been a rabbi ("he kept guard over holiness") "in the State of Germany - for about thirty years" before his arrival in Penzance around 1867. This is most likely a slightly inflated figure, in that he would have been only about 15 in 1837. However, the acquisition of some Talmudic knowledge in his youth might well have enabled him to make a start in carrying out some religious duties. The same headstone gives his father's Hebrew name as Zvi, most commonly rendered in the vernacular as Heinrich (German) or as Henry or Harry (English). From this it is likely that Isaac's father was Heinrich Bischofswerder, born around 1790. The forenames, Henry and Harry were passed down to five of Isaac's grandchildren.

Isaac Bischofswerder was a jeweller by trade, and may have continued this business from his home in Penzance to supplement his congregational salary. However, he only appears as a minister in the records above. At the time of the 1871 census, only a few years after he had arrived in the town, Isaac Bischofswerder was living in a modest, recently built property at 6, Belgrave Terrace, with his second wife, Rachel (Rahle Weile, 42), and Isaac's children, from his first

The Family of Isaac Bischofswerder of Penzance

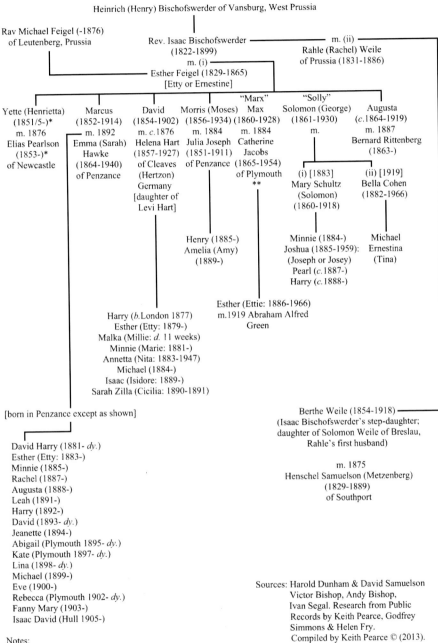

Heinrich (Henry) Bischofswerder of Vansburg, West Prussia

Rav Michael Feigel (-1876) of Leutenberg, Prussia

Rev. Isaac Bischofswerder (1822-1899)
m. (i) Esther Feigel (1829-1865) [Etty or Ernestine]
m. (ii) Rahle (Rachel) Weile of Prussia (1831-1886)

Yette (Henrietta) (1851/5-)*
m. 1876 Elias Pearlson (1853-)* of Newcastle

Marcus (1852-1914)
m. 1892 Emma (Sarah) Hawke (1864-1940) of Penzance

David (1854-1902)
m. c.1876 Helena Hart (1857-1927) of Cleaves (Hertzon) Germany [daughter of Levi Hart]

Morris (Moses) (1856-1934)
m. 1884 Julia Joseph (1851-1911) of Penzance

"Marx" Max (1860-1928)
m. 1884 Catherine Jacobs (1865-1954) of Plymouth **

"Solly" Solomon (George) (1861-1930)
m.

Augusta (c.1864-1919)
m. 1887 Bernard Rittenberg (1863-)

(i) [1883] Mary Schultz (Solomon) (1860-1918)

(ii) [1919] Bella Cohen (1882-1966)

Henry (1885-)
Amelia (Amy) (1889-)

Minnie (1884-)
Joshua (1885-1959): (Joseph or Josey)
Pearl (c.1887-)
Harry (c.1888-)

Michael Ernestina (Tina)

Esther (Ettie: 1886-1966)
m.1919 Abraham Alfred Green

Harry (b.London 1877)
Esther (Etty: 1879-)
Malka (Millie: d. 11 weeks)
Minnie (Marie: 1881-)
Annetta (Nita: 1883-1947)
Michael (1884-)
Isaac (Isidore: 1889-)
Sarah Zilla (Cicilia: 1890-1891)

[born in Penzance except as shown]

David Harry (1881- dy.)
Esther (Etty: 1883-)
Minnie (1885-)
Rachel (1887-)
Augusta (1888-)
Leah (1891-)
Harry (1892-)
David (1893- dy.)
Jeanette (1894-)
Abigail (Plymouth 1895- dy.)
Kate (Plymouth 1897- dy.)
Lina (1898- dy.)
Michael (1899-)
Eve (1900-)
Rebecca (Plymouth 1902- dy.)
Fanny Mary (1903-)
Isaac David (Hull 1905-)

Berthe Weile (1854-1918)
(Isaac Bischofswerder's step-daughter; daughter of Solomon Weile of Breslau, Rahle's first husband)

m. 1875
Henschel Samuelson (Metzenberg) (1829-1889) of Southport

Sources: Harold Dunham & David Samuelson Victor Bishop, Andy Bishop, Ivan Segal. Research from Public Records by Keith Pearce, Godfrey Simmons & Helen Fry.
Compiled by Keith Pearce © (2013).

Notes:
dy. Six of Marcus and Sarah Bischofswerder's children died in infancy.
*Public records differ significantly in the year of Henrietta's birth. Elias Pearlson's age in 1876 is given as 23 (*b.*1853) but he recorded the year elsewhere as 1847. ** Daughter of Mark Jacobs (*b.* London *c.*1840) Jeweller of Plymouth and Henrietta (*b.* Truro *c.*1845): (Helen Fry 2000).

245

marriage to Esther, or Ernestine Feigel (1829-1865), Yette (Henrietta, 20: see below) a Milliner, Marcus (18) a Hawker, David (16) a Hawker, Morris (Moses, 14) a Pawn-broker's Assistant, Marks (Max, 12), "Saly" (Solly or Solomon, 10, known as George), Augusta (8), and a step-daughter (written in the contemporaneous sense as "Daur. In Law"), Bert(h)a Waile (Weile) from Rahle's first marriage. By the time of the 1881 census, the Terrace had been re-named as Belgravia Street, and David Bischofswerder was then living a few doors away at No. 19. Isaac Bischofswerder's first wife, Esther, was the daughter of Rabbi Michael Feigel (-1876) who was the head of the Leutenberg Rabbinical Court (*Beth Din*) for 45 years. It would seem that Isaac and his wife soon migrated towards North West Germany, and all seven of their children were born there. Their third child, David, was born in Hamburg in 1854, and, around 1876, in London, he married a German Jewess, Helena Hart (1857-1927) of Hertzon. (She is not known to have been related to the Hart family of Penzance). Esther Feigel died in the summer (12th Av) of 1865 at the age of 36 in the town of Feinsburg.[466] These details are confirmed by the original Circumci-sion Register of Rabbi Eliayahu (Elias) Pearlson, at the front of which he wrote, in Hebrew, of his family background. He was to marry Isaac Bischofswerder's daugh-ter, Yette (Henrietta) in 1876.

Isaac Bischofswerder's second wife, Rahle Weile, was the widow of Solomon Weile of Breslau. She married Isaac very soon after Esther's death, and effectively brought up his children. Rahle had several children of her own from her first marriage, who may have been old enough to be independent by the time she came to Britain with the Bischofswerder family around 1867. Her youngest child, Berthe, then about thirteen, is the only one she is known to have brought with her, and it would seem that she did not have any more children from her second marriage. On her headstone in the Penzance cemetery, Rahle is given as "the daughter of Mann". The latter would normally be taken to be her father's Hebrew forename, and in view of the fact that a Manheim Bischofswerder, also from Prussia, lived in Plymouth in 1891 (see Max Bischofswerder, below) it is possible that Rahle was in some way related to another branch of the Bischofswerder family. *Bischofs* (*lit.* Bishop or Bishop's place or seat) can be found as a place-name across the German speaking regions of the continent, and also as a family name, sometimes as *Bischof-swerder* (*werder* = river islet, or holm), *Bischofsheim* (home or homeland), and *Bischofsberg* (hill), with other variations. Another, likely related Bischofswerder family, lived not far from Bydgoszcz, in what is now Ryczvol, Poland.[467] A Julius Bischofswerder was born there in 1856, his parents being a Marcus and Roeschen Bischofswerder. Marcus would have been a near contemporary of Isaac Bischof-swerder (1822-), possibly related as brothers or cousins, and Julius Bischofswerder was of the same generation as Isaac's children, one of whom (his second son) was named Marcus (1853-). Manheim Bischofswerder (*c.* 1850-), also a contemporary, may also have been a brother to Julius, and a cousin to Isaac's children. It may be of significance that Rahle Weile's daughter, Berthe (1854-) named her second son, born in 1878) as Julian, a likely variant of Julius.

Bertha Weile (1854-1918) does not appear to have been legally adopted by Isaac Bischofswerder, and she is not known to have used his family's surname. She left Penzance in 1875[468] to marry Henschel Samuelson, formerly Metzenberg (1829-

1889) of Southport, a man some 25 years her senior. His family had also originated from Breslau, Prussia (later Wroclaw, Poland). Henschel had emigrated from Breslau in the mid 1800s, together with his brother, Elias. Elias moved to Dublin, where, by 1846, he was living in Capel Street, an area where other Prussian-Polish Jews lived, including a Levy Metzenberg from Lissa, Prussia (Leszno, Poland), some fifty miles north of Breslau, who may have been a relative. (Capel Street still houses a significant Polish community today). Elias Metzenberg became a successful merchant and military Tailor, and President of the Dublin Hebrew Congregation in 1859 and 1865. In 1874, he moved with his family to Maida Vale, London, establishing his business in the exclusive Savile Row area. Henschel Samuelson's marriage to Bertha Weile took place on 21st December 1875 at Elias' home in Maida Vale, with the Chief Rabbi, Dr. N. Adler, officiating. Henschel is recorded on the marriage certificate as already resident in Southport, where he traded as a Tobacconist and Importer of Fine Havana Cigars. The 1881 Census[469] records the Samuelsons as living in North Meols, Lancashire. With them were Bertha's two sons, Julian (2) and Lawrence (10 months), and also resident in the household were a nurse, Bertha Arndt (22) from Prussia, and a servant, Caroline Rechner (22) from Austria. The couple were to have a total of five children, all born in Southport. A son, Sydney, born in 1876, died in his first year in 1877. Julian Ulrich, or "Wylie" (1878-1934) was to become a theatrical impresario, and died in London. Moses (Morris) Laurence (1880-c.1951) became a playwright. Rahleen May (1886-1949) lived in Birmingham, London and Brighton, and George Berthold, "Bertie" (1889-1947) was to become a pioneer film producer. Henschel Samuelson died on 25th August 1889, when his son, Bertie, was only six weeks old, and was buried in the Green Lane cemetery in Liverpool (now disused). Bertha Samuelson died in Birmingham in 1918, and she is buried in Liverpool.

Rev. Isaac Bischofswerder served the Penzance Congregation for a continuous period of at least 18 years from around 1868. In his later years as minister, he suffered from ill health, and he retired in the same month that his wife died (March 1886). He is likely to have resumed occasional duties after that, however, and his headstone in the Penzance cemetery refers to him as having officiated as "Cantor and Shochet here for more than twenty years". After 1886, he became financially (and most likely) physically dependant upon his children, and had moved in with the family of his son David, whose (albeit temporary) prosperity had allowed him to rent the lease to the substantial town mansion, "The Hollies", in Alverton Road. After David Bischofswerder's departure for South Africa, Isaac presumably lived with his son Morris, in Morrab Road. Isaac Bischofswerder's relative poverty is reflected in the fact that, toward the end of his incumbency, he had to ask the Penzance congregation for charitable assistance to supplement his salary on at least two occasions, and also to meet his medical bills. Despite searches, no Will or Grant of Probate has been identified for him.[470] Although this could be explained by his signing over of his personal assets to his family, it would more commonly suggest that, at his death in 1899, those personal assets were very low, and that the total value of his estate was below the level required for probate. Of his children, two, David and Morris, were to play a significant part in the town's commercial and social life.

Henrietta (Yetta) Bischofswerder: Milliner, 6, Belgrave Terrace (1871 Census). In the 1871 census, her age is given as 20, and her name appears above those of her siblings as the oldest child of the family. It is not clear if this age, which would give her birth year as 1851, is reliable, in that other census and public records consistently give an age that would make her birth year as *c*.1854-1855. Her marriage certificate in 1876 gives her age as 21, and the 1881 census (Elswick, Northumberland) as 26, from which her birth year would be 1855. In 1901 (Hull), her age is given as 48, suggesting *c*.1853-1854. When her mother, Esther, died in 1865, Henrietta would certainly have been a young girl, and, despite the arrival of her step-mother, Rachel, the following year, would, no doubt, have needed to assume responsibilities beyond her years. It cannot be known if this factor led to an inflation of her age, or whether the 1871 census recorder committed an administrative error from what he understood Isaac Bischofswerder had told him, filtered through the latter's German-accented English pronunciation. Henrietta was to marry Rabbi Elias (Eliayahu) Pearlson of Newcastle, the son of Abraham Pearlson, a Hebrew teacher. Elias Pearlson's detailed record of his family history, recorded in his circumcision register,[471] claims to trace his rabbinic origins back to 1499. He also noted that he had been born in Poland in 1847, had come to England in 1875, living in Oxford for 6 months, and was then appointed as *chazan* and *shochet* at Newcastle. The reliability of his birth year, is, again, uncertain, in that, on his marriage certificate (9th February 1876) his age is recorded as 23 (that is born *c*.1853), and subsequent records would support the latter. Unless an error has occurred in the computation and translation of the birth year from Pearlson's handwritten Hebrew script in his register, it is tempting to suppose that, in 1875, the Newcastle congregation would have looked more favourably upon the appointment of a man approaching 30, rather than one barely into his twenties. The marriage of Elias Pearlson to Henrietta Bischofswerder took place in the synagogue in Penzance, and was conducted by the bride's father.[472] Whether a false, or simply an inadvertent declaration was made by the couple as to their respective ages when they married, and subsequently in the 1881 census, cannot be known, but if Henrietta was indeed born in 1851, and Pearlson in 1853, she would clearly have been older than her husband, by two years, rather than younger, as the record shows; in the census of 1901 they were both 48. This example does illustrate, however, the difficulty that can arise in trying to establish dates, even from this later period, when documentary sources are plentiful. The couple were to play an important part in the future of the bride's siblings, in that they moved to the North-East of England, where, in 1877, their only child, Gustav was born. It would seem that Henrietta's younger sister, Augusta, age 17, may also have left Penzance to move in with them (1881 census for Elswick, Northumberland). Augusta does not appear in 1881 as a "visitor" at Elswick, nor on the same census for Penzance, as part of Isaac Bischofswerder's household. A few years later, on 10th August 1887, giving her age as 21, she married Bernard Rittenberg, who, like his father, Lewis Rittenberg, was a Pawnbroker of Hull. The ceremony took place in the synagogue there, and was conducted by Elias Pearlson. From 1875 to 1906, apart from his other ministerial duties as a Rabbi, Pearlson was to be in considerable demand as *Mohel*, travelling extensively across the region to perform 220 ritual circumcisions in

Newcastle, Hull and Sunderland, from which he earned a significant sum, and from 1883 to 1888, in Hull alone, he performed 164 circumcisions, the last there being in 1898. There can be little doubt that Pearlson's reputation and his contacts in Hull (where the census records him by 1901), led to Henrietta's brother, George, marrying Mary Schultz of Hull, and moving there himself in 1883. Eventually, he was joined by his brothers, Marcus and Morris Bischofswerder.

David Bischofswerder: Hawker, 6 Belgrave Terrace (1871 Census); Traveller in Jewellery, 19 Belgravia Street (1881 Census); Wholesale and Retail Jeweller and Diamond Merchant, Importer of Cigars, Watches, Clocks and Foreign Merchandise (*Cornishman* Newspaper advertisement, 11th March 1886); Traveller Pawnbroker and Jeweller, 13 & 14 Market Jew Street and Tobacconist, 111 Market Jew Street; Home: Alverton Road (Kelly 1889); Merchant, The Hollies, Alverton (1891 Census).

David, was Isaac Bischofswerder's second son, born in Hamburg around 1854. He was the only member of the family known to have become a wealthy man while living in the town, becoming a prominent figure in its affairs in the 1880s. He may have lived briefly in London, where he married [473] his wife, Helena Hart, who was from Cleaves (Herzon), Germany.[474] She had given birth to her first son, Harry in London in 1877 (1881 Penzance Census). In the same census David is recorded as a Traveller in Jewellery, at 19 Belgravia Street, with two children, Harry (4) and Esther (Hetty, 2). From this time, David Bischofswerder took an active part in the Jewish congregation, and his name appears for every subsequent year in the Minute-Book. Between 1880 to 1890, Helena gave birth to six more children. The 1891 census records Harry (then 14) Tobacconist's Assistant, Esther (Etty, 12), Minnie (10), Nita (Annetta, 8), Michael (7) and Isaac (Isidore, 2). Two children, Malka (Millie) and Sarah Zilla (Cicilia) died in 1880 and 1891 at 11 weeks and 14 months respectively, and were buried in the Penzance cemetery (6:1 and 7:4). On the birth certificate of his daughter, Nita, in 1883, David Bischofswerder is described as a Diamond Merchant, which, in his case, did reflect a significant improvement in his business interests, and from this time the local newspaper, *The Cornishman,* began to carry a weekly advertisement for his business, that extended to a staff of "experienced workmen kept on the premises for watch, clock and jewellery repairs". By the early 1880s he had moved from Belgravia Street to Alverton Road (Kelly's Directory 1883) eventually acquiring the lease to the grand detached town mansion of The Hollies, where the 1891 census records him as a "Merchant" living with his family and his father, Isaac. Also resident were three employees, Annie Harris (servant), Emily Brown (nurse) and Emily Mathews (under-nurse). It is possible that David Bischofswerder's prosperity was in part due to his astute purchase of a substantial quantity of items, including jewellery, that had eventually been released for open and legal sale as unclaimed salvage from the wreck of the *S. S. Schiller* in 1875, by the Receiver of Wrecks, J. T. Handley.[475] In the mid to late 19th century, the conduct of the importation of diamonds and gold was not subject to the much stricter controls that were introduced after the Great War, and it is possible that David Bischofswerder benefitted from the relatively liberal climate that surrounded the diamond trade in the 1870s to 1890s. It is not known if his trading in precious stones was in any way illicit, although the precise application of such a term is not itself self-evident in the context of the times. If he did secure a degree of financial improvement by his various commercial activities, he certainly continued to live in his small house in Belgravia Street for some years (1881 census) before moving to The Hollies by 1889, where the 1891 census locates him. It is likely that gains from further commercial ventures during the 1880s helped bring about that degree of social advancement.

Towards the latter part of the 1880s there occurred the affair of the disgraced manager of Barclays Bank at St. Just-in-Penwith, Richard Boyns, who had transferred funds from the bank to support local mines, and had done this without the knowledge or authorisation of the main bank. Upon discovery, he had absconded, and avoided bankruptcy only by a private arrangement with his creditors. He was forced to sell off the "Botallack Epergne", a large table ornament of solid silver, to pay off his debts. (Ironically, he had been awarded the Epergne for his services in supporting local mines, a cause that David Bischofswerder would also come to espouse). The purchaser of the Epergne was David Bischofswerder. It is not certain if he kept this ornament, or if he sold it on, but in any event, his ability to purchase it was indicative of his means. If sold, it may well have enabled him to negotiate a favourable lease on the Hollies, and to diversify his business interests sufficiently to occupy at least two premises in Market Jew Street by the turn of the decade. Kelly's Directory for 1889 records him as a Pawnbroker and Jeweller at Nos. 13 & 14, and the 1891 census as a Tobacconist at No. 11, where David's son, Harry, worked as an assistant. He was now a wealthy man, but he was also recognised for his charitable work, and as a philanthropist within the wider community.

The advent of the Queen's Jubilee in 1887 brought with it considerable public debate on how best the town could prepare for its celebration. On 10th February, the town's newspaper, *The Cornishman*, carried a lengthy report[476] that "a fully-attended meeting, comprising all classes on Penzance, was held at the guildhall on Friday to consider this subject". Amongst those present was D. Bischofswerder, alongside such prominent landowners as Admiral Borlase, Councillor Borlase and William Bolitho of Polwithen. There is no report that Bischofswerder contributed to the discussions, and as one of the "nouveaux riches" alongside the gentry, and the monopoly of "old money", he may have failed to gain any recognition or influence in this forum, because he is not recorded as present at the many subsequent meetings reported by the paper over the following months. However, the paper did report that "on jubilee morn" a patriotic "Jubilee Service at the Jew's (*sic.*) Synagogue, Penzance", was "convened by Mr. D. Bischofswerder", at which the Rev. Mr. Rubenstein had preached a sermon praising the "perfect freedom" the Jews had enjoyed under the Queen, and that the "national anthem was sung by the whole congregation".

But it would seem that he had decided to make his own mark with a commemorative civic gesture, and on 11th August 1887, the same paper reported the "Opening of Mr. D. Bischofswerder's New Jubilee Hall" built in Market Jew Street on the former site of shop premises. The "little hall" is described as "capable of seeting 450 persons" and as suitable for "the better display of his (David's) collection of paintings and other pictures, and for…his periodical auction sales" for which it was "especially adapted". It was also noted that it "will be found particularly suitable for entertainments of various kinds or an occasional dance". There followed a detailed description of the building's numerous facilities and the considerable range of craftsmen and local firms that had been involved in its construction. That David Bischofswerder had comfortably integrated into the local community is shown by the fact that he had invited a Christian Minister, the Rev. E. Townhend, vicar of St. John's, to formally declare the Hall open and to say grace. Townhend was not the vicar of the town's main church, St. Mary's, in Chapel Street (a prestigious incumbency sometimes occupied by those connected with the local landed classes) but of a sister church located in the Leskinnick area of the town, close to, and with its church schoolhouse adjacent to the Jewish cemetery. What is most striking in the report, however, is the impression that David Bischofswerder did not use the occasion to advance himself socially by exclusively, or even primarily, issuing invitations to the most prominent and influential members of the community. There is an absence of mention of the names of any of the local gentry, including those who had attended the various Jubilee meetings. The impression gained is that they may have boycotted the event, or had not been invited to it, because mention of such prominent people at such an event was common practice and even expected. However, there is mention of the fact that David had arranged a lavish banquet for the town's elderly and needy, with various choices of meats and "vegetables of all kinds, followed by puddings, tarts, cakes &c., Ales and tea and coffee for the abstainers". It would seem that, although David Bischofswerder and his family were known to be scrupulous in adhering to Jewish dietary regulations (a characteristic noted more than once in the local press) they did not insist that these should apply to their Gentile guests on such public occasions as this. There was music and singing for "one hundred and fifty of the aged of Penzance to dine with him…on Bank-holiday afternoon". Indeed, "there were many in Penzance who could testify to Mr. Bischofswerder's private acts of charity, he would not look coldly on a pressing case for relief". The Rev. Townhend, "loyalties to the Queen and royal family having been properly shewn, addressed the old people on kindness, especially eulogising that of their enterprising and benevolent host", and gave a proposal of thanks. After the two-hour celebration for the elderly, "Several, prevented by old age, infirmity or otherwise from attendance, were minded by Mr. B. in their own homes". Moreover, the "contractors, workpeople, and other friends, to the number of 100 or more, sat down to a similar spread at five o'clock (and) had a dance from eight until shortly before eleven. Five pounds of Jubilee shillings were also distributed among the guests". Noted as present at the event were David's son Harry, and the latter's uncle, Marcus. Marcus Bischofswerder (whose wife was to bear him a total of 17 children) does not appear to have been so successful in business as his brothers David and Morris, and his presence would suggest David's solicitous support for him. Also present were family friends from London, including "the Misses A. Hertzon and E. Myers". (The latter is likely to have been related to the J. Myers who was to be a witness at Marcus Bischofswerder's wedding in 1892).

That this was not an isolated event, but was characteristic of David Bischofswerder's generosity is shown by a report, "Entertaining the Poor at Penzance", in *The Royal Cornwall Gazette* of 21st January 1892: "Mr. and Mrs. Bischofswerder, and Harry Bischofswerder, their son, have entertained 350 of the poor of Penzance to a New Year's dinner. All who served were afterwards the guests of the same kind and hospitable people". A week earlier, *The Jewish Chronicle* had referred to this as an annual event, but, lacking close local knowledge of those involved, implied incorrectly (in an ambiguous and poorly constructed opening sentence) that the event was hosted solely by Harry Bischofswerder, who (although only 15 in 1892) is implied to have been the builder of the Jubilee Hall and a local mine-owner: "The annual dinner given to the poor of Penzance by Mr. Harry Bischof-swerder, son of Mr. David Bischofswerder, of Penzance, and proprietor of the Wheal Helena mine, took place on Wednesday last at the Jubilee Hall, Penzance, built by Mr. Bischofswerder in 1887... Those who were prevented coming by age, sickness or infirmity were allowed to send for their dinner and partake of it in their own homes".[477] It is evident that Harry's presence at these occasions shows that his father was concerned to develop his son's social conscience and to encourage his involvement in such charitable work in the wider community.

David Bischofswerder had also seen to it that his son should participate in the affairs of the Hebrew congregation, and Harry's name appears in the Minute-Book in 1890 and 1892, alongside his father, and his uncle, Morris. In August of 1889, Harry's *Bar Mitzvah* had taken place in the Penzance synagogue, conducted by Rev. Michael Leinkram, who had succeeded Isaac Bischofswerder as Rabbi. The ceremony was attended by "Jew and Gentile alike" and the occasion was given some prominence in the local press,[478] which gave its readers a colourful and very detailed description and explanation of the religious ceremony and the internal appearance and ritual artefacts of the "modest little synagogue" whose external appearance belied "so large a place of worship...for its usual congregation, small when compared with other places of worship in Penzance or Hebrew tabernacles elsewhere" (presumably a reference to the Falmouth or Plymouth synagogues). Various Gentile dignitaries were noted as present, including Alderman Wellington Dale (a particular friend of the Bischofswerder family), W. K. Baker C.C. (County Councillor), and various others given by name. Most noticeable is the positive tone with which the newspaper went on to extol the virtues of "the Jewish character" with its "wonderful uniformity of view" of "this extraordinary people through so many ages" as "a living and continuous miracle...and amongst these traits is hospitality – kindness to be freely extended to the stranger within the gates, and respect for his creed and nationality, even though no rule or custom be relaxed that is applicable to the entertainers". The festivities following the ceremony were also given considerable coverage, when "80 people dined at The Hollies later on – numbers increased to 100, and dinner gave place to dancing, (but) a hearty welcome to kindred and friends has in no ways departed from Hebrew domestic life". The festivities "seemed to include all, from highest to lowest, in any way connected with Mr. David Bischofswerder's large business".

David Bischofswerder did not own the freehold of the Hollies, but would have taken a lease on it, and the report noted a "Mr. Thorne" had been the previous tenant of the house, and had built an additional wing "the ground floor of which was used as a schoolroom". Joseph Thorne was a schoolmaster from Hampshire, and the 1881 Census indicates that he occupied it with his wife, four children, three male boarders, and three female servants, including a nurse. He was soon to expand this private school into a far larger enterprise, and by 1889, he was established in a more spacious house nearby (1891 Census). Thorne's original schoolroom at the Hollies had enjoyed a luxurious transformation by David Bischofswerder into a spacious dining-room. Elsewhere in the property was to be found a general wealth of "paintings, some of which are valued at many hundreds of pounds each and are, undoubtedly by masters" together with "rich carvings... rare china (and) ornaments" from all over the world. After Israel Oppenheim, a senior member of the congregation, a relatively successful businessman in the town, and a friend of the family had delivered an honorary speech to the young celebrant, Harry, Mr. Wellington Dale, in a lengthy and humorous speech, enumerated David Bischofswerder's qualities and accomplishments, including the fact that he "is proud of the fact that he began at the bottom and that by his persevering industry and bold speculation and wise realizations, he has surrounded himself with a large and lucrative business and raised himself to the position he occupies this day". The affectionate eulogy described his colourful and temperamental character, but that Dale had never known him to be "unkind or ungenerous...(but)... on the contrary, I have known him do many a kind and generous deed". It would seem that the occasion of Harry's coming of age was also to mark his father's "relaxation from business" and that he was able to consider at least partial retirement, to allow his family and employees to manage his various enterprises on his behalf. One speech by "Mr. Baker C.C. of Tredorwin" is of special interest in that it refers to David Bischofswerder as a neighbouring "landowner at Towednack", a hamlet between Penzance and St. Ives. This clearly indicates that he had begun to diversify his investments beyond his mercantile business interests in the town.

In 1891, David Bischofswerder headed a syndicate which, for only £1,600, bought at auction a mine at Tregurtha Downs,[479] at St. Hilary, near Marazion, saving it temporarily, and saving its workers from unemployment after it had closed. He renamed the mine *Wheal Helena,* after his wife. The syndicate included Wellington Dale, who secured the lease of the mine, together with the back wages of its employees. In the context of mining, the term *syndicate* was used from the 1870s to refer to two or more people who bought mining leases with a view to starting a mine and floating a company to work it for minerals, or to a group of dealers in mining shares. It was, therefore, a form of limited company for bringing out joint-stock schemes.[480] In the case of the Bischofswerder syndicate, it seems to have been an informal group without any legal existence or office of organisation, which was not intending to trade, but simply to support local industry. In the case of *Wheal Helena* this was a considerable financial risk, because the mine had had a troubled history. In the 18th and the first half of the 19th century, the mines in the Marazion area had been worked primarily for copper, but by 1850 were moving over to tin production. There were at least 27 mines in the St. Hilary and Marazion mining district, and the mine at Tregurtha Downs was worked jointly with another at Owen Vean. The instability of these two mines from around 1883 was influenced by a dramatic fall in the price of tin, and the especially high development costs these particular mines required. Although Tregurtha Downs' prospects improved in 1887-1888, a disastrous fire which severely damaged its engine-house on 5th

January 1889 saw the mine flooded. By 1891, however, production had recovered.

The *West Briton* newspaper reported the mine's re-opening: "Wheal Helena - Re-Starting the Engine....in the past failure and misfortune have been associated with the name Tregurtha Downs. In July last the limited liability company, which has carried on the mine for the last ten years, ceased working, and all the mining plant, machinery, and leases were sold on September 2nd to Mr. David Bischof-swerder of Penzance for £1,600". The paper noted that the mine was 120 fathoms deep, 110 fathoms below the adit, which had flooded, and might take up to a year to pump out. (The pumping engine, it was noted, that had been built many years ago, was one of the most powerful in the county). David Bischofswerder had arranged a "gigantic feast" to celebrate the re-starting of the pumping-engine, including a whole roasted ox and sheep. Hundreds gathered to witness the event, and four rows of tables for the workmen were set outside the carpenter's shop, which had been "fitted up as a dining room". David and his daughter Hetty (Esther, then 12) arrived in the afternoon, to be greeted by the strains of the Penzance Season Band, and Esther then "broke a bottle of wine on the nose of the bob, and re-chris-tened the mine Wheal Helena". "The ponderous machinery moved, and the water was lifted to the surface, accompanied with musical strains from the band, and cheer after cheer from the assembled multitude", after which "the whole party then adjourned to the carpenter's shop where 150 guests partook of an excellent cham-pagne dinner, presided over by Mr. Bischofswerder". There were various toasts and speeches praising those who had worked to ensure the mine's security and the miners' wages, and appreciation that David Bischofswerder "was prepared to spend such a large sum of money to prove the property". In reply, David acknowledged that it was "rather a biggish speculation upon which I have entered" and concluded by saying, "I hope that the miners will do their best for the mine, and I will my best for them".

In the event, it was all to be a vain hope. Over the next few years things did not go well for the mine. David Bischofswerder's flamboyant and incautious person-ality, inclined to lavish spectacular luxury on such occasions as these, may have played its part in over-extending his hand financially across too wide a range of projects in too short a period. It would certainly appear that he suffered serious financial damage as a result of this particular venture, from which he may never have entirely recovered. In December 1891, there was a quarrel with one of his partners, Joseph Prisk, who departed from the syndicate. In February and March 1892 , there was damage to the engines and pitwork, some of which was the result of an unknown saboteur. In April 1892, David Bischofswerder finally abandoned the syndicate, and moved to Plymouth. The mine eventually closed in 1895. Israel Oppenheim, who was also an investor in the syndicate, lost a great deal of money through his involvement in the scheme. It is not certain if he withdrew at the same time as David Bischofswerder, or if his losses were as great as Bischofswerder's, because Oppenheim was still trading in Penzance in 1897. However, the significant downturn in his fortunes from being another of the town's prosperous business-men, eventually led to his departure for Bristol, where he had settled by 1901.

Soon after 1892, David Bischofswerder moved temporarily to Plymouth, where his brother Max had settled some ten years earlier. It would seem that he travelled widely, attempting to revive his fortunes. In November 1894, appearing as a "diamond merchant of Plymouth", he was charged at Bradford Borough Police-court "with obtaining jewelry to the value of £615 from Joel Wacholder, of Hatton-garden, London, with intent to cheat and defraud". It was alleged that in June and July of that year, he had "a large sale" in St. George's Hall, Bradford. During that time he was said to have obtained jewellery from Wacholder, for which he had not paid him. He was also accused of refusing to settle a sum with the auctioneer at the sale, a Mr. Stansfield. Bischofswerder claimed that he was owed a total of £7,000 by various creditors, and that when he had received that amount from them, he would settle with the auctioneer. Enquiries showed that the sum of £7,000 was not due to Bischofswerder, and that he did owe the auctioneer £28. The case was referred to the civil courts.[481] Whatever the outcome of the case, it is likely to have further damaged David Bischofswerder's finances and his reputation, and to have hastened his decision to emigrate to South Africa with his family. His son, Harry, at least, did not accompany the rest of the family, and, in 1901, the census for Hanley, Staffordshire, records him there (age 24), as a "Wine Traveller", together with his wife Elvie (27), "from Warwick: Birmingham", and their infant daughter, Ettie (or Elsie) 7 months. It is likely that Harry Bischofswerder moved to Stoke-on-Trent, where a son, Michael Levi, was born in September 1906, and he was circumcised there by Rabbi Elias Pearlson, the husband of Harry's aunt, Henri-etta.[482] David Bischofswerder's brother, George, had already spent some time in the Cape from 1890-1892, and David may have established some connections there through him, although, as a Diamond Merchant, he is likely to have had his own business contacts there for some time. David Bischofswerder died, age 48, at Cape Town in 1902, and his wife Helena in 1927. They are buried opposite one another at Woltemade Cemetery, Maitland. [483]

George Bischofswerder: Picture Framer, 6, Belgravia Street (1881 Census). The youngest of Isaac Bischofswerder's sons, George Bischofswerder (1861-1930) appears on the 1871 census for Penzance, age 10, in the recorder's barely decipher-able hand as *Saby* or *Saly*, although possibly as *Laby* or *Gaby*. Of these alternatives, *Laby* could be "Little Grandfather" (from *Leb*?), and *Gaby* an abbreviation of *Gabriel* (sometimes used as a variant of George). However, in view of the fact that George was also known as *Solomon* (and appears as such on the birth certificate of his son, Joshua, where the family name is given as *Bishop*)[484] it seems most likely that the name should be read as *Saly*, intended as *Solly*. The recorder no doubt wrote what he heard, from Issac Bischofswerder's German and Yiddish-inflected pronuncia-tion. In 1876, George's sister, Henrietta, had married Rabbi Elias Pearlson of Newcastle. He acted as the official *Mohel* for that part of the North East, and regu-larly performed circumcisions in Hull, where, by 1901, the census records him as resident. In 1883, George Bischofswerder married Mary Schultz (Solomon: born *c.* 1859-60) of Hull, the daughter of Mark Schultz, a pawnbroker, whose family was originally from Poland. All of their children were born in Hull between 1884 to *c.*1888: Minnie (1884-1917), Joshua (Joseph or Josey: 1885-1959), Pearl or Pearly (*c.*1887-) and Harry (*c.*1888-). Initially, George traded as a general shopkeeper, but when this venture did not prove a success, he seems to have travelled widely, and may have retained some business interest in Penzance. From 1885-1887 it would seem that he was in Hull, but from November 1887 to September 1888, he appears to have returned to Penzance, where his name appears in the congregational minutes. From 1888-1890 he was back in Hull, but from June 1890 until 1892 he was at the Cape, South Africa, where he must have consolidated his finances, in that he soon returned to settle in Hull. Some confusion exists as to the date of his return. He is recorded as a witness at the marriage of his brother, Marcus, in Penzance on 12th June, 1892. His Naturalisation application (see below) states that he returned from South Africa "in 1892" but also that he had lived there "to the end of 1892". It acknowledges, however, that the applicant had "incorrectly stated" various "times and places of residence in the United Kingdom", but that these errors had "been committed through inadvertence, not with any intention to defraud". Initially, for a few weeks, he lived in Hull at the house of his father-in-law, who was a pawnbroker in Holderness Road, and then, up to 1895 at various addresses.

Throughout this period he had rented various houses, sometimes using the name of Solomon Bishop, and he was able to call upon the testimony of five local Gentiles as well as Estate agents and landlords (including an Abraham Moss) that he was completely reliable in the payment of rent. In 1895, in his application for Naturalisation Papers, he gave his reasons as a wish to purchase freehold property.[485] He gave his current address as 6, Saville Street, and his occupation as a Tobacconist. He eventually achieved considerable success in business, and bought a sizeable piece of land, on which he had a large house, called "St. Michael's Mount", built in Inglemire Lane (later Avenue), in the Newland district of Hull. It boasted seven bedrooms, a tennis court, a bowling green and extensive gardens. David Bischofswerder had kept a bull mastiff in his house in Penzance, and this family tradition was maintained by George at his new house, where, with security in mind, two mastiffs, *Hector* and *Lysander*, were trained as guard dogs, let loose to roam the grounds at night against intruders. Their vicious temperament with strangers was notorious, although they were friendly, docile and obedient with the family and with visitors. As *Bishop*, George worked for many years as a commercial traveller, representing the firm of Waterloo Mills and Ayre Brothers of Hull, manufacturers of Dairy Feeding Cakes and Cubes (linseed oil cakes as winter feed for cattle).[486] Of George and Mary Bischofswerder's children, Minnie married a Dr. Cutler, and Joshua married Violet Barnett (1889-) of West Hampstead (in 1915). Joshua and Violet Bishop had two sons, George (1917-1932) and Victor (1920-2004), the latter moving to Norwich. Victor Bishop became a prominent member of the Norwich Hebrew Congregation, and represented it on the Board of Deputies of British Jews for many years. In 1912, Pearl Bishop married Lionel Hiller of Carlisle, and Harry Bishop married a Sarah Goldstein. After the death of his wife, Mary, in 1918, George Bishop (Snr.) was married the following year to a much younger woman, Bella Cohen (1882-1966), the daughter of Benjamin Cohen, a watchmaker. There were two children from this marriage, Michael, who emigrated to New Zealand, where he became a teacher and a Justice of the Peace, and Ernestina (Tina) who remained in Hull. Like his brother, David, George Bishop has been remembered by family members as an ambitious and generous man, with a colourful and extrovert personality.[487]

Chapter 4.
"Mr. Levin". Henry Levin, or one of his sons, Alexander or Israel.
Courtesy the Morrab Library, Penzance.

Chapter 4.
Israel Levin's Watch, Clock, Jewellery & Plate Establishment in Market Jew Street.
Courtesy Penlee House Museum and Gallery.

Plate 17

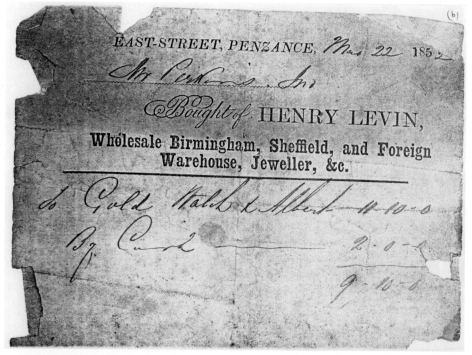

I. LEVIN'S
WHOLESALE & RETAIL
Watch, Jewellery, and Plate Establishment,
102, MARKET-JEW-STREET, PENZANCE.

Gold and Silver Watches, Gold Alberts, Neck Chains, Lockets, Ladies' Rings, Gents' Rings, Brooches, Ear Rings, and Scarf Pins. SILVER & ELECTRO PLATE.

A LARGE ASSORTMENT OF

PLATED AND JET JEWELLERY, CUTLERY, &c., &c.

SILVER WATCHES, 25s. GOLD WATCHES, 3 GUINEAS.

Chapter 4.
Advertisement for Israel Levin, Jeweller, from the *Cornishman* of July 18th 1878.
From an original copy courtesy of Eileen Nethercott of Penzance and courtesy of the *Cornishman*.

EAST-STREET, PENZANCE, *Mar 22* 185

Mr Perkins Snr

Bought of HENRY LEVIN,

Wholesale Birmingham, Sheffield, and Foreign Warehouse, Jeweller, &c.

Chapter 4.
An original receipt for a "Gold Watch & Albert" (1852) from Israel Levin's father, Henry Levin. In the private possession of and courtesy of Ronnie James of Penzance.

Plate 18

Chapter 4.
(Top) Samuel Oppenheim of Penzance, and his wife, Elizabeth (Beila) Levy of Truro. (Below) Their son, Israel Oppenheim, and his wife, Mathilda (born in Liverpool), daughter of Barnet Lyon Joseph of Falmouth.
From original photographs, courtesy of David M. Jacobs.

Plate 19

Chapter 4.
Mathilda Oppenheim in old age.
Courtesy of David Jacobs.

Plate 20

Chapter 4.
Oppenheim billboard and the shop at the top of Market Jew Street (right).
Both photographs from originals, courtesy the Penlee House Museum and Gallery.

Plate 21

Chapter 4.
From an original receipt,
Courtesy of John Bodilly.

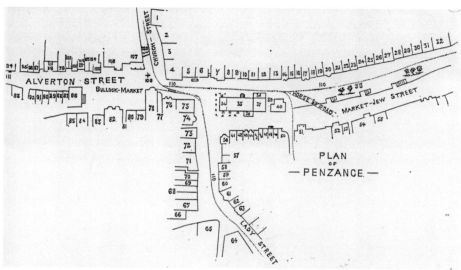

BA Simmons	Rabbi	21 "Market Jew ST."	Mi. 1878/80.
Oppenheim	Furniture Trader	22	
Henry Joseph	Pawnbroker	24	
Oppenheim		27	
Lemon Hart	Wine & Spirit Merchant	47	
Joseph	Pawnbroker	49 (possibly as 24)	
Simmons	Old Clothier	56 (Phoebe Simmons?)	
Ol(i)ver & Simmons	Drapers	59/60	
Harris	Jeweller	62	
Lemon Woolf	Spirit Merchant	70	

George Bown Millett: "Plan...abt 1805...of the Centre of Old Penzance, and Names of some of the Several Persons who occupied houses and shops...from about the commencement of this century to the present time. This list does not pretend to completeness or much accuracy...but it may be...an aid to memory." Courtesy of Penzance Public Library.

Note: The Drapers Ol(i)ver & Simmons were not Jewish.

Plate 22

Chapter 4.
Front page
advertisement
from an original
copy of the first
issue of the
Cornishman in
the possession
of Eileen
Nethercott.

THE CORNISHMAN, THURSDAY, JULY 18, 1878.

TRADE·ANNOUNCEMENTS.

OPPENHEIM'S
GREAT FURNISHING MART,
PENZANCE.

Oppenheim's Bedstead Department.

Over 500 BEDSTEADS constantly in Stock.

Iron Folding Bedsteads ....from 5s. 11d. each.
Full-size French Bedsteads, 4-ft 6-in
wide .... 11s. 9d. each.
Handsome Ornamented Bedstead,
(new design) 4-ft. 6-in. wide ... 10s. 6d. each.
Handsome Birch, Mahogany, and Brass Bedsteads
from £2 10s. to £15 15s. each.

Oppenheim's Bed Room Furniture Department.

Painted Deal Chest Drawers......from 21s. each.
Full-size Mahogany ditto....... ,, 30s. each.
Wardrobes, &c., &c.
Washstands ....from 4s. 11d. each.
Marble-top Mahogany Washstands ,, 21s. each.
Cane-seat Chairs .... ,, 3s. each
Toilet Glasses, &c., &c.
Bed Room Furniture in Pitch Pine, Enamelled, Birch,
Walnut, Mahogany, Ash, &c., &c.
Toilet Glasses, &c., &c.

Oppenheim's Dining Room Furniture.

Mahogany Dining Room Tables, with
extended patent screw ......from 70s. each.
Mahogany Couches in Hair Seating,
from .... 70s.
Mahogany Chairs to match ......from 16s.
Mahogany Easy Chairs to match, ., 50s.
Chiffoniers, Sideboards, Dinner Waggons, &c., &c.
Suites in Leather...................from £15 15s.
Fenders, Fire Irons, &c., &c.

Oppenheim's Drawing Room Furniture.

Handsome Walnut Suites in Green
Rep and Spring Stuffed—consist-
ing of Couch, Lady's Easy, Gent's
Easy, and Six Small Chairs ...... £9 9s.
Large-size Centre Walnut Loo Table,
carved Pillar and Claws, and
beautifully inlaid.................... £3 15s.
Handsome Suites in Silk, Velvet, &c., &c. Ebonized
Suites, Chiffoniers, Cabinets, Canterburys, Occasional
Tables, &c., &c.
Music Stools, patent screw, covered
in Leather............................. 12s. 6d.
A large assortment of Gilt Chimney Glasses, Fenders,
Fire Irons, &c., &c.

Oppenheim's Parlour Furniture.

Mahogany Loo Tables, pillar and block 50s.
Parlour Chairs, covered, in hair cloth 5s. 11d.
Easy Chairs .... 14s. 6d.
Couches .... 35s.

Oppenheim's Kitchen Furniture.

Strong Windsor Chairs, well polished 3s. 6d. each.
Strong Round Tea Tables .... 10s. 6d. each.
Kitchen Tables, &c., &c.

Oppenheim's Venetian Blinds.

Best Quality .... 7½d. per foot.
Send for Price List of Blinds of every Description.

Oppenheim's Bedding Department.

Full Size Palliasses.................... 8s. 6d. per pair.
Full Size Wool Mattresses .... 21s. each.
Full Size Feather Bed, Bolster and 2
Pillows .... 50s. the set
Full Size Spring Mattress .... 50s. each.
All Bedding Warranted, and Manufactured on the
Premises.

Oppenheim's Carpet Department.

Brussels Carpets .... 2s. 11d. per yd.
Tapestry Carpets....................... 1s. 11d. per yd.
All Wool, Kidderminster Carpets ... 2s. 6d. per yd.
Felt ditto ...... 10d. per yd.
Stair Carpets, &c., &c. Turkey's Wilton pile, &c.,
&c., to order. Cocoa Matting. Door Mats, &c., &c.
Passage Canvass. Bonlunkor Floor Cloth, &c.

Oppenheim's Drapery Department.

Blankets, Quilts, Sheets, Linens, &c., &c.

Oppenheim's Paper-hanging Department.
All New Patterns from 2½...

THE MOST COMPLETE
ESTABLISHMENT OUT...

OPPENH...
Great Furnish...
PENZAN...

ESTABLISHED 1836.

ISRAEL OPPENHEIM,
Cabinet Maker, Upholsterer,
DRAPER, CARPET FACTOR,
COMPLETE HOUSE FURNISHER, AND CONTRACTOR.

SHOW ROOMS AND OFFICES:—
3, 4, & 8 MARKET JEW STREET,
and Bread Street, PENZANCE.

DEPARTMENTS.

Iron and Brass Bedsteads | Gilt Cornices, Poles, &c.
Chest Drawers, and Wardrobes | Bedding, Carpets
Washstands and Toilet Tables | Mattings, Drapery
Wood Bedsteads | Blankets and Quilts
Dining, Loo, and other Tables | Linens, Damasks, &c.
Chiffoniers and Sideboards | Furnishing Ironmongery
Easy Chairs and Couches | Fenders and Fire Irons
Chairs of every description | Cutlery, Trays, &c.
Toilet and Chimney Glasses | Toilet Sets

AND EVERY REQUISITE FOR COMPLETELY FURNISHING A HOUSE THROUGHOUT.
Best Quality Venetian Blinds, Painted any Colour, 8d. per Sq. Foot.
SALESMEN SENT TO ANY PART TO WAIT ON CUSTOMERS.
GOODS DELIVERED FREE BY OWN VANS WITHIN 20 MILES.
All Goods sent Carriage Paid to any Railway Station (no Charge for Packing).
AN ILLUSTRATED CATALOGUE SENT POST FREE ON APPLICATION.
WHOLESALE & EXPORT ORDERS PROMPTLY EXECUTED.
Factory: Bread St., PENZANCE.

Chapter 4.
Advertisement *c.* 1880,
Courtesy of the *Cornishman.*

Plate 23

Chapter 4.
Cornishman,
March 11th 1886
(p.2; col. 4).

DaVID BISCHOFSWERDER,

WHOLESALE AND RETAIL JEWELLER AND DIAMOND MERCHANT.

IMPORTER OF CIGARS, WATCHES, CLOCKS, AND FOREIGN MERCHANDISE,

14, Market-Jew-Terrace, Penzance,

(the shop lately occupied by Mr. Kinsman, bookseller.)

———

Experienced workmen kept on the premises for watch, clock, and jewellery repairs.

CLEANING—Geneva, 1s. 6d.; Lever, 2s. 6d. ; main springs, 2s. 6d. ; glasses, 4d.

———

GOLD LEVER WATCHES, from £5. to £120.
SILVER ENGLISH PATENT LEVERS, from £2 10s.
to £8 8s.
Genevas (Gold) from £1 10s. upwards
,, (Silver) ,, 16s. 6d. ,,

Chapter 4.
David Bischofswerder (centre seated) with members of his family at his home *The Hollies* (*Chycelin*) *c.* 1889. His father, Rev. Isaac Bischofswerder, by this time a widower, is seated far right. Photo from an original in the possession of Victor Bishop.

Plate 24

Chapter 4.
David Bischofswerder's headstone
in South Africa. Photo by Paul Cheifitz.

Chapter 4.
(Left) Emma Hawke (Sarah Bischofswerder) and (right) her daughter, Leah (Segal).
Both photos courtesy of Barry Bishop and Ivan Segal.

Plate 25

Chapter 4.
The Headstones of Marcus and Morris Bischofswerder in Hull. Photos by Andy Bishop.

Plate 26

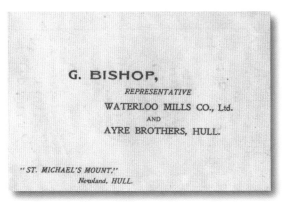

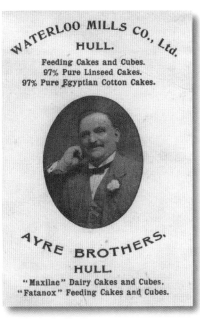

Chapter 4.
(Top) George (Solomon) Bishop
(Bischofswerder) of Hull, and (below) his son,
Joshua. From originals courtesy of Victor Bishop

Plate 27

Chapter 4.
The Wedding of Lionel Hiller (1886-1961) to Pearl (1887-1958), daughter of
George and Mary Bishop, in Hull in December 1912. Present also were Pearl's
siblings, Harry, Joshua and Minnie Bishop, together with Anita and Elsie
Bishop. Courtesy of Herbert A. Walford.

Chapter 4.
The marriage of Isaac Bischofswerder's grand-daughter, Ernestina Bishop,
daughter of George Bishop and his second wife, Bella Cohen. The groom was
Abraham Greenberg. Courtesy of Henrietta Jacobs.

Plate 28

Chapter 5.
(Top) Henry Harris and his wife Esther Jacob. (Bottom) Morris Hart Harris and his wife Rebecca Jacob. Courtesy of Brian and Paul Yule and Jacob Archive.

Plate 29

Chapter 5.
(Top Left) Morris Hart and Rebecca Harris with their sons Jacob Gerald and Henry.
(Top Right) Their daughter Rosetta. (Bottom) Their daughters Amelia (Millie: Left) and
Esther (Right) Courtesy of Brian and Paul Yule

Plate 30

Chapter 9.
Rabbi Joseph Rintel of Falmouth. Courtesy Jacob Archive

Plate 31

Right: Chapter 9.
Joseph Rintel's Birth
Certificate of 1809: this,
and the following, are all
from the original documents.
Courtesy of Godfrey Simmons.

Below left: Chapter 9.
Joseph Rintel's Travel
Pass issued to Joseph Bendix
Rentely in Hamburg in 1831.
Courtesy of Godfrey Simmons.

Below right: Chapter 9.
Joseph Rintel's
Naturalisation Papers
issued in London in 1861.
Courtesy of Godfrey Simmons.

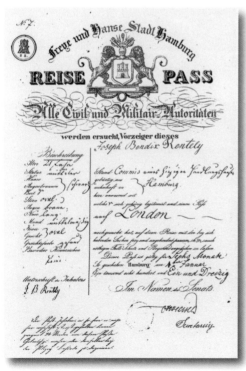

Plate 32

Max Bischofswerder: Traveller, 6, Belgravia Street (1881 Census). Isaac Bischofswerder's fourth son appears on the 1871 census for Penzance as *Marks,* which may, again, reflect what the census recorder took to be his name from his father's pronunciation. The 1881 census for Penzance records Max's age as 20, and his occupation as a *Traveller,* but, in the same year, the census for Plymouth[488] records him as a boarder (traveller, age 20) at 41 Union Street, in the home of Harriet Gabrielson from Cracow, Poland, whose husband was, like Max's brother, George, a picture framer. Max Bischofswerder had moved to Plymouth by 1884, where he was to settle permanently (adopting the surname *Bishop*). In September that year he married Catherine (Kate) Jacobs, age 21, daughter of Mark Jacobs (originally from London) a shopkeeper, Outfitter and Jeweller, and his wife Henrietta (who had been born in Truro).[489] Henrietta was the daughter of Nathaniel Schram from Holland, and his wife, Anna, from Gwennap, Cornwall (see Truro and Falmouth Trades). The 1891 Census records Max Bishop (30) a Jeweller, at 73 Union Street, with his wife, Kate (27) and their daughter, Ettie (5). (A Bernard Mass, Shopman and Assistant Jeweller, from Kielcach, Russia, was also resident). A few doors away, at 64 Union Street, the same census records: Manheim Bischofswerder (42), a Tobacconist, his wife, Augusta (39) and daughters, Elsa (or Elsie, 14) and Tova (8).[490] Both the Bischofswerder family of Penzance, and that of Manheim Bischofswerder of Plymouth had originally come from Prussia. Moreover, like Max's brother, David, Manheim also traded as a Tobacconist. It would seem most likely, therefore, that Max and Manheim Bischofswerder were related in some way, possibly as cousins or as nephew and uncle. It has been suggested earlier that Rahle Weile, Isaac Bischofswerder's second wife, who bore on her headstone, the Hebrew title "daughter of Mann", may have come from this branch of the family. As a "Merchant's Traveller", Max Bischofswerder, of 73 Union Street, East Stonehouse, Plymouth, applied for Naturalisation status in February of 1906.[491] Max and Catherine Bishop's only child, Esther (Etty), married an Abraham Alfred Green in 1919.[492] Max Bishop (-1928), his wife Catherine (-1954) and daughter Etty, or Ettie (-1966) are all buried in the Gifford Street Cemetery, Plymouth.

Marcus Bischofswerder: Hawker, 6 Belgrave Terrace (1871 Census); Traveller, 6, Belgravia St. (1881 Census); Jeweller, 22, Rosevean Rd. (1891 Census). Marcus Bischofswerder (1852-1914) was Isaac Bischofswerder's oldest son. In 1871, the entire family of ten were living at Belgrave Terrace, and by 1881, the household had also come to include a servant, a local girl of 18, Emma Hawke, who soon became Marcus' common-law wife, bearing him their first child, David Harry, who died at fourteen days old, in June 1881. Between 1883 to 1889, Emma gave birth to four other girls, Esther (Etty, or Hetty), Minnie, Rachel and Augusta. On the birth certificate for Hetty (born 19th July 1883; registered on 30th August that year) the father is not named, and Emma Hawke is given as living at Back Lane, Penzance. It would seem that she had moved from Isaac Bischofswerder's family home. On the birth certificate for her daughter, Rachel (18th October 1887; registered on 3rd December that year) Marcus is given as the father, and Emma (not yet married) incorrectly used Marcus' surname. The couple were then living at 17, St. James Street.[493] A fifth daughter, Leah, was born in July of 1891, by which time Marcus and Emma had moved with their children to 22 Rosevean Road.[494] Marcus and Emma did not marry until 12th June 1892, just before Emma was to give birth to their seventh child. Emma had converted to Judaism by this time, and, accordingly, the ceremony was conducted, at their home, by Rabbi Michael Leinkram. The groom is recorded on the civil certificate as *Batchelor,* and the bride as Emma Boramlagh Hawke, *Spinster,* daughter of Thomas Hawke (deceased), a Policeman.[495] The witnesses were a J. Myers, Marcus's brothers, George and David, and the latter's son, Harry. Isaac Bischofswerder did not officiate at the wedding, as he had done for every Jewish wedding since 1869, including those in the synagogue of his daughter, Henriettta, in 1876, and his son, Morris, in 1884, and he is not recorded on the certificate as a witness. It is possible that Isaac Bischofswerder did not approve of a relationship that had produced six children out of wedlock to a mother who was not of Jewish descent. For some time, Emma Hawke had been using the Hebrew forename, *Sarah,* presumably to facilitate her acceptance within the family, and this may also have been a preliminary to her conversion. The earlier birth certificates,[496] prior to the marriage, record her as *Emma,* but they are also unusual in that she is given as *Bischofswerder, formerly Hawke,* a declaration that was technically fraudulent. Because of her unmarried status, there was no provision at the time for the name of the father to be included, and it should not have been (as opposed to *need* not have been). Nevertheless, on all of the certificates, Marcus' name and signature appears. The couple would appear to have repeatedly perjured themselves on these certificates, and samples of other pre-marital (non-Jewish) births in those years, recorded by the same Registrar, do not reflect this practice. Clearly, the couple were very keen indeed to proceed as if they were legally married, despite the risks involved.

The attitudes taken by Jewish congregations to pre-marital births where both parties were Jews, or where a Jew had fathered a child with a Gentile mother, may not have been uniform. The extent to which the conversion of the mother, and the subsequent marriage of the couple, was viewed as legitimising the Jewish status of the children is also difficult to assess with certainty, but the acceptance of the family as a whole is likely. The treatment of unconverted wives, and of their Jewish partners by congregations is likewise unknown. No doubt principle and practice may have varied from place to place, and no general inference can be drawn from individual cases. In Stroud, in 1881, three Jews married Gentile women, and five in 1891. Two of the 1891 wives converted to Judaism and were married in the synagogue, and both of these couples had produced offspring before marriage.[497] Where, in records of Jewish births, the name of the father is given, he is normally assumed to be the husband, and the child legitimate, as is the case for such records in the South West from 1784-1867. However, in the six year period 1881-1887 in the Jewish community in Newcastle, Rabbi Elias Pearlson recorded four male births from unmarried mothers in ninety-four circumcisions. In the late 18th century, the Plymouth congregation laid down the special rule that "One who lives with a non-Jewess…may not come to any holy matter", which, in itself, implies that such cohabitation was not unknown. However, the fact that the same congregation did not have a similar rule to cover the cohabitation of or sexual relations between unmarried Jewish couples may suggest that such an occurrence was unknown, or, at the very least, extremely rare.[498]

Soon after their wedding, Sarah Bischofswerder's seventh child, Harry, was born, on 17ᵗʰ July 1892. Between 1893 and 1905, Sarah gave birth to another ten children, although several of them died in infancy. Marcus Bischofswerder was eventually to compile a complete list of their offspring, in a family Bible, dated 1906, with his address in Hull, although it is likely to be a later transcription of earlier records. It contains the dates and, in some cases, the place of birth of all of these seventeen children, including birth dates for himself and for his wife. Where births took place in Penzance, no place or address is given, except where there had been a return to the town, but births in Plymouth and Hull are specified. The handwriting throughout can be identified as that of Marcus from a comparison with his signature on his wedding certificate.[499] With such a large and growing family, it would seem that Marcus Bischofswerder's prospects were always precarious. The 1881 Penzance Census describes Marcus as a Traveller, and that of 1891 as *Jeweller Gold*. In July 1891, on the birth certificate of his daughter Leah, he is described as *Jeweller Master*, but by November 1900, on that of his daughter Eve, as *Commercial Traveller*. From 1895 to the early 1900s, the family led a peripatetic existence, alternating between Penzance and Plymouth, and living at various modest addresses in each place. Marcus' brother, Max, had settled in Plymouth, but his domestic circumstances were very different from those of his brother. The 1901 Plymouth Census[500] shows Max and with his wife, Kate, with their only child, and Kate's sister, at 74 Union Street, one of the city's principle thoroughfares, while Marcus' and Sarah's family of nine children were living in one of a small row of houses at 24, Edgar Terrace. Marcus is given in the census as a self-employed commercial traveller. His daughters, Abigail (1895-) and Kate (1897-), the latter dying in infancy of whooping cough, had, according to the family Bible record, been born in Plymouth, although the census gives Cornwall, which may be where their births were eventually registered.

Unlike his brothers, Marcus Bischofswerder is not known to have played any major part in the affairs of the Penzance Hebrew Congregation. An *M.* Bischofswerder is mentioned on several occasions in the Minute-Book between 1886 to 1890, but the forename *Marcus* is not recorded, and these entries are more likely to refer to his brother Morris, who is specifically given by name up to 1892. (Likewise, the *M.* Bischofswerder who was a member of the Penzance Masonic Lodge, was Morris: see below). Marcus was present, as a witness, at the wedding of his sister, Henrietta, in 1876, and, as has been noted, at the grand opening of his brother David's new Jubilee Hall in 1887. George Bischofswerder had settled in Hull soon after his marriage in 1883, and the Hull census for 1901 lists Marcus's oldest daughter, Esther (Etty) then 18, as a visitor at the home of her uncle. By 1905, Marcus and family had moved to Hull, where Sarah's last child, Isaac David, who was not to survive, was born on 14ᵗʰ May 1905 at 23 Cogan Street. Alongside the entry in the Bible is written, "God Bless him...*Amen.*" Marcus Bischofswerder died at 15 Cogan Street, aged 62, in July 1914. (The *Jewish Chronicle* Obituary, of 17ᵗʰ July, gives the date as 12ᵗʰ, but his headstone gives it as the 26ᵗʰ). He is buried in the Hull Jewish cemetery along with his brothers, George and Morris. Four of Marcus Bischofswerder's daughters, Rachel, Jeanette (Nita), Abigail and Eve, eventually moved to London. On 7ᵗʰ January 1909, Rachel married Moses (Morris) Kersh (1886-) a

Tailor from Hull. The wedding took place in the Hull Synagogue. Elias Pearlson and George Bischofswerder were witnesses. By 1916, when their daughter, Rose Marian, was born (on 18th March; the birth registered on 24th March), the couple lived in the East End, at 396, Commercial Road. Morris Kersh was employed as a "Tailor's Presser" at premises in 34 Alfred Street, Bow. It would seem that the Tailor was a *Markovitch*, in that Nita Bischofswerder married a Louis Markovitch, of that same address, an apprentice Cabinet Maker, and, presumably a son of Morris Kersh's employer. A son, Alfred, was born to Louis and Nita Markovitch on 7th January 1924.[501]

Morris Bischofswerder: Secondhand Clothes Dealer, 118 Market Jew Street (Kelly's Directory 1883); Home: 8 Cornwall Terrace (Kelly 1889). General Dealer (Kelly 1891); Jeweller, 118 Market Jew Street (1902 Kelly 1906 & 1910); General Merchant, dealer in Antique Silver and Curios, Watches, Jewellery Plate &c (1902 trade invoice[502]); Home: 47 Morrab Road (Kelly 1902 & 1911).[503] Morris (Moses) was the third of Isaac Bischofswerder's five sons. On the 1871 Census, he is recorded as a Pawnbroker's Assistant, and on the 1881 Census as a Traveller. By 1883 he was trading from a shop in Market Jew Street, and in 1884, he married Julia Joseph (1851-1911), a daughter of Henry Joseph, a prominent member of the Hebrew Congregation, and a successful pawnbroker in the town. The ceremony took place in the synagogue, conducted by Isaac Bischofswerder, with Marcus' brother, David, as one of the witnesses. They were to have two children, Henry, born in 1885, and Amelia (Amy) in 1889, by which time they were living at 8, Cornwall Terrace, a relatively modest house situated near the sea-front. In 1891, the census records them there with a resident servant, Martha Nicholls of Madron. In the same year, his name appears on the membership records of the Penzance Masonic Lodge. His business in Market Jew Street appears to have flourished, because later editions of Kelly's Directory, from 1902, indicate that the family had moved their home to 47, Morrab Road, a significantly larger property in one of the town's most prestigious areas. Morris Bischofswerder had been advertising his business regularly in the local press from the 1880s, and this identically worded entry was to appear in every issue of the daily edition of the *Cornish Telegraph*, from 1890 to 1900: "WANTED, LADIES' DRESSES (for cash). Morris Bischofswerder, 118, Market-jew St. Penzance, having large orders from the Colonies, can afford to give good prices for Ladies', Gentlemen's and Childrens' left-off clothing of every description. Mr. B. will call, or appointment made by letter, best market prices given for old Gold and Silver. All parcels strictly attended to, and P.O.O. sent by return of post. Note the address, next to the Star Hotel". His trade card and headed business paper for 1902[504] read: "Morris Bischofswerder, General Merchant. Also dealer in Antique Silver and Curios, Watches, Jewellery, Plate etc. 118 Market Jew Street, Penzance."

In his application for Naturalisation Papers that same year, Morris Bischofswerder gave his reason as "a desire to possess the right to vote". In a "Memorial" (testimonial) of 1st September 1902, supporting the application, the Mayor of Penzance, William Colenso wrote that he had known the applicant "ever since with his parents he came to Penzance about 33 years ago". He mentions that he is "one of our respectable Tradesmen carrying on his Business in one of the main streets and living in one of the principle Roads" (he had given his address as 47 Morrab Road). Colenso attests of his (very) good character, that he banks at "Bolitho's Consolidated Ltd." (the town's principle private bank), and that he has received the approval of employees of the bank, together with that of the main Referee, Percy Teague Chirgwin", a "merchant" of 7 & 8 Market Place, who traded a few doors from Bischofswerder's shop. Colenso closes by mentioning that Morris Bischofswerder has been "for many years" a member "of our Masonic Lodge", and that Mr. Chirgwin was also initiated into the Lodge when Colenso "occupied the Chair" (of Master) in 1886. (Most of the Mayors of Penzance, and the members of the Town Council were Freemasons).[505] Of particular note is Colenso's reference to Morris Bischofswerder's marriage to a "Native of this town". Colenso uses the term to denote a local Jewish family, that of Henry Joseph (1806-1881), originally from Falmouth, and his wife Amelia Jacob (1811-1891) who had been born in Camborne. Their daughter, Julia (1851-1911) the youngest of their twelve children, was the "Native" mentioned by Colenso.[506] Morris and Julia Bischofswerder's daughter, Amy (Amelia) attended the West Cornwall College, and her success in the Preliminary Cambridge Local Examinations was recorded in the Jewish Chronicle on 1st March 1901.

Morris Bischofswerder took an active part in the affairs of the Jewish Congregation, and his name appears every year in its Minute-Book from 1882. His brother David, appears to have taken charge of the affairs of the dwindling congregation, and, after his departure from the town around 1892, the responsibility fell to Morris, who tried in vain, with drastically reduced finances, to keep the synagogue open, but by 1906 it was sold. After David Bischofswerder's departure, his father, Isaac, would have taken up residence with his son Morris. When the town's (and the County's) last resident Rabbi died in 1899, Morris was the only member of his family left in Penzance. Morris' wife, Julia, died on 20th April 1911 at their family home, and her burial in the cemetery was to be the last of a member of the original Jewish community. Morris Bischofswerder remained in the town until 1913, when he left and moved to be near other members of his family in Hull. He died there, aged 78, on 20th July 1934.

Henry Bischofswerder: Apprentice Chemist (1902: Colenso's reference).[507] Born 1885, the son of Morris Bischofswerder. Colenso does not identify the chemist to whom Henry was apprenticed.

Penzance Jewish Marriage Registers, 1838-1892[508]

Marriages before 1838

Marriage entries before and after 1838 have been included here where at least one party is known to have been, or may have been, Jewish. From genealogical pedigrees and other records, such as parish and census returns (the latter from 1841) it is obvious that various marriages (where one or both parties were Jews) did take place in Penzance well before 1838. The lack of congregational records before 1808, or of any congregational marriage register prevents a wider identification. Where such marriages can be inferred they have been noted below or elsewhere. Census records in particular allow a retrospective calculation of the approximate year of a marriage from the ages of the children from the first born child.

7th April 1804. John Levi to Eleanor Dash, Parish of Madron (assumed to be in church).[509] It is not known if this is the **Jacob Levy**, merchant seaman, listed in the trades section for 1808-1812,[510] who may have been Jewish, but neither John Levi or Jacob Levy have been confirmed as being of Jewish descent.

31st January 1828. **Abraham Joseph** of Plymouth to **Eliza**, daughter of Lemon Woolf of Penzance,[511] and reported in the *Exeter Flying Post* on 14th February 1828.

28th February 1833. **H. L. Cohen**, late of Warsaw, to **Rosate Moses**, late of Falmouth. (*Exeter Flying Post; 7th* March 1833).[512] Rosate Moses may have been a daughter of Philip Moses (-1831), a son of Alexander Moses of Falmouth. It is possible that the **Bessy Cohen** who was born in Penzance *c.* 1836 was their daughter, although she may have been a member of the family of Emanuel Cohen (1766-1849) of Redruth. The 1851 Bristol census, for 39 College Green, records her age as 15, and as born in Penzance. In Bristol, she was an assistant in the household of Arabella Levy (widow), a jeweller.[513] The latter, Arabella Joseph (1803-1897) was the daughter of Lyon Joseph (1775-1825) and Judith Levy (1774-1846) of Bath, both formerly of Falmouth. Arabella Joseph was born in Falmouth, and her late husband, Solomon Levy (who was not related to the distinct Levy families of Falmouth and Truro, and who died in 1841), was the son of Joseph and Sophia Levy of Exeter. Solomon and Arabella Levy had nine children.

The errors in the Cornish genealogies compiled by William Jessop (1951) have been mentioned previously, and some are noted at various points in this text. The example above is an illustration of the consequences that such uncorrected errors can have. Jessop's confusion and conflation of the separate and unrelated Levy families of Exeter and Truro led him to record Solomon Levy (-1841) as a son of the (Truro) family of Israel Levy (-1824) and Hannah Moses (1758-1841), who he gives as "of Exeter". Further, Jessop records that one of Solomon and Arabella Levy's sons, Joseph (1834-1899) married Arabella Harris (1826-1904) of Truro (as his first wife). In fact, Joseph Levy married a Maria Davy, or Davis (1846-1917), and Arabella Harris of Truro married *another* Joseph Levi (1811-1880) of Portsea.[514] One of their children, George (1846-1877) married Sarah Kate Jacob (1849-1919), daughter of Moses "Moss"

Jacob Jacob (1812-1860) of Falmouth. Because there was another Cornish Levy family, that of Barnet Levy (1731-1791) and Esther Elias (- 1780) of Falmouth, it is likely that the Jessop pedigrees have led to the further erroneous assumption that *both* Solomon Levy and Arabella Joseph had been born in Falmouth.[515]

Circa. 1836: **Rose**, daughter of Lemon Woolf to **Josiah (Isaac) Solomon**, son of Isaac Jacob Solomon of Exeter.[516] The couple, who settled in Plymouth, had eleven children. Rose (Rosetta) Solomon died in 1870, and is buried in Plymouth Hoe cemetery.[517] Josiah Solomon had moved to New York by 1872. He was likely to have been the Josiah Solomon present at the marriage of his wife's sister, Amelia to the (unrelated) Phillip Solomon of Newcastle in 1842, although this may have been a relative of the bridegroom. Josiah Solomon of Exeter should not be confused with his namesake of Liskeard who traded in Penzance as a Tailor in 1871 (see above).

There were 18 Jewish marriages registered during this period, one of which involved a convert to Judaism. One other Jewish marriage was not registered locally, and at least one other civil marriage, not conducted as a Jewish religious ceremony, was between a Jew, Frederick Lazarus, and a non-Jew. As such, this marriage cannot strictly be regarded as a "Jewish" marriage, but is included here. Only 4 marriages were between partners where both lived in Penzance, and 4 were between members of the Penzance and Falmouth congregations. The remaining 8 marriages were between Penzance residents and partners from outside the locality. This in itself would indicate the trend for marriage to result in migration from the town. The synagogue was used for 9 of the marriages, 8 were in the family homes, and 1 took place at the Register Office. The abbreviation *ofa* indicates that *of full age* appears on the certificate; *Ma.* indicates that the couple were "married by...", who signed the certificate.

June 6th 1838. **Joseph Benedict Rintel**, Jewish Rabbi, of Killigrew Street, Falmouth, age 28, son of Benedict Jacob Rintel, Gentleman, married **Fanny Simmons**, 24, of Market Jew Street, Penzance, daughter of Rabbi Barnett Asher Simmons. Witnesses: I. Jacob and Henry Levin. (House). Ma. Rabbi Barnett Simmons. Of the witnesses, (unless the "I" is to be read as a "J") the "I. Jacob" would have been (Moses) Isaac Jacob (1820-1888) son of Jacob Jacob (1774-1853) of Redruth, and a grandson of Moses Jacob. Isaac Jacob's name appears in the Congregational Minute Book. Henry Levin (1798-1877), originally from Stockholm, was a prominent member of the congregation, and, later, its President. The marriage took place in the house of B. A. Simmons in Market Jew Street. Joseph Rintel (1810-1867) and Fanny Simmons (1814-1884) eventually moved to London. There were no children. In 1871, Fanny Rintel, by then a widow, was recorded in the census as a visitor at the house of her brother, Moses, in Islington.[518]

January 23rd 1839. **Samuel Oppenheim**, Jeweller, of 8 Market Street, age 34, son of Nathan Oppenheim, Merchant, married **Elizabeth Levy**, 38, daughter of Israel Levy, Jeweller. Both parties of Penzance. Witnesses: Henry Levin and Lemon

Woolf. Ma. B. A. Simmons. Nathan Oppenheim, Samuel Oppenheim's father, was German, and is not recorded as deceased on the certificate, although it is not certain that he was present, or that he had lived in Penzance. Elizabeth Levy (1798-1879) was a daughter of Israel Levy (-1823), a Jeweller of Truro, and his wife Hannah Moses (1758-1841) from Falmouth. It is not known how long Elizabeth Levy had been resident in Penzance, but her father was affiliated to the Penzance congregation. The marriage took place in the Synagogue.

June 9th 1841. **Bella Woolf**, 24, of Market Jew Street, daughter of Lemon Woolf, Merchant, married **Markis (Marks or Markes) Levy**, 29, Silversmith, of Plymouth, son of Abraham Levy, Merchant. Witnesses: Henry Joseph and Benjamin Selig. Ma. B. A. Simmons. The marriage took place in Lemon Woolf's house in Market Jew Street. Bella (or Betsy) Woolf (1817-1881) was the fourth daughter of Lemon Woolf and his wife Rebecca Jacob (1781-1853) who was from Redruth. The couple settled in Plymouth, where Markes (Mordecai) Levy (1812-1871) was a Jeweller and Navy Agent in 1851 at 50 Bedford Street, and a Pawnbroker at 38 Union Street (1861) and 190 Union Street (1871). Their children were Abraham (1841-), Sarah (1843-1858) who died at 15 and is buried in the Plymouth Hoe cemetery,[519] Julia (1843-), Esther (Ellen 1848-), Caroline (1849), Eliza (1851-), Asher (1852-), Bernard (1858-) and Albert (1860-). The family employed three household servants, and, in 1861, an Elizabeth Lyon (27) as a shop assistant, and also as a nurse, cook and housemaid. After 1871, Markes and Bella Levy moved to London, where they both died, in Islington, Markes in 1877, aged 64, and Bella in 1881, also aged 64.[520]

May 10th 1842. **Amelia Woolf**, (of full age), of Market Jew Street, Penzance, daughter of Lemon Woolf, Merchant, married **Phillip Solomon** (of full age), Hardwareman, of "Newcastle on Tine" (*sic.*), son of Isaac Solomon, Silversmith. Amelia Woolf (1813-1889) was Lemon Woolf's third daughter, and Phillip Solomon (1813-1894) was a son of Isaac Jacob Solomon (1772-1854) of Exeter. Witnesses: Josiah Solomon (likely Phillip's brother) and Lemon Woolf. Ma. B. A. Simmons. The marriage (which was reported in the *West Briton* on 20th May 1842) took place in Lemon Woolf's house. By 1851 until sometime after 1871, Philip and Amelia Solomon were living in Shoreditch, London, where Philip traded as a Carpet Bag Maker. By 1881 they had moved to Paddington, where Philip remained after the death of his wife in 1889, and until his own death in 1894. Their children were Solomon (1844-), Samuel (1847-), Sarah (1849-), Eliza (1850-), Lemon (1852-), and (possibly twins) Henry (1854-) and Rebecca (1854-). Four of the children, Samuel, Eliza, Lemon and Rebecca, remained unmarried well into their late 30s and early 40s. Philip and Amelia Solomon had at least two grandchildren, a girl, Moyelle (1879-) and a boy, Alfred (1880-), children either of Solomon, Sarah or Henry Solomon. It is of note that these two grandchildren were both born in Bombay (1891 Census). Rebecca Solomon became an artist in watercolours, and between 1893-1913 exhibited on at least a dozen occasions, including the Royal Society of Artists, Birmingham, the Royal Society of Portrait Painters, and the Royal Academy.[521] Amelia's older sister, **Rose (Rosa or Rosetta) Woolf** (1810-) married Phillip Solomon's brother, **Josiah (Joseph Isaac) Solomon** (1811-). This marriage most likely took place in Penzance before 1837-1838 (and the introduction of civil registration). It is not recorded in the Plymouth Congregational marriage register, which begins in 1837, although the couple settled there, where Josiah Solomon ran a Fancy Goods Warehouse at 22 Whimple Street. Rosetta is buried in Plymouth, and most likely died there sometime before 1871, in that her husband had moved to New York by 1872.[522]

June 10th 1846. **Moses Barnett Simmons**, (ofa), Gilder (*sic.*), of Market Jew Street, Penzance, son of Rabbi Barnett Asher Simmons, "Rabi" (*sic.*), married **Rosa Aaron**, (ofa), of Killigrew Street, Falmouth, daughter of Abraham Aaron, Merchant. Witnesses: Jonas Heilbron and Benjamin Aaron Selig. The couple were married by Rabbi B. A. Simmons in the house of M. B. Simmons. The marriage was noted in the *West Briton* (12th June 1846, Friday): "At Penzance, on Wednesday last, Mr. M. B. Simmons, to Miss Rosa Aaron".[523] Rosa (Rose) Aaron (*c.* 1816-) was the only daughter of Abraham Aaron (1767-1833) of Plymouth. She had seven older brothers, born between 1796 and 1814.[524] Her father had married Phoebe Joseph (-1832) a daughter of Abraham Joseph I (1731-1794) of Plymouth, but Rosa Aaron was born at Goodmans Fields, London. It is not known if Abraham Aaron had traded in Falmouth. Moses Barnett Simmons (1817-1876) and Rosa later moved to London, where Moses traded as a Carver & Guilder in Bury Street (1851 & 1861 Census). By 1851 he was employing three men and also working with his brothers, Levy (1828-) and Abraham (1831-) as Carvers & Guilders (a skill the three brothers would have learned from their father, Rabbi Barnet Asher Simmons) and also a Barnett Levy (age 18), who had been born in Bristol, as an apprentice Carver. Moses' unmarried sister, Amelia (age 25) was living in the household, and worked as an embroiderer. By 1861, Moses Simmons was employing seven men and seven boy apprentices, and by 1871 they had moved to Lonsdale Square, Islington.[525] Their children were Abraham (1848-), Phoebe (1852-), Barnett (1855-), Bessey (1858-) and Florence (Flora, 1961-).

Witnesses: Jonas Heilbron and Benjamin Aaron Selig. Ma. B. A. Simmons, in the house of M. B. Simmons.

August 5th 1846. **Jonas Heilbron**, (full age), Jeweller, of High Street, Falmouth, son of Isaac Heilbron, Merchant, married **Phoebe Simmons**, (full age), of Market Jew Street, Penzance, daughter of Rabbi Barnett Asher Simmons, Rabbi. Jonas, (Joseph) Heilbron (1806-), who was born in Germany, and Phoebe Simmons (1815-) may have moved to South Wales, but were in London by 1851, where Jonas Heilbron traded as a General Dealer.[526] They are believed to have emigrated to Australia. There were no children.

Witnesses: Henry Joseph and Benjamin Aaron Selig. Ma. B. A. Simmons in the home of M. B. Simmons.

November 11th 1846. **Solomon Teacher**, age 35, Shopkeeper, of Market Jew Street, Penzance, son of Markus Teacher, Merchant, married **Maria Selig**, age 32, of Causewayhead, Penzance, daughter of Aaron Selig, Watchmaker. Witnesses:

Henry Levin and Moses B. Simmons. Ma. B. A. Simmons. The marriage took place in the synagogue, and was noted in the *West Briton* (November 13ᵗʰ 1846, Friday): "At the synagogue, Penzance, on Wednesday last, by the Rev. B. A. Simmons, Mr. Solomon Teacher, shop-keeper, to Maria, only daughter of the late Mr. A. Selig, watchmaker and jeweller, of that town."

September 1st 1847. **Benjamin Aaron Selig**, age 33, Jeweller, of Causewayhead, Penzance, son of Aaron Selig, Watchmaker, married **Catherine Jacobs**, age 26, of Market Street, Falmouth, daughter of Samuel Jacob, Jeweller. Witnesses: Henry Levin and B. A. Simmons. Ma. B. A. Simmons in the synagogue. Catherine Jacob (1820-) was the daughter of Samuel Jacob (1778-1860) of Falmouth and Sarah Levy (1784-1868) of Truro. This branch of the Jacob family had moved to Penzance, and Catherine was a niece of Rabbi B. A. Simmons' wife, Flora Jacob (1790-1874). Benjamin Aaron Selig (1814-1872) was to become a rabbi, and is thought to have studied with B. A. Simmons in Penzance. After the death of his parents, Benjamin Selig emigrated with his family to Australia, where he became the minister of the Melbourne congregation, and later of the Canterbury congregation, South Island, New Zealand. The couple were to have three sons: Aaron and Lemon (*c.*1849-50), who may have been twins.[527] Aaron settled in London, and Lemon eventually emigrated to America. The third son, Phineas (Pinchas) Selig (1856-1941) was born in Melbourne (1856), and there were three other children, Hannah, Sarah and Henry.[528] Upon her husband's death, Catherine Seilg returned to Melbourne, Phineas remaining in New Zealand.[529]

June 12th 1850. **Hyman Fienburg** (Fienberg) (of full age), General Merchant, of Commercial Street, Newport, Wales, son of Moses Feinburg, Merchant, married **Catherine Simmons**, (of full age), of Penzance, daughter of Rabbi Barnett Asher Simmons. Hyman Fienburg (1812-1866) and Catherine Simmons (1819-1891) had a large family, many of whom emigrated to Australia, and others to South Africa. The variant spellings, *Fienburg* and *Feinburg* appear on the certificate. The groom signed himself with the first spelling, but his father's name is given with the second. Witnesses: Jonas Heilbron and David Levin. (Synagogue). Ma. B. A. Simmons. The marriage was noted in the *West Briton* (14ᵗʰ June 1850): "At the Synagogue, Penzance. On Wednesday last, Mr. Feinburgh of Newport, to Catherine, third daughter of the Rev. B. A. Simmons of Penzance." In 1851, the couple were in Newport, where Hyman Feinburg traded as a Broker. The census record gives "Cornwall" as the birth-place for both, although this may be an error in the case of Hyman Feinburg. By 1861, the family were in Birmingham, where Hyman was trading as a "Cap Maker", and his place of origin is given as "Poland, not naturalised". Their children were Deborah (1851-), Joseph (1853-), Lemon (1854-), Barnet (1856-), all born in Newport, Amelia Rose (1857-), born in Bristol, and David (1860-), born in Birmingham. Family records also give a Morris, a Minnie and a Fanny. In 1861 a Lyon Feinburg (40), a General Dealer, unmarried, also from Poland, most likely Hyman's brother, lived with the family.[530]

August 21st 1850. **Charles Goodman**, 23 years, Painter & Glazier, of Newbridge, Lamorna, son of George Goodman, Jeweller, married **Amelia Jacob**, 28 years, of 9 Leskinnick Terrace, Penzance, daughter of Samuel Jacob, Jeweller. Witnesses: Solomon Teacher and Simon B. Simmons. The marriage took place in the Synagogue, and Rabbi B. A. Simmons officiated. Amelia Jacob's age, as given on the certificate, is incorrect, in that her family birth register recorded [531] her birth as having taken place on 25th October 1817, which would have made her some ten years older than her husband. (Her sisters, Catherine and Phoebe, likewise, reduced their ages, each by one year, at the time of their respective marriages.) Amelia's "creative accountancy" in making a false declaration of her true age was technically an offence, although the absence of a formal birth certificate for her, allowed for a certain latitude, and may even have been regarded, by some at least, as a "Lady's Privilege". The wry comment has been made of Amelia (she died in 1921): "This raises the intriguing problem - of whether she died at 99, or whether she went on to 104 – it seems hard to become a centenarian without knowing it."[532] It is not inconceivable, however, that in a time well before the introduction of public records very elderly family members might not recall the exact year of their birth, and misremember or misrepresent it. Amelia (Goodman) had been named after her unmarried great aunt, Amelia Jacob. The register clearly gives *her* birth year as February 1786. She died on 23rd September 1864, likely within a new Jewish year. This would have made her 78 or 79. Yet it seems that she may have insisted that she was ten years younger, because her age on the headstone is given in English as 70, but in the Hebrew as 79. No doubt Amelia claimed to know her own age perfectly well, but her family knew otherwise, and may have preserved a private family joke on the headstone inscription. Charles Goodman was from Wales and was not a resident of Cornwall. The *Newbridge* given here is not the small village west of Penzance, on the road to St. Just, but a town of the same name north of Cardiff. It seems unlikely that Goodman was living at the time of his marriage at Lamorna, an isolated rural hamlet set above a cove, several miles to the south of Penzance, on the Land's End peninsula. The insertion of *Lamorna* may have been an erroneous clerical interpolation by the Registrar, on the assumption that the local Newbridge applied, although the latter is some five miles north of Lamorna itself. There were a number of Jewish *Goodman* families in South Wales, not all related, but often bearing the same forenames, *Harris, George* etc., and appearing in the same census records for Glamorgan. Charles Goodman's family were from Poland. By 1851, Charles Goodman (24) and his wife, Amelia (29) were living in Llantwit Pontypridd, where Charles traded as a Glazier and Clothier.[533] Charles Goodman was a naturalised British subject by 1861. Their children were Theodore Lionel (1852-), Rachel (1854-) and Sarah (1857-). From 1871, Amelia's sister, Betsy (Elizabeth) Jacobs (1824-), who was unmarried and had been a deaf mute since birth, lived with the family, and from 1881 (when Amelia Goodman is recorded as being deaf), so did Julia Goodman (*c*. 1859-), Charles' unmarried niece. While the family lived in Glamorgan, Charles Goodman traded as a Pawnbroker, in the High Street, Pontypridd. A David Goodman and a George Goodman were also Pawnbrokers in the town at this time, and the former was also a Watch and Clock Maker.[534] By 1891, when he was 64, Charles Goodman had retired from that

THE JEWS OF CORNWALL

trade, and the family had moved to London, where they lived in Willesden. Curiously, the 1901 Census for Willesden records Charles Goodman as a retired *builder*, and his son Theodore, and his wife, *Luida* (likely Louisa), together with Elizabeth Jacobs (Betsy) are given as *Johannesburg Refugees*. It is possible that, between 1891-1901, Theodore and Louisa Goodman, together with Betsy Jacob, had emigrated to South Africa and returned from there. In 1901, a Minnie Allen (26), a British Subject from Spain, is recorded as a Secretary to the Retired Builder. Charles Goodman has been taken to be a brother of the Ephraim Goodman (who married Amelia's sister, Phoebe in 1853), but the names of their respective fathers are distinct, despite the fact that both families shared the trade of Glazier. It may be that the two men were cousins.

February, 1853, but not listed in the Penzance Registry: *The West Briton*, Friday 25th February records "At the Synagogue Penzance, Mr. J. (*sic.*) Davidson, of London, to Amelia, youngest daughter of the Rev. B. A. Simmons, of the former place".[535] In fact, this marriage did not take place in Penzance, but in London, on 16th February at the Great Synagogue, St. James, Duke's Place. The service was conducted by the Chief Rabbi, Nathan Adler.[536] The bridegroom, **Isaac Davidson** (1830-1890) was a London watchmaker, originally from Falmouth, and lived at 75 St. George Street East in London. He was the son of Abraham Davidson, a clothier of Falmouth, and originally a Watch and Clockmaker (*c.* 1830). The bride, **Amelia Simmons** (1825-1919) was living at the time at 17a Bury Street, St. Mary Axe, the address of her sister, Fanny, who was married to Rabbi Joseph Rintel, a London *shochet*, and the former rabbi at Falmouth. Amelia's brother, Moses Barnett Simmons (1817-1876) also lived in London. Isaac Davidson and Amelia Simmons were first cousins once removed. The bride's father, Barnet Ascher (*sic.*) Simmons, is given as "Clerk", that is a clerk (or cleric) in Holy Orders. The witnesses were Simon Archer, Aaron Levy …(?), and Simeon Oppenheim, Secretary of the Great Synagogue.[537] The marriage was registered in St. Luke's Parish (Islington). Amelia and Isaac Davidson later emigrated to Australia, where Amelia's brother, Abraham Barnett Simmons (1831-1908) also settled, in Ballarat, Victoria.[538] Amelia and Isaac Davidson lived in Sydney, where they died. They had at least four children, Flora (named after her grandmother), Rose, Morris (Moses) and Abraham (after his grandfather).

May 8th 1853. **Ephraim George Goodman**, age 26, Glazier "Gen", of Merthyr Tydfil, Wales, son of Harris Goodman, Pawnbroker, married **Phoebe Jacob**, age 24, of Leskinnick Terrace, Penzance, daughter of Samuel Jacob, Jeweller. After Phoebe's death, Ephraim George Goodman married Rose Joseph in 1865 (see below). It is not certain if there were children from the first marriage. Witnesses: Benjamin Aaron Selig and Solomon Ezekiel. (Synagogue). B. A. Simmons. The *West Briton* noted the marriage (13th May 1853, Friday): "At the Synagogue, Penzance, on Sunday last, Mr. Ephraim George Goodman of Merthyr Tydvil, Wales, to Phoebe, third daughter of Mr. Samuel Jacob of Penzance." Ephraim Goodman's father, Harris Goodman (*c.* 1799-), a Pawnbroker, appears with his family in Census records for Merthyr from 1851.[539] His wife, Pauly (Paulina?) was from Russia. Harris Goodman's father, George (78) lived with the family. Ephraim George Goodman's older brother, Joseph (1822-) and his wife, Mary (1826-), also Polish, with their son, Barnett (6 months) also lived in the house, together with a younger brother, Moses (1833-) and a lodger, Israel Goodman (1830-), who was unmarried, and had been born in Merthyr. By 1861 Moses Goodman was married to a Phoebe (1837-), from Poland, and was still living in his parents' house, with a daughter, Elizabeth (11 months old). By 1871, Harris Goodman was a widower, but still trading as a Pawnbroker with a live-in clerk, Samuel Lazarus. Joseph Goodman's wife Mary, may have died soon after 1851. By 1881, his wife was a Jennet(te), age 40, who was from Germany and a British subject. Their children were Raphael (1854-) a Diamond merchant Jeweller, Hyman (14) and Sophia (12). Harris Goodman died *c.* 1886, at the age of 95. Phoebe Jacob (*c.*1827-1865) of Penzance was a daughter of Samuel Jacob (1778-1860) of Redruth and Sarah Levy (1784-1868) of Truro. She was a cousin to her older namesake, **Phoebe Jacob** (1823-1904) of Penzance, the daughter of Levy Jacob of Redruth (1788-1824), a younger brother of Samuel Jacob. Both brothers, sons of Moses Jacob of Redruth, had moved to Penzance. Levy Jacob was married to Sophia Mordecai (1781-1853) of Exeter. Phoebe, daughter of Levy and Sophia Jacob was married to an Abraham Kestenberg of Poland in Exeter on 8th June 1845. The Exeter Hebrew Congregation Marriage Register records her as *Phobe Jacobs of Penzance, age above 21*, of 11 North Street, Exeter.

The marriage of Phoebe Jacob and Ephraim George Goodman was the last marriage conducted by Rabbi B. A. Simmons before his retirement.

July 24th 1861. **Frederick Lazarus**,[540] age 24, Licensed Hawker, of Penzance, son of Jonas Lazarus, deceased, Licenced Hawker, married Emily Cock, age 22, Domestic Servant, of Penzance, daughter of Thomas Cock (deceased), Farmer. Witnesses: William Noy and John Easton Tonkin. (Register Office). Ma. John Trythall (Registrar). As noted, this is not a marriage which would be recognised under Jewish Law in that one of the parties was not Jewish. As such it was a civil marriage. It is also the first recorded marriage in Penzance of a Jew to a non-Jew. Although he later settled in Penzance, Frederick Lazarus appears to have been an itinerant hawker at this stage. At this time, he may have been a member of a Jewish Lazarus family resident in the town, but it is not known if he was related to the Hyman Lazarus who is mentioned in the Penzance Congregational Minute Books in 1843 and 1845, or to the Isaac Lazarus, who donated 4 shillings, and the "… Lazarus", who donated 1 shilling and 7 pence (both recorded in the original handwritten accounts) for the acquisition of a new *Sifre Torah* in 1828. Frederick Lazarus is not recorded on the certificate as a Jew, but he may not have been asked for his religion, and may not have had any affiliation with the Penzance Congregation. Neither of the witnesses to the marriage were Jews. On 23rd August 1862, the birth of Frederick and Emily's daughter, Annie, was registered in Redruth, where they were living in Penryn Street. Frederick Lazarus appears to have been illiterate, and gave his "mark" in place of a signature on both the marriage and birth certificates. Emily signed her name at the marriage. Frederick's illiteracy may suggest a background where his parents had become estranged from

Jewish society and communal life, where the education of children would have been a high priority and a traditional practice. Consequently, illiteracy was rare amongst Jews.

November 22nd 1865. **George Goodman**, age 37 (widower), Pawnbroker, of "Ponty Pridd" (*sic*.), Glamorganshire, son of Harris Goodman, Pawnbroker, married **Rose (Rosa) Joseph**, age 27, of 5 The Terrace, Market Jew Street, Penzance, daughter of Henry Joseph, Pawnbroker. Witnesses: Henry Levin and Michael Jacob. Ma. Rabbis Rittenberg (Rabbi of Penzance) and I. (Isaac Aryeh) Rubinstein (Rabbi of Falmouth). The groom was the Ephraim George Goodman (above). It is not known if any of the Goodman families had been resident in Cornwall for any length of time. (A Ruth Goodman had been charged with handing over stolen silver to Benjamin Levi, at Falmouth, in 1852, but may not have been related to this family.[541]) This marriage took place in the house of Henry Joseph. Rose Joseph (1838-1896) was Henry Joseph's 4th child, and two of her younger sisters also married into Welsh families (see below). The witness, Michael Jacob, may have been from Wales, although it is possible that he was the 15 year old son of Moses Jacob Jacob (1812-1860) of Falmouth. Alongside the signature of Michael Jacob are the initials *M.C.*. George and Rose Goodman appear in census records for Llantwit Vardre, Glamorgan, from 1871 to 1881. Their children were Esther (1867-) who may have died young, in that she does not appear in subsequent census records, Anna, or Annie (1870-), Selina (1874-), Albert Victor (1876-) and Abraham (1848-). In 1871, Rose Goodman's sister, Julia (1851-1911) was living with the family, at Goodman's Court. She was later to marry Morris Bischofswerder of Penzance (see below). In 1881, at 3 Davies Place, Rose's sister, Bessy, Elizabeth or Betsy, was living with the family as a Pawnbroker's Assistant. Her age is given incorrectly as 30 (she was then 33). Betsy Joseph (1848-1900) remained unmarried, and like her sister, Julia, she is buried in the Penzance cemetery. By 1891, George and Rose Goodman had retired to Swansea. George and Rose Goodman both died in Swansea in 1896, within a few months of one another.[542]

June 9th 1869. **Aaron Harris Mark Beirnstein**, age 21, Pawnbroker, of Dowlais (Merthyr Tydfil), Wales, son of Abraham Beirnstein, Pawnbroker, married **Esther Joseph**, age 26, of Penzance, daughter of Henry Joseph, Pawnbroker. Witnesses: Henry Levin, Jonas Levy, A. Abelson (Rabbi of Falmouth) and Henry Joseph. Ma. Rabbi Isaac Bischofswerder. The couple were married in Henry Joseph's house, 5 The Terrace, Market Jew Street. The bridegroom wrote his name in Hebrew, and it was transcribed into the certificate as Aaron Mark Beirnstein Harris (the last name appearing under Aaron), but he signed his name in English script as Harris Mark Beirnstein. Jonas Levy and A. Abelson (then the Rabbi in Falmouth) were, presumably, friends or relatives of the bridegroom, and Abelson was to become minister in Merthyr Tydfil in 1873. [*Levy* and *Harris Beirnstein* appear in the Congregational Minute Book for 1869: *Abelson* does not]. Esther Joseph (1843-) was the 7th child of Henry Joseph (1806-1881) who was originally from Falmouth, and Amelia Jacob (1811-1891) who had been born in Camborne. Like her older sister, Rose (1838-), above, Esther's younger sister, Kate (next marriage) also married into a Welsh family.

Although this marriage took place in a private house, Henry Joseph signed as the Synagogue's Secretary. By 1881, Esther and Harris Beirnstein were living in Nottingham, where Harris traded as a Money Lender. A Solomon Rubenstein from Russia, who was 21 and unmarried, lived with the family as a Money Lender's Clerk, together with two unnamed servants. Harris and Esther Beirnstein's four daughters were Sarah (1874-), Hannah (1876-), Florence (1878-) and Blanche (1881-).[543]

August 31st 1870. **Abraham Freedman**, age 28, (Widower), Pawnbroker, of Aberdare, son of Samuel Freedman, Pawnbroker, married **Kate Joseph**, age 23, of Penzance, daughter of Henry Joseph, Pawnbroker. Witnesses: B. H. Jos(eph), Henry Levin, Abel Abelson and Henry Joseph (Secretary). Ma. Isaac Bischofswerder. This marriage also took place in Henry Joseph's house. Kate Joseph (1847-) was the 10th of Henry Joseph's twelve children (her birth was noted by the *West Briton* (Friday April 23rd) in 1847).

February 9th 1876. **Elias Pearlson**, age 23, Jewish (*sic.*) Rabbi, of 34 Railway Street, Newcastle-on-Tyne, son of Abraham Pearlson, Hebrew Teacher, married **Henrietta Bischofswerder**,[544] age 21, of Belgravia Street, Penzance, daughter of Isaac Bischofswerder, Jewish Rabbi. Witnesses: Henry Levin, Marcus Bischofswerder and Henry Joseph (Secretary). Ma. Isaac Bischofswerder (in the Synagogue).

February 5th 1884. **Morris Bischofswerder**, age 27, Clothier, of 9 Belgravia Street, Penzance, son of Isaac Bischofswerder, Jewish Minister, married **Julia Joseph** (full age) of 5 The Terrace, Penzance, daughter of Henry Joseph (deceased), Pawnbroker.

Witnesses: B. H. Joseph, David Bischofswerder and Israel H. Levin (Sec.y). Ma. Isaac Bischofswerder (in the Synagogue). Julia (1851-1911) was Henry Joseph's youngest daughter and the last of his twelve children. She was also the last member of the original Jewish community to be buried in the cemetery.

June 12th 1892. **Marcus Bischofswerder**, age 39, Jeweller, of 22 Rosevean Road, Penzance, son of Isaac Bischofswerder, Retired Rabbi, married Emma Bramlaugh Hawke, age 27, of 22 Rosevean Road, Penzance, daughter of T(h)omas Hawke (deceased), Policeman. Witnesses: George Bischofswerder, J. Myers, David Bischofswerder (Secretary) and H. Bischofswerder. Ma. Rabbi M. Leinkram.

This is the last Jewish marriage recorded in Penzance at a time when the Jewish congregation was in terminal decline. It has been mentioned that, although Emma Hawke was not of Jewish descent, and had borne Marcus Bischofswerder several children out of wedlock, she had converted to Judaism by this time, taking the forename *Sarah*, by which she came to be known in the family. At the time of the marriage, therefore, both parties were Jews, and, accordingly, a Rabbi was able to officiate. On her birth certificate (19th November 1863; registered 18th December that year) Emma Hawke's second name is given as *Bramwell*, and her parents' address as *Jamaica, Madron*. Her mother, Jane Hawke was illiterate, and gave her mark. Her father, Thomas Hawke is given as Lawyer, that is law-officer. On the marriage certificate, Emma Hawke gave her age incorrectly as 27 (she was 29), and her signature records her second name as *Bramlaugh*. Unlike the other two Bischof-swerder family marriages, it did not take place in the Synagogue, but in the couple's home in Rosevean Road. Isaac Bischofswerder, who was by now in poor health, may not have been present and he did not sign the certificate as a witness.

From the mid-1850s, the following, all children of Rabbi B. A. Simmons of Penzance, married partners from outside Cornwall:

Sarah Simmons (1821-1892) married **Rabbi Harris Isaacs** (-1888) at Newport, South Wales in 1855. Harris Isaacs was from Poland, and by 1861 until some time after 1871, he was trading in Merthyr Tydfil as a Pawnbroker. Harris and Sarah Isaacs had three daughters, Flora (1860-1950), named after her grandmother, Fanny Phoebe (1863-) and Josephina (1868-19442). After the death of her husband, Rabbi B. A. Simmons in 1860, his wife, Flora, moved to live with this daughter in Merthyr Tydfil. Some years earlier, Barnett and Flora Simmons had moved from Cornwall to live in the household, but had returned to Penzance. Flora Simmons died in 1874 and is buried in Merthyr Tydfil. Some time after this, Harris and Sarah Isaacs moved with Phoebe and Josephina to Birmingham, where Harris Isaacs became a Teacher of Hebrew, and where they died.[545] Flora married a David Marcuson, and Josephina a Julius Marcuson.

Levy Barnett Simmons (1828-1899) married **Phoebe Levy** (1833-1890) in London.

Abraham Barnett Simmons (1831-1908) married **Leah Alman** (-1903) of Melbourne, in Australia.

Simon Barnett Simmons (1836-1918) married **Rachel Joseph** (1845-1901) in Portsea. By 1871 the couple were living at Westbury-on-Trym, Bristol, where they had named their house *Mount's Bay Villa*, after the bay at Penzance. Simon Simmons was trading as a Commercial Traveller in Jewellery. Their children were Florence (1866-1942), Bernard (1868-1956) who was to marry a Joanna Selig (1886-1940), and Lizzie (1870-1951), these three being born in Bristol. The fourth child, Isidore (1872-1952) was born in Birmingham. At the time of the 1871 census, a Rose Casper, Niece (age 15) was living with the family. The following year they moved to Edgbaston, Birmingham, where, by 1881, an Anne Levy (21) from Poland, lived with them as a Cook and Domestic Servant. Florence, Lizzie and Isidore Simmons remained unmarried. Bernard Simmons did not marry the much younger Joanna Selig until he was about forty. Of their children, Ruth (1913-) married Ernest Wolf, John (1915-2005), who became a Slavonic scholar and Fellow-Librarian of All Souls College, Oxford, married Fanny Craven (there were no children from the marriage), and Godfrey Simmons (1919-), whose research into the Cornish Jews began when he was a young man, married Winifred Nathan (1913-2003).[546]

The Branwell family of Penzance have been mentioned previously in relation to the Jewish community. They were not a Jewish family but, along with other influential Christian families connected with the locality, such as the Barham, Bolitho, Borlase and Rogers families, they were supportive of the Jewish community and helped them become established in the town. The motivation of these families may not have been entirely without financial self-interest but their role in facilitating the provision of land for the development of a burial ground and the building of both synagogues was crucial.

The Branwells, who lived in the vicinity of Chapel Street, were an extensive and prosperous family, and they were involved in the leasing and building of both the first and second synagogues of 1768 and 1807. By tradition they were Anglicans, but they possessed a long association with and sympathy towards Methodism, and also Congregationalism, and this came to extend to the Jewish Congregation. The Branwells were also Freemasons in the same Redruth Lodge the *Druids Lodge of Love and Liberality* as several of the leading members of the Jewish community, including Lemon Hart and Lemon Woolf. A Richard Branwell (1744-1812), or, possibly his son Richard (1771-1815) is named as a member of the lodge in 1808, and Thomas Branwell (b. 1801) in 1826.[547] Another Thomas Branwell (1746-1808) had married Anne Carne (1743-1809) in 1768, the year in which the first synagogue was built on Branwell land. Their daughter, Maria, was born in 1783.

Thomas Branwell (1746-1808) was a prominent member of the Town Corporation and a successful grocer and tea merchant who was involved in the import trade. He owned bonded warehouses and cellars on the Quay (near St. Mary's Church, and at the bottom of Chapel Street) where imported luxury goods (tea, brandy, wines and snuff) were processed through the Customs House before being sold in his shop in the Market Square. He had also invested in property around the town, including the Golden Lion Inn in the same square and a brewery.[548] These business interests would also have brought him into contact with Lemon Hart and Lemon Woolf. Lemon Hart occupied premises near St. Mary's churchyard, some of which may have extended to similar warehouses, and was involved in the import of Jamaica rum. As we have seen earlier, Thomas Branwell acted as Executor in Trust to the estate of Thomas Solomon, a former jeweller, in October 1793.

Members of the Branwell family were involved in the development of some of the town's most important buildings, including the former Assembly Rooms in Chapel Street (now incorporated into the Union Hotel), the Masonic Lodge (just across from the synagogue), and a large Millhouse, named after them. They also owned land in the Leskinnick area of the town, where the burial ground came to be established on plots owned by the Rogers and Barham families, later subleased to the Borlase family. The Penzance of the late 18th and early 19th century was, therefore, a far more prosperous and cultured town than its far-flung location might suggest. Sea trade, fishing and tin-mining had made it the most important banking centre in Cornwall. The Bolitho family bank held substantial investments for the Branwells as it did for most of the other traders in the town,[549] including Jewish traders, and it was also involved in the Jewish congregation's financial arrangements.

Thomas Branwell's wife, Anne Carne, was a Penzance silversmith's daughter. They had eleven children in all, at least three dying in infancy,[550] and possibly two

The Branwell Family of Penzance

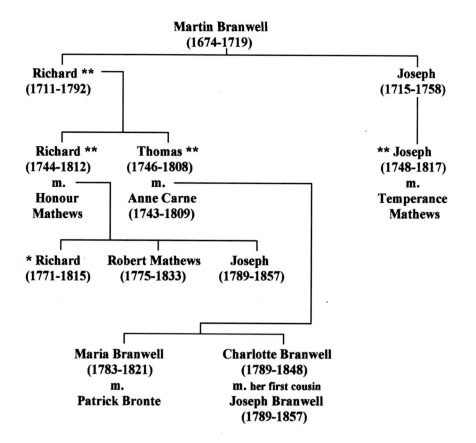

Joseph Branwell Sutherland (1777-1844), a contemporary of the three men
above*, and his son Joseph Branwell (1810-1850) may have been members of the
Branwell family. J. B. Sutherland is named in the Penzance Congregational
Accounts as the lessor and recipient of rental payments for the (second)
synagogue in 1808. The name of Joseph Branwell (died 1817) or possibly his
namesake (died 1850) also appear. The lessor of the first synagogue of 1768 could
have been any of the Branwell men above (**).

Source: P. A. S. Pool (1990)
Keith Pearce © (2013)

others in childhood. Soon after the second synagogue had been built, Thomas Branwell died in 1808 and his wife died the following year, both just after the completion of the second synagogue. Their son Benjamin continued his father's businesses and became Mayor in 1809. By 1841 the Branwells were still carrying on a flourishing and expanding business in the town.[551] There were four daughters, including Maria. In 1811, she moved to Yorkshire to live with her aunt, Jane Fennell, to work in the Methodist boarding school run by Jane's husband, the Rev. John Fennel. There, Maria met and married the Rev. Patrick Brontë, the minister of Hartshead, and they became the parents of the famous Brontë sisters.[552] It is not surprising, therefore, that the Branwell family with its free-thinking tradition, its links with Non-Conformists, and its close involvement with and sympathy towards the Jewish community of Penzance should have produced the independent-minded sisters who, for their day, were radical novelists.

---

[238] Defoe (1724) edit. Rogers (1986) p. 233. Pool (1974) p. 70, includes this passage, and references it to the Rogers edition of 1971: curiously, he gives "prosperous" for "populous". Rogers (1986) notes (p. 38) that "The errata to the first edition have been silently incorporated…".

[239] Pool (1974) p. 131.

[240] I have edited this passage from the report (see note below) in the interests of continuity.

[241] See Pool (1974) pp. 70-82, 88-89, 130-134 & 142-144. J. A. Paris, *Guide to Mount's Bay* (1816) p. 12; A. H. Moncure Sine, *Penzance Congregational Church* (1662-1936) p. 13; G. T. Clark, *Report on the Sanitary Condition of Penzance* (1849).

[242] Pool (1974) pp. 104-127, 132-133, 141-144, 149, & 158-162.

[243] Pool (1974) pp. 228, 230, 254 & 273.

[244] The eminent genealogist Sir Thomas Colyer-Fergusson is believed to have compiled an annotated family tree of the Harts in the early part of this century from information which he may, in part, have received from descendants of the Harts then living in London. To what extent the input of these family descendants can be regarded as accurate, or what sources, if any, they drew upon, is unknown. A copy of these documents, apparently in Colyer-Fergusson's handwriting, has survived, and the details given in this introductory paragraph are drawn directly from these documents as a tentative reconstruction of the family's origins. The Colyer-Fergusson Collection is owned by the Jewish Historical Society of England, and was formerly placed on long-term loan deposit at University College, London. It is now in the safekeeping of the Society of Genealogists where it is on indefinite loan. I am grateful to the Society of Genealogists for permission to draw extensively on Colyer-Fergusson's family tree of the Harts.

[245] Colyer-Fergusson states only that: "…..the present name of the family in Germany is Altstadter", and does not give a surname for the family before Abraham Hart (b. 1784).

[246] Colyer-Fergusson's handwritten family tree is difficult to decipher at this point, with a broken line that does not clearly link Abraham Hart with Moses and Asher Hart, and a double mark of descent that appears to link Joshua with Moses. The intention of the line-break may have been to indicate that

Moses was a son of Joshua (above) but that Asher should be taken as a continuation of the (sibling) link with Abraham. I have favoured the latter interpretation.

[247] Ledger in the Morrab Library, Penzance, p.115: Research by Godfrey Simmons. Rev. William Borlase was the first clergyman in Cornwall to be admitted as a member of the Masons, at the Falmouth *Lodge of Love and Honour*, on 26th September 1751: (Osb. FM p. 266). See later pp. 269-270.)

[248] They are to be found in the Royal Institution of Cornwall Library, Truro, p.56-96: research by Godfrey Simmons. Leslie Douch (2001) has also provided me with some of this information.

[249] David Stacey, *A Gentleman and a Miner, by John Opie*, in the Journal of the Royal Institution of Cornwall (2011) pp. 7-14.

[250] Earland, *John Opie and His Circle* (1911) pp. 30-33 & 350; *John Opie* (Arts Council Catalogue 1962-3); Viv Hendra, *The Cornish Wonder: A Portrait of John Opie* (2007) pp. 22-25, 33, 37, 45 & 53. Neither Earland or the Arts Council Catalogue refer to the painting as that of a Rabbi of Penzance, but simply as "The Old Jew", and none of the publications listed give a primary source reference that would confirm the ascription by Hendra (p. 58f.) that the painting is that of a Rabbi of Penzance. The Royal Institution of Cornwall, which exhibited the painting for many years, do not have any information in their records that would throw light on the identity of the sitter (Letter from Margaret Morgan, Documentation Officer, RIC Truro, to Godfrey Simmons, 17th November 2009).

[251] Hendra (2007) pp. 45-47.

[252] RIC Truro; ref. 26D / 66, p. 16 (Information from Leslie Douch).

[253] It was acquired by the Penlee Museum, Penzance in 2009, where its description as *probably* belonging to Abraham Hart is questionable.

[254] Susser (1993) p. 32. Obviously, Susser was unaware of the Borlase source. The clockface was for many years in the Head Office of Allied Domecq.

[255] Brown (1961) p. 69.

[256] Susser (1993) pp. 94 & 293.

[257] PRO.CUST. 68/11.

[258] H. Miles Brown (1961) pp. 68-70, mentions some of these men. Other sources, such as Insurance Policies (see below) confirm the further names given.

[259] See M. Cooper, *Robbing the Sparry Garniture, A 200 Hundred Year History of British Mineral Dealers 1750 to 1950* (Arizona 2006) pp. 17 & 112; P. A. S. Pool, *William Borlase* (RIC Truro 1986): various Index references, especially under *Cornish Diamonds, Costa, Minerals* and *Royal Society*.

[260] George Rude (1971) pp. 53-56, and Roy Porter (1982) p. 78.

[261] Geoffery Cantor, *The Rise and Fall of Emanuel Mendes da Costa*, in the English Historical Review, Vol. CXVI, No. 467 (June 2001) p. 587; Katz (2001) pp. 224-225, 269 & 271; Endelman (1979) pp. 125 & 262-264; (2002) p. 258.

[262] Cantor (2001) p. 600.

[263] Cantor (2001) p. 589.

[264] *Collectanea Cornubiensia*, 1501.

[265] Susser (1993) pp. 35, 38-9, 225, 236, 257-8 & 328.

[266] Cooper (2006) p. 33.

[267] Letter from Justin Brooke to Keith Pearce (3rd January 2000).

[268] Shakespeare, *Twelfth Night*, Act II, sc. iii, l. 27; *Henry IV* pt. II, Act V, sc. iii, l. 47; *The Merry Wives of Windsor*, Act IV, sc. ii, l. 171; Spenser, *Faerie Queene*, Book 1, Cantos i, 6, & vii, 14; Book 2, Canto v, 28; Book 3, Canto ii, 20 & viii, 40; Book 4, Canto i, 9; Book 5, Canto viii, 2.

[269] The Archives of Allied Domecq plc.; Research by Tony Pawlyn from Merchant Shipping Registers, Penzance (1786-1823); Green (1989) p. 203.

[270] Roth (1950) pp. 59 & 30.

[271] Susser (1993) p. 230; Berger (2004) pp. 202-203; Faber (1998) p. 241.

[272] PRO RG11; piece 0170; folio 96; p. 1.

[273] Colyer-Fergusson does not give a sister of Lemon Hart with the name Eddle, but only an aunt Edel (b. 1747); however Joseph (1975, facing p. 26) does give Eddle as Lemon Hart's sister. They are in agreement that his other sisters were Rebecca and Leah.

[274] Records of United Rum Distillers, the Company which once owned the LEMON HART ® rum Label. LEMON HART ® rum was still produced under its own name as a registered trade mark of Allied Domecq Spirits & Wine Limited in the 1990s. I received from this Company various information from

their records including a portrait of Lemon Hart, images of the LEMON HART ® rum label, and other illustrations commissioned by United Distillers as promotional material, and supplied by Allied Domecq from their archives. Letters and enclosures from Joanne Liddle of Allied Domecq to Keith Pearce (4th & 10th February 1999) summarising information from their cumulative archival records. The Lemon Hart brand was later acquired by *Pernod Ricard*, and in 2010 by the company *Mosaiq Inc.* based in Quebec, Canada.

[275] *The Times*, 3rd February 1820, page 3, col. G. (Research by Jackie Hill 2004).

[276] Anthony P. Joseph (1975) pp. 26-7.

[277] Faber (1998) pp. 74, 136, 159, 162-3, 203, 205, 208, 219, 222, 233-4, 244, 247 & 250. There are also various references to *Hart* in Jacob Andrade's *A Record of the Jews of Jamaica from the English Conquest to the Present Time* (1941).

[278] Faber (1998) pp. 129-130.

[279] Congregational Accounts of May 14th 1815.

[280] Letters to Godfrey Simmons from Bernard Hooker (11th January 1998) and Rev. Ernest H. de Souza of Kingston, Jamaica (14th August 1998).

[281] The information on ships and ship-owning in this chapter, as well as some other material, has been provided from extensive research by Tony Pawlyn, a Trustee of the Cornwall Maritime Museum at Falmouth where it is intended to establish a maritime research library.

[282] Merchant Shipping Registers, Penzance (CRO, MSR, Penzance 1786-1823). Of these co-owners, Thomas Love (-1812) was a merchant of the firm *Love, Ellis & Co.* (Bailey's Directory 1783). It is likely, but not certain, that *Ellis* was a John Ellis (of whom there were several). The will of Thomas Love (made in 1795) shows that he owned two houses with gardens in the vicinity of lower Chapel street (possibly near the Abbey Slip), and the (1803) will of John Ellis (1761-1809) of Lambessow rfers to a "dwelling house cellar and premises situate near the Quay in the town of Penzance now held by Mr. Lazarus Hart as tenant". I am grateful to Charlotte MacKenzie for permission to include this information from her research (2014).

[283] The Penzance Custom House Out-Port Letter Books do not contain the original documents, but are contemporary fair copies made by the Customs House Clerks. They exist in a very extensive range of 200 unnumbered folio volumes, copied roughly in date order. They appear to be the original copies kept at Penzance. They can be found at the Public Records Office at Kew where the Cornwall books are filed under PRO.CUST 66-69. The Penzance books are numbered PRO.CUST 68. The *Nancy & Betsy* plantation certificates are to be found as PRO.CUST 68/13 & 68/15.

[284] PRO.CUST 68/14: Research by Godfrey Simmons (1997).

[285] This reference may have led to the mistaken notion that Borlase had bought candlesticks from *Abraham* Hart.

[286] Leslie Douch (2000) provided this material from his research.

[287] Guildhall Library Manuscripts (GLM) MS11936 Vol. 257, Policy No. 383575 (Letter from Kathryn Atkin to Keith Pearce: 16th November 2000). Note: the year given for each policy presumes the renewal of the policy from the previous year. Hence the first policy of Lazarus Hart covers 1777-1778, and so on.

[288] GLM MS 11936 Vol. 331, No. 508170 (Helen Fry 2000).

[289] GLM MS 7253 Vol. 36, No. 168172 (HF 2000). George Rigal has also provided comprehensive details of all of these and other Hart family policies, together with Insurance details of a wide range of other Cornish Jewish policies (10th February 2000).

[290] PRO.CUST 68/18: Research by Godfrey Simmons (1997).

[291] Letter from Tony Pawlyn to Godfrey Simmons (8th December 1998).

[292] Lemon Hart's wife, Letitia Michael of Swansea, is recorded in the miscellaneous papers of Cecil Roth in the Brotherton Library in Leeds, in a letter addressed to Roth, dated 25th February 1955, from Geoffrey H. White, Editor of *The Complete Peerage*, and a descendant [research by Evelyn Friedlander 1999]. The information on the Michael family of Swansea has been provided from their research by Anthony P. Joseph, Godfrey Simmons and by Michael Jolles. See M. Jolles, *A Directory of Distinguished British Jews, 1830-1930* (2000) pp. 37-39.

[293] Roth (1950) p. 103 gives the year as 1741; Jolles (above) indicates the year as 1749. I am grateful to Godfrey Simmons for advising on the Hart-Michael connections.

[294] Colyer-Fergusson.

[295] Roth (1950) p. 103-104 (note).

[296] Angela Shire (1999) p. 30: ref. 88/43. Note: Colyer-Fergusson's pedigree and the *Collectanea Cornubiensia,* 325, give the date of the marriage, incorrectly, as *29th* July.

[297] *One and All,* November 1868 & *Collectanea Cornubiensis,* CC 325, RIC Truro (Note, as above that both of these sources contain errors). cf. also a letter from Wilfred Samuel to Alex Jacob, dated 14th March 1955 in the Jacob Archive.

[298] Shire (1999) pp. 14, 23 & 81: refs. 43/3, 67/5 & 231/34.

[299] Obituary: *The Gentleman's Magazine,* October 1852, p. 659 (Helen Fry 2000).

[300] Susser (1993) p. 253: his information is largely drawn, as he acknowledges (on p.331) from Charles Thomas (1959, pp. 11-12). See also Pool (1974) pp. 110-111.

[301] *The Royal Cornwall Gazette,* 12th November 1803 reporting from the War Office announcement of 8th November in the *London Gazette* (Tony Pawlyn).

[302] Letter to Keith Pearce from Michael Michell (January 2009).

[303] Susser, *op. cit.,* p. 236 & 323; c.f. *Jewish Chronicle,* 17th June 1881, and Colyer-Fergusson.

[304] For the information on the Pidwell family, I am greatly indebted to a descendant of the Pidwell family, Jackie Hill, for providing me with information from her research (from 2000).

[305] George Clement Boase (1829-1897) *Reminiscences of Penzance* (pub. 1976; edit Pool) pp. 31 & 61-70.

[306] Paul Parish Baptismal Records & Soc. Gen. Trans. CO/R4.49 (Evelyn Armitage 2003).

[307] Warn's Trade Directory for Falmouth (1864) p. 94.

[308] Guildhall Library Ref. Ms. 17827/2 (Research by Evelyn Armitage; Letter to Keith Pearce, 5th September 2003). Waltham Forest Records (London) refer, correctly, to Mary, aged 49 in 1863, as born in the Parish of Paul, near Penzance. Information has been provided by Josephine Parker, Archivist of the Waltham Forest Archives in a letter and enclosures to Helen Fry, 26th February 1999; and letter to Keith Pearce dated 23rd March 1999 from Christine North, County Archivist, CRO, Truro.

[309] Colyer-Fergusson.

[310] Jackie Hill (2008 & 2009).

[311] Colyer-Fergusson gives Rebecca's date of death as 1866; Anthony Joseph gives it as 1864.

[312] Colyer-Fergusson; Susser, *op. cit.,* p. 236 & 323; *Jewish Chronicle,* 17th June 1881.

[313] These details have been repeated (without substantiating evidence) in various minor publications and articles.

[314] Susser Census Survey (1995) p. 12.

[315] Jessop (1951) reprint Gent (2000) pp. 3, 4 (n. 52) & 11 (n. 19).

[316] Lemon Woolf's headstone in the Penzance cemetery bears this patronymic.

[317] Susser (1972) p. 34.

[318] Susser (1972) p. 37.

[319] Susser (1972) p. 39 & (1993) p. 105.

[320] Susser (1972) p. 9.

[321] Susser (1972) p. 39

[322] Susser (1995) p. 233; Nathaniel Hart does not appear in Susser's 1861 Census survey.

[323] Susser (1972) p. 37.

[324] Susser (1993) p. 211.

[325] Susser (1972) p. 37.

[326] Susser (1993) p. 232 & (1972) p. 39

[327] His Hebrew names, along with those of some of the others mentioned above, are listed in Susser's (unpublished) ledger of communal deaths in Plymouth, the *Pinkus* or *Pinkes,* which consists of 139 Hebrew patronymics, only 50 of which Susser was able to identify. The Ledger may be incomplete. I am grateful to Helen Fry for supplying me with a copy of the Ledger (April 2013).

[328] See Susser (1972) Hoe Cemetery Survey, pp. 31-32.

[329] Green (1989) p. 147. Lemon Hart's first wife has also been given as "Mary Wolf" (*d.* 10th October 1803), but I have not found independent evidence of this. It seems likely that this name reflects a confusion and conflation of the surname of Lemon Hart's mother (Rebecca Woolf), and the forenames of his second wife (Mary Solomon) and his daughter-in-law (Mary Pidwell). It is possible that an unconnected Mary Wolf died in Penzance on the same day as Letitia Michael. A daughter of Lemon Hart's son, David, was named Leitita (1838-) and Jessop (1951) suggests that Lemon Hart's sister, Rebecca (1766-1841) named a daughter *Letitia,* and his daughter, Rebecca (1796-1874) did likewise. The name *Letitia*

passed down in the Hart and Michael families, and *Lemon* (as a forename) and *Hart* (as a middle name) were passed down through the *Michael* family.

[330] Roth (1933).

[331] Evelyn Friedlander, *Lemon Hart,* in "The Jews of Devon and Cornwall"(The Hidden Legacy Foundation 2000) p. 37.

[332] See Peter Thorold's *The London Rich, The Creation of a Great City From 1666 to the Present* (New York 2000).

[333] George Rigal (Letter of 21st January 2000).

[334] PROB II/2052 (from a copy in Godfrey Simmons archive).

[335] Green (1989) p. 147.

[336] See the Insurance Policy in the Trades section, below.

[337] Green (1989) p. 193, nt. 1.

[338] A. Cecil Hampshire, *Just An Old Navy Custom* (William Kimber 1979) pp. 40-41; James Pack, *Nelson's Blood* (Maryland 1983) pp. 8-17, 82, 121, 135-136.

[339] C.f Joanne Liddle (*op.cit.,*) and Roth (Chapter 4, *op.cit.,*). Geoffrey Green (*op.cit.*, p.147); ref. extensive searches of the official Naval victualling records held at the PRO Kew (ADM 109-111; 111/270 & 284; 112/160-1, 197-8 & 212; & 113) and the National Maritime Museum, Greenwich (ADM: C 729-731 & DP 31 A&B.): research by Peter Towey (1997-1999). The Hart Business and Estate Papers (1806-1848) include an authenticated copy of the co-partnership agreement between Lemon Hart and his nephew Jacob James Jacobs (Ms. 10,622, Guildhall Library, London): research by Michael Gandy (December 1997), and Helen Fry (2000). The latter's transcript of the agreement has been made available to the present writer.

[340] Letter to Keith Pearce from George Rigal (6th April 2000).

[341] Geoffrey Green (1989) p. 147.

[342] Transcriptions by Helen Fry (2000).

[343] GHL Policy No. 968088 (George Rigal 2000).

[344] Joanne Liddle, *op. cit.*

[345] *Jewish Chronicle*, 31st October 1845 (p. 15).

[346] *Muirhead's Great Britain* (1930) p. 37.

[347] *Jewish Chronicle* (as above); *The Gentleman's Magazine*, 13th October 1845 (p. 662: Helen Fry 2000). It should be noted that the death certificate records Lemon Hart's age at the time of his death as 76, whereas the *JC* obituary notice gives 77. The Brady Street cemetery headstone appears to give 76 (although the barely legible digit could be 8). Colyer-Fergusson's genealogy records that Lemon Hart had been born in November of 1768. The *Collectanea Cornubiensia*, 325, gives the date, place of death and Lemon Hart's age at the time of his of death incorrectly as 7th October in Penzance, age 75.

[348] *The Times,* 7th June 1854, p. 11.

[349] *West Briton* 5th November 1852.

[350] See the case of Henry Branscombe, publican at Mile-end in *The Times*, 29th April 1858, p. 11); *The Times*, 27th October 1874, p. 4. I am grateful to Jackie Hill for her research into the various items from *The Times* from 1847-1874 relating to the Hart family firms.

[351] *The Times*, 26th November 1847, p. 5; 19th January 1849, p. 8, and 14th March 1849, p. 7; Green (*op. cit.*, p.147 & p. 193): *The Jewish Chronicle* of 31st August 1849; Letter from Geoffrey Green to Keith Pearce, 21st September 2004; *The Times*, 7th May 1852 & 3rd January 1860 for 40,000 gals. (p. 6).

[352] Green (1989) pp. 197-213.

[353] Roth (1933).

[354] *The Times*, 9th January 1863, p. 3. (See also *The Times*, 10th October 1862).

[355] *The Times*, 22nd November 1870, p. 5.

[356] *The Times*, Tuesday 27th October 1874, p. 9; *The Times*, 14th October 1874 (p. 6); 20th January 1875 (p.11); 2nd August 1875 (p. 10) and 5th February 1877 (p.11): *Ex Parte Young, Re Lemon Hart & Son; The Times*, 7th June 1854 (p. 11).

[357] The records of Allied Domecq.

[358] Jackie Hill (2004).

[359] By the Canadian company *Mosiaq Inc.* of Quebec.

[360] Pool (1974) pp. 101-102.

[361] *Collectanea Cornubiensia*, vol 3, c.c. 1510, 1534, 1563-4.

[362] See also Pool (1974) p. 262.

[363] Pool (1974) p. 275.

[364] A letter from Stephen Pyke to Alex Jacob, dated 13th April 1949, gives Abraham as the bankrupt, but, an earlier letter from W. S. Jessop of Chicago to Cecil Roth dated 20th July 1948 (in the Roth Collection, Leeds) states (incorrectly) that it was his father Joseph Joseph who was involved in the Woolf case. In fact, Joseph Joseph's bankruptcy had been fourteen years earlier, in 1816. Anthony Joseph (1975, p. 28) gives the year of Joseph Joseph's bankruptcy adjudication as 1821, but a bankruptcy after that of 1816 has not been identified.

[365] George Elwick, *The Bankrupt Directory 1820-1840* (1843) p. 233: research by John Simmons (2000). Letters from Abraham Joseph to B.A. Simmons, 29th May 1833 and 10th January 1834, in private archive of Godfrey Simmons.

[366] Susser (1972) pp. 30-31 & (1993) pp. 105-106.

[367] Susser (1972) pp. 31-32 & (1993) p. 106.

[368] Arthur P. Arnold *Apprentices of Great Britain 1710-1773*, in *TJHSE* vol. XXII (1970) pp. 145 & 155.

[369] Susser (1972) p. 90 (Index) and (1973) p. 359 (Index).

[370] Susser (1972) pp. 9 & 36, and (1973) p. 38.

[371] George Rigal & Helen Fry (2000): GHL Nos. 383575 & 508170 (MS 11936, Vols. 257 & 331); No. 168172 (MS 7253, Vol. 36, p. 146).

[372] George Rigal & Helen Fry (2000): GHL Nos. 119915 & 245214.

[373] CRO Truro Ref. FP 179/1/1; 1789-1812. I am grateful to Jackie Hill (Letter of 14th February 2006) for this burial entry, and to Deborah Tritton of CRO Truro for copies of the original entries (2nd March 2006: Letter to Keith Pearce).

[374] Raymond Lamont-Brown, *Humphry Davy* (Sutton 2004) pp. 11-12, 14-15, & 51.

[375] Pool (1974) pp. 84-85: Pool's dates for Coryton's incumbency are 1788-1806.

[376] The Gospel of John, Ch. 20 vv. 19-29.

[377] The Gospel of John, Ch. 11 vv. 1-44.

[378] H. Miles Brown (1970 ed.) p. 81.

[379] George Rigal & Helen Fry (2000): GHL Nos. 208744, 227621 & 236272.

[380] Green (*op.cit.* p.147).

[381] 1871 Census records.

[382] GR & HF (2000): GHL Nos. 235360, 247107 and 287589.

[383] Green (1989) p. 212.

[384] Original in the Archive of Godfrey Simmons.

[385] I am grateful to Tony Pawlyn for providing information from his research on the Cornish prisoners (Letter and enclosures to Godfrey Simmons 3rd August 2000).

[386] This genealogical information on the Magnus family has been supplied from research by Angela Shire from Dutch and English civil and synagogue records (Letters from Angela Shire, 23rd January 2000, 11th February 200 & 12th March 2000). I have taken the information on Elias Magnus' involvement in Penzance congregational and community life from local records.

[387] The *de Pass* family were members of this congregation, Alfred Aaron de Pass later buying the freehold of the Falmouth (Penryn) Jewish cemetery.

[388] *Collectanea Cornubiensia*, 1527 & 1548.

[389] George Rigal & Helen Fry (2000): GHL No. 282443.

[390] *Collectanea Cornubiensia*, 1536.

[391] Cooper (2006) pp. 197-8.

[392] Helen Fry (2000).

[393] Research by Godfrey Simmons from the original records at CRO Truro.

[394] Susser (1995) p. 58.

[395] Susser (1993) pp. 40, 48-9, 83 and 215; Exeter Directory (1792).

[396] Jackie Hill (2009).

[397] Helen Fry (2000).

[398] Jackie Hill (2005).

[399] Obituary notice in *The Jewish Chronicle* (26th August 1904): Anthony Joseph (2004).

[400] His will (proved 21st November 1877 in Bodmin) records effects under £4,000 (Helen Fry 2000).

[401] In *The Lost Jews of Cornwall* (2000) Lavin's upholstery store was incorrectly identified as a business

of Henry Levin and as belonging to the same family.

[402] Cooper (2006) p. 203.

[403] Helen Fry (2000).

[404] George Clement Boase *Reminiscences of Penzance* (edit. Pool 1976) p. 27; Cooper (2006) p. 203.

[405] Helen Fry (2000).

[406] John Simmons (2000).

[407] *The London Gazette*, 12th October 1816, p. 1967, and 28th December 1816, p. 2483; Green (1989) p. 148; Susser (1993) p. 106; & PRO ADM 15/2 Solicitors' Papers.

[408] Susser (1972) p. 22 & the *Exeter Flying Post* 14th February 1828 (Helen Fry 2002).

[409] Letters from Abraham Joseph to B.A, Simmons from Plymouth, dated 29th May 1833 & 10th January 1834; letter dated 1856 from Savile Row to the Chief Rabbi, Dr. Adler (to whom Abraham Joseph was distantly related). Originals in the possession of Godfrey Simmons. Susser (1993) pp. 105-106, & 247; Jessop (1951: reprint Gent 2000) pp. 10 & 13-17.

[410] Susser, Hoe Cemetery (1972) p. 22; Jessop (1951) pub. Gent (2000) pp. 13-17.

[411] Minute Book: entries from May to October 9th 1811.

[412] 1891 Census (RG/12/60 Folio 106 p. 10). Research by Jackie Hill (2005).

[413] Records of Anthony Joseph. Jessop (1951) gives her surname as *Solomon*.

[414] Jackie Hill (2009).

[415] Cornwall Online Census Project.

[416] Jackie Hill (2011).

[417] *Tapp's Plymouth Directory,* 1822; Susser (1993) pp. 55, 258 & 332, (1995) pp. 29 & 37; Plymouth Hebrew Congregational Marriage Register.

[418] Susser (1972) p. 20.

[419] The name occurs throughout the Book of Ruth, and also in I Kings 7:21; I Chron. 2:12; & 2 Chron. 3:17. It also appears in the Gospels in Mat. 1:5 & Lk. 3:32.

[420] G. Pawley White, *A Handbook of Cornish Surnames* (Third Edition 1999) p. 14.

[421] Susser (1972) p. 9.

[422] W. Cornish, *Directory of Penzance* (1864) p. 33.

[423] *Jewish Chronicle* 4th June 1869; Letter from David Jacobs 21st March 2000.

[424] Hugh Miners, *The Story of the Bristol Cornish* (1975, pp. 2-5, 8, 19 & 48-9) and the *Western Daily Press,* 4th & 21st October 1901; 16th October & 6th December 1902. Israel Oppenheim was, as noted, an only son. Miners (p. 8) is incorrect, therefore, in saying that Israel Oppenheim traded with a brother in Bristol. This is most likely a confusion with the oldest son, Henry, who was about thirty in 1901-02: Letter from David M. Jacobs to Keith Pearce, dated 2nd January 1989. David Jacob's maternal grandmother was Israel Oppenheim's daughter Annie. Judith Samuel: 1997, p.148-150 & 169). Letter from Anthony P. Joseph, 26th March 1999]. Research from the 1901 Census for Bristol by Jackie Hill (2005): ref. RG13/2401 Folio 39 p. 82; RG13/2376 Folio 66 p. 27 & RG13/2369 Folio 119 p. 8.

[425] Letter from David Jacobs 4th February 2000, in which he refers to photographs of the girls in his possession taken marked with addresses in Landau, and to a German-English dictionary belonging to his grandmother Hannah (Annie) inscribed with her signature, and dated, Landau 1880.

[426] This address in Causewayhead can be inferred from the marriage certificates of his daughter and his son, of 11th November 1846 and 1st September 1847.

[427] 1851 Census. In the 1901 Census for Tottenham, Alfred Selig is given as 57 years of age. This would give a birth year of 1844, and may be an incorrect entry.

[428] *West Briton* 8th July 1842 (Jackie Hill 2007).

[429] Anthony P. Joseph (1970, p. 32).

[430] Research from 1881 & 1901 Census records by Jackie Hill (2005).

[431] *West Briton*, 6th January 1843, 26th February 1847, & 2nd April 1847: Jackie Hill (2009).

[432] His Will (proved 7th February 1882 at Bodmin) records a personal estate of £1,506, left to his sons, Barnet Henry Joseph and Joseph Joseph, both Merchants, of 20 Frederick Street, Birmingham (Helen Fry 2000).

[433] *Collectanea Cornubiensia 437.*

[434] Archive of Alex Jacob, the register having been in the possession of a Mrs. Charles King of London.

[435] A note by Alex Jacob attached to the register, referring to information from his father.

[436] Temple Parish; Piece No. 1947; District 29; Folio 3: Household Schedule No. 12): research by Anthony

P. Joseph and Jackie Hill (2004).

[437] Letter from Jackie Hill to Keith Pearce (17th February 2004).

[438] (1871 Census): RG10/3083 Folio 16 (p. 26) & (1881 Census): RG 11/2203 Folio 64 (p. 35): Jackie Hill (2005).

[439] RG 12/913 Folio 80 (p. 18): Jackie Hill (2005).

[440] Anthony Joseph (1975) p. 36.

[441] (1871 Census): RG/10/515 Folio 68 (p. 24): Jackie Hill (2005).

[442] Roth (1933) and Jessop (1951).

[443] Susser (1993) p. 322.

[444] Jessop (1951) re-printed 2000, p. 69.

[445] Frank Gent in *The Jews of Devon and Cornwall* (2000) pp. 51-52 correctly identifies the Ezekiel family links from original sources, including the leases. The flawed Jessop pedigree of the Ezekiel family (pub. Frank Gent, Crediton 2000) is reproduced on p. 69 without amendment. See also Susser (1993) pp. 48, 94, 99, 128-129, 208, 213-215, 258, 306, n.116, 322 & 332.

[446] *Exeter Flying Post,* 3rd August 1815 (Helen Fry 2000).

[447] *Biblioteca Cornubiensis,* Vol. 1: 145.

[448] Reprinted in *The Cornish Telegraph* (13th March 1867) four days after the occasion of Solomon Ezekiel's death.

[449] Helen Fry (2000)..

[450] See the chapter on the Rabbis.

[451] *Exeter Flying Post,* 7th March 1833: Helen Fry (2000).

[452] M. Jolles (1999-2000): *A Directory of Distinguished British Jews 1830-1930,* p. 220.

[453] Helen Fry (2000).

[454] Ref. RG12/181 Folio 201 (p. 32) and RG12/913 Folio 80 (p. 18): Jackie Hill (2005).

[455] His Will (proved on 6th May 1887 in London) records a personal estate of £701, left to his brother, Alexander Levin of Birmingham, as next of kin: Helen Fry (2000).

[456] Pool (1974) pp. 121 & 156-157.

[457] Contrary to Sharman Kadish, *Jewish Heritage in England* (English Heritage 2006) p. 94, col. 2.

[458] Helen Fry (2000).

[459] A. L. Rowse, *Tudor Cornwall* (1941-57) p. 27; Berresford Ellis ((1974) pp. 74 & 91.

[460] George Rigal (2000).

[461] Letters and documents from his descendants: Esther Fishman (August 17th 1998 and 8th December 1999) and Stuart Raine (27th October 1998).

[462] Information drawn from research by David James (1999), a descendant of Frederick and Emily Lazarus, and Jackie Hill (2005).

[463] Apart from my own research, I have received information and copies of original documents relating to the Bischofswerder family from various descendants, including Victor Bishop (1920-2004) grandson of George Bischofswerder, Sidney Schultz, Ivan Segal, Barry and Mark Monk, Linda Graicher, Harold Dunham, David Samuelson, Keith and Marian Harper, Professor Peter Mittler and Andy Bishop. I am also grateful to those who have sent me details of the family from their research into census and other public records, including Helen Fry, Trudy Martin, and Jackie Hill.

[464] The information from Kelly's Directories 1883-1910 has been provided from research by Graham Rogers (1999).

[465] Dunham and Samuelson (1989-1999) p. 1.

[466] I am grateful to Mark Monk for providing me with a translation of the sections of the register that relate to the Bischofswerder family. See also Susser (1993) pp. 282 & 306.

[467] Information from Professor Peter Mittler, a descendant of this family (Letter of 13th December 2008).

[468] I am grateful to Harold Dunham and David W. Samuelson for making available a copy of their book, *Bertie: The Life and Times of G. B. Samuelson* (Privately produced 1889-1999) from which details of the Weile-Samuelson marriage have been drawn (pp. 1-37).

[469] PRO RG11; Piece 3750; Folio 45, p. 20 (Research by Jackie Hill 2002).

[470] Letter to Keith Pearce from T. Knowles, Court Service Probate Registry Searches, York, 16th December 1999.

[471] Details from Mark Monk (5th October 2000) and see Susser (1993) pp. 282, 288, 290 & 306.

[472] Susser (1993) p. 282 records that, in his register, Pearlson had written that he had married Yetta

Bischofswerder "In Newcastle on Tyne". It is possible that this phrase, in the original Hebrew, was intended to refer to some previous record, such as his appointment to that place, but could be read (without a break) as introducing the reference to the marriage.

[473] There is no record of a marriage certificate in Penzance.

[474] I am grateful to Helen Fry for this detail.

[475] Justin Brooke, an expert on Cornish Mining, and the Executor of the papers of the Cornish historian, the late A. K. Hamilton-Jenkin, recalled (in a letter to Keith Pearce, 3rd January 2000) that he had seen a note to the effect that David Bischofswerder had made "a fortune" from the purchase of the Schiller salvage, the note being in one of the deceased's notebooks from the 1920s that had been deposited at the County Record Office, Truro. He also refers to a note that David Bischofswerder was "an illicit diamond buyer". However, these items have not been identified amongst the Hamilton-Jenkin papers there (CRO ref. AD 621/2: Letter from David Thomas, Archivist, to Keith Pearce, 3rd January 2000). These claims concerning David Bischofswerder remain anecdotal and unsubstantiated.

[476] Found on p. 6, and spread over three columns.

[477] Susser (1993) pp. 213, 298 & 319 incorrectly identifies the proprietor and chief philanthropist as Harry. I incorporated this error from Susser into *The Lost Jews of Cornwall* (2000) pp. 193-4, although, after further investigation of the sources, I included an *erratum* upon publication. Curiously, Susser references both the *Royal Cornwall Gazette* report (from which the error could not arise) and that found in the *Jewish Chronicle* (from which it could), but appears not to have registered the discrepancy. There is no reason to suppose, however, that Susser had any familiarity with or detailed knowledge of the Bischofswerder family from which he could have identified the source-error as evident.

[478] *The Cornishman*, August 1st 1889, p. 4, cols 5 & 6; August 8th 1889, p. 8, col. 2. (I have slightly edited some of the extracts from the reports). I am grateful to Elizabeth Brock (1997) for drawing my attention to these two newspaper articles. See also *The Lost Jews of Cornwall* (2000) pp. 298.

[479] G.M.A. Trinnick: *The Tregurtha Downs Mine 1700-1965* (Industrial Archaeology Review Vol. II, No. 2, Spring 1978) pp. 111-127; *The West Briton*, 30th November 1884, 11th June 1885 and 29th October 1891; *Mining Journal*:- 25th April (476), 9th (532) & 28th (504) May 1885; 5th September (1008), 17th (1180) & 24th (1205) October 1891; 5th December (1372) 1891, and 23rd April (459) 1892. Trinnick describes not only the mine's history, but also David Bischofswerder's involvement in it.

[480] Letter from Justin Brooke to Keith Pearce (7th November 2000).

[481] *The Times*, 2nd November 1894, p.10 (Research by Jackie Hill 2004).

[482] The names of the two females in the census are indistinct: Rabbi Pearlson's Register (Letter from Mark Monk to Keith Pearce 5th October 2000).

[483] National Archives of South Africa, MOOC, Vol. 6/9/464; ref. 4423. Research, gravestone transcriptions and photographs by Paul Cheifitz (December 2002; via Saul Isroff).

[484] Joshua Bishop was born on 13th December 1885, but the birth was not registered until 8th July 1886. Original certificate in the possession of Victor Bishop.

[485] These details of his movements are confirmed by the Naturalisation Papers held at PRO KEW Ref. HO 144/374/B18105

[486] Copy of original business card and photographs in the possession of Victor Bishop. Letters from Sidney Schultz to Keith Pearce (10th and 20th January 1999). The letters from Victor Bishop and Sidney Schultz contain their personal recollection of George Bishop and their visits to "St. Michael's Mount", Hull.

[487] Letters from Victor Bishop to Keith Pearce (12th March and 19th June 2001).

[488] Susser (1995-6) p. 61. I am grateful to Helen Fry (2000) for identifying this item, and to Jackie Hill (2003) for a full transcription and source references (Piece RG12/1739; Folio 112, p. 27, Schedule 199).

[489] Plymouth Congregational Marriage Register, and 1881 census. (Susser 1995-6; Helen Fry 2000).

[490] Research by Jackie Hill (2003). The handwritten spelling of the girls' names on the original census sheets (Piece RG12/1739: Folio 74, p. 5, Schedule 34) is difficult to decipher, and the names given above have been inferred. Susser (1995-6) did not record this family in his survey of the 1891 census.

[491] PRO Kew Ref. HO 334/41

[492] Helen Fry (2001).

[493] Information form Keith and Marian Harper in a letter to Keith Pearce (19th June 2009).

[494] Leah had not been born at the time of the 1891 census.

[495] See Pool (1974) pp. 148-149 on the organisation of the Police in 19th century Penzance.

[496] Formerly held at the Penzance Registrar's Office (now at CRO Truro), with a separate file of Jewish marriages (1838-1892). Copies of these various certificates have been drawn from Godfrey Simmons' archive, and others have been provided by various descendants of the Bischofswerder family.

[497] Harold Pollins, *The Jewish Community of Stroud 1877-1908*, in *The Jewish Journal of Sociology,* vol. 38, no. 1 (June 1996) pp. 33-34.

[498] Susser (1993) pp. 82-85 & 236-238.

[499] Original in the possession of Ivan and Sheila Segal.

[500] I am grateful to Jackie Hill (2004) for copies of the original census entries.

[501] Information drawn from copies of family certificates in the possession of Keith Harper (2009).

[502] Public Record Office, Kew: ref. HO 144/657/B38710.

[503] *The Jewish Chronicle,* 28th April 1911 (p. 2). For Morris Bischofswerder, also see Penzance Masonic lists.

[504] Copy of an original provided by Victor Bishop.

[505] Penzance Masonic Lodge records.

[506] PRO Kew HO 144/657/B3871.

[507] PRO Kew HO 144/657/B3871. I am grateful to Anthony Joseph for providing me with information on some of the individuals who married Jews from Penzance (Letter to Keith Pearce of 1st March 2009).

[508] Secondary copies of all of these marriage certificates have been drawn from the Archive of Godfrey Simmons. I am grateful to John Lee, Marriages Section of the General Register Office for National Statistics, Southport for permission to use the personalised data contained in these documents: Letters to Keith Pearce, 12th October & 18th November 1998; also to Rita Collier the Registrar at Penzance who has provided further information on these marriages.

[509] *CFHSoc.Truro.*

[510] The forename *Jacob* was commonly anglicised to *John* by Jews, and *Levy* was a variant of *Levi.*

[511] Susser (1972) p. 22, B68.

[512] HF (2000).

[513] Piece No. 1951, Folio 37, Schedule 161: information from Anthony Joseph and Jackie Hill (2004).

[514] Genealogical records of Anthony Joseph.

[515] Judith Samuel (1997) p. 51.

[516] Plymouth Census returns 1841-1861 (Susser 1995, pp. 25, 36 & 47). The eleven children of Josiah and Rose (Rosetta) Solomon appear in the census returns.

[517] Susser (1972) p. 21, B60.

[518] Research by Jackie Hill (2009).

[519] Susser (1972) p. 21.

[520] Susser (1995) pp. 45 & 51; and research by Jackie Hill (2009): Census ref. HO107/1879 Folio 233 (pp. 28-9), RG9/1443 Folio 78 (p. 24), RG10/2119 Folio 111 (p. 30).

[521] Research from Census records and on British Artists 1880-1940 by Jackie Hill (2009): HO 107/1533 Folio 231 (p. 6), RG9/230 Folio 176 (p. 10), RG10/440 Folio 61 (p. 9), RG11/11 Folio 12 (p. 18) & RG12/5 Folio 70 (pp. 15-16).

[522] Susser (1972) p. 21.

[523] This, and several other items on these marriages from the *West Briton* have been provided by Jackie Hill (2009).

[524] Susser (1972) p. 9.

[525] Research by Jackie Hill (2009) from Census records: HO 107/1532 Folio 33 (p. 25), RG9/229 Folio 45 (p. 15), and RG10/255 Folio 19 (p. 32).

[526] Jackie Hill (2009): Census ref. HO 107/1524 Folio 193 (p. 35).

[527] Birth Register of Samuel Jacob's children (Alex Jacob Archive).

[528] Genealogical Records of Anthony Joseph.

[529] Anthony Joseph (1975) p. 32.

[530] Research by Jackie Hill (2009): Ref. HO107/2452 Folio 552 (p. 5) and RG9/2142 Folio 47 (p. 37), and the family records of Godfrey Simmons.

[531] Copy of an original handwritten family birth register (1778-1858). The compiler of the register is not certain, and the entries may not be contemporaneous, relying upon memory and family tradition: (Archive of Alex Jacob).

[532] Alex Jacob (Archive): in an extract from an undated letter to an unknown family member about the

details in the register

533 Jackie Hill (2009): HO197/2456 Folio 459 (p. 15). *Goodman* families can also be found in the records of the Glamorgan Family History Society.

534 Slater's Commercial Directory 1880 (Jackie Hill: 2009).

535 Jackie Hill (2005).

536 March Qtr 1853, St. Luke Registration District Vol. 1b (p. 651): Jackie Hill (2009).

537 From copy of original marriage certificate. A word following *Levy* is indecipherable.

538 Anthony Joseph (1975) p. 31.

539 Jackie Hill (2009): HO107/2458 Folio 379 (p. 46); RG9/4053 Folio 14 (p. 21); RG10/5395 Folio 15 (p. 22); Rg11/5313 Folio 3 (p. 4).

540 Family research by David James, great grandson of the couple, who has provided marriage and birth certificates and the information that Frederick Lazarus was Jewish: Letter to Keith Pearce (3rd September 1997).

541 *Royal Cornwall Gazette* of 22nd September 1852 (p. 5, col. 5).

542 Jackie Hill (2009) census records: RG10/5382 Folio 47 (p. 11); RG11/5299 Folio 110 (p. 5); RG12/4482 Folio 78 (p. 1).

543 Jackie Hill (2009): census records RG11/3366 Folio 23 (p. 8).

544 Details of the Bischofswerder family and their marriages have been given earlier.

545 Jackie Hill (2009): census records RG9/4053 Folio 30 (p. 15), RG10/5395 Folio 40 (p. 2) & RG11/2981 Folio 47 (pp. 28-9).

546 Family records of Godfrey Simmons, and research by Jackie Hill (2009) from census records (1871-1901): Ref. RG10/2567 Folio 72 (p. 41), RGT11/2956 Folio 104 (p. 70) and RG13/2816 Folio 53 (p. 49).

547 Osborne (1901, p.82 & 112); Pool (1990).

548 Barker (1995, pp. 48-49); Peter Pool (1990).

549 Barker, *op. cit.*, p. 49.

550 Barker, *op. cit.*, p. 48.

551 Barker, *op. cit.*, p. 844, note 72.

552 Barker, *op. cit.*, p. 51ff.

CHAPTER 5
The Jews of Truro

"Truro is a very considerable town…it stands up the water north and by east from Falmouth, in the utmost extended branch of the haven, in the middle, between the conflux of two rivers, which though not of any long course, have a very good appearance for a port. And make a large wharf between them in front of the town; and the water here makes a good port for small ships, though it be at the influx, but not for ships of burthen." (Defoe 1822)

There was a small Jewish population in Truro comprising at any one time of no more than a few families. Susser gives fourteen families in Truro for the period 1748-1844, though not all of these would have been there for any significant length of time, and itinerant hawkers may have been included.[553] Before the early 1800s, trade directories suggest isolated individual names, but it is during the period 1820-1850 that Jewish family businesses are mentioned most frequently. Any significant Jewish presence in Truro was comparatively short-lived from the late 18th to the mid-19th century. Even though such a small community would not have had a rabbi, it did have a *shochet* for a period in the 1820s, although he was most likely the visiting minister from Falmouth.[554] A small burial ground, which may have been a Jewish plot, established sometime around 1780-1800, was abandoned by the 1840s and is no longer to be seen. No documentary evidence of a synagogue in the town has been found. Nevertheless, worship could have taken place in private homes, but Jews would have looked to Falmouth as the nearest established congregation where family ties through marriage and business would draw them. Similar links existed with Penzance.

Trades and Occupations

Levy Emanuel: Silversmith 1748-1763.[555] He had been born in Weisendorf, Germany in 1732, and had landed at Harwich in 1748. He appears to have come to Truro in the same year, remaining there until 1763. After Truro he went to Plymouth, where he lived for 40 years (Plymouth Congregational Minute-Book).[556]

13th November 1770. Two Jews arrested in Truro on suspicion of being involved in the Chelsea murders; also a Jew at Falmouth, on suspicion of being Coshay, one of the gang.

30th December 1770. Sir John Fielding wrote to Truro and Falmouth that, although the arrested Jews probably took part in the robberies, no evidence could be produced, and they should be sent back to Holland.[557]

Isaac van Oven: Spectacle-maker (1771-85).[558] He was born in 1730 at Altona, near Hamburg, and he landed at Harwich in 1751. He lived in London until 1771. After leaving Truro he lived in Plymouth for 18 years.

Solomon Simmons, pedlar, was born in Truro, *c.* 1778 (Su.), and, later, he was in Falmouth (1851 census).
It is not known if he was related to the family of Samuel Simons (1740-1832) of Truro.

Sally (Sarah) Levy (later **Jacob**), was born in Truro, 1783 (Su.), and, later, was in Penzance, (1851 census).

Israel……. (1789 Rate Book).[559]. This likely the same as **Israel Levi** (1797 & 1816 Rate Book).

Symons……Jeweller (Un. 1791). It is possible that this is **Samuel (Solomon) Simons** (1740-1832), or a member of his family.

William Levis (1794), a tenant in Pydar Street (CRO EN337/2).[560] He is unlikely to have been Jewish.

"….son of **Libche**, Truro, shoemaker" (1796). Referenced by Susser as "a scrap of paper (in Hebrew) inserted in a note-book).

John Pentecost **Job** (Br. 1805) Watchmaker, Kenwyn Truro. *Royal Cornwall Gazette* (6th July 1805): a watch lost and returned to Mr. Job. An 1821 Bond upon administration of goods to Elizabeth his mother.[561] He is not known to have been Jewish, and a Jew, unless Christian convert, would not have used a name from a Christian festival. Most likely related to:-

Henrietta Job was born in Truro *c.* 1811. It is not known that she was Jewish, but in 1851 she was recorded as an unmarried Annuitant and a visitor at the home of Edward Banks, a Gentile, and a Draper by trade in Market Street, Falmouth. He was the 24 year old unmarried son of Anna Banks, who may have been a granddaughter of Isaac Polack of Penryn.

Samuel Jacob, son of Moses Jacob of Redruth, married Sarah (Sally), daughter of Israel Levy of Truro on 16th June 1813 (Jacob Archive).

"**Alexander, son of Samuel**, of Truro".[562] (Plymouth Hebrew Congregation Account- Book, 1815-22). He appears to have lived in Truro around 1815, and married Esther, daughter of Judah Moses (1741-1826) of Plymouth.[563] His occupation is not known, but it is possible that the Esther Samuel (45) who appears as a shopkeeper in the 1841 census for Plymouth, was his widow. Alexander Samuel was President of the Plymouth Congregation, and died on 1st August 1832, and was buried in the Hoe Cemetery (A18).[564]

Lyon Levy (1782-1836) a hardwareman and silversmith, from Plymouth traded in Truro from around 1821 to 1829, and he appears in Masonic records for Perranporth (see below). Lyon "Lipe" Levy (*Aryeh Judah ben Zvi*) was married to Leah, another daughter of Judah Moses of Plymouth. The marriage of their daughter, Sarah (a hawker) is listed in the Plymouth Congregation's Marriage Register for 3rd January 1838, where her (late) father's occupation is given as "salesman". Lyon Levy is buried in the Jewish cemetery on Plymouth Hoe.

Another **Lyon Levy**, a Stationer, was born in Truro *c.* 1783. It is not known if he was related to the family of Israel Levy of Truro. In 1861, this Lyon Levy, then 78, was living in Aston, Birmingham, with his wife, Maria (51) who had been born there (1861 Census for Birmingham).[565] The name of the first Lyon Levy appears in the Penzance Congregational Minute-Book in 1821, along with that of Simmons of Truro, the two being partners in a hardware business. *West Briton*: 6th March 1829 (advertisement): "The business partnership of Lyon Levy & Harman Semmons of the Borough of Truro, Jewellers & Hardwaremen, has been dissolved by mutual consent. All debts [outstanding bills] to be paid to Mr. Lyon Levy." (Harman Semmens: see below).

Jacob Levi (1833 & 1835 Rate Book). Not related to Israel Levi. (See below)

Israel ben Naphtali Hirsch, Truro (*c.* 1836). He was a Silversmith from Exeter.[566]

Levy Families of Truro

There were two main *Levy* (or *Levi*) families who were either Jewish or of Jewish descent in Truro. Most significantly, there was the Jewish family of **Israel Levy**, or **Levi** (-1823) [567] who married Hannah (1758-1841) daughter of Alexander Moses of Falmouth. Three of their children married into the Jacob, Levin and Oppenheim families of Penzance, where they settled. Unrelated to them was the family of **Jacob** (John) **Levi**, who married a non-Jew, all of their children being baptised. **Lyon Levy**, a Freemason and Silversmith, from Plymouth, traded in Truro in 1828, and a **Henry** and **Jane Levi**, hawkers, who may have been Jewish, are recorded on the 1841 Census as of "Foreign" origin, in Old Bridge Street. A "Levy" who was a Jeweller appears in Truro from the 1780s (Ba. 1783; Un. 1799), and a **Sally**, or **Sarah Levy**, was born in the town in 1783, later moving to Penzance (1851 census). There were at least two Jews named "Levi" who traded in Truro around the early 1820s: **Israel Levi**, Clothes Dealer, who was trading at 4 High Cross St. by the 1820s, (Pg. 1823/4), his son (?),[568] **Henry Levi** (known as **Levin**), a Clothes-Dealer at East Bridge St. (Pg. 1823/4). This Henry Levin has appeared on various genealogical pedigrees as a son of Israel Levy of Truro, but without dates or marital status. It is possible that he was associated with (rather than closely related to) the family of Israel Levy, and it may be that he is to be identified with Henry Levin (1798-1877) of Penzance, who was from Stockholm, and who married a Julia of Truro. Israel Levy's unmarried daughter, **Catherine** ("**Kitty**") **Levy** (-1864) traded as a Clothes

Levy of Truro (I)
[not known to be connected with Levy of Falmouth]

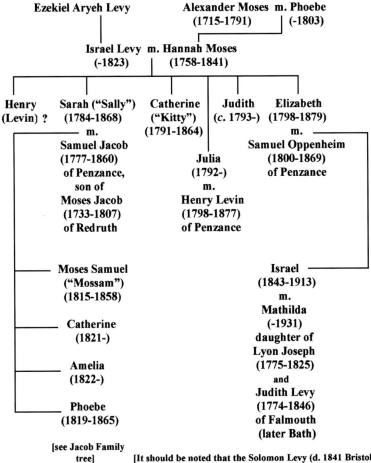

Ezekiel Aryeh Levy

Alexander Moses m. Phoebe
(1715-1791)   (-1803)

Israel Levy m. Hannah Moses
(-1823)   (1758-1841)

| Henry (Levin) ? | Sarah ("Sally") (1784-1868) m. Samuel Jacob (1777-1860) of Penzance, son of Moses Jacob (1733-1807) of Redruth | Catherine ("Kitty") (1791-1864) | Judith (c. 1793-) | Elizabeth (1798-1879) m. Samuel Oppenheim (1800-1869) of Penzance |

Julia (1792-) m. Henry Levin (1798-1877) of Penzance

Moses Samuel ("Mossam") (1815-1858)

Catherine (1821-)

Amelia (1822-)

Phoebe (1819-1865)

Israel (1843-1913) m. Mathilda (-1931) daughter of Lyon Joseph (1775-1825) and Judith Levy (1774-1846) of Falmouth (later Bath)

[see Jacob Family tree]

[It should be noted that the Solomon Levy (d. 1841 Bristol) who married Arabella Joseph, daughter of Lyon Joseph of Falmouth (later Bath), was not, a son of Israel and Hannah Levy, but of Joseph and Sophia Levy of Exeter.]

Unrelated to the family of Israel Levy of Truro: Jacob (John) Levi of Truro m. Elizabeth. Children: (b. from c. 1813): Charles Anna Jacob Elizabeth Henry. Also in Truro: Lyon Levy (Silversmith of Plymouth, c. 1828); Henry and Jane Levi (Hawkers: 1841 Census).

It is entirely my own conclusion that Julia was a daughter of Israel Levy and that she married Henry Levin. This is not firmly supported by independent genealogical information but I view it as a credible inference (KP).

Source: Anthony P. Joseph and Godfrey Simmons. Compiled by Keith Pearce © (2013).

Levy of Truro (2)

Jacob Levy may have been of Jewish descent, but his wife was not.

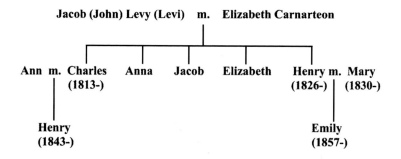

The marriage of Jacob Levi and Elizabeth Carnaerton took place in St. Mary's Parish Church, Truro on 1st June 1813, and their children were subsequently baptised there from 1813. Source: Godfrey Simmons and Bernard Susser (1993); Census Records 1841-1861 (Cornwall family History Society Truro). Compiled by Keith Pearce © (2013).

and General dealer in Calenick Street,[569] and later in Kenwyn St. (1841 Census). She may have moved to Falmouth. The 1861 census for Falmouth records a Kitty Levey, born in Truro, age 66, as a servant to a Mrs. Ronson (retired widow) in High Street. Catherine Levy died on the 14th July 1864, and is buried in the Penzance cemetery. Apart from this, little is known of the family of Israel Levy.

The unrelated **Jacob** (John) **Levi(y)**, a Watch & Clockmaker, traded at 5, King St. (5, St. Nicholas St.), (Br. 1822; Pg. 1823/24/30; Wi. 1847). Jacob Levi(y), who was to play a role in the establishment of the first municipal (non-denominational) burial ground in Truro, was married to a Gentile, Elizabeth Carnaerton. Their four children were Charles, Anna, Jacob and Elizabeth, born between 1813 and 1822, were baptised together on 22nd February 1822 in St. Mary's Church,[570] which was subsequently demolished for the building of the Cathedral. It was most likely Anna Levi who married a …. *Jolliffe*, but appears to have been widowed. On 16th August 1844, the *West Briton* carried the marriage notice: "At Kenwyn (church) on Sunday last, Mr. Timmins Neville Miller, confectioner, to Mrs. Jolliffe, eldest daughter of Mr. Jacob Levy, silversmith, Truro".[571] Jacob and Elizabeth had another son, Henry, after 1822. The eldest son, **Charles** was a Watch & Clockmaker, and Jeweller in Kenwyn St. (Pg. 1844; Sl. 1852/3) and at 6 King St. (Br. 1844). The 1841 census records a Jacob Levy (50) a watchmaker as having been born in the county, which could suggest that he may not have been of Jewish descent. His wife, Eliza (49) had been born in Helston. The oldest sons, Charles and Jacob, are not listed with the family, but their siblings appear as Hannah (24), Elizabeth (19), Henry (17), Emma (15), Matilda (10) and Harriet (8). From the early 1840s onwards the mass production of factory-made clock movements by cheap labour undercut the profitability of the work of master clock makers, who were forced into other more various commercial areas. Lower-skilled men could buy the ready made parts, fit them in a cheap, locally-made case, and sell them at a price that a wider range of people could afford. There was especially an influx of very cheap American clocks, one of the firms offering these clocks, *Ramsey & Devonport*, regularly advertised in the Cornish press. On 11th April 1845, the *West Briton* reported that Charles Levy was to open a further shop at 29 Boscawen St. On 29th January 1846, he relinquished these premises but continued to trade in Kenwyn St., where he sold ironmongery, toys, carpenters' and masons' tools, musical instruments, and American and Bracket Clocks (Br.). Charles Levy (and Morris Hart Harris of Penzance) both offered the American clocks at 17s 6d.[572] Charles Levy continued to trade as a watchmaker (1851 census) but also as a Silversmith (Wi. 1847), and **John Levy** (Charles' brother **Jacob**) was a Cabinet Maker in the same street (Wi. 1847). Kelly's Directory of 1856 indicates that this was a versatile family business, listing Charles, now as a Cabinet Maker at 7 Westbridge, and his brother **Henry** as a Jeweller, Silversmith, and the proprietor of a musical instrument warehouse in King St., (Slater, 1852/3). Henry Levy appears as a Watchmaker and Jeweller in the census records (1851-1861). The 1861 Census gives Charles as a Watch maker at Victoria Place, with his son, Henry, then 18, as his assistant. By 1871, Charles Levy had moved to Birmingham, where he traded as a Cabinet Maker.[573] The 1871 Census lists him with his wife, Ann, age 58, and a son, Henry, age 28, (single) who was Shopman to his father. All three are recorded as born in Truro. In 1881, Charles, then a widower, continued to trade with his still unmarried son at the same address. By 1891, Henry Levy, then 49, had married Annie, age 36, from Birmingham, and had moved to Kings Norton, Worcester, where he traded as an Upholsterer. The death of his father, Jacob Levy, was reported in the *West Briton* on 9th August 1850: "At Truro, on Friday last, Mr. Jacob Levy, clock and watch maker, aged 61 years".[574]

The Harris Family

Henry Harris: Watch & Clockmaker, 2 Lemon St. (Pg. 1823); Jeweller, 8, Lemon St. (Pg. 1830/44; Br. 1844); Silversmith, Silks & Haberdashery (Br. 1844; Wi. 1847; Sl. 1852/3). Henry Harris (1787-1872) was the son of **Samuel Harris** (1754-1824) and **Judith Solomon** (1763-1839), both of whom are buried in the Falmouth cemetery (3:12 and 4:7). The Harris family had originally come from Germany. Samuel Harris came from London to Cornwall around the mid to late 1700s, living for a while in Penzance, where Henry Harris was born. He then settled in Falmouth, where he traded in High Street as a Watchmaker until his death in 1824.[575] Judith Harris died on 5th March 1839 at the family home in High St. and she was described on her death certificate as the "widow of a merchant".[576] In 1819, Henry

Harris of Falmouth and Truro

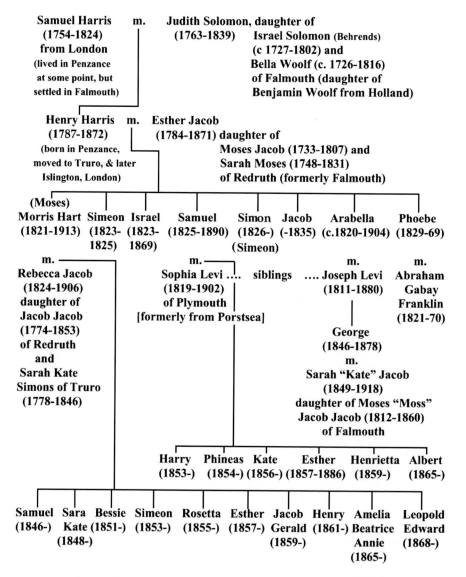

Samuel Harris m. **Judith Solomon, daughter of**
(1754-1824) **(1763-1839)** Israel Solomon (Behrends)
from London (c 1727-1802) and
(lived in Penzance Bella Woolf (c. 1726-1816)
at some point, but of Falmouth (daughter of
settled in Falmouth) Benjamin Woolf from Holland)

Henry Harris m. **Esther Jacob**
(1787-1872) **(1784-1871) daughter of**
(born in Penzance, Moses Jacob (1733-1807) and
moved to Truro, & later Sarah Moses (1748-1831)
Islington, London) of Redruth (formerly Falmouth)

(Moses)
Morris Hart **Simeon** **Israel** **Samuel** **Simon** **Jacob** **Arabella** **Phoebe**
(1821-1913) **(1823-** **(1823-** **(1825-1890)** **(1826-)** **(-1835)** **(c.1820-1904)** **(1829-69)**
1825) **1869)** **(Simeon)**

m. m. m. m.
Rebecca Jacob **Sophia Levi** .... siblings .... **Joseph Levi** **Abraham**
(1824-1906) **(1819-1902)** **(1811-1880)** **Gabay**
daughter of of Plymouth **Franklin**
Jacob Jacob [formerly from Porstsea] **(1821-70)**
(1774-1853)
of Redruth **George**
and **(1846-1878)**
Sarah Kate m.
Simons of Truro **Sarah "Kate" Jacob**
(1778-1846) **(1849-1918)**
daughter of Moses "Moss"
Jacob Jacob (1812-1860)
of Falmouth

Harry **Phineas** **Kate** **Esther** **Henrietta** **Albert**
(1853-) **(1854-)** **(1856-)** **(1857-1886)** **(1859-)** **(1865-)**

Samuel **Sara** **Bessie** **Simeon** **Rosetta** **Esther** **Jacob** **Henry** **Amelia** **Leopold**
(1846-) **Kate (1851-)** **(1853-)** **(1855-)** **(1857-)** **Gerald** **(1861-)** **Beatrice** **Edward**
(1848-) **(1859-)** **Annie** **(1868-)**
(1865-)

- Arabella Harris' date of birth is often given as 1826, but as she would only have been 15 in 1841, it may have been around 1820, or even before. All of the Harris family settled in London.
- Sources: W.S. Jessop, Alex M. Jacob, Anthony P. Joseph, Godfrey Simmons, Brian & John Yule. Compiled by Keith Pearce © (2013).

Harris married **Esther Jacob** (1784-1871), a daughter of Moses Jacob and Sarah Moses of Falmouth, who later moved to Redruth. By 1823, Henry and Esther Harris had moved to Truro where Henry established a successful business as a Jeweller in Lemon Street, where Esther ran a Lodging House from the same premises.[577] In 1833, Henry Harris was appointed by warrant as Jeweller to William IV,[578] and this was subsequently renewed by Queen Victoria, and reported in the *Royal Cornwall Gazette* in November 1837: "The Queen has been graciously pleased, by warrant of the Lord Chamberlain to appoint Mr. H. Harris, No. 8 Leman [Lemon] St. to be her Majesty's Jeweller in ordinary at Truro".[579]

Henry and Esther Harris had eight children, one of whom, Simon, was born around 1823, and died in infancy, in 1825. **Morris** (**Moses**) **Hart Harris** (1821-1913) married his cousin, **Rebecca Jacob** (1824-1906). Their children, born between 1846 and 1868, were Samuel, Sarah Kate, Bessie, Simeon, Rosetta, Esther, Jacob Gerald, Henry, Amelia (Millie) Beatrice Annie, and Leopold Edward.[580] **Israel Harris** (1823-1869), and **Samuel Harris** (1825-1890) who married (in July 1851) **Sophia Levi** (1819-1902) a daughter of Phineas (1784-1861) and Kitty Levi (1788-1851), both originally from Portsea, who lived and traded in Plymouth. (Kitty Levi's family name has been given both as *Aschenberg* and as *Mordecai*. It is possible that she was a sister to Mark Mordecai of Plymouth, in that, like Phineas and Kitty Levi, he was also from Portsea). Samuel and Sophia's children, born between 1853 and 1865, were Harry, Phineas, Kate, Esther, Henrietta and Albert.[581] (Joseph Levi, Sophia's brother, married Samuel Harris' sister, Arabella: see below). Kitty Levi died in Devonport (*c.* 1852) and was buried in the Hoe cemetery. Phineas Levi then moved to London, where he died. Two other sons of Henry and Esther Harris, **Israel** (1823-) and **Simeon or Simon Harris** (1826-) appear in the circumcision register of Rabbi B. A. Simmons of Penzance. Although the register contains some minor errors of dating, it appears that Israel and an earlier Simeon Harris may have been twins. Israel Harris was circumcised on 15th February 1823, and Simeon on 3rd April. The latter's circumcision may have been delayed because of the child's ill-health, and he died in his second year. **Morris Harris** (19) and his brother, **Simeon (as Simon)** (14) appear in the 1841 census, Morris as a watchmaker, and Simon as an apprentice watchmaker. **Israel Harris** was a watch and clockmaker at 9 St. Nicholas Street in 1844 (Br.). Henry Harris and his sons retained strong links with Penzance, and they were active members of the congregation there. From 1843, the signatures of Henry, Morris Hart, Samuel and (the second) Simeon (as *Simon*) appear in the minute book. Samuel, was, with Morris, and eight others, a warden and trustee of the Penzance burial ground in 1844, and Morris Hart Harris (who was living and trading in Penzance at this time) was President of the Penzance congregation from 1849-1850. Another son of Henry Harris, **Jacob**, whose year of birth is not known, died in 1835. There were two daughters: **Arabella** (*c.* 1820-1904) was married by "Rev. Mr. Rintle" (Rabbi Joseph Rintel of Falmouth) at No. 8 Lemon Street, Truro, to **Joseph Levi** (1811-1880) in August 1841,[582] and later moved to London. Her sister, **Phoebe**, died in 1869.[583] The 1851 Census for Truro records the Harris family still resident in Lemon Street, with Henry Harris recorded as a Jeweller and Silk Mercer, and his son, Israel, a Watchmaker.[584] Henry and Esther Harris moved to London where they lived in Islington. Esther died there on 1st August 1871 and Henry on 25th September 1872.[585]

In 1850, Morris Hart Harris went to Bristol, where, in 1851, he is recorded as a Visitor, in the house of Alexander and Israel Levin (both from Penzance) at 17 Bath Street, Temple.[586] In the same year, his wife, Rebecca, "Jeweller's wife", and her daughters, Sarah Kate and Bessy, were living with their father, Jacob Jacob, now retired, in Bell's Court, Falmouth, together with Rebecca's sisters, Esther and Amelia.[587] Presumably, Morris had gone to Bristol to seek advancement, but the family were to settle in London. By 1861, Morris Hart Harris was trading there, as a Commercial Traveller, in Bury Square, Saint Mary Axe, EC., where their household now consisted of eight children and two female servants, one of whom, Louisa Lawyer, had been born in Penzance. By 1871, the family had moved to 17, St. Augustine's Road in Camden (Kentish Town District) where they remained for over forty years.[588] (His brother Simeon, was living in the same road at that time). In 1871, Morris was working as a Clerk to a Bead Merchant (his brother Samuel), but by 1881, he is given as a General Dealer. The 1911 census records him as a Retired Jeweller. Samuel Harris is recorded on the 1861 census at 7, Finsbury Circus, as a Dealer in Fancy Goods. By 1871, he had moved to Houndsditch, trading as a Bead Merchant, although he is also given as "wholesale and export warehouse for jewellery, cutlery, combs & brushes; importer of beads, bugles & foreign fancy goods."[589] He became the Houndsditch representative on the Council of London, and on 28th October 1856 he was granted the Freedom of the City of London. His success and status can be seen from his official invitation "From the Right Honourable John Staples, Lord Mayor" to a banquet at the Guildhall on Monday 9th November 1885, addressed to "Samuel Harris Esq. & Lady".[590]

Another **Samuel Harris** (1813-1864) has been assigned, incorrectly, to the family of Henry Harris of Truro.[591] This Samuel Harris was the son of Henry Harris and Elizabeth Solomon of London, where he was born.[592] On 5th July 1832, when he was recorded as single, but with ten children, he was sentenced to seven years for stealing coins and banknotes worth more than 100 pounds from his employers, Elias Moses and Isaac Moses. Having been held in custody in the Hyde Park Barracks, he was transported to Australia, where he was imprisoned. His good behaviour during his incarceration led to his being granted a ticket of leave in 1833, and by 1839 he was released. He moved first to Melbourne, where, in 1840, he was one of the four readers at the first High Holyday service, and he became one of the early members of the Melbourne Congregation. He opened two drapery stores there, with a Jacob Marks, one of which was very successful until the economic depression of 1843, when the partnership of Harris and Marks was dissolved. In the meantime, his successful rehabilitation enabled the immigration of his sister, Hannah Marks, and his brother-in-law, Mark Marks, together with Rachel Ackman (also Samuel's sister) and her husband, Emanuel. In 1845, there was a donation of £5 towards the Sydney Synagogue building appeal from a "Henry Harris" (who may have been his father) and another of £2 from Samuel himself. On 26th March, as Samuel Henry Harris, he married Elizabeth Levey (1828- 1892) a daughter and eldest child of Isaac and Dinah Levey, originally from Liverpool, where Elizabeth had been born. By 1846, the couple settled in Melbourne and were to have ten children. In June of 1853, Samuel Harris was able to acquire land in Sydney in the form of five allotments for £4,102. He died in Sydney on 28th September 1867, and his estate was valued at £48,000.

Zelig Harris, who was not related to the Harris family of Truro, was trading there in 1841. He was then aged 30, and the census records him as "Jew, Foreign", together with another Harris "Jew, 45" (who may have been a relative) and a **Jacob Stafegan** (or Stafhagan) Jeweller, all three living in Kenwyn Street. Zelig Harris also traded in Falmouth (1861) and in Penzance (1871), as a hawker. He was from Poland, and the **Hyman Harris**, (24) a travelling Glazier from Poland, who was in Plymouth in 1861, may have been a relative. The **Bessy Harris**, whose name appears alongside that of Hyman Harris, may have been his wife. She was born in Plymouth. It is uncertain if the Jacob Stafegen, above, was connected with the family of **Rev. Myer Stadthagen** of Plymouth (1841-1861 census), who was from Prussia, and whose wife, Arabella Joseph, was born in Redruth.

The Simons Family of Truro and Falmouth

The Continental origins of the Simons family are uncertain, and it is not known if **Simon Simons** lived in this country or in Cornwall, but members of the family may have lived in London. Simon Simons' son, **Samuel (Solomon) Simons** (1740-1832) married **Rosa (Ann) Moses** (1757-1838), a daughter of Alexander and Phoebe Moses of Falmouth. The family name appears variously as *Symons, Symonds* and *Simmons*. (The family was not related to that of Rabbi B.A. Simmons of Penzance, whose surname was subject to similar variants.) It could be inferred [593] that Samuel Simons' marriage to Rosa Moses was his second. If there was an earlier wife, her name has not survived, and it is possible that the seven known children were all born to Rosa Ann Moses. If so, Samuel Simons had six sons, **Philip, Joseph** (1798-), **Eliezar, Moses** (Morris 1788-), **Walter** and **Isaac** (*c*.1796-), and one daughter, **Sarah Kate**, also known as Kitty (1778-1846). Initially, Samuel and Ann Simons lived in Falmouth, where they appear in trade directories (Bailey 1788 and Universal 1791) under separate entries as "Ann & Samuel Symons: Mercer, Draper and Shop-keeper". A *Symons* was trading as a Jeweller in Truro by 1791, and this may have been the year that Samuel Simons moved there. **Isaac Simons** married Rose, or Rosetta (*c*.1800-), the daughter of Lazarus Jacobs and Rebecca Hart of Penzance, and for a while the couple may have lived in that town, where (from 1819 to 1823) Isaac Simons' name (sometimes as *Simons of Truro*) appears regularly in the Penzance Minute Book as a subscriber to the congregation, together with an Alexander Symons, who may have been a relative. Between 1823 and 1840, Isaac and Rosetta Simons had at least eleven children, one dying in infancy, and nine of whom were to leave the County. Of Isaac's brother, Walter, little is known, but a sister, **Sarah Kate Simons**, married **Jacob Jacob** (1774-1853), a son of Moses Jacob of Redruth. The couple settled in Falmouth. Philip, Joseph, Eliezar and Morris Simons became some of the earliest Jewish settlers in Cincinnati, Ohio in the 1820s, that community having been established by Jews from Exeter.[594] **Joseph Simons** married a **Celia** (born *c.* 1808) who may have been from a **Zachariah** family of Portsea. It is possible, but not certain, that the child *Isaac ben Joseph* who was circumcised by Rabbi B. A. Simmons "in the congregation of Falmouth...on Monday Erev Pesach, 5581" (16th April 1821) was their son, and may have been named after his uncle.

Simons of Truro
(or Symons)

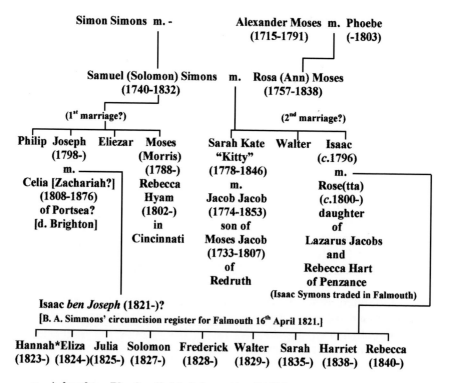

Simon Simons m. -

Alexander Moses m. Phoebe
(1715-1791) (-1803)

Samuel (Solomon) Simons m. Rosa (Ann) Moses
(1740-1832) (1757-1838)

(1st marriage?)

(2nd marriage?)

Philip Joseph Eliezar Moses
(1798-)
m. -
Celia [Zachariah?]
(1808-1876)
of Portsea?
[d. Brighton]

(Morris)
(1788-)
Rebecca
Hyam
(1802-)
in
Cincinnati

Sarah Kate Walter Isaac
"Kitty" (c.1796)
(1778-1846) m. -
m.
Jacob Jacob Rose(tta)
(1774-1853) (c.1800-)
son of daughter
Moses Jacob of
(1733-1807) Lazarus Jacobs
of and
Redruth Rebecca Hart
of Penzance
(Isaac Symons traded in Falmouth)

Isaac *ben Joseph* (1821-)?
[B. A. Simmons' circumcision register for Falmouth 16th April 1821.]

Hannah*Eliza Julia Solomon Frederick Walter Sarah Harriet Rebecca
(1823-) (1824-) (1825-) (1827-) (1828-) (1829-) (1835-) (1838-) (1840-)

- A daughter, Phoebe, died in infancy (April 1824).

Note: It is possible that Samuel Simons married twice and that the four sons, Philip to Moses, were from a first marriage. Conventionally, however, only the three children, Sarah Kate to Isaac, have been regarded as children of Rosa Ann Moses. Provisionally, all seven children are given here as family members.

Sources: W.S Jessop (1951, reprint Gent 2000, pp. 9 & 56); Bernard Susser (1993) p. 58-9, Anthony Joseph, Godfrey Simmons, & Jill Hyams (2005 & 2010).

Compiled by Keith Pearce © (2013).

However, the mother would have been barely 14 years old at the time, and it is not known when the couple married. They appear without other family in census records for Storr's Township in Hamilton County Ohio in 1850 and 1860. Joseph *Simmons* is given as 52 (1850) and 63 (1850) and Celia as 42 (1850) and 53 (1860). Eliezar and Morris *Symonds* were trading as merchants at separate addresses in the Lower Market by 1825 (*Cincinnati City Directory*), but there is little known of Philip and Joseph Simmons' life in Ohio. After Joseph Symonds' death, his wife returned to England. She died in Brighton in 1876.

Saul Symonds (-1886) who was born in London around 1821, has been taken as the son of Joseph and Celia Simons, but he was in fact the son of Blumah (Flora) Simons (*c*. 1791-) and Moses Jacobs of London. The latter died (or deserted the family) before 1841, and the children reverted to their mother's family name, as *Symonds*. Saul Symonds married a **Hannah Elkan.** He traded as a Master Embroiderer in Brighton, and later moved to London, where he ran a cigar manufacturing business in the Pentonville area, which his sons continued after his death (in London, at 252 Pentonville Road, Finsbury, Holborn district, on 13th February 1886).[595] It is not known if Blumah Simons of London was related to the Simons family of Truro, but there may have been a connection.[596] A Philip Symonds from Portsmouth, not known to be connected with Simons of Truro, Symonds of London or the family of Celia (Zachariah), left Liverpool with his family for Cincinnati in 1818.[597]

Before he emigrated to America, **Morris** (Moses) **Symons** (1788-) may have lived in a cottage adjoining the Falmouth synagogue (*c*.1811). Later, he married **Rebecca Hyam** (1802-), theirs being the first marriage amongst the new Jewish settlers in Cincinnati. In Cornwall, Isaac and Rosa Symons settled in Falmouth, where they traded in China and Glass in Market Street (Pigot 1830). Isaac Simons later traded in Falmouth as a Bullion Dealer. It has been noted that an Alexander Simons was a member of the Penzance congregation at the same time as Isaac Simons (1819-1824), and that both men were trading (separately) in Falmouth by 1830. It is possible that they were related. Samuel Simons, his wife, Rosa, and their children Isaac and Sarah Kate are all buried in the Falmouth cemetery, along with Isaac Simons' infant daughter, Phoebe (Feigele).

Abraham Aaron & Son. Surgeons. Lemon St. (Pg. 1830). The **Hyman Aaron**, a Doctor, age 35, who practised at East Bridge Street (1841 census) was most likely the son of Abraham Aaron. In the two newspaper items (below), the "Dr. Aaron", will be Abraham Aaron.

Henry and **Jane Levi**. Hawkers, Old Bridge Street (1841 Census). Both recorded as "Foreign". They are not known to have been related to the families of Israel or Jacob Levy.

Joseph Pfaff. Watchmaker, New Bridge St. (1841 Census: recorded as "Foreign"). Uncertain. He moved to Redruth (1851-1861 census records), and by 1864, he was trading as a Jeweller, in High Street, Falmouth. (Brown gives a Joseph Pfaff as a watchmaker in Truro as early as *c.* 1800, but this may be his father).

Lily Harris. Jeweller, Kenwyn. (1841 census). Uncertain. Age 30, she is listed as "Foreign", with another Harris (male, age 45: forename unclear, who may be the "Harris" recorded with Zelig Harris, above). They are not known to be related to the family of Henry Harris, and the Samuel Harris who emigrated to Australia (mentioned earlier) may have been from this family.

Henry Joseph Isaac. Itinerant (1841): "The public are cautioned against the impositions of a young Jew, calling himself Henry Joseph Isaac, apparently about twenty years of age, who has lately passed through Truro, it is thought on his way to Falmouth, and who, under the colour of being a convert to Christianity, is appealing to the charity, more particularly to the clergy of the county. His case has been thoroughly examined, and his papers have been proved by application to the gentlemen whose names appear therein, and reference to the register of the parish in which he pretends to have been baptised, to be nothing more or less than a series of gross forgeries." (*West Briton*, 21st May 1841).[598]

Hermon Semmons (variant spellings). Hardwareman (*c.*1821-1829), Watchmaker in New Bridge Street (Br. 1834) & Jeweller (1841). He is the Simmons of Truro listed with Lyon Levy as subscribers in the Penzance congregational records in 1821, with Semmens (only) listed in 1822. His partnership with Lyon Levy of Truro (above) was dissolved in 1829. The 1841 Census for Truro [599] gives Semmons as a Shopkeeper, of Castle Street, Kenwyn, age 45, "born in Foreign Parts". His wife, **Rose**, also 45, is given as born "In County". She may have been a member of one of the Cornish Jewish families, and five of their six children (also born in the County) had common Jewish forenames: **Pheby** (Phoebe, 15), **Israel** (14), Jane (12, the exception), **Joseph** (9), **Henrietta** (8) and **Benjamin** (2). There had been a daughter (younger than Henrietta) who had died on 16th May 1837,[600] and there may have been another son, Simon, absent from the 1841 census listing. It is possible that the **Soloman Sammons**, a pedlar from Truro (Falmouth 1841 census) was a relative of Hermon Semmons. In March of 1842,[601] Harman "Semmour" (Semmons) "a jew jeweller of Truro" had come into possession of two silver spoons, as part exchange for the purchase by William Morcomb, 21, of a silver chain. The spoons, that "were much rubbed, particularly about the initials, as if the object had been to erase them" were said by Morcomb to have been found by him under the flooring of a house. Morcomb, of St. Columb, had, in fact, stolen them from a Mrs. Phillips, landlady of the Indian Queen, in the same parish, the previous September. Semmons, who had been travelling in the parish to sell his wares, called at Mrs. Phillips' house, and she recognised the spoons as hers. Morcomb was found guilty, and sentenced to six months hard labour. Four months later, Semmons, described as "a jew jeweller, lately residing in Truro" appeared at the Insolvent Debtors' Court in Bodmin in July 1842. The court acknowledged that Semmons "had been in a large way of business - many years", and had known connections with the (reputable) firm of Oppenheim of London. Semmons was held to be in debt to Horatio Smith, a watchmaker, for the sum of £30. & 5 shillings, but had also contracted debts to a total of £508 during the years 1841-1842, although he held that he was himself owed some £327. Semmons had sold goods (he claimed "to support his…large family" and for their extensive medical bills) to "Mr. Oppenheim of Penzance" (whose connection, if any, to Oppenheim of London, is not known). These in turn were auctioned off for Oppenheim by Mr. Clyma of Truro, but only fetched some £46. Despite his claims to the contrary, the court found no evidence that Semmons had paid any of his creditors, and considered that he had altered some of his outstanding bills to reduce the amounts. (This included a bill from "Mr. Burlase", that is Borlase, a prominent merchant in Penzance.) Semmons was given a prison sentence of two months. (*West Briton*, 29th July 1842).[602] Semmons' much earlier business partnership with Lyon Levy had been dissolved in 1829, with debts (unpaid bills) to be paid to the latter (see below). Also in July of 1842, Semmons' fifteen year old son, Israel, was "charged with assaulting Semmons Semmons, his brother". This is likely to be a Simon Semmons, who, as noted above, does not appear on the 1841 census, although *Simon* may have been another name for Joseph (10) or the youngest, Benjamin (3). This Semmons was also charged with "threatening the lives of the family". The court was told that "The prisoner, the night before (Sunday 10th July) had loaded a pistol, and threatened to kill his mother". He was found guilty, fined £2 "with costs, and in default of payment, he was committed to the house of correction for one month, to be kept at hard labour".[603]

Moses Friedeberg. *West Briton* (12th May 1848): "Truro Police – On Wednesday last, Moses Friedeberg, a jew, from Posen, was committed for one calendar month for begging. He had a petition stating that he was in the greatest distress in a strange country, but on searching him the policeman found in his possession nine watches, three sovereigns, and 12s. 6d. in silver. He also had a pedlar's box at his lodgings, without possessing a hawker's licence".[604] Friedeberg was from Poland (*Posen* being the German for the Polish *Poznon*). The "petition" mentioned relates to the fact that he was deaf, and possibly a mute. The 1851 Census records him as a visitor in a house in the village of Latchford, near Warrington. He is given as a watchmaker and jeweller, and the recorder marked by his name in the column "blind, deaf, or dumb".

Israel Harris. Watch & Clockmaker, Jeweller. 9 St. Nicholas St. (Pg. 1844; 1851 census). This is a son of Henry Harris.

Henrietta Jacobs was born in Truro c. 1845. She was the daughter of Nathaniel Schram from Holland and his wife, Anna from Gwennap, Cornwall (see Falmouth Trades). Her sister, Angelina was also born in Truro in 1843. It is not certain that Nathaniel and Anna Schram's family were Jewish. Henrietta became the wife of **Mark Jacobs**, Jeweller, General Dealer & Outfitter, of Plymouth, who had been born in London (Plymouth Census 1881 & 1891). Their daughter, Catherine (b. 1865) married Max, fourth son of Rev. Isaac Bischofswerder (Rabbi of the Penzance congregation). The marriage of Henrietta, and that of her daughter, Catherine would indicate that conversion to Judaism (from the female Schram line) must have taken place at some point. The marriage of Catherine and Max Bischofswerder (Bishop), and their eventual burial in the new Jewish cemetery at Gifford Place are both recorded in the Plymouth Congregational Registers.

Berenger & **Schwerer**. Watchmakers and Jewellers, Church Lane. (Br. 1849; Sl. 1852/3)..

Jacob Schwerer. Watch and Clockmaker, Church Lane (Br. 1856). Both men were German in origin, but, as noted, only Schwerer was Jewish. Jacob Schwerer's brother, Joseph, traded in Lemon Street. In February 1851, a "lad called Henry Farr, living in Goodwives Lane" stole a watch from a neighbour, a shoemaker, William Wale, who, on a Friday evening had left his door unlocked and had gone into the town. Most likely before the theft had been reported to the police, that same evening Farr "sold the case to Mr. Schwerer for 3s. 6d. in the Church-lane; and Mr. Schwerer sold it next day to a Jew whom he did not know". Soon after, Farr made the mistake of selling "the body of the watch, and an accordion" to an Isaac Ludford (who was not Jewish) "keeper of a bazaar open near the White Hart". Ludford's wife took the watch body to another Truro jeweller, called Edwards, hoping to exchange it for a smaller one for her daughter, but, by this time, Edwards "having received information from the police that a watch had been stolen, detained this watch and sent it to the police station, in consequence of which the prisoner was afterwards arrested".[605] The incident is of interest for several reasons: such a reckless series of acts by Farr could hardly succeed in such a small town, no culpability attached to Jacob Schwerer, the presence of the Jew was unknown to him (most likely an itinerant pedlar), and that Schwerer, being open for business on a winter's Friday evening (when the Sabbath had begun) and again on the Saturday (before it had ended) was hardly a strict, observant Jew.

Frederick Levy was a boarder at a Church School in Pydar Street in 1851. He had been born in St. Keverne in 1841, and is most unlikely to have been of Jewish descent.

Oliver Gluyas Solomon. Jeweller, St. Nicholas Street (PO Directory 1856; 1861-1871 census).[606] Uncertain. It is not known if he was related to Isaac Soloman, to the T. Solomon (below) or to the Christian Solomon families of Bodmin and mid-Cornwall.

William Moses (24), a Papier-Mache Traveller, and his wife, Mary Ann, both from Helston, were trading in Truro in 1861. Unlikely.

Samuel Myers: (1861) a Corn Factor from Leeds, traded in River Street.

Isaac Soloman. Jeweller, Calenick Street (1861 Census). Aged 65, he is recorded as from Poland. His wife, Fanny, 47 was from Ireland. They may have been Jewish, but Isaac Soloman is not known to have been related to Solomon of Falmouth.

Morris Oppenheim: (1871) a Commercial Traveller in Glass, (35) from London. Not known to be related to Oppenheim of Penzance.

Paul Zizfel: (1861) unmarried (25) and a Clockmaker from Germany. He was working at **Joseph Schwerer's** Jeweller's shop in Lemon Street. Uncertain.

Simeon Simeons, Former Jeweller, Kea, Truro (1861 Census). He was 84 in 1861, and had been born in Truro (c. 1777). It is not certain that he was Jewish or that he was related to the family of Samuel Simons (1740-1832) of Truro. He may have been related to Hermon (Hyman) Semmons (above).

Henry Levey: (1871) a Commercial Traveller (36) from Scotland, boarding at a hotel in River Street. Uncertain.

Mary Ann Moses, (39) an unmarried cook from Probus, Ann Solomon (20) from Liskeard, James Solomon (15) from Truro, and Elizabeth Jewry (28) a housemaid from St. Agnes, were patients at the Royal Cornwall Infirmary (1861-1871). Unlikely.

T. Solomon. Plumber, Glazier, Carver, Gilder, Decorator, etc. 19 King Street (Kelly 1873). See also Truro Masonic record, below. A Thomas Solomon, who is not known to have been Jewish, was Mayor of Truro (*c.* 1867).

Two much earlier references may relate to temporary residence, in that travelling bazaars and surgeons were not uncommon:

Jones Mandoffsky (Jonas Mandovsy) opened a Bazaar in Truro in 1834. His brother, Moses Jones Mandoffsky had a similar establishment in Plymouth. A *Mandovsky* "offered comparatively large sums to the Plymouth Congregation in 1822" and the surname represents one of the first Eastern European names to occur in Plymouth. A Moses Jonas Mandovsky married a Sophia Simon in London on 12th September 1827.[607] A Jonas Mandovsky, 41, Merchant ("Foreign") appears on the 1841 Census for Plymouth with Sophia, 40, born in Devon, and a Henrietta Mandovsky, 28, also born in Devon. In view of her age, the latter is unlikely to be a daughter (unless the ages have been misrecorded). Another Sophia Mandovsky, age 30, a Toy Dealer's wife, born in Devonport, appears on the 1851 Census for Plymouth.

16th September 1826. The *Royal Cornwall Gazette* carried an advertisement that **Dr. Aaron** effects cures and could be contacted at Tippett's opposite Pearce's Hotel, Truro, where he sells a *Balm of Manheim*.[608] Dr. Aaron's medicinal trade included travelling to sell his cures. In 1828, "Dr. Aaron & Son of Truro - proprietors of the celebrated cordial *Balm of Manheim*" advertised their forthcoming visit to the city of Exeter, where they could be consulted at "Mr. Welch's, Silversmith, Bartholomew-Yard".[609] The advertisement carried eloquent testimony of "their superior Mode of Treatment" from an Elizabeth Poat of Kenwyn Street Truro, who testified to having been "restored from death to life" by Dr. Aaron's administering of his medicine, having "for a considerable time" been "afflicted with a dropsy of a most alarming nature" which, despite previous treatments by doctors who were "the most skilful (*sic.*) of the faculty" had shown every sign of worsening, until she had been persuaded by her friends to "apply to Dr. Aaron", whose attentions had so far lasted for three weeks. (Dr. Aaron's advertisement carries distinctive echoes of the miracle-healing stories from the Gospels,[610] which, no doubt, Christian readers would recognise). Twenty years earlier, on 24th May 1806, the *Royal Cornwall Gazette* carried a notice extolling the medicinal efficacy of a Dr. **Solomon's** *Cordial Balm of Gilead*, drawing attention to its availability from various traders in Cornish towns, and directly from Dr. Solomon of "Gilead House, Liverpool". It is not known if Dr. Solomon was ever resident in or travelled to Cornwall, nor if Dr. Aaron had taken supplies of "balm" from him. A business connection between the two men is not confirmed.

Isaac and Solomon Families in Truro

To avoid confusion with their Jewish namesakes, brief mention should be made of these Christian families, whose names (especially Solomon) appear widely in census and parish records for Truro and mid-Cornwall. None of them are known to have been of Jewish descent. Census records show the great majority of them and their families as having been born in Truro or in Cornwall, and parish baptismal, marriage and burial records confirm that they were Christians.

Isaac. Isaac men appear as masons, painters and gardeners. William Isaac, Scrivener, Carclew Street; Isaac Isaac;[611] Cordwainer, Bodmin Street; Fanny Isaac, a painter's widow, from Bristol, living in River Street; Jane Isaac (36) a widow with three sons and a daughter, living with an uncle, William Solomon, a Maltster, all born in Truro; Richard Isaac, an unmarried lodger (67), a Bellow-Maker from Tavistock, living at the George and Dragon.

Solomon. This surname was widespread across Cornwall, and appears frequently in Truro. Thomas Solomon, above, has been mentioned. All of the following were shoemakers in various locations in Truro: Henry Solomon, Edward Solomon, John Solomon, William Solomon (numerous), Richard Solomon, James Solomon, Elizabeth Solomon (bookbinder). Charles Solomon, Cabinet Maker, Calenick Street and Goodwives Lane; Edward B. Solomon, Solicitors' Writing Clerk from London; Sarah Solomon, Straw Bonnet Maker; Jane Solomon, Milliner, from London; William Solomon, Greengrocer, from St. Columb (his wife was from Penzance); Richard Solomon, Mason, Castle Street; James Solomon, Stonemason; Joseph Solomon, Lead Miner; George Solomon, Sailor, from St. Columb; Henry, John J. and Edward Solomon, Cordwainers; Farmers: Hercules Solomon, Thomas Solomon, and Nicholas Solomon.

[553] c.f. Susser, *op.cit.*, Table 10, p. 51. Although it is not clear how he has arrived at his figures for the towns listed, these are probably minimal estimates based on references compiled by the author over time. Source-references are not given on the Table for any of the totals.

[554] c.f. Chapter 4, edit 14.

[555] Lipman: Plymouth Aliens List p. 92. Some of these references were given by Bernard Susser in a letter to Godfrey Simmons, dated August 1994, in which Susser had extracted details from his earlier Ph.D. thesis (prior to the publication of his 1993 book). For Truro and some of the other Cornish towns see Susser (1993: given here as Su.) chapter 2, part 2, on "Towns of Minor Jewish Settlement.....", pp. 47-51.

[556] University of Southampton Library, Archives and Manuscripts; Ref. MS/116/125. The Minute-Book contains an analysis of trades, birth-places and ports of entry. This document, and the Lipman Aliens List, have formed the sources from which some details have drawn for other individuals in this chapter. I am grateful to Helen Fry for drawing my attention to these sources.

[557] Rumney, *Economic & Social Development of the Jews in England* (1933) p. 78.

[558] Lipman p. 191; Susser (1993) p. 48.

[559] Truro Rate Books researched by June Palmer. Correspondence with Godfrey Simmons August-September 1994.

[560] June Palmer (1994).

[561] Brown (1961) p. 79.

[562] It has not been possible to link an Alexander with the extant genealogical records of the Levy, Harris or Simons families of Truro. Samuel Simons (1740-1832) is not known to have had a son named Alexander, unless it is another forename for one of his other sons. *Solomon* and *Samuel* were sometimes interchanged as forenames: Alexander ben Samuel may have been a son of the Solomon Simmons, above.

[563] Susser (1972) pp. 9 & 34.

[564] Susser (1972) p. 9.

[565] RG9/2175 Folio 74, page 21: Jackie Hill (2005).

[566] Susser (1993) p. 218.

[567] It has been noted that W. S. Jessop (1951) confused and conflated the families of Israel Levy of Truro and Joseph Levy of Exeter. This Jessop pedigree (reprinted Frank J. Gent, 2000, without correction, p. 55) is unreliable, and since the 1950s it has led to errors in the allocation of individuals to both Levy families.

[568] Records of Anthony Joseph.

[569] An (undated) note from Bernard Susser to Godfrey Simmons.

[570] St. Mary's Church Register, p. 654, (Su).

[571] Jackie Hill (2009).

[572] H. Miles Brown (1961) p. 15.

[573] Z. Josephs, *Birmingham Jewry,* Vol. II (1740-1930) p. 51 (Birmingham Jewish History Research Group 1984). Research from the 1871-1891 census records by Jackie Hill (2005).

[574] Jackie Hill (2011).

[575] A copy of James Trathan's *The Ancient and Modern History of Falmouth* (1815) in the Archive of Godfrey Simmons is inscribed and endorsed (in French) and signed by "H. Harris", also as "Henri". In view of the fact that the book lists in its Trade Directory, a "Harris, J. attorney and notary" as well as a "Harris" who was an Innkeeper, it cannot be certain that this is Henry Harris, although it is likely to be in view of the fact that "Harris, H, watchmaker" is also listed in High St.(p. 84).

[576] Research by Carol P. Nicholson; Letter to Alex Jacob, 7th January 1972.

[577] Williams (1847).

[578] Letter from Arthur Barnett, JHSE, to Alex Jacob, 29th December, 1953.

[579] Duschinsky (1921) p.141). The original handwritten letter of notification of the appointment (through a magistrate) is still in the possession of his descendants Brian and John Yule (Copy to Keith Pearce: March 2013).

[580] I am grateful to Barbara Pearce (April 2013) for duplicates of the London Census records: RG9; Piece 229; Folio 49; p. 23 (1861); RG10; Piece 235; Folio 36; p. 17 (1871); RG11; Piece 210; Folio 4; p. 4 (1881); RG12; Piece 131; Folio 106; p. 3 (1891); RG13; Piece 149; Folio 87; p. 13 (1901); RG14; Piece 717 (1911).

[581] London Census Records: RG9; Piece 229; Folio 138; p. 17 (1861); RG10; Piece 413; Folio 4; p. 1 (1871); RG11; Piece 369; Folio 42; p. 29 (1881).

[582] *West Briton*, 27th August 1841 (Jackie Hill 2007).

[583] The 1841 Census for Truro records only four of the children at their home in Lemon Street. The ages given on the 1841 census are known to be subject to error, and in the case of the Harris family, they depart in most cases by several years from genealogical records: Henry Harris (45), his wife, Esther (50), sons Israel (18) and Samuel (15), and daughters Arabella (20) and Phoebe (12): See note below.

[584] Also resident were the other Harris children, Esther (64), Phoebe (23), a grandson, Samuel (5), son of their daughter, Arabella (c.1820-1904) who had married Joseph Levi (1811-1880) of Portsea, and an unmarried niece, Kate Alexander (35) who had been born in Plymouth. Kate Alexander was, presumably, the daughter of a sibling of Henry Harris.

[585] c.f. Nicholson, ibid; death certificates, and 1871 census.

[586] 1851 Census: Piece 1947; Folio 231; p. 3.

[587] 1851 Census: Piece 1911; Folio 231; p. 3.

[588] Research by Michael Gandy (Letter to Godfrey Simmons, January 30th 1999).

[589] Gandy, ibid.

[590] PRO Kew, Ref. 9095SO; Arthur Barnett, ibid. The original invitation is in the possession of Brian and John Yule.

[591] Jessop (1951). Jessop's tree of Harris of Truro does not include Henry Harris' son, Samuel Harris who married Sophia Levi.

[592] I am grateful to Liz James of the Australian Jewish Historical Society (28th & 29th March 2013) for detailed information on this Samuel Harris, and for providing copies of the religious marriage record (an image of the original) and the civil document (V184569 135/1845 NSW). See also, J. S. Levi & G. F. J. Bergman, *Australian Genesis, Jewish Convicts and Settlers 1788-1850*, Robert Hale, London (1974) p. 297.

[593] W.S. Jessop (1951).

[594] I am grateful to Jill Hyams for information from her research into the Jews of Cincinnati (Letters to Keith Pearce, 16th May & 16th June 2005 and further communication of 14th July 2010). Sources: 1850 & 1860 Census entries for Cincinnati; "Cincinnati: English Jews Settle", from *The Jewish Encyclopaedia* (1901-1906); "The Jews of Ohio" in *The Occident and American Jewish Advocate* (1843). Susser (1993) pp. 58-9.

[595] In Memoriam notice in the *Jewish Chronicle* 16th February 1894.

[596] Jill Hyams (2005-2010).

[597] Susser (1993) p. 58.

[598] Research by Jackie Hill (2007).

[599] HO107/147/15, Folio 28, p.1.

[600] *West Briton* 19th May 1837.

[601] *West Briton* 18th March 1842.

[602] Research by Jackie Hill (2007).

[603] *West Briton* 15th July 1842.

[604] Research by Jackie Hill (2011).

[605] *The West Briton*, Friday 7th February 1851: Jackie Hill (2011).

[606] HF (2000).

[607] IR 51.6; Stamp Office 1831. Letter from Betty Naggar to Keith Pearce (November 1998). Susser (1993) p. 38; Angela Shire 1999: Great Synagogue Marriage Records, p. 86; ref. GSM 248/45. Susser's Decennial Census Records (1995).

[608] In the letter to Godfrey Simmons (August 1994) Susser refers to Aaron's Balm of *Gilead*, whereas in his thesis, it appears as of *Manheim*. In the letter, Susser may have confused this item with the "Solomon" reference of 24th May 1806. Susser's notes record his observation that Aaron may have been a "quack".

[609] *Exeter Flying Post, 15th May 1828* (Helen Fry 2000).

[610] See Mark 5:25-28 & Luke 14:1-5.

[611] His unrelated Jewish namesake traded in Falmouth.

CHAPTER 6
Towns with Minor Jewish Settlement

"In these towns there is rarely evidence of more than two or three Jewish families resident at any one time, more often there was only one, but it should be borne in mind that there may have been several, or even many more. In spite of their small numbers, these isolated and scattered families represent an important factor in the development of provincial Jewish life, as they provided a kind of cross-country hostelry, always ready to welcome a Jewish hawker.....or simply to help a poor Jew on his way to the next Jewish community, where he would find food, shelter, the offer of a job, and financial help."[612]

An example, from Somerset, illustrates this: "A Jewish pedlar, down on his luck, making his way to Bridgwater in 1821, was asked if he had friends there. 'No, but there are Jews there and they will help me'." [613]

The Jews of Redruth

Only five or six Jewish families are known to have lived in Redruth from the 1760s to the 1860s. One of the earliest to settle in the town was the family of Moses and Sarah Jacob, from Falmouth.

Moses Jacob (1733-1807)

Although his birthplace is not known, Moses ben Jacob was most likely one of the earliest settlers in Falmouth, the family having originated from Germany. It is even possible that he was born in Cornwall, although such an early date for Jewish settlement in the County is uncertain, and it is not known if his parents ever came to England or, indeed, to Cornwall. His grave in the Penryn Jewish cemetery records him as *Moses ben Jacob*. An original handwritten family tree in the Jacob Archive, in the hand of Leah Myer (1846-1933), wife of Alexander Jacob (1841-1903) records that Moses Jacob's mother is buried "at Falmouth". There is no confirmation of this from any other source, although there are unmarked graves there.[614] Moses Jacob married **Sarah Moses** (1748-1831), a daughter of Alexander Moses (Zender Falmouth). Zender's strict religious observance meant that he would have been very selective in his approval of a prospective son-in-law, and it would seem that Moses Jacob was indeed a man of meticulous orthodoxy. Sarah Moses shared this inclination, and was said to lead the prayers in the synagogue in Zender's absence. By all accounts she was a formidable woman with a forceful personality. Sarah and Moses Jacob had a total of fifteen children, three of whom died in infancy. Three of the others were deaf mutes, a congenital tendency which affected, in varying degrees, some members of the family in succeeding generations.[615]

By 1766[616] Moses and Sarah Jacob had left Falmouth and were well established in Redruth, a growing industrial and mining town, where Moses Jacob began by trading as a "Silversmith, Toymaker & Dealer in Old Clothes",[617] setting up business in Cross Street where he remained for the rest of his life. From at least 1769, he also traded as a watch and clock maker,[618] which, together with his skills as a Jeweller, became his primary business. His landlord was Captain Richard Paynter, a mine manager, and from this connection, Moses Jacob became one of the first people to deal in mineralogical specimens as a second trade. When Paynter died in 1787 the property passed to his daughter, Ann, who was the wife of William Murdoch, the local manager of the firm of *Boulton and Watt*. James Watt (1736-1819) was so celebrated during his lifetime for his achievements that he became the first engineer to be commemorated in Westminster Abbey, and he was lauded by the former Penzance chemist, Humphry Davy, as an inventor of genius with a profound knowledge of practical application. Watt was born in Greenock, Scotland. As a young man he went to London to study instrument-making, and later worked repairing instruments in the University of Glasgow, where, after some years he improved the performance of the steam engine first produced by Thomas Newcomen in 1712, and widely used into the 1760s. Watt eventually moved to Birmingham, where he went into partnership with the entrepreneur, Matthew Boulton (1728-1809), and, with another engineer, John Wilkinson, they produced an engine powerful enough to be used throughout Britain for grinding, milling, spinning, and weaving, which was introduced in Cornwall in the 1780s for pumping water from the mines, the first engine being installed at Great Wheal Busy mine near Chacewater.[619] Watt and Boulton spent much time in Cornwall promoting their engines, and it was Boulton's practice to buy "...shares in the mines, which he supplied with engines, his object being partly to finance the purchase of his engines and partly to strengthen his position in dealings with the adventurers" (other mining investors), such as Thomas Daniell (1715-1793) of Truro, through whom he met Sir Francis and Lady Basset of Tehidy.[620] William Murdoch of Redruth was responsible for the installation of these pumping-engines in the mines as well as watching the financial interest of his employers. Moses Jacob remained Ann Murdoch's tenant, as did a Simon Levy, who lived in a house which another of Paynter's daughters (Sally) had inherited.[621]

Although Moses Jacob was known primarily as a Jeweller and Clockmaker,[622] the diversification of his interests into the specialist field of trading in mineralogical specimens deserves some mention. He first appears in records as a mineral dealer in 1790, although he may have started earlier, and this aspect of his business was continued by his sons, Levy and Jacob Jacob, the former in Penzance, and the latter in Falmouth. This trade, which Moses Jacob was to pursue for over forty years, required the development of considerable geological knowledge, as well as familiarity with the local mining industry. Potentially it was also a very lucrative trade, but Moses Jacob did not exploit it to the detriment of his customers. William Jenkin, a mining agent in late 19th century, recorded the tradition that Moses Jacob had been known as "Honest Moses",[623] and this reputation was confirmed by Moses Jacob's contemporary, the mineralogist Philip Rashleigh (1729-1811) who noted that some dealers charged more for specimens than Jacob.[624] He came to hold a vast stock of specimens of an extremely high quality. Gregory Watt (1777-1804), son of the engineer James Watt, bought specimens from Moses Jacob up to 1798, and Jacob was still buying specimens from the local mines in 1804. He was also renowned for the beauty of the jewel and mineral displays in his shop, a characteristic that applied particularly to Jewish jewellers and mineral traders, both locally and elsewhere. Consequently, to liken something to a *Jew's Shop*, or to say that it must have been fashioned by a *Jewish* Jeweller, became common expressions indicating items or sights of exceptional beauty, reflected, for example, in Herman Melville's story of 1855, *The Apple-Tree Table*, in which a bug, that had been causing a disconcerting noise in its woodwork, crawls out of a crack, its colours "flashing in the room's general dimness, like a fiery opal - a tiny necklace round its neck – a diamond necklace - it was a beautiful bug – a Jew Jeweller's bug - like the sparkle of a glorious sunset." Melville's maritime travels took him to many places, including the Middle East and Jerusalem, and he possessed considerable Biblical knowledge. He had also visited Europe, including Liverpool, and had lived for many years in New York.[625] In these places he would have seen for himself the displays in Jewellers' shops.

In the mid 1790s, William George Maton visited Redruth, and reported: "We found nothing interesting here…" (Defoe, some thirty years later was to say of the town that it was "of no consideration") but Maton continues, " except an extensive collection of minerals belonging to a dealer of the name of Moses Jacob, an Israelite."[626] Jacob's business must have prospered, because by 1769 he was able to employ a James Dawson as his "journeyman" watch and clockmaker. A French subject, Dawson had led a colourful and interesting life. In an examination[627] sworn on oath before the magistrate Joshua Howell in Redruth on 4th May 1769, he recounted how he had been born in Dieppe in Normandy some 40 years previously (around 1728), where he had learned his trade as a clock and watchmaker from his father. In 1747, from the age of 19 he had been conscripted and served in the French army for some years, before travelling and plying his trade across Europe, living, amongst other places, in Vienna, Berlin, Cologne, The Hague, Amsterdam and Rotterdam, never spending more than a year or two in any town, or indeed any country. He eventually travelled from Rotterdam to Harwich, coming to London around 1758, subsequently living in Wales and Ireland, in Swansea, Ilfracombe, Drogheda, Dublin, Newry, Fishguard, Pembroke, and Swansea again, before arriving in Plymouth around 1767-8, where "he wrought upward of one year with one Abraham Joseph at the wages of eighteen pound a year, with meat, drink, washing and shaving twice a week".[628] From Plymouth he had come to Redruth and worked in Moses Jacob's business for the rest of his career, settling at last into domestic life, and marrying Grace Pascoe, a widow of Redruth.[629] Working for Moses Jacob seems to have had its attractions, one of which was his contract of employment which paid him sixteen shillings a week for a five-day week, together with paid Jewish holidays, when of course, the business was closed.[630] The Jacob/Dawson agreement is an example of one of the earliest "holidays with pay" contracts, and Dawson's value to the business must have been considerable for Moses to consider such generous terms of employment.

Although maintaining his loyalty to Orthodox Judaism, Moses Jacob integrated with ease into the host community. The earliest record of his social activities is to be found in Masonic records. The first Masonic Lodge in Redruth was the Druid's Lodge, and his name is mentioned in the first list of Members, Midsummer Quarter 1777, where he is described as having been initiated previous to 1777. Certainly Freemasonry was one of the few activities where men of different religions, countries and backgrounds could mix socially without the problems which would have been encountered in the everyday world. In 1779, a number of prisoners of war were present at the Redruth Lodge: "March 18th, A.L. 5779 - the following Brethren being Prisoners of War, this evening favoured us with a visit". Their signatures, together with a note that they were French, are those of Jean Labrouche Garnier (or Gaynieight), Crepin Nicholar (Crespin Nicholas), Joseph Babein, Jean Duhart, Joseph Vernoi, Charles Gilbert, and Sebastian Fiumee. At a subsequent lodge meeting, on 22nd April 1779, these men "proposed themselves to become members of the lodge, which was unanimously agreed to" (another man, possibly an Italian, G. N. Peyabeni, was also present).[631] These examples of the liberality of the members of the Druid's Lodge, especially in a time of war, indicate the favourable climate enjoyed by Moses Jacob in this context. He was to display a similar disposition and character when at the next Lodge meeting on 6th May 1779, a French Gentleman, M. Martial Raillon, presumably another paroled prisoner-of-war, was proposed for membership by Jean Labrouche Garnier. Moses Jacob seconded the proposition which was "unanimously accepted".

Likewise, in Falmouth, in January of 1782, two "prisoners", a Peter Cogrel "at Kegillick", and a Benjamin Warogmer "a French prisoner", both applied to the Lodge for charitable relief, which they were granted in the form of one guinea each. In March that year, Cogrel, now described as a prisoner of war, held by the Americans "in the hospital at Boyer's Cellars, Falmouth" applied once more, and, because he was confirmed as "a proper object" of charity, the Lodge "appointed a committee of three members to examine into the wants of Bro. Cogrel, and ordered that such relief should be given him as they found necessary."[632] Although, these recipients of charity were not Jewish, they indicate the concern in these Cornish Lodges for the welfare of any Mason, that would have extended, if necessary to its Jewish members. It should not be assumed that Congrel was found "a proper object" for charity in the sense that he was confirmed to be a Mason, in that Masonic charitable activity extended into the wider community, irrespective of Masonic allegiance. On 12th November 1783, the secretary of the Falmouth Lodge "feelingly states that a poor man (James Singclear) an object of charity, evidently not a mason, applied to the lodge for relief, and the members thought it proper to give him five shillings, and the brethren present also gave him eleven shillings."[633] Clearly, whilst charity towards masons carried a weight of obligation, discretionary acts of charity towards others were not uncommon. It is, no doubt, characteristic that, on 5th February 1811, the Falmouth Lodge, along with other British Lodges, donated ten guineas towards the relief of British prisoners in France, and at the same time voted one guinea for the relief of "a very aged Mason".[634]

Upon his death in 1807, Moses Jacob's will (which valued his estate at £200)[635], signed in a cursive Hebrew script, left all the tools of his trade to his son, **Levy Jacob** (1788-1824), and the business to his wife Sarah, who continued to carry it on (with Levy and Dawson) until her death in 1831. An eight-day grandfather clock of Moses Jacob (c. 1780) still exists, with a dial depicting a rocking ship, and there is another clock with King Neptune riding the waves in the arch.[636] There are at least three references to Moses Jacob in contemporary documents. Between 1782 and 1784, a "Mr. Cornish", a Tin-Smith and leading Quaker in Redruth, kept an account-book of his various dealings, amongst which is listed "Jacob Moses, Clock-maker, Redruth". The Universal British Directory for 1791[637] lists him as a Watch-maker. In 1804, the cash-ledger of a Mr. Alfred Jenkin records: "Paid for mineral specimens, Moses Jacob, to pd Isaac the Jew - for 8 specimens of Wh Fanny Tin 16/-".[638] This "Isaac the Jew" was **Moses Isaac Joseph** (-1834) of Falmouth, who had married Moses Jacob's daughter, **Judith Jacob** (1768-1849).

On the 8th May 1903, the *Jewish Chronicle* published the obituary of **Alexander Jacob** (1841-1903) a descendant of Moses Jacob. The obituary mentioned that Alexander Jacob had been a founder-member of the Hampstead synagogue, and noted that he had originally come from Falmouth, where his father "Moss J Jacob", that is **Moses Jacob Jacob** (1812-1860), was for many years the Warden and "main support of the congregation". It also mentioned that the Falmouth cemetery contained the graves of four generations of the Jacob family. On the 15th May 1903, the *Jewish Chronicle* published a letter from Alexander Jacob's brother, Samuel Jacob (1838-1913):[639] "The Jacob Family of Falmouth, SIR, referring to the obituary of my brother in your issue of the 8th, the following details may be of interest to your readers. Prior to the last of us brothers leaving Falmouth in 1880, there were, living and dead, six generations of the family there; all in turn supported the congregation and many were the old tales told of their ancestors. The first was that of an old lady, an 18th century dame, who laid *Tephillin*, acted as parnass in the absence of her lord and perhaps master (our ancestor, Moses Jacob) fasted on Mondays and Thursdays a half-day in memory of Moses going and returning after receiving the Tablets of the Law, superintended the horsing and packing of the animals and departure of her spouse, who was accompanied by a pony and a boy leading a pack-horse. The husband was a very little man who rode a very big horse. Regularly every Monday this procession went forth, returning every Friday for the Sabbath. (At this stage Moses Jacob acted as his own journeyman). He was most orthodox, his mid-day prayers never omitted and said on horseback. He had taught the animal to stand perfectly still during the *Amidah* and even to step backwards (as ritual demands) when the proper time arrived for doing so.[640] This may be said to have been a truly Jewish beast. This ancestor settled his son (Levy) in Redruth as a clockmaker, who in turn placed his son in Camborne as a draper. Such was his (*Moses Jacob's*) integrity that people would wait on Saturday night for the appearance of the Three Stars, the sign of the finish of the Sabbath, to do business with him. (There were) - 12 brothers and sisters - one married a Reverend Mr. Simmons, a Londoner (appointed to Penzance by Dr. Hirschell, the then Chief Rabbi). His daughter married a Mr. Rintel of Bury Street, London, EC, a great Mohel - who was appointed to Falmouth (as rabbi) - and remained there for seventeen years. Such is the short account of our family who resided in Cornwall for about a century and a half".

The reference to Moses Jacob at first acting as his own "journeyman" would most readily suggest his activities of travelling as a salesman and workman out into the country districts, an aspect of his trade that was vital to his income, in that the town centre shop alone would not be sufficient to support the business. The term was used more strictly, however, to denote a former apprentice who had served his time, and had completed his "journey" to become a fully qualified and skilled craftsman, now eligible for permanent employment. Part of the duties of the new journeyman would be to travel as a representative of his employer. It was only after his move to Redruth that Moses Jacob was able to train an apprentice as his assistant. His sons would also have been trained in his trade.

Other Jewish Traders and Residents in Redruth

Reuben and Meyers. Mercers, Market Place (1792) Insurance Policy.[641] It is not known how long this business traded in Redruth. It is possible that it is Reubens' infant son, *Jacob ben Reuven*, who is buried in the Falmouth Jewish cemetery (1:9).

A "Myar" is mentioned in 1828 in the Penzance Minute Book as contributing towards a new *Sefer Torah*, although this may the Congregation's Rabbi Myer Stadthagen, who served there from 1827 to 1829. A "Brother Myers" (possibly unrelated) appears in the Falmouth Masonic records in 1861.

Wolfe. Draper (Univ. 1793-8; Vol. 4, Pt. 1, p. 312).[642] Uncertain.

Hannah Silverstone, later a dealer in shells and curiosities in Plymouth, was born in Redruth c. 1797.[643] It is not known if she traded in Redruth. In Plymouth census returns, her age is recorded variously as 45 (1841), 53 (1851) and 70 (1861). An earlier marriage may explain her childrens' surname, *Joseph*. Her original family name has not been identified, and it is not known if she was related to the family of Israel Silverstone of Exeter.

Simon Levy. Occupation unknown. c. 1787. (Ref. Richard Paynter's will, above).[644]

The Joseph Family in Redruth

The extensive Joseph family, the issue of the two marriages of Joseph Joseph of Alsace (who died in London) took up residence in St. Austell, Falmouth, Redruth and Penzance. The branch of the family that settled in Redruth were from Falmouth.

Isaac Joseph. Tin-man and mineralogical specimens; c. 1804-1820. This is "Isaac the Jew" referred to by Alfred Jenkin in 1804, that is, Moses Isaac Joseph (-1834) formerly of Falmouth, Moses Jacob's son-in-law, who had married the latter's daughter, Judith (1768-1849). Their son was Joseph Joseph, below.

Joseph Joseph. Watch & Clockmaker, and Jeweller. Fore St. (Pg. 1823/4 & 1830/44;

Br. 1823); (1838: Insurance Policy); [645] Silversmith (1841 Census) and Mineralogist (Wi. 1847). Joseph Joseph (1802-1879) specialised as a dealer in mineralogical specimens in Redruth from 1823 to 1849, although he may have been resident in the town from 1819. The earliest reference to him as a mineral trader is in 1837, in a letter to a John Williams, offering him a specimen of Chalcedony, recently raised from a local mine.[646] From 1838-1848 he was supplying specimens from Cornwall and from Australia to the Royal Institution of Cornwall at Truro, some of which remain there. From 1840 he is listed in various directories as a mineralogist, and he advertised his stock in the local press: "To be seen at the house of Mr. Joseph, Redruth, a most Perfect Block of what is termed *Jews' House* Tin, which was lately found in that neighbourhood, the age of which is variously stated to be from 1600 to 2000 years." (1844). "Sale of Mineral Specimens and Shells by J. Joseph, Redruth." (1846).[647]

At the trial, in March 1844, of a Philip Treglohan, Joseph Joseph, together with his fellow jeweller, Jacob Schwerer, gave evidence concerning silver items that had been brought to them by the accused, and which he was charged with stealing in a burglary. Joseph Joseph had refused to buy the silver, but would also not surrender it, in that "…it had the appearance of being stolen." After various interventions, including that of his brother, Thomas Treglohan, who was known to Joseph Joseph, Joseph offered to return the silver, but was persuaded to buy it. Philip Treglohan was, however, arrested, and at the preliminary hearing, the "magistrate complimented Mr. Joseph for the caution he observed in buying suspicious goods." Because of insufficient evidence, and numerous credible character references, at his trial the jury found the accused Not Guilty.[648]

In 1845, between May to October, Joseph Joseph corresponded with Robert Hunt of the Museum of Practical Geology. On 5th June 1845, he offered him "A Large specimen of Blistered copper in the shape of the Prince's feathers [emblem] weighing 32lbs - a large specimen of very rare Christials [*sic*.] of Yellow Copper - a Beautiful specimen of Buntcupferez - and the specimen of Cobalt reserved for you." The reference to "Buntcupferez" is of particular interest in that it illustrates the striking and rare displays of minerals that were found in the shops of mineral dealers, and especially in the shop of Joseph Joseph. "Buntc(k)upferez" is an early synonym of the mineral Bornite (copper iron sulphide), a massive metallic material with a copper-red colour when freshly exposed, but which is brittle and quickly tarnishes to purple and blue upon exposure to air and moisture. It will often have dark grey or black streaks, but it is rarely in crystals, which, if formed are tiny, sparkling like miniature diamonds, with four to eight faces. It was a much sought after mineral, being found in Cornwall, and also in Arizona. The mineral had been known since 1725, but it was only given its current name in 1845, the same year that Joseph wrote to Hunt, being named after the Austrian mineralogist, Ignaz von Born (1742-1791). Joseph is also likely to have known it as "Peacock Ore" because of its purple colour and its tendency towards an iridescence that reflected the spectrum of colours in the rainbow, and its particular characteristic of changing colour with its position.[649] His trade in this particular mineral indicates his keen knowledge of this specialised field.

Joseph Joseph married **Fanny Solomon** (1815-1855) a daughter of Lazarus

Solomon (-1835) of Plymouth. The Solomon family had come from Lublin, Poland, where Fanny had been born. The 1841 Census for Redruth records Joseph[650] and Fanny Joseph living in Fore Street, with their four children. When Joseph Joseph left Redruth for Plymouth in 1849, the esteem in which he was held by the people of the town "in which place he has carried on the business of a jeweller for the last thirty years", was reflected in a lavish feast, and "a large party of the principal tradesmen of Redruth met together at St. Andrew's Hotel...to pay him the compliment of a public supper...[and]...unexpectedly large numbers...embraced the opportunity of manifesting their respect for Mr. Joseph's honourable and consistent character".[651] In Plymouth Joseph Joseph continued to trade in Whimple Street as a Watchmaker, Silversmith and Mineralogist. Between 1858-1863 he was selling minerals, including calcite, to the British Museum.[652] Their children were **Solomon Lazarus** (1837-1939), who married an Amy Marks, **Phoebe** (1838-) who married a Van Nirop, **Henry Isaac** (1839-), **Abraham** (1840, d.y.), **Esther** (1843-) who became a singing teacher and married Moses Rosenberg (1830-) a traveller of Devonport (1851 Plymouth Census), **Sarah Rachel** (1845-) a governess, **Gertrude** (1846-1935) who married a Mark Nathan (1846-1936), and whose granddaughter was to marry a nephew of the conductor, Sir Thomas Beecham, **Rose** (1849-) and **Julia** (1850-1930), the latter having been born in Plymouth (1861 Census), who married a Montague de Lissa (1844-1914). Two further children, **Florence** and **Mathilda**, may have been twins (both were 9 in 1861) were born in Plymouth c.1851/2. Florence Joseph (1851-1946) was to marry a Solomon Barnet, a property developer in the Kilburn and Willesden areas of London. She moved there and her husband named many of the streets there after places in Devon where his wife had been born. (This marriage should not be confused with that of her relative and namesake to Solomon Barnard of Dublin.)[653] Two of the most striking features of this family were the longevity of its members (Solomon Lazarus Joseph lived to be 102) and their emigration to Melbourne, Australia, and subsequent settlement in Canada and South America. Some of these emigrants returned to England, and others travelled in the South Pacific as traders and mineral prospectors.[654] Joseph Joseph's sister, Arabella (1802-1862) also lived in Plymouth, where her husband Myer Stadthagen, who had been the Rabbi at Penzance from 1827 to 1829, was Minister of the Hebrew Congregation (1861 Census), a post which he held for over 30 years until his death in the same year as his wife,1862.[655] Fanny Joseph died in 1855, and is buried in the Plymouth Hoe cemetery.

Joseph Joseph continued to trade in the city (1861 Census), but his trade with London became sufficiently established and lucrative that he had moved there, possibly with his unmarried daughters, by 1868, taking up residence in central London, in Goodge Street, off Tottenham Court Road, being listed there in trade directories from 1868 to 1870. Upon his arrival in London he took out an advertising flyer as a "dealer in minerals and other articles of natural history - antiques, &c", saying he hoped "by continuing the same care in the selection of Specimens, and the preservation of their correct localities, which he has hitherto done, to merit the continuance of the support he has received for many years past at REDRUTH and PLYMOUTH. J. J. has an extensive collection of Minerals (especially those found in the mines of Cornwall and Devon) from which single specimens may be selected or collections of any size can be made up. J. J. also prepares Elementary Collections of Minerals for teaching the Rudiments of the Science of Mineralogy – each specimen being carefully selected to illustrate one or more of the most important physical properties of the species to which it belongs. These collections are arranged in Mahagany [sic.] Cabinets at the following prices: 200 Specimens in four drawers £5 – 5 – 0, 350 larger Specimens in …eight drawers £10 – 0 – 0, Private Collections Named and Arranged by Competent Persons."[656] This last reference indicates clearly that Joseph Joseph was able to employ staff to assist in his business. Joseph Joseph died in London in 1879, age 77, and he is buried in the Willesden cemetery.[657]

It has been mentioned that Joseph Joseph of Alsace, who died in London, married twice. From his first marriage, there were two sons, Henry (1760-1802) who settled in St. Austell, and Moses Isaac (-1834) who came to Falmouth, and was the father of Joseph Joseph of Redruth. From the second marriage, there were two sons, Abraham (-1828), father of the Joseph Joseph below, and Lyon (1775-1825), father of the Barnet, below. The identity and the families of these two men, both named Joseph Joseph, can easily be confused. Joseph Joseph of Redruth, was a half-first-cousin, to:

Joseph Joseph of Falmouth (1802-1877 [658]), a Jeweller, married to **Phoebe Alexander** (1801-1869) of Plymouth, who had moved to Liverpool by 1860. This Joseph Joseph, was a son of **Abraham Joseph** (-1827) a Pawnbroker and Watchmaker of Falmouth, and a nephew of Abraham's brother, **Lyon Joseph** (1775-1825), the Falmouth shipping merchant who died in Bath. Gore's Liverpool Directories[659] list Joseph Joseph as a Jeweller at 11 Clarence Street (1860, 1864 & 1867). In 1865 the "Misses Joseph, Milliners" are given at the address. In 1868 and 1870 he appears in the directories as a "gentleman" at 64 Hope Place, and in 1871 he was at 18 Daulby Street. One of Joseph Joseph's daughters, **Arabella** (1837-1883) married Zallul Coppel of Liverpool at the Seel Street synagogue in 1868.[660] She died on 11th September 1883, and was buried in the Deane Road cemetery of the Liverpool Old Hebrew Congregation. Another daughter, **Rose**, married Hyman Moses, secretary of the Liverpool New Hebrew Congregation,[661] and her sister **Florence** (1852-1946) married Solomon Barnard of Dublin. Two years after his wife's death,[662] the 1871 Census for Liverpool records Joseph Joseph as a Widower and Retired Jeweller, age 69 years, with his daughters **Esther** (29) and **Rachel** (25), both Dressmakers, **Julia** (22) and **Rose** (19) both Governesses. That four of these daughters bore the same forenames (Esther, Florence, Rose and Julia) as the daughters of Joseph Joseph of Redruth, can further confuse the identities of the two families. It has not helped to differentiate the respective daughters in that both Esthers (1842-3) and both Julias (1849-50) were born within a year of their namesakes, with only three years separating the two Roses (1849-52). Joseph Joseph died in Liverpool on 3rd June 1877 at 18 Daulby Street,[663] and he was buried in the Green Lane Cemetery, where his headstone bears his name as *Joseph ben Abraham.*[664]

Lyon Joseph's son, **Barnet Joseph** (1801-1880), who had married a Betsy Jacob (1801-1889) of Dartmouth, had left Falmouth in 1823 for Bristol, where he became President of the Hebrew Congregation at the age of 24. He traded in Bristol as a

Jeweller, Silversmith and Watchmaker. By 1835 he had moved to Liverpool, where he became a founder of the Hope Place Synagogue.[665] It seems likely that he was the first of the Cornish Joseph family to live in the city. Although Barnet Joseph and his wife eventually retired to Birmingham (where they died) at some point at least two branches of the Cornish Joseph family were living in Liverpool, all trading as Jewellers.

Other Traders

Emanuel Cohen (*c.* 1775[666]-1849). Watch & Clockmaker and Jeweller. (Pg. 1830/44).

He was born in Carlsberg near Mannheim in 1775, and came to England via Gravesend in 1801. He lived in London for about 18 months (1801-2) and then spent 6 months in Plymouth, which he left in 1803 for Cornwall.[667] Cohen traded in Redruth for some 30 years, and it was said, he could be seen waiting on Fridays (the Sabbath eve) for sunset so that he could close his shop, and again on Saturdays to re-open it.[668] On 17th March 1848, the *West Briton* carried the following report: "ATTEMPTED ROBBERY – About three o'clock on Friday morning, the 3rd instant, two Housebreakers commenced their operations by boring four holes in the shutters of the shop-window of MR. COHEN, silversmith, Redruth. Mrs. Cohen, hearing an unusual sound, jumped out of bed and lifted the window, when she saw the two scoundrels run up the street. She called "thieves", which awoke a neighbour; and as a description of the rascals has been sent to the police of the neighbouring towns, it is hoped they may be overtaken by justice."[669] In the last year of his life, Emanuel Cohen subscribed five shillings to starving Jews in Tiberias, and the *West Briton*, just after his death, carried a notice on 22nd June 1849 that his business was to be disposed of. In his will he left everything to his wife, Leah.[670] He was affiliated as a member of the Penzance congregation, where his name appears in the Minute-Book, and it is possible that he is buried in the Penzance Jewish cemetery, in an unmarked grave, although the graves that have lost their headstone are much earlier than 1849. No grave for Emanuel Cohen has been identified in Falmouth, or in Plymouth. An eight-day grandfather clock (c. 1820) and a silver pear-case watch (hallmark 1821) still exist as examples of his work.[671] The 1841 Census records him (age 60) as "Foreign" and resident in Fore Street, with his wife Leah (50) and a daughter, Sophia (15). A male (50) "Levi…", whose forename is indecipherable, is given as "Independent", and may have been related to the Levi below:

Elias Levi. Jeweller Fore Street. (1841 Census: given as "Foreign"; age 20). He is recorded as living with the family of James Thomas, Greengrocer.

Isaac Solomon: a Pedlar (45) from Poland, Penrose's Row (1851 census). His wife, Fanny (36) was from Dublin, and their son, Alexander Solomon (10) had been born in Jersey.

Jacob and **Joseph Schurer** (*sic.* **Schwerer**), with Joseph Beringer. Clock Makers,

13 Fore Street. (1841 Census) as below. The Census records the Jewish Joseph Schwerer as 25, and Jacob (presumably his brother) as 30. Joseph Beringer was 20, and all three are given as "Foreign". The Schwerers traded both in Redruth and in Truro. The 1851 census for Redruth gives Jacob Schwerer (45) as an unmarried watch and clock maker at 3, West End, with Frederick Beringer (28), a watch maker and silversmith, also unmarried, and Leo Beringer (19) as his cousins. Schwerer's nephew, Conrad (17) was also employed as an apprentice watch maker.

Jacob Schwerer was involved as a witness in two cases involving theft in July of 1842.[672] In the first, a youth, William Hicks, aged 13, had stolen a silver watch from an engine-house at the Wheal Buller mine in Redruth. The watch was the property of the engine-house keeper, Benjamin Tippet. Assuming the false name of Goldsworthy, Hicks had taken the watch, that he claimed his father wanted him to sell on his behalf, to Schwerer's shop, and part exchanged it for a smaller watch. After contact with Tippet, Schwerer handed the watch over to a police officer. He arrested Hicks, who was sentenced "To be once privately whipped". In the second case, Mary Ann Reed, aged 21, was found guilty of stealing a silver watch from the house of Christopher Bawden of Camborne. Schwerer stated that she had come to his shop in Redruth and sold it to him. Bawden identified the watch as his, and despite the fact that Mary Reed "denied ever having been in the neighbourhood of Redruth for four years", she was sentenced to six months' hard labour.

Berenger (Beringer) and **Schwerer**. Watch & Clockmakers and Jewellers. Fore St. & West End. (Pg. 1844; Br. 1844; Sl. 1852/3; Kelly 1856). By 1861, Fidelis Beringer, from Baden had joined the firm. He was then 38, and his wife, Jane (32) was from Truro. Their five sons were Francis, John Jacob, Cornelius, Richard Ernest, and Heinrich. A Catherine Beringer (45) an unmarried sister, and a stepbrother, Joseph Pfaff (41) also unmarried were living in the household. By 1871, a John G. Pfaff (30), unmarried, was trading with the firm as a Jeweller.

Joseph Frankinstein: a Licensed Hawker of Drapery (33) and unmarried (1861 census). He was from Poland.

Samuel, son of **Isaac Lazarus** of Hayle was born in Redruth in 1838. A **Solomon Lazarus**, likely to have been another son, was also born in the town in 1843.[673]

Frederick Lazarus. Hawker. Penryn St. (Birth certificate of his daughter, Annie, 1862).
(Not known to have been related to the above.)

Joseph Saum: a boarder (43), an unmarried watchmaker from Germany. Uncertain.

Solomon and Marks. These two surnames appear in census records for Redruth and Camborne for various Christian families who might be taken as Jewish, but were not: James and Thomas Solomon were Sawyers in Redruth, and families with the surname *Marks* were masons and copper miners: Elisha Marks, James Marks, Abraham Marks and Matthias Marks.

Camborne

John Joachim, Excise-Man (*c.* 1793). Unlikely. He married a Catherine Rosewarne on 22ⁿᵈ May 1793.[674]

Jacob Jacob. Draper. from *c.*1811-18 (Ref. Roth ibid.) A son of Moses Jacob of Redruth, Jacob Jacob (1774-1853) appears in the Penzance Minute-Book as a subscribing member at this time. He was married to **Sarah Kate ("Kitty") Simons** (1778-1846), a daughter of **Samuel Simons** of Truro. Their children Moses ("Moss") Jacob Jacob (1812-1860) and Amelia Jacob (1811-91) were born in Camborne. [675]

Harris Samuel.[676] Jeweller, Union Street (1841 Census). He may have been of Jewish descent, but this is not certain. The census records him as "Foreign", age 35.

All of the following are unlikely to have been of Jewish descent: Henry Harris. Shoemaker, College Street (1841 Census). He is not known to have been related to Henry Harris of Truro. Hannah Harris. Cabinet Makers. (Sl. 1852/3). She is not known to have been related to Henry Harris of Truro. She is most likely the wife of the James Harris, Carpenter, who lived at Basset Street, with their children Hannah and Eliza (1841 Census). Abraham Harris. Medical Practitioner (Masonic Records: see below). Michael Abrahams. Hotel Keeper (Masonic Records 1869: see below). Members of this family were buried in the parish church cemetery. Henry Abraham. Mining-Agent (Masonic Records, *Boscawen Lodge*, 1871).

Gwennap (a small village, near Redruth)

A **Levi** family, who may have been Jewish, lived here *c.*1800, although their residence could have been temporary. Winifred Levi married a non-Jew in 1803 (see Falmouth marriages). Anna (a tailoress) who may have belonged to this Levi family, married Nathaniel Schram, and later moved to Plymouth. Later marriages and burials in the Schram family confirm Jewish status (see Nathaniel Schram: Falmouth Trades).

Helston

The town is not known to have had any significant Jewish settlement, except for transient hawkers, and the following were Christians: Solomon Rafael. Tin Miner (1841 Census for Sithney). Unlikely, although both names might suggest possible Jewish descent. Samuel Symons. Coal Merchant, Porthleven (1841 Census for Sithney). The census records three sons, Samuel (15), Solomon (12) and Tobias (7). Amelia Abrahams: Draper (1841 Census). She was only 15 at the time, and was born in Cornwall. She may have related to Annie Abrahams (1871). William Marks: Confectioner (1851). Joseph Beringer. A Watch and Clock maker (31) from Neustadt, Germany. He was not Jewish, nor was his wife, Christina (29) from

Sithney. All of his children were born in Cornwall. The Beringer firm, of Jacob Beringer, traded with the Jewish Jacob Schwerer in Truro and Redruth. There were marriage connections between the two families. Joseph Beringer traded in Helston for many years from at least 1851. **W. B. Symons.** Watch and Clock Maker, Meneage Street (1856 Br.). **Samuel Symons.** Carpenter, Church Street; and **Samuel Symons.** Grocer's Labourer, Meneage Street (1861).

Nathaniel Schram. Herbalist (1871 Census). A Jew from Holland. He also traded in Falmouth. Also Albert Schram. Bootmaker (1871 Census). Born Prussia. Also in Falmouth. Uncertain.

St. Keverne

Nora Jordan was born at St. Keverne *c.* 1885. It is not known that she was Jewish, or if she was connected with **Phoebe Aaron** (read as *Jordan*) of Bodmin (*c.* 1849) or with **Sophy Jordan** (1869) and **Robert Jordan** (1874) who were married in the Plymouth synagogue (see below). The surname Levy also occurs here for Christian families.

St. Agnes

Isaac Jacob, a travelling Jew, had deposited his box of Chapman's Wares as a security for indemnifying the Parish of St. Agnes in respect of an illegitimate child of which he was reputed to be the father. He had failed to return as required and unless he did so (by October 18th 1770) in response to the published notice, his box would be opened and the contents appraised and sold towards maintenance of the child (*Sherborne Mercury*, 24th September 1770).

WEST CORNWALL

Hayle

Joanna (a non-Jew), wife of Henry Moses, was born in Hayle in 1812.[677]

Samuel Jacob (1778-1860). He was a watch and clockmaker, and a son of Moses Jacob of Redruth. He was married to **Sarah Levy** (1784-1868) a daughter of **Israel Levy** of Truro. Samuel and Sarah Jacob's son, Moses Samuel, known as "Mosam", was born in Copperhouse, Hayle in 1815 (1851 census for Falmouth).[678] He never married, and died in 1858. Samuel Jacob is mentioned in various locations at around this time, and even traded on the Isles of Scilly. He settled in Penzance.

Isaac Lazarus. Watch and Clockmaker, Hayle (Ro. 1839; Copperhouse, 1841 Census).[679] Isaac Lazarus (35) is listed in the 1841 census with his wife, Rachel (35).

Both were from Poland, but are given only as "Foreign", with their children Harriet (7), David Leo (4), Lazarus (3), Samuel (2) and (almost illegible) Francetta, or possibly Henrietta (1). The latter may have died young, in that she is not listed in subsequent census records. All of the children were born in Hayle. Samuel was born in 1838, and further census records indicate that he was, in fact, a year older than his brother, Lazarus. A daughter, Phoebe, and a son, Solomon, were also born in Hayle between 1842 to 1843. Isaac Lazarus appears in the Accounts of the Penzance Congregational Minute-Book for 3rd August 1828, as having made a donation of 4 shillings towards a new *Sefer Torah*. Pigot's (1844) Directory does not give Isaac Lazarus as a watchmaker, but as a Hardwareman. By 1851, the family had moved to Liverpool, where Isaac Lazarus traded as a Dealer in Watches, and where another daughter, Rebecca, was born around 1850. David Lazarus remained in Liverpool, and adopted the surname *Lawrence*. From 1861 onwards, he appears at several addresses as a lodger, unmarried, his occupation being given variously as a Gilder, Hawker and General Dealer. In 1871, he was living with another Polish family, that of Julius and Yeta Hyams. He is not recorded as married until the 1901 census. Isaac and Rachel Lazarus had moved with their family to London by 1861, where Isaac, then 61, traded as a Dealer in Trinkets in the vicinity of the City of London. By 1871, he had been widowed, and the census for that year records him as living alone, in Aldgate. Isaac Lazarus died in London at Houndsditch on 18th August 1879.[680] His son, Lazarus Lazarus, is not listed as living in London on census records, and on 26th January 1880, he emigrated from the Port of Liverpool to the United States.[681] Isaac Lazarus of Hayle should not be confused with his namesake, a Jeweller of Exeter, who married Eliza Jacobs in Plymouth in 1842. Eliza Jacobs was a daughter of Levy Jacob (-1824) of Penzance. She was born in Falmouth (*c.* 1814). Another Isaac Lazarus was married in Plymouth in 1888.[682]

Jacob Schurer (Schwerer). (25) Clock maker, with Joseph Beringer (20), Clock maker, and Fidelis Beringer (15). All given as Foreign (1841 Census).

None of the following are known to have been of Jewish descent: Josiah Symons. Mason, Bodriggy (1841 Census). Unlikely. The trade is not one associated with Jews. The census gives his wife, Esther, and children, Josiah, Martha and Esther. The girls' names were common among Gentiles, and were most likely taken directly from the family's familiarity with the Old Testament. Sisters Betsy and Mary Simons, Dressmakers (a trade commonly practised by both Jewish and Gentile women) also appear at Trevassack in 1841. Neither are likely to have been Jewish, which their brother's trade, "Engine Maker" would tend to reinforce. Benjamin Harris. Shoemaker, age 50 (1841 Census) given with his wife, Eliza (50), and sons, Anthony (20), Jacob (15) a "Boiler", and Joseph (15) a Ropemaker: unlikely. There were Christian Jordan and Marks families in Hayle. Thomas Marks was a Labourer, and Elisha Marks, a Mason (1841 Census). Harris Benjamin. Hair Dresser (Pigot 1844). Uncertain. Henry Wildman. Professor of Music from London, (58) married, and a lodger (1851 Census): uncertain. Jacob Sickerson. (1851 Census) Carpenter (31), with his wife, Sarah (30), and son, Henry (7). The family were from York. Uncertain. Samuel Hart. Copper Miner, from Marazion (1861 Census). He was not connected with the Jewish Hart family of Penzance. George A. Solomon. Miller, from Camelford (1871 Census). His wife, Eliza, was born in rural Devon, and his children in Devon and Cornwall. Unlikely.

St. Ives

1703. Two pedlars, who may have been Jews, were given charity by the borough of St. Ives.[683]

Wiseman ———— before 1752. (Br.[684]) Uncertain.

Gabriel Rosenthal. "Miscellaneous" (most likely a travelling hawker: Pg. 1830). His surname appears in the Penzance Congregational Minute-Book for 1828 as contributing 2s. 6d. towards a new *Sefer Torah*.

Henry Edwards Jacobs. Master Mariner (b. 1840). Unlikely. (Masonic Records).

Joseph Barnet. Dealer in Marine Stores, Fore Street (1841 Census) and 2 Pudding-bag Lane (1851 Census). In 1841 he was living (most likely as a lodger) with Grace Major, her daughter, Mary, son Ephraim(e), a Plumber, and two others, all five of whom were born in Cornwall. Joseph Barnet is recorded as "Foreign". In 1851 he was living alone, and was unmarried. The census records that he was born in Holland (but, curiously, "Devon" is written alongside the entry) and a British Subject . He died in 1856, and he was buried in the Penzance Jewish cemetery (8:2) at the Congregation's expense.

Alexander Singer: Herbalist (1851). He was 21, unmarried, a lodger, and, presumably, a travelling hawker. From Turkey, he may been a Turkish Jew.

Solomon Teacher (Techaur). Jeweller. He traded in Penzance (see earlier), but lived in St. Ives at some point, where he died on 10th March 1856. He was also buried in the Penzance Jewish cemetery (7:1) at the Congregation's expense.

Gentile Jacobs, Marks and Abraham Families: these surnames appear amongst Christians in St. Ives. The following represent selected examples: Philip Jacobs and Jacob Jacobs were fishermen, Grace Jacobs a fish dealer, and John Jacobs, a sailor (1841). Nicholas Jacobs was a fisherman (1861), Rebecca Jacobs a tailoress, Jacob Jacobs, a fisherman, and John Jacobs, a labourer (1871). Benjamin Marks was a sawyer, from Marazion (1851). Henry Marks was a tin miner from Mawgan, his wife, Hannah, from Cury. Of their children, Joseph Marks was a labourer, and Sydney Marks, a tin miner (1881). Joseph Abraham was a fisherman from Penryn, and his wife, Catherine, and four children were all born in St. Ives (1871). By 1881 he is recorded as a "Sweeper (Scavenger)", and his sons, John and Joseph, were both fishermen. The surname, **Hart**, was (and still is) widespread in St. Ives. There is no known connection with the Jewish Hart family of Penzance.

Isaac Bloomfield. A soldier from Wiltshire (1871). Unlikely.

The Isles of Scilly

Samuel Jacob. Occupation unknown. (*c*. 1820s).[685] This is the same as Hayle, above; see Penzance Trades and Freemasonry).

MID CORNWALL

St. Austell

Barnett Levy. Silversmith, 1758-1765.[686] This is not the Barnet Levy, from Holland, who settled in Falmouth. Barnett Levy of St. Austell was born at Widdleshofen, Ansbach, Germany in 1732. He had entered at Harwich in 1758, and after leaving St. Austell in 1765, he went to Portsmouth for 10 years, then to Plymouth for 28 years.

Samuel Solomon. Tailor. (Un. 1799). He may have been Jewish.

Phillip Samuel. Jeweller. *c*. 1815-1819.[687] Samuel was from Warsaw, and the son of the Secretary of the Great Synagogue there. He was highly educated in Hebrew. His early marriage in Poland, that produced one daughter, was not successful. He traded as a silk merchant, importing materials from Danzig, to which he travelled. He also lived in Vilna, and travelled through Poland, and to Russia, where he stayed in Moscow, but he fled the country to avoid bankruptcy and consequent imprisonment. Upon arriving in England, he secured, through the influence of the Chief Rabbi, Herschell, an interim appointment in the Penzance synagogue as a Reader in Prayers (from July 1810 to April 1811). In the Congregational Minute Book, his name appears as *Rav Feivel*. The incumbency appears to have included the responsibilities of *shochet* in killing cattle and poultry, "for which he was not fitted", and he soon found work with the merchant Lyon Joseph of Falmouth as an agent for buying gold. Lyon Joseph's business interests collapsed, and when Lyon Joseph moved to Bath in 1815, Samuel set up as a jeweller in St. Austell, "with a fellow countryman" whose identity is not known. However, this venture was not a success, and he was advised by Lyon Joseph to go to Portugal, where Lyon Joseph had business connections, and where Solomon Solomon of Falmouth had settled in Lisbon. Philip Samuel was in Lisbon when Solomon Solomon died there in 1819, and he remained in the city and traded as a jeweller.

J. Joseph. Watch & Clockmaker. (Br. 1820). This will not be a son of Henry Joseph (1760-1803) of St. Austell, whose son, Joseph (and his brother, Philip) died in infancy in 1790, and are buried in the Falmouth Jewish cemetery (6:1). The J. Joseph given by Brown is likely to be the Joseph Joseph (1802-1879), son of Moses Isaac Joseph (-1834) of Falmouth, who traded in Redruth from *c*.1823 until 1849. It is also possible that this is Joseph Joseph (1802-1877) son of Lyon Joseph (1775-1825) of Falmouth. Both Joseph Josephs lived in Plymouth after leaving Cornwall.

Samuel Harris. Tin-Man & Brazier. (Pg. 1830). Uncertain.

Martha Woolf may have been born in St. Austell (1832). See Bodmin.

Lyon Colman. Jeweller (c. 1839-1841). In July of 1839, Colman appeared as a witness at the trial of Josiah Anthony, who was accused of stealing a quantity of tin and other minerals from the Old Blowing House, the property of a Richard Davey of St. Austell. Colman did not usually deal in mineralogical specimens, but when approached by Anthony, agreed to try to seek an assessment of the tin's value by weight. He gave some money to Anthony as provisional payment, but then sent the tin elsewhere for assessment. The tin was eventually passed to the police. There was no implication that Colman was in any way complicit in the affair, and Anthony was found guilty of theft and was "transported to such of her Majesty's dominions as her Majesty in council may think fit for the term of seven years."[688] Of particular interest in the report are the references to Colman's excursions "into the country", a reminder that Jews resident in Cornish towns, such as jewellers and watch makers, whether trading from shop premises or from private houses, needed to spend much of their time travelling around the district to sell their wares and to offer their skills to repair items. In the 1841 census for St. Austell, Colman appears at Duck Street, as a jeweller, age 45, "born in Foreign Parts". He was most likely born around 1800, and was from Poland. He was in Callington by 1851 (see below).

Jacob Hyman. Watchmaker, Fore Street (1841 Census; born in Cornwall). Brown does not list a Hyman. His age in the Census is given as 77, and it is likely that he is to be identified with Brown's **Jacob Higman** (1763-1841) who had traded in the town since 1806, and died on 29th October 1841 age 78. In November 1841, his business was put up for sale. Brown records for Higman: a robbery (20th December 1811), advertises for an apprentice (26th February 1823) and a journeyman (25th November 1825) and a burglary (18th September 1835).[689] It is not certain that he was of Jewish descent. See also: Samuel Higman, Surgeon, of Falmouth (1768). A Frederick Higman was a clay merchant in St. Austell in 1871.

"A Travelling Jew. On Monday last an inquest was held at the Union House, St. Austell, on the body of **Barnard Youngman**, a travelling Jew, aged 51 years. It appeared in evidence that he was liberated from Bodmin gaol on Friday last, and that he was seen at various places on the road betwixt that place and St. Austell; and all agreed to the weak state he appeared to be in. At one place, a woman made some tea for him, but he refused to take it. He was found lying in the hedge, on Sunday morning early, about a mile from the town, and was conveyed in a cart to the Union House, where medical aid was procured; but he expired in less than an hour after he was brought in. Verdict, died from cold and exhaustion. 18th July 1845." [690]

Benjamin Michael (c.1768-1853). Watch and Clock Maker, Fore Street (1800-1847). Br. Pg. 1830 and 1841 Census. Also as "& Co." (1847). His name could suggest that he was of Jewish descent, but it is unlikely, and the family were Christians. He was born in Cornwall and was married in the parish in 1800. He was the Parish Clerk in that year. He was buried in the Parish churchyard on 18th August 1853,[691] after a Coroner's Inquest [692] of his sudden death in a public place. He had set out from St. Austell to walk to Mevagissey, a distance of some five to six miles, and had collapsed and died. At the time of his death, the Coroner's Report [693] noted that he "was the oldest tradesman in the town" (of St. Austell), and was about 85 when he died. William Michael. Watchmaker, Fore Street (1841 Census: age 25) The son of the above.

Thomas Jacob, Tailor, Joseph Jacobs, Tailor (both 1841 Census) and John Jacob, Tailor (Wi. 1847). Uncertain.

Aran (*sic.***Aaron) Moses**. Traveller (likely hawker), Tregonissey Street (1841 Census). He is recorded as "Foreign".

Solomon Levy. A Hawker (50) is recorded (1841) as having been born in the County. It is not certain that he was Jewish, and he has not been linked with the families of Barnet Levy of Falmouth or Israel Levy of Truro. It is possible that he was related to the Barnett Levy who traded much earlier in St. Austell, but who left Cornwall in 1765, eventually living in Plymouth from around 1785. Nor is it known if he was connected with Lyon Levy of Plymouth, who traded in Truro from 1821-1829. Solomon Levy appears in the 1841 Census with his wife, Mary (45), who was not born in Cornwall. Likewise, their first four children, Hannah (15), Harriet (15), Eleazar (15: the name is unclear and could be read as *Eleichazan*) a Tin Miner, and Emma (13) were not born in Cornwall, but the other six children were: Solomon (12), Rebecca (10), Eliza (8), Mary (6), Ellen (5) and Joshua (3). The childrens' names could suggest they were Jews, but no Jew has been identified by occupation as a tin miner elsewhere. An Alice Levey (20) also appears in the 1841 Census (in another location in St. Austell), and she had been born in the County.

John Joseph (1851). Grocer and Tea dealer from Devonport. Uncertain. George Isaac (1851). Grocer. Uncertain.

Joseph Ponisi (1851-1871). A Licensed Hawker from Italy. Uncertain. His wife and children were all born in St. Austell, and their names do not suggest Jewish descent. A son, Edmund Ponisi, was a Cordwainer's assistant in 1871.

George Spiegelhalter (1851). A Clockmaker from Plymouth. Uncertain. His wife, Sarah, is given as from St. Austell in 1851, but from Stoke Damerel, Devon in 1861. The surname appears among Jews in London, but also among Gentiles. A Spiegel-halter family, Jewellers and watchmakers, have run a business in Penzance until the present day, and are German in origin, but not Jewish. A Savory Spiegelhalter[694] was a clock cleaner in St. Austell in 1873.

Raphael and Isadore Zabor, and Raphael and Iago Silva from Guatemala, were advanced students at a small boarding school, Ledra House, run by Henry Drake from Nova Scotia and his wife Mary, from Falmouth (1861). The boys' ages ranged from 20 to 15. It is possible that the Zabor and Silva boys were from a Sephardic Jewish family, but their names were also common amongst Spanish colonial Christians.

Jacob, Solomon and Isaac families who were Christians appear in St. Austell: Thomas Jacobs (1841) and John Jacob (Wi. 1847), both Tailors. William Jacob. Boot & Shoemaker, Fore Street (Wi. 1847; 1851 Census). He was born in St. Austell and his wife, Mary, in Mevagissey. William Jacobs (55) and his sons, Benjamin (a Mason) and Joseph Jacobs (a Tailor) appear in the 1841 Census (and later). All of the family were born in St. Austell. William Thomas Jacobs (1851) was a Journeyman Carpenter, and other Jacobs men were china clay workers (1871). Joseph Jacob. Mercer & Tailor, Fore Street (1861 Census). He is recorded as employing "2 Men, 4 Females & 1 Boy". His family were all born in St. Austell. William Solomon (1841) was an Agricultural Labourer, born in Cornwall, together with all of the members of his family. A Nancy Solomon (1841) was a servant at Penrice House, and a Jane Solomon (1841) and her six children were resident at the St. Austell Workhouse. Ann Solomon (Solamon) was a lodger housekeeper, and another Jane Solomon from St. Columb was a kitchen servant (both 1851). A William Solomon from Mevagissey was a dock labourer (1861-1871). Charles Isaac and his son Richard were copper miners (1861) and George Isaac was a stone mason (1871). Various Isaac women in St. Austell were domestic servants. The surnames *Kippel* and *Kissel* might be taken as Jewish, but they are found amongst Gentile families who worked as copper and tin miners (1861).

Joseph Shephard, from Salop, whose name might also suggest a Jew, was, in fact a Primitive Methodist Preacher (1861).

"A Travelling Jew and his Box. It is generally thought a thing almost impossible for a Jew to part with his box; but on Wednesday last the town of St. Austell was greatly disturbed by that very occurrence. The Jew, in going from a jeweller's to his lodgings, finding his box heavy, placed it on a waggon that was passing, which carried it so far, and then took it off the waggon into a shop, saying, 'Let me leave this box, please, until I call for it.' He then went to his lodgings, and when he was about to leave, at ten p.m., he went for his box where he usually left it, namely the bedroom – but lo! the box was not there. He swore he had put it there, and told the landlord he should expect him to replace it, to the value of 80 pounds. The box was accidentally discovered the next day, at twelve o'clock, in a butcher's shop, but in the meantime, all the policemen in the town were in requisition; three or four houses were searched, and the characters of several honest men questioned by the Jew. 20th January 1865." [695]

Mevagissey

Israel Davies (1768) apprenticed to Thomas Cock, a Ropeworker. Uncertain. It has been assumed that he was Jewish.[696] The forename, Israel, was not uncommon amongst Christians.

St. Blazey

St. Blazey Benjamin Cohen. Seaman (1881 Census). He may have been of Jewish descent. He was born in Brighton (c. 1862).[697]

NORTH CORNWALL

Bude (Stratton)

The 1841 and 1848 Post Office Directories for London give a **George Simons** as a Watch Manufacturer at 49 King Square, Finsbury. He also appears as a Watchmaker at No. 49 King Square in the 1851 Census, born in Stratton, Cornwall (c. 1799-). Listed with him is a **Moses Simons,** also born in Stratton (c. 1796-), presumably George Simons' brother. The two men are listed as trading together in the 1852 Post Office Directory at the same address. A decade earlier, in 1841, the same directory lists an **Abraham Simons** (who may have been a relative) living at 56 King Square. It is not known if any of these men were Jewish, and variants of *Simons* appear as a common surname amongst non-Jews in Cornwall and elsewhere in England in the 18th and 19th centuries. The fact that in the later 1871 Census the Jewish family of **Saul Simons (Symonds),** cigar manufacturer, mentioned above, were living at 46 King Square may be coincidental.[698]

There was no resident community of Jews at Stratton or in Bude, and if a solitary Jewish Simons family did live there, they would have been affiliated to either the Exeter or Plymouth congregations, both about 50 miles away.

Bodmin

Martha, wife of **Henry Woolf** (the surname is given variously in census records as *Wolf, Woolf, Wolfe* & *Woolfe*). Martha Woolf's place of birth is uncertain: *Bodman* (*sic.*) in 1861, and St. Austell in 1891.[699] She was born in 1832, and died in 1891.[700] Her family surname is not known. Her husband, Henry Woolf was born in Exeter in 1820, the son of George Woolf of Exeter and his wife Rachel of Barnstaple. Both parents were travellers, selling stationary (Exeter Census 1851). Henry Woolf settled in Plymouth, and traded there as a Jeweller in Union Street, East Stonehouse (1861 Census), and later at 6, Windsor Street (1871 & 1881 Census). Henry Woolf was buried in the Gifford Place cemetery, Plymouth on 14th April

1886, age 66, and his wife, Martha Leah was interred there on 3rd August 1891, age 58. Henry Woolf of Plymouth was not related to Lemon Woolf of Penzance.

Jonson & Abraham. Watchmakers & Silversmiths. Fore St. (Br. 1844). Sale upon moving to Falmouth (*West Briton*, 6th September 1844; Pg. 1844). Jonson is likely to have been Jewish. It has been mentioned previously that immigrant Continental Jews sometimes adopted English surnames, especially if their own names were particularly difficult for English people to scan and pronounce, such as Eastern European (Polish and Russian) names. A nationally famous name, could be used, and *Nelson* was adopted in this way. This surname occurs amongst Jews in Plymouth in various census records from 1871.[701] A Harry (Hyman) Nelson, was a Jeweller in Union Street in 1906, and a Rachel Nelson was married to a Michael Jacobs in the Plymouth synagogue in 1907, and eight Jewish burials are listed for the Plymouth Gifford Place cemetery.[702] Names that were familiar locally, or characteristic of that area, were also used. Jews whose patronymic was *Jonah* adopted names such as *Jonas, Jones* or *Johnson*. There was a Jewish *Johnson* family in Devon. A "Mr. Johnson" is mentioned in Plymouth Congregational records in 1810. A Sarah Johnson married Mosley Hyman, a Mercer, in Plymouth in 1849.[703] Eliza Johnson (70) a former pawnbroker from Portsmouth, and who may have been related to David Israel Johnson from Portsmouth, was living with a Hyman family in Catherine Street, Plymouth in 1851. She had previously lived in Exeter.[704] A Joseph Johnson lived in Exeter in the mid 18th century, and earlier, a Phineas Johnson (c.1805) and a Moses Johnson (c. 1818) had lived in Exeter, Plymouth and Portsmouth. The name, *Jonas*, was also found among westcountry Jews. A Hannah Jonas, *Hannah bas Menhahem* the Levite, was buried in the Hoe cemetery in 1875, and two burials with this surname took place at Gifford Place.[705]

Phoebe Aaron (*c.* 1849) of Bodmin: a joint insurance policy with Hyman Aaron of Edinburgh, Louisa Marks of London, Rose Symons (no town) and Jane Moses of Cincinnati, U.S.A., on a house on The Quay, Stonehouse, Devon. The surname in the insurance policy is likely to be *Aaron*, but it has been read as *Jordan*: it is unclear in the original document. Phoebe Aaron was a daughter of Abraham Joseph I (1731-1794) of Plymouth and Rosy Abraham of London. Phoebe Joseph (who died in 1832) married an Abraham Aaron (who died in 1833), and an Abraham Aaron (who may have been the same) traded in Falmouth in the early 1830s. One of their eight children, was a Hyman Dov Aaron, who may be the name on the policy. Phoebe may have been his daughter or niece. Rose Symons is likely to be Phoebe and Abraham Aaron's only daughter, Rose (*c.* 1816-) who married Moses Simmons (1817-1876), a son of Rabbi B. A. Simmons of Penzance. Rosy Abraham's grandfather was a Michael Moses of London, and the Jane Moses of the policy may have been a descendant. Abraham Joseph I (1731-1794) had owned various leasehold and freehold properties in Plymouth, including three on this same Quay at the time of his death, and these were left jointly to his daughter, Phoebe, and her siblings, Joseph, Geller, Henel, Samuel and Brina. He also left in trust to Phoebe Aaron, a house in Pyke Street, in which she lived with her husband. Joseph Joseph, Phoebe's brother, or his son, Abraham Joseph II (1799-1868) may have sold a lease to those named in the policy above.[706] If the first name on the policy is to be read as *Jordan*, it is not known if Phoebe Jordan was related to the Sophy Jordan of Plymouth, daughter of Charles Jordan (a Doctor), who, on 27th October 1869, married Solomon Tucker, who like his father Charles, was a watchmaker. A Robert Jordan, Surgeon Dentist, son of Mark Jacob Jordan, on 28th January 1874, married Bella Joel, daughter of Asher Joel (1810-1880) an itinerant jeweller of Plymouth.[707] Plymouth census records from 1841 to 1871, and the Jewish Congregational Burial records for Gifford Place contain various *Joel* entries, but there are none for *Jordan*. Nor is there any reference to Bodmin.

George Solomon. Grocer & Tea Dealer. St. Leonard's St. (Wi. 1847) and George Solomon. Tailor, 57 Lower Bore St. (1861 Census). Both unlikely. The surname, Solomon, appears for families around the Bodmin area, but they may not have been of Jewish descent. These families were Christians, as various parish records of baptisms, marriages and burials show.

Liskeard

Edel, wife of **Joseph Joseph** of Plymouth, was born in Liskeard in 1771.[708] Joseph Joseph (1766-1846) is buried alongside his wife Edal "daughter of Abraham Zvi" in the Hoe cemetery. She may have been a niece of Minnele (-1811) wife of Henry Hart (c.1726-1808) of Plymouth. Jessop's speculation that this Edel (or Edal) was from the Hart or Woolf families of Penzance is not supported by genealogical information. Lemon Hart's aunt, Edel, was born in 1747, and his sister, Eddle (whose dates are not known) married Hyman Woolf (*c.* 1732-1820). The spurious connection of Edal Joseph (of Liskeard and Plymouth) with a Penzance family derives solely from the use of the forename by the Penzance Hart women, and also the fact that Edel Joseph's son, Abraham (1799-1868) married Eliza (Telza: 1808-1850) a daughter of Eddle and Lemon Woolf of Penzance. Edel Joseph of Plymouth and Eddle Woolf of Penzance were, therefore, related through marriage.

Nathan Harris. Apprenticed to Peter Pitt, a Gunsmith, 1760-62.[709] Unlikely, but this Harris has been taken to have been Jewish, in that others with the same name were Jews.

Sarah (also known as Betty ot Betsey) wife of **Abraham Abraham(s)**[710] of Plymouth, was born at Linkinhorne/Callington (between Liskeard and Tavistock) *c.*1800. Her family name was also Abraham, and she was the daughter of a John Abraham. Her father may have been a Jewish pedlar, but it is not certain that her family was of Jewish descent. Abraham Abraham (1794-), was the son of **Mordecai Abraham**[711] (1743-1811) a Plymouth silversmith, and his wife **Rachel**. Mordecai Abraham was from Gelheim, near Mannheim, Germany, and he arrived in England, via Harwich, in 1766. He is buried in the Hoe cemetery. Abraham and Betty Abrahams were living at 13, Morley Place, Plymouth in 1841, together with Abraham's mother, Rachel, then 83. Abraham Abraham is given as a watchmaker.

They already had seven children born from around 1829, but they were not married in a Jewish ceremony until 11th January 1846. The Plymouth Hebrew Congregation Marriage Register records that both bride and groom lived at Hicks Lane, Plymouth. In 1851, they were living at 99, Union Street, Stonehouse. Abraham does not appear on this census, and Betsey is given as a "sempstress, pensioner's wife". In 1861, they were living in a lodging house at 16 Finewell Street, Plymouth with their children Markes (19) and Rebecca (17). Abraham Abrahams, then 67, is given as "Chelsea" (pensioner), his son, Markes, as a tailor, together with a Joseph Abrahams (66) a traveller from Holland. Sarah and Abraham Abrahams may have been cousins, although the surname is so common amongst Jews that their families may not have been connected.

Josiah Abraham. Miller (-1810).[712] Uncertain. It is not known if he was related to his namesake, below, or to John Abraham, above. A Josiah Abraham was in Falmouth in 1751.

Webb & **Abraham**. Watch & Clockmakers. (Pg. 1823). It is likely that Webb (who is unlikely to have been Jewish) is to be identified with the Watchmaker John Webb of Liskeard (c. 1811-1815 Br.) or with the Watch and Clockmaker W. H. Webb (1856 Br.) both of whom traded in Lower Lux Street. For the partner Abraham, see below.

Joseph Beer. Groceries & Sundries, Dean Street. (Pg. 1830). Uncertain.

Josiah Solomon. Tailor, was born in Liskeard in 1834. It is not known if he traded in Liskeard, but he was a Tailor in Penzance in 1871. Uncertain.

Eli Levi, age 18, on 17th October 1845, pleaded guilty at Bodmin Quarter Sessions to the charge of stealing three pocket knives, the property of Thomas Brown of Liskeard, and was sentenced to two months (*West Briton* 16th-24th October 1845).[713] Eli Levi was most likely an itinerant, and he may have been Jewish. He is not known to have been related to the family of Israel Levi of Truro or Barnet Levy of Falmouth.

Josiah Abraham (1796-1879) Watch and Clockmaker, Church Street, Pike Street (Br.) Uncertain.

Solomon Cohen. General Dealer (1881 Census). Recorded as a lodger, he is likely to have been a hawker, and was born in London.[714]

Launceston

Solomon Hymes (**Hyams**). Silversmith (1805). A man with this name (who may not have been Jewish) was acquitted of rape at the Lent Assizes in April 1805. It is possible that he is to be identified with the Solomon Hyams who was born in Germany in 1740,[715] entering Harwich in 1762, and trading in Plymouth as a silversmith from 1793.[716]

Solomon Levy. General Shopkeeper. Southgate. (Pg. 1830). He may have been Jewish, but no connection with other Levy families in south Cornwall is known.

Joseph Zalmanson. Licensed to search for minerals in the Parish of Lezant (1885). Although it is likely that he was Jewish, he was not a resident of the County, but was from London. His home was at Highbury New Park, Middlesex. The licence, for one year from 12th October 1885, was issued in London, and drawn up there by a solicitor. It was issued jointly to C. T. H. Bennet, a resident of Launceston.[717]

Callington

The following are uncertain, but may have been of Jewish descent: F. Almond. Watch & Clockmaker (Pg. 1830). Benjamin Samuells. Tailor, Chapel Street (1841 Census). Jane Samuels. Dressmaker, Back Street (1841 Census). Henry Silberman. Stationer & Bookseller. Higher St. (Wi. 1847).

"**Alexander Morris**, 18, was indicted for stealing, on 22nd February last, at Callington, a silver watch, gold ring, six silver buttons, three sovereigns, two half-sovereigns, and two seals, the property of Thomas Lake. The prisoner, who was a Polish Jew, through an interpreter, pleaded Guilty to the charge, and was sentenced to Eight Months' hard labour. He cried bitterly on being informed of his sentence." (*West Briton*, 3rd April 1846).[717a]

Lyon Colman. Silversmith. Fore Street. He appears in the 1851 census as a Lodger, unmarried, age 51 "born Poland, Russia".

Lostwithiel

Aaron Abrahams. Watchmaker. (Br. 1821). Moved to Plymouth. It is not known if he is to be identified with Abraham Abrahams (above) or as a member of the family of Mordecai Abraham of Plymouth.

John Symons, Draper, and Charles Symons, Apprentice Tailor, Fore Street (1841 Census). Unlikely.

Morwenstow

Aaron Harris. Watchmaker. (Br. c. 1830). Uncertain.

Saltash

Selina, wife of Maurice Lazarus, a tailor, from Leigh in Essex, was born in Saltash in 1831. Her family name is not known, and it is not certain that she was Jewish. Census records show Maurice Lazarus (1821-) was living in Plymouth from at least 1851. In 1871 they were living at 22 Bedford Street, with three daughters, Alice (16), Eliza (14) and Ellen (12). It is likely that the couple were married *c.* 1854. Curiously, Maurice Lazarus alone appears in the 1861 Census.[718] There is no record of the couple's marriage in the Plymouth Congregational Register. No connection is known between this Lazarus family and that of Frederick Lazarus of Penzance (who was originally from Yorkshire), and Isaac Lazarus of Hayle. Other Jewish Lazarus families lived in Exeter.[719]

Itinerant

Mordecai Jacobs. Umbrella Maker, in Cornwall *c.* 1753-73. He was born in Prague in 1727, entering via Harwich in 1750. He spent three years in London, and then twenty in Cornwall. From 1773 he lived in Plymouth, where he died in 1806. He is buried in the Jewish cemetery on the Hoe. His son **Jacob Jacobs**, who was also interred there in 1811, was married to **Hannah**, daughter of **Hyam Barnett** of Gloucester. In his will, Jacob Jacobs left the sum of £100 to be invested, with the interest to be paid "to the poor Jews of Plymouth every year", on condition that "my late father Mordecai Jacobs, and myself, be commemorated forever at the Yizkor service." [720]

Unidentified

There may also have been an isolated Jewish family at each of Cawsand (1815), Stratton (1821) and Saltash (1831).[721]

---

[612] Susser, 1993. *op. cit.*, p. 47.

[613] Susser, *op. cit.*, p. 280.

[614] In notes attached to Leah Jacob's family tree, Alex M. Jacob confirms her handwriting, and that the tree is incomplete, with pencilled additions by her son, George (1877-1963). Alex Jacob notes there is no evidence for Leah Jacob's claims about the burial.

[615] For their twelve children, see the accompanying pedigree.

[616] Susser (1993) p. 48: says by 1767.

[617] Guildhall Library Insurance Policy No. 237892 (dated 1766): George Rigal (2000).

[618] H. Miles Brown (1966) p. 70.

[619] Adam Hart-Davis, *Britain's Head of Steam*, in *The Daily Telegraph* (8th March 2011) p. 29.

[620] See, G. M. A. Trinick, *Industrial Archaeology Review*, Vol. II, No. 2 (1978) p. 112; and W. Pryce, *Mineralogia Cornubiensis* (1778), 313; Stacey (2011) pp. 7-13.

[621] Mitchell (1985 edition) p.54.

[622] Universal British Directory Vol. 4 (1791) p. 311.

[623] Papers of A. K. Hamilton Jenkin, CRO Truro (Ref. 621/5).

[624] Cooper (2006) p. 29, 53-54, 197-199.

[625] Andrew Delbanco, *Melville* (Picador 2005): see in the Index (pp. 389-405) for various references to - biblical allusions, names, scholarship; *Clarel* and Zionism (Jews); Europe, Liverpool, Middle East and Judea; New York; xenophobia etc.

[626] Ref. Maton's *Observations of the Western Counties of England* (1794 & 1796); pub. 1797, J. Easton, Salisbury.

[627] The document can be seen at the Thurston Peter Collection: PET/24, RIC Truro.

[628] Mitchell, *op.cit.*, pp. 48-9. H. Miles Brown (1961) p. 25.

[629] H. Miles Brown (1961) p. 25.

[630] Susser, ibid. pp. 94-5 and 293.

[631] Hughan (1866) p. 81, and Osborne (edit. Hughan 1901) pp. 55-56. Hughan and Osborne do not entirely concur on the spelling of these names, which may have been difficult to decipher, and Osborne gives them with variant spellings (pp. 56 & 114). Hughan gives *G. N. Peyabeni*, but his name is not included by Osborne.

[632] Hughan (1866) pp. 481-482.

[633] Hughan (1866) p. 482, and (1867) p. 22.

[634] Hughan (1867) p. 221.

[635] The will was proved at Exeter on 8th June 1807. Ref. IR26/341/87: Helen Fry (1999).

[636] Mitchell, ibid. p. 48; Brown, ibid. p. 82.

[637] Vol. 4, pp. 311-2.

[638] Mitchell, ibid. pp. 52 and 69.

[639] Published simultaneously in *Jewish World*, 15th May 1903.

[640] Jacob family tradition has it that on one occasion the horse did so as required, only to deposit Moses Jacob in a ditch: (Jacob Archive).

[641] Rigal (2000): Guildhall Library Policy No. 128551.

[642] Helen Fry (2000).

[643] Susser (1995) Census returns, pp. 29, 33 & 43, & pp. 13, 16 & 21.

[644] Mitchell, ibid. p. 48.

[645] Guildhall Library Policy NO. 1268378 (Rigal 2000).

[646] Cooper (2006) pp. 199-200.

[647] Mitchell, ibid. pp. 124 and 129, quoting from the *West Briton*.

[648] *West Briton* 1st & 29th March 1844: Jackie Hill (2008).

[649] Letter to Keith Pearce (27th November 2008) from Sara Chambers, Assistant Director of Collections at the Royal Cornwall Museum, Truro, in which she cites the name from Max Hey's *Index of Mineral Species and their Varieties Arranged Chemically* (British Museum London 1955).

[650] The 1841 Census gives his age incorrectly as 30, when he was 40. The latter is confirmed by later census records.

[651] *West Briton* 25th May 1849: Jackie Hill (2011).

[652] Cooper (2006) p. 200; 1841 Census (Redruth) and the 1851 & 1861 Plymouth Census (Susser, 1995, pp. 35 & 46). Anthony Joseph (1975) p. 32: "Joseph and Fanny Joseph had a large family in Plymouth and decided to follow the example of their sisters and close cousins by moving to Melbourne at the time of the goldrush." This refers to some of their children, not to the parents.

[653] *Jewish Chronicle* 8th June 1877, and Letters from Anthony Joseph to Keith Pearce (5th December 2004 & 16th January 2005).

[654] Anthony Joseph (1975) p. 32.

[655] Susser (1993) pp. 57, 69, 152, 155, 157-8, 191, 199, 204-5, 233, 287, 309 & 314.

[656] Ludlam Archive, NHM (Cooper p. 200).

[657] Berger (1999) p. 286.

[658] Jessop's (1951) dates for him (as 1791-1872) are incorrect.

[659] Research by J. Wolfman (2004).

[660] Letter from J. Wolfman to Godfrey Simmons (27th May 2005).

[661] Letter from J. Wolfman to Keith Pearce (5th July 2005).

[662] Berger (2004) p. 188.

[663] Berger (1999) p. 286.

[664] Research by J. Wolfman (2004).

[665] Anthony Joseph (1975) p. 35; Judith Samuel (1997) pp. 103-4.

[666] Both H. Miles Brown and Mitchell give his year of birth incorrectly as 1766. This may be an error for 1776. In the 1841 Census, his age is given as 60, although the 1841 census tended to round ages up or down by 5 to 10 years. The birth year of 1775 is most likely. (From Brown and Mitchell's' dates, he would have been 75 at the time of the census, and 83 at the time of his death).

[667] Lipman, *Aliens List* No. 58 and Plymouth Congregational Minute-Book. Cohen's trade is not specified in either document.

[668] Brown (1970) p. 82.

[669] Jackie Hill (2009).

[670] Ref. PCC Cornwall, 1849, 329: (Helen Fry 2000).

[671] Brown, ibid. p. 82; Mitchell, *ibid.* p. 48.

[672] *West Briton* 8th July 1842: Report of Quarter Sessions: Jackie Hill (2007).

[673] Jackie Hill (2006).

[674] Phillimore Parish Registers, Vol. 12, p. 136.

[675] Susser (1993) p. 48 gives their birth years as 1813 & 1812 (not source referenced). Jessop (1951; pub. Gent. 2000, p. 54), Anthony Joseph (1975, p. 33 *et al.*) and Alex Jacob (Archive) give the dates as above.

[676] In the census his name is given as *Samuell.*

[677] Susser (1993) p. 48.

[678] HO 107/1911 Folio 233 p. 42.

[679] Isaac Lazarus is not recorded by Brown either as a watch or clockmaker. Robinson lists him as both, although census records refer only to his trade in watches.

[680] Doreen Berger, *The Jewish Victorian 1871-1880* (1999) p. 304. Compare also Susser Census Records (1995) pp. 12,13,15, 18 & 20.

[681] Jackie Hill (2000-6) has provided some of this information on the Lazarus family.

[682] Plymouth Hebrew Congregation Marriage Registers: entries 9 & 95.

[683] J. H. Matthews, *A History of St. Ives* (1892) p. 296 & quoted by Susser (1993) p. 30.

[684] Brown also references Wiseman to Baillie, *Watchmakers and Clockmakers of the World* (1947).

[685] Roth (1933).

[686] Lipman (1962) p. 192 & Susser (1993) p. 48. Susser, either misreading the Plymouth Congregational Minute-Book, or following an evident mis-print in Lipman, gives him, incorrectly, as in St. Austell from 1758-1775 (17 years). The Plymouth Congregational Minute-Book of Trades, however, gives 7 years for St. Austell (1758-65), followed by 10 in Portsmouth (1765-75: also Lipman) and 28 years in Plymouth (from 1775).

[687] The details in this section have been taken from Israel Solomon (1885-1887).

[688] *West Briton,* 12th July 1839.

[689] Brown's references are from *The West Briton.*

[690] Barton (1971) p. 121.

[691] St. Austell Burial Register, entry No. 1008. His age was crossed out and re-recorded as 85, suggesting some uncertainty of his exact year of birth. I am grateful to Les Douch and Angela Broome of the Courtney Library, RIC Truro, to Trudy Martin of the Cornwall Family History Society Truro, and to Alison Campbell, CRO Truro, for additional information on Benjamin Michael : Letters of January & February 2002.

[692] *The West Briton,* 19th August 1853, p. 5.

[693] *The Royal Cornwall Gazette* (dated as above).

[694] Brown (1970) p. 85.

[695] Barton (1972) p. 125.

[696] Arnold (1970) p. 253.

[697] Helen Fry (2000).

[698] Jill Hyams (2005-2010).

[699] The Plymouth Census Records.

[700] Susser (1993) gives the year incorrectly as 1829 (p. 48) but later, correctly as 1832 (p. 361).

[701] Susser (1995) p. 88 (various references) & (1993) pp. 230 & 259.

[702] Gifford Place Burial Records: 340-347 (Nelson).

[703] Plymouth Congregational Marriage Registers (Johnson & Nelson).

[704] Susser (1995) pp. 12 & 36.

[705] Susser (1993) pp. 58, 101, 207, 230, 232, 283 & 326 (*Johnson*); pp. 55, 58-60, 103, 129, 280, 282-3 & 314;

& Susser (1972) p. 25; Gifford Place Burial records: 241 & 242 (Jonas).

[706] Guildhall Library Policy No. 1600451/2 & Nos. 69052, 78918, 80086, 81507 & 94360; George Rigal (2000); Susser (1993) p. 105.

[707] Plymouth Hebrew Congregational Marriage Register. The bridegroom was resident in Devonshire Terrace, and the bride in Buckland Street.

[708] Susser (1993) p. 48.

[709] Susser (ibid.) pp. 94 & 292-93; Arnold (1970) p. 150.

[710] It should be noted that this name (both as forename and as surname) appears variously as *Abraham* and as *Abrahams*. Both variants are documented for the families of Sarah and Abraham Abraham(s). The Marriage Register and the 1841-1861 Census records give *Abrahams*, with *Abrahams Abrahams* for the husband in 1861: Susser (1995) pp. 24, 38 & 46.

[711] Lipman Plymouth Aliens List, no. 51, p. 194; Susser (1972) p. 35; Susser (1993) pp. 104, 276 & 294.

[712] His will proved on 29th June 1810 at Exeter (effects under £450) ref. IR26/341/650 (Helen Fry 2000).

[713] Jackie Hill (2008).

[714] Helen Fry (2000).

[715] Susser (1993) pp. 48 & 290; Lipman, Aliens List (No. 22, p. 191). Susser notes (with some delicacy) that the age of the Plymouth Samuel Hyams, 65 at the time of the alleged rape in Cornwall, may cast doubt on the identification.

[716] Lipman's Aliens List No. 22, p. 191.

[717] Helen Fry (2000): Exeter RO; Ref. 382/TC 280; & information from Chief Archivist, Exeter RO to Keith Pearce 12th November 2003.

[717a] Jackie Hill (2013).

[718] Susser (1995) pp. 34, 45 & 51.

[719] Susser (1995) pp. 83-84 (Index).

[720] Lipman, Aliens List no. 53, p. 194; Susser (1972) pp. 29 & 35; (1993) pp. 49, 53, 150 & 162.

[721] Susser (1993) p. 51.

CHAPTER 7

Jews in Cornish Freemasonry

The importance of Freemasonry to Jews, especially at a time when they were faced with various legal disabilities and a struggle to gain acceptance and advancement in Gentile society, cannot be underestimated. Through its charitable activities and its opportunities for social contact beyond the confines of Jewish congregational life, Masonry enabled Jews to establish themselves on a firm basis, and to make social connections with men drawn from a wide background, both from Cornwall and from overseas. Some members of the affluent and influential Cornish Gentile families, such as the Basset family of Tehidy, near Redruth, the Rogers family of Sithney, and the Branwell and Borlase families of Penzance were prominent Freemasons, and were especially supportive of the Jewish congregations. The Basset family, which owned land at Penryn and Falmouth, gave the Falmouth Jewish community a plot for its cemetery at Ponsharden. The Branwell family leased land to the Jews for the building of both of the synagogues in Penzance, and Canon Rogers of Sithney granted leases (and the Borlase family sub-leases) to land for the Jewish cemetery there. In these latter cases, both the named lessors (or their agents) and lessees were Freemasons. Jews comprised only a small proportion of the total membership of Cornish Masonry, and not all of the resident Cornish Jews were Freemasons, although the most significant Jewish families were members of Lodges. In view of the commercial links between Jews and shipping, both in Falmouth and Penzance, it is of significance that Mariners (referred to as "seafaring members" in the Falmouth Lodge records)[722] were well-represented in Masonic Lodges. On 28th July 1780, the Falmouth Lodge initiated a Mr. Stephen Sowel, Master of the *Hanover* Packet boat into its membership, and on 13th September that same year notes that the reason for postponing the last lodge meeting was "on account of the great number of people which were then in the House, who landed from a numerous fleet". It would seem that the obligations of hospitality that such an event laid upon the Lodge was a burden to its finances, and on 24th June 1784 it was proposed "that all brethren (not members of any lodge) residing at or sailing in vessels belonging to or hailing from the Port of Falmouth, who shall in future visit this lodge, shall on every such visit pay as a visiting fee four shillings". Other visitors who were members of a lodge were expected to pay only two shillings, or that which was customary in the lodges to which they belonged. In 1754, Thomas Dobree, Provincial Grand Master of the Channel Islands came from Guernsey to pay the Lodge a visit, and in 1763, his equivalent for the Scilly Isles, Isaac Head, did likewise. There were also visits from foreign masons, especially from France. On 31st March 1784 "Louis Videloup and Jean Carpentier, Frenchmen" attended the Falmouth Lodge, and on 27th April 1785, "John Penchant, belonging to a French ship, was initiated". On 13th July 1785, a more exotic visitor, "Bro. Mahamet Celiby - from the Kingdom of Algiers" appears in the records. A "Marceleony Dabelz" is recorded as another visitor to Falmouth (28th September 1785), and a "Brother D'Houvitte" of Truro, on 24th June 1788. Mention has been made of the seven French prisoners of war who visited the Redruth Lodge in 1779, and a Dane, Johan Christian Munster, was initiated there on 1797. In 1820, a Spaniard, "C. Suaerey", and two British seafaring men, had arrived in Falmouth from South America, where one of the Britons, named Hyslop, had suffered imprisonment and the threat of execution for not naming fellow Masons to a Spanish General, Morilla.[723] Earlier, in 1814, charitable relief had been granted to an Irish Mason, James Hingston, whose ship had foundered off Land's End in a gale, leaving him indigent. In the same year, so great was the call upon the generosity of the Falmouth Lodge, that its Master, James Tippett, complained that "Masonic tramps" were inclined to exploit Masonry's charitable nature, and travelled "the kingdom for that purpose from one end to the other". He urged the exercise of caution in the admission of such members who had rendered some lodges devoid of funds. In particular, he warned of the practice of Masons seeking elevation within the Craft, as a means of self-advancement and advantage prior to boarding the local packet boats as emigrants. There is little doubt, however, that the Jews who settled in the Cornish ports found acceptance and support by their membership of Cornish lodges, and that Masonry assisted their social and commercial integration into Cornish society.

Early Masonic records are not readily accessible, although it has been possible to gain some information from the original Lodge records.[724] Some of these records have been used to compile the names of Jewish Masons, although the original documents have not been referenced here. Likewise, Masonic members' handbooks have not been referenced. Published historical volumes, such as J. G. Osborne's invaluable "History of Freemasonry in West Cornwall, 1765-1828" contains various references to Masons who were Jews, and it is from this book that further information in this section has been drawn in some chronological sequence. Osborne also contributed a series of articles under the general title "Jewish Names" to the *Freemasons' Magazine* of 1866. Further articles on the history of Cornish Freemasonry by William James Hughan appeared in issues of the journal from 29th September to 31st August 1867. The first article is titled "A History of the Craft in Cornwall" and subsequent ones as "A History of Freemasonry in Cornwall". They rely, for much of their information, on the Minute-Book of the *Falmouth Love and Honour Lodge* (later No. 75), starting with 12th June 1751 and ending with 24th June 1771.[725] The dates of the formation of the Cornish lodges are taken from both Osborne and Hughan, the latter referring, in 1867, to "the present table published about 1766, being a 'new and correct list of all the lodges'". [726] Masonic activity in Cornish towns did take place in the 18th century, although it may have been irregular, in that Masonic organisations were often formed, disbanded and later revived.

FALMOUTH: The Lodge of Love and Honour. No. 75 (*est.* May 20th 1751).

This is the oldest Cornish Lodge, and its records have remained intact from 1751. Its original warrant was granted on 20th May 1751. The Lodge records for 10th

August 1785, note that another Masonic lodge was active in Falmouth, the *Lodge of Regularity and Reputation,* as well as the *Lodge of Peace, Joy and Brotherly Love* of Penryn. By 1815, the *Lodge of Love and Honour* is thought to have had about 70 members, and another Falmouth Lodge, the *Lodge* of *Love and Unity* (No. 244) had about 32 members, the latter being mentioned by the former in the context of a fraternal invitation to join a Civic Procession in 1814.[727]

12th June 1751: the date of the formal consecration of the Lodge, which met subsequently "…at the house of Edward Snoxell, being the sign of the King's Arms in Falmouth." **Alexander Moses** is recorded as a founder member of the Lodge, and as a Master Mason, suggesting that he had been a member of a Masonic Lodge previously, most likely in London. Upon its consecration, the Lodge Master was William Pye, the Deputy Master, George Bell, and Alexander Moses and Matthew Allison were appointed as Wardens. At this time, Alexander Moses was not living in Falmouth itself (see below). It is most likely that he was resident in or traded from Penryn, where there may also have been a Masonic lodge, or some form of Masonic society, either at this time or after 1751. The entry for 1758, below, suggests that Alexander Moses, may have left the Falmouth Lodge sometime after 1751, to join one elsewhere, such as Penryn, later moving to live in Falmouth and rejoining the lodge there. There is no explicit mention of Alexander Moses in the Falmouth lodge records from 1753-1757.

Note: the names Abraham Renfroy (1751), Elias Pomeroy (1751-53), Josias Cock (1754, of Redruth), Micon Meluss (Secretary of the Lodge in 1751; died 1757), Isaac Head (1763), Nathaniel Steel (1765-69), Thomas Hefferman (1766), Nathaniel Hicks (1769), Hosea Roberts (1780), William Job (1781), Malachi Laskey (1795) and Abel Dagge (1800) appear in the Lodge records, but they are not known to have had any Jewish connection.

18th & 24th June 1751. **Alexander Moses**, Warden. He visited the *Lodge of Antiquity* in London on at least three occasions (13th August 1751, 12th February 1754, and 14th January 1755). On the first occasion, the Falmouth Lodge Minutes record that… "As Bro. Moses was going to London he was asked to purchase jewels for the officers".[728] The Falmouth Lodge had resolved to delegate this task to Alexander Moses at an earlier meeting on 3rd August 1751. On 26th March 1752, the Lodge Minutes record that "Ordered unanimously that Brother Moses do write to his correspondent that furnished him with the Master's jewel, to send down jewels for the Master, Wardens, and two Stewards, with gold lace for hanging the Master and Wardens' jewels by…with handsome red ribband for the Stewards' jewels."[729] This correspondent may have been Philip Moses, a London Tailor, who traded at Duke's Place "nearly opposite (Sam) Moses' Coffee House".[730] He is likely to have been Alexander Moses' brother, or brother-in-law, in that Alexander Moses' wife, Phoebe, is believed to have had the identical surname, *Moses*.[731] Philip Moses was a member of this London Lodge in 1749. He was its Junior Warden in 1752, and its Master in 1754 and 1759. The last mention of him in the Lodge's records is in 1760, which could mark either the year of his death, or of his departure from Lodge membership.[732] The presence of Philip's son, Moses, a junior, at a lodge meeting on 17th January 1755 (when Alexander Moses was present as a visitor) suggests that Philip Moses may have been born around 1710, although there is no age recorded for him in 1749. It seems likely that Alexander Moses had also been a member of this *Lodge of Antiquity*, or some other in London, before coming to Cornwall, in that he was already a Master Mason in 1751. However, Alexander Moses is not recorded as a member of the *Lodge of Antiquity*, but only as a visitor.

18th June 1751. Josiah Abraham. Uncertain.

10th October 1751. Alexander Moses signs the Lodge Accounts as "Master". The Lodge Master, whose (illegible) signature appears for all other dates (1751-1752) was William Pye. It is likely that Alexander Moses was standing in for Pye on this occasion, but omitted to sign as "Acting Master", or as "Master Mason".[733] On all other occasions, Alexander Moses signed only as Warden or Senior Warden. A complete list of the Lodge's Masters hangs in its Temple, and a complete record of its serving masters (1751-2000) has been compiled by the Lodge Archivist. There are no Lodge records for its Masters from 1772 to 1779.

31st October 1751. Brother **Isaac**. This may be **Michael Isaac** or **Isaac Isaac**, both Falmouth traders. The former traded as a dealer in silver and hardware (*c.* 1802) and the latter as a clothes dealer (*c.* 1815-1841). Brother Isaac may, however, be a member of the previous generation, possibly father of one of the above. The reference may also apply to Isaac Polack, although there are no records of Lodge initiation or membership for him from this time.

9th April 1752. Brother Simon is paid two guineas for having brought an item to the lodge. It is not known if this man was Jewish.

12th October 1752. "Brother Meluss and Brother **Moses** were desired to bring their bills the next lodge night."

26th July and 13th September 1753. "Brother **Cohen**", and "Brother **Benjamin**", recorded as visitors.[734] They may be the P. Cohen [possibly the father of Emanuel Cohen (1766-1849) of Redruth] and the Isaac Benjamin who are recorded at the St. Ives Lodge in 1767 and 1772, respectively (see below). The latter was a visitor to the Falmouth Lodge on a number of occasions.

The records for 1753 also refer to a "**Raffael**…..", and much later, in 1847, but this name is not certain to refer to Jews .

10th January and 24th June 1754. Jos (Josiah?) Simon. Uncertain. A "Brother Simon" is also mentioned on 9th January 1752.

31st January 1754. Visitor **Isaac Benjamin**. He joined the Lodge in 1755,[735] from which year his name appears frequently in the records. Eventually, he was

"Obliged to resign on account of his increasing deafness". He was made an Honorary Member "for his long and diligent services" in 1787. Isaac (Wolf) Benjamin (1712-1790) was a Jeweller in the town.

1st February 1754. "Brother Mossam" entered the Lodge. This is likely to be **Moses Jacob** (1733-1807), later of Redruth, who married Sarah (1748-1831) daughter of Alexander Moses, above. Moses Jacob may have transferred his membership to the Redruth Lodge (see below).

26th September 1754. Brother Wolfe. This is likely to be the Jacob Wolfe of 1764.

24th June 1757. Josiah Abrahams.

26th January 1758. **Alexander Moses** rejoined the Falmouth Lodge: "as he is now resident in this town, was at his own request admitted a member of this Society."

31st August 1758. Brother J (or I) Lawrance. Uncertain. It is possible that this is **Jacob Lawrance**, the father of Moses Lazarus (Eliezer) Lawrance. The latter traded as a Money Broker (c. 1823) and was buried in the Penryn Jewish cemetery in 1841. A Joseph Lawrence lived next to the synagogue in 1861 (Census).

11th June 1761. **Isaac Polack** visited the Lodge, and appears to have been previously initiated (see 1762 below).

13th August 1761. **Alexander Moses**, Senior Warden.

29th October 1761. **Alexander Moses**, Senior Warden.

11th February 1762. Brother (Isaac) **Polack** was charged with a breach (unspecified) of his Masonic responsibilities, and it was unanimously agreed that "he be refused admittance in this lodge, until he has acquitted himself of a complaint laid against him of a breach of the degree of Master Mason, and that notice thereof be sent to the lodges in the county." At a meeting of the Lodge on 3rd May 1762, the Master, Thomas Yonge, proposed that a letter be sent to a Brother Street of Bideford (the complainant) to "inquire into the circumstances of the charge laid against Bro. P" and that Brother Street should answer "to the letter to support the charge" in that Polack "is to be entitled to a clearance of the same." The letter was sent to Bideford by the Falmouth Lodge Secretary, T. Horton, requesting Brother Street that he should write by return to Horton "whether he (Polack) has or has not been guilty of the breach laid to his charge. The neglect of your answer in due course will entitle him to a release of the expulsion, which in consequence of your charge, this lodge has inflicted upon him." It appears that no answer or satisfactory response was given, and Polack was re-instated by resolution of the Lodge.[736] There may have been a further controversy over his suitability, in that his application for membership of the Lodge was rejected in 1764. Polack is also recorded in 1762 as (Isaac Polack) on 10th & 24th June and on 18th August, and later in 1783. The very rare occurrence of the surname *Polack* has been noted previously, and the much later election, over two hundred years later, in 1983 of F. G. Pollock as Secretary of the Falmouth Lodge and in 1986 as its Master, may not be connected.

30th December 1762. **Alexander Moses** appointed Junior Warden.

11th August 1763. The Isaac Benjamin (above): "Bro. **Benjamin**, for some reasons refused to give his vote for the new election" i.e. of the new Master, Brother Hooten. At the same meeting, the new Master invested **Alexander Moses** as Senior Warden.

13th December 1764. Jacob Wolfe. He was a Mariner, a trade not associated with Jews. He became bankrupt in 1792. [737]

27th December, 1764. **Alexander Moses** was invested as Junior Warden by the new Master, Henry Pye.

9th June 1768. **Isaac Polack** becomes a member of the Lodge.

12th July 1768. As Senior Warden of the "Lodge of Peace, Joy and Brotherly Love" of Penryn (No. 449, closed in 1809, which met at the King's Arms, Broad Street) Polack attended the Provincial Grand Lodge meeting in Falmouth.

8th June 1769. "J. Pollock" (who may be Isaac Polack) appointed as Senior Warden, and also given as "J. Pollack" on 12th July 1769..

24th June 1769. Brother Hart. On 8th June, 12th July and 28th December 1769, a Josiah Hart is recorded as Secretary. It is not known if he was Jewish. Colyer-Fergusson's family tree of the Hart family of Penzance does not list a Josiah Hart: see 1858, below. It is possible that one of the references to a Brother Hart may refer to Eleazar (Lazarus) Hart (1739-1803) of Penzance, who had married Rebecca Woolf of Falmouth in 1763. His son, Lemon Hart (1768-1845) was a member of the Redruth Lodge. (See also reference to a Hart in 1785, below).

12th July 1769. "Jacobs" of Redruth. "Visiting". Likely **Moses Jacob**.

1770. Solomon Abraham.[738] His connection with a local Jewish family of that name is not certain.

24th June 1771. **M. Jacob** of Redruth Lodge, present at Masonic Procession for the festival of St. John the Baptist. It is noteworthy that no other Jewish names, including the Falmouth Lodge, appear.

After 1771, there is a gap in Lodge records of some nine years.[739]

11th April 1781. Benjamin Salmon (not a lodge member) was given one guinea as charitable relief. It is not known if he was Jewish.

c. 30th March 1782. **Aaron Delissa(ser)**, Junior Warden (see 1783).

27th December 1782. Elijah Goldsworth initiated. Uncertain.

12th March 1783. Brother **Polack** of Penryn Lodge.

9th July 1783. John Moss. It is possible that this is the grandfather of the **Henry Moss** who was a Dentist in Falmouth in 1877. The latter's marriage in August 1877 to a **Sophia Basch** is recorded in the Plymouth Synagogue's marriage register.

27th December 1783. Worshipful Master: **Aaron Delisser**.[740] It is possible that he was of Sephardic Jewish descent. He took over as Master from Thomas Williams. Lodge records for 1768 list his trade as a Jeweller.

9th March 1785. Brother Hart of Lodge of Unity Topsham (Exeter, Devon). He may not have been Jewish, and it is not known if he was connected with Josiah Hart (above).

25th May, 8th June and 12th October 1785. **Isaac Benjamin**, visitor. (See below: possibly a grandson of the Isaac Benjamin, above).

10th August 1785. Jacob Wolfe, visitor. Uncertain.

11th January 1786. **Isaac Benjamin** initiated (present at subsequent meetings on 26th April and 28th June). This cannot be the initiation of Isaac Benjamin (1712-) above, nor that of his son, Wolf Benjamin (1744-) in that both were members in 1768. It is possible that this initiation, and that below, were of sons of Wolf Benjamin. Alternatively it may be that the "initiation" here refers to entry into an higher Masonic level.

9th November 1786. **Wolf Benjamin** initiated. By 1789 he was the Senior Warden.

On the same date, four German visitors are recorded: Jacob Schwerer, P. Straatman, W. H. Geysen, and Franz Joseph Kreutzeven. Jacob Schwerer, as noted, was Jewish, and the family ran a successful Jewellery business, both in its own name and in partnership with that of the (non-Jewish) German family, Berenger, in several Cornish towns. It is not known if the three other German visitors were Jewish. A *Fidelis Berenger* (also as *Beringer*), Jeweller, appears on the membership lists of the *Mount Sinai Lodge*, Penzance (1865-1880). F. F. Beringer was a member of the *Meridian Lodge*, Redruth (No. 73, est. 1865) and a John Jacob Beringer of the *Mount Edgcumbe Lodge*, Camborne (No. 1544, est. 1875). The Jacob Schwerer of 1789 would be a father or grandfather of the Jacob Schwerer who traded in Falmouth from 1844. Confusion can arise over Wolf Benjamin's family and its members, in that both father (1712-) and son (1744-) carried both of the forenames *Isaac* and *Wolf*, the former as *Isaac Wolf*, and the latter as *Wolf Isaac*.

25th January 1787. It was agreed that "Bro. P (presumably **Polack**, as the 'Bro. P' of 3rd May 1762) be admitted into the lodge to defend himself of the charges alleged against him, consisting of two, viz., for initiating gentlemen into the mysteries of Masonry unconstitutionally" and "of his conduct towards Miss A". He was heard by the Lodge, and was subsequently re-instated.

In the years up to 1793, Isaac Polack appears as a member of the Penryn Lodge, comprising men who were involved in the shipping business, either directly as mariners or otherwise as lawyers, builders, brokers, customs officers, tailors and, a number of innkeepers and victuallers, whose customers always comprised a large number of sailors. The names, below, from the Penryn membership, are mainly those of mariners, those associated with the boat industry and members of the Penryn volunteer defence army, of which Sir Francis Basset of Tehidy, who had been the M.P. for Penryn in 1780, was the Commander, as Lieutenant Colonel. Polack's is the only Jewish name, and his linguistic skills as a translator and compiler of commercial and legal documents would have been of considerable value to this influential group of men: Sir Francis Basset, Baronet (Baronet Basset of Tehidy in 1779), James Babbidge, Lieutenant Army, Benjamin Hearne, Merchant (a Tallow Chandler from Penryn and Captain of the Penryn Volunteers), John Davis, Attorney (from Penryn), Francis Mulkins, Captain, Army (and Treasurer of the Penryn Lodge), Joseph Dillon, Captain, Packet (and member of the Penryn Corporation), Isaac Polack, Linguist (his daughter, Frances, was a Grocer in Penryn), Henry Dillon, Merchant (a Roper from Penryn), William Crowgey, Attorney (from Penryn, and Secretary of the Penryn Lodge), Rev. John Basset, Clerk (Cleric, brother of Sir Francis), Sampson Spargoe, Captain Packet, John Stona, Merchant (a Draper from Penryn), Rev. Robert Dillon, Cleric (and Chaplain to the Penryn Volunteers), Edward Penwarne, Attorney (Captain in the Penryn Volunteers), John Harris, Master Packet, Richard Rowe, Lieutenant Navy, Thomas Treeve, Merchant (from Penryn), John Penwarne, Attorney (from Penryn), William Roberts. Captain Packet, John Rusden, Master Packet.[741]

1st July & 7th October 1800. Benjamin Osler, who was the Lodge Secretary in 1802. He is not known to have been Jewish.

7th April 1801. J. Silver. It is possible that he was related to the family of **Emanuel Silver (Da Silva)** who had been a Mariner in Falmouth (*c.* 1785). A Thomas Anthony Silver, son of Thomas and Dorcas Silver, was baptised in Falmouth on 30th July 1763, and a Philip Silver, a Mariner, was a member of the Penryn Masonic Lodge (*c.* 1795). A Mary Silva (46) was living in High Street, Falmouth, at the time of the 1841 Census.

6th March 1801. H. Ralf. Possibly **Henry Ralph** of Penzance. See Penzance trades.

4th October 1808. Brother Absolom. David Absalom (b. 1746, Yarmouth) was a Mariner and is listed as a member in 1768. It is not certain that he was Jewish.

2nd June 1809. Jacob Beil, a "native of Hamburgh", who may have been a Mariner, although possibly a passenger, in that he was initiated at some short notice "In consequence of his daily expecting to sail". It is not known if he was Jewish.

12th July 1847. "....Raffael". The 1841 Census records a Charles Rafael (49) "Professor of Music", his wife Eliza (31) and daughters Claudine (11) and Emiline (16) at 7 Penwerris Terrace, Falmouth. Charles Rafael had been born in Exeter, his wife on The Lizard, and both daughters in Bideford, Devon. It is not known if Charles Rafael was of Jewish descent. The same census, for Sithney (Newtown) gives a Solomon Rafael (30) Tin Miner (an occupation not associated with Jews), with his wife and four children, all born in Cornwall.[742]

27th December 1849. I. Jacobs initiated. That is, **Moses Isaac Jacob** (below).

13th October 1851. Moses Jacobs initiated. This is **Moses ("Moss") Jacob** (1812-1860), a grandson of the Moses Jacob, above. Moses Jacob Jacob was Lodge Secretary in 1852.[743] His brother, **Moses Isaac Jacob** (1820-1888) appears as "I. Jacob" (as above) and in the records from 1850. He was Lodge Treasurer for 1852, and Secretary in 1862.[744]

12th July 1858: J. Hart. This cannot be the earlier Josiah Hart of 1769, although it may be a son, or grandson.

12th August & 10th September 1860. **Nathan Vos** (or Voss). His name appears only once until his re-admission in 1892.

11th November 1861. Brother Myers. It is not known if he was connected with the "Meyers" who traded with a Reuben in Redruth in 1792 (see Redruth trades). The 1861 Census gives a John P. Myers (59) and his wife Mary Ann (60) in Penzance (the former had been born in Cheltenham, and the latter in Dartmouth) and a Samuel Myers (50) in Truro, who had been born in Leeds.[745] A Charles Myers appears in the 1871 Census for Falmouth.

13th January 1862. Henry (Heinrich) **Herman**. It is not known if he was related to the family of father and son, Samuel and Abraham Herman from Konin, Poland, who served as Rabbis to the Falmouth congregation (c. 1850 to 1860). Samuel Herman's wife, Frances, was from Neustadt. A Mr. Herman, Rabbi, (and presumably at least some of his family) left Falmouth in 1860 to take up an appointment in Sheffield. It is possible that Henry Herman was a visitor to the Lodge.

17th January 1862. "Brother Jacob (Secry.)". Moses Isaac Jacob, above.

28th August 1867. Brother Hart. This is most likely the "J. Hart" of 1858. It is possible that this refers to Lemon Hart's son David Hart (1799-1868) a Victualler and Wine and Spirit Merchant of London, who had married a Mary Pidwell of Falmouth. Her mother, Elizabeth had lived in the Falmouth area until her death in 1855, and David and Mary Hart's son, Charles, was born in nearby Flushing in 1846. If David Hart was a Mason it is more likely that he would have been a member of a London Lodge, and would have been recorded in 1867 as a "visitor". A David Hart, Victualler, has been identified as a London Freemason in 1786, but there is clearly an error in the record in that the year is given both as his date of birth and the date of his membership of a Lodge.[746] Unless this date is in error, this cannot be Lemon Hart's son, David (b. 1799) nor the latter's son, also David (b. 1844). There were various unrelated Hart families, Jewish and Gentile, in London in the 18th and 19th centuries, but that another David Hart, also a Victualler, traded there is intriguing. It is possible that the year 1786 should be read as 1886.

The "J. Hart", above, who may have been a Gentile, Josiah Hart, was not related to the family of Lemon Hart.

9th September 1867. **Samuel Jacob.** The use of "initiated" is curious if he is to be identified with the Samuel Jacob who was a Mason in 1864 in Penryn (see below). It is possible that the entry intended to record admission to the lodge, or to a higher rank within it. Samuel Jacob (1838-1913) was the son of the Moses Jacob Jacob above. He ran a successful business in Falmouth, but left for London in 1880.

10th May 1892. **Nathan Vos**, Ships' Chandler, re-admitted as a member of the Lodge. He attended meetings irregularly until his death in November 1913.[747] In view of this reference to his re-admission to the Lodge, it is curious that there are no records of him between 1854 (the earliest date when he could have been admitted previously, at the minimum age of 21) and 1892 of his either joining or leaving the Lodge.

1905. Ernest H. Moss, Steward. It is not known if he was related to Henry Moss, who was a Dentist in Falmouth in 1877 (see trades).

After Falmouth, Masonic Lodges were established at Helston (April 4th 1752), Truro (September 22nd 1752), Redruth (February 14th 1754), Penzance (June 14th 1755) and St. Ives (July 16th 1765).

Penryn. The Three Grand Principles Lodge. No. 967 (revived 1863)

There had been several lodges in Penryn, but their presence was not continuous. Samuel Jacob, Deacon (1864).[748] "Deacon" would imply that he had been a Mason for some time. Another member of this lodge was a Thomas H. Lanyon. Samuel Jacob's brother, Alexander (1841-1903), was photographed with a Lanyon, and two others (c.1859), prior to an expedition to British Columbia.[749]

St. Ives. Ship Lodge. No. 240 (*est.* 1765; until 1786)

From late 1780, little or nothing is known of its history. This lodge appeared in the *Freemasons' Calendar* for 1784 (as Lodge No. 227), but does not appear in official Masonic lists between 1792-1799. In 1815, it became the lodge of *True Friendship* (No. 678) at Crowan, near Hayle, although it appears to have come under the auspices of the *St. Michael's* Lodge of Helston (originally constituted in 1752-56 as *The True and Faithful Lodge*) before its formal transfer to Crowan. Its first Master was Thomas Lean. (It is not known if this man was related to his later namesake, Thomas Lean of Marazion, who, in 1906, bought the former Penzance synagogue on behalf of the Plymouth Brethren). The last meeting of the Crowan lodge was on 28th December 1819, when its Secretary, Thomas Eva was elevated to the position of Master Mason. (In 1837, a William Eva of Gwinear, near Hayle, by trade a wheelwright, together with his wife, Barbara, had sold to the Penzance Jewish Congregation two cottages that Barbara Eva had inherited from her aunt, Temperance Branwell of Penzance. These cottages adjoined the Penzance synagogue, and were then incorporated into the enlarged synagogue building. A family connection with the later Mason Thomas Eva, above, is possible, but not certain). In 1838, a warrant was granted for the former Crowan lodge to be revived, although the new lodge did not open until 1848 as the *Cornubian* Lodge (No. 659) of Hayle.

Jewish members appear in the Minutes of the St. Ives lodge, but not at Crowan.

St. Ives

3rd March 1767. Brother P. **Cohen** presented three candles to the Lodge. This may be the father of Emanuel Cohen (1775-1849), watch and clockmaker.[750] An unmarried Jacob Phillip Cohen (Jacob ben Uri Shraga) who was a member of the Plymouth Congregation in 1819, died there in August 1832, and is buried in the Hoe Cemetery.[751] He would have been in his mid to late eighties in 1832, and there may not be any connection with the Brother P. Cohen, above.

3rd March 1772. Visitant, brother **Isaac Benjamin**, when his dues were reduced to 2/6 per quarter.[752]

Hayle. The Cornubian Lodge No. 659.[753]

The following are all listed in the lodge membership. It is not known if any were of Jewish descent:

Henry Harris (1848-49). It is not known if this was Henry Harris (1787-1872) of Truro, who was Jewish. The surname is very common in Cornwall. See *Phoenix Lodge*, Truro 1854.

26th January 1852. An unnamed Hungarian was admitted to the Lodge (see Guttman, below).

John Abraham, Crowan. Yeoman (1816-1887). Member from 1854. Unlikely.

Michael Abrahams, Camborne. Hotel Keeper. Joined from *Fortitude Lodge,* Truro in 1873. Resigned 1876. Unlikely. He is buried in Camborne Parish Churchyard.

Oscar Guttman, from Hungary. Member from 1889-1895. Uncertain.

Abraham Harris, Camborne. Medical Practitioner. Member from 1862. Unlikely.

Henry Edwards Jacobs, St. Ives. Master Mariner. Member 1867-1869. Unlikely.

Redruth. Druid's Lodge of Love & Liberality No. 176 (est.1754)[754]

The Lodge's original warrant was dated on 12th or 14th February 1754 to a Josias Cocke and others. In 1754, the lodge appears not to have had its later name, which was adopted in 1773-1777. The Minute Book from 1754-1777 is lost. The lodge membership declined during the early 19th century, and it became extinct for a few years but it was reconstituted in 1851. Although a lodge had been formed in Penzance in 1755, it appears to have disbanded after 1767. After this date, some Jewish Masons from Penzance joined the Redruth Lodge, at least until the Penzance Lodge itself was revived after 1810. The first list of members, Midsummer quarter, 1777, mentions **Moses Jacob**, with a record that he was initiated previous to 1777.

May 6th 1779: **Moses Jacob** seconds the proposal from Jean Labrouche, a prisoner of war, for initiation into the membership of a "French gentleman", Martial Raillon. There is no subsequent record of his initiation.

February 13th 1789. Visit by members of the Falmouth Lodge of Love and Honour, **Wolf Benjamin**, Senior Warden, and Jacob Wolfe. Jacob Wolfe may have been Jewish, but he is not known to have been related to the Jewish Woolf family of Falmouth and Penzance..

May 1st 1798: **Lemon Hart**, age 30, Merchant, Penzance. Initiated.

August 2nd 1799: **Lemon Hart** of Penzance present.

April 5th 1803: **Jacob Hart**, age 24, Merchant, Penzance. Initiated. This is Jacob (James) Jacobs (1784-1846), Lemon Hart's nephew, and the son of his sister, Rebecca Hart (1766-1841) from her first marriage to Lazarus Jacobs. As mentioned earlier, Jacob Jacobs adopted his mother's family surname for commercial reasons when he went to London to work in his uncle's business.

July 10th 1805: **Lemon Hart** proposed to the Royal Arch, and exalted on July 24th.

September 17th 1805: **Jacob Hart** exalted to the Royal Arch.

August 13th 1806: **Lemon Wolfe** (Woolf), age 24, Merchant, Penzance. Initiated.

On 4th October 1808. Richard Branwell of Penzance, whose family leased the land for the building of the second synagogue there in 1808, was initiated into the Lodge.

November 1st 1808: Four candidates from Penzance, including **Moses Isaacs**, "Gentleman". This is Rabbi Moses Isaac (*Rav Moshe*) who served the Penzance Congregation from April 1808 to September 1810. He remained in Penzance after that date, but for how long is not known. A **Lawrance Isaacs** is listed in the Penzance Lodge in 1815, and may have been related to Moses Isaacs.

October 10th 1809: **Moses Isaac**(s), age 30, Gent. [Rabbi], Penzance. Initiated.

August 2nd 1813: **Levi Jacobs**, age 24, Jeweller, Falmouth. Initiated.

August 27th 1817: **Lemon Woolf**, as one of the members, confirms the rules of the Chapter.

August 15th 1821: Druid's Royal Arch, meeting at Foss's (late Pearce's) Hotel, Redruth. Brother **Lemon Woolf**, Merchant, age 38, was proposed by Richard Pearce. Lemon Woolf paid his annual fees of 12/-.

August 16th 1826: **Lemon Woolf**, Royal Arch Mason, acting as "Junior Scribe".
Present at this occasion was Thomas Branwell, Attorney at Law, of Penzance, who was exalted to the Royal Arch, and in 1827 to the Order of Knights Templar.

Truro

Phoenix Lodge (Truro and Chacewater) No. 331 (est. 1810)

This Lodge was originally constituted in 1752. It ceased to function soon after, but revived between 1763-1786, only to decline once more. It was successfully reformed in 1810.

1854. **Henry Harris**. The son of **Samuel Harris** (1754-1824) from London, who lived in Penzance at some point, but settled in Falmouth, where he is buried. Samuel Harris married Judith Solomon of Falmouth. Their son, Henry (1787-1872) was born in Penzance, but moved to Truro, where he traded as a Jeweller and watch and clockmaker, eventually moving to London. He married Esther (1784-1871) a daughter of Moses Jacob of Redruth. Their son **Morris (Moses) Hart Harris** was a member of the Penzance Lodge in 1842 (see below).

Fortitude Lodge (Truro and Perranporth) No. 131 (est. 1772)

This lodge originally had military connections being associated with the 67th Regiment and the Royal Regiment of Devon and Cornish Miners.

1828. **Lion (Lyon) Levi** (1782-), Silversmith. He traded in Truro.

1859, 1864 & 1868. Edward B. Solomon (1819-), Accountant. It is not certain that he was Jewish, and he is not known to have been related to the Solomon family of Falmouth. William Solomon (not known to have been Jewish, nor to have been be related to Edward B. Solomon) was a member of the Callington Lodge (No. 557, est. 1848) in North Cornwall.

1865. Thomas Solomon, Decorator. Like Michael Abrahams, below, it is not certain that he was of Jewish descent. He may have been related to the above.

1869. Michael Abrahams (1824-) Hotel Keeper, Camborne. Uncertain. He left to join the *Cornubian Lodge,* Hayle in 1873.

Penzance

Mount Sinai Lodge No. 121 (est. 1813)[755]

The Penzance Lodge is the second oldest in the county. Its original warrant was dated 14th June 1755, but it is not noted in the minutes of the Falmouth lodge until 11th June 1767. It seems to have collapsed for a time, but efforts were made to revive it in 1810. It was formally established in 1813 by the transfer of a warrant from a defunct lodge which had closed, the *St. George's Lodge* of Georgetown, Granada, in the British West Indies.[756] Membership lists of the Penzance Lodge exist from 1813, but the earliest Minute Books (before 1822) are not in the possession of the Lodge.

21st February 1813. **Elias Magnus**, Wine Merchant. A member of the Penzance Hebrew Congregation, and its Treasurer in 1811, he is also listed in the Penzance Lodge records in 1814. Elias Magnus (1775-1850) was descended from a Dutch family. He married Lemon Hart's sister, Rebecca (1766-1841), then a widow. Magnus moved to London around 1820, and died in Shoreditch on 21st January 1850.[757]

1st June 1814. **Lemon Woolf**, Silversmith. Lemon Woolf (1783-1848) had also attended the Redruth Lodge, where he had been initiated in 1806.

July & August 1814. "**Mr. Ezekiel**" (see below for 1817-18).

18th June & 19th October 1814. **B. A. Simmons**, Silversmith. Barnet Asher Simmons (1784-1860), Rabbi of the Penzance Hebrew Congregation, holding office there as its Minister, intermittently, from 1811 until his death in 1860. Like Samuel Jacob, below, he had joined the *Godolphin Lodge* on the Isles of Scilly in 1814, and may have retained his formal membership there, while attending the Penzance Lodge, which he did not join until 1821. Soon after, in 1823, he is recorded there as a "defaulter" on his membership dues. By 1824, however, he is again listed as a contributing member.

John Abraham Bechtel, Merchant, age 29, was, at one time a member of the Scilly Lodge, but he is not known to have been Jewish.[758]

15th May 1815. Brother **Semmens** (as above) being raised to the 4th degree.

22nd & 27th June, 17th July 1815. **Samuel Jacob**(s) of Hayle, Mercer. Samuel Jacob (1778-1860) was a son of Moses Jacob of Redruth. He had traded in Camborne and also on the Isles of Scilly, and eventually settled in Penzance. He joined the *Godolphin Lodge* of Scilly in 1811. The Penzance Lodge also recorded him as a defaulter in 1823, and he appears to have withdrawn from membership thereafter. He died in 1860, and is, therefore, not to be confused with his namesake and much younger relative, Samuel Jacob (1838-1913) of the Falmouth Lodge, who also appears in the Penzance Lodge records (1872-1879). The latter was a great grandson of Moses Jacob of Redruth.

27th December 1815. **Lawrance Isaacs**. It is likely, but not certain, that he was Jewish, although he may have been related to the Rabbi Moses Isaacs, noted at the *Druid's Lodge* Redruth (1808-1809), who was Rabbi of the Penzance Congregation (1808-1810). Moses Isaac's name appears in the Penzance Congregational Minute Book; Lawrance Isaacs's name does not. There were also Jewish traders named *Isaac* (or *Isaacs*) in Falmouth from this time, but they may not have been related to Lawrance or Moses Isaac. Christian Isaac or Isaacs families traded in Truro.

17th January 1816. **Barnett A. Symons** (as above). Later in the year, on 17th December, he signed the Lodge accounts with Lemon Woolf.

1818. **Lemon Woolf**, Master. He is recorded as such on the table of Masters which hangs in the Lodge Temple.

From 1817-1818. **Solomon Ezekiel** (*c*.1786-1867). A tin plate and copper worker. Originally from Devon, he married Hannah Jacob (1775-1864) a daughter of Moses Jacob of Redruth. He remained in Penzance for the rest of his life. He may have had Masonic links with the (largely Jewish) *Hiram* Lodge of London.[759]

21st August 1819. **Levi Jacob** (1788-1824), Mineralist. He was a son of Moses Jacob of Redruth. Levi Jacob joined the Redruth Lodge from 1813, and was admitted as a member of the Penzance Lodge in 1821. By 1823, he was no longer a subscribing member, and he died in 1824.

29th June and 17th July 1821 . **Alex. Simmons**, Spirit Merchant. He is likely to be the Alexander Symons who appears in the Penzance Congregational Minute Book at this time. He is not known to have been related to B. A. Simmons, above. Alexander Simmons had joined the London *Hiram* Lodge in 1819.[760] His name continues to appear in the Penzance Lodge records from 1822, but in 1826 he is recorded as a "defaulter".

10th July 1821. **Samuel Jacobs**, Watchmaker. The same as 27th June 1815, above.

17th July 1821. **Barnett Ashur** (*sic*. Asher) **Simmons**, Jeweller. As previous entries.

21st August 1821. **Levi Jacobs**.

In 1822, **Lemon Woolf**, Spirit Merchant, appears in the records as the Lodge Secretary. His Masonic rank is given as Royal Arch.

11th March 1823. Johan **Salomon** Bergendahl, from Sweden. He may have been Jewish, but it is not certain. Henry (Hyman) Levin, the father of Israel Levin, below, was also from Sweden (Stockholm). Jews from Germany first settled in Sweden from the 1770s, the first community in Stockholm being established around 1775. From 1782, Jews were admitted to Gothenburg, Norrkoping and Kariskrona. (Sweden's Jews were not emancipated until 1870, when other communities were established in Malmo and elsewhere.)

30th October 1827. **Abraham Jacobowitch**, who is recorded as from "Russian Poland". It is possible that this is the **Abraham Jacobs**, tailor, from Poland who lived in Plymouth at the time of the 1871 Census,[761] when he was recorded as age 64 years. If so, he would have been just 21 at the time of his visit to the Penzance Lodge.

From 1827 to 1831. **Lemon Woolf** was the Lodge Treasurer.

In 1836. **Lemon Woolf** was the Lodge Secretary.

17th June 1837. Anthony Kistler, Clockmaker. It is uncertain if he was Jewish.

20th December 1842. **Morris Hart Harris**, Jeweller. M. H. Harris (1821-1913) was a son of Henry Harris (1787-1872) from Penzance, later of Truro and London. Morris Hart Harris had married into the Jacob family (of Falmouth and Redruth) and he was President of the Penzance Hebrew Congregation from 1850-1852.

17th August 1859. **Solomon King**. It is not certain that he was Jewish, but he is listed with Israel Levin, below:

17th August 1859. **Israel Henry Levin**, Merchant (and Jeweller). Israel Levin (1829-1887) was the son of Hyman (Henry) Levin (1798-1877). Both father and son occupied the Presidency of the Penzance Hebrew Congregation.

1863. **Israel Levin** was Lodge Master. His name appears regularly in the Lodge records.

1869. "At a Cornish Provincial Grand Lodge meeting in 1869, Israel Levin, Past Master of the Mount Sinai Lodge No. 121 of Penzance, and Samuel Jacob, Past Master of the Three Grand Principles No. 967 at Penryn, were honoured with Provincial rank".[762]

7th March 1870. Arie Behrens, from Holland, Mariner. The name suggests that he may have been of Jewish descent, but this is not certain.

2nd August 1872 (to 1879). **Samuel Jacob** of Falmouth, Outfitter & Jeweller. Samuel Jacob (1838-1913) was from an affluent family with diverse commercial interests in Falmouth. In 1880 he left for London, although his name continues in the Lodge records as "of London" until 1881, when he resigned his Lodge membership.

From 20th March 1889. **Israel Oppenheim**, Merchant. The son of Samuel Oppenheim (1800-1869), Israel (1843-1913) continued his father's general household store in Market Jew Street. He was President of the Penzance Hebrew Congregation (1868-9 & 1871-1872). He moved to Bristol, where he died.

From 20th May 1891. **M. Bischofswerder**, General Dealer. A son of one of the last Rabbis in Penzance, Isaac Bischofswerder (1822-1899), this is **Morris (Moses) Bischofswerder** (1856-1934) who had married Julia, a daughter of Henry Joseph, a leading member of the Penzance Hebrew Congregation, and its President for several terms between 1852-1881. Morris Bischofswerder left Penzance around 1913, after the death of his wife in 1911. [The names of his father, Rev. Isaac Bischofswerder (1822-1899), and his brothers, Max (1860-1928), who settled in Plymouth in 1884, George Solomon: (1861-1930), who settled in Hull in 1885, Marcus (1852-1914), who moved to Plymouth around 1895, and soon after to Hull, and David (1854-1902) who also moved to Plymouth after 1892, and then emigrated to South Africa, do not appear in the Lodge records.] A Christian friend of the Bischofswerder family, Alderman Wellington Dale (mentioned earlier in connection with David Bischofswerder) was a Lodge member in 1888. It has also been noted that Morris Bischofswerder's membership of the Lodge is also confirmed by a letter (dated 1st September 1902) from the Mayor of Penzance, William Colenso, to the Home Office in support of Morris Bischofswerder's application for Naturalisation, in which Colenso confirms that the applicant and his referee, Mr. P. Chigwin, "have both been for many years members of our Masonic Lodge", and that he (Colenso) had "occupied the chair in 1886".[763]

The following, whose names also appear in the Penzance Lodge records were not Jewish: Solomon Cock (1814), Josiah Teague (1815), Emmanuel Rogers (1874), Abraham Warren (1874), George William Wolfe (1899 & 1901).

From Cornwall, many Jewish families migrated to the developing towns and cities of the United Kingdom where their story can still be told and where the memory of their Cornish origins is still preserved, in many cases as proudly as the Continental origins of their forebears. More extensive still is the history of emigration from Cornwall where Jews, together with their Christian neighbours, travelled to the Americas, South Africa and Australasia. Many settled in those places for life and founded new communities and congregations. The role of Masonry in Cornish life, especially in the 19th century, has been emphasised by writers on Cornish history such as Sharron Schwartz who has visited Cornish settlements in the United States and has drawn attention to the fact that the majority of Cornish burials in public cemeteries are still to be found in the sections reserved for Freemasons, of which the following may serve as an example: "Carn Marth miner, Joseph Kemp, buried at the Glenwood Cemetery in Park City, Utah, has Masonic insignia on his headstone."[764] Likewise, Philip Payton, who has written extensively of Cornish emigration, says of the mining frontier towns of North America: "Masonic Lodges often behaved as surrogate Cornish associations or trade union branches, providing solidarity and security in an otherwise volatile environment - furthering the interests of the Cornish wherever possible. - The continuance of the Masonic tradition abroad - would also have strengthened the kin network. - Significantly, one of the first buildings erected in the overwhelmingly Cornish town of Gold Hill - in Nevada, was the Masonic Lodge".[765] For Jews, as a cultural and religious minority amongst these Cornish pioneers, the Masonic community of which many were members would have been of special importance in assisting their adaptation to an unfamiliar country and an uncertain future. And so, even as the Jewish congregations in Cornwall were drawing towards their close, they were at the same time bestowing new life upon Jewish communities abroad. The loss of the relatively short-lived Jewish communities in Cornwall must inevitably be a matter of regret, but theirs was of a transitional nature and their purpose, perhaps, was to give to their descendants the memory and confidence that Jewish life could indeed be lived out in the circumstances of peace, tolerance and security which Cornwall had given them.

Appendix: Documentary Sources for Chapters 3–7.

Directories:

1. Bailey's Western and Midland Directory, 1783 (Ba 1783).
2. Bailey's Universal Directory, 1791 (Ba 1791).
3. Universal British Directory of Devon and Cornwall, 1799 Vol. 4 (Un 1799).
4. Holden's Directory, 1811 (Ho 1811).
5. The Falmouth Guide, 1815 (Fa 1815).
6. Pigot's Directories: of 1823, 1824,1830 and 1844 (Pg etc.).
7. Williams' Commercial Directory of Cornwall, 1847 (Wi 1874).
8. Slater's Royal National and Commercial Directory of Cornwall, 1852-3 (Sl 1852/3).
9. Charles Coulson's Directory of Penzance, 1864 (Co 1864).

10. Warn's Directory, 1864 (Wa 1864).
11. Postal Directories, 1862 & 1873 (Po. 1862/1873).
12. Kelly's Directories, 1889 & 1902 (K. 1889/1902).

Publications:

13. G. B. Millet (Lecture, 1878): *Penzance, Past & Present* (1880) Beare & Sons (Mil).
14. J. G. Osborne "History of Freemasonry in West Cornwall, 1765-1828" by J. G. Osborne; Frederick Rodda, Penzance, 1901 (Os).
  Old Masonic members-handbooks, for individual Lodges, published annually and available only privately, can sometimes be found in second-hand bookshops, but they are not referenced here. Some Jewish names are to be found in them. Access to historic archival records can be obtained with permission from local lodge archivists.
15. H. Miles Brown, "Cornish Clocks and Clockmakers" David & Charles, 1970 (Br).
  (The dates given as Br. in brackets refer to the date given by Brown to the subject's work and activities, not the date of publication; ditto Jackson, below).
16. Frank Mitchell, "Annals of an Ancient Cornish Town" (Redruth) Dyllansow Truran, Trewolsta, Trewergie, Redruth, 1985 (Mit).
17. Jacksons Silver & Gold Marks of England, Scotland & Wales;
First Edition Pickford; Antique Collectors Club; 3rd. edition, 1994 (Ja).

Census lists, Aliens Lists (Lipman) and newspaper references are given individually. Various travel guides to Cornwall, to be found in most Public libraries, also make occasional reference to and carry advertisements for Jewish businesses in Cornish towns.

---

[722] Hughan (1866) p. 481. The various references to visitors in this section are all drawn from pages in Hughan and Osborne (1901).
[723] Hughan (1867) p. 345.
[724] I am grateful to R. John Hall of the Falmouth Lodge, and to Peter Luscombe of the Penzance Lodge for their invaluable help in allowing access to their historical records (prior to 1900), and providing guidance and assistance in reviewing them (2004). Items in this section not referenced to other writers, represent my own research from the original Lodge records in 2004.
[725] See also John M. Shaftesley, *Jews in Regular English Freemasonry 1717-1860*, and Morris Rosenbaum, *Jewish Freemasons in England* (18th and Early 19th Centuries: a Provisional List): both published in the Transactions of the Jewish Historical Society of England, Sessions 1973-1975, Vol. XXV, pp. 150-209 (London 1977), from which some of these names have been drawn; other sources include Shaftesley's *The Lodge of Israel No. 205, 1793-1968* (London 1968), Jacob Katz's *Jews and Freemasons in Europe 1723-1939* (Cambridge Mass. USA 1970)) and his *Out of the Ghetto: The Social Background of Jewish Emancipation 1770-1870* (Camb. Mass. 1973).
[726] Hughan (1867). p. 401.
[727] Trathen's *History of Falmouth* (1815) p. 65, and Hughan (1867) p. 282.
[728] R. John Hall's History of the Falmouth Lodge 1751-2001 (Published privately) p. 11.
[729] Hughan (1866) pp. 266 & 281, who comments that these details of elaborate gold lacing of regalia appear to have been unusual.
[730] George Rigal (Letter to Godfrey Simmons, 9th November 2004): Insurance Policy 13th January 1757

(No. 32741). An earlier policy No. 21342 has not survived, but would have been dated *c*.1746-7.

[731] Letter from Philip Levy to Godfrey Simmons (6th November 2004).

[732] Details concerning Philip Moses and Alexander Moses' visits to London have been extracted (November 2004) by Diane Clements (Director of the Library and Museum of Freemasonry, London) from C. W. Firebrace, *Records of the Lodge of Antiquity* (1911 & 1926) from the second volume (1926).

[733] R. John Hall's History of the Lodge (2001) Appendix pp. ii to iv.

[734] This expression indicates that they were not members of that Lodge, although membership of several lodges is possible.

[735] Rosenbaum (1977) p. 173.

[736] Hughan (1866) pp. 362 & 381.

[737] *Exeter Flying Post,* 10th May 1792 (Helen Fry 2000).

[738] Rosenbaum *Trans. JHSE* (1973-1975) p. 170.

[739] Hughan (1867) p. 21.

[740] R. John Hall (2001) Appendix, p. ii.

[741] I am grateful to Michael Michell (Letters of 13th December 2008 & 8th January 2009) for this information, drawn from the records of the Library of Freemasons' Hall, London; to David Thomas, Archivist CRO Truro; Letter of 2nd March 2009, and to Peter Aitkenhead, Assistant Librarian, the Library and Museum of Freemasonry, London (Letter to Godfrey Simmons of 16th April 2009).

[742] Trudy Martin (2004).

[743] R. John Hall (2001) Appendix p. v.

[744] Hall does not give a Secretary in 1862, but M.R. Ellis in 1859 and C.B. Scot in 1863. The Lodge records for 17th January 1862 refer to "Bro. Jacob (Secry.)".

[745] Trudy Martin (2004).

[746] Rosenbaum (p. 180).

[747] Letter from R. John Hall, Almoner and Archivist of the Lodge, to Eric Dawkins (1st February 1999).

[748] W. Warn, *Directory and Guide for Falmouth and Penryn and their Vicinities* (Falmouth 1864) p. 128.

[749] The original photograph in the Alex Jacob Archive is inscribed on the back with the name *Lanyon.*

[750] Osborne (pp. 6-8); Rosenbaum (p. 175).

[751] Susser (1972) p. 18.

[752] Osborne (p. 13).

[753] T. E. A. Stowell, *The Centenary History of the Cornubian Lodge* (1950). I am grateful to Dr. Roger Burt of Exeter University for drawing my attention to this private publication (Letter to Godfrey Simmons, 17th August 2000). A copy of the book can be found in the Cornish Studies Library, Redruth. Both Osborne and Hughan contain sections on this lodge.

[754] Stowell gives the Lodge number as 450, which may have been its original number. The Lodge was revived in 1851 as No. 589. Osborne contains a very detailed section on this lodge: pp. 38-213.

[755] Hughan (1866) p. 122.

[756] Letter from Stephen Leach of St. Just-in-Penwith to Keith Pearce (11th February 2004).

[757] Research by Godfrey Simmons from the Congregational Minute-Books, and by Angela Shire into Dutch and English records (civil and synagogue) copies of which are in her private Archive (Letters from Angela Shire, 23rd January 2000, 11th February 2000 & 12th March 2000).

[758] Rosenbaum (1973-1975). p. 173 (no date given for his membership).

[759] Rosenbaum, p. 178.

[760] Shaftesley, pp. 153 & 166.

[761] Susser (1995, p. 49).

[762] Transactions of Quatuor Coronati Lodge, Vol. 92.

[763] *The Cornishman,* 1st & 9th August 1889; and Ref. PRO Kew. HO 144/657/B38710.

[764] Sharron Schwartz and Roger Parker (1998, p. 152).

[765] Philip Payton (1999, pp. 37-8).

PART THREE
Congregational and Religious Life

⪮

CHAPTER 8
The Jewish Cemeteries

Based upon a survey (1975) by Nicholas de Lange and Jennifer Speake

Hebrew Transcriptions by Nicholas de Lange and Jennifer Speake
Translations by Herman Zeffertt

(i)
Jewish Cemeteries and Burial Rites

Jewish tradition and religious practice require that congregational cemeteries are held in and treated with the highest respect. A synagogue ceases to be a holy place once it has been vacated and is no longer required for religious worship. A cemetery, however, cannot be deconsecrated, and remains a sacred place in perpetuity. Burial grounds are so fundamental to Jewish religious life, that they have often been established well before the formal congregation itself, and certainly before the acquisition of a synagogue. In Hebrew, a cemetery is variously called *Bet Kevarot*, a House or Place of Graves, *Bet ha-Chaim,* the House or Garden of Life, and *Bet Olam*, the House of Eternity.[1] Clearly, these expressions reflect both a recognition of human mortality and a belief in its transcendence. The head should be covered when entering a cemetery, a prayer should be said for all of those laid to rest there, any disrespectful act or behaviour is prohibited, and the cemetery itself may not be used for any secondary or extraneous purposes. The Talmud itself states that the dead are to be guaranteed the eternal inviolability of their graves, and from this principle no grave can be used for more than one interment, and it should never be disturbed, re-used, or even walked upon. In Christian cemeteries, family members may be interred in the same grave, but the prohibition against this in Jewish tradition results in the practical consequence that in a Jewish burial ground the available land is likely to be used up more rapidly than in a Christian ground of the same area where there have been the same number of burials. In Plymouth the singularity of graves in the Old Cemetery on The Hoe may not always have been respected, and the proximity of certain tombstones could suggest that coffins had been buried on top of one another, a matter that was drawn to the attention of the Chief Rabbi in 1825, and which may have led to the suspension of further burials there, even in reserved plots that showed no obvious sign of previous use.[2] Where historically, upon a Jewish cemetery becoming full, and Jews might be forbidden to open a new one or to enlarge the existing one by the purchase of adjacent land (which did occur in Prague) Rabbinical authority has allowed headstones to be removed from graves but preserved on the site, and for the graves to be covered over with a depth of six handbreadths of earth interposing to allow a new burial to take place without disturbing the previous interment. However, such provisions have operated only in situations of *extremis*, but, in reinforcing the principle of inviolability, have meant that, where Jewish cemeteries have survived, their headstones are often much older than in Christian cemeteries that pre-date them. Where cemeteries were destroyed or had to be abandoned, headstones were sometimes transferred to a new cemetery.[3] Jewish headstones, known as *mazzevah*, are the only artefact connected with burial that may be expensive and elaborate, preserving the precious memory of both the individual laid there, but also reflecting and encompassing the totality of the departed of the family of Israel. The headstone will contain the names of the deceased and his, or her, father, and are often accompanied by some form of honorific title. Of these, for men, the term *rabbi*, "teacher" or "master" came to signify, not a minister as such, but an honorific or courteous term for a respected member of the congregation. For the office of Rabbi, the abbreviation *MHRR* may be found, signifying *Morenu ha-rab rabbi*, that is, *Our* (the congregation's) Teacher, sometimes accompanied by *dayyan*, or judge. Other titles that are found reflect some public office within the congregation, such as *gabbai* (Treasurer), *rosh* (Senior, or Head), and the most honorary *parnas*, the President or Chief Officer and Warden of the Congregation. Lower titles include *shamash* (sexton). For women, there are fewer titles, the most common being *marat* (married) or infrequently, in the case of a Rabbi's (minister's) wife or daughter, *rabbanit*. On the continent, for those who had died as a martyr in a pogrom, the term *Kadosh* (literally "Saint") was used (though without its Christian connotations). Later and elsewhere this term was used of any who had died an unnatural or tragic death, most likely preserving echoes of a propitiatory sacrifice. The headstone will contain formulaic blessings for and eulogies about the deceased. Of these the most common blessings are: "Cherished memory" or "The memory of the just is blessed" (Proverbs 10:7) and, most frequently, *Tehi Nishmato Ts'rurah Bitzor Ha-Chayim* - "Let (or May) his (her) soul be bound up in the bond of life" (from 1 Samuel 25:29).

The eulogies (often the lengthiest part of the inscription) tend to praise the character and noteworthy acts of the deceased, represented by such common attributes as sincerity, justice, wisdom, eloquence and generosity. The eulogies for men tend to focus on the qualities of congregational involvement and activity, whereas those for women display a greater variety of attributes, often reflecting a societal and domestic context, including virtue, honesty, sincerity, resolve, courage, comfort, charity, dedication, beauty and kindness. It is axiomatic that the reading of Hebrew headstones often requires some specialist linguistic and historical knowledge. The nature of the Hebrew quadratic alphabet evolved into forms that eventually stabilised, although the practice of engravature varied in time and location, and, in the absence of numerical icons in Hebrew script, dates require inference from the numerical value of letters according to their sequence in the alphabet, and the chronogrammatic addition of each of these values towards a sum value. Later headstones may contain additional miniature ciphers or icons, above or beneath letters to assist in such computation. The potential for error in interpretation is considerable, and the omission of such indicators from consideration could alter the meaning of words and the numerical value of specific sections of the script.

Historically, the inscriptions may contain oblique reference to persons or events not readily comprehensible without knowledge of the period and place in question.[4] Headstones commonly have, at the top point, the Hebrew letters *pey* and *nun*, an abbreviation for *po nikbar* or *po nitman*, "Here lies buried (the man or the woman)". Sometimes found on headstones is the Hebrew (or an abbreviation) for "Remember", being a solemn command to the living to recall and respect the memory of the departed, but also serving as a *memento mori,* acting as a reminder to the living to take heed of the sacred essence of life itself while it may still be lived. These themes of mortality and eternity constitute a powerful symbiosis, and inform the practices of understatement and solemnity that characterise Jewish funerary rites. The architectural development of continental headstones can be traced from the 7th century onwards in Southern Italy and France (Narbonne 668, Brindisi 832 and Lyon 1101) through the 13th and 14th centuries in the Rhineland Germany, Lower Austria, Bohemia and Moravia, and into the 16th to 18th centuries in Prague, where burial houses and sarcophagi or four walled horizontal tomb-stones, each known as *ohel* (shrine) or *hoysl* (little house). Later, decorative symbols appeared, such as a grapes, for wisdom and fertility, the Star of David, the *Magen David,* money-boxes for charity, blessing hands, representing the priestly Kohen tribe, and pitchers and musical instruments for the Levites, their assistants. Animals also appear, their Hebrew names mirroring family names, the most common being a lion, a deer, a bear and a wolf, and tools and implements for trades, the scissors (tailors), lancets (physicians), mortars (chemists), books (schol-ars and bookbinders), a quill (scribes), and even instruments for circumcision (the mohel).[5]

On the continent, where Jews were accustomed to discrimination and persecu-tion, the acquisition of suitable sites for the establishment of a cemetery was diffi-cult. The additional requirement that the burial ground should be near a source of fresh running water, for ritual and hygienic purposes, made the identification of an available site even more problematical. The concern for inviolability meant that, where possible, Jewish communities would try to purchase a site for permanent possession, although the costs could be extortionate and the sites themselves infe-rior. They were often remote, although their isolation and relative concealment may have contributed to the survival of some of the oldest cemeteries. Even where burial grounds were located in or close to towns "To protect the graves from dese-cration and damage, the cemeteries were surrounded by a tall stone wall and a gate (often double) in the form of a small house, which in small rural cemeteries also served as a mortuary."[6] It is of interest that this description of an historic conti-nental cemetery could be applied in its entirety to the intact structure of the burial ground in Penzance, and would seem to indicate that traditional practice was retained even in an entirely different and benign cultural context, where, in Cornwall, the Jews were welcomed and were readily provided with desirable, permanent sites to establish their cemeteries.

Jewish burial practice would have been under the care of the congregation's *Hevra Kaddishah*, the Holy Brotherhood, one of the oldest known forms of which was established in 1564 in Prague by Rabbi Eliezer Askenazy. The responsibilities of this society were shaped by the principle that no individual should benefit financially from the immediate necessities to care for the sick and the dying, or from their burial. The Society collectively took responsibility for all of the duties that would be carried out by an undertaker, but in addition visited, cared for and comforted the dying and their family. A *minyan* would recite all of the prescribed prayers for the occasion, including, at the moment of death itself, the *Shema Yisrael*, the communal affirmation of faith. These acts of final and ultimate kindness were held to be a sacred obligation of charity to be extended to all members of the community equally. The society's funds (to meet its material requirements) were provided by the individual subscriptions of congregational members, but, unlike payments that conferred full membership or seat tenure in the synagogue, the ministrations of the society extended to those in poverty who could not afford to make such contributions. The burial of the poor and the provision of their headstone could also be met from these communal funds, and from the situation that applied in Exeter and Plymouth in the 18th and 19th centuries it would seem that it was common practice for a member of the congregation to act as a Charity Warden, and another as a Cemetery Fund Treasurer. The former would defer general charitable expenses to needy members of the community for their treatment during sickness, and would devolve expenses to the latter, for the use of the Burial Society for the care and supervision of the dying and for their eventual preparation for burial. Some cemeteries set aside an area of the cemetery for the sole use of those who had not been able to purchase a burial plot. This area was sometimes known as that of the *Orchim*, literally "strangers", although this term does not denote unfamiliarity, but indicates those who were not full, subscribing members of the congregation. This area was available, however, for the burial of those who were by definition strangers, in that they were unfamiliar visiting Jews, such as itinerant hawkers, or those whose families could not be contacted in the event of a sudden death. It is possible that the Cornish Jewish cemeteries also set aside distinct areas for the burial of Gentiles married to Jews, of Jews married to Gentiles, and for suicides. This was certainly the custom in the Exeter and Plymouth cemeteries, where these areas set apart from the "regular rows" were referred to as "beyond the boards".[7] Any surplus funds of the society, held as profit, were to be used only to serve the community as a whole. The operation of this burial society can be traced throughout the accounts of the Penzance congregation in its Minute Book, including its charitable expenditure on the burial of several of its Poor. In Plymouth and Exeter, members of the society were even balloted to guard the corpse before burial and to stand guard for at least three nights afterwards to prevent the operation of body snatchers. Professional guards seem to have been hired in Devon on occasions, and the corruption that was rife amongst surgeons and sextons there extended to a coalition that included a Jewish accomplice, Israel "Izzy" Cohen.[8]

So fundamental was the Burial Society in Jewish religious tradition that it was often formed before any formal religious congregation had been established, the sacred obligation to bury the dead in a separated cemetery taking precedence over the building or acquisition of a synagogue. In this sense, the Society, and not the congregation itself formed the very basis of the idea of a religious community. In some congregations there would have been a restriction of formal membership of the society to senior married men, which may have reflected the recognition of respect for the domestic intimacy of the occasion with which only the married man would have direct experience as parent and spouse, but also mirrored their exclusive traditional role in the recitation of prayers, and their responsibility to convey the corpse to the grave at the *Levoyah* or funeral. The appropriate role of women in the society would, however, have been implicit, as it is today, in the attendance to the intimate needs of dying women and the washing (*Tahara*) of female corpses before burial.

Immediately after the death, Jewish tradition prescribes that the funeral should take place if possible on the same day, or if the death has taken place during the night, the very next morning. Interments would not occur, however, during the duration of the Sabbath (from Friday dusk to Saturday dusk), on the Day of Atonement, or on the first day of a major festival. The washing of the body, accompanied by prayer, is both an act of recognition of the dignity of the body, but is also a ritual purification, reflecting the fact that a child, given by God, is washed upon birth, and is washed again upon being returned to the Creator. The body is wrapped in a shroud of pure linen, and for men their *tallit* or prayer shawl, and is laid in a simple wooden coffin, without ornamentation, the latter symbolising the equality of death. The *Bet Tahorah* at the entrance to the cemetery would have been the traditional place for this rite, although in 19th century Exeter, at least, it took place in the deceased's home, as it might today, or, indeed, in a hospital.[9] Participation in a funeral procession and the burial is regarded in Judaism as *hesed shel emet*, a religious obligation of loving kindness, and not as an option or a matter left to personal disposition. Traditionally, the procession itself would be punctuated by seven pauses, said to represent the seven Hebrew forms of the word *hevel*, meaning death, the seven days of God's creation of the world, and also the idea of the seven stages of life that spread beyond Judaism itself and which Shakespeare drew upon so memorably in his play *As You Like It*.[10] At each of these moments of rest, and at the burial itself prayers are read and psalms recited, reflecting the brevity of life and the transition of the departed to eternity, and conclude with the *Kaddish* (which itself makes no mention of death). It would seem likely that the Jewish tradition of the processional seven stages influenced the Roman Catholic Easter ritual of the Stations of the Cross (doubled to fourteen).

The number seven also influences the period of mourning immediately after the burial, when members of the congregation visit the bereaved each day for a week, *shivah*, seven days, to say special prayers sitting on low stools, the practice being known as "sitting shivah". The mourning period for parents is 30 days, and for a parent, 11 months. Visiting graves is another sacred duty, and will be observed on the anniversary of the death, when a small stone or pebble is placed on the grave as a token of remembrance, a practice which may derive from the duty of

357

travellers to add a stone to grave mounds found in the desert.[11] In contrast to the simplicity required in the construction of coffins or the provision of a simple burial shroud, headstones are not only a precious family possession, but are also a respectful memorial, and are often very elaborate. The headstone to a grave will be added by the end of a year, when a special ceremony of stone-setting takes place.

Six handbreadths or "palms" also separate each grave from its neighbour, and family plots or areas, although more common today, were not customary, each person being interred "without any distinction, according to the sequence of funerals, in lines, side by side", although a space could be reserved for a close family member, but only then temporarily. However, some criteria of distinction could be applied in larger cemeteries, where space allowed it, such as the separation of the sinful from the righteous, and those who had "lived in mutual conflict or hostility", and also special rows of honour, usually containing especially elaborate headstones, for rabbis or congregational members of great honour, for descendants of the *Kohenim* (priestly families), often placed near the entrance, because their descendants should not be defiled by having to walk across the cemetery, and of the *Levites* (families of the temple assistants), although they were allowed to enter the cemetery, and, sometimes areas for the burial of infants and children, and the poor. Damaged or worn Torah Scrolls, withdrawn from use, were also buried in the cemetery.[12]

In the small Cornish Jewish cemeteries, some aspects of these arrangements may have been preserved, but any formal reconstruction of them is likely to be fragmentary.

(ii)
The Cornish Cemeteries

Nationally, there are only about twenty-five extant Jewish burial grounds predating the early 19th century. Seven of these are to be found in the South West, and, collectively, they form the best preserved regional group outside London. The Jewish burial grounds at Falmouth and Penzance represent the visible legacies of the 18th and 19th century Jewish communities in Cornwall. The synagogue buildings can still be viewed from the outside, but are no longer in use as synagogues. They are both now in private ownership. The cemeteries, however, are still under Jewish supervision with the Board of Deputies of British Jews as the Trustees. They represent a vital link with the past. They remain sacred Jewish sites even today after more than a century of disuse and can still be visited by appointment with the custodians. Time has taken its inevitable toll despite ongoing, if irregular, maintenance over the years. The Falmouth ground, especially, has suffered considerable decay. The Penzance cemetery, however, is the most perfectly preserved of the seven cemeteries of the South West, and is regarded as one of the finest examples of a walled Georgian Jewish cemetery in Britain.

Much of the credit for the survival of these grounds must go to the inconspicuous but devoted work of individuals who, over the years, have taken a personal interest in their protection and upkeep. Special mention should be made of the work of Alfred Dunitz (1917-2011) a Justice of the Peace and a former member of the Board of Deputies of British Jews in London, who, for many years, travelled extensively to supervise and check on the security and maintenance of the cemeteries. He initiated schemes for their necessary maintenance through the Probation and Community Services. This arrangement proved essential to their preservation. Penzance was fortunate in having Godfrey Simmons as the custodian for over twenty years; his great-grandfather, Barnett Asher Simmons, was the longest-resident Rabbi in Cornwall. Godfrey and his brother, John Simmons, ensured that a corner section of the Penzance cemetery's high surrounding wall (so important for its protection) was rebuilt when it required attention in the early 1990s, and Godfrey Simmons also paid himself for other necessary maintenance to the cemetery. Alfred Dunitz's successor, Michael Harris (1928-2006), successfully negotiated a maintenance agreement for the Penzance cemetery with the local Town Council. The latter, together with the Penlee House Gallery and Museum, now act as local guardians for the cemetery, and this has considerably enhanced its protection. For many years the Falmouth cemetery's custodian was Eric Dawkins, the town's former Clerk, and today, Anthony Fagin, formerly of the Museum at Masada, and members of *Kehillat Kernow* have taken an active interest in the protection and supervision of that cemetery. In Penzance, since 1997, I have taken over this role, and so both cemeteries have had non-Jews as custodians at some time. Maurice Minsky undertook to visit and oversee the Cornish cemeteries, until the Board of Deputies appointed a permanent Director of Community Issues, Colin Spanjar, who is now responsible for all disused historic cemeteries, which have been drawn under the auspices of BODHeritage, established in 2009.

Fortunately, the cemeteries have been surveyed and their tombstones recorded on several occasions over the course of the last century. These surveys have been combined to form the basis of this chapter. Without them, much of the inscription material would be lost to us today as, inevitably, some of the stones have disappeared or been weathered by time and are no longer legible. There was also a significant difference between the two cemeteries from the time when they were first established, in that it would seem that Falmouth burial ground was enclosed in some form around or soon after its inception, in the early 18th century, whereas the Penzance cemetery (roughly contemporaneous) was located on open ground for many years. It was only partially enclosed from around 1822, and not completely enclosed, by its present substantial and high wall until its enlargement in 1845. Because of this comparatively late enclosure, from 1822-1845, the earliest headstones in Penzance from the period *c.*1750-1820 have either disappeared or are in a fragmentary condition which prevents formal identification, and so the information they carried concerning some of the Jewish community's founding members has been lost. There are no named headstones in the Penzance cemetery earlier than 1823, and none which can be dated earlier than 1791, although there are a number of unmarked graves, and others with fragmentary headstones, in the vicinity of the 1791 grave. This is the earliest part of the cemetery, and it would be reasonable to assume that these unidentified graves are at least contemporaneous with, or may even predate the year 1791 by several decades. In fact the identities of a number of people who are known from other sources to have died in Penzance before or around this time, can be allocated to these graves, although not to specific plots. In the Falmouth burial ground, which, presumably, was in some way enclosed from very early on, there about a dozen headstones remain intact from the period 1790-1810. Two of these that have been listed as being of particular historical interest are those of Isaac ben Benjamin (1790) and Alexander Moses (1791),[13] but there is an earlier burial, that of the wife of Barnet Levy (1:4) Esther Elias (1:11), who is known to have died in 1780. A recently discovered granite headstone, virtually indecipherable, may be that of Esther Elias.

Barnet Lyon Joseph (1801-1880) compiled a list of the Falmouth headstones around 1850-60. This was eventually published in the *Jewish Chronicle* on 22nd July 1910. It was reprinted privately with some corrections and further details by Anthony P. Joseph in 1954. B.L. Joseph appears to have read the oldest surviving headstone, incorrectly, as 5534 (1774). This particular headstone, that of Giteleh Benjamin, has subsequently been confirmed as 1794. In 1938, John Simmons, Fellow and Librarian of All Souls College, Oxford (and brother of Godfrey Simmons) surveyed the Penzance cemetery, and in 1939, Alex M. Jacob carried out a complete survey of Falmouth. He converted the Hebrew dates on the headstones into their secular equivalents. Bernard Susser also surveyed the Falmouth cemetery on at least two occasions, around 1960-1970, and his notes on the Penzance cemetery, although incomplete as a survey, have also survived. He is undoubtedly correct in saying that such cemeteries would have been in use well before the dates of the earliest headstones.[14] These earlier surveys have proved invaluable, even though there are some discrepancies between them. There are, in fact, about twenty unidentified graves in the Falmouth cemetery, and, again, it would be reasonable to suppose that a significant proportion of these, and possibly most of them, are earlier than 1790. Some of the Falmouth headstones that have survived have at some time been displaced. The early surveys have helped to co-ordinate, and largely resolve issues of uncertain location and contradictory data, and so allow some progress towards the reconstruction of a complete record of burials. Moreover, a synoptic comparison of each of the surveys from 1850 to the present, allow for a plan of the original location of each grave, even if it does not mirror exactly the present appearance of the ground.

In 1975, Nicholas de Lange and Jennifer Speake carried out a wide-ranging general survey of Jewish cemeteries across the United Kingdom, with particular attention to Gloucester, Cheltenham, Canterbury, and the two Cornish burial grounds. This 1975 survey, which was part of a wider survey of older Jewish burial grounds in the British Isles, supported jointly by the Jewish Historical Society of England and Anglo-Jewish Archives[15], included the recording of the complete Hebrew headstone transcriptions for Falmouth and Penzance. In 1988, this part of the survey was updated by Godfrey Simmons, Keith Pearce, Rachel Stratton, Tracy Poulton and Mira Little, to take into account the correct re-allocation of misplaced headstones and to draw up plans of both sites. The survey also made cross-reference to the known familial connections between the two cemeteries and their communities. The recent translation of the Hebrew inscriptions on the headstones by Herman Zeffertt and the cross checking of the Hebrew dates with their secular equivalents by Yissochor Marmorstein now brings this collective enterprise to its completion and records for posterity all of those known to have been laid to rest in these cemeteries.

(iii)
Falmouth[15a]

The Falmouth cemetery lies outside the post-mediaeval town of Falmouth itself at Ponsharden, near the older borough and port of Penryn, on a steep incline beside a busy main road, overlooking the tidal mouth of the Penryn river. It adjoins a disused Christian (Congregational) cemetery, separated from it by a small hedge. The two cemeteries together share an area of about a third of an acre, and the Congregational cemetery is about three times the size of the Jewish burial ground. The Ponsharden area was once farmland, and in the Elizabethan period the area where the cemeteries are situated was one where the woodland deerpark of the mediaeval college and Bishop's palace of Glasney merged into fields. Near the cemeteries was a turnpike road, and, as the name Ponsharden suggests, a mediaeval bridge (from the Cornish *pons*, bridge) may have crossed a stream to a small promontory into the Penryn river in Elizabethan times. In 1788, this feature (now lost) was known as The Island. By the time the Jewish and "Dissenters" cemeteries were established (the former around the early to mid 18th century) the turnpike may have marked the border between the borough of Penryn and the town of Falmouth.[16] It is possible that these nonconformist cemeteries were required to be situated outside the town, although in Penzance, around the same time, the Jewish cemetery was established very close to the town centre itself. Over the years the Penryn cemetery has seen some considerable decay. Some of the headstones have inevitably disappeared or been weathered by the damp climate or pollution, and others have been vandalised and broken. However, the most serious threat to its preservation is represented by the mature, proliferate, overgrown trees which surround the cemetery. Their extensive root-systems have surfaced over the years, effectively destroying much of the Christian ground next to it and dislodging many of the headstones in the Jewish cemetery. The headstones are mostly of local slates but some are of a fine grained sandstone. Only one, likely the oldest, and recently rediscovered, is of granite. Most headstones have curvilinear upper edges, and are similar to local Christian headstones of the same period. The inscriptions before 1838 employ only a Hebrew script, but later, English is also found, and increasingly so towards the mid to late 1800s (a pattern similar those in the Penzance cemetery). The orientation of the Penryn graves is somewhat unusual, in that they face NNE-SSW, rather than towards Jerusalem, as is traditional.

On one of his visits, probably around the 1970s, Susser observed of the cemetery that "…only a fireplace against a wall indicates where the chapel stood."[17] The "chapel", the *Ohel*, or *Bet Torhorah* (Cleansing House) would have been where the Congregational Burial Society, the *Hebrah Kaddishah*, may have prepared the body for burial, washing it and wrapping it in a linen shroud (and for males the Tallith, or Prayer Shawl) and placing it in a simple, light coffin, although the chapel may have been used primarily as a vestibule, used for preparatory prayer. The fireplace would provide hot water, that would have been drawn, as Jewish tradition requires, from a nearby source of fresh running water. The small chapel may have been roofed. However, there is no documentary evidence from maps or plans of this feature, and there is no unambiguous visible trace of a fireplace today. It is possible, that this feature suffered decay after Susser's visit, or that Susser drew the inference of a fireplace (and a chapel) partly from his observation of the feature in other South West cemeteries, or, in Falmouth, from what appeared to suggest it. It is possible that the cemetery's present entrance is not the original, in that a redundant entrance with an arch lies along one side, now largely submerged and overgrown. This could give the appearance of an alcove,[18] and it is most likely this feature that Susser took to be the remnant of a fireplace, and so drew the conclusion that it had once been contained within a chapel. The Penzance cemetery certainly had an entrance chapel whose structure, without its roof survives today, although the location of the original fireplace, if there was one, is not obvious. The Exeter cemetery has a chapel that is still in use, and the Plymouth Hoe cemetery, according to Susser, also has a fireplace indicating the original chapel, and, in view of the prevalence of the feature in these cemeteries, it is likely that the Falmouth Congregation followed this common practice.

The cemetery was founded in the mid to late 18th century when the need for a burial ground became pressing. The first Jewish settlers came to Falmouth around the 1740s, encouraged to settle there by the leading figure of Alexander Moses (who was also known as Zender Falmouth). The community soon became well-established and therefore had a need for its own burial ground. It is possible that some of the earliest Jewish settlers lived both in the Penryn and Falmouth areas, although the latter eventually came to be the location of the synagogue and the focus of the Jewish community. It is likely that a site for a cemetery was initially sought in Falmouth itself, but the lack of availability of land there widened the search to Penryn.

The Basset Estate of Tehidy (near Redruth), whose head was Sir Francis Basset (-1769), owned various lands in the Penwerris area of Penryn. The Basset family had first come to Cornwall from Oxfordshire in the time of William the Conqueror, and the family house at Tehidy was not sold until 1916.[19] They settled in the Camborne-Redruth area, coming to own extensive lands that were rich in minerals, and these became a vast source of wealth from mining. The family enjoyed close links with the monarchy, and supported various kings in their wars, from the Welsh Wars of Edward I in 1227, up to the English Civil War. They gained possession of the Manor of Tehidy, near Illogan, and the castle on Carn Brea, during the reign of Edward IV (1461-1483), and became Sheriffs of the County. By 1640, Francis Basset had bought St. Michael's Mount, Marazion, which he fortified and held until his death in 1645, but, under the Commonwealth, their fortunes suffered under Cromwell, and the Mount was sold to the St. Aubyn family. The Basset family's recovery was slow, but the considerable income derived from the ownership of some of the richest mines in Cornwall enabled John Pendarves Basset (-1739) to restore Tehidy Manor and its parklands from 1734. Under John's brother, Francis (-1769), who had become the M.P. for Penryn, the small port of Portreath, near Redruth, was developed to export ore from the mines.

On 25th September 1751, the Basset Estate granted a lease to a Lazarus Steel[20], for nine years, of two fields of 6 acres and two houses for the tarring of yarn (a rope works formerly held by a Thomas Doubt of Budock) at a rent of £13. 9s. a year. Steel's forename might suggest a Jewish connection, in that it is a variant of the Hebrew *Eliezar*, commonly used by Jews, including the Hart family of Penzance. His surname could also be taken as an anglicised form of the German *Stiller* or *Stahl*, also common Jewish names. It is possible, but unlikely that Steel was of Jewish descent. There is no headstone in the Penryn Jewish cemetery for any such name (although Steel's death would likely have predated the earliest extant headstone of 1790.) The name *Lazarus* was often used by Christians, drawing upon both the Hebrew Bible and the New Testament. Over twenty baptisms of a *Lazarus* can be identified from the printed parish register of the church of King Charles the Martyr, Falmouth, from 1580 to 1830. Moreover, *Steel* was a common surname in the Falmouth area, and at least three men called Lazarus Steel (possibly related to the above) received Christian burials there between 1714 and 1729. A Lazarus Steel, whose dates are consistent with the issue of the Basset lease, married a Jane Whitehead (who may have been a widow) on 20th January 1728. Their five children (including a son, also Lazarus) were all baptised between 1732 and 1743. The two sons of a Nathanael Steel, whose forename might also suggest a Jewish origin, and who may have been a relative, had both been baptised as *Lazarus*, on 4th February, 1715, and 11th October 1720. A Lazarus Steel who may be the Steel of the lease, was interred in Falmouth parish churchyard, with no age given, on 11th June 1765, and the Nathanael Steel, who had been buried there the previous year on 3rd May 1764 (again, no age given) may have been his brother. Despite the uncertainty as to the ages of these two males, neither were infants, in that they left wills. Another Nathaniel Steel, likely to be related to this family, is mentioned in the records of the Falmouth Masonic Lodge for the years 1765-1769,[21] where he would have met and known Alexander Moses.

It is unlikely that the lease granted to Lazarus Steel in 1751 included the grounds that later comprised the Jewish and Congregational cemeteries, in that a few years later, an application was made by the Jews to the Basset Estate for a burial ground in the same vicinity. The Basset Memorandum and Proposal Book contains an entry dated 8th June 1759 under *Penwerris* 1,: "Moses, a Jew of Penryn[22], applies for leave to enclose a burying place for the Jews, 50ft. square, out of the green plot at Penwerris now in Dr. Turner's pos(ses)sion....to have an absolute term of 99 years."[23] Clearly, the "green plot" was not leased to Steel, and the Jew was presumably Alexander Moses (1715-1791) of the Falmouth congregation. There is no recorded answer to the proposal, and the calendar of Basset leases do not show that one was executed on this occasion. However, many of the Basset leases were lost or destroyed. As a result, a lease could have been issued around 1759, but is not recorded. Alternatively, the matter of the 1759 application may have lapsed.

That this *Moses* is given as "of Penryn" rather than "of Falmouth" at first may seem a little odd. However, Penryn was a thriving market town in its own right at this time, and had once been of greater significance and size than Falmouth. Moreover, "Penryn" could still be used as a term to include the neighbouring town. The latter was expanding rapidly, however, and by 1768, the Jewish community was largely centred there, with a synagogue by the harbour front. If the applicant is to be identified with Alexander Moses, then, together with other Jews, he is likely to have traded in Penryn, and may even have occupied premises there. It was common practice, no doubt partly born from their experience on the continent of the potential dangers of living in close proximity with their Christian neighbours, to seek burial grounds at some discreet distance from nearby towns. (Ritual considerations of separation may also have played their part). Situated as it is between the centres of Penryn and Falmouth, the *Penwerris* site may have been seen to meet this concern for privacy and relative obscurity. The distance from Penryn to Falmouth is negligible, and the transportation of the light, simple coffins (prescribed by Jewish tradition) by boat between the Penryn wharf and the Falmouth waterfront quays would have been easy. As for Lazarus Steel's adjacent lands, these continued to be used as a Hemp Works and a Wire Works, at least up to 1913, when, enlarged up to 31 acres, they became known as the *Ashfield Estate.* It is likely that Moses of Penryn and Lazarus Steel were not unknown to one another. Jews trading in Penryn would have had as customers those who worked in such a business as the local rope and wire making industry, as well as the boat making industry around the Penryn Wharf, and this may have facilitated the establishment of the cemetery in this locality.[24] Alexander Moses had been a founding member of the Falmouth Masonic Lodge in 1751, and a "Nathl. Steel, Brasier" (whose trade would be integral to a wire making business) was a member of this lodge in 1768. Lazarus Steel may not have been Jewish, but the notion that he would have enjoyed commercial and social contact (such as Masonry) with Falmouth's Jews is entirely credible. That Moses of Penryn applied for ground next to Steel's could be perceived as mere coincidence, but it cannot be entirely irrelevant that many of Falmouth's Jews and the men of the Basset family were prominent Freemasons.

Another Sir Francis Basset (1757-1835) the eldest son of the former Sir Francis (-1769) was still a minor when his father died, but he eventually inherited the title of the Baronet of Tehidy on reaching the age of 21, on 9th August 1778. In 1780, he became M.P. for Penryn, his father's old seat. The new Baronet strengthened his hold over various Cornish boroughs, including Penryn. He lost Truro, to Lord Falmouth, but gained Tregony from him. This Sir Francis was to become the richest and most influential man in the County, and a considerable patron of the arts, including the Cornish painter, John Opie. But Basset also possessed a ruthless and forceful political instinct, which he demonstrated all to clearly when he put down by force the Corn Riots of 1795 in Redruth. For this service, Pitt made him Lord de Dunstanville in 1796. Earlier, in 1782, he had been a founder member of the Penryn Masonic Lodge whose members, as we have seen, included mariners, shipbuilders, victuallers, surgeons, lawyers, and members of the Penryn defence volunteer corps that Sir Francis commanded. Included in its membership were a number of naval and Packet Boat Captains, reflecting the fact that Penryn and other ports were linked by a regular boat service and by maritime commercial interests. Two of the members of this Penryn lodge were Benjamin Hearne, a Tallow Chandler, and Henry Dillon, a Rope Maker. Isaac Polack is the only Jewish name to appear, as a

Linguist.[25] (His daughter, Frances ran a Grocers' shop in Penryn.). It is not clear if Polack was a practising Jew or if he was a member of the Hebrew congregation, and he may have been a Christian convert. No other Jewish name appears on the membership list of this lodge. Polack's skills as a translator would have been useful to these men, and suggest that they were engaged in foreign maritime trade, most likely with the Iberian peninsula and the West Indies.

At the time when Moses of Penryn had applied to the Basset Estate in 1759, it was not clear in English Law if Jews could hold property or land at all, leasehold or otherwise. It is quite possible that Sir Francis Basset (-1769), a High Tory and an Anglican, had been reluctant to venture into uncertain legal waters by granting a lease to a Jew, with the risk that its legitimacy might subsequently be challenged. (The fact that such a lease was granted to Lazarus Steel some eight years earlier, might further suggest he was not Jewish, unless, of course, overriding commercial considerations played a part in the case of the rope works, that did not apply in the case of a proposed cemetery). Moreover, in 1759, it may well have been that the size of the Jewish presence was perceived by the Basset Estate as negligible, with no guarantee that a settled community would establish itself in the locality for any length of time, even though, of course, a Jewish burial ground would in fact have encouraged such settlement. If conservative caution did play a part at this stage, it is not known how many years passed before a plot at Ponsharden was granted by the Basset estate. Roth, referring to consecration of the new synagogue in 1808, states "A Burial Ground, adjacent to the Congregational cemetery, was presented to the community *later on* [writers' italics] by Lord (de) Dunstanville" (*sic.*).[26] Roth gives no source for this claim. Alex Jacob, however, places the gift "some ten years before" the death of Alexander Moses' death (-1791), that is around 1780, when (or soon after which) Esther, the wife of Barnet Levy, is believed to have died, and is presumed to be interred in the cemetery in an unmarked grave. Although the earliest decipherable headstone, that of Isaac ben Benjamin, is dated 1790, the year 1780 is the earliest that Jacob could infer from genealogical information concerning Esther Levy's death. However, the fact that this plot would have been used for burial by this date does not in itself lead to the conclusion that the land had already been gifted. The 1759 application not only suggests that the need for a burial ground had arisen much earlier, but that burials could have taken place long before 1780. Indeed, the plot may have been used by the Jews under permission from the Basset Estate without a formal lease being granted, and transferred to them as a gift at a much later date. Neither the Basset Estate Proposal Book, nor the archive of Basset leases (Penwerris Barton) give the opening date of the Jewish burial ground, and there are no leases relating to the Jewish cemetery in the Basset records. Lands in the Penryn-Budock area, formerly belonging to R. Scott Bickford, passed into Basset ownership in the 1770s, but it is not known if the burial ground comprised any part of these lands. The Jewish cemetery does appear on a 1788 map of Penryn, as part of the Duke of Leeds' manor of Penryn Forryn, and also on a 1793 survey of the Basset Estate of the Barton of Penwerris. On both maps it appears alone. It is marked as "The Jews Burial Ground" in 1788, and as "Jew's Burying Place" in 1793.[27] It is further shown on Richard Thomas' 1814 Survey of Penwerris for the Tehidy Estate, with the "Jew's Bury'g Ground" marked alongside "Dissenter's Burying Gro'd".[28] The Budock parish tithe map of 1840[29] also shows the Jewish Cemetery (unnamed) as does the Ordnance Survey map of 1880, which indicates that trees had been planted along the periphery of the hedges which surrounded both burial grounds. When Sir Francis became Baronet of Tehidy in 1778, he could, at will, have been minded to grant what form of lease he chose to the Jews, or to have let a plot to them with or without formal lease or even rental. A date of around 1778-1780[30] would certainly coincide with the time of the first known burials, although, as noted, some may have been earlier. Eventually, Lord de Dunstanville did present a plot of land jointly to the Jewish and Congregational communities for them to divide into their respective burial grounds,[31] which came to be formally separated by a low rough built hedge, the whole site being enclosed by a wall.

Each of the Jewish and Christian grounds were held by their respective congregations on a different basis. The Congregational plot came to be held under lease by Indenture (from 28th May 1829 with a term of 400 years) on a "peppercorn" annual rent of 1 shilling.[32] There were six named Trustees to the lease, and it is possible that this was an extension of an original lease for fifty years from 1779, but there is no evidence of this as such, nor that the Trustees ever appointed successors, or that the holding was taken to be a possession in perpetuity. It would seem that the Jews, however, were not granted a lease to their plot. In 1793, Alexander Law of Exmouth undertook an audit and survey of the Basset holdings in the Barton of Penwerris. His map shows the "Jew's (sic.) Burying Place" (as "b" or "No. 2"), with the accompanying abstract page showing that the column for the usual annual rent was left blank, against which is the entry "No Lease".[33] The property was on Estate land, but no written agreement was entered into, no rent was charged, and no lease was issued (at least by this date). The Jews were allowed to use the plot for their burials, but had no legal entitlement to it, relying upon the continuing good will and protection of the Estate.

This situation contrasts starkly with the situation that had applied in Penzance, where, as early as 1808 (when records begin in the Congregational Minute Book) leases were issued directly and exclusively to named Jews by the Rogers Estate (or by those, such as the Borlase family, who came to hold sub-leases). The Penzance cemetery had been used for burials before 1808 (possibly for several decades) and so, presumably, even earlier leases or agreements had applied there. In Penzance, moreover, the congregation eventually bought the freehold of the ground, in 1844. In Plymouth, Jews had been using land in their private possession for burials since 1744, with the assistance of some prominent London Jewish merchants. This situation was legalized by lease in 1758. A lease had been granted to Abraham Ezekiel of Exeter for use as a cemetery in 1757. When, by 1811, the Plymouth congregation was flourishing and needed to acquire a further plot of land for burials, the land was conveyed to three Plymouth Jews and a non-Jew.[34] It is all the more surprising, therefore, and indicative of the comparatively conservative ethos that pervaded the Basset Estate, that, in Falmouth, where leases were issued for the neighbouring Congregationalist burial ground, such an "enabling lease", as the 1811 Plymouth lease, was, apparently, never issued to a named Christian (on behalf of the Jews) who would act as a signatory and, more importantly could operate as their legal guarantor. That no evidence has been found of Basset leases to the Jews does not, of course, in itself, prove that none were ever issued. However, it seems unlikely, and, even if they were, by 1913 (when the Ashfield Estate was sold) no leases applied to the transaction, although an expired lease was identified. But by this time, of course, the Jewish congregation had been dissolved for over thirty years. The Tithe Apportionment of 1841 does state that the Jews and Congregationalists were the owners and occupiers of their respective burial grounds, but the accuracy of this particular record may be questionable. If leases were never issued to the Jews for the Penryn burial ground, it must be assumed that where leases were subsequently issued to others to lands which incorporated the Jewish plot, that conditions were attached by the Basset Estate to prevent incursion into the site, and to protect the exclusivity of its use by the Jews.[35] On 19th June 1832 Lord de Dunstanville leased an area of 23 acres, comprising a house and fields, in the vicinity of (and possibly incorporating) the Jewish cemetery, to Elizabeth Lydia Tregelles and Rachel Tregelles (spinsters) of Budock for a rent of £100 per year. The "lives" on the lease were Thomas Smith Tregelles, aged 34, John Stephens, aged 13, and Esther Budge, aged 10. On 31st December 1895, this lease was surrendered to the Basset Estate by John Stephens, by which time the Jewish burial ground was effectively disused and, in the absence of adequate maintenance, vulnerable and decaying.

The decline of Falmouth's Jewish community since the 1850s, and the subsequent closure of the synagogue in 1880, led to the inevitable disuse of the cemetery, although one burial, that of Nathan Vos, did take place in 1913. Samuel Jacob of Falmouth, the last President, had kept the synagogue open for services up until 1879, but in 1880 he left with his family for London after carrying out repairs to the building. Communal life ceased and the synagogue building fell into deplorable disrepair. There may have been vague hopes that the community might revive, and the Lazarus family may have lived in, or in an adjoining cottage (now demolished), as caretakers of what came to be known as "Synagogue House". In 1892, the Chief Rabbi ordered the Trustees to sell it and to use the proceeds to help maintain the cemetery which had begun to fall into neglect. (It is not known if the synagogue was sold at this point, or if it was eventually acquired by default for renovation). In 1889, a solicitor, Lewis Emanuel of Finsbury Circus, London launched a Restoration Fund Appeal for the Jewish cemetery. Emanuel was probably related to Abraham Leon Emanuel, one of the late Trustees of the Synagogue, and Samuel Jacob's mother was from an Emanuel family of Portsea. The Fund Appeal estimated that 6 guineas was required for reclamation and repair, and 2 guineas annually for maintenance. Mrs. Charles and Mrs. George Goodman each donated 1 guinea, as did Alex Laurance, Samuel Jacob, Ray (Hyman) Joseph, and Walter Symons. All of the named subscribers were descended from the Cornish Jewish families, their relatives being interred in the cemetery. Mrs. Charles Goodman (1822-), the widow of Charles Goodman of South Wales, was a daughter of Samuel Jacob of Penzance (1778-1860). Her sister, Phoebe (1829-1865) had been the first wife of Ephraim George Goodman, also of South Wales. (The latter is not certain to have been related to Charles Goodman, so common was this surname amongst Jews in South Wales). Ephraim George Goodman's second wife, "Mrs.

George Goodman" was Rose Joseph (1838-1896), daughter of Henry Joseph of Penzance (1806-1881), and formerly of Falmouth. Walter Symons, or Simons (1829-) was a grandson of Samuel (Solomon) Simons (1740-1832) of Truro and Rosa (Ann) Moses (1757-1838) of Falmouth, a daughter of Alexander Moses. "Ray" (Hyman or Henry) Joseph (1815-1899) was a son of Lyon Joseph (1775-1825) of Falmouth. The Jacob, Joseph and Symons families could all trace descent from Alexander Moses. Alex Laurance may have been a son of the Joseph Laurance who lived next to the synagogue,[36] and the grandson of Lazarus (Moses Eliezer ben Jacob) Lawrence (-1841) from a first marriage. The latter had been a money broker in Falmouth, and became the second husband of Judith Moses (-1843), another of Alexander Moses' daughters. The sums raised by the Appeal, totalling about £1000 in today's currency, may have led to an immediate improvement, but the Falmouth Town Clerk wrote to Lewis Emanuel in 1896 implying that it was unlikely that anyone could be found "who would undertake to see to the disused Jewish cemetery being kept in order", although he offered the possibility that a (presumed) publican, "Mr. Nathan (that is Nathan Vos: 1833-1913), of Marine Hotel, Quay Hill" might be worth contacting. Whether the cemetery had ever been leased to the Jews of Falmouth, or whether as a plot it had fallen under Basset leases granted to local Christians, by 1913 it appears to have come under the possession of a "Mr. Bennett" (see below), who may have taken over the lease surrendered in 1895 by James Stephens.

Alfred de Pass and the de Pass Family

In 1897, a wealthy Jewish entrepreneur, Alfred Aaron de Pass (1861-1952) from a Sephardic background, and with long-established family connections in South Africa, came to live in Falmouth. He had visited Devon and Cornwall on his honeymoon in 1888, and in August 1895 he spent a summer holiday in Falmouth with his family. He was so taken with the town that he later bought a plot of land there, and commissioned the architects, W. E. and F. Brown of London to draw up plans for a house. The building of "Cliffe House", by the Cornish firm Trehearne of Liskeard, began in March 1896, and was completed within a year. Alfred de Pass and his wife moved into it in August 1897. It was not his sole residence, but he returned to it frequently, and appears to have regarded it as his main home. He also lived in London, in Finchley, later moving to a larger property in Lower Berkeley Street. He travelled widely after 1897, especially to South Africa, where, from 1926, he spent his winters, returning to Falmouth for the summer. In June 1924, his second wife, Nora, was to buy "two acres of land overlooking the river Gannel at Pentire, near Newquay, and they ordered a house to be built, called The Cottage".[37] During the Second World War, this house was requisitioned for evacuees, and Alfred's daughter, Myrtle, who had been widowed in 1932, and who had three children, lived in another house near there, named "Finchley". Although Alfred de Pass left Falmouth in 1939, Cliffe House was taken over by the Admiralty during the war to house Wrens from the Royal Navy. After the war, it was returned by the Admiralty, and sold in 1946. All of the family's property in Cornwall was sold by 1948.[38] Although the scope of this book has been limited to the Jews whose families lived in Cornwall in the 18th and 19th century, so important was Alfred de Pass' involvement in preserving the future of Falmouth's Jewish cemetery in the absence of a local Jewish community, and so considerable and unique was his contribution to the expansion of Cornwall's artistic holdings during his time in Falmouth, that some space should be given to him, and to his remarkable family.[39]

The De Pass (de Pas or de Paz) family were Marrano Jews from the Iberian peninsula, some of whom migrated to France, to Germany and to the Low Countries before the 15th century. The name *de Paz* is derived from the Spanish-Portuguese for "peace" or "peacefulness", *Pas* being a form of the French *Paix*, with *S(h)alom* (see below) being the Hebrew equivalent. The family can be traced back with some degree of accuracy to the 1500s, when they were landowners in Artois, France, but around the early to mid 16th century, they developed into two familial branches, most likely from the offspring of at least two brothers. The first of these became established in France, and was closely linked with the French Court. In 1548, Barbe de Pas, daughter of Jean de Pas, was married to Jerome de Verni, and another de Pas (*c.* 1542-) was created Baron St. Pol. Around 1570, Gideon de Pas was killed at Paris and Daniel de Pas at Doulans, both fighting in the King's army. Duarte de Paz (-1541) of Portugal was a soldier and diplomat, who went to Rome, and is said to have tried to protect the Marranos from the Inquisition, but was accused of duplicity and financial dishonesty by them, and incurred the displeasure of King John III (1521-1557) of Portugal. He went to Venice and then to Ferrara, where he was imprisoned. After this, he became an enemy of the Marranos, fled to Turkey and became a Moslem. Some members of this Iberian-French branch of the de Pas family went to Holland (as did the Alvarez branch, below), and others to Germany.

Cryspan van de Passe (the Elder) was born in Arnemuiden in 1564 and died in Utrecht in 1637. He invented a new method of engraving on copper, and published a book with his engravings on botany, the *Hortus Florida*, which was translated into French and English in 1611. There were two other engravers, Simon de Passe, born in Cologne in 1593, who died in Copenhagen in 1647, and Crispyn de Passe (the Younger), who may also have been from Cologne, but who died in Amsterdam in 1670. A William de Passe was born in Cologne in 1598, and came to London, where he was baptised in 1624, at the age of 26, in the Dutch Church. The Spaniard Enrique Enriquez de Paz, the son of a marrano, also known by his alias as Diego Enriquez de Villaneuva, was born in Segovia in 1590, and became a soldier, dramatist and poet. He was admitted as a visitor at the Spanish Court, and was decorated with the Order of St. Michael, but he fell under the suspicion of the Inquisition, fled to Bordeaux, and then to Paris. He eventually went to Amsterdam, where he openly practised his Jewish faith. He died there in 1662. In France, Francois de Pas (*c.* 1525-) was created the first Marquis de Fourquieres, and was killed at Ivry in 1590, and Manasses de Pas of Saumur (*c.* 1585-), the second Marquis, died as a prisoner of war in 1640. Isaac de Pas (-1688) was appointed ambassador to Spain, and Antione de Pas (1648-1711) became the governor of Verdun. From South West France, Abraham Salom Morenu de Paz, who had retained his Spanish name of

Luis de Paz, had come to England by 1663, trading as a merchant in London. It would seem that he converted to Christianity, although he reverted to Judaism before his death in 1684 at Bayonne near the Spanish border. His wife, Sarah, died in London in 1717, and the children settled there. Of these, Jacob Morenu de Paz (-c. 1735) was the first seatholder with this name at the Bevis Marks synagogue. His brother, Elias (Eliahu) known also as Elijah (c. 1670- d.1739) was one of the first of twelve Jews to be elected a member of the Royal Exchange. His wealth can be gauged by a bequest in his will (written in Spanish) of £1,200 for a *Jesiva* or Jewish day school of religious learning for the young, but this was the subject of a dispute in Chancery Court, which ruled that the money could not be donated to a non-Christian foundation. In 1754, George II allocated the money to the Christian Foundling Hospital.

Alfred de Pass came from the second branch of the French de Pas family which retained its Iberian name of Alvarez, and eventually migrated to Amsterdam, where the first synagogue had been established in 1551. An Alvarez de Pas (c. 1575-) married a Francisca of Amsterdam, and Rodrigo Alvarez de Pas, who may have been their son, also known as Josephus the Just of Amsterdam, married, first, Helen Gomes, and, second, Maria Nunes Mendes. There were two sons from the first marriage, both of whom may have been born in or settled in London. The younger son, Moses Alvarez de Paz (-1767) and his wife, Rebecca (-1756) had three children: Rebecca, who married Jacob Suares d'Aguilar in 1737, David (1738-1819) who, in 1776, married Simha (-1823) daughter of Mordechai Ancona, and Abraham, who settled in Jamaica. The older son of Alvarez de Pas, Abraham Alvarez de Pas (c. 1680- d. 1753) was also married twice, the name of his first wife being unknown, and his second wife being Sarah, daughter of Moses Lopez-Albin. There were no children from the second marriage, but from the first, there were five children, including his son Jacob Abraham Alvarez (1715-1783), known as de Paz, who was born in London and married Rebecca, daughter of Samuel Torres on 19th November 1732. The couple's first son, Raphael (c. 1740-) also went to live in Jamaica, where he may have settled. Raphael had four sons, Caleh (1770-), Ebenezer (1771-), Hiram (1772-) and Ralfe (1775-). His brother, Aaron (1741-1810) who adopted the family name as de Pass, married Hannah Dias (1762-1822) daughter of Jacob Dias of King's Lynn, Norfolk on 13th May 1781, when he was forty, at the Bevis Marks Synagogue in London, where the men of the de Pass family are recorded as members, and where their family marriages took place. De Pass family burials were also to be in London, at the Novo cemetery, Mile End. Members of these widespread and various de Pas families may have come to England as early as the time of Cromwell's re-admission of the Jews in 1656.

Aaron de Pass was fifty five when his son Daniel was born in the City of London in 1796. Aaron had various business interests. He was ship's captain and traded with Jamaica, where at least one of his sons was born, and where two of his sons, Abraham and Jacob worked for the rest of their lives. Aaron de Pass was to settle in King's Lynn, where there had been a Jewish presence since 1747, but where the small Jewish community was to be relatively short-lived. It has been noted that Aaron de Pass' family had once lived in Amsterdam, and Jews from there were in contact with the King's Lynn community.[40] Aaron and Hannah de

Pass were to have a large family, consisting of eleven children. In 1814, their son, Daniel Haim (1796-1857) was married to Rachel Davis (1798-1866) daughter of Michael (Meir) and Catherine Davis of King's Lynn. Michael Davis traded as a sugar merchant in Lynn, the cane sugar business later being one of the de Pass family's main commercial interests in South Africa. Daniel de Pass was a senior warden of the Lynn Hebrew congregation in the 1830s, but it had been in decline for some time. By 1811 the site of its early synagogue in Tower Street had been taken over for the construction of a new Methodist Chapel. Meetings of the remaining Jewish community took place privately for some years until a small building was found for services in 1826. A burial ground had been established some years earlier, presumably under lease, and this was extended, or the freehold purchased in 1830, the congregation's representatives, its senior members, being Hart Jones, a watchmaker and silversmith, who occupied a shop in the High Street and whose brother, Isaiah Jones, was a dentist who had come from Norwich to practise in Lynn, Judah Hynes, an optician from Exeter, who had moved to Lynn after his marriage, Isaac Sampson, tobacconist, and Daniel de Pass, who is recorded as a Clothier. In 1850, only fourteen headstones were visible, some dated before 1830. In 1842, the Jewish community consisted of only seven families, with some outlying members, but it was to enter its final decay soon after 1846.[41]

Daniel and Rachel de Pass were also to have a large family of nine children, born between 1815 and 1833. The oldest of these was Aaron Alfred de Pass (1815[42]-1877) who, in 1836, married Esther da Costa (1817-1891), daughter of Benjamin Gomez da Costa and Lucy ("Lucky") Foligno of London. Lucy Foligno da Costa's family came from Pisa, and the wedding took place at the house of Mr. Isaac Foligno, Esther's maternal uncle, a silversmith, who was married to a Hannah Gomes da Costa.[43] The men of the de Pass family were unable to make a living in the small and remote town of Lynn. Daniel de Pass began his working life as a pen, quill and pencil maker, next turning to drapery, and then opening a shoe shop, *The Golden Boot*, in the High Street, with a stock of thousands of articles.[44] The shop's business began to decline after 1839, and although it is still recorded in local trade directories up to 1846, by that time it may have ceased to trade altogether. In the meantime, Daniel and his family had moved to London, in 1834, to expand their business interests. The family then occupied a wholesale premises at 71 Wood Street, Cheapside, and later at 40, Cateaton Street, Cheapside, with a branch in the High Street, Wisbech. The Post Office Directory for 1856 records Daniel de Pass and Sons Merchants at 20 Finsbury Place, London.[45] In Lynn, the de Pass family ran another business in the High Street, the *London Clothes, Cloth and Hat Warehose*, or the *Lynn Mart*.[46] Despite this commercial diversification, the remuneration was insufficient, and a journal kept by Aaron de Pass from 1840 reveals the extent of his travels to find work.[47] In 1833 he had gone to France, but returned to live in London, lodging with a cousin, and it was in London where he first met his future wife. His father joined him there in 1834, and opened a shoe warehouse. In August of 1835, Aaron sailed to Jamaica "as a merchant", with his uncle Abraham, where family members had settled. (A Moses Garcia Depass, who may have been a relative, and who died in 1867, age 37, is buried in the Kingston Jewish cemetery).[48] He returned, via Ireland, in April 1836, and during that year he "travelled over a great part of England as a Commercial Traveller" and was in Liverpool in July with his father. The week after his marriage in Bevis Marks on 28th December, he had moved to Stroud,[49] where he tried to keep a shoe shop, but "lost money" and "Removed to Brighton in Sussex at the latter end 1837". His daughter, Hannah, was born there on 9th December, but he could not make a living in the town, and by February 1838 he was back in Lynn, where his son, Daniel (1839-1921) was born. He left Lynn again at the end of 1840 for London, and became engaged as a Commercial Traveller "through the West of England in the Leather & Shoe Trade". He does not mention if he reached as far as Devon and Cornwall in the South-West, but he also travelled along the whole of the South Coast, and up into East Anglia as far north as Lincolnshire. By 1842 he had "commenced the cigar trade" with his brother Abraham Daniel (1823-1897) at 36 Brown Street in Finsbury, London, together with a "commission in the shoe thread trade" held by his father, from a firm in Tooley Street, which Aaron de Pass was later to represent in Cape Town. Another brother, David (1817-1890) was to join the cigar business in Finsbury. In 1845 Aaron was in Paris, and in South Wales, and noted that "In this year I travelled 8 thousand miles".

The following year, he was to leave the country with his wife, Esther da Costa, their two young children, and Aaron's much younger brother, Elias (1829-1913), departing from Portsmouth in the ship *Mary Ann*. After a brief stay in Madeira, they sailed for the Cape of Good Hope, arriving on 27th April. The family appear to have been financially independent upon their arrival, and Aaron established himself as a shipping merchant and ship owner in Cape Town, at 2 Strand Street, with his own vessel, the *Osbourne*.[50] In October 1847 the family returned to England in the vessel, and after leaving Daniel at a school in London, they returned to the Cape in March 1848. Elias also returned to England in the *Osbourne* in 1849, and returned with their brother, Jacob (John: 1827-1905) the following year. In 1855, they were joined by Aaron's son, Daniel, who by then had completed his schooling. This pattern of travel between the Cape and England continued for the next decade, together with extensive journeys throughout South Africa, to Mauritius (1851), Sierra Leone, France and Germany (1852), and Australia (1857-58). Aaron de Pass was successful in a wide range of commercial enterprises as a shipping magnate, trading in salted fish from the family's own fisheries, in guano and sugar off the south-west coast of the Cape, as well as being involved in the whaling and sealing industry and the copper mining industry. He is said to have developed the first facilities for hauling ships up for repair, in Simonstown, having imported the first patent slipway, and also the first ice-making plant in the Cape.[51] He also helped to establish the Hebrew congregation in Cape Town, initially in a private house in 1849, and later in a newly built synagogue in 1862.[52] He became a Freemason in 1850[53], was appointed Justice of the Peace in 1860, and Commissioner for the Cape Town municipality in 1861, the year he retired from the family business. In 1862 Elias de Pass served with distinction as a lieutenant in the "Kaffir" or Xhosa War in the Eastern Cape Frontier. In these nine wars, which lasted from 1779-1879, the European settlers eventually deprived the indigenous amaXhosa people of their lands, incorporating them into the Cape Province. Elias de Pass was wounded during these wars and was commended for bravery. Like his brother, he was also active in Jewish congregational affairs. His wife was Floretta Moses, daughter of Henry Moses of London.

Aaron de Pass' sister, Hannah, who had been born in Kings Lynn in 1818, and who died in Brussels in 1874, had married Judah Moses Kisch (1810-1856) a shoe merchant of Norwich. Three of their sons were also to go to South Africa. Daniel Montagu Kisch, who was born in Wisbech in 1840, and who died at sea in 1898, arrived in South Africa in 1857. After a period as an explorer, he managed the De Pass sugar estates, and later settled in Pretoria, where he was a founder member of the synagogue in 1876. He also worked as a photographer and patent agent, and held various posts in President Kruger's government in the Transvaal. His brother, Benjamin (1843-) also worked as a photographer in Durban, as did the third brother, David Henry (1848-) in Pietermaritzburg.[54] The Kisch family had also been closely involved with the King's Lynn Hebrew congregation, and a Maurice Kisch managed the de Pass' *Lynn Mart* mentioned above.[55] A "B. Kisch" was an officer of the congregation in 1842, and earlier, in 1825 a Jacob Kisch, who may have been a relative, was authorised by the Chief Rabbi Solomon Hirschell to act as a *shochet* in Nottingham. In 1843, the surname *Kisch* of Wisbech appears as a seatholder in the King's Lynn synagogue.[56]

Aaron de Pass' son, Daniel (1839-1921) expanded the family's business interests and became a pioneer in the sugar cane industry in Natal, introducing an improved variety of cane, and developed locally manufactured machines to process his products. He was also active in the guano trade, and owned his own fisheries. He owned shares in copper-mining, and large interests in the diamond industry. He was also active in Jewish congregational affairs, and became respected as a philanthropist. Daniel de Pass married an Emily Luna Abecasis (1838-1867), daughter of Solomon Abecasis of London.[57] The couple settled in Cape Town, where their son, Alfred Aaron de Pass was born in 1861. (The name *Luna* is found amongst the Jews of Gibraltar. The Spanish radical Republican novelist, Vicente Blasco Ybanez (1867-1928), whose most famous work is *The Four Horsemen of the Apocalypse* (1916), was a frequent visitor to Gibraltar, where his two sons were at school. There, Ybanez met a local Jewish girl, on whom he based the main character of his novel *Luna Benamor* (1909). James Joyce knew this book, and it influenced the character of Molly Bloom, especially in the last chapter of *Ulysses*. Molly is the daughter of an Irish officer and Lunita Laredo, a Jewish girl from Gibraltar.)

In 1857, a John Spence "an experienced seaman and native of the Orkney Islands"[58], had joined Aaron and Elias de Pass in their business and the company was then renamed *De Pass, Spence & Co.* In 1860, Daniel de Pass also joined the business, and when Aaron retired in 1861, he left Daniel to work with Spence. Emily de Pass died of peritonitis at the age of 29 on 14th July 1867 at the Cape of Good Hope, a month after the birth of her fifth child, Mary.[59] Aaron de Pass returned to England in 1862, where he retired, living first in Bayswater at 7 Pembridge Crescent, and later in Southampton. He went back to the Cape in 1864 and 1867, returning to London in 1869. He died there on 29th August 1877, the *Times* recording his death "at his residence North Lodge, Crystal Palace…formerly of Good Hope, age 62". In South Africa, his obituary in the *Cape Argus* described him as "eminently benevolent in private…none can tell the extent of his charities secretly distributed, though in some cases, where large amounts were given, his unostentatious gifts came to light by accident". [60]

Daniel de Pass, with Alfred, then 9, had arrived in London in 1870 with all of his children (except Esther, who was living in London with her grandfather). They lived in Paddington, opening an office for the business at 128 Leadenhall Street as a "shipping, manure, diamond and commission merchant and Natal sugar planter".[61] In Paddington, Alfred attended a local school, run by the "Misses Belisaros", opposite the family's home at 9 Delamere Street. Later, during the academic year 1871-72, he went to University College School, where his father had been, but did not stay there for long, and was sent to a boarding school in Ramsgate run by Rev. Issac Myers. From 1875-1877 he lived in Gottingen, attending first the Commercial and Folk School, and then the University of Gottingen, where he studied chemistry, geology, mineralogy, botany and also worked in the agricultural chemical laboratories. In 1878 he returned to London, and appears to have completed his training at the School of Mines in South Kensington in 1878, and also under Anthony Nesbit in a city laboratory.[62] In 1879 he went to Natal with his father, to acquaint himself with the sugar-cane industry, and then returned to spend just over a year as a junior clerk in his father's firm. In November 1880 he went to Natal to involve himself directly in his father's business affairs, remaining there until 1883 during which time he assisted in introducing a disease resistant cane. On his return to London, he was given a twentieth share in the business.

In 1886 Daniel de Pass returned to Natal for some years, and was not present when, on 3rd September 1888, Alfred de Pass married an Ethel Phoebe Salaman, age 19, daughter of Myer Salaman of Bayswater. The latter was a wealthy man in his own right, who had built up a successful business with branches in Cape Town and Port Elizabeth, dealing in ostrich feathers. Ethel Salaman's family was a large one, of fourteen children, and Myer Salaman and his wife lived at 20 Pembridge Crescent, whilst later also buying an old country house, Wentworth House, at Mill Hill for holidays. Alfred's grandfather, Aaron de Pass, must himself have achieved significant success in his working life, because his widow, Esther, gave the couple the sum of £1000 on the occasion of their marriage. Daniel de Pass was to meet his daughter-in-law the following year in Paris, where he spent much of his time when he was not in South Africa, and where he had an apartment which he retained for a number of years. By 1895 he had severed his connections with South Africa, although he did not sell off all of his business interests there until 1920. By 1910, he had returned to England from South Africa and from Paris, and settled in Worthing, whilst also having a flat at Old Court Mansions, Kensington. He died at 13 Herne Terrace, Worthing on 5th April 1921, aged 82, leaving a lengthy will in which he established trusts for three generations of his family. He also left significant bequests to Jewish charities in London, and to the Guardians of the Poor of the parish of King's Lynn "where I was born".[63]

Alfred de Pass was able to capitalise on the success of his father's business by retiring from it in his thirties, after which he devoted himself to art collecting. His interest in art is likely to have derived from his mother's family. In Ethel de Pass' family there were maternal cousins named Solomon. These included the well known and respected painters Abraham (1823-1862), Rebecca (1832-1886) and

De Pass (de Paz) of London, King's Lynn, South Africa & Falmouth

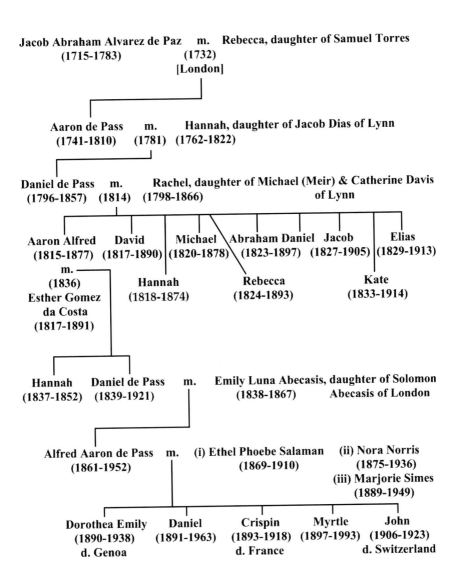

Jacob Abraham Alvarez de Paz m. Rebecca, daughter of Samuel Torres
(1715-1783)   (1732)
[London]

Aaron de Pass m. Hannah, daughter of Jacob Dias of Lynn
(1741-1810) (1781) (1762-1822)

Daniel de Pass m. Rachel, daughter of Michael (Meir) & Catherine Davis
(1796-1857) (1814) (1798-1866)   of Lynn

Aaron Alfred   David   Michael Abraham Daniel Jacob   Elias
(1815-1877) (1817-1890) (1820-1878) (1823-1897) (1827-1905) (1829-1913)

m.
(1836)   Hannah   Rebecca   Kate
Esther Gomez (1818-1874)   (1824-1893)   (1833-1914)
da Costa
(1817-1891)

Hannah   Daniel de Pass m. Emily Luna Abecasis, daughter of Solomon
(1837-1852) (1839-1921)   (1838-1867)   Abecasis of London

Alfred Aaron de Pass m. (i) Ethel Phoebe Salaman (ii) Nora Norris
(1861-1952)   (1869-1910)   (1875-1936)
                                 (iii) Marjorie Simes
                                 (1889-1949)

Dorothea Emily   Daniel   Crispin   Myrtle   John
(1890-1938) (1891-1963) (1893-1918) (1897-1993) (1906-1923)
d. Genoa   d. France   d. Switzerland

Source: Colyer-Fergusson, Archie de Pass, Ena Black, Phoebe Walker & Rebecca Coutts.
© Keith Pearce (2013)

De Pass and Joseph of Plymouth

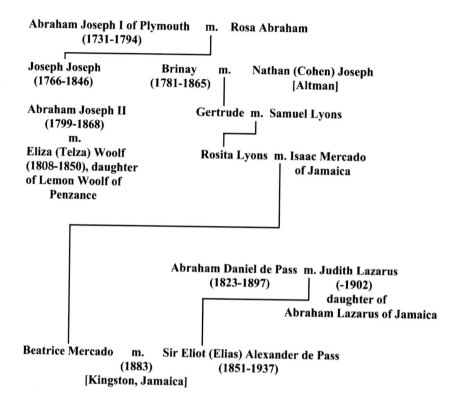

Abraham Joseph I of Plymouth   m.   Rosa Abraham
(1731-1794)

Joseph Joseph   Brinay   m.   Nathan (Cohen) Joseph
(1766-1846)   (1781-1865)   [Altman]

Abraham Joseph II   Gertrude m. Samuel Lyons
(1799-1868)
m.
Eliza (Telza) Woolf   Rosita Lyons m. Isaac Mercado
(1808-1850), daughter   of Jamaica
of Lemon Woolf of
Penzance

Abraham Daniel de Pass m. Judith Lazarus
(1823-1897)   (-1902)
daughter of
Abraham Lazarus of Jamaica

Beatrice Mercado   m.   Sir Eliot (Elias) Alexander de Pass
(1883)   (1851-1937)
[Kingston, Jamaica]

Source: Colyer-Fergusson, Ena Black, Anthony Joseph, Phoebe Walker & Rebecca Coutts.
© Keith Pearce (2013).

Simeon (1840-1905). In addition, several of Ethel's brothers and sisters were also artists, attending the Slade with Augustus John. Alfred de Pass was mainly preoccupied with painting and furniture. "His approach to collecting appears to have been dynamic, sometimes selling works in order to buy others as recorded in sales from his collections at Christie's in 1896, and Sotheby's in 1911."[64] His collecting was well established before Alfred moved to Falmouth with his wife. Ethel Salaman's brother, Michael, had married a Chattie Wake, who he had met when they were both students at the Slade. Augustus John (1878-1961) was also there at that time, and in 1899, he was to make a drawing of Alfred de Pass, who came to

Solomon of Exeter and De Pass

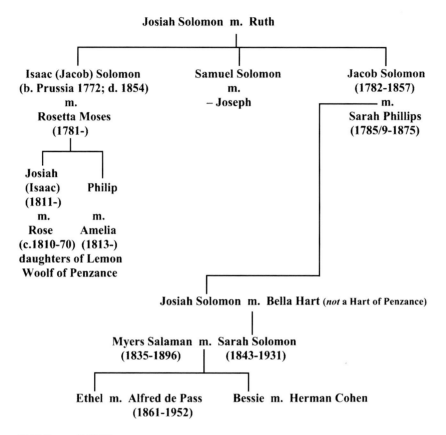

Josiah Solomon m. Ruth

Isaac (Jacob) Solomon
(b. Prussia 1772; d. 1854)
m.
Rosetta Moses
(1781-)

Samuel Solomon
m.
– Joseph

Jacob Solomon
(1782-1857)
m.
Sarah Phillips
(1785/9-1875)

Josiah
(Isaac)
(1811-)
m.
Rose
(c.1810-70)
daughters of Lemon
Woolf of Penzance

Philip
m.
Amelia
(1813-)

Josiah Solomon m. Bella Hart (*not* a Hart of Penzance)

Myers Salaman m. Sarah Solomon
(1835-1896) **(1843-1931)**

Ethel m. Alfred de Pass
(1861-1952)

Bessie m. Herman Cohen

Keith Pearce © (2013).

Notes: Isaac Solomon is buried in the Exeter cemetery; his wife Rosetta was the daughter of a Philip Moses from Kent (Susser 1993 p. 64) although she may have been born in Devon (1841 Exeter Census). Jacob Solomon does not appear in the Census. He may have moved away from Exeter if his wife came from elsewhere. Jacob and Sarah Solomon had 6 sons and 2 daughters: one son, Henry (1813-) married Sarah, daughter of Nathan Adler.

own some of John's paintings. Alfred and Ethel de Pass were to have five children, three of whom were to pre-decease their father. Dorothea Emily de Pass was born in 1890. In 1913 in Falmouth, she married a Captain in the Italian army. She went to live in Rome, and died in Genoa in 1938. Daniel de Pass (1891-1963)[65] became a Commodore in the Royal Navy and was based in Ceylon from 1944-1946. Crispin Asahel de Pass was born in 1893 and went to the University of Cambridge. He joined the army and trained in British Columbia, coming to fight in France as a corporal. He died in March 1918, age 24, at Mordier, Cambrai in France, on the front line, leading his troops into action. In 1921, Myrtle de Pass (1897-1993) married Gerald, son of Sir Alexander Prince. John de Pass was born in 1906 in London, and died in a skiing accident in Switzerland in 1923, age 17. He was buried at Lausanne. When her youngest child, John, was only a few years old, Ethel de Pass developed severe tuberculosis from which she never recovered. She was hospitalised in "a sanatorium in Birdlip, Gloucestershire [and] Alfred leased and furnished a house for her in the village there. When she became too ill for further treatment she moved to her house". She died there on 6th March 1910, age 40.[66] His older children were by now self-sufficient, at boarding school, or pursuing their own interests and careers, and, upon the death of his wife, Alfred de Pass sold his London home and spent the next year travelling in France with friends and the family's governess, Nora Norris (1875-1936). They also went to Venice and Egypt, where Alfred was to marry Nora Norris in the British Consulate in Cairo. From this time on, and especially after the death of John in 1923, Alfred de Pass spent much of his life travelling in Europe and to South Africa. In the Cape, he visited his mother's grave, and was alarmed by the lack of upkeep of the burial ground. Subsequently, he gave money (in 1931 and in 1935) for its improvement and maintenance. In 1935, he bought a house in South Africa for the winter, naming it "Norfolk Villa" after his grandfather's home county, but for some of the summer months he returned to Falmouth. It was there that Alfred's second wife died in the summer of 1936. In 1937 he married a Marjorie Anne Beatrice Simes (1889-), a retired nurse, who had friends in South Africa, and family in Falmouth. She died in South Africa on 15th December 1949.[67]

Some years before the visit to his mother's grave in South Africa, and some time after his arrival in Falmouth in 1896, Alfred de Pass had visited the Penryn Jewish cemetery, and was disturbed by its condition. His concern that its survival could be under threat eventually led him to make enquiries as to its ownership. What success he had over the ensuing years is not known, nor whether he involved himself financially in the cemetery's maintenance and upkeep during those years. The previous year, Lawrence Jacob must have made enquiries regarding the ceme- tery, in that a letter of December 15th 1912 from H Baynham Paull of the Tehidy Office of the Basset Estate, addressed to him at the Lodge, Randolph Crescent, Maida Hill, London, confirms that Lot 1 Penwerris had been sold to a Mr. Gilbert Stephens for £3700, although "No evidence could be found of the exact terms of letting".[68] On 24th July 1913, at the Royal Hotel, Falmouth, a sale took place of former leasehold Basset properties in the Penwerris Estate, belonging to Stephens of Ashfield near Falmouth, all to be sold with their freehold, amongst which (as Lot 1) was the Ashfield Estate "On which is erected the Modern and Extensive

Hemp and Wire Rope Factory, Valuable Building and Accommodation Land".[69] Included in the sale were the two cemeteries, both offered as freehold plots of land. Whilst the Christian (or "Independent") cemetery was subject to the limitation that its sole use continued to be for "the burial of persons belonging to the Religious Independent Congregations at Penryn and Falmouth", crucially, no such limitation accompanied the sale of "The Jew's Burial Ground", which is stated to be "In Hand", a term which would conventionally imply that the vendor's lease had expired. The prospective purchaser of the plots would acquire the lease which the Basset Estate had issued (presumably for the Congregational ground only) "for a term of 400 years from 28th May 1829 to Wm. Tucker and others" (as representatives of the Church). It would seem that the cemeteries were not sold on this occasion. The sale catalogue has a figure of £3000 (the reserve figure) entered against the Ashfield Estate, as Lot 1, and there is another note (which may refer to the cemeteries as parts 82 of the Lot) of "no bid". Within a month, however, both cemeteries had changed hands. Alfred de Pass seems not to have been aware of the original sale of 24th July, or the identity of the freeholder at that point, but the matter had come to his attention by 6th August 1913, when he wrote a letter from his home, Cliffe House in Falmouth, that does not indicate the addressee, but can be presumed to have been sent to Lawrence Jacob in London:[70] "Mr. [Nathan] Vos informs me that you might know whether the Jewish burial ground here is freehold property belonging to the Jewish Community, in which case the deeds must be somewhere, or whether it was leased by Mr. Bassett (*sic.*) only. The reason I ask is that it was recently sold by Mr. Bennett with the neighbouring cemetery and other land and I have agreed with the purchaser to take the [Jewish] burial ground off his hands".

If de Pass had seen the catalogue for the original sale he would have realised that the Jewish cemetery was the freehold property of the Basset Estate, not of the "Jewish Community", although he may have intended the sense of "used by them", or "leased to them". From his mistake in the spelling of *Basset*, it is possible that de Pass meant to write that name rather than "Bennett". It is also possible, however, that he had meant to write "sold *to* Mr. Bennett", that is, by the Basset Estate. Lawrence Jacob must have passed the enquiry to the Board of Deputies, and from 19 Finsbury Circus, Walter L. Emanuel, standing in during the absence of his brother, Charles, wrote on 21st August 1913 that, until his brother's return, he could provide no information on the Falmouth burial ground, although he would retain de Pass' letter. On 12th September 1913, Charles Emanuel, having investigated further by contacting de Pass directly, wrote to Lawrence Jacob that the "Trustees (of the synagogue) held a lease only and that this had either expired or had been legally put an end to before the property was sold". Aaron de Pass did step in and buy the freehold to the Jewish cemetery "as a portion of Mr. Basset's freeholds" at an auction sale by John H. Lake of Falmouth, who recorded de Pass as "a wealthy gentleman, a member of the Jewish church". De Pass then undertook the cemetery's maintenance, and would appear to have informed the Board of Deputies of the steps he had taken. In their next Annual Report, the Board registered the name of A. A. de Pass "a locally resident Jew" as its new owner, and confirms that the burial ground had been found to be "leasehold only, and the lease had expired". [71] From this it would seem that senior members of the Hebrew Congregation had held the lease.

Earlier in 1913, de Pass had given permission for what came to be the last Jewish burial in the cemetery, the first for 45 years (since that of Gershan Elias in 1868), that of Nathan Vos, who had run a public house in the town. Vos had married a non-Jew, and may not have been observant or connected with the former Hebrew Congregation. His son, however, made considerable efforts to ensure that he received a Jewish burial. The occasion became the little cemetery's "swansong" and was by all accounts "a deeply impressive service" as reported in the Jewish Chronicle on 14th April 1913: "Those present were: The Rev. D. Jacobs (Minister), The Rev. I. Slavinsky (Reader), Mr Joseph L. Jacobs of Plymouth, Mr. Max von Bosch (Nephew), Mr. A. Costa and Mr. E. Franks. The chief mourner was Mr. J. B. Vos (son), whilst amongst the many others present were Mr. C. S. Goldman M.P., The Mayor of Falmouth (Alderman A. W. Chard, J.P.) and many Freemasons, for Mr. Vos was a Brother of the "Love and Honour" Lodge, Falmouth."

Of those mentioned as present, Max von Bosch, was related to the Levi von Bosch who traded in Falmouth as a Ship's Chandler in 1871. His wife, Helena, was, like Nathan Vos, from Holland, and a relative. An A. G. de (da) Costa was in Falmouth, as "Traveller", in 1851. (Revs D. Jacobs and I Slavinsky were, respectively, the Rabbi and Cantor of the Plymouth congregation, and C. S. Goldman is mentioned in this book's conclusion). The occasion of this funeral was reported in the Jewish Chronicle, with some mention of de Pass' involvement, and this aroused some comment and controversy, despite the fact that de Pass was a Jew and the only person to have taken such responsibility for the cemetery's protection and survival. A Dr. James V. Albert wrote to the newspaper the following week, and in a letter entitled "Extinct Congregations: Falmouth and Penzance", asking "as to whom the power rests with to sell a Jewish Burial Ground? Who receives the purchase money? And to what purpose it is applied? Also whether the ancient Synagogue was sold at the same time? There is another extinct congregation in Cornwall, viz., that at Penzance. Are the Synagogue and Burial Ground there also to be sold to the highest bidder?". The writer also raised the question of "what has become of the ancient books and records of these two congregations?". Whilst this comment on a benevolent and well-intentioned act by de Pass may seem churlish, it raised important issues of religious concern, particularly in relation to the burial grounds which, unlike the synagogue buildings, remained as consecrated lands in perpetuity.

When Alex M. Jacob made a visit to Falmouth in 1939, he carried out another survey of the headstones in the cemetery. In his papers, he noted that he had obtained the key from a Mr. Vos of Falmouth. It would seem therefore that the remaining Vos family held this key on behalf of de Pass. They may also have arranged the cemetery's maintenance, although de Pass's subsequent bequest for this purpose may suggest that the key was entrusted to Mr. Vos primarily out of respect for his need to have access to the family grave. While de Pass had remained in the country, his efforts to maintain the cemetery no doubt continued, but in 1939 he left Falmouth for Cape Town with his third wife, Marjorie. The outbreak of the War prevented his return. In 1947, his son, also Daniel de Pass, wrote to the Board of Deputies of British Jews in London, asking them to take over the Burial Ground, (but they did not, in fact, take formal responsibility for the Ground as its Trustees until August 1962, most likely being reluctant to assume liability for such a far-flung site, where there was no Jewish community). He also gave one hundred pounds towards clearing the weeds and undergrowth. It is not known if Alfred de Pass had maintained contributions during his absence, or, if so, whether such contributions had been inadequate. On 15th December 1947, the Clerk to the Board of Deputies, a Mr. Levy, wrote to Alex M. Jacob to ask him to supply him with details of the names of those interred there, so they could try to trace descendants with a view to making an appeal for contributions. Levy had that summer visited the cemetery "which has been allowed to deteriorate to such a condition that it has become a wilderness of overgrown weeds and shrubs". He had not been able to secure any help locally in clearing the growth and repairing the walls, and asked Jacob if he could obtain "any help in Falmouth in the direction we desire". It would seem that the Board had received an offer from de Pass "to defray a certain amount of the cost, and also a sum towards the annual upkeep of the cemetery, but we cannot take advantage of this offer until the necessary work has been carried out".[77] It would seem that de Pass had placed these conditions upon any further payments he might make. On 10th December 1952, Alfred de Pass died in Muizenberg, Capetown, South Africa, leaving in his will a legacy of two hundred pounds for the cemetery. On 24th December, the Cape Times published an obituary notice referring to him as "a connoisseur, collector and patron of the arts. Of a Sephardic family, his grandfather, Elias, arrived in South Africa in 1846." The erroneous reference in the obituary to his great-uncle, Elias, as his grandfather, may have arisen because Aaron de Pass and his son Daniel had long before left the country, and the name of the man who had come to be one of the heroes of the Kaffir Wars was more familiar to the journalist. Simple journalistic error (or insufficient research) may have been the cause, however, because the business activities and the enormous charitable contribution of Aaron and Daniel de Pass were remembered and a matter of public record long after their departure.

After de Pass' death, Alex Jacob, recognising that the cemetery might again fall into decay, appears to have approached the Plymouth congregation with a view to asking them to take it over. His genealogical research enabled him to stress the familial links which existed between the two congregations, which he offered to elaborate further. On 22nd June 1953, the Secretary of the Plymouth Congregation wrote to Jacob: "I thank you for your letter of 7th inst., and for your offer to give us information in this matter. I would, however, inform you that my Congregation thought that this disused cemetery could be best administered by the Board of Deputies and arrangements are being made for the cemetery to be conveyed to them. However, certain legal formalities have to be overcome and it may be a short while before the land is actually conveyed." It is not clear if a formal legal conveyance ever took place, but the Board eventually took responsibility for the Penryn and Penzance cemeteries as Trustees. In fact, Alfred de Pass had no direct familial connection with the Jews of Falmouth, but there was a distant link through marriage with the Jews of Plymouth and Penzance. Alfred de Pass' grandfather, Aaron de Pass, had a younger brother, Abraham Daniel de Pass (1823-1897) who had married Judith Lazarus (-1902) daughter of Abraham Lazarus of Jamaica, in 1846 in Kingston. They were to have numerous children, one of whom, Eliot (Elias) Alexander (Arthur) de Pass (1851-1936), who was knighted in 1880, married Beatrice Mercado, daughter of Isaac Mercado of Jamaica, in 1883 at Kingston. She was a descendant of the Joseph family of Plymouth. Abraham Joseph I of Plymouth (1731-1794) had married a Rosa Abraham. Their daughter, Brinay, married a Nathan Joseph Cohen who took the surname *Altman*. Their daughter, Gertrude, married a Samuel Lyons, and their daughter, Rosita, married Isaac Mercado of Jamaica. Rosita Mercado was related, therefore, to Abraham Joseph's grandson, Abraham Joseph II (1799-1868) of Plymouth who had married Eliza Woolf (1808-1850) daughter of Lemon Woolf (1783-1848) of Penzance. Through his (first) marriage to Ethel Salaman, de Pass also came to be related to a Solomon family of Exeter and the Woolf family of Penzance.

Alfred Aaron de Pass not only helped to safeguard the Jewish cemetery during his time in Cornwall, but he was also became the County's most generous artistic benefactor, leaving to the Falmouth Museum and to the County Museum, The Royal Institution of Cornwall in Truro, what has become the most important and extensive single collection of art and artefacts to have been donated to the County. These gifts also included a number of sacred Hebrew religious texts, including a book of the Torah or Pentateuch printed in Hamburg in 1663-1664, a Prayer Book printed in Florence in 1752, and a Scroll of the Book of Esther.[73] It has been said of Alfred de Pass that, together with the Cornishman George Penrose (1876-1951): "what a debt we all owe to these two men who, in effect, made it possible for us to talk now about Truro as a Museum of some rank in both the county and the country, [they] were in a very real sense the creators of the Museum we have today. Some 80% of what the Museum now has was acquired by their efforts." De Pass in fact contributed almost two thirds of the increase in the size of the Museum's collections during the period 1901-1950, his first gift (of antique cut gems) being in 1914, and his last (of 25 pictures from Cliffe House) in 1949. "Only in the areas of mineralogy, natural history and Cornish material was de Pass a minor donor. In all other areas, notably European painting, drawing, sculpture, bronze work, ceramics and glassware, and in Egyptian, Chinese, Japanese, Greek and Roman objects, De Pass was almost single-handed the creator of the fine collections the Museum now possesses." The only area of collecting that de Pass did not embrace was that of antiquarian books and manuscripts,[74] although it has been noted that he did possess and donate some important Jewish religious manuscripts. Alfred de Pass himself confirmed that to Truro "…I gave pictures, drawings, early pottery, porcelain, bronze, objects d'art and went in from year to year until 1935 to form almost a complete collection of modern and old masters and drawings, furniture, silver, etc. besides building a gallery for the old masters pictures, making this in fact one of the model smaller galleries and museums in England."[75] His "dynamic" approach to collecting has already been noted, but his acquisitions were not primarily intended for private display, in that "some 80% of what he bought went straight from auction room to some designated museum, although, once there, he took a personal interest in how they were labelled, and pressed for their speedy public exhibition, even to the point of paying for the display cases, and, in some cases, actual galleries to hang them".[76]

Alfred de Pass' first donation was in 1905, to the National Gallery. At the suggestion of one of the gallery's trustees, Lord Gower, who was a visitor to Cliffe House, he gave a picture that hung in his home. In 1906, he contributed to help the Bodleian Library, Oxford, acquire an original Shakespeare manuscript. Whether his "dynamic" approach to collecting can be regarded as a form of obsession or compulsion is debateable, but it was characteristic of him that he was especially motivated to make sizeable donations to museums at times of bereavement. He lived through the passing not only of his parents, but also the loss of his three wives and three of his children. On some of these occasions his bequests were given expressly as memorials to the person who had died, and this also appears to have motivated his concern to preserve the Penryn Jewish cemetery as an act of respect. In 1910, he gave seven paintings to the Tate Gallery, London, in memory of his wife, Ethel, including works by William Blake, Ford Maddox Brown and Dante Gabriel Rosetti, and presented three more in 1913.[77] He also made gifts of works to the National Portrait Gallery, and to the British Museum. He became involved with the Truro Museum in 1914, and by 1936, he had donated over 500 drawings and paintings, including 16th and 17th Italian drawings, works by Corregio, Guardi and Tiepolo, 18th and 19th century French drawings, and Dutch and Flemish drawings by Van Dyck, Rembrandt, Rubens and others. Amongst English artists, he gave some sketchbooks by Romney, works by Constable, Rowlandson, Gainsborough, Turner, Hogarth, Waterhouse, Rosetti, Burne Jones and portraits by the Cornish painter, John Opie (1761-1807). A drawing, "Dorelia", of Augustus John's second wife was also donated by him. In 1928 alone he gave 192 paintings and drawings by Turner, Watteau, Delacroix, Gainsborough and others. Alfred de Pass knew the painters J. W. Waterhouse (1849-1917) and Thomas Cooper Gotch (1854-1931) and both were guests in Cornwall, either at his house and on his boat, but his closest friend was the painter Henry Scott Tuke (1858-1929).[78] De Pass had owned many of his paintings, and Tuke had painted portraits of Alfred's son Daniel (aged 4) in 1896, and also, from a photograph, his grandfather, Aaron de Pass. When Tuke died, Alfred de Pass gave one of his paintings to the Truro Museum. In 1933, after the death in France of his son Crispin, who had been at Trinity Hall, Cambridge, he gave pictures and ornamental china to the Fitzwilliam Museum there, and in 1920, fourteen old master paintings, including a Reynolds, to the National Gallery, London, where he had become an associate in 1917. Also in 1917 he was elected an Associate of the RIC, Truro, and in 1920 he became its Vice-President.

Alfred de Pass also gave generously to the Falmouth Public Library. In 1923, soon after the death of his son, John, in Switzerland, he presented some pictures to the Falmouth Reading Room in memory of both of his late sons. In 1926 he bought a large Burne Jones painting for Plymouth, and two Waterhouse paintings, one for Plymouth and one for Falmouth. He gave extensively to the Plymouth City Museum and Art Gallery, including French Porcelain, works by artists of the German, Flemish and Italian schools, and he also donated individual oil paintings by Girola da Trevise, Marten Jacobsz van Veen Heemskerck, Garbo del Raffaeilino, and Giovanni Battista Tiepolo. In addition Plymouth received from him watercolours by Mariano Fortuny, Jean Louis Forain and Jules Cheret, as well as drawings by Edgar Degas, Francesco Guardi, Jean Francois Millet, John Everett Millais and Edward Burne-Jones.[79] In 1927 he gave Falmouth gifts of pottery, glass, pewter, Greek and Roman coins, and a number of oil paintings. A decade later he donated several maritime paintings, and by then he had funded the building of an annexe to house the collection, which had also come to comprise prints by Durer, Rembrandt and Piranessi. As with Truro, he had become, in a short time, the Falmouth gallery's most important benefactor, having donated almost fifty pictures. He was remembered by the Librarian at the time as a "...most generous man, if his interest was aroused, and an implacable enemy if crossed".[80] In the summer of 1936, after the death of his second wife, Nora, he gave a total of 211 items to the Bristol Art Gallery, of "numerous paintings, drawings, furniture, ceramics, carved work, jewellery and carpets". He also financed the production of a catalogue for the collection.[81] Numerous works were also given to South Africa, to the National Gallery, Capetown, and he created a new gallery with pictures for the South African Government in the Groot Constantia, and provided Dutch furniture for the previously empty house. Amongst these various donations were 23 oil paintings in 1926-1927, including works by Daubigny, Fantin Latour, Boudin, Sisley and Rodin, and by 1948 he had given several hundred paintings, sculptures and prints. The prints themselves became a special collection with works by Durer, Canaletto, Millet, Whistler, Samuel Palmer and Augustus John. In his later years, from 1932, Alfred de Pass took up painting himself, producing a wide range of works, including watercolours. By 1948, he had given away nearly all of his collection of fine art and artefacts, apart from a few works by local, South African artists.

His ownership and supervision of Penryn's Jewish cemetery, is by comparison, a little known aspect to his generosity. When he acquired it in 1913, there had not been a sizeable Jewish community in Falmouth for several decades, and none at all since 1880. The Penzance congregation had ended by 1906, with its last member leaving the town in the same year that de Pass acquired the Penryn cemetery. The burial ground lay in a relatively exposed position, along a main road, and near the wharf's industrial activities. There is little doubt that the responsibility for the burial ground that de Pass assumed protected it for the next twenty five years until he left for South Africa, and most likely for the ensuing years while he retained the freehold. For some time after the death of Alfred de Pass it is likely that the cemetery was maintained irregularly, if at all. In 1973, George Wain, the General Manager of Dales Garage, adjacent to the cemetery, who had worked in Stamford Hill, London, and who had developed an interest in Jewish custom and tradition, influenced by his many Jewish customers there, wrote to the Board to offer to restore and maintain the cemetery grounds, to be the voluntary custodian and keyholder, and to show visitors around. This he did at his own expense until his retirement, employing a firm of landscape gardeners to restore the burial ground. When he died, an obituary notice, written by Alfred Dunitz, Chairman of the Disused Cemeteries Committee of the Board of Deputies, appeared in the Jewish Chronicle, on 29th August 1986, praising Wain as "a true friend of the Jewish people" who had "looked after the plot with utter devotion". The renamed Vospers Garage continued to act as a keyholder, but with the former Town Clerk of Falmouth, Eric Dawkins, as its official custodian. Alfred de Pass would have been gratified that his efforts have been continued by others.

Chapter 9.
Top: Portraits of Rabbi Barnett Asher Simmons of Penzance and his wife Flora Jacob of Redruth. Both oil on canvas by Richard T. Pentreath (1806-1869).

Bottom: Right: Portrait of their son, Simon Barnett Simmons (1836-1918).
Oil on canvas by W. H. Allcott. Left: his wife, Rachel Joseph (1845-1901). Oil on canvas (Anon.). All four portraits from a Private Collection, on loan to the Penlee House Gallery and Museum, Penzance. Courtesy of Bernard Simmons.

Plate 33

Chapter 9.
(Right) B. A. Simmons: A
Letter of Introduction (1811)
from Lemon Hart to Hyman
Woolf, President of the
Penzance Hebrew
Congregation.
Courtesy of Godfrey Simmons.

Chapter 9.
(Below left) B. A. Simmons: A
Report from the Chief Rabbi
Hirsch (1836) confirming
Simmons' satisfactory
examination as a shochet.
Courtesy of Godfrey Simmons.

Chapter 9.
(Right) A Presentation gift to B. A.
Simmons on his leaving Penzance in
1854, from his Gentile friend, Henry
Cornish, the Hebrew Inscription being
in the latter's hand.
Courtesy of Godfrey Simmons.

Plate 34

Chapter 9.
B. A. Simmons' headstone in the Penzance
Jewish Cemetery (1860).
Photo by Gordon Brown.

Chapter 9.
Flora Simmons' headstone in the Merthyr
Jewish Cemetery (1874).
Courtesy Godfrey Simmons.

Plate 35

Chapter 9.
(Left) Abraham Joseph II (1799-1868) of
Plymouth, in later life. He was Reader in
Prayers in Penzance from 1826 to 1827,
and lived for a few years in the town.
He married Eliza, daughter of Lemon
Woolf of Penzance.

Chapter 9.
(Below left) Their daughter, Sarah Joseph
(1836-1922) in 1919. She became the second
wife of Rev. Raphael Harris (1835-1911:
right) who was Chazan and Secretary of
the Bayswater Synagogue for 47 years
from 1864-1911.
Courtesy of David Lang.

Plate 36

Chapter 9.
Top left: Rev. Isaac Bischofswerder, after his retirement. Courtesy of Victor Bishop.
Top right: Amy Bischofswerder (right) one of Rabbi Isaac Bischofswerder's numerous
grandchildren, and daughter of Morris and Julia Bischofswerder, with her Gentile friend,
Kate ("Daisy") Uren (*c.* 1903). From the private collection of and courtesy of Graham Rogers of Penzance.

Chapter 9.
Rev. Michael Leinkram and his wife
Esther, *c.* 1910. Courtesy of Esther Fishman,
and Gail and Stuart Raine.

The graves of Michael and Esther
Leinkram in the Edmonton Federation
Cemetery. Courtesy Gail and Stuart Raine.

Plate 37

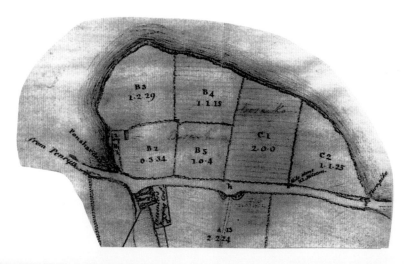

Chapter 9.
From Richard Thomas' 1814 survey for the Basset Estate with the Jews' and Dissenters' (Congregationalist) burial grounds marked. Courtesy of the CRO Truro (ref. AD 4/7/35).

Plate 38

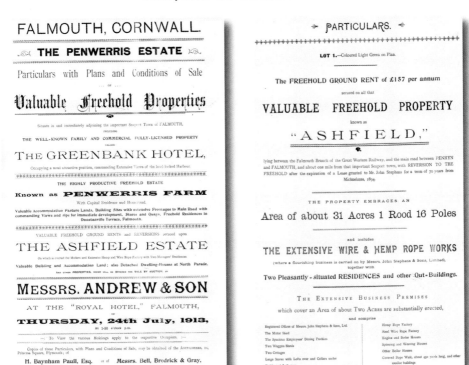

Chapter 9.
Sale advertisements for the
Ashfield Estate, including
the Jewish Cemetery (1913).
Courtesy the Cornwall Record
Office, Truro (Ref. WH6542).

Plate 39

Chapter 9.
Alfred de Pass. Courtesy of Phoebe Walker and Rebecca Coutts.

Chapter 9.
A recently discovered headstone which is likely to be that of Esther Elias who died in the late 1780s. It is the only headstone in the Penryn cemetery made of granite, and it may be the oldest surviving Jewish headstone in Cornwall.
Photo by Anthony Fagin (2013).

Plate 40

Chapter 9.
(Top) The Falmouth Jewish Cemetery: general View (1999).
(Bottom) Yakov Eliyahu (Hart Elias: 3:8), Killa daughter of Moses, wife of Abraham
Simeon Segal (Kitty Segal, or Solomon: 5:4) and Eliyahu ben Ezekiel Arieh (Israel Levy of
Truro: 3:11). Photos by David Sonin.

Plate 41

Chapter 9.
Isaac ben Benjamin (Wolf Benjamin: 1:2).
Photo by Karsten Berg.

Chapter 9.
Moses Jacob of Redruth (2:9).
Photo by David Sonin.

Chapter 9.
Tsvi ben Joseph (Henry Joseph of St.
Austell: 2:4). Photo by Karsten Berg.

Chapter 9.
Levi ben Issachar (Levy Levy: 1:6).
Photo by Karsten Berg.

Plate 42

Chapter 9.
Alexander Moses ("Zender Falmouth":
1:3). Photo by Karsten Berg.

Chapter 9.
Behr ben Joel (Barnet Levy, also known as
Barnard Beer and Bernard Jewell: 1:4).
 Photo by Karsten Berg.

Chapter 9.
The unmarried Leah, daughter of Israel
Aaron ha-Levi (1:10). Austell: 2:4).
Photo by Karsten Berg.

Chapter 9.
Feigeleh, daughter of Isaac ben Samuel
(Phoebe Simons: 3:10).
Photo by Karsten Berg.

Plate 43

Chapter 9.
Moses ben Israel ha-Levi
(Moses Segal, the son of
Israel Solomon: 1:8).
Photo by Karsten Berg.

Chapter 9.
Samuel ben Samuel
ha-Levi (Rabbi Saavil: 2:6).
Photo by Kartsen Berg.

Plate 44

Chapter 9.
Alexander ben Zvi (1:6) an infant son of
Henry Joseph (2:4) and Judith Joseph (nee
Moses, later Lawrence: 4:5). Photo by David
Sonin.

Chapter 9.
The headstone of Nathan Vos (6:2), the last
burial in the cemetery. The headstone was
photographed in 1999, and has since been
shattered. Photo by David Sonin.

Chapter 9.
Lewis Falkson (4:9).
Photo by Karsten Berg.

Plate 45

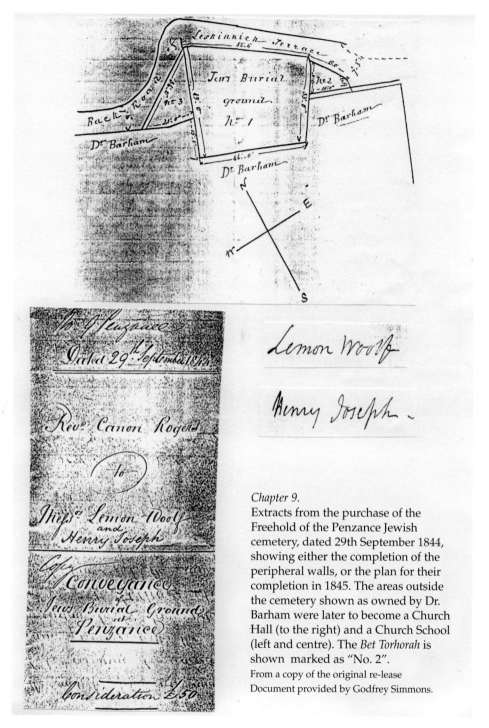

Chapter 9.
Extracts from the purchase of the Freehold of the Penzance Jewish cemetery, dated 29th September 1844, showing either the completion of the peripheral walls, or the plan for their completion in 1845. The areas outside the cemetery shown as owned by Dr. Barham were later to become a Church Hall (to the right) and a Church School (left and centre). The *Bet Torhorah* is shown marked as "No. 2".

From a copy of the original re-lease Document provided by Godfrey Simmons.

Plate 46

Chapter 9.
Penzance Jewish Cemetery: General Views (1999 & 2007). (Top, Bottom & Centre Left)
Photos by David Sonin (1999). (Centre Right) Photo by Maurice Minsky (2007).

Plate 47

Chapter 9.
(Top) Zvi ben Yekutiel (Henry Levin)
and his wife, Yuta bas Israel (Julia: 1:5 & 4).
(Bottom) their unmarried son, Israel Levin
(1:3). Right; the oldest dated headstone
(1791): after 4:4 (ii). It is not named, and is
in the oldest section of the cemetery, with
graves which are likely to be significantly
earlier. Photos by Mandy Pearce

Plate 48

Headstone Transcriptions

All headstones transcribed below are known to have been in place at the time of one or more of the various surveys from *c.*1850 up to 1998. The headstones transcribed in these surveys date from 1790 to 1868, and one stone from 1913. The transcriptions have been set out first with the full name of the person buried there to identify the grave, followed by a translation of the Hebrew inscription where known or legible. The translation from the original Hebrew inscription has been indicated for the reader by the use of *Heb.* On some of the headstones there is English as well as Hebrew. The English inscription has been indicated by being prefaced with *Eng.* I have added some biographical information where possible. Familial information and marriage connections have been included to allow individuals to be cross-referenced within each list, as well as between the Falmouth and Penzance lists. It is hoped that this will give the material as a whole, a degree of coherence. A full plan of the cemetery showing the original location of each interment and the surviving headstones up to 1998 has been included at the end of the chapter.

Earlier reference has been made to the displacement and loss of headstones in the cemetery, partly through the invasion of root systems from the surrounding trees. Moreover, the cemetery's position has never allowed it to be completely secured from public access. From 2000 onwards the displacement of headstones was especially marked, and several of the most elaborate were broken up as a result of vandalism. Amongst these shattered headstones were those of Sarah Kate Simons (5:2), Jacob Jacob (5:3) and Nathan Vos (6:2). Other headstones have been partially damaged, although still decipherable, including that of Moses Jacob (2:9), and there are significant gaps between surviving headstones where the originals have disappeared.[82] The exact position of each grave is in a few cases uncertain, and the general alignment of the headstones is not always regular. Consequently, later surveys can differ in some respects from earlier surveys, although a significant degree of consistency and coherence can be discerned from a synoptic, chronological comparison of the various surveys from 1850-1998, mentioned earlier. It is possible from these comparisons to identify topographical consistencies, and to infer where other burials, currently unmarked, were located. (The records of the Jewish Museum suggest that transcriptions were also made sometime before 1953 by a Mr. Stolloff, although these may have been taken from rubbings of the headstones provided by the Jacob family, rather than by Stollof *in* situ, and may not have included English translations).[83] The current location of some of the headstones in the Falmouth cemetery can be misleading, but their most likely original location is given here. Only in a few cases is that location speculative. Susser's reading of some of the dates also differs from earlier and later surveys. The Hebrew dates from both the Falmouth and Penzance headstones and from earlier surveys of these cemeteries have since been cross-checked by Yissochor Marmorstein of London from standard conversion calendars, including E.H. Lindo's (1838) *Jewish Calendar for Sixty Years*, and the *Kaluach* computer program conversion calendar of Yisrael Hersch (1997-2000). In the very few cases where transcriptions or conversion calendars do not correspond exactly with the original headstones, the latter have been retained. Where available, details from official death certificates have also been used. There can be occasional, minor errors in the original carving of the Hebrew script on the headstones, work carried out by local Gentile masons. The most notable of these was the Gentile family firm of Olver, the name inscribed at the base of some headstones. (The Olver firm may have built the Falmouth synagogue). Subsequent deciphering and transcription of the Hebrew, especially where decay to the surface may have taken place, could, in some cases, have resulted in error, especially for the Hebrew dates that are inferred from minute carved markings accompanying Hebrew letters. Secular days and dates of the Gregorian calendar are also given in the text, but this does not necessarily indicate that they are in every case to be found on the original headstones. Some minimal family detail, given earlier, has been repeated here for ease of reference.

ROW 1 (starting in the Upper Corner)

1. **GITELEH BENJAMIN** (Mrs Woolly Benjamin: Deborah Giteleh, wife of Isaac Menasseh).

Died 6 Ellul 5554 (Monday 1ˢᵗ September 1794).

Heb. Here lies the modest woman Deborah Gitteleh, wife of Isaac. The deceased was close to the Lord. She died on 6th and was buried on 7th Ellul, 5554. May her soul be bound up in the bond of eternal life. Wife of:

2. **WOOLF BENJAMIN** (Woolly Benjamin: Isaac, son of Benjamin).

Died 17 Cheshvan 5551 (Monday 25ᵗʰ October 1790).

Heb. Here lies an upright generous man who went in the path of the good. All his deeds were for the sake of heaven. Isaac the son of Benjamin. He died on Monday, 17ᵗʰ MarCheshvan and was buried on Tuesday, 5551. May his soul be bound up in the bond of eternal life.

Isaac Wolf Benjamin (1712-1790) was a Jeweller, a trade continued by his son Wolf Isaac Benjamin (1744-). Both men were members of the Falmouth Masonic Lodge. There is no Headstone for Wolf Isaac Benjamin in the Falmouth cemetery, and it is likely that he is to be identified with the son, renamed Benson, who moved to Bristol. A daughter of Isaac and Giteleh Benjamin lived in Haydon Square, London. This daughter married a Lyon Levy who committed suicide by throwing himself off the Monument circa 1809. This dramatic incident is mentioned in the *Ingoldsby Legends*.

3. **ALEXANDER MOSES** ("Zender Falmouth").

Died 24th Nisan 5551 (Thursday 28th April 1791).

Heb. May his soul be bound up in the bond of eternal life. Here dwells and takes delight a faithful man, a leader and guide; a shield to his generation with his body, his blood and his flesh. His house was open and his table laid for all. He stood righteously until the Lord, in whom he trusted, gathered him. Alexander the son of Moses. Died on the 24th and was buried on the 25th Nisan 5551.

Alexander Moses was married to Phoebe (2:3). There were two sons: (i) Philip (known as "Phill") Moses (2:2) who married Betsy Jacobs (3:9); (ii) Moses Moses who went to live in Le Havre and who may have become estranged from his family for marrying a non-Jewess. The daughters were: (i) Rosa (4:2), the wife of Samuel Simons (4:4); (ii) Hannah (Pz. 5:I) wife of Israel Levy (3:11); (iii) Judith (4:5), wife of (first) Henry Joseph (2:4) and then Lazarus Lawrence (4:6); (iv) and Sarah (4:1), wife of Moses Jacob (2:9).

Alexander Moses was the founder of the Falmouth Jewish community. His family became connected through marriage to most of the other resident families, and, as a result most Jews descended from them can trace their descent back to Alexander Moses.

4. **BARNET LEVY** (Behr, son of Joel).

Died 11 Iyar 5551 (Sunday 15th May 1791).

Heb. Here lies Behr the son of Joel. He died on the 11th and was buried on the 12th Iyar 5551. May his soul be bound up in the bond of eternal life.

Barnet Levy, also known as Bernard Beer or Jewell, was an immigrant from Alsace. He was by trade a soap-boiler but became a pedlar and prospered through Zender Falmouth's patronage. He married Esther Elias (1:11) from London, whose family were originally from Germany. Their sons were Levy Levy (1:6); Joel Levy who married Rachel Joseph; and Abraham Levy who married Zipporah Benjamin of Plymouth. Their daughters were Judith Levy (not 3:7 or 4:5) who married Lyon Joseph; Hendele (Hannah) Levy (Pz. 1:2) the wife of Abraham Joseph (3:5); Elizabeth (Betsy) Levy (not 3:9 or 5:1), who married Solomon Solomon (son of 2:1 and 3:2): she died in Bristol and her husband died in Lisbon [they were the parents of the Israel Solomon who emigrated to New York, and author of *Records of my Family* 1887]; Sally Levy; and Shevya Levy (Pz. 6:4) who married her uncle Hart Elias (3:8), the brother of Esther Elias.

5. JOSEPH JOSEPH.

This headstone has no dates.

This is the infant son of Lyon Joseph of Falmouth and Judith Levy (above).

6. LEVY LEVY (Levi, son of Issachar).

Died 1 Kislev 5552 (Sunday 27th November 1791).

Heb. Here lies Levi the son of Issachar. Died New Moon Kislev and was buried on the 2nd Kislev 5552. May his soul be bound up in the bond of eternal life.

The eldest son of Barnet Levy (1:4).

7. ALEXANDER (son of Zvi)

Died 5 Ab 5564 (Friday 13th July 1804).

Heb. Here lies Alexander the son of Zvi. He died on Friday, Sabbath eve and was laid to rest on Sunday 7th Av 5564. May his soul be bound up in the bond of eternal life.

Note: Susser (1963) placed 7 (above) and 8 (below) in Rows 2 and 3 respectively, with 8 next to Gershan Elias. De Lange (1975) identified an illegible headstone before 8 below.

8. MOSES (son of Israel Segal)

Died 5559 (1798-9).

Heb. Here lies the unmarried male, Moses the son of Israel Segal. 5559. May his soul be bound up in the bond of eternal life.

The son of Israel Solomon (2:1).

9. JACOB (son of Reuven)

Died 5561 (1800-1).

From genealogical records it is not possible to identify him with certainty. However, he may have been an infant son of the Reuben who traded with a Meyers, as Mercers, in Redruth in 1792.

10. **LEAH** (daughter of Israel).

Died 15 Tevet 5602 (Tuesday 28th December 1841).

Heb. Here lies the single woman Leah, the daughter of Israel Aaron Segal. She died on Tuesday, 15th Tevet and was buried the next day Wednesday, in the year 5602. May her soul be bound up in the bond of eternal life.

The daughter of Israel Aaron Segal (Israel Solomon, 2:1).
Note: This stone may have been displaced to 4:8 at some time.

11. **ESTHER ELIAS** (Esther wife of Behr).

She died *c.* 1780. She was the wife of Barnet Levy (1:4) and may have been one of the first to be buried in the Falmouth cemetery, although burials earlier than 1780 are likely. Her brother, Hart Elias, is buried in 3:8. In an addendum (1885) to his *Records of my Family*, compiled in the 1880s, but not published in New York until 1887, Israel Solomon (1803-1893), grandson of the below, claimed that Barnet Levy (1731-1791) died "within two or three years" of his wife, which would give a year *c.* 1788.

He also states that, when Esther died, her youngest son, Abraham, who was born in 1791, was a "very little boy" and his sister, Sally (Sarah) was "a baby in arms". From this it can be taken that a date of around 1780 is most likely for Esther Elias' death. Joseph (1860-1870) and Jacob (1939) recorded her headstone at the end of this line. A recently discovered granite headstone, with a virtually illegible inscription, may be that of Esther Elias.

ROW 2

1. **ISRAEL SOLOMON** (Israel Aaron Levi, son of Isaac Segal)

Died 23 Sivan 5562 (Wednesday 23rd June 1802), aged about 78.
Heb. Here lies an upright and perfect man. All his deeds he performed with propriety. "As strong as a lion, fleet as a deer and swift as an eagle" (Mishnah, Ethics of the Fathers 5:23). Israel Aaron Ha-Levi, the son of Isaac Segal. He died on Wednesday and was buried on Thursday, 24th Sivan 5562. May his soul be bound up in the bond of eternal life.

Israel Solomon was from Ehrenbreitstein, opposite Koblenz on the Rhine. His family name in Germany was Behrends. He was married to Bella Woolf (3:2) from Holland. Their daughters were Judith (4:7) who married Samuel Harris (3:12); Leah who was unmarried (4:8); and a daughter who eloped to India. Their sons were

Solomon who married Betsy Levy (see 1:4); and Simon (3:3) who married Kitty Jacob (5:4). Israel Solomon and Bella Woolf were the paternal grandparents of the Israel Solomon who emigrated to New York (see 1:4).

2. **PHILL MOSES** (Uri Shraga, son of Alexander).

Died 14 Kislev 5592 (Saturday 19th November 1831).

Heb. Here lies Uri Shraga, the son of the Manyah (? the teacher) Alexander - may his memory be for a blessing. Died on the 14th Kislev 5592. May his soul be bound up in the bond of eternal life.

The son of Alexander Moses (1:3) and Phoebe (2:3). He was married to Betsy Jacob (3:9). Their daughter Rosey was born *c*.1802.

3. **PHOEBE MOSES** (Feigele, daughter of Moses)

Died Yom Kippur 10th Tishri 5565 (Saturday 15th September 1804).

Heb. Here lies a woman of worth (Proverbs 31:10), Feigele, the daughter of Moses, the wife of Alexander. She died at the dawn of the Day of Atonement and was buried Sunday at the termination of the Day of Atonement, 5565. May her soul be bound up in the bond of eternal life.

The wife of Alexander Moses (1:3).

4. **HENRY JOSEPH** (Zvi, son of Joseph).

Died 3rd Adar 5563 (Friday 25th February 1803).

Heb. Here lies Zvi the son of Joseph. He died in the night (Tuesday), the 3rd and was buried on the 4th Adar 5563. May his soul be bound up in the bond of eternal life.

This is the Henry Joseph of St. Austell, not Henry Joseph of Penzance (Pz. 6:5). He was the first husband of Judith Moses (4:5) who was the daughter of Alexander Moses (1:3). They had three children: Alexander, Philip and Joseph who all died in infancy (see 2:6, 2:7 and 2:8).

5. **MOSES ISAAC JOSEPH** (Isaac, son of Joseph).

Note: There are no dates on this headstone, but Moses Isaac Joseph died in 1834.

This is the brother of Henry Joseph (2:4). He married Judith Jacob (3:7) who was a daughter of Moses Jacob (2:9). They had six children: Henry, unmarried, who died in Brazil; Rose who emigrated to Australia; Phoebe (3:6) who married Isaac Davidson; Joseph who married Fanny Solomon; Solomon who died unmarried in London; and Bella who married Rabbi Meyer Stadhagen of Plymouth (formerly minister in Penzance).

6. **ALEXANDER JOSEPH**.

There are no dates on the headstone.

He was the infant son of Henry Joseph (2:4) and Judith Joseph (née Moses, later Lawrence, of 4:5).

7 and 8 UNMARKED

These two graves are unmarked but they are likely to be the other two infant sons of Henry Joseph, Philip and Joseph. See 6:1 and 6:2.

9. **MOSES JACOB** of Redruth.

Died the first of the middle Days of Passover 17th Nisan 5567 (Saturday 25th April 1807).

Heb. Here lies an upright man. All his deeds he performed with propriety. He fed and supported the numerous members of his household with honour and not in need. Moses the son of Jacob of Redruth. He died on Sabbath, the first of the intermediate days of Passover and was buried on the second of the intermediate days of Passover 5567. May his soul be bound up in the bond of eternal life.

Note: This Moses Jacob should not be confused with 4:10 or 5:5.

Moses Jacob married Sarah Moses (4:1), a daughter of Alexander Moses (1:3). They had 12 children: Betsy (not 3:9 or 5:1) who died unmarried (see the note to Pz. 3:1); Judith (3:7) who married Isaac Joseph (2:5); Rose who married Alexander; Killa or Kitty (5:4) who married Simon Solomon (3:3); Jacob Jacob (5:3) who married Sarah Simons (5:2); Henne, or Hannah (Pz. 3:2) who married Solomon Ezekiel (Pz. 2:3); Samuel Jacob (Pz. 2:1) who married Sarah Levi (Pz. 1:9); Rebecca who married Lemon Woolf (Pz. 1:1); Esther who married Henry Harris (see 3:12); Mirele or Amelia (Pz. 3:1) who was unmarried; Levi who married Sophia Mordecai (1781-1853); and Flora (who is buried at Merthyr Tydfil) and who married Rabbi Barnett Asher Simmons (Pz. 1:8). Four other children died young. Moses Jacob was President of the Falmouth Congregation from 1791-1807.

An original handwritten document from the Jacob Archive, in the hand of Leah Jacob (1846-1933), wife of Alexander Jacob (1841-1903) records that the mother of Moses Jacob is buried in the cemetery. There is no confirmation of this from other sources, although there are unmarked graves, and Alex M. Jacob notes that there is no evidence of the burial in Falmouth.

10. UNKNOWN.

11. **"Rabbi SAAVIL"** (Samuel, son of Samuel Levi).

Died 1 Nisan 5574 (Tuesday 22nd March 1814) aged 73.

Heb. Here lies a generous man, going in righteousness. His actions were perfect in faith. He ate from the labour of his hands and stood in his righteousness until he was gathered to his rest on high. Samuel the son of Samuel Ha-Levi. He died on Tuesday, New Moon Nisan and was buried on Wednesday, 5574. May his soul be bound up in the bond of eternal life.

12. **GERSHAN ELIAS** (Gershom, son of Elijah).

Died 17th Adar 5628 (Wednesday 11th March 1868), aged 84.

Heb. Here lies a man who walked in uprightness. All his deeds were perfect in faith, and gave to the needy with joy according to his ability until he was gathered on high to his rest. Gershan the son of Elijah, died on Wednesday, 17th Adar and was buried the next day, Thursday, 18th Adar, 5628. May his soul be bound up in the bond of eternal life.

Eng. In memory of Gershan Elias who died 11th March 5628, 1868, aged 84.

It is possible that this stone has been displaced in view of the surrounding stones being much earlier. Susser placed this grave in the next row.

This was the last burial of a member of the extant congregation. Gershan Elias was a relative of Esther Elias (1:11) and Barnet Levy (1:4) and also of Shevya Levy (Pz 6:4) and Hart Elias (3:8).

<u>ROW 3</u>

1. A. H. H.

Died 5607 (1846/7).

There is no inscription. It is a small tombstone partly hidden by a hedge. This may be the infant son of Morris and Rebecca Harris.

2. **BELLA WOOLF** (Beila, daughter of Benjamin).

Died 2 Adar 5576 (Saturday 2nd March 1816).

Heb. Here lies Beila, the daughter of Benjamin (may his memory be for a blessing) the wife of Israel Segal. She died at dawn on the Sabbath and was buried on Sunday, 3rd Adar 5576. May her soul be bound up in the bond of eternal life.

She was born in Holland and was the wife of Israel Solomon (2:1).

3. **SIMON (Segal) SOLOMON** (Abraham Simeon, son of Israel Aaron Levi).

Died 4 Tevet 5586 (Wednesday 14th December 1825).

Heb. Here lies buried a man who was upright in generosity. He walked in the path of the good. All his actions he performed with propriety. His soul cleaved to the Lord with uprightness. He did not turn aside from all the commandments of the Lord. Abraham Simeon, the son of Israel Aaron Ha-Levi. He died on the 4th and was buried on the 5th of Tevet 5586. May his soul be bound up in the bond of eternal life. Amen.

He was a son of Israel Solomon (2:1) and Bella Woolf (3:2). He married Kitty Jacob (2:9 and 5:4) the daughter of Moses Jacob. He was a painter and had a brother and sister who were also painters.

4. **ISHAYA son of Moses** (Isaiah Hyman).

Died 1 Nisan 5587 (Thursday 29th March 1827) aged 17½ years.

Heb. Your God chose you to take delight in your soul, for day and night you meditated on your Torah, and you went in an upright way all the days of your life. You listened to the voice of your teachers, and in the resurrection you will be restored to life. Isaiah the son of Moses - may God preserve and protect him. Aged seventeen and half when he died on Thursday, New Moon Nisan and was buried on Sabbath eve, 2nd Nisan 5587. May his soul be bound up in the bond of eternal life. Amen.

This is the firstborn son of Rabbi Moses Hyman (4:3).

5. **ABRAHAM** (son of Joseph).

Died 6 Tishri 5589 (Sunday 14th September 1828) aged 60.

Heb. Here lies a man who was upright in generosity, who went in the way of the good. He gave charity generously to the needy. He was a tree of life to those who strengthen the hands of the learned. Righteous and upright. All his deeds he did with propriety. His soul cleaved to the Lord with uprightness. His body sleeps in the earth and his spirit was summoned to the Garden of Eden. All his deeds were for the sake of heaven. He himself cleaved to the living God. Abraham the son of Joseph. 60 years of age when he died on Sabbath night, and he was buried on Sunday, 8th Tishri 5589. May his soul be bound up in the bond of eternal life.

Note: The Sabbath was the 5th Tishri and the Sunday was the 6th, which would correspond with 13th and 14th September. It is likely, therefore, that he died either on the Sabbath eve (Sabbath *night* referring to the evening of the Friday 4th) and was buried on the 6th.

This is the son of Joseph Joseph of Alsace by his second marriage. Abraham Joseph was the husband of Hannah Levy (Pz 1:2) who was the daughter of Barnet Levy (1:4). Their son Henry Joseph is buried in the Penzance cemetery (6:5).

6. **PHOEBE JOSEPH** (Feigele, daughter of Joseph).

Died 25 Shevat 5590 (Thursday 18th February 1830), aged 24.

Heb. Here lies Feigele the daughter of Joseph. The wife of Isaac the son of Moses. She was 24 when she died, 25th Shevat 5590. May her soul be bound up in the bond of eternal life.

She was the daughter of Isaac Joseph (2:5) and Judith Jacob (3:7). She was the first wife of Isaac Davidson.

7. **JUDITH JACOB** (daughter of Moses).

Died 26* Kislev 5610 (Saturday 8th December 1849).

Heb. The woman who fears the Lord, she shall be praised (Proverbs 31:30). She stretched out her hand to the poor; she put forth her hand to the needy (Proverbs 31:20). Judith the daughter of Moses, wife of Moses Isaac. She died on Sabbath, 26th Kislev and was buried the next day, Sunday 5610. May her soul be bound up in the bond of eternal life.

Note: The Sabbath was the 23rd * Kislev. The second letters in the Hebrew for "23rd " and "26th " are slightly different, by a small mark, which could have become indistinct with time thus leading to an incorrect transcription.

Judith Rebecca Joseph was a daughter of Moses Jacob (2:9) and Sarah Moses (4:1). She married Moses Isaac Joseph (2:5), and was the mother of Joseph Joseph of Redruth, who left Cornwall in 1849. She was 82 at the time of her death, which was reported in the Cornish press.[84]

8. **HART ELIAS** (Jacob Elijah, son of Naphtali).

Died Kislev 5596 (late November to early December 1835).

Heb. Here lies Jacob Elijah the son of Naphtali. He died and was buried in the month of Kislev 5596. May his soul be bound up in the bond of eternal life.

He married his niece Shevya Levy (see 1:4 and Pz 6:4.)

9. **BETSY JACOB**.

Died 3rd Nisan 5598 (Thursday 29th March 1838).

This was the wife of Philip Moses (see 1:3 and 2:2). She is not to be confused with the unmarried daughter of Moses Jacob (2:9) or Betsy Jacob of 5:1, also unmarried.

10. **PHOEBE SIMONS** (Feigele, daughter of Isaac the son of Samuel).

Died the first day of Pesach 5584 (Tuesday 13th April 1824).

Heb. Here lies the girl Feigele the daughter of Isaac the son of Samuel. She died the first day of Passover and was buried on the second, 5584. May her soul be bound up in the bond of eternal life. Amen.

This was the infant grand-daughter of Rosa Moses (4:2) and Samuel Simons (4:4). Phoebe was the daughter of their son Isaac.

11. **ISRAEL LEVY** (Israel, son of Ezekiel Aryeh).

Died second day of Shavuot 5584 (Tuesday 3rd June 1824).

Heb. Here lies a generous man. He went uprightly. His deeds were perfect in faith. He ate from the labour of his hands. He stood in his perfection until he was gathered. Israel the son of Ezekiel Arieh. He died on the second day of the Feast of Weeks and was buried on the next day (Isru Hag) 5584. May his soul be bound up in the bond of eternal life. Amen.

Israel Levy of Truro was married to Hannah Moses (Pz 5:1), the daughter of Alexander Moses (1:3). Their children were Henry, Sarah (Pz 1:9) who married Samuel Jacob (Pz 2:1), Judith (*c.* 1793-), and Elizabeth (Pz 1:6) who married Samuel Oppenheim of Penzance (Pz 1:7).

12. **SAMUEL HARRIS** (Samuel, son of Naphtali).

Died 29 Tammuz 5584 (Sunday 25th July 1824).

Heb. Here lies an upright man in generosity. He walked in the way of the good. His soul cleaved to the Lord in uprightness. Strong as a lion and fleet as a deer, swift as an eagle (Mishnah, Ethics of the Fathers 5:23). He did not turn aside from any commandments of the Lord included in the ten commandments. Samuel the son of Naphtali. Died and was buried on 29th Tammuz, in the year 5584. May his soul be bound up in the bond of eternal life. Amen.

Samuel Harris was the husband of Judith Solomon (4:7) the daughter of Israel Solomon (2:1) and Bella Woolf (3:2). His family was German in origin, although he came from London. He was the father of Henry Harris of Truro, who married Esther Jacob (2:9) a daughter of Moses Jacob.

13. **ESTHER FALKSON** (Esther, daughter of Samuel).
Died 9th Av 5623 (Saturday 25th July 1863).

Heb. Here lies the woman Esther the daughter of Samuel. The wife of Judah the son of Joshua. She died on Sabbath Eve, the eve of Tisha (9th) b' Av, and was buried on Sunday 10th Av 5623. May her soul be bound up in the bond of eternal life.

Note: It may be that she died on the Saturday evening (after the Sabbath), although Sabbath *eve* could be taken to refer to the Friday (but this would be 8th Av).

Eng. In memory of Esther Falkson, who departed this life July 25th 5623, 1863.

Esther was the wife of Lewis Falkson (4:9). Her age at the time of her death is uncertain, although the 1851 census gives her age as 60 (b. 1791) this may not be accurate, in that the age of her husband (61) does not correspond with other records (see 4:9). Esther was born in Truro. It is possible that she was a daughter either of Samuel Harris (1754-1824) who is buried next to her, or of Samuel Simons (1740-1832) (of 4:4).

<u>ROW 4</u>

1. SARAH (Moses) JACOB.

Died 1 Shevat 5591 (Saturday 15th January 1831) aged 83 years.

Heb. Here lies the woman Sarah, the wife of Moses the son of Jacob - may his memory be for a blessing. She stored up the fear of the Lord. Charity and peace were the fruits of her deeds. Fullness of days were her years, for children and the children of children received kisses from her mouth (Song of Songs 1:2). She went to her everlasting rest to see the delight of the Lord on New Moon, Shevat 5591. May her soul be bound up in the bond of eternal life.

Sarah Moses was born in 1748 and her age was 83 years at the time of her death in 1831. The Hebrew inscription shows a dot above the letter *yod*, and it was recorded (de Lange and Speake) as such, giving an age of 93 years.

Sarah Jacob was a daughter of Alexander Moses (1:3) and the wife of Moses Jacob (2:9).

2. ROSA (Moses) SIMONS (Rosa, daughter of Alexander).

Died 15 Tevet 5598[85] (Friday 12th January 1838) in her 82nd year.

Heb. Here lies the woman Rosa the daughter of Alexander, the wife of Samuel. She died on Sabbath eve 15th Tevet and was buried on Sunday 17th Tevet 5598. May her soul be bound up in the bond of eternal life.

Rosa Simons was a daughter of Alexander Moses (1:3), the wife of Samuel Simons (4:4). She was the mother-in-law of Jacob Jacob (5:3) and sister to Sarah (4:1). Rosa and Samuel had at least two children, Isaac and Kitty (5:2).

This burial, being that of one of the last surviving children of the congregation's founder, was reported in the County press:

"At Falmouth, on Friday last, Mr. Symons' widow, aged 92 years. She was interred on Sunday last at the Jews' burying ground, at Ponsharden, and was followed to the grave by a large assemblage of her descendants".[86]

397

Her age is given incorrectly in this report, and her age at the time of her death, 82, accords with genealogical records. However, having been born some 80 years before the introduction of civil registration, her year of birth cannot be confirmed from public records. In this case, and others from this period, some degree of error is possible.

3. **Rev. MOSES HYMAN** ("Rabbi Mowsha": Moses, son of Hayyim).

Died 22 Ellul 5590 (Friday 10th September 1830).

The date of his death has been taken as 14th September, but conversion tables suggest that the Friday was the 10th. Alex Jacob (1949) transcribed this date incorrectly as 24th October 1832.

Heb. Here lies a perfect man; he went in the path of the good; righteous and upright, he performed his deeds with propriety. Moses the son of Hayyim, cantor - may his memory be for a blessing. From here Falmouth. He died on Friday 22nd Ellul 5590. May his soul be bound up in the bond of eternal life.

4. **SAMUEL SIMONS** of Truro (Samuel, son of Simeon).

Died 29 Tishri 5593 (Tuesday 23rd October 1832) aged 92 years.

Heb. Here lies Samuel the son of Simon. He died on Tuesday, the eve of the New Moon of Cheshvan, and was buried on Wednesday, New Moon of Cheshvan 5593. May his soul be bound up in the bond of eternal life.

Note: He died on the last day (29th) of Tishri, which was the eve of the New Moon of Cheshvan. He was buried the next day, 1st Cheshvan.

Samuel Simons was married to Rosa (4:2). Their children were Sarah Kate, known as Kitty, (1778-1846), Walter and Isaac (*c.*1796-). Samuel Simons may have had several children from an earlier marriage: Philip, Joseph, Eliezar and Moses (Morris).

Susser read this headstone as dated 11th Tishri.

5. **JUDITH MOSES** (Yetele, daughter of Alexander).

Died 6th Kislev 5604 (Wednesday 29th November 1843).

Heb. Here lies a woman of worth (Proverbs 31:10); the king's daughter is all glorious within (Psalms 45:14); her name is known in the gates for her hand she always stretched out to the poor. Yetele the daughter of Alexander. She died on Wednesday, 6th Kislev and was buried on Thursday 7th Kislev 5604. May her soul be bound up in the bond of eternal life.

Eng. Judith Lawrance. Died 29th November, 5604.

Judith was a daughter of Alexander Moses (1:3). She married Henry Joseph of St. Austell (2:4), who died in 1803. Their three infant sons died (see 2:6 to 2:8). She later married Lazarus Lawrance (4:6). There were no children to this second marriage, although Lazarus Lawrance may have had children from an earlier marriage.

6. **LAZARUS LAWRANCE** (Eliezer, son of Jacob).

Died 12 Ab 5601 (Friday 30th July 1841).

Heb. Here lies a generous man who went with perfection. All his deeds were perfect in faith. He gave amply to the hungry far and near. He was free with his wealth; his business dealings were with faith. At all times he was one of those who paid attention to the cry of the poor and needy. His name was known with love. Eliezer the son of Jacob who went to his eternal rest on Friday, Sabbath eve, 12th Av, and was buried on Sunday, 14th Av 5601. May you rest and bear your lot until the end of days. May your soul be bound up in the bond of eternal life.

Eng. Lazarus Lawrance, 5601.

There was a Lawrence (or Laurance) family which lived in the disused Falmouth synagogue as its caretakers. It was known at that time as "Synagogue House". This family may have been related to Lazarus Lawrence.

7. **JUDITH SOLOMON** (Yetele, daughter of Israel Aaron Segal).

Died 19th Adar 5599 (Tuesday 5th March 1839) aged 75.

Heb. Here lies a woman of worth, pious and upright. She did the righteousness of the Lord. The wise woman, her spirit went on high. All her days she proceeded on the right path. She observed the commandment of the Lord. Yetele the daughter of Israel Aaron Segal. She died on Tuesday, 19th Adar and was buried on Thursday 21st Adar 5599. May her soul be bound up in the bond of eternal life.

Eng. Mrs Judith Harris, 5th March 5599. Aged 75.

The daughter of Israel Solomon (2:1) and the wife of Samuel Harris (3:12).

8. **LEAH** (daughter of Israel Solomon; as 2:1).

The unmarried sister of Judith (4:7).

Note: Susser (1963) gave this headstone as dated 15th Teveth 5602 (December 1841/2).

9. **LEWIS FALKSON** (Judah, son of Joshua).

Died 19 Cheshvan 5613 (Monday 1st November 1852) aged 65 years.

Heb. Here lies a man upright in generosity, who went in the way of the good. He was strong as a lion in carrying out the will of his Father in heaven; and his spirit ascended to heaven amongst the beloved and delightful. Judah the son of Joshua. He died and was buried on Monday, 19th Cheshvan 5613. May his soul be bound up in the bond of eternal life.

Eng. Lewis Falkson, died 1852, aged 65 years.

Lewis was the husband of Esther (3:13). His age as given on the headstone does not correspond with the 1851 census (61: year of birth 1790) or his death certificate (68: year of birth 1784). The headstone implies 1787. He was born in London, and may have been related to Falkson families from Latvia, but this not certain.[87] The genealogical tables of the families of Ber (1797-1861) and Ette (Esther) Falkson (1803-1876), and Jankel (1781-) and Minna Falkson (1783-), together with detailed personal information relating to the latter family, are to be found in the Riga Record Office. It is not known if these particular Latvian families were related to the Falksons of Falmouth.

10. **MOSES SAMUEL JACOB** ("Mosam").

Died Falmouth 17 Ellul 5618 (Friday 27th August 1858) aged 43.

Heb. Here lies Moses the son of Samuel from Penzance. He died the eve of Sabbath, 17th Ellul and was buried on the 19th Ellul 5618. May his soul be bound up in the bond of eternal life.

Eng. Moses Samuel Jacob, son of S. & S. Jacob Penzance; died at Falmouth. August 27th 5618/1858, aged 43. The stone was erected to his memory by his cousin Moss. J. Jacob.

Moses Samuel Jacob was the unmarried son of Samuel Jacob (Pz 2:1) and Sarah Levy (Pz 1:9), the daughter of Israel Levy of Truro (3:11). "Mosam" was, therefore, a grandson of Moses Jacob of Redruth (2:9) and Sarah Moses (4:1), the daughter of Alexander Moses (1:3). He was a prominent Freemason and was elevated to the

Provincial Grand Lodge Honours at a very early age. His will[88] was not proved until 14th December 1864 at Bodmin "By the oath of Margaret Ann Callaway of Falmouth Spinster, the Sole Executrix". His Effects were under £100. Moses Samuel Jacob is described as a "Clerk to an Outfitter", being employed by his prosperous cousin Moses Jacob Jacob (1812-1860).

<u>ROW 5</u>

1. **BETSY JACOB** (Beila, daughter of Jacob of Falmouth).

Died 4th Nisan 5598 (c. Friday 29th March 1838) aged 16 years.

Heb. Here lies the unmarried woman, Beila the daughter of Jacob from Falmouth. She died on the eve of Sabbath, 4th Nisan and was buried on Sunday, 7th* Nisan 5598. May her soul be bound up in the bond of eternal life.

Eng. To the memory of Betsy, third daughter of J & K Jacob, Falmouth, who departed this life 29th March 5598. Aged 16 years. A dutiful child, an affectionate sister, beloved and esteemed by all of her acquaintances.

Note: * There may be an error here in the dating or the transcription. The 4th Nisan was a Friday and the Sunday would have been the 6th. However, if she died early on the Friday, and was buried late on the Sunday, the next day (7th Nisan) would have begun.

Betsy Jacob was the third daughter of Jacob Jacob (5:3) and Sarah Kate Jacob (5:2). She is not to be confused with the unmarried daughter of Moses Jacob (2:9) or the Betsy Jacob of 3:9.

2. **SARAH KATE SIMONS** ("Kitty" Jacob: Sarah Killa, daughter of Samuel).

Died 12th Kislev 5607 (Tuesday 1st December 1846), aged 69 years.

Heb. Here lies a pious and upright woman. Her deeds were pleasantness. Her husband's heart had trust in her because she planted a vineyard from the fruits of her hands. Her children rise up and call her happy. For fear of God her soul desired, and her spirit went on high, and her body will sleep in peace. The woman Sarah Killa, the daughter of Samuel. Wife of Jacob the son of Moses, who went to her eternal rest on Tuesday 12th Kislev and was buried on Thursday, 14th Kislev, in the year 5607. May her soul be bound up in the bond of eternal life.

Eng. To the memory of Sarah Kitty, the beloved wife of J. Jacob of Falmouth, who died on 1st December 5607, 1846. Aged 69 years.

She was known as "Kitty" Jacob, but should not be confused with her sister-in-law also "Kitty" Jacob (Segal or Solomon: 5:4). Her sister-in-law was a daughter of Moses Jacob (2:9) and was married to Simon Solomon (3:3). Sarah Kate Simons was the daughter of Samuel Simons (4:4) and Rosa Moses (4:2). She married Jacob Jacob (5:3), her first cousin. They had 10 children. Four died very young or in infancy: Alexander, Simon, Phoebe, and Henry. Betsy died aged 16 years (5:1); Esther, who was unmarried (and who died at the home of her brother Isaac Jacob at 164, Portsdown Road, Maida Vale, London, on 2nd June 1878, aged 69).[89] Amelia (Pz. 6:6) married Henry Joseph (Pz. 6:5); Moses Jacob Jacob (5:5) who married Frances Emanuel of Portsea; Isaac who married Sophia Lazarus; and Rebecca who married Morris Hart Harris (son of Henry Harris of Truro).

3. JACOB JACOB of Falmouth (Jacob, son of Moses).

Died 25th Shevat 5613 (Thursday 3rd February 1853), aged 79.

Heb. Here lies a God-fearing man, who kept his covenant.... in death and in life. On his death, in his piety he turned towards God (?) .... he called on his God with all his heart; he drew near to God humbly. Jacob with a good name; as with flute and drum.... he went and returned from the place (roundabout ?). Whilst still alive he generously opened doors to the wretched and poor. His hands supported the house of his Lord. He magnified it as a Sanctuary....How goodly are thy tents, O Jacob (Num 24:5). Loved ones, children, dear ones sent to the God of Jacob entreating him on behalf of the soul of Jacob, may his memory be for a blessing. By the God of the system he was given and was taken on Thursday, 25th Shevat and returned to dust on Sunday 28th of the same year {5}613. May his soul be bound up in the bond of eternal life.

Note: This headstone was extremely difficult to translate. It consists of many acrostics on the name Jacob and is a kind of Mediaeval poem. There are two unusual features of the Hebrew wording. Firstly, the name of God is given in the unusual form *Elokei* on several occasions rather than the usual *Elohei*. The former usage may denote a secular substitute name to avoid the association of *Elohei* with the strictly religious context. This may be linked with the extremely unusual phrase "God of the system". It is possible that this is a reference to Freemasonry. Jacob Jacob's father, Moses Jacob, was also a Mason.

Eng. To the memory of Jacob Jacob of Falmouth who died on the 3rd February 5617, 1853, aged 79 years.

Jacob Jacob was a son of Moses Jacob (2:9) and the husband of Sarah Kate Simons (5:2). Her sister, Kitty, is buried next to him (5:4). He was, apparently, a competent amateur painter. His sister, Kitty, also married into an artistic family (5:4 and 3:3). In an article, "A Journey's End" in the *Jewish Chronicle* (March 18th 1960), Florence Abrahams described how she had discovered, in an antique shop in Philadelphia, two miniature portraits painted by Jacob Jacob, of himself and his wife Sarah. On the back of one of the miniatures was inscribed "Drawn by me, July 1820, in my 46 year of age. J. Jacob" and on the other, "In her 42 year of age, Mrs. J. Jacob." (Jacob Jacob was born in 1774, and Sarah in 1778). These portraits must have left the possession of the family at some point. They were bought during the War by an American serviceman called Smith who took them back to the USA where he eventually sold them to an antique dealer. Florence traced the great, great grandson, Alex M. Jacob, from whose archives these details have been drawn. She purchased the portraits for him for 35 dollars, bringing them back to London in July 1958. Sadly, they were stolen when Alex Jacob's flat was burgled in the 1980s and have never been recovered.

4. **KITTY (Segal) SOLOMON** (Killa, daughter of Moses).

Died 19 Iyar 5514 (Wednesday 17th May 1854).

Heb. Here lies a God-fearing woman; she shall be praised; she stretched her hand out to the poor and she put out her hands to the needy (Proverbs 31:20). Killa the daughter of Moses, wife of Abraham Simeon Segal. She died Wednesday, and was buried on Sabbath eve, 21st Iyar, 5514. May her soul be bound up in the bond of eternal life.

She was a daughter of Moses Jacob (2:9) and the wife of Abraham Simeon (Segal) Solomon, or Simon Solomon (3:3), and was also a painter.

5. **"MOSS" JACOB JACOB** (Moses, son of Jacob of Falmouth).

Died 21st Shevat 5620 (Tuesday 14th February 1860), aged 47.

Heb. Here lies a man upright in generosity. He went in the path of the good; as a righteous man he walked in peace and may he repose in his resting place. Moses the son of Jacob, may his memory be for a blessing. Leader and guide of the Holy Congregation of Falmouth. He died on Tuesday 21st Shevat and was buried next day, Wednesday 22nd 5620. May his soul be bound up in the bond of eternal life.

Moss was a son of Jacob Jacob (5:3) and Sarah Kate Simons (5:2). He was married to Frances Emanuel (1812-1875) of Portsea.

ROW 6

1. **PHILIP JOSEPH and JOSEPH JOSEPH** (Uri and Joseph, sons of Zvi).

403

Philip Joseph died 4 Sivan 5550 (Monday 17th May 1790) and Joseph Joseph died 14 Ab 5550 (Sunday 25th July 1790) respectively.

Heb. Here lies Uri the son of Zvi. He died on 4th and was buried on the 5th Sivan.

Heb. Here lies Joseph the son of Zvi. He died on the 14th and was buried on 15th Av.

These were the infant sons of Henry Joseph (2:4) and Judith Moses (4:5).

Note: The early dates on these stones suggest that they may have been displaced from row 1.

2. NATHAN VOS.

Died 28 Tishri 5674 (Wednesday 29th October 1913), aged 80.

Heb. Here lies Nathan the son of Meir Vos. He died on Wednesday 28th Tishri. May his soul be bound up in the bond of eternal life.

Eng. In loving memory of my dearly beloved husband, Nathan Vos, born 25th April 1833, who died on 28th Tishri 5674, 29th October 1913, aged 80 years. Gone but not forgotten.

This was the last Jewish burial in Falmouth. Nathan Vos had been born in the Netherlands in 1834. Before coming to Cornwall, he had lived in South Wales, where he worked as a spectacle-maker. He was a Freemason, a Ships' Chandler and he also worked as an innkeeper, being associated with the Truscotts Pier Hotel in Quay Street (also known as the Marine Hotel, Quay Hill) and the Greyhound Hotel, Church Street, which he ran with his wife, Mary Ann Maclenaer, who was not Jewish. She had been born in Falmouth in 1840, and she already had a daughter, Marie Virginia Eleanor (b. 1863), when she married Nathan Vos. Nathan and Mary Vos may have become estranged, and Nathan Vos is believed to have co-habited with a Harriet Husham (it is not known if she was Jewish).[90] Mary Vos continued to run the hotel with her second son, John Blower (b. 1876) after Nathan's death, but she died soon after, on 18th March 1914. They had two other children, Frederick Nathan (b. 1868) and Rosalie (b. 1873). Nathan Vos' will (proved 6th May 1914 in London) left his estate, with Effects of £1,765, to his son John Blower Vos, Hotel Keeper. The will also contains conditions transferring the whole of his estate to the four children, from Mary, should she enter into a "second marriage". This standardised term could be read as "further" or "subsequent", and may not mean that her marriage to Nathan Vos was her first. In her own will (proved 7th May 1914 in London) she left her estate, with effects of £3,209, to John Blower, Licensed Victualler, and Walter Ainsworth Stevens, Meat Purveyor.

Plan of Falmouth Jewish Cemetery

Row 1.   1 2 3 4 5* 6 7*   8* 9* 10* 11*

2.   1*   2* 3 4 5* 6* 7* 8* 9* 10* 11*   12*

3. 1 2 3 4 5 6* 7* 8 9* 10* 11   12   13*

4. 1 2   3 4   5 6 7 8   9   10

5. 1 2   3 4 5

6. 1* 2

This burial ground has been maintained on an irregular basis over the last 130 years or so. Many stones have been displaced or lost. Some may have been buried beneath the grass, and later re-appeared, because surveys have noted stones not included in earlier surveys, and noted the loss of stones once present. Some headstones have been broken and damaged. * The asterisk marks the location of graves either unmarked, without a headstone, or marked with a damaged, displaced, or illegible headstone (1998-2000). Since this plan was drawn up, some other headstones have been displaced or damaged. The plan above represents the original location of the headstones, and does not reflect any recent changes to location or condition.

53 graves
33 graves with headstones.

(iv)
Penzance

Hidden in a triangle of back alleys in the heart of Penzance lies the Jewish cemetery. It is situated in a locked, enclosed and secure location, devoid of invasive trees and in a traffic-free location. Apart from the loss of its earliest headstones, it is one of the best preserved walled Jewish cemeteries from the Georgian period, and is regarded as the finest of the 25 from this period outside London. Unlike the Falmouth burial ground, it has not weathered with time. Most of the tombstones remain intact and the writing on most of them is as clear as the day that they were erected.

Jews first came to Penzance from the Rhineland area of Germany and from Holland in the early part of the 18th century, possibly around the 1720s, and at least by the 1740s. The size of the Jewish population of the town at this time is unknown, and, because the first synagogue was not built until 1768, their arrangements for worship would most likely have taken place in private houses. Because settlement would not have been viable without a separate Jewish burial ground, steps must have been taken to secure a plot for this purpose very early on. The Cornish historian and author of the official History of Penzance, Peter Pool, assumed in 1974 that there had been a Jewish burial ground earlier than the present site at Leskinnick, and that it had been located some distance from it in the Rosevean area of the town. He had drawn this conclusion from what appeared to him may have been a burial ground from a field name in a document of 1837 held in private possession.[91] At this time, an enclosed or clearly delineated plot set aside for some form of exclusive usage, or indicating the holdings of some party such as the freeholder or leaseholder, were sometimes indicated on tithe maps as a *gue*, from the Cornish word *gew* "an enclosure". The tithe maps relating to the putative Truro Jewish cemetery (see later) have this notation. Today, there is still a relatively self-contained enclave of cottages, nestling between higher ground and the harbour front, in the port of Porthleven, only a few miles from Penzance, that carries the address of *The Gue* or, in Cornish, *An Gew*, and in Marazion, on the main entrance road to Penzance, a large detached house enclosed in its own grounds also carries the name *The Gew*. It is clearly not possible to know with any certainty if the letter *g* in *gew* would have been pronounced as a hard consonant, as in "get", or as a soft consonant, as in "generous". If the latter was, or tended to be the case, then the potential for its meaning to be confused with the English *Jew* becomes obvious. By 1994 Pool had come to doubt that the 1837 map indicated a Jewish cemetery, in that the *gue* ground shown on it could have been understood simply to mean an enclosed area, rather than indicating a *jew* ground, and so he concluded that the Leskinnick cemetery was the only one that had been established and used by the historic Jewish community.[92] Certainly no evidence from old maps or records or leases has so far come to light to substantiate the existence of the "Rosevean cemetery" conclusively, and there are no visual signs today of what could have been a burial ground in the area.

It is likely that a plot of unenclosed land in or on the periphery of virgin fields in the Leskinnick area of the town was acquired (possibly by lease[93]) for a cemetery just before or around the 1740s. If formal leases were issued, they have so far not been identified. Indeed, they may not have been issued at all, in that in the 18th century, as we have seen with regard to Penryn, it was considered doubtful if Jews were legally entitled to possess land on any formal basis. Arrangements for Jews to use or rent land were, therefore, often informal, although these could in some instances be formalised with the passage of time. Non-Jews could take out leases on behalf of Jews, and Jews with some influence or standing with local landowners might succeed in acquiring the grant of a lease on this, or on some other basis. In Plymouth, a private garden on The Hoe was used for Jewish burials from about 1744, being expanded in 1758, when its use was officially declared on the lease that was purchased by three prominent London Jewish merchants. It would appear that at no time was there a formal application for permission to establish a Jews' cemetery in Plymouth, and it was not until 1811 that the land was formally conveyed to three Jews, but with a Christian, John Saunders "Gentleman" underwriting the contract by countersigning as an additional lessee. Presumably, his signature was deemed necessary in the event that the three Jews were found to be ineligible to hold land. It is of interest that the earliest known leases for the Penzance cemetery also date from the same time, from 1810, but that no Christian signatory was employed. This could well indicate a more liberal, tolerant and progressive approach in Penzance to the leasing of land to Jews, although the fact that the original freeholder of the land was a Canon of the Anglican church, and that another Christian minister acted as an intermediary with regard to sub-leases, may have been seen as conferring a degree of legal security upon the transactions.

Sadly, most of what can be presumed to be the very the earliest graves in the cemetery, located as they are in a small area that would have comprised the plot for the original burial ground (not at that time enclosed by a wall) have lost their headstones and remain unmarked. The earliest dated headstone, in the form of an anonymous fragment, comes from 1791,[94] but the surrounding unmarked graves, of which there are a number, can reasonably be presumed to predate this, perhaps by several decades, or at the very least to be contemporaneous. The same principle can be applied to the Penryn cemetery, and to others [95]. The phenomenon of unmarked graves pre-dating the earliest surviving headstone is a common feature of burial grounds from this period. The Plymouth Jewish cemetery was being used by 1750, but the oldest tombstone is dated 1776, and in Exeter, the cemetery was opened in 1757, but the oldest decipherable headstone is dated 1807. It would seem axiomatic, therefore, that the Penzance cemetery would have been used for burials before 1791, and this consideration would tend to confirm Pool's suspicions (of 1994) that there would not have been an earlier cemetery. Moreover, whilst the earliest identified headstone is from 1823 (that of Solomon Zalman) there are a number of Jews who died, or are likely to have died in Penzance, who would have been interred in the cemetery before 1791. The official genealogy of the Hart family[96] suggests that Abraham Hart (Solomon Lazarus) had come to Penzance as early as *c.* 1720, and that he died in the town on 3rd July 1784. It is not known if his father, Asher Hart, who died around 1745-1752, his mother (whose name is not known)· or his brothers, who included Lazarus (-1741), Elhanan (-1776) and Zalman, or Salman (-1779) also came to Penzance, but this possibility cannot be discounted. Salman Hart may have been the father of the Solomon Zalman (-1823) who is buried in the cemetery. Whilst the latter's headstone gives him as the son of Jacob Segal, the latter name is a variant of Solomon, and Abraham Hart was also known by this name. It is not known if *Jacob* was an element in his patronymic. Clearly, it can be assumed that Abraham Hart's (unidentified) wife lived in the town, and, although there is only explicit documentary evidence of Abraham Hart's son, Eleazar (Lazarus) Hart (1739-1803), trading in Penzance, he also had five siblings, Mordecai (1736-), Madel (1743-), Edel (1747-), Anna (1750-) and Lemel (1755-), all of whom are likely to have lived in, and at least some of whom may have died in Penzance, together with their spouses. Eleazar Hart's daughter-in-law (his son, Lemon Hart's first wife) Letitia Michael of Swansea [- 1803] died in Penzance, and, presumably, so did Lazarus Jacobs (d. *circa* 1809), the first husband of Lemon Hart's sister, Rebecca. A Solomon Jacobs[97], who died in Penzance in 1803, will also be buried in the cemetery. The cemetery will also contain the unmarked graves of a number of infants.

It is not surprising that the early Jewish settlers were concerned to have their own burial ground, and the fact that by the 1760s the Jewish community was size-able enough to contemplate the acquisition of its first purpose-built synagogue of 1768, in itself suggests that burials would have taken place well before 1791. Around the late 1700s or early 1800s, the freehold of the cemetery land was acquired by Canon John Rogers[98] who owned land and estates at Treassowe in Ludgvan, near Penzance, and at Penrose in Sithney near Helston. He also owned the Leskinnick and Lescudjack areas of Penzance. At a time when the value of arable land and woodland was falling, and the population of towns such as Penzance, with its rapidly expanding fishing, mining and maritime trade, was increasing and attracting new settlement, the leasing of plots for new building became a lucrative business. Before this process began in earnest, however, the Jews had successfully established a small burial ground in the Leskinnick area of the town, and were eventually taking steps to plan its eventual enclosure.

The cemetery lay on a boundary which divided land owned by Canon Rogers and land owned by the Barham family. Thomas Foster Barham (1766-1844) of Leskinnick, came to Penzance in 1806. His son, whose full name was identical to that of his father, Thomas Foster Barham (1794-1869), practised as a doctor in Exeter. Barham, the father, appears to have come into possession of land to the West and South of Leskinnick, which would have been passed to his son, who by 1834, had bought a further field from Canon Rogers. It was this Dr. Barham whose generosity enabled the Jews to complete their enlargement of the burial ground in 1844, by "ceding his rights in a contiguous strip which they required".[99] The devel-opment of the burial ground took place, therefore, in stages, and it would seem that, with each stage, some form of extended enclosure became necessary.

From 1808, when the congregation's detailed Minutes and Accounts begin, it is possible to trace the cemetery's development with some certainty. In 1808, the Jews were paying an annual rent of one guinea for the cemetery. On 31st March 1810, a "three life" lease for 99 years was granted to Lemon Hart by Canon Rogers at a rent of three guineas, which would not begin until Mary (Tyeth) Borlase died. Mary Borlase, who was to die in 1822, was the wife of Walter Borlase (1727-) of Penzance. Their daughter, also named Mary (1766-1849) married the Rev. John Foxell (1777-1852) who had come to Penzance in 1804, and was the town's Congre-gationalist minister until 1852, and Librarian of the Penzance Library from 1822 to 1852.[100] Foxell, like other Congregational ministers lodged with the Pidwell family,[101] whose members attended either the Anglican Church of St. Mary's or the Congregational Chapel in Market Jew Street. St. Mary's church was in the same locality as property known to have been held by (and possibly the family house of) Lemon Hart. Much later, in London, Lemon Hart's son, David (1799-1868) was to marry Mary Pidwell (1811-1894) a daughter of Thomas Pidwell (1778-1848) and Elizabeth Davies Edwards (-1855). From 1810 to 1822, the Jews continued to pay one guinea a year to "Mr. Foxhole" (*sic.*) who, as Mary Borlase's son-in-law, acted on her behalf in the matter of rent due to her. At this stage the "Jews Burying Field" consisted of the wedge-shaped plot (roughly row 3 on the plan) which has the oldest, anonymous graves. It has been noted that it is of particular interest that, unlike the situation in Plymouth in 1811, the 1810 Rogers lease, together with all of the subsequent leases were granted solely to Jews from the Penzance congregation, and were not subject to any condition to include a Christian countersignatory as guarantor lessee. The negotiations for the congregation's leases from 1811 to 1844 were also conducted solely by two Jews, Lemon Woolf and Henry Joseph. The 1810 lease was, however, overseen by the congregation's solicitors, Borlase and Scott, and the congregation's various leases to the synagogue and burial ground were deposited for security with local banks. By 1845 they were with the Union Bank, and by 1881 they were held at the Bolitho Bank.[102]

The 1810 Rogers lease reflects the practice that Landowners and Landlords would often grant leases for a period of 99 years, calculated as likely to end on the death of the last of three "lives". The tenant could name each of these "lives", for example, by picking three people known to him personally, such as a member of his family. It would seem that Walter Borlase held a lease from the Rogers family to a part of the Leskinnick area,[103] and nominated his wife Mary as one of the "lives". It was most likely a small section of this leased ground that the Jews obtained from the Borlase Estate as a sub-lease to establish their cemetery around 1750 or soon after. The new lease of 1810, however, was agreed directly with the Rogers family, and the congregation's accounts for 17th November 1810 record that the sum of 7 Guineas was paid to "Borlase & Scott for new lease of Burying Ground". In 1811 the Jews agreed to build a new wall around the cemetery "when the present lease or old life drops off", and to begin building when Mary died. In the synagogue records there is a note dated 14th April 1811 to the effect that a sum of 35 pounds, ten shillings, and eleven and a half pence had been put aside on deposit at 5% towards this eventual purpose, with any outstanding balance of the cost to be returned for the benefit of the congregation. By the end of 1815 this wall must have been completed, in that the accounts for 7th October that year record that the sum of £1. 14s. 4d. was paid to "Harvey" (the local carpenter regularly employed by the congregation) "for Door of Burial Ground". (This door may have been in a different location to the present one).

In 1823 the Jewish congregation paid Foxell rent of 7 shillings and 3 pence for the period up to the death of Mary Borlase, in August 1822. From then on their payments were direct to the Rogers estate, and by 1825 they paid a Mr. Dobb, presumably Rogers' agent, £1. 18s. for the period from August 1822 to March 1823, plus two full years of 3 guineas each, to March 1825. In 1827, the Congregation had to pay rental arrears in court for the difference between what they had paid, and the new rental, dating from Mary Borlase's death (1822). By this time the whole area around the cemetery had become known as the "Jews' Fields", lying on a gentle gradient falling towards the sea. In 1834 a meadow, called the Jews Field, together with the (higher) part of "Lower Jews Field" (probably in the area of rows 5 to 8 on the plan) was sold by Canon Rogers to Thomas Foster Barham (the younger). At this stage the Jewish cemetery was bounded to the West and South by Barham lands, further to the West and to the East and North by Rogers lands, and also to the South by lands held by Francis Paynter. On 13th August 1835 Canon Rogers granted a 99 year lease, to begin from 24th June, to Richard Rowe, a mason, to build a house on "...part of the Jews Burial Ground" (near row 3). In 1838 and 1841, Rogers agreed to the further development of Leskinnick Terrace (which subsequently became known locally as "Jerusalem Row"), and granted building leases for plots in the "Higher Jews Burial Ground Field" (near rows 1 and 2). The Congregation's New Regulations of 1844 indicate that this "High ground" was reserved for "privileged members" (*baal* batim, permanent paying seat-holders) and their wives "free of expence" (*sic.*). Their "children, parents, brothers and sisters" also received a "right of ground free of expence" in another section of the cemetery. This rule (No. 36) explains why husbands and wives are to be found alongside one another in this part of the cemetery, but other family members are interred elsewhere. Such reserved plots may exist in other parts of the cemetery, but the lack of space after enclosure and the passage of time would have limited the practice.

It is from 1841 that the cemetery first appears on a map, which clearly shows the burial ground in relation to adjacent properties.[104] To prevent the incursion of these various building projects, from late 1844 to early 1845, the Jews succeeded in negotiating the purchase of the freehold of the cemetery for fifty pounds (i.e. the whole area within rows 1 to 8 of the present ground). The process began with a release document dated 29th September 1844, that effectively renewed the congregation's lease to the "several plots or pieces of ground" that, as a whole, comprised the burial ground, and released it "in fee simple" of £50, as an "absolute purchase" and a conveyance into a freehold possession ("Inheritance"). Presumably the sale was either conditional upon the necessary completion of the ground's enclosure, and its complete separation from the track or road that lies adjacent to it, or it was assumed that such enclosure would take place. One of the "Trusts" or undertakings that applied to the new freeholders was that they should respect "a right of free passage over the said road to and from the said several plots of ground with horses, carts and carriages". This could suggest that the cemetery's plots had extended further west and north into and across the path of the road, and that the Congregation decided to relinquish potential usage of these extensions, drawing the cemetery's boundaries in by the construction of the wall, and so avoiding any intrusion into the cemetery by pedestrians, and "horses, carts and carriages" (the latter of a very small variety) which the narrow alleys, also known as "donkey tracks" came to accommodate. Certainly the land that comprised the burial ground was larger than its present size would suggest, although there is no evidence today that any burials took place outside its current perimeter.

Another salient condition of the conveyance was that Rogers reserved to himself and to his heirs any mineral rights to the burial ground, namely to "all mines, metals and minerals at any time hereafter to be found or gotten within or out of the said premises with liberty to enter and carry away the same." The conveyance incorporates previous leases to Lemon Hart, and, although it acknowledges that the ground had and would be used for burials, it does not appear to restrict the use of the land to that sole purpose, even though in Jewish religious practice it could and would only be used as such. Accordingly, Rogers states in the conveyance that he grants it "so long as (that is, for as long as) the said several plots or pieces and plots shall continue to be used as a burial ground for the people called Jews and from the time and when and as soon as the same shall be used for any other purpose whatsoever or shall cease to be used as such Burial Ground as aforesaid". This release of 1844 was negotiated by and granted to Lemon Woolf, "spirit merchant", and to Henry Joseph, "pawnbroker", "wardens of the congregation of the Jews of Penzance" as "The Jews burial ground, and adjoining triangular plots", in the presence of four named Gentile witnesses, Thos. P. Tyacke, John Pope, James Pascoe (likely the same monumental mason whose headstones in the cemetery, along with those by Scott and Angwin, are inscribed with the maker's name), and Reginald Rogers of Truro, Solicitor.

Subsequently, Henry Joseph made an application to the freeholder, Dr. Barham of Exeter, for another plot adjoining the burial ground, which he consented to present to the Jewish congregation as a gift. By July 1845, the entire perimeter of the ground had been enclosed with the completion of the building of a very substantial high wall, the work having been supervised by Henry Joseph. Over thirty years before this, as early as April 1811, the congregation had resolved to enclose the burial ground, and were allocating sums for this purpose. It seems likely that building work began in 1822, when, with the death of Mary Borlase, and as the 1810 Rogers lease agreement stipulated, the congregation would come into its possession. The congregation's minutes for 13th April 1845 record that "The burial ground having been purchased this quarter for the sum of £50", [the previous meeting having been in December of 1844] and notes that the deeds to the cemetery have been placed "at the Union Bank". On 6th July 1845, the minutes state that "The congregation having purchased the Fee Simple and Inheritance of the Burial Ground, Mr. H. Joseph made application to Dr. Barham of Exeter for a piece of ground adjoining it which he has kindly consented to give the Congregation". Crucially, these minutes presuppose that the burial ground was already enclosed (as it may have been for over twenty years) but that the gift of the additional strip of ground by Dr. Barham that year had made it "requisite to *rebuild part of the walls*" to incorporate this new portion, and that "the whole of the ground has been taken in & the walls rebuilt".

The foresight and wisdom of the congregation's plans from 1811 for the enclosure of the burial ground can be seen today, in that various buildings, originally a church school and community rooms, have encroached right up to the edge of the cemetery walls on two sides, and are only separated from houses on the other sides by a narrow pathway (one of the many "donkey tracks" used in the town for transport and the conveyance of goods).

These walls of 1845 were so well constructed that they remained intact until the 1940s. During the Second World War of 1939-1945, 867 German bombs fell in the Penzance area between 1940 and 1942: 16 people were killed, 48 houses were totally destroyed, 157 were seriously damaged,[105] but many more houses, almost 4000, received minor damage of some kind. One bomb destroyed part of the lower walls near the cemetery entrance, and also several headstones in the section of the cemetery which had been reserved by the Congregation for the Poor. Repairs were carried out, presumably by the Town Council or by the church authorities, to these damaged walls. The respect with which the cemetery was regarded at the time, especially in view of the fact that there had not been a Jewish community in the town for over fifty years, is reflected in the fact that the headstones that were damaged beyond repair were replaced with several miniature headstones.

They are in English script only (those of Solomon Teacher, 7:1; Catherine Levy, 7:2; and Joseph Barnet, 8:2). Further weakening to the walls may have resulted, and in the early 1990s several sections of the exterior-facing walls were substantially rebuilt.

Throughout the congregation's Minutes and Accounts from 1808, it is clear that the congregation were vigilant in their upkeep of both the synagogue and the burial ground, as the regular payments to numerous local tradesmen show. Builders were brought in for essential repairs to both. The synagogue building itself was insured. The early minutes of September to November 1810 record: "By half years insurance on Synagogue...8 shillings 9 pence." There are numerous such entries for ensuing years, and this may also have covered the cemetery as part of the congregation's property, as no separate insurance for the burial ground is specifically itemised. Frequent payments to local carpenters are mentioned, and their services would most likely have been used for the building of the simple coffins for burial. Builders may also have been employed to prepare the graves for burial. A groundsman for the cemetery, a Mr. Richards, was appointed as late as April 1891, at a point when the congregation, and its finances, were in decline. It is not known if the congregation employed a groundsman for the cemetery throughout the period from 1808-1892, nor if the position was a regular or an occasional one. It seems likely, however, that the George Foot who was "Retained at £2. 2s. per annum" in June of 1852, was the cemetery's caretaker. After the congregation's demise in 1906, and the last burial in 1911, arrangements for the cemetery's maintenance are unclear, although anecdotal evidence suggests that the Parish Church of St. John, and the Town or District Councils may have undertaken some supervision. Ground maintenance of the cemetery by individuals, including neighbouring residents of the parish also seems to have taken place. In the 1970s the custodian was a Mr. F. Potter who lived in Leskinnick Terrace.[106] The cemetery has continued to enjoy the voluntary (and unpaid) services of a permanent local custodian for over thirty years. Godfrey Simmons, a descendant of Rabbi B. A. Simmons, acted in this capacity for over twenty years and into the 1990s, after which, from 1997, the present writer has assumed this responsibility.

The cemetery contains forty nine identified headstones, many of which are in remarkably good condition with beautifully carved and elaborate Hebrew inscriptions, only five of which are decayed and unidentifiable. The last burials of members of the congregation were Bessie Joseph in 1900, and the family of the last Rabbi, Isaac Bischofswerder, who were interred between 1880 and 1911. There are two later graves not belonging to original members of the historic community, both from the late 1900s: that of Adolf Salzmann who may have been a refugee who had settled in Redruth, lies at the entrance in the front row, and behind it that of Dr. Arnold Levene of London (and Padstow), an internationally renowned specialist in skin cancer research. Despite the absence of a Jewish community in the town for almost a century, this walled Georgian cemetery is one of the finest surviving examples of the Anglo-Jewish heritage, and was listed by recommendation of English Heritage in 2004.[107] The listing, at Grade II, was applied to the entire boundary walls, and to four specific monuments (headstones), being the earliest (unidentified fragment) of 1791, and those of Solomon Zalman (1823), Judah ben

Moses (Levy Jacob, 1824) and Jacob James Hart (1846). All of the headstones in the cemetery are within the curtilage of listing, but since 2004, a number of other headstones have received a specific listing. The listing decision includes the observation that the cemetery "is thought to be the most complete Jewish cemetery outside London", and that "Of outstanding interest, is the rare survival of a *Bet Tohorah*" (cleansing house). The entrance porch, which may once have possessed a roof, contains a wedge shaped alcove to the right, which could accommodate a coffin, and where the original fireplace was most likely located. The latter feature is not itself visible, and may have been rendered into the wall after the cemetery's disuse. The body of the chapel itself was separated from the garden of the burial ground itself by a second door, and the appearance of the sides of walls suggest this. Along the side of two lengths of the listed walls, and along the numerous small alleys that dot the Leskinnick area, and other areas of the town, would have run the small *leats* or streams that ran through the valley, thus providing the cemetery with a source of fresh running water essential not only for hygienic purposes, but also for ritual cleansing.

A significant number of the headstones in the Penzance cemetery are of are a very fine quality both in respect of their engravature, which is sometimes very elaborate, and in the subtlety and refinement of the scholarship displayed in the composition of their Hebrew inscriptions which often effortlessly weave eulogistic formulae with scriptural quotation and reference. The latter features are frequently taken both from the Hebrew Bible and from traditional prayers, and the scholarship and skills to produce these particular inscriptions clearly existed within the Congregation itself. Some of these headstones represent some of the finest examples of their kind from this period.[108]

Headstone Transcriptions

ROW 1
reading from left to right

1. **LEMON WOOLF** (Asher, son of Hayyim: son of Hyman Woolf).

Died 9th Adar II 5608 (Tuesday 14th March 1848), aged 65 years.

Heb. Here lies a steadfast man, leader and guide who went in the ways of the good, strong like a lion, running like a deer (*Mishnah, Ethics of the Fathers* 5:24) to the sound of the Torah and prayers, evening and morning. His house was open wide (*Ethics of the Fathers* 1:5); he gave of his bread to the hungry. His body dwells with the holy ones who are in the earth, and his soul is in the garden of Eden. Our teacher, leader and guide, Asher the son of the leader of the community, Hayyim. Died 9th of Second Adar and was buried on the 10th 5608. May his soul be bound up in the bond of eternal life.

Eng. In memory of Lemon Woolf, aged 65 years.

Lemon Woolf [the son of Hyman Woolf and Eddle (Esther) Hart (5:5) the latter a daughter of Eleazar Hart, and a sister to Lemon Hart] was married to Rebecca Jacob, a daughter of Moses Jacob of Redruth (Fal. 2:9). He owned a wine and spirit business in Market Jew Street and another in Chapel Street. He may have occupied other premises (possibly in Causewayhead) as a pawnbroker. Lemon Woolf's sister, Hannah (Hindele: 1:10) married Aaron Selig (1:11) of Penzance. After Lemon Woolf's death, Rebecca Woolf went to live in Plymouth, where she is buried, and where several of her daughters had settled.

2. **HANNAH LEVY** (or Elra Joseph: Hendele, daughter of Issachar Jacob).

Died 28th Cheshvan 5612 (Saturday/Sunday 22nd/23rd November 1851), aged 82 years.

Heb. Here lies a woman of worth (Proverbs 31:10), the righteousness of the Lord she did. She perceived that her earnings were good (Proverbs 31:18); she was humble like a bee; her deeds were pleasant; the daughter of the king is all glorious within (Psalms 45:14), she the wise woman whose soul went up to the heights; she went on the straight path all her life; she kept the commandments of the Lord. Hendela the daughter of Issachar Jacob. She died on Saturday night, 28th Cheshvan and was buried on Tuesday, the eve of the New Moon of Kislev 5612. May her soul be bound up in the bond of eternal life.

The daughter of Barnet Levy of Falmouth (Issachar Jacob; Fal. 1:4). She was the widow of Abraham Joseph of Falmouth (Fal. 3:5). Her son Henry is buried in 6:5. This Hannah Levy should not be confused with Hannah Levy (nee Moses) of 5:1.

3. **ISRAEL LEVIN** (Israel, son of Zvi).

Died 9th Nisan 5647 (Sunday 3rd April 1887), aged 58 years.[109]

Heb. To the memory of Israel the son of Zvi. Died 9th Nisan 5647. Israel to the cradle of the Lord. And Israel did valiantly (Numbers 24:18). May his soul be bound up in the bond of eternal life.

Eng. Sacred to the memory of Israel Levin who died April 3rd 1887, aged 58 years. May eternal happiness be his portion.

Israel Levin was a contributor to the Penzance Dispensary (established in 1809) which was to become the forerunner of the Hospital (founded 1874). He continued his father's jewellery business at 102 Market Jew Street. He was also a Freemason, and Master of the Penzance Lodge, and President of the Hebrew Congregation.

He was the son of Henry (1:5) and Julia Levin (1:4). He died at 8, The Terrace. Note: he should not be confused with Israel Levy of Truro (Fal. 3:11).

4. **JULIA LEVIN** (Yuta, daughter of Israel).

Died 12th Tishri 5640 (Monday 29th September 1879), aged 87 years.[110]

Heb. Here lies a woman of worth. Her name - Yota the daughter of Israel. She died 12th Tishri 5640. May her soul be bound up in the bond of eternal life.

Eng. Sacred to the memory of Julia, relict of Henry Levin, who departed this life September 29th 1879, 5640, aged 87 years. Faithful to every duty of life, she is gone to receive her reward.

Julia was the widow of Henry Levin, and likely a daughter of Israel Levy of Truro.

5. **HENRY (Hyman) LEVIN** (Zvi, son of Yekutiel).

Died 12th Cheshvan 5638 (Friday 19th October 1877), aged 79 years.[111]

Heb. Here lies a man who in his active life chose righteousness and uprightness. His soul is bound up in the bond of eternal life. May his rest be with the righteous of the world. His Honour Rabbi[112] Zvi, the son of his Honour Rabbi Yekutiel. He was gathered to his People on the eve of Sabbath 12th Cheshvan and was buried on Monday 15th 5638. 79 years old. May his soul be bound up in the bond of eternal life.

Eng. Sacred to the memory of Henry Levin, who departed this life Friday October 19th 1877, 5638 in the 79th year of his age. Piety, faith and charity marked his pilgrimage on earth; may God in heaven grant him his due reward. His memory will ever be cherished and revered by his children.

The 1871 Census records that Henry Levin (1798-1877), a general dealer at 102 Market Jew Street, was from Stockholm. He had married Julia (1792-1879) of Truro (1:4). Her family and surname have not been identified with certainty. If Henry Levin was not a son of Israel Levy of Truro, it is possible that this Julia was another (unrecorded) daughter of his. Julia's birth year practically coincides with that of Israel Levy's daughter, Judith (*c.*1793) assumed to have been unmarried. It remains uncertain if Judith and Julia were connected in any way, or if they can be taken as one and the same. Henry and Julia Levin's children were Mathilda (1826-), Alexander (1828-1891) and Israel (1829-1887: 1:3). Their two sons, David (1833-1873) and Hyman (1830-1844) are buried in 5:7 and 5:8. Genealogical records[113] do suggest that a Henry *Levy* (no dates) was a son of Israel Levy (-1824) of Truro. The dates of this Henry Levy's siblings would be consistent with his birth year being *c.*1798.

415

The Penzance congregational Minute Books show that for Henry Levin, and for others, the surname was freely alternated as *Levy, Levi, Levin* and *Lavin*. The same Minute records show that Israel Levy of Truro subscribed to the Penzance congregation, and although he is buried in Falmouth (3:11), other members of his family are buried in Penzance, including his wife Hannah Moses (5:1), and his daughters Sarah (1:9), Elizabeth (1:6) and Catherine ("Kitty", 7:2). Israel Levy of Truro, however, is not known to have originated from Stockholm. Henry Levin's family may have originated from Germany, in that the first Jew to be granted the right to live in Stockholm in 1775, founding the Jewish congregation there in 1782, was an Aaron Isaac from Germany. Henry Levin served as President of the Penzance congregation for five terms between 1848 and 1877.

6. **ELIZABETH OPPENHEIM** (Beila, daughter of Israel).

Died 23rd Tammuz 5639 (Monday 14th July 1879), aged 81 years.

Heb. Here lies a cherished and important woman, Beila the daughter of Israel. She died on Monday, 23rd Tammuz 5639. She trod in the paths of uprightness all her days. Her soul has gone to God in heaven. May her soul be bound up in the bond of eternal life.

Eng. In affectionate remembrance of Elizabeth relict of the late Samuel Oppenheim who died on Monday July 14th 1879, 5639 in her 81st year. May all happiness be her portion.

Elizabeth Oppenheim was a daughter of Israel Levy (Fal. 3:11) and Hannah Moses (Pz. 5:1). She was the widow of Samuel Oppenheim.

7. **SAMUEL OPPENHEIM** (Samuel, son of Nathan).

Died 13th Sivan 5629* (Sunday 23rd May 1869), aged 69 years.

Heb. Here lies an honest and upright man. Samuel the son of Nathan, of blessed memory. He died on Sunday 13th Sivan 5629, aged 69. In his life and in his death he trusted in the loving kindness of his Father. In the courtyards of his God he will flourish for ever like a palm-tree (Psalm 92:13). May his soul be bound up in the bond of eternal life.

Eng. In affectionate remembrance of Samuel Oppenheim who died on Sunday May 23rd [114] 1869, 5630*, aged 69 years. May all happiness be his portion.

*Note: The Hebrew year is given correctly as 5629 in the Hebrew script, but is given incorrectly as 5630 on the headstone in English.

Samuel Oppenheim, as mentioned in the section on Penzance Trades, was a prosperous, bourgeois businessman who ran a family furniture and general household stores on the Terrace (opposite the present-day Humphry Davy statue). The business was continued by his only child, his son, Israel. Samuel Oppenheim died as the result of a burst blood vessel whilst in the Royal Baths on Penzance Promenade, and his death was recorded in *The Jewish Chronicle,* on June 4th 1869.[115]

8. BARNETT ASHER SIMMONS (Abraham Issachar, son of Asher).

Died 4 Kislev 5621 (Sunday 18th November 1860) aged 76 years.

Heb. "And Abraham died in good old age" (Gen 25:8).."this pile is witness and this tombstone is witness" (Gen. 31:51). Here lies a man true in spirit and fearing heaven; pure in heart and clean of hands. His honour, Rabbi Abraham Issachar the son of Asher of blessed memory, Cantor and Shochet, and Mohel. Died on Sunday 4th Kislev and was buried on Tuesday 6th 5621. Abraham returned to his place. There is a good reward for his deeds (*a play on his name - Issachar is split into two words - "there is" and "reward"*). (The son of) 77 years old. He was gathered to his people. Happy is he in his rest in the Garden of Eden (*"Happy is he" is a play on his father's name, Asher. Therefore the complete name is shown by quotations*). May his soul be bound up in the bond of eternal life.

Eng. B. A. Simmons died 4th Kislev 5621.

Barnett Asher Simmons served, intermittently, as rabbi and *shochet* in Penzance (from 1811 to 1859) and he was the County's longest-resident rabbi. He married Flora Jacob, a daughter of Moses Jacob of Redruth (Fal. 2:9). They had 11 children.

9. SARAH (Sally) LEVY (Sarah, daughter of Israel) Mrs. Sarah Jacob.

Died 10th Iyar 5628 (Saturday 2nd May 1868) aged 84 years.

Heb. Here lies a modest woman Sarah the daughter of Israel. 84 years old. She died on Sabbath, 10th Iyar and was buried on the 12th 5628. May her soul be bound up in the bond of eternal life.

She was the daughter of Israel Levy of Truro (Fal. 3:1) and Hannah Moses (5:1), and the widow of Samuel Jacob (2:1), who was deaf. They had a daughter Betsey, a dressmaker, who was deaf and dumb, a problem which in one form or both, afflicted a number of Moses Jacob's descendents (3:1), and may have affected some of those from other families where there had been intermarriage with the Jacob family, such as Harris of Truro. This may explain why several of the Jacob and Harris females remained unmarried. Sarah's spinster sister, Catherine, is buried in 7:2.

10. HANNAH SELIG (Hindele, daughter of Hayyim).

Died 17th Tammuz 5607 (Thursday 1st July 1847) aged 68 years.

Heb. Here lies a woman of worth (Proverbs 31:10), she perceived that her earnings were good (Proverbs 31:18). Her soul went to on high. She performed the commandments of the Lord. Hindele the daughter of Hayyim, of blessed memory. She died 17th Tammuz and was buried on the 18th 5607. May her soul be bound up in the bond of eternal life.

Eng. Sacred to the memory of Hannah Selig who died July 1st 5607 aged 68.

Hannah was the daughter of Hyman Woolf (-1821) and the widow of Aaron Selig (1:11).

11. AARON SELIG (Aaron, son of Phineas).

Died the eve of New Moon Av 5601 (Sunday 18th July 1841) aged 59 years.

Heb. Here lies a man of integrity and generosity, who walked in the path of the good; his soul cleaved to the Lord, and he caused friends to enter into the covenant and circumcised them. Rev. (Hechaver) Aaron the son of Pinchas who died on the eve of the New Moon Av and was buried on the New Moon 5601. May his soul be bound up in the bond of eternal life.

Eng. Sacred to the memory of Aaron Selig who died on 18th day of July 5601, aged 59 years. In life beloved, in death deeply regretted.

The honorary title given to Aaron Selig, that of *Hechaver*, suggests a man with some rabbinical knowledge, sufficient to act as its minister, and the congregational records indicate that as *Rav Aaron* he was employed from May 1811 to October the same year as *chazan* and *shochet*. Aaron Selig was by trade a watchmaker and jeweller. As a leading member of the congregation, his relations with them were fractious. He was married to Hannah Woolf (1:10). Their son, Benjamin, was also a watchmaker. After his parents had died, he emigrated to Australia in 1854 with his wife Catherine and their children, Aaron and Lemon. By 1872, he was Reader (minister) of the Wellington Hebrew Congregation in New Zealand.[116]

ROW 2

1. SAMUEL JACOB (Samuel, son of Moses).

Died 16th Kislev 5621 (Friday 30th November 1860) aged 83 years.

Heb. Here lies a perfect and upright man in his deeds, fearing his God, righteous in his faith. Samuel the son of Moses, peace be upon him. 83 years old. He died on the eve of Sabbath 16th Kislev and was buried with a good name on the same day. May his soul be bound up in the bond of eternal life.

Eng. Samuel Jacob died November 30th 5621, aged 83 years. He who pursues the way of righteousness will repose peaceably in the tomb.

Note: The 16th Kislev refers to the Friday *eve* of the Sabbath.

Samuel Jacob (1778-1860) was the second son of Moses Jacob of Redruth (Fal. 2:9). He was married to Sarah ["Betsy" or "Sally"] Levy (1784-1868:1:9) in Truro on 16th June 1813. The couple had lived in Hayle before they settled in Penzance. The births of their seven children as recorded by the Jacob family[117] were: Phoebe (1814-), Moses (1816-), Amelia (1817-), Catherine (1820-) Henry (1822-),[118] Elizabeth (1824-) and Phoebe (*c.*1827/9-).

2. Rev. HYMAN GREENBERG (Samuel Hillman: son of Simeon Greenberg).

Died 27th Nisan 5621 (late Saturday 6th April 1861), aged 24 years. Buried early 7th April (still Nisan 27th).

Heb. Here lies the man great in wisdom. His sun speedily set, hastening to evening. His tender shoot soon withered. 24 years old. God will guard him. He died with a good name on Saturday evening and was buried the next day, Sunday 27th Nisan 5621. Our teacher Rabbi Samuel Hillman the son of our honoured Master and Teacher Rabbi Simeon Greenberg. May his soul be bound up in the bond of eternal life.

Eng. Rev. H. Greenberg died 7th April 5621, aged 24 years.

Note: 27th Nisan is counted here as beginning on the Saturday night, with his burial early the next (secular) day Sunday 7th April.

A young man, possibly a recent immigrant. He may have been without trade, except some religious (Talmudic) knowledge and was therefore briefly employed by the community between 1859 and his untimely death in 1861. The 1861 Census records the death of "...a Jewish Rabbi....between the day of delivery and the day of the collection of the [census] schedule..." as a former occupant of 56 Adelaide Street. There is no mention of his family, and he appeared to live in only a part of the property. The mention of his father Rabbi Simeon Greenberg would seem to imply that he also had occupied some position in the congregation, although he is never mentioned in the Minute-Book, and there is no grave marked with his name in the cemetery.

3. **SOLOMON EZEKIEL** (Isaac, son of Ezekiel).

Died 2nd Adar II 5627 (Saturday 9th March 1867).

Heb. Here lies Isaac the son of Ezekiel. Died on Sabbath 2nd Adar II and was buried on the 4th 5627. May his soul be bound up in the bond of eternal life.

Eng. Solomon Ezekiel died March 9th 5627 (1867).

He was from an Ezekiel family of Devon, where he was born *c.*1781-6.[119] By 1811 he had moved to Falmouth, and to Penzance in 1813-14. He suffered bankruptcy, in 1815 and was imprisoned for debt at Bodmin. He was married to Hannah Jacob (3:2). Their only child, Eli (1817-1844) is buried in 6:2. Solomon Ezekiel was very active in the civil and cultural life of the town. He was also a Freemason.

Note: It can be seen that his headstone does not give either his year of birth or his age at the time of his death, which could imply that these precise details were uncertain.

ROW 3

1. **AMELIA JACOB** (Mirele, daughter of Moses).

Died 22nd Ellul 5624 (Friday 23rd September 1864) aged 70.

Heb. Here lies the spinster Mirele daughter of Moses. 79 years old. She died on 22nd Ellul 5624 and was buried on the 24th.

Eng. Amelia Jacob died September 23rd 5624, 1864 aged 70 years.

Note: The English inscription reads aged 70 years at the time of her death, but the Hebrew translates as 79 years, with a phrase which may mean "see age below". That she was a deaf mute may have led to uncertainty, and she may have maintained that she was a different age than that held by her sister, Flora, with whom she may have lived. She was, therefore, born either around 1785 or 1794. At least three of Moses Jacob's daughters were deaf mutes. Amelia remained unmarried. Her sister, Betsy, was also a spinster (Fal. 2:9). Their niece, also Betsy or Bessie, is buried in 7:5. Another unmarried niece, Selina, is buried in 4:3. This Amelia's niece, also called Amelia Jacob, is buried in 6:6 and was married to Henry Joseph (6:5).

2. **HANNAH JACOB** (Henne, daughter of Moses).

Died 29th Ellul 5624 (Friday 30th September 1864) aged 89.

Heb. Here lies the woman Hannah, the daughter of Moses. 89 years old. She died on Friday, 29ᵗʰ Ellul 5624.

Eng. Hannah the wife of Solomon Ezekiel, died Sept 30ᵗʰ 5624.

Hannah was another of Moses Jacob's daughters. She was the wife of Solomon Ezekiel (2:3). Mirele and Henne were granddaughters of Zender Falmouth (see also 5:1 below).

ROW 4

The first three graves in this row were all children of Henry Joseph (6:5) and Amelia Jacob (6:6)

1. **ABRAHAM JOSEPH** (Abraham, son of Zvi).

Died 22ⁿᵈ Sivan 5599 (Tuesday 4ᵗʰ June 1839) aged 5 years.

Heb. Here lies a delightful boy, charming and pleasant. The boy Abraham the son of Zvi who died on 22ⁿᵈ Sivan and was buried on Sabbath eve 25th 5599. May his soul be bound up in the bond of eternal life.

Eng. Abraham Joseph died June 4ᵗʰ 5599.

2. **SAMUEL JOSEPH** (Samuel, son of Zvi).

Died 29ᵗʰ Tishri 5605 (Saturday 12ᵗʰ October 1844), aged 5 months.

Heb. Here lies the boy Samuel the son of Zvi. May his soul be bound up in the bond of eternal life.

Eng. Samuel Joseph, Oct 12ᵗʰ 1844 aged 5 months.

Abraham and Samuel Joseph were sons of Henry Joseph (6:5).

3. **SELINA (Sarah) JOSEPH** (Sarah, daughter of Zvi).

Died 12ᵗʰ Ellul 5632 (Sunday 15ᵗʰ September 1872), aged 37 years.

Heb. Here lies the spinster, delightful and pleasant in her deeds; she found favour in the eyes of God and man, and in the eyes of all who saw (her). Hayye Sarah daughter of the important, honoured Master and Teacher Zvi, leader of our

421

community. She died on Sunday and was buried on Monday 13th Ellul 5632. May her soul be bound up in the bond of eternal life.

Eng. In affectionate memory of Selina Joseph who died on Sunday September 15th 5632, 1872, aged 37 years. The memory of the Just is blessed.

Selina Joseph was an unmarried daughter of Henry Joseph (6:5) and Amelia Jacob (6:6).

4. LEVY JACOB (Judah ben Moses).

Died 9 Ellul 5584 (Thursday 2nd September 1824).

Heb. Here lies a man upright in his generosity who went in the way of the good; his body will sleep in the ground but his soul was summoned to the Garden of Eden. He devoted himself to the living God. Yehuda the son of Moses who died on Thursday, 9th Ellul and was buried on Sabbath eve, 5584. May his soul be bound up in the bond of eternal life.

(Moses) Levy Jacob (1788-) was a son of Moses Jacob of Redruth, and like his father, was a watch and clockmaker, and he traded in Penzance. He was married to Sophia Mordecai (1781-1853), a daughter of Moses Mordecai, Silversmith and Engraver of Exeter. After her husband's death, Sophia traded as a clothes dealer in Penzance, later returning to her family in Devon. The death of Levy Jacob was recorded in the *Exeter Flying Post* on 9th September 1824.[120]

<u>4 unidentified headstones</u>

(a) *Heb.* Here lies a woman of worth.

(b) *Heb.* Bu(ried) on Sunday, 25th Shevat 5551. (Sunday 30th January 1791[121]).

Note: This is the earliest dated grave. In view of the fact that a number of adjacent graves are unmarked, it can reasonably be supposed that they are even earlier, possibly by several decades. This could suggest that Jewish settlement in Penzance was underway by the 1740s, and it may mean that some Jews had settled in the town before the establishment of the Falmouth community. It has been mentioned these early unmarked graves would cast doubt on the assumption that there had been an earlier Jewish cemetery at Rosevean, north of Leskinnick.

(c) *Heb.* A man upright in his generosity who went in the way of the good.........son of our honoured Master and Teacher, Rabbi Abraham... and was buried on Thursday, 19th Tishri 5583 (4th October 1822). May his soul be bound up in the bond of eternal life.

This may be a son of Abraham Hart who died in 1784. Three of his sons were Mordechai (1736-), Madel (1743-) and Lemel (1755-).

(d) *Hb.* ....the daughter who (was born) 25th Ellul .... (year?). She died on .... 21 Kislev 5556... (Tuesday 3rd December 1795) ..... Sabbath and he was buried......Kislev 5557 ...(December (1796). May their soul be bound up in the bond of eternal life.

This stone has at least two inscriptions for a male and female who died within a year of one another. Although this may be a husband and wife, surviving fragments suggest a pair of small headstones, and so these graves may be those of children, a brother and sister.

ROW 5

1. **HANNAH MOSES** (Henne, daughter of Moses) Mrs. Hannah Levy.

Died 2nd day of Pesach 5601 (Wednesday 7th April 1841) Aged 83 years.

Heb. Here lies a pious woman Hannah, the wife of Israel of Truro, who died the 2nd day of Passover 5601. May her soul be bound up in the bond of eternal life.

"On the 7th instant, at Penzance, Mrs. Levi, relict of the late Mr. Israel Levi, of the town (i.e. Hannah) aged 83 years" (*West Briton* 16th April 1841). Hannah was a daughter of "Zender Falmouth" (Fal. 1:3) and the wife of Israel Levy of Truro who died in 1824 and was buried at Falmouth (Fal. 3:11). She may have moved to Penzance to live with a relative, most likely one her daughters Sarah (1:9), wife of Samuel Jacob, or Elizabeth (1:6) wife of Samuel Oppenheim. Hannah Moses' unmarried daughter, Catherine, is buried in 7:2.

Note: This Hannah Levy should not be confused with her namesake (1:2).

2. **PESSIA SIMMONS** (Pessia, daughter of Abraham).

Died 14 Marcheshvan 5593 (Saturday 10th November 1832).

Heb. Here lies a most beautiful virgin. Our daughters are as polished corner stones (Psalm 144:12) in a grave; your soul is in the Garden of Eden; she died in an epidemic. To be raised to life at the resurrection of the dead. Pessia the daughter of Abraham Issachar. She died and was buried on the Sabbath, 14th Marcheshvan 5593. May her soul be bound up in the bond of eternal life.

Pessia was a daughter of Rabbi B.A. Simmons (1:8). Like her relative Ruth (6:7: the girls were related through marriage) she became ill with cholera in the Great Epidemic of 1832 and they both died within 24 hours of one another. Because of emergency regulations, she was buried on the sabbath. Pessia and Ruth are the only known Jewish victims of this epidemic. Strangely, Pessia was not listed by B. A Simmons in his register of the births of his children. She was probably about 8 years old at the time of her death.

The Burial Register for St. Mary's Church, Penzance contains the names of 57 victims of the cholera epidemic for the period from September to November 1831. Pessia Simmons is not named on this list, although the name of Ruth Joseph "a Jewess", does appear.

3. JACOB JAMES HART (Jacob ben Solomon Levi).

Died 24th Shevat 5606 (19th February 1846) aged 62.

Heb. And the days drew nigh that Jacob must die and he called to his friend (based on Gen 7:29) and said: I will lie with my fathers and you shall bury me in their burying place, give thirty pounds to my sister, (or) for a plot. The grave of Jacob ben Solomon Ha-Levi, who died Sabbath eve* 24th Shevat and was buried on Thursday*, the first day of the New Moon of Adar 5606.

Note: There is an obvious error here* in that he is given as dying on the Friday, and being buried on the Thursday. As Friday 24th Shevat was in fact 20th February, it seems likely that he died on the Thursday evening (23rd Shevat) 19th February, and was buried the next day (24th Shevat) 20th February.

Eng. Sacred to the memory of Jacob James Hart, esq. Late her Britannic Majesty's Consul for the Kingdom of Saxony and a native of this town, who departed this life in London on 19th February AM (*Anno Mundi*) 5606, aged 62 years.

Jacob Isaac (James) "Hart" (1784-1846) is mentioned in Israel Solomon's *Records*. He was a son of Lemon Hart's sister, Rebecca (1766-1841) and Lazarus Isaac Jacobs. His younger brother, was Frederick (1790-1853), also known as Asher Laemle, or Lemon Jacobs, who married his first cousin, Rebecca Hart (1798-1874/6) [a daughter of Lemon Hart] as her second husband. Jacob Hart's sisters were Rosetta, who married Isaac Simons of Truro, and Letitia, who married a combmaker, Glickenstein. Jacob Hart was, therefore, originally called "Jacobs" and took his surname from his uncle Lemon Hart whilst working in the latter's wine business, which his brother also joined. Jacob Hart fell out with his uncle, Lemon, left the firm and lived abroad. He also became estranged from his family. Jacob Hart requested in his will that he should be buried in the Penzance cemetery. He died at his home at 19, Brook Street, Grosvenor Square.[122]

4. **SOLOMON ZALMAN** (son of Jacob Segal).

Died 10th Iyar 5583 (Monday 21st April 1823).
Heb. Here lies a man …He died Monday, and was buried …11th Iyar 5583. May his soul be bound up in the bond of eternal life. Solomon Zalman the son of Jacob Segal.

It has been suggested earlier that Solomon Zalman may have been a member of the Hart family, and he may be the Solomon Solomon who traded in Penzance as a silversmith in 1781. He is not known to have been connected with the Solomon family of Falmouth (see Falmouth cemetery 2:1; 1:10 & 4:8. Also 1:8; 3:3 & 4:7).

5. **HYMAN and EDDLE WOOLF**.

Eng. In memory of Hyman and Eddle Woolf, parents of Lemon Woolf. Erected by the late Henry Harris of Truro.

There is no Hebrew inscription or date

Hyman Woolf, was born *c.* 1732, and died on 23rd December 1820, age 88.[123] Genealogical records have usually given the year of his death as 1821, which may represent an error in computation from the Hebrew calendar. He was originally from Falmouth, and his father Benjamin Woolf was from Holland. Hyman Woolf was the second President of the Penzance congregation, taking over from Lemon Hart in 1811, and serving until 1820, although in his later years, his son, Lemon Woolf, signed the congregational minutes on his behalf. Hyman Woolf's wife, Eddle (Esther) was a daughter of Eleazar Lazarus) Hart (-1803) of Penzance. The year of Eddle Woolf's death is not known.

6. **EDIL** (daughter of Asher).

Died 2nd Sivan 5607 (Monday 17th May 1847).

Heb. Here lies a young unmarried girl Edil the daughter of Asher the leader and guide of the community, who died 2nd Sivan 5607. May her soul be bound up in the bond of eternal life.

Edil was probably a daughter of Asher ben Hayyim (Lemon Woolf, 1:1).

7. **DAVID LEVIN** (David, son of Zvi).

Died 10th Marcheshvan 5634 (Friday 31st October 1873), aged 40 years.

Heb. Here lies a perfect and upright God-fearing man. David the son of Zvi. He was gathered unto his people on the Sabbath eve, 10th Marcheshvan 5634. May his soul be bound up in the bond of eternal life.

Eng. Sacred to the memory of David Levin who died October 31st 1873.

8. **HYMAN LEVIN** (Hayyim, son of Zvi).

Died 2nd day New Moon Tammuz 5604 (Tuesday 18th June 1844), aged 13 years 3 months.

Heb. Here lies. O passer-by look and see! Here lies a delightful young man, on the good path, he walked until he reached 14 years of age. The young man Hayyim the son of Zvi who died on Tuesday the second day of the New Moon Tammuz, and was buried on Wednesday 5604. May his soul be bound up in the bond of eternal life.

Eng. Hyman Levin died June 18th 1844 aged 13 years & 3 months.

Hyman Levin's death was recorded in the *West Briton* on 21st June 1844, where his age was given as 14 years.[124] Hyman and David were the sons of Henry and Julia Levin (1:5 and 1:4 respectively).

ROW 6

1. **SOLOMON (Samuel) LEVY** (Phineas, son of Menachem).

Died 4th Ellul 5601 (late Friday 20th August 1841), aged 56.

Heb. Here lies an upright man. He went in the path of the good. A good heart to strengthen the hand of the poor and needy. All his deeds he performed fittingly, and the commandments of the Lord he observed with uprightness. Pinchas the son of Menachem. 56 years old. He died and was buried on 4th Ellul 5601. May his soul be bound up in the bond of eternal life.

Eng. In memory of Solomon Levy, a native of Exeter who died Aug 20th 5601, 1841, Aged 56 years. May his soul rest in peace.

Note: the 20th August was in fact 3rd Ellul, a Friday, the 4th Ellul being a Sabbath (Saturday 21st). He may have been buried after the ending of the Sabbath.

Solomon Levy was the son of a Menachem (Emanuel) Levy of Exeter. Although his death and burial are given as 20th August, his death certificate is dated 21st. His occupation of Optician, suggests that he was a hawker and lens-grinder. His death, by a "Visitation of God in a natural way", took place at St. Ives. He is not known to have been related to any other Levy family resident in Cornwall. His name does not appear in the 1841 census, and he is not mentioned by full name in the congregational Minute-Book, although "…Levy" does appear.

This Solomon (Samuel) Levy *ben Menachem* of Exeter should not be confused with the Solomon Levy *ben Joseph,* also of Exeter, who committed suicide in Bristol, also in 1841. The latter had married Arabella Joseph (1803-1897), daughter of Lyon Joseph (1775-1825) of Bath, formerly of Falmouth. The potential for confusion with *Levy* families in Devon and Cornwall is not helped by the fact that William Jessop, in his pedigrees, incorrectly combined and conflated the families of Solomon ben Joseph of Exeter with the unrelated family of Israel Levy of Truro. Also, the Solomon Levy buried here is unlikely to be identical to, and is not known to have been related to the Samuel Levi who traded as a Jeweller in High Street, Falmouth in 1841 (Census). Another Solomon Levy, General Shopkeeper, who may have been Jewish, traded in Southgate, Launceston, North Cornwall in 1830 (Pigot's Directory). With reference to Solomon Levy's Hebrew patronymic of *Phineas (Pinchas) son of Menachem,* the *Exeter Memorbuch* (which contains no dates) gives a *Rev Pinchas son of Rev Menachem,* and there is also a *Rev Menachem son of Rev Naphtali the Levite.* Whilst *Rev/Rav* may be an honorific title, it is possible that Solomon Levy was from a family of rabbis. There is a gap in the Penzance Minutes from 1829-1843, so it is not known if Solomon Levy (as Pinchas ben Menachem) was employed by the congregation as an incumbent. Altogether, in the *Exeter Memorbuch* and the Exeter Jewish cemetery there are about twenty further names, none of which can be connected to this Solomon Levy with any certainty. Amongst these are (Memorbuch): *Rev Menachem ben Yehudah, Rev Menachem ben Tzev the Levite, Rev Shimon ben Rev Menachem the Levite, "The boy Shmuel ben Menachem the Levite and his brother Yosef"* (presumably child deaths), "[The women]…*Sarah* (and) *Esther* (daughters of) *Rev Menachem, Rev Menachem ben Ya'akov, Rev Eliezer ben Menachem the Cohen and his wife*; and in the Cemetery: Elizabeth Levy (no date) wife of the late Emanuel Levy, Samuel Levy (1824), Moses Horovitz Levy (1834), Catherine Levy (1834) wife of Moses Levy, Juliet Levy (1826) wife of Gershon Levy (1822) of Guernsey, and one later grave of Jonas Levy (1884).

2. **ELIAS (ELI) EZEKIEL** (Eliezer, son of Isaac).

Died 14th Sivan 5604 (Saturday 1st June 1844).

Heb. Here lies the young man Eliezer the son of Isaac who died on the Sabbath, 14th Sivan 5604. May his soul be bound up in the bond of eternal life.

This is Elias (Eli) Ezekiel, the son of Solomon Isaac Ezekiel (2:3) and Hannah Jacob (3:2). Elias Ezekiel, who was an only child, was born in 1817, and was only 27 years old at the time of his death.

427

3. **MILLIE BISCHOFSWERDER** (Malka, daughter of David).

Died 23rd Av 5640 (Saturday 31st July 1880), aged 11 weeks.

Heb. Here lies the girl Malka the daughter of David, she died in her illness on the Sabbath day 23rd Av 5640. May her soul be bound up in the bond of eternal life.

Eng. In memory of Millie, daughter of David & Helena Bischofswerder who died July 31st 1880, aged 11 weeks.

Millie was the infant daughter of David and Helena Bischofswerder, who lost another young child called Sarah (7:4). She was the granddaughter of one of the last Cornish Rabbis, Isaac Bischofswerder (8:3).

4. **SHEVYA LEVY** (Shevya, daughter of Issachar Jacob).

Died 6th Adar 5610 (Monday 17th February 1850) aged 84 years.

Heb. Here lies a pious and upright woman, the righteousness of the Lord she did like our mother Sarah; the prayer of the Lord she prayed with devotion; she observed the commandments of the Lord in the house in which she dwelt. Shevya, the daughter of Issachar Jacob, who died and was buried on Monday, 6th Adar 5610. May her soul be bound up in the bond of eternal life.
Eng. Mrs. Elias relict of Mr Hart Elias of Falmouth, Feb 17th 1850, aged 84.

Shevya was the daughter of Barnet Levy of Falmouth (Fal. 1:4). She is mentioned in Israel Solomon's *Recollections*. She married her uncle Hart Elias in London. Her husband's business failed and they returned to Falmouth where Hart Elias was buried in 1835 (Fal. 3:8). Like Hannah Levy (5:1), she may have moved to Penzance to live with relatives.

5. **HENRY JOSEPH** (Zvi, son of Abraham).

Died 28th Kislev 5642 (Tuesday 20th December 1881), aged 75.

Heb. Here lies an upright man; Zvi the son of Abraham. He was gathered to his people on Tuesday, 28th Kislev 5642, 75 years old. May his soul be bound up in the bond of eternal life.

Eng. In loving memory of Henry Joseph of this town, born at Falmouth March 18th 1806, died DecR 20th 1881, 5642.

Henry Joseph was the son of Abraham Joseph (Fal. 3:5) and Hannah Levy (1:2 above). His mother came to live with him after she was widowed. He was married to Amelia Jacob (6:6). At least five of his twelve children are buried in the Penzance cemetery: Abraham (1834-1839 of 4:1); Selina or Sarah (1835-1872 of 4:3); Lionel (1840), who died young, and who may be buried in the cemetery in an unmarked grave; Samuel (1844-) who died at five months (4:2); Betsey (Elizabeth or Bessie of 7:5, 1848-1900) who was unmarried, and Julia (1851-1911 of 7:6) who married Morris (1856-1934) son of Rev. Isaac Bischofswerder. Henry Joseph was an influential member of the Hebrew Congregation, served as its President for seven terms between 1850 and 1881, and was directly involved in negotiations for the purchase of the freehold of the cemetery.

6. **AMELIA JACOB** (Mirele, daughter of Jacob): Mrs. Amelia Joseph.

Died 3rd Nisan 5651 (Saturday 11th April 1891) aged 80 years.

Heb. Here lies an upright woman, Mirele the daughter of Jacob, the wife of Zvi the son of Abraham. She was gathered to her people on the 3rd Nisan 5651. 80 years old.

Eng. In loving memory of Amelia, wife of Henry Joseph, born at Falmouth March 18th 1811, died April 11th 1891 aged 80 years.

Amelia was the granddaughter of Moses Jacob of Falmouth. Her parents were Jacob Jacob (Fal. 5:3) and Sarah Kate Simons (Fal. 5:2). She married Henry Joseph (6:5 above). The Amelia Jacob of 3:1 was her aunt.

7. **RUTH JOSEPH**.

Died 13 Marcheshvan 5593 (Friday 9th November 1832), aged 20.

Heb. All who pass by look on me, the praiseworthy spinster Ruth, 20 years old, the daughter of Joseph, son of Rabbi Abraham Isaac, leader and guide in the holy community of Plymouth. Her heart was fearful and perfect; a pure heart to strengthen the hand of the poor and needy to the best of her ability. She died in the epidemic at the time when God punished the inhabitants of the world in his anger. (She died) on the eve of Sabbath, 13th Marcheshvan 5593. May her soul be bound up in the bond of eternal life.

Ruth Joseph had been born in Plymouth on 13th October 1812. She was a daughter of Joseph Joseph (1766-1846), a former President (*c.* 1815) of the Plymouth Hebrew Congregation (he should not be confused with Fal. 1:5 or Fal. 2:8), and his wife Edal (1771-1861). Ruth's grandfather was Abraham Joseph I (1731-1794: not to be confused with Pz. 4:1 or Fal. 3:5) a wealthy merchant, who had also been President of the Plymouth Congregation (*c.* 1780s). Ruth's brother, Abraham Joseph II (1799-1868) had been employed by the Penzance congregation as a reader in prayers for one year August 1826 to September 1827), and in 1828 had married Eliza (Telza:

1808-1850) a daughter of Lemon Woolf of Penzance (1783-1848). Ironically, Ruth Joseph had been sent by her family to Penzance to stay with Rabbi B. A. Simmons and his family, to escape the cholera outbreak in Plymouth. Her relative, Pessia (5:2) also died of cholera.

Note: The Josephs of Plymouth were later to become related through marriage to the Simmons family of Penzance: Ruth and Abraham's first cousin, Rosa Aaron married Moses Barnett Simmons (1817-1876) in June 1846. In a letter to B.A. Simmons, dated 10th January 1834, Abraham Joseph sent his congratulations on the engagement of Fanny Simmons to Rabbi Joseph Rintel (the marriage took place some four years later in June 1838). Eliza Joseph added a postscript to "Dear Uncle and Aunt Simmons and Fanny" and calls herself "your affectionate niece and cousin".[125]

8. **ISRAEL** (son of Moses).

Heb. Here lies the boy Israel the son of Moses.

There is no date on the child's headstone.

ROW 7

1. **SOLOMON TEACHER**.

Eng. Solomon Teacher died 10th March 5616, 1856. [Monday 3rd Adar II] Aged 45 years. There is no Hebrew on the headstone, which like those of Catherine Levy (7:2) and Joseph Barnet (8:2) are not the originals, which were destroyed by bomb damage during the Second World War.

Solomon Teacher, the son of Markus *Techauer* of Bavaria, was married to Maria Selig, the daughter of Hannah and Aaron Selig (1: 10 & 11). Solomon and Maria had three children, Hannah (1850-), David (1854) and Solomon (1856-). Solomon Teacher was a pawnbroker and jeweller, and a member of the Penzance congregation. The family lived at 35 Leskinnick Terrace (1851 census), although they were at some point resident in St. Ives, where Solomon died, at Fore Street, after a long illness. There is no headstone for his wife Maria in the Penzance cemetery, and she is not named on Solomon's death certificate. She may have left Cornwall after her husband's death, just before, or soon after the birth of their third child. Her brother, Benjamin and his family had emigrated in 1854, and lived in Australia. An infant son of Solomon Teacher died on 27th August 1848 (*West Briton*), and will be buried in the cemetery in an unmarked grave. Descendants of Solomon Teacher hold that the family may have originated from Spain[126] before migrating to Germany. The Teacher family have also held the tradition that Solomon Teacher's father-in-law, Aaron Selig, was a one-time Mayor of St. Ives. The latter is not known to have lived in St. Ives, and his surname does not appear in the complete historical records of the holders of the position of Mayor in that town, nor in Penzance. Neither does the surname *Teacher* appear in these records.

2. **CATHERINE LEVY**.

Eng. Catherine Levy died 14th July 5624, 1864. [Thursday 10th Tammuz] Aged 73 years.

"Kitty" Levy was an unmarried daughter of Israel Levy of Truro, where she had traded as a clothes and general dealer in Calenick Street and Kenwyn Street. Two of her sisters, Sarah (Sally: 1784-1868, 1:9) and Elizabeth (1798-1879, 1:6) had married into Penzance families, the former becoming the wife of Samuel Jacob (1778-1860, 2:1), a son of Moses Jacob of Redruth, and the latter the wife of Samuel Oppenheim (1800-1869, 1:7). Julia (1792-) may have been another sister, who married Henry Levin (5:8). After the death of Lewis Falkson of Falmouth in 1852, Kitty Levy went to live with his widow, Esther, where, in the 1861 census, she is recorded as a domestic servant. When Esther Falkson died in 1863, it seems that Kitty had come to Penzance to be near her sisters. Samuel Oppenheim was recorded as present at Kitty's death (at 8 Leskinnick Terrace, adjacent to the cemetery).

3. **RACHEL BISCHOFSWERDER** (daughter of Mann).

Died 4th Adar II 5646 (Wednesday 10th March 1886), aged 55 years.

Heb. Here lies the modest and important woman; praised for loving kindness and goodness. Rachel the daughter of Mann the wife of Rabbi Isaac, the Cantor and Shochet who was here twenty years. She was 55 years old. Her pure soul departed from her body on the 4th Adar II, and on the 5th she was led to her burial in the year 5646. May her soul be bound up in the bond of eternal life.

Eng. In loving memory of Rachel the beloved wife of the Rev. Isaac Bischofswerder, who died March 10th 1886 aged 55 years.

She was known by her German forename, Rahle, and was the widow of Solomon Weile of Breslau, with a daughter, Berthe, when she married Rev. Isaac Bischof-swerder.

4. **SARAH CICILIA BISCHOFSWERDER** (Sarah Zilla, daughter of David).

Died 16th Adar II, 5651 (Thursday 26th March 1891), aged 14 months.

Heb. Here lies the girl Sarah Tsilla (or Zilla) daughter of David. She died on 16th Adar 5651. May her soul be bound up in the bond of eternal life.

Eng. In memory of Sarah Cicilia beloved daughter of David & Helena Bischof-swerder who died March 26th 1891 aged 14 months.

Note: whilst *Cicilia* is clearly a phonetic derivation from the Hebrew *Tsilla* or *Zilla*, it has also been variously linked with the Latin *Coeli lilia*, "lily of Heaven", with *coelum* (the contemplation of Heaven) combined with the Hebrew name *Leah*, and with *coelum* and the Greek *leos*, "the people" (who gaze at heaven). These associations are mentioned by Chaucer in "The Second Nun's Tale": *Interpretatio Nominis Ceciliae*. A number of the Bischofswerder headstones carry the symbol of the lily, although this also applies to those of other families. The lily, and other flowers as symbols may also simply reflect the practice and trademark of the local Gentile stonemason.

5. **BESSIE (Betsy) JOSEPH** (Belia, daughter of Zvi).

Died 2nd Kislev 5661 (Saturday 24th November 1900).

Heb. Here lies the spinster Beila the daughter of Zvi. She died 2nd Kislev 5661. May her soul be bound up in the bond of eternal life.

Eng. In loving memory of Bessie Joseph born 1st DecR 1848, died 24th NovR 1900, 2nd Kislev 5661. May her soul rest in peace.

Bessie Joseph was born on 1st December 1848. She was an unmarried daughter of Henry Joseph (6:5) and Amelia Jacob (6:6). At the time of her death,[127] she lived at her parents' former home, 5 The Terrace. In her will, she left her modest estate to her brothers Barnet Henry (1837-1907) and Joseph (1846-) both of Birmingham.

6. **JULIA BISCHOFSWERDER** (Yittel).

Died 8th day of Passover 5671 (Thursday 20th April 1911).

Heb. May she come to her place in peace. Here lies a dear and important woman Yittel, wife of Moses Bischofswerder. She died on 8th day of Passover 5671. May her soul be bound up in the bond of eternal life.

Eng. In loving memory of Julia, wife of Morris Bischofswerder, born June 1st 1851, died April 20th 1911.

Julia Joseph, a daughter of Henry Joseph (6:5), was born on 1st June 1851. She was married to Morris Bischofswerder. This was the last burial of a member of the original community.

7. (see below).

ROW 8

1. JUDAH ben NAPHTALI LEVY.

Heb. Here lies Judah the son of Naphtali.

Although undated this is the grave of the *Mr. Levy,* whose death, on 9th April 1817, reputedly at the age of 100 and as the oldest Jew then living in the County, was recorded by the *Exeter Flying Post* on 17th April.[128] He is to be identified with the "infirm old man", *Leb Hanne* [Judah from Hanau, in Germany] who was maintained by regular charitable donations from the congregation, from 1809 onwards, and whose welfare and safety became a matter of concern to its members. On 1st October 1809, they resolved that he should be maintained by them and given 7 shillings a week subject to his remaining in Penzance every night "…to prevent any accident happening to him from travelling to distant places." From this it would seem likely that he had been an itinerant pedlar. Charitable donations were paid to him, initially through Lemon Hart, throughout the next eight years, and his burial was at the congregation's expense. He is buried in the section of the cemetery reserved for the Poor [7:1 & 2, and 8: 1 & 2], near Catherine ("Kitty") Levy, a daughter of Israel Levy of Truro. Judah Levy is not known to have been related to that family, nor to that of Barnet Levy of Falmouth. Neither is there any known relationship to Henry Levin [sometimes referred to as *Levy* in the Penzance Minute Book]. This (original) head-stone may have been displaced before the bomb-damage to surrounding stones [of 7:1, 7:2 and 8:2] because this one remains intact. Within recent memory it had been resting against the wall near 6:1. It was correctly re-positioned in 1995.

2. JOSEPH BARNET.

Eng. Joseph Barnet died 7th April 5616 (1856). [Monday 2nd Nisan].

There is no Hebrew on this headstone, which is not the original. Joseph Barnet, who was unmarried, was originally from Holland, and at some time had lived in Devon. He traded as a Marine Store dealer in St. Ives, lodging with the family of Grace Major, a widow, in Fore Street (1841 census [129]). By 1851 he was living alone at No.2, Puddingbag Lane. His death certificate of 1856 indicates that he died on 6th April in St. Ives, and that he was a pedlar. It would seem that he had fallen into relative poverty, in that his burial expenses were met from the congregation's charitable funds.[130]

3. Rev. ISAAC BISCHOFSWERDER.

Died 14th Cheshvan 5660 (Wednesday 18th October 1899), aged 77 years.

Heb. And Isaac entreated the Lord (Gen 25:21). Here lies a perfect and upright man,

Isaac the son of Zvi who was Cantor and Shochet here for more than twenty years, and also in the State of Germany he kept guard over holiness for about thirty years. He died on 14th Cheshvan 5660. May his soul be bound up in the bond of eternal life.

Eng. In affectionate remembrance of our dearly beloved father the Rev. Isaac Bischofswerder who departed this life on the 18th October 1899, aged 77 years. May his dear soul rest in peace.

One of the last and (continuously) the longest serving minister of the Penzance congregation, and the head of the Bischofswerder family. His story, and that of his family is detailed elsewhere in the book.

Neither of the below were connected with the historic Jewish Congregation.

4. ADOLF SALZMANN.

Died 9th Adar 5724 (Saturday 22nd February 1964), aged 65 years.

Heb. Here lies. To the memory of Avner the son of Hayyim Israel. He died on 9th Adar 5724. May his soul be bound up in the bond of eternal life.

Eng. In memory of Adolf Salzmann, died 22 February 1964 aged 65 years.

Adolf Salzmann lived at 66 Raymond Road, Redruth, with his wife Auguste, and is presumed to have been a refugee from Germany.[131] Special permission was given for this burial in 1964 when the cemetery had been classified as disused for many years. Adolf Salzmann had no known connection with the historical Jewish community.

IN ROW 7

7. ARNOLD LEVENE (Aharon ben Shlomo).

Heb. Here lies Aharon ben Shlomo. *Tet-Nun-Tsadi-Bet-Hey* (*Tehi Nishmato Ts'rurah Bitzor Ha- Chayim* – May his soul be bound up in the bond of Eternal Life).

Eng. Arnold Lawrence Levene, M.B., F.R.C.S., PhD. Born 7 December 1924, Died 18 July 1998. "What is man that he delighteth in life and loveth many days that he may see Good" (Ps. 34 v. 2).

Arnold Levene was an internationally renowned expert in the treatment of skin cancer, and the headstone bears at the top the Hippocratic symbol of his profession. He was Head of Histopathology at the Royal Marsden Hospital for many years, and was the chairman of the World Health Melanoma Committee. He also carried out medico-legal work on silicosis and asbestosis on behalf of miners and shipworkers in the North West of England and Belfast. He owned a considerable library of books, especially on history, Jewish history, medical history and botany. He died suddenly in London, and was buried there. His family also have homes in Padstow, and it was his wish to be laid to rest in Penzance. He was re-interred in this cemetery prior to his stone-setting in 1999. As with Adolf Salzmann, special permission was given for his interment here. He was survived by his wife, Leatrice, and his children, Simon, Caroline, Susannah and Rachel.

Plan of Penzance Jewish Cemetery

"Higher Jews' Burying Ground" for Senior Members of the Congregation

Row 1.	1	2	3	4	5	6	7	8	9	10	11
Row 2.	1	2	3								

Oldest Section ("Jews' Burying Field")

									Am	Au	
Row 3.	1	2	Au		Am		Au	Au			Am
Row 4.	1	2	3	4							
Row 5.	1	2	3	Au	4(2)		5		6	7	8

"Lower Jews' Burial Ground"

Row 6.	1	2	3	4	?		5	6	7	8	
Row 7.	1	2		3	4	?		5		6	(8:5)
Row 8.	1		2		3						4

Forecourt &
***Bet Torhorah* (House of Cleansing) – the Cemetery's entrance alcove**
Door

Au = Anon. unmarked grave.

Am = Anon. marked (broken or illegible grave).

? = a flat grave-size space, but no obvious mound as with Au/Am.

58 graves, 9 unknown. Some infant (unmarked) graves are likely to lie adjacent to other graves
Rows 3 and 4 probably represent the oldest part of the cemetery, first leased as the "Jews Burying Ground" (originally only partially, or nominally enclosed).
Rows 1, 2 and (parts of) 5 may have been added next as the "Higher Burial Ground".
Rows 6 to 8 were added last as the "Lower Burial Ground".
Some later graves are found in earlier sections.

(v) Truro[132]

The Jewish population of Truro in the 18th and 19th centuries was very small, and is unlikely to have comprised more than a few families. The names "Simons", 'Levy' (or 'Levi') and 'Harris' were the most common. No documentary evidence of the existence of a synagogue there has ever emerged and so it would seem that a private house or other premises may have been used for worship, although Jews would also have travelled to Falmouth to attend services, especially at the time of the various festivals that punctuated the Jewish Religious Year. At one time it was assumed that any burial of a Jew resident in Truro would have taken place in the Falmouth cemetery. Truro is only about 10 miles up river from Falmouth, and the Falmouth cemetery is only a few hundred yards from the Penryn wharf, and so it would have been relatively easy and inexpensive to transport coffins from Truro by boat.

In fact, what may have been a Jewish cemetery or small burial plot did exist in Truro sometime around the late 18th or early 19th century, but it was to all intents and purposes abandoned by the 1840s, and it is not known to what extent, or indeed, if it was ever used as a cemetery. By the time that the children of the family of John Levi were all baptised in 1842 (at St. Mary's Church, now the Cathedral) the Jewish presence in Truro had started to decline, although some Jews continued to trade there. The baptism of Levi's children may well have effectively marked the end of any significant Jewish settlement in Truro. Jacob (John) Levi (or Levy) was not related to the Jewish family of Israel Levy (-1824) and Hannah Levy (1758-1841) of Truro. John Levi appears to have been of Jewish descent, but he had married a Gentile, Elizabeth Carnaerton in St. Mary's Church, Truro on 1st June 1813. It is not certain that John Levi had himself converted to Christianity, or if he had any links with the Falmouth congregation, but he may have retained a sense of Jewish identity sufficient to want a Jewish burial for himself. (Also in Truro at this time, and unrelated to either Israel Levy or John Levi were Lyon Levy from Plymouth, a Silversmith, who lived in the town around 1828, and Henry and Jane Levi, presumably itinerant hawkers, who appear on the 1841 census).

The minute-book of what later became the Truro General (Municipal) Cemetery has survived.[133] On 21st February 1840, an initial meeting was called to discuss the proposal that a general, that is non-denominational, cemetery should be established, distinct from those of the Church of England. The issue had been provoked by the case of an irate non-conformist free-thinker who had been refused burial by a local parson. Present at the meeting was John Levi, when a committee of six was taxed with finding a suitable site for the general cemetery. John Levi's name does not appear on the subsequent list of initial subscribers of July 1840, but by 27th November that same year, he appears as a shareholder and a member of the committee. This committee was in existence for at least the next fifteen years, in that Levi took out an extra share in February 1841, but then sold both shares by July 1842. He had bought further shares, however, by 7th February 1843, and he is recorded as being present at meetings of the committee on 20th February 1851 and 24th August 1855. It would appear that land was eventually obtained for a Public cemetery from Edmund Turner, who had acquired numerous plots in the Trennick area, as a lessee of Lord Falmouth.[134] However, initial steps towards this goal were met with failure. Following the original meeting in February 1840, the sum of £2-10-0 was raised towards the cost of purchase, and at a provisional meeting of the committee on 9th March 1840, it was reported that "Mr. Edwards had applied to the steward of Mrs. Agar respecting what is called the Jews Burying ground, which is not to be obtained."[135]

From the fact that by 1840 this area of ground was named by association with Jews would seem to imply that it had been acquired by them some years before, possibly by as much as several decades. Susser suggested that the Jews of Truro may have obtained this plot, as designated for Jews, around the time of the 1832 cholera epidemic "in case any such died", and would need to be buried immediately, because emergency restrictions would not allow the transportation of bodies to Penryn for burial in the cemetery there. Such a place for Jewish cholera victims, a "small portion of Bury Meadow" was set aside in Exeter, but it was never used.[136] However, the Truro (St. Clement) Tithe Apportionment Document of 1844[137] shows plot 1082 titled as *Gue Burying,* owned by the Honourable Anna Maria Agar, who owned further plots in the adjacent areas of *Oxfords, Penhillick* and *Alverton.* Plot 1082 was in the possession of James Pascoe, who had been using the plot as *arable* land, which casts doubt on the existence of an earlier Jewish burial ground. This substantial lower section of a wedge of land at the junction of Trennick Lane and St. Clements Hill was, indeed, referred to as a "Gue Burying Field", and appeared as such in old survey documents. As *Gue* or *Gew* was the Cornish for an enclosure, it could reasonably be inferred that this land was so-named because it was set aside, or enclosed for burials, general or otherwise. The surveyor may well have written what he had heard from the lessee of the ground's usage as enclosure, and, therefore, recorded this precisely as *Gue,* but in time the Anglicised (phonetic) similarity of *Gue* to *Jew* may have given rise to the erroneous notion that this plot was a Jewish burial site. Such misapplication as this could have been common as the largely spoken Cornish language disappeared, leaving sometimes unintelligible words and place names.

In this case, however, it would seem that the Jews of Truro had, in fact, acquired a plot of land (presumably by lease) for Jewish burials. The plot in question (known as *gue*) appears on some old maps as plot 1082. The Jewish cemetery was, in fact, at the extreme corner of the wedge from plot 1082, adjoining a triangular parcel of land, plot 1081, known as the "Three Corner Close" belonging to the Earl of Falmouth and Truro Corporation as two enclosures used as Meadow (1081 and 1059), the other five enclosures (1060-1064, not belonging to Lord Falmouth) being allotment and waste land. During the 1840s these seven enclosures were in the possession of a John Rollins, but the "Three Corner Close" was eventually leased by Lord Falmouth to Sir Samuel Thomas Spry on 4th March 1852. The Edmund Turner Mortgage document in the Archive Department of Old County Hall in Truro contains the reference, "...three-cornered field and Sopers field, also Jews Burial Ground (Lr), near Trennick Lane in St. Clement... and the next of kin of James Trestrail dec.d of meadow in St. Clement (...1812) formerly in possession of William Moore. This ground and the Jews Burial Ground was then one close... ."[138] This would suggest that the Jews Burial ground was designated from this "one close" sometime after 1812. The meadow referred to above was left by James Trestrail to his daughter Mary Ann Julyan of Tregony. Upon her death in November 1849, her will refers, as part of her estate, to "All that part of a field called the Jews Burying ground consisting of about three roods of ground (the remainder being considered as Freehold and estimated at one rood) situate lying and being near the lane leading to Trennick in the Parish of Saint Clement, which said Field was then in the occupation of Mr. Nankivell and was held for the remainder of a Term of ninety nine years determinable on the death of a life aged about fifty years." [139]

It seems likely that the Jewish burial ground was abandoned by 1840, and the Company which founded the Public cemetery took over the site, which opened in 1841. The whole of this plot has long since been covered over and built upon, and today no sign exists that it may once have been set aside as a Jewish cemetery, and no records of names of those who could have been buried there have come to light. Burials in the new Municipal Public Cemetery included Jacob Beer (1849: plot 221), Jane Eliza Levis (infant 1852: plot 348) and Grace and George Beer (1855: plots 487 and 495). Although *Beer* occurs as a Jewish surname, as *Behr* or *Behrends,* and *Levis* could suggest a form of *Levi*, it is not known that these people were Jews. If records were kept of Jewish burials in Truro, they may have been transferred to Falmouth to be held in the congregation's records there, and have since been lost, or perhaps they may have been taken out of the County. To date no Jewish burial records for Truro have been identified. Although Jews resident in Truro were buried in the Falmouth cemetery, it would seem that the plot in Truro may have been set aside for this eventual purpose by its small Jewish population, perhaps in the hope that their numbers might grow sufficiently to merit some degree of autonomy. In the event, the nascent Truro community was short-lived, and it is uncertain if, and perhaps unlikely that the burial ground was ever used by the town's Jews. The plot, however, continued to bear their name.

(vi)
The Plymouth and Exeter Cemeteries

These burial grounds do not fall within the remit of this study, and they have received extensive coverage elsewhere.[140] However, because the Cornish Jewish congregations and their cemeteries lay in the South of the County, any Jews living in North Cornwall (such as Mordecai Jacob, resident there from 1753-1773) would most likely have been affiliated to the Plymouth Congregation, and some would have been buried there. Some Jews from South Cornwall, through marriage, migration and resettlement were buried in the Devonian Cemeteries. Some of these are given here, although there are numerous graves in the Plymouth Hoe Cemetery that have lost their headstones, and it is possible that a proportion of these may also be of Cornish Jews.

Plymouth: the Hoe Cemetery.

Lyon Joseph (1775-1825), the former President of the Falmouth Congregation, whose failure in merchant shipping led to his departure and resettlement in Bath, where he died. He was not buried there, and it could be expected that his senior position at Falmouth would have merited a burial plot there, but a possible rift with the Falmouth Congregation over the legal ownership of the synagogue may explain why he was not interred in Falmouth, but at Plymouth, some five days after his death.

Alexander Samuel (d. August 1832) was a President of the Plymouth Congregation, and had formerly lived in Truro. He was married to Esther, daughter of Judah Moses (1741-1826) of Plymouth.

Abraham Levy (1779-1834) was also a President of the Plymouth Congregation. He was a grandson of Alexander Moses, founder and first President of the Falmouth Congregation, and the son of Barnet Levy (1731-1791) of Falmouth. Abraham Levy had married Zipporah Benjamin (1784-1861). One of their children, Markes Levy (1812-1877) married Bella Woolf (1817-1881) a daughter of Lemon Woolf of Penzance.

Lyon Levy (1782-1836) was not related to the above, nor to any Levy family resident in Cornwall, but he had lived and traded there, in Truro, around 1828. He was married to Leah, a daughter of Judah Moses of Plymouth.

Rebecca Woolf (1781-1853) the wife of Lemon Woolf of Penzance, and the mother of Bella, and the women below. She was a daughter of Moses Jacob of Redruth (formerly of Falmouth, and a President of the Congregation there, where he is buried).

Eliza Joseph (1808-1850) the wife of Abraham Joseph (1799-1868) of Plymouth. She was a daughter of Lemon Woolf of Penzance.

Fanny Solomon (1815-1855), the daughter of Lazarus Solomon of Plymouth, and the wife of Joseph Joseph (1802-1879) of Redruth, died in Plymouth. She was from Poland, and lived in Redruth, Cornwall, for some time, where seven of her children were born. After her death, her husband moved to Liverpool.

Rosetta Solomon (1810-1870) the wife of Josiah (Isaac) Solomon of Plymouth (formerly of Exeter). Rosetta was another daughter of Lemon Woolf of Penzance. Two years after her death in 1870, her husband moved to New York.

Arabella Stadhagen (1802-1862) was the wife of Rev. Myer Stadhagen (1804-1862) minister of the Plymouth Congregation. The couple died within five days of one another, Myer on 21st April, and Arabella on the 26th. Arabella was the daughter of Moses Isaac Joseph (-1834) of Falmouth and Judith Rebecca Jacob (1768-1849) a daughter of Moses Jacob of Redruth.[141]

Plymouth: the Gifford Place Cemetery.

Max Bishop (Bischofswerder: 1860-1928) was a son of Rev. Isaac Bischofswerder (1822-1899) of Penzance. His wife, Catherine Jacobs (1865-1954) is also buried in this cemetery. Max Bishop's brothers migrated from Cornwall to Hull, and one, David, died in South Africa.

Henrietta Jacobs (Schram: 1846-1909) was the daughter of Nathaniel Schram (from Holland) and his wife Anna. Anna and Henrietta Schram were both born in Cornwall, the latter in Truro. It is not certain that the parents were Jewish, and Henrietta may have converted to Judaism when she married Mark Jacobs (1839-1913), who traded as a Clothier in Plymouth, and who was originally from London. He is also buried in this cemetery.

[Jack Gordon (*d.* 1944) "of St. Austell", and his wife, Freya (*d.* 1947) are not known to have been connected with earlier Cornish Jewish families].

Exeter

Andrew George Jacob (1874-1900) a son of Samuel Jacob (1838-1913) of Falmouth, is buried in the Exeter cemetery.[142]

---

[1] The first and third of these expressions are derived from Biblical references found in Nehemiah 2:3 and Ecclesiastes 12:5. A valuable and concise outline of the place of cemeteries in Jewish tradition by Arno Parik can be found in *Old Bohemian and Moravian Jewish Cemeteries*: Petr Ehl, Arno Parik and Jiri Fielder (Paseka, Prague 1991; pp. 5-21), from which some of these general introductory details have been drawn. See also Therese and Mendel Metzger, *Jewish Life in the Middle Ages* (Charwell Books 1982) p. 79 and pp. 75-78.

[2] Susser (1993) pp. 189 & 314.

[3] Parik (pp. 10-11)

[4] Parik (pp. 12-21). For a more specific guide, see Susser (Lonsdale Press 1995) *How to Read & Record a Jewish Tombstone.*

[5] Parik (pp. 14-21).

[6] Parik (pp. 6-7).

[7] Susser (1993) p. 189.

[8] Susser (1993) p.188.

[9] Susser (1993) p. 189.

[10] Act 11; scene V11; lines 139-166.

[11] Parik (p. 9).

[12] Parik (pp. 9-10).

[13] *Falmouth Packet,* 29th August 2002.

[14] Susser (1993) p. 129.

[15] The papers of this extensive survey of Jewish cemeteries in Britain are now lodged with the Anglo-Jewish Archives in the Library of the University of Southampton.

[15a] For *The Lost Jews of Cornwall* (2000) Eric Dawkins provided me with material from his research for the introductory section on the Falmouth cemetery. Since then, I have carried out extensive new research on the cemetery's background from various other sources. David Thomas, Archivist at

CRO, Truro, has also provided some of the new information, and I have rewritten and revised this composite and far more comprehensive introduction.

[16] Catherine Parkes, *Falmouth Jewish and Congregationalist Cemeteries, Cornwall, Archaeological Assessment* (Cornwall Council Historic Environment Project Report Number 2010R039, July 2010) pp. 14-58. I am grateful to Professor Charles Thomas for providing me with a copy of this report.

[17] Susser (1993) p. 129.

[18] In a letter to Keith Pearce (21st December 1998) Eric Dawkins, the cemetery's custodian, confirmed this feature.

[19] Crispin Gill (1995) *The Great Cornish Families*, pp. 7-10.

[20] For *Elieazar/Lazarus,* see, for example Gen. 15:2; 1Chron. 7:8; Ezra 8:16; Lk. 3:29; 16:20-25; John 11. The printed parish registers for the parish church of King Charles the Martyr, Falmouth from 1580 to 1830 (*Cornwall Family History Society records, Truro*). For *Steel* wills, see: Refs. *Jul 1765 Rushworth 273* and *Jun 1764 Simpson 241:* Cornish Wills, Somerset House and PRO Kew: Letters to Keith Pearce from Trudy Martin, *CFHSocTruro,* 28th November 2003; David Thomas, Archivist CRO Truro, 1st December 2003; Angela Broome, *RIC, Courtney Library Truro,* 13th December 2003.

[21] Noted by Keith Pearce (2003) from the original Minute Books, and mentioned by Hughan (1866) pp. 401-402, & 421.

[22] I am grateful to David Thomas for his tentative suggestion that a Penryn Jewish community could have had some connection with the local rope making industry (of Lazarus Steel, and others before him) making a burial ground there a viable and convenient option (Letter to Keith Pearce 24th October 2003).

[23] See TM, CRO, Truro, ref: AD 894/7/5, Manor No. in Rent-Book: 1754. I am grateful to Allen Buckley, and also to David Thomas, Archivist, County Record Office (Truro) for this information. David Thomas: Letter to Keith Pearce, of 19th March 1999. All of the information on the transfer of lands on the Penwerris area from 1751 to 1913 has been drawn from information provided by David Thomas (1999-2003).

[24] Letter from David Thomas, Archivist CRO Truro to Keith Pearce (24th October 2003).

[25] Research by Michael Michell (January 2009).

[26] In the 1975 survey, de Lange and Speake note Roth's date, after 1808, but feel that Jacob's date of *c.*1780 accords better with the actual headstones. The Basset proposal book and the Basset leases (Penwerris Barton), are both held at CRO Truro. Basset volume of destroyed leases, ref. B37, NO. 1536, p.115, Manor of Penwerris; CRO Truro, ref. AD894/7/35; Letter to Keith Pearce from David Thomas, Archivist, April 1999).

[27] CRO ref. RH 2938 and AD 894/7/52.

[28] CRO ref. AD 4/7/35.

[29] CRO ref. P/22/27/5.

[30] Roth, *The Rise of Provincial Jewry* (1950) p. 62; Jacob, *The Jews of Falmouth* (1949) p. 7 & ft. 18.

[31] Relative to the size of their respective congregations, the Jewish holding was about half the area of the Christian plot. (CRO ref. WH 6452).

[32] CRO WH 6452 indicates that "The Tithes according to the present averages amounting to £6. 17s. 1d. are paid by the Lessee".

[33] CRO ref. AD 894/7/52.

[34] Susser (1993) pp. 126-129.

[35] Sadly, the Basset (destroyed leases) volumes at CRO Truro (ref. B37) do not give such precise details.

[36] 1861 Census.

[37] Price (1982) p. 13.

[38] Walker (1979) p. 145; Price (1982) pp. 13-15: see note below.

[39] I am especially grateful to various descendants of the de Pass and Kisch families who have allowed me to have sight of copies of original family documents, genealogies and private research papers. Chief amongst these are various original documents and sources from the extensive family archive of Phoebe Walker, many of which have been made available by her to other family members and researchers. Specific documents include: (i) genealogies thought to have been compiled by Eliot Archibald (Archie) de Pass (1892-1841) from papers now held at the Hartley Library, University of Southampton (MS 116/13); (ii) an anonymous, untitled and undated paper (published privately) on

the De Pass family's history and origins, including genealogical and biographical data on various family members, most likely written by Alan de Pass (1899-); (iii) a privately published thesis by Rebecca Walker (now Coutts) on the De Pass family (1979, pp. 167) and (iv) updated family trees of the De Pass and Kisch families by Ena Black, who has given valuable information and advice on other published sources and original documents. Selective details from these various sources have been incorporated into these sections. Information has also been provided by Anthony Joseph relating to Sir Thomas Colyer-Fergusson's family tree of the de Pass family (The Jewish Genealogical Society of London) and by Saul Isroff. Other sources include B. D. Price's short biography of Alfred Aaron de Pass, Royal Cornwall Polytechnic Society, Falmouth (1982: pp.1- 16) and Norman Nail's (1993) essay which includes much information on Alfred de Pass' bequests to various museums has also been an important source, and is given below. Significant material on the de Pass family has also been provided by Jackie Hill (February 2010, Michael Jolles (2013) and (prior to 2000) by Eric Dawkins.

[40] See Brown, below, p. 226.

[41] Roth (1950) pp. 77-81. See also Malcolm Brown, *The Jews of Norfolk and Suffolk Before 1840* in the Transactions of the Jewish Historical Society of England (XXXII, 1990-1992: pp. 219-235).

[42] The circumcision registers for Bevis Marks give an Aaron de Pass in 1814, but the original diaries of Aaron de Pass (in the possession of Phoebe Walker and her daughter, Rebecca) gives the date of his birth as 4th July 1815. It is possible that the circumcision register gives an older son of Daniel de Pass, who died in infancy, a family relative, or a child of another family.

[43] Walker (1979) p. 39; and letter from Rebecca Coutts to Keith Pearce (9th April 2012). This information is from the original diaries of Aaron's father, Daniel, in the possession of the Walker family. Esther da Costa's maternal grandparents were Moses Zachariah Foligno, who was born in Pisa, and Rachel de Isaac Baquis (or Bajuis) who was born in Aldgate, London. Aaron de Pass' diaries record that a "Mr. I. Foligno" (most likely the same as Esther's uncle) presented "the necessary ornaments for the Sepher Torah" to the Jewish congregation in Cape Town. Further information on the Foligno family is contained in the Walker-Coutts archive, together with new research by Rebecca Coutts from census records (1841-1871).

[44] Malcolm Brown (1990-1992) p. 226.

[45] Letter from Rebecca Coutts to Keith Pearce (9th April 2012).

[46] Brown (1992) p. 227.

[47] A copy of the original from the archive of Phoebe Walker (provided by Ena Black).

[48] R. D. Barnett and P. Wright, *The Jews of Jamaica* (Jerusalem 1997: edit. Oroa Yoffe) p. 69. The Slave Registers of Former British Colonial Dependencies (1812-1834) give some 277 slaves against various de Pass owners. Whilst some of these owners may have been connected to the de Pass family of Kings Lynn, other de Pass names may be those of Christians: research by Jackie Hill (February 2010).

[49] There was not to be a Jewish presence in Stroud until 1877. It was short-lived and had ended by 1908. The census records of 1881 & 1891 reveal various Jewish families and travellers, many from Russia and Poland, some from Austria, Prussia and the Low Countries, trading as tailors: Susser (1995) pp. 93-107; with source references to Torode (1989) pp. 57-64, Pollins (1995 & 1996).

[50] The vessel registered with Lloyds of London (1850) as a brig of 1921 tons built at Plymouth in 1815 (Walker 1979: research note).

[51] Paul H. Emden, *The Jews of Britain: A series of Biographies* (1943) p. 387, & research by Ena Black (2009).

[52] Walker (1979) pp. 43 & 65.

[53] The year has sometimes been given as 1849, but is confirmed as 1850 from Aaron's own diary and from the South West African Journal (article 1971): research by Rebecca Coutts.

[54] Roth (1950) p. 80 omits a comma after Benjamin (implying two nephews only) and does not give the surname as Kisch. See also: S. A. Rochlin's articles on Daniel Montagu Kisch in *The Zionist Weekly* (September 1937, pp.49-50, and September 1947, pp. 27-28).

[55] Brown (1990-1992) p. 227.

[56] Roth (1950) p. 80 & 88.

[57] Mesod Benady, *The Settlement of Jews in Gibraltar, 1704-1783*; in the Transactions of the Jewish Historical Society of England (1974-1978) Vol. XXVI, pp. 87-110. R. D. Barnett and W. M. Schwab (edit.) *The Sephardi Heritage* (1989) pp. 167, & 174-5.

[58] Price (1982) p. 2.

[59] Walker (1979) p. 67; Berger (2004) p. 92.

[60] I am grateful to Jackie Hill (February 2010) for providing detailed information on various members of the de Pass family from Census records and birth, marriage and death records from 1841 up to 1911. Letter from Rebecca Coutts (9th April 2012).

[61] Post Office Directory (1879): Walker (1979) pp. 69 & 75.

[62] Walker (1979) pp. 73-75. Price (1982) p. 4, notes that "There is no record in the archives of Imperial College (which now incorporates the School of Mines) of Alfred having been there as a student".

[63] Walker (1979) pp. 101, 123 & 137.

[64] Walker (1979) p. 109.

[65] The year of his death has sometimes been given as 1962, but it has been confirmed by Rebecca Walker that he died on 9th August 1963.

[66] Price (1982) p. 10; Walker (1979) p. 111. This, and other information has also been drawn from the extensive family Archive of Phoebe Walker.

[67] Walker (1979) pp. 135 & 143; Price (1982) pp. 10-11 & 15. Recent research by Rebecca Coutts from shipping lists reveals the spelling of her name as *Simes* (and not *Symes*, as sometimes given) and her middle names.

[68] From the original letters in the Alex Jacob Archive, dated 15th December 1912 (Tehidy), 9th December 1913 (Falmouth) and 17th December 1913 (Plymouth).

[69] Whitford of St. Columb Solicitor's Collection (ref. WH 6452 CRO Truro).

[70] The original handwritten letter is in the Alex Jacob Archive.

[71] The 64th Annual Report of the Board of Deputies of British Jews (Session 1913-1916).

[72] Original letter in the Alex Jacob Archive.

[73] These Hebrew texts are still held at the museum where they can be seen, although they are not always on public display.

[74] Norman Nail, *The Cornish Curator and the Cosmopolitan Collector* in The Journal of the Royal Institution of Cornwall (New Series II) 1993, vol. 1, pt. 3, pp. 277-289. The records of the de Pass Collection can be viewed on the Museum's website. Details of Alfred de Pass' donations to various museums have also been selected from the de Pass family's records: Archive of Phoebe Walker and information from Ena Black (2009); Rebecca Walker (1979).

[75] An article in the *Cape Times* (19th April 1935), quoted by Nail (p. 277-78).

[76] Nail (1993) p. 281.

[77] Walker (1979) p. 111.

[78] Alfred de Pass' close friendship with Tuke is covered by Price (1982) pp. 6-14.

[79] Letter and enclosures (27th June 2011) from Alison Cooper, Plymouth City Museum and Art Gallery.

[80] Letter from Ms R. Beckett (29th November 1978) quoted by Walker (1979) pp. 133 & 139.

[81] Walker (1979) p. 143

[82] From a further survey made by Keith Pearce in January 2012.

[83] Letter from Wilfred S. Samuel to Alex Jacob (8th April 1953).

[84] *West Briton* 14th December 1849.

[85] Susser read this date as 5595 (1835).

[86] *The West Briton* 19th January 1838: Research by Jackie Hill (2011).

[87] Records of *Latvijas Valsts Vestures Arhivs*: Letter and enclosures (February 11th 2000) to Barry Graham, Raleigh USA. Letters from Marylin Graham of Chigwell, Essex to Keith Pearce (June 11th & 24th 2003).

[88] Helen Fry (2000).

[89] *Collectanea Cornubiensia*, 403.

[90] Some of the information on Nathan Vos has been drawn from notes provided by Derek Cousins (Letter to Keith Pearce, 4th May 2004), whose family was also from Holland. As recent Jewish arrivals in South Wales, and as Opticians, they employed Nathan Vos in their shop. Research into the Vos Wills by Helen Fry (2000).

[91] Pool (1974, p. 155; ftnt. 30).

[92] Letter from Peter Pool to Godfrey Simmons, June 1994. Much of the information in this introduction has been drawn from the original lease documents (some of which are held by the Morrab Library) and also from the Jewish congregation's Minute Books and Accounts. Complete copies of

the lease documents and Congregational Minute Books (the originals of the latter being in the Brotherton Library, University of Leeds) are in my possession. I am grateful to Anne Chappell for making available an original lease (dated 13th August 1835) containing a plan of the cemetery plots, to Harry Carter for information from aspects of his research into the cemetery's history, and especially to the late Peter Pool for advising Godfrey Simmons on the role played by the Barham, Borlase and Rogers families in the various lease negotiations (Letter to Godfrey Simmons, 25th June 1994).

[93] Susser (1993) pp. 126-128 & 299.

[94] The survey carried out by Nicholas de Lange and Jennifer Speake in April 1975, transcribed the Hebrew date, and, in this singular case, translated it incorrectly as 1741, having omitted a ciphermark which would have added to the date an additional 50 years. I am grateful to Eva Grabherr for drawing attention to this error from her reading of the original headstone, and to Nicholas de Lange for confirming the date as 1791 from photographs.

[95] See also Susser (1993) p. 129:

[96] Sir Thomas Colyer-Fergusson (compiled early 1900s): The Society of Genealogists, London. Further details of its compilation and sources are given in the sections on the Hart family in Penzance.

[97] The administration of his estate is among the records at the Family Record Office, Myddleton Street, London (Ref. IR26/341/42: research by Helen Fry, 2000).

[98] The documents from the Rogers family Archive relating to the cemetery were acquired by the Morrab (Gardens) Library around 1994. Pool's research into these documents form the basis of the information in this section.

[99] Roth (1933).

[100] Pool (1974) p. 89.

[101] Information from Jackie Hill in Letters of July and August 2002.

[102] Minute Book entries for 13th April 1845 and 25th December 1881. I am indebted to the late John Simmons for his detailed analysis of the complete set of congregational leases, copies of which have been drawn from Godfrey Simmons' archive.

[103] This is the provisional inference which Pool drew from his study of the Rogers' documents.

[104] Pool (1974) p. 155. The map is in the possession of the Morrab Library.

[105] Pool (1974) pp. 173 & 203 (Peter Laws).

[106] A note in the Archive of Alex Jacob, which records Potter as contemporary with George Wain (given by Jacob as Winn) in Falmouth.

[107] Schedule of Listing No. 490978. Decision (Inspector's Advice Precis) 8th January 2004): Department of Culture, Media & Sport, 23rd February 2004.

[108] From a detailed analysis of the headstones *in situ* by Rev. Elkan Levy (June 2008).

[109] See also *Collectanea Cornubiensia*, 498.

[110] See also *Collectanea Cornubiensia*, 498.

[111] See also *Collectanea Cornubiensia*, 498.

[112] Translation by Hermann Zeffert (1999).

[113] The genealogical records of Anthony P. Joseph.

[114] The family records of David M. Jacobs of St. Albans gives the date of death as 27th May 1869 (Letter to Keith Pearce of 21st March 2000).

[115] See also, *Collectanea Cornubiensia*, 643.

[116] *Collectanea Cornubiensia*, 885.

[117] Archive of Alex M. Jacob.

[118] Rabbi B. A. Simmons' Circumcision register.

[119] Roth (1933); *cf. Biblioteca Cornubiensis*, Vol. 1: 145; Susser (1993) pp. 129, 208, 213-5 & 346.

[120] Research by Helen Fry (2000).

[121] In the *Lost Jews of Cornwall*, the date of this stone was given incorrectly as 1741, as noted earlier.

[122] *The Gentleman's Magazine*, 19th February 1846, p. 439 (Research by Helen Fry 2000).

[123] The *Collectanea Cornubiensis*, 1290 (referencing the *Royal Cornwall Gazette*).

[124] Research by Jackie Hill (2008).

[125] Original letter in the Archive of Godfrey Simmons.

[126] Letters and documents from Kenneth Teacher to Keith Pearce (3rd June 1999 and 8th February 2000). Information from Malcolm Veal, St. Ives Town Clerk: 12th May 2003; Pool (1974) pp. 279-283: Mayors of Penzance 1614-1949).

[127] Her will, proved with probate, 21st October 1901 in London (Research by Helen Fry 2000). See also *Collectanea Cornubiensia,* 498.

[128] Research by Helen Fry (2000). See also G.C. Boase, *Collectanaea Cornubiensia* (1890), p. 498. I am grateful to Yissochor Marmorstein for his translation of the Hebrew and Yiddish sections of the Minute-Book, including those that relate to Leb Hanne.

[129] Information accessed from the records of CFHistSoc. Truro by Trudy Martin (December 2003).

[130] Congregational Minute Book for 1856.

[131] In his will (proved with probate on 6th April 1964 in Bodmin) his estate, with effects of £109, was left to his widow. Probate was also granted to Edith Smollet, wife of a Max Smollet. (Research by Helen Fry 2000).

[132] A substantial proportion of the content of this section is drawn from research by Godfrey Simmons.

[133] Courtney Library, RIC Truro. These details have been extracted by Godfrey Simmons from the Minute Book records (1995).

[134] Letter from June Palmer to Godfrey Simmons (4th January 1995), and Tregothan Estate Records.

[135] In a collection of unlisted deeds and leases arranged by Parish in the Clifden Collection at Old County Hall, Truro. The information in this section has been drawn from these documents, together with the Edmund Turner mortgage document, by Godfrey Simmons (Research at CRO and RIC Truro 1994 & 1995).

[136] Letter from Bernard Susser to Godfrey Simmons 30th April 1993. See also Susser (1993) pp. 89-90 and Thos. Shapter *The History of the Cholera in Exeter in 1832* (pub. 1849) pp. 55 & 169-170.

[137] Letter to Godfrey Simmons (28th November 1994) from the Tregothan Estate Office, Truro, from which this, and other lease details of the various plots have been drawn.

[138] DD.BRA.1623. Research by Godfrey Simmons 1994.

[139] AP. WR/73 CRO Truro. Research by Paul Brewer (Letter to Keith Pearce 13th August 2002). Extract collated by David Thomas, Archivist CRO Truro (27th August 2002).

[140] Susser (1972) *An Account of the Old Jewish Cemetery on Plymouth Hoe* (which contains some errors of dating and genealogy relating to the Cornish Jews); Susser (1993) pp. 126-128 (Plymouth), 30 & 128-9 (Exeter); Plymouth Congregational Burial Records (the Gifford Street cemetery); Exeter Congregational Burial Records.

[141] Susser (1972) p. 22 (B67) gives her parents incorrectly as Judith (Moses) and Henry Joseph. The latter was brother to Moses Isaac Joseph.

[142] I am grateful to Helen Fry for drawing this Exeter burial to my attention.

CHAPTER 9
The Rabbis

Although the Jewish communities in Cornwall survived for a little under two hundred years, some thirty or more ministers were associated with the Falmouth and Penzance congregations in the 18th and 19th centuries. Little is known of the Rabbis in the 18th century, but from the early 1800s onwards names appear more frequently. It is not possible to identify all the rabbis who served the Cornish Jewish congregations because formal congregational records do not exist for Falmouth, although some information there can be reconstructed indirectly from other sources. Details of the ministers in Penzance are uncertain before 1807, but it is fortunate that information after that date has survived in some detail and in various forms, including the Congregation's Minute-Books and other contractual documents. For both communities the cemetery headstones, census returns and newspaper reports are helpful. From these sources about thirty separate names have been identified: 17 for Penzance and at least 10 for Falmouth.[1]

Identifying the rabbis can be complicated by the fact that the term *Rav* appears frequently on Jewish headstones as an honorary or courtesy title for people who were not, in fact, ordained as rabbis or registered with the Chief Rabbinate. Some were senior lay members of the congregation such as the President (*Parnas*) or the Treasurer. They would have been respected men of wisdom, experience, and good character, without any special religious training, but competent in religious knowledge and practical religious matters. Consequently, such lay people were sometimes given the title *Rav* without having taken any formal religious training or possessing extensive learning in Talmudic study. In the case of others, this title would often denote some form of recognition in religious learning and subsequent suitability for a limited ministry, perhaps as a *chazan* or Reader in Prayers, or perhaps as a Teacher of Hebrew, but without further rabbinical qualifications,[2] and such men would not possess the specialist skills of a *shochet* or *mohel*. In the Penzance cemetery for instance there is only one known Rabbi (B. A. Simmons, 1:8) who was qualified in all of these areas, and two "Reverends" (Hyman Greenburgh, 2:2; and Isaac Bischofswerder, 8:3). However, several other men receive the title *Rabbi*, sometimes in effusive terms although they are known only to have been lay members of the congregation. The example of the headstone of Henry Levin illustrates this practice: "His honour Rabbi Zvi, the son of his honour Rabbi Yekutiel."[3]

The Penzance Minute-Book makes it clear where a man's appointment was in the capacity of *shochet*, and the terms *rav* and *chazan* are also used for such individual appointments. Where a member of the congregation (usually a former minister) was already qualified as a *shochet*, a minister without that skill might be appointed, perhaps as a stop-gap, and in any case there was not at all times a ready pool of candidates to fill vacancies. There was also a degree of variation and inconsistency in the use of the terms used of a minister. The case of the last minister appointed in Penzance in 1887, Michael Leinkram, illustrates the difficulty in gaining a clear perspective on this. He was appointed as *shochet* and *chazan*, and his marriage certificate at this time refers to him by the general term of "Jewish Minister". He did move to other positions in Belfast and London as a minister, but his headstone in the Edmonton cemetery does not have any mention of him as *rav* nor does it refer to his having had a religious vocation of any kind. It is entirely conceivable, of course, that the men appointed to congregations such as these might have developed and expanded their skills and formal standing over time, as they moved from place to place. Some of the earliest (and some of the later) men to have served the Cornish communities may not, therefore, have been rabbis in a formal sense, and the skills which they possessed would have varied from minister to minister. Care has been taken here to try to eliminate those lay members who received the title of *rav* as a courtesy, and to include only those who are known from other documentary sources to have been employed in a religious capacity. In some cases, however, men who were appointed in a religious capacity, such as Aaron Selig (in 1808, and again in 1811) and B. A. Simmons (who arrived in 1811) are recorded as *rav* and *shochet* in the Minute-Book. Selig's headstone inscription also confirms that he was a *mohel*, and B. A. Simmons' headstone refers to him as *Rebbe, Chazan, Shochet* and *Mohel.* Both men relinquished their office and remained in the congregation as lay members. It is striking that Aaron Selig is *not* referred to as *rav* on his headstone.

From the Penzance congregational documents it is obvious that the range of duties that, with varying degrees of success, the congregation sought to impose upon and extract from its ministers was considerable: "the one man had perforce to see to many matters. The main requirement was a reader and *shochet,* but activities extended, in fact, far beyond this. An agreement of 1817 lays down the functions of the communal factotum (the *Rav,* or *Rebbe,* as they called him) in detail. He was to slaughter animals for food whenever any of his employers should require it; to porge the meat (attending the market twice weekly for a couple of hours for this purpose, as we learn from another record); to instruct the children belonging to the congregation in Hebrew and cognate subjects; to supervise the cleaning of the Synagogue; to conduct Divine service; to read the Law; to prepare the Scrolls for the next day, on the eve of Sabbaths and Festivals; to bind the Palm Branches on the Feast of Tabernacles; and to produce the willow twigs on *Hosanna Rabba.* In addition, according to the original regulations, he was to collect week by week all offerings made by members. He had to recite the *Megilla* on Purim, and to supervise the preparation of the flour on Passover. Finally, every Sabbath, he was to conduct a lesson for adults in the forenoon. In return for all this, he enjoyed the princely salary of some £40, or a little less, per annum."[4]

The salary of Jewish ministers in the South West in the 19th century was very poor compared with their Christian counterparts, who could expect anything varying from £70 to £200 per year. The Jewish minister, however, was paid little more than an agricultural labourer, and about half that of a skilled artisan, especially in London. What has not been included in the range of responsibilities expected of the Rabbi are the other duties to circumcise, celebrate at weddings and *bar mitzvahs*, and to bury the dead, although they might receive "gifts in cash or kind" on such occasions, as well as donations from those called to read the Law, or payments from the congregation's charitable funds. Some ministers might give private lessons in Hebrew or German, and even take in pupils as boarders, but the opportunity to earn additional money was unpredictable and unreliable.[5] Some incumbents in Penzance were compliant, but others kicked against the onerous pressures from their congregations, contesting them and, in some cases, had them modified, or, at least on occasions, absented themselves or failed to comply, refusing to be intimidated by the congregational elders. "It is not surprising, under such circumstances, that there was a constant *va et vient* of incumbents, few of whom seem to have exceeded, or even completed, the term of two years for which they were engaged."[6] These were the conditions that prevailed in Penzance, and they may well have been distinctive of that community. From them we cannot assume that a similar atmosphere and ethos existed in Falmouth, but disputes there and in Penzance did arise, and they were also a feature of congregational life in Exeter and Plymouth.[7] Needless to say, such a wide range of expectations placed upon a young minister, some of whom had only recently arrived from the Continent, were unrealistic, and where the appointee's command of English was rudimentary, he might be quite unable to function effectively across the whole spectrum of his responsibilities. Some fortunate individuals who fell within this category might be appointed initially or primarily as a *shochet*, but only later progress to further duties,[8] but such arrangements seem rarely, if ever, to have applied in Penzance.

A simple audit of the incumbents of the positions of President and Minister in Falmouth and Penzance respectively is instructive, and provides a striking comparison between the two congregations, the first appearing to be characterised by a much greater degree of stability, and fewer internal disputes than the second. In Falmouth, from around 1760 to the congregation's demise in 1879, there were only six Presidents, each holding the Office for life (or, in the case, of Lyon Joseph, until his resignation). In Penzance, although the Presidency may have been held for life initially, it was held on a biannual basis, and in the period from 1760 to 1900 there were over twenty men in the Office, although some re-occupied it on a rotating basis. In the same period, Falmouth had at least ten ministers, most staying for several years, whereas in Penzance (excluding a period from 1830-1842, for which no records have survived, and during which there must have been several ministers) there were at least seventeen ministers, most of whom were only appointed on a short-term basis, and some, like B. A. Simmons, on several occasions.

Disputes from congregations were sometimes referred to the Chief Rabbi, who might intervene, and also supervise the appointment of new ministers. From the Penzance Minutes, we know that such involvement on the part of the Chief Rabbi was routine, especially in later years. Soon after his arrival in Penzance, Rabbi B. A. Simmons wrote to the Chief Rabbi for permission to marry, and it is likely that other single ministers did the same. The Chief Rabbis who were in office in London during the period of the Jewish communities in Cornwall were: in the 18th century, Aaron Hart (who served from 1704-1756), when the earliest Jewish settlers arrived in Falmouth and Penzance, Hart Lyon (Zevi Hirsch: 1758-1764), and David Tevele Schiff (1765-1791), these three being appointed from the Great Synagogue. (During

Schiff's tenure, the Hambro and New Synagogues appointed a rival Chief Rabbi, Meshullam Solomon, from 1765-1780, but Schiff was eventually reconfirmed as overall Chief Rabbi). From 1791-1802, the post was vacant, but during the 19th century, three men occupied the position: Solomon Hirschell (1802-1842), Nathan Marcus Adler (1845-1890) and his son, Hermann Adler (1891-1911), the latter being the delegated Chief Rabbi from 1879, due to the failing health of his father.

Falmouth.

As we have seen, the organisation of the earliest Jewish communal life in Falmouth was very much under the supervision and patronage of Alexander Moses (1715-1791). At first his efforts were focused on the development of a satisfactory economic climate which would enable the nascent congregation to become established. In those early days, it is unlikely that the community was able to contemplate the appointment of a salaried rabbi, and in these circumstances its senior members would have led the services. Tradition has it that Sarah Moses (1748-1831), apparently a most forceful personality, and a daughter of Alexander Moses, took a prominent part in congregational affairs, and even led services, either when the Parnas was absent (that office being first held by her father, and later by her husband, Moses Jacob), or when the men had not returned from their work or travels in time to make up the *minyan* for the Sabbath. She is even said to have laid *tephillin*.[9] In any event, such a small community could only support a rabbi if he were virtually self-sufficient with his own trade.

Isaac Polack (*c.* 1760-).

The only name which comes from this early period is that of Isaac Polack, who is known to have lived in Penryn in the 1760s and 1770s. Little is known of his background although his name suggests Eastern European origins. He may originally have come from London where some Polish Jews had settled, and where an Isaac Polack, possibly a relative, was licensed as a hawker from 1710-1714.[10] It has also been suggested that Isaac Polack of Penryn possessed family connections with Devon, in that he was a first cousin to both a Henry Marx of Exeter, and to the father of the Rosa Abrahams who married Abraham Joseph I (1731-1794) of Plymouth.[11] Polack was an early member of the Falmouth Masonic Lodge (from *c.*1760) and was well-educated and most certainly multi-lingual. There is no unequivocal evidence that he was qualified and skilled as a Rabbi, and there is no direct evidence that he served the Falmouth congregation in any formal capacity, but his various academic skills alone could have placed him to be of assistance to the congregation. Moreover, Isaac Polack may have been only loosely attached to the congregation and not entirely committed to Judaism. On 15th February 1760 he married Mary Stoughton, a widow, also of Penryn. Whether Isaac had by then (or later) converted to Christianity is not certain, but the wedding took place in the local church of St. Gluvias.[12] The Phillimore Parish registers refer to him as a

"Jewish priest".[13] This wedding may, however, indicate a trend towards cultural rather than religious "anglicization" for the purpose of social and commercial advantage rather than full assimilation and conversion. Even if Polack did convert, it is difficult to know how seriously the issue of conversion or marrying-out would have been taken in general by the Jewish community in such isolated places, even if some cases provoked ostracism and publicity, such as that, much later, of Harriet Hyman.[14]

The Phillimore reference to Polack as a "Jewish Priest" is unusual and raises a number of issues. It is unclear if Polack used this term of himself, either habitually or on the sole occasion of his church marriage, or if the Christian priest who officiated at the marriage took him to be an equivalent minister within the Jewish religion. If Polack did use the term of himself, it is not certain that he intended to identify himself as a Rabbi, in that the term would not have been employed within Jewish circles for that purpose, and Judaism's ancient ritual priesthood, long since extinct in practice, was quite distinct from the scholarly rabbinical traditions that developed subsequently. It is possible, however, that Polack was descended from a priestly line as a *Kohen*, and this may have led to the ascription. It is also most unlikely that Alexander Moses would have countenanced a man who had married a Christian in a church ceremony as an acceptable and suitable minister for the Falmouth Hebrew Congregation. There is no sign today of any headstone for Isaac Polack in the Penryn Jewish cemetery. When he died in 1794, he may have been buried there and the stone may not have survived, but earlier headstones, such as that of Alexander Moses of 1791 are still intact. Polack's daughter, Frances, who ran a shop in Penryn, was buried in a Christian churchyard.[15]

Polack's occupation was that of a translator and interpreter of commercial and legal documents. He was eager to promote and advance himself as a man of learning and expertise. He took full advantage of the commercial opportunities offered by Falmouth as an expanding centre for maritime trade. He realised the need for a translator and interpreter in this context. On 1st July 1776 he could afford to take out an elaborate advertisement in the *Dorset Sherborne Mercury*: "TRANSLATION OF LANGUAGES Isaac Polack, of Penryn, in Cornwall most respectfully acquaints those Mercantile Gentlemen who have connections in foreign countries, such as France, Germany, Holland, etc. that he writes and translates into English (and vice versa) letters, invoices, bills of lading, and other incidental circumstances of commercial intercourse, stiled in either the FRENCH, HIGH GERMAN, or LOW DUTCH Languages, with the utmost propriety, accuracy, and expedition. Also protests in the foregoing Languages carefully copied and translated for Attornies, Notaries, and Tabellions; and the greatest attention will be paid, so as to merit their kind favours. The said Isaac Polack begs leave to assure the Gentlemen above addressed, (or any other employer) that SECRECY will be the principal object attached to; and their respective commands from any part of this county assiduously accomplished at a reasonable charge. PETITIONS, MEMORIAL, etc, drawn for disabled seamen, sailors, widows, orphans, or other persons, to any public office in this kingdom, and to foreign Courts, or to their Ambassadors, Residentaries, and Ministers of State, at very moderate fees. Dated Penryn June 27, 1776".[16]

Isaac Polack was a Freemason, Warden of the Penryn Lodge, and eventually a member of the Falmouth Lodge. The Penryn Lodge had been founded in 1782, and membership was comprised mainly of men who, as mariners, shipbuilders and others such as lawyers and victuallers, were linked to seafaring. Others were members of the defence volunteers, from the Penryn area.[17]

Samuel ben Samuel Ha-Levi ("Rabbi Saavil") and Eliezar Lipman (*c.* 1790-*c.*1813).

Saavil has been taken[18] as the first known minister to have served the community for some years, although his status as a Rabbi is uncertain. He died on the 22nd March 1814, and his headstone in the Falmouth cemetery (2:11) does not refer to any formal position of leadership that he occupied but simply praises his right-eousness rather than his leadership. This could imply that the use of *Rabbi* for him was a courtesy title.

As for Eliezer Lipman, it is possible that the *Lipman* (or Liepmann) who was paid by the Penzance congregation (on 9th October 1811) to "come from Truro to kill" was in fact the Rabbi in Falmouth at this time. His name also appears, as Eliezar Lipman (son of Michael), most likely as the officiant minister at a wedding in Penzance in June of 1813. (It is not known if this Lipman was connected with the much later Rabbi Nachum Lipman of Falmouth, from 1871). It would not be surprising if the Falmouth *shochet* was a regular visitor to Truro, where there was a small Jewish presence of a few families, and more than one man with such qual-ifications may have resided in the south of the County at some time or other.

Rev. Moses Hyman ("Rabbi Mowsha", or Moses ben Hayyim: *c.*1813-1830).

The Rev. Moses Hyman, who was born around 1765, and who died on 10th September 1830, is referred to as the community's *Chazan* on his headstone in the Penryn cemetery (4:3). There is, in fact, some confusion between various sources over the date of Moses Hyman's death. The headstone gives "Friday 22 Ellul 5590" which conversion tables suggest would have been 10th September 1830.[19] It has been said that Moses Hyman served the Falmouth congregation for 27 years,[20] but this may be an error, and the length of his service may have been 17 years, beginning in 1813, after the departure of Eliezer Lipman. (Although "Rabbi Saavil" died in 1814, he may not have served formally as Rabbi, or for only a brief period before 1803).

Little or nothing is known of Moses Hyman's ancestry, or that of his wife, Sarah (Sally), who was born in Helston around 1776 (1851 Census).[21] There was no settled Jewish presence in Helston, and it seems likely that Sarah was the daughter of Jews who were travelling, but who may have settled in the Helston-Falmouth area. Moses and Sarah Hyman were to have at least eight children, all of whom were born in Falmouth. The first child, Zibiah Hyman, was born around 1806,[22] and she married an Israel Myers (*c.* 1791-1872), a General Dealer of Plymouth, who was from Bavaria.[23] Their children were Bessey (1833-), Myer (1836-), Isaiah (1838-), Rebecca (1841-), and Jacob (1845-).[24] Zibiah Myers was a seamstress. There is no record of a burial for Israel or Zibiah Myers in Plymouth. Moses and Sarah Hyman's second child was Isaiah (Ishaya). He was born around 1809. He died at the age of seventeen and a half on 30th March 1827, and is buried in the Penryn Jewish cemetery. The third child, Leah was born around 1810, and worked as a Dressmaker. She married a Woolf Solomon of London. Harriet Elizabeth Hyman was born on 22nd December 1811. Two months after her father's death, on 7th November 1830, she was baptised into the Methodist Church in Falmouth by the Rev. W. Lawry.[25] The names of her parents are given in the register, and her late father is recorded as "Jewish Rabbi". On 11th August 1834, she was married to a local Christian, Edward Pearce Morrall. Her brother, Jacob Hyman had been born around 1812, and he died on 10th June 1900. He married a Jewess, Frances Phillips (c. 1813-1886) of Spitalfields, likely to have been related to the Isaac Phillips (below). Jacob Hyman worked in Spitalfields as a Butcher from 1843. From 1851, he was also a Constable in the London Docks, and an Attendant at his local synagogue. By 1881 he was living in Paddington, and later at St. Petersburgh Place, W.2. Jacob Hyman's sister, Julia was born around 1814. On 2nd December 1840, she married Isaac Phillips (c. 1816-1877) of Spitalfields, who was the son of Phillip van Koln from Holland. The couple had at least four children: Phillip, Moses, Isaiah and Miriam. Julia Hyman died at Bell Lane, Christ Church, London on 3rd July 1871. Her younger sister, Rose (Rosetta), was born around 1822. She appears to have been unmarried, and traded as a Furrier in Whitechapel. She died in Hackney on 28th January 1892. The youngest child of Moses and Sarah Hyman was Abraham (1823-1891), who appears in the circumcision register of Rabbi B. A. Simmons: "Falmouth…Abraham, son of Moses on Thursday, Rosh Chodesh Ellul 5583" (The New Moon marking the end of the month of Av and the beginning of the month of Ellul: 7th/8th August 1823 [26]). Abraham Hyman married a Catherine Myers (-1877) of London, and he also traded there as a Furrier. It is likely that Catherine Myers was related to the Israel Myers who had married Zibiah Hyman.

If Moses Hyman's incumbency lasted for some 27 years, from around 1803, it would have coincided with the Presidency of three men over the Falmouth congregation: Moses Jacob (until 1807), Lyon Joseph (1807-1815) and Jacob Jacob (1816-1853). In 1827, the latter found need to seek the guidance of the Chief Rabbi, Solomon Hirschel, on a matter relating to an impending marriage. From Hirschel's letter of reply to "Mr. Jacobs",[27] dated Motzaei Shabbath (Saturday night) 20th Kislev 5588 (8th December 1827), and from other genealogical information,[28] it can be inferred that the parties concerned were Rose (Rosetta) Joseph (1806-) and Abraham Davidson. The intended bride was a daughter of Moses Isaac Jacob (-1834) of Falmouth, and his wife, Judith Rebecca Jacob (1768-1849). Judith Jacob was the sister of the President, Jacob Jacob (1774-1853), who, in writing to the Chief Rabbi, was raising a matter of some delicacy, in that the prospective bride was his niece. In the absence any surviving community records for Falmouth, the Chief Rabbi's reply affords not only a glimpse into the conduct of this aspect of congregational affairs, but also confirms the concern of the congregation to proceed with respect and caution with regard to religious practice. " I received the letter regarding the marriage and I will reply to your questions in order: Regarding the fact that the bride is pregnant from the bridegroom. First of all, we require three G-d fearing men who are not relatives of the bride or the bridegroom to sit down together and question the bride and the bridegroom carefully. If both admit that she became pregnant from him, they must take an oath (that this is true), that is the bride must swear that she was never with anyone else from whom she may have become pregnant and that she is sure that she is pregnant from him. He too must take an oath that he does not suspect her of being pregnant from anyone else and that the child is his. After this is carried out, she should be referred to in the kethuba as 'this Rosa daughter of…' (not the usual form 'this virgin Rosa…) with no mention made in the kethuba as to whether she is a virgin or not. As long as we know that she behaved decently and was not, G-d forbid, licentious, we can rely on their oaths. The sum pledged by the husband in the ketubah should be 100 (silver coins) not 200 (as in the case of a virgin). It appears to me that the name should be spelt (in Hebrew) 'Roisa', as this is how it is pronounced. If the above is in order, the marriage ceremony may be carried out by the learned Reb Moshe, the reader and (leader?) of your community, and it should be recorded in the community records that they both took an oath". It is not known if the couple's child survived, but their first child, Isaac (who may be the same) was born in Penzance (his year of birth having been given as 1830).[29] This Isaac Davidson was to marry a daughter of Rabbi B. A. Simmons of Penzance, Amelia Simmons (1825-) in London around 1853. Rosa and Abraham Davidson are known to have had three further children, Eliza, Henry and Annabel. Rosa Joseph's sister, Phoebe, was to marry Abraham Davidson's brother, Isaac, and both couples eventually emigrated to Australia (as did Isaac and Amelia Davidson).

The conversion of the late Rabbi Moses Hyman's nineteen year old daughter Harriet in 1830, was an event of some notoriety. She had become drawn to Christianity, and announced her intention to convert. A dispute broke out within her family, fuelled by the animosity of some people within the Jewish congregation to her proposed baptism. It became so bitter that the girl ran to the Town Mayor, James ("Jas") Cornish, for protection. He was obliged to adjudicate and summoned her family, who only agreed to take her back if she stopped going to Church. The domestic outcome is uncertain but her engagement was broken off. She remained resolved to convert and, eventually, it was reported in the *West Briton* and *Cornwall Advertiser* that she had been publicly baptised at the Wesleyan Methodist Chapel. Evangelical activity to gain converts was common at this time as Methodism expanded rapidly, and a case such as this gave a high profile to the issue of Jewish conversion, as Chapels sprang up and proliferated in both the main towns and country areas alike. Later, by 1864 two organisations for "Promoting Christianity among the Jews" had established offices in Falmouth. The small Jewish congregation would have felt particularly vulnerable to such a popular and enthusiastic movement, and the publicity and controversy surrounding the Harriet Hyman affair would have contributed to their sense of insecurity and initiated a period of acute self-awareness, and possibly alarm as a religious minority within the town.

Rabbi Joseph Benedict Rintel (*c*.1832-1849).

Rintel's birth certificate (issued in 1809), his *Reisepass* (1831), a six-month permit from the Hamburg authorities and his Naturalisation papers (1861) have all survived.[30] He was born in the Hanseatic town of Hamburg on 29th November 1809 to Benedict Jacob Rintel and Thérèse (née Kalman). Rintely, his father's family name, and Kalman are both Hungarian. His father's forename Benedict was a vernacular form of the Hebrew name *Baruch*. On his *Reisepass*, issued in Hamburg for a period of six months on 4th January 1831, his name is given as Joseph Benedix Rintely. He was then 21 years of age. The *Reisepass* records that he had black hair and beard, and brown eyes. This young rabbi arrived in England in 1831, and was appointed as his first position to the Falmouth congregation soon after. Later, he walked alongside the Mayor and the Roman Catholic Priest in a public parade to demonstrate for the implementation of the Reform Bill.[31] This has been taken to be the Reform Bill of 1832, but it is possible that the public parade in question relates to the petition to remove Jewish Disabilities and to allow Jewish Parliamentary representation in 1848.

The Quakers had been established in Cornwall for some time, and they built a Meeting House in Falmouth in 1805, a few years before the opening of the second synagogue. Most prominent amongst the Cornish Quaker families was the Fox family of Falmouth, which became a wealthy, charitable and well-connected family through their involvement in shipping, the fishing industry, and mining. In his journal, which he kept from 1832, Robert Barclay Fox (1817-1855), then 15, described in some detail and with accuracy his attendance at a Jewish wedding on 28th August 1833, and the "priest" who officiated at the occasion may well have been Rintel. The wedding was, in fact that of Henry Joseph of Bristol to Amelia Jacob, the second daughter of Jacob Jacob of Falmouth, and it was reported in the Cornish press.[32] Later, on 31st March 1836, Fox was to record in his Journal that he "visited nearly all the Jews in town with a French captain to sell some doubloons". In September 1839, he attended a lecture by a David Moses on "Peace", but he does not indicate if the speaker was Jewish. In December 1841, he refers to a "Jewess Mrs. Moses" who was a witness to an assault upon a ship's captain by three sailors.

During his years in Falmouth, Rintel supplemented his income by bookbinding and teaching Hebrew and German.[33] Not only would German have been the natural means of communication for the members of the Jewish community, but it would also have helped children in their study of the Torah portion for the week which would have had a Yiddish commentary. On 6th June 1838 at the age of 28, he married Fanny (1814-1884), a daughter of Rabbi Barnet Asher Simmons of Penzance. On the marriage certificate Rintel is identified by the rank of "Gentleman" rather than the profession of Rabbi. The couple subsequently lived in Killigrew Street in Falmouth. Rintel was a *mohel*, but it is not known whether he learned this skill before arriving in England, or in London, before his arrival in Falmouth, or later, either from B. A. Simmons, or upon moving to London (in 1849) where he became renowned for his skills as a *mohel*. He is mentioned in the Minute-Books of the Penzance community on several occasions, because he acted as a locum there when his father-in-law suffered ill-health. He remained in Falmouth for 17 years. Local family ties and his assistance to his father-in-law allowed him to lead a settled and agreeable life in the 1840s. He kept abreast of ideas and developments in the wider Anglo-Jewish world, however, because for 1842 and 1845 he is listed as a subscriber to the Jewish periodical *The Voice of Jacob*. Dr. Nathan Marcus Adler, the Chief Rabbi, issued a statistical audit "of all the Congregations in the British Empire", in which it was recorded that Rintel was the paid incumbent minister at Falmouth, as *shochet*, *chazan*, mohel, secretary and teacher, at a salary of £50 per annum. When he eventually left Falmouth in April 1849, the occasion was reported in the County's press: "Testimonial of Respect to a Hebrew Pastor – The Rev. JOSEPH RINTEL, Rabbi of the Jews at Falmouth, being about to leave that place after a ministry of eighteen years, for London, has been presented by his congregation, amongst whom he had much endeared himself by his general conduct, with a silver salver bearing the following inscription – Presented to the Rev. Joseph Rintel, by the members and friends of the Falmouth congregation, as a testimonial of their respect and esteem. A.M. 5609".[34]

He had served the Falmouth congregation during the last period of its existence as a sizeable and flourishing community. It was soon to decline with rapid speed. Rintel and his wife were to settle in London, where Fanny Simmons' brother, Moses (1817-1876), was well established, and was a member of the Great Synagogue in Duke's Place. Moses Simmons was well placed to keep Rintel informed of any opportunities which might arise in the city. Rintel and his wife Fanny took up residence (at No. 17a) in Bury Street, in the City, where Moses lived in the same row of houses as the Chief Rabbi. Joseph Rintel died on Monday 5th August 1867 at 33 Francis Street, Victoria Park "after a severe and protracted illness". He was 57 and was buried in the Jewish Burial Ground at West Ham. A year later, on 24th July 1868 "a numerous body of friends and relatives" were present in the cemetery for the setting up of his memorial headstone. The respect with which he was held was reflected in the presence of "Rev. A. Levy, Rev. A. L. Green, Dr. A. Asher, and representatives of the societies to which [the] deceased had belonged". It was noted that the inscription on the stone was "from the pen of Samson Rausack, Librarian to the Beth Hamidrash".[35] A Rev. Myer Rintel was minister in Edinburgh (1824-1827) and his son, Rev. Moses Rintel (who may have born in Edinburgh in 1823) was later *chazan* in Brighton. Eventually he left for Australia.[36] Myer Rintel and Moses Rintel may have been related to Joseph Rintel, but this is not certain.

Samuel Herman (*c.* 1850-1860).

By the time of the 1851 census, Falmouth had a new rabbi. The census shows Samuel Herman from Konin in Poland, age 49, as the Rabbi of the Hebrew Congregation. His son, Abraham David Herman, then 23, is described as a bookbinder. However, the following year Abraham is given as the incumbent Rabbi, and his father Samuel as "clergy".[37] Whilst it is possible that father and son were both rabbis, it is also possible that this is an error, or that Samuel Herman was also named *Abraham*. Samuel Herman's wife was from Neustadt, Poland. From this time the congregation was in serious decline, and its finances must have suffered as a result of falling numbers. Herman must have decided that he needed to look elsewhere for a secure incumbency. In 1860 a dispute broke out between the Falmouth community and Mr. Herman relating to a delay in the payment of his salary as *shochet*. The withholding of his salary was clearly a punitive response by congregational officials to his intention to leave for another position in Sheffield. Herman saw this as a form of intimidation and he wrote to the Chief Rabbi, Dr. Adler, who wrote to the President of the Falmouth congregation on his behalf: "Mr. Herman is leaving for Sheffield and complains you object to him leaving . I think you have no right to form an impediment to the man's promotion in life."[38] The extent to which the Chief Rabbinate was involved in the affairs of the Cornish congregations is difficult to assess, although, in the case of Penzance, there is direct evidence of such involvement, especially in the appointment of ministers during the 1800s.

Marks Morris (1860-1864).

Little is known about the Rev. "Marks Morris of Prussia" whose appointment as Rabbi of Falmouth Synagogue was announced in the *Royal Cornwall Gazette* on 5th November 1860.[39] In the 1861 census for Falmouth his name is given as "Morrice Marks" and his year of birth as 1827. He was married to Jebbeth (b.1831). They had three children who had by that time all been born in Prussia: Charlotte (b.1852), Willy (b. 1856) and Lena (b.1860). It is not known how long Morris remained in Falmouth, but he probably stayed until 1864, because from that year the Falmouth congregation no longer had a *shochet* and had to send to Penzance for kosher meat. By 1874, a Rev. Marks Morris, likely the same man, was Reader at the Great Synagogue, Manchester. It would seem unlikely that the Maurice Marks who laid the foundation stone of the Middlesbrough synagogue in 1937 was the same man, in that he would have been 90 years old by that time. This M. Marks was probably a relative of the Rev. Jacob Marks who was minister at Middlesbrough in 1874.[40]

Isaac Aryeh Rubinstein (*c.* 1864-1868)
and A. (Abraham) Abelson (*c.* 1868-1870/71).

Isaac Aryeh Rubinstein (who was from Russia) officiated (jointly) with Rabbi Rittenberg, the minister in Penzance at a wedding there in 1865. Much later, in 1886, he was living in Northampton (but was not its minister) and he then became the minister in Penzance. He may have been the minister in Falmouth from late 1864 or early 1865, being followed by A. Abelson, in or soon after 1868. It would seem that both men were associated with the Falmouth congregation, and were examined by the Chief Rabbi on their skills as *shochetim*, Rubinstein in 1868, and Abelson in 1872.[41] It seems that Abraham Abelson, or his family, were originally from Lithuania, but the 1871 Census for Falmouth (in which he appears as a

Teacher of Hebrew and German) gives his birth-place as Neustadt, Germany. There were several towns with this name in Germany and Poland. Abelson was a witness at the marriage in Penzance on 9th June 1869 of Aaron Harris Mark Beirnstein of Dowlais, Merthyr Tydfil, to Esther Joseph, a daughter of Henry Joseph. It is likely that Abelson left his post in Falmouth in 1871, and in 1873 he became the minister in Merthyr Tydfil, which was comprised of Jews from Russia and Poland.[42] His examination by the Chief Rabbi in 1872 may well have been preliminary to his being confirmed as suitable to take up the post in Merthyr. His son, Joseph was born there in 1873, and he was later to become a Rabbi, at Cardiff (1895-1899) and Bristol (1899-1906), and he was in Leeds by 1920.[43]

Nachum Lipman (*Nahum Eliahu b'HaRav R. Mordecai Lipman c.1871-1874/5*)

Nachum Lipman (*c.*1847-1921), son of Rabbi Marcus Lipman, came to England from Poland *c.* 1869, likely as a married man, with his wife Leah (*b.* 1850) and an infant, Deborah. Their second child, Rebecca, was born in London. He served in Falmouth for a short term only, and two of his daughters were born there. A close friend of the Chief Rabbi and his study circle, Lipman was appointed *Rosh Hashocetim* (Chief Shochet) *c.*1874, a post he held in London for 47 years.[44]

Samuel Orler (1875-1880).

The last known Rabbi was Samuel Orler, who was in Falmouth from around 1875 to 1880.[45] His family were from Russia, where Samuel Orler was born in 1853, and his wife, Leah in 1854. The young couple came to England in 1874, and arrived soon after in Falmouth, with their sons, Herman (who had been born in Russia in 1873) and Philip (born in London, Middlesex, in 1874). A daughter, Queene (Queenie, or Malkah) was born in Falmouth in 1879, in which year the congregation had all but ceased to exist. It seems most likely that Orler came to Falmouth despite the terminal condition of its congregation because his youth and comparative inexperience prevented him from finding a position with better prospects elsewhere. His duties as a minister cannot have been especially onerous, nor financially rewarding, and his appointment may well have been a charitable act on the part of Samuel Jacob, the congregation's President. When the family left Falmouth, Samuel Orler went to Stroud, where his daughter, Sarah, was born in 1880. The Stroud Jewish community, which was to enjoy only a brief existence, from 1877 to 1908, consisted mainly of young Jews from Poland and Russia, with a few from Germany. By trade they were almost exclusively tailors who had been recruited directly from Eastern Europe by the large local non-Jewish clothing firm of Holloway Brothers. From 1881 to 1891, census records show that the members of the Stroud congregation were nearly all in their twenties or thirties, with around 40 to 60 children below the age of 14 (all requiring Hebrew classes, and the males preparation for their *bar mitzvah*. There was a high proportion of unmarried men, several of whom married local non-Jews, one in church, but with two women converting to Judaism). The lack of potential Jewish marriage partners was a factor in migration to other places. From 1880 (or 1881) to 1890, Orler was the Stroud congregation's minister.[46] His family were settled in Stroud by the time of the 1881 Census, when Samuel Orler is given as "Min. of Religion", although a Samuel Shynman (52), from Poland, is also recorded on the census as "Jewish Minister". It is not known if Shynman was, or had ever been the Rabbi of the Stroud congregation, but he had previously lived in Middlesborough and Merthyr Tydfil. He may have made way for the younger Orler, or he may have been a temporary resident, perhaps awaiting an incumbency elsewhere. Samuel Orler appears on Stroud Jewish marriage records as Secretary or Celebrant from 1882 to 1889, and when he left in 1890, he was described as the "Minister to the Stroud Congregation for the last ten years [and] was the recipient of a handsome testimonial from his pupils upon leaving that town". His successor was a Rev. A. Rosenberg from the Longton congregation in Staffordshire.

Penzance

For the Penzance community there are various documentary sources that reveal the names and tenure of the congregation's ministers, chief of which are the congregational minutes and accounts (from 1808) which include formal contracts in Hebrew and Yiddish (some very detailed)[47] for each minister. In the 18th century, however, such records do not exist, and any reconstruction of the ministers must be tentative. In the early days of the Penzance community, members of the Hart family may have acted in some religious capacity. They had settled there just prior to the 1740s, and their influence within the Jewish community and over the Hebrew congregation was significant. Several members of the family were known by the title *Rabbi* including Abraham Hart, who died around 1720, his son, Asher Hart, who died between 1745-1752 (neither of whom are certain to have lived in the town), and Abraham Hart, also known as Solomon Lazarus (*d.* 1784), who was a resident of Penzance. Although the title of "Rabbi" may have been applied to these men in an honorary sense, indicating their status and experience in leadership of the congregational affairs, it remains possible that they were from a skilled and trained rabbinical background. Even if they were not rabbis, they would have conducted the religious services, and regulated congregational affairs in circumstances where it was not possible for a trained rabbi to be employed. The fact that the first synagogue was built in 1768 suggests that the Jewish community was by then large enough to need the services of a minister and *shochet*.

The Rabbis from 1808.

From 1808 and 1811 a series of incumbent ministers passed through Penzance, most remaining in the town only briefly. It is not known if they were all qualified sufficiently to be recognised by the Chief Rabbi. Some would have possessed knowledge in a limited area only, such as Talmudic study, or ritual slaughter, or in the skills of a cantor by virtue of a good voice, and so be of sufficient use to be hired for a short term only. It has been supposed that they were hired only for a two-year period,[48] but very few stayed for the full two years, or remained for longer, and eventually, even shorter, one-year appointments were made. The onerous duties which the senior members expected of their rabbis (formally ratified in a document of 1817) seem to have proved insupportable for many of the ministers in Penzance, and this combination of heavy duties and poor pay applied to other areas of the South-West.[49]

Aaron Selig (to 1808).

When the Penzance Minute Book opens in 1808, a *Rav Aaron* was the incumbent minister, and a note of 8th April records "By cash advanced to *Rav Aaron* Wages £15. By deficiency on the cost of *Matzos* for *Rav Aaron Selig* 16/8". This Aaron Selig had apparently come to Penzance from London, and he returned there after these payments due to him. He was to be re-engaged (from London) in May 1811.

Moses Isaac (1808-1810).

A few days after the departure of Aaron Selig, the Minutes of 11th April note:
"By paid *Rav Moshe* expenses from London £11", the sum suggesting that the expenses were for the transport of a couple or a family, in that the journey from London to Penzance by stage wagon (which took up to a week, or slightly longer) is recorded elsewhere in the Minutes as costing as much as £6 for one person, just under a sixth of the rabbi's annual wage. On 21st September, *Rav Moshe* was paid his "half years Salary £19-10", from which he was still expected to make regular offerings to the congregational fund, as on the 9th October, when he paid in six shillings. The signatures, in Hebrew, of the men who scrutinized and authorised the accounts and these payments also appear in 1808, and subsequently as: *Asher Laemle ben Eliezar* (Lemon Hart), *Hayyim ben Benyamin Wolf* (Hyman Woolf), *Moshe Hayim ben Avraham* (Henry Ralph), *Elimelech ben Yoseph* (Elias Magnus) and *Asher Laemle ben Hayim* (Lemon Woolf). Before the end of 1808, a new set of *Tikkunim* (Regulations) were drawn up for the administration of the congregation's affairs, and included specific rules relating to the Rabbi's duties to collect donations, to study before noon each day with the Gabbai (Treasurer), and his entitlements to receive half a crown as part of his salary: before reading Megillah, any portion of the Mishnah which relates to holy objects, at Passover and at Simchas Torah, and "after a woman gives birth".

The following year saw Moses Isaac's salary reduced, with two half-year payments of £18 each, on 9th April and 1st October 1809, and, on the latter date an increased offering by him of 11/9. The Minutes do not reveal what may have led to this, but it is clear that the Rabbi had decided to leave his post as soon as he was able. It seems that negotiations were already being made to replace him. A record of 1st October, "To M (presumably "Mr.") *Phillips* since recd. 14/6", would seem to be an offering from the next aspiring incumbent, *Feival* (Phillip Samuel) made with a view to secure the position. If the congregational elders had acted with a degree of frugality in paying Isaac, they were not without charity when it came to another of their community, and on the same date made a charitable payment from donations "towards *Leb Henna* (Judah from Hannau, Germany) an infirm old man, the sum of Seven Shillings per Week for his Maintenance, To be paid by Lemon Hart" (who would be re-imbursed by the other donors). It would seem, however, that Moses Isaac had achieved an improvement in his salary, most likely as a condition of post-poning his resignation, his successor's arrival being delayed. On 25th March 1810, there is the entry "By half Years Wage (Rabbi) £21", and on 30th June "By wages to this day Moses Isaac £7 – 10 – 0". This last sum was clearly not the equivalent of a further three months salary, and it would seem that Isaac must have disputed the payment. The entry of 30th June also notes that £6 had been paid "By expenses for *Rav Feival* coming from London" (to take up his post). Some two months later, an entry dated as Friday, the eve of the New Year 5571 (September 1810) Moses Isaac, signing in Hebrew as *Moshe ben Rav Isaac*, confirmed his acceptance of his severance wages of a further £10. Despite his resignation, he remained a member of the congregation for the time being, his name appearing until the Spring of 1811.

Rabbi Feival: Phillip Samuel (June 1810 - April 1811).

The Minute Book entries dated as 29th September and 28th October confirm that *Rav Feival* had been paid the sum (or possibly part sum) of £16 – 13 – 4, and that "Feival took office New Moon of Tammuz June 1810", Feival signing a receipt of wages for £12 as *Meshulam Feivush ben Rav S* (Samuel?). From these details, and the reference of 1st October 1809 to *Phillips* (above), Feival, whose brief tenure was less than a year, can be identified as the Phillip Samuel who is mentioned at some length by Israel Solomon (1803-1893) in his *Records of my Family* (1887).[50] Solomon was clearly intrigued by Phillip Samuel, of whom he says that "his life was full of romance".[51] Samuel, who was a native of Warsaw, was the son of the "secretary" (presumably the President, the *Rav S*, above) of the great synagogue there, and he was "highly educated in Hebrew…and well versed in Jewish literature". As was the tradition in Poland at that time, Jewish marriages were at an early age. The identity of Samuel's wife is not known, but they had at least one child, a daughter. The marriage was not a happy one, and may have ended in divorce, but certainly Samuel appears to have abandoned his family, and it would seem that, from then on, he remained single. He moved to Vilna, from where he travelled widely, trading as a silk merchant. He purchased his stock from importers in Danzig, and had to travel there regularly by caravan to purchase supplies. The strict religious regulations that operated in Poland required that he had to take ten men with him to make up a minyan for prayer, a practice that Samuel found "opposed to the activity required for commercial pursuit". When a "quicker means of transport came into vogue", that of the sledge, Samuel abandoned the former practice, which was even then an anachronism, travelling alone, and reaching Danzig within in a day. For this he was placed under a *cherem* (excommunication) by the rabbis.

Samuel travelled as far as Moscow, where he had "a good customer" in the form of an unusually liberal-minded and tolerant merchant, who "was at that time in advance of the general prejudices against foreigners and Jews in particular" (that were held by the merchant's family and his household) and he would invite Samuel to lodge with him on his visits. On one such occasion the merchant "told Phillip in confidence that his wife and servants would have the sleeping apartment, bedding and every chair on which he had sat scrubbed, washed and purified with the sprinkling of holy water to protect their Slavonic holiness from the pollution that a Jew might leave behind". Such anti-Semitism was rife in both attitude and action, and the assault and murder of solitary Jewish travellers was common. The rule of the rabbis that ten men should travel together for the purpose of prayer may in essence have had a ritual character, but it also served the interests of safety and security. Samuel was to discover this to his great cost when he encountered the perils of the Russian winter. While he was crossing a frozen river "with a train of wagons laden with silk and other merchandise...the ice gave way and the wagons sank into the river". Samuel escaped with his life, and with just enough money to flee from Russia, where his inevitable bankruptcy could result in a prison sentence.

How many years passed after this flight from Russia is not clear, but he did not stay in Eastern Europe and, eventually, he arrived in England, where the prospect of "the life of an ordinary Polish emigrant, supported by peddling, was disgusting to the educated Phillip", and he determined to seek a better life for himself. The fact that he was the son of a former President of the Warsaw synagogue (and, presumably, his suppression of the fact that a *cherem* had once been laid upon him in Poland) gave him a certain prestige, and he must have made contacts who assisted him to gain entry into the London house of the Chief Rabbi Herschell. It is not known if Samuel had ever trained as a *shochet* in Poland, or if he sought and obtained a licence in London to practise as such, but his Hebrew learning, and ability to lead services as a *chazan*, impressed the Chief Rabbi, who "got him the place as reader in prayers in the synagogue at Penzance". However, his appointment did not turn out well, because "For this he was not fitted. Attached to which office was then the slaughtering of cattle and poultry kosher". As *Rav Feival*, Samuel is not referred to as *shochet* in the Penzance Minutes, it is possible that he had been appointed solely as *chazan*, perhaps on condition that he should undertake training in these skills with Moses Isaac to secure a licence. However, it is likely that his brief tenure in Penzance was connected with the fact that the duties of *shochet* were either distasteful to him, or beyond his capacity. Alternatively, if Moses Isaac, who continued to live in the town, agreed to cover as *shochet* it is possible that Samuel, habituated to the life of a solitary traveller, found even the responsibilities of a *chazan* and teacher too great, and was unable to adapt to the demands that congregational life made of him. The Penzance minutes for the 25th March 1811 note that *Rav Feival* was paid what appears to have been his final wages of £8 - 6 – 8. *Rav Moshe* (Isaac) made an offering on 14th April, and Samuel's successor was in place by May.

In Falmouth, the congregation's President, Lyon Joseph, was an agent for the government's programme of collecting gold (purchased with paper money) to pay the troops engaged in the war with Napoleon, and to fund supplies for campaigns. The work of such a gold agent was potentially very profitable, especially for an enterprising man. Phillip Samuel went to Falmouth to work for Lyon Joseph soon after leaving Penzance. On 18th August 1811, a 26-year old Polish man, Isaiah Falk Valentine, originally from Wroclaw (Breslau), some 190 miles south-west of Warsaw, had been appointed as *shochet* to the Plymouth congregation. To supplement his salary he also acted as an agent for a London money exchange merchant, and he travelled through Devon and Cornwall buying up gold in exchange for paper money. Such agents would often "sub-let" their services to others, and at some point, it is said[52] that Phillip Samuel entrusted some money to him to buy gold on his behalf. Knowing that he would be carrying a considerable quantity of paper money, a man named Wyatt, "lured Valentine to Fowey and drowned him there"[53], on 11th November 1811. "Subsequently, a roll of sea-soaked notes amounting to £260 was found in a pile of dung in Wyatt's stables".[54] Wyatt was hanged for the crime, and the case was widely reported in the Cornish press.[55] Eventually, the government gold-buying programme ended. Lyon Joseph left Falmouth for Bath in 1815, and Phillip Samuel "and a fellow-countryman settled down in St. Austell...as jewellers". It was there that Israel Solomon, who was travelling by coach from Falmouth to London, stopped off while the coach was changing horses, and first met Samuel "at his shop and residence". Through Lyon Joseph, Samuel would have known Israel Solomon's father, Solomon Solomon (1764-1819) who, presumably, was in the coach party. This meeting must have made a great impression on the very young Solomon, then about thirteen, and it led to a friendship between Phillip Samuel and Israel Solomon.

Phillip Samuel's jewellery business in St. Austell was not a success. He was still in contact with Lyon Joseph, who advised him to go to Portugal, where the Joseph and Solomon families had business contacts. Samuel accepted the advice, and was provided with letters of recommendation to a Schemaya Cohen "the richest resident in Lisbon", and set sail for the Portuguese capital. Phillip Samuel was, apparently, "a handsome gentleman, wearing a black beard" and whilst on board ship, "he felt so impressed with the prejudice that his beard would arouse amongst the Portuguese rabble" that he shaved it off. Later he came to regret this when he became familiar with some of "the secret Jewish families", descended from the Marranos, from the time of the cruelties of the Inquisition, and who received him as a friend, and held fast to their Jewish faith in private. Israel Solomon himself was present in Lisbon in 1819, having sailed from Falmouth to tend to his terminally ill father. "I remember one Saturday evening two gentlemen came to Mr. Cohen's house to ask the date of Kippur and they bowed low to the Ark; one knelt and wept like a child". In 1820, after his father's death, Israel Solomon left Lisbon, but Phillip Samuel remained there, and, as an act of charity, he took in a Jewish orphan to live with him and work as his assistant. The youth deceived Samuel by stealing a stock of gold watches that had been imported from France. He was eventually found out, but he "converted to Christianity and was set free by the intercession of his god-father, an influential resident of Lisbon". It would seem that the solitary and childless Samuel had become fond of the boy and had trusted him, and he was shocked and distressed to be publicly insulted and taunted by the thief when, later, he met him in the street. The incident is said to have "killed poor Samuel, for he went home and died a few hours after from a broken heart". In later life, Israel Solomon looked back with fondness and sadness on the time he had spent with Phillip Samuel in Lisbon, where, at the Solomon house, he had witnessed his ability to talk and discuss with "so many educated Jews from Morocco and Arabia…over their books". He came to regret that he had not learned Hebrew from Samuel and from the Jewish visitors, so that he too could have enjoyed such an experience, and taken it with him for the future. The impression gained from Israel Solomon's recollection of Phillip Samuel is of an intelligent, cultured, and kindly man, but also of a lonely man, whose personal life was unsettled and unfulfilled.

Today, Lisbon has two synagogues. The largest is Sephardi, in the Rua Alexandre Herculano, and the smaller one is Ashkenazi, on the first floor of a building in the Rua Elias Garcia. In the early 1800s the Jewish population in Lisbon (and in Portugal itself) was small, but it was characterised by an especially close co-operation between the Sephardi and Ashkenazi communities, and between Jews and Marranos, both features of Israel Solomon's account. That Jews from Cornwall should have gravitated to Lisbon is not at all surprising in view of the daily Packet Boat services that linked Falmouth and Penzance to the Portuguese capital. In Penzance, at the bottom of Chapel Street, and immediately opposite St. Mary's Church a grand detached house with its own garden overlooking the harbour, was to become the town's Portuguese Embassy, so important was trade and commerce between Penzance and Portugal. The story of *Rav Feival* of Penzance and that of the Joseph and Solomon families of Falmouth would seem to reflect these connections.

Aaron Selig (1811).

Feival's early departure prompted the Penzance elders to re-engage Aaron Selig, and the Minutes for May 1811 record: "By cash paid in London to *Rav Selig* £3, paid him remainder of his expenses down & for Books". His contract follows: "On this day 15th Iyyar (May) we have employed Rav Aaron son of Pinchas as *shochet* and *chazan* and to teach children of the Penzance congregation. For 40 guineas per annum. [A half year's notice before leaving is required on either side], (signed) *Aaron ben Pinchas Selig, Shochet of Penzance*. The 29th July was to be the last entry of accounts drawn up by Lemon Hart as President. On 4th August, the accounts were drawn up by Elias Magnus, with a balance paid to the new President, Hyman Woolf. The entry notes: "On this day, Sunday 4th Av 1811 we paid Rabbi Aaron son of Pinchas three months wages 10 guineas, I have received from Elimelech ben Joseph [Elias Magnus] three months wages, [signed] *Aaron ben Pinchas Selig (shochet)*". Selig's incumbency may well have been a stop-gap, and he left the position early in October, when, on 9th, the Minutes read: "Mr. Magnus expenses paid by him for *Lipman* to come from Truro to kill, Paid Selig his [final 3 months] wages £9 – 12 – 2 and what he owed for offering making together ten Guineas £10 – 10, [and in the left column], By Selig his offering, 17/10". The reference to this *Lipman* is intriguing, especially as his name is associated with Truro. Truro had only a very small Jewish community, and its members were affiliated either to Falmouth or to Penzance. This Lipman is most likely to be identified with the Eliezar Lipman (son of Michael) who was named as a witness on the *Ketubah* (marriage contract) of Barnett (Abraham Issacher) Asher Simmons to Bluma (Flora) Jacob in June of 1813 in Penzance (see below). Lipman was, most likely, *shochet* and *rav* in Falmouth at this time.

Aaron Selig settled in Penzance and traded as a jeweller, and his contributions as a member of the congregation appear from this point, with his signature on the accounts of 23rd November 1812. He was to have a troubled and disputatious relationship with the congregational elders, especially during the 1820s, when, for a while, he lost his membership. From this it seems likely that his two brief periods as *shochet* were also marked with a degree of discord, and his successor was to fare no better. Aaron Selig's son, Benjamin (1814-1872), a watchmaker, was also to take an active part in congregational affairs, and at some point during his time in Penzance, he trained as a rabbi, under B. A. Simmons (below). After the death of his parents, Benjamin Aaron Selig emigrated to Australia, and became the minister of a congregation in Melbourne, and from there he moved to the new Canterbury Hebrew congregation at Christchurch on the South Island of New Zealand, where he died. His widow returned to Melbourne with her family, but a son, Phineas Selig (1856-1941) remained in Christchurch, and became the proprietor of the Christchurch Press, and the first President of the New Zealand Newspaper Proprietors' Association.[56]

Barnett Asher (Abraham Issachar) Simmons (December 1811 – June 1813).

Barnett Asher Simmons (Abraham Issachar ben Asher, 1784-1860) was the longest resident Rabbi in Cornwall from 1811 to 1860. He did not serve the congregation for the whole of that time, nor, it would seem, for any substantial continuous period, but he was employed by them, intermittently, over a period of some forty years.[57] His maternal grandfather, Abraham (Issachar) Michel (-1818) was the son of a Reb Michael Michel of Ostrowza, Poland. It is not clear when Abraham Michel arrived in London, and the name of his wife is not known, but the couple had daughters, one of whom, Sara (*bas Issachar*) married an Asher Simmons (*ben Simcha*) from Germany. Their son, Barnett Asher, was also named Abraham Issachar, after his maternal grandfather, although one of these names may also have belonged to his paternal grandfather. He was born in 1784 in London. When he was only seven years old, his mother, Sara, died, and was buried on 9th June 1791.[58] Soon after this, his young son went to live in the home of his grandfather, at 2, Duke's Place, adjacent to the Great Synagogue, where Abraham Michael was a member. Asher Simmons was to re-marry, although the name of the second wife is not known. There were at least two sons from this marriage, Joshua and Benjamin, who became half-brothers to Barnett Simmons.

Abraham Michel was also a prosperous man. An original extract from one of his accounts, dated 1st January 1804, indicates that, by then, his business held reserve profits of some £500, in partnership with "L. Abrahams", whose share that year was £169. On his death, Abraham left in his will (dated 1818) an estate worth some £6000, to his two remaining daughters, who are not named.[59] Whilst living with his grandfather, on the 6th June 1798, Barnett Simmons became formally apprenticed to Abraham Jacobs, "Japanner and Painter", of Denmark Court in the parish of St. Martin-in-the-Fields, from whom he learned his trade. At the time he was apprenticed, he lived in New Court, Dukes Place, in the Parish of St. James. His indenture fee of twenty one pounds (a considerable sum at that time) was paid by his maternal grandfather Abraham Michel, also of New Court. The document (of 6th June 1798) was witnessed by I. I. Bing and L. J. Abrahams, and clearly signed as "Barnett Simmons". His father's name, Asher, does not appear on the document, suggesting, perhaps, that he was deceased. Abraham Michel carried on a polishing business, catering for the needs of the many goldsmiths and silversmiths in the area, with L. J. Abrahams as his partner. I. I. Bing was secretary of the Great Synagogue in Duke's Place and it would have been the synagogue where the Simmons family worshipped. B.A. Simmons's name, however, does not appear on a list of charity apprenticeships sponsored by the synagogue. B.A. Simmons' employer, Abraham Jacobs, Japanner and Painter, of Denmark Court, in the Parish of St. Martin-in-the-Fields, Westminster, was closely connected with the Western Synagogue in its early days. He was well known as a sign-painter, a skill which would have been passed on to his apprentice, and it has been supposed (but not confirmed) that, later, Simmons may have applied such skills to paint some of the artefacts of the interior of the Penzance synagogue, such as the two panels of the Ten Commandments.[60] Abraham Jacobs was also said to have been extremely learned in Jewish religious matters. His influence may have determined his apprentice's eventual choice to become a Rabbi, and he could well have come to the attention of the Chief Rabbi through the influence of I.I. Bing.

Simmons completed his Articles in 1804, and little or nothing is known of his life at that time. Like Lemon Hart, a degree of mythology has grown around the man, and he has even, quite erroneously been given as "of Falmouth".[61] Soon after 1804, while still living in London, it has been said that he was press-ganged into the Navy (the abduction has even been transposed to Chapel Street, Penzance after his arrival in 1811, there being, of course, no evidence of any prolonged absence on his part in the congregational records). It has also been supposed that he was at the Battle of Trafalgar, but no direct evidence of any of these details has ever emerged. It is uncertain if his name ever appeared on the muster roll of any of the fleet which would have been registered at Greenwich. He certainly does not appear on the list of the holders of the Trafalgar medal, but as this was not issued until 1848, and had to be applied for, this is inconclusive. The tradition that he lost a finger at that famous battle is almost certainly apocryphal,[62] the lost finger having been the result of a boating accident, much later, in Penzance harbour. Whatever the exact circumstances of this accident, it is unlikely to have been connected with the dispute that came before the Mayor of Penzance, whose Journal for 30th December 1816 records a "Hearing Angwin against Symmons about boat and craft, advised them to refer it to arbitration of two fishermen". Some six months later, on 28th July 1817, the Mayor heard a similar boating complaint by a Henry Symons

Simmons of Penzance

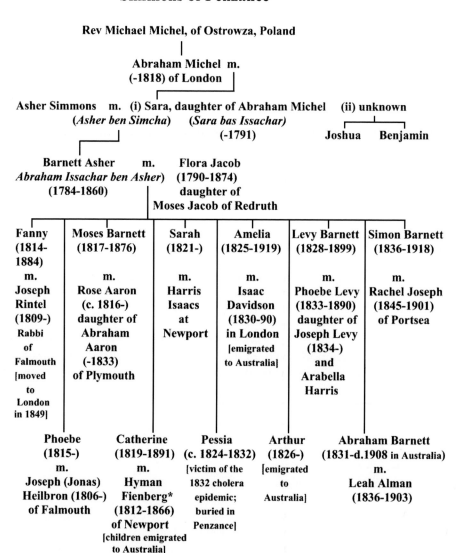

Rev Michael Michel, of Ostrowza, Poland

Abraham Michel m.
(-1818) of London

Asher Simmons   m. (i) Sara, daughter of Abraham Michel   (ii) unknown
(Asher ben Simcha)   *(Sara bas Issachar)*
(-1791)   Joshua   Benjamin

Barnett Asher   m.   Flora Jacob
Abraham Issachar ben Asher)   (1790-1874)
(1784-1860)   daughter of
Moses Jacob of Redruth

Fanny (1814-1884)	Moses Barnett (1817-1876)	Sarah (1821-)	Amelia (1825-1919)	Levy Barnett (1828-1899)	Simon Barnett (1836-1918)
m. Joseph Rintel (1809-) Rabbi of Falmouth [moved to London in 1849]	m. Rose Aaron (c. 1816-) daughter of Abraham Aaron (-1833) of Plymouth	m. Harris Isaacs at Newport	m. Isaac Davidson (1830-90) in London [emigrated to Australia]	m. Phoebe Levy (1833-1890) daughter of Joseph Levy (1834-) and Arabella Harris	m. Rachel Joseph (1845-1901) of Portsea

Phoebe
(1815-)
m.
Joseph (Jonas)
Heilbron (1806-)
of Falmouth

Catherine
(1819-1891)
m.
Hyman
Fienberg*
(1812-1866)
of Newport
[children emigrated
to Australia]

Pessia
(c. 1824-1832)
[victim of the
1832 cholera
epidemic;
buried in
Penzance]

Arthur
(1826-)
[emigrated
to
Australia]

Abraham Barnett
(1831-d.1908 in Australia)
m.
Leah Alman
(1836-1903)

Source: Godfrey Simmons & Anthony Joseph. [*or Feinburg]
Compiled by Keith Pearce © (2013).

against Angwin, from which an ongoing dispute between these two Cornishmen can be inferred.[63]

The Minutes of 10th October 1811 note: "To Mr. Magnus for expenses of New *shochet* to come down £5. Paid Further expenses for New *Rav Yissachar* £1". In December 1811, at the age of 27, Simmons came to Penzance to take up his post, having been engaged by Lemon Hart in London. Hart must have been all too familiar with the tensions that characterised the Penzance congregation, especially in regard to the controlling and authoritative way in which its senior members were inclined to treat its ministers. Simmons, as a very young Rabbi, would have been particularly vulnerable and potentially susceptible to such intimidation, and, to anticipate this, Lemon Hart took the trouble to see that two letters of recommendation were sent to the Penzance congregation, to arrive to coincide with Simmons' arrival. The first was from "The High Priest Solomon Hirshell", the Chief Rabbi, Hirschell, and the other was a brief, personal letter from Lemon Hart to Hyman Woolf, the new President. This letter, dated 22nd/23rd December 1811, refers to Simmons as a "respectable young man, I hope you will behave towards him properly, for you may rest assured that such articles are very scarce in this Market", a clear reference to the quality and range of the young Rabbi's skills.[64]

In view of the fact that Simmons' early years had been shaped by living in London, it may seem surprising that he should chose to go to such a far-flung community as Penzance, but the post of a Rabbi was not easy to find in larger and more established congregations, even for such a well-qualified man. In fact, the remote position of Penzance belied its flourishing and prosperous commercial and cultural life, and it was the County's main centre for sea-trade, fishing, banking and also a major area for mining. As Lemon Hart realised, Simmons' religious and occupational versatility (as a craftsman) made him something of a catch for a small community which lacked the financial resources to employ separate individuals to carry out the functions of teacher, *shochet*, *mohel* and *chazan*.

Despite B. A. Simmons' potential and Lemon Hart's recommendation and admonition to Hyman Woolf, either his temperament or the treatment he received from the Penzance congregational elders (and, likely, a combination of both factors) led to tensions and disputes that were to become a repeated feature of their relations for the rest of Simmons' life, because, surprisingly, he either did not seek, or failed to secure a position elsewhere. These difficulties are likely to have begun soon after his arrival. At the beginning of his incumbency the elders decided to pay Simmons on a regular monthly basis, and the accounts for 19th April 1812 list four occasions when he was paid £3 – 10, from January to *Nisan*/April 1812. This may have continued, but the records for the remainder of the year up to 23rd November, could be read as delayed payments: "Paid 4 months wages £14. Paid (ditto) 3 months wages to 5 Nov £10 – 0". From then on Simmons appears to have received nothing until 9th May 1813: "Paid Mr. Simmons 6 months Wages to April 1813 £21…[for which he signed]…Received of Simmons given up in consequence of being paid 13 months instead of 12, £1". Whether the issues were financial or personal (or both), the arrangement was to last for only one more month: "Paid Mr. Simmons 1 month wages £3 -10 -10 [and] 2 weeks wages for killing up to 10th

June when he left, £1 -15". He had been in office for 21 months, but he was to work in future as both *shochet* and *mohel*, and he was to be re-employed by the congregation as their minister on several occasions . There is no indication how, if at all, the congregation was able to secure *kosher* meat over the next six months, when no minister appears to have been in post. Simmons, Selig (or some other, perhaps from Falmouth) may have been paid as *shochet* on a week to week basis, but the Minutes are silent on this aspect of the congregation's arrangements for the next six months, until the arrival of a new Rabbi.

The month of Simmons' departure from his post coincided with his marriage to Bluma (Flora) Jacob (1790-1874) a daughter of Moses Jacob of Redruth, and originally from Falmouth. The original *Ketubah*[64a] confirms that the wedding took place in Penzance in June 1813 (22nd *Av* 5573). The witnesses were *Chaim son of Benjamin* (Hyman Woolf, the congregation's President) and (mentioned previously) Eliezar Lipman (son of Michael). The latter, being a *shochet*, was the Rabbi of Falmouth, where the Jacob family were members, and it was most likely Lipman who married the couple.

Elthanan Joseph Mortara (October 1813 to July 1814).

On 5th October 1813, a lengthy section of the minutes includes: "We have employed *Rav Elthanan*, as *shochet* for £40 per annum, he is obliged to teach children and the congregation and to act as *shochet* and *chazan* and whatever else the congregation expects of him. 3 months notice on either side, unless he is disqualified by the Chief Rabbi". Mortara agreed to these extensive and somewhat open-ended conditions, and signed himself, not in a cursive hand, but in Biblical script as: *Elthanan Yosef ben Hayim Schlemo Ha Levi Segal*. He was an Italian, the son of *Hayim Solomon Levi Mortara*, the Rabbi of Verona. His background as a Sephardic Jew may have placed him outside the usual orbit of the Chief Rabbi, and it is unclear what may have brought him to England and to such a remote place. The wording of the note, above, could well suggest that he may have been inexperienced and that his appointment was a matter of some desperation, but also that he was to be tested as to how much he could, or would do as minister. Although the Cornish Jews were almost exclusively from an Ashkenazi background, it has been mentioned that maritime contact between the Cornish ports and the Iberian Peninsula (and, indeed, beyond into the Mediterranean, and further still to the West Indies) was common, and the appearance of a visitor like Mortara was not unusual, even if they were not to settle. A "Dr. Messina", who may have been Italian, appears as a signatory of the Penzance Minutes from 1825-1827, and his forename, *John*, is likely to have been an Anglicised variant of *Giovanni*. When donations were being collected in 1818 towards the purchase of a new *sefer torah* one contributor was a "Mocato". There were Sephardic Jews in Plymouth and Exeter, and between 1757 and 1788, at least ten Sephardim landed in Cornwall, nine at Falmouth and one at Fowey.[65]

Three weeks after Mortara's appointment, on 24th October, his signature appears in the Minutes, along with that of Aaron Selig. The other signatories were

Samuel Jacobs of Hayle, B. A. Simmons, signing as *Avraham Yissachar ben Asher Yitzak*, and Jacob Jacobs of Camborne, signing as *Yakov ben Moshe Cambrun*, these three being admitted as members of the congregation. The following year, "Mr. Mortara" was paid his wages up to the 29th May 1814, of £20, but it is not clear how long he may have been kept waiting for the money to materialise. What is clear, however, is that he had never been reimbursed for his original expenses "coming down" eight months previously, and these were also paid to him as a separate sum on the same date as his half-year wages. It seems likely that Mortara was not satisfied with this situation, and the payment to him of wages of £7 – 10 (slightly more than two months salary) on 27th July 1814, may well have marked his departure, although no mention is made of his resignation in the Minutes, but his name does not appear again. It would seem that he served for only ten months (a factor that was to influence the contract of the next minister in 1815).

The name, *Mortara*, was, of course, a common surname in Italy. It is not known if Elthanan Joseph Mortara of Verona was related to the Jewish Mortara family of Bologna. In this notorious case of 1858, a young Jew, Edgardo Mortara, was secretly "baptised" with holy water and blessed with the appropriate formula by his nursemaid, without the knowledge of his parents, when he was seriously ill and the maid, "fearful of his soul", believed he would die. The child recovered, and the girl confessed to a priest what she had done. The child was seized by the Inquisition and taken to Rome on the grounds that he was a Christian child and could not remain with his Jewish parents. The case became a *cause celebre*, and resulted in interventions by Lord Rothschild, a Member of Parliament, and by Sir Moses Montefiore and the Board of Deputies. There was extensive coverage in the Jewish and secular press, governmental and diplomatic intervention, direct appeals to the Vatican, and a widely-circulated private petition of several hundred names protesting against the seizure. This petition carried the names of British Christians, "persons of rank and influence",[66] including Archbishops and Bishops, Peers, Knights of the Realm and MPs, Mayors, Magistrates, Bankers, Army and Naval Officers, and other private signatories. Signatories from Cornwall included the Mayors of Bodmin and Camelford, and a Mr. John Poole of Hayle. All of these avenues failed to secure the child's release, but it did highlight the issue of the forced baptism of Jewish children on the Continent. Edgardo Mortara eventually became a priest, and an ambassador for the Vatican. He attended his mother's Jewish funeral, but never reverted to his family's faith. "He retired to an abbey in Belgium and died there on 11th March 1940, a few weeks before German troops invaded Belgium and began rounding up those of Jewish blood".[67]

After the departure of Rabbi Elthanan Joseph Mortara, *Symons* (B. A. Simmons) resumed his duties as *shochet*, and, on 27th October he was paid "his wages for killing, same year ¼ [at] £30 a year £7 – 10". This annual wage, being £10 less than the minister's salary would indicate that he resumed duties as *shochet* only, and not as *chazan*, and he is not given that title, or that of *rav* in the minutes for 1815. On 27th January 1815 he received "December's wages to this day, £7 – 0" and on 14th May he was paid £5". On 24th August 1814, Simmons' wife, Flora, had given birth to a daughter, Fanny (who was later to marry Joseph Rintel, Rabbi of Falmouth, in 1838), and by the following year she was expecting her second child,

Phoebe, who was born on 4th December 1815.[68] Before this, however, Simmons' was finding it difficult to support his family, and a minute of 7th October would seem to confirm this, in that it introduces a rule to the effect that if the *shochet* has borrowed money from individual members of the congregation and has failed to repay the debts, the congregation is not to use its funds to reimburse them. Clearly, the elders did not see it as their responsibility to assist the young *shochet* and his growing family as an act of charity, but what is not known, of course, is the extent to which Simmons was indebted to his creditors, or for how long he had allowed his debts to accumulate. A further indication that the congregation did not have a minister at this time is found in a payment of 7th October 1815 to Jacob as *shammas*, beadle, or caretaker. As such he was responsible for the cleaning woman (*shabbos goia*), and for the upkeep and preparation of the synagogue for worship. This separate paid position lasted only for about fourteen months,[69] and it was abolished and subsumed into the role of subsequent rabbis as an additional responsibility.

Hyman Selig (November 1815 to *c.* January 1817).

It is not known if Hyman Selig was related to Aaron Selig. Their surnames suggest a German origin. November 3rd 1815: "Paid expenses to Rabbi Hyman Selig coming from London £6". This was an advance payment, and on 14th November - "Tuesday Hyman Selig left London from which time his wages begun arr. Penzance Monday 20th November 1815". Hyman Selig's contract of employment included the condition that he was to be employed as *shochet* and Teacher for one year for £36, and that if he were to leave before the end of the year he was to be paid only £27. Presumably, the stipulation of "one year" was included after the costly experience of Mortara's departure after only 10 months, together with the subsequent additional expenses involved in having to re-employ Simmons as *shochet*. The new Rabbi signed the contract as *Hayim ben Z (elig) from KH*, that is, Kobenhaven, Copenhagen.[70] Nothing is known of his tenure of office, but the reduction of his salary (from £40 to £36) cannot have escaped the new minister's notice, even though this was in order to employ a *shammas*. Selig's name appears the following year, on 20th April 1816: "Paid *Rav Hayim* at different times £15", from which it would seem that he was paid in instalments. Jacob (the *shammas*) was also paid "his half year 3/6". Selig was able to improve his income by repairing a scroll, for which he was paid £6, and the same accounts note that he was paid "his salary which will be due £3". In the left column Selig acknowledges receipt of his wages in Yiddish. Later in the year, *Rav Hayim* was paid "for wages to the 2nd Oct 5 months £15" and Jacob received his half-year of 3/6. When the Minutes open for 1817, it is clear that Selig had decided to leave: "Paid *Rav Hayim* full [that is, final] wages to 10th *Shevat* (January/February) being four months £12". Selig had stayed for just over one year. At the same time, the *shammas* also resigned: "Paid Jacob Moses wishes leaving alltogether (*sic.*) £1 – 7 – 0". The separate position of *shammas* was then effectively abolished, and, in future, the responsibilities it carried were written into the new Rabbi's contractual duties.

Moses Levi (1817-1820).

The same minutes for early 1817 suggest that the congregational elders continued to drive down costs: "Paid *Rav Moshe* expenses coming down £4 – 10". This considerable reduction from £6 to just over £4, could suggest that the new Rabbi had not travelled from London itself, although it would seem that he had done so, but that he had been expected to meet part of the travel expenses himself: "Advanced him to be paid by him out of his wages £5" and [in small script] "10/- pr week". Moses Levi was not related to Israel Levy of Truro, but he may be the same man who was in Bristol from 1798 to 1803. A Solomon Levy, who may have been a relative, was also in Bristol from 1829-1830.[71] After his arrival in Penzance, *Rav Moshe* was paid two weeks wages £1 – 4 – 0, and then for two months, £4. The new minister's elegant and detailed contract seems to have been drawn up in the hand of *Rav Moshe* himself, and it displays a degree of scholarly style.[72] Dated as "Penzance 1st *Adar* (February/March) 1817", *Moshe* accepted annual wages of only £30, £10 less than that of earlier incumbents, with the minimal fringe benefits of food "for *shabbos* and *Yom Tov*", suggesting, perhaps, that he was unmarried. The range of duties he agreed to undertake was considerable: to act as *shochet* when called upon by any member of the congregation; to be Porger, Teacher and Reader in Prayers; to act as *shammas* to ensure that the synagogue is kept clean every Friday eve and on Holy Days; to tie the Palm Branches for *Succot*, and to roll the Scrolls to the correct place every Friday and on Holy Days. Six months notice was to be given to terminate the contract. The new Rabbi signed as *Moshe ben Yehudah Leib, Dayyan Frankfort-on-Main, Chazan and Officer*. The signature confirms that his father was Rabbinical Judge (Dayyan).

September 1817 saw *Rav Moshe* make an offering of 5/-, and another on 18th October of twice that amount. The next day, he was paid his wages of £11 "having paid everything left to the congregation" (the deduction of his £5 advance of the previous February). It is possible that the Rabbi was susceptible to pressure from the elders, because the period from 26th April to 18th October 1818 saw not only the payment of his annual wages (in three instalments) but a further increase in his offerings, of 13/6 and 15/2. It would seem, however, that there was satisfaction with the Rabbi's performance of his duties. The 14th January 1819 saw his annual salary increased to £38, and on 28th February there was a "new agreement with Moses Levi our Rabbi, to serve us & the whole congregation for the space of two years from last Friday 26th Febry 1819, & to do his duty as a *Rav* as hitherto in all things belonging to this *Kehillah*". On 28th July, Moses Levi received his increased six-month wages of £19, and the same amounts in April and September of 1820, when he made a further increased offering of 19/-. He was not to continue in office for the full two years of the "new agreement", and he had left his position by September or October 1820, having been in office for three and a half years, a significantly longer period than his predecessors. It would seem that he remained in Penzance until 1827 (see below).

Hart (Hirsch) Symons (October 1820 to April 1826).

Like Moses Levi, the new Rabbi, Hart Symons was also to provide a period of stability for the congregation. On 25th October 1820 a contract was drawn up for: *Rav Hirsch ben Rabbi Shimon*, or Rabbi Hart (Simeon) Symons. He was to be employed as *shochet, chazan, shammas*, Reader of the Torah, Porger, teacher "and whatever else the congregation requires of him". The Minutes note that he "Arrived at Penzance [Hebrew script] Wednesday 25th October 1820 and was paid half month's Wage at the rate of £38 pr Annum or £3 - 3 - 4 pr Month being [£] 7.11.8 Up to 7 Nov 1820".

The previous year, the Minutes of 2nd April 1819 record that *Isaac Symons* (of Truro) had been admitted as a member of the congregation. Born around 1796, Isaac Symons was a son of Samuel (Solomon) Simons (1740-1832) of Truro and his wife, Rosa (Ann) Moses (1757-1838) of Falmouth. Isaac Symons was a bachelor when he joined the congregation, but he later married Rose (Rosetta) Jacobs (*c.* 1800-) daughter of Lazarus Jacobs and his wife, Rebecca Hart (1766-1841), a sister of Lemon Hart. Just before Hart Symons' appointment, on 17th September 1820, the name *A (Alexander) Symons* appears in the accounts, and continues up to late 1823. It is not known if Alexander Symons was related to Hart Symons, but neither man was connected with the family of Isaac Symons of Truro. However, on 29th April 1821, a subscription from *L (Lyon) Levy & (Harman or Hyman) Semmens (Symons?)* of Truro appears for the first time (Semmens given subsequently as *Hymon*). Lyon Levy was not related to any of the Levy families of Truro, but was a silversmith from Plymouth (where he is buried). His partnership (Jewellers and Hardware) with Harman Semmens was dissolved in March 1829. Harman Semmens was not related to the Symons family of Truro, and it is not known if he was connected with Alexander Symons.

Like his predecessor, Moses Levi, *Rav Hirsch*, was paid (retrospectively) partial expenses "from London" of only £3 - 4 – 6 on 29th April 1821, he received a further (retrospective) payment of "7 months wages £20 – 11 – 8". On 23rd September that year the accounts note: "Paid the *Rav* 6 months wages home to (*sic*. i.e. "up to")[73]… £19". (In a few sections from this point, the dates are given in Hebrew script, but written in Yiddish, with some errors in translating the text into numerals: in this case the Yiddish gives 5581, but it is incorrectly rendered as 5586).[74] At the same time, Hart's contract was renewed (whether for one or two years is unclear) with the same conditions as before, but with his salary increased to £40 per year. The record of payments of wages to *Rav Hirsch* continue from mid-1822 to mid-1824. In March of 1822 he was paid the additional sum of £3 "for repairing all the Scrolls as agreed with the congregation", and in April it was noted that he was away in London, but the purpose of his visit is not specified, although the reason may have been a medical matter, and Symons received medical treatment in Penzance in 1825 and 1826. From September 1822 to April 1824, his signature, in a cursive script, appears alongside that of other members in the Minutes.

Nothing is known for certain of Hart Symons' origins. Because his surname was commonly given as *Simmonds* or *Simmons*, it has been assumed that he may have been identical with Rabbi B. A. Simmons (whose name sometimes appears as *Symons*),[75] but there was no family connection, and the two men were simply resident in Penzance at the same time. Like B. A. Simmons, however, Hart Symons was a man of some education, and, in addition he was a gifted linguist. He most certainly possessed a strong and combative personality and a biting wit. He was also the author of a number of pamphlets on controversial or topical religious issues. In 1822 he entered into a literary debate over the interpretation of the Hebrew Bible with The Rev. Canon John Rogers, Rector of Mawnan. He wrote his text in Hebrew, out of principle rather than necessity, and it was translated into English by another local Jewish writer and lecturer, Solomon Ezekiel.[76] Both of these men were active and successful in opposing the activities of the *Society for Promoting Christianity amongst the Jews* which was active in Penzance (and also, as we have seen, in Falmouth). Solomon Ezekiel had been able to prevent Sir Rose Price, the Society's most influential spokesman in Penzance, from establishing a branch and an office in the town. It may have been to strengthen the faith and the resolve of Jews who might become objects of the Society's attentions that Symons had written his *Letter to a Jew* in 1818, published by R. Scantlebury, in Redruth. In 1823 he had his *Arguments of Faith: Incontrovertible Answers to Sophists and Epicureans* published in and distributed from London and addressed to the Society, refuting their arguments.[77]

In 1824 a satirical pamphlet was published in Penzance under the pseudonym of J.J. Rouseau (the French philosopher and author of the controversial *Confessions*) who represented himself as "Maître de Danse, a présent malade a Penzance".[78] It was written in a brilliant parody of a Frenchman's pidgin-English, filtered through the mannerisms of how Yiddish-speaking Jews might pronounce English words. It was addressed to the Rector of St. Mary's Church, Charles Valentine le Grice (1773-1858), who was curate from 1806 to 1831. Religious controversy and debate were in a state of ferment in Penzance at this time between and within the various Christian denominations, and le Grice had himself been in dispute with the Vicar of Madron, William Borlase, in 1808, and in 1824, he was instrumental in removing the "formidable Sir Rose Price of Trengwainton from the Presidency of the S.P.C.K. because of the heretical unitarian views held by Price".[79] The precise circumstances and issues which lay behind and gave rise to the Hart Symons pamphlet are not clear. Valentine le Grice was from an ancient Norfolk family, who had come to Cornwall from Essex, to be a tutor to William John Godolphin Nicholls of Trereife Manor, who died unmarried in 1815. Le Grice married into this family and inherited the Manor and Estates in 1821 (where his descendants have lived ever since). Le Grice had secured the permanent incumbency of St. Mary's, and he regularly published his sermons and other pamphlets for the edification and interest of the local populace. In 1824, le Grice, by now a wealthy man, had written to the Corporation to seek funds to repair and rebuild St. Mary's, and was promised the considerable sum of £1000. It is not known if this particular matter was the reason for Hart Symon's satire, or if some other controversy had arisen, such as the local activities of the Society for the Promotion of Christian Knowledge amongst the Jews, but Hart Symons had sent le Grice a Hebrew text (possibly of a previous publication), refuting or taking issue with his views in some respect. It is not known how, or if le Grice responded to this, or if the matter became a cause célèbre in Penzance, but the *Letter of Condolence* was subsequently published by Symons, and then included by le Grice himself in one of his own collections.[80]

The Letter of Condolence is remarkable from a literary point of view for the perfect taste and judgement which Symons shows in the use of the satirical genre. It is noticeable that he achieves his effects by satirising le Grice as the social-climber, together with his French surname with its aristocratic associations, living in some comfort in his grand rectory, with his enviable garden, somewhat detached from the town he "served", but unable to readily understand the Jew's Hebrew book. At the same time, in the person of the multi-titled "Maitre de Danse", he creates a picture of the reactionary absurdity of those who might sympathise with the stereotypes of the Jew which "Rouseau" expresses, and also be appalled and enraged to the point of apoplexy at the temerity of a Jew who dared contradict a Christian "Curé". *The Letter* shows clearly that the rabbis were often very well-educated men. It also shows the confidence and boldness of a Jew who is proud and secure in his religious and cultural identity, unafraid, as a minority voice, to express himself in scathing and trenchant terms. It also highlights the liberal tolerance of the society in which the Jews found themselves in Cornwall. Non-conformism was on the rise in the County at this point in the early 18th century. Only twelve years before, in 1812, the Wesleyans had broken away from the Church of England, and, in 1814, the first, very large Methodist Church was built only a few hundred yards from St. Mary's Anglican Church where le Grice was Rector. Members of the Branwell family lived between St. Mary's Church and the Rectory, and the family owned land elsewhere near the Market Place. The family was Anglican, but sympathetic towards the Non-conformists, with whom they had established a close association. They had also helped the Jews in the building of both of the synagogues, in 1768 and in 1807, and Branwell men had business and Masonic connections with members of the Jewish community. Hart Symons may well have realised that he did not speak only for his fellow Jews when he published his satire. It is difficult to assess the significance of the re-publication of the *Letter* in le Grice's own collection. It could point to his naivety in being taken in by it, supposing the Frenchman *J.J. Rouseau* to be an ally, but it could equally suggest that he saw the joke. Whatever the case may have been, this particular Rabbi had certainly raised the profile of the Jewish community in Penzance. It is likely that Symons relished the climate of open debate which flourished in the town, and some 40 years later, little had changed: "Opinions at Penzance are expressed without fear, and surrendered without bitterness".[81]

In April 1825, alongside the 6 months wages of the *Rav*, of £20, the *shabbos goia* (later given as Mary Kenefic) who Hart Symons would have supervised in his capacity as *shammas*, received her half year's wages of 10/-. On 23rd April, when payments for seats in the synagogue were received from the brothers Abraham and Isaac Davidson, from a Solomon Johnson (little being known about these three men, who may have been temporary residents) and from Henry Levi (possibly another visitor, although he may be the same as the congregation's Henry Levin), Rabbi Hirsch signed the Minutes as *Hart Symons*. Later in the year, on the 26th August, the name of a Dr. Messina appears in relation to the donation of a "Cocked Hat, Gown, [& another item, which is illegible] if you would permit them to be worn at all times of Public Devotion". Presumably, these items were to be worn by the Rabbi. Messina, who may have been Italian, was a doctor of medicine. The Minutes indicate that he was paid £1 – 7 – 6 for "attending" the Rabbi in August 1825. It is not clear where he had come from, or if his appearance in Penzance was at the request of Hart Symons, but he remained in the town for the time being. On 2nd September, Messina became a privileged member of the congregation, and his signature appears in the Minutes, together with his membership offerings up to, but not beyond, 1827. On 12th September 1825 (the Hebrew year is given incorrectly as 5886, and should have been written as 5586) the Rabbi was paid four and a half months wages of £15, but B. A. Simmons was also paid the sum of £5, suggesting that he had been standing in for Hart Symons as *shochet* during his illness. The text of the Minutes is barely legible at this point, and the figure indicating the duration for which Simmons was paid could be read either as "*17* (or as ½) month half of… ". From this, it cannot be known if illness had forced Hart Symons to suspend his duties as *shochet* on a temporary basis, or if he had relinquished them altogether, but the former seems most likely. No record is given of any further payment to B. A. Simmons, and on 16th April 1826, the accounts note: "Paid *Rav* 6 Months wages £20 Also for [one further] Month, £3 – 6 – 8: £23 – 6 – 8". Five weeks later, Symons was to leave: "Paid ½ months Wages to *Rav* Hart Symons from 8 May 5586 (1826) to 22 May [at] 16s 8d week, £1 – 13 – 4". The entry is followed by: "Paid B. A. Simmons for his trouble as *shochet*, 2 ½ Mo(nths), £4 – 5 – 0". This entry is of significance in highlighting what became a feature of B. A. Simmons' life in Penzance, supporting his family from the sale of general items, including crockery and bones,[82] accepting the call to serve the congregation as *shochet* when they were unable to secure another minister, but not venturing to seek a post elsewhere. Hart Symons, however, (as Hart Symonds) was the minister in Nottingham by 1827.[83]

Abraham Joseph (August 1826 – September 1827).

Abraham Joseph (1799-1868) was from the prominent Joseph family of Plymouth. He was the son of Joseph Joseph (1766-1846) and the grandson of Abraham Joseph I (1731-1794) of that city. His background has been described in detail in the pages on the Penzance Jewish community and the occupations of its residents. He was not related to the widespread Joseph family of Cornwall, and Henry Joseph (1806-1881) of Penzance, his contemporary, was a son of Abraham Joseph (-1827) of Falmouth. The family of Abraham Joseph II of Plymouth were accustomed to an affluent and comfortable existence, but their fortunes had taken a turn for the worse, and Abraham Joseph's father, Joseph Joseph, had been made bankrupt in 1816.[84] It is likely that contacts between the Penzance elders and the Plymouth congregation had resulted in an arrangement which suited both parties, but which included an element of charitable assistance on the part of the senior members in Penzance. Even so, they clearly wanted to fill the post of minister, albeit as a nominal and temporary one for a Reader in Prayers, before another *shochet* could be employed, and Abraham Joseph needed some form of income to offset his, and his family's financial difficulties. His father, Joseph Joseph was a mohel (but not a minister of the Plymouth congregation), and his register (from 1784-1834) records 76 circumcisions, the first when Joseph Joseph was 18. Most of the circumcisions recorded were of his family or close friends.[85] Later in life, Abraham Joseph was to achieve a reputation as a man of considerable religious learning, and such early signs of learning and competence may have been factors influencing his appointment at the age of 27.

There is no evidence that he was qualified or skilled as a *shochet*, and nowhere in the Minutes is he referred to as such, nor by the title of *Rav*. Another aspect of his character is in evidence from his letters, some of which were written at a later point to Rabbi B. A. Simmons, in which the young man adopts towards the older man, fifteen years his senior, a patronising tone and an undue self-regard in his eagerness to display his fund of religious knowledge.[86] Whether this was a product of his family upbringing or a particular trait in his character, the Minutes, after noting "Paid Abram Joseph Expenses coming down arrived at Penzance 22 August 1826....£3 – 3 – 0" (it is possible that he had come from London rather than Plymouth, having been in the capital to seek some employment), do not proceed to outline a detailed contract of duties similar to those issued to previous ministers, but instead, for 24th September, gives only the following, which is entirely consistent with the tone of the letter noted above: "Agrees in writing to give three months notice, at any time I shall feel inclined to quit my situation", to which he penned his signature. It is unlikely that he was entirely free to dictate his own terms to the elders, but he was paid the same, £40 per year, as the previous *Rav* and *shochet*, and for this sum he may well have been expected to act as *shammas*. He was admitted as a member of the congregation on 4th May 1827, and he did make the customary offerings, £1 – 4 – 3, on 11th April 1827, and a similar amount on 22nd September (when he left his position). It seems likely that B. A. Simmons filled in as *shochet* on some occasions during this period, but that Rabbi Moses Levi (who had remained in the town) also did so for most of the time. The accounts for 24th September 1826 note: "Paid for New Killing Knife 13/- Carriage 7/9, £1 – 0- 9", and on 22nd September 1827, "Paid Simmons 3/7 [for a single "killing"?], Paid *Rav Moshe* who went to London to be a *shochet*, £3 – 0 – 0, Another being sent in his Room", (*sic.* "in his place").

Abraham Joseph's signature and offerings continued to 1829. He remained in the town, marrying Eliza (Telza) Woolf (1808-1850), a daughter of Lemon Woolf. He set up in business as a Corn Merchant and a dealer in flour, but he was made bankrupt in 1830.[87] (It has been mentioned earlier that, after travelling, most likely to Gibraltar, where his father had previously sought to improve his fortunes, and where Abraham's older brother, Henry, had established himself, he returned to Plymouth, from where he wrote to B. A. Simmons, whose family had taken in his wife, Eliza, during his travels. By 1851 he was trading as a Bill Broker in Plymouth, and he eventually became a prosperous and well-connected man, with a second home in Savile Row, London. He became the Plymouth congregation's representative to the Board of Deputies of British Jews in London, and was also a partner in the Devon and Cornwall Bank. He died in Plymouth in 1868, leaving his extensive library of books to the Chief Rabbi, Dr. Adler, to whom he was distantly related through marriage).[88]

Myer Stadthagen (October 1827 – May 1829).

The Minutes note: "Paid Expenses of *Rav Myar* coming from London £3, arrived at Penzance 12th October 1827, Paid him One Weeks Wages to 21 October, 8/- from which time his salary begins to commence at twenty five pounds [per] Year". This is a significant salary reduction from the £40 that had been paid to the 26 year old Abraham Joseph, and would seem to reinforce the suspicion that the latter had been treated with a measure of charity and favouritism by the Penzance elders. Stadthagen had been born around 1804, and he would have been only 23 when he arrived in Penzance. His youth and inexperience might well explain the low salary, but it is likely that he was appointed primarily as a *shochet*, and when he left in 1829 to go to Plymouth, his appointment there was initially in that capacity only, although he assumed further duties as time went on.[89] However, his contract in Penzance read as previous contracts, for a "shochet, teacher and whatever else is required", and it was for one year. The new Rabbi signed as: *Myer ben Rabbi Yitzak Isaac Stadthagen*. Some misinformation has attached to Myer Stadthagen's arrival in England, and to his marriage into a Cornish Jewish family. It has been said [90] that he "arrived in England as a bachelor in 1828 when he was 24 years old", which would give his year of birth as 1804. These details are derived from a post-1844 naturalisation record, in which the original year of arrival in England would have been determined from the applicant's memory, with an error of at least one year being possible, especially if some confusion had arisen over the secular equivalent of a Hebrew year. Clearly, he had arrived by 1827. It has further been held that he was appointed as *shochet* in Plymouth in 1828, when, in fact, he was still minister in Penzance, and was to remain there until April 1829. (It is not known if Penzance and Plymouth shared his services as *shochet* from 1828, or if his appointment to Plymouth was made well in advance of his departure from Penzance). More significantly, incorrect information has been given by Susser concerning Myer Stadthagen's later marriage to a girl from a Cornish Jewish family: "He had married Arabella, daughter of Judith Moses and Isaac Joseph. Isaac was a comfortable merchant, and Judith was the granddaughter of Moses Jacob who was well settled in Redruth by 1767 and great-granddaughter of the founder of the Falmouth Congregation… [that is Alexander Moses]…around 1750".[91] Unfortunately, this passage reflects the errors all too common in attempting to unravel the complex genealogies of the Jewish families of Cornwall. It confuses the Cornish *Joseph* and *Jacob* families. Judith *Moses* (1768-1843) was a *daughter* of Alexander Moses of Falmouth. She did not marry Isaac Joseph, but *Henry* Joseph (1760-1803) of St. Austell. The relevant "Judith" was Judith (Rebecca) *Jacob* (1768-1849) who was a *daughter* (not granddaughter) of Moses Jacob of Redruth. This Judith Jacob married (Moses) Isaac Joseph (-1834) of Falmouth, and it was *their* daughter, Arabella (1802-1862) who married Myer Stadthagen. (They were to die within a few days of one another in 1862). Judith Jacob was, therefore, a *grand*daughter (not "great-grand-daughter") of "the founder of the Falmouth Congregation".

The Penzance Minutes reveal little of substance regarding Stadthagen's ministry. On 25th March 1828, he was paid 5 months wages, and on 4th May, B. A. Simmons was elected as *Gabbai Tsedek* (Charity Officer), for one year. *Myar* is listed on 3rd August as contributing 2/- towards a new *Sefer Torah*, and on 29th September he was paid 6 months wages of £12 – 10 (including a sum as arrears), from which he made an offering of £1. 9s. & 6d. The congregation were either satisfied with his service, or he may have requested a review of his salary, because the Minutes for 12th October note: "It is agreed that *Rav Myer* shall have his Salary increased from twenty pounds to Thirty Pounds payable to him by monthly payments.". By April 1829, Stadthagen had been paid what seems to have been his final 7 months wages of £17, and in May he made an offering of £1. 15s. After this, he must have left for Plymouth, where there was already a *shochet*, an "H. Harris", who left in 1831. Stadthagen remained in Plymouth for 33 years, until his death in 1862.[92] Unlike his short time in Penzance, his career in Plymouth has been well documented.[93] He was to return to Penzance at least on one occasion, to perform a circumcision in 1856.

1830 to 1842.

There are no Congregational Minutes or Accounts for this period. In view of the regularity of the record-keeping for the earlier and later periods, it would seem unlikely that the practice was abandoned altogether, and it would be reasonable to assume that these accounts were mislaid. It is not known how many rabbis officiated during this period, but one name, that of **Rabbi Simeon Greenberg**, may have been the congregation's minister at this time. His son, **Hyman Greenberg,** or Greenborough (also known as Samuel, or Solomon Hillman) served as Rabbi from 1859 until 1861, in which year he died, at the age of 24. He is buried in the Penzance cemetery, and his headstone records that he was "Our Teacher, Rabbi Samuel Hillman, the son of our honoured Master and Teacher Rabbi Simeon Greenberg". There is no headstone for Simeon Greenberg in the cemetery, and he may have left Penzance for another appointment. It is not known when Simeon Greenberg officiated, or if his son succeeded him. (It is possible, of course, that the term "honoured" may indicate that "Rabbi" was an honorific title in the case of Simeon Greenberg).

B. A. Simmons (-1853).

It was certainly the case that B. A. Simmons continued to live in the town after 1830. He was the congregation's *shochet* in 1837, and is likely to have been its minister before and after this year, although his term of office is not known. The congregation continued to find Simmons' performance as *shochet* to be wanting, both technically and in the lack of concern he sometimes showed in recognising that regularity and consistency were needed to supply the community with kosher meat. It can only be supposed that some personal factor led Simmons' to underperform. His personal dissatisfaction with the congregational elders and his resentment of them (justified or otherwise) may have led to a lack of pride in the task, or to a lack of motivation to carry it out to the best of his abilities. It is possible that his delicate health played a part. But he was certainly not deficient in the technical skills required of a *shochet*, even though the congregation sent him to London on several occasions to be re-assessed. A letter from the Chief Rabbi Hirsch, dated May 31st 1837, and sent to "Mr. Wolf President" confirms that Simmons had been thoroughly tested in his skills as a *shochet*: "I appointed him immediately to begin his examination his being rather fatigued from his journey. Detained him untill (*sic*.) this morning when he finished his examination, in Whitechaple with the knife and serging and is cappable (*sic*.) of his situation". (The reference to "serging" is barely legible in the original, and may be an idiosyncratic term for the surgical skills required in porging: or what appears to be an "s" may have been intended as a "p", as "perging"). A further letter, dated 16th September 1845, signed by the new Chief Rabbi Nathan Marcus Adler ("*M Adler Dr.*") indicates that the Penzance elders had again felt it necessary to send Simmons to London, but that Adler confirmed that Simmons "has passed his examination satisfactorily and that I sanction his continuance in office on the usual conditions of *shochetim* [in Hebrew]".[94] Some six months before this, on 13th April 1845 the congregational elders "resolved in future Mr. Simmons should receive the sum (of £32. 10s. pr year) which sum is to include all perequisites & grants". It is possible that this was, in fact, a reduction in his salary, reflecting further dissatisfaction with his performance, because the same meeting imposed the condition upon him that "in future Mr. Simmons to attend Market for the purpose of porging on Thursdays from 9 in the morning until 11 o'clock & on Tuesdays from 9 to half past 9 o'clock". But, very soon after the visit to London, and the receipt of the letter from Adler, on 27th September, from which Simmons must have felt vindicated, "Mr. Simmons requested that the hour for attending the Market on Thursdays should be altered during the winter resolved the time should be from half past nine to half past ten". The following year, on 20th September 1846, he "made an application to have an increase of salary" which was "To be considered at the next meeting". On 11th November, "In answer to Mr. Simmons' application it was resolved that he should have an increase of £5 pr year – making his salary £37 – 10 – 0 Pr Year". By this time, on his limited and intermittent salary, B. A. Simmons and his wife, Flora, had raised a family of eleven children, and Simmons' health was precarious. The same meeting, of 11th November notes: "letter of thanks should be sent to Mr. Rintel for his kind services during Mr. Simmons' illness". (Rintel, it has been mentioned was Rabbi and *shochet* in Falmouth from 1832 to 1849, and he was also Simmons' son-in-law). How long this illness lasted is not known, and although a meeting of 28th March 1847 saw the issue raised that Simmons' previous salary increase had not been subject to the customary ballot, it was confirmed, with 11 to 1. In 1848, on 23rd January, Simmons was present at a meeting convened to petition Parliament for the Removal of Jewish Disabilities, but on 16th April, at the Annual Meeting of the Congregation he is not listed as a "present seatholder", and his salary was reduced to £32 per year. On 24th September, a second letter of thanks was sent to Rintel for his services as *shochet* during another period of illness for Simmons. A year later, on 16th September 1849, he was given notice that his salary was to be further reduced to £32 -10 per year. The reasons for this are not given, but whether his attendance to his duties as *shochet* were still regarded as technically deficient, or irregular, his ill-health would have incurred costs for the congregation. Clearly, an immediate replacement for Simmons could not be found, and the congregation's numbers and its income were falling. In March 1850, two of its most active and prominent members, Morris Hart Harris, its President and Treasurer, and B. A. Simmons' son, Moses B. Simmons, left Penzance.

On 31st March 1851, Simmons filled in the (Ecclesiastical) Census Return for Places of Public Religious Worship, signing as the synagogue's "Minister, Barnett A. Simmons". He declined to fill in any optional information under "Remarks", and his record of the year when the building was erected is given incorrectly as 1838, instead of 1808 (although he may have been indicating when he believed that it had been extended). On 13th April he made an application "for a Grant", and was voted the sum of ten shillings, which was, in effect, a nominal charitable payment which Simmons may well have regarded as derisory. Matters were clearly far from satisfactory, but they continued for another fourteen months, until they reached a crisis point in 1852, when the Minutes for 17th June note: "Mr. Simmons having Resigned his situation as *shochet* which the *kahal* (congregation) has accepted". On 29th June, a letter "Signed by the Whole of the Congregation" was sent to the Chief Rabbi: "Mr. Simmons our Late *shochet* having resigned his situation on Thursday last at a moment's notice I think it most advisable to make you acquainted with the circumstances as occurred to which the Whole Congregation will bear Witness by affixing their Signatures to the following – On Sunday last being a meeting of our Benefit Society in case of Sickness of which Mr. Simmons is also a Member he grossely (*sic.*) insulted a Member of the Congregation in fact a Senior Member, so much so he requested me to call a meeting of the Congregation & summon Mr. Simmons to attend and substantiate what he said or Retract, otherwise if he would not do so the Matter would have been referred to a court of Justice. Instead of doing as a person ought in a Public office of his description after receiving my Notice to attend a Meeting to be held this day he called on me on Thursday for his quarters salary I immedeately (*sic.*) paid him, he then Resigned his Situation. I convened a Meeting of the Congregation the same evening and altho Mr. Simmons left us at a moments notice the Decision was postponed until this day so as to afford him ample time to reconsider himself & do his duties. Instead of which Friday being killing day he neglected to do so, we were compelled to send to Falmouth for Meat we leave you to Judge his Conduct, (signed) Benj Aaron Selig President".

Although the individual insulted is not named, and the precise nature of the accusation made by Simmons is not identified, it would seem to have involved an imputation of dishonesty or deceit which might qualify as a civil offence. Simmons was certainly in dispute with Solomon Teacher during this period, as various minutes show. The latter's family was effectively in a state of poverty, and in 1856 he was to be buried at the congregation's expense, suggesting that he was a beneficiary of the congregation's charitable payments, and possibly of the Benefit Society mentioned. Simmons would also have been in receipt of similar payments during his periods of illness, and his salary had been reduced. It is not fanciful to speculate that some mutual resentment between the two men may have centred around their respective financial situations and the individual sense of entitlement each held regarding charitable support. The letter clearly reveals the intensity of such disputes within the congregation, and the irascibility and unpredictability of Simmons' character. There is no indication of any formal response from the Chief Rabbi, but he may have issued some ultimatum to Simmons, who, for whatever reason, performed a *volte face* within the space of a few days. "At a Special Meeting of the Congregation held June the 27th 5612 Mr. Simmons made application for the situation as *shochet* & *rav*. Having agreed to do away with his vow & Sign the Rules, was duly elected at a Salary of £30 per Annum, Including all Grants. Education Excluded. A vote of thanks was proposed & seconded & unanimously Responded to the President for his conduct in the Matter". From this, it is obvious that Benjamin Aaron Selig must have brought about a resolution to the dispute with considerable powers of diplomacy and persuasion, whatever the nature of Simmons' "vow". The incident also shows that there was no realistic way of securing another *shochet* to replace Simmons. He was not present at the meeting, which closed "by notifying the same to the *rav*". During the week-long dispute, it was Rabbi Herman of Falmouth who would have supplied kosher meat to Penzance, and some six months later, on 12th December 1852, he was paid the sum of 10/- for that service.

A consequence of these ongoing disputes with Simmons, resulting in the letter of complaint, was that in future the Chief Rabbi was drawn more closely than before into the congregation's affairs. In particular, Dr. Adler placed conditions upon the appointment of ministers to Penzance, and Simmons' retraction of his "vow" and his signing the "Rules" may well have been an example of Adler's conditions for his re-employment. The Chief Rabbinate would have been aware that the congregation's difficulties with Simmons had persisted for, or at least resurfaced over a period of some forty years. Even though other ministers seem to have experienced similar problems in Penzance, the particular bitterness of this case may have influenced Adler's decision to formalise an initial 12 month trial contract in Penzance, with a three (later one) month period of notice. Matters did not improve, however, and on 10th July 1853, there were further formal complaints about "Mr. Semons Conduct as regards his bad Porching [porging of meat] & several other things". He was to be informed of the congregation's resolve to "desmiss" him (with three months notice) if further complaints were substantiated. A proposal by Solomon Teacher for his instant dismissal was only narrowly defeated. Two weeks later, on 24th July he sent in his resignation as *shochet*. This effectively marked his retirement. He remained in the town for the time being, but he was to be re-engaged in 1857 once more because a replacement as *shochet* could not be found, and he was available. On 24th July, the same meeting decided to advertise in the *Jewish Chronicle* and to "send to the Chief Rabbi for a Reader at a Salary of £35 pr year".

B. A. Simmons' Circumcision Register (1821-1847).

Although Simmons became the County's only permanent *mohel*, others would have practised both in Penzance, Falmouth and Truro. At least seven circumcisions are believed to have been carried out in Falmouth,[95] but only two appear in B. A.

Simmons' register. The other circumcisions may have been performed by Simmons before or after the dates in the register, or by other ministers. B. A. Simmons' original register is contained in a calf-bound book, leather book-binding being another of his skills. He would have been able to obtain the materials for this during the course of his work as a *shochet*, from which he also collected bones which he sold from his shop.[96] The register records a total of only sixteen circumcisions: nine in Penzance (including four of his own sons and a grandson), two in Falmouth and five in Truro. These are likely to significantly under-represent the number of male births during the 19th century, but even so it would not be unreasonable to infer that the register itself "…is an indication that the communities were hardly self-generating".[97]

A curious feature of the Register is that the days and dates given by Simmons do not in every case coincide with the record of the actual Hebrew calendar found on standard conversion tables.[98] From these errors it would seem that, at least in some cases, Simmons may not have entered the details in the register at the time of the circumcision itself. If this was the case, he may well have been mistaken in his recollection of the precise day or date when it took place, or he may have relied upon the recollection of others. Alternatively, he may have written the date incorrectly, or failed to complete it. In this way, "2 Ellul" may in fact have been "20 Ellul". What must also be taken into account is that the precise day or date of the month may in fact have been the next (or previous day) in that the Hebrew reckoning fell from dawn to dusk, while the civil reckoning fell at midnight. Direct identification of the child and the family is not always certain, and possible only with reference to extraneous sources, such as headstones, genealogical information and other records. Another factor requiring caution is that the Hebrew names recorded may have been used exclusively for that ritual occasion, and may not have been the names used by them in a social context. The parallel with headstone inscriptions is obvious. In several examples, the register gives the father's name as *Naphtali*, while he was in fact known as Henry. The *Sondek* (who is named in most of the entries) was the person given the honour of holding the child during the circumcision, this would normally be the grandfather or another elderly relative, an uncle, a rabbi or a scholar.

1. "Mazzel Tob! The circumcision in the congregation of Falmouth of the child Isaac son of Joseph on Monday, Erev Pesach, 5581".

This is the first day of Passover (14th Nisan) which fell on Monday 16th April 1821. The child's father may have been Joseph Simons (1798-), a (presumed) son of Samuel (Solomon) Simons (1740-1832) of Truro and Rosa Ann Moses (1757-1838) of Falmouth. Much later census records for Cincinnati (1850 and 1860) where Joseph Simons emigrated, indicate that he was married to a Celia, whose year of birth would have been around 1807-1808, in that she is recorded as 42 (1850) and 52 (1860), and her death certificate of 15th May 1876, gives her age as 68. She may have been from a Zachariah family of one of the South Coast communities in Brighton or Southampton. The informant at her death is recorded on the certificate as an "A. J. Zachariah", who may have been her nephew. In 1855 Esther Meyer married Samuel Zachariah in London, and the 1861 Census for Southampton gives Samuel Zachariah (49) as a Jeweller, born in Poland and a British Subject, with his wife, Esther. Two years after Celia Simons' death in Brighton, the 1878 Post Office Directory records Esther Zachariah there as the proprietor of a boarding house, in the same district of the town where Celia had died.[99] It is possible that Joseph Simons, who was about 23 years old in 1821, had been married previously, and his wife may have died. However, if Celia was this child's mother, she would have been underage, and only about 13 or 14 years at the time. It is not known when the couple married. On the American census records, Joseph and Celia *Symonds* are not listed with any children. If this Isaac was their child, he would have been an independent adult by 1850. Joseph Simons did have a brother, or half-brother, Isaac (*c.* 1796-), and this child may have been named after him. Unlike Joseph Simons' other brothers, Philip, Eliezar and Moses, who also emigrated to Cincinnati, Isaac Symons remained in Falmouth, where he traded. He was married to Rose (Rosetta) Jacobs (*c.* 1800-) a daughter of Lazarus Jacobs and Rebecca Hart of Penzance. Isaac *Symons'* name appears in the Penzance congregational minutes from 1819 to 1823.

2. "place of Truro, Moses son of Naphtali on Friday, 17 Ellul, 5581. Sondek: Samuel Harris".

This is the 14th September 1821. The child is Morris (Moses) Hart Harris, the son of Henry Harris (1787-1872) who had been born in Penzance but who moved to Truro. His wife was Esther Jacob (1784-1871) a daughter of Moses Jacob of Redruth.

3. "Penzance, Haim son of Asher Isaac on Wednesday, 3 Tishri, 5582".

This date as given cannot be correct. The 3rd Tishri fell on Saturday 29th September. If Simmons recorded the day with reasonable accuracy, it is most likely that the Hebrew date should be 13th Ellul (= Tuesday 9th October). Both the 23rd and 30th Ellul fell on a Friday, the 23rd on 19th October, and the 30th on 26th October. The child is Hyman, son of Lemon (Asher) Woolf (1783-1848) and Rebecca Jacob (1781-1853). The Sondek's name is absent from the record.

4. "Penzance, Tseve son of Samuel on Saturday, 13 Tammuz, 5582. Sondek: L. Jacob".

The 13rd Tammuz fell on Tuesday 2nd July 1822, and the 3rd Tammuz, fell on Saturday 22nd June. However, the family birth register of Samuel Jacob's children records that Henry (Tseve) was born on Saturday 29th June.[100] The circumcision would have taken place a week later on Sunday 7th June, and the Hebrew date given by Simmons (as 13th) should be read as 18th Tammuz. The child's parents were Samuel Jacob (1778-1860) and Sarah (Sally) Levy (1784-1868). The Sondek was Samuel Jacob's brother, Levy Jacob (1788-1824).

5. "Truro, Israel son of Naphtali on Saturday, 4 Adar 5583. Sondek: L. Jacob".

The date is Saturday 15th February 1823. The child was another son of Henry Harris. The Sondek was Esther Harris' brother, Levy Jacob (above). The child's twin brother is the subject of the next entry in the register.

6. "Truro, Simeon son of Naphtali on Thursday. Last day of Pesach, 5583. Sondek: L. Levy".

The date is 22nd Nisan (= Thursday 3rd April 1823). The child's circumcision, some six weeks after his brother, will have been delayed because of fears for his health. He was to die in 1825. The Sondek was Lyon Levy (1782-1836) a silversmith from Plymouth who traded in Truro from around 1821, and who returned to Plymouth around 1829.

7. "Falmouth, Abraham son of Moses on Thursday, Rosh Chodesh Ellul, 5583. Sondek: Mr. Larance".

The New Moon in 5583 fell on 30th Av (= 7th August 1823). The child was the son of Rabbi Moses Hyman of Falmouth. The Sondek was Lazarus (Moses Eliezar) Lawrance (-1841) who was a Money Broker in Falmouth. He was the second husband of Judith Moses (1768-1843) the widow of Henry Joseph (1760-1803) of St. Austell.

8. "Truro, Samuel son of Naphtali on Tuesday 11 Adar 5585. Sondek: Jacob Jacob".

The date is Tuesday 1st March 1825. This is another son of Henry Harris of Truro. The Sondek was Jacob Jacob (1774-1853) who was married to Sarah Kate (Kitty) Simons (1778-1846) a daughter of Samuel Simons of Truro. Samuel Harris was to marry Sophia Levi of Plymouth, whose family came from Portsea.

9. "Truro, Simeon the son of Naphtali on Sunday 11 Tammuz [the year has been omitted], Sondek: L. Larance".

The date is 11th Tammuz 5586 (= Sunday 16th July 1826). Henry Harris named the child after his son, Simeon, who had died in 1825.

10. "Penzance, my son, Asher, son of Abraham Issachar on Friday 2 Ellul 5586. Sondek: Dr. Meune".

The child was Arthur Barnett Simmons, who appears in B. A. Simmons' family birth register, born on 21st September 1826. The circumcision register should read "27 Ellul (= Friday 29th September). The identity of the Sondek is not certain, but the name may have been written incorrectly or indistinctly, and be that of Dr. John Messina who was a member of the congregation from 1825-26. Messina attended Rabbi Hart Symons, the incumbent minister at this time during an illness, and he may also have delivered Flora Simmons' child. Messina was to leave the town at the end of November 1826. Arthur Simmons emigrated to Australia.

11. "Penzance, my son, Judah son of Abraham Issachar on Monday 8 Ellul 5588. Sondek: Abraham Joseph".

The date is Monday 18th August 1828. The child was Levy (Judah) Barnett Simmons (1828-1899). The Sondek was Abraham Joseph (1799-1868) of Plymouth who had been Reader in Prayers in Penzance for one year, 1826-1827, and who married Telza (Eliza) Woolf (1808-1850) a daughter of Lemon Woolf of Penzance.

12. "Penzance, Israel son of Tseve on Saturday 16 Adar Shine 5589. Sondek: L. Woolf".

The date, 16 Adar Shine (II) is 21st March 1829. The child was a son of Henry Levin (1798-1877) who was from Stockholm. Israel Levin (-1887) remained unmarried. His brother, Alexander, had been born the previous year, but his circumcision (like that of other children born to members of the congregation) does not appear in the register, illustrating the point that it cannot be taken as an accurate measure of male births. The Sondek was Lemon Woolf.

13. "Penzance, Abraham son of Abraham Issachar on Saturday, 2 Adar 5590. Sondek: L. Woolf".

The year 5590 cannot be correct: 2 Adar 5590 = Thursday 25th February 1830. B. A. Simmons' birth register records that his son, Abraham, was born on 26th February 1831 = Saturday 13th Adar 5591. The child would have been circumcised on Saturday 20th Adar (5th March) 1831 ("2 Adar" having been written as an incomplete date). Abraham Barnett Simmons also emigrated to Australia.

14. "Penzance, Simeon, my son, son of Abraham Issachar on Monday 17 Shebat Feby. 1st 5596. Sondek: M. B. Simmons".

The child (Simon Barnett) was born on Tuesday 26th January 1836 (= 7th Shevat 5596). If he was circumcised on 1st February (which was a Monday) this would be the 13th (not the 17th) Shevat. The Sondek was B. A. Simmons' oldest son, Moses Barnett (1817-1876).

15. "Mazzel Tob! Born on the 1st Day of Rosh Chodesh Tammuz. Penzance, Israel son of Samuel Hoffenheim on Wednesday, 3rd Tammuz 5603. Sondek: Alex. Levin".

3rd Tammuz 5603 fell on Saturday 1st July 1843. The date was most likely the 13th Tammuz (= Tuesday 11th July). The child was the son of Samuel Oppenheim (1800-1869) and his wife, Elizabeth (Beila) Levy (1798-1879). Elizabeth Levy was a daughter of Israel Levy (-1824) of Truro and Hannah Moses (-1841) of Falmouth. The Sondek was Alexander Levin (1828-1891).

16. "Thursday 2nd Tammuz, June 16th 5607, Penzance, my grandson Abraham son of Moses, on Thursday 9th Tammuz 5607. Sondek: Moses Giddin: Moses Woolf".

The first date will be the birth date. Wednesday 23rd June approximates to 9th Tammuz. The Sondek, Moses (Gideon?) Woolf was born in 1815, and was the son of Lemon Woolf.

Solomon Cohen (*c.* 1853-1856/7).

An Eleazar Cohen is believed to have emigrated from Poland and to have come to Penzance with several sons in the 1830s.[101] There is no reference in the Penzance Congregational Account to a *Cohen* at this point, and other records do not confirm a trader by that name in the town. Eleazar Cohen's three sons were Ephraim and Manasseh (presumed twins) and S. Cohen (most likely, Solomon or Samuel), who died in 1884. When Manasseh Cohen, age 24, "Minister of the Cardiff Hebrew Congregation" was married to Henrietta Moses, age 23, of Swansea on 20th April 1852, Cohen's father was given as *Eliaga*, or *Eliaza* (the "z" written with a flourish) Cohen, "Clothes Shop", implying a current trader in Cardiff. All three sons were Jewish Ministers, and titled as "Rev.".[102] It is very likely that the Solomon Cohen who was appointed to Penzance was this third brother.

There is no official record in the Minutes of Solomon Cohen's appointment, but it can be inferred that he took office in September 1853 or early 1854 from the entry for 20th September 1854: "agreed that Mr. Cohen be taken at 14/- Pr Week as *shochet* and to perform other services of the *kahal* as heretofore & continue 12 months with 3 months notice", with the new minister signing the agreement as *Solomon Cohen*. Before this, his surname (only) appears in late 1853, most likely for December (dated 17th Kislev 5614) on a list of subscribers to a charitable fund set up by Sir Moses Montefiore for the Jews of Jerusalem. His name does not appear again, up to 1856, but the following was noted in the Cornish press: "BIRTHS. At Penzance, on 19th instant, the wife of MR. COHEN, Rabbi of Penzance, a daughter" (*West Briton*, April 27th 1855). During Cohen's period of office it would seem that the congregation excluded B. A. Simmons from the vestry as a senior member: an entry dated 1st January 1854 notes that "Mr. Simmons sent a message offering 21/- per Year seat money in addition to paying his offerings which the congregation declined to accept". It would also seem that the elders were concerned to give Solomon Cohen full recognition as the *rav* and to ensure that no one (perhaps with Simmons in mind) should encroach upon the prerogatives of his office. A rule was drawn up on 9th April 1854 stating that "no one but the *chazan* shall on ordinary occasions read the Prayers". If indeed Simmons was marginalised by the congregation, this may have led to his decision to leave Penzance with his wife Flora in March 1854 to live with a married daughter in Merthyr Tydfil, where he remained for the next three years. There is no official record of Solomon Cohen's departure, and it is not known if he was able to act as a *mohel*, but the minutes for 13th April 1856 record that it had been necessary to pay a former minister, Myer Stadthagen, now the Rabbi in Plymouth to perform a circumcision in Penzance: "Mr. Staalhagen (*sic.*) for coming down for the *brit milah* of Mrs. Teacher's child & other expenses, £2 -15 – 5". The mother, Maria (Selig) Teacher was a widow at the time of the circumcision of her second son, Solomon, named after his father who had died in St. Ives on 10th March. His burial, at the congregation's expense, reflects the family's poverty, and would explain that the "other expenses" incurred were in the form of charitable assistance to cover the costs of the celebration of the occasion. Solomon Teacher's enmity towards B. A. Simmons has already been mentioned. If Simmons had been in Penzance at the time, it would seem likely that the congregation would have wanted him to carry out the circumcision rather than pay Stadthagen's fee and travel costs, but it is not certain that Simmons continued as a *mohel* after 1847, the year of the last entry in his Circumcision Register. As to Solomon Cohen, he may have left Penzance in 1856, or remained until 1857, but he was later to be Reader and Shochet in Coventry from 1860 to 1869.[103]

B. A. Simmons (*c.* 1857-1859).

If Cohen had left Penzance in 1856, it would seem that the congregation found itself once more unable to find an immediate replacement. Yet again, they were forced to resort to B. A. Simmons to carry out the essential functions of *shochet* and minister. It is not certain if Simmons returned to Penzance in 1856, soon after the Teacher circumcision, but the following entry, for 23rd November 1857 might suggest an unrecorded appointment in the previous year: "B. A. Simmons re-engaged as *shochet* &c. at a salary of 14/- Pr week, the same to continue for 12 months, the permission of Dr. Adler being only for that time". Simmons' signature appears accepting the conditions of re-appointment. There are no further details of his period of office in the Minute-Book, and his name does not appear again. This was the final stage in his long period of residence, and of his intermittent and largely unhappy career in Penzance. The periods of interruption in B. A. Simmons' incumbency were the result of dissatisfaction on both sides, and the ill-health which he experienced in later life, especially from 1846 onwards did not help matters. He was not so much suspended from his duties, but that he "suspended" himself by walking out in the wake of some dispute or other. Simmons accepted or endured these breaks, and remained available if and when the congregation should decide to re-appoint him. That he was prepared to do so for many a decade, when other rabbis were moving on quickly to seek better opportunities and more amenable situations elsewhere, most certainly ran counter to the pattern set by most of the rabbis in Cornwall. In total he was to spend 44 years in the town in this way.

Two years after he first arrived in Penzance, Simmons wrote in 1813 to the then Chief Rabbi, Solomon Hirschell, asking permission to marry Blumah (Flora) Jacob of Redruth, one of the many children of Moses Jacob. In this letter, to jog the Chief Rabbi's memory, he reminds him that his nickname was *Little Bera*, being short in stature (a family attribute that has come down the generations in the Simmons family). Apart from this singular reference to his stature, two fine family portraits of B. A. Simmons and his wife have survived, and hang today in the Penlee House Gallery and Museum Penzance.[104] They were painted by the Cornish artist, Richard Thomas Pentreath (1806-1869) who was born in Mousehole, but lived in Clarence Street, Penzance. He began life as a sign painter, but became a versatile artist in watercolours, pastels and oils, and he eventually exhibited various works, including local landscapes and portraits at the Royal Academy.[105] The Simmons portraits were painted in 1834, to celebrate the Rabbi's 50th birthday. After his marriage, with the responsibility of providing for his growing family, he turned at some point to setting up some kind of small shop as an alternative and occasional source of income. The Simmons family lived in Market Jew Street (up to 1848), then moved to Leskinnick Terrace, adjacent to the cemetery, in 1849, and eventually to the Rosevean area of the town in 1857. While B. A. Simmons held his posts as rabbi for several brief periods, he could calculate that he would always find himself in demand as a minister eventually and he could be in a position to make himself indispensable to the little congregation as the need arose. From 1818 to 1854, he was the congregation's most frequently employed incumbent, even though disagreements continued and ill-health intervened. While he was on hand as *shochet*, and prepared to act as such, there was no need for the congregation to look elsewhere or to import the necessary supplies of kosher meat. That the congregation came to rely on him almost exclusively during the periods he did serve, or when other incumbents left their post or another minister could not be found has been indicated by the fact that he was formally reprimanded when he occasionally neglected to butcher sufficient meat for the Friday Sabbath eve, or did so carelessly, and that when he fell ill, kosher meat had to be sent for from Falmouth.

The numerous tensions within the Penzance congregation persisted for much of Simmons' tenure. The congregation's Minute Book allows glimpses of a fractious and occasionally very tense atmosphere amongst the synagogue's administrators, worsened, no doubt, by ongoing difficulties of financing the community's religious needs from such limited resources. It is clear that too much came to be expected of the incumbent minister, and even in his duties as *shochet* alone he was expected to slaughter twice a week in the winter months and three times a week in the summer.[106] It would seem that the senior members who administered the congregation's affairs were themselves overbearing and domineering, and their failure to retain other incumbents for more than very brief periods would suggest a failure on their part to create good relations with their ministers, on whom they placed unreasonable demands. The Minute-book records various occasions when Simmons was reprimanded for dereliction of duty, incivility and even physical assault upon a member of the congregation, suggesting that he had a fiery temperament.[107] He was suspended from his duties on at least one occasion, although for how long is unknown. Whether these criticisms were justified or not, we cannot be certain. His salary was inadequate and was often a fundamental bone of contention.

To supplement his inadequate and unpredictable income when he was employed as the rabbi, B.A. Simmons ran a small huckster's shop at 21 Market Jew Street where he (and, presumably, his wife, Flora) sold crockery and other small household and personal items, including clothing, and even bones, the latter most likely obtained from his work as a *shochet*. He may also have sourced animal hide to carry out book-binding, and a range of early 19th century hand-bound vellum pocket-books and prayer books have been handed down through the Simmons family and are believed to have been produced by him. Of particular interest are several of his original accounts, stocklists and receipts.[108] One of these, dated "Penzance, the 30th January 1825 Sunday the week of the Torah reading "Yisro" [Jethro] [5]585", consists of an "Account of Mr. Simmons", written in Yiddish, in a cursive Hebrew script.[109] The account mentions several seals, keys and chains, a ring, broaches, and a small number of stones "amethyst 5/-, turquoise 6/6, black garnet (?) and, rubies(?)". The impression given is that Simmons had not received payment for some of these items, and that he was not making any significant profit: Total £8….goods taken to the value of 1-2-4, total adds up to 9-4-4, I received goods to the value of 1-1-6, Total left owing sum of 8-2-10, over the course of two months I received £4-00". Barnett Simmons' wife, Flora, had been raised as the daughter of Moses Jacob in Redruth, where he became established not only as a jeweller, and clock and watchmaker, but also as a significant, successful and expert trader in precious stones and mineralogical specimens. While there is no evidence that B. A. Simmons was skilled or experienced in these respects, his wife would have possessed some knowledge of her father's occupation, and the listing of some precious stones may indicate that she retained useful and relevant contacts in this field. A further (undated) inventory lists various items of clothing "from Stock" to the value of £3-7-8 and £2-17, including "Scarlit, Perpil, Shalls and Cloaks". Another more detailed invoice, dated 10th October 1827, from Dillwyn & Co. of the Cambrian Pottery, Swansea, made out to "Mr. Lemon Woolfe" (then President of the Penzance Congregation) indicates that he had ordered (or received) a wide range of crockery to the value of just over £49, and that a supplementary order "for Mr. B. Simmons" of "supper plates, jugs, bowls, soap boxes" and other items came to £33-7. A brief letter from Dillwyn to Lemon Woolfe, of 13th November 1827 includes another "Letter for Mr. Simmons' Complete Account £33-7-0", which may indicate either that it was sent as a receipt of payment, or as a reminder that payment was due.

It is not certain that B. A. Simmons was the incumbent Rabbi during the period 1830-1847 (for which there are no surviving congregational records) but the archives of the Chief Rabbi Solomon Hirschell contain a "Copy of a notice by the 'Wherry Town Mining Company, Mount's Bay, Penzance, Cornwall', informing shareholders that 'the third call of 30s. per share is now made', dated Nov. 27, 1837, discloses that the Rabbi must have had some interest in these shares".[110] It is not known if he applied his various artistic skills as a sign-painter in the wider community, or if he taught Hebrew beyond the parameters of the Jewish community to interested Christian students, such as Henry Cornish, mentioned later.

The tense relationship between Simmons and the Penzance congregation was especially bitter, but it was not unique, and it has been noted that there were also disputes at Exeter, Plymouth and Falmouth, where, in each case, the incumbent minister was supported by the Chief Rabbi.[111] The ministers, who were often better educated men than their congregants, whose servants they were, could find themselves treated as such. Whether or not the complaints, resignations and re-engagements of B. A. Simmons reported in the Minute Book were justified, it is certain that steps were taken to ensure that the rabbi was not overpaid. The "article" (as Lemon Hart had previously referred to Simmons in his letter of recommendation) had become significantly devalued in this "market." It is difficult to understand why Simmons was prepared to endure this ongoing situation for a period of 43 years when he could have moved to another post; especially after his children had left the town. He may have possessed a temperament lacking in ambition or characterised by insecurity or apathy, although genuine attachment to the locality and its people could have played a part, particularly since his wife Flora, who came from an extended family, had lived in the County all her life. There are also indications in the Minutes that he may have suffered from a delicate constitution and from worsening health in later years. Simmons was not the only minister or member to be the object of disapproval and reprimand. Faults no doubt existed on both sides, and Simmons' ongoing poor health, subsequent indisposition and inability to sustain his duties did not help. It has been assumed in the Simmons family that, like his sponsor, Lemon Hart, B. A. Simmons was of a relatively liberal temperament. Whether this led to suspicion and distrust within the Penzance congregation cannot be known. Lemon Hart was a leading member of a local volunteer force, and, like other Jews in Penzance, he was also a Freemason (as was Simmons). Whilst three of Lemon Hart's children married non-Jews after leaving Penzance, none of B. A. Simmons children did so. However, Simmons must have had Gentile friends, and, when Simmons retired he was presented with a gift, inscribed with the dedication:

"Presented to the Revd. B. A. Simmons in his leaving Penzance after a residence of nearly half a century – His courteous and amiable disposition in imparting knowledge will always be remembered by his sincere friend – Henry Cornish". March 20th 1854. To the dedication has been added several lines of carefully written Biblical Hebrew script. Presumably, this Hebrew was penned by Cornish himself, perhaps having been tutored in Hebrew by Simmons, and the imparted knowledge may well have extended to discussion of religious matters.

In 1854, the decision to leave Penzance had been made, and Simmons and his wife went to live with in Merthyr Tydfil with a married daughter, most likely Catherine (1819-1891) who, in 1850 in Penzance, had married Hyman Fienburg (1812-1866) of Newport, South Wales. Several marriages were contracted between Jews of Penzance and South Wales, and in 1855, another daughter of B. A. Simmons, Sarah (1821-) married Rabbi Harris Isaacs at Newport. He is likely to be the same as the Harris Isace (sic.) who was Rabbi at Merthyr in 1851. The Jewish community in Merthyr was a young one. Although there had been a small Jewish presence there from the 1830s, the congregation itself was not founded until 1848, with its first synagogue being built in 1851, and a new one around 1852.[112] The domestic arrangement in Merthyr was not an unqualified success. Simmons and Flora may have missed the town of Penzance where they had spent so much of their life, and in 1857, they returned to Penzance to take a cottage in the peaceful Rosevean area just outside the town centre. In a letter to a member of the family,[113] the rabbi described how he would go down to the cemetery in Leskinnick to say his prayers each day, suggesting perhaps, that he was not inclined to visit the synagogue itself. Obviously relations with the Jewish congregation could not have been so bad that they would not countenance re-employing Simmons once more as their rabbi. He was re-engaged on a renewable 12 month contract. He served two final years there from 1857 to 1859.

He died in 1860 at the age of 76 years and was buried in the cemetery of the community where he had served for so long. The original receipts, made out to Flora Simmons' oldest son, M . B. (Moses Barnett) Simmons (1817-1876), for the funeral expenses give an insight into the congregational arrangements for burial at this time. The Coffin and Headstone were provided by John T. Fleming, "Cabinet Maker, Undertaker, Turner & Bed Pillar Manufacturer, Below the Independent Chapel, Market Jew Street, Penzance", at the cost of £1. 10. 0. "Tom", who may have been the gravedigger, was paid 7 shillings, and the "Drivers" 10 shillings. "B. Mathews" received 1 shilling (for unspecified services, possibly as an attendant) and "Walace" (Constable, or chief attendant) was paid 2 shillings. Moses B. Simmons made three offerings to the congregation through Henry Levin, the President, and the new Rabbi, Hyman Greenberg, most likely for "staying up", the recitation of prayers, and the preparation and supervision of the body prior to the burial: 21 shillings came from each of "M. Semons", Moses Barnett, and his brother "Simeon", Simon Barnett (1836-1918), and 5 shillings from another brother, "Levy", Levy Barnett (1828-1899). "To Baal (Bill)", that is the invoice from a William Ball, for Brandy at 7/6 and Gin at 3/6, on 19th November, and the Hearse & 3 Carriages, on 20th at £1. 10. 0. The obituary in the *Cornish Telegraph* (which cost 10 shillings) referred to B. A. Simmons as "highly esteemed and respected by his own friends and neighbours in this place,[114] but, significantly, made no mention of the congregation. The total cost of B. A. Simmons' funeral was £7 and 8 shillings, the equivalent of four months of his previous wages.

A few days later on 8th December, the newspaper published an anonymous tribute in the form of a letter from a local non-Jew, entitled paradoxically "The Christian Jew", which for its day suggests the genuine respect and affection with which he came to be held in the wider community in Penzance, where, for example, he was a member of the Masonic Lodge: "SIR - I observed in the obituary of your last week's paper the report of the death of the Rev. B. A. Simmons - for nearly half a century the Rabbi of the Jewish congregation in this town. He was a man much to be admired for his uprightness of character; well read in the writings of his profession, yet without bigotry, or bitterness towards those holding religious opinions differing from his own; and an example for many professing Christians of this day in this respect. I as an old friend of his, though of another creed, have often wished in my heart that a man so estimable had professed Christianity. He rested firmly on the promise made to Abraham and his seed. Sir, yours respectfully, HOMO. - Penzance, Dec. 8th, 1860". The similarity of the opening words to those of the dedication of 1854, suggest that this was written by the same Henry Cornish, who would have been more than aware of the history of animosity towards B. A Simmons in the Hebrew congregation, and the treatment he had received from its elders over many years. The writer was obviously determined that his friend's contribution to the life of the local community should receive some wider, public recognition, and that the positive aspects of his character should not be forgotten. In complete contrast, no such record has been found of any printed tribute to him from the Jewish community, and there is no mention in the Minutes of his death or of a letter of condolence having been sent to his family (although the Minutes themselves become fragmentary at this time). His widow Flora returned to

Merthyr Tydfil in the same year to live with her family there. She died on 2nd December 1874 at the age of 84, and she is buried in the Merthyr Jewish cemetery. Her children migrated to London, Birmingham, and three emigrated to Australia, where, later, several grandchildren also settled.

Hyman Greenberg (Samuel Hillman: September 1859-1861).

The Minutes for 25th and 29th September 1859 confirm that Hyman Greenborough (Greenberg) also known as Samuel or Solomon Hillman (*Samuel ben Simeon*) replaced Simmons as *"shochet &c"*, significantly at an increased salary of £40 per year. In a signed agreement he accepted the situation of *"shochet & chazan,* to perform all duties of same as former Rabbis". He also agreed to a clause of 3-months notice "except in the case of being deprived of licence by Dr. Adler – in that case this agreement is cancelled". The Rev. Hyman Greenberg was engaged by the congregation while he was still a young man of around 22 years of age. B. A. Simmons had been five years older, at 27, when he was appointed in 1811, but he is likely to have come already trained as a *shochet*, and Greenberg's skills in this area, together with the other responsibilities expected of a minister, had not yet been fully tested. Moreover, he may not have completed his training in all of the skills ideally required of an incumbent rabbi, but he would have undergone suffi-cient training for a *shochet's* licence, and would have possessed some background in Talmudic study. Even if he was a comparative novice, he was at least judged to have the religious knowledge to enable him to fulfil the congregation's ceremonial needs. As things turned out he seems to have been a considerable success, and his tenure seems to have been a happy one.

From 1860 he was elected to act as the congregation's Secretary, some of the minutes being in his hand, and he delivered at least one discourse in the synagogue on the Sabbath preceding the Passover of 1860, the minutes for the annual meeting of 1st April recording that "a vote of thanks was proposed and carried unanimously to Mr. Greenborough for his able and instructive lecture". So impressed was the President that "Mr. Levin has presented a clerical hat to be worn by the Rabby (*sic.*) on all Religious Occasions". B. A. Simmons, nearing the end of his life, may well have been present on this occasion, and one cannot help but think that the laurels bestowed on the young Rabbi served partly to make a telling point. The young man may well have shown considerable promise, and to act as secretary would in itself require a reasonable education. He appears to have carried out the duties of secretary voluntarily, and there is no mention of his being paid for a tedious and time-consuming task which others would, no doubt, have been more than eager to relinquish or avoid. He may have been ambitious or eager to please, and his youth and relative inexperience may have rendered him to be adaptable and pliable to the requirements of the senior members of the congregation. He held the post for only 18 months, and he died, tragically young, at the age of 24 in 1861.[115] The 1861 Census for Penzance mentions the death of "a Jewish rabbi, between the day of delivery and the day of collection of the schedule", and records him as a former occupant of No. 56 Adelaide Street. There is no mention of his death in the minutes, but he is buried in the Penzance cemetery, and it has been noted above, that his headstone refers to his father, "our Honoured Master and Teacher Rabbi Simeon Greenberg", who may have been an earlier minister, perhaps during the period 1829-1843, for which there are no records. If Simeon Greenberg remained in the town, he may be buried in one of the graves without a headstone. However, if he lived beyond 1843, one would have expected some mention of him, or at least of his son, in the minutes from 1844-1859, but these later minutes are not in the form of detailed accounts (which would itemise the names of subscribers) but only summaries of meetings. Even so, it could be expected that such honoured Teachers, especially Rabbis, would have taken a prominent role in meetings. From this, that possibility mentioned earlier, that Simeon Greenberg had left the town, and his son, Hyman, was recruited from elsewhere, might seem more likely. It is not known if the Rabbi Samuel Isaac Hillman who was at the South Portland Street (later Great Central) Synagogue in Glasgow around 1910 was related.[116]

A. Lupshutz (May 1861-*c*.1862).

The Minutes for 18th May 1861 contain Lupshutz's handwritten agreement "to take the situation of *chazan* and *shochet* [in Biblical Hebrew script] to the Penzance Congregation & to perform all the duties requisite at a salaray of Forty pounds Pr. Year to be settled quarterly at Midsummer, Michelmas (*sic.*) Xmas & Ladyday & to give & take three months notice at the end of Twelve months." It is of interest that the dates for the payment of his salary are given in relation to the secular and Christian calendar, a practice that occurs elsewhere, especially in the early minutes and accounts. Nothing more is known of Lupshutz's tenure, or if he was re-engaged after May 1862.

Marcus Spiro (September 1862-1865).

On 13th September 1863, the minutes record: "Mr. Spiro Salary to be one Pound a week, and to give a month notice". The salary increase is significant, and also the reduction from 3 to 1 month's notice. There is no contract for his appointment in the minutes, and the above may have been the renewal of his post from 1862. On 17th April 1864, it was "agreed by all members to give 10/6 to Mr. Spiro for *matzas*". A few months later, the minutes of 31st July record that one Friday evening he left the town without any warning or prior notice, leaving the congregation on the eve of the Sabbath, "neglecting those duties you might be called upon to perform", presumably, failing to prepare kosher meat (although he may have slaughtered on the Thursday) and to lead the services as *chazan*: "At a Special Meeting held this Day to take into considaration (*sic.*) the Conduct of our *shochet* Rev Mr. Spiro in leaving the Congregation on his own Business for Plymouth and staying away on *shabbos* without permission of the President". He was severely reprimanded in a letter drawn up by the President, Henry Levin, and was asked to explain himself in writing. There is no mention of the outcome, but matters cannot have been resolved to the satisfaction of the congregation, because, on 1st October it is noted that "Salary of Mr. Spiro to be reduced as original 16/- per week to commence the 5th December 1864". This indicates that he had indeed been appointed in 1862 at the "original", lower salary, but having shown promise and given satisfaction to the congregation at the start of his incumbency, received the increase to £1 per week in 1863. The salary reduction following his reprimand led to Spiro's resignation by 9th April 1865[117]: "Mr. Spiro has sent a Months Notice to leave his situation as *shochet* wich (*sic.*) the Congregation has accepted and resolved to engage another *shochet* ".

Rittenberg (1865-1868).

The date of his appointment is not given in the minutes, but he was in the town by late 1865, when, on 22nd November he officiated, jointly with Rabbi I. Rubinstein, at the marriage of George Goodman of Glamorgan to Rose Joseph, a daughter of Henry Joseph of Penzance. The presence of Rabbi Rubinstein at the Goodman-Joseph wedding is somewhat surprising, in that he is not recorded as the official incumbent for Penzance until 1886-1887. He may, therefore, have been resident in the town for some considerable time before his appointment, unless, in the meantime, he had left for another post and returned in 1886. Rittenberg stayed in his post for several years, and he too had his salary reduced by the withdrawal of an annual allowance towards the end of 1867, the minutes for 14th April that year noting: "at the end of six months the extra allowance of 30/- to Mr. Rittenberg should be discontinued". It is not clear from the Minute Books if this was the result of financial restrictions or for disciplinary reasons. Soon after this, Rittenberg left his position, although there is no record of the resignation. A Rev. Bernhard Rittenberg (1843-1917) was minister in Edinburgh from 1864 to 1873. Unless these dates are incorrect, it seems unlikely that he can be identified with Rittenberg of Penzance, but there may have been a family connection. Much later, in 1898, a J. B. Rittenberg was minister in Exeter for the brief tenure of six months.[118]

Isaac Bischofswerder (c. 1868-1886).

The arrival of Rabbi Isaac Bischofswerder in the late 1860s with a large family breathed fresh life into the congregation and certainly gave it some stability. There is no mention of his formal appointment, but this was most likely in 1868, and he officiated at his first wedding on 9th June 1869. He served the congregation for 21 years until his retirement in 1886, but he lived in Penzance for a total of 30 years, until his death in 1899. His headstone in the Jewish cemetery (8:3) reads in Hebrew: "was *chazan* and *shochet* here for more than twenty years". After 1886, he was in poor health, but he may have served on an occasional basis after the departure of the last official Rabbi, Michael Leinkram, in 1895. In the 1860s he had come to England from Vandsburg in Prussia where he was born in 1822 (now Bydgoszoz in Poland, between Gdansk and Warsaw). His first wife was Esther (Etty or Ernestine) Feigel (1829-1865), the daughter of Rav Michael Feigel (-1876) of Leutenberg, Prussia. Esther had seven children, all born in Germany: the first was most likely, Yette, or Henrietta, who may have been born around 1851 (public records, such as census returns and registry certificates differ significantly on her birth year and age), Marcus (1852-1914), David (1854-1902), Morris 1856-1934), Max (1860-1928), George, or Solomon, known as "Solly" (1861-1930) and Augusta (c.1864-1919).[119] Their mother died in 1865, possibly giving birth to Augusta, or soon after from complications arising from her birth. With a large and very young family to raise, within a short time after Esther's death, Isaac Bischofswerder married Rahle (Rachel) Weile (1831-1886), who was also a native of Vandsburg, and the widow of Solomon Weile. She had at least one daughter from her first marriage, Berthe, who came to live with the Bischofswerder family. Eventually, the whole family arrived in England, and then came to Penzance.[120]

Isaac Bischofswerder officiated at his first Jewish wedding in Penzance on 9th June 1869: that of Aaron Beirnstein of Dowlais in South Wales to Esther Joseph, a daughter of Henry Joseph. He officiated at another wedding on 31st August 1870 of Abraham Freedman of Aberdare to Kate Joseph, another daughter of Henry Joseph. However, it was not until April 1874 that he is first mentioned in the Minute Books, when it was "resolved that Mr. Bischofswerder should be allowed this year 30/- for Passover", and on 23rd May he is listed as donating 2/6 to the Bengal famine and Jerusalem Relief funds. A year later, on 19th April 1875, it was agreed that "Mr. Bishopswarder (sic.) be allowed 21/- for *matzah*" and "that Dr. Harvey's Bill of £1 – 12 – 4 be paid for Medical attendance on Mr. Bishopswarder". On 9th April the congregation had drawn up an account of subscriptions received towards the Sir Moses Montefiore Testimonial Fund. That Isaac Bischofswerder's name is not listed suggests that he was finding it difficult to manage on his salary with such a large family to support. The 1871 census confirms that he had been living with his whole family in a small recently-built house[121] at 6, Belgrave Terrace (later Belgravia Street). He was to remain there, at least until his wife died, in 1886. Clearly, he could not manage on the salary he received, and the minutes of 25th July 1875 record that "At a Special Meeting held this Day to consider an application made by our Rabi (sic.) Mr. Bishopswarder for an increase of Salary Resolved that the salary be increased from £47. 12. 0 pr Annum to Fifty two Pounds £52 pr Annum including £2. 12 .0 for Killing Beast to commence from this date". The congregation must have been satisfied with their rabbi to allow this, because finance had become a growing problem for the congregation in the latter part of the 19th century. Isaac Bischofswerder, like rabbis such as B. A. Simmons before him, would have needed a small shop or a private business outlet from his home to supplement his income. He was by trade a jeweller. His sons were not yet fully established in the town, although later they were sufficiently successful in local business to invest in the Bolitho Bank, to shore up the congregation's finances during its period of final decline, and to support their widowed father. In his last years, sometime after 1886, he moved from Belgravia Street into "The Hollies", a very large and imposing house in the Alverton area of the town, on which his son, David, would have taken out a temporary lease on the strength of his personal, recently-acquired wealth, which he was soon to lose. After this, Isaac Bischofswerder became dependant on the family of his son Morris.

A decade before Isaac Bischofswerder's wife died in their Belgravia Street house in 1886, there occurred, in 1875, the most serious accident at sea in living memory, when the German mail-steamer the *S .S. Schiller*, at that time one of the largest vessels afloat, left Hoboken Pier, New York on 27th April, being hove-to off Long Island until the 28th. It was scheduled to arrive in Plymouth on the 7th May, but due to delays the ship was almost a day behind. The ship foundered on the Retarrier Ledges off the Isles of Scilly on the 7th May.[122] Nearly 350 lives were lost, and only 43 people survived. The incident was reported extensively in the National and Cornish press as early as the 8th and 9th May, and shocked the local community in West Cornwall. The Board of Trade Enquiry and the Coroner's Inquest went on for many months. Arising from this tragic event, and most likely originating some time later from a cocktail of confused, mistaken (and possibly anti semitic) local rumour, claims have survived that Rev. Isaac Bischofswerder used unscrupulous means to benefit from the aftermath of the disaster. He is supposed to have been appointed the Receiver of Wrecks for the *Schiller* in 1875, and local people (sometimes identified specifically as fishermen) who had scoured the sea and coast for wreckage are thought to have brought it to Bischofswerder, who is portrayed as appropriating the valuables for himself, selling them on and, in so doing, accumulated a fortune. In this colourful scenario, the angry and aggrieved smugglers tarred and feathered ornamental golden eagles at the entrance to his (supposed) town mansion, the Hollies. If these extensive claims of dubious acquisition and resale of salvage could be substantiated, they would seriously damage Isaac Bischofswerder's posthumous reputation, in that they amount to behaviour which is at the very least highly immoral, but which would also have constituted a criminal offence. They deserve to be closely examined, because they are, in fact, entirely without foundation.

Crucially, Isaac Bischofswerder was most certainly not (or ever) the Receiver of Wrecks, nor would he (nor any other Rabbi, or Christian minister) have been appointed to such a position. The Customs Officer at Penzance was also (as part of his permanent duties) the Receiver of Wrecks. His position was strictly regulated by the Government Department at the Board of Trade responsible for all aspects of shipping and maritime incidents. In the case of wrecks, the Receiver had to record the depositions of survivors and witnesses, co-ordinate and oversee all salvage operations, record and regulate the retention of all salvage, and he was also required to appear before the Coroner's Inquest and to report to the Board of Inquiry into the incident. Any Customs Officer in this position would find himself under particular scrutiny and, in any event, he would not have been entitled to retain or receive any of the salvage for his private use or profit. Even if he did attempt this, he would not have been capable of doing so openly, nor without considerable risk, when salvage or luggage was brought to him by his officers or by others. It is also most unlikely that sufficient quantities of gold and jewellery would have come his way to enable him to make a fortune for himself. Inevitably, some items of valuable salvage were appropriated and dishonestly concealed locally and on the Isles of Scilly, and these cases did include some quantities of dollars, bought up illicitly by dealers from the mainland, but these incidents were rare and there is no evidence that the practice was widespread, nor that the value of stolen items (except for the dollars) was considerable.[123]

The various enquiries and the supervision of the aftermath of the disaster were extensive and rigorous, and covered a period of many months. The identity of the Receiver of Wrecks for the *Schiller* incident is clearly stated in official Government communications and in the local press at the time as "Mr. Handley" the "Collector of Customs and Receiver of Wrecks".[124] It fell to James T. Handley to supervise the enormous task of recovering and recording all of the bodies, the property found on them, the cargo and other salvage, and he did so meticulously,[125] with the result that almost all of the gold and cargo was recovered. Some small items were exempted from recording by the Board of Trade, but Handley recorded them, nevertheless. The numerous items recovered were either handed in to the Receiver or his clerk directly, or to his officers, or to the Coastguard, who then passed them on.[126] The wreck was viewed so seriously by the Government that Handley imposed very strict rules of procedure on his officers locally, and refused to countenance the payment of the customary reward money to those local people who brought salvage to him. This caused considerable anger and resentment, especially among some of the inhabitants of the fishing-village of Newlyn, and their protest and opposition to Handley's regulations became the subject of several local newspaper reports at the time (and the Newlyn fishermen were to protest again, on an entirely unrelated matter, in the famous "Newlyn Riots" of May 1896).[127] Local jewellers and shopkeepers would also have been subject to the restrictions that applied to the retention and reception of salvage items, and there are a sufficient number of examples on record of Jewish Jewellers and pawnbrokers in Cornwall (who may have been especially concerned to be seen to operate with honesty) reporting their suspicions to the police when they were offered items which they suspected might be stolen. They followed this practice in the ordinary course of events,[128] and they would have been especially alert and cautious after the wreck of the *Schiller*, when there was a much greater likelihood that dubious practice would come to light.

After a period of time, the little salvage which remained unclaimed, or could not be allocated to its legal owners (in the case of survivors) or their heirs, was released by Handley and allocated to a Marine Store dealer in the town for lawful sale. From then on any member of the public could purchase the items. However, any further salvage from the wreck that was washed up was to be brought to the Receiver's notice, and, if it could not be allocated as before, an application could be made for a grant of "Rights of Salvage" to the finders. Upon reception of the grant the salvage items could then be lawfully retained or sold on. Handley continued to place the local area under surveillance for some time, and in January 1876 a legal injunction was sought and granted over some fishermen at Sennen (some miles from Penzance) who had recovered a quantity of dollars (known as "Eagles") from the wreck.[129] Such individual items of salvage could appear years after the wreck, and any resident of Penzance could have come into possession of them, although in reality little remained to be recovered, and certainly not in sufficient quantities to be of any great value.

At the time of the wreck, newspapers reported services of burial and remembrance in various local Churches, including a formal service at Paul attended by Handley and many dignitaries and representatives of local organisations. The names of the victims and those of the survivors were published in various reports, and a comprehensive list of the crew, passengers, cargo and rescuers can be identified. Detailed statements and depositions from the surviving passengers and crew were also collated in full. It is clear from these sources that a significant number of the passengers were Jews, which was also noted by the Jewish press in America and England at the time. Two such press reports mention that a Mr. Kornblum and his family were on the *Schiller*, having embarked at New York, on an extended tour of Europe: "a large concourse of friends and representatives of the benevolent societies of New York assembled on the steamship 'Schiller' to bid Mr. Kornblum and his family farewell on their departure for Europe. Unfortunately, neither the name of Mr. Kornblum nor that of any member of his family are included in the list of those saved from the vessel. We hear that there were several other Jewish persons on board".[130] Michael Kornblum was wealthy Jewish businessman from Brooklyn with premises in Manhattan. After setting up a branch of his business in London, he intended to take his family on an extended tour of Europe, and when they returned to New York, he would remain in London for two years to manage the new branch. The family were travelling first class, and in their luggage there were 85 gold watches, £500 in coin and a considerable quantity of diamond jewellery.[131] Many other first class passengers would have carried such valuable items, if not in the same quantities, but many other bodies were recovered with similar items on them: "Many had large sums of money in coin or banknotes, expensive jewellery and watches upon them. Every possession was registered and placed in the care of James Handley, or his clerk, for eventual return to relatives of the dead person".[132] Many of the bodies that were recovered were embalmed and returned to America for burial. Others were interred in collective graves on the Scilly Isles and in Penzance, and these graves may have held the bodies of unidentified Jews. Some separate graves were set aside for identified and related individuals, and some of these may have been Jews.[133] There is no mention in any of the press or official reports of Isaac Bischofswerder (who, as we have seen, had recently been in ill-health) or any other member of the Jewish congregation having been connected with the incident, involved with any of the relatives of the dead, or officiating at any ceremony for them. There were no burials in the Jewish cemetery at this time, and it would seem that no attempt was made to contact the Jewish congregation or its minister to arrange for the local burial of any Jewish victim. The name *Bischofswerder*, or any likely variant of it, is entirely absent from the numerous, contemporaneous local and national newspaper reports, and from the relevant Board of Trade records.[134]

The congregational minutes clearly show that the Rabbi was in need of financial assistance and support around the time of the wreck in 1875, and although the congregational minutes are lacking in detail from this point on, with little mention of the Rabbi, it is likely that he continued to be reliant on the congregation in this way for some years. The congregational elders were parsimonious to a degree, and they would not have countenanced the payment of additional money to support a minister claiming hardship if he had become a very wealthy man. Moreover,

Isaac Bischofswerder would not have been able to conceal such a change in his fortunes from the congregation in such a small and parochial community. When he died in 1899, he did not leave a will and there is no record of a grant of probate for him. This would be inconceivable had he made a fortune during his lifetime, and the most likely explanation for the absence of probate is that his personal estate was worth so little that it fell below the value required for the grant. Local census and directories from 1871 to 1883 show that he lived modestly at Belgrave Terrace at the time of the wreck and that he and his wife remained there until she died in 1886. He is not recorded as resident at the Hollies until 1891, sixteen years after the wreck, and he may well have made over or disposed of the little capital he possessed to his family before or when he moved there.[135]

In fact, no member of the Bischofswerder family lived at the Hollies at the time of the wreck, when it was most likely occupied by a Mr. Thorne, the tenant who is known to have extended it some years before 1891 to run part of the building as a private school. Isaac Bischofswerder was never the legal occupier or owner of the Hollies, and his son is highly unlikely to have acquired the freehold to it at a time when only a very small percentage of property was available on a freehold basis. David Bischofswerder, like Mr. Thorne, would most likely have acquired a short-term lease to the property, sometime from 1885 to 1891, and not before 1881.[136] The entrance to the house did indeed have eagles mounted on its pillars. The putative tarring of these eagles made in the claims cannot have been motivated by the anger of fishermen in 1875 against Isaac Bischofswerder, because he did not live there at that time, nor for some years to come. This spurious notion may reflect a confusion and conflation of the protests of the Newlyn fishermen against Handley's restrictions of May 1875, with the 1876 injunction against the Sennen fishermen's retention of the "Eagles" (dollars) from the wreck. In 1875, David Bischofswerder may well have bought judiciously from the sale of the remaindered salvage at the Marine Store, but if he did so, such purchase was entirely legitimate. Whether he came into possession of any valuable items by illicit and dubious means is unknown, but in any event it is improbable that *he* could have made a fortune from this incident alone. He was eventually to become an experienced and successful diamond importer, when that particular trade was not regulated so strictly as it was in the twentieth century, and he was in a position to fully benefit from that source.

David Bischofswerder continued to live in Belgravia Street for several years after 1875, and his significant wealth was not acquired until the early to mid 1880s. When this eventually allowed him to move into the Hollies, he used much of his resources to support local charitable and civic causes. However, he was a flamboyant and colourful character, and, for a time he lived well and enjoyed the benefits of *un nouveau riche*. He may well have courted controversy and become the focus of local resentment and envy, and even anti-Jewish prejudice, at a time when many local people were very poor. Whatever his local reputation for business practice, if the eagles at the Hollies were tarred after he moved there, in local tradition this later occurrence may have been retrospectively and erroneously transferred to the incident of the wreck of the *Schiller*, and, by association, to Isaac Bischofswerder himself, who was by then also living there. David Bischofswerder lost his wealth and the Hollies in an unwise investment in a failing local mine, and he may well have overextended himself by making unwise investments in other areas. Later, after he left Penzance, he was accused of dishonest business practice and was involved in a court case in the North of England, subsequent to which he emigrated to South Africa, but none of this, in itself, is evidence of any earlier malpractice on his part in Penzance. After the departure of his son, David, from Penzance, Isaac Bischofswerder would have lived as a dependant with his remaining son, Morris. There is, therefore, no known link between Rev. Isaac Bischofswerder and the wreck of the *Schiller*, no evidence that he was ever a wealthy man, and no cause to cast doubt upon his integrity.

On 9th February 1876, at the age of 21, Henrietta Bischofswerder married Rabbi Elias Pearlson, age 23, from Newcastle and moved there.[137] He became the Rabbi in Newcastle and they later moved to Hull. Their son, Gustav, became a professional pianist. He was also a gifted linguist, and is said to have written a book on Jewish history at the age of 18.[138] Eventually, Isaac Bischofswerder's son, George, moved to Hull, where he became established and built a large house, giving it the name "St. Michael's Mount". Michael (1899-), the son of Marcus and Sarah Bischofswerder, joined his uncle's household there, and later, his parents also moved to Hull. Of the Hull family house, a descendant has recalled: "I remember going to the house which was huge by any standards. My grandmother [Sarah, who was a Gentile by birth] always had a pronounced Cornish accent, and made Cornish pasties".[139] Another of Isaac Bischofswerder's sons, Max, married a Catherine Jacobs of Plymouth, where the couple remained. On 5th February 1884, at the age of 27, Morris Bischofswerder married Julia Joseph, aged 33, the daughter of a prosperous local pawnbroker, Henry Joseph of Queen's Square. They were the only members of the Bischofswerder family to remain in the town, where Julia died in 1911, Morris leaving in 1913.

Ill-health may well have continued to take its toll on Isaac Bischofswerder throughout the period from 1875-1886. He is not recorded in the Minutes after 1875, and he seems not to have taken an active part in vestry meetings, in that his signature does not appear in the minutes, although his sons were signatories. Isaac Bischofswerder continued as minister and *shochet*, as the minutes for 17th September 1876 indicate: "Mr. Sam. Jacob of Falmouth is supplied with meat from this congregation for 10 [guineas? - the script is unclear] we have decided on charging him 2/- Pr week". The Falmouth congregation was in terminal decline, and was only to survive with Samuel Jacob's family as its last members until 1880. On 1st April 1877, the minutes note that: "Mr. Jacob of Falmouth has declined having meat from here". Although it seems most likely that financial restraint might have been the key factor in Samuel Jacob's decision, he was from a relatively affluent family, and he was to continue to live in Falmouth for several years. He may have sent for kosher meat from Plymouth at a better rate, but it is also possible that he was not satisfied with the quality of the supplies from Penzance. This is conjectural, but if Isaac Bischofswerder's health was deteriorating, his performance as *shochet* may also have been affected. On 10th March 1886 at the age of 55, Isaac Bischofswerder's wife, Rachel, died. This blow prompted the rabbi to hand in his resignation, on the grounds of ill health, a few days later on 14th March. The congregation resolved to "advertise in the Jewish Chronicle & World for Reader,

Bal Korah & *Shochet*, we write the President of the Plymouth Congregation that [we] shall have meat during the time we are without a *shochet*. Resolved the weekly payments be discontinued until the appointment of a new Reader & Shochet". Isaac Bischofswerder lived in the town for a further 13 years, and died on 18th October 1899 age 77 years. His grave and headstone is at the front of the cemetery in a section of graves mainly occupied by members of his family. He has the distinction of having been the longest continuously serving Jewish minister in Penzance, and possibly in Cornwall.

Isaac Aryeh Rubinstein (June 1886 to *c.* September 1887).

On 25th April 1886 the Minutes note: "Resolved that Mr. B. H. [Barnet Henry] Joseph's kind offer of visiting Northampton & having an interview with the Revd. I. Rubinstein & reporting same to congregation be accepted". B. H. Joseph "Birm'm" [Birmingham] was present at this meeting, together with Isaac Bischofswerder's sons, David and Morris. The Rev. Rubinstein (or Rubenstein) had a previous connection with Penzance, in that, he had been the joint officiant with the minister of the Penzance congregation, Rev. Rittenberg, at the wedding of Rose Joseph, a daughter of Henry Joseph of Penzance in 1865. Rubinstein was the minister and *shochet* in Falmouth at that time, and until 1868, and he appears to have been connected with the Joseph family there, and in Penzance. Rubinstein was not the incumbent minister at Northampton in 1886, where, in 1885, the Reader and Shochet was the Rev. A. H. Echmann. A Sydney Baruch Rubinstein appears in records for the Northampton congregation in 1888 and 1894,[140] and this may be the same family. It is not known if the Chief Rabbi, Dr. Adler, advised on Rubinstein's suitability, but B. H. Joseph's report to the congregation must have been positive and was accepted. The congregational elders acted swiftly, and on 9th May Rubinstein was elected as "Reader & Shochet" with a salary of 21/- per week. He took up his appointment on 1st June, receiving his first payment.

Having been in Penzance some 20 years earlier, when Rubinstein arrived in the town he was mystified by the scale of the congregation's decline and the exodus of Jews from the locality. In contrast to the restrictions, persecution and prejudice which were familiar to him in Russia, in that he kept in communication with his homeland and his fellow-countrymen, he marvelled at the open, tolerant and affluent society where opportunities seemed to flourish. Nowhere was this more so for him than in Penzance. After six months in his post, he decided to write an open letter from Penzance, and on 25th November 1886, this was printed in the popular and widely-circulated Russian-Jewish journal *Ha-Melitz*. He says: "Many Jews flourished here in abundant plenty and some acted in a representative capacity in local and national government equally with Christians. Moreover those who live here today live on the fat of the land and enjoy unhindered and uninterrupted peace. In spite of this, our brethren have forsaken this place. Why, I know not. It is a riddle without interpretation, they leave a blessed land, without any compelling reason."[141] The tone of this letter was typical of the "panegyric" of East European Jewish immigrants extolling the opportunities to be found in their new country of residence, but it resulted in some disquiet and concern amongst the Russian-Jewish community in London, and the Russo-Jewish Committee responded by advertising the reasons why Jews should not leave the East End of London for the provinces. These included problems of isolation, fear of prejudice, language barriers and lack of opportunities for Jewish education. These reasons, although significant, do not entirely explain away Rubinstein's puzzlement. The reasons for the decline were not primarily social, civil or economic, but numerical. The Jewish communities in Cornwall, even at their prime, fell below the critical level that would allow for self-generation and permanent settlement. It is unlikely that the Cornish Jewish population, even at its highest, was ever more than 50-60 people in each of Penzance and Falmouth, and it was very low by 1886. If one removes from this the children, then there was little room for exclusive marriage between local Jews, and especially within the same congregation. Most Jewish marriages in Penzance were to Jewish partners from outside the area, resulting in some cases in the migration of whole families of offspring from Penzance. Conversion to Christianity or marriage to non-Jews was not common, but it was not unknown, and was an ever-present threat. The modest size of the Cornish Jewish congregations made them intrinsically non-viable in the long-term without a continuous and increasing influx of new members, and this did not happen in the numbers or with the regularity needed to re-invigorate local Jewish life.

On 8th April 1887, the Annual Meeting recorded the death of Mr. Israel Levin, and resolved that his name should be replaced with that of David Bischofswerder "on the Deed" (to the synagogue's property, held in the Bolitho Bank) and as a Trustee. In the wake of this newly acquired status he decided to organize a special service to celebrate the Queen's forthcoming Jubilee, having already funded the building of a grand Jubilee Hall in the main street of the town, together with a Jubilee festival meal for the town's inhabitants. The local press recorded both events, and in the service, Rubinstein again held forth on the virtues of English life for Jews: "Jubilee Service at the Jew's [sic.] Synagogue, Penzance, Special services convened by Mr. D. Bischofswerder, were held in the Jew's synagogue, Penzance on Jubilee morn, when special prayers, prepared by Rev. Dr. Adler, chief-rabbi, were offered by Rev. Mr. Rubenstein. In the course of his sermon, referring to the history of the Jews in England, he pointed out the numerous advantages and the perfect freedom they had enjoyed under the reign of Queen Victoria, as compared with former times, and contrasted the favourable circumstances they were in to what their brethren were experiencing in other countries. The national anthem was sung by the whole congregation." [142] Two months later, on 8th September, the vestry met "To consider the resignation sent in by Rev. I. A. Rubenstein which was accepted in favour of his accepting situation in Cardiff, we have also unanimously aggreed (sic.) to give Rev. Rubenstein a written Testimonial in consideration of his services both as shochet & rav which duties he has carried out most satisfactory (sic.)". The same minutes record that the congregation had "engaged services temporary recomended (sic.) through Dr. Adler by Telegram Sallery (sic.) to be considered at a future meeting of his arrival". Five years after Rubinstein's departure for Cardiff, a Rev. E. Rubenstein was minister in Sheffield (1892).[143] It is not known if he was connected with I. A. Rubinstein.

Michael Leinkram[144] (September 1887 to 1894/5).

Leinkram's exact date of birth is unknown but he was born in Krakow in Poland sometime between 1852 and 1854. His birth name was Mikael ben Schloma, the son of Solomon Leinkram, also known as Solly Barnett, who was a teacher by profession. Michael was one of four sons, at least two of whom emigrated to America. When Michael emigrated to England, his father remained in Poland. The East End of London contained a large Polish-Jewish community in the late 19th century and so he was able to live at 6 Wentworth Street, Spitalfields, with the Polish family of Moses (Morris) Riesenfeld who was a tinker (1881 Census), whose sons, David and Abraham emigrated to Virginia. At the age of 33 Michael Leinkram was to marry Moses Riesenfeld's daughter, Esther, age 27, at Sandys Row synagogue, with Rabbi V. Rosenstein officiating, on 7th December 1887. There is no mention on Michael Leinkram's headstone (see below) that he was a rabbi or acted in any religious capacity, and it has been supposed by his descendants that Michael Leinkram was never formally a rabbi, but an observant man who could conduct services as well as teach Hebrew and religion classes to the children.[145] However, the Congregational Minute Book records that Michael was appointed to Penzance at the age of 33, taking office on 12th September 1887 as "Shochet & Chazan"[146] at a salary of 20/- per week. He was formally elected on 25th September, and his appointment was confirmed on 23rd October. Six weeks later, he returned to London for his wedding, describing himself on the certificate as "Jewish minister". His father was recorded as deceased. Esther was illiterate, giving her mark on the marriage certificate in place of a signature. In 1888, the minutes for March 17th note that the meeting "unanimously agreed to give the Rev. Mr. M. Leinkram £1 for Pesach". By this time, Esther Leinkram was expecting her first child. On 23rd September, the congregation agreed that "two guineas shall be given to the Rebba on account of his wife's coming accouchement." It seems that the couple lost this baby because family records do not show a first-born child for several years. Esther Leinkram was to lose a number of children through miscarriage, at birth or in infancy.

David Bischofswerder had married Helena Hart (1857-1927) of Cleaves (Herzon) in Germany.[147] She was the daughter of Levi Hart, who is likely to have lived in London, where her first child, Harry, was born in 1877. In August 1889, the *bar mitzvah* of Harry Bischofswerder took place in the synagogue, with Michael Leinkram officiating, and Harry's grandfather, Rev. Isaac Bischofswerder also present. During Leinkram's tenure, B. H. Joseph of Birmingham and David Bischofswerder must have made a disproportionate contribution to the congregational finances at a time of dwindling membership and income. By 1890, the finances of the dwindling community were such that the services of a rabbi were formally dispensed with, and the minutes of 5th October that year presuppose that a "Minion" (minyan) was not always possible for the Sabbath Service. There is no mention of Leinkram in the Minutes from 1888 to this point, and his signature does not appear. He remained in the town, however, and may have carried out some occasional or minimal duties as a minister, and he is listed on the 1891 Census, living with his family at No. 16 Alverne Buildings. On 27th March 1892 the minutes note: "Resolved that £1 be given to the Reader as a gift for Passover". He was to officiate at the last Jewish wedding in the town; namely that of Marcus Bischof-swerder to Emma Hawke on 12th June 1892. Leinkram was to stay for only a few years after this.

Several of Michael and Esther Leinkram's children were born in Penzance: Anna (1890), who died in Newport, Virginia in 1901, and sons (likely twins) *Bitzall*, K and L were born in 1891, one of whom, Blazelle Bear Leinkram, known as Samuel or Solly (Solomon), named after his grandfather. (He died on 6th September 1967 in Euston, London).[148] Another son, Maurice, or *Moses* (who may also have been named *Joseph*, or had a twin by that name) was born in Penzance in 1892 or 1894.[149] Twins, Carrie (Clara) and Lewis (Louis) were born to a Leinkram family in Whitechapel, London in late 1895. They died in Belfast in 1895 and 1896 respectively.[150] Another daughter, Sadie, was born in Belfast in 1897, and may also have been the survivor of twins, her sister being Rebecca. By 1897 Michael Leinkram had been appointed as a minister in Belfast, at 77 Hopewell Street, where his daughter, Caroline (Crozy or Krusha, also known as Carrie) was born in 1898, and a son, Samuel in 1900. In 1901, on 20th June, the Leinkram family sailed from Liverpool to New York aboard the *SS Teutonic*. On arriving at Ellis Island, they were refused entry on the grounds of carrying an infectious disease. They returned to Liverpool, but then sailed again on 11th July 1901 on the White Star Liner, *SS Majestic*, gained entry and gave their destination as Esther's brother, David Reisfeld in Virginia. During their brief stay, their daughter, Annie died, and is buried there. On 15th May 1902, the family returned to Liverpool aboard the *SS Majestic*.[151] Their daughter, Gertrude was born in Belfast in 1904. They moved back to South East London, to Woolwich, where from 1906 Michael Leinkram traded as a draper and general shopkeeper at 33 Beresford Street (the trade and address given on his Will of 1918). He was buried on 26th November 1923, age 71, at the Edmonton Federation Cemetery in north London.[152] His wife Esther died on 30th June 1932, age 72, and is buried next to him.

After Michael Leinkram's departure from Penzance in 1895, Isaac Bischofswerder, albeit retired and in poor health, remained in Penzance as the County's last resident Jewish minister. He may have been able to assist with ministerial duties on an occasional basis, and the affairs of the vestigial congregation were by now almost entirely in the hands of four or five people. David Bischofswerder's financial ruin led to his departure from the town in the early 1890s. His signature, and that of his son, Harry, appear on the final surviving Minutes of the congregation on March 27th 1892, together with those of Israel Oppenheim and B. H. Joseph. The former was also was also to leave Penzance. Isaac Bischofswerder died in 1899, at the age of 77. Morris Bischofswerder remained in Penzance after his father's death to try to keep the synagogue open. By the beginning of a new century, it had become obvious that the congregation was no longer sustainable. The synagogue was used for the Sabbath and then eventually only for the High Holy Days and Festivals. Business meetings were conducted in Morris' home. Finally in 1906 the synagogue was sold. On 20th April 1911, Morris lost his wife Julia. By 1913 he had left the town. There are today at least five impressive graves in the Penzance cemetery, taking up much of the area at the front of the burial ground. They are a reminder of the importance which Rabbi Isaac Bischofswerder and his family had in the life of the declining congregation and the wider life in the town.

---

[1] Susser (1993, p.156 and 307) gives only 8 for Penzance and 6 for Falmouth.

[2] Letter from Herman Zeffertt to Keith Pearce (17th September 1998).

[3] Pz. 1:5: transcription by Nicholas de Lange and Jennifer Speake (1975), and translation by Herman Zeffertt (1999).

[4] Roth (1933).

[5] Susser (1993) pp. 149-157.

[6] Roth (1933).

[7] Susser (1993) pp. 158-159.

[8] Susser (1993) p. 157.

[9] *The Jewish World*, 15th May 1903, p.153.

[10] Naggar (1992) p. 15; from The Hawkers' and Pedlars' Office Accounts held at PRO Kew.

[11] W. Jessop (1951) *A Coat of Many Colours* (pub. Frank Gent 2000; pp. 22 & 6).

[12] Phillimore Parish registers, vol 13, p.87.

[13] Phillimore, *op. cit.*

[14] Susser (1993, p. 95, 238, and 243).

[15] Full details of the Polack family are given in the sections on Falmouth Trades.

[16] Susser (1993, p. 95 and 293) refers to this same advert. It appeared on the same date in the *Western Flying Post*. At the time, these newspapers were the only two circulating in the South West. Advertisements could be placed locally in Falmouth, Penryn and Truro.

[17] Michael Michell (January 2009).

[18] Jacob (1949/53).

[19] Alex Jacob's archive contains his own (unpublished 1939) survey notes of the Penryn (Falmouth) cemetery: he translates this date as 14th September 1830 (which has tended to influence other genealogical sources). However, in his article on the Jews of Falmouth (written in 1949 and published in 1953) he gives the date as 24th October and the year (incorrectly) as 1832. Susser in an article in the *Cornishman* (Thursday 16th July 1964) gives the month as September. He places the conversion of Hyman's daughter Harriet some six weeks later, which would roughly coincide with 7th November. In his book (1993 p. 307) he gives the date (incorrectly) as 24th October 1830.

[20] Susser, the *Cornishman* (16th July 1964).

[21] David Liss and Gary Kent: detailed information from their research into the Hyman family (various letters from 2000-2004).

[22] In the Plymouth Census records her age is given as 30 (1841), 43 (1851, where she appears as *Tibiah*) and 56 (1861).

[23] In the Plymouth Census records his age is given as 40 (1841), 60 (1851) and 72 (1861).

[24] These birth years are approximate and have been inferred from the same Census records where some of the ages given for the parents and their children are inconsistent, varying from census to census.

[25] Church Baptismal entry No. 147 (Eric Dawkins, 2000).

[26] I am grateful to Yissochor Marmorstein for identifying this date.

[27] Letter Book if the Chief Rabbi's Archive (Solomon Hirschel, page 164), translated from the cursive Hebrew script by Yissochor Marmorstein (December 2002) from a copy in the possession of Godfrey Simmons. The letter is quoted here with some minor interpolation (in brackets).

[28] Genealogical Records of Anthony Joseph and Letter to Keith Pearce (5th December 2010).

[29] Records of Anthony Joseph.

[30] Documents in Godfrey Simmons' archive. His great aunt was married to Rintel. I am grateful to Roger Ainsworth for translating these documents.

[31] Letter in *Jewish World*, 15th May 1903, p.153. See also Jacob (1949-53) and Roth (1933).

[32] *Royal Cornwall Gazette* (31st August 1933).

[33] Susser (1993, p.248).

[34] *Royal Cornwall Gazette* and *The West* Briton, 27th April 1849: Research by Jackie Hill (2011).

[35] Berger (2004) p. 313.

[36] Jolles (199) pp. 217 & 222.

[37] Information supplied by Lewis Falkson; also Slater's *Royal National & Commercial Directory*, 1852, see the section "Places of Worship" and "Clergy".

[38] Susser (1993, p.158).

[39] RCG, 5th October 1860, p.5, col. 6.

[40] Michael Jolles (1999) p. 230 & 231.

[41] Frank Gent, in *The Jews of Devon and Cornwall* (2000) p. 30.

[42] Bellany (1998) p. 12; Jolles (1999) p. 231.

[43] Jolles (1999) pp. 218-219.

[44] Jacob (1949) and Roth (1950) p. 63. Roth assumed that Lipman officiated in Falmouth in the 1860s. Nachum Lipman was the grandfather of the late scholar and historian, Dr. Vivian Lipman, who may have given information to both Roth and Jacob. Jacob (1949), Roth (1950) and Susser (1993) give him only as "N. Lipman". In 2000 I gave him (incorrectly) as *Nathan*. The 1881 Census for Whitechapel records *Nieman*, Leah and Deborah Lipman "born Poland", but the 1891 Census gives "born Russia" (he was from Suwalk on the north eastern borders). The 1881 Census confirms that Caroline and Henrietta Lipman were born in Falmouth, later census records suggesting Henrietta in 1875 (the birth was registered in Falmouth in the second quarter of 1875) and Caroline in 1873 (although that registration was in 1871). It is possible that their ages may have been given incorrectly in each census, and the same records suggest Lipman's year of birth as 1843, not 1847. The 1875 registration of birth suggests that Lipman may not have taken up his (1874) appointment as Chief Shochet until the following year. Five more children (Isabella, Rosa, Samuel, Isadore and Sylvia) were born in London from c.1878. Nachum Lipman is buried in the Willesden Jewish Cemetery. Lipman's obituary makes no mention of his years in Falmouth. I am grateful to Dr. & Mrs. Harold Davis and to Dr. Michael Jolles for this information on Lipman (February 2014).

[45] c.f. Susser (1993, p.307). Letter from Lord Mishcon to Bernard Susser, 10th March 1993.

[46] Susser (1995) pp.93-107; Pollins (1995) *The Jewish Community of Stroud, Gloucestershire* (Oxford Menorah, issue 136, pp. 17-18; Pollins (1996) *The Jewish Community of Stroud 1877-1908* (Jewish Journal of Sociology, vol. XXXVIII, No. 1, pp. 27-41; Brian Torode (1999 rev. of 1989), *The Hebrew Community of Cheltenham, Gloucester and Stroud*, pp. 95-96; Letter from Brian Torode to Keith Pearce (7th January 2001) with corrections and further information ref. Orler, including the Stroud Census 1881 & 1891 and Stroud Marriage Registers 1882-1889; *Jewish Chronicle* 27th June 1890, p. 19.

[47] These have not been reproduced here, either in full or in significant detail, but salient details have been extracted from them. I am grateful to Yissochor Marmorstein for his translation and explanatory comments on these contracts and on the sections of the complete minutes where references to the ministers' names, duties and employment occur in Hebrew script. Cecil Roth's (1933) study of the documents has also been used in this reconstruction.

[48] Roth (1933).

[49] Susser (1993, p.136-159, 169).

[50] Roth (1933) clearly saw that this was the case from his comparison of Solomon's *Records* with the sections of the Minute Book (1810-1811).

[51] The quotations that follow are taken directly from Israel Solomon's words.

[52] According to Israel Solomon, although it has not been confirmed by other sources.

[53] Israel Solomon states incorrectly that the murder was "at Plymouth Dock".

[54] Susser (1993) pp. 36, 151, 165 & 306.

[55] *Royal Cornwall Gazette*: 30th November 1811, 28th March 1812 & 3rd April 1812.

[56] Anthony Joseph (1975) p. 32.

[57] I am much indebted to Godfrey Simmons for much of the information on B. A. Simmons.

[58] Great Synagogue Burial records (Letter from Angela Shire to Godfrey Simmons, 24th April 2000).

[59] Originals of the Accounts, the Will and the Indenture in the Archive of Godfrey Simmons.

[60] Held in the Jewish Museum, London.

[61] Jessop (1951) repub. Gent (2000) pp. 59-60.

[62] Repeated by Jacob (1949-53) & Susser (1993) p. 254. It has also been said that Simmons changed his

name. This is clearly based on a lack of understanding of the same person having both Hebrew (patronymic) names and an Anglicised equivalent.

[63] *Collectanea Cornubiensia*, 1548.

[64 and 64a] From the Archive of Godfrey Simmons.

[65] Susser (1993) pp. 34, 38, & 276-77.

[66] *The Times*, 19th October 1858.

[67] Raphael Langham, *The Reaction in England to the Kidnapping of Edgardo Mortara* (Transactions of the Jewish Historical Society of England (Vol. 39, 2004) pp. 79-101. Langham gives detailed sources and other studies of the affair.

[68] The original Birth Register of B. A. Simmons in the possession of Godfrey Simmons.

[69] See also Roth (1933).

[70] I am grateful to Yissochor Marmorstein, Nicholas de Lange and Herman Zeffertt for translating these sections of the Minute Books.

[71] Jolles (1999) p. 218.

[72] Roth (1933).

[73] The expression "home to" occurs several times in the accounts in the sense of "up to".

[74] I am grateful to Yissochor Marmorstein for identifying these errors in the Yiddish.

[75] Roth (1933).

[76] *Collectanea Cornubiensis B. C.* vol i, p.145.

[77] Susser (1993, p. 244-5).

[78] The complete text of the original is to be found in the Morrab (Gardens) Library, Penzance. It was transcribed by Godfrey Simmons.

[79] Pool (1974) p. 85, & 88-94.

[80] Le Grice (1824): Morrab (Gardens) Library, Penzance.

[81] Pool (1974) p. 149 (citing a likely but uncertain source).

[82] Susser (1993) p. 151.

[83] Jolles (1999) p. 234.

[84] *The London Gazette,* 12th October 1816, p. 1967 and 28th December 1816, p. 2483; Green (1989) p. 148; Susser (1993) p. 106.

[85] *Collectanaea Judaica Plymouthensis* (edit. Frank Gent 2000); Susser (1993) pp. 72-73.

[86] Originals (29th May 1833 & 10th January 1834) in the Archive of Godfrey Simmons.

[87] George Elwick, *The Bankrupt Directory 1820-1840* (1843) p. 233. (Research by John Simmons 2000).

[88] *Jewish Chronicle* (May 1868); Susser (1972) p. 22; Jessop (1951; publ. Gent 2000) pp. 13-17.

[89] Susser (1993) p. 157.

[90] Susser (1993) pp. 69 [nt. 287], 152, 155, & 157.

[91] Susser (1993) p. 152.

[92] Susser (1993) p. 155.

[93] Susser (1993) - various index references, and also by name in his Census records (1995) and Hoe cemetery survey (1972).

[94] The letters are not in the Minute-Book, but the originals are in the family archive of Godfrey Simmons.

[95] Jacob (1949-53).

[96] The register and a collection of bound prayer-books are in the possession of Godfrey Simmons.

[97] Susser (1993) p. 73. On page 72, Susser states that the register's 16 names refer to Penzance, but he itemises the entries correctly on p. 73.

[98] Numerous such conversion tables exist in manual form and on-line. I have cross-checked all of the dates in the register with on-line conversion tools from *Chabad* and the Jewish Genealogical Society.

[99] Research by Jill Hyams (2010).

[100] Archive of Alex M. Jacob.

[101] These details, which are derived from the family tradition of descendants, are not certain: Letters & enclosures from Alan Tyler to Keith Pearce (12th & 24th May 1997).

[102] Copies of original certificate and obituary notice for S. Cohen from the *Jewish Chronicle* in the possession of Alan Tyler.

[103] Jolles (1999) p. 220.

[104] The portraits are on permanent loan to the Museum, courtesy of Godfrey Simmons' son, Bernard Simmons.

[105] Algernon Graves, *The Royal Academy of Arts, A Complete Dictionary of Contributors and their work from its foundation in 1769 to 1904*, Vol. VI (1906) p. 104.

[106] Susser (1993, p.149).

[107] C.f. Penzance Minute Books, 17th & 20th June 1852 (Letter to the Chief Rabbi); and 10th & 24th July 1853.

[108] All of the items mentioned are in the Archive of Godfrey Simmons.

[109] The Account (some of which is barely decipherable) has been translated by Yissochor Marmorstein (January 2011).

[110] Duschinsky, *The Rabbinate of the Great Synagogue, London, from 1756-1842* (London 1921) p. 141, referencing the *Royal Cornwall Gazette*.

[111] C.f. Susser (1993, p.157-9).

[112] Roth (1950) p. 25; Wendy Bellany, *The Jews of Merthyr Tydfil*, in *Shemot* (September 1998) pp. 11-13: ref. note 1: Anthony Glaser & Ursula Henriques, *The Jews of South Wales* (Historical Studies, University of Wales Press 1993); Jolles (1999) p. 231.

[113] The original is in Godfrey Simmons' archive.

[114] *Cornish Telegraph*, 5th December 1860.

[115] Not in 1863 as suggested by Susser (1993, p.156).

[116] Jolles (1999) p. 224.

[117] Not in 1863, as suggested by Susser (1993) p. 156, where dates for several Rabbis have been conflated.

[118] Jolles (1999) pp. 222-223; Susser (1993) p. 156.

[119] Full details of the seven children are given in the sections on the Jewish Communities.

[120] Much of the information about the Bischofswerders and the photographic records have been provided in letters and other documentary material by various descendants; including Lilly, Sheila and Ivan Segal, and David, Andy and Victor Bishop. I am also grateful to David Samuelson and Harold Dunman for access to relevant sections of the text of their book entitled "Bertie, the Life and Times of G. B. Samuelson".

[121] Penwith District Council records confirm that this street was constructed from around the mid to late 19th century, and this has been confirmed in research by Peter Laws, published in *A Review of the Architecture of Penzance* in Pool (1974) p. 193.

[122] A comprehensive account of the wreck can be found in Richard Larn's *Shipwrecks: The Isles of Scilly* (1971, pp.38-41), but the definitive study of the loss of the *Schiller* is Keith Austin's *The VictorianTitanic* (Halsgrove 2001, pp. 240). Of the many newspaper reports, the following are perhaps the most detailed: *Western Morning News*, 10th May; *Falmouth Packet*, 15th and 22nd May (the latter reporting the account from *The Times* of 12th May); *The Cornish Telegraph*, 12th and 19th May; *The West Briton*, 10th, 12th, 17th, 20th, 27th May; 3rd, 7th, 10th, 17th June; and 5th July. Reports continued until the end of the year and beyond.

[123] Austin (2001) p. 171.

[124] Board of Trade Telegram, 14th May 1875, PRO KEW: CUST 68/163 (all PRO Kew references from Peter Towey's research); *Cornish Telegraph*, 12th and 19th May; *Falmouth Packet*, 15th May.

[125] PRO Kew: Lloyd's List, from 11th May to 31st March 1876; CUST 68/158 Isles of Scilly: Wreck letter book 1857-1886; CUST 68/163 Isles of Scilly: Board of Trade Letter books 1868-1908; SS *Schiller* Droit (Recovered Property) Book. See also Keith Austin, *The Victorian Titanic, The Loss of the S.S. Schiller in 1875* (Halsgrove 2001) pp. 159, 165 & 209.

[126] Austin (2001) pp. 158-176.

[127] Pool (1974) pp. 163-166.

[128] These examples can be seen in the sections on the Jewish Community and Jewish Trades.

[129] Records of Tony Pawlyn.

[130] Austin (2001) pp. 223-237 also gives a comprehensive list of bibliographical sources; *The Jewish Chronicle* (May 14th 1875) p. 105, referencing "a mournful paragraph in one of the American Jewish papers": I am grateful to David Dale for providing me with this item; Letter from Keith Austin to Keith Pearce (30th September 2007).

[131] Austin (2001) p. 58. I have slightly edited out some of the original wording for convenience.

[132] Austin (2001) p. 159.

[133] Austin (2001) pp. 162-174.

[134] The Board of Trade and other Shipping records are held at PRO Kew. Keith Austin has also confirmed

that his research, preliminary to the publication of his book on the wreck, revealed no mention of any such name (Letter of 30th September 2007).

[135] Letter from T. Knowles, Probate Registry, York (16th December 1999).

[136] Kelly's Directory (1883) refers to him as at Alverton (where the Hollies is situated) and the 1891 Census as resident there.

[137] Henrietta's age, clearly stated on the marriage certificate, would make her year of birth 1855. However, Samuelson (*op. cit.*, chapter 2:6, p.10) gives the year as 1850/1 on a genealogical tree. I have assumed that this is an error in that the other Samuelson dates (for Morris and Marcus/Marks) are consistent with marriage certificate details.

[138] Samuelson.

[139] Letter from Ivan Segal to Keith Pearce dated 9th September 1998.

[140] Jolles, *A Short History of the Jews of Northampton 1159-1996* (1996) pp. 50, 53, 69 & 72; Jolles (1999) p. 233.

[141] Vol. XXVI, 155, 25th November 1886. Susser (1993, p.42-44 & 279) quotes from this letter at greater length. I have slightly edited this extract.

[142] *The Cornishman*, 30th June 1887, p. 6.

[143] Jolles (1999) p. 237.

[144] Information on Michael Leinkram has been provided in letters and supporting documents by his descendants: Esther Fishman, and Mr. and Mrs. Stuart Raine. I have sourced other details from public records and from the Congregational Minute-Book.

[145] Stuart Raine (14th March 2013).

[146] His family believe that he possessed a fine singing voice, and may have visited America as a very young man, where his brothers may have settled. He is said to have taught singing there, being offered a position at the New York Opera, which he declined because he could not take part in performances on the Sabbath (Esther Fishman).

[147] Helen Fry (2000).

[148] Letter from Stuart Raine to Keith Pearce (27th October 1998).

[149] The tombstone of Maurice Leinkram gives his birth date as 4th October 1892, but he may have been sickly infant, his birth registered at a later date, and his name changed to mark his recovery (Stuart Raine) .

[150] Some of the previous births are listed in the records of the General Registrar's Office (Cornwall Studies Centre, Redruth).

[151] Research from the Immigration and Emigration Ellis Island Records by Stuart Raine.

[152] Grave 31, Block P, Row 1: Letter from Stuart Raine to Keith Pearce (27th October 1998).

CHAPTER 10
Congregational Life

Social contact between members of the Jewish communities and Cornish Christians would have been common through trade and business, through charitable activity, volunteer groups and civil organisations (such as Freemasonry). Jewish religious life, however, would have taken place in privacy and separation. Whilst Christians might embrace the Hebrew Scriptures (in translation, as the Old Testament), Jews could not reciprocate by approving Christian worship or the New Testament. Although non-Jews could be welcomed as guests at synagogue services, it is doubtful if many were ever present, except at special occasions, and most local people would never have seen the interior of the two Cornish synagogues. Moreover, Jewish liturgical worship was in Hebrew, a language to which Christians would not have ready access.

Jews could refer with respect to their "Christian Brethren" as their friends, but, as we have seen, the Christian conversionist movement, the *Society for the Promotion of Christianity amongst the Jews,* was very active in the late 18th and early 19th centuries, with influential Christian supporters, such as Sir Rose Price in Penzance. The threat to the two Jewish congregations was real enough, especially as Jews comprised a very small proportion of the total population of the Cornish towns. In Penzance, Solomon Ezekiel and Rabbi Hart Symons established their own counter-offensive through education and publications. The fact that they could do so, without fear, and with a strong sense of their own civic integrity speaks for itself of the general tolerance of their neighbours. The conversion of a Rabbi's daughter (albeit after his death), that of Harriet Hyman in Falmouth in 1830, and her subsequent marriage to a Christian, led to anxiety and tension there. However, of the many hundreds of marriages involving Cornish Jews, known from public and genealogical records, the vast majority were between Jews, as Jewish tradition required, and the impression gained is that the Cornish Jewish congregations were conservative and observant of tradition in this regard. The examples of the marriages of three of Lemon Hart's children to Christians, in church (in one case, that of David Hart, the marriage was to a Cornish girl) are atypical, in that they took place in London, long after the Hart family had left Cornwall. None of the Hart family returned to live in the County, and these cases cannot, therefore, be regarded as evidence of Jewish integration into Cornish society through Christian marriage (although they could, of course, be seen as later integration into English society). The few cases that have been identified in Cornwall of Jews marrying Christians, or of formal baptism and conversion, do not reveal any general or widespread pattern of integration through these means. Nor, as we have seen, does the contemporaneous, widespread usage of "Jewish" (Hebrew) names amongst the Cornish population afford evidence of Jewish assimilation into the Christian population. Where integration did occur to some extent, it was through the secular and civil forms of involvement, though even here, the requirements of *kosher* dietary regulations would have limited Jewish social contacts with Christians.

The pattern and rhythm of Jewish religious life was not synchronous with that of the Christian population, and this would also have set the Jews apart from their neighbours. The Jewish day, which is solar, begins and ends at sunset, its exact timing being seasonal. The Sabbath, a strict day of rest and cessation from work and business, begins on Friday Eve, and ends at sunset on the Saturday. The Jewish year, however, is lunar, beginning and ending in September, and the festivals which mark its passage are quite distinct in character from those celebrated in Christian churches, although some, like *Pesach* (Passover) and *Hanukah* (Lights) occur around the time of Easter and Christmas, in the Spring and at Midwinter respectively.

The Jewish congregations also maintained their exclusive and enclosed cemeteries. The two Jewish congregations were self-regulating, self-financing, and sustained by the donations and contributions of their members. Each employed its own minister and *shochet* under private contract, and each congregation would have had its own culture of administration, regulation and organisation. Whilst maintaining connections with the Chief Rabbinate, local congregations were not part of a formal national organisation or hierarchy, like the established Anglican Church or the Roman Catholic Church. If anything, they shared a similar character and ethos to the Nonconformist or free churches.

Anecdotal and unsubstantiated claims have sometimes been made to the effect that there were other synagogues in Southern Cornwall. A non-conformist chapel in the hamlet of Tredavoe (Cornish, *Trewordhavow*) on the outskirts of Newlyn, near Penzance, has a small Hebrew inscription beneath a high window arch just below the roof, and above the entrance porch. This feature has been taken, quite erroneously, to indicate a former synagogue. The inscription bears the Hebrew characters *Yud – Hey –Vav – Hey* (Yahweh/Adonai), and *Yud – Resh – Alef – Hey* (Yireh), that is "The Lord/God will see".[1] The inscription reflects the Binding of Isaac in Genesis (*Bereshith*) Chapter 22 vv. 8 & 14, where, on Mount Moriah, Abraham was saved from sacrificing his son, Isaac, by the voice of an angel and the appearance of "a ram caught in a thicket" which he sacrificed instead. "And Abraham named that site Adonai-yireh", that is "The Lord will see", which may be intended in the sense of "see to it" or "provide" (as in v. 8: "God will see to the sheep for His burnt offering"). God's "seeing" into the human heart, over the actions of men and his providential power are all evoked by the expression. The setting of the inscription beneath the chapel's window is likely to represent God's Eye.[2] The chapel (which was also used as a day school) was built in the mid-1840s, extended in 1899. It was leased to the Bible Christians, a Methodist denomination formed originally in 1815 in North Cornwall, which spread into Devon and beyond. Around a quarter of the Bible Christian chapels came to be based in Cornwall. The Hebrew inscription is a very unusual feature for Cornish churches, but there was no connection with the Jewish community in Penzance. Such an inscription would not have been carved by a Jew, but by a local Christian mason, in that it includes the Four Letter Name of God that is never pronounced or written by Jews. Bible Christians and some other groups, such as Baptists and Congregationalists, gave particular attention to

Old Testament study, and often called their chapels after Biblical names, such as Bethel ("House of God"), Salem ("Place of Peace"), or Ebenezer ("The Stone/Rock of Help"). This was a practice also common in Wales. It is possible that the Tredavoe chapel (which may have been called "Moriah" or "Mount Moriah", ("The Fear of God") once had Hebrew inscriptions inside the building, although this would also be unusual, and there is no sign of this today.[3] The British and Foreign Bible Society, which was formed in 1804, eventually produced Bibles in Hebrew and Greek for the use not only of students of Theology, but also for study by church groups, and this may have influenced the placement of the inscription.

Putative synagogue buildings have also been claimed to have existed in St. Ives and Truro, together with a community of Jews (unspecified in size or date) at Sennen, near Land's End, all without conclusive or credible evidence. The most curious of these notions has been that the Basset Estate of Tehidy, near Camborne, used Jewish workers from Germany to build and install furnaces and smelting houses, and because of the time-consuming nature of the project, a synagogue was built for them (the location is not specified), with, apparently, accommodation provided for these Jews on the site of what is now the Lamb and Flag Inn near St. Erth. There is, in fact, no record in the extensive, surviving Basset papers of any Jewish workers ever being employed in such a capacity or of any such religious building being built. Moreover, the Bassets did not possess any estates or land south of the Hayle River. All of these claims would seem, therefore, to be spurious, and despite extensive searches in public records and private archives, no specific documentary evidence has been found of a synagogue (other than those in Falmouth and Penzance) in any other part of Cornwall, even where Jews are known to have lived in small numbers.[4] (This does, of course, not exclude the possibility that where small numbers of Jews lived, albeit on a temporary basis, private houses may have been used for worship when travel to Falmouth or Penzance was impractical). The fact, therefore, that there were only two small synagogues in Cornwall throughout the 18th and 19th centuries,[5] at a time when there were many hundreds of Christian churches in the County's chief towns and scattered across its many rural communities, is indicative of how small the Jewish population was, even at its peak in the early to mid 19th century.

1
Falmouth

The Falmouth Jewish community was formed around 1740 with the arrival of Alexander Moses and his wife, Phoebe. The couple were probably recent immigrants from the Continent, although they may well have lived in London for some years, where they had family members. Alexander Moses may well have been the first Jewish settler in the town. He either became known as *Zender Falmouth*, "Zender" being a common Jewish abbreviation or diminutive for "Alexander". This secondary name was either given to him by others, or it was self-styled. In either case, it acknowledged his primary settlement in the town and his seniority and supervisory position over the nascent Jewish community. Other examples of

Chapter 9.
(Top) The Higher Ground: the Graves of the Senior Members of the Congregation.
(Bottom) Facing towards the entrance and the *Bet Torhorah.*
Photos by Maurice Minsky (2007).

Plate 49

Chapter 9.
Penzance Jewish Cemetery (*c.* 1980). Photos by Mandy Pearce.

Plate 50

Chapter 9.
Asher ben Hayim
(Lemon Woolf: 1:1).

Chapter 9.
Hendele bas Issachar
Jacob (Elra Joseph,
daughter of Barnet Levy,
and widow of Abraham
Joseph of Falmouth: 1:2).
Except where indicated, all
of the following photos were
taken by Mandy Pearce.

Plate 51

Chapter 9.
(Top) Samuel ben Nathan and Beila bas Israel (Samuel and Elizabeth Oppenheim: 1:7 and 1:6). Photos by Mandy Pearce (Bottom) Hindeleh bas Hayim and Aaron ben Phineas (Hannah and Aaron Selig: 1:10 and 1:11). Photo by Michael Shapiro.

Plate 52

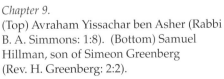

Chapter 9.
(Top) Avraham Yissachar ben Asher (Rabbi B. A. Simmons: 1:8). (Bottom) Samuel Hillman, son of Simeon Greenberg (Rev. H. Greenberg: 2:2).

Chapter 9.
(Top) Isaac ben Ezekiel (Solomon Ezekiel: 2:3). (Bottom) Samuel ben Moses (Samuel Jacob: 2:1).

Plate 53

Chapter 9.
(Top) Avraham ben Zvi (Abraham Joseph, died at 5 years: 4:1). (Bottom) Samuel ben Zvi (Samuel Joseph, died at 5 months: 4:2).

Chapter 9.
(Top) Mirele bas Moses (Amelia Jacob: 3:1). (Bottom) Henne bas Moses (Hannah Jacob, wife of Solomon Ezekiel: 3:2).

Plate 54

Chapter 9.
(Top) Hannah, a daughter of Alexander Moses of Falmouth, and the wife of Israel Levy of
Truro (5:1). Right) Pessia, daughter of Abraham (B. A. Simmons) who died in the cholera
epidemic of 1832. (Bottom) Left: Jacob ben Solomon Ha-Levi (Jacob James Hart, or Jacobs:
5:3). Photo by David Sonin. Right: Judah ben Naphtali Levy (Mr. Levy, *Leb Hanne,* Judah
from Hanau, who was reputed to be the oldest Jew living in Cornwall when he died in
1817: 8:1).

Plate 55

Chapter 9.
(Top) Zvi ben Avraham and Mirele ben Yakov (Henry Joseph and his wife Ameila Jacob: 6: 5 & 6). (Bottom) Yizak ben Zvi (Rev. Isaac Bischofswerder: 8:3) and his grand-daughter, Malka ben David (Millie, daughter of David and Helena Bischofswerder. She died at 11 weeks: 6:3).

Plate 56

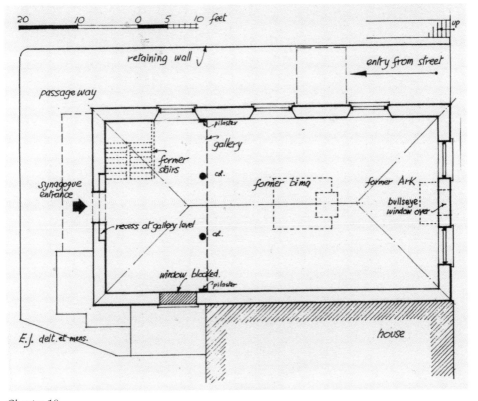

Chapter 10.
(Top) Left the former Falmouth Synagogue (1939) and right (1998). Photos by Alex M. Jacob and Helen Fry. (Bottom) Architectural plan (1958), courtesy of Edward Jamilly.

Plate 57

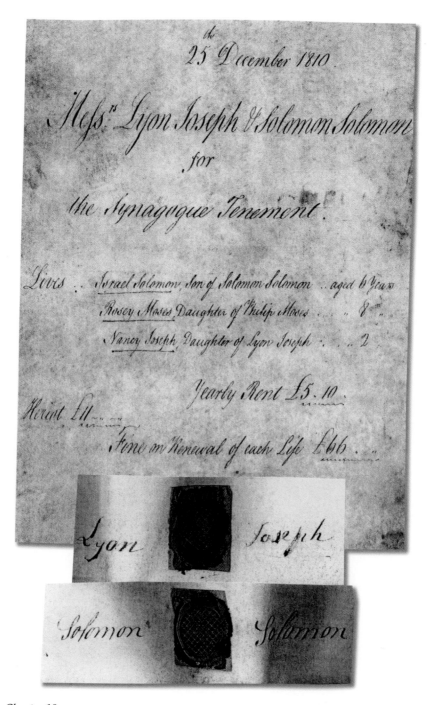

Chapter 10.
Falmouth Synagogue, Original Lease (1810). Archives of the Wodehouse Family
(Earl of Kimberley Collection, Courtesy of the Cornwall Record Office, Truro; Ref. K58).

Plate 58

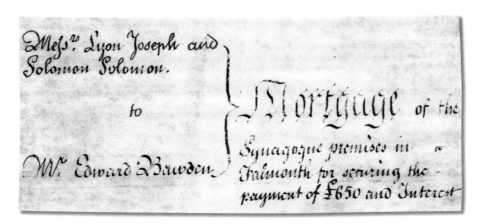

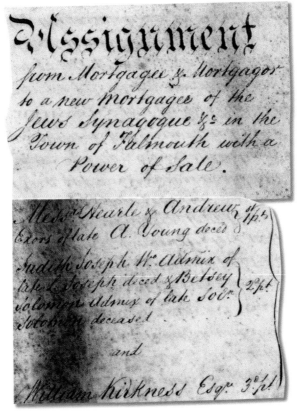

Chapter 10.
(Top) Mortgage Agreement (1811) with Edward Bawden, and (Below) Mortgage
Agreement (1827) with William Kirkness. Both Courtesy CRO Truro (Ref. K.58).

Plate 59

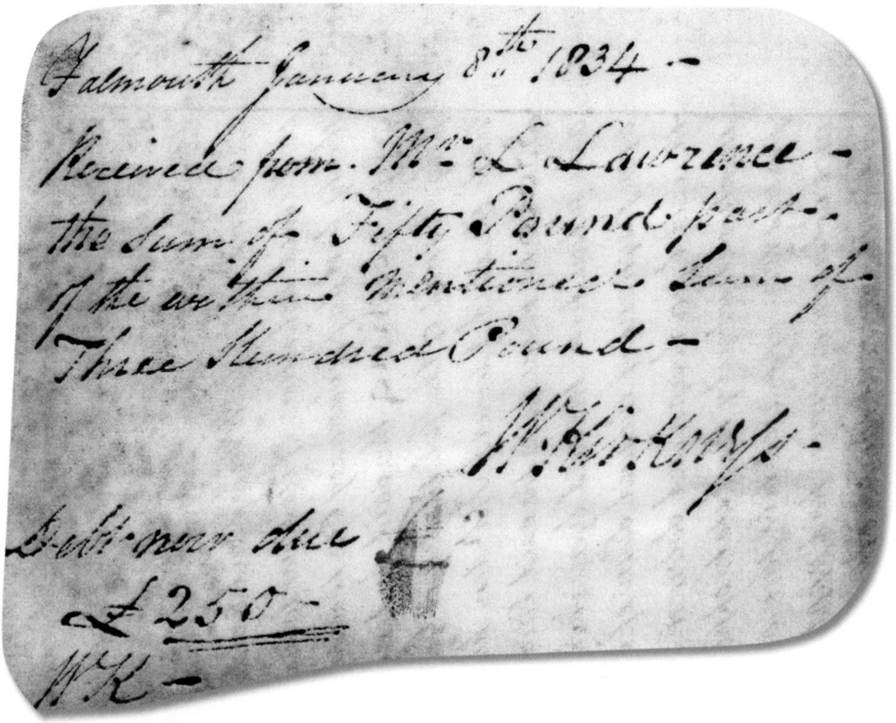

Chapter 10.
(Top) Mortgage payment receipt (1834) and (below) Arwenack Manor Record (1871) of the named Lives of the synagogue Lease. (CRO Truro, Ref. K.58).

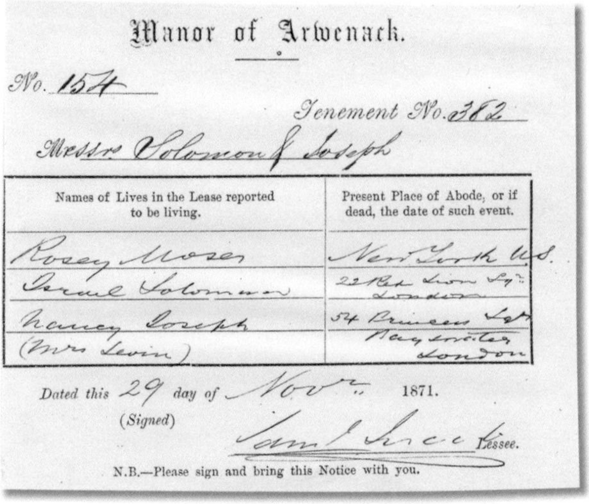

Plate 60

Chapter 10.
The exterior of the former Penzance synagogue (1998).
Photo by Helen Fry.

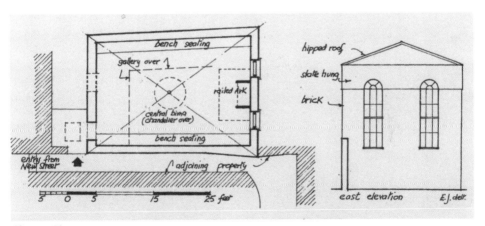

Chapter 10.
Architectural plans (1958).
Courtesy of Edward Jamilly.

Chapter 10.
The Tablets of the Ten Commandments.
Courtesy of the Jewish Museum, London.
Photo by Keith Pearce (c. 1985: Courtesy of the
Jewish Museum, London).

Plate 61

Chapter 10.
(Left) The interior of the former Penzance Synagogue (*c.* 1970), when it was a place of Christian worship, showing the position of the Ark of the Covenant, located between two windows (which are not the originals of 1807, but Victorian replacements of 1865). Above the Ark are the two tablets of the Ten Commandments, and beneath, a panel inscribed "Open to us the Gates of Mercy". The tablets are now in the Jewish Museum, London, and the panel remains in private ownership in Penzance. (Below) A view from the Ladies' Gallery. Photos by David Giddings.

Plate 62

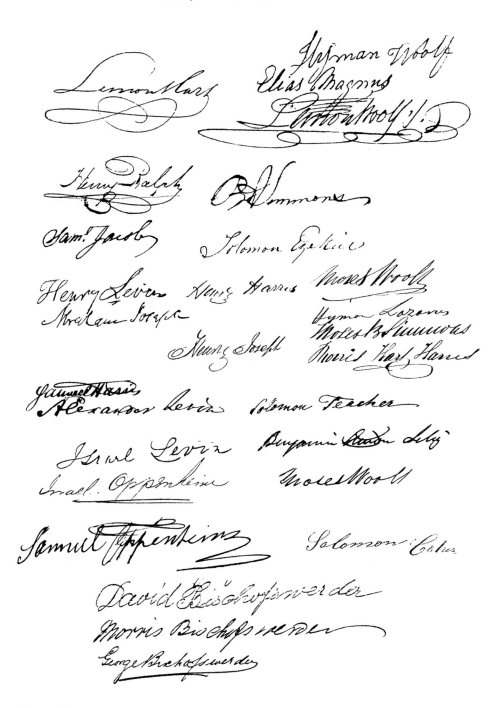

Chapter 10.
Signatures of Senior Members of the Penzance Congregation from 1808 to 1892.
Roth Collection, Courtesy of the Brotherton Library, the University of Leeds.

Plate 63

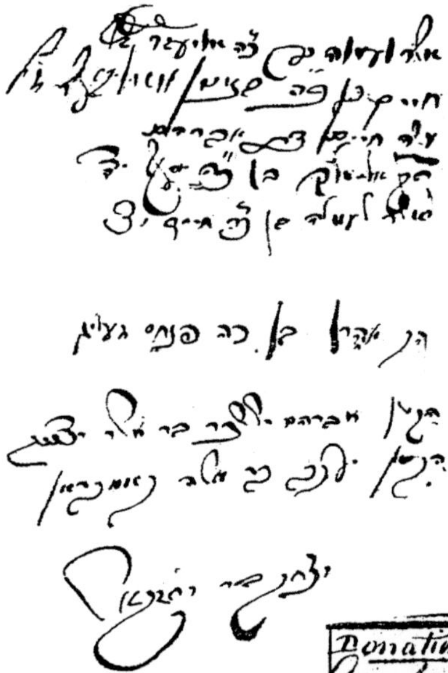

Asher Leamle ben Eliezar (Lemon Hart)

Hayim ben Benyamin (Hyman Woolf)

Moshe Hayim ben Avraham (Henry Ralph)

Elimelech ben Yosef (Elias Magnus)

Asher Laemle ben Hayim (Lemon Woolf)

Aaron ben Pinchas Selig (Aaron Selig)

Avraham Yissachar ben Asher Yitzak (B. A. Simmons)

Yakov ben Moshe Cambron (Jacob Jacob)

Yitzak ben Ezekiel (Solomon Ezekiel)

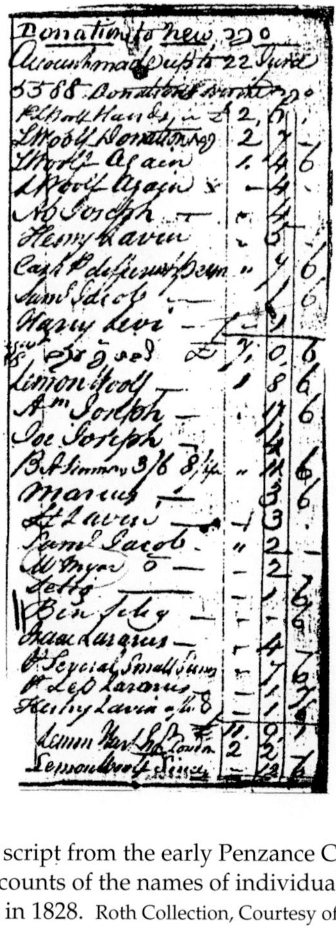

Chapter 10.
Signatures in cursive Hebrew script from the early Penzance Congregational Minute Book (1808-1811). (Below): Accounts of the names of individual donations towards a new *Sefer Torah,* (Scroll of the Law) in 1828. Roth Collection, Courtesy of the Brotherton Library, the University of Leeds.

Plate 64

such topographical personal names can be found amongst the Jews of Angevin England, and also from the period of the early 18ᵗʰ century, such as Moses Lazarus of Rochford (*c.* 1740-1814), known as *Moshe Rochford*, and Simon Hyam of Ipswich (*c.* 1740-1824), known as *Simcha Ipswich*.[6] This practice, whilst identifiable, may not have been widespread, even within the same locality, and there is no evidence that Abraham Hart, Alexander Moses' contemporary in Penzance, adopted such a locational name.

Alexander Moses can be assumed to have been the Falmouth congregation's first President, and he may well have led worship in the very early days. Ministers would have been appointed to act as *shochet*, *mohel* and religious teachers of the young, but the names of the earliest are not known, nor are their dates of service, apart from a few individuals, such as *Rabbi Saavill*, Samuel ben Samuel ha-Levi, who died in 1814. The early members of the congregation were pedlars and travellers, who may have been away from Falmouth during the week, trading in the outlying towns as far as Helston, Redruth, Truro and their surrounding villages, returning to Falmouth on Fridays to make up the *minyan* for worship. As time went on, and members of the Jewish community had established a viable trade, they opened shops in Falmouth and Penryn, and this helped to secure for the congregation a more settled pattern of weekly worship.

Unlike Penzance, original documentary sources relating to the Falmouth synagogue and its congregation, such as the congregational Minute-Book, have either been presumed as lost, or remained unidentified. It would appear that Jacob Jacob (1774-1853) did pass a copy of the Congregation's marriage register to the Exeter Registry after the introduction of Civil Registration, but a letter to Alex Jacob dated 11ᵗʰ November 1946 confirms "All the records of the Registry were destroyed by enemy action".[7] Various historical studies, and also guide books to Falmouth suggest that the first synagogue was established in a building in Hamblyn's Court (subsequently known as Dunstan's or Jeffery's Court, by the harbour on Fish-Strand, around 1766-68. A Cornish oven (or range) that was once in this building was transferred to the Falmouth Museum. The oven may have been used for the making of *matzoth* (unleavened bread) at Passover.[8] A second, purpose-built synagogue was erected in an elevated position overlooking Falmouth Sound, on Porham Hill (or Fish-Street Hill) in the first decade of the 19ᵗʰ century. The date has been given as 1806 by some later sources,[9] but as 1808 by earlier ones.[10] The later date of 1808 has generally been adopted, and would appear to be confirmed by an item in the *Royal Cornwall Gazette,* of Saturday 13ᵗʰ August 1808: "…a new Jewish synagogue was opened at Falmouth on Friday, and consecrated with great pomp."[11] This item, which represents the full report, does not identify the synagogue's location, but it is likely to be the same building that came to stand on Porham Hill. From other mortgage records (see below) it could be inferred that the latter building was erected around 1810-1811, although a date of 1808 is not inconsistent with financial arrangements being finalised a few years after the building's completion, and it was not unknown for builders and tradesmen to complete work well in advance of payment.

Whilst the congregation's Minute-Book remains unidentified, a secondary fragment from it, in the form of a copied extract, and some of the original congregational leases and mortgage agreements have survived.[12] Together with details from the Ecclesiastical Census of 1851, which included the synagogues at Falmouth and Penzance, these documents allow a glimpse into the Falmouth congregation's affairs. However, the extent of congregational property in the form of the synagogue's religious artefacts is uncertain, and (unlike Penzance) no document itemising the congregation's disposable assets has survived. The only account available is very late, and compiled from distant memory, well after the congregation had been dissolved and the artefacts from the second synagogue dispersed: "In the Congregation's possession were five scrolls with two sets of silver bells and pointers; a curtain for the Ark; and Notice Boards recording donations of ten guineas and more, together with two wooden panels, one displaying the Commandments and the other the Prayer for the Royal Family. Prominent amongst the building's decorations were four or five elaborate and massive candelabra."[13]

The land which was given to the Falmouth congregation for its burial ground was part of the estates of Lord De Dunstanville, of the Basset family of Tehidy, near Redruth. The cemetery land adjoined land owned by Lord Wodehouse, the Earl of Kimberley of Norfolk, whose Cornish seat was Arwenack Manor. Sir John Wodehouse was born in 1741, and was elevated to the peerage in 1797. He had married a descendant of the landed Killigrew family of Falmouth, which had as its home Arwenack Manor, together with estates extending to Pendennis Point.[14] The Killigrew title itself had become extinct in 1704, and with the Killigrew-Wodehouse marriage, the Kimberley estates eventually incorporated much of the town of Falmouth, including the prestigious area formerly called Porham Hill, later Smithick Hill, where the synagogue came to be built. The area itself was originally known as *Smithick,* and its cluster of houses represented some of the earliest to spring up in the town from around 1600. It might be assumed that the rising fortunes and affluence of this area of Smithick, as a part of central Falmouth, was reflected in its other name in the English vernacular as *Penny-come-quick* (later extended into adjacent parts of the town), but, in fact, as noted previously, the expression can be construed from a combination of the Cornish *Pen-y-cwm* (head of the vale) and the Saxon *wick* (village or town): hence "the village at the head of the valley". (Falmouth stands, not on an estuary, but on a river-valley, drowned by the sea). The Killigrew family had procured a market for Smithick in 1652, and the Custom House was then moved there, from Penryn. The trade which this encouraged, together with its auspicious location overlooking the vast natural harbour (today known as Falmouth Sound) led to its rapid expansion.

There are no relevant documents for the period 1806-1809, but the original lease [and counterpart] dated 25th December 1810, presupposes that the synagogue premises and its adjoining tenement is "…now erected and built on the West side of Porham Hill Lane …" Although, strictly, this does not suggest a date for the building as early as 1806-1808, and, indeed, appears to imply that the synagogue had only recently been completed, it could also reflect a period of administrative delay between the earlier erection of part of the synagogue and the eventual granting of a lease upon its completion. It seems likely, therefore, that, from 1808 to the end of 1810, at least some part of the Porham Hill building was used by the congregation on an informal basis. The lease, however, marked their lawful tenancy and possession of the whole premises, commencing in January of 1811. However, in the Ecclesiastical Census for 31st March 1851, the synagogue's then President, Jacob Jacob (signing himself, *J. Jacob*, "Secretary")[15] records the year of its erection as 1811. The year given by Jacob may either represent the building's completion, or, after a gap of 40 years, be an error for 1808. He also records that it possessed a "Free Space or Standing Room" for 80 (likely the men's area on the ground floor) and sittings for 60 persons (the ladies' gallery).[16] Even if the figure 140 represents the full capacity of the building, including the seating, a building of this size would have required the permission and involved the supervision of the Wodehouse estate. As soon as the lease had been granted and signed, the Jewish congregation secured a private mortgage to purchase the property. The securing of this mortgage could explain the delay from 1808 to 1811, in that the Estate may have required finance to be in place, before issuing a formal lease.

The architect and builders of the synagogue have not been identified,[17] but there were several prominent families of builders in Falmouth in the early years of the 19th century, named Devonshire, Olver, Earle, Harvey, Mankin and Roberts. Two of the most important were the Devonshires and the Olvers, and between them they were responsible for much of the building in old Falmouth.[18] It is likely, therefore, that they would have been contracted to the Wodehouse estate. It has been mentioned that the name *Olver* appears on some headstones in the Penryn cemetery, and so this family of builders may have acquired some particular connection with the Jewish congregation. In later years, in the 1860s, the Olver family had considerable commercial interests in Falmouth. Jacob Olver, of Olver & Sons, Green Bank, Falmouth (and also Lemon Street, Truro) was a builder, cabinet maker, upholsterer, undertaker and auctioneer. He had been the Mayor of Falmouth (1859-1861), a Town Councillor (until 1866), Vice Chairman of the Falmouth Poor Law Union, a Magistrate, Treasurer of the Falmouth Volunteers (the 3rd Cornwall Rifles), and a member of the Burial Board, along with W. Slade Olver, an ironmonger and commission agent. Thomas Rickard Olver (also of Olver & Sons) was also a builder and auctioneer, and, with Charles L. Olver, Accountant, an Income Tax Assessor, for the Budock Division. Slade Olver and Charles Olver were also Insurance Agents.[19]

The original 99 year lease (which came to be the Manor Office lease No. 382[20]) was drafted on behalf of the Rt. Hon. John Lord Wodehouse, the Rt. Hon. Sophia Lady Wodehouse, both of Kimberley in the County of Norfolk, and Sir Charles Mordaunt of Walton, Warwick. The lease was further countersigned by Margaret Cox, James Symmonds, Letitia Wodehouse, Thomas Clive, Robert Simmons, Susan Mordaunt, Wm. Hodder and Wm. Kite, all of whom can be taken to have been Trustees of the Arwenack Estate. There were two signatories for the Jewish congregation, who were related through marriage. The first was Lyon Joseph, "Merchant" (1775-1825), the third President of the Falmouth Congregation, from 1807 to 1815. (He was married to Judith, a daughter of Barnet Levy of Falmouth, and his brother, Abraham, was married to her sister, Hannah). The second signatory was Solomon Solomon, "Shopkeeper" (1764-1819), who was a Tailor, General Hardwareman and Navy Agent, and he was in a business partnership with Lyon Joseph. Solomon Solomon was a son of Israel Solomon (-1802), and he was also married to one of Barnet Levy's daughters, Elizabeth (or Betsy) Levy. The lease stipulated the names of three children as "lives", as was customary. These were: Israel Solomon, aged 6 years (born *c.* 1803, died New York *c.* 1893), the son of the Solomon Solomon, above; Rosey Moses, aged 8 years, daughter of Philip Moses (-1831), the eldest son of Alexander (Henry) Moses (1715-1791), the Congregation's first President; (Philip Moses continued his father's business as a pawnbroker, and he was married to a Betsy Jacobs who died in 1838. Her relationship to other *Jacobs* families is not certain. Rosey Moses eventually moved to New York, but she should not be confused with her aunt, also Rose Moses (1757-1838) who married Samuel Simons (1740-1832) of Truro; and Nancy (Hannah) Joseph, aged 2 years (a daughter of Lyon Joseph), who married a Moses Levin (1801-1885) and moved to London (see below). The yearly rent under the lease was £5 10s, and payable in four equal and even quarterly parts on or within twenty-one days of Lady Day (25th March), Midsummer Day (24th June), Michaelmas Day (29th September) and Christmas Day (25th December). The heriot was £11 (the heriot being the fine due to the Lord of the Manor upon the death of a tenant: by this time it was levied in monetary value, but it was originally the deceased man's best beast or chattel). The fine for the renewal of each life was £66 "together with lawful interest". (Where one of the extant "lives" was withdrawn, and a new life was to be nominated and added, and this sum was to be paid within twelve calendar months; upon the death of a nominated "life", it was to be paid within twenty-four months.)

The provisions and stipulations of the lease required that the lessees must "at their own proper costs and charges, well and sufficiently repair, sustain and maintain and keep the roof or roofs with slate (in character with the other buildings in the town) and (eventually upon determination) yield and give up (the) Piece or Parcel of ground together with the said tenement, Erections and Buildings". The "Steward or Agent" of the Wodehouse estate was to be allowed " with workmen or without, from time to time and at all Times to enter into the premises to view search and examine into the state and condition thereof". If the lessees were to "permit or suffer the said premises to be out of repair or in decay to the value of forty shillings or more, and shall not within two months next after Notice Thereof given in writing then (the estate's) Steward, Agent or Attorney (will) well and sufficiently repair the same" (at the lessees cost). If they should "commit or cause or suffer to be done or committed any waste on the said premises, or any Act, Matter or Thing whatsoever whereby the same shall or may be prejudiced or impaired",[21] then the Wodehouse estate could re-possess the property.

The Lessees were further bound to appear "from time to time" before the "Courts" of Lord Wodehouse at Arwenack (also known as "Roskrow"), with "reasonable notice thereby given, and shall and will also execute the Office of Reeve [that is, a Bailiff or Steward: at one time a high official or chief magistrate of a district] and perform all such other suits and services as other Tenants of the said Manor have been accustomed or used to do and will also grind at the Mill of and belonging to the said Manor all such Corn, Malt and Grain as shall be used in or upon the said Premises (during the term of the lease) and will (pay) such Market

Toll or Money as would have been payable for the same if brought into the Market of Falmouth on a Market Day."

These early leases do not restrict the use of the building to religious worship, whereas the much later freehold conveyance of 1878 (see below) does contain this stipulation. This is explicable in that the use of the building is taken for granted in 1810-11 at a time when the Jewish community was flourishing. By 1878 (the synagogue was to close a year later) the congregation's decline was all too obvious, and the Wodehouse Estate, anticipating its demise, and aware of its potential market value for alternative use, pre-empted the congregation's Trustees from selling the building for any purpose other than its previous use without the Estate's knowledge and permission. The 1810 lease, however, had also protected the Estate's interests by the incorporation of a "surrender" clause.

On 31st January 1811 the synagogue was mortgaged to an Edward Bawden of Gwinear, ("Yeoman") to secure the payment of £650 and interest, with Lyon Joseph and Solomon Solomon again as the signatories. (A William Eva of Gwinear, and his wife Barbara Mathews of Penzance were to be involved in a similar way with the Penzance congregation.) On 4th January 1785, an Edward Bawden (d.1825) of Talland married Elizabeth Young (1763-1805) in Falmouth. The groom was a Mariner. His bride was sister to the Andrew Young who later took on the Congregation's mortgage (see below). Elizabeth's death at the age of 42 may have led to her husband's eventual re-marriage. On 15th May 1814, an Edward Bawden of Gwinear, near Camborne, married Margaret Trewhella in the parish of Ludgvan, near Penzance (there is no mention in the register of the bridegroom's status, *bachelor* or *widower*, although these details were not always recorded). Records for the subsequent baptism of their three children, Mary, Edward and Eliza, in the parish of Gwinear (1816 to 1819) give the father's occupation as *labourer*, on 5th May 1816, and later as *miner*, on 3rd August 1817 and 30th May 1819.[22] In view of the description, *Yeoman,* in the mortgage document, it cannot be certain that the Mariner who married in Falmouth, and the Labourer/Miner of Gwinear were one and the same, although they may have been related. If they are to be identified, then re-marriage was far from being a rare occurrence in a time of high and early mortality. *Bawden* (or *Bowden* as a variant spelling) was and still is a common Cornish name, but no other Edward Bawden of Gwinear appears in the relevant parish records for this period. It was also common for men to change both trade and location during their lifetime, and Edward Bawden may have become affluent through such a varied and resourceful occupational career. His marriage to Elizabeth Young, who appears to have come from an established and secure family, would also have helped to consolidate his financial position.

The mortgage agreement of 1811 was based upon the terms of the Wodehouse lease indenture with its "divers other payments, covenants, conditions, reservations and agreements" relating to the "Piece or Parcel of ground by admeasurement forty four poles or thereabouts…(drawn in the margin of the said indenture, and shown as a small sketch of an almost rectangular plot)… together with the messauge or tenement erected thereon, part of which is used as a synagogue and the other parts occupied by Moses Simon and John Ellis". Moses Simon (whose dates are not known) was most likely a son of Samuel Simons (1740-1832) of Truro and Rosa (Ann) Moses (1757-1838), a daughter of Alexander Moses. Samuel and Ann Simons (or Symons) traded in Falmouth as Mercers and Drapers from c.1788 to 1791.[23] John Ellis, an auctioneer,[24] was not Jewish. There is no indication in the mortgage document itself of the trade of either occupant, or if their use of the cottages, attached to the side of the synagogue premises, was commercial, or purely domestic. The mortgage may have been in the form of a relatively short "bridging loan" in that there is no extended term of years mentioned for its repayment, beyond the stipulation that there would be a "penal sum (of) £1,300, (as) one Bond or Obligation" for the £650 "with the interest thereof (of) five pounds per cent per annum to be paid on 13th April next, on or before". Bawden reserved the right to lawfully enter the premises "from thenceforth (to) quietly and peaceably to have hold, use, occupy, possess and enjoy", and to receive his "Rents, issues and profits thereof without any manner of let, suit, trouble, eviction, ejection, molestation, disturbance, hindrance or denial whatsoever."

Despite the fact that this agreement gave the Congregation until "13th April next" (barely two months if this means 1811, but just over a year if "next" implies 1812) to pay the £650, six years later, at the end of 1817, Lyon Joseph and Solomon Solomon had failed to pay off the debt of £650 to Edward Bawden, and the amount still owing was £500. It is not known if Bawden had levied the "penal sum", in whole or in part, but, in view of the considerable time lapse, it seems most likely that he had shown the forbearance which was also characteristic of the Congregation's later creditors. This forbearance may well have involved an element of resignation on Bawden's part, in that such an onerous penalty was simply unrealistic in view of the Congregation's limited finances. In fact, Lyon Joseph had left Falmouth in 1815 for Bath after the failure of his business, a misfortune that would have been shared by Solomon Solomon as his business partner, and these factors may have affected their management of the Congregation's mortgage. Before the end of 1817, Lyon Joseph and Solomon Solomon took steps to resolve matters, and applied to an attorney and notary public, Andrew Young (1772-1822) of Falmouth[25] to discharge the debt, which he did in a new loan agreement with them, on 1st January 1818.

During the ensuing year, concerns had grown within the Jewish congregation that the synagogue buildings might be deemed in law the personal property of Lyon Joseph and Solomon Solomon as the original signatories to the indenture and the mortgages. These concerns would, no doubt, have been aggravated by the failure of their business partnership and the fear that the synagogue could be accounted as part of their assets, and even sold to offset their financial losses and debts. Moreover, the mortgage payments were in arrears, despite the fact that the various members contributed significant annual sums to the congregational finances. It is not known if either of the signatories had asserted their right to ownership, but to clarify the principle of communal ownership an agreement was drawn up between the members in January 1819: "At a meeting held at Falmouth in January 1819 at the vestry belonging to the Congregation of Falmouth. Present –

Mr. Abm Joseph £12. 0. 0
Solomon Solomons[26] £9. 0. 0
Samuel Harris £6. 0. 0
Simon Solomon £9. 0. 0
Jacob Jacobs £12. 0. 0
Henry Harris £6. 0. 0".

Of those present, "Mr. Abm" is Abraham Joseph (-1828), Lyon Joseph's brother, and Solomon Solomons (who was to die the following year in Lisbon) the second lease signatory already mentioned, Samuel Harris (1754-1824) was originally from London, and was the father of the Henry Harris (1787-1872) listed below him. Both men were jewellers, and the latter traded in Truro, before moving to London. Simon Solomon (-1825) was Solomon Solomon's brother. Jacob Jacob (1774-1853) was a son of Moses Jacob (1733-1807) and Sarah (1748-1831) a daughter of Alexander Moses. Jacob Jacob had succeeded Lyon Joseph as President of the Congregation, serving in that post until 1852. Simon Solomon was married to Jacob Jacob's sister, Kate (1772-1854).

The account of the meeting continues – "When it was unanimously agreed that in order for the support of the synagogue they agreed to pay the following sums Pr.Year as annexed against their respective names, and also that Mr. Lyon Joseph is to pay twelve pounds per year. It is also hereby agreed and declared that although the synagogue was purchased in the sole clames (sic.) of Mr. Lyon Joseph and Solomon Solomons, and the deeds made put accordingly in their names, that the sale and purchase then made was done only as trustees, and that the synagogue is the property and also the dwelling houses adjoining with the appertenance thereto of the whole body of Jews at Falmouth as above described and named and that as soon as it can conveniently be done fresh deeds are to be made in the name of the whole congregation."

If such "fresh deeds" were drawn up, they are not among the papers in the Wodehouse Archive. The fact that a further mortgage was drawn up in 1827 with only two named individuals (both women, Judith Joseph and Betsy Solomon) does not preclude that the synagogue was by then secured in some form under Congregational proprietorship. However, the lease continued to be issued formally to specified representatives of the Joseph and Solomon families, in that it was decided that it could not be issued "in the name of the whole congregation" as an abstract entity. It may well be that the widows of the original signatories were retained, either because they possessed or insisted upon this as their legal entitlement, or at the insistence of the Manor Estate itself: as noted earlier, the Estate was entitled to levy a "fine" of £66 "together with lawful interest" if one of the lives was withdrawn, or upon death. The replacement of new names would have incurred this fine, but the retention of the widows may have enabled the Congregation to negotiate its avoidance. In view of the fact that the widows were absentees by 1827 (see below) and would not, therefore, in practice be involved in the running of the Congregational affairs, the nomination of the two women may indicate that this was a formality, and, indeed, the most convenient option.

The agreement continues with the following: "It is also hereby declared and agreed that Mrs. Abraham Joseph [Hannah Levy, 1769-1851] is to have the seat belonging to Mrs. Lyon Joseph [Judith Levy, 1774-1846, her sister] that is her during her absence, and should she return to reside in the Town she is to have her seat again restored to her, and in order to prevent controversy on Mrs. Lyon Joseph ('s) return it is hereby agreed that a seat is to be made above the present seat she now occupies, the Entrance to be closed up accordingly for her accommodation; but no young ladies or any other person is to sit up above Mrs. Joseph ('s) present seat."

By this time Lyon and Judith Joseph had moved to Bath. There had been a small and sporadic Jewish presence in Bath since 1738, but no proper Jewish organisation existed until a community was established soon after 1800, with a synagogue appearing in local directories from 1826, and a new one being opened in 1841.[27] Lyon and Judith Joseph remained members of the Falmouth Congregation, and are presumed to have had "seating rights". Judith Joseph's seat, in the Ladies' Gallery, was, no doubt, in a superior position because of her husband's former Presidency. The reference to "any controversy" relating to preferential occupancy of seats, together with the measures to safeguard Mrs. Joseph's interests to the extent of sealing off her seat, does suggest that there may well have been a dispute with the family of Lyon Joseph. It has been noted that when Lyon Joseph died in Bath, on 2nd May 1825, he was not buried there, but in Plymouth[28] on the following Sunday. He may not have been a member of the Bath congregation (its first synagogue having been opened soon after the year of Lyon Joseph's death), and the Bath Jewish Burial Ground was not established until the early part of the 19th century. That Lyon Joseph was not interred in the Falmouth cemetery, with other family members, where it would be reasonable to assume that a plot would have been reserved for him as one of the congregation's most senior, privileged members, may well be an indication of a dispute with the Falmouth congregation, although the Plymouth cemetery was the resting place of Lyon Joseph's mother, and this factor may have dictated the decision to take him there for burial. It is not known if this particular instance of 1819 of seat occupancy as a competitive issue was characteristic of the congregation at a time when its numbers were healthy, but some thirty years later, in 1851, the Ecclesiastical Census records the number of "Free Sittings" as 54, and "Other Sittings" (taken to be "paid" or reserved) as only 6. (In the same year, in Penzance, the reverse was the case: 6 "Free" and 30 "Other"). In the event, Judith Joseph is not known to have returned to Falmouth to live, although after her husband's death she may have revisited. (She is not to be identified with the Judith Joseph who was trading as an earthenware dealer in Market Street in 1823. This could have been either Judith (Rebecca) Jacob (1768-1849: another daughter of Moses Jacob), the wife of Isaac Joseph (-1834) or Judith Moses (1768-1843: daughter of Alexander Moses) widow of Isaac's brother, Henry Joseph (1760-1803) of St. Austell.)

The entry concludes – (It was) "agreed and declared that Mr. Jacob Jacobs be requested to take up the Treasuryship which he has accepted accordingly. In witness whereof we have hereunto subscribed our Names firmly to these presents (sic.) Witness- Abraham Joseph, B. Mordecai - for Lyon Joseph, S. Solomon, A. S. Solomon, Jacob Jacob." From the fact that Jacob Jacob had been the President since 1816, it is clear that this resolution served at this juncture to vest financial responsibility in the Congregation's highest office, and is an indication that he was respected and regarded as a trustworthy man. Of the witnesses, "B. Mordecai" is likely to be a relative of Sophia Mordecai (1781-1853) of Exeter, who had married Levy Jacob (1788-1824), Jacob Jacob's brother. "A.S. Solomon" is Simon Solomon, who signed using the initials of his Hebrew name, *Abraham Simeon*. In the absence of the original Minute Book and Accounts (of which this item would originally have comprised a part), this is the only document to date to have emerged from the records and proceedings of the Falmouth Congregation, and as such, it is of considerable importance, even though it is in the form of a secondary copy, in one hand throughout, including the names of the signatories. (It would appear to have been a clerical record of the Estate Office, lodged with that Office as notice of the Congregation's intention to re-negotiate the lease.)

If the Vestry Meeting of 1819 does indicate a dispute within or a complaint by the Congregation regarding the security and ownership of its property, it is likely to have been a comparatively rare event. During the later Presidency of Moses ("Moss") Jacob Jacob from 1852-1860 it would seem that Falmouth was a relatively stable and settled congregation (and may always have been so). "Moss" Jacob Jacob made an annual visit to London where he would call upon the Chief Rabbi, "when Dr. Adler would welcome him as representing one of the few Congregations which never had disputes to bring before him".[29] The absence of a Minute-Book for Falmouth does not make it possible to know if harmony had always been the state of affairs in Falmouth. However, its administrative arrangements certainly helped to sustain an ethos of stability. The Congregation's Presidents were appointed for extended periods of office, and held the position for life, or until they left the town. The first President, Alexander Moses served for 50 years, his son-in-law, Moses Jacob, for 16, Lyon Joseph for 15 (leaving for Bath), Jacob Jacob for 38 years, Moss Jacob for 8 years, dying in Office, and Samuel Jacob for 17 years, until 1879-1880, after which he left for London. The length of service of Falmouth's ministers also suggests a degree of stability: Moses Hyman, who died in 1830, is said to have been the rabbi for 27 years[30] (although his ministry or residence may have overlapped with that of his predecessor), Joseph Rintel was rabbi for 17 years, and Samuel Herman and Morris Marks each served about ten years. It has been mentioned that the Penzance Minute-Book, on the other hand, shows the Office of President changing hands every 2-3 years (albeit often rotating amongst the same select few) and the majority of ministers being appointed on a short term basis, and only staying in post for about 2-3 years. Although B. A. Simmons held the distinction of being the longest *resident* Jewish minister in Cornwall (from 1811 to 1860) and was employed as *shochet* and *rav* during that period, he only served intermittently, others being employed in his place, and his relations with the Penzance Congregation were particularly fractious. Only Rev. Isaac Bischof-swerder served for an extended period of about 20 years, from around 1868 to 1886. The Penzance Minute-Book certainly reveals that the Congregation there was characterised by internal dispute, resignation, dismissal and the imposition of fines and sanctions, with the Chief Rabbi being called in to adjudicate in disputes and also to authorise the appointment of ministers.

On 5th June 1822, Andrew Young died. Upon probate of his will, on 19th October that year, the congregation still owed his estate £300. The executors to Young's will, and the trustees of his estate, were Thomas Hearle of Falmouth,[31] "Gentleman", and Thomas Andrew of Penryn,[32] "Common Brewer". Like the Edward Bawden who had married Elizabeth Young, Hearle was also from Talland, having been baptised there either on 16th March 1782 or 24th January 1785.[33] His family was widely dispersed in the Penryn area. He was a landing surveyor, or "land-waiter" at the Customs House, responsible for searching incoming cargoes for illegal goods, and later, he was to become Comptroller of Customs at Falmouth. In his work, therefore, he would have come into regular contact with members of the Jewish Congregation who traded in Marine Supplies, or as Money or Navy Agents, and especially with Lyon Joseph, who had been involved in merchant shipping, linked to the Iberian Peninsula. (Thomas Hearle's son, also Thomas, was later a Solicitor in Falmouth). The second executor, Thomas Andrew (1774-1855) had also worked, much earlier, as a land-waiter in the Office of Customs. By 1841, the Census for Quay Street, Penryn would suggest that he was a widower, and his wife is not listed.[34] The same Census records that, of his children, three were born around 1811. Of these, two of his sons, George and William, were also Clerks in the Office of Customs. The first Trustee, Thomas Hearle appears to have treated the Jewish congregation with considerable tolerance at this juncture, and for some years to come, in that by the end of 1826, the debt of £300 was still owed. During the interim, Solomon Solomon had died in Lisbon in 1819, and his wife had moved to Bristol. Lyon and Judith Joseph had already left Falmouth for Bath, where Lyon died in 1825. It is not known if the Hearle family possessed a particular sympathy towards the Jewish community, but, later, a family member, George Michael Hearle (1922-2008) was to marry an American Jewess, Lilian Marie Jaffa (1926-1998) of New York. Their son, David was born in Brooklyn in 1948, and he married Anne Sicher (b. Paris 1952). Anne Sicher's family originated from Bohemia, and her great-uncle, Dr. Gustav Sicher (1880-1960) was Chief Rabbi of Prague (and Bohemia) from 1947 until his death. David and Anne Sicher Hearle were founding members of *Kehillat Kernow* in 1999, and remain active in that congregation today.

The ensuing confusion and uncertainty surrounding the nominal lessees may have contributed to the hiatus in resolving matters, but, eventually, the outstanding congregational debt was taken over by William Kirkness (1783-1851)[35] of Budock. His paternal family was from Orkney, and his maternal family, the Matthews, from Wales, had married with some Cornish families. Kirkness was born in Stepney, London, in 1783, and had married Jane Saunders in Falmouth in 1803. He had gained a permanent command in the Packet Service, and as captain of the *Queen Charlotte*, he had distinguished himself in several engagements with privateers. He also gained command of the *Countess of Chichester*. A new mortgage document with Kirkness, dated 1st January 1827, was drawn up in Bristol by Jacob Strickland, Attorney at Law, and it was signed by and issued to "Judith Joseph, Widow and Administrator of Lyon Joseph of Bath", and "Betsy Solomon of Bristol, Widow of Solomon Solomon of Falmouth". Judith Joseph's son, B. L. (Barnet Lyon) Joseph (1801-1880) also appears as counter-signatory and witness. B. L. Joseph, who had married a Betsy Jacob (1801-1889) of Dartmouth, had been born in Falmouth, but had left for Bristol in 1825. He subsequently lived in Liverpool, and then Birmingham, where he died. The mortgage carried the condition that the signatories were to be given no more than 40 days to pay the entire sum owing. Failure to comply with these terms gave Kirkness the entitlement to the property "to sell and dispose by public auction or otherwise."

Barnet Lyon Joseph, by then a fairly prosperous man, may have underwritten the debt, so that its eventual repayment to Kirkness was assured. The strict condition does seem to have been waived by Kirkness, and some alternative term of years for repayment negotiated, because the synagogue remained in the hands of the Jewish congregation. However, it may well have been that no payments were made for the next seven years, because, on 8th January 1834, Kirkness issued a receipt: "Received from Mr. L. Lawrence the sum of Fifty Pounds part of (the) sum of Three Hundred Pounds - Debt now due £250 - WK." This "Mr. Lawrence" was Moses Lazarus (Eliezar) Lawrence, who traded as a Money Broker in Church Street. He had married Judith Moses, widow of the Henry Joseph mentioned above. There were no children of this marriage, and Moses Lawrence died in 1841. In the 1861 census, a Joseph Lawrence, who may have been a relative, was living in "Synagogue House", adjoining the synagogue, as one of twenty-one residents. Further to the sum of £50, another payment must have been made within the next few years, because a receipt for 8th January 1839 records: "Received Two Hundred & Ten Pounds being the principal and interest due to me WK. Clear of all demands."

These financial arrangements indicate a leniency and patience towards the Jewish Congregation which not only reflects a social tolerance, but also, no doubt, a shrewd business sense, in that the Jewish community was making a significant contribution to the town's economy, and the commercial interests of the various parties were inter-dependent. In the late 1820s, Philp had noted of the Jews that "Their numbers are considerable and respectable; and a great deal of commercial business has been transacted by them for a series of years in this town." Beyond this however, there appears to have been a far greater respect for Jews *per se* than might be expected. Although a certain nostalgia for the passing of an era may have played a part at a time when the Jews had left Falmouth, and it cannot be taken as axiomatic that it represented a widespread Philosemitic sentiment. However, much later, on 9th April 1881, *The Falmouth and Penryn Weekly Times* carried an impassioned item which included the words "what do people mean when speaking of a Jew, as one of the Jewish *persuasion* – a Jew is not a Jew by persuasion any more than a Gentile by persuasion. A Jew is a Jew by birth and grand lineage and he will glory in being called a Jew." The passage continues by calling the term *persuasion* "a disgrace" which lowers the "individuality of the Jew - a character as being from principle."

In 1845, Dr. Nathan Marcus Adler was elected as Chief Rabbi, and shortly after he issued a detailed questionnaire *Statistical Accounts of all the Congregations in the British Empire*. It revealed that Falmouth had nine *Baalei Batim* (senior or privileged members), three seat holders and fifty Jewish residents. On 3rd January 1845, the journal *The Voice of Jacob* published a list of ten donors from Falmouth to the Mogador relief fund, the total received from them being £5. 7s. A few years later, in 1850 the Packet Boat Service that had been established in 1688 was withdrawn, and, upon its removal, the whole of the mail service was transferred to Liverpool and Southampton. The result was a dramatic reduction in the number of ships which would have called, and docked at Falmouth. Together with other local traders who were engaged in the service sector, the Jews were highly dependent on the custom that the packet boats brought to the town. Although none of the twelve Packet Agents in Falmouth,[36] from 1689 to 1845, were Jews, some Jews did operate as bullion brokers, in money exchange, and as naval agents. In 1847,[37] just a few years before the removal of the Packet Service, the figures for the Falmouth congregation were the same as in 1845 (and in Penzance, the figure was very similar). These numbers were to fall off significantly after 1850, when directories list fewer Jewish traders. Improved rail communications to Plymouth and London soon followed, and led to a further decline of the Jewish community. In the Ecclesiastical Census of 28th – 29th March 1851, Jacob Jacob recorded the "Estimated Number of Persons attending Divine Service" as a mere 8 (for each of Friday Evening and Saturday Morning only), and the average number of attendants for each service during a six month period as 10. He added to this his remarks that "Since the breaking up of the foreign packet establishment here, the Congregation has decreased with the inhabitants generally."[38] The equivalent figures for other South West congregations are instructive, (where a Saturday Afternoon service was also counted): Exeter, 28 – 48 - 12 and 35 – 55 – 15, Plymouth, 40 – 50 – 24 (average attendance not stated) and Penzance, 14 – 16 - 5 and 5-12 – 16-25 and 5-12.[39] The Board of Deputies' return for Falmouth in 1852 showed only three members, but there may have been more Jewish residents in the town than this figure implies.

Even before 1851, Jacob Jacob would have been acutely aware of the scale of decline in the Jewish community and the likelihood that his family would eventually leave Falmouth to seek better opportunities elsewhere. Christian, especially nonconformist evangelical activity was still a prominent feature of Cornish religious life. It is not known if Jacob Jacob actively sought to oppose Christian missionary activity directed specifically at the Jews (as Solomon Ezekiel and Rabbi Hart Symons had done in Penzance), but, as President of the small congregation, he was concerned to oppose and clarify that Jews had not been the murderers of Christ, and to assert the perpetual validity of the Jewish religion. Two original note-books, written in Jacob Jacob's hand, not long before his death, and dated 30th January 1850 (dated 5610),[40] when he was 76, and 3rd November 1851 (5612) reveal his close reading of both the Hebrew Bible and the New Testament. The note-books suggest that they may have been prepared for a talk, or to answer questions from Christians at a meeting, although they may only represent Jacob's private reflections on the relationship between Judaism and Christianity. They may also, of course, have been used by him within the context of the synagogue service, or for educational purposes. What is of particular interest is that Jacob drew upon a range of passages from the New Testament to illustrate his belief that both Jesus and the Apostle Paul defended the integrity of the revelation to the Jews, and that the Romans were the true murderers of Christ. Jacob argues against "notions regarding the death of Jesus that he was not actually put to death but in appearance", and he notes the gospel details which would suggest the reality of Christ's death as "tribulation, vexation, distress, persecution, anguish, excessive pain of body or mind" (the notes also suggest that he intended these features to reflect the Jewish historical experience of persecution). He comments that "(In) My opinion Christ never suffered death by Jews but by Romans - the governor that tried him - but to destroy the Jews as they (presumably, the Gospel writers, or later Christian tradition) expected it would it was thrown on them." (It is clear that Jacob had read the gospels with care, and he focussed on passages from each gospel, especially Matthew and John, which he felt had been used to malign the Jews for Christ's death). His notes continue with what seems to be a contemporaneous reference: "something similar occurred in Damascus a few years since with Father Mathews", and concludes with the rhetorical comment "Has not every thing been done to destroy the Jews as a Nation, but our Heavenly Father ordained it in other ways". There are three notes which may have been intended to address or answer anticipated questions: (i) "What is your opinion did Christ willingly dye" (sic.); (ii) "I am aware that Christians says (sic.) there is a Trinity and the three are one. I can't find any thing of the kind in the Bible"; and (iii) from an article or letter in *The Times* "Decr. 1850, The Bishop of London says the Bible alone is the Religion of Protestants, I could have told the Bishop that the Bible alone is the Religion of Jews". However fragmentary, personal or partial these notes may be, they do illustrate that Jacob Jacob, and likely the Jewish congregation itself, was far from isolated from the wider religious environment, nor ignorant or unaware of the Christianity of its neighbours.

By the 1860s, the original trustees of the synagogue had died, and the existing lessees, Judith Joseph and Betsy Solomon, had moved away. Responsibility for the synagogue now rested largely in the hands of the Jacob family, whose head, Moses ("Moss") Jacob Jacob (1812-1860), a clothes dealer and pawnbroker in Market Street, had been its president from 1853 until his death in 1860, when his eldest son, Samuel (1838-1913)[41] assumed the presidency until the synagogue's closure in 1879. Restricted income from a declining congregation led to a deterioration in the building's maintenance, which had been subject to explicit provisions in the original lease of 1810. Although the synagogue had become the property of the congregation upon the final payment to William Kirkness, it was not owned by them on a freehold basis, as the original Wodehouse lease was still in force, and by this time, Samuel Jacob had become the sole official lessee. (A later notice, dated 29th November 1871, records the lease as No. 154, and the tenement number as 382. The Lessee's signature is that of Samuel Jacob). It would seem that concerns in the Arwenack Manor Office and in the congregation led to a search to trace the whereabouts of the original nominated "lives", and also for descendants of those involved in the various agreements. Samuel Jacob's brother, Michael (1840-) was by this time acting as the Synagogue Secretary (he was also Treasurer of the Falmouth Debating Society). On 24th July 1866, Michael Jacob[42], most likely acting as Treasurer to the congregation, wrote on its behalf to a J. J. Skinner at the Manor Office, which had sent out a "circular", which, presumably, enquired if individuals still lived, and, if so, where. Michael Jacob replied: "In reply to your circular - Mr. Israel Solomon lives at 32 Red Lion Square Holborn London. Nancy Joseph (Mrs. M. L. Levin) 2 Bevis Marks London and Rosey Moses[43] Mrs. Cohen is at present living in New York U.S. and has been heard from within the last three months".[44]

The letter ends with a reference to "particulars of lives in houses in Market Street", which may refer to other properties leased to Jews (although the occupants are given as "Renfree and others"). Of those mentioned by Michael Jacob, Israel Solomon (as mentioned earlier), who was the author of *Records of my Family* (1887), was to die in New York (*c.*1893). He was the son of the original lessee, Solomon Solomon. "Nancy" is Hannah Joseph. "Mrs. Cohen" was Lyon Joseph's daughter Kate (1811-1897) who had married a Moses Cohen (1799-1879) of London. Rosey Moses, would have been 64 in 1866, and may have been unmarried. As such she may have once lived with Kate Cohen in London.

The final known correspondence relating to the Falmouth congregation and the Wodehouse lease takes the form of a card sent from London, on 24th November 1871, by Henry Joseph (1815-1899), a son of the late Lyon Joseph. Henry Joseph had married Maria Samuel (1816-1897) daughter of Abraham Samuel of London. (To avoid potential confusion, it should be noted that this Henry Joseph should be distinguished from Henry Joseph (1760-*c.*1802), of St. Austell, who was a son of Joseph Joseph from his first marriage, and also from the Henry Joseph (1806-1881), who married Amelia Jacob (1811-1891), and moved to Penzance. Henry Joseph of Penzance was a son of Abraham Joseph (-1828), brother of Lyon Joseph, mentioned in the earlier vestry meeting of January 1819. Abraham and Lyon Joseph were both sons of Joseph Joseph from his second marriage. Henry Joseph of Penzance was, therefore, a nephew of Lyon Joseph, and a cousin to Henry Joseph of London). The card was sent by Henry Joseph to Samuel Jacob, updating him on details of two of the "lives": "Israel Solomon's address is 22 Red Lion Square London and Nancy or Nanny Joseph now Mrs Levin resides at 54 Princes Square Bayswater London. Yours Truly, Kind regards to all - Henry Joseph." Whatever the outcome of these searches, it would seem that those identified were either unavailable or unwilling to assume further responsibility for the synagogue. However, two new names were eventually found to act as Trustees with Samuel Jacob: Simeon Solomon Harris, Commercial Traveller, of 117 St. Augustine Road, Camden Town, London, and Abraham Leon Emanuel, Court Jeweller, of Ordnance Row, Portsea (Portsmouth).[45] The former was Simon Harris (*c.* 1826-) a Watchmaker and Jeweller, formerly of Truro, but by now living in London. He was the grandson of Samuel Harris of Falmouth, and a son of Henry Harris of Truro (later of London), both of whom were mentioned in the vestry note of January 1819. The latter would have been related to Frances Emanuel (1812-1875) of Portsea who had married Moses Jacob Jacob (1812-1860), Samuel Jacob's father. It is also likely that this A.L. Emanuel was related to the London Solicitor, Lewis (Leon) Emanuel, who launched a Restoration Appeal for the Jewish cemetery in 1889. That A. L. Emanuel was a "Court Jeweller" indicates that he traded by Royal Warrant. The Jeweller, Henry Harris of Truro had also traded by Royal Warrant, to William IV in 1833, and to Queen Victoria in 1837. Such warrants could be renewable. Samuel Jacob (soon to move to the Capital), Simeon Harris, and Abraham Emanuel (the latter through his Warrant) all had family, and similar commercial connections in London.

Subsequently, there was a formal renewal of the lease on 25th April 1878[46], in the form of the conveyance of the "fee simple in possession" (the freehold) of the synagogue, although this was hedged around with contractual exclusions and conditions, including a clause of reversal to the Estate, in the event of failure in contractual compliance: "the said synagogue shall not at any time or times here-after be used for any other purpose than as a place of religious worship or for the performances of religious rites by the Jews without the permission or consent in writing of the said Earl of Kimberley, his heirs (etc.) [otherwise] the interest of (the three named Trustees) in the same piece of land and heredity (freehold) shall cease and become void, and thereupon shall as a distinct freehold Tenement become the property of the Earl of Kimberley." From this, the closure of the synagogue as a place of worship, could, in the absence of permission from the Estate for alternative usage, be deemed "a failure of contractual compliance". Clearly, the Estate Office was by now fully aware of the Congregation's terminal condition, but also of the considerable resale value of the building in its particular location. The papers, amongst which this conveyance is found, contain other contracts of conveyance for the building of domestic dwellings. The size and location of these plots in such an elevated position with panoramic views would have brought considerable revenues to the Wodehouse Estate. In the event, the sum paid by the synagogue's Trustees for the fee simple was £50. This final conveyance is of special interest in that the freehold possession carried with it a scale plan of the building and the land which bordered it. The plan site, "containing by admeasurement nine Perches and three quarters of a Perch" (a perch, pole or rod, was equivalent to five and a half yards, which, squared, gives approximately thirty yards) shows a vestibule or side room of 12ft. 8ins. and a main body of the synagogue as 30ft. (front facing) by 47ft. (sides). On the outside of the building, the front extends to a space of approx. 45ft. by 20ft., and to the side a strip of land approx. 7ft. 8ins. in width.[47] (The land behind the synagogue rose on a gradual gradient.)

In the event, the congregation's decline was such that the building was not to be occupied for much longer. Before Samuel Jacob closed the synagogue in 1879 he ensured that essential repairs required by the lease (which still had 30 years before expiry) were made to the building. After he left for London in 1880[48], although the synagogue did not fall into immediate decay it became the target for vandals, and by the spring of 1881, the local press carried the following item[49] from its regular columnist, "A Rambler: Have any of my readers noticed the (I believe) total disappearance from our town of Jewish families. I recollect in years agone Falmouth contained more resident Jews than were to be found in all Cornwall (in fact, not strictly true).[50] Those were the times of the mail packets [i.e. before 1850]. There were then families in the town representing Abram, Isaac, Jacob, Joseph and Moses besides other names of strict individuality. The last representative of the (sic.) jewish residents, himself a descendant from the most honoured and honourable of Falmouth Jews [i.e. Alexander Moses] was Mr. Samuel Jacob, who left us some few months since for London. Mr. Jacob did a very creditable thing before he left - he thoroughly repaired the synagogue and placed it on a lasting holding from the lord of the manor - but, alas, the synagogue is closed and deserted; at once an evidence of Jewish prosperity and Jewish decline in Falmouth. Also, the Jews' synagogue, in its deserted state, is unfortunately made one of the targets of mischievous urchins who glory in trying the effect of stones on glass. It is a pity and a shame that such a state of things exists in Falmouth -

would not covering the windows with a close meshed wire-netting be a good preventative….(?)"

The state of the synagogue eventually became deplorable, and, in 1892, the Chief Rabbi ordered its sale. It was either sold by the Jacob family, or reverted to the Wodehouse Estate, by some form of agreement or by repossession. By the time that Samuel Jacob moved to London, his being the sole remaining family to have sustained the vestiges of congregational life, it would seem that the former contentious issue of the collective ownership of property had become a purely academic matter. Consequently, he took the synagogue's remaining religious artefacts with him. Some of these he later donated to the Royal Institution of Cornwall, in Truro.[51] The donation (which may have comprised all of the following) consisted of four Torah scrolls, all of which originated from the German-speaking areas. It is not known if they had been brought to England from the Continent by the families of Alexander Moses or Moses Jacob, and then to Falmouth, but it is possible. One of these scrolls would seem to be about 350 years old, and may have been produced around 1660, but it is also possibly much older. The other scroll appears to be between 250 to 300 years old, from around the early 1700s. Their age is, therefore, consistent with the arrival of the earliest Jewish families in Cornwall in the 1740s. The first scroll, which bears the name *Jacob*, is highly unusual, in that it has 68 lines, when the maximum allowed by the halachic authorities was usually 60. In this sense it may well be unique. Its use of a Hebrew variant of the letter *Pey* (the *Pey Parpuot*), and other markings, suggests that the scroll may have been produced for or by a Kabbalistic mystical movement. It is not clear, however, if this scroll, or all four, had been passed down in perpetuity through the Jacob family. Two of the scrolls are today beyond viable repair, and the fifth scroll which the congregation may have possessed (mentioned) may have been taken out from usage at some point.

In January 1933, George Grenville Jacob (1877-1963), son of Alexander Jacob (1841-1903) and grandson of "Moss" Jacob Jacob (1812-1860), wrote to the Manor Office, Arwenack with an enquiry relating to the synagogue, and he received the following reply, dated 10th January 1933, from a Percy O. Fell, and addressed to him at 29, Upper Hamilton Terrace, London NW8: "I have searched the rentals as far back as 1854 and can find no mention of the Synagogue. It would appear that payments of rent ceased before 1854. The building was used as a cabinet maker's shop in 1904 and has since been sold to a local auctioneer (H. J. R. Corlyon) who uses the premises as a sale room and store."[52] It would seem that Jacob pursued his enquiries further, and wrote to another Falmouth Auctioneer, John Julian & Co. Ltd., whose firm had recently bought the building[53] and used it under the name of "Synagogue Premises"[54]. W. J. Opie from the firm replied to him on 15th July 1933: "with reference to the stone tablet which was fixed in the Hebrew Synagogue. We have made enquiries, and believe the tablet, together with Sacrifice Knife and another Hebrew tablet is in the hands of the previous owner of the synagogue." Jacob was referred to a local resident, Mr. A. H. Moss (who may have been Jewish) for further details. Moss knew the owner of the tablets, Corlyon, and after talking to him, reported that "a Jewish gentleman saw them some time since & told him that if he were to advertise them in the "Jewish Journal" that he would realise 50

Guineas on the Hebrew Prayer Tablet alone. The owner would not state any figure but asked for an offer." Jacob was clearly displeased with this report, and replied by return, rejecting out of hand the valuation of £50, stating that "They are actually worth nothing at all. To me, as the grandson of the gentleman who ran the synagogue for a good many years, they have a sentimental value. I understand there are four Tablets and a Knife. If an offer of five guineas is of any use I shall be pleased to pay same, but would not consider anything beyond this amount." A later handwritten note from Jacob dated "Aug. 1935" records "Corlyon & Sons Auctioneers have prayer for Royal family (insert 1854) in Hebrew from Falmouth Synagogue also Shochet's Knive (*sic.*) - asking £5." From this it is likely that the sum of £5 refers only to the Knife, and there is no further correspondence, suggesting that George Jacob decided to drop the matter.

In 1949, Alex Jacob made contact with Corlyon (who was ill and retired from the business), and received a reply from his wife, dated 31st January: "I have been making enquiries about the Wooden Panel, which I remember very well; my husband had it stored & I am hoping to trace it. I will let you know as soon as I can. I remember your father wanting to buy it many years ago. We also have a corner stone with an inscription in Hebrew - also the Knife that was used at the Synagogue & these might be of interest to you." Alex Jacob referred this to Wilfred Samuel, Chairman of the Jewish Museum, who wrote in February "about the Falmouth synagogue's relics, if Big Money is being asked for them they ought to supply snapshots so we can see what is being offered. I should think that Mrs. Corlyon is entitled to regard as landlord's fixtures the foundation stone and the Royal Family Tablet, but surely the Knife (circumcision or slaughterer's) was left behind inadvertently and should be surrendered gratis." Samuel noted that a Mr. Dangelowitz had come into possession (and presumably purchased, but from whom is unclear) the "Falmouth Commandments Board - (in fact two boards, which he presented to the Museum as a gift) -which we have here - was recently admired by an 18th century furniture expert who commended its purity of line and good finish." Samuel concluded his reply by hoping that Jacob would likewise purchase the foundation stone and Royal Family Tablet and donate them to the Museum. There is nothing to suggest that Alex Jacob did so, but he recorded that year: "In the Congregation's possession were five scrolls with two sets of silver bells and pointers; a curtain for the Ark; and Notice Boards recording donations of ten guineas and more; together with two wooden panels, one displaying the Commandments and the other the Prayer for the Royal Family. Prominent amongst the building's decorations were four or five elaborate and massive candelabra."[55]

The architect, Edward Jamilly, visited the Cornish synagogues in 1958, making detailed drawings of their arrangement and design. On Falmouth, he comments on the building "half as big again as Penzance synagogue - presenting to the street an east wall of red brick, patterned with vitrified headers, granite-quoined and set on a stone plinth. Rules of orientation dictated entry from the rear. Internally vestiges of woodwork point to a panelled dado of some delicacy (on the ground floor), the little fluted wooden pilasters identical to those at Plymouth (above the men's seating there). A gallery at the back was carried on (timber) Tuscan columns." The Great Synagogue in Duke's Place, founded in 1692, London was rebuilt between 1788 and 1790, only twenty years before the Falmouth synagogue of 1808, and showed some similar, if grander features, including full height Corinthian columns, pilasters to carry the roof, and smaller Doric columns to support the women's galleries. In addition "Giant Ionic columns supported the galleries at mid height and continued upwards to carry a bold cornice above them".[56] It is possible that some account was taken of these details when designing the Falmouth building. For some years prior to 1933, the building had been a cinema, and Jamilly observed that a door had then been added to the east end as a quick way to the street: "I am sure this would never have existed in the original synagogue, as it would have been immediately to the left of the Ark. I assume that entry to the synagogue was by way of the side passage to main doors at the rear (under the present corrugated annexe) in the west wall".[57] Unlike the former Penzance synagogue, the Falmouth building has been well preserved. It is now an artist's studio and a private residence. A plaque, commemorating its former use as a synagogue, was erected in April 2000.[58] Since 1975 it has been a grade II listed building.

The Presidents (Wardens) of the Falmouth Congregation.

Alexander (Henry) Moses, "Zender Falmouth" (*c*. 1740-1791).

Moses Jacob (1791-1807)
The Presidency did not pass from Alexander Moses to his son, Philip, but to his son-in-law, Moses Jacob. He was married to Sarah Moses, who, it has been said, took an active part in congregational affairs.

Lyon Joseph (1807-1815)

Jacob Jacob (1815-1853)
Son of Moses Jacob.

Moses ("Moss") Jacob Jacob (1853-1860)
Son of Jacob Jacob.

Samuel Jacob (1860-1879)
Son of Moses Jacob Jacob.

Congregational Names.

While no detailed record of congregational membership has survived for Falmouth, isolated records, such as the leases, allow for the reconstruction of a core membership. Other names can be derived from the local burial ground, and further names have been preserved in fragmentary form in genealogical sources, and most of these can be linked with Jewish residents in Falmouth or to visitors:

Aaron, Abrahams, Alexander, Arieh, Beer, Benjamin, Benson, Chayim (or *Hayim*), *David-son, Elias, Elijah* (*Elyahu*), *Ezekiel, Falkson, Ha Levi, Harris* (or *Harriss*), *Hirschell* (Chief Rabbi), *Isaac, Israel* (Solomon, or Levy of Truro), *Issachar, Jacob* (or *Jacobs*), *Jewell* (Barnet Levy, also known as Bernard Baer), *Joel* (perhaps as Jewell), *Joseph* (or *Josephs*), *Joshua, Lawrence, Levi* (or *Levy/Levin*), *Manassah, Moses, Mowsa* (or *Mowshay*, Rabbi Moses Hyman) [the photograph of a Morrise Shawyer, or Shire, who died in 1868, age 78, appears in the Jacob Archive, but this man may not have been a resident of Falmouth], *Naphtali, Oppenheim* (Penzance), *Reuben, Rintel* (Rabbi), *Saavill* (Rabbi), *Samuel, Segal, Simeon, Simmons* (Rabbi of Penzance), *Simon* (or *Simons*), *Solomon, Vos, Woolf, Zevi* (possibly as Henry or Alexander Moses).[59]

2
Penzance

In the case of Penzance, a detailed Minute-Book of congregational meetings, accounts and membership has survived.[60] It consists of 330 pages, intended to be read as 165 open (double) pages in the form of an accountant's ledger. The earlier accounts (1807-1829) are arranged in strict ledger form, with income to the left (*verso*) and expenditure to the right (*recto*). These are mainly in English, but with a cursive Hebrew script for some congregational names, ritual items and liturgical references. There are detailed sections entirely in Hebrew (with some Yiddish) and these relate mainly to the appointment of incumbent ministers, but also to the decisions taken at vestry meetings. The signatures of those attending the meetings are found both in Hebrew and English, and the accounts and minutes were usually written in the hand of the presiding President. The later Minutes are not arranged in this way, but are mainly a summary of meetings, and copies of letters. There are some details of finance, but there are no detailed accounts. Signatures are mainly in English, but Hebrew is used for the same ritual references as before. The Minutes also contain the names of local people, including tradesmen and builders. Various leases and conveyances relating both to the synagogue and the cemetery have also survived and these contain important information on the congregation's affairs. From these sources a detailed picture of the life of the congregation during the 19th century can be reconstructed with some confidence.[61]

The earliest records from the 1700s have not survived. Presumably, there would have been conveyances and leases between the Congregation and the Branwell family of Penzance, the owners of the land on which the first synagogue was built in 1768, and also with the Rogers family of Sithney (and later, the Barham family of Exeter and Penzance) in relation to the earliest plots to comprise the burial ground in the Leskinnick area of the town. However, at a time when there was considerable uncertainty as to the legality of issuing leases to Jews, it is possible that, at first, some property may have been held by the congregation on an informal rental basis, although the one time existence of a formal lease of 1768 for the synagogue (see below) suggests otherwise. Leases may also have been issued for the cemetery during the 18th century, and certainly by 17th November 1810 the accounts refer to a payment of 7 Guineas made to "Borlase & Scott for new lease of Burying Ground". This lease is also mentioned as having a ninety-nine year term beginning on 31st March 1810, issued from (Rev.) John Rogers to Lemon Hart as "Plot No. 1". (The reference occurs in a much later conveyance of 29th September 1844, when Rogers released the freehold of this plot, together with adjoining triangular plots, "Nos. 2 & 3", to Lemon Woolf and Henry Joseph, for the sum of £50.)

No records of congregational meetings and administration have come to light from the 18th century. However, the building of the second synagogue in 1807-1808 (on the same site as the former) appears to have marked a more formalised system of congregational record-keeping, in the accounts book, where (at least until 1829) all expenditure and income from members' subscriptions were kept with meticulous care and balance. The minutes also reveal a glimpse of the ongoing issues that concerned the congregation, including the appointment of and salaries paid to its ministers.

The congregation's records consist of:

Various leases retained by the congregation from 1807 until 1906, originally lodged with the Bolitho Bank, but later with local solicitors.[62]

The early congregational minutes, consist of detailed accounts from 25th May 1807 through to the end of 1829 (with two fragments as entries for March 1830 and October 1831). Amongst these minutes and bi-annual accounts (in Yiddish and English) there are:

The synagogue conveyance of December 1807 (renewed with the synagogue's extension in 1837).

A formal set of Regulations (Tikkunim; lit. accounts) in Yiddish for the administration of the congregation's religious life, drawn up and ratified in 1808.

Leases relating to the cemetery (1835 and 1844), which culminate in the purchase of the freehold to the enclosed burial ground.

For the period 1829-1842, no detailed accounts have survived.

The later congregational minutes (but not detailed accounts) resume from 12th March 1843. With the exception of the period 1883-1884, these minutes, mostly in English, continue for some fifty years, up to 7th March 1892. They contain:

An extensive revised set of Regulations (1844).

A retrospective registration document for the synagogue (June 1872).

Two further conveyances in the form of financial transactions between congregational members (1880 and 1901).

The final conveyance of the synagogue's closure and sale (1906).

In the years before the building of the first synagogue, in 1768, the small congregation, which is likely to have consisted of only a few families, including those of Hart (from Germany) and Woolf (from Holland) would, no doubt, have met for worship in a private house, or some other temporary accommodation.[63] Roth notes correctly, that the "Polish rite of prayers" had been used by the congregation "from its earliest days", but his inference that this indicates that the "…earliest members originated exclusively, or almost exclusively, from Poland"[64], is misconceived and cannot be justified. The "Polish Rite" was not confined to Jews from Poland (whose borders at that time differed from those which apply today). This rite consisted of variations in texts and prayers between Polish and German custom, and it was used by Jews in Western, as well as parts of Eastern Europe. It came to be used widely in the 18th century by Jews in Britain. Some congregations (such as Plymouth) were composed of some Jews of Polish extraction, but the members of the Cornish congregations were mainly from Germany and the Low Countries.

Well before the opening of the first synagogue, however, the Jews had acquired the unenclosed plot at Leskinnick for their exclusive use as a burial ground (without which they could hardly settle permanently), and, it would seem, a *Mikveh,* or ritual bath (without which they could not observe the obligations of ritual cleansing). As later records from 1808 show, the *Mikveh* was located, not adjacent to the synagogue itself, but in the private house of Hyman Woolf, whose dates (c.1732-1820) would suggest that he had settled in the town before the first synagogue was built. It would seem that, with the building of the second synagogue, the congregation saw no need to construct a new *Mikveh* at the synagogue itself. In Falmouth, arrangements for a *Mikveh* before 1808 are not known, but the second synagogue there had a *Mikveh* adjoining the building. In Penzance, at least, these early measures indicate what the later minutes and regulations confirm, which is that the isolated community was anxious not to lose its traditional character, but strove to regulate its religious life as strictly as it could, and "was punctilious in its attachment to tradition", even at the considerable costs which could be involved for such a small community with a limited income.[65]

The oldest synagogue conveyance for 1768, related to a plot of land in New Street, and this document was in existence until the early 1980s.[66] The original had not been copied, but this lease was from a member of the Branwell family, who was a butcher by trade. The plot was referred to in the document as "adjoining a killing place", presumably where Branwell slaughtered. The date for the building of the first synagogue is further confirmed by several published sources. In the years prior to 1939, the stationer, Saundry of Chapel Street, published an annual *Almanac*. The editions for 1933 and 1936 note "1768: Old Jews' Synagogue built".[67] Much earlier, Thomas, in his *History of Mount's Bay* (1820) had stated that "the Jews have a synagogue which was built in 1807; but prior to this, they had one that was erected in 1768."[68] Almost contemporaneous, however, *The Universal British Directory for Devon and Cornwall* (1799) in its section on Penzance, mentions that "the Jews have a synagogue", obviously referring to the existing structure which had been built some thirty years earlier.[69] The Branwell family,[70] which had considerable commercial interests in Penzance from the 17th to the late 19th century, sustained a financial involvement with the Jewish congregation well into the mid-1800s, in that they provided leases for land for the building of both synagogues. Consequently, the family name receives mention in the minute-book from 1807, although it is not always possible to identify specific individuals with certainty. The genealogy of the Branwell family is complicated by the fact that several of the male line married twice. Moreover, male forenames were duplicated across the generations, and maternal surnames were sometimes adopted as an additional surname (which, today, would most commonly appear in a "double-barrelled" form).

Martin Branwell (1674-1719) was a butcher who married twice. His first wife, Margery, died in 1703. Her surname is not known, although it may have been *Sutherland,* appearing as it does in a later generation. Their son, also Martin, and whose dates and descendants are not known, continued his father's business, and in 1719 he inherited a large plot of land from his father. This plot is thought to have included the section leased to the Jews for the building of the 1768 synagogue, and its 1807 successor. The name of the lessor on the 1768 lease has been recollected[71] as Joseph Branwell Sutherland (died 3rd December 1844), but this man was not born until 1777 (he died in 1844 age 67). However, he was involved in the lease and rental arrangements for the *second* synagogue of 1808 (named either as J. B. Sutherland, or simply as *Sutherland*). It is possible that one of his forbearers, possibly his father or an uncle was the lessor of 1768, and he may also have been related to Martin Branwell who took possession of the 1719 plot, or to his first wife, whose surname may have been *Sutherland.* (A John Sutherland appears in the 1841 Census as a butcher.) The headstone of Joseph Branwell Sutherland can be seen today opposite the main entrance to St. Mary's Church in Chapel Street, and it records, in turn, his son, Joseph (c. 1801-1850), who may have been the Joseph Branwell, or *Branwell,* also named in the congregational minutes in relation to rental payments for the second synagogue, although this name most likely refers to the Joseph Branwell who died in 1817 (see below). From the second marriage of Martin Branwell (senior, d. 1719), the children included a Richard (1711-1792) who was a mason, and a Joseph (1715-1758) whose trade is uncertain, although an association with the family's building or butchery trades is likely. Their sons were, respectively, Richard (1744-1812) a builder, who married an Honour Mathews in 1771, and his cousin Joseph (1748-1817) who married her (presumed) sister, Temperance, in 1772. Although the original bond has not survived, the Accounts and Resolutions of the Mayor (1793-1835) confirm that, on 14th February 1814, the Corporation borrowed from Temperance Branwell the sum of £200.[72] Some of her former property, adjacent to the synagogue, was later purchased by the Jewish congregation. It is conceivable, therefore, that the mason, Richard Branwell (father) had some financial involvement in the building of the first synagogue in 1768, and his builder son Richard, in the second, in 1807, although for the latter, a "Mr. Wallis" and various other local tradesmen (who could have been sub-contracted) are named in the minute-book (see below) as completing the building. Richard Branwell's name does not appear.

Arrangements for the congregation's payment of rent from 1768 are not known, but the minute-book shows that between 1807 to the end of 1817, various entries record that rent for the new synagogue was paid to a Mr. Joseph Branwell (sometimes given simply as *Branwell*). These entries would most likely refer to the husband of Temperance Matthews. Joseph Branwell had known the congregation's

President, Lemon Hart, for some years, and the Hart and Branwell families were near neighbours, both occupying properties in the vicinity of Chapel Street. In 1805, Joseph Branwell, along with four other local men, had joined Hart in a business venture involving co-ownership of the cargo ship, *Speculation*, which was registered by them to work out from Penzance harbour. Upon Joseph Branwell's death in 1817, and that of his widow, Temperance in 1818, rent was paid, for one year only, to J. B. Sutherland, presumably a Joseph Branwell Sutherland, likely to have been the son of the Sutherland of 1768, whose headstone is mentioned, above. It seems likely that J. B. Sutherland had taken out a short-term sub-lease on the synagogue. From 1819 onwards (in 1829 the congregational minutes break off) rent was paid to a Mr. (William) Eva, a wheelwright from a long-established family of Gwinear, between Camborne and Hayle. He had married a Barbara Mathews of Penzance in 1817, and his involvement came about in that his wife had inherited from her aunt, Temperance Branwell, both the freehold title to the synagogue, and that of a two houses adjoining it. This inheritance and the financial relationship with William Eva were to benefit the congregation some two decades later, in 1837.

By the early 1800s, however, the Jewish congregation must have found the original synagogue building of 1768 too small for their requirements and they had resolved to rebuild another on the same site. The first entry in the minute-book dates from May 25th 1807, and shows that work on the new building was well underway, and may have begun in 1806. Further entries indicate that it had been completed before the end of 1807. Just over thirty years later, in 1839, 1807 is given as the official year of its completion in Edmonds' *Statistical Account of Madron and Penzance*.[73] On 11th December 1807, the senior representatives of the congregation signed a lease: "Joseph Branwell of Penzance demises and lets to Lemon Hart, Hyman Wolf, Henry Ralph, Elias Magnus and Lemon Wolf, all also of Penzance, the Meeting House or Synagogue lately erected and built by the assignees, L. Hart *et al*. In the courtilege behind the Dwelling House of the said Joseph Branwell in New Street Penzance and on a place where there was sometime a killing shop and slaughterhouse used by the said Joseph Branwell, to have and to hold for twenty-one years from 25th December next subject to an annual rent of £6. 6s. paid quarterly and with an obligation to keep the fabric in good repair." [74] The accounts show that the congregation took this obligation very seriously, as, indeed they did the management of their finances in general. The Minutes and Accounts are drawn up in the conventional form of income (to the left) and expenditure (to the right), and were recorded twice each year. It is striking that for every half-year from May 1807-1829 (when the accounts break off) the sums for income and expenditure are identical.

The lease of 1807 was signed by all of the parties concerned, with the exception of Elias Magnus. From this extract it would seem that the assignees had built a synagogue on Branwell's land on the understanding that they would then lease it from him. To accommodate a larger structure than the former building, Branwell, who was sixty years old by this time, must have decided to retire from his trade, and had agreed to the demolition of a slaughterhouse previously on this site. The minutes for November 1807 show that the congregation had received "benefactions and subscriptions towards the New Synagogue" to the total of £28. & 6s., together with a further balance of £24. 6s. & 9d. Joseph Branwell had also provided a sum to the congregation, effectively in the form of an advance loan, of £20.00, and received his first rental payment of £4.14s. & 6d at the end of January 1808, recorded as "3/4 Year Rent due 25 December last". It seems likely that Lemon Hart also made a loan to the congregation towards the synagogue. He was by this time a comparatively wealthy man, and had already opened a branch of his Wine and Spirit business in London, under the supervision of his nephew Jacob James Jacobs (or Hart), providing the considerable sum of £5,000 as initial capital. The congregational accounts for 1807, which were kept by Hart as President and Treasurer until 1811, record an opening balance of £24. 6s. & 9d. Together with the subscriptions for the synagogue mentioned earlier, the total amounted to over £52. In addition to this, Hart's half-year subscription, of about £12.00 was twice that of Hyman Woolf and Henry Ralph (who paid about £6.00) with other senior members paying less again. On 26th June 1808, Hart recorded in his own hand that the "Ballance (*sic.*) due to me" of £32. 16s. & 11d. had been re-paid. The same sum was again noted as expenditure "By Ballance due to LH" on 21st September 1808, and a further sum of £3. 18s. & 11d. was paid "By Ballance forward dew (*sic.*) to LH" on 9th October that year.

The accounts for 1807-8 record payments totalling nearly £100 to various local tradesmen, which afford an intriguing glimpse into the course of the synagogue's construction: "1807: May 25 Henry Bottrell for Oak; Brewer halling (*sic.*) 3 loads of hay; June 28 Thos. Nichol for Stones; 1808: Jan 1 Peter Roberts for Earth; Mr. Wallis towards his Bill; Jan 29 Peter Richards Mason Bill; Bolitho & Sons for Lime; Feb 1 Joseph Tonkins Bill (unspecified); March 15 Robt. Edwards Tin Man; April 8 Richard Coulson Painter; July 15 Paid Mr. Wallis Ballance of his acct. Building Synagogue". Further improvements were made to the completed building over the ensuing year, with payments, on 9th October 1808, to "Tonkin" (likely the Joseph Tonkin, above) for candlesticks (the synagogue's only form of lighting) and in April 1809 to "E. Hornblower Painter", and to "Mrs. Broad for Greencloth". Insurance cover for the building was in place from 1808 to 1809, consisting of "Premiomms" (*sic.*) of £1, but this cover may not have been maintained. However, from this point on, the accounts do not contain regular mention of expenditure on the leases for the synagogue and the burial ground. Occasional mention is made of payments to a cleaning woman for the synagogue (sometimes recorded as the *shabbos goia*) who, in 1811-1812, was paid an annual salary of 16 shillings. This same woman or another caretaker was later recorded in 1818 as being paid to light the candles on the Sabbath in the synagogue.

It might be expected that these early accounts would reflect an over riding preoccupation with the material aspects of the synagogue's construction and equipment, but this is not the case, and care was taken to ensure that the costs of meeting the ritual aspects of the congregation's religious life were not neglected at a time when finances were sorely stretched. Amongst the various payments from 1808 (and characteristic of those which appear in the minutes for subsequent years) are those to Rabbi Aaron (Selig) in April, "By cash advanced (as) Wages £15.", and also to him, "By deficiency on the cost of *Pesach Matsos* (bread for Passover) £16s. 8d." In September that year, for the festival of *Succot* (Tabernacles or Booths) he received a similar payment (of 9s. 8d.) for the purchase of an *Etrog,* or citron fruit, one of the four species of plant used during the festival's ritual celebrations. The significant cost to the congregation of buying the *Citron*, which had to be perfect in stem and body, and the difficulty of acquiring one for such a far-flung community, indicates the concern to maintain a strict observance of Jewish tradition. The traditional practice of ensuring donations from members at the time of being called up to the Reading of the Torah (Law) at Sabbaths and Festivals was also followed, and seven of these are listed for June 1808. Also from 1808, the concern to uphold ritual practice is reflected in the entries of "sundry expenses" to "Mr. [Hyman] Woolf", which included those incurred in the maintenance of the *Mikveh*, which was located (most likely in Causewayhead) in his private house, at or near which there must have been an adequate supply of water, either from free-running "leats", or from standing pumps (which accessed underground streams), both sources being located around the town. Woolf charged two guineas yearly (subsequently doubled) for this service, which would have involved regular cleaning of the baths, the replenishment of the water, and, most likely, the superintendence of his wife, or other female members of the congregation.

Throughout the Minutes there is clear evidence that the members of the congregation were concerned to maintain the traditional devotion to study, and they organised weekly lessons for adults each Sabbath, as well as the routine instruction in Hebrew and religion for the children. Also observed was the watch night of learning on the eve of Passover and on Hoshanna Rabba, when the Rabbi was paid an additional fee, and, as fortification, spirits and refreshments were provided from the congregational funds. The Rabbi was also paid to oversee the preparation and provision of the Passover bread, and the cleansing and sweeping of the synagogue beforehand. Charitable donations took up a considerable proportion of the congregation's relatively small budget, and the Treasurer was even authorised to make such payments without consulting the President, provided that the sum involved did not exceed half a crown on any particular occasion. The members also operated a rota system to provide meals for itinerant beggars, and, sometimes the Rabbi (some of whom were single) also received this complimentary nourishment.[75]

The *Tikkunim* or Regulations of 1808.

On 19th October 1808, the senior members of the congregation formally ratified a set of regulations (eventually totalling about 18) drawn up in Yiddish. These show a community, anxious to order itself along strict lines, and its geographical isolation may have intensified and influenced this concern. The scope and detail of the 1808 regulations are relatively modest, compared with the larger congregations in Devon. From 1779, Plymouth had 64 regulations (increased to 26 pages in 1835), and in 1823, Exeter was to have 48 (revised in 1833). However, in 1844, the Penzance *Tikkunim* were to be revised and developed into a total of 95 rules for the benefit of only 11 full members.[76] The disproportion of these later arrangements would suggest that the Penzance congregation possessed an over-bureaucratic ethos, and such a culture may well have contributed to the tensions and fractiousness which came to characterise the congregation's meetings, especially as reflected in the later minute-books.

Penzance followed other congregations in its oligarchic structure, which distinguished between:

Baalei Batim - full members who possessed *Hezkat HaKehillah,* permanent congregational rights and vestry membership;

Toshavim - seatholders, paying an annual rental;

Orchim - strangers or guests, that is, all others who were not regular paying members, even though they may have been long term residents.

By 1845, while Exeter and Falmouth had a balance across these three categories, in Plymouth, the full members (19) comprised only a quarter of the total numbers, with seatholders (33) and strangers (on estimate, 30). In complete contrast to these congregations, Penzance was the exception with 11 full members, *no* seatholders, and 9 strangers.[77] This clearly suggests that the congregation was run and owned by an exclusive, and presumably, relatively affluent elite. It would seem inevitable, that in such a situation, congregational procedure came to serve the interests, primarily of its senior members.

The Penzance *Tikkunim:* a Summary Translation from the Yiddish.

"The Scroll of the Law and the holy objects belong to the Holy Congregation of Penzance.

Obligation on those called up to the reading of the Law to make a donation to the synagogue.

Obligation of every resident to attend synagogue at the stated times.

The Rabbi's obligation to collect donations, and when they are to be collected.

Obligation of the congregation to make a donation at the time of Yahrzeit (the anniversary of a death), and to come to prayers, or to pay a fine of half a guinea.

The whole congregation is obliged to attend personal celebrations (weddings, circumcision, bar Mitzvah), or to pay a fine of half a guinea.

The Rabbi is obliged to study before noon each day with the Gabbai (Treasurer).

The Rabbi is entitled to receive half a crown as part of his salary: before reading the Megillah (the Scroll of Esther read at the festival of Purim, but also a portion of the Mishnah or Oral Tradition, which relates to holy objects), and at Passover (for matzoth, unleavened bread) and after a woman gives birth (regarding aspects of ritual purity).

The Hatan Torah (the last man called to read the final section of the Torah at the end of the annual cycle of reading) and the Hatan Bereshith (the first man called to begin the reading of the first section of the new cycle) must donate (at Simchas Torah, the festival of Rejoicing in the Law) two shillings to charity and half a crown to the Rabbi.

On the eve of Shavuot (the festival of Weeks) and Hoshana Raba (during the festival of Tabernacles) congregants must come to study.

The Parnas (President of the synagogue) authorises donations for charity.

Hayim ben Benyamin (Hyman Woolf) to be President for life.
(Woolf did not, in fact, become President until 1811, after Lemon Hart left for London. This may suggest that some regulations, such as this one, were added after 1808, and the system of life-presidency was to be abandoned).

The congregation is obliged to give guests or visitors who come to it, food and drink, and these named householders (witnessed and signed by each), in an agreement between them: R. (*Rav*, as a term of respect) Hayim ben Benyamin (Hyman Woolf), R. Elimeleh ben Joseph (Elias Magnus) and R. Asher ben Hayim (Lemon Woolf) must give the guest two shillings if he comes on a Friday (Sabbath eve: to make up the minyan).

The names of householders,[78] each of which is obliged to make an annual payment:

President: Asher Laemle ben Eliezer (Lemon Hart) 20 pounds;

Treasurer: Hayim ben Benyamin (Hyman Woolf) 10 pounds;

Moses Hayim ben Abraham (Henry Ralph) 10 pounds;

Elimeleh ben Joseph (Elias Magnus) 4 pounds & 10 pence;

Asher Laemle ben Hayim (Lemon Woolf) 4 pounds & 10 pence;

The unmarried Asher (Laemle Isaac Jacobs; Frederick Hart, Lemon Jacobs) [blank];

Laemle ben Solomon Aharon ha-Levi (Lazarus Isaac Jacobs) I Guinea.

(It seems likely that these sums were reviewed annually, in that a later note in the regulations repeats the sums relating to Lemon Hart and Hyman Woolf.)

All householders promise to give (amounts unclear) to charity and for the repair of the cemetery.

Hayim ben Benyamin has allowed his Mikveh for the use of the congregation for

2 pounds every year. He agrees to give the key over to the women on the day of their immersion, and that he will keep it at all times in good order. He also agreed to keep the copper to heat water for the women who need it. The Parnas (President) is obliged every year to send (to London or to Israel) for an Etrog (citrus fruit) at the festival of Tabernacles for the congregation. When it is more than 1 guinea it must be paid for from the charity fund, but up to 1 guinea, every member of the congregation must pay from his pocket proportionately."

The regulations are signed by:
Hayim ben Benyamin, Elimeleh ben Joseph and Asher Laemle ben Hayim.

Of the seven members listed as annual subscribers, it has been noted that Lemon Hart (1768-1845), the President, was to leave for London in 1811. It seems likely that he had held the office of President before 1808, and that his grandfather, Abraham Hart (Solomon Lazarus, d.1784) and father, Eleazar (Lazarus) Hart (1739-1803) held senior positions in the congregation when it occupied the first synagogue of 1768. Lemon Jacobs, Lemon Hart's nephew, known as Frederick Hart (1790-1853) also left at some point to work in Lemon Hart's business in London. Frederick's brother, Jacob (1784-1846) also took the name *Hart* and joined the Hart firm in London. Their father, Lazarus Isaac Jacobs, is likely to have died in 1811, in that his name does not appear in the list of members' subscriptions after August that year. He may be buried in the Jewish cemetery, but, if so, his headstone has not survived. Hyman Woolf (c. 1732-1820) and his son, Lemon Woolf (1783-1848) remained in Penzance for the rest of their lives.

Of the other signatories, Henry Ralph had been trading in Penzance as a Grocer and Pawnbroker from at least 1804, and he was a licensed Navy Agent by 1809. His name and signature appear frequently in the minutes and accounts in the early 1800s, but not after 1811, when he may have left Penzance. By 1814 he had moved to Plymouth Dock (Devonport) where he is said to have become a leading member of the "Dock Minyan" of Jews who traded there, and met privately for their own worship.[79] He may have been related to Abraham Ralph of Barnstaple (-1805), who had traded in that town as a silversmith for over forty years, hosting the "synagogue assemblies" in his house. At least two of his children were also silversmiths, and one, Lewis, a Naval Agent in Plymouth in 1812.[80] Before Henry Ralph left Penzance, on 19th October 1810, he formally donated three ritual items to the synagogue "for ever". These were two curtains for the Ark, one for general use, and a white one for use on the High Holy Days, and another white cover for the reading desk, also for use on the High Holy Days. On the same occasion, Lemon Hart donated a Scroll of the Law with a silver *yad*, or hand, for reading the script, both of which had belonged to his deceased father-in-law, Lazarus Solomon of London. Together with these Hart signed over "Six large Brass Candlesticks, two large Chandaliers (*sic.*) & one Curtain of Red Sattin (*sic.*) with white borders.".

The remaining signatory, Elias Magnus (1775-1850) who traded as a Wine and Spirit Merchant in the town, was to become the second husband of Lemon Hart's sister, Rebecca (1766-1841) after the death of Lazarus Jacobs. By 14th April 1811 the minutes record that Magnus had become the congregation's Treasurer, responsible for the collection of subscriptions. On 6th October 1811 he was paid 12 shillings and 6 pence in expenses for bringing a *shochet* from Truro. Although he is not named, the *shochet* was most likely Eliezar Lipman, the Rabbi of Falmouth from around 1790-1813. It would seem that Magnus' business in the town was not as profitable as Lemon Hart's, and from 1813 Magnus began to fall into debt with the congregation. However, he re-paid his subscription ("and other owings") of almost 7 pounds on 23rd September 1816, and remained an officer of the congregation until at least July 1817. On 18th April 1819, the minutes record that "Elias Magnus, having withdrawn from this congregation without any cause, and withheld payment due, the sum of three pounds & three shillings, shall no longer be considered to have any right or title". This rupture in relations appears to have been final, and he is not mentioned in the minutes thereafter. It is at this time that he is likely to have moved with his family to London, where Rebecca Magnus died in November 1841, and Elias in 1850.[81]

The congregation's income came from members' subscriptions, donations from visiting "strangers" (often from Cornish towns, but sometimes from family members who had migrated from Penzance), and additional offerings from members and others who attended regularly. The accounts also show the precise figures paid for seat rentals. This pattern was to continue throughout the life of the congregation and was just sufficient to keep heads above water, and even at this early stage allowed scope for charitable purposes. An early note made on 1st October 1809 committed Lemon Hart, Henry Ralph, Elias Magnus and Lemon Woolf to contribute a total of 7 shillings a week "towards *Leb Henna* [Judah from Hannau] an infirm old man for his maintenance", subject to the condition that he "is to be at Penzance every night if possible to prevent any accident happening to him from travelling to distant places." Leb Henna, also known as "Mr. Levy" was to receive these charitable payments until 1817, when the accounts of 26th April that year show that the congregation met his burial costs. He was interred in the Jewish cemetery, in the section reserved for the poor, with a simple headstone, as *Judah ben Naphtali*, and he was reputed to have been the oldest Jew in Cornwall at the time of his death.[82] It seems likely that he had no immediate family. Later, the congregation was also to meet the burial costs of other local Jews. Leb Henna was not the only recipient of the congregation's charity, however, and regular offerings are recorded for the "charity box" and for another unnamed "poor man" (on 23rd November 1812). "Charitable donations appear to have taken up quite a considerable portion of the slender budget of the Community." [83]

It would seem that the congregation's charity extended even to its miscreants, and much later, on 29th April 1821, an intriguing entry in the accounts records that 14 shillings had been paid out "in achieving Godfrey from Prison". He remains unidentified, and the circumstances and justification for his incarceration are not known. His imprisonment would have been an extremely unpleasant experience. Records for the Corporation of Penzance from as far back as June 1662 refer to an "Accompt of Disbursements", to include the sum of 4 shillings "For clensinge the prisons".[84] In 1803, James Neild, a campaigner for the improvement of prison conditions, had reported: "Penzance Borough Prison (generally and more properly called the Black Hole) is a dark room with a double door at the end of the Corn

Market, a great part of which is not of sufficient height for the prisoner to stand upright in. Straw on the floor. The only light or ventilation it receives is from an aperture 12ins by 5½ins, which opens to the staircase, and being a borrowed light, serves only to make the darkness visible. The annoyance of rats in this place is terrible; so that the wretched prisoner, ever on the watch, may perhaps dose (*sic.*) in feverish anxiety, but never knows the balm of peaceful sleep." Neild also visited the Penzance Debtors' Prison in the Green Market: "This wretched prison, which is in the back yard of a public house, is about twelve feet square and six feet high, with a necessary in one corner, the floor extremely damp…without a fireplace, and lighted and ventilated by one small iron-grated window, without casement or glass to keep out the cold."[85]

The financial regulation of the small congregation's affairs was no easy matter, and the issue of loans, debts and fines indicates this. In April and October of 1815, two such matters are recorded (in extensive detail, in Hebrew script). In the early part of the year, the difficulty in maintaining a *minyan* for the Sabbath is reflected in the comment (in Yiddish) that some members appeared to prefer spending their time in the "coffee-house" (written in Yiddish) to attendance at the synagogue. It was agreed that when no minyan is possible, each member who does attend pays 6 shillings to charity. Presumably absentees are to be fined. In October, the *shochet* (then Barnet Asher Simmons, but not named in the accounts) must have found himself in financial difficulties, and had borrowed some money from a member (or members) of the congregation, but had failed to repay it. The loan may have been repaid from congregational funds, because the instruction was drawn up that this method of repayment was not permitted. Funds were also raised by the congregation through members' purchase by auction of "honours", such as that of being last to read the Torah, or on the occasion of other special readings (1818). Bachelors, however, were not permitted to do so, and those who had previously enjoyed this privilege could be exempted from doing so.

On 14th April 1811, in anticipation of Lemon Hart's imminent departure for London, the Minutes acknowledged the role that the Hart family had played in the founding of the congregation by drafting the following regulation (in cursive Hebrew script):

"It is agreed the Penzance Congregation will mention the following names wherever Prayer for the Souls of the Departed is recited in the Synagogue –

Rabbi Abraham ben *He'chaver* [Learned Man] Asher [Abraham Hart];
Rabbi Eliezar ben Rabbi Abraham [Eliezar or Lazarus Hart];
A Special Blessing on every Sabbath and Yom Tov for Honourable Asher Laemle ben Eliezer [Lemon Hart] and his wife and children.
All future members of the Penzance Congregation are bound by this".

Lemon Hart left for London in 1811, but his name appears as a subscriber to the congregation up to the end of that year, but not beyond. His duties as Parnas were taken over by Hyman Woolf. Lemon Jacobs (Frederick Hart) and his brother Jacob Hart continued as subscribers from London until 1812. The loss of Lemon Hart, together with his son, David, then about twelve, together with the earlier departure of Lemon Hart's nephews, Jacob James Jacobs and Frederick Jacobs (who became *Hart* in the family firm) may well have placed the congregation's *minyan*, or quorum of 10 adult men for Prayers, under threat. It may be that for this reason, on 24th October 1813, the congregation added another regulation to their Minutes [again, in Hebrew script]: "It is agreed that it is the duty of the *Shamas* [Beadle] or the Rabbi that they should inform each member of the congregation every Friday when Prayers are going to be held and whoever fails to attend is to be fined five shillings, but those members who live elsewhere are exempt unless they are in the town for *Shabbos* or *Yom Tov*".

It is noticeable in the accounts that from 1810 subscriptions were recorded for men who lived outside Penzance. Initially these were from the Jacob and Joseph families from Redruth: Samuel Jacob (1778-1860) who lived for a time at Hayle, his brother, Jacob Jacob (1774-1853) in Camborne, signing himself, in Hebrew, as of "Cambron", and (Moses) Isaac Joseph (-1834) who had originally lived in Falmouth. The two Jacob brothers were admitted as full members in October 1813. In 1815, the name of Israel Levy (-1824) of Truro also appears. Solomon Ezekiel (*c.*1786-1867) of Penzance became a member of the congregation in 1817, and Levy Jacob (1788-1824) a brother of the two Jacob men, above, in 1819. These men would have helped the congregation's numbers and finances, and such applications were addressed in a regulation marked as "No. 14", on 6th July 1817: "Any one applying for membership must have been approved by a majority of the members of the congregation & pay 2 Guineas unless the son of an existing member, then ½ Guinea". It has been mentioned previously that from 1819 the congregation's accounts show that they paid rent for the synagogue to William Eva of Gwinear, the sum being recorded as 3 guineas per half-year, 6 guineas per year being the sum paid to the previous leaseholder, J. B. Sutherland. The separate rental for the burial ground is recorded as "Paid Rent (of I guinea) [for the] House of Life up to 25th March 1819". In April 1820, Isaac Simons of Truro became a member of the congregation, although his name appears as a subscriber in 1819. The youngest son of Samuel (Solomon) Simons (1740-1832) and Rosa Ann Moses (1757-1838), he had been born around 1796, and had married Rosetta Jacobs (*c.*1800-) the daughter of Lazarus Jacobs and Rebecca Hart (1766-1841) the sister of Lemon Hart. Isaac Simons (who was trading in Falmouth by 1841, and is likely to have remained there) appears in the minutes as Symons, and in the same year the name of an Alexander Symons, who is not known for certain to have been a relative, is also recorded. (A Samuel Symons was resident in Penzance from at least 1835 to 1860.[86] He may have been related to Alexander Symons, although this Samuel Symons may not have been Jewish). Alexander Symons may have been connected with Harman Semmens (Hyman Simmons) of Truro, and his business partner, Lyon Levy, whose names appear from 1820, as does that of E. (Emanuel) Cohen of Redruth. These new members helped to some extent to improve the congregation's income, but this was offset by the failure of others to pay their contributions. The expulsion, in April 1819, of the congregation's former Treasurer, Elias Magnus, has been mentioned. In 1821, the same form of expulsion was imposed upon another congregation member, Aaron Selig (1782-1841) a Jeweller, and one of its former incumbent ministers. He had likewise "withdrawn from the Congregation and also attempted to make a great disturbance amongst them and withheld paying two pounds and ten shillings due to them after having demanded the Same Several times." He was eventually reinstated, but his conflicts with the congregation were to resurface over the next ten years, and indicate that, despite its growth, there were ongoing tensions within the Penzance congregation. 1821 may well have brought further problems in the practice of allocating the honours for reading in the synagogue for special occasions, because further regulations were drawn up regarding their distribution.

Apart from the salaries of the incumbent ministers, and the congregation's rental payments, the upkeep and maintenance of congregational property remained a priority throughout this time. In 1813 a "Copper Sistern" and a "New Lock" were fitted, and another lock in 1814, one of these requiring "testting"(sic.) in 1815. The same year records a payment to Harvey, a carpenter, of £3 7s., and in 1816 the sum of £6.00 to *Hayyim* (the rabbi Hyman Selig) for repairs to a Torah Scroll, further repairs to it being carried out in 1818. 1816 saw a payment to a local tradesman for unspecified repairs, and to another, Mr. Edmonds, a painter. John Wallis, who had been involved in the construction of the 1808 synagogue, was paid for work in 1818, and a bill from Harvey the carpenter was settled in 1819. In 1820 a mason was paid for repairs to a wall and for stones, although this may have been in the burial ground. 1822 again saw payments to Wallis, for unspecified "Repairs", as well as the routine payment to the *shabbos goia* for candles and cleaning materials, and the regular purchase of "12 Wax Lights". Year by year, the congregation was also meticulous in observing the ritual and celebratory aspects of congregational life, and sums were always set aside for the various items required at the time of the festivals. The obligation to accumulate a fund for charitable purposes was strictly administered by a Charity Officer (*gabbai* or *tsedek*), charitable donations and payments being recorded each half-year in the accounts. When the Minute Book begins in 1808, it is noticeable that the balance held in the Congregational Fund shows a healthy credit balance in double figures, with some of the approximate sums recorded[87] as £18 to £35 (1810), £16 to 28 (1811), £27 to £30 (1813), £51 (1814), £31 to £52 (1815), £27 to £33 to £17 (1816) and £32 (1818). Naturally there would be a fluctuation throughout the year, and some of the higher figures may reflect the income generated from loans secured from the Bolitho Bank to carry out the improvements to the new synagogue building. Another factor in the solvency of the Congregation's finances at this stage may be the input from the relatively prosperous Hart family, even after their departure for London. However, from 1819 onwards (until the accounts end in 1829) there is a marked decline in the size of the Fund, and the balance in hand rarely exceeds single figures. It is not surprising that the supervision of the Congregation's finances became a vital factor in its survival, and when much later, in 1844, the New Regulations were drawn up, there were eleven rules given to the matter of Revenue.

On 24th January 1823, on the Friday Sabbath Eve (12th Shevat 5583) a Service of Dedication of the Synagogue took place, during which the Scrolls of the Law were taken around the synagogue seven times (as they would be at the festival of Simhat Torah, or Rejoicing in the Law, held in October). It would seem likely that the occasion marked the fifteenth anniversary of the new synagogue, and possibly the installation of a new Ark of the Covenant, or the acquisition of new *rimmonim*, torah scroll caps or bells. A handwritten note on a copy of the original order of service, gives the names of "I. Isaacs" and "J. Myers", both of Plymouth. The handwriting appears to give the abbreviation *Cat*, that is "Ca(bine)t, although this could be read as *Cap* or *Cab*. Isaacs is recorded as a Maker, and the latter as a Manufacturer. An original copy of the service is likely to have been preserved by Rabbi B. A. Simmons, although he was not the incumbent minister at the time.[88] Curiously, no specific mention is made in the congregational accounts of expenditure for this occasion, but the following year saw extensive repairs to the synagogue, payments being made to four or five local tradesmen, including work on the windows, damaged during a storm ("broken by hail Weather"), further repairs to a lock, and for a quantity of lime for masonry work to the walls and roof. New "Socketts" were also purchased for the synagogue's brass candlesticks, together with a new *shofar*. Repairs to or the replacement of locks occur throughout the accounts at this time, and in 1825, a local blacksmith was called in, apparently to install a new padlock (part of the entry is illegible). From these references, it seems possible that the synagogue's security was at risk, although other properties in the town may have experienced similar problems.

From 1823, some existing members, including Isaac Symons and Samuel Jacob, entered into a formal written agreement to purchase seating rights. At the same time, the former also became responsible for the administration of the congregation's charity fund. On 12th April 1825, Henry Levin (1798-1877), originally from Stockholm, and an existing member of the congregation, became a privileged member, or *bal*, upon the initial payment of 1 guinea, and agreed to pay yearly the sum of 4 guineas "to be paid monthly if demanded". On 23rd April, Abraham and Isaac Davidson (who may have been brothers), Henry Levi (possibly a son of Israel Levy of Truro) and Solomon Johnson became new members. Henry Levi's signature does not appear, but he is recorded subsequently amongst subscribers as *Harry Levy*, and is distinguished in the accounts from Henry Levin (or Lavin) who became a privileged member on 12th April 1825. In 1824, Levi Jacobs had died, and from 1825 the name of his widow, Sophia Jacobs, appears in the list of offerings. Her reduced circumstances are reflected in that, in place of her late husband's offering of 2 guineas, she makes a contribution of 15s, and then, regularly of 10s 6d up to 1828, increasing this to 1 guinea in 1829 (when the records break off). Another name to appear, once only, for September 1825, is that of an Isaac Pollack. It is not known if he was related to his namesake who had lived in Penryn in the 1760s, and he may have been a visitor.

On 26th August 1825, a letter was received by the congregation from a Dr. Messina, who was a physician and, possibly, an Italian Jew: "To Mr. L. Woolf and the Instituted Members of the Penzance Synagogue – Gentlemen, I beg your Acceptance of a Cocked Hat, Gown and Cuffs [barely legible] as a Donation, and if you permit them to be worn at all times of Public Devotion you will oblige the donor". Presumably, Messina was already living in the town, and may have been known to the congregation. On 2nd September, he agreed "to become a member or a full (privileged) member" paying one guinea "entrance" and four guineas annu-

ally for a seat. During the next year he made a voluntary offering to the congregation of £1 7s 10d, and took an active part in vestry meetings, his signature appearing on several occasions to ratify the Minutes. Very soon after his admission
Messina was present at a meeting at the beginning of September when a memorandum was drawn up relating to the "calling up" of Aaron Selig's son (Benjamin
Aaron), who was born around 1814, and would have been approaching the time
for his bar mitzvah. Aaron Selig's unreliable record in the making payments to the
congregation is reflected in the fact that an offering was to be made to charity upon
the occasion by the father, and it was also to be made in advance. This condition is
clearly stated, and in the event of non-payment, the son would "not be allowed to
be called up". It would seem that this may have resulted in resentment on the part
of Aaron Selig, who might have raised it as a cause for controversy in the wider
Jewish community. An addendum notes that "It is agreed that any Member that
shall divulge or disclose any of the proceedings this day shall be fined 10/6." The
memorandum and addendum were signed separately by six members, including
Messina. The conditions laid upon Aaron Selig were, in fact, rescinded on 16th April,
when, at the same meeting it was decided that when members' subscriptions were
sufficient to take the accounts "out of debt, that the seats in the Synagogue shall be
reduced [in cost] in proportion". Messina's name appears in the accounts of 16th
April 1826, when he was paid for his services in attending the rabbi, Hart Symons,
who had been ill. The same accounts of 16th indicate another payment to an "Eva"
(not the synagogue's freeholder) a local painter, for his bill, and reveals the name
of the *shabbos goia*, the cleaning lady, as a Mary Kenefic, who appears in the accounts
for 24th September that year as "the woman", but is subsequently named.[89] That
year, Bodilly, a Glazier was paid, presumably for replacing a broken pane, and a
new "Killing Knife" for the *shochet* was purchased at 13 shillings, with carriage costs
of 7s 6d, most likely from London. Sometime towards the end of 1826, an undated
note indicates that Aaron Selig had once more suffered expulsion from the congregation, having been "at variance" with it, but was to be readmitted, with "his
former rights which he possessed" restored and "all former agreements which was
[*sic.*] entered into as relating to him shall be considered as null & void". On the 24th
September 1826, Selig's formal membership payment was agreed, including his
purchase of the seat of John Messina, whose next, and last subscription was paid
up, when the accounts note that he left on 30th November that year. Very soon after
this a Dr. Messina, said to have been a former physician to the Emperor Napoleon
I, appeared in Portsmouth, and can be taken as the same person.[90]

1827 saw payments made to a Mr. Nicholls for "One Year's Insurance Aliance
250" (the latter figure being the amount of cover for the synagogue), to a Mr.
Thomas, Mason, to Ellis, Carpenter for repairs and for "various times varnishing",
and to Mr. Batten for Timber. A curious, unexplained and un-itemised payment was
made to "Constable", and another to Selig, who may have become the Charity
Officer, who paid out 3 guineas to a poor family. The former minister and *shochet*,
B. A. Simmons, appears twice in the minutes for 1828. The congregation appears to
have operated a system of bidding for the renewal of seats. Accordingly, members
who could afford to do so, albeit temporarily, could increase the sum they had
previously paid for their seat, to move to a better one. On 4th May 1828, for an

annual fee of £3 15s, Henry Levin took over the seat of B. A. Simmons, who then, for £4 10s, took the seat of Abraham Joseph, a former Reader in Prayers (1826-1827. The latter moved to a seat vacated by Samuel Jacob, for £5 10s. Presumably, Jacob had found his annual outlay was not viable. B. A. Simmons was also appointed Charity Officer. In 1828 the congregation raised funds for the purchase of a new *Sifre (Sefer) Torah* (Scroll). Several previous references in the accounts indicate that it had been necessary to repair the congregation's *Sefer* on a number of occasions. By the end of August, the sum of £14 13s 1d had been raised, mainly from members of the congregation itself, but also from local Jews. Most of the names of subscribers are familiar from the accounts, and most members gave donations several times. The new rabbi, Myer Stadthagen ("Mr. Myar"), who had arrived the previous autumn is noted as a subscriber, along with an unknown *Marcus*, an Isaac Lazarus (who is known to have traded as a watchmaker and hardwareman in Hayle from 1839), a second reference to a Lazarus, although the forename, in abbreviation, appears to be *Leb*, a "Mr. Rosenthall" (Gabriel Rosenthal from St. Ives) and a "Mr. Macato". It is not known if the last named was from the affluent Mocatto family of London.[91] This period in the Jewish community's history would seem to mark its highpoint in terms of membership and resources. The new *Sefer* was not the only item of major expenditure. The accounts for August also indicate unspecified payments to local tradesmen: £12 to a Mr. Ansell and £3 to L. Moyle, further minor payments for locks and roof repairs, and an agreement on 12th October to increase the rabbi's salary from £25 to £30 per annum. Why the accounts and minutes break off in 1829 is not clear. Two fragments of income are given for 1830 and 1831, but nothing more. Whether the accounts lapsed, because of a serious fall in the congregation's fortunes, or were indeed kept, but have been lost, is not known. Sadly, the final item to end the period up to 1829 is a record of yet another controversy with Aaron Selig. He had "sent a message that it was his determination (underlined) not to pay" [presumably his seat rental] "having also told that he would (underlined) not pay". The reasons for this are not given, and it does not seem that he was expelled, but his right to be called as a reader during the service was withdrawn.

From 1830 to 1842.

Although minutes and accounts for the congregation have not been identified for this period, it is possible from other sources to outline some details of its affairs. There would have been discussions with local land owners regarding the site of the cemetery. It has been mentioned previously that, in 1834, Canon John Rogers, Rector of Mawnan, sold off part of the land around the burial ground in the Leskinnick Terrace area to Thomas Barham. This included a meadow which was called the "Jews Field", and a section (the higher part) of the "Lower Jews Field". The following year, Rogers granted a 99 year lease to Richard Rowe, a mason, to build a house on "part of the Jews Burial Ground", at an annual rent of 13 shillings. In 1838 and 1841, Rogers agreed to the further development of Leskinnick Terrace, and granted building leases for plots in the "Higher Jews Burial Ground Field". The Jewish congregation may not have used these areas for burials, or have had any direct claim upon them under their previous leasehold agreements. The adjacent "fields" may well have acquired their name by association with the burial ground, but it does seem likely that the cemetery was only partially enclosed at this time. The danger of incursion into the cemetery from the building development, and the consequent proximity of dwelling-houses, where, before, there had been open land, presented the congregation with the need to consider what action should be taken to protect the cemetery's integrity. The population of the town had been increasing for some time, and it would have been obvious to the congregation for some years that such development was in prospect. They must have been setting aside funds to meet the eventuality of buying the freehold to the burial ground and completely enclosing it, and negotiations with Rogers and Barham would have taken place well before the congregation acquired the cemetery's freehold in 1844-1845.

The concern to acquire freehold possession of their property also extended to the synagogue itself. On 27th December 1837 a release of conveyance of the freehold was signed between William Eva of Gwinear and his wife Barbara to "Lemon Woolf, merchant, Aaron Selig, jeweller, Henry Levin, jeweller, Moses Woolf, brewer, and Benjamin Selig, watchmaker, all of Penzance." The consideration was the sum of £160, and the sale included a "dwelling-house in New St, Penzance, together with an adjoining house (formerly two messuages)". These houses (built most likely in the 18th century and, possibly contemporaneous with the first synagogue of 1768) were added to the synagogue from 1838. It would seem that the house which was adjacent to the rear of the synagogue was incorporated into it to enlarge its seating capacity and to extend the Womens' Gallery. The Adjoining house appears to have been retained to provide rooms for a communal Vestry, kitchen, washroom, lavatory and storage facilities, and presumably, some form of connecting access was opened up between this house and the newly-enlarged synagogue itself. The congregation had set up a building fund for all of these works, most likely in 1836. The 1808 synagogue had been built to accommodate only a small number of people, and the third, enlarged building only held about fifty people. In 1839, Richard Edmonds published an important statistical analysis of Penzance.[92] In this he gave the expanded synagogue's "sittings" as fifty, most likely meaning the maximum that it could hold, rather than the actual number of seats. He also gave the average "Sunday" (sic.) i.e. "Sabbath" congregation as 25, stated that weekday attendance was seldom 10, and that the total number of the congregation was "14 men, excluding women and children". On Friday 2nd October, 1840, the West Briton carried the notice:

"NEW SYNAGOGUE – On Sunday last, the Jews of Penzance consecrated their splendid new Synagogue. It was said to be a very interesting ceremony, and was witnessed by a great number of the most respectable inhabitants, who appeared highly delighted." Neither of the two houses that were added to the congregation's property was retained as a dwelling-place, and there is no evidence that one of the houses ever became "the rabbi's house".[93] The ministers who do appear in public records have residential addresses elsewhere in the town. The only exception to this might seem to be that of Marcus Spiro, who in 1864 appears in Cornish's trade directory as the synagogue's rabbi at 2, New Street, but this is by association with his profession, and his residential address is given as Causewayhead.

In 1845, J. S. Courtney published his *Guide to Penzance*, in which he listed seven religious buildings, including the synagogue, and dismissed them collectively as functional, but lacking in any architectural merit (he had, in fact, referred to the synagogue previously in 1839).[94] He says in his guide that he will give further details of these buildings in an appendix, but, curiously, did not do so. He did not include a description of the exterior or interior of the synagogue, which of course, he may not have entered.[95] No description appears in any of the other town guides of the time. By 1847, it would seem that the total Jewish population of Penzance was about fifty, and that in 1851 the number attending the synagogue for worship was 30, with 6 seat-holders, that is, permanent paying members.[96] On 31st March 1851, B. A. Simmons, then the "Minister" completed the return for the Ecclesiastical Census of Places of Public Religious Worship. He recorded, in a somewhat misleading entry, that the building had been erected in 1838, meaning the third extension. His figures for seating and attendance are given as 30 Sittings and 6 Free (paid) seats, with further free space or standing room as 20 by 6 feet. He recorded the last attendance[97] as 16 (morning), 5 (afternoon) and 14 (evening), and the average attendance[98] as 16 to 25 (morning), 5 to 12 (afternoon) and 5 to 12 (evening). These figures give some impression of the size and resources of the Jewish congregation from 1830 to the resumption of the minutes in 1843, and up to 1851. The enlarged synagogue of 1838-1840 was still a relatively modest building. Edward Jamilly visited the building in 1958 when it was used as a Christian place of worship, but when "it had only been partially dismantled". He has described its exterior so: "Roughly rectangular and quite lofty it had thick walls of stone rubble, the upper part hung with slates, covered by a low-pitched roof hipped four ways". Internally, it had "a pair of tall sash windows with semi-circular heads set about 6 feet apart in the east wall...Bench seats, each with a locker underneath to store prayer books, ran along the north and south walls, which were panelled to a height of 5 feet and plastered above. A gallery extended along the north and west walls, over the entrance, its front plain-panelled to half height, with a carved wood lattice above. In the centre of the ceiling, from an ornamental panel about 6 feet in diameter, hung an elaborate candelabrum over the reading desk; both objects have now disappeared". The contrast with the more ornate synagogue of the more populous and prosperous Falmouth congregation is striking, but although "The synagogue was only about 24 feet square and 29 feet high, yet by a miracle of orderly planning completely fitted in every detail".[99]

The Regulations of 1844 and the Minute Books 1843-1892.

The records of the congregation resume on 12th March 1843 and continue to 1882, and include the detailed revised regulations of 1844. There is a break in the record from 1882 to 1885, but with one item of inventory for May 1883. The records then cover the last years of the congregation from 1885 to 1892. The early accounts contain extensive pages in Hebrew script, especially when detailing the appointment and conditions of service for each incumbent minister. There is a distinct change in the character and form of the later records from 1843 in that they are mainly in English with very little use of Hebrew script, and they consist of summary outlines of meetings and of copies of letters rather than detailed accounts. The strict use of the two columns of accounts, balancing income against expenditure, so characteristic of the records from 1807, has been abandoned entirely. This might not seem at first to be of any great consequence, and, if the later Minutes had been recorded in much greater detail, the transition to narrative summary might have compensated for the abandonment of the previous practice. However, the meticulous detail of the earlier accounts allow a surprisingly colourful and substantive picture to emerge of the Congregation's ongoing life, practice and social development, which the later documents do not provide with such precision or consistency.

If there had been a cessation of congregational record-keeping from 1829, or a decline in its regularity, it would seem that this situation came to be regarded as unsatisfactory, possibly resulting in a deterioration in the congregation's affairs and arrangements, because one of the first decisions noted in the new 1843 minutes is that a select committee of five members should be charged with the task of "forming a code of Rules for the better government of the Congregation". The first meeting of all of the seat-holding members was held on 12th March 1843 "for the purpose of determining the Amount to be Subscribed towards the Salary of the Chief Rabbi. It was agreed that the amount should be Five Pounds Pr year – the same to be raised by a tax of Twelve Shillings – on every Seat Holder". Those present were Lemon Woolf, Henry Joseph, Henry Levin, Moses Woolf, Moses. B. Simmons and Morris Hart Harris. There seems to have been a determination that meetings should be held more frequently, and another took place the next month on 9th April "for the purpose of auditing the Acts. & The ballance (*sic.*) in hand being £11: 2: 9 it was agreed to pay into the Bank Ten Pounds". The bank, most likely the Bolitho Bank, also held the congregation's leases. At the same time Henry Joseph was re-elected as Treasurer and the resolution was passed that "all members are bound to attend every Quarterly and especial meetings under the penalty of 2/-6". It has been noted that it was a feature of the Penzance congregation's membership that it drew subscriptions and enjoyed donations from Jews who lived in other towns, including Hayle, Camborne, Redruth and Truro. The congregation authorised its President, Lemon Woolf to write, on 23rd May to Henry Harris (1787-1872) of 8, Lemon Street, Truro, who had once lived in Penzance. He was the son of Samuel Harris (1754-1824) who had come from London and had settled in Falmouth. In his letter, Lemon Woolf acknowledged "The uniform kindness that you have always shown towards our Congregation & the many donations received" and offered him privileged membership. Henry Harris replied on 25th May accepting the honorary membership "more enhanced by me by Penzance being my native town".

On 16th September, the accounts were again audited (but details not recorded in the minutes) and the "flourishing state of the finances, it was resolved that £10 should be paid into the Bank – reducing the amount to - £70". It would seem that the congregation had taken out a mortgage to complete its purchase of the freehold of the synagogue and the two adjoining houses from William Eva in 1837, and, no doubt, to complete its extension and refurbishment. On 25th December, Henry Harris's privileged membership saw his sons (Morris Hart and Samuel) being considered for this status "having a seat 12 months & paying for the same". The same meeting again saw an audit of the accounts, and (Samuel) "Mr. Oppenheim"

(1800-1869) was fined for non-attendance "unless he can show good cause", which, later, he did, and was excused upon his apology. His absence from vestry meetings is noted in future years.

On 31ˢᵗ March 1844 "it was resolved to pay £15 off the mortgage", and the committee was formed "for the purpose of framing a code of Rules". At the same time a rota was drawn up to cover the next ten years (5605 to 5615 in the Jewish calendar) for members' participation in the Festival of *Simchat Torah* (Rejoicing in the Law) held in October. Two men were chosen from the seat-holders for each year, one to read the end of the Torah cycle (the *Hatan Torah*) and the other to read the beginning (the *Hatan Bereshith*). It is notable that more signatures (ten in all) appear in the minutes for this meeting than for any other in the congregation's records.

The New Regulations of 1844.

The Committee began work on these soon after 31ˢᵗ March, and they were completed by 3ʳᵈ August. They proved themselves over-zealous to a degree and produced a total of 95 detailed rules to regulate a dwindling congregation of fewer than 12 seat-holders.[100] Traditionally, the congregations at Exeter and Plymouth had managed on fewer regulations for significantly larger congregations. It is an irony that by the middle of the 19ᵗʰ century, Jewish communities in the South-West began to decline rapidly in numbers. The Exeter congregation had disbanded by 1880, and although Plymouth declined in the 1840s it had revived by 1881. In Penzance it would seem that by 1849, the total number of seat holders was 8, falling to 4 by 1874, and in the same period, in Falmouth (where congregational records have been lost, where the synagogue held about 80 seats) the number of Jewish families has been estimated as falling from 14 in 1842, to 3 in 1874.[101]

Where in the Regulations the terms for officials, festivals and ritual items or practices occur in Hebrew script, they are indicated below in italics. The original numbering has been retained, although, after the cancelled items, this was not amended by the committee's scribe.[102]

Rules

1. "It is the duty of every (indistinct, possibly "Jew") regularly to attend Divine Service in the Synagogue, to treat the Prayers with due devotion and to perform the Ceremonies with suitable reverence".

2. The second rule establishes that the synagogue's traditional liturgy "that termed *Minhag Poland* (the Polish Rite) "is to be continued according to that system. The *schul* (synagogue) shall be opened for Divine Service every Friday evening, *shabbos* (Saturday) Morning, Afternoon and Evening and every Holiday (Holy Day): also on (the Festivals are all listed in Hebrew) and for *milah* (a circumcision) [and] *yahrzeit* (the anniversary of a death)". The times of opening of the synagogue are given in relation to the *shabbos* before *Pesach* (Passover, in the spring) to the end of

Simchat Torah (Rejoicing in the Law, in October) as eight in the morning from Spring, and from half past eight from the beginning of Winter.

Government

3. The Congregation shall be governed by its Warden (*Parnas*) and Privileged Members (*Baal Baatim*).

4. The Warden "shall have the general superintendence of the affairs of the Congregation, whether relative to the state of the community in general or to the Synagogue in particular, the whole according to the Laws, Resolutions & Regulations established for such purpose".

5. "The Parnas shall have the charge of all monies coming into his hands for the use of the Congregation & its expenditure & shall dispense the Charitable Donations to the poor such relief not to exceed 5/- within six months to one individual".

6. In the absence of the Parnas, his duty is devolved to the *Gabbai* (Treasurer), "the last past officer" (a previous Warden or Gabbai) or the oldest privileged member.

Congregation

7. "The Congregation forming the Community is classed thus":
Privileged members (*Baal Baatim*);
Full members (permanent or established paying seat-holders);
Jewish residents (*Toshavim*) who may hold a seat for 12 months;
Strangers (*Orachim*): "all other descriptions of Persons" (this would include the poor and visitors).

Duties of the Honorary Officers

8. The President (Parnas) is responsible for assuming the duties of the *Segan* (who calls people up to read the Torah during the service) "on all occasions when the same is not otherwise disposed of".

9. The *Segan* is to "issue orders for the celebration of Marriages and for the Burials belonging to the Congregation & as well regulate the payment of debts due from the parties to the Congregation at such periods".

10. "Proclamations (which must at all times be in English) shall not be made in the Synagogue without the special licence of the *Segan* nor shall any paper be affixed to the Synagogue or the buildings attached thereto without the like permission".

11. The *Segan* is also made responsible for the allocation of special honours, specifically *aliyot* (being called up to read the Torah) and readings on festivals and special days (*yom tov*). When allocating these honours he must do so "according to the seniority of members excepting such members who are in arrears whose cases come under the consideration of the Congregation".

12. "No person shall (make) more than one blessing (after the calling up to the Torah) where a donation is offered".

13. "It is the duty of the *Parnas* to attend to the letting and regulating of the seats in the synagogue; vacant seats shall be let at any time when application is made for the same".

14. "It is also his province to superintend and order all repairs immediately required in the Synagogue or other premises belonging thereto provided the expence (*sic.*) do (*sic.*) not exceed Two Pounds. It is also his duty to purchase any article required provided the expence do not exceed Two Pounds, *ethrogim* [citrus fruits for *Succot*, or Tabernacles] and candles excepted."

15. "He shall keep an Inventory of all of the property of the Synagogue belonging to the Congregation and deliver the same to his successor in office."

16. "He must render his Accounts at each quarterly meeting."

17. "It is also his duty to [note: in conjunction with his colleagues – scored through] to superintend the distribution of *mitzvos* (charitable payments) to the poor".

18. "In case of the demise of any person in the *kehillah* (congregation) it is the duty of the *Parnas* to have everything arranged in due time for the Funeral, which it is his province to see conducted with all possible respect and decorum".

19. "It is his duty to see that the Burial Ground is kept in proper order & to direct any repairs that may be required not exceeding Ten Shillings & Sixpence".

20. "All donations collected at a funeral must be immediately distributed to the Poor".

Election of the Officers

21. This regulation was scored through with two lines, and marked in bold as "Cancelled". "No More being perpetual, the *Parnas* [and] the *gabbai* shall be elected at our yearly meeting by...." (illegible, with the Hebrew scored through). This seems to suggest that the President's office, no longer being perpetual ("There no more being a perpetual *Parnas*, the *gabbai*...") the office of the Treasurer should follow suit. Presumably, the election was to be by a quorum of senior or seat-paying members.

22. "The officer, after being duly elected, should he refuse to accept office he shall pay a fine of ten Shillings & sixpence".
23. "In all cases where the persons elected to any Honorary offices decline accepting the same a new election shall take place as early as possible".

24. "Members related to each other in the following degrees of consanguinity cannot be elected for *Parnas* & *Gabbai* [Treasurer] at one and the same time. *Viz.* Father & Son, Father & Son-in-Law or Two Brothers". (Only the last line is scored through, although the single score is taken to the end of the line, and Cancelled is written across the whole section).

One subsequent Rule was cancelled in its entirety (No. 94) but this was re-written. Because the final Rule in the manuscript is No. 94, this could suggest that the Rule above was retained in some modified form. However, the numbering up to 94 may be in error, and only 93 Rules may have been finalised.

25. "Any member may be elected to an honorary office but shall not be fined for refusing the same, nor shall he be liable to a fine if re-elected within a period of three years".

26. "Any person accepting office, and before the expiration of the year refusing to continue serving the same, shall pay double the amount of the original fine".

27. "Any member of the vestry who shall be elected to an office in the Service of the Congregation, to which a salary is attached, suspends his rights as a member of the vestry".

28. "In case of the demise of any of the Honorary Officers, the vacancy for the remainder of the year to be immediately filled up by the vestry, the non-acceptance of which office incurs a Penalty of Ten Shillings & Sixpence".

29. "On the first day of *Pesach* (Passover) after the Reading of the Law (Heb.) a Special Blessing (Heb.) shall be made in the Synagogue proclaiming the names of the Honorary officers elected for the following year".

30. "Any person who shall insult an officer while on duty, shall be liable to a fine, subject to the approval of the vestry."

Of a Privileged Member (*Baal Bayit*)

31. A *Baal Bayis* is entitled to the following rights & privileges: he is eligible to be a member of the vestry; to vote on all occasions; to be elected an Honorary Officer of the *Kehillah* (Congregation) and also to officiate as *Hatan Bereshith* and as *Hatan Torah*".

32. "He has the right to officiate as *Segan* on the occasion of the marriage [and written above] on the *shabbos* after his marriage, or the confirmation *bar mitzvah* of any of his children, and the day of his wife's attending Synagogue after childbirth; also on a *brit milah* [circumcision] (Holidays excepted)".

33. "Members under the following circumstances are entitled to be called to the *Seger* [Reading of the Torah]: On *Yom Tov*, the *shabbos* before and after the marriage, [inferred "on the occasion"] of a child's *brit millah* or [at] *yahrzeit*; the day of his wife's appearance from her confinement, the day of his son's *bar mitzvah*, or when in duty bound to say *gomel*" - (a Blessing or Thanksgiving after travel or sickness).

34. "He has the right to the attendance of the *Hazan* [Cantor] on the occasions of a *brit milah* or [during a period of] *shiva* [mourning]".

35. "He has the right to read prayers as the Leader of Prayers, except on *Shabbos* or *Yom Tov*, unless objected to by the *Parnas*".

36. "He has the Right of Burial on the High ground belonging to the Congregation, free of expence (*sic.*) for himself & wife and right of ground free of expence for his children, parents, brothers and sisters". (The "High Ground" refers to the most elevated section at the rear of the cemetery, consisting of at least the whole of the first row, and possibly the left section of the second row).

37. "The whole of these rights and privileges belonging to the *baal bayit* are only to be understood as available upon the payment of all debts due to the Congregation if demanded by order of the Vestry".

38. "If two or more privileged members have the honour (*lit.* simcah, "joy") of Reading the Law [at *Simchat Torah*] or on a *shabbos*, the senior is to stand (or) the *segan* (shall decide) the number of those to be called divided among the parties".

Modes of acquiring Rights of a Privileged Member

39. "Every free person being the son of a *baal bayit* or marrying the daughter of a *baal bayit*, shall be ballotted (*sic.*) for & if elected to pay not less than £2. 2. 0. Anually (*sic.*) for (a) seat, having paid thereunto for Twelve Months".

40. "Every other free person wishing to be a *b//b* (*abrev.*) must be proposed at a vestry & seconded to be balloted for, and if admitted to pay £2. 2. 0. (as) entrance".

41. "Any person not residing in the *kehillah* may continue being a *baal bayit* by the annual payment of Ten Shillings & sixpence, unless he continue to pay for a seat in the Synagogue: Should he however be in arrears three years payments and refuses paying the same all rights to be forfeited".

42. "Everyone admitted a Member shall affix his Signature to the Book of Laws and his name shall be entered in the general register of Members".

43. "Any Member who shall have become reduced in circumstances, and hence unable to make the usual payments, may make application to the vestry in writing for a remission of part or whole of the same, which may be granted on such terms as the Vestry may decide upon; the person making the application not to vote in reference to it". (The signature of Solomon Teacher appears last on the final page of the Regulations. He is recorded as being in debt in at the end of 1854, and the congregation paid for his funeral and burial expenses in 1856).

44. "No person to vote for officers unless his last quarter's account is paid".

45. "In case anyone departing this life should be indebted to the Congregation, the officers for the time may use their discretion to ask or obtain payment of the same".

Meetings

46. "The President [& Treasurer: scored through, see below] shall have the power to call Vestry Meetings under a fine if requisite".

47. "At the hour appointed for taking the Chair the President shall call over the names of the members when all those who are absent shall be considered as fined, unless the party shall send an apology in writing which must be approved of by a majority of members present".

48. "Any person quitting the meeting previous to its termination, without permission of the President is liable to be fined equally as if he had altogether been absent".

49. "All matters proposed for consideration shall be decided by ballot, by the majority of the members present".

In the next rule it had originally been drafted to give the *gabbai* (Treasurer) the casting vote, but this word (in Hebrew) was scored out and replaced by what appears to be *Parnas* (in English, but barely legible). Also scored out from the original are the final, somewhat confused words: "in addition to his own, but not at the meetings, the *parnas* (Heb.) shall preside". The amended rule reads:

50. "At the four quarterly meetings in case the votes be equal the *Parnas* (?) shall have the casting vote…(final deleted section)".

The wording of the next rule is unclear. It seems to reflect some dispute and debate over the respective roles of President (Lemon Woolf) and Treasurer (Henry Joseph). It opens with "The *gabbai*" (in Hebrew, and not scored through, but with what appears to be the addition of *Parnas and…* written in bold Hebrew script above it).

The original ending was "the Officers", but this was written over to become "that Officer". It seems to have been the case in 1843 that it was the Treasurer who wrote up the record of meetings (they are in Henry Joseph's hand) and signed them in addition to the President. It is possible that this new rule is to be seen in the light of those above (46 & 50) where the President had taken over sole responsibility for matters previously shared with the Treasurer. In the same way, Lemon Woolf may have wanted to obtain complete control over the draft record of meetings and to be their sole signatory, but the committee was persuaded that the recording of meetings should be the responsibility of the Treasurer and that they must be countersigned by him. This is the arrangement that the minutes reveal from 1844 onwards. Whether the members suspected that the President might modify the records at his discretion if he were the sole signatory must remain a matter of speculation, but this rule does appear to be a limitation of the President's growing powers (and may mark the transition to the rotation of the office). The rule may well have been drafted to emphasise the words "**and** Treasurer", "**must**" (twice), "**all**" and "**each**".

51. "The President and Treasurer must attend and take minutes in English in the Book appropriated to that purpose of all the transactions of each meeting which must be signed by that Officer".

The following rule also suggests the wish to give the members more power over the President:

52. "It is in the power of any three members to require the *Parnas* to convene a vestry for any special purpose; such requisition to be in writing and signed by all the parties; the time of compliance of the *Parnas* must not exceed seven days".

Revenue

53. "The revenue of the Congregation consists of the sums received for the occupation of seats in the Synagogue, for the appropriation of [Hebrew, and scored through] voluntary donations and legacies".

54. "The several seats in the Synagogue occupied by *baal baatim* to be let as under, the payment of which must be [half yearly: scored through] quarterly, all other seats to be rated at the discretion of the Officers. The four *mizrach* (east wall-facing) seats to be let for Five Guineas each Three top seats on each side Three Guineas the lower seats at Two Guineas Pr Annum".

55. "If a seat becomes vacant it shall be offered to the senior free *baal baatim* and if he be not willing to occupy it, it shall be offered to the next free *baal baatim* and so on in rotation until an occupier be found".

56. "On the decease of any *baal baatim* his son shall have the right to his seat in the synagogue".

57. "Any person residing in the *kehillah* for six months, and after that time neglecting or refusing to engage a seat in the Synagogue, shall nevertheless be debited for one at the rate the vestry may think proper".

58. "On any person declining to continue renting the seat he holds in the Synagogue, it is in the power of the vestry to deprive his wife or other relative of such seat as she may occupy in right of his holding such seat".

59. "Any person renting a seat in the Synagogue shall be entitled to a seat for his Wife, Mother, Daughter or Sister, Without any additional charge. Widows or Married Ladies who may have no such claim, and are desirous of renting a seat shall be charged as agreed by Vestry".

60. "The Vestry is authorised to receive money from Benefit Societies, giving a receipt for the same, and for which they shall pay such interest as is received from the savings Bank".

This rule indicates an interesting feature of the congregation's financial arrangements, in that the social and charitable responsibilities towards its members and the Jewish community were not funded exclusively from a private fund, but incorporated a wider investment plan. The Mutual Benefit Societies mentioned here had developed in Europe and Britain in the 17th and 18th centuries, their roots being the burial societies of Ancient Greek and Roman times, and the Guilds of Mediaeval Europe. In England from about 1760 they grew rapidly, and by the 19th century they had become very numerous, acting as "Friendly" social societies for working men. In return for a small weekly or monthly contribution paid into a common fund, they provided various benefits for their members' security, including life insurance, sickness and health care insurance, assistance in securing employment, help during unemployment, financial help in business, and the costs of burying the dead. Many societies accepted both men and women equally. Originally small local institutions, from the 1840s they had begun the process of developing into large national organisations, with lodges such as the *Oddfellows, Foresters, Druids* and *Rechabites.* A few decades after the 1844 rule, above, they were to have about 4 million members, and under the 1911 National Insurance Act they were given a formal role as agents in the state scheme for health insurance.

61. "Any person not being a *baal bayit* and holding a seat at the rate of Two Guineas annually, shall after having held such a seat for Twelve Months & paid for the same and being free of the Books in every other respect be eligible to vote for the election of officers and also for *Chazan & Shochet*".

62. "All persons making application for seats to pay one quarter in advance".

63. "Non residents occupying seats in the Synagogue to pay for them at the rate fixed by the Vestry".

Service of the Synagogue

The detailed wording of the following regulations which apply to the combined office of *chazan* and *shochet* are likely to reflect the tensions and difficulties that had characterised the incumbency of B. A. Simmons, and possibly other ministers. The congregation expected the incumbent rabbi's responsibilities to cover a wide range of duties for a very limited remuneration. Rule 94, below, is a further reflection of this situation.

64. "The *Chazan* must at all times be present in the Synagogue previous to the commencement of prayers: it is also his duty to prepare the *Sifre Torah* conveniently for the reading of the portions ordained for every particular day. It is also his positive duty to attend in the Synagogue on the day prior to every *Shabbos* & *Yom Tov* for the purpose of rehearsing the portion allotted for the occasion, and to be careful in noticing and correcting any error that may have occurred in the manuscript of the Scripture, which might altogether desecrate the *Sifre Torah* or require correction the omission of such practice shall make him liable to severe censure".

65. "The *Chazan* must perform all Marriage Ceremonies, and write all the necessary documents & must attend on the requisite occasions for all of which he is to receive a fee of Twenty Six Shillings. Should the parties be unable to pay the fee, it may be lessened at the discretion of the officers".

66. "It is the duty of the *Chazan* strictly to attend to the observance of all of the laws & regulations as established for the Congregation & to remind the officers thereof as occasion may require".

67. "The *Chazan* must collect all monies due to the Synagogue according to the direction of the Officers & must pay over the same to the [*Gabbai* is scored through, and written above is] *Parnas* prior to the quarterly meetings". (See the rules above in Meetings where the Parnas assumed responsibilities once the remit of the Gabbai).

68. "The *Chazan* must take especial care that all the property belonging to the Synagogue is kept in proper order & must punctually attend to all his duties according to the agreement entered into with the *Kahal* [congregation]".

69. "It is the duty of the *Shochet* is to *shecht* (slaughter) twice every week during the winter months & three times every week from the first of May until the first of October".

70. "It is the duty of the *Chazan* to open and close the Synagogue at the appointed periods in due time".

The following rule is scored across as "Recinded":

71. "He must be in attendance at all Vestry & committee meetings, execute all orders & deliver letters & messages as he should be directed".

72. "Should the *Chazan* request leave of absence for a limited time he may obtain the same by the permission of the officers".

General Order

73. "It being indispensable that order & decorum should reign in the House of God, every person must, therefore, during divine service remain at his place & conduct himself with propriety; every act of defiance to this rule will subject the offender to a fine".

74. "On *Hoshanah Rabbah* [in the month of Tishri, early October: the last interme-diate day of *Succot*, Tabernacles, and a minor festival within *Succot* itself] & *Simchat Torah* [Rejoicing in the Law, at the end of *Tishri*] the *Sifre Torah* [Scrolls of the Law] shall be taken out from the Ark for circuits which shall be disposed of in the follow-ing order: *Hatan Torah* [then] *Hatan Bereshith*. The officers elect the free *Baal Baatim* according to seniority".

75. "The *Parnas* has the power of allowing anyone otherwise than the *Chazan* to read on *Yom Tov* or *Shabbos* and also to hold any public discourse in the Syna-gogue".

76. "No one [is] to officiate as *Baal Segan* except a married *Baal Bayit* who cannot depute any other to act for him".

77. "Every person who is obliged to be called up [to read the Torah] on any partic-ular *Shabbos* or *Yom Tov* must, on or before the previous Thursday, give notice thereof to the *Chazan* whose duty it is to make the *Parnas* acquainted therewith, as well as to give information of the amount of arrears such person is indebted to the Congregation in order that the same (if thought expedient) may be claimed and settled to the satisfaction of the *Parnas*".

78. "Any person being obliged who on account of arrears due has by the *Parnas* been refused the privilege of being called to the *Sifre Torah* cannot obtain the same by being presented therewith through the medium of any person purchasing the last reading [Heb.] or in any other mode whatsoever".

79. "It is imperative that any one being called to the *Sifre Torah* to cause the *Rav* & officers of the *Kehillah* to be announced in his first Blessing [Heb.]".

80. "Any person is at liberty to make offerings by means of a Blessing without having been called to the Torah which on *Shabbos* and *Yom Tov* must be declared before *Ashre* [Prayer] which offerings to be Cash".

81. "A special Benediction may be expressed for the ill or for a safe journey as well as mentioning the souls of the departed on *Yahrzeit* for each of which offerings must be made & paid for".

Although the prerogative powers of the President are mentioned in the previous rules, it is noticeable that greater emphasis is placed upon the executive role of the officers of the *Kahal* (the senior members of the Vestry) in the regulations that follow.

Hatan Torah and Bereshith[103]

82. "Every year on the first day of *Succos* the officers shall draw lots [Heb.] from the names of the *Baal Baatim* the senior member to be *Hatan Torah* the junior *Hatan Bereshith* to be declared in a special blessing before *Ma'ariv* [Evening Prayer] every person declining the same to be fined 10/6".

83. "In the event of one or both parties refusing to serve such office a drawing shall take place anew as soon as convenient; and any person accepting the office of *Hatan Torah* or *Hatan Bereshith* and not attending *Schul* at the appointed time on *Simchas Torah* and *Shabbos Bereshith* shall be fined at the discretion of the Vestry".

84. "It is incumbent on the *Hatan Torah* and *Hatan Bereshith* to offer on *Simchas Torah* not less than 2/6 in the [for] charity [Heb.] and Two shillings & Sixpence to the *Chazan* which sums must be paid".

Marriage

85. "The requisite notice of every intended Marriage must be given to the *Chazan* in due time previous to the celebration who shall communicate the same to the *Parnas* and all arrears due from the parties to the Synagogue must be settled to the satisfaction of the *Parnas* a week previous to the celebration of the Marriage".

Burials

86. "In the case of the decease of any *orach* [visitor, *lit.* "stranger"] a charge shall be made for burial at the discretion of the Officers".

Orachim also included members of the congregation who had fallen into poverty, and the congregation retained a section of the cemetery for these burials that were paid for as an obligation of charity. The section for *Orachim* is in the lowest corner of the burial ground to the left of the entrance. Solomon Teacher, a privileged member, was to be interred there in 1856. (The "High Ground" reserved for *Baal Baatim* was not full by that time, but he must have fallen into severe poverty).

Obedience to Laws

87. "Any person wilfully violating these laws (the penalty of which not being expressed) shall be summoned to attend and answer for the same at a meeting of the *Kahal* who shall deliberate on the same, and to the best of their judgement inflict such fine as they shall think proper, which is unalterable unless otherwise resolved by a similar meeting".

88. "Any person guilty of offending any of the Honorary Officers in their official capacity shall be summoned to appear at a meeting of the *Kahal* to answer & make satisfaction for the same in such manner as shall be determined by them".

89. "Any person who may conceive himself aggrieved by the act of any of the Honorary Officers may apply for redress in writing to the *Kahal* who shall enquire into the circumstances of the case at the first meeting after such application and award justice accordingly; should, however, the charge prove to be frivolous and vexatious it is in the power of the *Kahal* to inflict a proper fine on the complainant".

90. "No person can be deprived of his full membership [Heb.] but at a special meeting called for that purpose under a fine (i.e. for non-attendance) which must consist of a Vestry of all the ["Eight" scored through] members; the concurrence of at least three fourths of the persons present at that meeting is necessary in order to make its determination valid".

Alteration of Laws

91. "Propositions for the making any new Law, or the alteration of any law already contained in this code, can only be by means of a motion made at a meeting of the Vestry; due notice of which must be given at a preceding Vestry Meeting".

92. "That at all Vestry Meetings [the original number which is scored out and is illegible has been replaced by -] three members including the Officers shall be considered a quorum for the transaction of any business except where the Laws provide to the contrary".

93. "The person wishing to be appointed *Baal Tokea* [blows the *shofar*] (&) *Baal Tefillah* [Leader of Prayers] shall give eight days notice previous to *Yamim Noraim* [The Days of Awe: *Rosh Hashanah*, New Year, and *Yom Kippur*, The Day of Atonement, in the month of *Tishri*, early-mid September] to the *Parnas* for the approval of the *Kahal*".

The following rule was completely scored through and cancelled:

94. "Any person belonging to the Congregation shall not be allowed to *shecht* [slaughter] for himself or (for) any person (except by the sanction of the officers) and should

such an occurrence take place, such member shall forfeit all his privileges as a member of this congregation, and be deprived of his seat in the *Schul*; and if any person belonging to the congregation should be detected as aiding or otherwise encouraging such person, he or she shall be subject to the like punishment (this rule does not apply to persons duly authorised by the *rav* to kill poultry for themselves only)".

This rule would seem to reflect the difficulty for the congregation in monitoring the community's adherence to the *kosher* regulations. It was not uncommon for Jews other than the appointed *shochet* to receive a licence from him, or another so qualified, to kill small animals (such as chicken), subsequent to demonstrating that they were able to fulfil all of the skills needed. B. A. Simmons was the *shochet* at this time, and had held the post, intermittently, since 1811 and from 1822 to 1842. At this time, licenses were issued to *shochetim* by the Chief Rabbi, R. Solomon Hirschell. Simmons' skills had apparently been called into question by the congregation, and they had sent him to London to be examined in them. During this period, because Simmons' skills may have been regarded as suspect, and, later when he was absent altogether, abuses in the regulation of the system of ritual slaughter may have taken place. The New Regulations were finalised on Sunday 3rd August 1844, and on 16th September a letter was sent to the President of the Penzance Hebrew Congregation from the Office of the Jewish Ecclesiastical Administration in London. The new Chief Rabbi, Dr. Nathan Marcus Adler, issued a certification (No. 296) to "Mr. Simmons...I beg to inform you that he has passed his examination satisfactorily and that I sanction his further continuance in office". Upon receiving this, it would seem that the rule above was cancelled, and Simmons' resumed his duties.

The final rule (re-numbered as 94) relates to the conferring of the honour of conveyance of the Torah scrolls during worship: opening the Ark, taking a scroll out of the Ark and returning it, or to the person who lifts up the open scroll at the end of reading, or rolls it back together and covers it. The honour is given in Hebrew.

94. "Any one refusing to accept [this honour] presented to him in the *Schul* incurs a penalty of five shillings".

The completed regulations end with thanks to the committee "who in revising and framing these Laws were activated by that sole motive which must be the bond of all society". Whatever dispute or difficulty there may have been in composing the rules, the Hebrew word *Shalom* (Peace) was affixed in a clear scribal form to the end of the document, together with the signatures of Lemon Woolf [*Parnas*], Moses Woolf, Henry Joseph [Gabbai], Morris H [Hart] Harris, Henry Levin, Alexander Levin, Benjamin Aaron Selig, Simon Harris, Moses B. Simmons, Samuel Oppenheim, L (Lazarus) Hyman and Solomon Teacher. (The Simon Harris who appears as a signatory was the alternative name of Simeon Harris (1826-) a son of Henry Harris (1787-1872) of Truro, and a brother to Morris Hart Harris (1821-1913). Henry Harris' other son, Simeon, died in infancy in 1825, and "Simon" Harris was given his late brother's name. At the meeting below of 20th October, the signature of *Samuel* Harris appears, and not that of a *Simon* Harris).

On 29th September 1844, the congregation purchased the freehold of the cemetery for the sum of £50, and at a special meeting convened on 20th October "It was resolved that the Deeds of the Penzance Hebrew Burial Ground should be drawn in the names of Messrs. L. Woolf & H. Joseph the present wardens of the Congregation and the succeeding wardens as Trustees for ever", ten members signing the resolution. At this time it is possible that the issue of B. A. Simmons' treatment by the congregation in having to submit to re-examination of his skills as *shochet* may have caused resentment within his family. The following meeting of 15th December records that "Mr. M. B. [Moses Barnett) Simmons, not having attended the meeting is subject to a fine of 2/-6 unless he can show good cause for his non-attendance". In fact, B. A. Simmons' son failed to attend the next meeting on 13th April 1845, and was fined again. (There is no indication if the fines were ever paid). Whatever difficulties lay behind this, it would seem that it was felt necessary to retain the services of B. A. Simmons by increasing his future salary to "£32:10:0 pr year which sum is to include all perquisites & grants". However, it would seem that not all members were satisfied that he would attend punctually and adequately to one aspect of his role as *shochet*, and it was proposed "that in future Mr. Simmons should attend the Market for the purpose of *porging* [stripping the meat of those parts forbidden under kosher rules] on Thursdays from 9 in the morning until 11 o'clock & on Tuesdays from 9 to half past 9 o'clock". The matter of congregational contributions towards the salary of the Chief Rabbi also arose, and it was resolved that this should no longer be taken as a discrete sum from each individual member, but should be paid from the congregation's general fund. There are also two items of particular interest regarding the congregation's property. The first is that "The Burial Ground having been purchased this quarter for the sum of £50 including the back arrears of rent etc. it is agreed that the Deeds be placed for security in the Union Bank". The second item notes that "the officers be empowered to get a steps (*sic.*) now in the passage to the *Schul* to be removed".

The cemetery also features in the next meeting of 6th July, when it was noted that "The congregation having purchased the Fee simple and inheritance of the Burial Ground, Mr. Joseph made application to Dr. Barham of Exeter for a piece of ground adjoining it which he has kindly consented to give to the Congregation. It being requisite to rebuild a part of the walls, the whole of the ground has been taken in and the walls rebuilt". It was resolved that a letter of thanks should be sent to Dr. Barham. A John Barham (1774-1856) whose family name was *Abraham* was a renowned tenor and cantor in London during the early 19th century.[104] There were Jewish *Braham* families in Plymouth, Bath and Bristol.[105] It is not known if Dr. Barham was of Jewish descent. His gift of the land might suggest this, but religious empathy may have played no part in the gift, which he may simply have regarded as a minor courtesy. By 27th September 1845 it would seem that B. A. Simmons had accepted the terms of his attendance at the market, but he "requested that the hour for attending the market on Thursdays should be altered during the winter". The meeting "resolved that the hour should be from half past nine until half past ten during the winter". The meeting also formally recorded "That a new code of Rules for the better regulation of the affairs of the Congregation has been this day brought forward & passed into Law", and the "indefatiguable [*sic.*] labour in framing the rules" was acknowledged in a vote of thanks to the members of the committee that drew it up.

On 4th January 1846, there is an intriguing insight into the realities of the congregation's "better regulation" of its "affairs" when the Vestry meeting called to audit the accounts fell into disarray. Samuel Oppenheim interrupted the meeting on several occasions, and "was at length fined 2/-6". (At the same time "Mr. Hyman" received the same fine for non-attendance). "The Treasurer, not being able to command silence was obliged to adjourn the meeting". It was resumed a few days later, on 11th January when the only item noted was that Mr. Hyman was found to be "very much in arears (*sic.*) (lenity having been extended to him on account of illness) it was resolved by the Congregation unless he pay up his arrears before *Pesach* that the Rule respecting non payment shall be put in forse (*sic.*)". It cannot be known if Samuel Oppenheim's disruption of the previous meeting was in any way connected with this particular issue, and his name is not mentioned in this second meeting. A special meeting was convened on 22nd February 1846 to discuss a letter sent by "Frederic Hart Esq." that is Frederick "Lemon" Jacobs (1790-1853), a nephew of Lemon Hart, who worked in his uncle's firm in London. The letter informed the congregation of the death of his (unmarried) brother, Jacob James Hart (*b.* 1784) who had died, and whose wish had been that he should be buried in the Penzance cemetery. Jacob Hart, "late her Britanic Majestys (*sic.*) Consul general for the Kingdom of Saxony" had been a wealthy man, and the cost of his funeral and burial would have been met from his estate. The congregation agreed to the burial, and Jacob Hart was interred in the cemetery in a grave which is unique there in that it has a raised coffin-shaped surround characteristic of some found in the Brady Street cemetery of the Great Synagogue in London. (Lemon Hart's grave is in the same cemetery). This comparatively elaborate feature, together with the very fine quality of the headstone and its particularly detailed inscription,[106] reflect the success and affluence of the Hart family in London. Jacob Hart's grave is in marked contrast to the others in the Penzance cemetery, a distinction which, no doubt, he intended.

On the 5th and 19th April, the meetings note the payment of £45 into "the Bank towards the Mortgage on the *Schul*" and that the more expensive seats in the synagogue (at three guineas) were not being filled and "it was proposed that a stand be made outside the upper seats & let at Two Guineas pr year until more Three guinea seats are required". The upper seats were to be retained until required and then offered at the original rental. Meetings on the 25th and 28th June again suggest that the new regulations had not succeeded in improving administrative efficiency or attendance at the Vestry, with two members "Mess M. H. & S. Harris" being fined for absence, to which they formally objected "not considering they had suffiscient (*sic.*) notice". The new rule 71, which required that the *shochet* (B. A. Simmons) should attend the quarterly and special meetings, was cancelled (noted previously). Later in the year, on 20th September, he applied for an increase in his salary, which was not granted for another three months, when an increase was approved on 27th December 1846 of "£5 pr year – making his sallary (*sic.*) £37 Pr year". During the year Simmons had been ill, and his son-in-law, Joseph Rintel, Rabbi in Falmouth, had taken over his duties as *shochet*, for which he was sent a letter of thanks from the congregation. Simmons was to fall ill again in 1849, when Rintel gave further assistance.

From 1847 to 1853 it is striking that the names of women appear for the first time at Vestry Meetings. It is difficult to draw any clear inference from this, but some link with the introduction of the new regulations, their scope and application, seems likely. Whether the rules had aroused concern and debate in the wake of their application, or whether financial constraints and the implication of this for members', and their families' contributions had been factors cannot be known. While it is not recorded as such, the issue of the legal ownership of the synagogue and its contents would have been a concern as numbers began to fall. (It has been mentioned that this appears to have been an issue in Falmouth, some time earlier). The need to encourage better attendance at meetings may also have played a part. After 1853, the meetings seem, again, to have consisted only, or mainly of males, with attendance showing a marked decline.

At the beginning of 1847 the vestry met on 15th February to adopt "the rules laid down by our worthy Chief Rabbi". These were mainly concerned with the sale of privileges, *mizvas* (offerings) and the requisite number of not less than five privileged members to be called up to read the Torah and lead prayers on the Sabbath in a strict rotation. These were put into effect on 21st March for a period of six months, but issue of purchase of privileges led to some dispute later in the year (at the meeting of 20th June). On 28th March the Treasurer, Henry Joseph, was authorised to make a payment of £10 "to Messrs Bolitho & Sons towards the Forty Pounds borrowed on the Deeds". The following month, it was decided that a further "Ten Pounds should be paid to Messrs Bolithos & Co. in liquidation of part of the amount due to them". B. A. Simmons' salary increase was formally confirmed in a ballot, with the result that his wife, Flora Jacob ("Mrs. Simmons Senr.") was able to apply for and be granted a better seat in the gallery. The Chief Rabbi's new rules were again the subject of discussion on 15th August, when the meeting was held "for the purpose of settling the issue (of privileges) & also considering those rules & regulations of the Chief Rabbi which the meeting might think proper". All of the rules were approved, with the exception of five that were held over for discussion at the next quarterly meeting, when three "were rejected & all the others to be considered as laws of the Congregation". The rotation of those to lead prayer was allocated to six privileged members, and the rota of their names recorded (in English) together with the specific prayers they were to recite (written in Hebrew).

It is likely that at this time financial constraints were beginning to be a serious matter for concern within the congregation. The earlier accounts from 1843 show a fluctuating balance in the Fund, suggesting that the level and flow of income was becoming unstable: £11 (1843), £4 to £16 to £34 (1844), £46 to £52 (1846) and in 1847, £14. In addition, there are frequent references to members failing to pay their subscriptions on time, with a figure (in single figures) being the "balance due to the Treasurer". From 1848, the Fund (the balance in hand) rarely exceeds a few pounds.

On 17th October 1847, a special meeting was convened at which "it was resolved that the Congregation discontinue the £5 per year towards the funds for the support of the Chief Rabbi & a letter to that effect be written to Mr. S. Oppenheim Secretary to the Great Synagogue" (not to be confused with Samuel Oppenheim of Penzance) . There was also disquiet in relation to the (unnamed) local butcher used by the Congregation, and another special meeting was called on 14th November "in consequence of a complaint preferred by Mr. M. H. Harris against the Butcher". It is tempting to suppose that this may have been linked with the Congregation's finances, and he may not have been paid on time or in full, but this is conjectural, and the nature of the complaint against the butcher is not specified. However, "it was resolved that the officers caution him against acting in future in the manner complained of & if not complied with, they be empowered to kill with another Butcher". This meeting is the last where Lemon Woolf is recorded as present. Soon after this he was most likely incapacitated by illness, and he died on 14th March the following year. During this period Lemon Woolf retained the Presidency, with Henry Levin, the Treasurer, taking the chair at meetings. Moses Woolf appears to have represented his father. The President's Office was not filled until Henry Levin was elected on 6th April 1848. The quarterly meeting of 19th December notes that Simon Harris had "resigned his seat in the *schul* in consequence of leaving the Town". The minutes also note that "Mr. Joseph has agreed on behalf of Miss Jacob of Falmouth to let the house in New Road to the Congregation for the sum of Five Pounds per year which was accepted". Simon Harris would have been living in this house which was in the possession of his older cousin, Esther Jacob (1809-1878) an unmarried daughter of Jacob Jacob (1774-1853) of Falmouth and Sarah Kate Simons (1778-1846) from Truro.

At the beginning of 1848, on 23rd January, the Congregation took the unusual step of holding "a Public Meeting for the purpose of petitioning Parliament for the Removal of the Jewish Disabilities". The campaign for Jewish emancipation had been active for decades in France and the German states, but it had been late in coming to Britain, largely because earlier generations of Jews had been satisfied with the relative toleration shown to them in England. Another factor was the gradual achievement of middle-class status by a substantial number of Jews and their adaptation to British culture and society. Gradualism also characterised the way in which emancipation was granted to Jews in "piecemeal fashion between 1830-1871, rather than in a single comprehensive legislative act...some Jewish disabilities were discarded by local bodies without recourse to parliamentary action".[107] In fact, the Jews played little part in political consciousness before the issue of emancipation became linked with the challenge by Non-conformists, together with Roman Catholics (who had been allowed to hold national and local offices since 1829) to the predominant position of the Established Church. The Philo-Judean Society and evangelical Christians had long espoused the cause of the Jews, and although they wished that the Jews would ultimately embrace Christianity, they opposed the aggressive stance of the London Missionary Societies that pushed actively for the conversion of Jews. Although Jewish emancipation was opposed by the Tory High Church faction and by ultra-conservative evangelicals (they had opposed Catholic emancipation), support was to come from Whigs, progressive and evangelical Tories, together with other Radicals. Jewish emancipation was to receive passage in the Commons followed by defeat in the Lords in

1834, 1836, 1841 and (the case of the Petition in the Penzance Congregational Minute Book) in 1848, with subsequent defeats from 1849 to 1857. Despite the likelihood of defeat, the Penzance Congregation presented its Petitions to both Houses of Parliament and "signed by the Wardens of the Congregation on their behalf". The Petition to the Lords was sent to the Secretary of the Board of Deputies of British Jews "for their disposal" and that to the Commons to E. W. W. Pendarves MP "to be presented by him". In addition, it was "Proposed by Mr. B. Selig & seconded by Mr. M. Woolf…That a Memorial be drawn up & forwarded to the Member of Parliament, presenting the Petition, soliciting his support & interest". It was noted that "Mr. Harris of Truro having forwarded to his son in this Town Petitions for the Removal of Disabilities to be signed by the Christians, which precluded the possibility of this Congregation getting up one, a letter be written to him requesting the favor (*sic.*) of his allowing the said Petitions (now in the hands of his son) to remain with the Congregation for the presentation". The minutes conclude: "That the thanks of this meeting is due to our Christian Brethren of Penzance in having so readily & nobly supported the petition for the Removal of Jewish Disabilities, being the last Vestige of Religious Intolerance now remaining on the Statute Book of this free and enlightened Nation".

The annual meeting of 16th April gives the first indication of a decline in numbers, and it was noted that the "Congregation having sustained the loss of several members which caused a deficiency in the income". The situation was addressed by introducing several "austerity measures". These included an increase in individual seat rental and offerings, the reduction in the salary of the *shochet*, B. A. Simmons, from £37 to £32 per year, and the combining of the offices of President and Treasurer, Henry Levin being re-elected to the position "for the ensuing year". It has been noted that the new minute book (from 1843) unlike the earliest minutes (from 1808) is not in the form of detailed accounts, but in this instance, the precise sums that each member would now pay are itemised. The meeting closed with the resolution that a letter of condolence be sent "to Mrs Woolf on the heavy bereavement she has met with in the demise of her lamented & respected Husband who had been a great number of years the worthy *Parnas* of this Congregation". In the letter, written by Henry Levin, he refers to Lemon Woolf's "strict adherence to his religious and moral duties in private as well as in public", and concludes that he prays that the "Almighty [may] grant you many years of happiness in the bosom of your dear children and friends". Rebecca Woolf had gone to Plymouth, where she would have lived with one of her three daughters who had married and settled there. Her letter of thanks to the Congregation for their condolences was sent to Henry Levin and was included in full in the minutes.

On 2nd July and on 24th September the meetings record that the congregation had managed to restore its accounts with the Treasurer reporting a credit balance, and one member, Morris Hart Harris, took possession of the more expensive seat of the late Lemon Woolf. The meeting also sent a letter of thanks to "Mr. Rintel", the Rabbi at Falmouth, "for his kind services to the Congregation during the illness of Mr. Simmons", the *shochet*. The letter of thanks and Rintel's reply are included in the minutes. The Treasurer's finances may not have been able to cover this eventuality, and it is possible that Rintel, B. A. Simmons' son-in-law, had given his services either without payment or for a minimal consideration. In the letter of thanks, of the 22nd October, Henry Levin writes of Rintel's "important services" and of his regret "that at present it is not in our power of testifying the same by presenting you with any other token of respect". Rintel's gracious reply of the 30th refers to "the little services I have done", and offers to do so again if required. In the event, he was to leave Falmouth for London the following year. On 31st December the Minutes record that "A communication having been received from the London Committee of Deputies of British Jews of the sufferings of our brethren at Tiberias in the Holy Land arising from Pestilence & more particularly from the outbreak of Cholera amongst them, which has already carried off many, & exposed the survivors to the worst horrors of destitution it was resolved that £1: 1: 0 be given from the Congregation Fund towards alleviating their afflictions, & also that a private subscription amongst the Jewish residents be made for the same object". In addition to the amount drawn from the Fund, the minutes record the names of the vestry members and their additional donations. The modest total of £2:12:0 was duly sent to London, and an acknowledgement of receipt was sent by Sampson Samuel of the Board, conveying the thanks of Sir Moses Montefiore (1784-1885).

By the time of the next meeting, on 1st April 1849, the Minutes note the loss of another member, "Mr. A. Levin", Alexander Levin (1828-1891) son of the retiring President, Henry Levin. Alexander Levin, a watchmaker and jeweller, had assisted his father by keeping the accounts for the previous two years, during which time, the minutes appear to have been written in his hand, and "being about to leave the Town tendered his resignation of the Seat he has held". He left the accounts with a balance of only 6 shillings. He first went to Bristol, and later to Edgbaston, Birmingham. He married Rachel Joseph (1831-1891) formerly of Falmouth. Despite his departure, the accounts of 1st July continued to show a "ballance (sic.) in hand", but only of some 13 shillings, and the vestry was forced to accept that the limited family income of members required a reduction in the rental of seats from 16th September. B. A. Simmons, became a victim of this worsening situation, and suffered yet another blow to his family's income, in that his salary was again reduced, from £32.10.0 to £30 a year. By 16th September, however, the Fund was again in credit at just over £6: 13s.

From 1849 to early in 1850, Morris Hart Harris had been the President and Treasurer, but by 17th March, he had decided to leave the town, but "said although he was about to leave Penzance he did not wish to relinquish his Congregational rights & would therefore pay…10/6 Pr year". His stewardship of the accounts "gave great satisfaction to the Members there being in his hands a Ballance of £11:7:6. Like his parents, who lived in Truro, he was eventually to go to London. There was also regret expressed "at Mr. M. B. Simmons leaving them". Moses Barnett Simmons (1817-1876), son of B. A. Simmons, had also gone to London. By 23rd June, the Fund had accumulated the sum of £18: 2: 5, and, later in the year, on 1st September, "the amount was broken in on in consequence of sundry repairs & other expenses". The depletion in the accounts was minimal, however, and the year closed with the Treasurer, Henry Joseph, holding the sum of £16: 12: 0. This sum had increased to almost twenty pounds by 13th April 1851, and the solvency of the congregational Fund appears to have been secured. It is at this point that the minutes reveal what appears to be a private and internal investment system: "it was proposed by Mr Teacher & unanimously agreed to that "15 be placed to Interest application being made to Mr Joseph he consented to take it at 5 Pr. Cent." Henry Joseph was a successful and prosperous pawnbroker in the town. This arrangement would have been in no way unusual, in that, in the absence of a comprehensive and affordable banking system, pawnbrokers operated as surrogate banks and investment agencies. They were also an important source of social security at a time when social provision against unemployment, bankruptcy and illness was either undeveloped or unavailable. At the same meeting, the impact of the reduction in his salary upon his family can be seen in that "Mr Simmons having made application for a Grant the Congregation voted him 10/-." Simmons' reliance upon the congregation's charity as he approached his old age contrasts sharply with Henry Joseph's position, and that of Henry Levin's son, David, then only 18 years of age, of whom the minutes note: "Mr D. Levin has this day taken a seat at 30/- Pr year".

The summer and autumn of 1851 saw painting and repair work carried out in the synagogue. On 6th July "currant expences" were paid out of the Fund for painting the *schul*, and on 21st September, for further repairs (possibly to a Torah scroll)[108] "it was requisite to draw £7: 0: 0 from Stock to meet the expences". Despite this, on 28th March 1852, a further £20 was "placed to Interest" with Henry Joseph, who signed a receipt the next day[109] for that amount "for which I agree to pay five pr cent Interest pr annum & also agree to pay on demand a part or the whole of the amount if required to do so, the request to be signed by a majority of the members & by the President for the time being." It would seem that B. A. Simmons' resentment at the reduction that had been made in his salary by the vestry members resulted in a rash decision on his part to resign his position as *shochet* and *rav* without any prior warning. The deterioration in relations between the congregation and their minister had reached a crisis point, and the Chief Rabbi was informed, but within ten days, matters had been resolved, with Simmons reverting to his previous responsibilities and to the same salary. From this point on, however, the Penzance congregation appears to have been drawn into a closer supervisory relationship with the Chief Rabbi. Previously, it would seem that this far-flung congregation had proceeded with comparative independence in the hiring of their incumbent ministers, and in drawing attention to their internal conflicts by letter, found themselves as a focus of the Chief Rabbi's concern and attention. News of the frequency of disputes and the tense atmosphere within the congregation may also have reached the Chief Rabbi from former members who had moved to London. From now on, and until the end of the century, the Chief Rabbinate was to be involved far more closely in the appointment of ministers to Penzance. Unconnected with this issue, the same Minutes note that "George Foot to be Retained at £2: 2: 0 p(er). Annum with the usual Perquisites (sic.)". It is most likely that this entry refers to the cemetery caretaker and grounds man, and the additional costs which his maintenance of the burial ground would incur.

Solomon Teacher (1811-1856) was to take a proactive role at meetings from 1852 to 1853. He is likely to have been particularly critical of B. A. Simmons in these meetings, and there must have been a degree of antagonism between the two men, in that, at one point Teacher called for his instant dismissal. Teacher also proposed a review of several of the Rules: that Nos. 8 and 11 (the *Parnas* to act as *Segan* on certain occasions, and the duties of the latter) should be revised, that No. 13 (the *Parnas'* regulation of seats in the synagogue) should be reconsidered, that No. 15 (the *Parnas'* duty to keep an inventory of congregational property) should be repealed, that No. 24 (the prohibited degrees of consanguinity for the office of *Parnas* and *Gabbai*) should be "Strongly adhered to", and that with Nos. 29 and 36, the former (the proclamation in the synagogue at Passover of the elected officers for the year) should be reconsidered, and that the latter (the free burial of a privileged member and his family) should be enforced. Benjamin Aaron Selig (1814-1872) was both President and Treasurer at this time. The Simmons' issue and the President's supervision and speedy resolution of it, may have provoked Teacher's proposition relating to the rules in question, in that they are concerned with the President's powers, the criteria for his election to office, and his conduct of affairs, all of which Teacher may have sought to restrict as a result of his own more aggressive stance in the Simmons' affair. Teacher may also have had a personal interest in the final rule, in that he was in financial difficulties by this time, and could anticipate that he might die in relative poverty. At his death his burial was at the congregation's expense. On 12th September 1852, almost three months after Simmons' reinstatement, "Mr Teacher withdrew his propositions Respecting the Rules". At the end of this eventful year, on 12th December, the Treasurer "handed over Two Pounds to Mr Joseph in Trust" (and a further three pounds was given to him in April 1853). "Twenty one Shillings was also voted toward the Rebuilding of a School at Symarna (*sic.*) was duly sent off". The second reference to the Smyrna Schools relates to the Jewish community in the second largest city in the Turkish Empire. In 1825, it had been estimated that some 14,000 Jews lived there.[110] A vote was also passed to pay "10/- for Mr Herman of Falmou(th)" (the Rabbi there). This was to cover his expenses in stepping in to replace B. A. Simmons as *shochet*.

The meeting on 10th July 1853 was an especially busy one. After a general discussion and approval of an earlier proposal of Solomon Teacher's that offerings on the occasion of *Yizkor* (the memorial Prayer for the Departed) should be made to the General Charity Fund, it was recorded that "A Letter has being (*sic.*) received from the Board of Brittish (*sic.*) Jews inviting us to send A Member to the Board wich (*sic.*) the Conragation (*sic.*) declined on Account of the small Number". It was also noted that "the Congragation has Voted 10/- for Mr Colenso [a local Christian] for his services in collecting Names for the Jewish Petition likewise it has being agreed to send our worthy Chiff (*sic.*) Rabbi A Letter of Condolence on the Demise of his Lady". (A copy of the very long letter of 14th July was attached to the Minute Book). It would seem that relations between the members and B. A. Simmons had in no way improved and the minutes record that "Messrs Joseph Selig & Teacher having complained of Mr Semons Conduct as regards his bad Porching [porging of meat] & severall other things Mr Joseph proposed that the President please to inform Mr Semons of the Congragations determination that in future Mr Semons conduct is brought before them & proved he will be desmissed at once. Mr. S.

Teacher proposed a Amendment that Mr. Semons be desmissed at once (under-lined) after giving him 3 Months Notice wich being put to the vote was 2 for the Amendment & 3 against it Mr Josephs Proposition being carried". Again it would seem that Solomon Teacher's antipathy towards B. A. Simmons had to be moder-ated by the members in voting, common sense dictating that a replacement for the *shochet* could be difficult to find if he were to be dismissed (or should he resign) in too short a time scale. In the event, on 24th July, "the Resignation of Mr Semons our *shochet* has send [i.e. having been sent] to the Congragation it was resolved that it be Accepted and that the President be pleased to Advertise in the Jewish Croncele (*sic.*) and to send to the Chiff Rabbi for Reader at a Salary at £35 pr Year". This increase in the new "Reader's" salary is especially significant in the light of the reduction in that of B. A. Simmons. His resignation effectively marked his retirement, although he continued to live in the town. A new *shochet*, Solomon Cohen had been found by September. The meeting of 24th ended by noting that "Mr. Samuel Solomon of Poland St. London has being uniomsly (*sic.*) Elected A Deputi of Brittish Jews for our Congragation A Letter being send to him by the President wich has being coutosly replied". It is a striking feature of the minutes for these particular meetings that they contain so many grammatical and spelling errors. The new President was Henry Levin, whose very precise handwritten script from earlier years is hardly recognisable in this or in future meetings (where the deterioration is very marked). It seems likely that his capacities were in some way impaired by this stage. The formal letter of condolence is clearly not in his hand, and is unsigned, ending with President Warden of the Penzance Congregation" (the last word in its correct spelling).

Towards the end of 1853 (and unusually) the Minutes are dated according to the New Jewish Year, as 17th Kislef 5614, when a special meeting was convened "for the purpose of taking in consideration (*sic.*) a communication having been received from the London Committee of British Jews of the sufferings of our Brethren in Jerusalem". £1: 5: 0 was drawn from the Congregational Fund and donations "being colected amongst the Residend Jews in this town" brought the total to £3, "wich amount the President have (*sic.*) forwarded to Sir Moses Monte-fiore Brt.". The names and amounts donated are drawn up as a formal account, and it is striking that although the two most affluent (and senior) members, Henry Levin and Henry Joseph donated 10 shillings and 6 pence each, B. A. Simmons and his wife, Flora, gave a total of 4 shillings, despite the reduction in their family income. All of the other names are familiar from earlier meetings, with the excep-tion of "Lionel & Morris", sons of Henry Joseph, who, had been born in 1840 and 1841 respectively, and would have attained the age of eligibility for membership. The new Rabbi, given simply as "Cohen" donated 1 shilling, but one name that is not at all familiar from the Congregational records is that of "Scrann", who donated 2 shillings and 6 pence. This is likely to be Nathaniel Schram, a Dutch Jew who had lived with his family in Falmouth in the 1840s, but then moved to Plymouth. He travelled widely, and may have been a temporary resident in Penzance. In 1871, he was in Helston, between Penzance and Falmouth.

Either B. A. Simmons' financial difficulties or his resentment at his recent treat-ment by the congregation appear to be the reason for a minute of 1st January 1854:

"Mr. Simmons sent a message offering 21/- per Year seat money in addition to paying his offerings which the Congregation declined to accept." The meeting voted that he should pay 42/-, but the outcome is not recorded. During the year, however, the Congregation's own financial problems began to surface. On 24th September it was noted: "The income not being sufficient (*sic.*) to meet the expenditure, £2: 5: 2 was taken from Stock". The appointment of a new Rabbi, "Mr. Cohen" was made, however, "at 14/- Pr Week – as *shochet* and to perform other services of the *kahal* as heretofore & continue 12 months with 3 months notice". The 24th December saw Solomon Teacher fall behind with his subscription, and the accounts once more revealed "a defisciency" of £2; 14; 5, this amount being "drawn from the stock", which still held a balance of fifteen guineas. To regulate income more closely, it was proposed that "in future the payments be made weekly". The following Spring, on 8th April 1855, fines for "all persons being in arrears at the end of the Quarter" were introduced on a sliding scale from six to twelve months of arrears. Decline in income, membership and financial security from this point may also have played a part in the decision that Vestry meetings should no longer be held on a quarterly basis, but every six months. In some years (1857, 1858 and 1861) there is only one entry.

The following year saw an even greater drain on the dwindling resources, with two burials in the cemetery being paid from Congregational funds. Solomon Teacher's worsening health and finances had forced him to leave the town to live in St. Ives, where he may have been offered a place to live and some assistance with his condition. His pregnant wife, Maria, may have remained in Penzance. Another Jew, Joseph Barnet, who was unmarried, also lived there. Both men died within a few weeks of one another, Teacher on 10th March, and Barnet on 7th April. The congregation was also without the services of a *mohel*, and Maria Teacher's child, Solomon, had been born not long after his father's death. B. A. Simmons had been the County's chief *mohel,* but from March 1854 he had left the town with his wife to live with a married daughter in Merthyr Tydfil, and was not available to act in that capacity. Consequently, one of the congregation's former ministers, "Mr. Staalhagens" (Rev Myer Stadthagen) the rabbi in Plymouth had come down to perform the circumcision. These various expenses meant that a further £7: 1: 6 had to be drawn from Stock. Despite his resignation in July of 1853, Simmons was re-engaged as the congregation's *shochet* on 23rd November 1856, after returning from Wales.

By 5th April 1857, the accounts were again in balance by £32: 10s: 5d, and the vestry "resolved that the *schul* should be cleaned up after *Pesach* the Walls & ceiling sized & the paintings [the inscribed wooden panels] varnished. A year later, on 28th March 1858, with a similar balance in hand, it was decided "to carry [the sum] to Stock making it £10". How this financial recovery took place is uncertain, but the leading members, Henry Joseph, Henry Levin and Samuel Oppenheim were comparatively prosperous businessmen, and they may have increased their offerings to compensate for the state of the Stock. If this was the case, any recovery was temporary, and the minutes for 17th April 1859 note that the balance had fallen into a few shillings, with "£10 due from Mr. H. Joseph" the outgoing President. The 25th September saw little improvement, but weekly seat payments were revised sufficiently to allow a new *shochet* and *chazan*, "Mr. Greenbourgh" on an annual salary of £40. April 1st 1860 saw a healthier balance of just over £2, and "It was agreed on to have iron launders for the shule". (The "launders" refer to a Cornish dialect expression for roof-gutters.) On 9th September, a subscription of £1 was made "from the charity-boxes" to the "Syrian fund". Matters continued to show an improvement throughout 1861 to 1862, when the balance increased from £3: 4: 9 to £14: 2: 11 (when £10 was added to Stock), and was found to be £12: 15: 4 by 19th April 1863 and £15: 18: 0 on 13th September that same year, when the salary of the new Rabbi, "Mr Spiro" was increased to "one Pound a week". On 17th April 1864, the accounts showed a balance of "£14: 11: 1 and £20: 0: 0 at Interest of 5 pr Cent at Mr. Hy. Joseph". The same meeting recorded that "Mr Samuel Jacob of Falmouth has agreed to Pay the Congragation Two Pounds two shillings pr Year for supply of meat Poultry & wich the Congragation has accepted to commence March 1st 1864." These payments, which appear to be back-dated, reflect the final decay of the Falmouth congregation, which was to close in 1879. Samuel Jacob was its last President, and earlier, in 1852, Falmouth had temporarily supplied Penzance with *kosher* meat. There may have been an interim in the appointment of a *shochet* at Falmouth, or one or more of the last ministers that were appointed there may not have had the skills or licence to kill.

At this point in the Minute Book, entries appear in the form of a series of displaced fragments which relate to accounts for previous years from 1852-1862. After this there is an Inventory of Congregational property and religious artefacts, also displaced, in that it appears to have been drawn up later than 1864. Most of the inventory is in the hand of Henry Joseph (1806-1881), but its compilation cannot be dated with certainty. Only the final entry (in the hand of Israel H. Levin) is dated (May 3rd 1883) and relates to a single item, the gift of three Torah Mantles. The numerous items include artefacts made of brass, coverings and curtains of silk, velvet, items for the festivals, and damask, and various items for funerals. Of particular interest is a note that the deeds to the burial ground were held privately in a box "kept by the Treasurer", whilst the deeds to the synagogue itself were secured "at Messrs Bolitho & Sons" (mentioned earlier in the Minutes). It seems likely that the inventory was drawn up when the dwindling congregation was evaluating its assets against the likelihood of closure.

The Minute Book from 1864.

From 1864, the dates of the arrival and departure of ministers are no longer recorded. The meetings on 31st July and that of 1st October dealt with a dispute with the *shochet* regarding his unauthorised absence.[111] The accounts continued to improve, and by 9th April 1865, they showed a credit of just over £32. The same meeting noted the resignation of the *shochet*, and also that "the Congragation having but one *sefer* it is agreed on to buy a New or second hand *sefer* the Congragation has agreed on to make a *tikkun* [regulation or order] for that purpose". The cost of purchase was to be met by members' stipulated offerings when "called before the *sefer torah*". On 31st May, the accounts note that the *sefer torah* and two volumes of a Prayer Book for the Whole Year had been purchased at a total cost of eleven guineas. In July, the accounts received a welcome bequest of five pounds from the "wife of the late Mr. George Goodman of New Bridge in Wales". Their son, Charles, had married Amelia, daughter of Samuel Jacob (1778-1860) of Penzance.[112] On 24th September, the accounts allowed a charitable gift of one guinea to be sent to "the distressed Poor at Jerusalem".

Late in 1866, the congregation found itself "being in want of one for *minyan*, Mr. Levin offered to pay 10/- provided the other members would make up 15/-. Mr. Oppenheim proposed taking it from the funds, which was objected to – Messrs I. Levin, I. Oppenheim & H. Joseph paid 5/- each and had a person down from Plymouth for *Rosh Hashanah*". Clearly, numbers were by now a matter of critical concern. From 1867 to 1869, the accounts continued to show a credit balance, with some £20 being set aside on interest. On 25th April 1869, the vestry decided to raise money "in aid of the poor Jews of Russia & Poland". Although £2 was collected, this came from only six members, three being from the Levin family, and the total was reached after being "Taken from Stock". At the same meeting the Minutes record that the congregation had been left a legacy of £50 from the estate of the "Late Mr. Gorfenkle will be paid next October". Jacob Gorfenkle was a wealthy Liverpool businessman, dealing in the importation of sponges,[113] who travelled widely across the north of England in the course of his business. Some members of the Joseph family of Falmouth had moved to Liverpool, and they were related to Henry Joseph of Penzance. It is most likely that it was through these men from the Joseph family that Jacob Gorfenkle came to know about the Cornish Congregations and their respective circumstances. He may have had other West Country connections, however, and he died in Torquay on 13th October 1868. In his will he left various bequests to Jewish organisations, including congregations, schools, orphanages, and also to several hospitals in London and elsewhere. One bequest was for £500 to a former Mayor of Falmouth, Jacob Olver (who was not Jewish) to be paid by him to the Life-Boat Society. With this money, a life-boat was provided for a new station at Portloe in Veryan Bay, which had been established in 1870 to provide cover between Falmouth and Mevagissey. The new boat was named the *Jacob Gorfenkle*, but when the station closed in 1887, the boat had never been launched. It was initially placed in the reserve fleet, and was sold out of service in 1893. Gorfenkle may have decided not to leave a bequest to the Falmouth congregation, which had gone into rapid decline after 1865. Penzance, however, was to continue for several more decades, and other Cornish Jews, apart from the Joseph family, retained connections with Liverpool through family marriages. Moreover, when the Penzance congregation was dissolved and its synagogue was sold, a member of the Joseph family, resident in Birmingham, was a recipient of the conveyance. Such connections between Penzance, Birmingham and Liverpool were to become invaluable to the declining congregation. However, unlike Falmouth, the Penzance congregation was saved from premature decline by the arrival of a new minister, Isaac Bischofswerder, whose extensive family increased the numbers and helped the little community to survive until the very beginning of the twentieth century. (Bischofswerder's appointment is not recorded in the Minute Book). With Gorfenkle's £50 the vestry proposed that they "should have the *Schul* painted – 2 large windows put in & all other repairs required to be done as well have the Gas brought in unless they consider the expence to (*sic.*) great". Gas was installed at some point, and was certainly in service by 1889.[114] Two ornate 19th century brass synagogue lamps, found in a Penryn antique shop in 2003, and now in the Jewish Museum in London, may have come from the Penzance synagogue, although they were originally acquired from a source on the Devon-Cornwall border, and their origin may lie in another synagogue closure elsewhere in the country. The following year, on 10th April, after receiving the Gorfenkle legacy, the minutes note that "Sundry alterations were made in the synagogue".

On 9th June 1869, Isaac Bischofswerder officiated at the wedding of Esther Joseph (1843) the seventh of Henry Joseph's twelve children. She was married to Aaron Harris Mark Beirnstein of Dowlais, South Wales, and on the same day he became a paying seat-holder. At the same time, the congregation had lost another member, with the death of Samuel Oppenheim, and the payments from the other members were recalculated to offset this. When another of Henry Joseph's daughters, Kate (1847-) was married to Abraham Freedman, a young widower aged 28, of Aberdare on 31st August 1870, he also became a member of the congregation. It seems likely that these marriages may have been contracted with the express condition that the groom should become a paying member of the Penzance congregation. Nothing of consequence can be found in the minutes for 1871, beyond the bare notice of accounts, but the following year, there is a document which, at first sight, would seem to be very surprising. On 21st June 1872, signing himself as "A Trustee", Henry Joseph, as the congregation's President, "under and by virtue of an Act passed in the Nineteenth year of Her Majesty Queen Victoria" (that is 1856) registered the synagogue as a Place of Religious Worship "by a Congregation or Assembly of persons calling themselves Jews". The second synagogue had been a place of worship for over sixty years by then, and this registration is very late for a "chapel" which fell within the Nonconformist sphere. However, places of worship had been recorded from the mid-18th century, but there had been no systematic recording or registration. Even at the beginning of the 19th century, recording was uneven, but the collation of statistical records had improved from the 1850s. It seems likely that B. A. Simmons' completion of the 1851 census when the synagogue was recorded as a place of public worship may not have been transferred to the Registrar General's records, and this oversight may have led to the new registration of 1872.[115] The Minute Book itself makes no mention of the document.

Minutes for 1873 and the first half of 1874 consist solely of brief items of accounts. The meeting of 23rd May 1874, however, shows that charitable donations were not confined to Jews: "An Apeal (*sic.*) from the Chief Rabbi Dr. Adler for Subscription towards the famine now raging so severely in the Presidence of Bengal in India likewise an apeal on behalf of our Breathren Coreligionists in Jerusalem who are now suffering a severe distress owing to a severe Winter and a great Dearth". The amounts collected from each member were allocated between the two funds, with £2. 4s. 6d. to the Bengal Fund, and the same amount for the Jerusalem Fund, to which there was added an additional 2/6 (the donor is unclear), 10 shillings from the "Holy land Box" and a further 3 shillings from the "Charity Box". The Jerusalem donation was sent to "L. Emanuel Esq Secratery (*sic.*) the

Board of Deputies" (a guinea had been sent previously to Jerusalem on 24th September 1865) and the Bengal donation to the Chief Rabbi. ("L. Emanuel" is likely to be the Lewis A. L. Emanuel, a London Solicitor, who launched a Restoration Fund Appeal for the Falmouth Jewish cemetery in 1889). Despite these donations, the congregation's finances had improved, with a total balance of £45: 5: 10 by the 15th September. The impression remains that the more affluent members were sustaining the congregation from their private resources.

In April 1875 the congregation made a significant contribution towards the Testimonial Fund of Sir Moses Montefiore, who, as a prominent and affluent London Jew, was not only active in Jewish affairs in England, being President of the Board of Deputies for most of the period from 1835-1874, but had devoted a considerable amount of his time to assist those persecuted and impoverished in other countries.[116] The congregation donated three guineas from its general fund, and this was supplemented by members' contributions and most significantly four donations from local Christians, "Alderman J. B. Coulson, Councilor (sic.) Mapwell, Mr. Cornish, [and] Mr. Mounder". The total amount of £8: 19: 0 was sent to "Mr. Emanuel" Secretary to the Board. The terminal decline of the Falmouth community is reflected in a note of 17th September 1876, that Samuel Jacob of Falmouth had again paid for the supply of meat and that this was to continue at a charge of two shillings per week. By 1st April 1877, however, whether through increased charges or simply the inconvenience of doing so, the minutes note that "Mr. S. Jacobs of Falmouth has declined having meat from here". By 1880, Samuel Jacob had left Falmouth for London, and only the Penzance congregation remained as the most remote and isolated in the South West, the nearest Jewish community being at Plymouth in South Devon. It was to this congregation that the Penzance congregation was to turn and become reliant for some of its needs during its final years.

Just before Falmouth's final closure, on 14th April 1878, the Penzance minutes record that "the vestry payments not being sufficient to pay the expences (sic.) of the congregation, we the undersigned have agreed to pay each 6/- weekly - H. Joseph, Israel Levin & Israel Oppenheim". Clearly, matters were reaching a critical point, and the cost of running the synagogue itself was becoming impractical. There are no minutes for 1879, but on 29th August 1880, the congregation had recognised that its current members could not support the synagogue indefinitely, and that some might move away, without anyone younger to replace them. Therefore, they "resolved in consequence of the most of the trustees being no more of having other names placed on the Deeds as trustees viz.- Mr. I. Levin, Mr. Oppenheim, & Mr. B. H. Joseph". The latter was a son of Henry Joseph who had moved to Birmingham. In the event, Israel Levin (who was soon to leave the town) decided that his name should not be included. The previous names to the deeds, Lemon Woolf, Aaron Selig, and Henry Levin are given as deceased, and on 24th September 1880 the freehold of the synagogue was conveyed from "Henry Joseph, jeweller of Penzance, and Israel Levin, wholesale jeweller of Penzance to Barnett Henry Joseph of Birmingham, wholesale jeweller, and Israel Oppenheim of Penzance, merchant" for the peppercorn fee of ten shillings. It was not until a year later, on 25th December 1881 that the minutes record "the receipt from Messrs Bolitho Sons

& Co Mounts Bay Bank for the Deeds of the Synagogue & Burial Ground & all Books & papers connected with and belonging to the Congregation".

Henry Joseph had died in 1881, and in 1882, on 13th February, Israel Levin was unanimously selected to succeed him as Secretary (President). On 5th March, Issac Bischofswerder's son, David, is recorded as present, together with Barnett Joseph and his brother, Joseph Joseph of Birmingham. Weekly payments were again increased, with Israel Levin and Israel Oppenheim each paying 6/6, and David Bischofswerder paying 4/-. His brothers, Morris and George also became seatholders paying 1/- weekly. David Bischofswerder had become an affluent man through the importation of diamonds and cigars.[117] His brother, Morris was also a reasonably successful local merchant. To encourage further increase in income, "all rights and privileges of membership" were to be offered at 2/- per week. The congregation was by this stage increasingly reliant on financial help from the Joseph family of Birmingham, and both Barnett and Joseph Joseph undertook that each would subscribe 6/6 per week "in lieu of the amount paid by the late Henry Joseph", their father. Barnett Henry Joseph (1837-1907) had married Isabelle Blackensee (1839-1912) and they were to have a large family. Joseph Joseph (1846-) was married to Emily Jacob (1851-1937), a daughter of Isaac Jacob (1820-1888) of Falmouth. Further unspecified repairs were required to the synagogue, and an estimate had been received from "A. Pooley" for £9: 3: 0, "it be left the President to accept that or any other tender & see the same properly carried out". The cost of this work may well have been met, at least in part, by the Joseph brothers. The same minutes continue with the resolution that "the thanks of the congregation be given to Mess. Barnett & Joseph Joseph Birmingham for their many kindnesses & assistance". It is possible that one or both of the brothers had taken temporary residence in the town, or that they travelled from Birmingham for the vestry meetings, each taking turns to attend. At least one of their names is given as present from this point on.

On 10th September, Morris Bischofswerder "was accepted as a privileged member by paying 2/- per week for his seat. The meeting noted that a letter had been received from "A. Cohen Esq. M.P. President of London Committee of Deputies of the British Jews wishing to know if we are desirous of being represented at the Board". The vestry decided that was "not in a position" to have a representative, the cost of travel alone, no doubt being prohibitive for such a small and struggling congregation. The congregation must have fully realised that the prospect of closure was more than likely, and further departures of members were soon to take place, only the Bischofswerder family remaining. The future sale of the synagogue was always a viable option, but the burial ground possessed a sacred integrity for all time, and it could never be relinquished, even if it was inevitable that it would one day be abandoned by the demise of the Jewish community itself. At the meeting "Mr. Joseph Joseph introduced the subject of the present & future condition of the Burial Ground & desired that some person shall be employed to keep it in good condition. It was resolved that the President be empowered to do what he thinks best & report same at next meeting". Sadly, there is no indication of that meeting, and there are no minutes for 1883 to 1884, apart from a fragment dated May 1883, noting the gift of "3 Handsome Mantles for the

3 Scrolls of the Law presented by Mr. Barnet & Mrs Barnett H. Joseph Birmingham to commemorate the Barmitzvah of their son Selim".

Mrs. (Isabelle) Joseph was to make a further gift a few years later. It is possible that formal vestry meetings were suspended between 1883 and 1885, because the official thanks of the congregation for the three mantles was not recorded until 5th April 1885. March 1886 saw the resignation through ill health of the *shochet* Isaac Bischofswerder, and the need arose to advertise for a new minister. In the meantime, the vestry "Resolved that we write the President of the Plymouth Congregation if he is agreeable that the members of our congregation shall have meat during the time we are without a shochet". The additional cost involved in this arrangement (which is not mentioned subsequently) was met by discontinuing the payments previously made to Isaac Bischofswerder, who by then was most likely being supported by his son, David. On 25th April, Barnett Henry Joseph offered to travel to Northampton to interview a prospective replacement, the Rev. I. Rubenstein, whose appointment was agreed on 9th May, to begin on 1st June.

On 8th April 1887, much of the meeting was taken up with the accounts. The President, Israel Levin, who was unmarried, had died on 3rd April, at the age of 58. The meeting resolved that "Letters of Condolence should be sent to Mr. Alex Levin and also [to] Mrs. I. Aarons – Brother & Sister…". Alexander Levin (1828-1891) had married Rachel Joseph (1831-1891) of Bristol (formerly of Falmouth) and had moved there by the 1850s. His brother, Israel also lived there for some years, working in his brother's hardware business, before returning to Penzance to work with their father, Henry Levin. Alexander and Rachel Levin had moved to Birmingham before Israel Levin's death. Their sister, Mathilda Levin (1826-) had married Isaac Aaron (1811-) of Birmingham. David Bischofswerder was subsequently elected President in place of Israel Levin, initially for twelve months. There is little doubt that his considerable, albeit temporary, affluence helped to shore up the congregational finances at this crucial stage, together with significant donations from B. H. Joseph of Birmingham. The minutes of 8th September 1887 note the departure of yet another minister (for Cardiff) and the arrival of a replacement (from London), and in another meeting two weeks later, on the 25th September the accounts reveal that four members had subscribed towards repairs and decorating in the synagogue, David Bischofswerder's contribution of £5 being the lion's share of a total of £7: 1: 0. Despite this modest amount, Bischofswerder must have made up the remainder from his President's fund and from his private resources, in that the official accounts show an income of only 22 shillings and six pence. "The Estimate for the Decorating & alterations of the Shool (*sic.*) have been received & it was decided that Mr. Wallis should do the work according to the Architects's / Mr. Wear's (barely legible) specifications for the sum of £38: 15: 0. It was also proposed that the president should make enquiries regarding the cost for making a New Lavatory & W.C. in addition to the specifications – for the Repairs stated." It would seem that the congregation were more than eager to take advantage of David Bischofswerder's *largesse*, and he was well known at this time as a major contributor to a range of charitable and civic causes in the town. The various improvements to the synagogue may reflect a vague hope that the community might survive, although continued migration from the town suggested otherwise, and there were no Jewish arrivals to add to congregational numbers. The size and growing numbers of the Bischofswerder family may have engendered some confidence, but its members, including David Bischofswerder himself, were to leave the town within a few years, with only Morris Bischofswerder remaining, until 1913. It has been mentioned that David Bischofswerder was to lose most of his money, after 1891, following an unwise investment in a failing local mine which was to go out of production, and he left the town in 1892 for Plymouth, where his younger brother, Max (1860-1928) had settled. He then spent some time in the north of England, but then he emigrated to South Africa around 1895, dying there in 1902. While he was in a position to do so, however, his continuing support towards the maintenance of the building's fabric and the additions to its facilities would have helped to secure its value as a saleable asset some twenty years later.

Throughout 1888, the congregation still enjoyed the services of a minister, although the vestry fund showed only a few pounds. The charges of the architect, "Mr. Wear", for the work of two years earlier, were not submitted until the meeting of 29th September 1889, and were "considered accessive (sic.) & has been left to Mr. I. Oppenheim to settle". The outcome is not recorded, but it is noted that "Mrs. Joseph on her own acct. (account) and her daughters" had given some white "covering" for the "Sephurim", the Torah Scrolls. David Bischofswerder continued to be elected as President during this period. The accounts were still in a credit balance of almost nine pounds by 5th October 1890, when the President was thanked "for the very handsome Curtain for the Ark & covering for the Scroll of the Law which he presented to the Shool on the occasion of his son's Barmitzva". Harry Bischofswerder was formally elected a member at this same meeting, although his barmitzvah had been celebrated in the synagogue a year earlier in August 1889, reported in some detail in the local paper, *The Cornishman*. Present at that event were various guests and prominent dignitaries from the local Christian population. The general appearance of the synagogue's traditional interior, the unfolding of the ceremony, and the building's most striking features received particular mention, including "the ark or chest of the Law" with its "veil of damask" and an eight branched lamp, tall candlesticks with massive candles".[118] The congregation's other religious artefacts were always used on the Sabbath morning service, and the minutes note "That the service on Saturday morning shall commence at 9.a.m. & at half past nine (9.30) the Scrolls of the Law shall be taken out if there is a Minion, should there not be Minion, at 9.40, the scrolls of the law are not to be taken out, but the service proceeded with".

By 13th April 1891, the congregation was still concerned to maintain their cemetery, and it was "Resolved that the offer of 21/- per annum from Mr. Richards be accepted to keep the burial ground in order". The final entry in the Minute Book is a meeting of the 27th March 1892. It was held at David Bischofswerder's town mansion, "The Hollies" in the Alverton area of the town, and it is possible that meetings had moved to there from the synagogue some time before. David Bischofswerder was soon to surrender the lease on this palatial house, which he could no longer afford to occupy, and was soon to leave the town. The congregation may not have been fully aware of his forthcoming departure, or of the extent of his financial losses, and he was elected President for yet another year. The accounts still showed a modest balance of about six pounds. Morris Bischof-swerder was present at the meeting, and it has been mentioned that he was to remain in the town until 1913. His brother, Marcus was admitted a member at this final (recorded) meeting, although, with a very large family, he was the least successful brother of the family, and he too was soon to leave the town, for Hull, where his brother, George (Solomon) had settled and had become a prosperous businessman.

Whether meetings were held at all after 1892 is not clear, but they appear not to have been recorded. Israel Oppenheim then left Penzance for Bristol, leaving Barnett Henry Joseph and Morris Bischofswerder as the sole remaining members. The last incumbent minister, Michael Leinkram left around 1895, and he was not replaced. The infirm Isaac Bischofswerder still lived in the town, most likely with the family of his son, Morris, and he may have been able to officiate on an occasional basis. Sole responsibility for the synagogue, which may rarely have been used, now fell to Morris Bischofswerder, of whom it has been supposed that "On the High Festivals he would open the synagogue and recite his prayers in melancholy solitude".[119] On 11th October, an attempt was made by several of the surviving members to secure at least a temporary reprieve for the synagogue by executing a conveyance between them as the named parties. Barnett Henry Joseph and Israel Oppenheim (both living elsewhere) added Morris Bischofswerder to their names on the deeds. The end came a few years later when, on 31st May 1906, Thomas Lean of Marazion bought the building at a public auction in Penzance for £172, and the freehold was formally conveyed to him on 23rd June that year. When he died, on 1st July 1908, Lean's will (of 11th March that same year) appointed "his friend William James Bazeley, Merchant, and his nephew James Jewill Hill, Solicitor", both of Penzance, as the Trustees of the freehold property "to permit the same to be used and occupied for Divine Worship, Prayer, study of the Holy Scriptures and similar religious purposes by persons belonging to the connexion now known as the Brethren of which he was a member Subject to their keeping the same in repair and paying the Trustees the yearly rent of £8 payable quarterly and so long only as the said Brethren should continue to use and occupy the same for the religious purpose aforesaid". The will also stipulated that the Trustees should convey the yearly rental to the Treasurer of the British and Foreign Bible Society of London".

Unlike the Falmouth synagogue, where the Jacob family continued to take an interest in the building after their departure, there would seem to be no subsequent record of descendants of the Penzance Jewish community attempting to retrieve the synagogue's internal fixtures or of their making further enquiries about it. However, the Brethren, while using the former synagogue for Christian worship, retained its interior with considerable respect for many years. Visits to the building by the architect, Edward Jamilly (1958) and the historian, Bernard Susser (1964) resulted in detailed and impressive descriptions and plans of its appearance. Photographs taken in the 1970s, and reproduced in this book, confirm the integrity of the interior's former Jewish usage.[124] Around 1970, the ownership of the building was conveyed from the British and Foreign Bible Society to local Christians for use as a Meeting House for Worship, and they also continued to conserve its interior with care for some years. Eventually, the building was acquired by the Devenish Brewery of Redruth, and later by other national brewing companies. At some point, the synagogue was stripped of any vestige of its original interior features, but even then, some of the former Christian occupants were able to save two large inscribed Hebrew panels which had been above the Ark. They were conveyed into the safekeeping of the Jewish Museum in London, and another small panel was retained privately in Penzance. The synagogue itself was incorporated into the Star Inn, and its two main windows which had been replaced by the congregation with some pride in 1865, were boarded over and the interior used for storage. Although the synagogue has not been used as a place of collective Jewish worship for almost 125 years, its former congregants would have been gratified that their "Christian neighbours" who had supported them on various occasions and with whom they had lived in harmony, had come to play such an honourable part, while they were able to do so, in cherishing both the place of worship and the memory of the Jews who had once lived and worked in the town, contributing so much to its character and to its prosperity over so many years.

Morris Bischofswerder continued to trade in the town after the sale of the synagogue. His wife, Julia, the youngest daughter of the Congregation's former President, Henry Joseph (1806-1881), died on 20th April 1911, and not long after, in 1913, Morris Bischofswerder left the town for Hull. With his departure, the Penzance Jewish community passed into history.

The Presidents of the Penzance Hebrew Congregation.

Before the congregational minutes begin in 1808, it can be assumed that the leading family within the congregation was that of **Abraham Hart** (-1784) who, like his contemporary in Falmouth, Alexander Moses (-1791) is likely to have been the congregation's first President, followed by his son, **Eleazar Hart** (-1803) Hart, and then by his son, in turn, Lemon Hart (until 1811). This familial or "dynastic" pattern of tenure is reflected in the fact that, when Lemon Hart relinquished the Presidency, it was passed to his relative, Lemon Woolf. The Presidents below assumed office from the date when their predecessor either died or relinquished the post. From 1848, the approximate time of the spring festival of *Pesach* (late March to early April) became the traditional point during the year for re-election to the Presidency.

Lemon Hart: to August 1811 (when he left for London).
Hyman Woolf: to April 1820.
Lemon Woolf: to February 1848.

The New Regulations of 1844, brought in during Lemon Woolf's Presidency, reveal some disquiet with his sole assumption of responsibility for various matters that, previously, had been shared amongst members, and that a number of regulations appear to be have been designed to limit that drift of power away from the members themselves. This trend led to a more fundamental review of the system of the life-long tenure of the office, and a new system of the short-term rotation of the President's office, albeit amongst a "vestry elite", was introduced upon Lemon Woolf's death.

Henry Levin: to April 1849.
Morris Hart Harris: to March 1850.
Henry Joseph: to March 1852.
Benjamin Aaron Selig: to March 1853.
Henry Levin: to April 1854.
Henry Joseph: to April 1859.
Henry Levin: to March 1860.
Henry Joseph: to April 1863.
Henry Levin: to April 1865.
Henry Joseph: to April 1868.
Israel Oppenheim: to April 1869.
Henry Joseph: to April 1871.
Israel Oppenheim: to April 1872.
Henry Joseph: to April 1874.
Henry Levin: to April 1875.
Henry Joseph: to April 1881.
Israel Levin: to April 1887.
David Bischofswerder: to March 1892.
Morris Bischofswerder: to 1906. There are no minutes to confirm it, but it is most likely that when David Bischofswerder left Penzance in 1892, his brother **Morris** became the *de facto* President, a post which was, in effect, a nominal position at a time when the congregation was in rapid and terminal decline.

Congregational Names.

The names given here are mentioned in the Penzance Congregational Minute Books for the periods 1808-1829 and 1843 to 1892.[120] This does not imply that every person was present at a vestry meeting, and some would have been recorded in relation to the business under discussion. Clearly, the Chief Rabbi and Sir Moses Montefiore would not have been present, and neither would the local tradesmen or councillors who are named. Non-Jews are given in square brackets. Other bracketed names indicate congregational members whose forenames do not occur at that point in the minutes, but these have been added for clarification. Some names occur only in a cursive Hebrew script.

1808: [Joseph Branwell], Lemon Hart, Hyman Woolf, Henry Ralph, Lemon Woolf, (Elias) Magnus, ...Levy, L. (Lemon) Jacobs, Sam(uel) Joseph, Mr. Johnson (Plymouth: Moses or Phineas Johnson[121]), [Henry Bottrell, ...Brewer, Thos. Nichols, Peter Roberts, Jno. Wallis, Peter Richards, Bolitho & Sons, Joseph Tonkin, Robt. Edwards, Richd. Coulson], ...Michael (Swansea: connected to the Harts through marriage), *Rav Aaron* (Selig).

1809: Mr. Woolf, Mr. H. Ralph, Mr. Magnus, L. Jacobs, H. Woolf, [E. Hornblower], Lemon Hart, [Thos. Broad], *Rav Moshe* (Moses Isaac).

1810: Lemon Hart, H. Woolf, H. Ralph, E. Magnus, L. Woolf, L. Jacobs, (Rav) Moses Isaac, Lazarus Solomon (deceased), J. (Jacob) Jacobs (Camborne), *Rav Feival* (Phillip Samuel).

1811: Lemon Hart, Jacob Hart (London), Saml. (Samuel) Jacobs (Scilly), H. Woolf, Mr. Ralph, Elias Magnus, L. Woolf, L. Jacobs, J. Jacobs, A. (Alexander) Symons, ... Cohen (Emanuel Cohen of Redruth), ...Alexander (uncertain), Jacob Hart, Lemon Jacobs, Isaac Joseph (Redruth), Sam(uel) Jacobs, (Aaron) Selig, Mr. Margues (Margoulis?), Mr. Simmons (*Rav Yissochar*, B. A. Simmons), (Rav) *Lipman, Rav Feival, Rav Selig.*

1812: H. R....(possibly Henry Ralph, or a local tradesman), E. Magnus, Lemon Woolf, Samuel Jacob, Lemon Jacobs (London), Jacob Hart (London), Jacob Jacobs (Camborne), Isaac Joseph (Redruth), ...Jacobs (Exeter), Aaron Selig, (B.A.) Simmons, H. Woolf, *Leb Henna* (Mr. Levy: *Yakov ben Naphtali*).

1813: H. Woolf, E. Magnus, L. Woolf, Samuel Jacobs (Hayle), Aaron Selig, Jacob Jacobs (Camborne), Isaac Joseph (Redruth), Jacob Hart (London), B. A. Simmons, *Rav Elthanan* (Joseph Mortara, or Mortera).

1814: H. Woolf, S. Jacobs, A. Selig, B. A. Simmons, J. Jacobs (Camborne), I. Joseph (Redruth), (Elias) Magnus, Mortera.

1815: H. Woolf, L. Woolf, A. Selig, S. Jacobs (Hayle), B. A. Simmons, J. Jacobs (Camborne), I. Joseph (Redruth), Israel Levy (Truro), Mortera, [Branwell], ... Simons (possibly Simon Simons of Truro or, more likely, his son, Isaac, whose name appears later, together with an Alexander Simons, to whom he was not related), Hyman Woolf, Joseph Barrow (Jamaica), Lemon Hart (now in London, but possibly as a visitor), A. Selig, B. A. Simmons, Samuel Jacob (Hayle), I. (*sic.* J) i.e. Jacob Jacob of Camborne, Isaac Joseph (Redruth), Israel Levy (Truro), [...Foxwell, i.e. Rev. John Foxell; Harvey, tradesman], (*Rav Hayyim*) Hyman Selig (from KH, i.e. Copenhagen), *Jacob* (Jacob Moses, *shammas*).

1816: Hyman Woolf, L. Woolf, A. Selig, B. van Oven[122] (likely a relative of Isaac van Oven, spectacle-maker of Truro *c.* 1771-1785), B. A. Simmons, Samuel Jacob, [Harvey, Branwell], Jacob, Magnus, [Bryan, Williams], *Moses* (Jacob Moses).

1817: H. Woolf, E. Magnus, L. Woolf, A. Selig, B. A. Simmons, Samuel Jacob, Jacob Moses, [Mr. Edmonds, Joseph Wallis], Solomon Ezekiel, *Rav Hayyim, Rav Moshe* (Moses Levi), *Leb Henna* (burial).

1818: Hyman Woolf, L. Woolf, E. Magnus, A. Selig, B. A. Simmons, J. Jacob, Solomon Ezekiel, [Mrs. Branwell, John Wallis].

1819: [J. B. (Branwell) Sutherland, Harvey], (Rabbi) Moses Levi, Levi Jacob, Elias Magnus, H. Woolf, Lemon Woolf, B. A. Simmons, Solomon Ezekiel, Samuel Jacob, Isaac Symons (of Truro), [Mr. Wallis, Willam Eva].

1820: Isaac Symons, H. Woolf, L. Woolf, A. Selig, B. A. Simmons, Samuel Jacobs, Solomon Ezekiel, Levi Jacob, [Wallis, Foxhall *sic*.], (Emanuel) Cohen (Redruth), Mrs. I. Joseph (Judith Rebecca Jacob, wife of Moses Isaac Joseph of Falmouth, later Redruth), *Rav Hirsch ben Rav Shimon* (Hart Symons).

1821: L. Woolf, A. Selig, B. A. Symons (Simmons), Samuel Jacob, Isaac Symons, Levy Jacob, A. S. Solomon (Abraham Simeon, or Simon, Solomon of Falmouth, married to Kate, or Kitty Jacob of Redruth), Alex(ander) Symons, E. Cohen (Redruth), I. Levy (Truro), Simmons (Isaac Simons of Truro), [Eva], Godfrey (unknown, but possibly a secondary name for a congregational member: he was "achieved" from the local prison, presumably on payment of a fine), [Foxhall], Lyon Levi (Truro), Hyman (Harman Semmens of Truro), Mrs. Joseph (Redruth), Mord(ecai), which may be a reference to a relative of Sophia Mordecai of Exeter who was married to Levi Jacob, Henry Levin, John Mortara, *Rav. Hirsch*.

1822: Lemon Woolf, B. A. Simmons, Samuel Jacob, Isaac Symons, Levi Jacob, A. (Alexander) Symons, Symons (Truro), [Eva, Foxhole], *Rav Hirsch.*

1823: L. Woolf, B. A. Simmons, Samuel Jacob, Isaac Symons, Levi Jacob, Alex Symons, [Eva, Foxhole, Mary Borlase], Henry Levin, *Rav Hirsch.*

1824: Samuel Jacobs, Alexander Symons, Lemon Woolf, B. A. Simmons, A. Selig, Levi Jacob, H. Lavin (Levin), [Eva, Tho. Thomas, Alice…(possibly a cleaner), William Small, John Ellis, William Eddy, Samuel John].

1825: Lemon Woolf, Samuel Jacobs, B. A. Symons (Simmons), Henry Lavin, Sophia Jacobs (Mordecai, wife of Levi Jacobs), Aaron Selig, Abraham Davidson, Isaac Davidson, Harry Levi (likely a son of Israel Levy of Truro), [Eva, I. Dobb], (Dr.) John Messina, Solomon Johnson, Solomon Ezekiel, Isaac Pollack, (Rabbi) Hart Symmonds (Symons).

1826: Lemon Woolf, Samuel Jacobs, B. A. Simmons, Henry Lavin, John Messina, Solomon Ezekiel, Sophia Jacobs, A. B. (Abraham) Davidson, Isaac Davidson, Solomon Johnson, Harry Levy, Hart Symons, [Eva, Mary Kenefic, cleaner], Abraham Joseph (from Plymouth, Reader in Prayers), [Bodilly[123]], Henry Levin, Aaron Selig.

1827: Lemon Woolf, A. Selig, Samuel Jacob, B. A. Simmons, Henry Lavin, John Messina, Sophia Jacob, Harry Levi, B. (Benjamin Aaron) Selig, H. (Henry) Joseph, Mr. Joseph (Abraham Joseph of Plymouth), [Nicholls, Thomas Mason, Mary Kenefic, Ellis], Solomon (Johnson), [Mr. Batten], *Rav Moshe* (Moses Levi), *Rav Myer ben Rav Yitzak* (Rev, Isaac Myer Stadthagen, who came from London, and later served in Plymouth).

Note: The father of Henry Joseph of the Penzance congregation was Abraham Joseph (-1828) of Falmouth, and he should not be confused with Abraham Joseph of Plymouth who was, briefly, Reader of Prayers in Penzance, and who remained in the town for a few years. Henry Joseph of Penzance had a son, also named Abraham (1834-1839) who is buried in the Penzance cemetery.

1828: Lemon Woolf, Aaron Selig, Samuel Jacob, Abraham Joseph, B. A. Simmons, Henry Levin, Henry (likely Harry) Levi, Sophia Jacob, B (Benjamin) Selig, [Eva, Mary Kenefic, W. Ansell, L. Moyle], Joseph Joseph (Henry Joseph's brother), M. Marcus (likely a visitor), (Rabbi) Myar, Isaac Lazarus, Lemon Hart, W. Meyer (a Myer, or Meyer traded in Redruth), Mr. Gabriel Rosenthal (St. Ives).

1829: Lemon Woolf, Moses Woolf (son), Aaron Selig, Samuel Jacob, Henry Lavin, Abraham Joseph, Harry Levy, Sophia Jacob, Joseph Joseph, Rabbi My(er), B. A. Simmons, [Nicholls], Rose(n)thal, Simon (likely a Simons of Truro).

The minutes break off for the next thirteen years, and resume in 1843.

1843 (31st March): A meeting of the Select Committee to draw up a revised set of Rules for the congregation – L. Woolf, H. Joseph, H. Levin, M. H. (Morris Hart) Harris (of Truro, now resident in Penzance), M. B. (Moses Barnett) Simmons (son of B. A. Simmons).

1843 (3rd August): A Vestry Meeting to sign the Revised Rules (later read to the whole congregation) – Signatories – Lemon Woolf, Henry Joseph, Henry Levin, Benjamin Aaron Selig, Moses B. Simmons, L. (Lazarus) Hyman, Moses Woolf, Morris H. Harris, Alexander Levin, Simon (Simeon) Harris, Samuel Oppenheim, Solomon Teacher.

1843 (remainder): Henry Harris (of Truro), Morris H. Harris (son, and brother of Simon Harris), Henry Joseph, Hyman Lazarus, Henry Levin, Samuel Oppenheim, Moses B. Simmons, Lemon Woolf, Moses Woolf.

Note: it is possible that Lazarus & Hyman are inversions, although there may have been two men: Hyman Lazarus, and Lazarus Hyman.

1844: (Solomon) Ezekiel, Morris H. Harris, Samuel Harris, Simon Harris (three brothers), Henry Joseph, Alexander Levin, Henry Levin, Samuel Oppenheim, Benjamin Aaron Selig, Moses B. Simmons, Lemon Woolf, Moses Woolf.

1845: [Dr. Barham of Exeter: cemetery lease], Morris H. Harris, Henry Joseph, Hyman Lazarus, Alexander Levin, Samuel Oppenheim, Benjamin A. Selig, (Rabbi) Barnett A. Simmons, Moses B. Simmons, Lemon Woolf, Moses Woolf.

1846: Morris H. Harris, S. (Simon or Samuel) Harris, Frederick Hart (Jacobs), Jacob (James) Hart (Jacobs), both men from Penzance and now representatives of the

Lemon Hart firm in London; ....(likely Lazarus) Hyman, Henry Joseph, Hyman Levin, Samuel Oppenheim, (Rabbi) Joseph Rintel (of Falmouth, and B. A. Simmons' son-in-law), Benjamin A. Selig, Barnett A. Simmons, Solomon Teacher, Lemon Woolf.

1847: Morris H, Harris, Samuel Harris, Simon Harris, ...Hyman, Miss Jacob (of Falmouth: either Esther or Betsy Jacob, both unmarried daughters of Jacob Jacob), Henry Joseph, Henry Levin, Samuel Oppenheim, Benjamin A. Selig, Barnett A. Simmons, Mrs. B. A. Simmons (Flora Jacob, also known as "Blume"), Moses B. Simmons, Solomon Teacher, Lemon Woolf.

1848: S. Ezekiel, Henry Harris, Morris H. Harris, Henry Joseph, Mrs. H. Joseph (Amelia Jacob, daughter of Jacob Jacob), Alex. Levin, Henry Levin, Israel Oppenheim, Samuel Oppenheim, [E. W. Pendarves M.P.], (Rabbi) Joseph Rintel, Mrs, J. Rintel (Fanny Simmons), Benjamin A. Selig, Barnett A. Simmons, Moses B. Simmons, [...Somers], Solomon Teacher, Mrs. L. Woolf (Rebecca Jacob of Redruth), Moses Woolf.

1849: Morris H. Harris, Henry Joseph, Mrs. H. Joseph, Alex. Levin, Henry Levin (Sir Moses Montefiore, Sampson Samuel, Secretary to M.M: neither present), Samuel Oppenheim Benjamin A. Selig, Moses B. Simmons.

1850: Morris H. Harris, Henry Joseph, Samuel Oppenheim, Benjamin A. Selig, Moses B. Simmons, Solomon Teacher.

1851: Henry Joseph, David Levin (youngest son of Henry Levin), Samuel Oppenheim, Barnett A. Simmons, Solomon Teacher.

1852: [George Foot, caretaker], (Rabbi) Herman (of Falmouth), David Levin, Benjamin A. Selig, Barnett A. Simmons, Solomon Teacher.

1853: (Dr. Adler, Chief Rabbi, not present), [Colenso], (Rabbi Solomon) Cohen, Miss Jacobs, Henry Joseph, Mrs. H. Joseph, Miss Joseph (of Henry Joseph's six daughters, the three older, and not married at this time, were Sarah, Rose and Esther), Henry Levin, Israel Levin, Mrs. Levin (Julia from Truro, her surname being uncertain), Miss Levin (Mathilda), (Sir Moses Montefiore), Samuel Oppenheim, Mrs. Oppenheim (Elizabeth Levy of Truro), ...Scrann (likely Schramm of Falmouth), Benjamin A. Selig, Mrs. Selig (Catherine, daughter of Samuel Jacob), Lionel and Morris (sons of Henry Joseph), Barnett A. Simmons, Mrs. Simmons, Samuel Solomon (London), Solomon Teacher, Mrs. Teacher (Maria, daughter of Aaron Selig).

1854: (Rabbi) Solomon Cohen, Henry Joseph, Henry Levin, Israel Levin, Samuel Oppenheim, Benjamin A. Selig, Barnett Asher Simmons, Solomon Teacher.

1855: Henry Joseph, Henry Levin, Israel Levin, Samuel Oppenheim.

1856: Joseph Barnett (of St. Ives), (Dr. Adler, Chief Rabbi), …Hyman, Henry Joseph, Barnett A. Simmons,…"Staalhagens" (Rev. Myer from Plymouth, possibly with his family, to perform a circumcision), Mrs. Teacher, (Solomon) Teacher (infant son): Solomon Teacher had died before his son's birth.

1857: Henry Joseph.
1858: Henry Joseph. As with 1862, below, it is not clear if minutes were not kept, or if there were no vestry meetings.

1859: (Dr. Adler), Hyman Greenborough (Rev. Samuel Hillman, *Shmuel ben Simeon*), Henry Levin, Israel Levin, Henry Joseph, Samuel Oppenheim, Barnett A. Simmons.

1860: Hyman Greenborough, Henry Levin. Rabbi B. A. Simmons died in this year. There is no reference to this in the minutes.

1861: Henry Joseph, Henry Levin, (Rabbi) A. Lupp(s)hutz.

1862: Henry Joseph.

1863: Barnet H. Joseph (son of), Henry Joseph, Henry Levin, Israel Oppenheim, Mr. Spiro (Rabbi Marcus Spiro).

1864: Samuel Jacob (of Falmouth), Barnet H. Joseph, Henry Joseph, Henry Levin, Israel Oppenheim, Mr. Spiro.

1865: H. Levin, Henry Joseph, Mr. Spiro, Samuel Oppenheim, Israel Levi, Israel Oppenheim, Mrs. George Goodman of New Bridge, South Wales (a widow, her son, Charles had married Amelia Jacob, a daughter of Samuel Jacob).

1866: Henry Joseph, I. Levin, I. Oppenheim, B. H. Joseph.

1867: Israel Oppenheim, Mr. Rittenberg (Rabbi), H. Joseph.

1868: H. Levin, H, Joseph, I. Oppenheim.

1869: H. Levin, Israel Levin, Henry Joseph, S. Oppenheim, Harris Beirnstein (Dowlais, South Wales, married to Esther Joseph), Levy (uncertain), Mr. Gorfunkle (Gorfenkle of Liverpool: a bequest).

1870: Mr. Freeman (Aberdare: Abraham Freedman married Kate Joseph), Henry Joseph, Mr. Oppenheim.

1871: H. Levin, H. Joseph, I. Oppenheim.

1872: H. Joseph, I. Oppenheim.

1873: H. Joseph.

1874: Mr. (Rev.) Bischofswerder, Mr. Levin snr. (Henry), Henry Joseph, Israel Levin, Israel Oppenheim.

1875: Henry Levin, Henry Joseph, Mr. Bischofswerder, [Dr. Harvey], I. Oppenheim, [Alderman I. B. Coulson, Councillor Marwell, Mr. Cornish, Mr. Mounder], (Sir Moses Montefiore, Mr. Emanuel).

1876: Henry Levin, Henry Joseph, Israel Levin, Samuel Jacob (Falmouth), Israel Oppenheim.

1877: H. Joseph, Samuel Jacob (Falmouth). (Henry Levin died in 1877).

1878: H. Joseph, Israel Levin, Israel Oppenheim.

1879: no minutes.

1880: Henry Joseph, I. Levin, Mr. Oppenheim (Israel), Mr. B. H. Joseph.

1881: Mr. J. (Joseph) Joseph (a son of Henry Joseph, and married to Emily Jacob, daughter of Isaac Jacob of Falmouth), Mr. I. Oppenheim, Mr. I. Levin, Mr. David Bischofswerder, Israel Levin.

1882: Israel Levin, Barnett Joseph, Joseph Joseph, David Bischofswerder, Morris Bischofswerder, George Bischofswerder, Henry Joseph (deceased), [A. Pooley], (A. Cohen M.P.).

1883-1884: no minutes.

1885: B. H. Joseph (Birmingham), Mrs. (Isabelle) Joseph (Birmingham), I. Oppenheim, I. Levin, David Bischofswerder, Morris Bischofswerder.

1886: I. Oppenheim, D. Bischofswerder, M. Bischofswerder, I. H. (Israel Henry) Levin, B. H. Joseph, (Rabbi) I. Rubinstein.

1887: I. Levin, David Bischofswerder, Israel Oppenheim, Morris Bischofswerder, I. A. Rubinstein, (Dr. Adler), B. H. Joseph, J. Joseph, Alexander Levin, Miss Jacobs, [Mr. Wallis, builder], George Bischofswerder, Rev. Michael Lancrom (Leinkram).

1888: David Bischofswerder, I. Oppenheim, G. Bischofswerder, M. Bischofswerder, Rev. M. Lancrom.

1889: D. Bischofswerder, I. Oppenheim, M. Bischofswerder, B. H. Joseph.

1890: D. Bischofswerder, I. Oppenheim, M. Bischofswerder, J. Joseph, Harry Bischofswerder (son of David).

1891: D. Bischofswerder, I. Oppenheim, J. Joseph, B. H. Joseph.

1892: David Bischofswerder, Morris Bischofswerder, Harry Bischofswerder, B. H. Joseph, Israel Oppenheim.

---

[1] Translations and observations from Rabbi Neil Kraft, Hedy Parry-Davies (both 8th July 2013) and Dr Sharman Kadish (10th July 2013). Rabbi Dr. Nicholas de Lange has also confirmed these details.

[2] Hedy Parry-Davies (8th July 2013).

[3] I am grateful to John Probert for his information on the chapel and his observations on Bible Christian practice (8th July 2013) and to Rev. Julyan Drew, the chapel's minister, for his comments (8th-10th July).

[4] Letters and search information from: David Thomas, Archivist CRO Truro (February 1999), who has catalogued and researched all of the surviving Basset papers; Leslie Douch, the Courtney Library, RIC Truro (March 1999), and Allen Buckley (March 1999), both of whom possess a considerable knowledge of the same papers.

[5] See Sharman Kadish, *The Synagogues of Britain and Ireland* (Yale University Press 2011) pp. 32-33.

[6] Jacob (1949); Roth (1950) pp. 17 & 72.

[7] It is not known if Jacob Jacob retained a secondary copy of this register, although its equivalent was retained in Penzance, and this was lodged with the Penzance Registry.

[8] Roth, *The Rise of Provincial Jewry* (1950) p. 62.

[9] Gay: *Old Falmouth* (1903) p. 231; *Falmouth and Penryn Directory & Guide* (1864) p. 45.

[10] Lake's *Falmouth Guide* (1815) p. 48; Trathen: *History of Falmouth* (1815) pp. 46-47; Thomas: *History of Falmouth* (1827) p. 86; Philp: *Panorama of Falmouth* (1828) p. 49. See also Friedlander & Fry in *The Lost Jews of Cornwall*, pp. 292-295.

[11] English Heritage - National Monuments Records, Swindon (Ref. SW8032NE: Letter to Keith Pearce, 10th October 1997) give the date as 1808, although they have been unable to confirm an official source for the year; also Jacob (1949) [in Pearce & Fry Ed. (2000) pp. 55-56] ; & Roth (1933). Roth (1950 p. 62) identifies the *RCG* item incorrectly as 16th August: there was no issue of the *RCG* for that date, but it is possible that the item was reprinted in a national newspaper. I am grateful to Helen Fry for drawing my attention to the *RCG* reference in Roth, and to Angela Broome of the Courtney Library, RIC Truro, for identifying it from source (Letter to Keith Pearce, 12th December 2005).

[12] The analysis of the content of these documents has been compiled by Keith Pearce at the County Record Office, Truro. I am greatly indebted to H.C. Faulkner for his advice in helping to identify the location of these items, and to David Thomas, Archivist at CRO for his preliminary summary of their content. An extensive archive of the Wodehouse family has been deposited by the Arwenack Manor Office at the CRO Truro, and is to be found in *The Earl of Kimberley Collection*. There are several documents, and minor enclosures (Refs. K.58, K.121 and K.350/8) which relate to the Falmouth congregation.

[13] Jacob (1949) citing (i) a letter of 3rd June 1914 from Lawrence Jacob (1843-1923) to Charles H. L. Emanuel, Secretary to the Board of Deputies and (ii) the 64th Annual Report (1913-1916 Session) of the Board of Deputies. Some of these items are held at the RIC, Truro, and the Jewish Museum, London. Friedlander and Fry in *The Lost Jews of Cornwall* (2000) pp. 292-306.

[14] Gay (1903) pp. 18, 83 & 175.

[15] Susser (1993) p. 42 misread the name as *Andrew Jacobs* and his source reference (PRO HO 129/12/309) should read as *308*.

[16] PRO HO 129/308 (Copies of the original Census entry, courtesy of David Thomas & Deborah Tritton, CRO Truro 18th November 2005), and Ordinance Survey (1880): information from Helen Fry (1998).

[17] The National Monuments Record at Swindon, and the Royal Institute of British Architects in London (February 2001) have been unable to identify information on the architect and builders.

[18] This information has been provided by H.C. Faulkner: Letter to Keith Pearce 9th February 2001. CRO Truro cannot locate any business or personal papers of these builders amongst its holdings:

Letter from David Thomas, Archivist, to Keith Pearce, 15th February 2001.

[19] Warn's Directory (1864) pp. 24-26, 31, 70-71, 148-149, 231 & (Insurance Directories Section) pp. 6 & 34.

[20] There are two copies of this lease at CRO Truro. No. 382 applies to all subsequent leases and conveyances relating to the synagogue.

[21] I have edited these extracts, and others quoted subsequently throughout this chapter.

[22] The first three children were baptised on 5th May 1816, 3rd August 1817 and 30th May 1819. I am grateful to H.C. Faulkner, and also to Trudy Martin of the Cornwall Family History Society for this information (March 2001). The third child, Eliza, may have died in infancy, in that two further baptisms are recorded, for another Eliza, on 29th April 1821, and for Emma, on 13th March 1825 (the year of Edward Bawden's death).

[23] Bailey's Directory (1788) p. 234 & the Universal Directory (1791) Vol. 2, p. 99.

[24] Later, he appears as such in Pigot's Directory (1833) p. 141.

[25] Letter from H.C. Faulkner to Keith Pearce, 15th March 2001; and further records from Trudy Martin, from which this information and some details relating to Thomas Hearle and William Kirkness (below) have been drawn. Andrew Young, son of Andrew and Thomasina Young was baptised in Falmouth on 8th October 1772, and was buried there on 17th July 1822.

[26] The additional s often appears at the end of names such as *Solomon* or *Jacob* as a free variant spelling. Solomon Solomons is clearly identified with the second original signatory, who signed his name on the lease and mortgage documents as – *Solomon*.

[27] Roth (1950) pp. 27-29.

[28] Susser (1972) p. 8 (A13).

[29] Alex Jacob (1949) in *The Lost Jews of Cornwall* (2000) p. 59.

[30] Susser, in *The Cornishman* (16th July 1964).

[31] Pigot's Directory 1830, p. 143.

[32] The Universal Directory 1791, vol. 2, p. 97, lists a Thomas Andrew at Customs.

[33] The former date is consistent with his age, given as 59, in the 1841 Census for Falmouth. The Baptismal records for Talland give his parents as Nathaniel and Eulia Hearle. Two years later, on 24th January 1785, a Thomas Hearle, son of Nathaniel and *Eulalia* Hearle was also baptised there. However, the 1841 Census is known to be subject to error regarding ages, and although it appears to give Hearle's age correctly (in relation to a birth date of 1782), it may be that the second baptism (of 1785) is that of the above. Thomas Hearle had married a Grace Pearse in 1811, and records again show two sons for them, both named Thomas, baptised in 1815 and 1821 respectively.

[34] In the 1851 Census, Thomas Andrew, Former Brewer, is listed as a visitor at the home of John Tresidder, a Scrivener, of Broad Street, St. Gluvias.

[35] Pigot's Directory 1830, p. 40; Gay 1903, pp. 134-135; Letter from H.C. Faulkner, March 2001.

[36] Gay (1903) p. 203.

[37] Roth, *The Rise of Provincial Jewry* (1950) pp. 63 & 111. For Penzance, Roth gives six paying members. Roth gives his sources for these figures as *The Jewish Chronicle* (1842), Margoliouth's *History* (1851), and a vote in the Chief Rabbinate (1844).

[38] PRO HO 129/308 (VIII & IX). It has been noted that Susser (1993: pp. 42 & 279) has either misread or failed to recall this census entry correctly, in that he ascribes the entry to an *Andrew* Jacobs. In fact, it is clearly signed as "J. Jacob", and the name *Andrew* does not appear on the original (Andrew, son of Samuel Jacob, was not born until 1874). Further, Susser's wording of the "remarks" does not accord verbatim with the original.

[39] Vivian D. Lipman, *A Survey of Anglo-Jewry in 1851*, in *TJHSE* vol. XVII (1953) pp. 171-188.

[40] These are in my possession, having been passed to me, together with the Archive and Papers of Alex M. Jacob, by Philip Levy, legal executor of the Jacob Estate.

[41] Samuel Jacob was a founder member and a Deacon of the *Three Grand Principles* Masonic Lodge (No. 967) of Falmouth. Another member was Thomas H. Lanyon, who may have been a friend of the Jacob family: a photograph in the Jacob family Archive shows Samuel's brother Alexander (1841-1903) with three Cornishmen, one of whom is identified on the back of the photograph as a Lanyon.

[42] Warn's 1864 *Directory and Guide to Falmouth and Penryn* lists Michael Jacob as the Secretary of the Jews' Synagogue (p. 27) and the Treasurer of the Falmouth Debating Society (p. 31).

[43] The writing is not punctuated and proceeds without a break at this point to "Mrs. Cohen".

[44] These circumstantial details for Rosey Moses, Israel Solomon and Nancy Joseph subsequently appeared on the Arwenack Manor Notice (No. 154) of 1871.

[45] See Cecil Roth, *The Portsmouth Community and its historical background,* in Transactions JHSE, vol. XIII, p. 157.

[46] Ref. K.350/8.

[47] See Edward Jamilly, *The Georgian Synagogue,* JMC London (1999) pp. 20-21.

[48] As mentioned previously, the congregation's records, including the Minute-Book may well have been taken to London by Samuel Jacob. If it was passed down in the family, it is not to be found amongst the papers in the archive of the historian, the late Alex Jacob.

[49] *The Falmouth and Penryn Weekly Times,* April 9th 1881: information from Tony Pawlyn (2000). An abbreviated version of this item appeared in *The Cornubian* on 15th April 1881.

[50] Whilst Falmouth, with Penryn, is likely to have possessed the largest single community of Jews in Cornwall, it is doubtful if the statement can be taken as literally true. Penzance had its own signifi-cant Jewish population, and towns of minor settlement in mid-Cornwall, such as Truro, St. Austell, Redruth, Camborne and Hayle, together with scattered families across the county could have accounted collectively for numbers in excess of those living in Falmouth. Although some of these outlying families would have been members of the Falmouth congregation, others appear as paying members in the Accounts of the Penzance Congregation. However, in the early 1800s, it may well be that Falmouth's Jewish population was by far the largest in the County, and it must be acknowl-edged that the Falmouth synagogue had been built to accommodate 80 persons, whilst that in Penzance housed only 50.

[51] Friedlander and Fry, in *The Lost Jews of Cornwall*, p. 302.

[52] This original letter and the others mentioned here are from the Alex Jacob Archive.

[53] In a letter to Alex Jacob of 31st August 1958, Edward Jamilly describes a visit made to Falmouth and a conversation concerning the synagogue with John Julian and Co. "who own it and a good many other "dissenting" chapels for the purposes of storing furniture - bought it (25 years ago)".

[54] Letter from Alan I. Lewis in the *Jewish Chronicle* (9th April 1983).

[55] Alex M. Jacob, *The Jews of Falmouth 1740-1860* (JHSE 1949, Vol XVII p. 68). See also Friedlander & Fry, in *The Lost Jews of Cornwall* (2000) pp. 293-295 and 302-305. Edward Jamilly, *The Georgian Syna-gogue* (Jewish Memorial Council London 1999) pp. 20-21.

[56] Edward Jamilly *The Georgian Synagogue* (1999). pp. 7 & 20-21 and Letter to Alex Jacob (31st August 1958).

[57] Ref. Jamilly's letter to Alex Jacob of 1958.

[58] *The Falmouth Packet,* 8th April 2000. Friedlander and Fry, *The Lost Jews of Cornwall,* p. 295.

[59] These names are recorded in the Hyamson Papers held at the Jewish Genealogical Society of Great Britain, Kinloss Gardens, London (research by Helen Fry, February 2000).

[60] The original is to be found in the Roth Collection at the Brotherton Library, the University of Leeds. It was preserved by the Joseph family of Birmingham (mentioned towards the end of this account) and passed on by George L. Joseph to Cecil Roth. Roth's perceptive analysis of the original minute-book formed the basis of his two-part study *Penzance, the Decline and Fall of an Anglo-Jewish Commu-nity,* published in *The Jewish Chronicle* in 1933, and reproduced in *The Lost Jews of Cornwall.*

[61] I have drawn upon complete secondary copies of these source documents. Of these, major sections of the minute-book have been newly translated by Yissochor Marmorstein of London (2002-3). The leases and conveyances were analysed by John Simmons of All Souls' College, Oxford (1998).

[62] At some later point, these documents passed into the care of the firms J. Jewell Hill, and Lacey, Moffat & Saunders. The latter firm, at one time, held a lease for the first (1768) synagogue.

[63] Roth (1933) states, incorrectly, that this would have been the case up to 1807-8. He was, apparently, unaware that there had been an earlier synagogue.

[64] Roth (1933).

[65] Roth (1933).

[66] The document's existence (with the firm Moffat *et.al.*) was confirmed by an accountant who had sight of it, in a conversation with Godfrey Simmons in 1983.

[67] *Saundry's Almanacs* 1933 (p.35) & 1936 (p.33).

[68] Thomas (1820) p. 47. There were at least two editions of this work: the 2nd edition of 1820, and the 3rd of 1831, titled *Ancient & Modern History of Mount's Bay.* Both were printed as "Thomas' *History* etc.

Printed & Sold by J. Thomas of Penzance." The *Bibliotheca Cornubiensis* (Bowes & Courtney 1878, p. 173) suggests that the book was not written by Thomas, but is reported to have been compiled by a William Colenso, who was apprenticed to J. Thomas.

[69] The Eva MSS (RIC Truro) gives the date as 1768: Pool (1974) p. 89.

[70] Peter Pool's *The Branwells of Penzance* (1990: private publication) contains information on the family, and I have drawn on this study in this section.

[71] See note 66 above.

[72] CRO Truro DCPEN/307.

[73] The years 1768 and 1806-1807 are given correctly by Pool in his History of Penzance (1974) p. 89.

[74] As an extracted precis by John Simmons (1998).

[75] Roth (1933).

[76] Susser (1993) p. 169.

[77] Susser (1993) pp. 136-144.

[78] I have amended the names where they were identified incorrectly in *The Lost Jews of Cornwall* (p. 88).

[79] Green (1989) p. 147.

[80] Susser (1993) pp. 31, 72, 96 & 218; and (1996: Hoe Cemetery Inscriptions) pp. 13, 16, & 24. Roth, *The Rise of Provincial Jewry* (1964) p. 22. Details of the Ralph family can also be found in the Roth Collection, the Brotherton Library, University of Leeds (Letter from Walter Samuel to Cecil Roth, 3rd January 1933). See also Helen Fry (pp. 61-62) in *The Jews of Devon and Cornwall* (2000).

[81] I am grateful to Angela Shire for providing some of the information on Elias Magnus used here and elsewhere.

[82] See his details in the Penzance cemetery (8:1).

[83] Roth (1933) in *LJC* p. 77.

[84] Pool (1974) pp. 227 & 229

[85] Pool (1974) p. 104.

[86] Ward Lists of the Penzance Borough 1835-1868 (CRO Truro ref. DCPEN/121-124): research by Godfrey Simmons.

[87] The figures have been rounded up or down for convenience.

[88] The original Hebrew copy and translation were passed down in the family of Rabbi Simmons, and have been provided by Godfrey Simmons.

[89] Her family appear in later Census records from 1841.

[90] Roth (1933).

[91] Todd Endelman, *The Jews of Britain 1656-2000* (2002) pp. 93 & 193; David Katz, *The Jews in the History of England* (2001) pp. 335, 341 & 381.

[92] Richard Edmonds, *A Statistical Account of the Borough of Penzance and of the Parish of Madron, Cornwall* (The Statistical Society of London; July 1839) p. 230.

[93] This misconception has found currency in local tradition and in some printed texts. As noted, the cottages are likely to be significantly earlier than the second synagogue of 1807, but this is not certain.

[94] 7th *Annual Report to the Royal Polytechnic of Cornwall* (1839) p. 22.

[95] J. S. Courtney, *Guide to Penzance* (London: E. Rowe, Longman, Brown, Green 1845) p. 44.

[96] Roth, *The Rise of Provincial Jewry* (1950) p. 111.

[97] The form only allowed for "Estimated Number of Persons attending Divine Service on Sunday, March 30, 1851.

[98] The form asked the compiler to refer to the attached Instructions VIII to record the average attendance during the last (specified period of) months. Simmons did not fill in the time-period that applied to his figures. Nor did he attach any "Remarks" to the form's section X.

[99] Edward Jamilly *The Georgian Synagogue* (1999) pp. 19-20; see also Friedlander and Fry in *The Lost Jews of Cornwall*, pp. 295-301.

[100] Susser (1993) p. 169 gives the year of the New Regulations incorrectly as 1884 (presumably a typographical error).

[101] Susser (1993) pp. 39-43 (with primary source-references).

[102] I have made some minor alterations to the wording, by omitting some superfluous words, and by adding punctuation to assist the sense.

[103] This is the only subsection where the title is in Hebrew script.

[104] Todd M. Endelman, *The Jews of Georgian England 1714-1830* (1979) p. 261.

[105] Susser (1993) p. 304 (note 72) and (1995) p. 74; Judith Samuel (1997) pp. 62, 71, 86, 104-111 & 118-121.

[106] This particular headstone has been Grade II listed by English Heritage.

[107] Endelman (2002) p. 101; & pp. 100-110, 112, 123-24, 150-51, 260, 266; see also Endelman (1979) pp. 46, 83, 103 & 113.

[108] Yissochor Marmorstein notes that the Hebrew word may have been written incorrectly, and that it could refer to the stitching of the parchment sheets of a Torah scroll.

[109] The receipt is not placed in the Minutes following those of 28th March, but appears to have been displaced, appearing in an Addendum at the end of the book, together with a number of fragmentary accounts for isolated dates from December 1852 up to April 1862.

[110] David S. Katz, *The Jews in the History of England 1485-1850* (Oxford 2001) pp. 381-382.

[111] This is covered in detail in the chapter on the Rabbis.

[112] Not the Samuel Jacob of Falmouth mentioned above.

[113] I am grateful to Godfrey Simmons, and to Joseph Wolfman of Liverpool, for providing extensive information on Jacob Gorfenkle from their research: Letters to Godfrey Simmons (1st September & 8th November 2004) and to Barry Cox, Honorary Librarian, the Royal National Lifeboat Institution (23rd September 2004); see also *The Life-Boat* (November 1st 1871) pp. 182-183. Berger (2004) p. 130 quotes a contemporary newspaper report of Gorfenkle's death and his bequests. The report contains some incorrect and uncertain details: he did not die in Plymouth and there is no record of his burial there; the lifeboat bequest was not made to the Mayor of Plymouth.

[114] *The Cornishman*, 1st August 1889, p. 4; correspondence between Jennifer Marin of the Jewish Museum London and Keith Pearce (October 2003); articles in *The London Jewish News* (9th January 2004) and *The Jewish Chronicle* (16th January 2004).

[115] I am grateful to John Probert for his observations on this registration document, a copy of which has been provided from Godfrey Simmons' archive.

[116] Katz (2001) pp. 336-338; Endelman (2002) pp. 121-123. For a detailed study of his life see Abigail Green, *Moses Montefiore, Jewish Liberator, Imperial Hero*, Belknap Press, Harvard (2010).

[117] See the section on Penzance Trades relating to the Jewish Communities and People.

[118] A more detailed account of the synagogue's interior by Friedlander and Fry in *The Lost Jews of Cornwall* (pp. 295-300), including Rabbi Bernard Susser's 1964 description of what then was a Christian place of worship.

[119] Roth (1933).

[120] These names were compiled by Godfrey Simmons in 1998. I have added some names of ministers where they appear in Hebrew. Some names have been omitted where they are indecipherable. Variant forms of the same person's name are common in the original.

[121] Susser (1993) pp. 101, 207, 232 & 283 (nt. 83

[122] This name may have been carried over from 1815.

[123] It is possible that this man was of the same family as John Bodilly of Penzance, who provided me with an original receipt (dated January 28th 1869) from Israel Oppenheim's furnishing store. The receipt had been passed down through his family.

[124] These descriptions and images of the synagogue and its artefacts were included by Evelyn Friedlander and Helen Fry in both *The Lost Jews of Cornwall* and in *The Jews of Devon and Cornwall* (2000). Preliminary to applying for listed status for the synagogue, Susan Soyinka has compiled a supporting document *The Penzance Synagogue – A Brief History* (2013 unpublished). I am grateful to her for providing me with a copy of this document, which I have referenced in the Bibliography, but because it does not fall within my temporal remit to deal with this post-community period in relation to Penzance (when the former Jewish families of the town were not involved in the synagogue in any way) and because, as stated in my Preface, I have not chosen to cover architectural or ritual aspects of the synagogues (*vide* Jamilly, Susser, Friedlander, Fry and Kadish) I have not drawn upon the writer's new and most interesting (post-1906) research in this book, but I have confined myself to selected details only from pre-published texts.

Conclusion

It has not been within my chosen remit to continue the story of Jewish settlement beyond the demise of the historic congregations and their former communities. In 1913, Morris Bischofswerder left Penzance, and the burial of Nathan Vos took place in Penryn. Jewish congregational life had come to an end in Falmouth by 1880 and in Penzance it was effectively over by 1892-1895, the synagogue there being sold some ten years later. However, it is likely that Jewish life in Cornwall was not extinguished altogether. Some Jews, scattered widely across the County may have remained, and, in the 20th century others eventually came to live here. The new arrivals are not known to have had familial links with the Cornish Jews of the 18th and 19th centuries, and some may have stayed only briefly. I mention here only a few who were distinguished either by individual achievement, or by circumstance.

Charles Sydney Goldman (1868-1958) was a businessman, journalist and author. He was born in the Cape, South Africa, spending much of his early life in the Transvaal, and he made a fortune as a young man in mining. He came to own estates and properties in South Africa, British Columbia and England. He was a correspondent during the Second Boer War (1899-1902), and subsequently wrote a book about his wartime experiences. During the First World War he served as a major in the Cornwall Royal Garrison Artillery. He served as the Unionist MP for Penryn and Falmouth from 1910 to 1918, and lived in Trefusis House, Falmouth, until the late 1920s.[1]

Arthur Blok (1882-1974) who was born in the East End, and whose father was of Dutch extraction, was an engineer who had some momentary contact with Cornwall. He was an assistant to Ambrose Fleming, the inventor of radio equipment, and in 1901, Blok was involved in some of the earliest moments in radio transmission from Poldhu Cove on the Lizard peninsula to America. Apart from his numerous achievements in the field of engineering, he was an accomplished conchologist and malacologist, amassing a huge collection of shells (13,000) and thousands of books, 600 on molluscs alone. He died in Brighton.[2]

Charles Singer (1876-1960), the son of Rev. Simeon Singer (the Hebraist of the "Singer's Prayer Book" from the 1890s onwards) was born in Camberwell. He was educated at University College, London and Magdalen College, Oxford, and was a historian of science, technology and medicine. He held university posts in London and America. After his retirement in 1942 (and possibly before) he lived in Cornwall near Fowey. He is remembered as being involved in the education of children who were evacuees during the Second World War. He died at Par.[3]

Piet Mendels (1901-1996) was born into a Jewish family in the Netherlands, although he maintained little contact with Jewish tradition. He worked for many years in the china clay industry. In June 1973, as managing director and chairman of the New Consolidated Mines of Cornwall Ltd, he received the MBE for his services to exports. He contributed greatly to the local community, especially in charitable activities, and set up the Piet Mendels Foundation. He became the chairman of the Fowey Hospital and its welfare committee, and he was also involved in the Cornwall Heritage Trust. He funded the publication of the Lanhydrock Land Atlas, and donated Castle Fields in Fowey to the National Trust.[4]

Albert Reuss (1889-1976) was born (as Reiss) in Budapest, and moved to Vienna in 1907. He was the son of a butcher, and as a young man he was an actor and singer. Painting was originally a passionate hobby for him, and his early works are full of vivid colours. Later, he became a distinctive painter of surrealist and figurative subjects, which are characterised by a restrained use of colour, and a pervading sense of ambiguity, dislocation and estrangement. Whilst his paintings are essentially melancholic in atmosphere, they are also serene and gentle in mood. When Hitler's troops marched into Austria in the *Anschluss* of March 1938, like many other Jews, Reuss fled the country and was given asylum in England. At first, with his wife, Rosa, he lived in Gloucestershire, and, for a time, was an art teacher at the Dean Close School in Cheltenham. In 1947 he was granted British citizenship, and he moved to Cornwall, where he settled in the village of Mouse-hole, near Penzance, living there for the rest of his life. He led a reclusive life, especially in later years, when his paintings, which he called his "works of loneliness",[5] became increasingly sombre. Reuss stood apart from the school of abstraction of the Cornish painters of his day, but his individuality, stature and the considerable scale of his achievement is now widely recognised. Around two hundred of his paintings constitute what is arguably the most significant and extensive collection held by the Newlyn Art Gallery.[6] There are many others in private ownership.

Hyman Segal (1914-2004) was born in London to Russian-Jewish parents. He attended the Jewish Free School in Camden Town. At the age of twelve he won a scholarship to attend the St. Martin's School of Art, where he studied painting, sculpture and design. In 1935 he designed posters for London Transport. During the Second World War, he served in Africa, and upon his return in 1946, he came to Cornwall. He lived for a while at St. Agnes, and provided art therapy for TB patients at the Tehidy Sanatorium. He settled in St. Ives, where he lived for the rest of his life. He worked at the famous Porthmeor Studios, and he was a founder member of the Penwith Society of Arts. A colourful and sociable character, his accomplished and often amusing drawings of local people, fishermen and cats became very popular. An exhibition of pub-goers in St. Agnes from the 1950s, was exhibited in the museum there in 2012. Copies of his caricatures of St. Ives locals can still be seen on the walls of the Sloop Inn, by the harbour-side in St. Ives.[7]

Norman Levine (1923-2005), novelist, short story writer and poet, was born in Rakov, Poland, into an Orthodox Jewish family. With the rise of anti-Semitism, the family fled to Canada, where his father worked as an impoverished fruit-seller in Lower Town, Ottawa. During the Second World War Levine served as a pilot in the Canadian division of the Royal Air Force. Returning to Canada, he studied at McGill University, in Montreal, Quebec, and in 1949 he won a fellowship to study at King's College, London. For about thirty years he lived in St. Ives, where he became friends with the painters Ben Nicholson, Patrick Heron, Terry Frost and Peter Lanyon. Levine also became a friend of the London painter Francis Bacon (1909-1992). Bacon was an instinctive city-dweller, and the subjects of his paintings were always given an interior setting. Surprisingly, he stayed in St. Ives for some four months from late September 1959, occupying one of the Porthmeor studios. Bacon was not associated with the St. Ives School of painters as such, and, as a resolutely figurative artist, he harboured a life-long distrust of abstract art. Loathing the countryside, he was also disinclined towards subjects based upon landscape, and he appears to have been indifferent to the renowned qualities of the Cornish marine light and to its seascape. (Of the twenty or more canvases Bacon completed during his stay, he destroyed all but six, and he never referred to this Cornish period). In fact, Bacon had little if anything in common with these Cornish painters, and, it seems, possessed little interest in or empathy towards their work. However, the sculptress, Barbara Hepworth, "had a positive opinion" of Bacon both as a man and as an artist "despite their widely differing views",[8] and Norman Levine greatly admired his paintings. In one of his most popular novels, "From a Seaside Town" (1970)[9] the character of the painter Charles Carter is based on him. Levine also wrote a short story (1983)[10] based upon his visit to the Jewish cemetery in Penzance, and his meeting with a Hebrew scholar, a Cambridge professor "Rabbi Jonathan Singer". This character was based upon a real-life meeting between Levine and Rabbi Dr. Nicholas de Lange, who surveyed the Cornish cemeteries in 1975, and who went to St. Ives to find Levine. From the 1980s, Levine lived in Canada, but eventually he returned to England. He died in Darlington.

Mark Rothko (1903-1970), the American abstract painter, made a fleeting three-day visit to St. Ives in August 1959, staying with the local painter, Peter Lanyon. Rothko was of Latvian Jewish descent, spoke Russian, Yiddish and Hebrew, and had studied the Talmud as a young man. During his brief stay (during which it has been said that he considered buying a disused chapel in Lelant to house some of his own works) he met other painters, including Patrick Heron, Terry Frost and also Paul Feiler, who was of German descent. It may seem perverse to include mention of such a transient incident, but, because of Rothko's great fame the visit has assumed the quality of an iconic moment in 20th century Cornish painting, preserved as it was by his being photographed with some of those he met. These Cornish painters, and others, have since achieved their own reputation and status, and Rothko's supposed influence upon and relationship to the St. Ives and Newlyn Schools has since come under scrutiny and has been subject to revision, having been characterised as "a footnote in the history of St. Ives abstraction".[11]

Prior to the outbreak of the Second World War some Jews arrived in Cornwall as refugees. One of these was Greta Glucksman from Vienna, a nurse, who lived in Redruth for a number of years.[12] The much later burial in the Penzance Jewish Cemetery (1964) of Adolf Salzmann, who also lived in Redruth, has been mentioned, but the date of his arrival in the County is uncertain. During the War itself numerous people came to Cornwall as evacuees. Jewish children were housed with Cornish families in many parts of the County, and several accounts of their memories have been published. Children from the Jews' Free School (JFS) in the East End of London came to Mousehole, outside Penzance, where they were educated at the village school,[13] and, further to the Blitz of 7th September 1940, evacuees also came to Helston from the West Ham Synagogue.[14] Devonians were also hosts to Jews during the War.[15]

After the War, Jews continued to settle in Cornwall, but without concentration in any particular towns, and, for several decades, without communal focus. Those who were concerned to be observant of the festivals would most likely have returned to their home towns and cities on those occasions, or visited the synagogues at Plymouth or Exeter. Eventually, in 1999, from a few contacts established between Jews, a new congregation *Kehillat Kernow* was formed, and it has grown steadily in numbers. I would hope that, one day, the story of this new community will merit a history of its own.

---

[1] W. D. Rubinstein, Michael Jolles & Hilary L. Rubinstein, *The Palgrave Dictionary of Anglo-Jewish History* (2011) p. 335.

[2] Michael Jolles, *Biographical Notes on 1200 British Jews* (preparatory notes: to be published).

[3] *Palgrave* (as note 1) p. 923.

[4] Michael Jolles (personal communication to Keith Pearce, 12th April 2013). Dr. Jolles and his family were well acquainted with Mendels.

[5] Kunsthandel Widder Gallery, Vienna.

[6] Melissa Hardie, *100 Years in Newlyn – Diary of a Gallery* (Patten Press, Cornwall 1995); David Buckman, *Artists in Britain Since 1945 Vol. 2* (Art Dictionaries Ltd. 2006); Melissa Hardie (edit.), *Artists in Newlyn and West Cornwall 1880-1940* (Art Dictionaries Ltd. 2009).

[7] Cornwall Artists Index (Melissa Hardie 2009, as above).

[8] Michael Peppiatt, *Francis Bacon* (Weidenfeld and Nicolson, London 1996) p. 181.

[9] Norman Levine, *From a Seaside Town* (Macmillan 1970).

[10] Norman Levine, *In a Jewish Cemetery* (Jewish Chronicle publications 1983). In this story, Levine incorrectly identifies the headstone of James Jacob Hart as that of Lemon Hart's *father*. Whilst Eliezar Hart will be buried in the cemetery (in an unmarked grave) the headstone is that of Lemon Hart's *nephew*. I am grateful to Nicholas de Lange for providing me with a copy of this story some years ago.

[11] Iain Gale in *The Independent* (13th August 1996); Chris Stephens, *Mark Rothko in Cornwall* (Tate Gallery St. Ives 1996).

[12] Information from John Probert (8th July 2013).

[13] Susan Soyinka, *From East End to Land's End* (Eliora Press 2013).

[14] Howard Bloch, *Earlham Grove Schul - One Hundred Years of West Ham Synagogue and Community* (London 1997) pp. 43-44 & 50-53.

[15] Helen Fry, *Jews in North Devon During the Second World War* (Halsgrove 2005).

Postscript

Kehillat Kernow

The Revival of Jewish Life in Cornwall

Harvey Kurzfield

I first came to Cornwall on holiday from London at the age of 14 with a Jewish friend whose family had often spent their summer holidays at Newquay. In 1972, after qualifying as a primary school teacher I secured a post at St. Agnes, and later I moved to Camborne, where I did meet one Jewish man, but, like me, he knew of no other Jews living in the area. For some years, the only time I met with other Jews was when I returned to London to visit my family, or when I went to other places outside Cornwall where there was a synagogue. Sometimes I would visit other schools to talk about Judaism, and, occasionally, I would meet children who said that one of their parents was Jewish, but for at least twenty years I had no real contact with Jewish people in the County.

Eventually, I became a member of the Cornwall Standing Advisory Council for Religious Education, as its first Jewish member, and some years later, David Hampshire, a new RE Advisor was appointed who also happened to be Jewish. Through his travels throughout Cornwall, he came into contact with various Jewish people who lived here. This led to his organising a small group of us to meet at his home in Truro, including Gloria and Milton Jacobson, Anne and David Hearle, Vera Collins, and Bonnie and Wilf Rockley. We agreed that we should try to organise occasional Sabbath services, and David agreed to do this. Over time, more people joined us, and, eventually, there grew the idea of re-establishing a Jewish congregation in Cornwall on a more formal basis. In this way, Kehillat Kernow, the Jewish Community of Cornwall, came about in 1999, and I had the honour of being elected as its first chairman, a post I still hold today.

From these small beginnings of about a dozen people, we have grown steadily year by year, and we now have around 100 members, consisting of 60 adults, who come from all over Cornwall, and some of their children also attend regularly. We hold fortnightly Sabbath services and observe all of the major Jewish festivals. Although we do not have a Rabbi, we run the services ourselves, and often welcome Jewish visitors.

The historic Jewish communities, which have been the focus of this book, lived exclusively in a few towns in south and mid Cornwall, centred primarily in Falmouth and Penzance. They had their own synagogues, their own burial grounds and their own ministers, and they were members of traditional, orthodox organisations. Today, our community is affiliated to the Movement for Reform Judaism but our members embrace many different forms and ideas and come from different backgrounds. Everyone is welcome and we hope to remain a growing and dynamic force within the expanding diversity that is modern Cornwall for many years to come.

This book by Keith Pearce on the history of the Jews of Cornwall provides a huge amount of new information relating to the historic communities, and its importance as a significant historical work should not be underestimated. Those of us who live here now continue to be informed and affected by the habits, preoccupations and religious observances of those former communities, whose members, for mainly practical reasons, chose to leave this County for ever. The Jews of the 18th and 19th centuries were mainly trades-people with skills and expertise that helped to shape some aspects of Cornwall's commercial life. In contrast, today's Jewish community includes teachers, lawyers, doctors and business people.

Cornwall today is a land of immense cultural diversity, and the recently formed Inter-Faith Forum includes representatives of many different faiths. Three centuries ago the Cornish welcomed the Jewish community; now it plays host to many, and we Jews who have settled here and who have formed Kehillat Kernow are proud and honoured to play a small part in the publication of this book.

Bibliography

Where information has been drawn from public or private archives this has been accredited in the notes accompanying the text.

Various Primary Sources include:

The Cornishman, The Cornish Advertiser, The Cornish Echo, The Cornish Telegraph, The Cornubian, The Daily Telegraph, The Dorset Sherborne Mercury, The Exeter Flying Post, Falmouth Packet, The Gentleman's Magazine, The Jewish Chronicle, Jewish World, Journals and Account Books of William Borlase (Courtney Library, RIC Truro), The London Gazette, The Mining Journal, The Royal Cornwall Gazette, The Times, The West Briton, The Western Daily Press, The Western Flying Post, The Western Morning News.

Secondary Sources: Essays, Articles and Chapters.

Michael Adler, "The Medieval Jews of Exeter" in *The Transactions of the Devonshire Association for the Advancement of Science, Literature and Art* (1931) Vol. lxiii, pp. 221-240.

Israel Abrahams, "Joachim Gaunse: A Mining Incident in the Reign of Queen Elizabeth", in *The Transactions of the Jewish Historical Society of England (TJHSE)*, vol 4 (1889).

C. K. Croft Andrew, "The Arms of the Duchy of Cornwall – Some New Facts", in The Journal of the Royal Institution of Cornwall Vol. XXV, parts 1 & 2 (1937-1938) pp. 75-83.

Shimon Applebaum, "Were there Jews in Roman Britain?", in *TJSHE* vol. XVII (1953).

Arthur P. Arnold, "Apprentices of Great Britain 1710-1773", in *TJHSE* vol. XXII (1970).

J. Bannister, "Jews in Cornwall", in *The Journal of The Royal Institution of Cornwall (JRIC)*, vol II (1867).

W. I. Bellany, "The Jews of Merthyr Tydfil", in *Shemot*, vol 6:3 (September 1998).

Mesod Benady, "The Settlement of Jews in Gibraltar 1704-1783", in *Transactions JHSE* Vol. XXVI (1979) pp. 87-110.

Reva Berman Brown and Sean McCartney, "David of Oxford and Licoricia of Winchester: glimpses into a Jewish family in thirteenth-century England", in *Transactions JHSE* vol. 39 (2004) pp. 1-34.

Malcolm Brown, "The Jews of Norfolk and Suffolk before 1840" in *The Transactions of the Jewish Historical Society of England* (1990-1992) Vol. XXXII pp. 219-235.

Allen Buckley and Charles Thomas (edit.) "Solomon the Tributer" in the Journal of the Royal Institution of Cornwall (2012) pp. 45-56.

Geoffery Cantor, "The Rise and Fall of Emanuel Mendes da Costa", in The English Historical Review Vol. CXVI, No. 467 (June 2001).

G. T. Clark, *Report on the Sanitary Condition of Penzance*, (HMSO, 1849).

J. S. Courtney, "Chronological Memoranda", in the *7th Annual Report to the Royal Polytechnic Society of Cornwall, 1839*, Courtney Library, RIC, Truro.

H. L. Douch, "Thomas Tonkin - an Appreciation of a Neglected Cornish Historian", in *JRIC* New Series Vol. IV 2 (1962).

S. J. Drake, "Politics and Society in Richard II's Cornwall", in the Journal of the RIC (2013) pp. 23-48.

Alfred Dunitz, "The Rise and Decline of Jewish Communities in Georgian England," in *Le'ela*, (September 1993).

Henry Hawkin, "The Jews in Cornwall", in *Through West Cornwall with a Camera* (London: Thomas Mitchell *c.* 1897).

C. W. Firebrace, "The Records of the Lodge of Antiquity, London (1911 & 1926), The Library and Museum of Freemasonry, London.

Andrew Foot, "Burchard Cranach in Cornwall", in *JRIC* (2002) pp. 64-84.

Evelyn Friedlander, "Lemon Hart", in *The Jews of Devon and Cornwall* (The Hidden Legacy Foundation 2000).

Evelyn Friedlander and Helen Fry, "The Disappearing Heritage: the Synagogues and their Ritual Artefacts", in *The Lost Jews of Cornwall* (2000) and in *The Jews of Cornwall and Devon* (as above) pp. 76-78 & 80-82.

William James Hughan, "Freemasonry in Cornwall", in *The Freemasons' Magazine*, (1866-1867).

Alex M. Jacob, "The Jews of Falmouth", in *Transactions JHSE,* vol. XVII (1953) pp. 63-72.

Henry Jenner:

"The Manx Language: its grammar, literature and present state" in the Transactions of the Philological Society *TPS* (1875-76);

"Cornish Place-Names", in the Journal of the RIC, *JRIC* vol. xviii (1910-11);

"A History of Cornish Place-Names", in the Journal of the Royal Cornwall Polytechnic Society vol. ii (1911-13);

"Cornwall – a Celtic Nation", in the Celtic Review *CR* vol. 1 (1905);

"Cornish Drama", in *CR* (1907);

"The Cornish Language" in *TPS* (1873-74);

"Traditional Relics of the Cornish Language in Mount's Bay", in *TPS* (1875-76);

"Descriptions of Cornish Manuscripts", in *JRIC* vol. xix 1912), and

"The History and Literature of the Ancient Cornish Language", in the Journal of the British Archaeological Society *JBAS* vol. xxxiii (1877).

Anthony P. Joseph, "Genealogy and Jewish History", *TJHSE*, vol 34 (1994-6).

Anthony P. Joseph, "Jewry of the South-West and some of its Australian Connections", in *TJHSE*, vol 24, (1970-73, pub. 1975).

Z. Josephs, "Birmingham Jewry", Vol. II (1740-1930), in the *Birmingham Jewish History Research Group* (1984).

Raphael Langham, "The Reaction in England to the Kidnapping of Edgardo Mortara", in the *Transactions of JHSE* Vol. 39 (2004).

Vivian D. Lipman, "A Survey of Anglo-Jewry in 1851", in *TJSHE* vol. XVII (1953).

Vivian D. Lipman, "The Development of London Jewry", in *A Century of Anglo-Jewish Life 1870-1970* (edit. Salmon. S. Levin) United Synagogue Publications (1970)

Vivian D. Lipman, "The Plymouth Aliens List, 1789 and 1803", in *TJHSE* (1962) Miscellanies Part VI, pp. 187-194.

Vivian D. Lipman, "The Anatomy of Medieval Anglo-Jewry", in *TJHSE* (1968) pp. 64-77.

Charlotte MacKenzie, "Ellis Trading Partnerships and Quayside Properties at Penzance" (2014 unpublished).

Charlotte MacKenzie, "The Mine Merchants of Hayle: Commerce and Family in an Early Industrial Port", Journal of the RIC Truro (2007).

Norman Nail, "The Cornish Curator and the Cosmopolitan Collector", in *JRIC* (New Series II), vol 1, pt. 3, (1993).

R. Morton Nance, "A Guide to Cornish Place Names", Federation of Old Cornwall Societies, Marazion (editions from 1951).

BIBLIOGRAPHY

R. Morton Nance, "When was Cornish last Spoken Traditionally?", in *JRIC*, vol 7, (1973).

R. Morton Nance, "John Davey of Boswednack and his Cornish Rhyme" in *JRIC* , XXI Pt.2 (1923).

Venetia Newall, "The Jews of Cornwall in Local Tradition", in *TJHS,* vol. XXVI (1979) pp. 119-121.

Plymouth Congregational Minute Book of Trades (1747-1801); University of Southampton Library Archives & Manuscripts: MS 116/125.

H. Pollins, "The Jewish Community of Stroud, Gloucestershire", in *Oxford Menorah,* No. 136, (1995).

Keith Pearce, "The Jews Houses" and Cornish Place-Names, in *The Lost Jews of Cornwall* (2000) pp.35-48.

H. Pollins, "The Jewish Community of Stroud, 1877-1908", in the *Jewish Journal of Sociology,* vol. XXXVIII, No.1, (June 1996).

P. A. S. Pool, "William Borlase, the Scholar and the Man", in *JRIC* NS V 2 (1966).

B. D. Price, "A Short Biography of Alfred Aaron de Pass (1861-1952), Art Benefactor Extraoridinary", *Royal Cornwall Polytechnic Society, Falmouth* (1982).

J. C. C. Probert (edit.), "1851 Religious Census, West Cornwall and the Isles of Scilly" (Redruth 1988).

Gerald Retlinger, "The Changed Face of English Jewry at the end of the Eighteenth Century", in *TJHSE* vol. XXIII (1971).

Francis Rodd, on the finding of a "Jews House", in the *Annual Report of the Royal Institution of Cornwall*, (1850 Courtney Library, RIC).

Cecil Roth, "Jew's Houses," in *Antiquity*, vol XXV (June 1951).

Cecil Roth, "Penzance: The Decline and Fall of an Anglo-Jewish Community", in *The Jewish Chronicle* (May and June 1933).

Cecil Roth, "The Portsmouth Community and its Historical Background", in *Transactions JHSE,* Vol. XII (1936) pp. 157-187.

John Rowe and C. T. Andrews, "Cholera in Cornwall," in *The Journal of the RIC*, vol 7, part 2 (1974).

Morris Rosenbaum, "Jewish Freemasons in England (18th & 19th Centuries): a Provisional List", and John M. Shaftesley, "Jews in English Regular Freemasonry 1717-1860", in the *Transactions of the Jewish Historical Society of England* (1973-1975) vol. XXV, pp. 150-209.

Edgar R. Samuel, "New Light on the Selection of Jewish Children's Names", in *TJHSE* vol. XXIII (1971).

Godfrey Simmons and Keith Pearce, "The Penzance Community Records", "The Jewish Cemeteries", "The Rabbis", and "The People", in The Lost Jews of Cornwall (2000) pp 86-94 & 307-311, and 100-278.

William Schonfield, "The Josephs of Cornwall" (1938: unpublished).

Susan Soyinka, *The Penzance Synagogue – A Brief History* (2013 unpublished).

David Stacey, "A Gentleman and a Miner by John Opie", in *JRIC* (2011).

Bernard Susser, "When Jews Worshipped in Penzance", in *The Cornishman* (16th July 1964).

C. Thomas, "A Cornish Mine Captain – Josiah Thomas 1833-1901" in *Camborne School of Mines Journal* 86 (1986) pp. 69-76.

C. Thomas, "Cornish Volunteers in the Eighteenth Century", in *Devon and Cornwall Notes and Queries*, vol. XXVIII, (1959).

G.M.A Trinnick, *The Tregurtha Downs Mine, Marazion 1700-1965,* in the *Industrial Archaeology Review,* vol.II, no. 2 (1978).

John N. Tyacke, " Life Insurance in Early 19th Century Cornwall", in the *Cornwall Family History Society Journal,* No. 69 (September 1993).

Rebecca Walker, "The de Pass Family" (unpublished thesis 1979).

Simon Young, "Five Notes on Nineteenth-Century Cornish Changelings", in the RIC Journal (2013).

The Exeter Congregational *Memorbuch*.

The Plymouth Congregational Marriage Registers 1837-1933 (Susser Archive).

The Plymouth Congregational Minute Book of Trades, Birth Places and Ports of Entry from 1745: University of Southampton Library, Archives and Manuscripts Ref. MS/116/125.

The Burial Register of the Plymouth Hebrew Congregation, Gifford Place Cemetery (Susser Archive).

Books.

Some books referenced in the main body of the text have been listed in the final section on General reading.

Peter Ackroyd, *Foundation,* The History of England Volume 1 (Macmillan 2011).

Michael Adler, *Jews of Medieval England* (JHSE London 1939).

Keith Austin, *The Victorian Titanic, The Loss of the S. S. Schiller in 1875* (Halsgove 2001).

John Bannister, *A Glossary of Cornish Names* (Williams & Norgate, London & Edinburgh; J. R.Netherton, Truro 1871).

Fisher Barham, *Yesterday and Today around Falmouth and Penryn* (Falmouth, Glasney Press 1981).

Juliet Barker, *The Brontës* (London: Phoenix, 1995)

D. Barrington, *On the Expiration of the Cornish Language* (*Archaeologica* III) (1776) & Additional notes (*Archaeologica* V) (1779).

R. D. Barnett and W. M. Scwab (edit.), *The Sephardi Heritage* (Gibraltar Books 1989).

R. D. Barnett & P. Wright, *The Jews of Jamaica, Tombstone Inscriptions 1663-1880* (Jerusalem, Ben Zvi Institute 1997).

R. M. Barton (edit.), *Life in Cornwall in Mid/Late/at End of the Nineteenth Century* (Truro, D. Bradford Barton, vols 1971, 1972 & 1974).

Thomas Beare, *The Bailiff of Blackmoor*, ed. J.A. Buckley (Camborne, Penhellick Publications 1994).

Doreen Berger (edit..), *The Jewish Victorian, Genealogical Information from the Jewish Newspapers 1871-1880* (Witney: Robert Boyd, 1999).

Bruno Bettelheim, *The Uses of Enchantment* (Alfred A. Knopf/Random House, 1976; Penguin 1991).

S. Bird, *Cornish Tales of Mystery and Murder* (Countryside Books, Berkshire 2002).

C. W., G. C. and F. Boase, *The Family of Boase* (1893).

George Clement Boase, *Reminiscences of Penzance* (edit Pool 1976).

William Borlase, *Antiquities of Cornwall* (Oxford 1754).

William Borlase, *Natural History of Cornwall (1758)* (London: E and W Books Ltd, 1970).

W. Bottrell, *Traditions and Hearthside Stories of West Cornwall* (1870 & 1873).

W. Bottrell, Stories and Folklore of West Cornwall (1880).

Mrs. Bray, *The Borders of the Tamar and the Tavy* (London, 1838).

H. Miles Brown, *Cornish Clocks and Clockmakers* (Newton Abbot: David and Charles, 2nd. Edition, 1970); ref. 1769 and 1790/1.

Allen Buckley, *Dolcoath Mine: A History* (Trevithick Society 2010).

J. Buller, *Statistical Account of the Parish of St. Just in Penwith* (Penzance 1842).

Burke's *Genealogical and Heraldic History of the Landed Gentry* (Burke's Peerage, London 1972; vol. III).

William Camden, *Britannia* (1607 and London: Edmund Gibson, 1695 ed).

Richard Carew, *Survey of Cornwall (1602)* (edit. F. E. Halliday. London: Andrew Melrose, 1953).

Bibliotheca Cornubiensis (Boase & Courtney) Vols I (1874) & ii (1878) and

BIBLIOGRAPHY

Collectanea Cornubiensa (Boase: 1890). (Courteney Library, RIC Truro).

Collectanea Judaica Plymouthensis (Susser *et al*. Ed. F. Gent. Crediton 2001).

David Cesarani (edit.), *Port Jews – Jewish Communities in Cosmopolitan Maritime Trading Centres 1550-1950* (Frank Cass, London & Portland Oregon 2002). Note: although this book does not cover the ports of the South-West, it is a indispensable study of how important ports were for Jewish settlement.

Nora K. Chadwick, *The Celts* (Penguin 1970).

John Chynoweth, *Tudor Cornwall* (Tempus 2002).

M. Cooper, *Robbing the Sparry Garniture, A 200 Hundred Year History of British Mineral Dealers 1750 to 1950* (Arizona 2006).

H. R. Coulthard, *The Story of an Ancient Parish - Breage with Germoe* (Camborne Printing & Stationary Co. Ltd., 1913)

J. S. Courtney, *Guide to Penzance* (London: E. Rowe, Longman, Brown, Green, 1845).

M. A. Courtney, *Cornish Feasts and Folklore* (Penzance 1890).

Barry Cunliffe, *The Celtic World* (London 1979).

J. J. Daniell, *Geography of Cornwall* (1854).

Tony Deane and Tony Shaw, *The Folklore of Cornwall* (London: Batsford, 1975).

Daniel Defoe, *A Tour Through the Whole Island of Great Britain* 1722 (Penguin 1971).

T. F. G. Dexter, *Cornish Names* (D. Bradford Barton Truro 1968).

N. Denholm-Young, *Richard of Cornwall* (Oxford: Blackwell, 1947).

H. L. Douch, *Old Cornish Inns* (Truro: D. Bradford Barton, 1966, 1st ed).

C. Duschinsky, *The Rabbinate of the Great Synagogue, London, 1756-1842* (London, 1921).

A. Earland, *John Opie and his Circle* (1911).

Richard Edmonds, *The Land's End District* (London: J. Russel Smith, 1862).

Richard Edmonds, *A Statistical Account of the Borough of Penzance and of the Parish of Madron, Cornwall* (The Statistical Society of London, 1839).

Petr Ehl, Arno Parik and Jiri Fiedler, *Old Bohemian and Moravian Jewish Cemeteries* (Paseka Prague 1991).

Eilert Ekwall, *The Concise Oxford Dictionary of English Place-names* (Oxford, 1960).

George Elwick, *The Bankrupt Directory 1820-1843* (London, Simpkin, Marshall & Co. 1843).

Todd M. Endelman, *The Jews of Georgian England, Tradition and Change in a Liberal Society* (Jewish Publication Society of America Philadelphia 1979).

Todd M. Endelman, *The Jews of Britain 1656-2000* (University of California 2002).

Eli Faber, *Jews, Slaves and the Slave Trade* (New York University Press, 1998).

Frank Felenstein, *Anti-Semitic Stereotypes: A Paradigm of Otherness in English Popular Culture 1660-1830* (Baltimore USA 1995).

Jan Filip, *Celtic Civilisation and its Heritage* (Prague 1962).

Helen Fry, *The Jews of Exeter* (Halsgrove 2013).

Helen Fry, *The Jews of Plymouth* (Halsgrove 2014).

A. Gasquet, *Henry VIII and the English Monasteries* (2 Vols. London 1888).

Susan Gay, *Old Falmouth* (London, Headley Bros. 1903).

Susan E. Gay & Mrs. Howard Fox, *The Register of Baptisms, Marriages and Burials of the Parish of Falmouth 1663-1812* (Exeter: Devon and Cornwall Record Society, 1914).

C. S. Gilbert, *Survey of Cornwall* (Plymouth Dock: J. Congdon, 1817, vol I).

D. Gilbert, *The Parochial History of Cornwall* (London: J. B. Nicholls and son, 1838).

Peter Gilson, *Falmouth in Old Photographs* (Stroud, Alan Sutton, 1990).

Bernard Glassman, *Anti-Semitic Stereotypes without Jews: Images of Jews in England 129-1700* (Detroit 1975).

Anthony Glaser and Ursula Henriques, *The Jews of South Wales* (University of Wales Press, 1993).

R. Glover, *The Ancient World* (Penguin 1953).

Algernon Graves, *The Royal Academy, A Complete Dictionary of Contributors and Their Works from its Foundation in 1769 to 1904* (Vol. VI 1906).

Abigail Green, *Moses Montefiore, Jewish Liberator, Imperial Hero* (Harvard 2010)

Geoffrey L. Green, *The Royal Navy and Anglo-Jewry, 1740-1820* (London: 1989).

G. V. le Grice, *Pamphlets Published in 1824*, no 24, Morrab Gardens Library, Penzance.

Arthur Grigg, *Place-Names in Devon and Cornwall* (Plymouth 1988).

W. Hals, *History of Cornwall* (1750).

A. Cecil Hampshire, *Just An Old Navy Custom* (William Kimber 1979).

J. Hatcher, *English Tin Production and Trade before 1550* (Oxford: Clarendon Press, 1973).

Jacquetta and Christopher Hawkes, *Prehistoric Britain* (Penguin 1958).

H. O'Neill Hencken, *The Archaeology of Cornwall and Scilly* (Methuen 1931).

R. Heath, *Account of the Isles of Scilly* (1750).

Viv Hendra, *The Cornish Wonder, A Portrait of John Opie* (Truran 2007).

Yisrael Hersch, *Kaluach* (Ginot Shomrom Israel 1997-2000: a computer program conversion calendar for Hebrew dates).

History of the Jewish Wars (Whiston's Josephus: London, 1811).

History of the Worthies of England (London: F. C. and J. Rivington, 1811).

R. Hunt, *British Mining* (London: Crosby Lockwood, 1884).

Robert Hunt, *Popular Romances of the West of England* (London 1871).

A. R. Hyamson, *A History of the Jews of England* (London: Chatto and Windus, 1908).

E. Hoffman, *Shtetl, The History of a Small Town & an Extinguished World.* (Secker & Warburg, London 1997).

D. Endean Ivall, *Cornish Heraldry and Symbolism* (Dyllansow Truran 1988).

Joseph Jacobs (edit.) *The Jews of Angevin England* (London 1893).

F. W. P. Jago, *English-Cornish Dictionary* (1887).

Edward Jamilly, *The Georgian Synagogue: an architectural history* (Jewish Memorial Council, London 1999).

Henry Jenner, *A Handbook of the Cornish Language* (London 1904).

W.S. Jessop, *Coats of Many Colours: Joseph Families* (Written Chicago 1951: pub. Crediton, Frank J. Gent 2000).

Michael Jolles, *A Directory of Distinguished British Jews 1830-1930* (London 2000-2001).

Michael Jolles, *A Short History of the Jews of Northampton 1159-1996,* Jolles Publications London (1996).

Sharman Kadish (edit.), *Building Jerusalem: Jewish Architecture in Britain* (London: Valentine Mitchell, 1996).

Sharman Kadish, *Jewish Heritage in England, An Architectural Guide* (English Heritage 2006).

Sharman Kadish, *Jewish Heritage in Britain and Ireland: An Architectural Guide* (revised edition, Swindon, to be published in 2015).

Sharman Kadish, *The Synagogues of Britain and Ireland* (Yale University Press 2011).

David S. Katz, *The Jews in the History of England* (Clarendon Press Oxford 1996).

Jacob Katz, *Jews and Freemasons in Europe 1723-1939* (Cambridge, Mass. USA 1970).

Jacob Katz, *Out of the Ghetto: The Social Background of Jewish Emancipation 1770-1870* (Camb. Mass. 1973).

W. S. Lach-Szyrma, *History of Penzance, St. Michael's Mount etc.* (Truro 1878).

Lake's *Falmouth Guide* (1815).

Raymond Lamont-Brown, *Humphry Davy* (Sutton 2004).

Robert Latham (edit.) *The Shorter Pepys* (Penguin 1993).

Richard Larn, *Cornish Shipwrecks, the Isles of Scilly* (Newton Abbot: David & Charles, 1971).

G. R. Lewis and G. Randall, *The Stannaries* (Cambridge: The Riverside Press, 1908).

R. Lewis, *The Victoria County History of Cornwall* (London: James Street, 1906).

Jeremy Lewis, *Tobias Smollett* (Jonathan Cape London 2003).

J. S. Levi and G. F. J. Bergman, *Australian Genesis, Jewish Convicts and Settlers 1788-1850* (Robert Hale London 1974).

H. Lindo, *A Jewish Calendar for Sixty Four Years* (London: 1838)

Vivian D. Lipman (edit.), *Three Centuries of Anglo-Jewish History* (London, 1961).

E. Lluyd, *Archaeologica Britannica* (1707).

D & S. Lysons, *Magno Britannia* (London: Caddell and Davies, 1814, vol. III).

Moses Margoliouth, *The History of the Jews in Great Britain* (London: R. Bentley, 1851, vol. III).

William George Maton, *Observations of the Western Counties of England* (1794 and 1796: Published 1797, J. Easton, Salisbury).

J. H. Matthews, *History of St. Ives* (1892).

Therese and Mendel Metzger, *Jewish Life in the Middle Ages* (Chartwell Books 1982).

Hugh Miners, *The Story of the Bristol Cornish* (St. Austell 1975).

Frank Mitchell, *Annals of an Ancient Cornish Town;* Dyllansow Truran, Trewolsta Trewergie, Redruth (1946, 2nd ed. 2nd imp. 1985).

R. J. Mitchell and M. D. R. Leys, *A History of London Life* (Longmans Green & Co. 1958).

Friedrich Max Müller, 'Are there Jews in Cornwall?', *Chips from a German Workshop* (London, 1867).

Pat Munn, *The Charlotte Dymond Murder* (Bodmin Books 1978).

Betty Naggar, *Jewish Pedlars and Hawkers 1740-1940* (Porphyrogenitus 1992).

Venetia Newall, *The Encyclopaedia of Witchcraft and Magic* (London, 1974).

Cyril Noall, *Geevor* (Geevor Tin Mines Ltd. Cornwall, 1983).

George Oliver, *Monasticon Dioecesis Exoniensis,* (Exeter 1846-54)

C. T. Onions, ed., *Oxford Dictionary of English Etymology* (Oxford: Clarendon, 1966).

J. G. Osborne, *History of Freemasonry in West Cornwall* (Penzance: Rodda, 1901).

James Pack, *Nelson's Blood, The Story of Naval Rum* (Naval Institute Press Annapolis Maryland 1982).

O. J. Padel, *Cornish Place Names Elements* (Nottingham: English Place Name Society, 1985).

J. A. Paris, *Guide to Mount's Bay* (1816).

Philip Payton, *The Cornish Overseas* (Alexander Associates: Fowey, 1999).

Keith Pearce and Helen Fry (edits.) *The Lost Jews of Cornwall* (Redcliffe Bristol 2000).

T. Pearce *The Laws and Customs of the Stannaries of Cornwall & Devon* (London 1725).

R. D. Penhallurick, *Tin in Antiquity* (London: Institute of Metals, 1986).

W. P. W. Phillimore, *An Index to Changes of Names* (1905).

Philp, *Panorama of Falmouth* (1828).

J. Picciotto, *Sketches of Anglo-Jewish History* (London, 1875).

Polwhele, *History of Cornwall* (London: Caddell and Davies; Law and Whitaker, 1808, vol III).

J. H. Plumb, *England in the Eighteenth Century 1714-1815* (Penguin 1960).

P. A. S. Pool, *The Branwells of Penzance* (Penzance: Penlee House Museum, 1990).

P. A. S. Pool, *The Death of Cornish* (Cornish Language Board, Penzance, 1982).

P. A. S. Pool, *William Borlase* (RIC Truro 1986).

Roy Porter, *English Society in the Eighteenth Century* (Penguin 1990).

W. Pryce, *Archaeologica Cornu-Britannica* (1790).

H. G. Richardson, *The English Jewry Under Angevin Kings* (London: Methuen, 1960).

I. A. Richmond, *Roman Britain* (Penguin 1958).

Jonathan A. Romain *The Jews of England* (Michael Goulston & JCP 1988).

Cecil Roth, *A History of the Jews in England* (Oxford: Clarendon Press, 1964).

Cecil Roth, *A History of the Marranos* (Jewish Publication Society of America, Philadelphia 1932).

Cecil Roth, *The Rise of Provincial Jewry* (London, 1950).

Cecil Roth, *History of the Great Synagogue* (London, 1950).

Alfred Rubens, *A History of Jewish Costume* (London, 1973).

D. and H. Rubinstein & M. Jolles (edits.) *The Palgrave Dictionary of Anglo-Jewish History* (Macmillan 2011).

Rumney, *Economic and Social Development of the Jews in England* (1933).

George Rude, *Hanoverian London 1714-1808* (Sutton 2003).

V. Russell, *West Penwith Survey* (Truro: Cornwall Archaeological Society, 1971).

A. B. M. Serfaty, *The Jews of Gibraltar under British Rule* (Gibraltar 1958).

Judith Samuel, *Jews in Bristol: The History of the Jewish Community in Bristol from the Middle Ages to the Present Day* (Bristol: Sansom & Co, 1997).

David Samuelson et al, *Bertie, the Life and Times of G. B. Samuelson* (pub. privately).

Saundry, *One and All Almanac* (Penzance: 1933 & 1935; Courtney Library, RIC).

A. H. Sayce, *Patriarchal Palestine* (London SPCK 1895).

Sharron Schwartz and Roger Parker, *Lanner: a Cornish Mining Parish* (Halsgrove: Tiverton, 1998).

John Shaftesley, *The Lodge of Israel No. 205, 1793-1968* (London 1968).

T. Shapter, *The History of the Cholera Epidemic in Exeter in 1832* (1859).

Angela Shire (edit.), *Great Synagogue Marriage Records 1791-1830* (Crediton: Frank J. Gent 1999).

Patricia Skinner (edit.), *Jews in Medieval Britain, Historical, Literary and Archaeological Perspectives* (Boydell Press 2003).

Israel Solomon, *Records of My Family* (New York: Stettiner, Lombert and Co, 1887).

John Steegman, *Cambridge* (Batsford 1949).
John Stow, *A General Chronicle of England* (London 1631).

T. E. A. Stowell, *The Centenary History of the Cornubian Lodge* (Privately published 1950).

Bernard Susser, *The Decennial Census* (Privately published, 1995)

Bernard Susser, *The Jews of South-West England* (Exeter: The University of Exeter Press, 1993).

Bernard Susser, *An Account of the Old Jewish Cemetery on Plymouth Hoe* (Privately published, 1972).

Charles Swainson, *The Folklore and Provincial Names of British Birds* (London, 1885).

Tapp's *Plymouth Directory 1822.*

H. Taylor, *St. Michael's Mount, Cornwall* (1932).

The Biography of Samuel Drew (London and Bodmin 1861).

The Jews of Devon and Cornwall (Exhibition Catalogue: Hidden Legacy Foundation, Redcliffe Press Bristol 2000).

Thomas, *History of Mount's Bay* (Penzance: J. Thomas, 1820; Courtney Library, RIC).

Charles Thomas, *Celtic Britain* (Thames and Hudson 1997).

R. Thomas, *History and Description of the Town & Harbour of Falmouth* (Falmouth, 1828).

Peter Thorold, *The London Rich, The Creation of a Great City From 1666 to the Present* (New York 2000).

Brian Torode, *The Hebrew Community of Cheltenham* (Cheltenham 1999, revised ed.).

James Trathen, *The Ancient and Modern History of Falmouth* (Falmouth, 1815).

E. S. Tregoning, *History of Falmouth and its Vicinity* (Falmouth, 1865).

J. L. Vivian, *The Visitations of the County of Cornwall, 1530, 1573 & 1620* (William Pollard, London 1887).

Anthony R. Wagner, *Historic Heraldry of Britain* (Oxford University Press 1939 & 1948).

J. Wake, *Guide to St. Michael's Mount* (1934).

Herbert A. Walford, *My Family* (published privately: Principat d'Andore 1994).

W. R. Ward, *Religion and Society in England 1790-1850* (London 1972).

W. Warn, *Directory and Guide for Falmouth & Penryn and their Vicinities* (1864).

R. Warner, *A Tour through Cornwall in 1808* (1809).

Craig Weatherhill, *Cornovia: Ancient Sites of Cornwall and Scilly 4000 BC to 1000 AD* (Halsgrove 2009).

Joseph Wright (edit.), *The English Dialect Dictionary* (London, 1902).

I. Pawley White, *A Handbook of Cornish Surnames* (Dyllansow Truran 3rd Edition 1999).

Thomas Witherby, *An Attempt to Remove Prejudices Concerning the Jewish Nation* (London 1804).

Thomas Witherby, *A Vindication of the Jews* (London 1809).

Conclusion.

Howard Bloch, *Earlham Grove Schul, One Hundred Years of West Ham Synagogue and Community* (London 1997).

David Buckman, *Artists in Britain Since 1945, Vol. 2* (Art Dictionaries Ltd. 2006).

Helen Fry, *Jews in North Devon During the Second World War* (Halsgrove 2005).

Melissa Hardie, *100 Years in Newlyn – Diary of a Gallery* (Patten Press, Cornwall 1995) and (edit.) *Artists in Newlyn and West Cornwall 1880-1940* (Art Dictionaries Ltd. 2009).

Michael Jolles, *Biographical Notes on 1200 British Jews* (to be published).

Michael Jolles, W. D. & H. L. Rubinstein, *The Palgrave Dictionary of Anglo-Jewish History* (Macmillan 2011).

Norman Levine, *From a Seaside Town* (Macmillan 1970), and *In a Jewish Cemetery* (Jewish Chronicle Publications 1983).

Michael Peppiatt, *Francis Bacon* (Weidenfeld and Nicolson, London 1996).

Susan Soyinka, *From East End to Land's End* (Eliora Books 2013).

Chris Stephens, *Mark Rothko in Cornwall* (Tate Gallery St. Ives 1996).

General.

Those readers unfamiliar with Cornish history may wish to read further to place the Jews of Cornwall against the County's cultural and historical background. Some of the books listed above are suitable for this purpose and they are included in this personal selection.

P. Berresford Ellis, *The Cornish Language and its Literature* (Routledge and Kegan Paul 1974).

Allen Buckley, *The Story of Mining in Cornwall* (Cornwall Editions Fowey 2007).

Roger Burt (Editor), *Cornish Mining – Essays on the Organisation of Cornish Mines and the Cornish Mining Economy* (David and Charles 1969).

H. Miles Brown, *The Church in Cornwall* (Truro 1964).

Bernard W. Deacon, *Cornwall, A Concise History* (University of Wales 2007).

L. E. Elliot-Binns, *Medieval Cornwall* (Methuen 1955).

R. Fletcher, *A Short History of Saint Michael's Mount* (edit. John Fletcher 1951).

Crispin Gill, *The Great Cornish Families* (Cornwall Books 1995).

E. Halliday, *A History of Cornwall* (Duckworth 1959 & 1963; House of Stratus 2000).

F. E. Halliday (Introduction and Editor), *Richard Carew of Anthony 1555 – 1620, The Survey of Cornwall Etc.* (Andrew Melrose, London 1953).

Charles Henderson (edit. A. L Rowse and M. L. Henderson), *Essays in Cornish History* (Oxford, the Clarendon Press 1935).

A. K. Hamilton Jenkin, *The Cornish Miner* (George Allen and Unwin, London 1948).

Alan M. Kent, *Celtic Cornwall* (Halsgrove 2013).

G. R. Lewis, *The Stannaries* (Bradford Barton, Truro 1965).

O. J. Padel, *A Popular Dictionary of Cornish Place-Names* (Alison Hodge 1988).

Tony Pawlyn, *The Falmouth Packets 1689-1851* (Truran 2003).

Philip Payton, *Cornwall: A History* (Cornwall Editions Fowey 2004).

Caradoc Peters, *The Archaeology of Cornwall* (Cornwall Editions Fowey 2005).

P. A. S. Pool, *Cornish for Beginners* (Cornish Language Board 1970).

P. A. S. Pool, *The History of the Town and Borough of Penzance* (1974).

John Rowe, *Cornwall in the Age of the Industrial Revolution* (1953, 1993 & 2006).

A. L. Rowse, *A Cornish Anthology* (Macmillan 1968).

A. L. Rowse, *Tudor Cornwall* (Jonathan Cape, editions from 1941).

Charles Thomas and Joanna Mattingly, *The History of Christianity in Cornwall AD 500-2000* (RIC Truro 2000).

Christine Truran, *A Short Cornish Dictionary: Gerlyver Ber* (Truran 1998).

Thomas Shaw, *A History of Cornish Methodism* (D. Bradford Barton 1967).

Craig Weatherhill, *Cornovia, Ancient Sites of Cornwall and Scilly 4000BC to 1000 AD* (Halsgrove 2009).

James Whetter, *Cornwall in the 13th Century* (Lyfrow Trelyspen 1998).

Nicholas Williams, *A Complete Guide to Cornish* (Evertype 2012).

Selective Index and Genealogical Guide

There are so many names of people and places in this text that any Index which included them all would amount to a small volume in itself. This Index is selective, and it concentrates on names and topics which I regard as central, such as the resident Cornish Jewish families, although, I have not given these on every page where the names appear. Where Cornish Christians and others are integral to the main story or serve some exemplary function, they have also been given, but other names (of Jews and Christians) which are incidental and peripheral or which serve a merely illustrative function have not been included. Many names are included in collective references, such as "Jews in Medieval England", "Christians, with Hebrew or Biblical Names" etc. I have highlighted the name of males, which accords with the practice in most public records, such as census returns, trade directories and, crucially, the patronomic practice of Jewish nomenclature. The wives, sisters and daughters, as well as other males are to be found within the pages given, and on the family trees. Namesakes have been distinguished in the text, but I have tried to repeat some of these distinctions in this Index where I feel that confusion is most likely. The names given can also be found within the collective family pages, the trees, and often in the cemetery chapter. I have given either the original family name of women or their married surname, or both. Cross-references to individuals can also be found in the cemetery chapter.